A MANUAL OF GREEK LITERATURE,

FROM

THE EARLIEST AUTHENTIC PERIODS TO THE CLOSE OF THE BYZANTINE ERA.

BY

CHARLES ANTHON, LL.D.,

PROFESSOR OF THE GREEK AND LATIN LANGUAGES IN COLUMBIA COLLEGE,
RECTOR OF THE GRAMMAR SCHOOL, ETC., ETC.

NEW YORK:
HARPER & BROTHERS, PUBLISHERS,
329 & 331 PEARL STREET,
FRANKLIN SQUARE.
1853.

PREFACE.

A course of Lectures on Greek Literature is one of the duties connected with the department of Ancient Languages in Columbia College, and, in fulfilling this requirement, the author of the present work has, for many years past, read a series of lectures on the subject to the senior classes of the institution. Each of these lectures being invariably followed by a written examination, on the plan pursued in foreign universities, and the student being called upon, in the course of such examination, for additional information obtained by private reading, a difficulty has long been felt with regard to the proper sources whence this information was to be derived. The principal works on the history of Greek Literature are not, in general, of easy access to American students, some by reason of the expense connected with them, but by far the greater part from their being written in foreign languages with which few of our youth are familiar. To obviate, therefore, in some degree, these two difficulties, the present work has been prepared, and, should it meet with a favorable reception, it will be followed by a similar manual of Roman Literature.

The introductory portion of the volume commences with a brief abstract of what is termed Linguistic, so far as this has a bearing on the Indo-European chain of languages, to which the Hellenic tongue belongs; a subject naturally possessing great interest for the young student, and well calculated to impart a liberal tone to academical researches. In preparing this part of the work, rich materials have been obtained from the stores of German erudition, and others of no less value from the productions of Donaldson, Prichard, Winning, and Mure, among English scholars.

The main work itself embraces in its plan the whole range of Greek Literature, from the earliest periods down to the close of the Byzantine era, and, besides a brief account of each successive stage of development in the history of the Grecian mind, will be found to contain biographical sketches of all the most eminent writers who flourished within the limits just mentioned. To the list of their works there is also appended, in the case of each writer, a condensed account of the principal editions, prepared from the best bibliographical sources, and which, though necessarily brief, may not prove without its value. A rapid survey is also taken of the different schools of Greek philosophy, of the medical systems of Greece, and likewise of the advances made in the cultivation of the mathematical sciences.

The earlier part of the work is based, in a great measure, upon the admirable history of Greek Literature by C. O. Müller, left unfinished at his death, and upon the labors of Mure and Ihne, from the latter of whom, in particular, the history of the Homeric controversy has chiefly been drawn. In general, the language and arrangement of these writers have been carefully retained, as far as was compatible with the system of condensation required throughout the work. The biographical sketches are taken, for the most part, from the excellent Dictionary of Greek and Roman Biography, edited by Dr. Smith, a work the high price of which places it almost entirely out of the reach of American students. It is but fair, however, to state, that, in giving these sketches, additions have frequently been made from other sources, and not a few errors have been corrected in matters appertaining to chronology and literary history. Valuable materials have also been obtained from Clinton, Schöll, Bernhardy, Bode, and many others of the most eminent European scholars. Indeed, the main object of the author has been to give, as far as possible, a complete *résumé* of the History of Greek Literature, and he presents the work as such to the students of his own country, in the earnest hope that it may lead them to a more intimate acquaintance with that noble field of mental culture, from which the literature of the civilized world almost exclusively derives its origin.

The subject of Sacred Literature forms no part of the present work, and only a few, therefore, of the ecclesiastical writers, such as Justin Martyr, Clemens of Alexandrea, and Origen, have been briefly mentioned under the head of the Neo-Platonic school.

The following is a list of the principal works from which materials have been obtained, or which have been consulted in the preparation of the present work:

1. Bopp, Vergleichende Grammatik, &c., Berlin, 4to, 1833, &c.
2. " Comparative Grammar of the Sanscrit, Zend, &c., translated by Eastwick, London, 3 vols. 8vo, 1845-50.
3. Pott, Etymologische Forschungen, Lemgo, 2 vols. 8vo, 1833–36.
4. Marsh, Horæ Pelasgicæ, Cambridge, 8vo, 1815.
5. Hug, Die Erfindung der Buchstabenschrift, Ulm, 8vo, 1801.
6. Donaldson, New Cratylus, London, 8vo, 2d ed., 1850.
7. Prichard, Researches into the Physical History of Mankind, London, 5 vols. 8vo, 1841–7.
8. Eichhoff, Parallèle des Langues de l'Europe et de l'Inde, Paris, 4to, 1836.
9. Eichhoff, Vergleichung der Sprachen, &c., von Kaltschmidt, Leipzig, 4to, 1840.
10. Chavée, Lexiologie Indo-Européenne, Paris, 8vo, 1849.
11. Winning, Manual of Comparative Philology, London, 8vo, 1838.
12. Pictet, De l'Affinité des Langues Celtiques avec le Sanscrit, Paris, 8vo, 1827.
13. Dankovszky, Die Griechen als Stamm- und Sprachverwandte der Slawen, Pressburg, 8vo, 1828.
14. Ahrens, De Linguæ Græcæ Dialectis, Götting., 2 vols. 8vo, 1839–43.
15. Prichard, Eastern Origin of the Celtic Nations, Oxford, 8vo, 1831.
16. Dieffenbach, Celtica, Stuttgart, 2 vols. 8vo, 1839–40.
17. Pococke, India in Greece, London, 8vo, 1852.
18. Latham, The Germania of Tacitus, with Ethnological dissertations and notes, London, 8vo, 1851.

19. Fabricii, Bibliotheca Græca, Hamb., ed. 3, 14 vols. 4to, 1718–28.
20. " " " " ed. Harless, 12 vols. 4to, 1790–1811.
21. Harless, Brevior Notitia Literaturæ Græcæ, Lips., 12mo, 1812.
22. Vossius, De Historicis Græcis, ed. Westermann, Lips., 8vo, 1838.
23. Müller, History of the Literature of Ancient Greece, London, 2 vols. 8vo, 1840–1.
24. Müller, Griechische Literatur, Breslau, 2 vols. 8vo, 1841.
25. Mure, Critical History of the Language and Literature of Greece, London, 4 vols. 8vo, 1850–3.
26. Schöll, Histoire de la Litérature Grecque Profane, Paris, 8 vols. 8vo, 1825.
27. Schöll, Geschichte der Griechischen Literatur, &c., Berlin, 3 vols. 8vo, 1828–30.
28. Bernhardy, Grundriss der Griechischen Literatur, Halle, 2 vols. 8vo, 1845–52.
29. Bode, Dichtkunst der Hellenen, Leipzig, 6 vols. 8vo, 1838–40.
30. Mohnike, Geschichte der Lit. der Griechen und Römer, Greifswald, 8vo, 1813.
31. Smith, Dictionary of Greek and Roman Biography, &c., London, 3 vols. 8vo, 1843–9.
32. Gräfenhan, Geschichte der Klassischen Philologie, Bonn, 4 vols. 8vo, 1843-50.
33. Roulez, Manuel de l'Histoire de la Lit. Grecque, Bruxelles, 8vo, 1837.
34. Jouffroy, Manuel de la Litérature Ancienne, Paris, 8vo, 1842.
35. Munk, Geschichte der Griechischen Literatur, Berlin, 2 vols. 12mo, 1849–50.
36. Tregder, Handbuch der Gr. und Röm. Literaturgeschichte, Marburg, 12mo, 1847.
37. Matthiæ, Manual of the History of Greek and Roman Literature, Oxford, 12mo, 1841.
38. Pierron, Histoire de la Lit. Grecque, Paris, 12mo, 1850.
39. Talfourd, History of Greek Literature, London, 8vo, 1850.
40. Matter, Histoire de l'Ecole d'Alexandrie, Paris, 2 vols. 8vo, 2d ed., 1840–44.
41. Egger, Histoire de la Critique chez les Grecs, Paris, 8vo, 1849.
42. Brucker, Historia Critica Philosophiæ, Lipsiæ, 6 vols. 4to, 1767.
43. Degerando, Histoire comparée des Systèmes de Philosophie, Paris, 4 vols. 8vo, 1823.
44. Tennemann, Grundriss der Geschichte der Philosophie, Leipzig, 8vo, 1829.
45. Tennemann, Manual of Philosophy, by Morell, London, 12mo, 1852.
46. Ritter, History of Philosophy, translated by Morrison, Oxford and London, 4 vols. 8vo, 1838–46.
47. Finlay, Greece under the Romans, London, 8vo, 1844.
48. " Mediæval Greece, and Trebizond, London, 8vo, 1851.
49. Clinton, Fasti Hellenici, Oxford, 3 vols. 4to, 1834–51.

50. Clinton, Epitome of the Civil and Literary Chronology of Greece, Oxford, 8vo, 1851.
51. Donaldson, Theatre of the Greeks, London, 8vo, 6th edition, 1849.
52. Wieseler, Theatergebäude, &c., bei den Griechen und Römern, Götting., 4to, 1851.
53. Browne, History of Classical Literature, London, 2 vols. 8vo, 1851.
54. Blackie, On Greek Pronunciation, Edinburgh, 8vo, 1852.
55. Grote, History of Greece, London, 10 vols. 8vo, 1846–52.
56. Thirlwall, History of Greece, London, new ed., 8 vols. 8vo, 1845–52.

CHARLES ANTHON.

Columbia College, April 5th, 1853.

CONTENTS.

CHAPTER XXVIII.

CHAPTER XXIX.

CHAPTER XXX.

CHAPTER XXXI.

CHAPTER XXXII.

CHAPTER XXXIII.

CHAPTER XXXIV.

CHAPTER XXXV.

CHAPTER XLIII.

CHAPTER XLIV.

CHAPTER XLV.

CHAPTER XLVI.

CHAPTER XLVII.

CHAPTER XLVIII.

CHAPTER XLIX.

CHAPTER L.

CHAPTER LI.

CHAPTER LII.

CHAPTER LIII.

CHAPTER LIV.

CHAPTER LV.

CHAPTER LVI.

CHAPTER LVII.

HISTORY

OF

GREEK LITERATURE.

INTRODUCTORY REMARKS.[1]

I. The Greek language forms a branch of the great family of languages, known by the name of the Indo-Germanic, and extending from India to the British Isles.

II. Some writers,[2] in speaking of this chain of languages, prefer the appellation *Indo-European;* but the term *Indo-Germanic* is decidedly preferable, since it points at once to the two most important branches of the family, namely, the Indian and Teutonic languages, and is also free from the vagueness which attaches itself to the name Indo-European; for there are languages in Europe which have no established affinity with this family.[3]

III. The languages included under the title of Indo-Germanic are the following: 1. The *Sanscrit*[4] and its derivative dialects. 2. The *Zend*,[5]

[1] *Donaldson's New Cratylus*, 2d ed., p. 108, *seqq.; Penny Cyclopædia*, vol. xi, p. 427, *seqq.; Müller, History of Greek Literature*, p. 3, *seqq.; Winning's Manual of Comparative Philology*, p. 20, *seqq.; Mure, Critical History of the Language and Literature of Greece*, vol. i., p. 37, *seqq.; St. John, The Hellenes*, vol. i., p. 3, *seqq.; Bernhardy, Grundriss der Griechischen Literatur*, vol. i., p. 160, *seqq.; Browne, History of Classical Literature*, vol. i., p. 9, *seqq.*

[2] *Winning's Manual*, &c., p. 20. Compare *Prichard, Eastern Origin of the Celtic Nations*, p. 17.

[3] *Donaldson, New Cratylus*, p. 108, 2d ed.

[4] The term *Sanscrit* is an epithet employed by the Brahmins to designate the language in which their books of law and religion are written. The original word *San-s-krĭta* is a compound: the first syllable is the preposition *sam*, "with" (compare the Greek σύν and ἅμα); the second is the passive participle *krita*, of the verb *krĭ*, "to make" (compare the Latin *cre-are*, and the Greek κραίνω), with a silent *s* interposed between the two. Hence *Sanskrita* is equivalent to the Latin *confectus*, and means "done, made, or formed completely." It indicates, therefore, a perfect, highly-polished, regularly inflected language, one possessing all its flexions and grammatical forms; in other words, a classical language, or one removed from the corrupting influences of every-day use.—*New Cratylus*, p. 121, 2d ed.

[5] The term *Zend* seems to be the ancient Parsee word for "book," and to have been specially applied to the volume of Zoroaster's sacred writings, in the same way as we use the word *Bible* (*Burnouf, Comm.*, p. 16). It was first applied by Anquetil to the language in which the Scriptures of the Parsees are written, and in this sense it has been generally adopted throughout Europe. The Zend language belongs to the Median branch of the Indo-Germanic family of languages (*Penny Cyclop.*, xxvii., p. 760). Some writers have regarded the Zend as merely a dialect of the Sanscrit, but this is evidently erroneous. Consult the remarks of Donaldson, *New Cratylus*, p. 126, 2d ed.

and the other ancient dialects of Persia. 3. The *Teutonic* languages, comprising the Gothic, German, Anglo-Saxon, Icelandic, Swedish, &c. 4. The *Latin* and *Greek*. 5. The *Sclavonic* languages, including the Lithuanian, Prussian, Polish, Bohemian, &c. 6. The *Celtic* languages.[1]

IV. The affinity which exists between all the languages of the Indo-Germanic family is evident, not merely from the number of words which are common to them all, but likewise from the similarity of their grammatical forms. The same words, only slightly disguised, are used in most of these languages for the pronouns, the numerals, and the most simple of the prepositions.

V. On the other hand, the Indo-Germanic languages are distinguished from those of the Semitic family (to which latter class the Hebrew, Syriac, Arabic, Ethiopic, and other kindred tongues belong) by a different mode of inflection, by different words for the pronouns, numerals, and prepositions, and by the power of forming compound words, which are not found, with the exception of a few instances, in the Semitic tongues.[2]

VI. While the Semitic branch occupies the southwest of Asia, the Indo-Germanic languages run almost in a straight line from southeast to northwest, through Asia and Europe. A slight interruption, however, occurs in the case of the latter in the country between the Euphrates and Asia Minor, which appears to have been occasioned by the pressure of Semitic or Syrian races from the south; for it seems probable that originally the members of this national family succeeded one another in a continuous line from the great parent source or home.[3]

VII. This home or parent source of the Indo-Germanic race appears to have been a region called *Irân*, bounded on the north by the Caspian, on the south by the Indian Ocean, on the east by the Indus, and on the west by the Euphrates. Within these limits were spoken, so far as we can discover, two languages, which bore the same relation to one another that we recognize as subsisting between Low and High German, a language analogous to the former being spoken in the low countries, in the north and east of the district, and one analogous to the latter in the more mountainous regions of the south. The southern one of these languages has been called by philologists the High Iranian, the northern and eastern the Low Iranian.[4]

VIII. The surrounding nations to the north and east belonged to the Turanian or Sporadic family, who appear to have scattered themselves over Europe long before the great Indo-Germanic migration commenced, and to have been either conquered by the latter races in their subsequent onward progress, or to have been driven by them to the mountainous extremities of the continent of Europe.[5]

---

1 On the claims of the Celtic to a place among the Indo-Germanic languages, consult *Prichard, Eastern Origin of the Celtic Nations*, Oxford, 1831, and *Pictet, De l'Affinité des Langues Celtiques avec le Sanscrit*, Paris, 1837.

2 *Penny Cyclopædia*, xi., p. 428.

3 *Müller, Hist. Gr. Lit.*, p. 4.

4 *Donaldson, New Cratylus*, p. 117, 2d ed.

5 By the term "Turanian," which has been borrowed from the old Persian legends of Iran and Turan, countries engaged from the earliest times in perpetual enmities, modern writers designate all the tribes to the north of Iran, or, in other words, the races dwelling to the northward of the Oxus and the range of Imaus. Among these, the

IX. When the mighty people confined within the comparatively narrow limits of Iran had become too numerous for the country they lived in, the eastern and northern tribes sent off emigrations to the southeast and northwest, breaking through or driving before them the tribes by which they were hemmed in. Those, however, who went off to the northwest were more powerful or more enterprising than the emigrants who took a southeasterly course; for while the former carried the Low Iranian dialect over all Asia and Europe to the islands of the West, the latter mastered only the northern part of Hindostan, and perhaps also, to a certain extent, a few of the islands of the Polynesia.[1]

X. Although we have no good reason to doubt the great antiquity of the Sanscrit language, and though the writings in which it is contained are the modern representatives of a school of epic and didactic poetry, probably older than the earliest specimens of Greek literature, we must not suppose that it was as we have it now, the same old Iranian idiom which was taken into Europe; on the contrary, it bears evident marks of those changes which long usage introduces into every language, and which have not operated to so great an extent in some of the sister tongues of Europe, for instance, in the Low German, the Latin, and the Greek. However, as we do not possess any memorials of the primeval language from which it sprung, and as it does present most remarkable correspondences with the oldest European languages of the Indo-Germanic family, we must be content to take it as the representative of the old Low Iranian.[2]

XI. If we consider the elements of the population of Europe, according to the order in which they were successively added to the first sprinkling of scattered Turanian tribes that had preceded them, we can hardly fail to arrive at the following results. The first emigrants from Asia were the sons of Gomer—Celts and Cimmerians—who entered the continent of Europe from the steppes of the Caucasus, and, passing round the northern coasts of the Black Sea, not only spread over the whole of Europe, especially to the south and west, but also recrossed into Asia by the Hellespont, and conquered or colonized the countries bordering on the southern shore of the Euxine.[3]

XII. The next invaders were the sons of Magog — Sarmatians or Sclavonians—who are generally found by the side of the Celts in the earliest settlements. They more fully occupied the east of Europe; but though they largely contributed to the population of Greece and Italy, they do not appear to have spread beyond the Oder in the North, or to have established themselves permanently in the Alps, or in the middle highlands of Germany. The Sclavonian is the most widely-extended idiom of the Indo-Germanic family. It is spread over a wide surface of

---

Scythians, or Mongoles and Kalmuks, are particularly meant. The Finns and the Esquimaux also belong to this great division, and it has been supposed that a Finnish population was spread over Europe when the great Celtic immigration commenced. Compare *Prichard*, *Researches into the Physical History of Mankind*, vol. i., p. 257, *seqq.*

[1] *Donaldson*, *New Cratylus*, p. 117, 2d ed.

[2] *Id. ib.*, p. 124.

[3] *Id. ib.*, p. 108.

Europe and Asia, from the Pacific to the Baltic, from the Adriatic to the Arctic Sea.[1]

XIII. Next in order after the Sclavonians came the Teutonic races, consisting, first, of the Low Germans, who, starting from the regions between the Oxus and the Iaxartes, burst through the Sclavonians, and finally settled themselves in the northwest of Europe; and, secondly, of the High Germans, who subsequently occupied the higher central regions. The High Germans, like the High Iranians, we so name from their inhabiting the mountainous districts of the south; and the Low Germans from their occupying the low countries toward the north.[2]

XIV. The people whom we call *Greeks*, from the Latin appellation *Græci*, but who styled themselves *Hellēnes* (῞Ελληνες),[3] were not the earliest inhabitants of the country which bore their name (*Græcia*, Ἑλλάς). Various tribes are said to have occupied the land previous to the arrival of the Hellenic race, the most celebrated among which was that of the *Pelasgi* (Πελασγοί), although some writers are of opinion that all these tribes were connected together, and merely formed so many parts of one great Pelasgic race.[4]

XV. Who the Pelasgi were must ever remain a matter of uncertainty.[5] Even the Greeks themselves appear to have had no definite information on the subject. Some accounts represent them as little better than mere savages, strangers even to the simplest arts of life, and to the first necessaries of civilized society, ignorant even of fire; while other legends made them, in the very earliest period of their settlement in Greece, to have already reached a comparatively high stage of social refinement. These latter accounts assigned unto them tillage and the useful arts as their proper and original pursuits. We are told that they loved to settle on the rich soil of alluvial plains, that they built towns which they fortified with walls of a colossal size, and zealously worshipped the pow-

---

[1] *Donaldson, New Cratylus*, p. 113. Compare *Schafarik, Slavische Alterthümer*, vol. i., p. 33, *seqq.*

[2] *Donaldson, l. c.* Compare *Mannert, Geschichte der alten Deutschen*, p. 4, *seqq.*; *Menzel, Gesch. der Deutschen*, p. 5.

[3] The name ῞Ελληνες is supposed to mean "warriors." Compare Müller's note on the Doric form Ἀπέλλων for Ἀπόλλων (*Dorians*, ii., 6, 6). Some, however, on the authority of Aristotle (*Meteorol.*, i., 14), find a relation between the ῞Ελληνες and the Σελλοί of Dodona, called Ἑλλοί by Pindar, the sanctuary of Dodona having itself been termed *Hella*. Compare *Niebuhr, Rom. Hist.*, vol. i., p. 47, note 143.

[4] This latter is the true opinion. Niebuhr asserts, not as a mere hypothesis, but as a matter, with him, of historical conviction, that there was a time when the Pelasgi, then, perhaps, more widely spread than any other people in Europe, extended over Italy and Greece, from the Po and Arno to the Bosporus (*Rom. Hist.*, vol. i., p. 52). The remarks of Grote on this assertion of Niebuhr are exceedingly flippant and unfair (*Hist. of Greece*, vol. ii., p. 347, note).

[5] The derivation of the name Πελασγοί from πελαργοί, "storks," in allusion to their migratory habits, quoted by Dionysius of Halicarnassus (i., 28) from Myrsilus of Lesbos, is simply absurd. Some modern attempts at etymology are not much better. Röth (*Gesch. abendländ. Philos.*) makes the term one of Phœnician origin, *Plashi*, "the wanderer," while Donaldson, on the other hand, makes Πελ-ασγός (following the analogy of Πέλ-οψ, "swarthy of face") mean "the swarthy Asgian, or Asiatic" (*Varronianus*, p. 24. Compare *Philolog. Mus.*, ii., p. 353). On the subject of the Pelasgi generally, consult *Lepsius, Ueber die Tyrrhen. Pelasger*; *Annali dell' Inst. Archæol.*, 1836, p. 186.

ers of heaven and earth, who made their fields fruitful and their cattle prolific.[1]

XVI. The language spoken by the ancient Pelasgi is described by one of the Greek writers as a barbarous tongue, that is, not Hellenic;[2] and this opinion has also been adopted by several modern inquirers. It appears exceedingly improbable, however, if the Pelasgic and Hellenic languages had either no relation to each other, or else only a very slight one, that these two tongues should have so readily amalgamated in all parts of Greece; and still more strange that the Athenians and Arcadians, who are admitted to have been of pure Pelasgic origin, should have both lost their original language, and learned the pure Hellenic tongue. It is reasonable, therefore, to suppose that the Pelasgic and Hellenic languages were different dialects of one common tongue, and formed by their union the Greek language of later times.[3]

XVII. But, what is of most importance with regard to the Pelasgian language, it appears that the old inhabitants of Italy were also Pelasgi, and there is certainly no radical difference between the Latin and the Greek. It is probable, therefore, that the Pelasgic and Hellenic tongues resembled each other as much as the Swedish and German, or the Spanish and Italian. In each of these cases the difference is such as to constitute, in the familiar sense, the one a foreign tongue as compared with the other, although in each the critical inquirer discovers a close affinity.[4]

XVIII. It has already been stated that the origin of the Pelasgic race is involved in utter uncertainty. Some modern scholars, however, think it probable that they were a Low Iranian people, and a branch of the great Sclavonic nation;[5] and what has been regarded as a strong argument in favor of this opinion has been drawn from the striking agreement of even the modern Sclavonic with the Latin, and also with the oldest element of Greek.[6]

XIX. The additional or Hellenic element of the Greek, which afterward pervaded the whole language, and gave a High German character to its entire structure, seems to have come from the East by the way of Asia Minor; at any rate, we find that the Hellenes make their first historical appearance in the south of Thessaly, or the northeastern part of

---

[1] *Herod.*, ii., 52; *Guigniaut, Religions de l'Antiquité*, vol. ii., pt. i., p. 289, note; *Müller, Hist. Gr. Lit.*, p. 8; *Thirlwall, Hist. of Greece*, vol. i., p. 38, *seqq.*, ed. 1845; *St. John, Hellenes*, vol. i., p. 12.

[2] *Herod.*, i., 55.

[3] *Donaldson, New Cratylus*, p. 128. Compare the remark of Niebuhr: "The farther we look back into antiquity, the richer, the more distinct, and the more broadly marked do we find the dialects of great languages. They subsist, one beside the other, with the same character of originality, and just as if they were different tongues" (*Hist. Rom.*, vol. i., p. 54).

[4] *Donaldson, New Crat.*, p. 129.

[5] *Id. ib.*

[6] The resemblance of the Russian to the Latin is said to be so striking, that a modern traveller has not hesitated to assert that the founders of Rome spoke the Russian language! (*Italy and its Inhabitants*, by J. A. Galiffe, of Geneva, vol. i., p. 356, *seqq.*). The student may consult the two following works on the affinity between the early Greek and the Sclavonic. "*Homerus Slavicis dialectis cognata lingua scripsit: ex ipsius Homeri Carmine ostendit Gregorius Dankovsky*," Vindob., 1829; and "*Der Griechen als Stamm- und Sprachverwandte der Slaven. Historisch und Philologisch dargestellt, von Gregor. Dankovsky*," Pressburg, 1828.

Greece. Aristotle, indeed, makes the original seat of the Hellenic race to have been near Dodona, in Epirus, but on what authority he gives this statement we do not know.[1] The general feeling of the Greeks, however, was different, connecting the Hellenes, primarily and specially, with the territory called Achaia Phthiotis, between Mounts Othrys and Œta. The region here meant was first called Hellas, a name extended afterward to the whole of Greece.[2]

XX. This new or Hellenic element is supposed by some eminent modern scholars to have been High Iranian or Persian.[3] The striking resemblance between the High German, on the one hand, and the ancient Greek and modern Persian on the other, was pointed out in the infancy of comparative philology.[4] The resemblance which the Greek bore to the Persian, in particular, must have been much greater formerly; so much so, indeed, that a Greek could learn Persian without any difficulty, as appears from the examples of Democedes and Themistocles, the former of whom made a witty remark in Persian before he had been long at Susa;[5] while the latter, an elderly man, who had never learned a foreign tongue in his life, made himself a proficient in the language within a year.[6]

XXI. In accordance with the usual method pursued by the Greeks, of inventing names to account for the origin of nations, the Hellenes are said to have descended from Hellen, the son of Deucalion. Hellen had three sons, Dorus, Xuthus, and Æolus; and Xuthus, again, had two sons, Achæus and Ion. From Dorus, Æolus, Achæus, and Ion, the Dorians, Æolians, Achæans, and Ionians were said to have descended, who formed the four great tribes into which the Hellenic nation was for many centuries divided.

XXII. According, however, to the ingenious and more satisfactory explanation of some modern scholars, the name *Hellenes*, as already remarked,[7] means "the warriors;" the *Dorians* (Δωριεῖς) are "Highlanders," from δα and ὄρος; the *Æolians* (Αἰολεῖς) are "the mixed men," from αἰόλος, "varied," a name which arose when the Dorians first descended from their mountains in the region of Thessaly, and incorporated themselves with the Pelasgi of the Thessalian plains. So, again, the *Ionians* (Ἴωνες) are "the men of the coast," from ἠιονία, or ἠϊών, "the coast or shore," called also Αἰγιαλεῖς, or "Beachmen," from αἰγιαλός, "the beach," and the Ἀχαιοί are "seamen," from a root in the Greek language answering to the Latin *aqua*.[8]

XXIII. It is a curious fact, noticed by some modern scholars, that the Grecian race which made the earliest and most rapid progress in civilization and intellectual attainments was the one in which the Pelasgian

---

[1] *Aristot.*, *Meteorol.*, i., 14.

[2] *Grote*, *Hist. of Greece*, vol. ii., p. 356. Aristotle very probably alludes to the first Hellenic settlement in the land, after which they may have moved south into Thessaly, and then first became known to history.

[3] *Donaldson*, *New Cratylus*, p. 131.

[4] *Lipsii Epist. Henrico Schottio*, *Op.*, vol. ii., p. 41, *seqq.*, Cent. iii., ed. 1614; *Salmas.*, *De Ling. Hellen.*, p. 331, *seqq.*

[5] *Herod.*, iii., 130.

[6] *Plut.*, *Themist.*, c. 29.

[7] Page 4, note 3.

[8] *Kenrick*, *Phil. Mus.*, vol. ii., p. 367; *Donaldson*, *New Cratylus*, p. 134.

blood was least adulterated by foreign admixture, namely, the Ionians of Attica and of the settlements in Asia; and that we probably owe to the Pelasgic element in the population of Greece all that distinguishes the Greeks in the history of the human mind. The Dorians, on the other hand, who were the most strictly Hellenic, long disdained to apply themselves to literature and the fine arts.[1]

XXIV. Before proceeding farther, however, one point naturally remains to be settled, namely, why the Hellenes were known to the Romans only under the appellation of *Græci* or *Graii*. The best solution of the difficulty appears to be, that the early Pelasgian colonists of central Italy were the *Græci* or *Graii*, who retained in their transmarine possessions their early name, which became obsolete in the mother country. Hence may be explained the practice so inveterate with the Latin poets, from Ennius downward, of calling the Greeks, even of the purely Hellenic age, Pelasgians, while the name Hellenes rarely, if ever, occurs in their text in its generic sense.[2]

XXV. During the century subsequent to the fall of Troy (1184 B.C.), extensive changes took place in the dialectical as well as political relations of the Hellenic states. About sixty years after that event (1124 B.C.), dissensions among the Æolic tribes in northern and central Greece produced a large emigration from Bœotia, and the neighboring districts, to the conquered coasts and islands of Asia Minor, already partially occupied by the sons or followers of the victorious chiefs. As the colonists were chiefly of Æolian race, the expedition bears the familiar name of Æolian, and the region occupied that of *Æölis*. About twenty years afterward, the Peloponnesus was overrun by the Dorians (1104 B.C.). This catastrophe was followed, at some interval (1044 B.C.), by a similar settlement of the greater part of the ejected population of the peninsula on the Asiatic coast, to the south of the district possessed by their Æolian kinsmen. Through these convulsions, the ties, social and political, which had previously united the Hellenic nation, were in a great measure dissolved, and the subsequent wider separation of domicile and interests interposed serious obstacles to their renewal.[3]

XXVI. From this period, accordingly, may be dated the more specific distinction of dialects, which becomes so important in the subsequent stages of Greek literary culture. The Hellenic tongue, prior to that distinction, might be divided into two comprehensive varieties; first, the *Ionic*, indigenous in the more civilized states, namely, Attica, the lowlands of the Peloponnesus, and probably other coasts and islands subject to or politically connected with these provinces; and, secondly, the *Æolic*, in the wider sense, embracing the whole remaining body of less cultivated dialects.[4]

XXVII. That the *Ionic* originally comprised secondary forms of dia-

[1] *Malden, Hist. of Rome*, p. 70.

[2] Compare *Niebuhr, Hist of Rome*, vol. i., p. 56, note 162.

[3] *Mure, Crit. Hist.*, vol. i., p. 107. Compare *Thirlwall, Hist. Gr.*, vol. i., p. 282, *seqq.*; *Grote, Hist. Gr.*, vol. ii., p. 434, *seqq.*; *Clinton, Fast. Hell.*, vol. i., p. 107, *seqq.*

[4] *Mure, Crit. Hist.*, vol. i., p. 108.

lect, as the Æolic did, may be inferred from the account given by Herodotus of those prevalent in his own time among the Ionians of Asia. We possess, however, no positive knowledge either from traditional or literary sources, of these particular varieties. The old Epic dialect, or, as it is also called, the old poetical Ionic, which was carried to perfection by Homer, exhibits the efforts of a nation pre-eminently gifted with poetical and musical genius, and as yet neither aided nor shackled by grammatical refinements, to embody its conceptions in the most expressive and harmonious forms. That this branch of the Ionic is, in a great degree, of poetical formation, its own internal evidence betrays. Many of its characteristic features originate in a tendency to adapt the structure of words to the exigencies of hexameter verse, the earliest, and, for a long time, the only measure in which the Greek poets are known to have composed.[1]

XXVIII. Under the name *Æolic* the Greek grammarians included dialects very different from one another, as in later times every thing was comprehended under that term which was not Doric, Ionic, or Attic. According to this acceptation of the name, about three fourths of the Greek nation consisted of Æolians, and dialects were classed together as Æolic, which, as is evident from the more ancient inscriptions, differed more from one another than from the Doric; as, for example, the Thessalian and Ætolian, the Bœotian and Elean dialects. The three most marked and distinguished varieties of the Æolic dialect were the *Lesbian*, the *Thessalian*, and the *Bœotian*;[2] the Thessalian forming a mean between the other two. A modern scholar[3] has shown, in fact, that the ancient grammatical critics are accustomed to affirm peculiarities as belonging to the Æolic dialect generally, which in truth belong only to the Lesbian variety of it, or to the poems of Alcæus and Sappho, which those critics attentively studied. Lesbian Æolic, Thessalian Æolic, and Bœotian Æolic, are all different; and if, abstracting from these differences, we confine our attention to that which is common to all three, we shall find little to distinguish this abstract Æolic from the abstract Doric, or that which is common to the many varieties of the Doric dialect.[4]

XXIX. On the whole, it may be said of the Æolic dialect, that it bears an archaic character, and approaches nearest to the sources of the Greek language. Hence the Latin, as being closely connected with the most ancient Greek, has a strong affinity with it, and, in general, the agreement with the other languages of the Indo-Germanic family is almost always perceptible in Æolic. It is distinguished from the Doric, as already remarked, by trifling differences; chiefly, however, by the so-called Æolic digamma.[5]

XXX. The superiority of the Lesbian Æolic to the other branches of that dialect may be accounted for as follows: The colonists of Lesbos, and of the neighboring Æolian coast, united with the taste for sensual enjoyment, common to their Ionian neighbors, a peculiar fervor and excitability of temperament. There sprung up, accordingly, among them a

[1] *Mure, Crit. Hist.*, vol. i., p. 112.
[2] *Müller, Hist. Gr. Lit.*, p. 9.
[3] *Ahrens, De Dial. Æol.*, § 51.
[4] *Grote, Hist. of Greece*, vol. ii., p. 448.
[5] *Müller, Hist. Gr. Lit.*, p. 10.

school of lyric poetry, pre-eminent above all others in impassioned composition, especially that of the amatory or voluptuous order. The adaptation of their language to such subjects actually involved a refinement of the old rustic features which it retained in the mother country. This was effected with little sacrifice of its native simplicity, partly by softening down its ruder asperities, and partly by an infusion of more liquid forms from the Homeric fountain-head of pure poetical idiom.[1]

XXXI. In Attica, the ancient population, with its pure Ionic idiom, remained undisturbed by any political movements from without. In the Peloponnesus, however, the change of inhabitants, consequent upon the Dorian invasion, was accompanied by a corresponding revolution of dialects. A remnant of the old Achæan population kept its ground on the narrow strip of territory between the Corinthian Gulf and the Cyllenian Mountains; and some other petty tribes of Ionians here and there, submitting to the conquerors, retained their possessions in a state of vassalage. But the language and habits of the subdued race became, in later times, more or less assimilated to those of the dominant states. Elis, on the eastern coast, was assigned to a body of Ætolian adventurers, who had joined the Dorian armament on its passage through their country. As, however, the previous dialect of both Ætolia and Elis was Æolic, no essential change was here produced. The Arcadian mountaineers, moreover, preserved, together with their independence, their proper Æolian tongue, which, itself closely allied to that of their new Dorian neighbors, had not participated in the culture of the expelled tribes.[2] The districts immediately occupied by the Dorians were Argolis, Laconia, and Messenia. In the sequel, however, their conquests, with their language, were gradually extended over Corinthia and Megaris to the Attic frontier, and subsequently, by settlers from Epidaurus, to the neighboring island of Ægina.[3]

XXXII. The peculiarities by which the Doric dialect was distinguished from the other varieties of the Greek language, are to be attributed to the mountain life of the Dorians in their earliest settlements. We always find a tendency to the formation of broad vowel sounds in the language of mountaineers, and this fondness for the α and ω, which letters the Dorians generally used where η and ου were employed in other dialects, and also their aversion to sibilants, is analogous to what we frequently observe in the languages which are spoken by both Highlanders and Lowlanders. The use of the article, also, in the Greek language is attributed to the Dorians, the poetry of Alcman having first introduced it into the literature of Greece, the older language, like the Latin, being entirely without it.[4].

XXXIII. The Doric dialect was rudest among the Spartans, the enemies of all change. It was spoken in the greatest purity by the Messe-

[1] *Mure, Crit. Hist.*, vol. i., p. 116. [2] *Strab.*, p. 333. Compare *Herod.*, viii., 73.

[3] *Mure, Crit. Hist.*, vol. i., p. 110.

[4] *Müller, Dorians*, vol. ii., p. 488; *Penny Cyclop.*, vol. ix., p. 90; *Matthiæ, G. G.*, vol. i., p. 5; *Ahrens, De Dial. Dor.*, p. 395, *seqq.* Müller has given a very full account of the Doric dialect, in *Appendix* viii. to his work on the Dorians (vol. ii., p. 484, *seqq.*), which is well worthy of perusal. But he carries the Doric peculiarities too far, and makes too wide a distinction between Doric and Æolic.

nians. The grammarians notice two epochs in it, according to which they divide it into the old and new Doric dialects. In the old, the comic poet Epicharmus, and Sophron, author of the Mimes, were the principal writers. In the new, which approached nearer the softness of the Ionic, the chief writer is Theocritus. Besides these, the first Pythagorean philosophers wrote in Doric.

XXXIV. The ejected inhabitants of the Peloponnesus first sought refuge among their Ionian kinsmen of Attica. Afterward, however, under the auspices of Athenian leaders, they crossed the Ægean, and occupied the coast of Asia, southward from the Æolian settlements, as far as the headland of Miletus, together with the adjacent islands of Chios and Samos. Here they appear in later times, under the distinctive name of *Ionians*. Their subsequent celebrity under this title, and the still greater celebrity of the metropolitan state of Athens on the opposite continent, caused the appellation of Ionian, in after ages, to be so exclusively restricted to the colonies, that the terms *Athenian* and *Ionian*, or *Attic* and *Ionic*, instead of being identical, as with Homer, were henceforward pointedly distinct. The southwestern extremity of the same Asiatic coast, with the adjacent islands, was afterward occupied, in like manner, by Dorian settlements.[1]

XXXV. During the long separation of interests between the two great bodies of the same Ionian race, consequent on the Dorian revolution, the previous common dialect was subjected in each to other changes, offering an interesting analogy to those in their national character. In the Asiatic colonies many causes conspired, not only to soften the ferocity of the old heroic spirit, but also to diminish the sense of political independence, and to promote effeminate habits. The enervating influence of Oriental luxury, with which they were brought into closer contact, was aided by a seductive climate, increase of commerce and wealth, and by their position in regard to the powerful nations of the interior, whose favor they were under the frequent necessity of courting, and toward whom they latterly stood on the footing of vassal to liege lord. Hence the new or later Ionic became the softest of the dialects, on account of the frequent meeting of vowels, producing a liquidness of sound, and the deficiency of aspirated letters.[2]

XXXVI. On the other hand, among the people of Attica, or the European descendants of the Ionic race, opposite causes produced as opposite effects. In Athens, with a less rapid advance in science or wealth, a complete political independence was accompanied by greater integrity of manners. The importance of that state, as a member of the old national confederacy, was also increased by the rivalry into which she was brought with the new Dorian dynasties. It was under these circumstances, therefore, that the intellectual powers of the Athenians, naturally of the highest order, were called forth; combining acuteness of conception with fertility of invention and purity of taste, they exhibit, during the flourishing ages of the republic, all the proper excellences of the Hellenic genius in the highest perfection. The Attic dialect, accordingly, offers the most ex-

[1] *Mure, l. c.*

[2] *Mure, Hist. Crit.*, vol. i., p. 11.

cellent model of a language for the familiar usage of social life, or the more practical and intellectual branches of letters.[1]

XXXVII. As the varieties of dialect were met by a corresponding variety of taste or talent, certain styles of composition came to be considered the more immediate province of one dialect than of another. The Doric became the favorite language of the higher branches of lyric composition, and of the primitive schools of philosophy; the Æolic of the amatory ode; the old Ionic retained its former privilege in regard to the epic style and hexameter verse; the new Ionic for a long time was the favorite dialect for prose, and especially historical composition, until supplanted by the Attic, which last also was regarded as the model in one particular department of poetry, namely, the dramatic, with the exception, however, of the choruses and lyric portions generally, in which a species of Doric predominates, the most eminent lyric poets having written in the Doric dialect. Most of the great works of antiquity which have been transmitted to our times are written in the Attic dialect.[2]

XXXVIII. Some writers have made two, and some three divisions of the Attic dialect, with reference to extant writers; but the general division of the Attic dialect into *old* and *new* seems to be sufficiently exact. To the former division belong Æschylus, Sophocles, Euripides, Antiphon, Thucydides, &c.; to the latter, Demosthenes, Æschines, and the contemporary orators. The language of Xenophon, Plato, and indeed Aristophanes also, may be considered as possessing a character somewhat intermediate between the two classes, and the name of *middle* Attic may consequently be given to it; but it would be difficult to say exactly how a writer of this middle class is to be distinguished from the writers of the *new* Attic.[3]

XXXIX. After the time of Alexander the Great, when the Greeks were more united as a nation, the superiority of Athenian literature made the language of Athens the common language of those who wrote pure Greek. Aristotle may be regarded as the earliest extant writer, not an Athenian by birth, who adopted the language of Athens. The Attic dialect, then somewhat modified under Macedonian influence and by local circumstances, became the common written language of the educated Greeks. We find, accordingly, under the successors of Alexander, and afterward under the Romans, a series of Greek prose writers, belonging to various countries, but all attempting to write one common language. This common language of the learned Greeks was called the *common* dialect (ἡ κοινὴ, or ἡ Ἑλληνικὴ διάλεκτος), and was marked, of course, by numerous deviations from the pure old Attic standard. Polybius, a native of the Peloponnesus; Strabo, of Asia Minor; Diodorus, of Sicily; and others, belong to the writers who use the common dialect.[4]

XL. Poetry, however, was not written in this common dialect. The peculiarities of the Homeric language were imitated by those who composed in hexameters, as the epic, didactic, and elegiac; and this became

---

[1] *Mure, Hist. Crit.*, vol. i., p. 115.

[2] *Id.*, p. 121; *Buttmann, G. G.*, p. 4, § 110, *Robinson's transl.*

[3] *Penny Cyclop.*, vol. iii., p. 62.

[4] *Ibid*

therefore, just as the Attic for prose, the prevailing dialect or universal language for these forms of poetry, and remained current even in the Alexandrine and later ages, when it was no longer understood by the common people, but a learned education was necessary for the full comprehending and enjoyment of such poems. The most celebrated poets of this class are, in the Alexandrine period, Apollonius, Callimachus, Aratus; and later, Nicander, Oppian, Quintus Smyrnæus,[1] &c.

XLI. In the mean time the Doric dialect was not entirely excluded from poetry, even in the later periods. It maintained itself in some of the minor species, especially in rural and sportive poems; partly because there were even here certain earlier models; and partly, also, because in many of these poems it was essential to imitate the tone and language of the countryman and of the lower classes, whose dialect was almost every where the Doric, in consequence of the very general spread of the Doric tribe. Hence the works of the idyllic writers, Theocritus, Bion, and Moschus, are Doric, though their later Doric differs much from that of Pindar.[2]

XLII. Out of the common language arose what was called the *Alexandrine* dialect, to which partial allusion has already been made. This was the common dialect, interspersed with peculiarities, which the grammarians designate as Macedonian forms, and deriving its name from the city of Alexandrea, the centre of later literary culture. The Septuagint version of the Old Testament was written in this dialect; but it can hardly be considered a fair specimen of the language spoken at Alexandrea, since the Jewish translators have introduced into the version many Hebrew phrases and constructions. The New Testament was written in the same dialect, whence it passed, with some variations, into the writings of the Fathers, and has hence been called *Ecclesiastical* Greek. The Greek spoken at Constantinople subsequently assumed a still more corrupt form, and so many foreign words were introduced into the language that a glossary is necessary for understanding many of the writers of the Eastern empire.[3]

XLIII. No one of the sister tongues can compete with the Greek in regard to sound, or in fertility of composition and flection, in luxuriance of grammatical forms, and in many delicate phases assumed by the primary parts of speech; characteristics reflecting a singular acuteness of the discriminating faculty, and affording in return a rich fund of materials for its exercise. The nearest approach in these respects is made by the Sanscrit. The vowel-sounds of the Sanscrit, however, are comparatively monotonous, occasionally harsh and constrained. Those of the Greek, on the other hand, are distinguished for variety and euphony. In the combination of consonants and vowels, the Greek, also, exhibits the same happy blending of uniformity and versatility, the same just medium between redundancy and poverty, which characterizes all the productions of Hellenic genius.[4]

XLIV. Another remarkable feature, which distinguishes the Greek

---

[1] *Buttmann*, p. 4, § 12; *Mure, Crit. Hist.*, vol. i., p. 126.
[2] *Buttmann, l. c.*; *Mure, l. c.*
[3] *Penny Cyclop.*, vol. ix., p. 428.
[4] *Mure, Crit. Hist.*, vol. i., p. 97, *seqq.*

from all the other European dialects, is the extreme delicacy and subtlety of its metrical and musical development, as shown in the distinction which obtained in familiar pronunciation, between accent and quantity, and in the nicety of the laws by which the two were adjusted in their relation to each other, or to the language at large. In the modern European tongues this distinction is unknown. Accent and quantity, the long syllable and the accentuated syllable, are, in the poetry of the present day, as identical, as they were essentially distinct in that of Greece.[1]

XLV. One more characteristic of the Greek language remains to be mentioned, and to which, also, no parallel can probably be found in any other cultivated language, namely, its anomaly. This feature may be classed under two heads; anomaly of structure, and anomaly of syntax. The former, in particular, is familiar to the classical scholar in the elementary rules of his grammar: that no Greek verb possesses, for example, its full complement of forms derived from the same root; and that many of the verbs in most universal use are dependent, even for certain of their more fundamental forms, on radically distinct sources. Both peculiarities constitute important elements of that richness and variety which form such prominent characteristics of the Greek language.[2]

[1] *Mure, Crit. Hist.*, vol. i., p. 97, *seqq.*

[2] *Id. ib.*

GREEK LITERATURE.

CHAPTER I.

DIVISION OF THE SUBJECT.

I. The literature of Greece may be divided most conveniently into Seven Periods; namely, 1. The *Mythical;* 2. The *Poetical;* 3. The *Early Prosaic*; 4. The *Attic;* 5. The *Alexandrine;* 6. The *Roman;* and, 7. The *Byzantine.*[1]

II. The *First* or *Mythical Period* comprises the origin and early cultivation of the art of poetry, with the legendary notices of those bards and sages to whom popular belief ascribed the first advances in literary culture, but of whose existence or influence no authentic monuments have been preserved.

III. The *Second* or *Poetical Period* extends from the epoch of the earliest authenticated productions of Greek poetical genius, through those ages in which poetry continued to be either the only, or else the most assiduously cultivated branch of composition, and terminates about the period of the Persian war.

IV. The *Third* or *Early Prosaic Period* begins, in fact, before the full termination of the preceding one, with the first attempts at prose composition, and extends to and includes the era of Herodotus.

V. The *Fourth* or *Attic Period* commences with the rise of the Attic drama, and of the fuller culture of prose literature, and closes with the establishment of the Macedonian ascendency, and the consequent extinction of republican freedom in Greece.

VI. The *Fifth* or *Alexandrine Period* may be dated from the foundation of Alexandrea, and ends with the fall of the Græco-Egyptian empire.

VII. The *Sixth* or *Roman Period* succeeds, and extends to the foundation of Constantinople.

VIII. The *Seventh* or *Byzantine Period* comprises the remaining ages of the decay and corruption of ancient civilization, until the final extinction of the classical Greek as a living language.

IX. Some divide the history of Greek literature into *three periods* merely; the *first* extending from the earliest times to the rise of Athenian literature; the *second* comprising the flourishing period of Athenian literature; and the *third* comprehending all the writers from the time of Alexander to the fall of the Eastern empire. This arrangement, however, is open to serious objections, and is by no means equal, in point of precision and clearness, to the one which we have first given, and which will be followed in the present work.

---

[1] *Mure, Crit. Hist.*, vol. i., p. 6. Compare *Bernhardy*, vol. i., p. 148.

CHAPTER II.

FIRST OR MYTHICAL PERIOD.

I. Many centuries[1] must have elapsed before the poetical language of the Greeks could have attained to the splendor, copiousness, and fluency which so strongly excite our admiration in the poems of Homer. The first outpourings of poetical enthusiasm were doubtless songs describing, in few and simple verses, events which powerfully affected the feelings of the hearers.

II. It is probable that the earliest date may be assigned to the songs which referred to the seasons and their phenomena, and expressed with simplicity the notions and feelings to which these events gave birth. They appear to have been sung by peasants at the corn and wine harvests.

III. It is remarkable that songs of this kind often had a plaintive and melancholy character; which circumstance, however, is explained when we remember that the ancient worship of outward nature (which was preserved in the rites of Ceres and Proserpina, and also in those of Bacchus) contained festivals of wailing and lamentation, as well as of rejoicing and mirth.

I. THE LĬNUS.

IV. To the number of these plaintive ditties belongs the song Lĭnus (*Λίνος*), mentioned by Homer,[2] the melancholy character of which is shown by its fuller names, *Αἴλινος*[3] and *Οἰτόλινος*[4] (literally, "Alas! Linus," and "Death of Linus"). It was frequently sung in Greece, according to Homer, at the grape-picking. From a fragment of Hesiod,[5] it would appear probable that the song of lamentation began and ended with the exclamation *Αἶ Λίνε*.

V. Linus was originally the subject of this song, the person whose fate was bewailed in it; and there were many districts in Greece (for example, Thebes, Chalcis, and Argos) in which tombs of Linus were shown.

VI. According to the very remarkable and explicit tradition of the Argives, Linus was a youth who, having sprung from a divine origin, grew up with the shepherds among the lambs, and was torn in pieces by wild dogs. Similar legends are found in other parts of Greece, and also in Asia Minor, wherein boys in the bloom of youth, and of divine parentage, are supposed to have been drowned, or devoured by raging dogs, or destroyed by wild beasts, and whose death is lamented in the harvest, or other periods of the hottest season of the year.[6]

VII. The real object of lamentation, however, both in the Linus and

---

1 *Müller, Hist. Gr. Lit.*, p. 16, *seqq.*

2 *Il.*, xviii., 569, *seqq.*

3 *Æsch.*, *Ag.*, 121; *Soph.*, *Aj.*, 627; *Pausan.*, ix., 29, 8.

4 *Pausan.*, ix., 29, 3.

5 *Ap. Eustath.*, p. 1163 (fragm. 1, ed. *Gaisf.*).

6 *Fabric.*, *Bibl. Græc.*, vol. i., p. 110, *seqq.*, ed. *Harles*

in all these other dirges, was the tender beauty of spring destroyed by the summer heats, and other phenomena of the same kind, which the imagination of these early times invested with a personal form, and represented as being of a divine origin. These popular dirges, therefore, originally the expression of grief at the premature death of nature, through the heat of the sun, were transformed into lamentations for the death of youths, and were sung on certain religious occasions.

VIII. It was a natural confusion of the tradition that Linus should afterward become a minstrel, one of the earliest bards of Greece,[1] who begins a contest with Apollo himself, and overcomes Hercules in playing on the cithara. Even, however, in this character, Linus meets his death, having been killed by Hercules,[2] and we must probably assume that his fate was mentioned in the ancient song.

IX. Plaintive songs of this same kind, in which not the misfortunes of a single individual, but a universal and perpetually recurring cause of grief, was expressed, abounded in ancient Greece, but more particularly in Asia Minor, the inhabitants of which latter country had a peculiar fondness for mournful tunes. The Ialĕmus (Ἰάλεμος)[3] seems to have been nearly identical with the *Linus*, as, to a certain extent, the same mythological narrations are applied to both. At Tegĕa, in Arcadia, there was a plaintive song called Scephrus (Σκέφρος), which appears, from the fabulous relation in Pausanias,[4] to have been sung at the time of the summer heat. In Phrygia, a melancholy song called Lityerses (Λιτυέρσης)[5] was sung at the cutting of the corn. At the same season of the year, the Mariandȳni, on the shores of the Euxine, played the mournful ditty called Bormus (Βῶρμος)[6] on the native flute. Of similar meaning are the cries for the youth Hylas (Ὕλας),[7] swallowed up by the waters of the fountain, which, in the neighboring country of the Bithȳni, re-echoed from mountain to mountain. In the southern parts of Asia Minor we find, in connection with the Syrian worship, a similar lament for Adōnis (Ἄδωνις),[8] and in Egypt a like dirge for Manĕrōs (Μανέρως).

II. PÆANS.

X. A very different class of feelings is expressed in the Pæans (Παιᾶνες: in Homer, Παιήονες). These songs were originally dedicated only to Apollo, and were closely connected with the ideas relating to the attributes and actions of this deity. They were chants, of which the tune and words expressed courage and confidence. "All sounds of lamentation" (αἴλινα), says Callimachus, "cease when the Ie Pæan, Ie Pæan (ἰὴ Παιῆον) is heard."[9] As with the Linus the interjection αἴ, so with the Pæan the cry of ἰή was connected;[10] exclamations, unmeaning in themselves, but made expressive by the tone with which they were uttered.

XI. Pæans were sung, not only when there was a hope of being able,

---

1 *Eudocia*, Ἰωνιά, p. 277. Compare *Diod. Sic.*, iii., c. 66.
2 *Diod. Sic.*, *l. c.*; *Fabric.*, *l. c.*
3 *Æsch.*, *Supp.*, 116; *Eurip.*, *Phœn.*, 1034.
4 *Pausan.*, viii., 53, 2.
5 *Ilgen*, *Scol. Gr.*, p. xvi., *seq.*
6 *Athen.*, xv., p. 620, A.
7 *Ap. Rhod.*, i., 131, 1350.
8 *Apollod.*, iii., 14.
9 *Hymn. ad Apoll.*, 20.
10 *Athen.*, xv., p. 696, E, *seqq.*

by the help of the gods, to overcome a great and imminent danger, but when the danger was happily past; they were songs of hope and confidence, as well as of thanksgiving for victory and safety. The custom at the termination of the winter, when the year again assumes a mild and serene aspect, and every heart is filled with hope and confidence, of singing *vernal pæans* (εἰαρινοὶ παιᾶνες), recommended by the Delphic oracle to the cities of Lower Italy, is probably of very high antiquity.

XII. The Pæan was sung by several persons, one of whom probably led the others, and the singers either marched onward or sat together at table. Thus Achilles, after the death of Hector, calls upon his companions to return to the ships, singing a pæan on account of the glory they had gained;[1] and the Achæans, after restoring Chryseis to her father, are represented as singing a pæan to Apollo at the end of the sacrificial feast, in order to appease his wrath.[2]

XIII. The Pæan was also sung, in a later age, as a battle song, both before an attack on the enemy and after the battle was finished.[3] This practice seems to have prevailed chiefly among the Dorians, but it was also common among the other Greek states. The origin of it is said to have arisen from the fact that Apollo sang a pæan after his victory over the Pythian serpent. It must be remarked, however, that the Pæan was, in later times, sung to the honor of other gods besides Apollo. Thus Xenophon relates that the Lacedæmonians on one occasion sang a pæan to Neptune, to propitiate him after an earthquake,[4] and also that the Greek forces in Asia, under the younger Cyrus, sang a pæan to Jove.[5]

III. THE THRĒNUS AND HYMENÆUS.

XIV. Not only the common and public worship of the gods, but also those events of private life which strongly excited the feelings, called forth the gift of poetry. The lamentation for the dead, which was chiefly sung by women, with vehement expressions of grief, had, at the time described by Homer, already been so far systematized, that singers by profession stood near the bed where the body was laid out, and began the lament; and while they sang it, the women accompanied them with cries and groans.[6] This lament was called the THRĒNUS (Θρῆνος) or "*Dirge.*"

XV. Opposed to the Threnus is the HYMENÆUS (Ὑμέναιος), the joyful and merry bridal song, of which there are descriptions by Homer[7] in the account of the designs on the shield of Achilles, and by Hesiod in that of the shield of Hercules.[8] Homer speaks of a city, represented as the seat of bridal rejoicing, in which the bride is led from the virgin's apartment through the streets by the light of torches. A loud *hymenæus* arises: young men dance around, while flutes and harps (φόρμιγγες) resound.

---

1 *Il.*, xxiii., 391.
2 *Ib.*, i., 473.
3 *Thucyd.*, i., 50; iv., 43; ii., 91; vii., 44; *Xen.*, *Anab.*, i., 8, 17.
4 *Xen.*, *Hell.*, iv., 7, 4.
5 *Id.*, *Anab.*, iii., 2, 9.
6 *Il.*, xxiv., 720, *seqq.*
7 *Ib.*, xviii., 492, *seqq.*
8 *Scut.*, 274, *seqq.*

IV. EARLY BARDS.[1]

XVI. After this brief sketch of the kinds of poetry which existed in Greece before the Homeric era, with the exception of the epic, we will now proceed to give some account of the early composers of sacred songs and hymns, as far as any reliable information can be obtained respecting them from the confused mass of statements contained in later writers. The best accounts of these early bards were those which had been preserved in the temples, at the places where hymns were sung under their names. Hence it appears that most of these names are in constant connection with the worship of peculiar deities; and it will thus be easy to distribute them into certain classes, formed by the resemblance of their character and their reference to the same worship.

(A.) SINGERS BELONGING TO THE WORSHIP OF APOLLO IN DELPHI, DELOS, AND CRETE.

XVII. Among these, one of the most conspicuous is OLEN (Ὠλήν). According to the ancient legend,[2] he was a Lycian or Hyperborean, that is to say, sprung from a country where Apollo loved to dwell. Many ancient hymns, attributed to him, were preserved at Delos, which are mentioned by Herodotus,[3] and which contained remarkable mythological traditions, and significant appellatives of the gods; also *nomes* (νόμοι), that is, simple and antique songs, combined with certain fixed tunes, and fitted to be sung for the circular dance of a chorus. The Delphian poetess Bœo called him the first prophet of Phœbus, and the first who, in early times, founded the style of singing in epic metre (ἐπέων ἀοιδά).[4] His name, according to Welcker, signifies simply the *flute-player*.[5] Of the ancient hymns which went under his name, Pausanias mentions those to Juno, to Achæïa, and to Ilithyia. The last of these was in celebration of the birth of Apollo and Diana.

XVIII. Another of these bards is PHILAMMON (Φιλάμμων), said to have been a son of Apollo,[6] and who became, by the nymph Argiope, who dwelt on Parnassus, the father of Thamyris and Eumolpus.[7] He is closely associated with the worship of Apollo at Delphi, and with the music of the cithara. To him also was referred the formation of the Delphian choruses of virgins, which sang the birth of Latona, and that of her children, Apollo and Diana; and some ascribe to him the invention of choral music in general. According to Pherecydes,[8] it was Philammon, and not Orpheus, who accompanied the Argonauts.

XIX. Another bard of this class was a Cretan, named CHRYSOTHĔMIS (Χρυσόθεμις), who is said to have sung the first chorus to the Pythian

---

1 *Müller, Hist. Gr. Lit.*, p. 24, *seqq.*
2 *Suid.*, *s. v.*; *Fabr.*, *Bibl. Gr.*, vol. i., p. 134, ed. *Harles.*
3 *Herod.*, iv., 35. Compare *Pausan.*, i., 18, 5; ii., 13, 3; v., 7, 8, &c.
4 *Pausan.*, x., 5, 8.
5 *Welcker, Europa und Kadmos*, p. 35.
6 *Tatian. adv. Græc.*, 62, *seq.* Compare *Ovid*, *Met.*, xi., 317.
7 *Apollod.*, i., 3, 3; *Pausan.*, iv., 33, 3.
8 *Ap. Schol. ad Apoll. Rhod.*, i., 23. Compare *Fabric.*, *Bibl. Gr.*, vol. i., p. 214.

Apollo, clothed in the solemn dress of ceremony, which the citharœdi, in later times, wore at the Pythian games.[1]

(B.) SINGERS IN CONNECTION WITH THE COGNATE WORSHIPS OF CERES AND BACCHUS.

XX. Among these were the EUMOLPĬDÆ (Εὐμολπίδαι), of Eleusis in Attica, a race which, from early times, took part in the worship of Ceres, and, in the historical age, exercised the chief sacerdotal function connected with it, namely, the office of Hierophant.[2] These Eumolpidæ evidently derived their name, which means "beautiful singers," from their character (εὖ μέλπεσθαι), and their original employment was the singing of sacred hymns. Popular tradition, however, made them to be the descendants of a Thracian named EUMOLPUS (Εὔμολπος), who is described as having come to Attica either as a bard, a warrior, or a priest of Ceres and Bacchus. As Eumolpus is evidently a mythic personage, the various legends respecting his origin and history need not be given here. It will be sufficient to state that he was regarded as an ancient priestly bard, and that poems and writings on the mysteries were fabricated and circulated at a later period under his name. One hexameter line of a Dionysiac hymn, ascribed to him, is preserved in Diodorus.[3] The legends connected him, also, with Hercules, whom he is said to have instructed in music, or initiated into the mysteries.[4]

XXI. Another Attic house, the LYCOMĬDÆ (Λυκομίδαι), which likewise had, in later times, a part in the Eleusinian worship of Ceres, were in the habit of singing hymns, and, moreover, hymns ascribed to Orpheus, Musæus, and Pamphos.

XXII. Of the songs which were attributed to PAMPHŌS (Πάμφως[5]), we may form a general idea by remembering that he is said to have first sung the strain of lamentation at the tomb of Linus.[6] Besides this Linus-song, he is said to have composed hymns to Ceres, Diana, Neptune, Jove, and Eros. Pausanias places him later than Olen, and much earlier than Homer.[7] Philostratus[8] has preserved for us two remarkable verses ascribed to this bard, which remind us forcibly of the symbol (the *scarabæus*) under which the Egyptians represented the Creator of the universe, or the author of animal life.

Ζεῦ κύδιστε, μέγιστε θεῶν, εἰλυμένε κόπρῳ
μηλείῃ τε καὶ ἱππείῃ καὶ ἡμιονείῃ.

"O Jove, most glorious, most mighty of the gods, enveloped in the dung of sheep, and horses, and mules."

XXIII. The name of MUSÆUS (Μουσαῖος), which, in fact, only signified a singer inspired by the Muses, is in Attica generally connected with songs for the initiations of Ceres, and the legend represented him as pre-

1 *Pausan.*, x., 7, 2.

2 *Hesych.*, *s. v.* Εὐμολπίδαι; *Tac.*, *Hist.*, iv., 82; *Arnob.*, v., 25; *Clemens Alex.*, *Protrept.*, p. 16, *seqq.*

3 *Diod. Sic.*, i., 11. Compare *Suid.*, *s. v.* Εὔμολπος.

4 *Hygin.*, *Fab.*, 273; *Theocrit.*, xxiv., 108; *Apollod.*, ii., 5, 12.

5 Often incorrectly written Πάμφος.

6 *Pausan.*, ix., 29, 3. Compare *Bernhardy*, *Grundriss der Griech. Lit.*, vol. i., p. 248.

7 *Pausan.*, *l. c.*

8 *Heroic.*, p. 693. Compare *Bernhardy*, *l. c.*

siding over her rites in the time of Hercules.[1] Among the numerous works ascribed to him, a hymn to Ceres is alone considered by Pausanias as genuine.[2] Musæus, in tradition, is commonly called a Thracian. He is also reckoned as one of the race of Eumolpidæ, and stated to be the disciple of Orpheus.[3] Pausanias mentions a tradition that the Μουσεῖον in the Piræeus bore that name from having been the place where Musæus was buried.[4]

We find the following poetical compositions accounted as his among the ancients:[5] 1. Χρησμοί, *Oracles*.[6] Onomacritus, in the time of the Pisistratidæ, made it his business to collect and arrange the oracles that passed under the name of Musæus, and was banished by Hipparchus for interpolating in the collection oracles of his own making.[7] 2. Ὑποθῆκαι, or *Precepts*, addressed to his son Eumolpus, and extending to the length of 4000 lines.[8] 3. A hymn to Ceres, mentioned above as, according to Pausanias,[9] the only genuine production of Musæus extant in his day. 4. Ἐξακέσεις νόσων.[10] 5. Θεογονία.[11] 6. Τιτανογραφία.[12] 7. Σφαῖρα.[13] What this was is not clear. 8. Παραλύσεις, Τελεταί, and Καθαρμοί.[14] Aristotle quotes some verses of Musæus, but without specifying from what work or collection.[15] The poem on the loves of Hero and Leander is by a very much later author of the same name. Nothing remains of the poems attributed to Musæus but the few quotations in Pausanias, Plato, Clemens Alexandrinus, Philostratus, and Aristotle.[16]

XXIV. The Thracian singer Orpheus (Ὀρφεύς) is unquestionably the darkest point in the entire history of the early Greek poetry, on account of the scantiness of the information respecting him which has been preserved in the more ancient writers. This deficiency is ill supplied by the multitude of marvellous stories concerning him which occur in later writers, and by the poems and poetical fragments which are extant under his name.

The name of Orpheus does not occur in the Homeric or Hesiodic poems, but during the lyric period it had attained to great celebrity. Ibycus, who flourished about the middle of the sixth century B.C., mentions him as "the renowned Orpheus" (ὀνομακλυτὸν Ὄρφην).[17] Pindar enumerates him among the Argonauts as the celebrated harp-player, father of songs, and as sent forth by Apollo.[18] In the dramatic poets, also, there are several references to Orpheus.

Many poems ascribed to Orpheus were current as early as the time of the Pisistratidæ, and they are, moreover, often quoted by Plato. The allusions in them to later writers are very frequent; for example, Pau-

1 *Diod. Sic.*, iv., 25.
2 *Pausan.*, i., 22, 7. Compare iv., 1, 5.
3 *Diod.*, *l. c.*; *Serv.*, *ad Virg. Æn.*, vi., 667.
4 *Pausan.*, i., 25, 8.
5 *Fabric.*, *Bibl. Gr.*, vol. i., p. 120, *seqq.*
6 *Aristoph.*, *Ran.*, 1031; *Paus.*, x., 9, 11; *Herod.*, viii., 96.
7 *Herod.*, vii., 6; *Pausan.*, i., 22, 7.
8 *Suid.*, *s. v.* Μουσαῖος.
9 *Pausan.*, i., 22, 7.
10 *Aristoph.*, *Ran.*, 1031; *Plin.*, *H. N.*, xxi., 8, 21.
11 *Diog. Laert.*, *Proœm.*, 3.
12 *Schol. ad Apol. Rhod.*, iii., 1200; *Eudocia*, Ἰωνιά, p. 248
13 *Diog. Laert.*, *l. c.*
14 *Schol. ad Aristoph.*, *l. c.*; *Plat.*, *De Repub.*, ii., p. 364, *extr.*
15 *Aristot.*, *Polit.*, viii., 5; *Hist. An.*, vi., 6.
16 *Fabric.*, *Bibl. Gr.*, *l. c.*
17 *Ap. Prisc.*, vi., 18, 92, vol. i., p. 283, ed. *Krehl* (fragm. 22, ed. *Schneidewin*).
18 *Pind.*, *Pyth.*, iv., 315.

sanias speaks of hymns of his which he believed to be still preserved by the Lycomidæ, of whom we have already made mention, and which hymns, he says, were only inferior in beauty to the poems of Homer, and held even in higher honor, on account of their divine subjects. He also speaks of them as very few in number, and distinguished by great brevity of style.[1]

Considering the slight acquaintance which the ancients evidently possessed with these works, it is somewhat surprising that certain extant poems which bear the name of Orpheus should have been generally regarded by scholars, until a very recent period, as genuine, that is, as works more ancient than the Homeric poems, if not the productions of Orpheus himself. It is now, however, fully established that the bulk of these poems are the forgeries of Christian grammarians and philosophers of the Alexandrean school; but still that among the fragments, which form a part of the collection, are some genuine remains of that Orphic poetry which was known to Plato, and which must be assigned to the period of Onomacritus, or perhaps a little earlier. The Orphic literature, which, in this sense, we may call genuine, seems to have included *Hymns*, a *Theogony*, an ancient poem called *Minyas*, or the *Descent into Hades*, *Oracles*, and *Songs for Initiations* (Τελεταί), a collection of *Sacred Legends* (Ἱεροὶ λόγοι), ascribed to Cercops, and perhaps some other works.[2]

The apocryphal productions which have come down to us under the name of *Orphica* (Ὀρφικά), are the following:[3] 1. Ἀργοναυτικά, an epic poem in 1384 hexameters, giving an account of the expedition of the Argonauts. It is full of indications of its late date. 2. Ὕμνοι, eighty-seven or eighty-eight hymns in hexameters, evidently the productions of the Neo-Platonic school. 3. Λιθικά, the best of the three apocryphal Orphic poems, which treats of the properties of stones both precious and common, and their uses in divination. 4. Fragments, chiefly of the *Theogony*. It is in this class that we find the genuine remains, above referred to, of the literature of the early Orphic theology, but intermingled with others of a much later date.[4]

The chief editions of Orpheus, after the early ones of 1517, 1519, 1540, 1543, 1566, and 1606, are those of Eschenbach, Traj. ad Rhen., 1689, 12mo; Gesner and Hamberger, Lips., 1764, 8vo; and Hermann, Lips., 1805, 8vo, by far the best.

The genuine fragments are collected by Lobeck in his Aglaophamus, vol. i., p. 410, *seqq.*, Regimont., 1829.

(C.) SINGERS AND MUSICIANS, WHO BELONGED TO THE PHRYGIAN WORSHIP OF THE GREAT MOTHER OF THE GODS, OF THE CORYBANTES, ETC.[5]

XXV. The Phrygians, allied indeed to the Greeks, yet a separate and distinct nation, differed from their neighbors in their strong disposition to an orgiastic worship, that is, a worship which was connected with a tumult and excitement produced by loud music and violent bodily movements, such as occurred in Greece at the Bacchanalian rejoicings; where,

---

[1] *Pausan.*, ix., 30, 5.

[2] *Smith's Dict. Biogr.*, *s. v.*

[3] *Fabric.*, *Bibl. Gr.*, vol. i., p. 148, *seqq.*

[4] *Smith's Dict. Biogr.*, *s. v.* Compare *Bernhardy*, *Grundriss d. Griech. Litt.*, vol. ii., p. 266, *seqq.*

[5] *Müller*, *Hist. Gr. Lit.*, p. 26.

however, it never, as in Phrygia, gave its character to every variety of divine worship. With this worship was connected the development of a peculiar kind of music, especially of the flute, which instrument was always considered in Greece to possess a stimulating and passion-stirring force. This, in the Phrygian tradition, was ascribed to the demi-god MARSYAS,[1] who is known as the inventor of the flute, and the unsuccessful opponent of Apollo, to his disciple OLYMPUS,[2] and, lastly, to HYAGNIS,[3] to whom also the composition of nomes addressed to the Phrygian deities in a native melody was attributed.

V. ANCIENT THRACIAN MINSTRELS.[4]

XXVI. By far the most remarkable circumstance in these accounts of the earliest minstrels of Greece is that several of them, especially from the second of the three classes just described, are called THRACIANS. It is utterly inconceivable that, in the later historic times, when the Thracians were contemned as a barbarian race, a notion should have sprung up that the first civilization of Greece was due to them; consequently, we can not doubt that this was a tradition handed down from a very early period. Now, if we are to understand it to mean that Eumolpus, Orpheus, Musæus, and others, were the fellow-countrymen of those Edonians, Odrysians, and Odomantians, who, in the historical age, occupied the Thracian territory, and who spoke a barbarian language, that is, one unintelligible to the Greeks, we must despair of being able to comprehend these accounts of the ancient Thracian minstrels, and of assigning them a place in the history of Greek civilization.

XXVII. When we come, however, to trace more precisely the country of these Thracian bards, we find that the traditions refer to *Pieria*, a district to the east of the range of Olympus, to the north of Thessaly, and the south of Emathia or Macedonia. In other words, they refer to a narrow slip of country, on the southeastern coast of Macedonia, extending from the mouth of the Penēus to the Haliacmon, and bounded on the west by Mount Olympus and its offshoots. In Pieria, likewise, was Libethra, where the Muses are said to have sung the lament over the tomb of Orpheus. The ancient poets, moreover, always make Pieria, not Thrace, the native place of the Muses, which last Homer clearly distinguishes from Pieria. It was not until the Pierians were pressed in their own country by the early Macedonian princes that some of them crossed the Strymon into Thrace Proper, where Herodotus mentions the castles of the Pierians at the time of the expedition of Xerxes.[5]

XXVIII. It is, however, quite conceivable that, in early times, either on account of their close vicinity, or because all the north was comprehended under one name, the Pierians might, in Southern Greece, have been called Thracians. These Pierians, from the intellectual relations which they maintained with the Greeks, appear to have been a Grecian

---

1 *Apollod.*, i., 4, 2; *Diod.*, iii., 58, 59.

2 *Suid.*, *s. v.* Ὄλυμπος.

3 *Plut.*, 2, p. 1132, F.; *Anthol. Pal.*, 9, 266.

4 *Müller*, *l. c.*

5 *Herod.*, vii., 112.

race; which supposition is also confirmed by the Greek names of their places, rivers, fountains, &c., although it is probable that, situated on the limits of the Greek nation, they may have borrowed largely from the neighboring tribes.[1]

XXIX. These same Thracians or Pierians lived, up to the time of the Doric and Æolic migrations, in certain districts of Bœotia and Phocis. That they had dwelt about the Bœotian mountain of *Helicon*, in the district of Thespiæ and Ascra, was evident to the ancient historians, as well from the traditions of the cities as from the agreement of many names of places in the country near Olympus, such as *Libethrion*, *Pimplēïs*, *Helicon*, &c. At the foot of Parnassus, moreover, in Phocis, was said to have been situated the city of *Daulis*, the seat of the Thracian king *Tereus*, who is known by his connection with the Athenian king Pandion, and by the fable of the metamorphosis of his wife Procne into a nightingale. From what has been said, then, it appears sufficiently clear that these Pierians or Thracians, dwelling about Helicon and Parnassus, in the vicinity of Attica, are chiefly signified when a Thracian origin is ascribed to the mythical bards of Attica.

XXX. With these movements of the Pierians was also connected the extension of the temples of the MUSES in Greece, who alone among the gods are represented by the ancient poets as presiding over poetry, since Apollo, in strictness, is only concerned with the music of the cithara. Homer calls the Muses the *Olympian;* in Hesiod, at the beginning of the Theogony, they are called the *Heliconian*, although, according to the notion of the Bœotian poet, they were born at Olympus, and dwelt at a short distance from the highest pinnacle of this mountain, where Jove was enthroned; whence they only go at times to Helicon, bathe in the Hippocrēnē, and celebrate their choral dances around the altar of Jove, on the top of the mountain. Now, when it is borne in mind that the same mountain on which the worship of the Muses originally flourished was also represented in the earliest Greek poetry as the common abode of the gods, it seems highly probable that it was the poets of this region, the ancient Pierian minstrels, whose imagination had created this council of the gods, and had distributed and arranged its parts.

XXXI. The poetry of these Pierian minstrels, moreover, was doubtless not concerned merely with the gods, but contained the first germs of the *Epic* or *Heroic* style. More especially should Thamyris, who in Homer is called a Thracian,[2] and in other writers a son of Philammon[3] (by which the neighborhood of Daulis is designated as his abode), be considered as an Epic poet, although some hymns were ascribed to him; for in the account of Homer, that Thamyris, while going from one prince to another, and having just returned from Eurytus of Œchalia, was deprived of both his eyesight and his power of singing and playing on the cithara by the Muses, with whom he had undertaken to contend,[4] it is much more natural to understand a poet, such as Phemius and Demodocus, who entertained kings and nobles at meals by the narration of heroic adventures,

[1] *Müller*, *Dorians*, vol. i., p. 472, 488, 501.
[2] *Il.*, ii., 594, *seqq.*
[3] *Apollod.*, i., 3, 3; *Pausan.*, iv., 33, 4; x., 7, 2.
[4] *Il.*, ii., 594, *seqq.*

than a singer devoted to the pious service of the gods and the celebration of their praises in hymns.

These remarks lead naturally to the consideration of the Epic style of poetry, or, in other words, to the *second division* of our subject, namely, the *Poetical Period.*

CHAPTER III.

SECOND OR POETICAL PERIOD.

INTRODUCTORY REMARKS.[1]

I. The *Second* or *Poetical Period* of Grecian literature extends, as we have already remarked, from the period of the earliest authenticated productions of poetical genius, or, in other words, from Homer and the Homeric poems, down to about the period of the Persian war.

II. The whole poetical literature of Greece was familiarly classed by the native critics under three comprehensive heads: *Epic, Lyric,* and *Dramatic.* The compositions of this period, however, fall strictly under the two former alone; the Drama being yet so completely in its infancy as not to supply materials for a separate subdivision.

III. The term *Epic,* in its literal acceptation, denotes what is narrated or recited; *Lyric,* what is sung to the lyre. This, however, like some other similar distinctions, invented at a later stage of the arts to which they apply, will be found defective in regard to the origin or more flourishing epochs of those arts Epic poems were, during the earlier and better days of Greek heroic minstrelsy, chanted to an instrumental accompaniment little less habitually than lyric odes. The epithet lyric, therefore, might, in so far, appear as applicable to the Iliad and Odyssey as to a song of Sappho's or an elegy of Mimnermus's. The distinction, however, is justified, even in its extension to this early period, by the more artificial nature of the accompaniment, and the more vital connection between the music and the words, in the case of the lyric than in that of the epic poems. The nice distinction of terms may have originated about the period when lyric composition first acquired importance as a branch of cultivated literature; epic poetry being then on the decline, and the practice of its musical recital gradually falling into disuse.

IV. But although, in point of origin, these two branches of composition may be classed as coeval, yet the Epic invariably enjoys a priority of cultivation wherever the progress of letters, as in Greece, is spontaneous and free from secondary influence. This is a consequence of the more direct medium through which it appeals to the sympathies; the mass of mankind, in all ages, being more interested in the study of facts than of opinions, in listening to accounts of great or marvellous adventures than to commentaries on the admiration of which they may be deserving.

---

1 *Mure, Crit. Hist.,* vol. i., p. 168, *seqq.*

V. The difference of the mode, too, in which the epic and lyric styles are embodied, corresponds to that of their characters. In the epic, an exclusive preference is given to prolonged metrical forms in harmony with the continuity of the narrative. The lyric, on the other hand, offers a greater subdivision and a more varied combination of numbers, adapted to its more lively and versatile expression of thought or feeling.[1]

VI. Under these two general heads of Epic and Lyric have been here comprised various works but partially marked by the proper features on which the distinction just drawn depends, and which might, therefore, appear, in a more accurate classification, to require a separate allotment. To the Epic head, for example, have been referred the "Works and Days" of Hesiod, and the so-called Homeric Hymns. The former poem, in a more artificial age of literature, would be assigned to the Didactic rather than the Epic style. At the period, however, in which this distinction of terms takes its origin, and, indeed, more or less, throughout the flourishing ages of Grecian art, the phrase Epic familiarly denotes any descriptive or narrative work, any thing told or recited, as distinct from what is sung or dramatically represented. The Homeric Hymns, on the other hand, might seem, both in right of their title and their subject, to belong to the Lyric order. The epic character, however, in the narrower sense, really predominates in them to such an extent as to warrant the arrangement here adopted.

VII. From deference to a parallel law of custom, various works have been embraced in the Lyric division of the subject which, on a more subtle principle of distinction, might appear to belong more properly to the Epic. The Elegiac measure, for example, though, in its origin and early use, familiarly ranked as lyric, was frequently employed in narrative or didactic poems of considerable compass. It may, indeed, be considered as an intermediate stage between the one style and the other, being compounded of purely dactylic elements, with such modification as was requisite to adapt the old heroic hexameter to compositions of a more fugitive nature. The Iambic trimeter, on the other hand, appropriated, during its earlier stages of cultivation, to the same class of poems as the elegy, and, like it, comprehended under the general head of lyric poetry, possesses epic qualities only inferior to the hexameter.[2]

VIII. Upon the above general data, therefore, the whole poetic Greek literature of this period may be classed as follows:

First. *Epic Composition*, comprising, in addition to heroic poems properly so called, every work in hexameter verse possessing reasonable claims to date prior to the period of the Persian war.

Second. *Lyric Composition*, comprising every poetical work not embodied in hexameter verse, and, by consequence, the whole elegiac and iambic, in addition to the melic and choral poetry of the period.

Each class will be made the subject of a separate treatment.

[1] *Mure, Crit. Hist.*, vol. i., p. 172.

[2] *Id. ib.*, vol. i., p. 174.

CHAPTER IV.

SECOND OR POETICAL PERIOD—*continued.*

HOMER.

I. PERSONAL HISTORY OF HOMER.[1]

I. The various dates assigned to Homer's age offer no less a diversity than 500 years, namely, from B.C. 1184 to B.C. 684. Crates and Eratosthenes state that he lived within the first century after the Trojan war; Aristotle and Aristarchus make him a contemporary of the Ionian migration, 140 years after the war; the chronologist Apollodorus gives the year 240, Porphyrius 275, the Parian Marble 277, Herodotus 400 after that event; and Theopompus even makes him a contemporary of Gyges, king of Lydia.[2] It seems most probable that the events he celebrated took place at a considerable distance from his time, because, as observed by Velleius Paterculus, he represents men in his age as far inferior in strength to the heroes whom he celebrates.

II. The place of Homer's birth was the subject of great controversy, even among the Greeks. Seven cities are enumerated as contending for this honor in the following distich:

ἑπτὰ πόλεις μάρναντο σοφὴν διὰ ῥίζαν Ὁμήρου,
Σμύρνα, Χίος, Κολοφών, Ἰθάκη, Πύλος, Ἄργος, Ἀθῆναι.

But, in fact, there were more than seven cities which claimed Homer for their countryman; for if we number all those that we find mentioned in different passages of ancient writers, we have seventeen or nineteen mentioned as his birth-place. The claims, however, of most of them are so suspicious and feeble, that they easily vanish before a closer examination.

III. *Athens*, for instance, alleged that she was the metropolis or parent city of Smyrna, and had, therefore, a right to number Homer among her citizens;[3] and the opinion of Aristarchus, the Alexandrine critic, which admitted her claim, was probably qualified with the same explanation. Even *Chios* can not establish its right to be considered as the original source of the Homeric poetry, although the claims of this island are supported by the high authority of Simonides. It is true that in Chios lived the race of the *Homeridæ*. These, however, were not a family, but merely a society of persons who followed the same art, and therefore worshipped the same gods, and who placed at their head a bard-hero, from whom they derived their name. A member of this body of Homeridæ was probably the "blind poet," who, in the Homeric Hymn to Apollo, relates of himself that he dwelt on the rocky Chios, and whom even Thucydides erroneously took for Homer himself.

---

[1] *Ihne* (*Smith's Dict. Biogr.*, *s. v. Homerus*), p. 500. Compare *Grote*, *Hist. Gr.*, vol. ii., p. 175, *seq.*

[2] *Nitzsch*, *Melet. de Histor. Hom.*, fasc. ii., p. 2; *De Hist. Hom.*, p. 78.

[3] *Bekker*, *Anecd. Gr.*, vol. ii., p. 768.

IV. The best claim seems to have been advanced by Smyrna, and the opinion that Homer was a Smyrnæan appears to have been the prevalent one in the flourishing times of Greece. It is also adopted by the generality of modern scholars.[1]

V. Smyrna was founded by an Ionian colony from Ephesus, or from an Ephesian village called Smyrna. These Ionians were followed, and afterward expelled, by Æolians from Cyme. The expelled Ionians fled to Colophon, and Smyrna thus became Æolic. Subsequently, however, the Colophonians drove out the Æolians from Smyrna, which from henceforth was a purely Ionic city. Now the Æolians were originally in possession of the traditions of the Trojan war, which *their* ancestors had waged, and in which no Ionians had taken part.[2] It has been supposed, therefore, and with no small degree of probability, that Homer, himself an Ionian, and belonging to one of the families which went from Ephesus to Smyrna, received these traditions from the Æolian colonists who came to Smyrna after the Ionians had settled there, and who subsequently, as above remarked, expelled them from that city; and hence, too, perhaps we may explain the peculiarities of the Homeric dialect, which is different from the pure Ionic, and contains a large mixture of Æolic elements.

VI. According to this view of the subject, the time of Homer would fall a few generations after the Ionic migration to Asia; and with this the best testimonies of antiquity agree.

VII. The parentage also of Homer is involved in doubt. According to the writer of the Life of Homer, falsely attributed to Herodotus,[3] the name of the poet's mother was Crithēïs, and he was born on the banks of the Meles, near Smyrna, from which circumstance his parent gave him the name of *Melesigenes* (Μελησιγενής). The bard, according to this same authority, was of illegitimate origin. These and various other particulars that are related of him by the writer of the life in question are equally unworthy of belief. Thus, for instance, we are informed that Critheïs subsequently married Phemius, a schoolmaster of Smyrna, and that, on the death of his step-father, Homer succeeded him in his school, and became celebrated for his wisdom. He subsequently travelled in many countries, and in the course of his wanderings became afflicted with total blindness. Finally, he settled at Chios, where he acquired great wealth by reciting his poems. He died at the island of Ios, while on a voyage to Athens.

VIII. Whatever credit, however, we may refuse to these details, it certainly would appear from the Iliad and Odyssey that Homer had actually travelled much, and that in the course of his travels he had visited and accurately observed all the principal places in Greece.

IX. As to the blindness of Homer, no one need extend to this part of

---

1 *Welcker*, Episch. *Cyclus*, vol. i., p. 153; *Müller*, *Hist. Gr. Lit.*, p. 41, *seqq.*

2 *Müller*, *Æginet.*, p. 25; *Orchom.*, p. 367.

3 There are many lives of Homer, all of which, whatever truth is mixed up with them, derive their materials from early legendary history. Two of these are attributed to Plutarch. The one ascribed to Herodotus, however, is by far the most circumstantial.

the story a moment's credence. The character of his compositions, as has been correctly remarked, seems rather to suppose him all eye than destitute of sight; and if they were even framed during his blindness, they form a glorious proof of the vivid power of the imagination, more than supplying the want of the bodily organs, and not merely throwing a variety of its own tints over the objects of nature, but presenting them to the mind in a clearer light than could be shed over them by one whose powers of immediate vision were perfectly free from blemish.[1]

X. The *name of Homer* (Ὅμηρος) is supposed by many not to have been the poet's original appellation, but to have been given to him to denote some quality of his mind or incident of his life. Etymology has, therefore, been employed to develop its meaning, in the hope that some light might thus be thrown upon his history. In the life falsely ascribed to Herodotus, he is said to have been called Homer (Ὅμηρος) from his blindness, the term ὅμηρος, in the Cumæan dialect, being equivalent to the Attic τυφλός. According to others, he was so named from ὅμηρος, "a hostage," having been delivered in that character in a war between Smyrna and Chios. The derivation which favors the theory of Wolf (to which we shall presently refer) is from ὁμοῦ, "together," and ἄρω, "to fit." This etymology proceeds on the assumption that such a poet as Homer never had any real existence, but that the Iliad and Odyssey are merely collections of rhapsodies or lays by different bards, united into two large poems.

II. PRODUCTIONS OF HOMER.[2]

XI. This Homer, then (of the circumstances of whose life we know so little), was the one who gave epic poetry its first great impulse. Before his time, in general, only single actions and adventures were celebrated in short lays, such as, in later times, were produced by several poets of the school of Hesiod. Occasionally, if it was desired, a longer series of adventures of the same hero was formed from these, but they always remained a collection of independent poems on the same subject, and never attained to that unity of character and composition which constitutes one poem. It was an entirely *new* phenomenon, therefore, which could not fail to make the greatest impression, when a Homer selected a subject of the heroic tradition, which had in itself the means of awakening a lively interest, and of satisfying the mind; and which, at the same time, admitted of such a development that the principal personages could be represented as acting each with a peculiar and individual character, without obscuring the chief hero and the main action of the poem.

XII. One legendary subject of this extent and interest Homer found in the *anger of Achilles*, and another in the *return of Ulysses*; the first producing the ILIAD, and the second the ODYSSEY.

ILIAD.—SKETCH OF THE POEM.[3]

XIII. The *Iliad* (Ἰλιάς, *scil.* ποίησις), or Poem of Troy, consists of 24

---

[1] *Talfourd, Early Greek Poetry*, p. 36.
[2] *Müller, Hist. Gr. Lit.*, p. 47, *seqq.*
[3] *Mure, Crit. Hist.*, vol. i., p. 268, *seqq.*

books, and contains, strictly speaking, a simple episode of the Trojan war. The poet sings of the events which took place during the compass of fifty-one days, from the quarrel between Agamemnon and Achilles to the obsequies of Hector.

XIV. From the notices interspersed throughout the poem, it appears that the first nine years of the siege of Troy had passed without any event of a decisive character. After a vigorous attempt to frustrate the landing of the Greeks, the Trojans, unable to cope with them in the field, shut themselves up within the walls of the city, where, by the strength of its fortifications, they baffled every assault of the enemy.[1] The Greeks naturally shaped their tactics by those of the besieged, and, in order to wear out their resources, occupied themselves in ravaging the country, and reducing other cities of the hostile confederacy.[2]

XV. In the tenth year, however, events occurred to alter the Trojan policy. Dissensions between Agamemnon and Achilles, the hero on whose valor the Greeks mainly relied for success, caused the secession of the latter. In proportion as this event tended to discourage the one party, already somewhat disheartened by a long and unprofitable warfare, it revived the hopes of the other. The city was at this epoch crowded with Asiatic auxiliaries, who, however valuable their services, pressed heavily on the resources of Priam,[3] and rendered some desperate effort the more indispensable.

XVI. Such a combination of circumstances obviously marked out this as the moment for a bold attack on the invaders. The quarrel, therefore, between the chiefs, as the immediate cause of a change in the languid character of the war, and of a series of fierce engagements, involving the death of Hector, the main bulwark of his country, but, above all, from the fine field it afforded for developing the character of Achilles, the heart and soul of the Iliad, could not fail to offer itself to the genius of Homer as the centre or pivot of action in any poem founded on the siege of Troy.

XVII. Nor does the peculiar nature of these events mark out the completion of the design less clearly than its commencement. From the quarrel of the heroes down to the restoration of Hector's body, the whole series of occurrences follow each other by a constant chain of cause and effect. On the withdrawal of Achilles depend the unwonted boldness and success of the Trojans. The disasters of the Greeks excite the sympathy of Patroclus, whose successful mediation with Achilles leads to his own death by the hand of Hector. Grief, anger, and remorse procure the immediate restoration of Achilles to the field, and the infliction of death on the destroyer of his friend. The duties of friendship and of religion indispensably require a performance of the last honors to the remains of the two fallen warriors, and with this the poem concludes.

ODYSSEY.—SKETCH OF THE POEM.[4]

XVIII. The *Odyssey* (Ὀδύσσεια, *scil.* ποίησις), also in 24 books, recounts the adventures of Ulysses (Ὀδυσσεύς) returning to his island home from

---

[1] *Il.*, viii., 5, &c.
[2] *Id.*, ix., 328.
[3] *Id.*, ii., 130; xvii., 220; xviii., 288, *seqq.*
[4] *Müller, Hist. Gr. Lit.*, p. 57, *seqq.*

Troy. It is indisputably, as well as the Iliad, a poem possessing a unity of subject; nor can any one of its chief parts be removed without leaving a chasm in the development of the leading idea; but it differs from the Iliad in being composed on a more *artificial* and more *complicated* plan. This is the case, partly because, in the first and greater half, up to the sixteenth book, two *main actions* are carried on side by side; partly because the action, which passes within the compass of the poem, and, as it were, beneath our eyes, is greatly extended by means of an *episodical narration*, by which the chief action itself is made distinct and complete, and the most marvellous and the strangest part of the story is transferred from the mouth of the poet to that of the inventive hero himself.

XIX. The subject of the Odyssey is the return of Ulysses from a land lying beyond the range of human intercourse or knowledge, to a home invaded by bands of insolent intruders, who seek to rob him of his wife and to kill his son. Hence the Odyssey begins exactly at that point where the hero is considered to be farthest from his home, in the island of Ogygia,[1] at the navel, that is, the central point of the sea, where the nymph Calypso (Καλυψώ, "the concealer") has kept him hidden from all mankind for seven years. Thence having, by the help of the gods, who pity his misfortunes, passed through the dangers prepared for him by his implacable enemy, Neptune, he gains the land of the Phæacians, a careless, peaceable, and effeminate nation on the confines of the earth, to whom war is only known by means of poetry.

XX. Borne by a marvellous Phæacian vessel, he reaches Ithaca sleeping; here he is entertained by the honest swineherd Eumæus, and having been introduced into his own house as a beggar, he is there made to suffer the harshest treatment from the suitors, in order that he may afterward appear with the stronger right as a terrible avenger.

XXI. With this simple story a poet might have been satisfied, and we should even in this form, notwithstanding its smaller extent, have placed the poem almost on an equality with the Iliad. But the poet to whom we are indebted for the Odyssey in its complete form has interwoven a second story, by which the poem is rendered much richer and more complete; although, indeed, from the union of two actions, some roughnesses have been produced, which, perhaps, with a plan of this kind, could scarcely be avoided; for, while the poet represents the son of Ulysses, stimulated by Minerva, coming forward in Ithaca with newly-excited courage, and calling the suitors to account before the people, and then afterward describes him as travelling to Pylos and Sparta to obtain information of his lost father, he gives us a picture of Ithaca and its anarchical condition, and of the rest of Greece in its state of peace after the return of the princes, which produces the finest contrast, and, at the same time, prepares Telemachus for playing an energetic part in the work of vengeance, which by this means becomes more probable.[2]

[1] Ὠγυγία, from Ὠγύγης, who was originally a deity of the watery expanse which covered all things.

[2] *Müller*, *l. c.*

CHAPTER V.

SECOND OR POETICAL PERIOD—*continued.*

HOMERIC CONTROVERSY.[1]

I. The whole of antiquity unanimously viewed the Iliad and the Odyssey as the productions of a certain individual called Homer. No doubt of this fact ever entered the mind of any of the ancients; and even a large number of other poems were attributed to the same author. This opinion continued unshaken down to the year 1795 of our era, when *Wolf* wrote his famous *Prolegomena*, in which he endeavored to show that the Iliad and Odyssey were not two complete poems, but small, separate, independent epic songs, celebrating single exploits of the heroes, and that these lays were *for the first time* written down and united, as the Iliad and Odyssey, by Pisistratus, tyrant of Athens.

II. This opinion, however, startling and paradoxical as it seemed, was not entirely new. Casaubon had already doubted the common belief respecting Homer, and the great Bentley had said expressly that "Homer wrote a sequel of songs and rhapsodies. These loose songs were not collected together in the form of an epic poem till about 500 years after."[2] Some French writers, Perault and Hedelin, and the Italian Vico, had made similar conjectures, but all these were forgotten, and overborne by the common and general opinion, and the more easily, since these bold conjectures had been thrown out almost at hazard, and without sound arguments to support them.

III. When, therefore, Wolf's Prolegomena appeared, the whole literary world was startled by the boldness and novelty of his positions, and great opposition was, of course, excited. The publication of his work took place during a crisis in the intellectual as well as the political destinies of Europe. A bold spirit of speculative inquiry was then abroad, the valuable effects of which, in exploding error and prejudice, have been too often counterbalanced by the spread of groundless or mischievous innovation. Wolf himself professed the scope of his argument to be rather to subvert the ancient fabric of opinion, than to erect any solid edifice in its place. The result, however, has not fully justified the accuracy of the figure; for, while no one has to this day been able to refute some of the principal arguments of the great critic, and to re-establish fully the old opinion which he overthrew, yet his views have been materially modified by protracted discussions, and a considerable portion of the old way of thinking has been revived.

IV. We will first state Wolf's principal arguments, and the chief objections of his opponents, and will then endeavor to discover the most probable result of all these inquiries.

---

1 *Ihne (Smith's Dict. Biogr., s. v. Homerus)*, p. 501, *seqq.*

2 *Letter by Phileleutherus Lipsiensis*, § 7.

In 1770, Wood published a book *On the Original Genius of Homer*,[1] in which he mooted the question whether the Homeric poems had originally been *written* or not. This idea was caught up by Wolf, and proved the foundation of all his inquiries. But the most important assistance which he obtained was from the discovery and publication by Villoison, in 1788, of the famous Venetian scholia on Homer. These valuable scholia, in giving us some insight into the studies of the Alexandrine critics, furnished materials and an historical basis for Wolf's inquiries.

WOLF'S FIRST ARGUMENT.[2]

V. The point from which Wolf started was, as we have said, the idea that the Homeric poems were originally not written. To prove this, he enters into a minute and accurate discussion concerning the age of the art of writing. He sets aside as groundless fables the traditions which ascribed the invention or introduction of this art to Cadmus, Cecrops, Orpheus, Linus, or Palamedes. Then, allowing that letters were known in Greece at a very early period, he justly insists upon the great difference which exists between the *knowledge* of the letters and their general *use* for works of literature. Writing is first applied to public monuments, inscriptions, and religious purposes, centuries before it is employed for the common purposes of social life. This is still more certain to be the case when the common ordinary materials for writing are wanting, as they were among the ancient Greeks. Wood, lead, brass, and stone are not proper materials for writing down poems consisting of 24 books. Even hides, which were used by the Ionians, seem too clumsy for this purpose, and, besides, we do not know *when* they were first in use.

VI. It was not, according to Wolf, before the sixth century B.C. that papyrus became easily accessible to the Greeks, through King Amasis, who first opened Egypt to Greek traders. The laws of Lycurgus were not committed to writing; those of Zaleucus, among the Locri Epizephyrii, in the 29th Olympiad, or 664 B.C., are particularly recorded as the *first* laws that were ever written down.[3] The laws of Solon, seventy years later, were written on wood, and after the fashion called *βουστροφηδόν*.

VII. Wolf allows that all these considerations do not prove that no use at all was made of the art of writing as early as the seventh and eighth centuries B.C., which would be particularly improbable in the case of the lyric poets, such as Archilochus, Alcman, Pisander, and Arion, but that before the time of the seven sages, that is, the time when prose writing first originated, the art was not so common that we can suppose it to have been employed for such extensive works as the poems of Homer. Wolf refers, in support of his position, to the testimony of Josephus,[4] and to a scholiast cited by Villoison in his Anecdota.[5]

---

1 "*An Essay on the Original Genius and Writings of Homer*," &c. Lond., 1775, 4to.

2 *Ihne*, p. 501.

3 *Scymn. Perieg.*, 313; *Strab.*, vi., p. 259.

4 *C. Apion.*, i., 2: Ὀψὲ καὶ μόλις ἔγνωσαν οἱ Ἕλληνες φύσιν γραμμάτων. . . . Καί φασιν οὐδὲ τοῦτον (i. e., Ὅμηρον) ἐν γράμμασι τὴν αὐτοῦ ποίησιν καταλιπεῖν, ἀλλὰ διαμνημονευομένην ἐκ τῶν ᾀσμάτων ὕστερον συντεθῆναι.

5 *Schol. ap. Villois.*, *Anecd. Gr.*, ii., p. 182.

VIII. But Wolf draws still more convincing proofs from the poems themselves. In the seventh book of the Iliad (v. 175), the Grecian heroes decide by lot who is to fight with Hector. The lots are marked by each respective hero, and are all thrown into a helmet, which is shaken until one lot is jerked out. This is handed round by the herald till it reaches Ajax, who recognizes the mark he had made on it as his own. If this mark had been any thing like writing, the herald would have read it at once, and not have handed it round. Again, in the sixth book of the Iliad (v. 168, *seqq.*) we have the story of Bellerophon, whom Prœtus sends to Lycia,

πόρεν δ' ὅγε σήματα λυγρά,
γράψας ἐν πίνακι πτυκτῷ θυμοφθόρα πολλά,
δεῖξαι δ' ἠνώγει ᾧ πενθερῷ, ὄφρ' ἀπόλοιτο.

Wolf here shows that *σήματα λυγρά* are a kind of conventional marks, and not letters, and that this story is far from proving the existence of writing.

IX. Throughout the whole of Homer, indeed, remarks Wolf, every thing is calculated to be heard, nothing to be read. Not a single epitaph, nor any other inscription, is mentioned; the tombs of the heroes are rude mounds; coins are unknown. In the eighth book of the Odyssey (v. 163, *seqq.*) an overseer of a ship is mentioned, who, instead of having a list of the cargo, must remember it; he is *φόρτου μνήμων*. All this seems to prove, according to Wolf, without the possibility of doubt, that the art of writing was entirely unknown at the time of the Trojan war, and could not have been common at the time when the poems were composed.

ANSWER TO WOLF'S FIRST ARGUMENT, WITH REMARKS.

X. Among the opponents of Wolf, there is none superior to *Nitzsch* in zeal, perseverance, learning, and acuteness. He wrote a series of monographies[1] to refute Wolf and his supporters, and he has done a great deal toward establishing a solid and well-founded view of this complicated question. Next to Nitzsch may be mentioned Kreuser, Clinton, and Thirlwall.

XI. Nitzsch opposes Wolf's conclusions concerning the later date of written documents. He denies that the laws of Lycurgus were transmitted by oral tradition alone, and were for this purpose set to music by Terpander and Thaletas, as is generally believed, on the authority of Plutarch.[2] The Spartan *νόμοι*, which those two musicians are said to have composed, Nitzsch declares to have been hymns, and not laws, although Strabo calls Thaletas a *νομοθετικὸς ἀνήρ* (by a mistake, as Nitzsch ventures to say!). Clinton also remarks, that it would have been an unnecessary provision for Lycurgus to have enacted that his laws should not be committed to writing, if writing had not been practiced.

XII. In answer to Strabo's statement, as quoted by Wolf, that the Epizephyrian Locrians were the first Greek people that received a code

[1] *Quæstion. Homeric. Specim.*, i., 1824; *Indagandæ per Odyss. Interpolationis Præparatio*, 1828; *De Hist. Homeri*, fascic. i., 1830; *De Aristotele contra Wolfianos*, 1831; *Patria et Ætas Homeri*, 1834.

[2] *De Mus.*, 3.

of written laws, Nitzsch gives a different explanation of Strabo's meaning, and maintains that the point in which the novelty consisted was, not that the laws were reduced to writing, but that the discretion of the Locrian magistrates was limited by a penal code.

XIII. To Wolf's argument, drawn from Bellerophon's *σήματα λυγρά*, no satisfactory answer has ever been given, though this has been attempted by Nitzsch, Kreuser, Thirlwall, and many others. Writing materials, however, were, according to Nitzsch, not wanting at a very early period. He maintains that wooden tablets and the hides (*διφθέραι*) of the Ionians were employed, and that even papyrus was known and used by the Greeks long before the time of Amasis, and was brought into Greece by Phœnician merchants. Amasis, according to Nitzsch, only rendered the use of papyrus more general (sixth century B.C), whereas previously its use had been confined to a few.

XIV. Thus Nitzsch comes to the conclusion that writing was common in Greece full one hundred years before the time which Wolf had supposed, namely, about the beginning of the Olympiads (eighth century B.C.), and that this is the time in which the Homeric poems were committed to writing. Even if this is granted, however, it does not follow that the poems were also *composed* at that time. Nitzsch can not prove that the age of Homer was so late as the eighth century. The best authorities place Homer much earlier, so that we again come to the conclusion that the Homeric poems were composed and handed down for a long time without the assistance of writing. In fact, this point seems indisputable. The nature of the Homeric language is alone a sufficient argument, but into this consideration Nitzsch never entered.[1] The Homeric dialect could never have attained to the softness and flexibility which render it so well adapted to versification—that variety of longer and shorter forms, which existed together—that freedom in contracting and resolving vowels, and of forming the contractions into two syllables—if the practice of writing had at that time exercised the power, which it naturally possesses, of fixing the forms of a language.[2]

XV. Moreover, the state of the Iliad and Odyssey in respect to the letter called the digamma affords a proof that they were recited for a considerable period before they were committed to writing, insomuch that the oral pronunciation underwent during the interval a sensible change. At the time when these poems were composed, the digamma was an effective consonant, and figured as such in the structure of the verse; at the time, however, when they were committed to writing, it had ceased to be pronounced, and therefore never found a place in any of the manuscripts, insomuch that the Alexandrine critics, though they knew of its existence in the much later poems of Alcæus and Sappho, never recognized it in Homer. The hiatus, and the various perplexities of metre, occasioned by the loss of the digamma, were corrected by different grammatical stratagems; but the whole history of this lost letter is very curious, and is rendered intelligible only by the supposition that the Iliad

1 *Hermann, Opusc.*, vi., 1, 75; *Giese, d. Æol. Dialect.*, p. 154.

2 *Müller, Hist. Gr. Lit.*, p. 38.

and Odyssey belonged for a wide space of time to the memory, the voice, and the ear exclusively.[1]

XVI. It is necessary, therefore, to admit Wolf's first position, that the Homeric poems were originally not committed to writing. We now proceed to examine the conclusions which he draws from these premises, regarding them, for convenience' sake, as so many successive arguments.

WOLF'S SECOND ARGUMENT, WITH AN ANSWER TO THE SAME.

XVII. However great the genius of Homer may have been, says Wolf, it is quite incredible that, without the assistance of writing, he could have conceived in his mind and executed such extensive works.

XVIII. But it is difficult to determine, as Müller remarks in reply to this argument,[2] how many thousand verses a person thoroughly impregnated with his subject, and absorbed in the contemplation of it, might produce in a year, and confide to the faithful memory of disciples devoted to their master and his art. We have instances of modern poets who have composed long poems without writing down a single syllable, and have preserved them faithfully in their memory, before committing them to writing. And how much more easily could this have been done in the time anterior to the use of writing, when all those faculties of the mind, which had to dispense with this artificial assistance, were powerfully developed, trained, and exercised.

XIX. Again, we must not look upon the old bards as amateurs, who amused themselves in leisure hours with poetical compositions, as is the fashion nowadays. Composition was their *profession*. All their thoughts were concentrated on this one point, in which and for which they lived. Their composition was, moreover, facilitated by their having no occasion to invent complicated plots and wonderful stories; the simple traditions, on which they founded their songs, were handed down to them in a form already adapted to poetical purposes. If now, in spite of all these advantages, the composition of the Iliad and Odyssey was no easy task, we must attribute some superiority to the genius of Homer, which caused his name and his works to acquire eternal glory, and covered all his innumerable predecessors, contemporaries, and followers with oblivion.[3]

WOLF'S THIRD ARGUMENT, WITH AN ANSWER TO THE SAME.

XX. Wolf's third argument, or second deduction from his main premises, is of more weight and importance. When people neither wrote nor read, the only way of publishing poems was by oral recitation. The bards, therefore, of the Heroic Age, as we see from Homer himself, used to entertain their hearers at banquets, festivals, and on similar occasions. At such times they certainly could not recite more than one or two rhapsodies or books. Now Wolf asks what could have induced any one to compose a poem of such a length that it could not be heard all at once.

XXI. To refute this argument, the opponents of Wolf were obliged to seek for occasions which afforded at least a possibility of reciting the

[1] *Grote, Hist. of Greece*, vol. ii., p. 196, *seq.*

[2] *Müller, Hist. Gr. Lit.*, p. 62.

[3] *Ihne*, p. 502.

whole of the Iliad and Odyssey. Banquets and small festivals were not sufficient; but there were musical contests (ἀγῶνες), connected with great national festivals, at which thousands assembled, anxious to hear and patient to listen. If, says Müller,[1] the Athenians could at one festival hear in succession nine tragedies, three satyric dramas, and as many comedies, without ever thinking that it might be better to distribute this enjoyment over the whole year, why should not the Greeks of earlier times have been able to listen to the whole Iliad and Odyssey, and perhaps other poems, at the same festival. Such occasions, we know, did occur at the Panionian festival, where poetical contests of the bards were held; at Sicyon, during the contests of the rhapsodists in the time of Clisthenes; and also in many other parts of Greece.[2]

XXII. Besides, it is not inconsistent with the theory, that each of these poems was composed with a unity of subject and design, to suppose that some of the parts or episodes might have been recited separately; that the plan of the whole, and the gradual unfolding of the story, should be so well known, from familiarity with it, that the hearers could delight in the recitation of a part, and their imaginations readily place and arrange it in the frame-work which fully occupied their minds. In later times, it was essential to the idea of Greek tragedy that the histories which the poet developed should be well known to the audience, and this probably was the case with the legends of the Trojan war, which were the original foundation of the Iliad and Odyssey.[3]

XXIII. Again, to refer, by way of illustration, to the habits of modern times, the popularity of those works of fiction, which are periodically published in parts, shows that, even with long intervals between the publication of the parts, it is possible to sustain the interest of a tale, and to keep awake the attention of the reader. In the same manner, those who listened to the divine poems of Homer might have been delighted to receive, book by book, his inspired strains.[4]

WOLF'S FOURTH ARGUMENT,[5] WITH AN ANSWER TO THE SAME.

XXIV. Wolf observes that Aristotle first derived the laws of epic poetry from the examples which he found laid down in the Iliad and Odyssey. It was for this reason, says Wolf, that people never thought of suspecting that those examples themselves were destitute of that poetic unity which Aristotle, from a contemplation of them, drew up as a principal requisite for this kind of poetry. It was transmitted, says Wolf, by old traditions, how once Achilles withdrew from the battle; how, in consequence of the absence of the great hero, who alone awed the Trojans, the Greeks were worsted; how Achilles at last allowed his friend Patroclus to protect the Greeks; and how, finally, he avenged the death of Patroclus by killing Hector.

XXV. This simple course of the story, Wolf thinks, would have been treated by any other poet in very much the same manner as we now read it in the Iliad; and he maintains that there is no unity in it, except a

[1] *Müller*, *Hist. Gr. Lit.*, p. 62. [2] *Browne*, *Hist. Class. Lit.*, vol. i., p. 48.
[3] *Id.*, *l. c.* [4] *Id.*, *l. c.* [5] *Ihne*, p. 503.

chronological one, in so far as we have a narration of the events of several days in succession. Nay, he continues, if we examine closely the last six books, we shall find that they have nothing to do with what is stated in the introduction as the object of the poem, namely, the *wrath of Achilles*. This wrath subsides with the death of Patroclus, and what follows is a wrath of a different kind, which does not belong to the former.

XXVI. The composition of the Odyssey is not viewed with any greater favor by Wolf. The journey of Telemachus to Pylos and Sparta, the sojourn of Ulysses in the island of Calypso, the stories of his wanderings, were originally, according to him, independent songs, which, as they *happened* to fit into one another, were afterward connected into one whole, at a time when literature, the arts, and a general cultivation of the mind began to flourish in Greece, supported by the important art of writing.

XXVII. These bold speculations of Wolf have met with almost universal disapprobation. Still, this is a subject on which reasoning and demonstration are very precarious and almost impossible. The feelings and tastes of every individual must determine the matter. But to oppose to Wolf's skeptical views the judgment of a man whose authority on matters of taste is as great as on those of learning, we proceed to give what Müller says on this same subject.

REMARKS OF MÜLLER ON THE UNITY OF THE ILIAD.[1]

XXVIII. All the laws which reflection and experience can suggest for the epic form are observed in Homer with the most refined taste; all the means are employed by which the general effect can be heightened.

XXIX. The anger of Achilles is an event which did not long precede the final destruction of Troy, inasmuch as it produced the death of Hector, who was the defender of the city. It was, doubtless, the ancient tradition, established long before Homer's time, that Hector had been slain by Achilles in revenge for the slaughter of his friend Patroclus, whose fall in battle, unprotected by the son of Thetis, was explained by the tradition to have arisen from the anger of Achilles against the other Greeks for an affront offered to him, and his consequent retirement from the contest. Now the poet seizes, as the most critical and momentous period of the action, the conversion of Achilles from the foe of the Greeks into that of the Trojans; for as, on the one hand, the sudden revolution in the fortunes of war, thus occasioned, places the prowess of Achilles in the strongest light, so, on the other hand, the change of his firm and resolute mind must have been the more touching to the feelings of the hearers.

XXX. From this centre of interest there springs a long preparation and gradual development, since not only the cause of the anger of Achilles, but also the defeats of the Greeks, occasioned by that anger, were to be narrated; and the display of the insufficiency of all the other heroes, at the same time, offered the best opportunity for exhibiting their several excellencies It is in the arrangement of this preparatory part, and its connection with the catastrophe, that the poet displays his perfect acquaintance with all the mysteries of poetical composition; and in his con-

[1] *Müller, Hist. Gr. Lit.*, p. 48.

tinual postponement of the crisis of the action, and his scanty revelations with respect to the plan of the entire work, he shows a maturity of knowledge which is astonishing for so early an age.

XXXI. To all appearance, the poet, after certain obstacles have been first overcome, tends only to one point, namely, to increase perpetually the disasters of the Greeks, which they have drawn on themselves by the injury offered to Achilles; and Jupiter himself, at the beginning, is made to pronounce, as coming from himself, the vengeance and consequent exaltation of the son of Thetis. At the same time, however, the poet plainly shows his wish to excite, in the feelings of an attentive hearer, an anxious and perpetually increasing desire not only to see the Greeks saved from destruction, but also that the unbearable and more than human haughtiness and pride of Achilles should be broken. Both these ends are attained through the fulfillment of the *secret counsel of Jove*, which he did not communicate to Thetis, and through her to Achilles (who, if he had known it, would have given up all enmity against the Achæans), but only to Juno, and to her not till the middle of the poem;[1] and Achilles, through the loss of his dearest friend, whom he had sent to battle not to save the Greeks, but *for his own glory*, suddenly changes his hostile attitude toward the Greeks, and is overpowered by entirely opposite feelings. In this manner the exaltation of the son of Thetis is united to that almost imperceptible operation of destiny which the Greeks were required to observe in all human affairs.

XXXII. To remove from this collection of various actions, conditions, and feelings any substantial part, as not necessarily belonging to it, would, in fact, be to dismember a living whole, the parts of which would necessarily lose their vitality. As in an organic body life does not dwell in one single point, but requires a union of certain systems and members, so the internal connection of the Iliad rests on the union of certain parts; and neither the interesting introduction, describing the defeat of the Greeks, up to the burning of the ship of Protesilaus, nor the turn of affairs brought about by the death of Patroclus, nor the final pacification of the anger of Achilles, could be spared from the Iliad, when the fruitful seed of such a poem had once been sown in the soul of Homer, and had begun to develop its growth.

UNITY OF THE ODYSSEY.[2]

XXXIII. If we yield our assent to these convincing reflections, we shall hardly need to defend the unity of the Odyssey, which has always been admired as one of the greatest master-pieces of Grecian genius, against the aggressions of Wolf, who could more easily believe that chance and learned compilers had produced this poem, than that it should have sprung from the mind of a single man.

[1] Thetis had said nothing to Achilles of the loss of Patroclus (*Il.*, xvii., 411), for she herself did not know it. Jove also long conceals his plans from Juno and the other gods, notwithstanding their anger on account of the sufferings of the Achæans. He does not reveal them to Juno until after his sleep upon Ida (*Il.*, xv., 65). The spuriousness of the verses (*Il.*, viii., 475, *seq.*) was recognized by the ancients, although the principal objection to them is not mentioned.

[2] *Ihne*, p. 504.

XXXIV. Nitzsch[1] has endeavored to exhibit the unity of the plan of this poem. He has divided the whole into four large sections, in each of which there are again subdivisions facilitating the distribution of the recital for several rhapsodists and several days. Thus, 1. The first part treats of *the absent Ulysses* (books i.–iv.). Here we are introduced to the state of affairs in Ithaca during the absence of Ulysses. Telemachus goes to Pylos and Sparta to ascertain the fate of his father. 2. *The song of the returning Ulysses* (books v.–xiii., v. 92) is naturally divided into two parts; the first contains the departure of Ulysses from Calypso, and his arrival and reception in Scheria; the second, the narration of his wanderings. 3. *The song of Ulysses meditating revenge* (books xiii., 92–xix.). Here the two threads of the story are united; Ulysses is conveyed to Ithaca, and is met in the cottage of Eumæus by his son, who has just returned from Sparta. 4. *The song of the revenging and reconciled Ulysses* (books xx.–xxiv.) brings all the manifold wrongs of the suitors and the sufferings of Ulysses to the desired and long-expected conclusion.

CHAPTER VI.

SECOND OR POETICAL PERIOD—*continued.*

HOMERIC CONTROVERSY—*continued.*

PROOF FROM INTERNAL EVIDENCE THAT THE HOMERIC POEMS ARE THE WORK OF ONE AUTHOR.[2]

I. In order to prove from internal evidence that the Homeric poems are the works of one author, it is necessary to establish three points. I. General similarity of style, taste, and feeling. II. Unity of plan. III. Consistency in the characters. The second of these points has already been anticipated in the previous chapter. The remaining two will now occupy our attention.

I. GENERAL SIMILARITY OF STYLE, TASTE, AND FEELING.

II. The language of the Iliad is throughout evidently that of one period; it does not exhibit so much variation as might be supposed to take place during the course of two successive generations; but, more than this, the propriety of expression, the adaptation of the descriptions to the things described, bear such marks of undesigned and natural resemblance, that it is scarcely possible to imagine them to have proceeded from more than one mind. Such, it must be confessed, is the general impression produced upon the reader, unless biased and inclined toward the contrary belief by other arguments and considerations.

III. The same words, the same phrases, the same modes of illustration, are constantly recurring. Some favorite similes, for instance, such as those of the lion and the boar, are frequently used. Their details are

[1] *Hall. Encyclop., s. v. Odyssee; Anmerk. z. Odyss.*, vol. ii., præf.

[2] *Browne, Hist. Class. Lit.*, vol. i., p. 52, *seqq.*

sufficiently similar to show probable identity of authorship, without wearying by too much repetition.

IV. The same musical rhythm and metrical arrangement are preserved throughout. The Homeric verse is *sui generis*, it can be compared to that of no other poet in any age. And this phenomenon, be it remembered, occurred when the laws of metre must have been simply the suggestions of a delicately organized ear and a naturally refined taste. They could not have been reduced to rule in so remote an age, and therefore there were no means of attaining resemblance to one great and perfect model by study and imitation.

V. There is a characteristic of the Homeric poetry which, in the manner of its treatment, is without parallel, although it has been imitated by countless poets since his time: this is the Simile.[1] It is evidently the favorite figure of the bard, full of knowledge gathered from observation of nature, animate and inanimate. Apposite, however, as the Homeric similes are, it is not that quality which strikes the reader as constituting their especial beauty; we almost lose sight of its intention to illustrate, in the profusion and variety of the images presented to us. This is not the case with the similes of any other author, except where they are palpable imitations of those of Homer. As no poet ever possessed the same graphic power, so none could venture, without danger of producing weariness, to introduce this figure so frequently. Every part of the Iliad abounds with them, except the commencement and conclusion of the poem; and this fact is to be accounted for by the busy character of these portions; the rapid succession of events left no room for illustration.

VI. Again, dramatic power pervades the whole poem.[2] Every character describes himself, and tells his own story. The poet is never seen, his sentiments are never known but through the medium of his actors: he is never subjective, he seems to forget himself. Although he is describing his own feelings, and enforcing his own sentiments, he never personally appears upon the stage, but leaves it to his characters to express his thoughts; and this is not only the case sometimes, but universally. Is it probable, then, that more than one poet, in one age, should have possessed this dramatic faculty in so eminent a degree?

VII. Uniformity on other points of this nature seems to stamp the poem as the work of one mind. Stories the most different from one another are told precisely in the same way; conversations and councils are carried on after the same plan. The sentiments on all important subjects, whether religious, political, or social, are uniform and without variation. One high tone of moral principle and willing obedience to law, both human and divine, pervades the whole work.

VIII. It is, doubtless, possible to conceive that a school of poets, such as the bards of the Homeric Age must have been, venerated for their inspiration, and respected for their moral and religious worth, would have resembled each other in mental culture, taste, and sentiments; but they could not have been equal in that mental power, which would have been necessary to produce the uniformity in these points observable in the Ho-

[1] Compare *Mure*, *Crit. Hist.*, vol. ii., p. 89, *seqq.*

[2] *Id. ib.*, p. 57, *seqq.*

meric poems. Throughout the Iliad no more inequality of talent is to be discerned than in great works which are known to have had but one author; at any rate, no more than would result from interpolations and additions, the introduction of which, to a certain extent, it is impossible to deny.

IX. The language of the Odyssey is throughout the whole poem as uniform in its structure and its principles as the Iliad. The versification never varies, it has always the same mechanical structure and the same harmonious flow, which is so difficult to arrive at, without betraying a palpable attempt at imitation. There can be traced also, from beginning to end, a consistent moral and religious principle, dramatic power, fidelity in describing, and taste in appreciating the beauties of nature; and lastly, spirit and picturesqueness in the use of similes and illustrations. These considerations are in favor of the hypothesis that the Odyssey, like the Iliad, had but one author, and was not formed by collecting together lays and episodes by different poets.

II. CONSISTENCY IN THE CHARACTERS.[1]

X. In his heroes the poet evidently intended to typify some striking phase of the heroic character. They all have their points of resemblance, but the points of contrast are more fully dwelt upon. Each is a representative man. Standing out, therefore, thus in bold relief, the slightest inconsistency would be at once detected. So strong, in fact, was the poet's impression of the distinct individuality of his heroes, that frequently the same distinctive epithet is applied to each, on the majority of occasions, throughout his whole career. Opposite as are the traits which mark the character of Achilles, they are all, vices as well as virtues, such as may be found united in noble and impetuous natures. Revengeful as he is, even to ferocity, his warm and passionate heart can sympathize with deep sorrow, and feel compassion for the vanquished. He is haughty and reserved, and yet a devoted and affectionate friend; unrelenting under a sense of injustice, yet, when satisfaction is offered, he is generously and unconditionally forgiving.

XI. Agamemnon[2] has all the regard for his subjects which marks the sovereign of a free people, but his generosity proceeds from impulse rather than principle, and therefore he is generally dignified, but sometimes vacillating. Menelaus,[3] though not kingly, possesses the virtues of royal race. He is brave and gentle, and has an unfeigned respect for the regal authority. Nestor[4] is an old man, and an experienced statesman; he has all the garrulity of the one, and the long-sighted wisdom of the other. He is too cheerful to betray much of the querulousness of age, although he can not forbear comparing the virtue of former days with the degeneracy of the present generation.

XII. Ajax[5] and Diomede[6] are thoroughly soldiers. The former has all

---

[1] *Browne, Hist. Class. Lit.*, vol. ii., p. 78, *seqq.* Compare *Mure, Crit. Hist.*, vol. i., p. 304, *seqq.*

[2] Compare *Mure, Crit. Hist.*, vol. i., p. 314, *seqq.*

[3] *Id. ib.*, p. 324, *seqq.*

[4] *Id. ib.*, p. 329, *seqq.*

[5] *Id. ib.*, p. 334, *seqq.*

[6] *Id. ib.*, p. 320, *seqq.*

the physical strength and animal courage which fit a man for the perils of war; the latter, the moral firmness and well-disciplined coolness which render him fit either to command or obey. Ulysses possesses every qualification, bodily as well as mental, for influencing men's minds; he is of noble figure and graceful bearing, sound-judging and discreet; an accurate observer of men and things. His intimate knowledge of the human heart, and its crooked ways, causes the policy, which is his favorite weapon, to appear at times crafty and dishonest, but it is only appearance, for he is benevolent, and has a strong sense of justice.

XIII. Hector unites moral with physical courage, but his warlike spirit sometimes degenerates into rashness. He is domestic and affectionate, and shows that tenderness toward women and children which characterizes true bravery. Priam is an Oriental sovereign, whose yielding yet amiable temper allows things to take their own course. He is too careless and self-indulgent to have any high moral principle, and yet he has strong affections, and impulses toward good. At length the depth of his despair awakens his energy, and in his old age, for the first time, he acts with vigor and heroism. Paris is an effeminate and conceited fop, but brave notwithstanding, as those often are who have been brought up in refinement and luxury.

XIV. Helen, though a light wanton, who has left her husband and child for an adulterer, is full of fascination. She is neither bold nor depraved; she can admire chastity, she feels remorse for her sin; to her seducer she is tender and faithful; but even when restored to her husband, there remains that voluptuous self-indulgence which perhaps paved the way to her weakness and her fall.

XV. Hecuba is a woman of strong passions, whose ferocity is increased, and not softened, by affliction; she can never look on Helen in any other light than as the cause of all her sorrows, and of course her revengeful temper can never forgive her. Andromache, the affectionate wife and mother, has not a spark of selfishness in her character. In his lifetime she was wrapped up in her husband, and after his death, though overwhelmed with the weight of her sorrows, she thinks more of her husband's fame, her child's irreparable loss, and the ruin of her country.

XVI. Such are the principal characters of the Iliad. Those who play an important part in the Odyssey[1] are very few. Helen and Ulysses have already been described, and in the luxurious matron, restored to her place in society, and the patient, strong-willed voyager, struggling with adverse fortune, the same points of character which were depicted in the Iliad are plainly discoverable, modified, as they necessarily must be, by change of circumstances.

XVII. Telemachus is a modest, ingenuous, and promising youth, full of consideration for his mother, and although not yet able to act for himself, willing to act with decision and energy at the suggestion of a wise counsellor, and with a strong sense of filial duty and obedience to his father's will.

XVIII. Penelope appears to possess the cool diplomatic policy which

[1] Compare *Mure, Crit. Hist.*, vol. i., p. 413, *seqq.*

distinguishes her husband, alloyed with somewhat of duplicity. Exposed as she is to the solicitations of the suitors, she has doubtless a difficult part to play; but the false hopes with which she deceives them, and the stratagem with which she puts off the fulfillment of her promise, while she permits their riot and extravagance, are scarcely consistent with a high tone of morality. She remains, however, faithful to her husband, even when his return scarcely seems probable; and when her fidelity is rewarded by his return, her coldness gradually melts, her caution gives way to conviction, and at length all her calculating shrewdness vanishes. The mask and restraint under which she had so long lived are removed, and her true woman's nature shines forth at once in all its tenderness and affection. Such a change, at first sight, may appear inconsistent, but the skillful and gradual manner in which it is managed by the poet renders it perfectly natural.

XIX. Euryclea is a model nurse; she continues the same attention to Telemachus when he is a youth which she paid him in infancy; nor is her kindness unreturned by her foster-child, for she it is to whom he applies in his difficulty, when a ship is refused him by the suitors.

XX. The elegant and unaffected simplicity of Nausicaa is most charming; and the noble swineherd Eumæus, the keeper of the king's swine, the principal wealth of his rocky isle, presents an inimitable picture of that sturdy, yeoman-like independence which is fostered and nurtured by the pursuits of rural life.

XXI. Such is the internal evidence in favor of both the great Homeric poems having been the works of one mind, and to this evidence may be added the following considerations. It is not too much to assert that the conditions requisite for denying the personality of Homer have never been fulfilled in any nation or in any times. The separators[1] of the Iliad from the Odyssey require the belief that, during a period extending over no very wide space, there should have lived two poets, whose talents and genius were of so high an order, and so nearly equal, as to have produced these two great poems. And yet the history of the world proves that no nation, during the whole period of its existence, has ever possessed more than one great epic poet. Rome had one Virgil, modern Italy one Dante, England one Milton.[2]

XXII. If the separators demand that which is improbable, those, on the other hand, who attribute the poems to a large number of original bards, argue in favor of a moral impossibility. To adopt their view implies the belief that at a period when all the rest of the world was destitute of literature, except the Semitic nations inhabiting Palestine, Greece and her colonies were so fruitful in poets as to give birth, almost simultaneously, to a vast number; that this phenomenon never occurred in that country either before or since; that they all chose for their theme different parts of the same subject; and that these, by accident or design, were so portioned out among them as to be capable of being welded together into one harmonious whole. This whole, moreover, was so complete as to contain all that so acute a critic as Aristotle, and many schol-

[1] *Vid.* p. 53.

[2] *Browne, Hist. Class. Lit.*, vol. i., p. 83.

ars of the most accomplished taste since his time, deemed essential to an epic poem. And again, those who arranged and set in order these separate poems, whether rhapsodists or others, must have possessed such exquisite skill and judgment that the places where they are joined together never present the appearance of abrupt transition from one part to another. And as this union could not have been effected without the composition of some fresh passages, they must have been poets and imitators nearly equal to the original composers themselves ![1]

CHAPTER VII.

SECOND OR POETICAL PERIOD—*continued.*

HOMERIC CONTROVERSY—*continued.*

HOMERIC INTERPOLATIONS.[2]

I. Although we maintain the unity of both the Homeric poems, we can not deny that they have suffered greatly from interpolations, omissions, and alterations; and it is only by admitting some original poetical whole that we are able to discover those parts which do not belong to this whole.

II. Wolf, therefore, in pointing out some parts as spurious, has been led into an inconsistency in his demonstration, since he is obliged to acknowledge something as the genuine centre of the two poems, which he must suppose to have been spun out more and more by subsequent rhapsodists. This altered view, which is distinctly pronounced in the preface to his edition of Homer, appears already in the Prolegomena, and has been subsequently embraced by Hermann and other critics. It is, as we have said, a necessary consequence from the discovery of interpolations.

III. These interpolations are particularly apparent in the first part of the Iliad. The catalogue of the ships has long been recognized as a later addition, and can be omitted without leaving the slightest gap. The battles from the third to the seventh book seem almost entirely foreign to the plan of the Iliad. Jove appears to have quite forgotten his promise to Thetis, that he would honor her son by letting Agamemnon feel his absence. The Greeks are far from feeling this. Diomede fights successfully even against gods; the Trojans are driven back to the town. In an assembly of the gods, in the beginning of the fourth book, the glory of Achilles is no motive to deliver Troy from her fate; it is not till the eighth book that Jupiter all at once seems mindful of his promise to Thetis.

IV. The preceding five books are not only loosely connected with the whole of the poem, but even with one another. The single combat between Menelaus and Paris, in the third book, in which the former was on the point of dispatching the seducer of his wife, is interrupted by the treacherous shot of Pandarus. In the next book all this is forgotten. The Greeks neither claim Helen as the prize of the victory of Menelaus, nor do they complain of the breach of the oath: no god avenges the perjury.

---

1 *Browne*, p. 84.

2 *Ihne* (*Smith's Dict. Biogr.*, *s. v. Homerus*), p. 505.

Paris, in the sixth book, sits quietly at home, where Hector severely upbraids him for his cowardice and retirement from war; to which Paris makes no reply, and does not plead that he had only just encountered Menelaus in deadly fight.

V. The tenth book, containing the nocturnal expedition of Ulysses and Diomede, in which they kill the Thracian king Rhesus, and take his horses, is avowedly of later origin.[1] No reference is subsequently made by any of the Greeks or Trojans to this gallant deed. The two heroes were sent as spies, but they never narrate the result of their expedition; not to speak of many other improbabilities. To enumerate all those passages which are reasonably suspected as interpolated would lead us too far.

VI. The Odyssey has experienced similar extensions and interpolations, which, far from inducing us to believe in an atomistical origin of the poem, only show that the original plan has been here and there obscured. Nitzsch[2] has tried to remove these difficulties, but he does not deny extensive interpolations, particularly in the eighth book, where the song of Demodocus concerning Mars and Venus is very suspicious. In the nineteenth book, the recognition of Ulysses by his old nurse, and, most of all, some parts near the end, appear to be also interpolated. All that follows after verse 296, book twenty-three, was declared spurious even by the Alexandrine critics, Aristophanes and Aristarchus.[3] The second *Necyia* (in the beginning of book twenty-four) is evidently spurious, and, like many parts of the first *Necyia*, in book eleven, most likely taken from a similar passage in the Νοστοί, in which was narrated the arrival of Agamemnon in Hades.[4]

VII. Considering all these interpolations and the original unity, which has only been obscured and not destroyed by them, we must come to the conclusion that the Homeric poems were originally composed as poetic wholes, but that a long oral tradition gave occasion to great alterations in their original form.

RHAPSODISTS.[5]

VIII. Wolf, from the premises laid down by him, and which we have already examined, came to the conclusion that the Homeric poems originated as small songs, unconnected with one another, which, after being preserved in this state for a long time, were at length put together. The agents to whom he attributed these two tasks of composing and preserving on the one hand, and of collecting and combining on the other, are the rhapsodists and Pisistratus. Originally, the bard sang, enlivening the song with occasional touches of the harp. His successor, the rhapsodist, merely recited the words, depending for effect upon voice and manner; a species of musical and rhythmical declamation, which gradually increased in vehement emphasis and gesticulation until it approached to that of the dramatic actor.

IX. The subject of the rhapsodists (ῥαψῳδοί) is one of the most compli-

---

1 *Schol. Ven. ad Il.*, x., 1.

2 *Anmerk. z. Odyss.*, vol. ii., præf., p. xliii.

3 *Spohn, Comment. de extrem. Odysseæ parte*, 1816.

4 *Pausan.*, x., 23, 4.

5 *Ihne*, p. 506.

cated and difficult of all; because the fact is, that we know very little about them, and thus a large field is opened to conjecture and hypothesis.[1] Wolf derives the name of rhapsodist (ῥαψῳδός) from ῥάπτειν ᾠδήν, which he interprets "*breviora carmina modo et ordine publicæ recitationi apto connectere.*" These *breviora carmina* are the *rhapsodies* of which the Iliad and Odyssey consist, not indeed containing originally one book each, as they do now, but sometimes more and sometimes less. The nature and condition of these rhapsodists may be learned, according to Wolf, from Homer himself, where they appear as singing at the banquets, games, and festivals of the princes, and are held in high honor.[2] In fact, the first rhapsodists were the poets themselves, just as the first dramatic poets were the first actors. Therefore Homer and Hesiod are said to have rhapsodized.[3]

X. We must imagine, continues Wolf, that these minstrels were spread over all Greece, and that they did not confine themselves to the recital of the *Homeric* poems. One class of rhapsodists at Chios, the Homeridæ,[4] who called themselves, without any good ground however, descendants of the poet, possessed these particular poems, and transmitted them to their disciples by oral teaching, and not by writing. This kind of oral teaching was most carefully cultivated in Greece, even when the use of writing was quite common. The tragic and comic poets employed no other way of training the actors than this oral διδασκαλία, with which the greatest accuracy was combined. Therefore, says Wolf, it is not likely that, although not committed to writing, the Homeric poems underwent very great changes by a long and oral tradition; only it is impossible that they should have remained quite *unaltered.* Many of the rhapsodists were not destitute of poetic genius, or they acquired it by the constant recitation of those beautiful lays. Why, he asks, should they not have sometimes adapted their recitation to the immediate occasion, or even have endeavored to make some passages better than they were?

XI. We can admit almost all this without drawing from it Wolf's conclusion. Does not such a condition of the rhapsodists agree as well with the task which we assign to them, of preserving and reciting a poem which already existed as a whole? Even the etymology of the name of rhapsodist, which is surprisingly inconsistent with Wolf's general view, favors that of his adversaries. Wolf's fundamental opinion is, that the original songs were unconnected, and singly recited. How, then, can the rhapsodists have obtained their name from *connecting* poems? On the other hand, if the Homeric poems originally existed as wholes, and the rhapsodists *connected* the single parts of these wholes for public recitation, they might, perhaps, be called "connecters of songs." But this etymology has not appeared satisfactory to some, who have thought that this process would rather be a *keeping* together than a *putting* together. They have therefore supposed that the word was derived from ῥάβδος, the staff

[1] *Wolf, Proleg.*, p. 96; *Nitzsch, Prol. ad Plat. Ion.; Heyne*, 2 *Excurs. ad Il.*, xxiv.; *Böckh ad Pind. Nem.*, ii., 1; *Isthm.*, iii., 55; *Nitzsch, Indagandæ*, &c., *Histor. Crit.; Kreuser, d. Hom. Rhapsod.*

[2] *Od.*, iii., 267; xviii., 383.

[3] *Plat., De Rep.*, x., p. 600; *Schol. ad Pind. Nem.*, ii., 1.

[4] *Harpocrat.*, *s. v.* Ὁμηρίδαι.

or ensign of the bards;[1] an etymology which seems countenanced by Pindar's expression ῥάβδον θεσπεσίων ἐπέων.[2] But Pindar in another passage gives the other etymology;[3] and, besides, it does not appear how ῥαψῳδός could be formed from ῥάβδος, which would make ῥαβδῳδός. Others, therefore, have thought of ῥάπις, "a stick," and have formed ῥαπισῳδός, ῥαψῳδός. But even this will not do; for, leaving out of view that ῥάπις does not occur in the signification of ῥάβδος, the word would be ῥαπιδῳδός. Nothing is left, therefore, but the etymology from ῥάπτειν ᾠδάς, which is only to be interpreted in the proper way.

XII. Müller says[4] that ῥαψωδεῖν signifies nothing more than the peculiar *method of epic recitation*, consisting in some high-pitched, sonorous declamations, with certain simple modulations of the voice, not in singing regularly accompanied by an instrument, which was the method of reciting lyric poetry. Every poem, he remarks, can be rhapsodized, which is composed in an epic tone, and in which the verses are of equal length, without being distributed into corresponding parts of a larger whole, strophes, or similar systems. Müller, therefore, thinks that ῥάπτειν ᾠδήν denotes the coupling together of verses, without any considerable divisions or pauses; in other words, the even, continuous, and unbroken flow of the epic poem.

XIII. But it has been justly objected to this explanation of Müller's that ᾠδή does not mean a *verse;* and besides, that a reference to the manner of epic recitation, as different from that of lyric poetry, could only be imparted to the word ῥαψῳδός at a time when lyric composition and recitation originated, that is, not before Archilochus. Previous to that time, the meaning of rhapsodist must have been different. It has been suggested, therefore, that ῥάπτειν ᾠδάς may have been used in the signification of planning and making lays, just as ῥάπτειν κακά is to plan or make mischief.

XIV. But whatever may be the right derivation of the word, and whatever may have been the nature and condition of the rhapsodists, so much is evident, that no support can be derived from this point for Wolf's position.

THE COLLECTION OF THE HOMERIC POEMS ASCRIBED TO PISISTRATUS.[5]

XV. Solon[6] made the first step toward that which Pisistratus accomplished. He is described as having checked the prevailing irregularities of recital, and having compelled the rhapsodists to adhere to the regular order of the text. Pisistratus went farther, and collected the poems, previously in a state of disorder, into a single body or volume.[7] Wolf explains this tradition respecting Pisistratus in a manner well calculated to favor his own peculiar views. He held this to have been the first move that was made in order to connect what, according to him, were before this loose and incoherent songs, into continued and uninterrupted

---

1 *Hes., Theog.*, 30. 2 *Isthm.*, iii., 5. 3 *Nem.*, ii., 1. 4 *Hist. Gr. Lit.*, p. 33.

5 *Ihne*, p. 506. Compare *Mure, Crit. Hist.*, vol. i., p. 203, *seqq.*

6 *Diog. Laert.*, i., 57.

7 *Cic., De Or.*, iii., 34; *Pausan.*, vii., 26; *Joseph. c. Ap.*, i., 2; *Ælian., V. H.*, xiii., 14; *Liban., Paneg. in Julian.*, i., p. 170, ed. *Reiske*, &c.

stories. Pausanias mentions associates (ἑταῖροι) of Pisistratus, who assisted him in the undertaking. These associates Wolf thought were the διασκευασταί mentioned sometimes in the scholia; but in this he was evidently mistaken. Διασκευασταί are, in the phraseology of the scholia, *interpolators*, and not arrangers.[1]

XVI. Another weak point in Wolf's reasoning is his saying that Pisistratus was the first who committed the Homeric poems to writing. This is expressly stated by none of the ancient writers. On the contrary, it is not unlikely that before Pisistratus, persons began in various parts of Greece, and particularly in Asia Minor, which was far in advance of the mother country, to write down parts of the Iliad and Odyssey. Whom Pisistratus employed in this undertaking Wolf could only conjecture. The poet Onomacritus lived at that time in Athens, and was engaged in similar pursuits respecting the old poet Musæus. Besides him, Wolf thought of a certain Orpheus of Crotona; but nothing definite was known on this point till Professor Ritschl discovered, in a MS. of Plautus at Rome, an old Latin scholion translated from the Greek of Tzetzes (published in Cramer's *Anecdota*). This scholion gives the names of four poets who assisted Pisistratus, viz., Onomacritus, Zopyrus, Orpheus, and a fourth, whose name is corrupted, Concylus.[2]

XVII. These four persons may have interpolated some passages, as it suited the pride of the Athenians or the political purposes of their patron Pisistratus. In fact, Onomacritus is particularly charged with having interpolated *Od.*, xi., 604.[3] The Athenians were generally believed to have had no part in the Trojan war; therefore *Il.*, ii., 547, 552–554, were marked by the Alexandrine grammarians as spurious, and for similar reasons *Od.*, vii., 80, 81, and *Od.*, iii., 308. But how unimportant are these alterations in comparison with the long interpolations which must be attributed to the rhapsodists previous to Pisistratus!

XVIII. It must be confessed that these four men accomplished their task, on the whole, with great accuracy. However inclined we may be to attribute this accuracy less to their critical investigations and conscientiousness than to the impossibility of making great changes on account of the general knowledge of what was genuine, through the number of existing copies; and although we may, on the whole, be induced, after Wolf's exaggerations, to think little of Pisistratus, still we must admit that the praise bestowed on him by the ancient writers is too great and too general to allow us to assent to Nitzsch's opinion that he only compared and examined various MSS.

XIX. If, then, it does not follow, as Wolf thought, that the Homeric poems never formed a whole before Pisistratus, it is at the same time undeniable that to Pisistratus we owe the first written text of the *whole of the poems*, which, without his care, would most likely now exist only in a few disjointed fragments.

---

[1] *Heinrich., De Diask. Homericis; Lehrs, Aristarchi Stud. Hom.*, p. 349.

[2] *Ritschl, Die Alex. Bibl. u. d. Sammlung d. Hom. Gedichte durch Peisistr.*, 1838; *Id., Corollar. Disput. de Bibl. Alex. deque Pisistr. Curis Hom.*, 1840.

[3] *Schol. Harlei.*, ed. *Porson*.

CHAPTER VIII.

SECOND OR POETICAL PERIOD—*continued.*

HOMERIC CONTROVERSY—*concluded.*

GENERAL SUMMARY.[1]

I. Having taken this general survey of the most important arguments for and against Wolf's hypothesis concerning the origin of the poems of Homer, the following may be regarded as the most probable conclusion. There can be no doubt that the seed of the Homeric poems was scattered in the time of the heroic exploits which they celebrate, and in the land of the victorious Achæans, that is, in European Greece. An abundance of heroic lays preserved the records of the Trojan war. It was a puerile idea, which is now completely exploded, that the events are fictitious on which the Iliad and Odyssey are based, and that a Trojan war never was waged.

II. Europe must necessarily have been the country where these songs originated, both because here the victorious heroes dwelt, and because so many traces in the poems still point to these regions. It was here, moreover, that the old Thracian bards had effected that unity of mythology which, spreading all over Greece, had gradually absorbed and obliterated the discrepancies of the old local myths, and substituted one general mythology for the whole nation, with Jove as the supreme ruler, dwelling on the snowy heights of Olympus. Impregnated with this European mythology, the heroic lays were brought to Asia Minor by the Greek colonies, which left the mother country about three ages after the Trojan war.

III. In European Greece, a new race gained the ascendency, the Dorians, foreign to those who gloried in having the old heroes among their ancestors. The heroic songs, therefore, died away more and more in Europe; but in Asia the Æolians fought, conquered, and settled nearly in the same regions in which their fathers had signalized themselves by immortal exploits, the glory of which was celebrated, and their memory still preserved by their national bards. Their dwelling in the same locality not only kept alive the remembrance of the deeds of their fathers, but gave a new impulse to their poetry, just as, in the Middle Ages in Germany, the foundation of the kingdom of the Hungarians in the East, and their destructive invasions, together with the origin of a new empire of the Burgundians in the West, awakened the old songs of the Niebelungen, after a slumber of centuries.[2]

IV. Now the Homeric poems advanced a step farther. From unconnected songs they were for the first time united by a great genius, who, whether he was really called Homer, or whether the name be of later

[1] *Ihne*, p. 507, *seq.*

[2] *Gervinus*, *Poetical Lit. of Germ.*, vol. i., p. 108.

origin, and significant of his work of uniting songs,[1] was *the one individual* who conceived in mind the lofty idea of that poetical unity which we can not help acknowledging and admiring. What were the peculiar excellencies which distinguished this one Homer among a great number of contemporary poets, and saved his works alone from oblivion, we do not venture to determine; but the conjecture of Müller[2] is not improbable, that Homer first undertook to combine into one great unity the scattered and fragmentary poems of earlier bards, and that it was this task which established his great renown.

V. We can now judge of the probability that Homer was an Ionian, who in Smyrna, where Ionians and Æolians were mixed together, became acquainted with the subject of his poems, and moulded them into the form which was suited to the taste of his Ionian countrymen. But as a faithful preservation of these long works was impossible in an age unacquainted with, or, at least, not versed in the art of writing, it was a natural consequence that, in the lapse of ages, the poems should not only lose their purity, but should also become more and more dismembered, and thus return into their original state of loose, independent songs. Their public recitation became more and more fragmentary, and the time at festivals and musical contests, formerly occupied by epic rhapsodists exclusively, was encroached upon by the rising lyric performances and players on the flute and lyre.

VI. Yet the knowledge of the unity of the different Homeric rhapsodies was not entirely lost. Solon, himself a poet, directed the attention of his countrymen toward it; and Pisistratus at last raised a lasting monument to his high merits, in fixing the genuine Homeric poems by the indelible marks of writing, as far as was possible in his time and with his means. That, previous to the famous edition of Pisistratus, parts of Homer, or the entire poems, were committed to writing in other towns of Greece or Asia Minor is not improbable, but we do not possess sufficient testimonies to prove it. We can, therefore, safely affirm that from the time of Pisistratus the Greeks had a written Homer, a regular text, the source and foundation of all subsequent editions.[3]

---

[1] *Welcker, Ep. Cycl.*, vol. i., p. 125, 128; *Ilgen, Hymn. Hom.*, præf., p. 23; *Heyne ad Il.*, vol. viii., p. 795, &c.

[2] *Hist. Gr. Lit.*, p. 47. Compare *Nitzsch, Anm.*, vol. ii., p. 26.

[3] The following list of the principal authors who have advocated, in whole or for the most part, the doctrines of Wolf, may not be unacceptable to the student. It is from Mure (*Hist. Crit.*, vol. i., p. 202), and will be found complete enough for all ordinary purposes: *C. F. Françeson, Essai sur la question, si Homère*, &c.; *F. Schlegel, Gesch. der Ep. Dichtk.*, viii.; *Heyne, Obs. ad Il.* (who claims, however, the right of prior discovery); *W. Müller, Homer. Vorschule; B. Thiersch, Urgestalt der Odyssée; Hermann, Opusc.*, vol. v., p. 52, *seqq.*; vol. vi., p. 70, *seqq.*; *Ritschl, Die Alexandrin. Biblioth.*; *Lachmann, Betrachtungen über die Ilias; Grote, History of Greece*, vol. ii., ch. 21.

The following are such as have entertained middle or opposite views: *Ste. Croix, Refutation, &c., de M. Wolf; Hug, Erfindung der Buchstabenschrift; Kreuser, Vorfragen über Homer; Clinton, Fast. Hell.*, vol. i., p. 366, *seqq.*; *Coleridge, Introd. to the Study of the Gr. Classics; Quarterly Review*, vol. xliv., p. 121, *seqq.* (article by Milman); *Welcker, Der Epische Cyclus*, vol. i., p. 122, *seqq.*; *K. O. Müller, Hist. of Gr. Lit.*; *Ihne* (*Smith's Dict Biogr.*); *Thirlwall, Hist. of Greece*, appendix to vol. i., 2d ed.; *Payne Knight, Prolegom in Hom.*; *Nitzsch, De Hist. Homeri* (and other works already cited by us).

CHAPTER IX.

SECOND OR POETICAL PERIOD—*continued.*

HOMERIC HYMNS AND MINOR POEMS.[1]

I. As certain hymns, which were known and admired in a more advanced literary period, were ascribed to the mythical bards, such as Olen, Orpheus, Linus, and Musæus, so many minor poems, consisting of hymns and humorous effusions, have been attributed to the author of the Iliad and Odyssey. Besides these there are a few short addresses to cities or private persons, which have been entitled Epigrams.

II. The Hymns, including the hymn to Ceres and the fragment to Bacchus, which were discovered in the last century at Moscow, and edited by Ruhnken, amount to thirty-three. There are six longer, and twenty-seven shorter ones. They were called by the ancients *προοίμια*, i. e., *overtures* or *preludes*, and were sung by the rhapsodists as introductions to epic poems at the festivals of the respective gods, to whom they are addressed. To these rhapsodists the hymns most probably owe their origin. According to Müller,[2] they exhibit such a diversity of language and poetical tone, that in all probability they contain fragments from every century, from the time of Homer to the Persian war.

III. Still, most of them were reckoned to be Homeric productions by those who lived in a time when Greek literature still flourished. This is easily accounted for. Being recited in connection with Homeric poems, they were gradually attributed to the same author, and continued to be so regarded more or less generally, till critics, and particularly those of Alexandrea, discovered the differences between their style and that of Homer. At Alexandrea they were never reckoned genuine, which accounts for the circumstance that no one of the great critics of that school is known to have made a regular collection of them.[3]

IV. Of the hymns now extant five deserve particular attention, on account of their greater length and mythological contents; they are those addressed to the Delian and Pythian Apollo, to Mercury, Ceres, and Venus. The hymn to the Delian Apollo, formerly regarded as part of the one to the Pythian Apollo, is the work of a Homerid of Chios, and approaches so nearly to the true Homeric tone, that the author, who calls himself the blind poet, who lived in the rocky Chios, was held even by Thucydides to be Homer himself. It narrates the birth of Apollo in Delos, but a great part of it is lost.

V. The hymn to the Pythian Apollo contains the foundation of the Pythian sanctuary by the god himself, who slays the serpent, and, in the form of a dolphin, leads certain men to Crissa, whom he establishes as priests of his temple.

VI. The hymn to Mercury, which, on account of its mentioning the

[1] *Ihne*, p. 508. [2] *Hist. Gr. Lit.*, p. 74. [3] *Wolf, Proleg.*, p. 266.

seven-stringed lyre, the invention of Terpander, can not have been composed before the 30th Olympiad, relates the tricks of the new-born Mercury, who, having left his cradle, drove away the cattle of Apollo from their pastures in Pieria to Pylos, there killed two, and then invented the lyre, made of a tortoise-shell, with which he pacified the anger of Apollo.

VII. The hymn to Venus celebrates the birth of Æneas in a style not very different from that of Homer. The hymn to Ceres, first discovered in 1778, in Moscow, by Matthæi, and first published by Ruhnken in 1780, gives an account of Ceres's search after her daughter Proserpina, who had been carried away by Pluto. The goddess obtains from Jupiter that her daughter should pass only one third part of the year with Pluto, and return to her for the rest of the year. With this symbolical description of the corn, which, when sown, remains for some time under ground, and then springs up, the poet has connected the mythology of the Eleusinians, who hospitably received the goddess on her wanderings, afterward built her a temple, and were rewarded by instruction in the mysterious rites of Ceres.

VIII. Another poem, of quite a different nature from the hymns, was also erroneously ascribed to Homer. This was the *Margītes* (Μαργίτης), a poem which Aristotle regarded as the source of comedy, just as he called the Iliad and Odyssey the fountain of all tragic poetry. From this view of Aristotle we may judge of the nature of the poem. It ridiculed a man who was said "to know many things, and to know all badly." The subject was nearly related to the scurrilous and satirical poetry of Archilochus and other contemporary iambographers, although in versification, epic tone, and language it imitated the Iliad. The iambic verses which are quoted from it by the grammarians were most likely interspersed by Pigres, brother of Artemisia, who is also called the author of this poem, and who interpolated the Iliad with pentameters in a similar manner.

IX. The same Pigres was perhaps the author of the *Batrachomyomachia* (Βατραχομυομαχία), or the Battle of the Frogs and Mice,[1] a poem frequently ascribed by the ancients to Homer. It is a harmless, playful tale, without a marked tendency to sarcasm and satire, amusing as a parody, but without any great poetical merit which could justify its being ascribed to the author of the Iliad and Odyssey. Knight[2] infers, from the employment of the word δέλτος as a writing tablet, instead of διφθέρα, a skin, which, according to Herodotus, was the material employed by the Asiatic Greeks for that purpose, that this poem was an offspring of Attic ingenuity; and, moreover, that the familiar mention of the cock (v. 191) affords a strong argument in favor of its late origin.

X. Besides these poems there were a great many more, most of which we know only by name, which we find attributed to Homer with more or less confidence. But we have good reason for doubting all such statements concerning lost poems, whose claims we can not examine, when we see that even Thucydides and Aristotle considered as genuine not only such poems as the Margites, and some of the hymns, but also all those passages of the Iliad and Odyssey which are evidently interpolated, and

[1] *Suid.*, *s. v.*; *Plut.*, *De Malign. Herod.*, 43.

[2] *Prolegom. in Homerum*, § 6.

which at the present day nobody would dream of ascribing to their reputed author.[1]

XI. The time in which Greek literature flourished was not adapted for tracing out the poems which were spurious and interpolated. People enjoyed all that was beautiful, without caring who was the author. The task of sifting and correcting the works of literature was left to the age in which the faculties of the Greek mind had ceased to produce original works, and had turned to scrutinize and preserve former productions. Then it was not only discovered that the cyclic poems and the hymns had no title to be styled "Homeric," but the question was mooted and warmly discussed whether the Odyssey was to be attributed to the author of the Iliad. Of the existence of this interesting controversy we had only a slight indication in Seneca,[2] before the publication of the Venetian scholia. From these we know now that there was a regular party of critics, who assigned the Iliad and Odyssey to two different authors, and were therefore called *Chorizontes* (Χωρίζοντες), "the Separators."[3] The question has been again opened in modern times, and we have already considered it.

CHAPTER X.

SECOND OR POETICAL PERIOD—*continued.*

HISTORY OF THE HOMERIC POEMS.[4]

I. The history of the Homeric poems may be divided conveniently into two great periods: one in which the text was transmitted by oral tradition, and the other of the *written* text after Pisistratus. Of the former we have already spoken; it, therefore, only remains to treat of the latter.

II. The epoch from Pisistratus down to the establishment of the first critical school at Alexandrea, that is, to Zenodotus, presents very few facts concerning the Homeric poems. Oral tradition still prevailed over writing for a long time; though in the days of Alcibiades it was expected that every schoolmaster would have a copy of Homer with which to teach his boys.[5] Homer became a sort of ground-work for a liberal education; and as his influence over the minds of the people thus became still stronger, the philosophers of that age were naturally led either to explain and recommend, or to oppose and refute the moral principles and religious doctrines contained in the heroic tales.[6]

III. It was with this practical view that Pythagoras, Xenophanes, and Heraclītus condemned Homer as one who uttered falsehoods, and degraded the majesty of the gods; while Theagenes, Metrodorus, Anaxagoras, and Stesimbrotus expounded the deep wisdom of Homer, which was disguised from the eyes of the common observer under the vail of an apparently insignificant tale. So old is the allegorical explanation, a folly at which the sober Socrates smiled, which Plato refuted, and Aristarchus

---

1 *Nitzsch, Anm. z. Odyss.*, vol. ii., p. 40.
2 *De Brevit. Vitæ*, 13.
3 *Grauert, über d. Hom. Choriz. Rhein. Mus.*, vol. i.
4 *Ihne*, p. 510, *seqq.*
5 *Plut.*, *Alcib.*, p. 194, D.
6 *Gräfenhan, Gesch. der Philologie,* vol. i., p. 202.

opposed with all his might, but which, nevertheless, outlived the sound critical study of Homer among the Greeks, and has thriven luxuriantly even down to the present day.

IV. A more scientific study was bestowed on Homer by the sophists of Pericles's age, Prodicus, Protagoras, Hippias, and others. There are even traces which seem to indicate that the *ἀπορίαι* and *λύσεις*, such favorite themes with the Alexandrine critics, originated with these sophists. Thus the study of Homer increased, and the copies of his works must naturally have been more and more multiplied. We may suppose that not a few of the literary men of that age carefully compared the best MSS. within their reach, and, choosing what they thought best, made new editions (*διορθώσεις*[1]). The task of these first editors was not an easy one. It may be concluded from the nature of the case, and it is known by various testimonies, that the text of those days offered enormous discrepancies, not paralleled in the text of any other classical writer. There were passages left out, transposed, added, or so altered as not easily to be recognized; nothing, in short, like a smooth vulgate existed before the time of the Alexandrine critics.

V. This state of the text must have presented immense difficulties to the first editors in the infancy of criticism. Yet these early editions were valuable to the Alexandreans, as being derived from good and ancient sources. Two only are known to us through the scholia, one of the poet Antimachus, and the famous one of Aristotle (*ἡ ἐκ τοῦ νάρθηκος*), which Alexander the Great used to carry about with him in a splendid case (*νάρθηξ*) on all his expeditions. Besides these editions, called in the scholia *αἱ κατ' ἄνδρα*, there were several other old *διορθώσεις* at Alexandrea, under the name of *αἱ κατὰ πόλεις*, or *αἱ ἐκ πόλεων*, or *αἱ πολιτικαί*. We know six of them, those of Massilia, Chios, Argos, Sinope, Cyprus, and Crete. It is hardly likely that they were made by public authority in the different states whose names they bear; on the contrary, as the persons who had made them were unknown, they were called, just as manuscripts are now, from the places where they had been found.

VI. All these editions, however, were only preparatory to the establishment of a regular and systematic criticism and interpretation of Homer, which began with Zenodotus at Alexandrea. For such a task the times after Alexander were quite fit. Life had fled from the literature of the Greeks; it was become a dead body, and was very properly carried into Egypt, there to be embalmed, and safely preserved for many ensuing centuries. It was the task of men, who, like Aristarchus, could judge of poetry without being able to write any themselves, to preserve carefully that which was extant, to clear it from all stains and corruptions, and to explain what was no longer rooted in and connected with the institutions of a free political life, and therefore was become unintelligible to all but the learned.

VII. Three men, who stand in the relation of masters and pupils, were at the head of a numerous host of scholars, who directed their attention either occasionally or exclusively to the study and criticism of the Ho-

[1] Compare *Wolf*, *Prolegom.*, p. 174.

meric poems. Zenodotus laid the foundation of systematic criticism by establishing two rules for purifying the corrupted text. He threw out: 1st, whatever was contradictory to, or not necessarily connected with, the whole of the work; 2d, what seemed unworthy of the genius of the author. To these two rules his followers, Aristophanes and Aristarchus, added two more; they rejected, 3d, what was contrary or foreign to the customs of the Homeric Age; and, 4th, what did not agree with the epic language and versification.

VIII. It is not to be wondered at that Zenodotus, in his first attempt, did not reach the summit of perfection. The manner in which he cut out long passages, arbitrarily altered others, transposed, and, in short, corrected Homer's text as he would have done his own, seemed shocking to all sober critics of later times, and would have proved very injurious to the text, had not Aristophanes, and still more Aristarchus, acted on sounder principles, and thus put a stop to the arbitrary system of Zenodotus. Aristophanes of Byzantium, a man of vast learning, seems to have been more occupied with the other parts of Greek literature, particularly the comic poets, than with Homer. He inserted in his edition many of the verses which had been thrown out by Zenodotus, and in many respects laid the foundations for what his pupil Aristarchus executed.

IX. The reputation of Aristarchus as the prince of grammarians was so great throughout the whole of antiquity, that, before the publication of the Venetian scholia by Villoison, we hardly knew how to account for it. But these excellent scholia, which have chiefly enabled us to understand the origin of the Homeric poems, teach us also to appreciate their great and unrivalled interpreter, and have now generally led to the conclusion that the highest aim of the ambition of modern critics with respect to Homer is to restore the edition of Aristarchus, an undertaking which is believed to be possible by one of the most competent judges, chiefly through the assistance afforded by these scholia.[1]

X. The *Obelus* (ὀβελός), one of the critical marks used by Aristarchus (÷), and invented, like the accents, by his master Aristophanes, was used for the ἀθέτησις, i. e., to mark those verses which seemed improper and detrimental to the beauty of the poem, but which Aristarchus dared not throw out of the text, as it was impossible to determine whether they were to be ascribed to an accidental carelessness of the author, or to interpolations of rhapsodists. Those verses which Aristarchus was convinced were spurious he left out of his edition altogether. Aristarchus was in constant opposition to Crates of Mallus, the founder of the Pergamenian school of grammar. This Crates had the merit of transplanting the study of literature to Rome.

XI. In the time of Augustus, the great compiler, Didymus, wrote most comprehensive commentaries on Homer, copying mostly the works of preceding Alexandrean grammarians, which had swollen to an enormous extent. Under Tiberius, Apollonius Sophista lived, whose *Lexicon Homericum* is very valuable. Apion, a pupil of Didymus, was of much less

[1] *Lehrs, De Aristarchi Studiis Homericis*, 1833.

importance than is generally believed, chiefly on the authority of Wolf. he was a great quack and an impudent boaster. Longinus and his pupil, Porphyrius, of whom we possess some tolerably good scholia, were of more value. The Homeric scholia are dispersed in various MSS. Complete collections do not exist, nor are they desirable, as many of them are utterly useless. The most valuable scholia on the Iliad are those already referred to, which were published by Villoison from a MS. of the tenth century, in the library of St. Mark at Venice, together with the scholia to the Iliad previously published, Ven., 1788, fol. These scholia were reprinted with additions, edited by Bekker, Berlin, 1825, 2 vols. 4to, with an appendix, 1826, which collection contains all that is worth reading. A few additions are to be found in Bachmann's *Scholia ad Homeri Iliadem*, Lips., 1835. The most valuable scholia to the Odyssey are those published by Buttmann, Berl., 1821, mostly taken from the scholia originally published by Mai, from a MS. at Milan, in 1819. The extensive commentary of Eustathius is a compilation destitute of judgment and of taste, but contains much valuable information from sources which are now lost.

EDITIONS OF HOMER.[1]

XII. The old editions of Homer, as well as the MSS., are of very little importance for the restoration of the text, for which we must apply to the scholia. The Editio Princeps, by Demetrius Chalcondylas, Flor., 1488, fol., was the first large work printed in Greek, one psalm only, and the Batrachomyomachia, having preceded This edition was frequently reprinted. Wolf reckons scarcely seven critical editions from the Editio Princeps to his time. That of H. Stephanus, in *Poet. Græc. Princ. her. Carm.*, Paris, 1566, fol., was one of the best. In England, the edition of Barnes, Cantab., 1711, 2 vols. 4to; and that of Clarke, who published the Iliad in 1729, and the Odyssey in 1740, were generally used for a long time, and often reprinted. The latter was published, with additions by Ernesti, Lips., 1759–1764, 5 vols. 8vo. This edition was reprinted at Glasgow, with Wolf's Prolegomena, in 1814, and again at Leipzig, in 1824.

XIII. A new period began with Wolf's second edition, *Homeri et Homeridarum Op. et Rel.,Halis*, 1794, the first edition (1784 and 1785) being merely a copy of the vulgate. Along with the second edition were published the Prolegomena. A third edition was published from 1804–1807. It is very much to be regretted that the editions of Wolf are without commentaries or critical notes, so that it is impossible to know in many cases on what grounds he adopted his readings, which differ from the vulgate. Heyne began in 1802 to publish the Iliad, which was finished in eight volumes, and was most severely and unsparingly reviewed by Wolf, Voss, and Eichstädt, in the *Jenaer Literatur Zeitung*, 1803. A ninth volume, containing the Indices, was published by Græfenhan in 1822.

XIV. The best recension of the text of Homer is that by Bekker, Berlin, 1843. A very good edition of the Iliad, with critical notes, was given by Spitzner, Gotha, 1832–1836, but the author did not live to publish his explanatory commentary. There is an excellent commentary to the two first books of the Iliad by Freytag, Petersburg, 1837, and a more extensive one by Stadelmann, of which two volumes have appeared, Leipzig, 1840–1844. But the best of all commentaries which have yet appeared on the Homeric poems are those of Nitzsch on the Odyssey, Hanover, 1825, &c., of which the three volumes now published extend only as far as the twelfth book. The latest edition of Homer for general readers is that from the press of Didot, Paris, 1838, containing also the Cyclic fragments. It has a corrected Latin version, but no commentary. There is a good school edition of the Iliad and Odyssey, with German notes by Crusius, Hanover, 1840, 1842.

XV. The most valuable of the separate editions of the Hymns are those by Ilgen, Hal., 1791, and Hermann, Lips., 1806. The *Lexicon Novum Homericum (et Pindaricum)* of Damm, originally published at Berlin in 1765, and reprinted at London, 1827, is still of

[1] *Ihne*, p. 511.

some value, though the author was destitute of all sound principles of criticism. But a far more important work for the student is Buttmann's *Lexilogus*, Berlin, 1825 and 1837, translated by Fishlake, London, 1840, 2d ed. A complete account of the literature of the Homeric poems will be found in the *Bibliotheca Homerica*, Hal., 1837, and in the notes to the first volume of Bode's *Geschichte der Hellenischen Dichtkunst.*

CHAPTER XI.

SECOND OR POETICAL PERIOD—*continued.*

CYCLIC POETS.[1]

I. The Iliad and Odyssey contained only a small part of the copious traditions concerning the Trojan war. A great number of poets undertook to fill up, by separate poems, the whole *cycle* (*κύκλος*) of the events of this war, from which circumstance they are commonly styled the *Cyclic* poets (Κυκλικοί). The series terminated with the death of Ulysses, this event being regarded as the closing scene of the cycle.

II. The Cyclic poems, both in their character and conception of the mythical events, were very different from the Iliad and Odyssey. These Cyclic authors can not even have been called Homeridæ, since a class of persons bearing this name existed only in Chios, and not one of the Cyclic bards is called a Chian. It is probable that they were Homeric rhapsodists by profession, to whom the constant recitation of the ancient Homeric poems would naturally suggest the notion of continuing them by essays of their own in a similar tone.

III. From a close comparison of the extracts and fragments of these poems, which we still possess, it is evident that their authors had before them copies of the Iliad and Odyssey in their complete form, or, to speak more accurately, comprehending the same series of events as those current among the later Greeks and ourselves, and that they merely connected the action of their own poems with the beginning and the end of these two epopees. But, notwithstanding the close connection which they made between their own productions and the Homeric poems, and notwithstanding that they often built upon particular allusions in Homer, and formed from them long passages of their own poems, still their manner of treating and viewing mythical subjects differs so widely from that of Homer, as of itself to be a sufficient proof that the Homeric poems were no longer in progress of development at the time of the Cyclic poets, but had, on the whole, attained a settled form, to which no additions of importance were afterward made.

IV. The Cypria[2] (τὰ Κύπρια ἔπη), in eleven books, was the first, in the order of the events contained in it, of the poems of the Epic Cycle relating to the Trojan war. It embraced the period antecedent to the beginning of the Iliad, to which it was evidently designed to form an introduction. From the outline given by Proclus, and from the extant fragments, a good idea may be formed of its structure and contents. The Earth,

---

1 *Müller, Hist. Gr. Lit.*, p. 64, *seqq.* Compare *Mure, Crit. Hist.*, vol. ii., p. 248, *seqq.*; *Welcker, Der epische Cyclus*, &c.

2 *Smith, Dict. Biogr.*, *s. v.* Stasinus; *Welcker*, vol. ii., p. 85, *seqq.*

wearied with the burden of the degenerate race of man, entreats Jupiter to diminish their numbers. He grants her request, and prepares two chief agents to accomplish it, Helen and Achilles, the beauty of the former furnishing the cause of the contest, and the sword of the latter the instrument of extermination. The events succeeding the birth of Helen, or, rather (for the form of the myth is varied), her being sent by Jupiter to Leda to bring up, and the marriage of Peleus, down to the sailing of the expedition against Troy, were related at great length, and the incidents of the war itself much more briefly, the latter part being apparently occupied chiefly with those previous adventures of the heroes which are referred to in the Iliad. It concluded with the following somewhat clumsy contrivance to connect it with the opening of the Iliad: the war itself is not found to be murderous enough to accomplish the object prayed for by Earth, and in order to effect it more surely, the fresh contention between Achilles and Agamemnon is stirred up by Jupiter.

V. The *Cypria* was attributed by some of the ancient writers to STASĪNUS (Στασῖνος) of Cyprus, but the statements on the subject are so various, and partake so much of conjecture, that no certain conclusion can be drawn from them. In the earliest historical period of Greek literature, and before critical inquiries began, the poem was accepted without question as a work of Homer. It is not till we come down to the times of Athenæus and the grammarians that we find any mention of Stasinus, and even then the *Cypria* is ascribed to him in a very hesitating and indefinite manner.[1] Proclus, who is our chief authority for the history of the epic cycle,[2] not only tells us that the poem was ascribed to Stasinus, or Hegesinas, or Homer, but what he and others say of Stasinus only adds new doubts to those which already beset the subject, and new proofs of the uncertainties of the ancients themselves respecting it.

VI. Stasinus was said to have been the son-in-law of Homer, who, according to one story, composed the *Cypria*, and gave it to Stasinus as his daughter's marriage portion; manifestly an attempt to reconcile the two different accounts, which ascribed it to Homer and Stasinus.[3] Considering the immense range of mythological stories which we know the poem to have embraced, there is much probability in the opinion of Bernhardy, that it was a work of many times and many hands. Its title also was not, as we are told, derived from the native island of Stasinus, but may be explained by the conspicuous part which Venus (Κυπρίς) has in the general action.

VII. Proceeding next to the Cyclic poems which *continued the Iliad*, we come to ARCTINUS of MILETUS,[4] who was confessedly a very ancient poet; nay, he is even called by Dionysius of Halicarnassus[5] the oldest Grecian poet, whence some writers have placed him even before the time of Homer; but the ancients who have assigned to him any certain date agree in placing him about the commencement of the Olympiads. He is

---

1 *Athen.*, ii., p. 35, *c*; viii., p. 334; xv., p. 682, *e*.

2 *Procl.*, *Chrestom.*, in Gaisford's *Hephæst. et Procl.*, p. 471, *seqq.*

3 *Procl.*, *l. c.*; *Ælian.*, *V. H.*, ix., 15.

4 *Smith*, *Dict. Biogr.*, *s. v.*; *Welcker*, vol. i., p. 211, *seqq.*

5 *Ant. Rom.*, i., 68, *seqq.*

called a disciple of Homer; and, from all we know about him, there was scarcely a poet in his time who deserved this title more than Arctinus. He was the most distinguished among the cyclic poets. There were in antiquity two epic poems belonging to the cycle, which are unanimously attributed to him, namely, the *Æthiopis* (Αἰθιοπίς) and Ἰλίου πέρσις.

VIII. The *Æthiopis* was in five books. It was a kind of continuation of the Iliad, and its chief heroes were Memnon, son of Aurora, king of the Æthiopians, and Achilles, who slew him. The substance of it has been preserved by Proclus. The Ἰλίου πέρσις, or *Destruction of Ilium*, was in two books, and contained a description of the taking and destruction of Troy, and the subsequent events, until the departure of the Greeks. The substance of this poem has also been given by Proclus. A third epic poem, called Τιτανομαχία, that is, the fight of the gods with the Titans, and which was probably the first poem in the epic cycle, was ascribed by some to Arctinus, by others to Eumelus of Corinth.[1]

IX. Lesches, or Lescheus[2] (Λέσχης, Λεσχεύς), was a native of Pyrrha, in the island of Lesbos, and in the neighborhood of Mytilene.[3] Hence he is called a Mytilenean or Lesbian. The best authorities concur in placing him in the time of Archilochus, or about the 18th Olympiad. The account, therefore, which we find in ancient authors of a contest between Arctinus and Lesches, can only mean that the later competed with the earlier poet in treating the same subjects, and not that they were contemporaries, which would be an anachronism. His poem, which was attributed by many to Homer, and, besides, to various other authors, was called the *Little Iliad* (Ἰλιὰς ἡ ἐλάσσων, or Ἰλιὰς μικρά). It consisted of four books, according to Proclus, who has preserved an extract from it. It was evidently intended as a supplement to the Homeric Iliad; consequently, it related the events after the death of Hector, the fate of Ajax, the exploits of Philoctetes, Neoptolemus, and Ulysses, and the final capture and destruction of Troy.[4] The connection of events was necessarily loose and superficial, and without any unity of subject.[5]

X. Between the poems of Arctinus, and Lesches, and the Odyssey, came the epic of Agias,[6] the Trœzenian, divided into five books, and entitled *Nostoi* (Νόστοι). His poem was celebrated in antiquity, and gave the history of the return (νόστοι) of the Grecians from Troy, and consisted of five books. The poem began with the cause of the misfortunes which befell the Greeks on their way home and after their arrival, that is, with the outrage committed upon Cassandra and with the seizure of the Palladium. Agias wrote about B.C. 740. Some writers attributed the Νόστοι to Homer.[7] Similar poems, and with the same title, were written by other poets also.[8] Wherever the Νόστοι, however, is mentioned without a name, we have generally to understand the work of Agias.[9]

XI. The continuation of the Odyssey was the *Telegonia*[10] (Τηλεγονία).

1 *Athen.*, i., p. 22; vii., p. 277. 2 *Smith, Dict. Biogr.*, *s. v.* 3 *Pausan.*, x., 25, 5.
4 *Arist.*, *Poet.*, 23, ed. *Bekker.* 5 *Müller, Hist. Gr. Lit.*, p. 66. 6 *Smith, Dict. Biog.*, *s. v.*
7 *Suid.*, *s. v.* *νόστοι*; *Anthol. Planud.*, iv., 30.
8 *Schol. ad Pind.*, *Ol.*, xiii., 31; *Athen.*, iv., p. 157; ix., p. 466.
9 The name was formerly written Augias, through a mistake of the first editor of the Excerpta of Proclus. 10 *Müller, Hist. Gr. Lit.*, p. 70; *Welcker*, vol. ii., p. 301, *seqq.*

It consisted of two books or rhapsodies, and formed the conclusion of the epic cycle. EUGAMON (Εὐγάμων) of CYRENE, who did not live before the 53d Olympiad, is named as the author. It contained an account of all that happened after the fight of Ulysses with the suitors of Penelope, until the death of Ulysses. The substance of the poem is preserved by Proclus. As Eugamon lived at so late a period, it is highly probable that he made use of the productions of earlier poets; and Clemens of Alexandrea expressly states that Eugamon incorporated in his Telegonia a whole epic poem of Musæus, entitled "*Thesprotis.*" The name Telegonia was formed from Telegonus, a son of Ulysses and Circe, who killed his father.

XII. With the exception of the events of the Trojan war, and the return of the Greeks, nothing was so closely connected with the Iliad and Odyssey as the *war of the Argives against Thebes;* since many of the principal heroes of Greece, particularly Diomede and Sthenelus, were themselves among the conquerors of Thebes, and their fathers before them, a bolder and wilder race, had fought on the same spot, in a contest which, though unattended with victory, was still far from inglorious. The *Thebaïs*, which consisted of seven books, or 5600 verses, took this war for its subject, and originated from Argos. The *Epigŏni* (Ἐπίγονοι) was so far a second part of the *Thebaïs*, that it was sometimes comprehended under the same name. Its subject was the second expedition against Thebes, in which the Epigoni proved successful.[1]

CHAPTER XII.

SECOND OR POETICAL PERIOD—*continued.*

HESIOD.

I. HESIOD (Ἡσίοδος)[2] was one of the earliest Greek poets, and we possess respecting his personal history little more authentic information than respecting that of Homer, together with whom he is frequently mentioned by the ancients. The names of these two poets, in fact, form, as it were, the two poles of the early epic poetry of the Greeks; and as Homer represents the poetry, or school of poetry, belonging chiefly to Ionia, in Asia Minor, so Hesiod is the representative of a school of bards, which was developed somewhat later at the foot of Mount Helicon, in Bœotia, and spread over Phocis and Eubœa.

II. The only points of resemblance between the two poets, or their respective schools, consist in their forms of versification and in their dialect, but in all other respects they move in totally different spheres; for the Homeric takes for its subjects the restless activity of the Heroic Age, while the Hesiodic turns its attention to the quiet pursuits of ordinary life, to the origin of the world, the gods and heroes. The latter thus gives to its productions an ethical and religious character; and this circumstance alone suggests an advance in the intellectual state of the ancient Greeks upon that depicted in the Homeric poems; though we do not mean to assert that the elements of the Hesiodic poetry are of a later date

[1] *Müller, Hist. Gr. Lit.*, p. 71.

[2] *Smith, Dict. Biogr.*, *s. v.*

than the age of Homer, for they may, on the contrary, be as ancient as the Greek nation itself.

III. But we must, at any rate, infer that the Hesiodic poetry, such as it has come down to us, is of later growth than the Homeric; an opinion which is confirmed also by the language and expressions of the two schools, and by a variety of collateral circumstances, among which we may mention the range of knowledge being much more extensive in the poems which bear the name of Hesiod than in those attributed to Homer. Herodotus and others regarded Homer and Hesiod as contemporaries, and some even assigned to the latter an earlier date than the former;[1] but the general opinion of the ancients was that Homer was the elder of the two.

IV. Most modern critics assume that Hesiod lived about a century later than Homer, which is pretty much in accordance with the statement of some ancient writers, who place him about the eleventh Olympiad, that is, about B.C. 735. Respecting the life of the poet we derive some information from one of the poems ascribed to him, namely, the Ἔργα καὶ ἡμέραι. We learn from that poem[2] that he was born in the village of Ascra, in Bœotia, whither his father had emigrated from the Æolian Cyma, in Asia Minor. The poet describes himself[3] as tending a flock on the side of Mount Helicon, and from this, as well as from the fact of his calling himself an ἀτίμητος,[4] we must infer that he belonged to an humble station, and was engaged in rural pursuits. But subsequently his circumstances seem to have been bettered, and after the death of his father he was involved in a dispute with his brother Perses about his small patrimony, which was decided in favor of Perses.[5]

V. Hesiod seems after this to have migrated to Orchomenus, where he spent the remainder of his life.[6] At Orchomenus he is also said to have been buried, and his tomb was shown there in later times. What we have thus far stated is all that can be said with any degree of certainty about the life of Hesiod. Among the apocryphal stories related of the bard is one respecting a poetical contest between him and Homer, which is said to have taken place at Chalcis during the funeral solemnities of King Amphidamas, or, according to others, at Aulis or Delos.[7] The story of this contest gave rise to a composition still extant under the title of Ἀγὼν Ὁμήρου καὶ Ἡσιόδου, the work of a grammarian who lived toward the end of the first century of our era, in which the two poets are represented as engaged in the contest, and answering each other in their verses. The author of this production pretends to know the whole family history of Hesiod, and traces his descent from Orpheus, Linus, and Apollo himself. These legends, though they are mere fictions, show the connection which the ancients conceived to exist between the poetry of Hesiod (especially the Theogony) and the ancient schools of priests and bards, which had their seats in Thrace and Pieria, and thence spread into Bœotia, where

---

1 *Gell.*, iii., 11; xvii., 21; *Suid.*, *s. v.* Ἡσίοδος.
2 v. 648, *seqq.*
3 *Theog.*, 23.
4 *Op. et Dies*, 636.
5 *Id.*, 219, 261, 637.
6 *Pind. ap. Procl.*, γένος Ἡσιόδου, p. xliv.; *Hes.*, *ed. Göttl.*
7 *Proclus*, *l. c.*, p. xliii.; *Plut.*, *Conv. Sep. Sap.*, 10.

they probably formed the elements out of which the Hesiodic poetry was developed.

VI. The differences between the Homeric and the Hesiodic schools of poetry are plain and obvious, and were recognized in ancient times no less than at present, as may be seen from the Ἀγὼν Ὁμήρου καὶ Ἡσιόδου.[1] In their mode of delivery the poets of the two schools likewise differed; for while the Homeric poems were recited under the accompaniment of the cithara, those of Hesiod were recited without any musical instrument, the reciter holding in his hand only a branch of bay, or a staff (ῥάβδος, σκῆπτρον).[2] Another point of difference between the Homeric and Hesiodic poetry is produced by certain grammatical forms in the language of Hesiod, although the dialect in which the poems of both schools are composed is, on the whole, the same, namely, the Ionic-epic, which had become established as the language of epic poetry through the influence of Homer.

VII. The ancients attributed to Hesiod a great variety of works; that is, all those which in form and substance answered to the spirit of the Hesiodic school, and thus seemed to be of a common origin. We shall subjoin a list of them, beginning with those which are still extant.

1. Ἔργα καὶ Ἡμέραι, or Ἔργα simply, commonly called *Opera et Dies*, or "Works and Days." In the time of Pausanias,[3] this was the only poem which the people about Mount Helicon considered to be a genuine production of Hesiod, with the exception of the first ten lines, which certainly appear to have been prefixed by a later hand. There are also several other parts of this poem which seem to be later interpolations; but, on the whole, it bears the impress of a genuine production of very high antiquity, though in its present form it may consist only of disjointed portions of the original. It is written in the most homely and simple style, with scarcely any poetic imagery or ornament, and must be looked upon as the most ancient specimen of didactic poetry. It contains ethical, political, and economical precepts, the last of which constitute the greater part of the work, consisting of rules about choosing a wife, the education of children, agriculture, commerce, and navigation.

A poem on these subjects was not, of course, held in much esteem by the powerful and ruling classes in Greece at the time, and made the Spartan Cleomenes contemptuously call Hesiod the poet of Helots, in contrast with Homer, the delight of the warrior.[4] Afterward, however, when the warlike spirit of the Heroic Ages subsided, and peaceful pursuits began to be held in higher esteem, the poet of the plough rose from his obscurity, and was looked upon as a sage; nay, the very contrast with the heroic poetry may have contributed to raise his fame, except, indeed, with such martial spirits as Cleomenes. At all events, the poem, notwithstanding its want of unity, and the incoherence of its parts, gives us an attractive picture of the simplicity of the early Greek mode of life, of their manners, and their domestic relations.

The conclusion of the poem, from v. 750 to 828, is a sort of calendar, and was probably appended to it in later times; and the addition καὶ ἡμέ-

[1] p. 248, *ed. Göttling*.
[2] *Hesiod.*, *Theog.*, 30; *Paus.*, ix., 30; x., 7, 2.
[3] *Paus.*, ix., 31, 3.
[4] *Plut.*, *Apophth. Lac. Cleom.*, i.

ραι, in the title of the poem, seems to have been added in consequence of this appendage, for the poem is sometimes simply called Ἔργα. It would farther seem that three distinct poems have been inserted in it, namely: 1. The fable of Prometheus and Pandora (v. 47–105); 2. On the Ages of the World, which are designated by the names of metals (v. 109–201); and, 3. A Description of Winter (v. 504–558). The first two of these poems are not so much out of keeping with the whole as the third, which is manifestly the most recent production of all, and most foreign to the spirit of Hesiod. That which remains, after the deduction of these probable interpolations, consists of a collection of maxims, proverbs, and wise sayings, containing a considerable amount of practical wisdom; and some of these γνῶμαι or ὑποθῆκαι may be as old as the Greek nation itself.[1]

2. Θεογονία, or "*Theogony*." This poem was, as we have already remarked, not considered by Hesiod's countrymen to be a genuine production of the poet's. It presents, indeed, great differences from the preceding one, its very subject being apparently foreign to the homely author of the Ἔργα. The Alexandrine grammarians, however, especially Zenodotus and Aristarchus, appear to have had no doubt about its genuineness,[2] though their opinion can not be taken to mean any thing else than that the poem contained nothing that was opposed to the character of the Hesiodic school; and thus much we may therefore take for granted, that the "Theogony" is not the production of the same poet as the Ἔργα, and that it probably belongs to a later date.

The "Theogony" gives an account of the origin of the world and the birth of the gods, explaining the whole order of nature in a series of genealogies, for every part of physical as well as moral nature there appears personified in the character of a distinct being. The whole concludes with an account of some of the most illustrious heroes, whereby the poem enters into some kind of connection with the Homeric epics. The whole poem may be divided into three parts: 1. The Cosmogony, which widely differs from the simple Homeric notion,[3] and afterward served as the ground-work for the various physical speculations of the Greek philosophers, who looked upon the Theogony of Hesiod as containing in an allegorical form all the physical wisdom that they were able to propound, though Hesiod himself was believed not to have been aware of the profound philosophical and theological wisdom which he was uttering. The Cosmogony extends from v. 116 to 452; 2. The Theogony, in the strict sense of the word, from v. 453 to 962; and, 3. The last portion, which is, in fact, a heroogony, being an account of the heroes born from mortal mothers, whose charms had drawn the immortals from Olympus. This part is very brief, extending only from v. 963 to 1021, and forms the transition to the *Eœæ*, of which we shall speak presently.

If we ask for the sources from which the author of the Theogony drew his information respecting the origin of the world and the gods, the answer can not be much more than a conjecture, for there is no direct information on the point. Herodotus asserts that Homer and Hesiod made

[1] *Isocr. c. Nicocl.*, p. 23, ed. *Steph.*; *Lucian.*, *Dial. de Hes.*, i., 8.

[2] *Schol. Venet. ad Il.*, xviii., 39.

[3] *Il.*, xiv., 200.

the Theogony of the Greeks; and, in reference to Hesiod in particular, this probably means that Hesiod collected and combined into a system the various local legends, especially of northern Greece, such as they had been handed down by priests and bards. The assertion of Herodotus farther obliges us to take into consideration the fact that, in the earliest Greek theology, the gods do not appear in any definite forms, whereas Hesiod strives to anthropomorphize all of them, the ancient elementary gods, as well as the later dynasties of Saturn and Jove. Now both the system of the gods and the forms under which he conceived them afterward became firmly established in Greece, and, considered in this way, the assertion of Herodotus is perfectly correct.

Whether the form in which the Theogony has come down to us is the original and genuine one, and whether it is complete or only a fragment, is a question which has been much discussed in modern times. There can be little doubt but that in the course of time the poets of the Hesiodic school and the rhapsodists introduced various interpolations, which produced many of the inequalities, both in the substance and form of the poem, which we now perceive; many parts, also, may have been lost. Hermann has endeavored to show that there exist no less than seven different introductions to the Theogony, and that, consequently, there existed as many different recensions and editions of it. But as our present form itself belongs to a very early date, it would be useless to attempt to determine what part of it formed the original kernel, and what is to be considered as later addition or interpolation.[1]

3. Ἠοῖαι, or ἠοῖαι μεγάλαι, also called Κατάλογοι γυναικῶν. The name ἠοῖαι was derived, according to the ancient grammarians, from the fact that the heroines, who, by their connection with the immortal gods, had become the mothers of the most illustrious heroes, were introduced into the poem by the expression ἢ οἵη, "or such as." The poem itself, which is lost, is said to have consisted of four books, the last of which was by far the longest, and was hence called ἠοῖαι μεγάλαι, whereas the titles κατάλογοι, or ἠοῖαι, belonged to the whole body of poetry, containing accounts of the women who had been beloved by the gods, and had thus become the mothers of the heroes in the various parts of Greece, from whom the ruling families derived their origin. The work thus contained the genealogies or pedigrees of the most illustrious Greek families. Whether the Eœæ or Catalogi was the work of one and the same poet, was a disputed point among the ancients themselves.[2]

4. Ἀσπὶς Ἡρακλέους, or "*Shield of Hercules*," a poem on the combat between Hercules and Cycnus, containing a description of the hero's shield. This description is an imitation of the Homeric account of the shield of Achilles, but is done with much less skill and ability. It is generally supposed that this poem, or perhaps fragment of a poem, originally belonged to the Eœæ.

5. Αἰγίμιος, an epic poem, consisting of several books or rhapsodies, on

[1] Compare *Creuzer und Hermann*, *Briefe über Hom. und Hes.*, Heidelb., 1817, 8vo, *Sickler*, *Cadmus*, &c., Hildburg., 1818, 4to.

[2] *Schol. ad Apoll. Rhod.*, ii., 181; *Schol. ad Hes.*, *Theog.*, 142.

the story of Ægimius, the famous ancestral hero of the Dorians, and the mythical history of the Dorians in general. Some of the ancients attributed this poem to Cercops of Miletus.[1] A few fragments alone remain.

6. Μελαμποδία, an epic poem, consisting of at least three books, and containing the stories about the seer Melampus. It was thus of a similar character with the poems which celebrated the glory of the heroic families of the Greeks. Some of the ancients denied that this was an Hesiodic poem.[2] Fragments alone have reached us.

7. Ἐξήγησις ἐπὶ τέρασιν. This is mentioned as an Hesiodic work by Pausanias,[3] and is distinguished by him from another entitled ἔπη μαντικά; but it is not improbable that both were identical with, or portions of, an astronomical work, ascribed to Hesiod, under the title of ἀστρικὴ βίβλος, or ἀστρολογία.[4] We have some fragments remaining.

8. Χείρωνος ὑποθῆκαι. This seems to have been an imitation of the Ἔργα. A few fragments remain.

VIII. The poems of Hesiod, especially the Theogony, were looked up to by the Greeks from very early times as great authority in theological and philosophical matters, and philosophers of nearly every school attempted, by various modes of interpretation, to bring about a harmony between the statements of Hesiod and their own theories. The scholars of Alexandrea and of other cities, such as Zenodotus, Aristophanes, Aristarchus, Crates of Mallus, Apollonius Rhodius, Seleucus of Alexandrea, Plutarch, and others, devoted themselves with great zeal to the criticism and explanation of the poems of Hesiod; but all their works on this poet are lost, with the exception of some isolated remarks contained in the scholia on Hesiod, now extant. These scholia are the productions of a much later age, though their authors made use of the works of the earlier grammarians. The scholia of the Neo-Platonist Proclus (though only in an abridged form), of Joannes Tzetzes, and Moschopulus, on the Ἔργα, and introductions on the life of Hesiod, are still extant. The scholia on the Theogony are a compilation from earlier and later commentators. The most complete edition of the scholia on Hesiod is that in the third volume of Gaisford's *Poetæ Græci Minores*.

EDITIONS OF HESIOD.[5]

IX. The Greek text of the Hesiodic poems was first printed at Milan in 1493, fol., together with Isocrates and some of the idylls of Theocritus. The next edition is that in the collection of gnomic and bucolic poems, published by Aldus Manutius, Venice, 1495. The first separate edition is that of Junta, Florence, 1515, and again 1540, 8vo. The first edition that contains the Greek scholia is that of Trincavellus, Venice, 1537, 4to, and more complete at Cologne, 1542, 8vo, and Frankfurt, 1591, 8vo. The most important among the subsequent editions are those of Dan. Heinsius, Amsterdam, 1667, 8vo, with *lectiones Hesiodeæ* and notes by Scaliger and Guietus: it was reprinted by Leclerc in 1701, 8vo; of Th. Robinson, Oxford, 1737, 4to; reprinted at Leipzig, 1746, 8vo; of Loesner, Leipzig, 1778, 8vo, containing all that his predecessors had accumulated, together with some new remarks; of Gaisford, in the first volume of his *Poetæ Græci Minores*, where some new manuscripts are collated; and of Göttling, Gotha and Erfurt, 1831, 8vo (2d ed., 1843), with good critical and explanatory notes. A revision of the text by Loers, with Latin version, is given in the Bibl. Græca of Didot, Paris, 1840. The Ἔργα were

[1] *Apollod.*, ii., 1, 3; *Diog. Laert.*, ii., 46. [2] *Paus.*, ix., 31, 4. [3] *Id. ib.*
[4] *Athen.*, xi., p. 491; *Plut.*, *De Pyth. Orac.*, 18. [5] *Smith, Dict. Biogr.*, *s. v.*

edited also by Brunck, in his *Poetæ Gnomici* and other collections. The Theogony was edited separately by F. A. Wolf, Halle, 1783, and by Van Lennep, Amsterdam, 1843, 8vo, with a very useful commentary. There are also two good editions of the 'Ασπίς, the one by Heinrich, Breslau, 1802, 8vo, with an introduction, scholia, and commentary; and the other by Ranke, Quedlinburg, 1840, 8vo.

CHAPTER XIII.

SECOND OR POETICAL PERIOD—*continued*.

MISCELLANEOUS EPIC POETRY OF THIS PERIOD.[1]

I. Great as was the number of poems which in ancient times passed under the name of Homer, and were connected in the way of supplement or continuation with the Iliad and Odyssey, and also of those which were included under the all-comprehensive name of Hesiod, yet these formed only about one half of the entire epic literature of the early Greeks. Of the others, some appear to have aimed at a certain amount of Homeric unity of structure, others were but metrical chronicles. Their authors appear, for the most part, both in the selection of their mythical subjects and in general style and phraseology, to have conformed to the old conventional standard of epic mannerism.

II. Toward the close of this period, however, efforts are observable on the part of Pisander, Epimenides, and other poetically gifted disciples of the popular schools of religious mysticism, who availed themselves of the Epic Muse in promulgating their doctrines, to enliven the prevailing monotony, partly by the introduction of new materials, partly by bolder methods of working up those transmitted by their predecessors. Few of these works, however, enjoyed any great celebrity or popularity with the later Hellenic public. Several had perished even during the flourishing ages of Greek literature, or were no longer familiar in the original text to the authors by whom they were cited; and with the exception of a limited stock of fragments, the whole are now entirely lost. We subjoin a brief account of the principal ones among these writers.

III. 1. Cinæthon[2] (Κιναίθων), of Lacedæmon, is placed by Eusebius[3] in B.C. 765. He was the author of: 1. *Telegonia* (Τηλεγονία), which gave the history of Ulysses, from the point where the Odyssey breaks off to his death.[4] 2. *Genealogies*, which are frequently referred to by Pausanias,[5] and which must consequently have been extant in A.D. 175. 3. *Heraclea* ('Ηράκλεια), containing an account of the adventures of Hercules.[6] 4. *Œdipodia* (Οἰδιποδία), the adventures of Œdipus; ascribed to Cinæthon in an ancient inscription, but other authorities speak of the author as uncertain.[7] 5. *The Little Iliad* ('Ιλιὰς μικρά), attributed by some to Cinæthon, though more correctly by others to Lesches, whom we have already mentioned among the Cyclic poets.

2. Eumelus (Εὔμηλος), of Corinth, a member of the noble house of the

---

1 *Müller, Hist. Gr. Lit.*, p. 100; *Mure, Crit. Hist.*, vol. ii., p. 445, *seq.*

2 *Smith, Dict. Biogr., s. v.* 3 *Chron.*, Ol. 3, 4. 4 *Euseb., l. c.*

5 *Paus.*, ii., 3, 7; ii., 18, 5; iv., 2, 1, &c. 6 *Schol. ad Apoll. Rhod.*, i., 1357.

7 *Paus.*, ix., 5, 5; *Schol. ad Eurip., Phœn.*, 1760.

Bacchiadæ, flourished about 761–744 B.C. Eusebius makes him contemporary with Arctinus. Those of the poems ascribed to him which appear pretty certainly genuine were genealogical and historical legends. To this class belonged his *Corinthian History* (Κορινθιακά);[1] his *Europia* (Εὐρώπια), or legend of Europa; and his Προσόδιον ἐς Δῆλον,[2] a strain which he had composed for the Messenians, for a sacred mission to the temple of Delos. He also wrote *Bougonia* (Βουγονία), a poem on bees, which the Greeks called βουγόναι and βουγενεῖς.[3] Some writers ascribed to him a Τιτανομαχία, which was also attributed to Arctinus. The Cyclic poem on the return of the Greeks from Troy is ascribed to Eumelus by a scholiast on Pindar, who writes the name wrongly, Eumolpus.

3. Antimăchus (Ἀντίμαχος), of Teos, an epic poet of great antiquity, but of little celebrity. Plutarch[4] cites him as having mentioned, contemporaneously it must be understood, the eclipse which happened on the 20th of April, in the third year of the sixth Olympiad, B.C. 753, the date assigned to the foundation of Rome. The title of no work by this poet has been preserved, and but a single verse is quoted, in condemnation of bribery.

4. Asius (Ἄσιος), of Samos,[5] ranks among the more ancient epic poets of the genealogical order, but no specific date is connected with his name, nor are his works mentioned under any other titles than the general one of genealogies. He lived in all probability about B.C. 700. He seems to have treated a variety of subjects, as episodes, it may be presumed, illustrative of local and family history. The longest extant passage gives a glowing and vivid description of the brilliant appearance of the Samian ladies advancing in procession to the temple of Juno, and is distinguished by a festive pomp of diction in good keeping with the subject.[6]

5. Pisander (Πείσανδρος), of Camirus, in Rhodes, is the most celebrated epic poet of this period next to Homer and Hesiod, and he ranks, accordingly, next to them in the epic canon of Alexandrea. He appears to have flourished about B.C. 648–645. Pisander was the author of a poem in two books on the exploits of Hercules. It was called *Heraclea* (Ἡράκλεια), and Clement of Alexandrea[7] accuses him of having taken it entirely from one Pisinus of Lindus. In this poem, Hercules was for the first time represented as armed with a club, and covered with the lion's skin, instead of the usual armor of the heroic period; and it is not improbable, as Müller suggests, that Pisander was also the first that fixed the number of the hero's labors at twelve.[8] Only a few lines of this poem have been preserved; two are given us by the scholiast on Aristophanes,[9] and another by Stobæus.[10] Other poems which were ascribed to Pisander were, as we learn from Suidas, spurious, having been composed chiefly by Aristeas. Pisander of Camirus must not be confounded with Pisander of Laranda, who flourished in the reign of Alexander Severus, A.D. 222–235.[11]

---

1 *Paus.*, ii., 1, 1; ii., 3, 8; *Schol. ad Apoll. Rhod.*, i., 148. 2 *Paus.*, iv., 4, 1; v., 19, 2.
3 *Varro, R. R.*, ii., 5, 5, ed. *Schneid.* 4 *Vit. Rom.*, 12. 5 *Athen.*, iii., p. 125.
6 *Müller, Hist. Gr. Lit.*, p. 102. 7 *Strom.*, vi., p. 266, ed. *Sylburg.*
8 *Strab.*, xv., p. 688; *Suid.*, *s. v.* Πείσανδρος. 9 *Nub.*, 1034.
10 *Floril.*, xii., 6. 11 *Smith, Dict. Biogr.*, *s. v.*

6. EPIMENIDES[1] (Ἐπιμενίδης) was a poet and prophet of Crete, whose biography[2] is partly connected with the realities of history, and partly enveloped in the mists of fable. Numerous works, both in prose and verse, were attributed to him, though few, if any, can be considered to have been genuine productions of Epimenides; the age in which he lived was certainly not an age of prose composition in Greece. All that tradition has handed down about him suggests that we ought to rank him in the class of priestly bards and sages, who are generally comprised under the name of Orphici; for every thing we hear of him is of a priestly or religious nature: he was a purifying priest, of superhuman knowledge and wisdom, a seer and a prophet, and acquainted also with the healing powers of plants. These notions about Epimenides were propagated throughout antiquity, and it was probably owing to the great charm attached to his name that so many works were ascribed to him. Diogenes Laertius[3] notices as prose works of his, one on sacrifices, and another on the political constitution of Crete. Among his poetic productions were Χρησμοί, "Oracles," and Καθαρμοί,[4] "Hymns of Purification." It is, however, very doubtful whether he wrote the Γένεσις and Θεογονία of the Curetes and Corybantes in 5000 verses, the epic on Jason and the Argonauts in 6500, and the epic on Minos and Rhadamanthys in 4000 verses; all of which works are mentioned by Diogenes. There can not, however, be any doubt but that there existed in antiquity certain old-fashioned poems written upon skins; and the expression Ἐπιμενίδειον δέρμα was used by the ancients to designate any thing old-fashioned, obsolete, and curious. An allusion to Epimenides seems to be made in St. Paul's Epistle to Titus.[5]

7. ARISTEAS (Ἀριστέας), of Proconnēsus, appears to belong to the same mysterious class with Epimenides, and his age, in so far as a real personality can be assigned him, nearly coincides with that of the latter. The accounts of his life are full of fable. Herodotus calls him the inspired bard of Apollo (φοιβόλαμπτος). He is said to have travelled through the countries north and east of the Euxine, and to have visited the Issedones, Arimaspæ, Cimmerii, Hyperborei, and other mythic nations, and on his return to have written an epic poem in three books, called τὰ Ἀριμάσπεια, in which he seems to have described all that he had seen or pretended to have seen. This work appears to have been full of marvellous stories, but was nevertheless looked upon as a source of historical and geographical information. Still it was an epic poem, and is frequently mentioned by the ancients; but it fell into oblivion at an early period. Thirteen hexameter verses from it are preserved by Longinus.

EDITIONS.—The most complete collection of the fragments of the minor Epic poets is by Düntzer, *Die Fragmente der epischen Poesie der Griechen bis zur Zeit Alexander's des Grossen*, Köln, 1840; and *Nachtrag*, &c., Ib., 1841: others are given by Dübner in the edition of Hesiod and the minor Epic poets in Didot's Bibl. Græca; and by Marckscheffel in his collection of the fragments of Hesiod, Eumelus, Cinæthon, &c., Leipzig, 1840.

---

[1] *Smith, Dict. Biogr.*, *s. v.*
[2] *Diog. Laert.*, i., 10; i., 109; *Plut.*, *Vit. Sol.*, 12.
[3] *Diog. Laert.*, i., 112.
[4] *Suid.*, *s. v.* Ἐπιμενίδης.
[5] Chap. i., v. 12.

CHAPTER XIV.

SECOND OR POETICAL PERIOD—*continued.*

LYRIC POETRY.

INTRODUCTORY REMARKS.[1]

I. According to the subdivision that has been laid down by us, Lyric composition is considered to comprise every poetical work not embodied in hexameter verse, and, consequently, the whole elegiac and iambic, in addition to the melic and choral poetry of this period.

II. Until the beginning of the seventh century before our era, or the 20th Olympiad, the epic was the only kind of poetry in Greece, and the hexameter the only kind of metre which had been cultivated by the poets with art and diligence. Doubtless there were, especially in connection with different worships, strains of other kinds, and measures of a lighter movement, according to which dances of a sprightly character could be executed; but these as yet did not form a finished style of poetry, and were only rude essays and undeveloped germs of other varieties, which hitherto had only a local interest, confined to the rites and customs of particular districts.

III. In all musical and poetical contests, the solemn and majestic tone of the epopee and the epic hymn alone prevailed; and the soothing placidity which these lays imparted to the mind was the only feeling which had found its satisfactory poetical expression. As yet the heart, agitated by joy and grief, by love and anger, could not give utterance to its lament for the lost, its longing after the absent, its care for the present, in appropriate forms of poetical composition. These feelings were still without the elevation which the beauty of art can alone confer. The epopee kept the mind fixed in the contemplation of a former generation of heroes, which it could view with sympathy and interest, but not with passionate emotion. And although, in the economical poem of Hesiod, the cares and sufferings of the present time furnished the occasion for an epic work, yet this was only a partial descent from the lofty career of epic poetry; for it immediately rose again from this lowly region, and celebrated in solemn strains the order of the universe.

IV. This exclusive prevalence of epic poetry was also doubtless connected with the political state of Greece at the time. The ordinary subjects of the epic poems must, as we have already remarked, have been peculiarly acceptable to the princes who derived their race from the heroes of the mythical age, as was the case with all the royal families of early times. This rule of hereditary princes was the prevailing form of government in Greece, at least up to the beginning of the Olympiads, and from this period it gradually disappeared; at an earlier date and by more violent revolutions among the Ionians, than among the nations of Peloponnesus.

---

[1] *Müller, Hist. Gr. Lit.*, p. 104.

V. The republican movements, by which the princely families were deprived of their privileges, could not be otherwise than favorable to a free expression of the feelings, and, in general, to a stronger development of each man's individuality. Hence the poet, who, in the most perfect form of the epos, was completely lost in his subject, and was only the mirror in which the grand and brilliant images of the past were reflected, now comes before the people as a man with thoughts and objects of his own; and gives free vent to the struggling emotions of his soul in elegiac and iambic strains. As the elegy and the iambic, those two contemporary and cognate species of poetry, originated with Ionic poets, and (as far as we are aware) with citizens of free states, so again the remains and accounts of these styles of poetry furnish the best image of the internal condition of the Ionic states of Asia Minor and the Islands, in the first period of their republican constitution.[1]

I. ELEGIAC VERSE.[2]

VI. We may safely assume, by reference both to the general law of human invention, and to the discriminating taste which marks the development of art among the Greeks, that the elegiac distich, namely, an hexameter followed by a pentameter, was called into existence by the object to which it was best adapted, that of modifying the old dactylic metre to familiar epigrammatic purposes; for the obvious effect of this combination of the longer and shorter measures, enhanced by a peculiar abruptness in the central cæsura of the latter, and in its closing foot, or catalexis, is to impart a certain emphatic point to the entire period.

VII. The Elegy or elegiac poem (ἐλεγεία) is but a repetition of the distich in numbers proportioned to the extent of the subject; and the scope and tendency of this branch of composition is to express concisely and emphatically, in the case of the single distich, a certain statement or maxim; in that of the prolonged elegy, a series of similar statements or maxims.

VIII. Each pentameter couplet ought obviously, in the true spirit of the Elegiac Muse, either itself to comprise a distinct clause or period of the sense, or at least to form a subdivision of another more comprehensive clause or head of argument, terminating in a pentameter verse; in other words, every full pause in the sense ought to coincide with a full pause in the measure. Where a continuous head of the subject runs through the close of one distich into the commencement of another, there results a palpable incongruity, which becomes the more glaring when the ensuing pause takes place in the body of the distich, whether at the close of the hexameter or in the middle of either verse. Not only, therefore, is the elegy disqualified by its epigrammatic spirit for continuous narrative, but even in its own proper sphere comparative brevity is essential to the full effect of an elegiac poem. However carefully, therefore, this real impropriety may be smoothed over by the ingenuity of the poet, the discerning critic must, in his own experience, have felt how much superior is the effect of the elegiac measure in the pointed epigram, and other concise

[1] *Müller, l. c.*

[2] *Mure, Crit. Hist.*, vol. iii., p. 16, *seqq.*; *Müller, l. c.*

and pithy compositions, than in prolonged poetical narratives or moral dissertations.[1]

IX. The word ἐλεγεῖον, as used by the best writers, like the word ἔπος, refers not to the *subject* of a poem, but simply to its *form*, and in this sense, therefore, means nothing more than the combination of an hexameter and a pentameter, making together a distich; and an *elegeia* (ἐλεγεία) is a poem made up of such distichs. The word ἐλεγεῖον, however, is itself only a derivative from a simpler word, namely, ἔλεγος. This parent term ἔλεγος, as we learn from the united testimony of the ancient critics, although its own etymology is quite uncertain, denoted, in its earliest usage, what had reference to mourning or sorrow. It means, properly, a strain of lament, without any determinate reference to a metrical form; thus, for example, in Aristophanes, the nightingale sings an *elegos* for her lost Itys; and in Euripides, the halcyon, or kingfisher, sings an *elegos* for her husband Ceÿx; in both which passages the word has this general sense.[2]

X. To this view, however, it has been objected that the extant elegiac compositions of remote antiquity are for the most part in a style quite opposite to either the funebrial or the epigrammatic, being chiefly martial or patriotic appeals, often of considerable length, addressed to the poet's fellow-citizens in times of public emergency. These poems, however, while possibly the oldest ascertained specimens of pentameter style, can not reasonably be assumed to represent the taste or practice in which that style originated. The distinction between what may formerly have existed and what has been preserved to posterity, is one of essential importance in questions of this nature. The elegy in the works of Callinus, Archilochus, and Tyrtæus, its earliest professional votaries, already appears in an advanced state of cultivation, implying a long course of previous practice, and consequent modification of its primitive use. Their compositions stand to its first beginnings in the same relation as the Iliad and Odyssey to the earlier efforts of the Epic Muse.[3]

XI. It were as reasonable to argue from the actual priority of the Iliad that the first poem in hexameter verse was a finished epopee, as from the existing compositions of Callinus, admitting him to be the most ancient author in this style, that the first elegy was a martial or political ode. For the great antiquity of the elegy, however, in its application to what has here been assumed to be its original object, appeal may be made to Archilochus, an author of the same age as Callinus, but of far more varied genius. The remains of Archilochus, while exhibiting the measure in its adaptation to every variety of subject, plaintive, martial, and satirical, offer, together with several elegies of a funebrial character, a general predominance of those of the epigrammatic order.

XII. But, even did the works of these earlier poets furnish no distinct proof of this presumed original destination of the measure, there remains another more competent source of illustration in the sepulchral or votive dedications of the same era. The existing relics of this class, though scanty in the ratio of their antiquity, yet form a more or less continuous series of evidence, that, during this whole early period, from an epoch equal or lit-

[1] *Mure, l. c.* [2] *Müller, l. c.* [3] *Mure, l. c.*

tle inferior to that of the poets above cited, the pentameter was the measure exclusively preferred in monumental inscriptions.[1] We will now proceed to give a brief account of the most eminent elegiac writers.

1. CALLINUS[2] (Καλλῖνος), of Ephesus, ranks among the earliest elegiac poets of whose compositions any portions are still extant. As regards the time in which he lived, we have no definite statement, and the ancients themselves endeavored to determine it from the historical allusions which they found in his elegies. From Strabo,[3] it is evident that Callinus, in one of his poems, mentioned Magnesia, on the Mæander, as still existing, and at war with the Ephesians. Now we know that Magnesia was destroyed by the Treres, a Cimmerian tribe, in B.C. 727, and, consequently, the poem referred to by Strabo must have been written previous to that year, perhaps about B.C. 730, or shortly before Archilochus, who, in one of his earliest poems, mentioned the destruction of Magnesia. Callinus himself, however, appears to have long survived that event; for there is a line of his[4] which is usually referred to the destruction of Sardis by the Cimmerians about B.C. 678. If this calculation be correct, Callinus must have been in the bloom of life at the time of the war between Magnesia and Ephesus, in which he himself, perhaps, took a part. We possess only a very few fragments of the elegies of Callinus, but among them there is one of twenty-one lines, which forms part of a war-elegy, and is, consequently, the most ancient specimen of this species of poetry extant.[5] In this fragment the poet exhorts his countrymen to courage and perseverance against their enemies, who are usually supposed to be the Magnesians, but the fourth line of the poem seems to render it more probable that Callinus was speaking of the Cimmerians. This elegy is one of great beauty, and gives us the highest opinion of the talent of Callinus. It is printed in the various collections of the "Poetæ Græci Minores." All the fragments of Callinus are collected in Bach's *Callini, Tyrtæi, et Asii Fragmenta*, Leipzig, 1831, 8vo, and Bergk's *Poetæ Lyrici Græci*, p. 303, *seqq.*

2. TYRTÆUS[6] (Τυρταῖος or Τύρταιος), contemporary with Callinus, and probably a few years younger. His age is determined by the second Messenian war, in which he bore a part. According to the older tradition, the Spartans, during the second Messenian war, were commanded by an oracle to take a leader from among the Athenians, and thus to conquer their enemies, whereupon they chose Tyrtæus as their leader.[7] Later writers,[8] however, embellish the story, and represent Tyrtæus as a lame schoolmaster, of low family and reputation, whom the Athenians, when applied to by the Lacedæmonians, in accordance with the oracle, purposely sent as the most inefficient leader they could select, being unwilling to assist the Lacedæmonians in extending their dominion in the Peloponnesus, and but little thinking that the poetry of Tyrtæus would achieve that victory which his physical constitution seemed to forbid his aspiring to. Many modern critics reject altogether the account of the Attic origin

[1] *Mure, l. c.* [2] *Smith, Dict. Biogr., s. v.* [3] *Strab.*, xiv., p. 647.
[4] Fragm. 2. Compare fragm. 8, ed. *Bergk.* [5] *Stobæus, Floril.*, li., 19.
[6] *Smith, Dict. Biogr., s. v.* [7] *Lycurg. c. Leocr.*, p. 211, ed. *Reiske.*
[8] *Paus.*, iv., 15, 3; *Justin.*, iii., 5, &c.

of Tyrtæus, and maintain that the extant fragments of his poetry actually furnish evidence of his being a Lacedæmonian. But it is impossible to arrive at any positive decision on the subject. Most probably, however, he was a native of the Athenian town of Aphidnæ, which is placed by the legends about the Dioscuri in very early connection with Laconia. The statement that he was a lame schoolmaster is rejected by all modern writers. It may simply mean that he was, like the other early musicians and poets, a teacher of his own art; and his alleged lameness may possibly be connected with some misunderstanding of expressions used by the earlier writers to describe his metres, namely, the pentameter in conjunction with the hexameter, compared with which the former is short of a foot.

The poems of Tyrtæus exercised an important influence upon the Spartans, allaying their dissensions at home, and animating their courage in the field. In order to appease their civil discords, he composed his celebrated elegy, entitled Εὐνομία, "Legal Order,"[1] which appears to have had a wondrous effect in stilling the excited passions of the Spartans. But still more celebrated were the poems by which he animated the courage of the Spartans in their conflict with the Messenians. These poems were of two kinds; namely, elegies, containing exhortations to constancy and courage, and descriptions of the glory of fighting bravely for one's native land; and more spirited compositions in the anapæstic measure, which were intended as marching songs, to be performed with the music of the flute. He lived to see the success of his efforts in the entire conquest of the Messenians, and their reduction to the condition of Helots.[2] He therefore flourished down to B.C. 668, which was the last year of the second Messenian war.

The extant fragments of Tyrtæus are contained in most of the older and more recent collections of the Greek poets, and, among the rest, in Gaisford's *Poetæ Minores Græci*, Schneidewin's *Delectus Poësis Græcorum*, and Bergk's *Poetæ Lyrici Græci*. The best separate editions are those of Klotz, Bremæ, 1764, 8vo; of Francke, in his edition of Callinus, 1816, 8vo; of Didot, with an elegant French translation, a Dissertation on the poet's life, and a modern Greek version by Clonaras, Paris, 1826, 8vo; and of Bach, with the remains of the elegiac poets Callinus and Asius, Lips., 1831, 8vo.

3. Archilŏchus (Ἀρχίλοχος). The biography of this poet belongs properly to the head of Iambic poetry, since it was on his satiric iambic poetry that his fame was founded. This union of elegiac and iambic poetry, however, in the same person, often appears after this. The same poet who employs the elegy to express his joyous and melancholy emotions, had recourse to the iambus, where his cool sense prompts him to censure the follies of mankind. The elegies of Archilochus, of which considerable fragments are extant, had nothing of that bitter spirit of which his iambics were full, but they contain the frank expression of a mind powerfully affected by outward circumstances. Nor are they quite wanting in the warlike spirit of Callinus, although he was not ashamed to avow in verse

[1] *Aristot.*, *Polit.*, v., 7, 1; *Paus.*, iv., 8, 2. [2] *Paus.*, iv., 14, 3.

that he had on one occasion incurred the disgrace of having lost his shield in an engagement with the Thracian foe.[1]

4. SIMONĬDES (Σιμωνίδης), of Amorgus, like Archilochus, properly belongs to the iambic school of poetry, and will be more fully noticed under that head. He composed an elegy in two books, which appears, from all that we can ascertain respecting it, to have been akin to the *Eunomia* of Tyrtæus.

5. MIMNERMUS (Μίμνερμος),[2] a celebrated elegiac poet, generally called a Colophonian,[3] but, from a fragment of his poem entitled *Nanno*, it appears that he was descended from those Colophonians who reconquered Smyrna from the Æolians,[4] and that, strictly speaking, Smyrna was his birth-place. Mimnermus flourished from about B.C. 634 to the age of the seven sages (about B.C. 600). He was a contemporary of Solon, who, in an extant fragment of one of his poems, addresses him as still living.[5] No other biographical particulars respecting him have come down to us, except what is mentioned in a fragment of Hermesianax,[6] of his love for a flute-player named Nanno, who does not seem to have returned his affection.[7]

The numerous compositions of Mimnermus were preserved for several centuries, comprised in two books, until they were burned, together with most of the other monuments of the erotic poetry of the Greeks by the Byzantine monks. A few fragments only have come down to us; sufficient, however, when compared with the notices contained in ancient writers, to enable us to form a tolerably accurate judgment of the nature of his poetry. These fragments belong chiefly to a poem entitled *Nanno*, and addressed to the flute-player of that name. The compositions of Mimnermus form an epoch in the history of elegiac poetry. Although the elegy had, from its first beginnings, a mournful tendency, and had been awarded a preference in odes of a funebrial and melancholy character by Archilochus and other early poets, Mimnermus is the first author who peculiarly and systematically adapted it to the more tender class of plaintive subjects. Though warlike themes were not altogether unnoticed by him, and though the subjection of a large part of Ionia, and especially of his native city, to the Lydian yoke, could not fail to produce a strong feeling of melancholy, yet he seems, on the whole, to have spoken of valorous deeds more in a tone of regret, as things that had been, than with any view of rousing his countrymen to imitate them. The instability of human happiness, the helplessness of man, the cares and miseries to which life is exposed, the brief season that man has to enjoy himself in, the wretchedness of old age, are plaintively dwelt upon by him, while love is held up as the only consolation that men possess, life not being worth having when it can no longer be enjoyed. The latter topic was most frequently dwelt upon, and as an erotic poet he was held in high estimation in antiquity.[8]

---

1 *Müller, Hist. Gr. Lit.*, p. 113.
2 *Smith, Dict. Biogr.*, *s. v.*; *Müller*, p. 115.
3 *Strab.*, xiv., p. 643.
4 *Id. ib.*, p. 634.
5 *Diog. Laert.*, i., 60; *Bergk, Poetæ Lyrici Græci*, p. 331.
6 *Athen.*, xiii., p. 597.
7 Compare, however, *Mure, Crit. Hist.*, vol. iii., p. 334, where a different opinion is expressed.
8 *Hor.*, *Epist.*, ii., 2, 100; *Propert.*, i., 9, 11.

From the general character of his poetry, Mimnermus received the appellation of Λιγυστιάδης or Λιγυαστάδης. He was a flute-player as well as a poet,[1] and in setting his poems to music he made use of the plaintive melody called the *Nomos kradias*.

So highly appreciated, indeed, were the claims of Mimnermus to novelty, if not to absolute originality, as regards the plaintive character of his elegies, and so marked the terms in which they were asserted by his admirers, as to have led superficial critics, both ancient and modern, to admit him, in the face of insuperable chronological difficulties, to a competition with Callinus and Archilochus for the honor of inventing the elegiac measure itself. Setting aside, however, this more fanciful title to priority, Mimnermus enjoys, perhaps deservedly, the same pre-eminence among erotic poets of the elegiac order, as Sappho among the cultivators of the melic branches of erotic poetry.[2]

The fragments of Mimnermus have been several times published, in the collections of Stephens, Brunck, Gaisford, Boissonade, and Bergk. There is a separate edition by Bach, Lips, 1826.

6. Solon (Σόλων), the celebrated legislator of Athens, also appears in the list of elegiac poets, but, like Archilochus, and Simonides of Amorgus, he belongs to that class which cultivated iambic verse as well as elegiac, and will therefore be considered under both heads. Of his poems several fragments remain. The whole number of extant verses is about two hundred and seventy-five. Of these upward of two hundred are in elegiac measure; between thirty and forty are iambic trimeters; of the remainder, sixteen are trochaic tetrameters; five alone are in purely melic style. The two hexameter verses, which make up the sum total of the collection, are of questionable authenticity. They are cited by Plutarch in reference to a tradition, of which he himself appears to make but little account, that Solon had originally intended to draw up his code in a metrical form; and of this legislative poem they profess to be the exordium.[3]

The longest passage of the collection, comprising seventy-six elegiac verses, in essentially gnomic[4] style, may be considered as a fair and favorable sample of the general character of Solon's poetry. It contains a summary of his views relative to the tenor of his life and conduct, forming evidently a portion of his "Reflections on his own Affairs," which last was the title of one of the works ascribed to him by the ancients. The doctrines inculcated are sound, often original and striking; are expressed with a vigor and terseness sometimes bordering on abruptness, and are illustrated by some spirited imagery. He comments, in equally emphatic but less querulous terms than Mimnermus, on the ephemeral nature of human enjoyments; dwells on the blessings of a clear conscience and a contented mind; condemning the insatiable thirst of mortals for the possession of a happiness beyond their reach, and their wayward caprice in its pursuit. The whole is pervaded by a deep tone of religious feeling and dependence [5]

[1] *Strab.*, iv., p. 643; *Hermesianax ap. Athen.*, *l. c.* [2] *Mure, Crit. Hist.*, vol. iii., p. 339.
[3] *Id. ib.*, p. 363. [4] This term will be explained under the article *Theognis*.
[5] *Mure, Crit. Hist.*, vol. iii., p. 364. Compare *Müller, Hist. Gr. Lit.*, p. 119.

Another bulky text, or series of texts, of a more strictly political tendency, composed, it would appear, about or shortly prior to the epoch of his legislative undertaking, describes in the same elegiac measure, and in equally spirited language, the evils which led his fellow-countrymen to resort to his healing interposition.[1]

Of the Salaminian ode, the most remarkable of all Solon's productions, and by which, as is well known, he sought to stimulate the Athenians to reconquer the island of Salamis, only eight elegiac verses are extant, composed in a spirited vein of patriotism.

The merits of Solon as an encourager of literature are chiefly concentrated around his regulations for the more orderly recital of the Homeric poems in the public festivities, to which we have already alluded. He has also the credit of having interpolated verse 558 of the Catalogue of the Forces, in support of the claims of Athens to the possession of Salamis. It was in the time of Solon that Thespis introduced his improvements in the drama, according to the commonly received account, and on this assumption is founded the story told by Diogenes Laertius[2] of Solon's having expressed great anger at these dramatic entertainments, on the ground of the deception connected with them. That the whole account, however, is a mere fable, is sufficiently clear even upon chronological grounds, since the first introduction of these entertainments at Athens (535 B.C.) took place twenty years after the death of Solon.[3]

The fragments of Solon are usually incorporated in the collections of the Greek gnomic poets, as, for example, in those of Sylburg, Brunck, and Boissonade. They are also inserted in the collections of Gaisford and Schneidewin, and in Bergk's *Poetæ Lyrici Græci*. There is likewise a separate edition by Bach, Lugd. Bat., 1825. The select correspondence of Solon with Periander, Pisistratus, Epimenides, and Crœsus, with which Diogenes Laertius has favored us, is of course spurious.

7. THEOGNIS (Θέογνις) of Megara was an elegiac and gnomic poet, whose reputed works form the most extensive collection of gnomic poetry that has come down to us under any one name; but, unfortunately, the form in which these remains exist is altogether unsatisfactory. The term "Gnomic" (from γνῶμαι, "maxims," or "apophthegms") appears to have been originally invented, as it was exclusively employed, to denote a school of elegiac poetry, the object of which was to inculcate moral doctrines, rather than express mental emotions; to enforce maxims of worldly wisdom in their more immediate bearings on objects of special interest to the author or his public. The characteristic, consequently, of the gnomic style was a sententious gravity, savoring often more of philosophy than of poetry.[4]

Most of our information respecting the life of Theognis is derived from his own writings. He was a native of Megara, the capital of Megaris, and flourished B.C. 548 or 544. It is evident, from passages in his po-

---

1 *Mure, l. c.*

2 *Diog. Laert.*, i., 59.

3 *Mure, Crit. Hist.*, vol. iii., p. 359, where the error of Grote (vol. iii., p. 194) and of Smith (*Dict. Biog.*, *s. v.*) is noted, both of whom place this very palpable fable respecting Thespis among the ascertained historical facts of Solon's life.

4 *Mure, l. c.*

ems, that he lived till after the commencement of the Persian wars, B.C. 490. Theognis was born and spent his life in the midst of a series of conflicts between the aristocracy and the popular party in Megara, producing several revolutions and counter-revolutions, and the consequent banishing and return of exiles. Theognis belonged to the party of the nobility, being himself noble by birth. In one of these revolutions, when a division was made of the property of the nobles, Theognis lost his all, and was cast out as an exile, barely escaping with his life. In his verses he pours out his indignation upon his enemies, laments the folly of the bad pilots by whom the vessel of the state had been often wrecked, and speaks of the common people with unmeasured contumely. It is interesting to observe in him, on these occasions, the employment of certain terms in their early or political meaning, as contradistinguished from their later and ethical one, although, even in his own verses, this ethical meaning is not absolutely unknown, but only rare. Thus, by ἀγαθοί, ἐσθλοί, χρηστοί, &c., are commonly meant the noble or upper classes, and by κακοί, δειλοί, &c., the lower orders, the mean.[1]

Most of these political verses are addressed to a certain Cyrnus, the son of Polypas, for it is now generally admitted that the name Πολυπαΐδης, which has been sometimes supposed to refer to a different person, is to be understood as a patronymic, and as applying to Cyrnus. From the verses themselves, as well as from the statements of the ancient writers, it appears that Cyrnus was a young man toward whom Theognis cherished a warm and firm friendship.

The other fragments of the poetry of Theognis are of a social, most of them of a festive character. They place us, as Müller remarks, in the midst of a circle of friends, who formed a kind of eating society, like the *philitia* of Sparta, and like the ancient public tables of Megara itself.[2] All the members of this society belonged to the class whom the poet calls "the good." The collection of gnomic poetry, which has come down to us under the name of Theognis, contains, however, many additions from later poets. The genuine fragments contain much that is highly poetical in thought, and elegant as well as forcible in expression.

There are two standard modern editions of the remains of Theognis, that of Bekker, who has preserved the order of the MSS., Lips., 1815, and 2d ed., 1827, 8vo; and that of Welcker, who has rearranged the verses, Francof., 1826, 8vo. There is also an edition of the text, with critical notes, by Orelli, Turic., 1840, 4to. The poems are also contained in several modern collections, and particularly in Schneidewin's *Delectus Poesis Græcorum*, Götting., 1838, 8vo; Bergk's *Poetæ Lyrici Græci*, Lips., 1843, 8vo, and in Gaisford's *Poetæ Minores Græci*, Oxon., 1814–1820; Lips., 1823, 8vo.

8. PHOCYLĬDES (Φωκυλίδης) of Miletus, an Ionian poet, was contemporary with Theognis, both having been born, according to Suidas, in the 55th Olympiad, B.C. 560, which agrees with Eusebius, who places Phocylides at Ol. 60 (B.C. 540) as a contemporary of the lyric poet Simonides.

---

[1] *Welcker, Prolegom. ad Theogn.* Compare *Grote, Hist. Gr.*, vol. iii., p. 62, note.

[2] *Müller, Hist. Gr. Lit.*, p. 123.

According to Suidas, he wrote epic poems and elegies, among which were Παραινέσεις or Γνῶμαι, which were also called Κεφάλαια. This gnomic poetry shows the reason why Suidas calls him a philosopher. Most of the few fragments we possess are of this character; and they display that contempt for birth and station, and that love for substantial enjoyment, which always marked the Ionian character. The didactic character of his poetry is shown by the frequent occurrence of verses beginning Καὶ τόδε Φωκυλίδεω. These words no doubt formed the heading of each of those sections (κεφάλαια), in which, as we have seen from Suidas, the poems of Phocylides were arranged. We possess only about eighteen short fragments of his poems, of which only two are in elegiac metre, and the rest in hexameters. They have been included in all the chief collections of the lyric and gnomic poets, from that of Constantine Lascaris, Venet., 1494, 1495, 4to, down to those of Gaisford, Schneidewin, and Bergk. There is a separate edition by Schier, Lips., 1751.

9. Xenophănes (Ξενοφάνης) of Colophon, who, about the 68th Olympiad (508 B.C.), founded the celebrated Eleatic school of philosophy,[1] at an earlier period, while he was still living at Colophon, gave vent to his thoughts and feelings on the circumstances surrounding him in the form of elegies. These elegies were symposiac in their character. There is preserved in Athenæus a considerable fragment, in which the beginning of a symposium is described with much distinctness and elegance. In his elegies, also, we see exhibited the direction of his mind toward investigation, and his earnest view of life. He derides in them the Pythagorean doctrine of the migration of souls;[2] makes good the claims of wisdom in opposition to the excessive admiration of the bodily strength and activity by which the victory was gained in athletic games;[3] lashes the effeminate luxury of the Ionians, which they had imitated from the Lydians,[4] &c. The fragments of Xenophanes are contained in the collections of Schneidewin and Bergk: there is a separate edition by Karsten, Bruxell., 1830.[5]

10. Simonĭdes (Σιμωνίδης) of Ceos, one of the most celebrated lyric poets of Greece, was the perfecter of the elegy and epigram, and the rival of Lasus and Pindar in the dithyramb and the epinician ode. As a lyric poet, however, he will be considered elsewhere. He is stated to have been victorious at Athens over Æschylus himself, in an elegy in honor of those who fell at Marathon, the Athenians having instituted a contest of the chief poets. The ancient biographer of Æschylus, who gives this account, adds in explanation that the elegy requires a tenderness of feeling which was foreign to the character of Æschylus. To what degree Simonides possessed this quality, and, in general, how great a master he was of the pathetic, is proved by his celebrated lyric piece containing the lament of Danaë, and by other remains of his poetry. Simonides likewise, like Archilochus and others, used the elegy as a plaintive song for the deaths of individuals; at least the Greek Anthology contains several pieces of Simonides, which appear to be not entire epigrams, but frag-

[1] *Plat.*, *Soph.*, p. 242; *Arist.*, *Met.*, ii., 5. Compare *Cousin*, *Nouveaux Frag. Philos.*, p. 9, *seqq.* [2] Frag. xviii. [3] Frag. xix. [4] Frag. xx.
[5] *Müller*, *Hist. Gr. Lit.*, p. 124; *Smith*, *Dict. Biogr.*, *s. v.*

ments of longer elegies lamenting with heartfelt pathos the death of persons dear to the poet. Among these are the verses concerning Gorgo, who, dying, utters these words to her mother: "Remain here with my father, and become, with a happier fate, the mother of another daughter, who may tend you in your old age."[1]

XIII. This place is the most convenient for mentioning a subordinate kind of poetry, namely, the *Epigram*, as the elegiac form was the best suited to it, although there are also epigrams composed in hexameters and other metres.

EPIGRAM.[2]

XIV. The *Epigram* (ἐπίγραμμα) was originally, as its name imports, an *inscription* either on a tombstone, or on a votive offering in a temple, or on any other object which required explanation. Afterward, from the analogy of these real epigrams, thoughts excited by the view of any object, and which *might* have served as an inscription, were called epigrams, and expressed in the same form. That this form was the elegiac may have arisen from the circumstance that epitaphs appeared closely allied to laments for the dead, which, as we have before remarked, were composed in this metre. However, as this elegy comprehended all the events of life which caused a strong emotion, so the epigram might be equally in place on a monument of war, and on the sepulchral pillar of a beloved kinsman or friend.

XV. The unexpected turn of thought and the pointedness of expression, which the moderns consider as the essence of this species of composition, were not required in the ancient Greek epigram; in this nothing more is requisite than that the entire thought should be conveyed within the limits of a few distichs; and thus, in the hands of the early poets, the epigram was remarkable for the conciseness and expressiveness of its language; differing in this respect from the elegy, in which a full vent was given to the feelings of the poet.

XVI. Epigrams were probably composed in an elegiac form, shortly after the time when the elegy first arose; and the collection which has come down to us contains some under the celebrated names of Archilochus, Sappho, and Anacreon. No peculiar character, however, is to be observed in the genuine epigrams of this early period. It was Simonides of Ceos who first gave to the epigram the perfection of which, consistently with its purpose, it was capable. In this respect Simonides was favored by the circumstances of his time; for, on account of the high consideration which he enjoyed both in Athens and throughout the Peloponnesus, he was frequently employed by the states which had fought against the Persians, to adorn with inscriptions the tombs of their fallen warriors. The best and most celebrated of these epitaphs is the inimitable inscription on the Spartans who died at Thermopylæ, which actually existed on the spot: "Stranger, tell the Lacedæmonians that we are lying here in obedience to their laws."[3] Never was heroic courage expressed with such calm and unadorned grandeur.

[1] *Müller, Hist. Gr. Lit.*, p. 125. [2] *Ib.*, p. 126, *seqq.* [3] *Simonides*, Frag. 27, ed. *Gaisf.*

XVII. There are, besides, not a few epigrams of Simonides, which were intended for the tombstones of individuals; among these we will mention only one, which differs from the others in being a sarcasm in the form of an epitaph. It is that on the Rhodian lyric poet and athlete Timocreon, an opponent of Simonides in his art: "Having eaten much, and drunk much, and said much evil of other men, here I lie, Timocreon the Rhodian."[1]

XVIII. With the epitaphs are naturally connected the inscriptions on sacred offerings, especially where both refer to the Persian war; the former being the discharge of a debt to the dead, the latter a thanksgiving of the survivors to the gods. Among the best of these is one referring to the battle of Marathon, which, from the neatness and elegance of the expression, loses its chief beauty in a prose translation. It was inscribed on the statue of Pan, which the Athenians had set up in a grotto under their Acropolis, because the Arcadian god had, according to the popular belief, assisted them at Marathon. "Miltiades set me up, the cloven-footed Pan, the Arcadian, who took part against the Medes, and with the Athenians." The original runs as follows:

Τὸν τραγόπουν ἐμὲ Πᾶνα, τὸν Ἀρκάδα, τὸν κατὰ Μήδων,
τὸν μετ' Ἀθηναίων, στήσατο Μιλτιάδης.[2]

XIX. But Simonides sometimes condescended to express sentiments which he could not have shared, as in the inscription on the tripod consecrated at Delphi, which the Greeks afterward caused to be erased, "Pausanias, the commander of the Greeks, having destroyed the army of the Medes, dedicated this memorial to Phœbus." These verses express the arrogance of the Spartan general, which the good sense and moderation of the poet would never have approved. The form of nearly all these epigrams of Simonides is the elegiac. Simonides usually adhered to it, except when a name (on account of a short between two long syllables) could not be adapted to the dactylic metre, as, for instance, Ἀρχεναύτης, Ἱππόνικος: in which cases he employed trochaic measures. The character of the language, and especially the dialect, also remained, on the whole, true to the elegiac type, except that, in inscriptions for monuments designed for Doric tribes, traces of the Doric dialect sometimes occur.

XX. The term *Anthology* is peculiarly appropriated to a collection of epigrams. The largest portion of those collected in the Greek Anthology, as it exists at the present day, was written in honor of the dead, introducing their names and characters, or occupations; or as tributes to beauty, in gratitude for acceptance, or in complaint on account of rejection; some of them are panegyrics on living and illustrious virtue; others contain brief records of remarkable events; others, again, consist of observations on human life, for the most part in a dark style of coloring. The weariness of old age, the shortness and unsatisfactory tenor of human life, the murmurs of sickness, and the miseries of poverty, are favorite topics. Bacchanalian poetry is mixed up with exhortations to eat and drink, for to-morrow we die. This prevailing tendency must be ascribed to the vague notions, undefined prospects, and differently sustained hopes respecting

[1] Frag. 58.

[2] *Ib.*, 25.

our transition into some other state of existence, by which the philosophers, poets, and ordinary men of those times were equally perplexed. But, however gloomy this view of things might be, it was compatible with a not unpleasing pathos, and raised their amatory and convivial effusions above vulgar voluptuousness or mere festive riot.[1]

LITERARY HISTORY OF THE GREEK ANTHOLOGY.[2]

I. The earliest known collection of inscriptions was made by the geographer Polemon (B.C. 200), in a work *περὶ τῶν κατὰ πόλεις ἐπιγραμμάτων*.[3] He also wrote other works on votive offerings, which probably contained the epigrammatic inscriptions on them. Similar collections were made by Alcetas, *περὶ τῶν ἐν Δελφοῖς ἀναθημάτων*;[4] by Menetor, *ἐν τῷ περὶ ἀναθημάτων*;[5] and perhaps by Apellas Ponticus. These persons collected chiefly the inscriptions on offerings (*ἀναθήματα*). Epigrams of other kinds were also collected, as the Theban Epigrams, by Aristodemus;[6] the Attic, by Philochorus; and others by Neoptolemus of Paros,[7] and Euhemerus.[8]

II. The above compilers chiefly collected epigrams of particular classes, and with reference to their use as historical authorities. The first person who made such a collection solely for its own sake, and to preserve epigrams of all kinds, was Meleager, a Cynic philosopher of Gadara, in Palestine, about B.C. 60. His collection contained epigrams by no less than forty-six poets of all ages of Greek poetry, up to the most ancient lyric period. He entitled it the *Garland* (*Στέφανος*), with reference, of course, to the common comparison of small beautiful poems to flowers; and, in the introduction to his work, he attaches the names of various flowers, shrubs, and herbs, as emblems, to the names of the several poets. The same idea is kept up in the word *Anthology* (*ἀνθολογία*), or "nosegay," which was adopted by the next compiler as the title of his work. The *Garland* of Meleager was arranged in alphabetical order, according to the initial letters of the first line of each epigram.

III. In the time of Trajan, as it seems, Philip of Thessalonica compiled his *Anthology* (*Ἀνθολογία*), avowedly in imitation of the *Garland* of Meleager, and chiefly with the view of adding to that collection the epigrams of more recent writers. The arrangement of this work was the same as that of Meleager. It was also entitled *στέφανος*, as well as *ἀνθολογία*. Another title by which it is quoted is *συλλογὴ νέων ἐπιγραμμάτων*. Shortly after Philip, in the reign of Hadrian, the learned grammarian, Diogenianus of Heraclea, compiled an Anthology, which is entirely lost. It might, perhaps, have been well if the same fate had befallen the very polluted, though often beautiful collection of his contemporary, Straton of Sardis. About the same time, Diogenes Laertius collected the epigrams, which are interspersed, in his lives of the philosophers, into a separate book, under the title of *ἡ πάμμετρος*. This collection, however, as containing only the poems of Diogenes himself, must rather be viewed as

[1] *Penny Cyclop.*, vol. ii., p. 95. [2] *Smith, Dict. Biog.*, *s. v. Planudes.*
[3] *Athen.*, x., p. 436, *d.*; p. 442, *e.* [4] *Id.*, xiii., p. 591, *c.* [5] *Id. ib.*, p. 594, *d.*
[6] *Schol. in Apoll. Rhod.*, ii., 906. [7] *Athen.*, x., p. 454, *f.*
[8] *Lactant.*, *Instit. Div.*, i., 9; *Cic.*, *N. D.*, i., 42.

among the materials of the later Anthologies than as an Anthology in itself.

IV. During the long period from the decline of original literature to the era when the imitative compositions of the Constantinopolitan grammarians had reached their height, we find no more Anthologies. The next was the Κύκλος ἐπιγραμμάτων of AGATHIAS SCHOLASTICUS, who lived in the time of Justinian. It was divided into seven books, according to subjects, and was the earliest Anthology so arranged. The poems included in it were those of recent writers, and chiefly those of Agathias himself and of his contemporaries, such as Paulus Silentiarius and Macedonius.

V. Next in order is the Anthology of CONSTANTINUS CEPHALAS, called also the *Palatine Anthology*. Constantinus Cephalas appears to have lived about four centuries after Agathias, and to have flourished in the tenth century, under the Emperor Constantinus Porphyrogennetus.[1] The labors of preceding compilers may be viewed as merely supplementary to the *Garland* of Meleager; but the Anthology of Cephalas was an entirely new collection from the preceding Anthologies and from original sources. Nothing is known of Cephalas himself. Modern scholars had never even heard his name till it was brought to light by the fortunate discovery of Salmasius. That great scholar, when a very young man, visited Heidelberg about the end of the year 1606, and there, in the library of the Electors Palatine, he found the MS. collection of Greek epigrams, which was afterward removed to the Vatican, with the rest of the Palatine library, in 1623, and has become celebrated under the names of the *Palatine Anthology*, and the *Vatican Codex of the Greek Anthology*. This MS. was transferred to Paris upon the peace of Tolentino in 1797; and, after the peace of 1815, it was restored to its old home at Heidelberg, where it now lies in the University library.

VI. Salmasius at once saw that it was quite a different work from the Planudean Anthology (to be mentioned presently). He collated it with Weichel's edition of the same work, and copied out those epigrams which were not contained in the latter. The work thus discovered soon became known among the scholars of the day as the *Anthologia inedita codicis Palatini*. The MS. is written on parchment, of a quarto form, though somewhat longer than it is broad, and contains 710 pages, without reckoning three leaves at the commencement, which are stuck together, and which are also full of epigrams. The writing is by different hands, of different ages. The most ancient handwriting is supposed to be of the eleventh century. The time of the others can not be fixed with any certainty. Of the compiler Cephalas, and his labors, the only mention made is in the MS. itself. In one passage (p. 81) a marginal scholium states that Cephalas arranged the *Garland* of Meleager, dividing it into different chapters; namely, amatory, dedicatory, monumental, and epideictic. The work itself, however, shows that this is not all that Cephalas did, and that the mention of Meleager, and of the titles of each section, are only given by way of example.

VII. The Anthology of Cephalas seems to have been compiled from the

[1] *Smith, Dict. Biogr.*, p. 387.

old Anthologies, as a basis, with the addition of other epigrams. He appears to have extracted in turn from Meleager, Philip, Agathias, &c., those epigrams which suited his purpose, and his work often exhibits traces of the alphabetical order of the *Garland* of Meleager. With respect to arrangement, he seems to have taken the Κύκλος of Agathias as a foundation, for both works are alike in the division of their subjects, and in the titles prefixed to the epigrams. The order of the books, however, is different, and one book of Agathias, namely, the descriptions of works of art, is altogether omitted by Cephalas. It is also to be observed that the Palatine Anthology contains ancient epigrams which had not appeared in any of the preceding Anthologies, but had been preserved in some other way.

VIII. Last in order is the Anthology of Planudes, a learned monk of the last age of the Greek empire. It is arranged in seven books, each of which, except the fifth and seventh, is divided into chapters, according to subjects, and these chapters are arranged in alphabetical order. The chapters of the first book, for example, run thus: 1. Εἰς Ἀγῶνας. 2. Εἰς ἄμπελον. 3. Εἰς ἀναθήματα, and so on, to 91. Εἰς ὥρας. According to Brunck and Jacobs, Planudes did little more than abridge and rearrange the Anthology of Cephalas. Only a few epigrams are found in the Planudean Anthology which are not in the Palatine. From the time of its first publication at the end of the fifteenth century, down to the discovery of the Palatine Anthology in the seventeenth, the Planudean Anthology was esteemed one of the greatest treasures of antiquity, and was known under the name of the *Greek Anthology*. Planudes, however, was but ill qualified for the duties of editor of such a work. Devoid of true poetical taste, he brought to his task the conceit and rashness of a mere *literatus*. The discovery of the Palatine Anthology soon taught scholars how much they had over-estimated the worth of the Anthology of Planudes. On comparing the two collections, it is manifest that Planudes was not only guilty of the necessary carelessness of a mere compiler, but also of the willful faults of a conceited monk, tampering with words, "expurgating" whole couplets and epigrams, and interpolating his own frigid verses. He reaped the reward which often crowns the labors of bad editors who undertake great works. The pretensions of his compilation insured its general acceptance, and prevented not only the execution of a better work, which in that age could scarcely be hoped for, but, what was far more important, the multiplication of copies of the more ancient Anthologies; and thus modern scholars are reduced to one MS. of the Anthology of Cephalas, which, excellent as it is, leaves many hopeless difficulties for the critic.

IX. The last and most perfect of the editions of the Planudean Anthology is that which was commenced by Hieronymus de Bosch, and finished after his death by Van Lennep, in 5 vols., 4to, Ultraj., 1795–1822. This splendid edition is not only useful for those who wish to read the Greek Anthology in the form in which it was compiled by Planudes, but it is valuable on account of the large mass of illustrative matter which it contains, including the notes of Huet, Sylburg, and other scholars; but above all for the metrical Latin versions of Grotius, which are esteemed by far the best of his productions in that department of scholarship, and which have never been printed except in this edition. The Greek text, however, is only a reprint of the Wechelian edition of 1600,[1] with many of its worst errors uncorrected.

X. In the years 1772–1776, appeared the *Analecta Veterum Poetarum Græcorum* of Brunck, Argentorati, 3 vols. 8vo, which contains the whole of the Greek Anthology, besides some poems which are not properly included under that title. The epigrams of the Anthology were edited by Brunck, from a careful comparison of the Planudean Anthology with various copies of the Vatican Codex; and they now appeared for the first time revised by a scholar competent to the task. Brunck also adopted a new arrangement, which certainly has its defects, but yet is invaluable for the student of the history of Greek literature. Discarding altogether the books and chapters of the early Anthology, he placed together all the epigrams of each poet, and arranged the poets themselves in chronological order, placing those epigrams, the authors of which were unknown, under the separate head of ἀδέσποτα.

XI. Important, however, as Brunck's edition was when it was published, it has been entirely superseded by the edition of Jacobs. The original plan of the last mentioned scholar was only to form a complete commentary on Brunck's *Analecta*, but the scarceness of copies of that work induced him to reprint it, omitting those parts which do not properly belong to the *Greek Anthology*, and carefully re-editing the whole. The result of his labors was a work which ranks most deservedly as the standard edition of the Greek Anthology. It is in 8 vols., or 13 parts, 8vo, viz., 4 vols. of the text, one of Indices, and three of Commentaries, divided into eight parts. In editing his *Anthologia Græca*, Jacobs had the full benefit of the *Palatine Anthology*. Not content with the almost perfect transcript made by Spalletti in 1776, and which, from its having been purchased by Ernest II., duke of Gotha, for the library at Gotha, is commonly called the *Apographum Gothanum*, Jacobs availed himself of the services of Uhden, then Prussian ambassador at Rome, who collated the copy once more with the original codex in the Vatican. The important results are to be found in Jacobs' emendations of Brunck's text, in his corrections of many of Brunck's errors in the assignment of epigrams to wrong authors, and in his Appendix of 213 epigrams from the Vatican MS., which are wanting in the *Analecta*. In the mean time, he formed the design of rendering to scholarship the great service of printing an exact and complete edition of this celebrated codex. After the printing of the text was completed, the unlooked-for restoration of the MS. to the University library at Heidelberg afforded an opportunity for a new collation, which was made by Paulssen, who has given the results of it in

[1] The Wechelian edition (*Francofurti, apud Claudium Marnium et Jo. Aubrium*, 1600, fol.) is, in the text, a mere reprint of that of Stephanus, with few of its errors corrected, and many new ones introduced. It is, however, of considerable value, as it contains, besides some new scholia, and the notes of Obsopæus and Stephanus, the whole of the excellent commentary of Brodæus. In spite of its faults, it remained for nearly two centuries, until the publication of Brunck's *Analecta*, the standard edition of the Greek Anthology.

an Appendix to the third volume of Jacobs' *Anthologia Palatina.* This work may, therefore, be considered an all but perfect copy of the Palatine Codex, and is hence invaluable for the critical study of the Anthology. It was published at Leipsic, 1813–1817, in 3 vols. 8vo.[1]

XII. Immense, however, as were Jacobs' services for the Greek Anthology, much has still been left for his successors to accomplish, in the further correction of the text, the investigation of the sources and forms of the earlier Anthologies, the more accurate assignment of many epigrams to their right authors, and the collection of additional epigrams, especially from recently-discovered inscriptions. The great scholars of Germany, such as Hermann, Welcker, Meineke, and others,[2] have not neglected this duty, and, in particular, a new edition of the Anthology is said to be in preparation by Meineke, who is, perhaps, better qualified for the task than any other living scholar.

CHAPTER XV.

SECOND OR POETICAL PERIOD—*continued.*

LYRIC POETRY—*continued.*

II. IAMBIC VERSE.[3]

I. THE invention of Iambic verse, the rival of the Elegy in antiquity and early popularity, was familiarly ascribed by the ancients, as was that of many other metrical forms, to Archilochus.[4] In the *Margites,* however, a poem of very early date, and assigned by Aristotle to Homer himself, iambic verses were introduced with heroic hexameters. It must be presumed, therefore, either that the respectable authors who attribute the invention of the former measure to Archilochus, differed from Aristotle as to the genuine antiquity of the *Margites,* or that the term *Invention,* as here applied by them, relates merely to the regular poem of continuous trimeters, to which, in popular usage, the phrase Iambic measure was appropriated.

II. But the nature and spirit of Iambic verse, still more, perhaps, than of the Elegy, entitle us to look, for its first beginnings at least, to the spontaneous effort of the primitive muse, rather than to the artifice of a politer age. The component elements of the elegy were contained in the old hexameter. It might very naturally occur, therefore, to an ingenious master of later times to invent a new form to suit a new purpose, by curtailing two syllables of every alternate verse; for such, in fact, is the

---

1 The following is its title: *Anthologia Græca, ad fidem Codicis Palatini, nunc Parisini, ex Apographo Gothano edita. Curavit, Epigrammata in Codice Palatino desiderata et Annotationem criticam adjecit F. Jacobs,* &c.

2 *Welcker, Sylloge Epigramm. Græc.,* Bonn., 1828, 8vo, with Hermann's review in the *Ephem. Lit. Lips.,* 1829, Nos. 148–151; and Welcker's reply, *Abweisung der verunglückten Conjecturen des Herrn Prof. Hermann,* Bonn, 1829, 8vo; Cramer, *Anecd.,* vol. iv., p. 366–388, Oxon., 1838, &c.

3 *Mure, Crit. Hist.,* vol. iii., p. 23, *seqq.*

4 *Plut., De Mus.,* xxviii.; *Clem. Alex., Strom.,* p. 308, &c.

whole amount of change in the mechanical structure of the measure. The Iambic, on the other hand, bears, perhaps above all other metres, in its very essence, the stamp of popular origin. It is, as Aristotle and other ancient critics have pointedly remarked, the metre of familiar discourse.[1] Hence, as the same critics observe, the frequency of its spontaneous occurrence in prose compositions, the justice of which remark may be easily verified by the test of experiment. The iambic measure, therefore, suggested itself instinctively to primitive genius, in any attempt to impart to the poetical treatment of a subject, not so much dignity or solemnity, as emphatic pungency and smartness.

III. In its further cultivation, however, iambic verse, or, rather, the iambic trimeter, for in that form alone is its full excellence displayed, not only embraces, like the elegy, the treatment of every variety of subject, but as possessing, in a degree little short of the hexameter, the principle of continuity, which is wanting in the elegy, is qualified to treat those subjects with similar, if not the same ease, amplitude, and dignity as the hexameter itself. The perfection of iambic versification is the text of Aristophanes, where it will ever remain unsurpassed and unrivalled in variety and brilliancy of dramatic effect.

IV. We will now proceed to give a brief sketch of the lives and works of the most eminent among the early iambic poets of Greece.

1. Archilochus (Ἀρχίλοχος), of whom some mention has already been made under the head of elegiac verse, but whose fuller biography belongs more properly to this place, was descended from a noble family who held the priesthood in the island of Paros. His father was Telesicles, and his mother a slave named Enipo. He flourished about 714–676 B.C. In the flower of his age, between 710 and 700 B.C., and probably after he had gained a prize for his hymn to Ceres,[2] he went from Paros to Thasos, with a colony, of which one account makes him the leader. The motive for the emigration can only be conjectured. It was most probably the result of a political change, to which cause was added, in the case of Archilochus, a sense of personal wrongs. He had been a suitor to Neobūle, one of the daughters of Lycambes, who first promised and afterward refused to give his daughter to the poet. Enraged at this treatment, Archilochus attacked the whole family in an iambic poem, accusing Lycămbes of perjury, and his daughters of the most abandoned lives. The verses were recited at the festival of Ceres, and produced such an effect that the daughters of Lycambes are said to have hung themselves through shame.

The bitterness, moreover, which he expressed in his poems toward his native island seems to have arisen, in part, from the low estimation in which he was held, as being the son of a slave. Neither was he more happy at Thasos. He draws the most melancholy picture of his adopted country, which he at length quitted in disgust.[3] While at Thasos, he incurred the disgrace of losing his shield in an engagement with the Thracians of the opposite continent; but, like Alcæus, under similar cir-

[1] *Arist.*, *Rhet.*, iii., 1; *Poet.*, xxiv.

[2] *Schol. in Aristoph.*, *Av.*, 1762.

[3] *Plut.*, *De Exil.*, 12, p. 604; *Strab.*, xiv., p. 648; viii., p. 370, &c.

cumstances, instead of being ashamed of the disaster, he recorded it in his verse. Plutarch states[1] that Archilochus was banished from Sparta the very hour that he had arrived there, because he had written in his poems that a man had better throw away his arms than lose his life. But Valerius Maximus says that the poems of Archilochus were forbidden at Sparta because of their licentiousness, and especially on account of the attack on the daughters of Lycambes.[2]

The fact that the fame of Archilochus was spread in his lifetime over the whole of Greece, together with his unsettled character, render it probable that he made many journeys of which we have no account. It seems that he visited Siris, in Lower Italy, the only city of which he speaks well.[3] At length he returned to Paros, and in a war between the Parians and the people of Naxos, he fell by the hand of a Naxian named Calondas, or Corax.

Of the merits of Archilochus in elegiac verse we have already spoken. His fame, however, principally rested on his satiric iambic poetry, the first place in which was awarded to him by the consent of the ancient writers, who did not hesitate to compare him with Sophocles, Pindar, and even Homer; meaning, doubtless, that, as they stood at the head of tragic, lyric, and epic poetry respectively, so was Archilochus the first of iambic satirical writers; while some place him next to Homer, above all other poets.[4] The Emperor Hadrian judged that the Muses had shown a special mark of favor to Homer in leading Archilochus into a different department of poetry. The Iambics of Archilochus expressed the strongest feelings in the most unmeasured language. The license of Ionian democracy, and the bitterness of a disappointed man, were united with the highest degree of poetical power to give them force and point. In countries and ages unfamiliar with the political and religious license which at once incited and protected the poet, his satire was blamed for its severity; and the emotion accounted most conspicuous in his verses was "rage," as we see in the line of Horace,[5] "*Archilochum proprio rabies armavit iambo*," and in the expression of Hadrian, λυσσῶντας ἰάμβους, and his bitterness passed into a proverb, Ἀρχίλοχον πατεῖς.

But there must have been something more than mere sarcastic power; there must have been truth and delicate wit in the sarcasms of the poet, whom Plato does not hesitate to call the "very wise" (τοῦ σοφωτάτου).[6] Quintilian also ascribes to him the greatest power of expression, displayed in sentences sometimes strong, sometimes brief, with rapid changes (*quum validæ, tum breves vibrantesque sententiæ*), the greatest life and nervousness (*plurimum vitæ atque nervorum*), and considers that whatever blame his works deserve is the fault of his subjects, and not of his genius.[7] In the latter opinion the Greek critics seem to have joined.[8] The best opportunity we have of judging of the structure of Archilochus's poetry, though not of its satiric character, is furnished by the Epodes of

---

1 *Inst. Lacon.*, p. 239, *b.* 2 *Val. Max.*, vi., 3, ext. 1. 3 *Athen.*, xii., p. 523, *d.*
4 *Dion Chrysost.*, Orat. 33, vol. ii., p. 5; *Longin.*, xiii., 3; *Vell. Paterc.*, i., 5; *Cic.*, *Orat.*, 2, &c. 5 *Ep. ad Pis.*, 79 6 *Plat.*, *Repub.*, ii., p. 365.
7 *Quint.*, x., 1, 60. 8 *Plut.*, *De Aud.*, 13, p. 45, *a.*

Horace, as we learn from that poet himself. Some manifest translations of Archilochus may be seen in the Epodes.

The fragments of Archilochus are collected in Jacobs' *Anthologia Græca*, Gaisford's *Poetæ Græci Minores*, Bergk's *Poetæ Lyrici Græci*, and by Liebel, in his *Archilochi Reliquiæ*, Lips., 1812, 8vo (2d edit., Vienna, 1819).

2. Simonĭdes (Σιμωνίδης) of Samos, or, as he is more usually designated, of Amorgos, has already, like Archilochus, been briefly alluded to under the head of the elegiac poets. He was the second, both in time and reputation, of the three principal iambic poets of the early period of Greek literature, namely, Archilochus, Simonides, and Hipponax.[1] He was a native of Samos, whence he led a colony to the neighboring island of Amorgos, where he founded three cities, Minoa, Ægialus, and Arcesine, in the first of which he fixed his own abode.[2] He flourished about B.C. 664. The iambic poems of Simonides were of two species, gnomic and satirical; and he is remarkable for the peculiar application which he made of the iambic metre; that is to say, he took not individuals, but whole classes of persons as the object of his satire. The most important of his extant fragments is a satire upon women, in which he derives the various, though generally bad qualities of women from the variety of their origin; thus, the uncleanly woman is derived from the swine; the cunning woman from the fox, the talkative woman from the dog, and so on. There is only one race created for the benefit of men, the woman sprung from the bee, who is fond of her work, and keeps faithful watch over her house.[3]

The fragments of Simonides of Amorgos have been edited, intermixed with those of Simonides of Ceos, and almost without an attempt to distinguish them, in the chief collections of the Greek poets; in Brunck's *Analecta*, and in Jacobs' *Anthologia Græca.* There is an edition of the fragment on women by Koeler, with a prefatory epistle by Heyne, Götting., 1781, 8vo. But the first complete edition was that of Welcker, published in the *Rheinisches Museum* for 1835, 2d series, vol. iii., p. 353, *seqq.*, and also separately, under the title of *Simonidis Amorgini Iambi qui supersunt*, Bonn., 1835, 8vo. The text of the fragments is also contained in Schneidewin's *Delectus Poesis Græcorum*, and in Bergk's *Poetæ Lyrici Græci.*

3. Solon (Σόλων) of Athens has been already mentioned, like the preceding, under the head of elegiac poets. After Solon had introduced his new constitution, he soon found that, although he had attempted to satisfy the claims of all parties, or, rather, to give to each party and order its due share of power, he had not succeeded in satisfying any. In order to shame his opponents, he wrote some iambics, in which he calls on his censors to consider of how many citizens the state would have been bereaved, if he had listened to the demands of the contending factions. As a witness of the goodness of his plans, Solon calls the great goddess Earth, the mother of Saturn, whose surface had before this time been

[1] *Proclus, Chrestom.*, 7; *Lucian.*, *Pseudol.*, 2.

[2] Compare *Strab.*, x., p. 487; *Steph. Byz.*, *s. v.* Ἀμοργός.

[3] *Müller, Hist. Gr. Lit.*, p. 140.

covered with numerous boundary-stones, in sign of the ground's being mortgaged; these he had succeeded in removing, and in restoring the land in full property to the mortgagers. This fragment is well worth reading, since it gives as clear an idea of the political situation of Athens at the time as it does of Solon's iambic style. It shows a truly Attic energy and address in defending a favorite cause, while it contains the first germs of that power of speech which afterward came to maturity in the dialogue of the Athenian stage, and in the oratory of the popular assembly and of the courts of justice. In the dialect and expressions, the poetry of Solon retains more of the Ionic cast.[1] The editions of the fragments of Solon have already been mentioned on page 76.

4. Hipponax (Ἱππῶναξ), a native of Ephesus, was, after Archilochus and Simonides, the third of the classical iambic poets of Greece. He flourished B.C. 546–520. Like others of the early poets, Hipponax was distinguished for his love of liberty. The tyrants of his native city having expelled him from his home, he took up his abode at Clazomenæ, for which reason he is sometimes called a Clazomenian.[2] He lived at the latter place in great poverty, and, according to one account, died of want. In person Hipponax was little, thin, and ugly, but very strong.[3] The two brothers Bupalus and Athenis, who were sculptors of Chios, made statues of Hipponax, in which they caricatured his natural ugliness, and he, in return, directed all the power of his satirical poetry against them, and especially against Bupalus.[4] Later writers add that the sculptors hanged themselves in despair. This, however, is probably a mere attempt to improve upon the resemblance between the stories of Archilochus and Hipponax, since Pliny contradicts the account of the suicide of Bupalus by referring to works of his which were executed at a later period. As for the fragment of Hipponax,[5] Ὦ Κλαζομένοισι Βούπαλος κατέκτειθεν, if it really be his (for it is only quoted anonymously by Rufinus),[6] instead of being considered a proof of the story, it should more probably be regarded as having formed, through a too literal interpretation, one source of the error.

The satire of Hipponax, however, was not concentrated entirely on certain individuals; from existing fragments it appears rather to have been founded on a general view of life, taken, however, on its ridiculous or grotesque side. He severely chastised the luxury of his Ionian brethren; he did not spare his own parents; and he ventured even to ridicule the gods. His language is filled with words taken from common life, such as the names of articles of food, clothing, and of ordinary utensils current among the working people. He evidently strives to make his iambics local pictures full of freshness, nature, and homely truth. For this purpose, the change which Hipponax devised in the iambic metre was as felicitous as it was bold; he crippled the rapid agile gait of the iambic, by transforming the last foot from a pure iambus to a spondee, contrary

[1] *Müller, Hist. Gr. Lit.*, p. 140, *seq.*
[2] *Sulpicia, Sat.*, v., 6.
[3] *Athen.*, xii., p. 552, *c, d; Ælian, V. H.*, x., 6.
[4] *Plin., H. N.*, xxxvi., 5, 4; *Horat., Epod.*, vi., 14; *Lucian., Pseudol.*, 2.
[5] Frag. vi., p. 29, *Welcker*, where Bergk gives Ὦ Κλαζομένιοι, Βούπαλός τε κἄθηνις.
[6] p. 2712, *Putsch.*

to the fundamental principle of the whole mode of versification. The metre thus maimed and stripped of its beauty and regularity, and technically made ἄῤῥυθμος, was a perfectly appropriate rhythmical form for the delineation of such pictures of intellectual deformity as Hipponax delighted in. As this new species of verse had hence a sort of halting movement, it obtained the name of *Chōliambus* (χωλιαμβός), "lame iambic," or *Iambus Scazōn* (ἴαμβος σκάζων), "limping iambic." Iambics of this kind are still more cumbrous and halting when the fifth foot is also a spondee; which, indeed, according to the original structure, is not forbidden. These last were called *Ischiorrhogic*, "broken-backed" (ἰσχιοῤῥωγικοί), and were invented by another iambographer named Ananius. They are very rarely used by Hipponax. The choliambics of Hipponax were imitated by many later writers; among others by Babrius, whose Fables are composed entirely in this metre.[1]

Hipponax wrote also a parody on the Iliad. He may be said to occupy a middle place between Archilochus and Aristophanes. He is as bitter, but not so earnest as the former, while, in lightness and jocoseness, he more resembles the latter. There are still extant about a hundred lines of his poems which are collected by Welcker (*Hipponactis et Ananii Iambographorum Fragmenta*, Götting., 1817, 4to), Bergk (*Poetæ Lyrici Græci*), Schneidewin (*Delectus Poesis Græcorum*), and by Meineke, in Lachmann's edition of Babrius, Berol., 1845.

5. Ananius (Ἀνάνιος), a Greek iambic poet, contemporary with Hipponax, flourished about 540 B.C. He is generally regarded as the inventor of ischiorrhogic iambics, of which we have just made mention. Ananius has hardly any individual character in literary history distinct from that of Hipponax. In Alexandrea their poems seem to have been regarded as forming one collection; and thus the criterion by which to determine whether a particular passage belonged to the one or the other was often lost, or never existed. Hence, in the uncertainty which is the true author, the same verse is occasionally ascribed to both.[2] The few fragments which are attributed with certainty to Ananius are so completely in the tone of Hipponax, that it would be a vain labor to attempt to point out any characteristic difference. These fragments appear with those of Hipponax in the edition of Welcker, and in the collections mentioned in the previous article.[3]

FABLE AND PARODY.[4]

V. Akin to the Iambic are two kinds of poetry, which, though differing widely from each other, have both their source in the turn for the delineation of the ludicrous, and both stand in a close historical relation to the iambic: 1. Fable, originally called αἶνος, and afterward, less precisely, μῦθος and λόγος; and, 2. Parody.

VI. With regard to *Fable*, it is not improbable that in other countries, particularly in the north of Europe, it may have arisen from a child-like, playful view of the character and habits of animals, which frequently sug-

[1] *Müller, Hist. Gr. Lit.*, p. 142; *Smith, Dict. Biogr.*, *s. v.*
[2] *Athen.*, xiv., p. 625, *c.*
[3] *Müller*, p. 143; *Smith, Dict. Biogr.*, *s. v.*
[4] *Müller, l. c.*

gest a comparison with the nature and incidents of human life. In Greece, however, it originated in an intentional travestie of human affairs. The *αἶνος* is, as its name denotes, an admonition, or rather a reproof, veiled, either from fear of an excess of frankness, or from love of fun and jest, beneath the fiction of an occurrence happening among beasts. Such is the character of the *αἶνος* at its very first appearance in Hesiod.[1] Archilochus employed the *αἶνος* in a similar manner in his iambics against Lycambes.[2] In like manner Stesichorus cautioned his countrymen, the Himeræans, against Phalaris, by the fable of the horse, who, to revenge himself on the stag, took the man on his back, and thus became his slave.[3]

VII. It is probable that the taste for fables of beasts, and numerous similar inventions, found their way into Greece from the East, since this sort of symbolical and veiled narrative is more in harmony with the Oriental than with the Greek character. Indeed, the very names given by the Greeks contain a distinct avowal of this. Thus, one kind of fable was called the *Libyan*, which we may, therefore, infer was of African origin, and was introduced into Greece through Cyrene. To this class belongs, according to Æschylus, the beautiful fable of the wounded eagle, who, looking at the feathering of the arrow with which he was pierced, exclaimed, "I perish by feathers drawn from my own wing."[4] From this example, we see that the Libyan fable belonged to the class of fables of animals. So also did the sorts to which later teachers of rhetoric give the names of the *Cyprian* and the *Cilician*. The contest between the olive and the bay, on Mount Tmolus, is cited as a fable of the ancient *Lydians*.[5]

VIII. The *Carian* stories or fables, however, were taken from human life, as, for instance, that quoted by the Greek lyric poets, Timocreon and Simonides. A Carian fisherman, in the winter, sees a sea-polypus, and he says to himself, "If I dive to catch it, I shall be frozen to death; if I don't catch it, my children must starve."[6] The *Sybaritic* fables, mentioned by Aristophanes, have a similar character.[7] Both the Sybaritic and Æsopian fables are represented by Aristophanes as jests or ludicrous stories (γελοῖα). As regards Æsop himself, Bentley has shown that he was very far from being regarded by the Greeks as one of their poets, and still less as a writer. They considered him merely an ingenious fabulist, under whose name a number of fables, often applicable to human affairs, were current, and to whom, at a later period, nearly all that were either invented or derived from any other source were attributed. His history has been dressed out by the later Greeks with all manner of droll and whimsical incidents. What can be collected from the ancient writers down to Aristotle is, however, confined to the following:

IX. Æsop (Αἴσωπος) was a slave of the Samian Iadmon, who lived in the time of the Egyptian king Amasis, the reign of which monarch begins B.C. 569. According to the statement of Eugeon, an old Samian historian, he was a native of the Thracian city of Mesembria, which existed

---

1 *Op. et D.*, v. 202, *seqq.* 2 Frag. xxxviii., *Gaisf.* 3 *Arist.*, *Rhet.*, ii., 20.
4 *Frag. Myrmid.* 5 Frag. xciii., *Bentl.*
6 *Walz*, *Rhet. Gr.*, vol. ii., p. 11. 7 *Aristoph.*, *Vesp.*, 1259, 1427, 1437.

long before it was peopled by a colony of Byzantines in the reign of Darius. According to a less authentic account, he was from Cotyæum, in Phrygia. It seems that his wit and pleasantry procured him his freedom; for, though he remained in Iadmon's family, it must have been as a freedman, or he could not, as Aristotle relates, have appeared publicly as the defender of a demagogue, on which occasion he told a fable in support of his client. It is generally received as certain that Æsop perished at Delphi; the Delphians, exasperated by his sarcastic fables, having put him to death on a charge of robbing the temple.[1] The fables now extant in prose, bearing the name of Æsop, are unquestionably spurious. Of these there are three principal collections, the one containing 136 fables, published first A.D. 1610, from MSS., at Heidelberg. This is so clumsy a forgery, that it mentions the orator Demades, who lived 200 years after Æsop, and contains a whole sentence from the book of Job. Some of the passages Bentley has shown to be fragments of choliambic verses, and has made it tolerably certain that they were stolen from Babrius. The second collection was made by Maximus Planudes, the monk of Constantinople, living in the fourteenth century. The third collection was found in a MS. at Florence, and published in 1809. Its date is about a century before the time of Planudes.[2]

The two best editions of Æsop are, that of De Furia, containing the new fables from the Florentine MS., Florent., 1809, 8vo, reprinted at Leipsic, and also by Coray, at Paris, in the following year; and that of Schneider, Breslau, 1810, 8vo.

X. Attempts were probably made at an early period to give a poetical form to the Æsopian fable. Socrates is said to have thus beguiled his imprisonment. Demetrius Phalereus, following his example (B.C. 320), turned Æsop's fables into verse, and collected them in a book; and, after him, an author whose name is unknown, published them in elegiacs, of which some fragments are preserved by Suidas. But the only Greek versifier of Æsop, of whose writings any whole fables are preserved, is Babrius (Βάβριος), called also Babrias (Βαβρίας), and sometimes Gabrias (Γαβρίας), an author of no mean powers, and who may well take his place among fabulists with Phædrus and Lafontaine. He lived, in all probability, a little before the age of Augustus, and made his version in choliambics. This version consisted of ten books, of which only a few fragments were known until within a few years, when a manuscript, containing 123 fables, was discovered on Mount Athos. Later writers of Æsopean fables, such as Maximus Planudes, probably turned the poems of Babrius into prose, but they did it in so clumsy a manner, that many choliambic verses may still be traced in their fables, as Bentley has shown in his Dissertation on the Fables of Æsop,[3] and as Tyrwhitt has proved still more clearly.[4] The latest editions of Babrius are, that of Boissonade, Paris, 1844, 8vo; in which the newly-discovered fables first ap-

---

[1] *Müller, Hist. Gr. Lit.*, p. 146. [2] *Smith, Dict. Biogr.*, *s. v.*

[3] Appended to the Dissertation on the Epistles of Phalaris.

[4] "*De Babrio, Fabularum Æsopearum Scriptore*," Lond., 1776, reprinted at Erlangen, 1785, ed. *Harles*.

peared; that of Lachmann, Berol., 1845; of Orelli and Baiter, Turic., 1845; and of Lewis, Lond., 1847.

XI. The other kind of poetry to which we referred was *Parody* (παρῳδία). This was understood by the ancients, as it is by ourselves, to mean an adoption of the form of some celebrated poem, with such changes in the matter as to produce a totally different effect; and generally to substitute mean and ridiculous for elevated poetical sentiments. This contrast between the grand and sublime images suggested to the memory, and the comic ones introduced in their stead, renders parody peculiarly fitted to place any subject in a ludicrous, grotesque, and trivial light. The purpose of it, however, was not, in general, to detract from the reverence due to the ancient poet (who, in most instances, was Homer) by this travesty, but only to add zest and pungency to the satire.[1]

CHAPTER XVI.

SECOND OR POETICAL PERIOD—*continued.*

LYRIC POETRY—*continued.*

CONNECTION OF LYRIC POETRY WITH MUSIC.[2]

I. In the Elegiac and Iambic styles of poetry, the former suited to the expression of grief, the latter to the expression of anger, hatred, and contempt, Greek poetry entered the domain of real life. Still, however, a great variety of new forms of poetry was reserved for the invention of future poets. The elegy and the iambic versification contained the germs of the lyric style, but the principal characteristic of lyric poetry, *strictly so called*, was its connection with *music*, vocal as well as instrumental. This connection, indeed, existed, to a certain extent, in epic, and still more in elegiac and iambic poetry; but singing was not essential in those styles. Such a recitation by a rhapsodist, as was usual for epic poetry, also served, at least in the beginning, for elegiac, and in great part for iambic verses.

II. Singing, however, and a continued instrumental accompaniment, are appropriate where the expression of feeling or passion is inconsistent with a more measured and equable mode of recitation. Moreover, as the expression of strong feeling required more pauses and resting-places, the verses in lyric poetry, strictly so called, naturally fell into *strophes* of greater or less length, each of which comprised several varieties of metre, and admitted of an appropriate termination. This arrangement of the strophes was, at the same time, connected with *dancing*, which was naturally, though not necessarily, associated with lyric poetry in this its stricter sense.

III. The Greek lyric poetry, therefore, in the stricter sense in which we are now considering it, was characterized by the expression of deeper and more impassioned feeling, and a more swelling and impetuous tone,

---

1 *Müller, Hist. Gr. Lit.*, p. 146.

2 *Ib.*, p. 149.

than the elegiac or iambic metre; and, at the same time, the effect was heightened by appropriate vocal and instrumental music, and often by the movements and figures of the dance. In this union of the sister arts, poetry was indeed predominant, and music and dancing were only employed to enforce and elevate the conceptions of the higher art. Yet music in its turn exercised a reciprocal influence on poetry; so that, as it became more cultivated, the choice of the musical measure decided the tone of the whole poem.

IV. In order, therefore, that the character of the Greek lyric poetry, strictly so called, may be more clearly understood, some account must be given of early Grecian music. Not, indeed, a technical analysis of the art, which would be here quite out of place, but some remarks merely on its elementary history, in connection with brief sketches of the history of the primitive improvers of Greek musical science.

V. The mythical traditions respecting Orpheus, Philammon, Chrysothĕmis, and other minstrels of the early times, being set aside, the history of Greek music begins with Terpander, the Lesbian,[1] who appears to have been properly the founder of it. He first reduced to rule the different modes of singing which prevailed in different countries, and formed out of these rude strains a connected system, from which the Greek music never departed throughout all the improvements and refinements of later ages. It is probable that Terpander belonged to a family who derived their practice of music from the ancient Pierian bards of Bœotia. The Æolians of Lesbos had their origin in Bœotia, the country to which the worship of the muses and the Thracian hymns belonged; and they probably brought with them the first rudiments of poetry. This migration of the art of the muses is ingeniously expressed by the legend, that, after the murder of Orpheus by the Thracian Mænads, his head and lyre were thrown into the sea, and borne upon its waves to Lesbos, whence singing and the music of the cithara flourished in this the most musical of islands. The grave supposed to contain the head of Orpheus was shown in Antissa, a small town of Lesbos;[2] and it was thought that in that spot the nightingales sang most sweetly. In Antissa, also, according to the testimony of several ancient writers, Terpander was born. In this way, the domestic impressions and the occupations of his youth may have prepared Terpander for the great undertaking which he afterward performed.

According to the best opinion, Terpander flourished between B.C. 700 and 650. Of his early life in Lesbos nothing is known. We find him subsequently removing from Lesbos to Sparta, where he introduced his new system of music, and established the first musical school or system (κατάστασις) that existed in Greece.[3] Terpander's connection with Lacedæmon is said to have originated in an invitation by the Spartan rulers to visit their city during a period of intestine discord. This step was taken by them in obedience to an injunction of the Delphic priestess, by whom the Lesbian musician had been pointed out as the destined means of rec-

[1] *Pind. ap. Athen.*, xiv., p. 635, *d; Plut.*, *De Mus.*, 30, p. 1141, *c; Suid.*, *s. v.*

[2] *Steph. Byz.*, *s. v.* Ἄντισσα.

[3] *Plut.*, *Mus.*, 9, p. 1134, *c.*

onciling the hostile factions. Such is said to have been the effect of his music on the Spartans, that the contending parties, dissolved in tears, embraced each other, and buried all previous differences in oblivion.[1] Fixing his abode in that city, he fulfilled, during the remainder of his life, the functions of state poet and musician amid universal admiration and esteem. After his death his memory was revered, and his compositions were regarded as models to all succeeding professors of citharœdic art. His system continued to flourish up to the time of his countryman Phrynis, whose innovations, about the period of the Persian war, were regarded as corruptions of the genuine Hellenic music.[2]

Great as was Terpander's fame, however, as an original genius, his merits would yet appear, from the more authentic notices, to have consisted less in actual discovery than in the adaptation, to Greek tastes and habits, of refinements of art already familiar to the cultivated nations of Asia. The most celebrated novelty for which he obtained credit was the invention of the seven-stringed lyre,[3] by the addition of three chords to the old tetrachord instrument. This, however, can not be considered, nor has it been so understood by the more critical even of his own countrymen, as indicating the first actual construction of a stringed instrument with the compass of an octave. There can be no doubt that the more civilized nations of Asia possessed, before his time, instruments of equal or greater compass; and Terpander is stated, on no less authority than that of Pindar, to have founded his improvements of the Greek cithara on a Lydian instrument of two octaves, called a *magadis*, which, under the Greek name of πηκτίς or βάρβιτον, he had also the merit (though this some modern critics doubt) of first introducing into Europe.[4]

Terpander is also the accredited inventor of the art of writing music;[5] and there can be little doubt of his having possessed a system of notation, forming the basis of that still in use. Here again, however, his services are probably to be understood rather in the way of adaptation to native Greek practice than of original discovery. Plutarch tells us that he set his own verses and those of Homer to certain citharœdic nomes, and sang them in the musical contests; and that he was the first who gave names to the various citharœdic nomes. These nomes were simple tunes, from which others could be derived by slight variations; and these latter were called μέλη. That the nomes of Terpander were entirely of his own composition is not very probable, and, indeed, there is evidence to prove that some of them were derived from old tunes, ascribed to the ancient bards, and others from national melodies. The remains of Terpander's poetry, which no doubt consisted entirely of religious hymns, consist of a few fragments, contained in the collections of Bergk and Schneidewin.

VI. Another ancient master, the Phrygian Olympus, so much enlarged the system of the Greek music, that Plutarch considers him, and not Terpander, to have been the founder of it. The date, and, indeed, the whole history of this Olympus, are involved in obscurity, by a confusion

---

[1] *Mure, Crit. Hist.*, vol. iii., p. 39. [2] *Id. ib.*

[3] *Frag. Terpandri*, 1, *ap. Schneidewin.*, *Del. Poes. Gr.*, p. 237.

[4] *Böckh, De Metr. Pind.*, p. 261; *Frag. Pind.*, ix.; *Mure*, p. 41. [5] *Plut.*, *Mus.*, 3.

between him (who is certainly as historical as Terpander) and a mythological Olympus, who is connected with the first founders of the Phrygian religion and worship. Even Plutarch, who, in his learned treatise upon music, has marked the distinction between the earlier and the later Olympus, has still attributed inventions to the fabulous Olympus which properly belong to the historical one. The ancient Olympus is quite lost in the dawn of mythical legends; he is the favorite and disciple of the Phrygian Silenus, Marsyas, who invented the flute, and used it in his unfortunate contest with the cithara of the Hellenic god Apollo.[1]

The later Olympus, whom we are here considering, was a Phrygian, and perhaps belonged to a family of native musicians, since he was said to be descended from the first Olympus. He is placed by Plutarch at the head of auletic music, as Terpander stood at the head of the citharœdic; and, on account of his inventions in the art, Plutarch even assigns to him, rather than to Terpander, the honor of being the father of Greek music, as we have already remarked (ἀρχηγὸς τῆς Ἑλληνικῆς καὶ καλῆς μουσικῆς).[2] With respect to his age, Müller places him, for satisfactory reasons, after Terpander and before Thaletas, that is, between the 30th and 40th Olympiads, B.C. 660–620. Though a Phrygian by origin, Olympus must be reckoned among the Greek musicians, for all the accounts make Greece the scene of his artistic activity, and his subjects Greek; and he had Greek disciples, such as Crates and Hierax.[3] He may, in fact, be considered as having naturalized in Greece the music of the flute, which had previously been almost peculiar to Phrygia.

Of the particular tunes (νόμοι) ascribed to him, the most important was the Ἁρμάτειος νόμος, a mournful and passionate strain, of the rhythm of which we are able to form an idea from a passage in the *Orestes* of Euripides, which was set to it, as the passage itself tells us. A dirge also, in honor of the slain Python, was said to have been played by Olympus, at Delphi, and in the Lydian style. Olympus was a great inventor in rhythm as well as in music. To the two existing species of rhythm, the ἴσον, in which the *arsis* and *thesis* are equal (as in the dactyl and anapæst), and the διπλάσιον, in which the *arsis* is twice the length of the *thesis* (as in the iambus and trochee), he added a third, the ἡμιόλιον, in which the length of the *arsis* is equal to two short syllables, and that of the *thesis* to three, as in the Cretic (–́ ⏑ –), the Pæons (–́ ⏑ ⏑ ⏑, &c.), and the Bacchius (⏑ –́ –). There is no mention of any poems composed by Olympus.[4]

VII. Thalētas (Θαλήτας), or Thales (Θαλῆς), marks the third epoch in the history of Greek music. A native of Crete, he found means to express in a musical form the spirit which pervaded the religious institutions of his country, by which he produced a strong impression upon the other Greeks. He seems to have been partly a priest and partly an artist; and from this circumstance his history is veiled in obscurity. He is called a Gortynian, but is also said to have been born in Cnossus or

---

[1] *Müller, Hist. Gr. Lit.*, p. 156.
[2] *Plut., Mus.*, p. 1133, *e;* 1135, *c.*
[3] *Id. ib.*, p. 1133, *e;* 1140, *d; Poll.*, iv., 79.
[4] *Smith, Dict Biogr., s. v.*

Elyrus.[1] In compliance, according to tradition, with an invitation which the Spartans sent to him in obedience to an oracle, he removed to Sparta, where, by the sacred character of his pæans, and the influence of his music, he appeased the wrath of Apollo, who had visited the city with a plague, and he composed the factions of the citizens, who were at enmity with one another.[2] He introduced from Crete certain principles or elements of music and rhythm which did not exist in Terpander's system, and thereby founded the second of the musical schools which flourished at Sparta. The date of Thaletas is uncertain; he seems to have flourished about B.C. 670 or 660, and how much before or after these dates can not be determined. It appears not unlikely that he was already distinguished in Crete, while Terpander flourished at Sparta. We have no remains of his poetry. Plutarch and other writers speak of him as a lyric *poet*, and Suidas mentions, as his works, *μέλη* and *ποιήματά τινα μυθικά.*

VIII. Terpander, Olympus, and Thaletas are distinguished by the salient peculiarities which belong to inventive genius. But it is difficult to find any individual characteristics in the numerous masters who followed them between the 40th and 50th Olympiads. By the efforts of these masters, however, music appears to have been brought to the degree of excellence at which we find it in the time of Pindar.[3]

CHAPTER XVII.

SECOND OR POETICAL PERIOD—*continued.*

LYRIC POETRY—*continued.*

SCHOOLS OF LYRIC POETRY,[4] ETC.

I. The *Lyric Poetry proper* of the Greeks, or Lyric poetry in the stricter sense of the term, is of two kinds, which were cultivated by different schools of poets, the name which is commonly given to poets living in the same country, and following the same rules of composition. Of these two schools one is called the *Æolic*, the other the *Doric*.

II. The *Æolic* school is so called because it flourished among the Æolians of Asia Minor, and particularly in the island of Lesbos. The *Doric* school was so called because, though it was diffused over the whole of Greece, yet it was first and principally cultivated by the Dorians in the Peloponnesus and Sicily. The difference of origin appears also in the dialects of these two schools. The Lesbian school wrote in the *Æolic* dialect, as it is still to be found in inscriptions in that island, while the Doric employed almost indifferently either a mitigated Dorism or the epic dialect, the dignity and solemnity of which was heightened by a limited use of Doric forms.

III. These two schools differ essentially in every respect, as much in the subject as in the form and style of their poems. To begin with the

[1] *Suid.*, *s. v.*; *Müller*, p. 159.
[2] *Pausan.*, i., 14, 4; *Plut.*, *Lycurg.*, 4.
[3] *Müller*, *Hist. Gr. Lit.*, p. 161.
[4] *Müller*, p. 164.

mode of recitation: the Doric lyric poetry was intended to be executed by choruses, and to be sung to choral dances, whence it is sometimes called choral poetry. On the other hand, the Æolic is never called choral, because it was meant to be recited by a single person, who accompanied his recitation with a stringed instrument, generally the lyre, and with suitable gestures. The structure of the Doric lyric strophe is comprehensive, and often very artificial, inasmuch as the ear, which might perhaps be unable to detect the recurring rhythms, was assisted by the eye, which could follow the different movements of the chorus; and thus the spectator was able to understand the intricate and artificial plan of the composition. The *Æolic* lyric poetry, on the other hand, was much more limited, and either consisted of verses joined together, or else it formed, of a few short verses, strophes in which the same verse is frequently repeated, and the conclusion is effected by a change in the versification, or by the addition of a short final verse.

IV. The strophes of the Doric lyric poetry were also often combined, by annexing to two strophes corresponding with one another (the first technically called *strophe*, and the second *antistrophe*) a third and different one, called *epode*. The origin of this (according to the ancients) is that the chorus, having performed one movement during the strophe, returned to their former position during the antistrophe, and then remained motionless for a time, during which the epode is sung. The short strophes of the Æolic lyric poetry, on the other hand, follow each other in equal measure, and without being interrupted by epodes. The Æolic strophe is sometimes called, for distinction' sake, the *Melic* strophe; the Dorian, in like manner, the *Choric* strophe.

V. It must not be inferred, however, from what is here stated, that poems for choral exhibition were never composed by the Æolic poets; for choruses were undoubtedly performed in Lesbos, as well as in other parts of Greece. Several of the Lesbian lyric poems, of which we have fragments and accounts, appear to have been composed for choral recitation. But the characteristic excellence of this lyric poetry was the expression of individual ideas and sentiments with warmth and frankness. These sentiments formed a natural expression in the native dialect of these poets, the ancient Æolic, which has a character of simplicity and fondness; the epic dialect, the general language of Greek poetry, being only used sparingly, in order to soften and elevate this popular dialect. Unhappily, the works of these poets were allowed to perish at a time when they had become unintelligible from the singularity of their dialect, and the condensation of their thoughts. To this cause, and not to the warmth of their erotic descriptions, is to be attributed the oblivion to which they were consigned. For if literary works had been condemned on moral grounds of this kind, the writings of Martial and Petronius, and many poems of the Anthology, would not now exist, while Alcæus and Sappho would probably be extant.[1]

VI. Before entering, however, upon the biographies of the poets belonging to the two schools which we have just been considering, it will

[1] *Müller*, p. 166.

be proper to give a brief sketch of the orders and occasions of lyric performances, more particularly as many terms connected with these will occur in the course of those biographies, which it will be less convenient then to explain.

ORDERS AND OCCASIONS OF LYRIC PERFORMANCE.[1]

VII. The various modes of adapting lyric poetry to those festive rites, public or private, with which its higher cultivation was so vitally connected, have special claims on our attention, since they supply one of the most striking illustrations of the fertile genius and discriminating taste of the Greek nation. From Olympus down to the work-shop or the sheepfold, from Jove and Apollo to the wandering mendicant, every rank and degree of the Greek community, divine or human, had its own proper allotment of poetical celebration. The gods had their *hymns*, *nomes*, *pæans*, and *dithyrambs;* great men their *encomia* and *epinicia;* the votaries of pleasure their *erotica* and *symposiaca;* the mourner his *threnodia* and *elegies;* the vine-dresser his *epilenia;* the herdsmen their *bucolica;* even the beggar his *eiresione* and *chelidonisma.* The number of these varieties of Grecian song recorded under distinct titles, and most of them enjoying a certain benefit of scientific culture, amounts to upward of fifty.[2]

VIII. A portion, indeed, of this number no longer exist but in name; and, with the exception of those immediately connected with the great public festivals, few have been described with such precision, or are so clearly illustrated by existing specimens, as to supply materials for treatment as distinct heads of subject. Those which in this more tangible capacity chiefly claim attention are the following: the *Hymn*, *Nome*, *Pæan*, *Hyporchem*, *Prosodium*, *Parthenia*, *Dithyramb*, *Threnus*, *Symposiaca*, *Encomia*, *Epinicia*, *Erotica*, *Gamelia*, *Embateria*. This catalogue may be ranged under two general heads, of Sacred, and Profane or Secular:[3] the former comprising poems in exclusive honor of the gods; the latter, those devoted, in whole or in part, to human concerns or interests. To the former head belong the hymn, nome, pæan, hyporchem, prosodium, dithyramb; to the latter, the symposiaca, encomia, epinicia, erotica, gamelia, embateria. As an intermediate class, partaking of both characters, may be ranked the threnus and parthenia. We will now proceed to offer a brief account of each, with the exception of the pæan, of which we have already treated.

IX. The first two names in the above list, *Hymn* and *Nome*, are rather generic terms applicable to every more dignified species of lyric compositions, than designations of any particular class of ode. The pæan, for example, was the hymn of rejoicing or triumph; the prosodium, the processional hymn; the prooemium, the introductory hymn to the sacred office in the sanctuary. In later times, however, the title Hymn appears to have attached, in a peculiar sense, to the odes sung by the chorus during the sacrifice, when stationary around the altar. *Nome* (νόμος), in its orig-

---

[1] *Mure, Hist. Crit.*, vol. iii., p. 63, *seqq.*

[2] Compare *Ilgen, Scolia sive Carmina convivialia Græc.*, p. xiv., *seqq.*

[3] *Proclus, Chrestom.*, ed. *Gaisf.*, p. 380, *seq.*

inal more comprehensive signification, denoted simply that more definite adaptation of musical to poetic numbers, which forms the essence of all lyric composition, as distinct from the continuous chant or recitative of the old epic minstrelsy. In the more advanced stages of lyric art, however, the term is restricted, in a proper sense, to a certain more solemn order of hymn or anthem, the older specimens of which were marked by a peculiar simplicity and dignity of style, and passed generally current as productions of the earliest and purest periods of lyric art.[1]

X. The term *Hyporchem* (ὑπόρχημα) denotes, in familiar usage, both a lively kind of mimic dance, and the branch of lyric composition by which that dance was accompanied.[2] The musical or poetical element of the hyporchem, from the earliest period of its cultivation, appears in style and numbers to have closely resembled the pæan. Both performances were connected preferably, during their best period, with the worship of Apollo; and a favorite measure of both was the Cretic or pæonic. Much similarity is, accordingly, observable between existing specimens of each order of composition; and among the ancient critics themselves it was often matter of doubt under which denomination an ode was to be ranked.[3] The main difference seems to have been, that the pæan was characterized by a pervading dignity and propriety, the hyporchem by a greater degree of vivacity, tending at times to levity or license.[4] Another feature of distinction was the greater prevalence in the hyporchem, when combined with dancing, of that mimetic action which entered more or less into all such solemnities among the Greeks. A third distinction was, that the pæan, during the best ages, was exclusively addressed to the gods, whereas hyporchems appear to have been, though rarely, composed and performed in honor of men.[5] The first poet to whom hyporchems are ascribed was Thaletas. In the fragments of the hyporchems of Pindar, the rhythms are peculiarly light, and have a very imitative and graphic character.[6] These characteristics must have existed in a much higher degree in the hyporchematic songs of Thaletas.[7] The chief recorded author of hyporchematic productions during the earlier period, besides Thaletas, was Xenodamus of Cythera. But no remains of the works of either of them have been preserved. The extant specimens of the immediately succeeding period emanate from its most celebrated poets, Simonides, Pindar, Pratinas, and Bacchylides, with several of whom the hyporchem was a favorite style.[8]

XI. The *Prosŏdium* (προσόδιον, *scil.* μέλος) was the hymn sung by the choristers in their procession to the altar or sanctuary. Although this order of composition must have been connected with the service of every deity of whose rites processional movements formed a part, its early culture and chief popularity were concentrated around the worship of Apollo. The prosodium, accordingly, is classed under the general head of Pæan,

---

1 *Plat.*, *De Leg.*, p. 700; *Proclus*, *Chrestom.*, ed. *Gaisf.*, p. 383.

2 *Proclus*, p. 384, *Gaisf.*

3 *Plut.*, *Mus.*, 9. Compare *Böckh*, *De Metr. Pind.*, p 201.

4 See a hyporchem of Pratinas, *ap. Athen.*, xiv., p. 617.

5 *Böckh*, *Frag. Pind.*, p. 596, *seq.*

6 *Böckh*, *De Metr. Pind.*, p. 201, *seqq.*; p. 270.

7 *Müller*, *Hist. Lit. Gr.*, p. 23, *seqq.* Compare p. 160, *seqq.*

8 *Mure*, *Crit. Hist.*, p. 72.

by the special title of Prosodiac, or Processional, pæan. Like the kindred order of sacred odes, the nome and pæan proper, it was composed, in the earlier epochs of its cultivation, in hexameter measure. Afterward, however, when the lyric school of art acquired the ascendant, and the dance became popular even in these graver processional solemnities, lyric numbers were exclusively preferred. The prosodia of Pindar, the oldest of which any considerable remains have been preserved, are chiefly in the same grave Dorian measure as the greater part of his epinician odes. The accompaniment of the flute, as usual in festive movements, was preferred to that of the harp, customary in the stationary choral rites.[1]

XII. To the head of Prosodia belongs in part the order of composition entitled *Parthenia*,[2] or "virginal songs." This title, however, comprises two different kinds of ode: first, processional or sacrificial songs, sung, as their name denotes, by virgins, in honor of certain deities; secondly, songs in honor of those same youthful members of the female sex.[3] The parthenia of the first class may, therefore, be characterized as sacred; those of the second as profane or secular. The sacred parthenia were substantially hymns, pæans, or prosodia, as the object or occasion might require. Their distinctive feature was a blending of feminine grace and tenderness with devotional solemnity.[4] Hence may be explained the great popularity of this style of composition with most of the leading lyric poets from Alcman downward.[5]

XIII. The *Dithyramb* (*διθύραμβος*), which comes next in order, is a celebrated branch of composition, and, as the parent of the Attic tragedy, assumes a still greater degree of importance and interest, than would even otherwise justly attach to it on account of its great popularity, and its extensive influence on the style and taste of every period of Greek poetical literature. The dithyramb, in its earliest form, was the hymn of Bacchus,[6] as the pæan was the hymn of Apollo. Its character was always, like that of the worship to which it belonged, impassioned and enthusiastic; the extremes of feeling, rapturous pleasure and wild lamentation, were both expressed by it. The existing notices of this order of composition are of comparatively recent date; nor, indeed, is there any allusion by Homer, Hesiod, or other primitive authorities, to the festive rites of Bacchus as popular in their day. That the dithyramb, however, in its simpler melic form of Dionysiac hymn or pæan, was already a cultivated branch of lyric art in the age of Archilochus, appears from a still extant distich of that poet,[7] in which he mentions it by name as the "beautiful song of Dionysus," and prides himself on his skill in its execution. These verses are in a lively vein of trochaic tetrameter, the same measure which Aristotle describes as originally proper to the dithyramb; and they may hence be presumed to have been themselves the exordium of a dithyrambic ode or chorus. In the generation subsequent to Archilochus, a more extended and artificial character was imparted to this branch

---

1 *Plut.*, *Mus.*, 18; *Mure*, p. 74.
2 *Athen.*, xiv., p. 631.
3 *Schol. in Aristoph.*, *Av.*, 920; *Suid.*, *s.v.*; *Proclus*, *Chrestom.*, p. 380, *Gaisf.*
4 *Dion. Hal.*, ed. *Reiske*, vol. iii., p. 1073. Compare *Plut.*, *Mus.*, 17.
5 *Mure*, p. 74.
6 *Plat.*, *De Leg.*, p. 700.
7 Frag. 72, *Bergk.* Compare *Athen.*, xiv., p. 628.

of lyric performance by Arion, the celebrated Lesbian musician, and by means of which the dithyramb was raised to a regular choral song.[1] But of this change we will speak more fully in our remarks on the origin of tragedy.

XIV. The term *Threnus* (θρῆνος) denotes in its origin any species of lamentation, more properly the dirge or lament for the death of kinsmen or dear friends. In later usage, the title became nearly equivalent to the more familiar one of elegy. When sung over the corpse at its laying out or entombment, the threnus acquired the distinctive name of *Epicedīum* (ἐπικήδειον), or funeral song.[2] The only two occasions on which the threnus is mentioned by Homer were of the latter description. To the threnus belongs also the song of Linus, which we have already considered. The measure of the threnus was probably at first the dactylic. With the advance of lyric art, however, a great variety of metrical forms was admitted. The reputed author of the extension was the Phrygian Olympus.[3]

XV. We come next to the *Symposiaca*, or convivial poetry of the Greeks. Convivial songs were classed by the ancients under three heads:[4] first, those sung in chorus by the whole company; secondly, those sung by each guest in succession; thirdly, such as were sung also in succession, but under certain peculiarities of arrangement, and with a limitation in ordinary cases to the more gifted members of the company. The *songs of the first class* appear to have been chiefly those inaugural odes familiarly called Pæans, sung as grace or proœmium to the whole entertainment, and usually addressed to Apollo, sometimes to Jove, Bacchus, Mercury, or such other deity as the occasion suggested. The *next* more varied order of symposiac performances, in which all took part, though not all simultaneously, very much resembles the modern custom of laying each guest under an obligation to sing his song,[5] whether his own composition or some popular ode of the day. On these occasions a lyre or myrtle branch,[6] less frequently a drinking cup,[7] was handed round as a temporary badge of office from guest to guest, each, in his turn, receiving it from his predecessor, and passing it on to his neighbor at the close of his own part. The lyre was probably destined for those alone who, together with a musical voice, possessed skill in the use of the instrument. When these qualifications, one or both, were wanting, the myrtle branch was preferred, as the ancient and proper symbol of the more simple styles of poetic recitation. The songs thus circulated bore no distinctive title, but that of *Paroenia* (παροίνια, *scil.* μέλη), "wine songs," or *symposiaca*, "drinking songs," common to all those of the convivial order.[8]

The *third* more complicated and more celebrated species of *Paroenia* were those called *Scolia* (σκολιά). The performance was here reserved for the more scientific and experienced musicians of the party. The chief

[1] *Mure*, p. 78. [2] *Proclus, Chrestom.*, p. 385, *Gaisf.*; *Etym. Mag.*, *s. v.* θρῆνος.
[3] *Mure*, p. 94, *seqq.*
[4] *Dicæarch. ap. Suid.*, *Hesych. et Phot.*, *s. v.* σκολιόν; *Plut.*, *Sympos.*, i., 1, 5.
[5] *Plut.*, *Sympos.*, p. 214, *seqq.* Occasionally prose was substituted for poetry, each guest telling a story, or offering a short essay on some pleasant topic. *Plut.*, *l. c.*
[6] *Aristoph.*, *Nub.*, 1358; *Schol. ad loc.*; *Vesp.*, 1214–1220; *Schol. ad loc.*; *Plut.*, *Sympos.*, i., 1, 5, &c. [7] *Athen.*, xi., p. 503. [8] *Mure*, p. 100.

of the qualified guests led off with a short stave or sonnet, whether an entire ode or a part of some longer composition, marked in either case by some lively spirit or point. He then handed the symbol of office to the person who, it had been arranged, should follow, or whom he thought fit to select as his successor, who passed it on, in his turn, to a third, and so on; each being expected at once to carry on the strain, whether in the way of continuation or repartee, in the same or a closely congenial style of subject or measure. The notion that the name of the song arose from its irregular course around the table (σκολιόν, "crooked") is not probable. It is much more likely (according to the opinion of other ancient writers) that in the melody to which the scolia were sung certain liberties and irregularities were permitted, by which the extemporaneous execution of the song was facilitated; and that on this account the song was said to be *bent*. The rhythms of the extant scolia are very various, though, on the whole, they resemble those of the Æolic lyric poetry, only that the course of the strophes is broken by an accelerated rhythm, and is in general more animated.[1]

The Lesbians were the principal composers of scolia. Terpander, who, according to Pindar, invented this kind of song, was followed by Alcæus and Sappho, and afterward by Anacreon and Praxilla of Sicyon, besides many others celebrated for choral poetry, as Simonides and Pindar. Among the preserved scolia are many of the more popular current in the best ages of Greece. Some of these are also, as may be supposed, among the most brilliant specimens of Greek epigrammatic or didactic poetry, and are constantly quoted and commented upon as such by the leading critics and moralists of every period. Even where the sense itself is not remarkable for point or spirit, the structure and rhythm are usually distinguished by a certain combination of emphasis with harmony, and by an alternate rapidity in the flow and abruptness in the termination of the rhythmical clauses, peculiar to these compositions, and singularly conducive to that mixture of elegance and pungency which it was clearly the object of their authors to impart to them.

Although scolia were mostly composed of moral maxims, or of short invocations to the gods, or panegyrics on heroes, there exist two, of great length and interest, the authors of which are not otherwise known as poets. The one beginning, "My great wealth is my spear and sword," and written by Hybrias, a Cretan, in the Doric measure, expresses all the pride of the dominant Dorian, whose right rested upon his arms; the other is the production of an Athenian named Callistratus, and was written probably not long after the Persian war, as it was a favorite song in the time of Aristophanes. It celebrates the liberators of the Athenian people, Harmodius and Aristogīton, for having, at the great festival of Minerva, slain the tyrant Hipparchus, and restored equal rights to the Athenians.[2]

XVI. The term *Encōmium* (ἐγκώμιον, *scil.* ἔπος) denoted originally the ode sung at the *Cōmus* (κῶμος), which latter term, in the wider sense, comprehended every convivial meeting accompanied by dance, song, and

[1] *Müller, Hist. Gr. Lit.*, p. 188. [2] *Id. ib.*, p. 189.

Bacchanalian festivity. In its more dignified application, however, the term *Comus* denoted a higher order of festive entertainment. Such were the public banquets held in honor of distinguished personages, of a warrior after a victory or successful campaign, of a magistrate on entering office; and, in later habitual practice, of the conquerors in the Olympian, Pythian, and other great national games. In every variety of the comus, a main part of the ceremony was performed in the open air; it being customary, even for private bands of revellers, when flushed with the pleasures of the table, to sally forth with music, song, and dance, sometimes to the sound of the trumpet,[1] into the streets and public thoroughfares.[2] The term thus became more peculiarly appropriated to this latter part of the entertainment, which in its turn assumed the character of a distinct ceremony. Such was the escort home, or serenade to a mistress,[3] or, after a banquet, to some favorite guest; such, in a nobler sense, the triumphal procession of the victorious hero or chief to the temple or banqueting-hall; such, by a still wider extension of the analogy, the deputation or mission which escorted the victor in the national games back to his native city.

The title *Encomium*, or song of the *comus*, is limited in its classical acceptation, as denoting an order of lyric poetry, solely, or chiefly to the panegyrical odes performed in the *comi* of a more dignified character. It is hence defined by the ancients as bearing the same relation to the praises of men as the hymn to those of the deity. No work of this class, prior to the age of Pindar, has been preserved. The leading poets, from Pindar downward, left large collections of encomia, of which the most celebrated were those addressed to the victors in the national games. These are usually ranked under the separate head of *Epinicia* (ἐπινίκια), or triumphal encomia. No such distinction, however, seems to have been recognized by their authors. Pindar, in his frequent appeals to his own Epinician odes, avails himself more frequently of the phrase *Encomia*, and other cognate derivatives of *comus*, than of their proper title.[4]

XVII. The *Erōtica* (ἐρωτικά), or love-songs, require no explanation. The most celebrated authors in this department, during the period we are at present considering, were: Alcman, of the Dorian school; Sappho and Alcæus, of the Æolian or Lesbian; and Mimnermus, of the Ionian school. The erotic odes of the three former poets are almost exclusively of the purely melic order, and in monostrophic forms, that is, with one form of strophe continually repeated. Mimnermus composed solely or chiefly in elegiac measure. Such effusions, though called forth by human objects of adoration alone, occasionally in so far partake of a sacred character as to assume the form of addresses to the deities whose countenance and favor were invoked. Such, for example, is the most brilliant of all love-songs, the Invocation of Venus, by Sappho.[5]

XVIII. *Gamēlia* (γαμήλια), or bridal songs, are classed under two heads: first, those called *Hymenæa*, sung at the marriage festival; secondly, the

[1] *Aristot.*, *De Aud.*, 49.
[2] *Hesiod*, *Scut. Herc.*, 281; *Aristoph.*, *Plut.*, 1040; *Thesmoph.*, 104, &c.
[3] *Hermesianax*, v. 38, 47, *ap. Athen.*, xiii., p. 598. [4] *Mure*, p. 112. [5] *Id.*, p. 114.

Epithalamia, or bed-chamber songs, performed on the night of the ceremony, as a serenade or vigil, in front of the door or below the window of the newly-wedded couple. The epithalamia are again subdivided into the *Lulling song* and the *Waking song*,[1] the former sung during the early part of the night, the latter toward the hour of rising. These songs, as may be supposed, formed, from a very early period, a popular branch of lyric composition, whether in honor of hero or heroine, living or dead, real or imaginary. The earliest-mentioned example is Hesiod's Epithalamium of Peleus and Thetis. Alcman[2] also availed himself of this, among other modes of honoring the sex, which formed the favorite subject of his muse; and Sappho left an entire book of hymenæa,[3] several of which seem to have partaken of the dramatic character. In the metre of these compositions no definite rule is observable. Hesiod, it need scarcely be remarked, uses the hexameter; Sappho occasionally employs the same measure, in addition to her own favorite combinations of more purely melic rhythm. The hexameter is also preferred by Theocritus. The invocations, "O Hymen! O Hymenæus!" addressed to the patron deity of the rite, were habitually introduced, as a sort of burden or epode, in all these varieties of metrical arrangement.[4]

XIX. Under the general head of *Embateria* (ἐμβατήρια, *scil.* μέλη) may be distinguished two kinds of military music; the first comprising every species of ode or song adapted, on ordinary festive occasions, to inspire or maintain warlike enthusiasm; the second may be defined as war music in the narrower sense, marches, charges, &c. In Homer mention is made of the first kind alone. The celebration of the exploits of the heroes of the olden time is described as a favorite recreation of the Homeric warriors. To the first kind also belong the elegiac odes of Callinus, and most of those of Tyrtæus. The latter were sung, consistently with Spartan usage, at the meals of the soldiers, after the ordinary convivial pæan, sometimes in chorus, sometimes by single performers in competition, the victor receiving as his prize from the polemarch an extra ration of butcher-meat.[5] They were also chanted in chorus before the tent-door of the king or commander-in-chief.[6]

The military music of the second kind was little cultivated, even in historical times, except among the Spartans. Their *pæan embaterius*, or hymn invoking the god of war, or other patron deities, commenced immediately after the order to advance, and continued during the charge and assault. The air was called the Castorean melody,[7] after the Tyndarid Castor, one of the popular martial demigods of Sparta, and was accompanied by wind instruments, disposed in different parts of the line. Its character was impressive, rather than wild or turbulent; the object being, in unison with the genius of Spartan warfare, to inspire steady determination, rather than furious ardor for the attack. The measure preferred was the anapæstic, as the most natural march time, and peculiarly ex-

---

1 *Schol. ad Theocrit. Id.*, xviii.; *Procl.*, *Chrest.*, p. 385, *Gaisf.*

2 *Welcker*, *Præf. ad Fragm.*, p. iii.

3 *Sapph.*, Frag. xxxvi., *seqq.*, *Gaisf.*

4 *Mure*, p. 116.

5 *Philoch. ap. Athen.*, xiv., p. 630.

6 *Mure*, p. 117.

7 *Plut.*, *Lycurg.*, 22; *De Mus.*, 26; *Schol. in Pind. Pyth.*, ii., 127, *seqq.*

pressive in its cadence of stern, energetic resolution. The custom of attacking in regular march-step, to the sound of music, is frequently noticed by the ancients as a peculiarity of Spartan discipline;[1] nor is there any allusion to the same practice in any other Grecian state, with the partial exception of the kindred Dorian republics of Crete.[2]

CHAPTER XVIII.

SECOND OR POETICAL PERIOD—*continued.*

LYRIC POETRY—*continued.*

POETS OF THE ÆOLIC SCHOOL.

I. Alcæus (Ἀλκαῖος) of Mytilene, in the island of Lesbos, the earliest of the Æolian lyric poets, began to flourish about B.C. 611. He belonged to a noble family, and a great part of his public life was employed in asserting the privileges of his order. These privileges were then endangered by democratic factions, which appear to have placed ambitious men at their head, and to have given them powerful support. A tyrant of this kind in Mytilene was Melanchrus, who was opposed by the brothers of Alcæus, Antimenidas and Cicis, in conjunction with Pittacus, the wisest statesman of the time in Lesbos, and was slain by them B.C. 612.[3] At this time the Mytileneans were at war with foreign enemies, the Athenians, who had conquered and retained possession of Sigæum, a maritime town of Troas. The Mytileneans, among whom was Alcæus, were defeated, and the poet incurred the disgrace of leaving his arms behind on the field of battle; these arms were hung up as a trophy by the Athenians in the temple of Minerva, at Sigæum.[4] His sending home the news of this disaster, in a poem addressed to his friend Melanippus,[5] seems to show that he had a reputation for courage such as a single disaster could not endanger; and, accordingly, we find him spoken of by ancient writers as a brave and skillful warrior.[6]

Alcæus afterward appears as an adherent of the aristocratic or constitutional party, in the resistance offered by them to the attempts made by a new series of demagogues. The most formidable of these leaders was Myrsilus, whose death the poet celebrates in a still extant passage of his works. In the sequel of the same political vicissitudes, Alcæus and his brothers appear in their turn as usurpers, or disturbers of the repose of the state. They were expelled, in consequence, by their old ally Pittacus, the only stanch and disinterested patriot, it would seem, among these political chiefs, and who was supported by the mass of the better disposed citizens. At last, as the most effectual stop to these disastrous

---

1 *Thucyd.*, v., 70; *Polyb.*, iv., 20; *Athen.*, xiv., p. 626, 630, *F*, &c.
2 *Heracl.*, *Polit.*, iii.; *Athen.*, xii., p. 517, *A*; *Mure*, p. 119.
3 *Diog. Laert.*, i., 74, 79; *Strab.*, xiii., p. 617.
4 *Herod.*, v., 95; *Plut.*, *De Herod. Malig.*, *s.* 15, p. 858; *Strab.*, xiii., p. 599, *seq.*
5 Frag. 56, p. 438, *Blomf.*
6 *Anthol. Palat.*, ix., 184; *Cic.*, *Tusc.*, iv., 33; *Hor.*, *Carm.*, i., 32, 6, &c.

series of civil broils, the same Pittacus was elected by the unanimous voice of the people, as Alcæus himself admits, to the dignity entitled among the Æolians αἰσυμνήτης, or constitutional chief, with dictatorial powers, for the preservation of the laws and liberty of the state. This measure is said to have been chiefly directed against the machinations of Alcæus and the other malcontents.[1]

The poet's muse, following the bent of his passions, was speedily directed against Pittacus, with an animosity as fervid as the zeal with which the cause of that patriot had formerly been lauded and supported. Imputed failings were now described in terms of vituperation expressly invented for the purpose, such as Archilochus himself might not have been ashamed to employ in his most withering iambic sallies. This is one of the worst features in the character or history of Alcæus; the moderation of Pittacus, and the purity of his motives, being admitted and eulogized by every impartial authority. But the hostility of Alcæus was not confined to words. In an armed attempt to re-establish their influence, his party was defeated, and himself made prisoner; when his generous adversary restored him to liberty.[2] His ultimate fate is unknown. By some authorities he is supposed to have been permanently reconciled to Pittacus, and to have passed the remainder of his life in tranquillity at Mytilene, under the mild sway of that patriotic ruler; by others, to have ended his days a discontented wanderer in foreign lands. In the course of his peregrinations, and of the maritime disasters with which Horace describes them as having been attended,[3] he visited Egypt;[4] and, about the same time, his brother Antimenidas, his steady companion, it would seem, in good or bad fortune, entered into the service of the Babylonian monarch Nebuchadnezzar, where he distinguished himself by his valor.[5]

The poems of Alcæus were chiefly addressed to particular friends, and at first they seem not to have been much known beyond the island of Lesbos, partly because they were written in the Æolic dialect, and partly, perhaps, because they had only a local and temporary interest. But subsequently they were considered by all the Greeks as master-pieces; and among the nine lyric poets in the Alexandrean canon, Alcæus occupied, according to some authorities, the first, and, according to others, the second place. Aristophanes and Aristarchus prepared the first correct editions, in which the poems were divided into at least ten books, and great care was taken to insure the correct representation of the metre. It is not known how the poems were arranged in these editions, except that the hymns formed the commencement. Besides these hymns, the poems of Alcæus consisted of odes, patriotic war-songs, erotic and symposiac songs, and epigrams. All were characterized by strong passion and enthusiasm. With Alcæus, as with most poets of the Æolic school, poetry was the outpouring of his deepest emotions, excited by the occurrences of the times in which he lived. Independent of their high poetical merits, the loss of the poems of Alcæus is much to be regretted, as they

[1] *Smith, Dict. Biogr.*, *s. v.* [2] *Diog. Laert.*, i., 76; *Val. Max.*, iv., 1, 6.
[3] *Carm.*, ii., 13, 28. [4] *Strab.*, i., p. 37. [5] *Alc.*, Frag. 33, p. 433, *Blomf.*

would have enabled us to gain a clearer insight into the public and private life of the Æolians.[1]

The metrical forms used by Alcæus are most light and lively; sometimes with a softer, sometimes with a more vehement character. They consist principally of Æolic dactyls, which, though apparently resembling the dactyls of epic poetry, are yet essentially unlike. Instead of depending upon the perfect balance of the Arsis and Thesis, they admit the shortening of the former; whence arises an irregularity, which was distinguished by the ancient writers on metre by the name of *disproportioned dactyls* (ἄλογοι δάκτυλοι). These dactyls begin with the undetermined foot of two syllables, which is called *a base*, and they flow on lightly and swiftly, without alternating with heavy spondees. The choriambics of the Æolic lyric poets are composed on the same plan, as they have also the preceding base; yet this metre always retains something of the stately tone which belongs to it. The Logacœdic metre also belongs peculiarly to the Æolic lyric poets. It is produced by the immediate junction of dactylic and trochaic feet, so that a rapid movement passes into a feebler one. This lengthened and various kind of metre was peculiarly adapted to express the softer emotions, such as tenderness, melancholy, and longing. Hence this metre was frequently used by the Æolians, and their strophes were principally formed by connecting logacœdic rhythms with trochees, iambi, and Æolic dactyls. Of this kind is the Sapphic strophe, the softest and sweetest metre in the Greek lyric poetry, and which Alcæus seems sometimes to have employed, as in his hymn to Hermes. But the firmer and more vigorous tone of the metre, called after him the Alcaic, was better suited to the temper of his mind. The logacœdic elements of this metre have but little of their characteristic softness, and they receive an impulse from the iambic dipodies which precede them. Hence the Alcaic strophe is generally employed by these poets in political and warlike poems, and in all in which manly passions predominate.[2]

The fragments of Alcæus were first collected by Neander in his *Aristologia Pindarica*, Basil, 1556, 8vo, then by Henry Stephens in his collection of the fragments of the nine chief lyric poets of Greece (1557), of which there are several editions, and by Fulvius Ursinus, 1568, 8vo. The more modern collections are those by Iani, Halæ Sax., 1780–1782, 4to; by Stange, Halæ, 1810, 8vo; by Blomfield, in the *Museum Criticum*, vol. i., p. 421, *seqq*., Camb., 1826, reprinted in Gaisford's *Poetæ Græci Minores;* by Schneidewin, in his *Delectus Poesis Græcorum*, and by Bergk in his *Poetæ Lyrici Græci*. Of separate editions, that of Matthiæ, Lips., 1827, used to be regarded as the most complete, until the appearance of Bergk's work. This last-mentioned is now deemed the most complete collection, since it contains the additions and supplements made by Welcker, Seidler, Osann, and others, in several philological journals in Germany, as well as those contained in Cramer's *Anecdota Græca*, vol. i., Oxon., 1835.

II. Sappho (Σαπφώ, or, in her own Æolic dialect, Ψάπφα) was a native

[1] *Müller*, p. 170, *seqq*.

[2] *Id. ib.*

of the island of Lesbos, though the exact place of her birth is uncertain, for, according to some, she was born in Eresus, but according to others in Mytilene. The time of her birth is also unknown, and there are few events of her life which can be exactly ascertained. Her own fragments, as well as those of Alcæus, show that these two greatest poets of the Æolic school were contemporaries, though Sappho must have been younger than Alcæus, for she was still alive in 568 B.C., as may be inferred from the ode which she addressed to her brother Charaxus, in which she reproached him for having purchased Rhodopis, the courtesan, from her master, and having been induced, by his love for her, to emancipate her.[1] Now Charaxus bought Rhodopis at Naucratis, in Egypt, and in all probability not before the reign of Amasis, who ascended the throne in 569 B.C. Before this time, and while she was still in the prime of life, Sappho is said to have left her country for Sicily, but the cause of this flight is unknown.

It was formerly a common belief that Sappho destroyed herself by leaping into the sea from the Leucadian promontory, in despair at her love being unrequited by a youth named Phaon. This story, however, vanishes at the first approach of criticism. The name of Phaon does not occur in one of Sappho's fragments, and there is no evidence that it was once mentioned in her poems. It first appears in the Attic comedies, and is probably derived from the legend of the love of Venus for Adonis, who, in the Greek version of the myth, was called Phaethon or Phaon, "the bright or shining one." How this name came to be connected with that of Sappho it is now impossible to trace. There are passages in her poems referring to her love for a beautiful youth, whom she endeavored to conciliate by her poetry; and these passages may perhaps be the foundation for the story. As for the leap from the Leucadian rock, it is a mere metaphor, which is taken from an expiatory rite connected with the worship of Apollo, and which seems to have been a frequent poetical image; it occurs in Stesichorus and Anacreon, and may have been used by Sappho, though it is not to be found in any of her extant fragments. A remarkable confirmation of the unreal nature of the whole legend is the fact that none of the writers who relate it go so far as positively to assert that Sappho died in consequence of her frantic leap.[2]

At Mytilene, Sappho appears to have been the centre of a female literary society, most of the members of which were her pupils, and her character for purity, in connection with this association, appears, if we credit the ancient accounts, to have been seriously marred. Advocates have, indeed, been found in more modern days who strive to vindicate the personal character of the poetess; and one of their principal arguments in her favor is as follows: that Sappho belonged to the Æolic race, which, at the time when the state of society in Attica had assumed a totally different aspect from that of the Heroic Age, still retained much of the simplicity of early Greek manners: that at Athens, on the contrary, women

[1] *Herod.*, ii., 135; *Strab.*, xvii., p. 808; *Athen.*, xiii., p. 596, *B.*
[2] *Smith, Dict. Biogr.*, *s. v.*

lived in the strictest seclusion, and that hence the free intercourse of women of ability, such as Sappho and her numerous friends, would lead to the opinion among Athenians that she pursued an immoral life. Plausible, however, as this reasoning is, it is very far from being satisfactory; and it is impossible to read the fragments which remain of Sappho's poetry without being forced to come to the conclusion that a female who could write such verses could not be the pure and virtuous woman which her modern apologists pretend.[1]

But whatever doubt there may be as to the moral character of Sappho, there can be only one opinion as to her poetic genius. It is almost superfluous to refer to the numerous passages in which the ancient writers have expressed their unbounded admiration of her productions. In true poetic genius she appears to have been fully equal to Alcæus, and far superior to him in grace and sweetness. Of all Greek lyric poets, she is the one, perhaps, who, in her own peculiar branch of inspiration, was held to have attained most nearly to perfection. She was complimented with the title of the "Tenth Muse," and already in her own age, if we may believe an interesting tradition, the recitation of one of her poems so affected Solon that he expressed an earnest desire to learn it before he died (*ἵνα μαθὼν αὐτὸ ἀποθάνω*).[2] Strabo speaks of her as *θαυμαστόν τι χρῆμα*,[3] and the praises and imitations of her by Catullus and Horace are too well known to require any mention here. The fragments that survive of her poetry, though some of them are exquisite, barely furnish a sample of the surpassing beauty of the whole. They are chiefly of an erotic character; and at the head of this class must be placed that splendid ode to Venus, of which we possess the whole, and next to it the shorter one to a beloved female.

Sappho is described, by the only authors who have transmitted any distinct notices on the subject, as not distinguished for personal beauty, but as short in stature, and of dark, it may be understood swarthy, complexion. The laudatory commonplace of *καλή*, or "fair," which Plato and others connect with her name, implies nothing more, perhaps less, than does the English term by which the Greek epithet has here been rendered, and which is as frequently bestowed, in familiar usage, on plain as on handsome women. Alcæus describes her simply as "dark-haired," and sweetly smiling.

The lyric poems of Sappho formed nine books. She appears also to have composed a large number of hymeneals, or nuptial songs, of which we possess some very beautiful fragments. Her hymns invoking the gods (*οἱ κλητικοὶ ὕμνοι*) are mentioned by the rhetorician Menander,[4] who tells

---

[1] Consult, on this subject, *Welcker*, *Sappho von einem herrsch. Vorurth. befreyet*, Gött., 1816, and in his *Kleine Schr.*, vol. ii., p. 80, *seqq.*; *Müller*, *Hist. Gr. Lit.*, p. 172, *seqq.* *Bode*, *Gesch. der Hell. Dichtk.*, vol. ii., pt. ii., p. 411, *seqq.*; *Neue*, *Sapphonis Fragmenta*; *Ulrici*, *Gesch. der Hell. Dichtk.*, vol. ii., p. 359, *seqq.*; *Richter*, *Sappho und Erinna.* We have adopted in the text the views of Mure, who gives the whole matter a very careful and fair examination (*Crit. Hist.*, vol. iii., p. 290, *seqq.*, and *Appendix F*, p. 497, *seqq.*). In the larger Biographical Dictionary of Smith, Sappho's character is warmly defended, in the abridgment of the same work it is condemned.

[2] *Ælian. ap. Stob.*, *Serm.*, xxix., 58. [3] *Strab.*, xiii., p. 617. [4] *Encom.*, i., 2.

us that among them were many to Diana and Venus, in which the various localities of their worship were mentioned. Suidas also ascribes to her epigrams, elegies, iambics, and monodies. The Greek anthology contains three epigrams under her name, but their genuineness is doubtful. Her poems were all written in her native Æolic dialect, and form with those of Alcæus the standard of the Æolic dialect of Lesbos. The rhythmical construction of her odes was essentially the same as that of Alcæus, though with many variations, and in harmony with the softer character of her poetry.[1]

A few remarks may not here be amiss respecting the musical and rhythmical forms in which the poetry of Sappho was embodied. Herodotus calls her generically μουσοποιός. Suidas uses the specific terms λυρική and ψάλτρια. Her instrument was the harp, which she seems to have used both in the form of the Æolian *barbiton* and the Lydian *pectis*. The invention of the latter was ascribed to her by some of the ancients. Her chief mode of music was the Mixolydian, the tender and plaintive character of which was admirably adapted to her erotic poems, and the invention of which was ascribed to her by Aristoxenus, although others assigned it to Pythoclides, and others to Terpander.[2]

Of the metres of Sappho, the most important is that which bears her name, and which only differs from the Alcaic by the position of a short syllable, which ends the Sapphic and begins the Alcaic verse; thus, for example,

	Grāndĭnīs mīsīt pătĕr ēt rŭbēn	*tĕ*
Vĭd	*ēs ŭt āltā stēt nĭvĕ cāndĭdūm.*	

From the resemblance between the two forms, and from the frequent occurrence of each of them in the fragments of Sappho and Alcæus, and in the odes of Catullus and Horace, we may fairly conclude that in these two verses we have the most characteristic rhythm of the Æolian lyric poetry. A new and manifestly more correct mode of reading the Sapphic verse is now beginning to prevail, the nature of which may be understood from the authorities mentioned in the notes.[3]

The fragments of Sappho have appeared in numerous collections, particularly in Brunck's *Analectă*, vol. i., p. 54, *seqq.*; vol. iii., p. 8, *seqq.*; in the *Museum Criticum*, vol. i., by Blomfield; by Gaisford, in his *Poetæ Græci Minores;* by Schneidewin, in his *Delectus Poesis Græcorum;* in Ahren's treatise, "*De Linguæ Græcæ Dialectis;*" and in Bergk's *Poetæ Lyrici Græci*. The best separate edition is that of Neue, Berol., 1827, 4to.

III. Erinna (Ἤριννα), a contemporary and friend of Sappho (about B.C. 612), who died at the age of nineteen, but left behind her poems which were thought worthy to rank with those of Homer. Her poems were of the epic class; the chief of them was entitled Ἠλακάτη, "The Distaff;" it consisted of three hundred lines, of which only four are extant.[4] It

[1] *Smith, Dict. Biogr., s. v.* [2] *Id. ib.*

[3] *Journal of Education*, vol. iv., p. 356; *Penny Cyclopædia, s. v. Arsis.* Compare *Donaldson's Varronianus*, p. 275. The prior claim to the discovery, or, rather, introduction of this new mode of reading Sapphics, gave rise to a pamphlet warfare between Dr. Donaldson and Professor Key of the London University.

[4] *Stob.,Flor.*, cxviii., 4; *Athen.*, vii., p. 283, *D*; *Bergk, Poet. Lyr. Græc.*, p. 632.

was written in a dialect which was a mixture of the Doric and Æolic, and which was spoken at Rhodes, where, or in the adjacent island of Telos, Erinna was born. She is also called a Lesbian and a Mytilenean, on account of her residence in Lesbos with Sappho.[1] There are several epigrams upon Erinna, in which her praise is celebrated, and her untimely death is lamented.[2] Three epigrams in the Greek Anthology are ascribed to her,[3] of which the first has the genuine air of antiquity, but the other two, addressed to Baucis, seem to be a later fabrication.[4]

IV. We come next to ANACREON (Ἀνακρέων), whose poetry may be considered as akin to that of Alcæus and Sappho, although he was an Ionian, a native of Teos, and his genius had an entirely different tone and bent. The accounts of his life are meagre and confused, but he seems to have spent his youth in his native city, and to have removed with the great body of the inhabitants to Abdera, in Thrace, when Teos was taken by Harpagus, the general of Cyrus, about B.C. 540.[5] If this statement be true, Anacreon can not have remained long at Abdera, for it was about this same time that Polycrates became tyrant of Samos; and it is said that Anacreon was invited from Teos, by the father of Polycrates, at the request of the latter, and before he became tyrant, to be his instructor and friend. Hence the account of his emigration to Abdera is rejected by some critics. Anacreon remained in Samos till after, or, at least, till shortly before the murder of his friend and patron, in B.C. 522. He then went to Athens, on the invitation of the tyrant Hipparchus,[6] where he became acquainted with Simonides and other poets. After the death of Hipparchus in B.C. 514, Anacreon appears to have returned to Teos. He died at the age of 85, probably about B.C. 478, but the place of his death is uncertain. Simonides wrote two epitaphs upon him, the second of which appears to say clearly that he was buried at Teos, but there is also a tradition that, after his return to Teos, he fled a second time to Abdera, in consequence of the revolt of Histiæus. This tradition, however, very probably arose from a confusion with the original emigration of the Teians to Abdera.[7]

The death of Anacreon is said to have been occasioned by a dried grape, which choked him, an account, however, which looks too like a poetical fiction. The statement that he was a lover of Sappho is, if not impossible, at least in the highest degree improbable, and arose from the practice, so common among writers of antiquity, of placing persons of the same character in some sort of relation to each other. His native town, proud of the poet, placed sometimes his full figure, sometimes his bust only, on its coins, some of which are still extant.

As a man, Anacreon has often been viewed in a false light, both in the later periods of antiquity and in modern times, being regarded, in fact, as a most consummate voluptuary. The ancients, however, considered his

---

1 *Suidas, s. v.; Eustath. ad. Il.*, ii., 726, p. 326.
2 *Brunck, Anal.*, vol. i., p. 241, n. 81; p. 218, n. 35; vol. ii., p. 19, n. 47, &c.
3 *Id. ib.*, p. 58; *Jacobs*, vol. i., p. 50.
4 *Smith, Dict. Biogr., s. v.*
5 *Strab.*, xiv., p. 638; *Herod.*, iii., 121.
6 *Plat., Hipparch.*, p. 228.
7 *Smith, Dict. Biogr., s. v.*

residence at the court of Polycrates as one of the greatest favors that fortune bestowed upon this prince. It is attested by the best authorities that Anacreon, although courted by the powerful and the rich, did not use his influence for purposes of base gain. He even rejected the munificent presents of Polycrates, declaring that they were not worth the trouble of keeping. Enjoying his talent of song, he lived a simple and happy life. In his enthusiasm for love and song, he never transgressed the boundaries of a pure poetical feeling. There have always been persons unable to understand how a poet can sing of drunken revelry, and yet be a sober man, and how the mere sight of the beautiful can raise enthusiasm. All the writers of the best times of Greece speak of Anacreon, as a man, in the same high terms in which they record his merit as a poet; and a poet whom Plato calls the wise, was assuredly not a lover of licentiousness.[1]

We still possess numerous fragments of the genuine poems of Anacreon, which enable us to form a notion of the character of his poetry, and which justify the universal admiration of antiquity. The praise of beauty, love, and wine was the substance of his poems from his earliest to his latest age; and the cheerful and joyous old man, as Anacreon describes himself in some of his latest productions, has made so strong an impression, that we can scarcely picture him to ourselves in any other form than that of an aged person, although the greater part of his fragments belong to the period which he spent at Samos and Athens. Simonides, his contemporary, in a fragment still extant, gives a most lively picture of Anacreon's character, and says that his whole life breathed the Graces, Bacchus, and Love. It was part of the poet's Ionic nature that his poems on these subjects were more light and playful than the deep and impassioned songs of Sappho and Alcæus. The collection of these songs, which was probably made long after his time, consisted of at least five books: they were extremely popular, and we have evidence that in the time of Plutarch and Athenæus they were sung on every joyous and festive occasion, to tunes composed by the poet himself. Besides these lighter poems, he also wrote elegies, iambic poems or satires, epigrams (of which several are still extant in the Greek Anthology), and hymns. All his poems were composed in the Ionic dialect.[2]

Besides the numerous fragments of the genuine poems of Anacreon preserved in ancient writers, there is a collection of fifty-five odes which have been generally considered as poems of Anacreon, most of which, however, are productions of a much later age. This collection was first published by Henry Stephens, Paris, 1554, 4to, from two manuscripts which he describes very vaguely, and which no one else has seen. The same poems, however, were subsequently found in the Codex Palatinus (now at Heidelberg) of the Greek Anthology, though arranged in a different order from that in the edition of Stephens. These poems have been subsequently published in numerous editions, but the best are those of Brunck, Strasb., 1786; Fischer, Lips., 1793; Mehlhorn, Glogau, 1825; and Bergk, Lips., 1834. The genuine fragments are given along with them.

[1] *Biograph. Dict. of Soc. for Diff. of Useful Knowledge*, vol. ii., pt. ii., p. 529. [2] *Ib.*

H

Most of these fifty-five poems are pretty in their way, but exhibit very little of the character and spirit which we perceive in the genuine fragments of Anacreon; and all modern critics are agreed that they are not the work of this poet, although they have been translated into all European languages, and have, with the majority of persons, been the groundwork upon which they have formed their notions of Anacreon. In order to understand how it was possible for such a number of poems to be attributed to him, we must recollect that, down to the third century of our era, the poems of Anacreon enjoyed extraordinary popularity, and that many poets attempted to write in his style. In proportion as such imitations suited the taste of their age, they became popular under the name of Anacreontic songs. Those who collected such popular poems in later times were frequently unable to judge of their merits, and they admitted into their collections what was most popular or most suited to their taste. It would seem, therefore, that the poems, now commonly known under the name of Anacreon, were a collection of this kind, made many centuries after the time of that poet. They are very unequal, and some may have been written soon after the time of Alexander the Great, while others bear strong marks of belonging to that description of poetry which was written during the fourth and fifth centuries. The chief reasons why they can not be attributed to Anacreon are briefly these: 1. Among the numerous passages cited by ancient writers from Anacreon, there is only one, and that in a very late writer, which refers to any poem contained in the collection published by Stephens. 2. The genuine poems of Anacreon were full of allusions to circumstances and persons around him, whereas, in the odes of Stephens's collection there is scarcely any thing that suggests the circumstances of the author's life; they rather resemble modern poems, written in the closet, than the ancient Greek lyrics, which are all drawn from the freshness of real life. 3. They contain ideas which were altogether foreign to the age of Anacreon. One example may suffice. The god of Love (Eros), down to the time of Alexander, and even later, was always represented as a full-grown youth; but in this collection he is always described as a wanton and mischievous little boy. 4. The language in some of the odes is barbarous, the versification faulty, and the sentiments trivial. For further particulars on all these points, the student can consult Fischer's preface to his second edition of Anacreon.[1]

In Anacreon we see plainly how the spirit of the Ionic race, notwithstanding the elegance and refinement of Ionian manners, had lost its energy, its warmth of moral feeling, and its power of serious reflection, and was reduced to a light play of pleasing thoughts and sentiments. The Ionic softness and departure from strict rule which characterizes his poetry may also be perceived in his versification. His language approached much nearer to the style of common conversation than that of the Æolic lyric poets, so as frequently to seem like prose embellished with ornamental epithets; and his rhythm is also softer and less bounding than that of the Æolians, and has an easy and graceful negligence, which

[1] *Biograph. Dict. of Soc. for Diff. of Useful Knowledge*, vol. ii., pt. ii., p. 529.

Horace has endeavored to imitate. Sometimes he makes use of logaœdic metres, as in the Glyconean verses, which he combines into strophes, by subjoining a Pherecratean verse to a number of Glyconeans. Sometimes, like the Æolic lyric poets, he used long choriambic verses; and again, an alternation of choriambics with iambic dipodies. Another measure much used by him was the Ionic a minore, the expression of which, however, he changed by combining two Ionic feet, so that the last long syllable of the first was shortened, and the first short syllable of the second foot was lengthened, by which change the second foot became a trochaic dipody. By this process, called by the ancients ἀνάκλασις, "a bending," or "refraction," the metre obtained a less uniform, and, at the same time, a softer expression, and thus, when distributed into short verses, it became peculiarly suited to erotic poetry. The only traces of this metre before Anacreon's time occur in two fragments of Sappho. Anacreon, however, formed upon this plan a great variety of metres, particularly the short Anacreontic verse (an Ionic dimeter), which occurs so frequently both in his genuine fragments and in the later odes imitated from his style.[1]

V. With Anacreon ceased the species of lyric poetry in which he excelled; indeed, he stands alone in it, and the tender softness of his song was drowned by the louder tones of the choral poetry. The poem (or melos) destined to be sung by a single person, never, among the Greeks, acquired so much extent as it has since attained in the modern English and German poetry. By modern poets it has been used as the vehicle for expressing almost every variety of thought and feeling. The ancients, however, drew a more precise distinction between the different feelings to be expressed in different forms of poetry, and reserved the Æolic melos for lively emotions of the mind in joy or sorrow, or for impassioned overflowings of an oppressed heart. Anacreon's poetry contains rather the play of a graceful imagination than deep emotion; and among the other Greeks, there is no instance of the employment of lyric poetry for the expression of strong feeling; so that this kind of poetry was confined to a short period of time, and to a small portion of the Greek territory.[2]

CHAPTER XIX.

SECOND OR POETICAL PERIOD—*continued.*

LYRIC POETRY—*continued.*

POETS OF THE DORIAN OR CHORAL SCHOOL.[3]

I. The characteristic features of the Doric lyric poetry have been already described, for the purpose of distinguishing it from the Æolic. These were: recitation by choruses, the artificial structure of long strophes, the Doric dialect, and its reference to public affairs, especially to the celebration of divine worship. The origin of this kind of lyric poetry can be traced to the earliest times of Greece; for, as has been already shown, choruses were generally used in Greece before the time of

[1] *Müller, Hist. Gr. Lit.*, p. 185. [2] *Müller*, p. 187, *seqq.* [3] *Id.*, p. 190, *seqq.*

Homer; although the dancers in the more ancient choruses did not also sing, and therefore an exact correspondence of all their motions with the words of the song was not requisite.

II. The production of those polished forms in which the style of singing and the movements of the dance were brought into perfect harmony, coincides with the last advance in musical art; the improvements in which, made by Terpander, Olympus, and Thaletas, have formed the subject of a particular notice. In the first century subsequent to the epoch of these musicians, choral poetry does not, however, appear in its full perfection and individuality, but approaches either to the Lesbian lyric poetry or to the epos; and thus the line which separated these two kinds (between which the choral songs occupy a middle place) gradually became more distinct. Among the lyric poets whom the Alexandrean grammarians placed in their canon, Alcman and Stesichorus belong to this period of progress; while finished lyric poetry is represented by Ibycus, Simonides, with his disciple Bacchylides, and Pindar.[1]

III. We shall now proceed to take a view of these poets separately, classing among the former the dithyrambic poet Arion, and among the latter Pindar's instructor, Lasus, and a few others who have sufficient individuality of character to distinguish them from the crowd.

IV. Alcman (Ἀλκμάν), called by the Attic and later Greek writers *Alcmæon* (Ἀλκμαίων), of which *Alcman* is merely the Doric form, the chief lyric poet of Sparta, was by birth a Lydian, and a native of Sardis. He was brought into Laconia as a slave, evidently when very young. His master, whose name was Agesidas, discovered his genius and emancipated him, and he then began to distinguish himself as a lyric poet.[2] To what extent he obtained the rights of citizenship is not known. Suidas calls him a Laconian of Messoa, one of the quarters or divisions of Sparta, meaning probably that he was enrolled as a citizen of Messoa after his emancipation. Alcman probably flourished from about 671 to about 631 B.C. The period during which most of his poems were composed was that which followed the conclusion of the second Messenian war. During this period of quiet the Spartans began to cherish that taste for the spiritual enjoyments of poetry, which, though felt by them long before, had never attained to a high state of cultivation while their attention was absorbed in war. In this process of improvement Alcman was immediately preceded by Terpander. But besides the aid which he derived from the important changes introduced by the latter, he had also an intimate acquaintance with the Phrygian and Lydian styles of music, and he was himself the inventor of new forms of rhythm, some of which bore his name.[3]

A large portion of Alcman's poetry was erotic. In fact, he is said by some ancient writers to have been the inventor of erotic poetry.[4] From his poems of this class, which were marked by a freedom bordering on licentiousness, he obtained the epithets of "sweet" and "pleasant" (γλυκύς, χαρίεις). Among these poems were many hymeneal pieces. But the

[1] *Müller*, p. 191. [2] *Suid.*, *s. v.*; *Heraclid.*, *Polit.*, p. 206; *Vell. Pat.*, 1, 18.
[3] *Smith*, *Dict. Biogr.*, *s. v.* [4] *Athen.*, xiii., p. 600; *Suid.*, *s. v.*

Parthenia, which form a branch of Alcman's poems, must not be confounded with the erotic. They were so called, as we have already remarked, because composed for the purpose of being sung by choruses of virgins, and not on account of their subjects, which were very various, sometimes, indeed, erotic, but often religious. Alcman's other poems embrace hymns to the gods, pæans, prosodia, songs adapted for different religious festivals, and short ethical or philosophical pieces. It is disputed whether he wrote any anapæstic war-songs, or embateria; but it seems very unlikely that he should have neglected a kind of composition which had been rendered so popular by Tyrtæus.[1]

His metres are very various. He is said by Suidas to have been the first poet who composed any but dactylic hexameters. This statement, however, is incorrect; but Suidas perhaps refers to the short dactylic lines into which Alcman broke up the Homeric hexameter. In this practice, however, he had been preceded by Archilochus, from whom he borrowed several others of his peculiar metres; others he invented himself. The Cretic hexameter was named Alcmanic from his being its inventor. The poems of Alcman were chiefly strophes, composed of lines sometimes of the same metre throughout the strophe, sometimes of different metres. His dialect was the Spartan Doric, with an intermixture of Æolic. The popular idioms of Laconia appear most frequently in his more familiar poems. The Alexandrean grammarians placed Alcman at the head of their canon of the nine lyric poets. The few fragments that remain of his poetry, though some of them are very beautiful, scarcely warrant the admiration which the ancients have expressed of him; but this may be owing to their extreme shortness, or because they are very unfavorable specimens. Müller endeavors to shield Alcman from the charge of licentiousness, but the terms in which the ancients speak of this are so strong that we can not well acquiesce in so favorable a representation of the character of his erotic poetry.[2]

Alcman's poems comprised six books, the extant fragments of which are included in the collections of Neander, H. Stephens, Fulvius Ursinus, Schneidewin, and Bergk. The latest and best edition is that of Welcker, Giessen, 1815.

V. Stesichorus (Στησίχορος) of Himera, in Sicily, a celebrated poet, was contemporary with Sappho and Alcæus, later than Alcman, and earlier than Simonides. He is said to have been born B.C. 632, and to have died at the age of eighty, or, according to Lucian, eighty-five.[3] The Parian marble says that Stesichorus the poet came into Greece at the same time at which Æschylus gained his first tragic victory, B.C. 475. But this statement refers, no doubt, to a later poet of the same name and family. Of the events of the life of Stesichorus we have only a few obscure accounts. Like other great poets, his birth is fabled to have been attended by an omen: a nightingale sat upon the babe's lips, and sang a sweet strain.[4] He is said to have been carefully educated at Catana, and

[1] *Smith, l. c.*
[2] *Id. ib.*
[3] *Suid., s. v.; Aristot., Rhet.,* ii., 20, 5; *Lucian., Macrob.,* 26.
[4] *Christod. Ecphr. ap. Jacobs, Anth. Græc.,* vol. i., p. 42; *Plin., H. N.,* x., 29.

afterward to have enjoyed the friendship of Phalaris, the tyrant of Agrigentum. Many writers relate the fable of his being miraculously struck with blindness after writing an attack upon Helen, and recovering his sight when he had composed a recantation or palinodia.[1] The statement that he travelled in Greece appears to be supported by some passages in the fragments of his poems, by the known usage of the early Grecian poets, and by the confused tradition preserved by Suidas, that he came to Catana as an exile from Pallantium, in Arcadia. For his connection with Catana, and his burial there, we have several testimonies. Suidas says that he was buried by a gate of the city, which was called after him the Stesichorean gate, and that a splendid octagonal monument was erected over his tomb, having eight pillars, and eight sets of steps, and eight angles; whence, according to some, was derived the name *Στησίχορος ἀριθμός,* applied to the throw "all eight" in gaming.[2]

Stesichorus lived at a time when the serene tone of the epos, and an exclusive devotion to a mythical subject no longer sufficed; the predominant tendency of the Greek mind was toward lyric poetry. He himself was powerfully affected by this taste, and consecrated his life to the transplantation of all the rich materials, and the mighty and imposing shapes, which had hitherto been the exclusive property of the epos, to the choral poem. His special business was the training and direction of choruses, and hence, it is said, he was called, or more properly assumed the name of, *Stesichorus*, or "leader of choruses," his original name having been *Tisias.* Hence Suidas remarks: *ἐκλήθη δὲ Στησίχορος, ὅτι πρῶτος κιθαρῳδίᾳ χορὸν ἔστησεν, ἐπεί τοι πρότερον Τισίας ἐκαλεῖτο.* In other words, it was he who first broke the monotonous alternation of the strophe and antistrophe through a whole poem, by the introduction of the epode. So great was the celebrity of this invention in later times, that the "Triad of Stesichorus" (*τὰ τρία Στησιχόρου*), denoting the strophe, antistrophe, and epode, passed into a proverb for the fundamental elements of a liberal education. The chorus of Stesichorus seems to have consisted of a combination of several rows or members of eight dancers; the number eight appears indeed, from various traditions, to have been, as it were, consecrated to him, a number which we have already mentioned in speaking of his tomb.[3]

As the metres of Stesichorus approach much more nearly to the epos than those of Alcman, as his dialect also is founded on the epic, to which he gave a different tone only by the most frequent and current Dorisms, so also, with regard to the matter and contents of his poems, Stesichorus makes, of all lyric poets, the nearest approach to the epic. According to the elegant language of Quintilian, he sustained the weight of epic poetry with the lyre.[4] The subjects of his poems were chiefly heroic. He transferred the subjects of the old epic poetry to the lyric form, dropping, of course, the continuous narrative, and dwelling on isolated adventures of his heroes. He also composed poems on other subjects. His extant re-

---

[1] *Pausan.*, iii., 19, 11.

[2] *Suid.*, *s. v.* *πάντα ὀκτώ*; *Pollux*, ix., 7; *Smith*, *Dict. Biogr.*, *s. v.*

[3] *Müller*, *Hist. Gr. Lit.*, p. 199.

[4] *Quint.*, x., 1, 62; *Müller*, p. 200.

mains have been classified under the following heads: 1. Mythological poems; 2. Hymns, Encomia, Epithalamia, Pæans; 3. Erotic poems and Scolia; 4. A pastoral poem entitled *Daphnis;* 5. Fables; 6. Elegies. From what we have remarked, it would appear that the poetry of Stesichorus was not employed in expressing his own feelings, or describing the events of his own life, but that he preferred the past to the present. This character seems to have been common to all the poems of Stesichorus. Thus, he did not, like Sappho, compose Epithalamia having an immediate reference to the present, but he took some of his materials from mythology. The beautiful epithalamium of Theocritus, supposed to have been sung by the Laconian virgins before the chamber of Menelaus and Helen, is, in part, imitated from a poem of Stesichorus.[1]

The fragments of Stesichorus have been printed with the editions of Pindar published in 1560, 1566, 1567, &c., and in the collections of the Greek poets published in 1568 and 1569, and recently in the collections of Schneidewin and Bergk. They have also been edited by Suchfort, Götting., 1771, 4to; by Blomfield, in the *Museum Criticum*, vol. ii., p. 256, *seqq.;* in Gaisford's *Poetæ Minores Græci;* and by Kleine, Berol., 1828, 8vo. The last mentioned is by far the most useful edition of his fragments, and the authorities respecting the life and writings of the poet are collected and discussed in a preliminary dissertation.

VI. Our information respecting Arīon (Ἀρίων) is far less complete and satisfactory, yet the little that we do know of him proves the wide extension of lyric poetry in the time of Alcman and Stesichorus. Arion was the contemporary of Stesichorus; he is called the disciple of Alcman, and (according to the testimony of Herodotus) flourished during the reign of Periander at Corinth, between 628 and 585 B.C. He was a native of Methymna, in Lesbos, a district in which the worship of Bacchus, introduced by the Bœotians, was celebrated with orgiastic rites and with music. The remarkable adventure of which he became the hero, and the preservation of his life by the music-charmed dolphin, which is narrated with so much attractive simplicity by Herodotus, has contributed nearly as much to his posthumous fame as the brilliancy of his musical compositions.[2]

Arion was chiefly known in Greece as the perfecter of the dithyramb,[3] of which we have already given a general account. According to the concurrent testimonies of the historians and grammarians of antiquity, he was the first who practiced a chorus in the representation of a dithyramb, and therefore gave a regular and dignified character to this song, which before had probably consisted of irregular expressions of excited feeling and of inarticulate ejaculations. This improvement was made by Arion at Corinth, the rich and flourishing city of Periander. The choruses which sang the dithyramb were *cyclic* or *circular choruses* (κύκλιοι χόροι), and were so called because they danced in a circle round the altar on which the sacrifice was burning. Accordingly, in the time of Aristophanes, the expressions "dithyrambic poet" and "teacher of cyclian choruses" (κυκλιοδιδάσκαλος) were nearly synonymous.

[1] *Smith, Dict. Biogr., s. v.; Müller*, p. 203.
[2] *Müller*, p. 203.
[3] *Herod.*, i., 23; *Schol. ad Pind., Ol.*, xiii., 25.

With regard to the musical accompaniments of the dithyrambs of Arion, it may be remarked that the cithara was the principal instrument used in it, and not the flute, as in the boisterous comus. Arion was himself the first cithara-player of his time, and the exclusive fame of the Lesbian musicians was fully maintained by him. He is also stated to have composed, like Terpander, *prooemia*, that is, hymns to the gods, which served as an introduction to festivals.[1] A fragment of a hymn to Neptune, ascribed to Arion, is contained in Bergk's *Poetæ Lyrici Græci.* Modern critical opinion has been much divided as to its genuineness. The negative appears to be the stronger side.

VII. In descending to the choral poets who lived nearer the time of the Persian war, we meet with two of very peculiar character, the vehement Ibycus and the tender and refined Simonides.

IBYCUS (Ἴβυκος), the fifth lyric poet of the Alexandrine canon, was a native of Rhegium, the city near the southernmost point of Italy, and which was closely connected with Sicily, the country of Stesichorus. Rhegium was peopled partly by Ionians from Chalcis, partly by Dorians from the Peloponnesus; the latter of whom were a superior class. The peculiar dialect formed in Rhegium had some influence on the poems of Ibycus; although these were in general written in an epic dialect with a Doric tinge, like the poems of Stesichorus. Ibycus spent the best part of his life at Samos, at the court of Polycrates, about B.C. 540. Suidas erroneously places him twenty years earlier, in the time of Crœsus, and the father of Polycrates. We have no farther accounts of his life except the well-known story, about which even some doubt has been raised, of the manner of his death. While travelling through a desert place near Corinth, he was attacked by robbers and mortally wounded; but before he died he called upon a flock of cranes that happened to fly over him to avenge his death. Soon afterward, when the people of Corinth were assembled in the theatre, the cranes appeared, and, as they hovered over the heads of the spectators, one of the murderers, who happened to be present, cried out involuntarily, "Behold the avengers of Ibycus!" and thus were the authors of the crime detected. The phrase αἱ Ἰβύκου γέρανοι passed into a proverb.[2]

The poetry of Ibycus was chiefly erotic, and partook largely of the impetuosity of his character. Others of his poems were of a mythical character and heroic caste, but some of these, also, were partially erotic. In his poems on heroic subjects he very much resembled Stesichorus, his immediate predecessor in the canon, and hence the ancient critics often doubted to which of the two a particular idea or expression belonged. The metres of Ibycus also resemble those of Stesichorus, being in general dactylic series, connected together into verses of different lengths, but sometimes so long that they are rather to be called systems than verses. Besides these, Ibycus frequently uses logaœdic verses of a soft or languid character; and in general his rhythms are less stately and

[1] *Müller*, p. 205.

[2] *Suid.*, *s. v.*; *Antip. Sid.*, *Epig.*, 78 *ap. Brunck*, *Anal.*, vol. ii., p. 27; *Smith, Dict Biograph.*, *s. v.*

dignified, and more suitable for the expression of passion, than those of Stesichorus. Suidas mentions seven books of his lyric poems, of which only a few fragments now remain. The best edition of the fragments is that of Schneidewin, Götting., 1835, 8vo.[1]

VIII. Leaving Ibycus in the obscurity which envelops all the Greek lyric poets anterior to Pindar, we come to a brighter point in *Simonides.* This poet has already been described as one of the greatest masters of the elegy and the epigram, but a fuller account of him has been reserved for this place.

SIMONIDES (Σιμωνίδης) was born at Iulis, in the island of Ceos, which was inhabited by Ionians. His birth-year was about B.C. 556, and he lived, according to a precise account, 89 years. He belonged to a family which sedulously cultivated the musical arts;[2] his grandfather on the paternal side had been a poet; Bacchylides, the lyric poet, was his nephew; and Simonides the younger was his grandson. He himself exercised the functions of a chorus-teacher in the town of Carthæa, in Ceos, and the house of the chorus (χορηγεῖον), near the temple of Apollo, was his customary abode. This occupation was to him, as to Stesichorus, the origin of his poetical efforts. He appears, indeed, to have been brought up to music and poetry as a profession. From his native island he proceeded to Athens, probably on the invitation of Hipparchus, who attached him to his society by great rewards.[3] After remaining at Athens for some time, probably even after the expulsion of Hippias, he went to Thessaly, where he lived under the patronage of the Aleuadæ and Scopadæ.[4] He afterward returned to Athens, and soon had the noblest opportunity of employing his poetic powers in the celebration of the great events of the Persian war. In 489 B.C., he conquered Æschylus in the contest for the prize which the Athenians offered for an elegy on those who fell at Marathon.[5] Ten years later, he composed the epigrams which were inscribed upon the tomb of the Spartans who fell at Thermopylæ, as well as an encomium on the same heroes;[6] and he also celebrated in verse the battles of Artemisium and Salamis, and the great men who commanded in them. He had completed his 80th year when his long poetical career at Athens was crowned by the victory which he gained with the dithyrambic chorus, being the 56th prize which he had carried off.[7] Shortly after this, he was invited to Syracuse by Hiero, at whose court he lived until his death.

Simonides was in high honor at Syracuse, and a great favorite with Hiero, who treated him with lavish munificence. He still continued, while at Syracuse, to employ his muse occasionally in the service of other Grecian states. Throughout his whole life he appears to have been attached to philosophy; and his poetical genius is characterized rather by versatility and purity of taste than by fervid enthusiasm. Many ingenious apophthegms and wise sayings are attributed to him, nearly re-

---

[1] *Smith, l. c.*

[2] *Chamælion ap. Athen.*, x., p. 456, *c.*

[3] *Plat., Hipparch.*, p. 228, *c; Ælian, V. H.*, viii., 2.

[4] *Theocrit., Id.*, xvi., 34; *Cic., De Orat.*, ii., 86; *Stes.*, Frag. 71, *Bentl.*

[5] Frag. 58, Epig. 149.

[6] Epig. 150–155, Frag. 9.

[7] Epig. 203, 204.

sembling those of the seven sages; for example, the answer to the question, What is God?[1] is ascribed both to him and to Thales: in the one anecdote the questioner is Hiero, in the other Crœsus. Simonides himself is sometimes reckoned among the philosophers, and the Sophists considered him as a predecessor in their art. He is said, moreover, to have been the inventor of the mnemonic art, and of the long vowels and double letters in the Greek alphabet.

Simonides made literature a profession, and is said to have been the first who took money for his poems; and the reproach of avarice is too often brought against him by his contemporary and rival, Pindar, as well as by subsequent writers, to be altogether discredited.[2] The chief characteristics of his poetry were sweetness (whence he obtained the surname of *Melicertes*) and elaborate finish, combined with the truest poetic conception and perfect power of expression, though in originality and fervor he was far inferior, not only to the early lyric poets, such as Sappho and Alcæus, but also to his contemporary Pindar. He was probably both the most prolific and the most generally popular of all the Grecian lyric poets. Among the poems which he composed for public festivals were hymns and prayers (*κατευχαί*) to various gods, pæans to Apollo, hyporchemes, dithyrambs, epinicia, and parthenia. In the hyporchemes, Simonides seemed to have excelled himself; so great a master was he of the art of painting, by apt rhythms and words, the acts which he wished to describe. His dithyrambs were not, according to the original purpose of this branch of composition, dedicated to Bacchus, but admitted subjects of the heroic mythology. His epinicia appear to have been distinguished from those of Pindar mainly in this, that the former dwelt more upon the particular victory which gave occasion to his song, and described all its details with great minuteness; whereas Pindar passes lightly over the incident, and immediately soars into higher regions.[3]

The following is a list of those of the compositions of Simonides of which we possess either the titles or fragments: 1. A poem, the precise form of which is unknown, on "The Empire of Cambyses and Darius" (*ἡ Καμβύσου καὶ Δαρείου βασιλεία*). 2, 3. Elegies on the battles of Artemisium and Salamis (*ἡ ἐν Ἀρτεμισίῳ ναυμαχία· ἡ ἐν Σαλαμῖνι ναυμαχία*). 4. Eulogistic poems in various metres (*ἐγκώμια*). 5. Epinician Odes (*ἐπίνικοι ᾠδαί*). 6. Hymns or Prayers (*ὕμνοι, κατευχαί*). 7. Pæans (*παιᾶνες*). 8. Dithyrambs (*διθύραμβοι*, also called *τραγῳδίαι*). 9. Drinking songs (*σκόλια*). 10. Parthenia (*παρθένια*). 11. Hyporchemes (*ὑπορχήματα*). 12. Laments (*θρῆνοι*). 13. Elegies (*ἐλεγεῖαι*). 14. Epigrams (*ἐπιγράμματα, ἀποσχεδιάσματα*).[4]

The fragment of his *Lament of Danaë* is one of the finest remains of Greek lyric poetry that we possess. The general character of the dialect of Simonides is, like that of Pindar, the Epic mingled with Doric and Æolic forms. The fragments of Simonides are contained in the chief collections of the Greek poets, in Brunck's *Analecta*, who gives with them those which belonged to the other poets of the same name; in Jacobs'

---

1 *Cic., N. D.*, i., 22.

2 *Schneidewin*, p. xxiv.–xxxii.

3 *Müller, Hist. Gr. Lit.*, p. 210.

4 *Smith, Dict. Biog.*, *s. v.*

Anthologia Græca; in Schneidewin's standard edition, Brunsw., 1835, and in his *Delectus Poesis Græcorum;* and in Bergk's *Poetæ Lyrici Græci.*

IX. Bacchylĭdes (Βακχυλίδης), the nephew of Simonides, and, like him, a native of Iulis, in Ceos, adhered closely to the system and example of his uncle. He flourished about B.C. 470, toward the close of the life of Simonides, with whom he lived at the court of Hiero, in Syracuse. He wrote, in the Doric dialect, Hymns, Pæans, Dithyrambs, &c., but all his poems have perished, with the exception of a few fragments, and two epigrams in the Greek Anthology. That his poetry was but an imitation of one branch of that of Simonides, cultivated with great delicacy and finish, is proved by the opinions of ancient critics, among whom Dionysius adduces perfect correctness and uniform elegance as the characteristics of Bacchylides. His genius and art were chiefly devoted to the pleasures of private life, love and wine, and, when compared with those of Simonides, appear marked by greater sensual grace and less moral elevation.[1] Bacchylides, like Simonides, transfers the diffuseness of the elegy to the choral lyric poem, although he himself composed no elegies, and followed the traces of his uncle only as an epigrammatist. The structure of his verse is generally very simple; nine tenths of his odes, to judge from the fragments, consisted of dactylic series and trochaic dipodies, as we find in those odes of Pindar which were written in the Doric mode. We find also in his poems trochaic verses of great elegance. Like his predecessors in lyric poetry, he wrote in the Doric dialect, but frequently introduces Attic forms, so that the dialect of his poems very much resembles that of the choruses in the Attic tragedies.[2] The fragments of Bacchylides have been collected by Neue, "*Bacchylidis Coi fragmenta,*" Berol., 1823; and by Schneidewin and Bergk.

X. The universal esteem in which Simonides and Bacchylides were held in Greece, and their acknowledged excellence in their art, did not prevent some of their contemporaries from striking into various other paths, and adopting other styles of treating lyric poetry. Lasus (Λᾶσος) of Hermione, in Argolis, was a rival of Simonides, during his residence in Athens, and likewise enjoyed high favor at the court of Hipparchus.[3] It is, however, difficult to ascertain, from the very scanty accounts which we possess of this poet, wherein consisted the point of contrast between him and his competitor. He was more peculiarly a dithyrambic poet, and was the first that introduced contests in dithyrambs at Athens, probably about B.C. 508. He is celebrated as the teacher of Pindar. The dithyrambic style predominated so much in his works, that he gave to the general rhythms of his odes a dithyrambic turn, and a free movement, in which he was aided by the variety and flexibility of tone of the flute, his favorite instrument.[4] He was also a theorist in his art, and investigated the laws of music, that is, the relation of musical intervals to rapidity of movement. Plutarch says that Lasus invented various new adaptations of music to dithyrambic poetry, giving it an accompaniment of several flutes, and using more numerous and more varied voices.

[1] *Müller*, p. 213.
[2] *Id. ib.*
[3] *Aristoph.*, *Vesp.*, 1410. Compare *Herod.*, viii., 6.
[4] *Plut.*, *Mus.*, 39.

Lasus wrote a hymn to Ceres, who was worshipped at Hermione, in the Doric dialect, with the Æolic harmony, of which there are three lines extant, and also an ode, entitled Κένταυροι, both of which pieces were remarkable for not containing the letter Σ, the hissing sound of which he avoided as dissonant.[1]

XI. Timocrĕon (Τιμοκρέων), of Rhodes, was a genius of an entirely peculiar character. Powerful both as an athlete and a poet, he transferred the pugnacity of the palæstra to poetry. He is celebrated for the bitter and pugnacious spirit of his works, and especially for his attacks on Themistocles and Simonides. From fragments of his poetry which are preserved by Plutarch,[2] it appears that he was a native of Ialysus, in Rhodes, whence he was banished on the then common charge of an inclination toward Persia (μηδισμός); and in this banishment he was left neglected by Themistocles, who had formerly been his friend, and connected with him by the ties of hospitality. What made the cause of offence greater was, that Themistocles had obtained their recall for other political fugitives. This distinction Timocreon ascribed to pecuniary corruption. Timocreon seems to have ridiculed and parodied Simonides on account of some tricks of his art, as where the latter expresses the same thought in the same words, only transposed, first in an hexameter, and then in a trochaic tetrameter. Of his poetry only a few fragments remain, which are given in the collections of Schneidewin and Bergk.[3]

XII. Pindărus (Πίνδαρος), the greatest lyric poet of Greece, was a native of Bœotia, but the ancient biographies leave it uncertain whether he was born at Thebes or at Cynoscephalæ, a village in the territory of Thebes. His parents, it is well ascertained, belonged to Cynoscephalæ, and may, perhaps, have resided at Thebes, which would serve to reconcile the two accounts. Pindar was born, as we know from his own testimony, during the celebration of the Pythian games. Clinton places his birth in B.C. 518, Böckh in B.C. 522, but neither of these dates is certain, though the latter is perhaps the more probable. He appears to have died in his 80th year, though other accounts make him much younger at the time of his death. If he was born in B.C. 522, his death would fall in B.C. 442. He was in the prime of life at the battles of Marathon and Salamis, and was nearly of the same age as the poet Æschylus. But the causes which determined Pindar's poetical character are to be sought in a period previous to the Persian war, and in the Doric and Æolic parts of Greece rather than in Athens; and thus we may separate Pindar from his contemporary Æschylus, by placing the former at the close of the early period, the latter at the head of the new period of literature.[4]

The family of Pindar ranked among the noblest in Thebes. It was sprung from the ancient race of the Ægidæ, who claimed descent from Cadmus. The family seems to have been celebrated for its skill in music, though there is no authority for stating, as Böckh and Müller have done, that they were hereditary flute-players, and exercised their profession regularly at certain great religious festivals. The ancient biogra-

[1] *Müller*, p. 214; *Smith, Dict. Biogr.*, *s. v.*

[2] *Themist.*, 21.

[3] *Müller*, p. 215; *Smith, Dict. Biogr.*, *s. v.*

[4] *Smith, Dict. Biogr.*, *s. v.*

phies relate that the father or uncle of Pindar was a flute-player, and we are told that Pindar, at an early age, received instruction in the art from the flute-player Scopelinus. But the youth soon gave indications of a genius for poetry, which induced his father to send him to Athens to receive more perfect instruction in the art; for it must be recollected that lyric poetry among the Greeks was so intimately connected with music, dancing, and the whole training of the chorus, that the lyric poet required no small amount of education to fit him for his profession. At Athens Pindar became the pupil of Lasus of Hermione, the founder of the Athenian school of dithyrambic poetry, and who was at that time residing at Athens, under the patronage of Hipparchus. He returned to Thebes before he had completed his twentieth year, and is said to have received instruction there from Myrtis, and Corinna of Tanagra, two poetesses, who then enjoyed great celebrity in Bœotia.[1]

Corinna appears to have exercised considerable influence over the youthful poet, and he was not a little indebted to her example and precepts. It is related by Plutarch,[2] that she recommended Pindar to introduce mythical narrations into his poems, and that when, in accordance with her advice, he composed a hymn (part of which is still extant), in which he interwove almost all the Theban mythology, she smiled and said, "We ought to sow with the hand, and not with the whole sack" (*τῇ χειρὶ δεῖν σπείρειν, ἀλλὰ μὴ ὅλῳ τῷ θυλάκῳ*). With both these poetesses Pindar contended for the prize in the musical contests at Thebes. But Corinna was five times victorious over him.

Pindar commenced his professional career as a poet at a very early age, and acquired so great a reputation that he was soon employed by different states and princes in all parts of the Hellenic world to compose for them choral songs for special occasions. He received money and presents for his works; but he never degenerated into a common mercenary poet, and he continued to preserve to his latest days the respect of all parts of Greece. His earliest poem which has come down to us (the 10th Pythian) he composed at the age of twenty. It is an Epinician ode in honor of Hippocles, a Thessalian youth, belonging to the powerful family of the Aleuadæ, and who had gained the prize at the Pythian games. The next ode of Pindar in point of time is the 6th Pythian, which he wrote in his twenty-seventh year. It would be tedious, however, to relate at length the different occasions on which he composed his other odes. It may suffice to mention that he composed poems for Hiero, tyrant of Syracuse; Alexander, son of Amyntas, king of Macedonia; Theron, tyrant of Agrigentum; Arcesilaus IV., king of Cyrene, and besides for many free states and private persons. He was courted especially by Alexander, king of Macedonia, and by Hiero of Syracuse; and the praises which he bestowed upon the former are said to have been the chief reason which led his descendant, Alexander, son of Philip, to spare the house of the poet when he destroyed the rest of Thebes.[3] About B.C. 473, Pindar visited the court of Hiero, in consequence of the pressing invitation of

[1] *Smith, Dict. Biogr.*, *s. v.*

[2] *De Glor. Athen.*, 14.

[3] *Dion Chrysost.*, *Orat. de Regno*, ii., p. 25.

that monarch; but it appears that he did not remain more than four years at Syracuse, as he loved an independent life, and did not care to cultivate the courtly arts which rendered his contemporary, Simonides, a more welcome guest at the table of their patron.[1]

But the estimation in which Pindar was held by his contemporaries is still more strikingly shown by the honors conferred upon him by the free states of Greece. Although a Theban, he was always a great favorite with the Athenians, whom he frequently praised in his poems, and whose city he often visited. In one of his dithyrambs[2] he called it "the support (ἔρεισμα) of Greece, glorious Athens, the divine city." The Athenians testified their gratitude by making him their public guest (πρόξενος) and giving to him 10,000 drachmæ;[3] and at a later period they erected a statue to his honor,[4] but this was not done in his lifetime, as the pseudo-Æschines states.[5] The inhabitants of Ceos employed Pindar to compose for them a προσόδιον, or processional song, although they had two celebrated poets of their own, Bacchylides and Simonides. The Rhodians had his seventh Olympic ode written in letters of gold in the temple of the Lindian Minerva.[6]

Pindar's stated residence was at Thebes, though he frequently left home in order to attend the great public games, and to visit the states and distinguished men who courted his friendship and employed his services. In the public events of the time he appears to have taken no share. Indeed, the praises which he bestowed upon Athens, the ancient rival of Thebes, displeased his fellow-citizens, who are said even to have fined him in consequence. It is farther stated that the Athenians paid the fine, but the tale does not deserve much credit.

The poems of Pindar show that he was penetrated with a strong religious feeling. He had not imbibed any of the skepticism which began to take root at Athens after the close of the Persian war. The old myths were for the most part realities to him, and he accepted them with implicit credence, except when they exhibited the gods in a point of view which was repugnant to his moral feelings; and he accordingly rejects some tales, and changes others, because they are inconsistent with his conceptions of the gods. Pindar was a strict observer of the worship of the gods. He dedicated a shrine to the mother of the gods near his own house at Thebes.[7] He also dedicated to Jupiter Ammon, in Libya, a statue made by Calamis,[8] and likewise a statue in Thebes to Mercury of the Agora.[9] He was in the habit of frequently visiting Delphi, and there, seated in an iron chair, which was reserved for him, he used to sing hymns in honor of Apollo.[10]

The only poems of Pindar which have come down to us entire are his *Epinicia*, or triumphal odes, commemorating victories at the games (ἐπινίκια, *scil.* ἄσματα, from ἐπί and νίκη). But these were only a small portion of his works. Besides his triumphal odes, he wrote *hymns* to the

---

[1] *Smith, Dict. Biogr., s. v.*
[2] *Dithyr.*, Frag. 4.
[3] *Isocr.*, περὶ ἀντιδ., p. 304, ed. *Dind.*
[4] *Pausan.*, i., 8, 4.
[5] *Epist.*, 4.
[6] *Smith, l. c.*
[7] *Pausan.*, ix., 25, 3.
[8] *Id.*, ix., 6, 1.
[9] *Id.*, ix., 17, 1.
[10] *Pausan.*, x., 24, 4.

gods, *pæans*, *dithyrambs*, *prosodia*, or processional odes ; *parthenia*, or songs of maidens ; *hyporchemes*, or mimic songs ; *scolia*, or convivial songs ; *threni*, or dirges ; and *encomia*, or panegyrics on princes. Of these we have numerous fragments. Most of them are mentioned in the well-known lines of Horace :[1]

> Seu per audaces nova *dithyrambos*
> Verba devolvit, numerisque fertur
> Lege solutis :
> Seu deos (*hymns* and *pæans*) regesve (*encomia*) canit deorum
> Sanguinem :
> Sive quos Elea domum reducit
> Palma cœlestes (*Epinicia*) :
> Flebili sponsæ juvenemve raptum
> Plorat (*dirges*).

In all of these varieties Pindar equally excelled, as we see from the numerous quotations made from them by the ancient writers, though they are generally of too fragmentary a kind to allow us to form a judgment respecting them. Our estimate of Pindar as a poet must be formed almost exclusively from his *Epinicia*, which were all composed, as already remarked, in commemoration of some victory in the public games, with the exception of the eleventh Nemean, which was written for the installation of Aristagoras in the office of Prytanis at Tenedos. The *Epinicia* are divided into four books, celebrating respectively the victories gained in the Olympic, Pythian, Nemean, and Isthmian games. In order to understand them properly, we must bear in mind the nature of the occasion for which they were composed, and the object which the poet had in view. A victory gained in one of the four great national festivals conferred honor not only on the conqueror and his family, but also on the city to which he belonged. It was accordingly celebrated with great pomp and ceremony. Such a celebration began with a procession to a temple, where a sacrifice was offered, and it ended with a banquet and the joyous revelry called by the Greeks κῶμος. For this celebration a poem was expressly composed, which was sung by a chorus, trained for the purpose, either by the poet himself, or some one acting on his behalf. The poems were sung either during the procession to the temple, or at the comus at the close of the banquet.[2]

Those of Pindar's Epinician odes which consist of strophes without epodes, were sung during the procession, but the majority of them appear to have been sung at the comus. For this reason, they partake to some extent of the joyous nature of the occasion, and accordingly contain at times jocularities which are hardly in accordance with the modern notions of lyric poetry. In these odes Pindar rarely describes the victory itself, as the scene was familiar to all the spectators, but he dwells upon the glory of the victor, and celebrates chiefly either his wealth (ὄλβος) or his skill (ἀρετή)—his *wealth*, if he had gained the victory in the chariot-race, since it was only the wealthy that could contend for the prize in this contest ; his *skill*, if he had been exposed to peril in the encounter. He frequently celebrates, also, the piety and goodness of the victor ; for,

---

[1] *Carm.*, iv., 2.

[2] *Smith*, *Dict. Biogr.*, *s. v.*

with the deep religious feeling which pre-eminently characterizes Pindar, he believed that the moral and religious character of the conqueror conciliated the favor of the gods, and gained for him their support and assistance in the contest. For the same reason, he dwells at great length upon the mythical origin of the person whose victory he extols, and connects his exploits with the similar exploits of the heroic ancestors of the race or nation to which he belongs. These mythical narratives occupy a very prominent feature in almost all of Pindar's odes; they are not introduced for the sake of ornament, but have a close and intimate connection with the whole object and purpose of each poem, as is clearly pointed out by Dissen, in his admirable essay, "*De Ratione Poetica Carminum Pindaricorum*," &c., prefixed to his edition of Pindar.[1]

Every Epinician ode of Pindar has its peculiar tone, depending upon the course of the ideas and the consequent choice of the expressions. The principal differences are connected with the choice of the rhythms, which again is regulated by the musical style. According to the last distinction, the epinicia of Pindar are of three sorts, Doric, Æolic, and Lydian, which can be easily distinguished, although each admits of innumerable varieties. In respect of metre, every ode of Pindar has an individual character, no two odes having the same metrical structure. In the Doric ode the same metrical forms occur as those which prevailed in the choral lyric poetry of Stesichorus, namely, systems of dactyls and trochaic dipodiæ, which most nearly approach the stateliness of the hexameter. Accordingly, a serene dignity pervades these odes; the mythical narrations are developed with greater fullness, and the ideas are limited to the subject, and are free from personal feeling; in short, their general character is that of calmness and elevation. The language is Epic, with a slight Doric tinge, which adds to its brilliancy and dignity.[2]

The rhythms of the Æolic odes resemble those of the Lesbian poetry, in which light dactylic, trochaic, or logaœdic metres prevailed; these rhythms, however, when applied to choral lyric poetry, were rendered far more various, and thus often acquired a character of greater volubility and liveliness. The poet's mind also moves with greater rapidity; and sometimes he stops himself in the midst of narrations which seem to him impious or arrogant. The Æolic odes, moreover, from the rapidity and variety of their movements, have a less uniform character than the Doric odes; for example, the first Olympic, with its joyous and glowing images, is very different from the second, in which a lofty melancholy is expressed, and from the ninth, which has an expression of proud and complacent self-reliance. The language of the Æolic epinicia is also bolder, more difficult in its syntax, and marked by rarer dialectical forms. Lastly, there are the Lydian odes, the number of which is inconsiderable; their metre is mostly trochaic, and of a particularly soft character, agreeing with the tone of the poetry. Pindar appears to have preferred the Lydian rhythms for odes which were destined to be sung during a procession to a temple or at the altar, and in which the favor of the deity was implored in an humble spirit.[3]

1 *Smith, l. c.* 2 *Müller*, p. 227. 3 *Id. ib.*

The Editio Princeps of Pindar was printed at the Aldine press at Venice, in 1513, 8vo, without the scholia; but the same volume contained likewise the poems of Callimachus, Dionysius, and Lycophron. The second edition was published at Rome, by Zacharias Calliergi, with the scholia, in 1515, 4to. These two editions, which were taken from different families of manuscripts, are still of considerable value for the formation of the text. The other editions of Pindar published in the course of the sixteenth century were little more than reprints of the two above named. The first edition containing a new recension of the text, with explanatory notes, a Latin version, &c., was that published by Erasmus Schmidius, Vitembergæ, 1616, 4to. Next appeared the edition of Benedictus, Salinurii, 1620, 4to; and then the one published at Oxford, 1697, fol. From this time Pindar appears to have been little studied, until Heyne published his celebrated edition of the poet at Göttingen, in 1773, 4to. A second and much improved edition was published at Göttingen, in 1798–1799, 3 vols. 8vo, containing a valuable treatise on the metres of Pindar, by Hermann. Heyne's third edition was published after his death, by Schäfer, Lips., 1817, 3 vols. 8vo. But the best edition of Pindar is that by Böckh, Lips., 1811–1821, 2 vols. 4to, which contains a most valuable commentary, and dissertations, and is indispensable to the student who wishes to obtain a thorough insight into the musical system of the Greeks, and the artistic construction of their lyric poetry. The commentary on the Nemean and Isthmian odes in this edition was written by Dissen. Dissen also published, in the *Bibliotheca Græca*, a smaller edition of the poet, Gotha, 1830, 2 vols. 8vo, taken from the text of Böckh, with a most valuable explanatory commentary. This edition is the most useful to the student from its size, though it does not supersede that of Böckh. A second edition of Dissen's, by Schneidewin, appeared, Gotha, 1843, *seq.* There is also a valuable edition of Pindar by Fr. Thiersch, Lips., 1820, 2 vols. 8vo, with a German translation, and an important introduction; and a very useful one by Cookesley, Etonæ, 1851, 2 vols. 8vo. The text of the poet is given with great accuracy by Bergk, in his *Poetæ Lyrici Græci.*[1]

CHAPTER XX.

THIRD OR EARLY PROSAIC PERIOD.

INTRODUCTORY REMARKS.

I. The *third period* of Greek literature is also denominated the *early prosaic* one, and, as we have already remarked, begins, in fact, before the full termination of the preceding one, with the first attempts at prose composition, and extends to and includes the era of Herodotus. In considering this period, it will be necessary to distinguish between the philosophical and historical writers; and as prose writing, according to some, originated among the former, we will consider them first in order, although some of the writers to be mentioned by us in this enumeration will be found to have written in philosophic verse, not in prose. Our object in making mention of these writers is to give a continuous view of early Greek philosophy.

I. EARLIER GREEK PHILOSOPHY.[2]

II. Philosophy, for some time after its origin in Greece, was as far removed from the ordinary thoughts, occupations, and amusements of the people, as poetry was intimately connected with them. Poetry ennobles and elevates all that is characteristic of a nation; its religion, mythology, political and social institutions, and manners. Philosophy, on the other hand, begins by detaching the mind from the opinions and habits in which it has been bred up; from the national conceptions of the gods and the

[1] *Smith, l. c.*

[2] *Müller, Hist. Gr. Lit.*, p. 239, *seqq.*

universe; and from the traditionary maxims of ethics and politics. The philosopher attempts, as far as possible, to think for himself; and hence he is led to disparage all that is handed down from antiquity. Hence, too, the Greek philosophers from the beginning generally renounced the ornaments of verse; that is, of the vehicle which had been previously used for the expression of every elevated feeling.

III. Philosophical writings were nearly the earliest compositions in the unadorned language of common life. It is not probable that they would have been composed in this form if they had been intended for recital to a multitude assembled at games and festivals. It would have required great courage to break in upon the rhythmical flow of the euphonious hexameter and lyric measures, with a discourse uttered in the language of ordinary conversation.

IV. The most ancient writings of Greek philosophers were, however, only brief records of their principal doctrines, designed to be imparted to a few persons. There was no reason why the form of common speech should not be used for these, as it had long before been used for laws, treaties, and the like. In fact, prose composition and writing are so intimately connected, that we may venture to assert that, if writing had become common among the Greeks at an earlier period, poetry would not have so long retained its ascendency. We shall, indeed, find that philosophy, as it advanced, sought the aid of poetry, in order to strike the mind more forcibly; but this philosophical poetry may, without any impropriety, be classed with prose composition, as being a limited and peculiar deviation from the usual practice with regard to philosophical writings.

V. However the Greek philosophers may have sought after originality and independence of thought, they could not avoid being influenced in their speculations by the peculiar circumstances of their position. Hence the earliest philosophers may be classed according to the *races* and *countries* to which they belonged; the idea of a *school* (that is, of a transmission of doctrines through an unbroken series of teachers and disciples) not being applicable to this period.

VI. The earliest attempts at philosophical speculation were made by the Ionians; that race of the Greeks which not only had, in common life, shown the greatest desire for new and various kinds of knowledge, but had also displayed the most decided taste for scientific researches into the phenomena of external nature. From this direction of their inquiries, the Ionic philosophers were called by the ancients "physical philosophers," or "physiologers." With a boldness characteristic of inexperience and ignorance, they began by directing their inquiries to the most abstruse subjects; and, unaided by any experiments which were not within the reach of a common man, and unacquainted with the first elements of mathematics, they endeavored to determine the origin and principle of the existence of all things.[1]

VII. If we are tempted to smile at the temerity with which the Ionians at once ventured upon the solution of the highest problems, we are, on the other hand, astonished at the sagacity with which many of them con-

[1] *Müller*, p. 240.

jectured the connection of appearances, which they could not fully comprehend without a much greater progress in the study of nature. The scope of these Ionian speculations proves that they were not founded on *à priori* reasonings, independent of experience. The Greeks were always distinguished by their curiosity and their powers of delicate observation. Yet this gifted nation, even when it had accumulated a large stock of knowledge concerning natural objects, seems never to have attempted more than the observation of phenomena which presented themselves unsought, and never to have made experiments devised by the investigator.

VIII. Pherecȳdes (Φερεκύδης),[1] a native of Syros, one of the Cyclades, deserves mention before we pass to the individual philosophers of the Ionic school (taking the term in its most extended sense), because he forms an intermediate link between the sacerdotal enthusiasts, Epimenides, Abaris, and others, and the Ionic physiologers. He is, according to some, the earliest Greek of whose prose writings we possess any remains, and was certainly one of the first who, after the manner of the Ionians (before they had obtained any papyrus from Egypt), wrote down their unpolished wisdom upon sheep-skins. But his prose is only so far prose, that it has cast off the fetters of verse, and not because it expresses the ideas of the writer in a simple and perspicuous manner. His ideas and language closely resembled those of the Orphic theologers, and he ought rather to be classed with them than with the Ionic philosophers. He maintained that there were three *principia* (Zeus or Æther, Chthona or Chaos, and Cronos or Time), and four elements (fire, earth, air, and water), from which were formed every thing that exists. Pherecydes lived about B. C. 544.[2] According to some, he was not the first who wrote any thing in prose, this honor being reserved for Cadmus of Miletus, but merely the first who employed prose in the explanation of philosophical questions.

IX. Thales (Θαλῆς), of Miletus,[3] was the first in the series of the Ionic physical philosophers. He was born, according to Apollodorus, in the 35th Olympiad, and lived in the age of the Seven Sages, one of whom he himself was. These seven sages were not solitary thinkers, whose renown for wisdom was acquired by speculations unintelligible to the mass of the people; their fame, on the contrary, which extended over all Greece, was founded solely on their acts as statesmen, counsellors of the people in public affairs, and practical men. This is also true of Thales, whose sagacity in affairs of state and public economy appears from many anecdotes. Thales is also said to have predicted the eclipse of the sun, which happened in the reign of the Lydian king Alyattes, B.C. 609;[4] and, under Crœsus, to have managed the diversion of the course of the Halys.[5] For calculating the eclipse in question, he doubtless employed astronomical formulæ, which he had obtained, through Asia Minor, from the Chaldæans, the fathers of Grecian, and, indeed, of all ancient astronomy; for his own knowledge of mathematics could not have reached as far as the Pytha-

1 *Müller*, p. 240, *seq.*
2 *Diog. Laert.*, i., 121; *Smith, Dict. Biogr.*, *s. v.*
3 *Müller*, p. 241; *Smith, Dict. Biogr.*, *s. v.*
4 *Oltmann, Abhandl. der Königl. Akad. der Wiss. in Berlin*, 1812, 1813.
5 *Herod.*, i., 75.

gorean theorem. He is said to have been the first teacher of such problems as that of the equality of the angles at the base of an isosceles triangle. In the main, the tendency of Thales was practical; and, when his own knowledge was insufficient, he applied the discoveries of nations more advanced than his own in natural science. Thus he was the first who advised his countrymen, when at sea, not to steer by the Great Bear, which forms a considerable circle around the pole, but to follow the example of the Phœnicians (from whom, according to Herodotus, the family of Thales was descended), and to take the Lesser Bear for their polar star.[1]

Thales was not a poet, nor, indeed, the author of any written work, and, consequently, the accounts of his doctrine rest only upon the testimony of his contemporaries and immediate successors; so that it would be vain to attempt to construct from them a system of natural philosophy according to his own notions. It may, however, be collected from these traditions that he considered all nature as endowed with life. "Every thing," he said, "is full of gods;"[2] and he cited, as proofs of this opinion, the magnet and amber, on account of their magnetic and electrical properties.[3] It also appears that he considered water as a general principle or cause of things. What may have led him to this last opinion was, according to Aristotle, that the fruit and seeds of things are moist, and that warmth is developed out of moistness. What we have here said is sufficient to show that Thales broke through the common prejudices produced by the impressions of the senses, and sought to discover the principle of external forms in moving powers which lie beneath the surface of appearances.[4]

X. Anaximander (Ἀναξίμανδρος),[5] also a Milesian, is next after Thales, whose pupil he is said to have been. He was born B.C. 610.[6] It seems pretty certain that his little work "upon nature" (περὶ φύσεως), as the books of the Ionic physiologers were mostly called, was written in B.C. 547, when he was sixty-three years old. This may be said to be the earliest philosophical work (strictly so termed) in the Greek language; for we can scarcely give that name to the mysterious revelations of Pherecydes. It was probably written in a style of extreme conciseness, and in language more befitting poetry than prose, as indeed appears from the few extant fragments. The astronomical and geographical explanations attributed to Anaximander were probably contained in this work. Anaximander possessed a gnomon, or sun-dial, which he had doubtless obtained from Babylon;[7] and, being at Sparta (which was still the focus of Greek civilization), he made observations, by which he determined exactly the solstices and equinoxes, and calculated the obliquity of the ecliptic. According to Eratosthenes, he was the first who attempted to draw a map; in which his object probably was rather to make a mathematical division of the whole earth, than to lay down the forms of the different countries composing it.

---

1 *Müller, l. c.*
2 *Aristot., De Anima*, i., 5.
3 *Id. ib.*, i., 2.
4 *Müller, l. c.; Smith, Dict. Biogr., s. v.*
5 *Müller*, p. 242; *Smith, Dict. Biogr., s. v.*
6 *Apollod. ap. Diog. Laert.*, ii., 1, 2.
7 *Plin., H. N.*, ii., 8; *Herod.*, ii., 109.

According to Aristotle,[1] Anaximander thought that there were innumerable worlds, which he called gods; supposing these worlds to be beings endowed with an independent power of motion. He also thought that existing worlds were always perishing, and that new worlds were always springing into being; so that motion was perpetual. According to his views, these worlds arose out of the eternal, or, rather, indeterminable substance, which he called *τὸ ἄπειρον;* he arrived at the idea of an original substance, out of which all things arose, and to which all things return, by excluding all attributes and limitations.

XI. Anaximĕnes (Ἀναξιμένης),[2] another Milesian, according to the general tradition of antiquity, was third in the series of Ionic philosophers. With both Thales and Anaximander he had personal intercourse; for, besides the common tradition, which makes him a disciple of the latter, Diogenes Laertius[3] quotes at length two letters said to have been written to Pythagoras by Anaximenes; in one of which he gives an account of the death of Thales, speaking of him with reverence as the first of philosophers, and as having been his own teacher. In the other he congratulates Pythagoras on his removal to Crotona from Samos, while he was himself at the mercy of the tyrants of Miletus, and was looking forward with fear to the approaching war with the Persians, in which he foresaw that the Ionians must be subdued. There is no safe testimony as to the exact period of the birth and death of Anaximenes; but since there is sufficient evidence that he was the teacher of Anaxagoras, B.C. 480, and he was in repute in B.C. 544, he must have lived to a great age.[4]

Like the other early Greek philosophers, he employed himself in speculating upon the origin, and accounting for the phenomena of the universe; and as Thales held water to be the material cause out of which the world was made, so Anaximenes considered air to be the first cause of all things, the primary form, as it were, of matter, into which the other elements of the universe were resolvable.[5] The elementary principle of the Ionians was always considered as having an independent power of motion, and as endowed with certain attributes of the divine essence.[6] Hence it appears that Anaximenes, like his predecessors, held the eternity of matter: nor, indeed, does he seem to have believed in the existence of any thing immaterial; for even the human soul, according to his theory, is, like the body, formed of air;[7] and he saw no necessity for supposing an Agent in the work of creation, since he held that motion was a natural and necessary law of the universe.[8]

XII. A person of far greater importance in the history of Greek philosophy, and especially of Greek prose, is Heraclītus (Ἡράκλειτος),[9] of Ephesus. The time when he flourished is ascertained to be about the 69th Olympiad, or B.C. 505.[10] After travelling extensively in his youth, he

---

[1] *Aristot., Phys.*, iii., 4.
[2] *Müller*, p. 243; *Smith, Dict. Biogr., s. v.*
[3] *Diog. Laert.*, ii., 3, *seqq.*
[4] *Strab.*, xiv., p. 645; *Cic., N. D.*, i., 11; *Origen*, vol. iv., p. 238; *Philol. Museum*, vol. i., p. 86, *seqq.*
[5] *Aristot., Metaph.*, i., 3.
[6] *Stobæus, Eclog.*, p. 296.
[7] *Plut., De Plac. Phil.*, i., 3.
[8] *Smith, l. c.*
[9] *Müller*, p. 244; *Smith, Dict. Biogr., s. v.*
[10] *Diog. Laert.*, ix., 1. Clinton (*F. H.*, vol. ii.) places him under B.C. 513.

appears to have led the life of a complete recluse, and at last to have retreated to the mountains, where he lived on pot-herbs; but, after some time, he was compelled, by the sickness consequent on such meagre diet, to return to Ephesus, where he died. The common story, that he was continually shedding tears on account of the vices and follies of mankind, is as little entitled to sober belief as that of the perpetually-laughing Democritus.

The philosophical system of Heraclitus was contained in a work which received various titles from the ancients, of which the most common is περὶ φύσεως. Some fragments of it remain, and have been collected and explained by Schleiermacher, in Wolf and Buttmann's *Museum der Alterthumwissenschaft*.[1] From the obscurity of his style, Heraclitus gained the title of σκοτεινός, and with his predilection for this method of writing was probably connected his aristocratic pride and hauteur (whence he was called ὀχλολοίδορος), his tenacious adherence to his own views, which, according to Aristotle, had as much weight with him as science itself,[2] his contempt for the opinions of previous writers, and the well-known melancholy of his disposition, whence originated the story already alluded to of his weeping for the follies and vices of mankind.[3] With regard, however, to his obscurity, we must also take into account the cause assigned for it by Ritter, that the oldest philosophical prose must have been rude and loose in its structure; and since it had grown out of a poetical style, would naturally have recourse to figurative language.[4]

The cardinal doctrine of his natural philosophy seems to have been, that every thing is in perpetual motion,[5] that nothing has any stable or permanent existence, but that every thing is assuming a new form or perishing. Seeking in natural phenomena for the principle of this perpetual motion, Heraclitus supposed it to be *fire*,[6] but by fire he meant only a clear light fluid, self-kindled and self-extinguished, and therefore not differing materially from the air of Anaximenes. Thus, then, the world is formed, "not made by God or man," but simply evolved by a natural operation from fire, which, also, is the human life and soul, and, therefore, a rational intelligence guiding the whole universe. With his physical theories his moral ones were closely connected. Thus, he accounted for a drunkard's incapacity by supposing him to have a wet soul; and he even pushed this so far as to maintain that the soul is wisest where the land and climate are driest, which would account for the mental greatness of the Greeks. He held man's soul to be a portion of the divine fire, though degraded by its migration to earth; and he considered the eyes more trustworthy than the ears, as revealing to us the knowledge of fire.

The Greek epistles bearing the name of Heraclitus, published in the Aldine collection of Greek letters, Rome, 1499, and Geneva, 1606, and also in the edition of Eunapius, by Boissonade, p. 425, are the invention of some later writer.

1 Vol. i., part 3.
2 *Aristot.*, *Eth. Nic.*, vii., 5.
3 *Juv.*, *Sat.*, x., 34.
4 *Ritter*, *Gesch. der Phil.*, vol. i., p. 267, *seqq.*
5 *Müller*, *l. c.*
6 *Maxim. Tyr.*, *Diss.*, xxv., p. 260.

XIII. Anaxagŏras (Ἀναξαγόρας)[1] of Clazomenæ, in Ionia, was born about B.C. 499. He is said to have gone to Athens at the age of twenty, during the contests of the Greeks with Persia, and to have lived and taught in that city for a period of thirty years. He became here the intimate friend and teacher of the most eminent men of the time, such as Euripides and Pericles; but, while he thus gained the friendship and admiration of the most enlightened Athenians, the majority, uneasy at being disturbed in their hereditary superstitions, soon found reasons for complaint. The principal cause of hostility toward him must, however, be looked for in the following circumstance. As he was a friend of Pericles, the party which was dissatisfied with the administration of the latter seized upon the disposition of the people toward the philosopher as a favorable opportunity for striking a blow at the great statesman. Anaxagoras, therefore, was accused of impiety, and it was only owing to the influence and eloquence of Pericles that he was not put to death. He was sentenced, however, to pay a fine of five talents, and to quit Athens. The philosopher now went to Lampsacus, and during his residence here a charge of μηδισμός, or partiality to Persia, was brought against him at Athens, in consequence of which he was condemned to death. He is said to have received the intelligence of his sentence with a smile, and to have died at Lampsacus, at the age of seventy-two.[2]

The treatise on Nature by Anaxagoras (which was written late in life) was in the Ionic dialect, and in prose, after the example of Anaximenes. We have copious fragments remaining of it, consisting of quotations made from it by later writers, such as Plato, Aristotle, Plutarch, Diogenes Laertius, Cicero, and others. These fragments exhibit short sentences connected by particles (*as*, *and*, *but*, *for*), without long periods. But though his style was loose, his reasoning was compact and well arranged. His demonstrations were synthetic, not analytic, that is to say, he subjoined the proof to the proposition to be proved, instead of arriving at his result by a process of inquiry.[3]

The Ionic philosophers had endeavored to explain nature and its various phenomena by regarding matter in its different forms and modifications as the cause of all things. Anaxagoras, on the other hand, conceived the necessity of seeking a higher cause, independent of matter, and this cause he considered to be νοῦς, that is, mind, thought, or intelligence. This νοῦς, however, is not the creator of the world, but merely that which originally arranged the world and gave motion to it; for, according to the axiom that out of nothing nothing can come, he supposed the existence of matter from all eternity, though, before the νοῦς was exercised upon it, it was in a chaotic confusion. In this original chaos there was an infinite number of homogeneous parts (ὁμοιομερῆ), as well as heterogeneous ones. The νοῦς united the former, and separated from them what was heterogeneous, and out of this process arose the things we see in this world. This union and separation, however, were made in such a manner that each thing contains in itself parts of other things or heterogeneous elements, and is what it is only on account of the preponder-

[1] *Smith*, *Dict. Biogr.*, *s. v.*; *Müller*, p. 246. [2] *Diog. Laert.*, ii., 3, *seqq.* [3] *Müller*, *l. c.*

ance of certain homogeneous parts which constitute its character.[1] Anaxagoras thus adopted the doctrine of atoms, and excluded the idea of creation from his explanation of nature. No doctrine of his, however, gave so much offence, or was considered so clear a proof of his atheism, as his opinion that the sun, the bountiful god Helios, who shines upon both mortals and immortals, was a mass of red-hot iron. How startling must these opinions have appeared at a time when the people were accustomed to consider nature as pervaded by a thousand divine powers! And yet these new doctrines rapidly gained the ascendency, in spite of all the opposition of religion, poetry, and even the laws which were intended to protect the ancient customs and opinions. A hundred years later, Anaxagoras, with his doctrine of νοῦς, appeared to Aristotle a sober inquirer, compared with the wild speculators who preceded him; although Aristotle was aware that his applications of his doctrines were unsatisfactory and defective.[2]

The fragments of Anaxagoras have been collected by Schaubach, *Anaxagoræ Fragmenta collegit*, &c., Leipzig, 1827, 8vo, and much better by Schorn, *Anaxagoræ Fragmenta dispos. et illustr.*, &c., Bonn, 1829, 8vo.

XIV. Diogenes Apolloniātes[3] (Διογένης ὁ 'Απολλωνιάτης), a native of Apollonia, in Crete, was not equal in importance to Anaxagoras, but is still too considerable a writer upon physical subjects to be here passed over in silence. Without being either the disciple or the teacher, he was a contemporary of Anaxagoras; and in the direction of his studies he closely followed Anaximenes, expanding the main doctrines of this philosopher rather than establishing new principles of his own. He wrote a work in the Ionic dialect, entitled περὶ Φύσεως, "Upon Nature" (a common title with the Ionic philosophers, as we have already seen), which consisted of at least two books, and in which he appears to have treated of physical science in the largest sense of the words. Of this work only a few short fragments remain, preserved by Aristotle, Diogenes Laertius, and Simplicius.

Diogenes, like Anaxagoras, lived at Athens, and is said to have been exposed to similar dangers.[4] He maintained that air was the primal element of all things; that there was an infinite number of worlds, and an infinite void; that air, densified and rarefied, produced the different members of the universe; that nothing was produced from nothing, or was reduced to nothing; that the earth was round, supported in the middle, and had received its shape from the whirling round of the warm vapors, and its concretion and hardening from cold. He also imputed to air an intellectual energy, though without recognizing any distinction between mind and matter.[5]

The fragments of Diogenes have been collected and published, with those of Anaxagoras, by Schorn, Bonn, 1829, 8vo, and alone by Panzerbeiter, Leipzig, 1830, 8vo, with a copious dissertation on his philosophy.

XV. A third Ionic physical philosopher of this time, Archelāus ('Αρχέ-

---

1 *Smith*, *l. c.*
2 *Müller*, *l. c.*
3 *Müller*, p. 248; *Smith*, *Dict. Biogr.*, *s. v.*
4 *Diog. Laert.*, ix., 57.
5 *Id. ib.*

λαος) of Miletus,[1] who followed the manner of Anaxagoras, is chiefly important from having established himself permanently at Athens. It is evident that these men were not drawn to Athens by any prospect of benefit to their philosophical pursuits; for the Athenians at that time showed a disinclination to such studies, which they ridiculed under the name of *meteorosophy*, and even made the subject of persecution. It was undoubtedly the power which Athens had acquired as the head of the confederates against Persia, and the oppression of the states of Asia Minor, which drove these philosophers from Clazomenæ and Miletus to the independent, wealthy, and flourishing Athens. And thus these political events contributed to transfer to Athens the last efforts of Ionic philosophy, which the Athenians at first rejected as foreign to their modes of thinking, but which they afterward understood and appreciated, and used as a foundation for more extensive and accurate investigations of their own.[2]

XVI. But before Athens had reached this pre-eminence in philosophy, the spirit of speculation was awakened in other parts of Greece, and had struck into new paths of inquiry. The *Eleatics* afford a remarkable instance of independent philosophical research at this period; for, although Ionians by descent, they departed very widely from their countrymen on the coast of Asia Minor. Elea (afterward Velia, according to the Roman pronunciation) was a colony founded in Italy by the Phocæans, when, from a noble love of freedom, they had delivered up their country in Asia Minor to the Persians, and had been forced, by the enmity of the Etruscans and Carthaginians, to abandon their first settlement in Corsica; which happened about B.C. 536. The three most eminent philosophers of the Eleatic school were Xenophanes, Parmenides, and Zeno.[3]

XVII. XENOPHĂNES[4] (Ξενοφάνης), a native of Colophon, and who flourished between the 60th and 70th Olympiads,[5] was concerned in the colonizing of Elea, and lived at least for some time in that place. He had quitted Colophon as a fugitive or exile. Xenophanes was a poet in earlier life, and did not attach himself to philosophy until he had settled at Elea. But even as a philosopher he retained the poetic form of composition: his work upon nature was written in epic language and metre, and he himself recited it at public festivals after the manner of a rhapsodist. Xenophanes, from the first, adopted a different principle from that of the Ionic physical philosophers; for he proceeded upon an ideal system, while their system was exclusively founded upon experience. He began with the idea of the godhead, and showed the necessity of conceiving it as an eternal and unchanging existence. The lofty idea of an everlasting and immutable God, who is all spirit and mind, was described in his poem as the only true knowledge. Xenophanes was universally regarded by antiquity as the originator of the Eleatic doctrine of the oneness of the universe.[6] The deity was, in his view, the animating power of the universe,

---

1 Ritter and others incline to regard him as a native of Athens, considering the fact as nearly established on the authority of Simplicius. We have preferred, however, following the common account with Müller. 2 *Müller*, p. 249. 3 *Id. ib.*
4 *Id.*, p. 250. 5 *Smith, Dict. Biogr., s. v.* 6 *Plat., Soph.*, p. 242; *Aristot, Met.*, ii., 5.

which is expressed by Aristotle in the words that, directing his glance on the whole universe, Xenophanes said, "God is the One."[1]

The fragments of Xenophanes have been collected by Karsten: "*Xenophanis Colophonii Carminum Reliquiæ*," &c., Bruxell., 1830.

XVIII. Xenophanes was followed by PARMENĬDES[2] (Παρμενίδης) of Elea. According to Plato, Parmenides, at the age of sixty-five, came to Athens to the Panathenæa, accompanied by Zeno, then forty years old, and became acquainted with Socrates, who at that time was quite young. Supposing Socrates to have been nineteen or twenty years of age at the time, we may place the visit of Parmenides to Athens in B.C. 448, and, consequently, his birth in 513.[3] Parmenides was regarded with great esteem by Plato[4] and Aristotle;[5] and his fellow-citizens thought so highly of him, that every year they bound their magistrates to render obedience to the laws which he had enacted for them.[6] The philosophical opinions of Parmenides were developed in a didactic poem in hexameter verse, entitled περὶ Φύσεως,[7] of which only fragments remain. In this poem he maintained that the phenomena of sense were delusive, and that it was only by mental abstraction that a person could attain to the knowledge of the only reality, a One and All, a continuous and self-existent substance, which could not be perceived by the senses. But, although he believed the phenomena of sense to be delusive, he nevertheless adopted two elements, Warm and Cold, or Light and Darkness.[8] The best edition of the fragments of Parmenides is by Karsten. It forms the second part of the first volume of *Philosophorum Græcorum Veterum Oper. Reliquiæ*, Amstd., 1835.

XIX. ZENO (Ζήνων), of Elea, was the favorite disciple of Parmenides. He was born about B.C. 488, and at the age of forty accompanied Parmenides to Athens. He appears to have resided some time at this latter place. Zeno developed the doctrines of Parmenides in a prose work, in which his chief object was to justify the disjunction of philosophical speculation from the ordinary modes of thought. This he did by showing the absurdities involved in the doctrines of variety, of motion, and of creation, opposed to that of an all-comprehending substance.[9]

XX. Before we turn from the Eleatics to those other philosophers of Italy, to whom the name of *Italic* has been appropriated, we must notice a Sicilian, who is so peculiar both in his personal qualities and his philosophical doctrines, that he can not be classed with any sect, although his opinions were influenced by those of the Ionians, the Eleatics, and the Pythagoreans. EMPEDŎCLES[10] (Ἐμπεδοκλῆς) of Agrigentum, in Sicily, flourished about B.C. 444. He was held in high honor by his countrymen of Agrigentum, and also apparently by the other Doric states of Sicily. He reformed the constitution of his native city by abolishing the oligarchical

1 *Aristot.*, *l. c.* Compare *Timon ap. Sext. Emp. Pyrrh. Hyp.*, i., 224.
2 *Müller*, p. 251; *Smith, Dict. Biogr.*, *s. v.*
3 *Plat.*, *Parmen.*, p. 127, *B*; *Id.*, *Soph.*, p. 217, *G.*
4 *Id.*, *Theæt.*, p. 183, *E*; *Soph.*, p. 237.
5 *Aristot.*, *Metaph.*, *A.* 5, p. 986; *Phys. Auscult.*, i., 23.
6 *Diog. Laert.*, ix., 23. Compare *Strab.*, vi., p. 252. 7 *Plut.*, *De Pyth. Orac.*, p. 402.
8 *Smith*, *l. c.* 9 *Müller*, p. 253. 10 *Ibid.*, *l. c.*; *Smith, Dict. Biogr.*, *s. v.*

council of the Thousand; which measure gave such general satisfaction, that the people are said to have offered him the regal authority.[1] The fame of Empedocles was, however, principally acquired by improvements which he made in the physical condition of large tracts of country. He destroyed the pestiferous exhalations of the marshes about Selinus, by carrying two small streams through the swampy grounds, and thus draining off the water. In other places he blocked up some narrow valleys with large constructions, and thus screened a town from the noxious winds which blew into it, by which he earned to himself the title of "wind averter" (κωλυσανέμας).[2] It is probable that Empedocles did not conceal his consciousness of possessing extraordinary intellectual powers, so that we need not wonder at his having been considered by his countrymen in Sicily as a person endowed with supernatural and prophetic gifts.

The works of Empedocles were all in verse. The two most important were a didactic poem on nature (περὶ Φύσεως), of which considerable fragments are extant, and a poem entitled Καθαρμοί, which seems to have recommended good moral conduct as the means of averting epidemics and other evils. Lucretius, the greatest of all didactic poets, speaks of Empedocles with enthusiasm, and evidently makes him his model. Empedocles was acquainted with the theories of the Eleatics and the Pythagoreans; but he did not adopt the fundamental principles of either school, although he agreed with the latter in his belief in the migration of souls, and in a few other points. With the Eleatics he agreed in thinking that it was impossible to conceive any thing arising out of nothing. Empedocles first established the number of four elements, which he called the roots of things.[3]

The first comprehensive collection of the fragments of Empedocles was made by Sturz, *Empedocles Agrigentinus*, Lips., 1805. Karsten also has greatly distinguished himself for what he has done for the criticism and explanation of the text, as well as for the light he has thrown on separate doctrines. (*Philosophorum Græcorum veterum Reliquiæ*, vol. ii.) A collection of the Fragments by Stein, Bonn, 1852, has also appeared.

XXI. We now turn to that class of ancient philosophers which in Greece itself was called the *Italic*;[4] the most obscure region of the Greek philosophy, as we have no accounts of individual writings, and scarcely even of individual writers, belonging to it. The most conspicuous name here is that of *Pythagoras*, which will alone occupy our attention. Pythagŏras[5] (Πυθαγόρας) was a native of Samos.[6] The date of his birth is uncertain, but all authorities agree that he flourished in the times of Polycrates and Tarquinius Superbus (B.C. 540–510).[7] He studied in his own country under Creophilus, Pherecydes of Syros, and others, and is said to have visited Egypt and many countries of the East for the purpose of acquiring knowledge. We have not much trustworthy evidence either as to the kind and amount of knowledge which he acquired, or as to his

---

1 *Diog. Laert.*, viii., 63, *seqq.*
2 *Id.*, viii., 60, 70, 69; *Plut.*, *De Curios. Princ.*, p. 515.
3 *Müller*, *l. c.*; *Smith*, *l. c.*
4 *Müller*, p. 255.
5 *Id. ib.*; *Smith*, *Dict. Biogr.*, *s. v.*
6 *Isocr.*, *Busir.*, p. 227, ed. *Steph.*
7 *Clinton*, *Fast. Hell.*, vol. ii., p. 19–21.

definite philosophical views. It is certain, however, that he believed in the transmigration of souls.[1] He is also said to have discovered the propositions that the triangle inscribed in a semicircle is right-angled, and that the square of the hypotenuse of a right-angled triangle is equal to the sum of the squares on the sides.[2] Discoveries in astronomy are also attributed to him; and there can be little doubt that he paid great attention to arithmetic, and its application to weights, measures, and the theory of music.[3]

Apart from all direct testimony, however, it may safely be affirmed, that the very remarkable influence exerted by Pythagoras, and even the fact that he was made the hero of so many marvellous stories, prove him to have been a man both of singular capabilities and of great acquirements. It may also be affirmed with safety that the religious element was the predominant one in the character of Pythagoras, and that religious ascendency, in connection with a certain mystic religious system, was the object which he chiefly labored to secure. It was this religious element which made the profoundest impression upon his contemporaries. They regarded him as standing in a peculiarly close connection with the gods. The Crotoniats even identified him with the Hyperborean Apollo.[4] And, without viewing him as an impostor, we may easily believe that he himself, to some extent, shared the same views. He pretended to divination and prophecy;[5] and he appears as the revealer of a mode of life calculated to raise his disciples above the level of mankind, and to recommend them to the favor of the gods.[6]

When we come to inquire what were the philosophical or religious opinions held by Pythagoras himself, we are met at the outset by the difficulty that even the authors from whom we have to draw possessed no authentic records bearing upon the age of Pythagoras himself. If Pythagoras ever wrote any thing, his writings perished with him, or not long after. The probability is that he wrote nothing.[7] Every thing current under his name in antiquity was spurious. It is all but certain that Philolaus was the first who *published* the Pythagorean doctrines, at any rate in a written form. Still, there was so marked a peculiarity running through the Pythagorean philosophy, that there can be but little question as to the germs of the system having, at any rate, been derived from Pythagoras himself.[8] Pythagoras resembled the philosophers of the Ionic school, who undertook to solve, by means of a single primordial principle, the vague problem of the origin and constitution of the universe as a whole. His predilection for mathematical studies led him to trace the origin of all things to number, his theory being suggested, or at all events confirmed, by the observation of various numerical relations, or analogies to them, in the phenomena of the universe.

Musical principles likewise played almost as important a part in the

---

1 *Diog. Laert.*, viii., 36; *Pausan.*, ii., 17.
2 *Diog. Laert.*, viii., 12.
3 *Id. ib.; Plin., H. N.*, ii., 8.
4 *Porph., Vit. Pythag.*, 20; *Iamb., Vit. Pythag.*, 31, 140.
5 *Cic., De Divin.*, i., 3, 46; *Porph., l. c.*, 29.
6 *Grote, Hist. Gr.*, vol. iv., p. 129.
7 Compare *Plut., De Alex. fort.*, p. 329; *Porph., l. c.*, 57.
8 *Brandis, Gesch. der Griech. Rom. Philos.*, p. 442.

Pythagorean system as mathematical or numerical ideas. We find running through the entire system the idea that order, or harmony of relation, is the regulating principle of the whole universe. The intervals between the heavenly bodies were supposed to be determined according to the laws and relations of musical harmony.[1] Hence arose the celebrated doctrine of the harmony of the spheres; for the heavenly bodies, in their motion, could not but occasion a certain sound or note, depending on their distances and velocities; and as these were determined by the laws of harmonical intervals, the notes altogether formed a regular musical scale or harmony. This harmony, however, we do not hear, either because we have been accustomed to it from the first, and have never had an opportunity of contrasting it with stillness, or because the sound is so powerful as to exceed our capacities for hearing.[2]

The ethics of the Pythagoreans consisted more in ascetic practice and in maxims for the restraint of the passions, especially of anger, and the cultivation of the power of endurance, than in scientific theory. What of the latter they had was, as might be expected, intimately connected with their number-theory.[3] Happiness consisted in the science of the perfection of the virtues of the soul, or in the perfect science of numbers.[4] Likeness to the Deity was to be the object of all our endeavors,[5] man becoming better as he approaches the gods, who are the guardians and the guides of men.[6] Great importance was attached to the influence of music as a means of controlling the force of the passions.[7] Self-examination was strongly insisted upon.[8] The transmigration of souls was viewed apparently in the light of a process of purification. Souls under the dominion of sensuality either passed into the bodies of animals, or, if incurable, were thrust down into Tartarus, to meet with expiation or condign punishment. The pure were exalted to higher modes of life, and at last attained to incorporeal existence.[9] As regards the fruits of this system of training or belief, it is interesting to remark, that wherever we have notices of distinguished Pythagoreans, we usually hear of them as men of great uprightness, conscientiousness, and self-restraint, and as capable of devoted and enduring friendship.

II. EARLIER GREEK HISTORIANS.[10]

I. It is a remarkable fact that a nation so intellectual and cultivated as the Greeks should have been so long without feeling the want of a correct record of its transactions in war and peace.

II. From almost the earliest times, the East appears to have had its annals and chronicles, whereas the Greeks, on the other hand, evinced a careless and nearly infantine indifference about the registering of pass-

---

1 *Nicom.*, *Harm.*, i., p. 6; ii., 33; *Plin.*, *H. N.*, ii., 20.
2 *Aristot.*, *De Cœlo*, ii., 9; *Porph. in Harm. Ptol.*, 4, p. 257.
3 *Aristot.*, *Eth. Mag.*, i., 1; *Eth. Nic.*, i., 4; ii., 5.
4 *Clem. Alex.*, *Strom.*, ii., p. 417; *Theodoret.*, *Serm.*, xi., p. 165.
5 *Stob.*, *Ecl. Eth.*, p. 64.
6 *Plut.*, *De Def. Or.*, p. 413
7 *Plut.*, *De Is. et Os.*, p. 384; *Porph.*, *Vit. Pyth.*, 30.
8 *Cic.*, *De Sen.*, 11.
9 *Aristot.*, *De An.*, i., 2, 3; *Herod.*, ii., 123; *Diog. Laert.*, viii., 31.
10 *Müller*, *Hist. Gr. Lit.*, p. 258, *seqq.*

ing events, almost to the time when they became one of the great nations of the world, and waged mighty wars with the ancient kingdoms of the East. The celebration of a by-gone age, which imagination had decked with all its charms, engrossed the attention of the Hellenic race, and prevented them from dwelling on more recent events. Besides this, the division of the nation into numerous small states, and the republican form of the governments, prevented a concentration of interests on particular events and persons.

III. No action, no event, before the great conflict between Greece and Persia, could be compared in interest with those great exploits of the Mythical Age, in which heroes from all parts of Greece were supposed to have had a share; certainly none made so pleasing an impression upon all hearers. The Greeks required that a work read in public, and designed for general instruction and entertainment, should impart unmixed pleasure to the mind; but, owing to the dissensions between the Greek republics, their historical traditions could not but offend some, if they flattered others. In short, it was not till a late period that the Greeks outgrew their poetical mythology, and considered contemporary events as worthy of being thought of and written about.

IV. From this cause, the history of many transactions prior to the Persian war has perished; but then, without its influence, Greek literature could never have become what it was. Greek poetry, by its purely fictitious character, and its freedom from the shackles of particular truths, acquired that general probability, on account of which Aristotle considers poetry as more philosophical than history. Greek art, likewise, from the lateness of the period at which it descended from the ideal representation of gods and heroes to the portraits of real men, acquired a nobleness and beauty of form which it could never have otherwise attained. And, in fine, the intellectual culture of the Greeks in general would not have taken its liberal and elevated turn, if it had not rested on a poetical basis.

V. Writing was probably known in Greece some centuries before the time of Cadmus of Miletus, the earliest Greek historian;[1] but it had not been employed for the purpose of preserving any detailed historical record. The lists of the Olympic victors, and of the kings of Sparta and the prytanes of Corinth, which the Alexandrean critics considered sufficiently authenticated to serve as the foundation of the early Greek chronology; ancient treaties and other contracts, which it was important to perpetuate in precise terms; determinations of boundaries, and other records of a like description, formed the first rudiments of a documentary history. Yet this was still very remote from a detailed chronicle of contemporary events. And even when, toward the end of the age of the Seven Sages, some writers of historical narratives in prose began to appear among the Ionians and the other Greeks, they did not select domestic and recent events. Instead of this, they began with accounts of distant times and countries, and gradually narrowed their view to a history of the Greeks

[1] Compare the opinions of Wolf and Nitzsch on this subject, in relation to the Homeric controversy, as already given by us, p. 32, 34, of the present work.

of recent times. So entirely did the ancient Greeks believe that the daily discussion of common life and oral tradition were sufficient records of the events of their own time and country.

VI. The Ionians, who throughout this period were the daring innovators and indefatigable discoverers in the field of intellect, took the lead in history. They were also the first who, satiated with the childish amusement of mythology, began to turn their keen and restless eyes on all sides, and to seek new matter for thought and composition. The Ionians had a peculiar delight in varied and continuous narration. Nor is it to be overlooked that the first Ionian who is mentioned as a historian was a *Milesian*. Miletus, the birth-place of the earliest philosophers; flourishing by its industry and commerce; the centre of the political movements, produced by the spirit of Ionian independence; and the spot in which the native dialect was first formed into written Greek prose, was evidently fitted to be the cradle of historical composition in Greece. If the Milesians had not, together with their neighbors of Asia Minor, led a life of too luxurious enjoyment; if they had known how to retain the severe manners and manly character of the ancient Greeks in the midst of the refinements and excitements of later times, it is probable that Miletus, and not Athens, would have been the teacher of the world.

VII. Cadmus (Κάδμος), of Miletus, is mentioned as the earliest historian, and, together with Pherecydes of Syros, whom we have already treated of, as the earliest writer of prose. It remains an unsettled point which of the two was the earliest prose writer, but there can be no doubt of the fact that Cadmus was the earliest Greek historian. There is every probability that he lived about B.C. 540.[1] He wrote a history of the foundation of Miletus, embracing the earliest history of Ionia generally, in four books (Κτίσις Μιλήτου καὶ τῆς ὅλης Ἰωνίας). The subject of this history lay in the dim period, from which only a few oral traditions of an historical kind, but intimately connected with mythical notions, had been preserved. The genuine work of Cadmus seems to have been lost at a very early period, for the book that bore his name in the time of Dionysius of Halicarnassus (that is, in the Augustan Age) was considered a forgery.[2] When Suidas and others[3] call Cadmus of Miletus the inventor of the alphabet, this statement must be regarded as the result of a confusion between the mythical Cadmus, who emigrated from Phœnicia into Greece, and the writer under consideration.

VIII. Acusilāus (Ἀκουσίλαος),[4] of Argos, is the next historian in order of time. Although by descent a Dorian, he wrote his history in the Ionic dialect, because the Ionians were the founders of the historical style. He probably lived in the latter half of the sixth century B.C. Acusilaus confined his attention to the mythical period. His object was to collect into a short and connected narrative all the events from the period of chaos to the end of the Trojan war. It was said of him that he translated Hesiod into prose, an expression which serves to characterize his work. He appears, however, to have related many legends differently from

[1] *Smith, Dict. Biogr., s. v.*
[2] *Dion. Hal., Jud. de Thucyd.*, 23.
[3] *Bekker, Anecd.*, p. 781.
[4] *Müller*, p. 261.

Hesiod, and in the tone of the Orphic theologers of his own time. The fragments of Acusilaus have been published by Sturz, Geræ, 1787, 2d ed., Lips., 1824; and also in the *Museum Criticum*, vol. i., p. 216, *seqq.*, Camb., 1826; and in Didot's *Fragmenta Histor. Græc.*, by C. and T. Müller, vol. i., p. 100, *seqq.*, Paris, 1841.

IX. HECATÆUS (Ἑκαταῖος)[1] of Miletus, the Ionian, was a man of a very different character of mind from the preceding. He belonged to a very ancient and illustrious family. We have only a few particulars of his life. In B.C. 500 he endeavored to dissuade his countrymen from revolting from the Persians; and when this advice was disregarded, he gave them some sensible counsel respecting the conduct of the war, which was also neglected. Previous to this, Hecatæus had visited Egypt and many other countries. He survived the Persian wars, and appears to have died about B.C. 476.[2] Hecatæus wrote two works: 1. Περίοδος γῆς, or Περιήγησις, divided into two parts, one of which contained a description of Europe, and the other of Asia, Egypt, and Libya. Both parts were subdivided into smaller sections, which are sometimes quoted under their respective names, such as Hellespontus, &c. 2. Γενεαλογίαι, or Ἱστορίαι, in four books, containing an account of the poetical fables and traditions of the Greeks. His work on geography was the more important, as it embodied the results of his numerous travels. Herodotus knew the works of Hecatæus, and frequently controverts his opinions. Hecatæus wrote in the Ionic dialect, in a pure and simple style, which sometimes became animated through the vividness of his descriptions. The fragments of his works have been collected by Clausen, *Hecatæi Milesii Fragmenta*, Berlin, 1831, and are also given in Didot's *Fragmenta Histor. Græc.*, by C. and T. Müller, vol. i., p. 1, *seqq.*, Paris, 1841.

X. PHERECȲDES (Φερεκύδης) of Leros, a small island near Miletus, also wrote on genealogies and mythical history, but did not extend his labors to geography and ethnography. He is sometimes called the Athenian, from having spent the greater part of his life at Athens.[3] He flourished about the time of the Persian war. His writings comprehended a great portion of the mythical traditions; and, in particular, he gave a copious account, in a separate work, of the ancient times of Athens. He was much consulted by the later mythographers, and his numerous fragments must still serve as the basis of many mythological inquiries. By following a genealogical line, he was led from Philæus, the son of Ajax, down to Miltiades, the founder of the sovereignty in the Chersonesus. He thus found an opportunity of describing the campaign of Darius against the Scythians, concerning which we have a valuable fragment of his history.[4] The fragments of Pherecydes have been collected by Sturz, *Pherecydis Fragmenta*, Lips., 1824, 2d ed.; and they are also given in Didot's *Fragmenta Histor. Græc.*, by C. and T. Müller, vol. i., p. 70, *seqq.*, Paris, 1841.

XI. CHARON (Χάρων),[5] a native of Lampsacus, a Milesian colony, also belongs to this generation, although he mentioned some events which fell

[1] *Müller*, p. 261.
[2] *Smith, Dict. Biogr.*, *s. v.*
[3] *Vossius, De Hist. Græcis*, p. 24, ed. *Westermann.*
[4] *Suid.*, *s. v.*; *Müller*, p. 263.
[5] *Müller*, p. 263.

in the beginning of the reign of Artaxerxes, B.C. 465.[1] Charon continued the researches of Hecatæus into Eastern ethnography. He wrote (as was the custom of these early historians) separate works upon Persia, Libya, Ethiopia, &c. He also subjoined the history of his own time, and he preceded Herodotus in narrating the events of the Persian war, although Herodotus nowhere mentions him. From the fragments of his writings which remain, it is manifest that his relation to Herodotus was that of a day chronicler to a historian, under whose hands every thing acquires life and character. Charon wrote, besides, a chronicle of his own country, as several of the early historians did, who were thence called *Horographers* (Ὡρογράφοι). The fragments of Charon, together with those of Hecatæus and Xanthus, have been published by Creuzer, *Hist. Græc. Antiquiss. Fragmenta*, Heidelb., 1806, 8vo, and also in Didot's *Fragm. Histor. Græc.*, by C. and T. Müller, vol. i., p. 32, *seqq.*, Paris, 1841.

XII. Hellanīcus (Ἑλλάνικος)[2] of Mytilene, in the island of Lesbos, was almost a contemporary of Herodotus, since we know that at the beginning of the Peloponnesian war he was sixty-five years old,[3] and still continued to write. The character of Hellanīcus as a mythographer and historian is essentially different from that of the early chroniclers, such as Acusilaus and Pherecydes. He has far more the character of a learned compiler, whose object is not merely to note down events, but to arrange his materials, and to correct the errors of others. Besides a number of writings upon particular legends and local fables, he composed a work entitled "the Priestesses of Juno of Argos," in which the women who had filled this priesthood were enumerated up to a very remote period (on no better authority than of certain obscure traditions), and various striking events of the heroic times were arranged in chronological order, according to this series. Another work, the *Carneonīcæ* (Καρνεονῖκαι), contained a list of the victors in the musical and poetical contests of the *Carnea* at Sparta. It was, therefore, one of the first attempts at literary history. Hellanicus was a very prolific writer, and, if we were to look upon all the titles that have come down to us as titles of genuine productions and distinct works, their number would amount to nearly thirty. But the recent investigations of Preller[4] have shown that several works bearing his name are spurious and of later date, and that many others, which are referred to as separate works, are only chapters or sections of other productions. Among the works deemed spurious, we may mention the accounts of Phœnicia, Persia, and Egypt, and also a description of a journey to the oracle of Jupiter Ammon. Thucydides[5] charges Hellanicus with want of accuracy in chronology. In his geographical view, also, he seems to have been greatly dependent upon his predecessors, and gave, for the most part, what he found in them. But the censure for falsehood, and the like, bestowed on him by such writers as Ctesias,[6] Theopompus,[7] Ephorus,[8] and Strabo,[9] is evidently one-sided, and should not bias us in

[1] *Smith, Dict. Biogr.*, *s. v.*; *Plut.*, *Themist.*, 27. [2] *Müller*, p. 264.
[3] *Pamphila ap. Gell.*, xv., 23. [4] *De Hellanico Lesbio Historico, Dorpat*, 1840, 4to.
[5] *Thucyd.*, i., 97. [6] *Ctes. ap. Phot.*, *Bibl. Cod.*, 72. [7] *Theopomp. ap. Strab.*, p. 43.
[8] *Ephor. ap. Joseph. c. Apion.*, i., 3. [9] *Strab.*, x., p. 541; xi., p. 508; xiii., p. 602.

forming our judgment of his merits or demerits as a writer; for there can be no doubt that he was a learned and diligent compiler, and that, so far as his sources went, he was a trustworthy one. The fragments of Hellanicus have been collected by Sturz, *Hellanici Lesbii Fragmenta*, Lips., 1826, and by C. and T. Müller, in Didot's *Fragm. Hist. Gr.*, vol. i., p. 45, *seqq.*, Paris, 1841.

XIII. Among the historical writers that remain, the most celebrated, and the only one deserving of mention, is Xanthus[1] (Ξάνθος), the Lydian. Suidas makes him to have been a native of Sardis, but this point is a doubtful one, as is also the period when he flourished. His date, however, is commonly fixed by modern scholars at B.C. 499. Xanthus, though a Lydian by birth, received a Greek education, and wrote a history of Lydia in that language, of which some considerable fragments have come down to us. The genuineness of the work, however, which went under his name, was questioned by some of the ancient grammarians themselves, and at the present day, also, opinions are divided. Among modern scholars, Creuzer, in his edition of the fragments of Xanthus, has maintained the genuineness of the work, while Welcker has constructed an elaborate argument against it.[2] C. Müller adopts the opinion of Welcker. It is certain that much of the matter in the extant fragments is spurious; and the probability appears to be that the work from which they are taken is the production of an Alexandrean grammarian, founded upon the genuine work of Xanthus. C. Müller has pointed out those passages which, in his opinion, are most probably portions of the original work. They are of great value. A work on the Magian religion (Μαγικά) was also ascribed to Xanthus, but was indubitably spurious. The fragments of Xanthus are collected in Creuzer's *Histor. Græc. Antiquiss. Fragmenta*, Heidelb., 1806, and by C. and T. Müller, in Didot's *Fragm. Hist. Græc.*, vol. i., p. xx., *seqq.*; p. 36, *seqq.*, Paris, 1841.

XIV. To the Greek historical writers before Herodotus modern scholars have given the common name of *logographers* (λογογράφοι), which is applied by Thucydides[3] to all historians previous to himself, including thus even Herodotus in the number. The appellation is a convenient one, though perhaps not very correct; for the term had not so limited a meaning as this among the ancients, since λόγος signifies any discourse in prose, and accordingly the Athenians gave the name to persons who wrote judicial speeches or pleadings, and sold them to those who were in want of them. These persons were also called λογοποιοί. Be this, however, as it may, the term logographer, as applied to the historical writers previous to Herodotus, is meant to indicate a class of persons who seem to have aimed more at amusing their hearers or readers than at imparting accurate historical knowledge. They described in prose the mythological subjects and traditions which had previously been treated of by the epic, and especially by the cyclic poets. The omissions in the narratives of their predecessors were probably filled up by traditions derived from other quarters, in order to produce, at least in form, a con-

---

[1] *Smith, Dict. Biogr.*, *s. v.*

[2] *Seebode, Archiv.*, 1830, p. 70, *seqq.*

[3] *Thucyd.*, i., 21.

nected history. In many cases, as we have already seen, they were mere collections of local and genealogical traditions.[1] The first Greek to whom the title of historian properly and truly belonged was *Herodotus*, the *Homer* of history.

CHAPTER XXI.

THIRD OR EARLY PROSAIC PERIOD—*continued*.

HERODOTUS.[2]

Herodotus (Ἡρόδοτος), the earliest Greek historian (in the true sense of the term), was, according to his own statement at the beginning of his work, a native of Halicarnassus, a Doric city in Caria, which, at the time of his birth, was governed by Artemisia, a vassal-queen of the great king of Persia. Our information respecting the life of Herodotus is extremely scanty, since, besides the meagre and confused article of Suidas, there are only one or two passages of ancient writers that contain any direct notice of the life and age of the historian, and the rest must be gleaned from his own work. He was born about B.C. 484. His family was one of the most distinguished in Halicarnassus, and thus became involved in the civil commotions of the city. Artemisia had been succeeded by her son Pisindelis, and he, in his turn, by his son Lygdamis. This last-mentioned ruler was hostile to the family of Herodotus. He put to death Panyasis,[3] who was probably the maternal uncle of the historian, and who will be mentioned hereafter as one of the restorers of epic poetry; and he obliged Herodotus himself to take refuge abroad. His flight must have taken place at an early age. Müller places it about B.C. 452, but this is too late a period. Herodotus repaired to Samos, the Ionic island, where probably some of his kinsmen resided, since Panyasis, too, is called a Samian. In Samos, he cultivated the Ionic dialect, and here too he imbibed the Ionic spirit which pervades his history. Before he was thirty years of age, he joined in an attempt made from Samos to effect the liberation of his native city from the yoke of Lygdamis. The attempt proved successful; but the banishment of the tyrant did not give tranquillity to Halicarnassus, and Herodotus, who himself had become an object of dislike, again left his native country, and settled at Thurii, in Magna Græcia, where, excepting the intervals of his travels, he spent the remainder of his life. Whether he went to Thurii with the first Athenian colonists, in B.C. 445, or whether he followed afterward, is a disputed point. The better opinion appears to be that he did not go with the first settlers to Thurii, but followed them many years after, perhaps about the time of the death of Pericles. The grounds for this opinion are a passage in his own work (v., 77), from which we must, in all probability, infer that in B.C. 431, the year of the outbreak of the Peloponnesian war, he was at Athens, for it appears from that passage that he saw

---

[1] *Thirlwall, Hist. Gr.*, ii., p. 126, *seqq.*; *Müller, Hist. Gr. Lit.*, p. 206, *seqq.*

[2] *Smith, Dict. Biogr.*, *s. v.*; *Müller, Hist. Gr. Lit.*, p. 266, *seqq.*

[3] *Suid.*, *s. v.* Πανύασις.

the Propylæa, which were not completed till the year in which that war began; and also the circumstance of his being well acquainted with and adopting the principles of policy followed by Pericles and his party, which leads us to the belief that he witnessed the disputes at Athens between Pericles and his opponents.[1]

The time when Herodotus wrote his history has been a matter of considerable discussion; the following, however, may be regarded as the fairest view of the case. The narrative of the Persian war, which forms the main substance of the whole work, breaks off with the victorious return of the Greek fleet from the coast of Asia, and the taking of Sestos by the Athenians, in B.C. 479. But numerous events, which belong to a much later period, are alluded to or mentioned incidentally, and the latest of them refers to the year B.C. 408, when Herodotus was at least 77 years old. Hence it follows that, with Pliny, we must believe that Herodotus wrote his work in his old age, during his stay at Thurii, where, according to Strabo, he also died and was buried, for no one mentions that he ever returned to Greece, or that he made two editions of his work, as some modern critics assume, who suppose that at Thurii he revised his work, and among other things introduced those parts which refer to later events. The whole work makes the impression of a fresh composition; there is no trace of labor or revision; it has all the appearance of having been written by a man at an advanced period of his life. Its abrupt termination, and the fact that the author does not tell us what in an earlier part of his work he distinctly promises (e. g., vii., 213), prove almost beyond a doubt that his work was the production of the last years of his life, and that death prevented his completing it. Had he not written it at Thurii, he would scarcely have been called a Thurian, or the Thurian historian, a name by which he is sometimes distinguished by the ancients.[2] There are, lastly, some passages in the work itself, which must suggest to every unbiased reader the idea that the author wrote somewhere in the south of Italy.[3]

Herodotus presents himself to our consideration in two points of view; as a traveller and observer, and as an historian. The extent of his travels may be ascertained pretty clearly from his History, but the order in which he visited each place, and the time of visiting, can not be determined. His travels, however, must have occupied a considerable period of his life, and he would seem to have first entered upon them in the full strength of body and mind, and after having been completely educated. The story of his reading his work at the Olympic games, which has found its way into most modern narratives, has been ably discussed by Dahlmann,[4] and we may say disproved. This story is founded on a small piece by Lucian, entitled "Herodotus or Aëtion," which apparently was not intended by the writer himself as an historical truth; and, in addition to this, Herodotus was only about twenty-eight years old when he is said to have read to the assembled Greeks at Olympia a work which was the

---

1 *Smith, Dict. Biogr.*, *s. v.*

2 *Aristot.*, *Rhet.*, iii., 6; *Plut.*, *De Exil.*, 13; *De Malign. Herod.*, 35.

3 *Smith, Dict.*, *s. v.*

4 *Life of Herodotus*, p. 8, *seqq.*, Engl. transl

result of most extensive travelling and research, and which bears in every part of it evident marks of the hand of a man of mature age. Some critics have recourse to the supposition that what he recited at Olympia was only a sketch or a portion of his work; but this is in direct contradiction to the statement of Lucian, who asserts that he read the whole of the nine books, which, on that occasion, received the names of the Muses. If the story in question had been known at all in the time of Plutarch, this writer surely would not have passed it over in silence, when he tells of Herodotus having calumniated all the Greeks, except the Athenians, who had bribed him. There is one tradition, indeed, which mentions that Herodotus read his work at the Panathenaic festival at Athens, in B.C. 445 or 446, and that there existed at Athens a psephisma, granting to the historian a reward of ten talents from the public treasury.[1] This tradition, however, is not only in contradiction with the time when he must have written his work, but is evidently nothing more than part and parcel of the charge, which the author of that contemptible treatise on the Malignity of Herodotus makes against the historian, namely, that he was bribed by the Athenians. The source of all this calumnious scandal is nothing but the petty vanity of the Thebans, which was hurt by the truthful description of their conduct during the war against Persia.[2]

With a simplicity which characterizes his whole work, Herodotus makes no display of the great extent of his travels; and he is so free from the ordinary vanity of travellers, that, instead of acting a prominent part in his narrative, he very seldom appears at all in it. Hence it is impossible for us to give any thing like an accurate chronological succession of his travels. In Greece Proper, and on the coasts of Asia Minor, there is scarcely any place of importance with which he is not perfectly familiar from his own observation, and where he did not make inquiries respecting this or that particular point; we may mention more especially the oracular places, such as Dodona and Delphi. In many quarters of Greece, such as Samos, Athens, Thebes, and Corinth, he seems to have made a rather long stay. The spots where the great battles had been fought between the Greeks and barbarians, as Marathon, Thermopylæ, Salamis, and Platææ, were well known to him, and on the whole route which Xerxes and his army took, on their march from the Hellespont to Athens, there was probably not a place which he had not seen with his own eyes. He also visited most of the Greek islands, not only in the Ægean, but even those in the western waters of Greece, such as Zacynthus. As for his travels in foreign countries, we know that he sailed through the Hellespont, the Propontis, and crossed the Euxine in both directions; with the Palus Mæotis he was but imperfectly acquainted. He further visited Thrace[3] and Scythia.[4] The interior of Asia Minor, especially Lydia, was well known to him, and so was also Phœnicia. He visited Tyre for the special purpose of obtaining information respecting the worship of Hercules. Previous to this he had been in Egypt, for it was in Egypt that his curiosity respecting Hercules had been excited.[5]

[1] *Plut., De Malign. Herod.*, 26. [2] *Smith, l. c.* [3] ii., 103.
[4] iv., 76, 81. [5] *Smith, l. c.*

What Herodotus has done for the history of Egypt surpasses in importance every thing that was written in ancient times upon that country, although his account of it forms only an episode in his work. There is no reason for supposing that he made himself acquainted with the Egyptian language, which was, in fact, scarcely necessary on account of the numerous Greek settlers in Egypt, as well as on account of that large class of persons who made it their business to act as interpreters between the Egyptians and Greeks; and it appears that Herodotus was accompanied by one of these interpreters. He travelled to the south of Egypt, as far as Elephantine, every where forming connections with the priests, and gathering information upon the early history of the country and its relations to Greece. He saw with his own eyes all the wonders of Egypt, and the accuracy of his observations and descriptions still excites the astonishment of travellers in that country. The time at which he visited Egypt may be determined with tolerable accuracy. He was there shortly after the defeat of Inarus by the Persian general Megabyzus, which happened in B.C. 456; for he saw the battle-field still covered with the bones and skulls of the slain,[1] so that his visit to Egypt may be assigned to about B.C. 450. From Egypt he appears to have made excursions to the east into Arabia, and to the west into Libya, at least as far as Cyrene, which was well known to him. It is not impossible that he may have even visited Carthage. From Egypt he crossed over by sea to Tyre, and visited Palestine; that he saw the Rivers Euphrates and Tigris, and the city of Babylon, is quite certain.[2] From thence he seems to have travelled northward, for he saw the city of Ecbatana, which reminded him of Athens. There can be little doubt that he visited Susa also, but we can not trace him farther into the interior of Asia. His desire to increase his knowledge by travelling does not appear to have subsided even in his old age, for it would seem that during his residence at Thurii he visited several of the Greek settlements in Southern Italy and Sicily, though his knowledge of the west of Europe was very limited, for he strangely calls Sardinia the greatest of all islands.[3]

A second source from which Herodotus drew his information was the literature of his country, especially the poetical portion, for prose had not yet been cultivated very extensively, as we have just had occasion to observe. With the poems of Homer and Hesiod he was perfectly familiar, though he attributed less historical importance to them than might have been expected. He placed them about 400 years before his own time, with the paradoxical assertion that they had made the theogony of the Greeks, a subject to which we have alluded in a previous part of the present work. He was also acquainted with the poetry of Alcæus, Sappho, Simonides, Æschylus, and Pindar. He farther derived assistance from the Arimaspēa, the epic poem of Aristeas, and from the works of the historical writers or logographers who had preceded him, such as Hecatæus, though he worked with perfect independence of them, and occasionally corrected mistakes which they had committed; but his main sources, after all, were his own investigations and observations.[4]

[1] iii., 12. [2] i., 178, *seqq.*; i., 193. [3] i., 170; v., 106; vi., 2. [4] *Smith, l. c.*

The object of the work of Herodotus is to give an account of the struggles between the Greeks and Persians, from which the former, with the aid of the gods, came off victorious. The subject, therefore, is a truly national one, but the discussion of it, especially in the early part, led the author into various digressions and episodes, as he was sometimes obliged to trace to distant times the causes of the events he had to relate, or to give a history or description of a nation or country, with which, according to his view, the reader ought to be made familiar; and having once launched out into such a digression, he usually can not resist the temptation of telling the whole tale, so that most of his episodes form each an interesting and complete whole by itself. He traces the enmity between Europe and Asia to the mythical times. But he rapidly passes over the mythical ages to come to Crœsus, king of Lydia, who was known to have committed acts of hostility against the Greeks. This induces him to give a full history of Crœsus and the kingdom of Lydia. The conquest of Lydia by the Persians under Cyrus then leads him to relate the rise of the Persian monarchy, and the subjugation of Asia Minor and Babylon. The nations which are mentioned in the course of this narrative are again discussed more or less minutely. The history of Cambyses and his expedition into Egypt induce him to enter into the detail of Egyptian history. The expedition of Darius against the Scythians causes him to speak of Scythia and the north of Europe. The kingdom of Persia now extended from Scythia to Cyrene, and an army being called in by the Cyreneans against the Persians, Herodotus proceeds to give an account of Cyrene and Libya. In the mean time, the revolt of the Ionians breaks out, which eventually brings the contest between Persia and Greece to an end. An account of this insurrection, and of the rise of Athens after the expulsion of the Pisistratidæ, is followed by what properly constitutes the principal part of the work, and the history of the Persian war now runs on in a regular channel until the taking of Sestos.[1]

In this manner alone was it possible for Herodotus to give a record of the vast treasures of information which he had collected in the course of many years. But these digressions and episodes do not impair the plan and unity of the work, for one thread, as it were, runs through the whole, and the episodes are only like branches that issue from one and the same tree: each has its peculiar charms and beauties, and yet is manifestly no more than a part of one great whole. The whole structure of the history thus bears a strong resemblance to a grand epic poem. The work, however, has an abrupt termination, and is probably incomplete. This opinion is strengthened, on the one hand, by the fact that in one place the author promises to give the particulars of an occurrence in another part of his work, though the promise is nowhere fulfilled (vii., 213); and, on the other hand, by the story that a favorite of the historian, of the name of Plesirrhous, who inherited all his property, also edited the work after the author's death.[2] The division of the history into nine books, each bearing the name of a muse, was probably made by some

---

[1] *Smith, l. c.*

[2] *Ptol. Hephæst. ap. Phot., Bibl. Cod.*, 190.

grammarian, for there is no indication in the whole work of the division having been made by the author himself.[1]

There are two passages[2] in which Herodotus promises to write a history of Assyria, which was either to form a part of his great work, or to be an independent treatise by itself. Whether he ever carried his plan into effect is a question of considerable doubt; the probability is that he never did. Layard is wrong when he says, in the introduction to his work on Nineveh, that Aristotle[3] had seen this history of Assyria. Aristotle merely mentions a fact in natural history of which a certain author was ignorant, for that author, in his account of the taking of Nineveh, describes an eagle drinking. But the name of that author, in the best MSS., is Ἡσίοδος, which reading is retained by Bekker; and however it may seem more probable that Herodotus should have described the taking of Nineveh than Hesiod, yet, even if so, there is nothing to show that Aristotle did not cite from memory, or copy from some other less accurate writer.[4]

The life of Homer in the Ionic dialect, which was formerly attributed to Herodotus, and is printed at the end of several editions of his work, is now universally acknowledged to be a production of a later date, though it was undoubtedly written at a comparatively early period, and contains some valuable information.

It now remains to add a few remarks[5] on the character of the work of Herodotus, its importance as an historical authority, and its style and language. The whole work is pervaded by a profoundly religious idea, which distinguishes Herodotus from all other Greek historians. This idea is the strong belief in a divine power existing apart and independent of man and nature, which assigns to every being its sphere. This sphere no one is allowed to transgress without disturbing the order which has existed from the beginning in the moral world, no less than in the physical; and by disturbing this order,man brings about his own destruction. This divine power is, in the opinion of Herodotus, the cause of all external events, although he does not deny the free activity of man, or establish a blind law of fate or necessity. The divine power with him is rather the manifestation of eternal justice, which keeps all things in a proper equilibrium, assigns to each being its path, and keeps it within its bounds. Where it punishes overweening haughtiness and insolence, it assumes the character of the divine Nemesis, and nowhere in history had Nemesis overtaken and chastised the offender more obviously than in the contest between Greece and Asia. When Herodotus speaks of the *envy of the gods* (φθόνος τῶν θεῶν), as he often does, we must understand this divine Nemesis, who appears sooner or later to pursue or destroy him who, in frivolous insolence and conceit, raises himself above his proper sphere. Herodotus every where shows the most profound reverence for every thing which he conceives as divine, and rarely ventures to express an opinion on what he considers a sacred or religious mystery, though now and then he can not refrain from expressing a doubt in regard to the

[1] *Smith, l. c.*
[2] i., 106, 184.
[3] *Aristot., De An.*, viii., 18.
[4] *London Quarterly Review*, vol. lxxxiv., p. 138, note.
[5] *Smith, l. c.*

correctness of the popular belief of his countrymen, commonly owing to the influence which the Egyptian priests exercised on his mind, but in general his good sense and sagacity were too strong to allow him to be misled by vulgar notions and errors.[1]

It would be vain to deny that Herodotus was, to a certain extent, credulous, and related things without putting to himself the question as to whether they were possible at all or not; his political knowledge, and his acquaintance with the laws of nature, were equally deficient; and, owing to these deficiencies, he frequently does not rise above the rank of a mere story-teller, a title which Aristotle bestows upon him.[2] But, notwithstanding all this, it is evident that he had formed a high notion of the dignity of history; and, in order to realize his idea, he exerted all his powers, and cheerfully went through more difficult and laborious preparations than any other historian either before or after him. In order to form a fair judgment of the historical value of the work of Herodotus, we must distinguish those parts in which he speaks from his own observation, or gives the results of his own investigations, from those in which he merely repeats what he was told by priests, interpreters, guides, and the like. In the latter case he undoubtedly was often deceived; but he never intrudes such reports as any thing more than they really are; and, under the influence of his natural good sense, he very frequently cautions his reader by some such remark as "I know this only from hearsay," or "I have been told so, but do not believe it." The same caution should guide us in his account of the early history of the Greeks, on which he touches only in episodes, for he is generally satisfied with some one tradition, without entering into any critical examination or comparison with other traditions, which he silently rejects. But, wherever he speaks from his own observation, Herodotus is a real model of truthfulness and accuracy; and the more those countries of which he treats have been explored by modern travellers, the more firmly has his authority been established.[3]

The dialect in which Herodotus wrote is the Ionic, intermixed with epic or poetical expressions, and sometimes even with Attic and Doric forms. This peculiarity of his language called forth a number of lexicographical works of learned grammarians, all of which are lost, with the exception of a few remnants in the Homeric glosses (λέξεις). The excellencies of his style do not consist in any artistic or melodious structure of his sentences, but in the antique and epic coloring, the transparent clearness, the lively flow of his narrative, the natural and unaffected gracefulness, and the occasional signs of carelessness. There is, perhaps, no work in the whole range of ancient literature which so closely resembles a familiar and homely oral narration as that of Herodotus. Its reader can not help feeling as though he was listening to an old man, who, from the inexhaustible stores of his knowledge and experience, tells his stories with that single-hearted simplicity and *naïveté* which are the marks and indications of a truthful spirit.[4]

[1] *Smith, l. c.* [2] *Aristot., De Animal. Gener.*, iii., 5. [3] *Smith, l c.*
[4] *Smith, l. c.* Compare *Dahlmann, Life of Herodotus*, p. 127, *seqq.*, Eng. transl.

Notwithstanding, however, all the merits and excellencies of Herodotus, there were, as we have already remarked, certain writers of antiquity who attacked the historian on very serious points, both in regard to the form and the substance of his work. Besides Ctesias, Ælius Harpocration, Manetho, and one Pollio, are mentioned as authors of works against Herodotus; but all of them have perished, with the exception of one bearing the name of Plutarch, and entitled Περὶ τῆς Ἡροδότου Κακοηθείας, "On the Malignity of Herodotus," which is full of the most futile accusations of every kind. It is written in a mean and malignant spirit, and is probably the work of some young rhetorician or sophist, who composed it as an exercise in polemics or controversy.[1]

EDITIONS OF HERODOTUS.

Herodotus was first published in a Latin translation by Laurentius Valla, Venice, 1474; and the first edition of the Greek original is that of Aldus Manutius, Venice, 1502, fol., which was followed by two Basle editions, in 1541 and 1557, fol. The text is greatly corrected in the edition of H. Stephens, Paris, 1570 and 1592, fol., which was followed by that of Jungermann, Frankfort, 1608, fol., reprinted at Geneva in 1618, and at London in 1679, fol. The edition of James Gronovius, Leyden, 1715, fol., has a peculiar value, from his having made use of the excellent Medicean MS.; but it was greatly surpassed by the edition of P. Wesseling and L. C. Valckenaer, Amsterdam, 1763, fol. Both the language and the matter are there treated with great care; and the learned apparatus of this edition, with the exception of the notes of Gronovius, was afterward incorporated in the edition of Schweighaeuser, Strasburg and Paris, 1806, 6 vols. in 12 parts (reprinted in London, 1824, in 6 vols., and again in 1830, in 5 vols. 8vo), with a valuable *Lexicon Herodoteum*. The editor had compared several new MSS., and was thus enabled to give a text greatly superior to that of his predecessors. The best edition after this is that of Gaisford, Oxford, 1824, 4 vols. 8vo, who incorporated in it nearly all the notes of Wesseling, Valckenaer, and Schweighaeuser, and also made a collation of some English MSS. A reprint of this edition appeared at Leipzig in 1824, 4 vols. 8vo. The last great edition, in which the subject-matter also is considered with reference to modern discoveries, is that of Bähr, Leipzig, 1830, &c., 4 vols. 8vo. An edition with valuable English notes has been commenced in the *Bibliotheca Classica*, under the superintendence of Professor Long, London, 8vo. A revised text, with Latin translation, and a valuable dissertation on the Ionic dialect by W. Dindorf, forms one of the volumes of Didot's Bibliotheca Græca, Paris, 1844, royal 8vo. Among the school editions, which are numerous, we may especially mention those of Matthiæ, Leipzig, 1825, 2 vols. 8vo; Steger, Gissæ, 1827–29, 3 vols. 8vo; Long, London, 1830, 8vo; Bekker, Berlin, 1833 and 1837, 8vo; Stocker, London, 1843, 2 vols. 12mo, 2d ed., containing merely a continuous history of the Persian wars; and that of Lhardy, in the collection of Haupt and Sauppe, Leipzig, 1850, &c., 12mo.

To these may be added the translation of Larcher's Notes by Cooley, London, 1844, 2 vols. 8vo, and a selected commentary on the whole of Herodotus by Dawson Turner, Oxford, 1848, 8vo.

---

[1] *Smith, l. c.* On the whole subject of the Life and Writings of Herodotus, consult the excellent work of Dahlmann just cited.

CHAPTER XXII.

FOURTH OR ATTIC PERIOD.

INTRODUCTORY REMARKS.[1]

I. GREEK literature, so far as we have hitherto followed its progress, was a common property of the different races of the nation; each race cultivating that species of composition which was best suited to its dispositions and capacities, and impressing on it a corresponding character. In this manner the city of Miletus in Ionia, the Æolians in the island of Lesbos, the colonies in Magna Græcia and Sicily, as well as the Greeks of the mother country, created new forms of poetry and eloquence. The various sorts of excellence thus produced did not, after the age of the Homeric poetry, remain the exclusive property of the race among which they originated. A *national literature* was early formed; every literary work in the Greek language, in whatever dialect it might be composed, was enjoyed by the whole Greek nation.

II. But the literature of Greece necessarily assumed a different form, when Athens, raised as well by her political power and other external circumstances as by the mental qualities of her citizens, acquired the rank of a *Capital* of Greece with respect to literature and art. Not only was her copious native literature received with admiration by all the Greeks, but her judgment and taste were predominant in all things relating to language and the arts, and decided what should be generally recognized as the classical literature of Greece, long before the Alexandrine critics had prepared their canons. There is, in fact, no more important epoch in the history of the Greek intellect than the time when Athens obtained this pre-eminence over her sister states.

III. The character of the Athenians peculiarly fitted them to take this lead. Energy in action and cleverness in the use of language were the qualities which most distinguished the Athenians in comparison with the other Greeks, and which are most clearly seen in their political conduct and their literature. The consciousness of dexterity in the use of words, which the Athenians cultivated more than the other Greeks, induced them to subject every thing to discussion. Hence, too, arose a copiousness of speech, very striking as compared with the brevity of the early Greeks; a copiousness which subsequently displayed itself in so marked a degree both in the field of literature and the arena of eloquence, though chastened at the same time, and stripped of all false and meretricious ornament by the severity of Attic taste.

IV. Before the Persian war, however,[2] Athens had contributed less than many other cities, her inferiors in magnitude and in political importance, to the intellectual progress of Greece. She had produced no artists

[1] *Müller, Hist. Gr. Lit.*, p. 275, *seqq.*
[2] *Thirlwall, Hist. Gr.*, vol. iii., p. 28, ed. 1846, 8vo.

to be compared with those of Argos, Corinth, Sicyon, Ægina, Laconia, and of many cities both in the eastern and western colonies. She could boast of no poets so celebrated as those of the Ionian and Æolian schools. But her peaceful glories quickly followed, and outshone her victories, conquests, and political ascendency. In the period between the Persian and the Peloponnesian wars, both literature and the fine arts began to tend toward Athens, as their most favored seat. For here, above all other parts of Greece, genius and talents were encouraged by an ample field of exertion, by public sympathy and applause, as well as by the prospect of other rewards, which, however, were much more sparingly bestowed. Accordingly, it was at Athens that architecture and sculpture reached the highest degree of perfection which either ever attained in the ancient world, and that Greek poetry was enriched with a new kind of composition, the drama, which united the leading features of every species before cultivated in a new whole, and exhibited all the grace and vigor of the Greek imagination, together with the full compass and the highest refinement of the form of the language peculiar to Attica.[1]

V. The Drama, indeed, was the branch of literature which peculiarly signalized the age of Pericles. The steps by which it was brought through a series of innovations to the form which it presents in its earliest extant remains are still a subject of controversy among antiquarians; and even the poetical character of the authors by whom these changes were effected, and also of their works, is involved in great uncertainty. We have reason to believe that it was no want of merit or of absolute worth which caused them to be neglected and forgotten, but only the superior attraction of the form which the drama finally assumed.[2]

VI. We now proceed to the history of the Drama, its origin and progress, and will endeavor to show how the utmost beauty and elegance were gradually developed out of rude, stiff, antique forms:

I. ORIGIN OF TRAGEDY.[3]

VII. The Tragedy (τραγῳδία) of the ancient Greeks, as well as their Comedy (κωμῳδία), confessedly originated in the worship of Dionysus or Bacchus. This worship was of a two-fold character, corresponding to the different conceptions which were anciently entertained of Dionysus, as the changeable god of flourishing, decaying, or renovated nature, and the various fortunes to which in that character he was considered to be subject at the different seasons of the year.

VIII. Hence the festivals of Dionysus at Athens and elsewhere were all solemnized in the months nearest to the shortest day, coincidently with the changes going on in the course of nature, and by which his worshippers conceived the god himself to be affected. His mournful or joyous fortunes, his mystical death, symbolizing the death of all vegetation in the winter, and his birth[4] indicating the renovation of all nature in the spring, and his struggles in passing from one state to another, were not only represented and sympathized in by the dithyrambic singers and

---

1 *Thirlwall, l. c.*

2 *Id.*

3 *Müller, Hist. Gr. Lit.*, p. 288; *Smith, Dict. Ant.*, *s. v.*

4 *Plat., De Leg.*, iii., p. 700.

dancers, but they also carried their enthusiasm so far as to fancy themselves under the influence of the same events as the god himself, and, in their attempts to identify themselves with him and his fortunes, assumed the character of the subordinate divinities, the Satyrs, Nymphs, and Panes, who formed the mythological train of the god.

IX. Hence arose the custom of the disguise of satyrs being taken by the worshippers at the festivals of Dionysus; from the choral songs and dances of whom the Grecian tragedy originated, being from its commencement connected with the public rejoicings and ceremonies of Dionysus in *cities*, while comedy was more a sport and merriment of the country festivals. In fact, the very name of *Tragedy* (τραγῳδία), far from signifying any thing mournful or pathetic, is most probably derived from the goat-like appearance of the satyrs, who sang or acted with mimetic gesticulations (ὄρχησις) the old Bacchic songs, with Silenus, the constant companion of Dionysus, for their leader.[1] From their resemblance in dress and action to goats, they were sometimes called τράγοι, and their song τραγῳδία, "the goat-song." According to another opinion, the word τραγῳδία was first coined from the goat that was the prize for the best ode or song in honor of Dionysus.[2] This derivation, however, as well as another, connecting it with the goat offered on the altar of the god, around which the chorus sang, is not equally supported by either the etymological principles of the language or the analogous instance of κωμῳδία, "the revel-song."[3]

X. But the Dionysian dithyrambs were not always of a gay and joyous character: they were capable of expressing the extremes of sadness and wild lamentation, as well as the enthusiasm of joy; and it was from the dithyrambic songs of a mournful cast, probably sung originally in the winter months, that the stately and solemn tragedy of the Greeks arose. It must be borne in mind, however, that in the most ancient times the dithyrambic song was not executed by a regular chorus. A crowd of worshippers, under the influence of wine, danced up to and around a blazing altar, led probably by a flute-player, the subject of the song being, as already remarked, the birth and adventures of Dionysus.[4] It is a reasonable conjecture that the coryphæus, or leader of this irregular chorus, occasionally assumed the character of the god himself, while the rest of the train or comus represented his noisy band of thyrsus-bearing followers.[5]

XI. The first improvement in the mode of performing the dithyramb was introduced by Arion, a celebrated citharœdus of Methymna in Lesbos, who flourished in the days of Stesichorus and Periander, and to whom we have already alluded. He is generally admitted to have been the inventor of the *Cyclic chorus* (κύκλιος χορός), in which the dithyramb was danced, after a more regular fashion, around the blazing altar by a band of fifty men or boys, to a lyric accompaniment. The idea seems to have been borrowed by him from the Dorian choral odes, with their regular lyric movements, since Arion travelled extensively in the Dorian states

[1] *Bode, Gesch. d. Hell. Dichtk.*, vol. iii., p. 31.
[2] *Bentley, Phalar.*, p. 249.
[3] *Etym. Mag.*, p. 764; *Eurip., Bacch.*, 131; *Ælian, V. H.*, iii., 40.
[4] *Plat., Leg.*, iii., p. 700, *B.*
[5] *Donaldson, Theatre of the Greeks*, p. 25, 6th ed.

of Hellas, and had ample opportunities of observing the varieties of choral worship, and of introducing any improvement which he might wish to make in it.[1]

XII. Previous to the time of Arion, the leaders of the wild, irregular comus, which danced the dithyramb, bewailed the sorrows of Bacchus, or commemorated his wonderful birth in spontaneous effusions, accompanied by suitable action, for which they trusted to the inspiration of the wine-cup. This is the meaning of Aristotle's assertion, that this primitive Tragedy was "extemporaneous" (αὐτοσχεδιαστική).[2] Arion, however, by composing regular poems to be sung to the lyre, at once raised the dithyramb to a literary position, and laid the foundations of the stately superstructure which was afterward erected. He turned the comus also, or moving crowd of worshippers, into a standing chorus, of the same kind as that which gave Stesichorus his surname. He was the inventor, also, of the *tragic style* (τραγικοῦ τρόπου εὑρετής), that is, he introduced a style of music or harmony adapted to and intended for a chorus of Satyrs.

XIII. Next in order was Thespis, the celebrated contemporary of Pisistratus, to whom the invention of Greek tragedy has been generally ascribed. He was born at Icarius,[3] an Attic deme,[4] at the beginning of the sixth century B.C.[5] His birth-place derived its name, according to tradition, from the father of Erigone;[6] it had always been a seat of the religion of Bacchus, and the origin of Athenian tragedy and comedy has been confidently referred to the drunken festivals of the place; indeed, it is not improbable that the name itself may point to the old mimetic exhibitions which were common there.[7]

XIV. Thespis is said to have introduced an actor for the sake of affording an interval of rest to the Dionysian chorus.[8] The actor was called ὑποκριτής, from ὑποκρίνεσθαι, "to answer," because he answered, as it were, the songs of the chorus. This actor was generally, perhaps always, the poet himself. He invented a disguise for the face by means of a pigment, prepared from the herb purslain; and afterward constructed a linen mask, in order, probably, that he might be able to sustain more than one character.[9] He is also said to have introduced some important alterations into the dances of the chorus, and his figures were known in the days of Aristophanes.[10] He did not, however, as an actor, confine his speech to mere narration; he addressed it to the chorus, which carried on with him, by means of its leaders, a sort of dialogue. The chorus, when not dancing, stood upon the steps of the *thymĕle* (θυμέλη), or altar of Bacchus; and in order that he might address them from an equal elevation, he was placed upon a table (ἐλεός),[11] which was thus the predecessor of the stage, between which and the thymele, in later times, there was always an intervening space. The wagon of Thespis, of which Horace writes, must

---

1 *Donaldson*, p. 29.
2 *Aristot.*, *Poet.*, c. 4.
3 *Suid.*, *s. v.*
4 *Leake*, *Demi of Attica*, p. 194.
5 Bentley, however, fixes the time of Thespis's first exhibition at 536 B.C.
6 *Steph. Byz.*, *s. v.* Ἰκαρία; *Hygin.*, *Fab.*, 130.
7 *Athen.*, ii., p. 40; *Donaldson*, p. 47.
8 *Diog. Laert.*, ii., 66.
9 *Welcker*, *Nachtrag*, p. 271; *Thirlwall*, *Hist. Gr.*, vol. ii., p. 126.
10 *Vesp.*, 1479.
11 *Welcker*, *Nachtrag*, p. 248.

have arisen from some confusion between this standing-place for the actor and the wagon of Susarion.[1]

XV. The custom introduced by Thespis was continued by Phrynichus. But as it was clear that, if the chorus took an active and independent part in such a play, it would have been obliged to leave its original and characteristic sphere, Æschylus, in consequence, added a second actor, so that the action and the dialogue became now independent of the chorus, and the dramatist, at the same time, had an opportunity of showing two persons in contrast with each other on the stage. A third actor was added by Sophocles; and it is said that Cratinus was the first to make this addition in comedy. A fourth actor, except, perhaps, in the *Œdipus Coloneus*,[2] was never added; but if a fourth character had to be introduced, one of the three present on the stage retired, and came in again personating this fourth one. Any number of mutes, however, might appear upon the stage.

XVI. The three regular actors were distinguished by the technical names of *πρωταγωνιστής*, *δευτεραγωνιστής*, and *τριταγωνιστής*, which indicated the more or less prominent part which an actor had to perform in the drama. Certain conventional means were also devised, by which the spectators, at the moment an actor appeared on the stage, were enabled to judge which part he was going to perform. Thus the *protagonistes* always came on the stage from a door in the centre, the *deuteragonistes* from one on the right, and the *tritagonistes* from a door on the left hand side. The protagonistes was the principal hero or heroine of a play, in whom all the power and energy of the drama were concentrated; and whenever a Greek play is called after the name of one of its characters, it is always the name of the character sustained by the protagonistes. The female characters of a play were always performed by young men.

II. ORIGIN OF THE SATYRIC DRAMA.[3]

XVII. The first writer of satyric dramas was PRATINAS, of Phlius, a town not far from Sicyon. For some time previous to this poet, and probably as early as Thespis, tragedy had been gradually departing more and more from its old characteristics, and inclining to heroic fables, to which the chorus of satyrs was not a fit accompaniment. But the fun and merriment caused by them were too good to be lost, or displaced by the severe dignity of the Æschylean drama. Accordingly, the *satyric* drama, distinct from the recent and dramatic tragedy, but suggested by the sportive element of the old dithyramb, was founded by Pratinas, who, however, appears to have been surpassed in his own invention by Chœrilus.

XVIII. It was always written by tragedians, and generally three tragedies and one satyric piece were represented together, which, in some instances at least, formed a connected whole, called a *tetralogy* (*τετραλογία*). The satyric piece was acted last, so that the minds of the spectators were agreeably relieved by a merry after-piece, at the close of an earnest and

[1] *Welcker*, *Nachtrag*, p. 247; *Gruppe*, *Ariadne*, p. 122; *Donaldson*, p. 48.
[2] *Müller*, *Hist. Gr. Lit.*, p. 305. Consult, on the opposite side, *Donaldson*, p. 164.
[3] *Smith*, *Dict. Ant.*, *s. v. Tragœdia.*

engrossing tragedy. The distinguishing feature of this drama was the chorus of *satyrs*, in appropriate dresses and masks, and its subjects seem to have been taken from the same class of the adventures of Bacchus and of the heroes as those of tragedy; but, of course, they were so treated and selected, that the presence of rustic satyrs would seem appropriate. In their jokes, and drollery, and naïveté, consisted the merriment of the piece; for the kings and heroes who were introduced into their company were not of necessity thereby divested of their epic and legendary character, though they were obliged to conform to their situation, and suffer some diminution of dignity from their position. Hence the satyric drama is not unaptly called "a playful tragedy" (παίζουσα τραγῳδία), being both in form and materials the same as tragedy.[1]

XIX. It must, however, be observed, that there were some characters and legends which, as not presenting any serious or pathetic aspects, were not adapted for tragedy, and therefore were naturally appropriated to the Satyric drama. Such were Sisyphus, Autolycus, Circe, Callisto, Midas, Omphale, and the robber Sciron. Hercules, also, as he appears in Aristophanes (*Ranæ*) and in the Alcestis of Euripides, was a favorite subject of this drama, as being no unfit companion for a drunken Silenus and his crew.[2] The only extant satyric drama is the Cyclops of Euripides, though we possess numerous fragments of others. A list of satyric pieces is given by Welcker.[3]

III. REPRESENTATION OF GREEK PLAYS.[4]

XX. If the Greek plays themselves differed essentially from those of our own times, they were even more dissimilar in respect to the mode and circumstances of their representation. We have theatrical exhibitions of some kind every evening throughout the greater part of the year, and in capital cities many are going on at the same time in different theatres. In Greece, however, the dramatic performances were carried on for a few days only in the spring; the theatre was large enough to contain the whole population, and every citizen was there, as a matter of course, from daybreak to sunset.[5] With us, a successful play is repeated night after night, for months together; in Greece the most admired dramas were seldom repeated, and never in the same year. The theatre with us is merely a place of public entertainment; in Greece it was the temple of the god, whose altar was the central point of the semicircle of seats or steps from which some 30,000[6] of his worshippers gazed upon a spectacle instituted in his honor. Our theatrical costumes are intended to convey an idea of the dresses actually worn by the persons represented, while those of the Greeks were nothing but modifications of the festal robes worn in the Dionysian processions.[7] Finally, the modern playwright has only the approbation or disapprobation of his audience to look to, whereas no Greek play was represented until it had been approved by a board appointed to decide between the rival dramatists.

1 *Welcker, Nachtrag*, p. 331. 2 *Müller, Hist. Gr. Lit.*, p. 295. 3 *Nachtrag*, p. 284, *seqq.*
4 *Donaldson, Theatre of the Greeks*, p. 141, *seqq.* 5 *Æschin. c. Ctes.*, p. 488, *Bekker.*
6 *Plat., Sympos.*, p. 175, *E.* 7 *Müller, Eumeniden*, § 32; *Id., Hist. Gr. Lit.*, p. 296.

XXI. Theatrical exhibitions formed a part of certain festivals of Bacchus. In order, then, to ascertain at what time of the year they took place, we must inquire how many festivals were held in Attica in honor of that god, and then determine at which of them theatrical representations were given. There have been great diversities of opinion in regard to the number of the Attic Dionysia, or festivals of Bacchus. It appears, however, to be now pretty generally agreed among scholars that there were four Bacchic feasts, in the sixth, seventh, eighth, and ninth months respectively of the Attic year. These were the "country Dionysia," the "Lenæa," the "Anthesteria," and the "great Dionysia."

XXII. The "*country Dionysia*" (τὰ κατ' ἀγροὺς Διονύσια) were celebrated all over Attica in the month Poseideon, which included the latter half of December and the first half of January. This was the festival of the vintage, which is still in some places postponed to December.[1] The *Lenæa* (Λήναια), or festival of the wine-press, was held in the month Gamelion, which corresponded to part of January and February. It was, like the rural Dionysia, a vintage festival; but it differed from them in being confined to a particular spot in the city of Athens, called the *Lenæon*, where the first wine-press (ληνός) was erected. The *Anthesteria* (τὰ 'Ανθεστήρια, τὰ ἐν Λιμναῖς) were held on the eleventh, twelfth, and thirteenth days of the month Anthesterion, corresponding to part of February and March. This was not a vintage festival like the former two. The new wine was drawn from the cask on the first day of the feast (Πιθοίγια), and tasted on the second day (Χόες): the third day was called Χύτροι, on account of the banqueting which went on then. The *great Dionysia* (τὰ ἐν ἄστει, τὰ κατ' ἄστυ, τὰ ἀστικά) were celebrated between the eighth and eighteenth of the month Elaphebolion, corresponding to part of March and April. This festival is always meant when the Dionysia are mentioned without any qualifying epithet.

XXIII. At the first, second, and fourth of these festivals, it is known that theatrical exhibitions took place. The exhibitions at the country Dionysia were generally of old pieces; indeed, there is no instance of a play being acted on those occasions for the first time, at least after the Greek drama had arrived at perfection. At the Lenæa and the great Dionysia, both tragedies and comedies were performed;[2] at the latter, the tragedies, at least, were always new pieces; the instances in the *didascaliæ*, which have come down to us, of representations at the Lenæa are indeed always of new pieces, but from the manner in which the exhibition of new tragedies is mentioned in connection with the city festival, we must conclude that repetitions were allowed at the Lenæa, as well as at the country Dionysia. The month Elaphebolion may have been selected for the representation of new tragedies, because Athens was then full of the dependent allies, who came at that time to pay the tributes; whereas the Athenians alone were present at the Lenæa. It does not appear that there were any theatrical exhibitions at the Anthesteria; it is, however, at least probable that the tragedians read to a select audience at the Anthesteria the tragedies which they had composed for the

[1] *Philol. Mus.*, ii., p. 296.

[2] *Demosth.*, *Mid.*, p. 517.

festival in the following month, or perhaps contests took place then, and the intervening month was employed in perfecting the actors and chorus in their parts.[1]

XXIV. In considering next the *means* of performance, we must recall to mind the different origins of the two constituent parts of a Greek drama—the chorus and the dialogue. Choruses were originally composed of the whole population. When, however, in process of time, the fine arts became more cultivated, the duties of this branch of worship devolved upon a few, and ultimately upon one, who bore the whole expense, when paid actors were employed.[2] This person, who was called the *Choragus*, was considered as the religious representative of the whole people, and was said to do the state's work for it (λειτουργεῖν). It was the business of the choragus[3] to provide the chorus in all plays, whether tragic or comic, and also the lyric choruses of men and boys, cyclian dancers, &c.; he was selected by the managers of his tribe (ἐπιμεληταὶ φυλῆς) for the choragy which had come round to it. His first duty, after collecting his chorus, was to provide and pay a teacher (χοροδιδάσκαλος), who instructed them in the songs and dances which they had to perform, and it appears that the choragi drew lots for the first choice of teachers. The choragus had also to pay the musicians and singers who composed the chorus, and was allowed to press children, if their parents did not give them up of their own accord. He was obliged to lodge and maintain the chorus till the time of performance, and to supply the singers with such aliments as conduce to strengthen the voice.

XXV. In the laws of Solon, the age prescribed for the choragus was forty years; but this rule does not appear to have been long in force. The relative expense of the different choruses, in the time of Lysias, is given in a speech of that orator.[4] We learn from this that the tragic chorus cost nearly twice as much as the comic, though neither of the dramatic choruses was so expensive as the chorus of men, or the chorus of flute-players.[5] The actors were the representatives, not of the people, but of the poet; consequently, the choragus had nothing to do with them. If he had paid for them, the dramatic choruses would surely have exceeded in expensiveness all the others; besides, the actors were not allowed to the choragi, but to the poets; and were, therefore, paid either by these, or, as is more likely, by the state.

XXVI. When a dramatist had made up his mind to bring out a play, he applied, if he intended to represent at the Lenæa, to the king-archon, and if at the greater Dionysia, to the chief archon, for a chorus, which was given to him if his piece was considered worthy of it. Along with this chorus he received three actors by lot, and these he taught independently of the choragus, who confined his attentions to the chorus. If successful, he chose his own actors for the following year.[6] When the day appointed for the trial came on, they united their efforts, and endeavored

---

1 *Philol. Mus.*, ii., p. 292, *seqq.*

2 *Buttmann ad Demosth. Mid.*, p. 37.

3 *Böckh, Public Econ. of Athens*, vol. ii., p. 207, *seqq.*, Engl. transl.

4 *Lys.*, 'Απολ. δωροδ., p. 698; *Bentley*, *Phal.*, p. 360.

5 *Demosth.*, *Mid.*, p. 565.

6 *Hesych.*, *s. v.* νέμησις ὑποκριτῶν.

to gain the prize by a combination of the best-taught actors with the most sumptuously dressed and most diligently exercised chorus. That the exertions of the choragus and the actors were often as influential with the judges as the beauty of the poem, can not be doubted, when we have so many instances of the ill success of the best dramatists.

XXVII. The judges were appointed by lot, and were generally, but not always, five in number.[1] The archon administered an oath to them; and, in the case of the cyclian chorus, partiality or injustice was punishable by fine.[2] The successful poet was crowned with ivy (with which his choragus and performers were also adorned),[3] and his name was proclaimed before the audience. The choragus who had exhibited the best musical or theatrical entertainment generally received a tripod as a reward or prize. This he was at the expense of consecrating, and in some cases built the monument on which it was placed. Thus the beautiful choragic monument of Lysicrates, which is still standing at Athens, was undoubtedly surmounted by a tripod, and the statue of Bacchus, in a sitting posture, which was on the top of the choragic monument of Thrasyllus, probably supported the tripod on its knees. Such, at least, seems to have been the intention of the holes drilled in the lap of the figure. The choragus, in comedy, consecrated the equipments of his chorus. The successful poet commemorated his victory with a feast. As, however, no prize drama was permitted to be represented for a second time (with an exception in favor of the three great dramatists, which was not long in operation), the poet's glory was very transient. The time allowed for the representation was portioned out by the clepsydra, and seems to have been dependent upon the number of pieces represented. What this number was is not known. It is probable, however, that about three trilogies might have been represented on one day.

XXVIII. The place of exhibition was, in the days of the perfect Greek drama, the great stone theatre erected within the Lenæon, or inclosure sacred to Bacchus. The building was commenced in the year 500 B.C., but not finished until about 381 B.C., when Lycurgus was manager of the treasury. In the earlier days of the drama, the theatre was of wood, but an accident having occurred at the representation of some plays of Æschylus and Pratinas, the stone theatre was commenced in its stead.[4] The student who wishes to acquire an adequate notion of the Greek theatre must not forget that it was only an improvement upon the mode of representation adopted by Thespis, which it resembled in its general features. The two original elements were the θυμέλη, or altar of Bacchus, round which the cyclic chorus danced,[5] and the λογεῖον, or stage, from which the actor spoke; it was the representative of the wooden table from which the earliest actor addressed his chorus,[6] and was also called ὀκρίβας. But in the great stone theatres, in which the perfect Greek dramas were represented, these two simple materials for the exhibition of a play were

[1] *Maussac., Diss. Crit.*, p. 204.
[2] *Æschin. c. Ctes.*, § 85.
[3] *Blomfield, in Mus. Crit.*, ii., p. 88.
[4] *Liban., Arg. Demosth. Olynth.*, i.
[5] *Müller, Anhang zum Buch, Æsch. Eumen.*, p. 35.
[6] *Pollux*, iv., 123.

surrounded by a mass of buildings, and subordinated to other details of a very artificial and complicated description.

XXIX. In building a theatre,[1] the Greeks always availed themselves of the slope of a hill, which enabled them to give the necessary elevation to the back rows of seats, without those enormous substructions which we find in Roman theatres. If the hill was rocky, semicircles of steps, rising tier above tier, were hewn out of the living material. If the ground was soft, a similar excavation of certain dimensions was made in the slope of the hill, and afterward lined with rows of stone benches. Even when the former plan was practicable, the steps were frequently faced with copings of marble. This was the case with the theatre of Bacchus at Athens, which stood on the southeastern side of the rocky Acropolis. This semicircular pit, surrounded by seats on all sides but one, and in part filled by them, was called the *κοῖλον* (in Latin, *cavea*), and was assigned to the audience. At the top it was inclosed by a lofty portico and balustraded terrace (marked *c* in the subjoined plan):

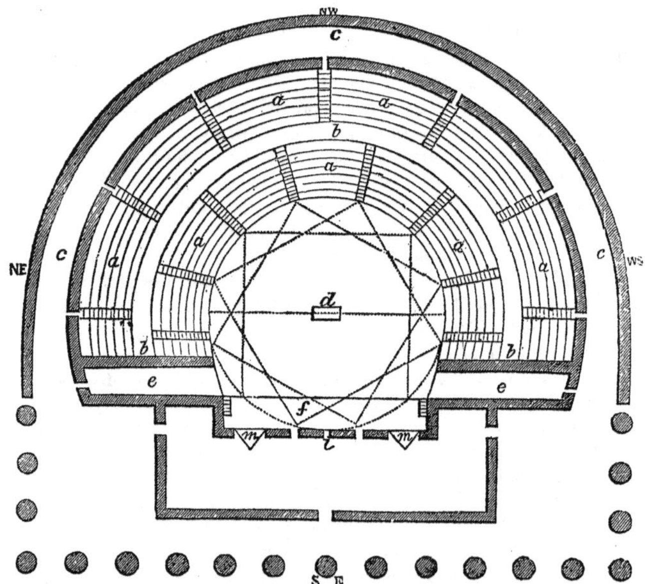

XXX. Concentric with this circular arc, and at the foot of the lowest range of seats, was the boundary line of the orchestra (*ὀρχήστρα*), or "dancing-place," which was given up to the chorus. If we complete the

[1] On the structure of ancient theatres generally, consult *Wieseler, Theatergebäude*, &c. Götting., 1851, 4to.

circle of the orchestra, and draw a tangent to it at the point most removed from the audience, this line will give the position of the scene, *σκηνή*, or "covered building," which presented to the view of the spectators a lofty façade of hewn stone, susceptible of such modifications as the different plays rendered suitable. In front of this scene was a narrow stage, called, therefore, the *προσκήνιον* (*proscenium*), and marked *f* in our plan. It was indicated by the parallel side of a square, inscribed in the orchestral circle, but extended to the full length of the scene on both sides. Another parallel, at a greater distance behind the scene, gave the portico, which formed the lower front of the whole building.

XXXI. The *κοῖλον*, or *cavea*, was divided into two or more flights of steps or seats by the *διαζώματα* (in Latin, *præcinctiones*), marked *bbb* on the plan, which were broad belts, concentric with the upper terrace, and with the boundary line of the orchestra, and which served both as lobbies and landings. The steps or seats of the *κοῖλον* were again subdivided transversely into masses called *κέρκιδες* (*cunei*), or "wedges," marked *aaa*, by stairs, *κλίμακες*, running from one *διάζωμα* to another, and converging to the centre of the orchestra. Different parts of the theatre received different names from the class of spectators to whom they were appropriated. Thus the lower seats, nearest to the orchestra, which were assigned to the members of the senate (*βουλή*) and others who had a right to reserved seats (*προεδρία*), were called the *βουλευτικὸς τόπος*,[1] and, again, the young men sat together in the *ἐφηβικὸς τόπος*.[2] The spectators entered either from the hill above by door-ways in the upper portico, or by staircases in the wings of the lower façade.

XXXII. The orchestra was a levelled space, twelve feet lower than the front seats of the *κοῖλον*, by which it was bounded. Six feet above this was a boarded platform, which did not cover the whole area of the orchestra, but terminated where the line of view from the central *cunei* was intercepted by the boundary line. It ran, however, to the right and left of the spectators' benches till it reached the sides of the scene. The main part of this platform, as well as an altar of Bacchus (*d*) in the centre of the orchestral circle, was called the *θυμέλη* (*thymĕle*). The segment of the orchestra not covered by this platform was termed the *κονίστρα* (*arena*), or "place of sand." In front of the elevated scene, and six feet higher than the platform in the orchestra (that is, on the same level with the lowest range of seats), was the *προσκήνιον*, already mentioned, and called also the *λογεῖον* (in Latin, *pulpitum*), or "speaking-stage." There was a double flight of steps (*κλιμακτῆρες*), from the *κονίστρα* to the platform in the orchestra, and another of a similar description from this orchestral platform to the *προσκήνιον*, or real stage. These last are seen in our plan on either side. There were also two other flights of steps leading to the orchestral platform from the chambers below the stage. These were called *χαρώνιοι κλίμακες*, or "Charon's stairs," and were used for the entrance of spectres from the Lower World, and for the ghostly apparitions of the departed. The regular entrances of the chorus were by the *πάροδοι*, or broad passages, on each side, between the projecting wings of the

[1] *Aristoph. Av.*, 794. [2] *Schol. ad Aristoph.*, *l. c.*

stage and the seats of the spectators, and which are marked *ee* on our plan.

XXXIII. It does not appear that the stage (προσκήνιον, λογεῖον) extended farther to the right or left than the scene or elevated centre of the façade. The parts of the façade on either side of the stage were called παρασκήνια,[1] a name which was also given to the chambers behind the whole range of scene-buildings. The front and sides of the λογεῖον were called ὑποσκήνια, and this name was given also to the chambers below the stage. The walls of the παρασκήνια and ὑποσκήνια were not liable to change of decoration, but were constantly adorned with statues and other architectural adjuncts.[2] The scene itself was altered to meet the emergencies of the case. As a general rule, it represented a public building with three entrances (εἴσοδοι). That in the centre belonged, as we have already remarked, to the principal personage in the play; that on the right introduced the second personage; while the inferior characters entered by the door on the left hand. Behind the central εἴσοδος was a chamber, which might be opened to the spectators' view by a contrivance called the ἐκκύκλημα or ἐξώστρα. Thus the actions or spectacles which belonged to the interior of the house were sometimes openly exhibited. For example, in the *Agamemnon* of Æschylus, Clytemnestra was seen standing over the body of her murdered husband; and in the *Acharnians* of Aristophanes, Euripides was discovered in his study.

XXXIV. Before the πάροδος, on either side, stood a triangular prism, or side-scene, called περίακτος,[3] which moved on a pivot, and not only indicated the different regions supposed to lie in the neighborhood of the scene, but was also made use of as a machine for introducing suddenly sea and river gods, and other incidental appearances. The theatre at Athens, being built on the southeastern side of the Acropolis, was so situated that a person standing on the stage saw the greater part of the city and the harbor on his left, and the country of Attica on his right. Hence a man who entered on the right by the parascenia was invariably understood to come from the country, or from afar; on the left, from the city or the neighborhood. As the right-hand passage, or δρόμος, therefore, represented the road to the country, and the left-hand one that which led to the city, the changes of scene effected by the revolutions of the right-hand περίακτος were distant views painted in perspective; while those on the left were pictures of single objects supposed to be close at hand. Changes of scene were very seldom necessary in ancient tragedy. The Greek tragedies are so constructed, that the speeches and actions of which they are mainly composed might with perfect propriety pass on one spot, and, indeed, ought generally to pass in the court in front of the royal dwelling. The actions to which no speech is attached, and which do not serve to develop thoughts and feelings (such as Eteocles' combat with his brother; the murder of Agamemnon; Antigone's performance of the obsequies of Polynices, &c.), are imagined to pass behind or without the scene, and are only related on the stage. Hence the import-

---

[1] On the παρασκήνια, consult *Meineke*, *Frag. Com. Græc.*, vol. iv.; *Epim.*, vii., p. 722, *seqq.*

[2] *Pollux*, iv., 124.

[3] *Vitruv.*, v., 7; *Pollux*, iv., 126.

ance of the parts of messengers and heralds in ancient tragedy. The poet was not influenced only by the reason given by Horace,[1] namely, that bloody spectacles and incredible events excite less horror and doubt when related, and ought, therefore, not to be produced on the stage · there was also the far deeper general reason, that it is never the outward act with which the interest of ancient tragedy is most intimately bound up. The action which forms the basis of every tragedy of those times is internal and spiritual; the reflections, resolutions, feelings, the mental or moral phenomena, which can be expressed in speech, are developed on the stage. For outward action, which is generally mute, or, at all events, can not be adequately represented by words, the epic form —narration—is the only appropriate vehicle. Exceptions, such as the chaining of Prometheus, and the suicide of Ajax, are rather apparent than real, and, indeed, serve to confirm the general rule; since it is only on account of the peculiar psychological state of Prometheus when bound, and of Ajax at the time of his suicide, that the outward acts are brought upon the stage. Moreover, the costume of tragic actors was calculated for impressive declamation, and not for action. The lengthened and stuffed-out figures of the tragic actors would have had an awkward, not to say a ludicrous effect in combat or other violent action. From the sublime to the ridiculous would here have been but one step, which ancient tragedy carefully avoided risking.[2]

XXXV. The theatre at Athens was well supplied with machinery calculated to produce startling effects. Besides the περίακτοι, which were used occasionally to introduce a sea-deity on his fish-tailed steed, or a river-god with his urn, there was the θεολογεῖον, a platform surrounded by clouds, and suspended from the top of the central scene, whence the deities conversed with the actors or chorus. Sometimes they were introduced near the left *parodus*, close to the *periaktus*, by means of a crane turning on a pivot, which was called the μηχανή.[3] The γέρανος was a contrivance for snatching up an actor from the stage and raising him to the θεολογεῖον, and, by means of the αἰῶραι, an arrangement of ropes and pulleys, Bellerophon or Trygæus could fly across the stage. Then there was the βροντεῖον, a contrivance for imitating the sound of thunder. It seems to have consisted of bladders full of pebbles, which were rolled over sheets of copper laid out in the ὑποσκήνια. Again, the appearance of lightning was produced by means of a *periaktus*, or triangular prism of mirrors placed in the θεολογεῖον. This place was called the κεραυνοσκοπεῖον. It may be inferred, too, that the orchestra near the stage was occasionally supposed to represent water. Thus, in the "Frogs," Bacchus rows in front of the λογεῖον to the melodious croakings of the chorus which swims around his boat. From the enormous size of the theatre at Athens, which is said to have contained 30,000 spectators,[4] it became necessary to employ the principles of acoustics to a considerable extent. All round the κοῖλον were bell-shaped vessels of bronze, called ἠχεῖα, placed in an inverted position, and resting on pedestals, which received

[1] *Ep. ad Pis.*, 180, *seqq.* [2] *Müller, Hist. Gr. Lit.*, p. 307, *seq.* [3] *Pollux*, iv., 128.
[4] *Plato, Sympos.*, 175, *E.* Compare *Wordsworth, Athens and Attica*, p. 92, *seqq.*

and distributed the vibrations of sound. In some theatres, though not in that of Athens, these ἠχεῖα were placed in niches excavated for the purpose. The difficulty of hearing must have been greatly increased by the want of a roof to the κοῖλον.

XXXVI. The chorus was supposed to be a lochus of soldiers in battle array. In the dithyrambic or cyclic chorus of fifty, this military arrangement was not practicable; but when the original choral elements had become more deeply enrooted in the worship of Bacchus, and the three principal Apollonian dances were transferred to the worship of that god, the dramatic choruses became, like them, quadrangular, and were arranged in military rank and file. The number of the tragic chorus for the whole trilogy appears to have been 50; the comic chorus consisted of 24. The chorus of the tetralogy was broken into four sub-choruses, two of 15, one of 12, and a satyric chorus of 8, as appears from the distribution in the remaining trilogy. When the chorus of 15 entered in ranks three abreast, it was said to be divided κατὰ ζυγά: when it was distributed into three files of five, it was said to be κατὰ στοίχους. The same military origin explains the fact that the anapæstic measure was generally, if not always, adopted for the opening choral song; for this metre, as we have before seen, was also used in the Dorian marching-songs. The muster of the chorus round the Thymele shows that the chorus was Bacchic as well as military; the mixture of lyric and flute music points to the same union of two worships; and in the strophic and antistrophic form of most of the choral odes we discern the traces of the choral improvements of Stesichorus.

XXXVII. In the life of antiquity, every thing great and important, all the main actions of family or political interest, passed in the open air and in the view of men. Even social meetings took place rather in public halls, in market-places and streets, than in rooms and chambers; and the habits and actions, which were confined to the interior of a house, were never regarded as forming subjects for public observation. Accordingly, it was necessary that the action of the drama should come forth from the interior of the house; and tragic poets were compelled to comply strictly with this condition in the invention and plan of their dramatic compositions. The heroic personages, when about to give utterance to their thoughts and feelings, came forth into the court in front of their houses. From the other side came the chorus, out of the city or district in which the principal persons dwelt; they assembled, as friends or neighbors might, to offer their counsel or their sympathy to the principal actors on the stage, on some open space; often a market-place designed for public meetings; such as, in the monarchical times of Greece, was commonly attached to the prince's palace. Far from shocking received notions, the performance of choral dances in this place was quite in accordance with Greek usages. Anciently these market-places were specially designed for numerous popular choruses; they even themselves bore the name of chorus.[1] As regards the chorus itself, considered in the light of an element of the drama, we must conceive of it, with Schlegel, as the person-

[1] *Müller, Hist. Gr. Lit.*, p. 302.

ification of the thought inspired by the represented action ; in other words, it often expresses the reflections of a dispassionate and right-minded spectator, and inculcates the lessons of morality and resignation to the will of heaven, taught by the occurrences of the piece in which it is engaged. Besides this, the chorus enabled the poet to produce an image of the "council of elders," which existed under the heroic governments, and under whose advice and in whose presence the ancient princes of the Greek tragedy generally acted. This image was the more striking and vivid, inasmuch as the chorus was taken from the people at large, and did not at all differ from the appearance and stature of ordinary men ; so that the contrast or relation between them and the actors was the same as that of the Homeric *λαοί* and *ἄνακτες*. Lastly, the choral songs produced an agreeable pause in the action, breaking the piece into parts, while they presented to the spectator a lyrical and musical expression of his own emotions, or suggested to him lofty thoughts and great arguments. As Schlegel says, the chorus was the spectator idealized.[1]

XXXVIII. The great size of the theatre gave occasion to another remarkable difference between the exhibitions of the ancients and our own. Every one of the actors in tragedy wore the thick-soled cothurnus or hunting-boot (*κόθορνος, ἀρβύλη*). This gave additional height to the person, while his body and limbs were also stuffed and padded to a corresponding size, and his head was surmounted by a colossal mask suited to the character which he bore. Masks (*πρόσωπα, προσωπεῖα*) appear to have originated in the taste for mumming and disguises of all sorts prevalent at the Bacchic festivals. In the earlier periods of the drama, as we have already seen, the actors smeared their faces with the lees of wine, then substituted a species of pigment, and subsequently adopted a mask of linen. The regular mask was introduced by Æschylus, and still farther improved by Sophocles. With regard to the material of which it was composed, a difference of opinion exists. According to some, it was made of bronze or copper. This, however, is scarcely credible, since, when taken in connection with the other parts of the mask, which actually covered the whole head and came down as far as the shoulders, it would make the entire apparatus too unwieldy. According to others, the part which covered the face was of a light kind of wood, which seems the more reasonable opinion. Others are in favor of thin pipe-clay or terra cotta. One thing is pretty certain, that such metallic specimens as have come down to us are rather to be regarded simply as model masks, or as works of art, designed by the artist as mere ornaments.[2]

XXXIX. The ancient mask was so constructed as not only to add to the height of the actor, but also to give greater power to the voice. The first of these objects was effected by means of the *ὄγκος*, a species of top-knot, forming a prolongation of the mask, the hair being arranged in a pyramidal form, like the roof of a house, or the Greek letter Λ, and having sometimes a bonnet superadded. For the purpose, again, of giving more power to the voice, the mask was connected with a tire or periwig (*πηνίκη, φενάκη*), of which the *ὄγκος* formed part, which covered the whole

[1] *Smith, Dict. Ant., s. v. Tragœdia.*

[2] *St. John, Hellenes*, ii., p. 265.

head, and left only one passage for the voice, indicated by the half-opened mouth, and answering, in fact, all the ends of a speaking-trumpet, whence the Latin name for a mask, *persona a personando.*

XL. The mask not only concealed the individual features of well-known actors, and enabled the spectators entirely to forget the performer in his part, but it gave to his whole aspect that ideal character which the tragedy of antiquity demanded. The tragic mask was not, indeed, intentionally ugly and caricatured, like the comic, but the half-open mouth, the large eye-sockets, the sharply-defined features, in which every characteristic was presented in its utmost strength, the bright and hard coloring, were calculated to produce the impression of a being agitated by the emotions and the passions of human nature in a degree far above the standard of ordinary life. The unnatural effect which a set and uniform cast of features would produce in tragedy of varied passion and action like ours, was much less striking in ancient tragedy, wherein the principal persons, once forcibly possessed by certain objects and emotions, appeared throughout the whole remaining piece in a state of mind which was become the habitual and fundamental character of their existence. It is possible to imagine the Orestes of Æschylus, the Ajax of Sophocles, the Medea of Euripides, throughout the whole tragedy with the same countenance, though this would be difficult to assert of Hamlet, or any other character in a modern drama. But, in truth, there is no necessity for supposing that the actors appeared throughout a whole play with the same countenance, for, if circumstances required it, they might surely change masks during the intervals between the acts of a piece. Thus, in the tragedy of Sophocles, after King Œdipus knows the extent of his calamity, and has executed the bloody punishment upon himself, he appeared in a different mask from that which he wore in the confidence of virtue and of happiness.[1]

XLI. Not only, however, were the masks intended to personify historical or mythological personages, designed in imitation of some well-known type, handed down through ages by the poets, painters, and sculptors, but every age and condition of life, from youth to decrepitude, or from the hero to the slave, was represented by an appropriate mask, the characteristics of which were sufficiently well known for the quality and condition of the personage represented to be immediately recognized by the spectators on his appearance upon the stage; and even the ὄγκος belonging to each particular mask had a settled style of coiffure, as well known as the features it accompanied. The color of the hair, also, was fixed in each particular case. No wonder, therefore, that the greatest possible care was bestowed upon the manufacture of masks. Julius Pollux divides the tragic masks into twenty-six classes;[2] the comic masks, however, were much more numerous.

XLII. The performers wore long striped garments reaching to the ground (χιτῶνες ποδήρεις, στολαί), which were serviceable also in concealing a portion of the cothurnus. Over these were thrown upper robes (ἱμάτια, χλαμύδες) of purple, or some other brilliant color, with all sorts

[1] *Müller, Hist. Gr. Lit.*, p. 298.

[2] *Pollux*, iv., 133, *seqq.*

of gay trimmings and gold ornaments, the ordinary attire of Bacchic festal processions and choral dances. Nor was the Hercules of the stage represented as the sturdy athletic hero, whose huge limbs were only concealed by a lion's hide; he appeared in the rich and gaudy dress we have described, to which his distinctive attributes, the club and the bow, were merely added. The dress of the chorus was not different in kind from that of the actors, and the choragus took care that it was equally splendid. But as the actors represented heroic characters, whereas the chorus was merely a deputation from the people at large, and in fact stood much nearer to the audience, the mask was omitted, and moreover, while the actors wore the cothurnus, the chorus appeared in their usual sandals. The comic actors, for the same reason, were content with the *soccus*, or thin-soled shoe, and their mask had no *ὄγκος*. They often, too, wore harlequinade dresses, with trowsers fitting close to the leg.[1]

XLIII. Aristotle, or the grammarian by whom his treatise on Poetry has been interpolated, informs us[2] that every Greek tragedy admitted of the following subdivisions: the *prologue*, the *episodes*, the *exode*, which applied to the performances of the actors, and the *parodus* and *stasima*, which belonged to the chorus. The songs from the stage (*τὰ ἀπὸ σκηνῆς*), and the dirges (*κομμοί*), are peculiar to some tragedies only. Besides these, it seems that there was occasionally a dancing song or canzonet of a peculiar nature.[3] The proper entrance of the chorus, as already remarked, was from the *parascenia*, by one of the *parodi*. The *parodus* was the song which the choreutæ sang as they moved, probably in different parties, along the side entrances of the orchestra. It was generally either interspersed with anapæsts, as is the case in the *Antigone;* or preceded by a long anapæstic march, as in the case of the *Supplices* and *Agamemnon*. Sometimes this anapæstic march was followed by a system of the cognate Ionics a minore.[4] This we find in the *Persæ*. In some tragedies there was no *parodus*, but the opening of the play found the chorus already assembled on the *thymele*, and prepared to sing the first *stasimon*. Such is the case in the *Œdipus Tyrannus*. It seems probable that they then entered by the passage under the seats.

XLIV. The *stasima* were always sung by the chorus when it was either stationary or moving on the same limited surface around the altar of Bacchus, and with its front to the stage. The places of the choreutæ were marked by lines on the stage (*διαγράμματα*). The comic chorus sang its *parodus* and its *stasima* in the same manner as the tragic; but they were, as pieces of poetry, much less elaborate, and generally much shorter. The main performance of the chorus in comedy was the *parabasis*. It was an address to the audience in the middle of the play, and was the most immediate representative of the old trochaic or anapæstic address by the leader of the phallic song, for which the personal lampoons of Archilochus furnished the model, and to which the old comedy of Athens was mainly indebted for its origin. This *parabasis*, or "countermarch," was so called because the chorus, which had previously stood facing the

[1] *Müller, Hist. Gr. Lit.*, p. 296, *seqq.; Id., Eumen.*, 32.
[2] *Arist., Poet.*, 12.
[3] *Donaldson, Introd. to Antig.*, p. xxxi.
[4] *Id., Gr. Gr.*, § 650.

stage, and on the other side of the central altar, wheeled about, and made a movement toward the spectators, who were then addressed by the coryphæus in a short system of anapæsts or trochees, called the κομμάτιον, and this was followed by a long anapæstic system, termed πνῖγος, "suffocation," or μακρόν, "long," from the effort which its delivery imposed upon the reciter. The *parabasis* is often followed by a lyric song in honor of some divinity, and this by a short system, properly of sixteen trochaic tetrameters, which is called the ἐπίῤῥημα, or "supplement." It contains some joking addition to the main purport of the *parabasis*.

XLV. There were regularly never more than three actors (ὑποκριταί, ἀγωνισταί), who were designated as respectively the *first*, *second*, and *third* actor (πρωταγωνιστής, δευτεραγωνιστής, τριταγωνιστής). The third actor in tragedy, as we have already remarked, was first added by Sophocles, an addition which Cratinus was the first to make in comedy. Any number of mutes (κωφὰ πρόσωπα) might appear on the stage. If children were introduced as speaking or singing on the stage, the part was undertaken by one of the chorus, who stood behind the scene, and it was, therefore, called a παρασκήνιον, from his position, or παραχορήγημα, from its being something beyond the proper functions of the chorus. It has been concluded by Müller,[1] that a fourth actor was indispensable to the proper performance of the *Œdipus Coloneus*, an opinion which, though opposed by some eminent scholars,[2] seems extremely probable.

XLVI. The narrowness and distance of the stage rendered any grouping unadvisable. The arrangement of the actors was that of a processional bas-relief. Their movements were slow, their gesticulations abrupt and angular, and their delivery a sort of loud and deep-drawn singsong, which resounded throughout the immense theatre. They probably neglected every thing like *by-play*, and *making points*, which are so effective on the modern stage. The distance at which the spectators were placed would prevent them from seeing those little movements, and hearing those low tones which have made the fortune of many a modern actor. The mask, too, precluded all attempts at varied expression, and it is probable that nothing more was expected from the performer than was looked for from his predecessor the rhapsodist, namely, good recitation.

XLVII. The rhythmical systems of the tragic choruses were very simple, and we may conclude that the music to which they were set was equally so. The dochmiac metre, which is regularly found in the κομμοί and τὰ ἀπὸ σκηνῆς, would admit of the most inartificial of plaintive melodies. The comic choral songs very frequently introduce the easy asynartete combinations,[3] which were so much used by Archilochus; and we find in Aristophanes a very curious form of the antispastic metre, the invention of which is attributed to Eupolis.[4]

XLVIII. We shall conclude with a few observations on the audience, and on the social position of the actors. For the first few years after the commencement of theatrical performances no money was paid for admission to them; but after a time (probably about B.C. 501) it was found

[1] *Hist. Gr. Lit.*, p. 305.
[2] *Donaldson, Theatre of the Greeks*, p. 164.
[3] *Id.*, *Gr. Gr.*, § 666.
[4] *Id. ib.*, § 677.

convenient to prevent the crowds and disturbances occasioned by the gratuitous admission of every one who chose to come. The charge[1] was two oboli; but lest the poorer classes should be excluded, the entrance-money was given to any person who might choose to apply for it, provided his name was registered in the book of the citizens (ληξιαρχικὸν γραμματεῖον). The lowest and best seats were set apart for the magistrates, the members of the βουλή, or senate, and all such persons as had acquired or inherited a right to front seats (προεδρία). It is probable that those who were entitled to reserved places at the theatre had also tickets of admission provided for them. The entrance-money was paid to the lessee of the theatre (θεατρώνης, θεατροπώλης, ἀρχιτέκτων), who paid the rent and made the necessary repairs out of the proceeds. The distribution of the admission money, or θεωρικόν, as it was called, out of the public funds, was set on foot by Pericles, at the suggestion of Demonides of Œa; its application was soon extended, till it became a regular largess from the demagogues to the mob at all the great festivals; and well might the patriot Demosthenes lift up his voice against a practice, which was in the end nothing but an instrument in the hands of the profligate orators, who pandered to the worst passions of the people.

XLIX. The lessee sometimes gave a gratuitous exhibition, in which case tickets of admission were distributed.[2] Any citizen might buy tickets for a stranger residing at Athens.[3] The question whether in Greece, and more especially at Athens, women were present at tragedies, is one of those which have given rise to much discussion among modern scholars, as we have scarcely any passage in ancient writers in which the presence of women is stated as a positive fact. But Jacobs[4] and Passow[5] have placed it almost beyond a doubt, from the various allusions made by ancient writers, that women were allowed to be present during the performance of tragedies. This opinion is now perfectly confirmed by a passage in Athenæus,[6] which has been quoted by Becker[7] in corroboration of the conclusion to which the above-mentioned scholars had come. We have, however, on the other hand, every reason to believe that women were not present at comedies, while boys might be present both at tragedy and comedy.[8] The seats which women occupied in the Greek theatres were in the highest row of benches, and separated from those of the men.[9]

L. Theatrical representations at Athens began early in the morning, or after breakfast;[10] and when the concourse of people was expected to be great, persons would even go to occupy their seats in the night. The theatres had no roofs. The sun, however, could not be very troublesome to the actors, as they were in a great measure protected by the buildings surrounding the stage, and the spectators protected themselves against it by hats with broad brims.[11] When the weather was fine, especially at

[1] *Böckh, Pub. Econ. of Athens*, vol. i., p. 289, *seqq.*, Engl. trans.
[2] *Theophrast., Charact.*, xi.
[3] *Plat., Gorg.*, p. 502, *D*; *Id., Leg.*, ii., p. 658, *D*
[4] *Vermischt. Schriften*, iv., p. 272.
[5] *Zeitschr. für die Alterth.*, 1837, n. 29.
[6] *Athen.*, xii., p. 534.
[7] *Charikles*, ii., p. 560.
[8] *Theophr., Char.*, ix.; *Aristoph., Nub.*, 537.
[9] *Göttling, Rh. Mus.*, 1834, p. 103, *seqq*
[10] *Æschin. c. Ctes.*, p. 466; *Athen.*, xi., p. 464.
[11] *Suid., s. v.* πέτασος and Δράκων.

the Dionysiac festivals in the spring, the people appeared with garlands on their heads; when it was cold, as at the Lenæa in January, they used to wrap themselves up in their cloaks.[1] When a storm or a shower of rain came on suddenly, the spectators took refuge in the porticoes behind the stage, or in those above the uppermost row of benches. Those who wished to sit comfortably brought cushions with them.[2] As it was not unusual for the theatrical performances to last from ten to twelve hours, the spectators required refreshments, and we find that, in the intervals between the several plays, they used to take wine and cakes.[3]

LI. The Athenian performers were much esteemed all over Greece; they took great pains about their bodily exercises, and dieted themselves in order to keep their voices clear and strong.[4] They appear to have been generally paid by the state; in the country exhibitions, however, two actors would occasionally pay the wages of their τριταγωνιστῆς.[5] The salary of actors was often very high, and Polus, who commonly acted with Tlepolemus in the plays of Sophocles, sometimes earned a talent by two days' performances. The histrionic profession was not thought to carry with it any degradation. The actor was the representative of the dramatist, and often the dramatist himself. Sophocles, who sometimes performed in his own plays, was a person of the highest consideration; the actor Aristodemus went on an embassy, and many actors took a lead in the public assembly. In some cases, the actors were not only recognized by the state, but controlled and directed by special enactments. Thus, according to the law brought forward by the orator Lycurgus, the actors were obliged to compare the acting copies of the plays of the three great tragedians with the authentic manuscripts of their works, preserved in the state archives; and it was the duty of the public secretary to see that the texts were accurately collated.[6]

CHAPTER XXIII.

FOURTH OR ATTIC PERIOD—*continued.*

GREEK TRAGEDIANS.

I. Chœrĭlus (Χοιρίλος) or Chœrillus (Χοίριλλος), of Athens, was a tragic poet, contemporary with Thespis, Phrynichus, Pratinas, Æschylus, and even with Sophocles, unless, as Welcker supposes, he had a son of the same name, who was also a tragic poet.[7] His first appearance as a competitor for the tragic prize was in B.C. 523, in the reign of Hipparchus, when Athens was becoming the centre of Greek poetry by the residence there of Simonides, Anacreon, Lasus, and others. This was twelve years after the first appearance of Thespis in the tragic contests; and it is, therefore, not improbable that Chœrilus had Thespis for an antagonist.

---

1 *Suid.*, *l. c.*
2 *Theophr.*, *Charact.*, ii.
3 *Athen.*, xi., p. 464; *Aristot.*, *Eth. Nicom.*, x., 5.
4 *Cic.*, *Orat.*, 4.
5 *Demosth.*, *De Coron.*, p. 345, *Bekker.*
6 *Plut.*, *Vit.* X. *Orat.*, p. 841, *D*, p. 377, *Wyttenb.*
7 *Griech. Trag.*, p. 892.

It was also twelve years before the first victory of Phrynichus (B.C. 511). After another twelve years, Chœrilus came into competition with Æschylus, when the latter first exhibited (B.C. 499); and since we know that Æschylus did not carry off a prize till sixteen years afterward, the prize of this contest must have been given either to Chœrilus or to Pratinas. Chœrilus was still held in high estimation in the year 483 B.C., after he had exhibited tragedies for forty years. Of the character of Chœrilus we know little more than that, during a long life, he retained a good degree of popular favor. The number of his tragedies was 150, of his victories 13,[1] being exactly the number of victories assigned to Æschylus. The great number of his dramas establishes an important point, namely, that the exhibition of tetralogies commenced early in the time of Chœrilus; for new tragedies were exhibited at Athens only twice a year, and at this early period we never hear of tragedies being written and not exhibited, but rather the other way. In fact, it is the general opinion that Chœrilus was the first who composed written tragedies, and that even of his plays the greater number were not written. The poetical character and construction of the plays of Chœrilus probably differed but little from those of Thespis, until Æschylus introduced the second actor. Of all his plays we have no remnant, except the statement by Pausanias[2] of a mythological genealogy from his play called Ἀλόπη.[3]

II. Phrynĭchus (Φρύνιχος), an Athenian, was one of the poets to whom the invention of tragedy is ascribed. He was a scholar of Thespis.[4] The dates of his birth and death are alike unknown. He gained his first tragic victory B.C. 511, twenty-four years after Thespis (B.C. 535), twelve years after Chœrilus (B.C. 523), and twelve years before Æschylus (B.C. 499), and his last in B.C. 476, on which occasion Themistocles was his choragus,[5] and recorded the event by an inscription. Phrynichus must, therefore, have flourished at least 35 years. He probably went, like other poets of the age, to the court of Hiero at Syracuse, and there died. Various improvements in the ancient drama are ascribed to Phrynichus. He introduced female masks, paid particular attention to the dances of the chorus, and for the light, ludicrous Bacchanalian stories of Thespis, he substituted regular and serious subjects, taken either from the Heroic Age, or the heroic deeds which illustrated the history of his own time. In these he aimed not so much to amuse the audience as to move their feelings; and so powerful was the effect of his tragedy on the capture of Miletus, which city had recently been taken by the Persians, B.C. 494, that the audience burst into tears, and Phrynichus was fined 1000 drachmæ for having recalled so forcibly a painful recollection of the misfortunes of a kindred people.[6] Phrynichus seems to have been chiefly remarkable for the sweetness of his melodies, and the great variety and cleverness of his figure-dances. The Aristophanic Agathon speaks generally of the beauty of his dramas, though, of course, they fell far short of the grandeur of Æschylus, and the perfect skill of Sophocles. In the dramas of Phrynichus the chorus still retained the principal place,

---

1 *Suid., s. v.* 2 *Paus.*, i., 14, 2. 3 *Smith, Dict. Biogr., s. v.*
4 *Suid., s v.* 5 *Plut., Themist.*, 5. 6 *Herod.*, vi., 21.

and it was reserved for Æschylus and Sophocles to bring the dialogue and action into their true position. The names of several tragedies attributed to Phrynichus have come down to us, but it is probable that some of these belonged to other poets. The few fragments of Phrynichus are given by Wagner, in his *Trag. Græc. Fragm.* (in Didot's *Bibliotheca*).[1]

III. PRATĪNAS (Πρατίνας),[2] one of the early tragic poets at Athens, was a native of Phlius, and therefore by birth a Dorian. It is not stated at what time he went to Athens, but he was older than Æschylus, and younger than Chœrilus, with both of whom he competed for the prize about B.C. 500. The step in the progress of the art which was ascribed to Pratinas was the separation of the satyric from the tragic drama,[3] to which we have already alluded. His plays were much esteemed. Pratinas also ranked high among the lyric as well as among the dramatic poets of the day. He cultivated two species of lyric poetry, the hyporcheme and the dithyramb, of which the former was closely related to the satyric drama by the jocular character which it often assumed, the latter by its ancient choruses of satyrs. Pratinas may, perhaps, be considered to have shared with his contemporary Lasus the honor of founding the Athenian school of dithyrambic poetry. The fragments of Pratinas are contained in Wagner's *Tragic. Græc. Fragm.* (in Didot's *Bibliotheca*).

IV. ÆSCHȲLUS (Αἰσχύλος)[4] was born at Eleusis, in Attica, B.C. 525, so that he was thirty-five years of age at the time of the battle of Marathon, and contemporary with Simonides and Pindar. His father Euphorion was probably connected with the worship of Ceres, and Æschylus himself was, according to some authorities, initiated in the mysteries of that goddess. At the age of 25 (B.C. 499) he made his first appearance as a competitor for the prize of tragedy against Chœrilus and Pratinas, without, however, being successful. Afterward, with his brothers Cynægirus and Aminias, he fought at the battle of Marathon (B.C. 490), and also at those of Salamis (B.C. 480) and Platææ (B.C. 479). In B.C. 484, sixteen years subsequent to his first defeat in the tragic contest, Æschylus gained his first dramatic victory. The titles of the pieces which he brought out on this occasion are not known, but his competitors were most probably Pratinas and Phrynichus, or Chœrilus. Afterward, in B.C. 472, he gained the prize with the Persæ, the earliest of his extant dramas. In B.C. 468, a remarkable event occurred in the poet's life: he was defeated in a tragic contest by his younger rival Sophocles, and, if we may believe Plutarch,[5] his mortification at this indignity, as he conceived it, was so great, that he quitted Athens in disgust the very same year, and went to the court of Hiero at Syracuse, where he found Simonides the lyric poet. Of the fact of his having visited Syracuse at the time alluded to there can be no doubt; but whether the motive alleged by Plutarch for his doing so was the only one, or a real one, is a question of considerable difficulty, though of little practical moment. It has been conjectured by some that the charge of ἀσέβεια, or impiety, brought against Æschylus

[1] *Smith, Dict. Biogr., s. v.*
[2] *Id., s. v.*
[3] *Suid., s. v.* πρῶτος ἔγραψε Πρατίνας.
[4] *Smith, Dict. Biogr., s. v.*
[5] *Plut., Cim.*, 8.

for an alleged divulging of the mysteries of Ceres,[1] but possibly from political motives, was in some way connected with his retirement on this occasion from his native country, but this charge belongs rather to a subsequent period of his life.

Shortly before the arrival of Æschylus at the court of Hiero, that prince had built the town of Ætna, at the bottom of the mountain of that name, and on the site of the ancient Catana. In connection with this event, Æschylus is said to have composed his play of the "Women of Ætna," in which he predicted and prayed for the prosperity of the new city. At the request of Hiero, he also reproduced the play of the "Persæ," with which he had been victorious in the dramatic contests at Athens (B. C. 472). Now we know that the trilogy of the "Seven against Thebes" was represented soon after the "Persæ," and hence it follows that the former must have been first represented not later than B.C. 470.[2] Besides the "Women of Ætna," Æschylus also composed other pieces in Sicily, in which are said to have occurred Sicilian words and expressions not intelligible to the Athenians.[3] From the number of such words and expressions which have been noticed in the later extant plays of Æschylus, it has been inferred that he spent a considerable time in Sicily on this his first visit. It may be remarked here, that, according to some accounts, Æschylus had even visited Sicily before this, about B.C. 488, in consequence of the victory gained over him by Simonides, to whom the Athenians had adjudged the prize for the best elegy on those who had fallen at Marathon. The truth of this statement, however, has been greatly questioned.[4]

In B.C. 467, his friend and patron Hiero died; and in B.C. 458 it appears that Æschylus was again at Athens, from the fact that the trilogy of the Orestēa was produced in that year. In the same or the following year (B.C. 457), Æschylus again visited Sicily for the last time, and the reason assigned for this his second visit to that island is both probable and sufficient. He was accused of impiety before the court of the Areopagus, and would have been condemned but for the interposition of his brother Aminias, who had distinguished himself at the battle of Salamis.[5] What the specific nature of the charge was is not known; but it is supposed to have been founded on his having either divulged or spoken profanely in some of his plays concerning the mysteries of Ceres. At any rate, from the number of authorities all confirming this conclusion, there can be no doubt that toward the end of his life Æschylus incurred the serious displeasure of a strong party at Athens, and that after the exhibition of the Orestean trilogy he retired to Gela in Sicily, where he died, B.C. 456, in the 69th year of his age, and three years after the representation of the Eumenides, on which play, according to some, the charge of impiety was founded. On the manner of his death the ancient writers are unanimous.[6] An eagle, say they, mistaking the poet's bald head for a stone, let a tortoise fall upon it to break the shell, and so fulfilled an

---

[1] *Aristot.*, *Eth.*, iii., 1.
[2] *Welcker*, *Trilogie*, p. 520; *Schol. ad Aristoph.*, *Ran.*, 1053.
[3] *Athenæus*, ix., p. 402, *b*.
[4] *Bode*, *Gesch. d. Dichtk.*, iii., p. 215.
[5] *Ælian*, *V. H.*, v., 19.
[6] *Suid.*, *s. v.* Χελωνημνῶν.

oracle, according to which Æschylus was fated to die by a blow from heaven.

The inhabitants of Gela showed their regard for his character, by public solemnities in his honor, by erecting a noble monument to him, and inscribing it with an epitaph written by himself,[1] in which, strangely enough, he describes the field of Marathon as the scene of his glory, without any allusion whatever to his success as a dramatist. In Sicily the memory of Æschylus was long held in the highest veneration; and in Attica, although he had parted from its shores with bitter feelings, the next generation appears to have prized the works of Æschylus very highly, for what we read about him in the "Frogs" of Aristophanes must be regarded as the judgment of the ablest Athenian critics at the time. Not only were the dramas which had been performed in his lifetime repeated after his death, and treated like new compositions, so as to be allowed to come into competition with new dramas, the state, by a special decree of the people, providing a chorus at the public expense, for any one who might wish to exhibit his tragedies a second time,[2] but pieces which had not been brought out by the poet himself were produced upon the stage by his son Euphorion, and gained prizes. In this way Euphorion was victorious with a tetralogy in B.C. 431, over Sophocles and Euripides. Philocles, also, the son of a sister of Æschylus, was victorious over the King Œdipus of Sophocles, probably with a tragedy of his uncle's. From and by means of these persons arose what was called the Tragic school of Æschylus, which continued for the space of 125 years.[3]

The style of Æschylus is bold, energetic, and sublime, full of gorgeous imagery and magnificent expressions, such as became the elevated characters of his dramas, and the ideas he wished to express.[4] In the turn of his expressions the poetical predominates over the syntactical. He was peculiarly fond of metaphorical phrases and strange compounds, and of obsolete language, so that he was much more epic in his manner of expression than either Sophocles or Euripides, and he excelled in displaying strong feelings and impulses, and in describing the awful and the terrible, rather than in exhibiting the workings of the human mind under the influence of complicated and various emotions. But, notwithstanding the general elevation of his style, the subordinate characters in his plays, as the watchman in the Agamemnon, and the nurse of Orestes in the Choëphoræ, are made to use language fitting their station, and less removed from that of ordinary life. The characters of Æschylus, like his diction, are sublime and majestic; they were gods and powers of colossal magnitude, whose imposing aspect could be endured by the heroes of Marathon and Salamis, but was too awful for the contemplation of a later age, who complained that Æschylus's language was not human. Hence the general impression produced by the poetry of Æschylus was rather of a religious than a moral nature; his personages being both in action and suffering superhuman, and therefore not always fitted to teach practical lessons.[5]

[1] *Paus.*, i., 14, 4; *Athen.*, xiv., p. 627, *D.* [2] *Aristoph.*, *Acharn.*, 102, *Æschyl. Vit.*
[3] *Hermann.*, *Opusc.*, ii., p. 158. [4] *Aristoph.*, *Ran.*, 934. [5] *Smith*, *Dict. Biogr.*, *s. v.*

The Greeks justly regarded Æschylus as the father of tragedy. Before his time the art scarcely deserved the name of drama, and the progress which it made under the direction of his genius was far greater than any which it owed to his successors. It required much more power to raise the drama from the state in which it was in the hands of the poets previous to Æschylus, to the condition in which we find it in his works, than merely to continue what he had commenced. Before the time of Æschylus, as we have before remarked, only one actor appeared on the stage at once, who carried on the dialogue with the chorus, or told his story to them. Æschylus introduced a second actor, which was the first step toward making the dialogue and the action independent of the chorus. The dialogue now became more free and animated, and the contrast between a principal (*protagonistes*) and a secondary character (*deuteragonistes*) enabled the poet to interest his audience in the action, which before his time was of secondary importance, the chorus being then the principal part of the drama. But still the action in the dramas of Æschylus is yet not altogether independent of the chorus, which takes a considerable part in the events of the piece. The complete separation of these two elements was reserved for Sophocles.[1]

An innovation like the above was undoubtedly adopted by the contemporaries of Æschylus, just as he himself, at a later period, adopted that of Sophocles, by which a third actor was introduced. There are, it is true, dramas of Æschylus in which three persons appear on the stage at once; but in this case the dialogue is carried on by only two of them. A third actor who takes part in the dialogue does not occur in any drama written before the year B.C. 468, when Sophocles showed the advantage of a third actor. The part of the protagonistes was in most cases performed by Æschylus himself, and the names of two celebrated actors are known who were trained and instructed by the poet, and probably acted the parts of deuteragonistæ. They were Clearchus and Myniscus of Chalcis. Before the time of Æschylus, the poets generally acted their own dramas, and were obliged to perform the parts of the several characters of a piece, one by one, in succession. This inconvenience was obviated, in some degree, by the introduction of a second actor, though the same actor was still obliged to perform several parts. There are, however, several points in the dialogue of the Æschylean drama which remind us of what the art was before his time. The dialogue is sometimes carried on between the actor and the chorus, and in this, as well as in other cases, it proceeds with great regularity, which to a modern critic would appear stiff and unnatural: the verses are mostly distributed in certain proportions between the speakers, and the protagonistes, in most cases, uses more verses than the deuteragonistes. This is, indeed, a peculiarity of all Greek tragedies, but in Æschylus it is more striking than in any of his successors.[2]

Æschylus also introduced great improvements in the choral dance. He invented several dances himself, instructed the dancers without the assistance of a teacher, and paid the most anxious attention to the or-

[1] *Biograph. Dict. of Soc. for Diff. of Useful Knowledge*, vol. i., p. 408. [2] *Ibid.*

chestral performances of the chorus. He was also the first who saw the propriety of adapting the dress of the actors and the scenery to the characters which they represented. He introduced the cothurnus, or high-soled buskin, and the other artificial means already mentioned, to raise the figure of the actors above the standard of ordinary men; the masks were greatly improved by him, and he bestowed the utmost care and attention upon the whole of the theatrical wardrobe. The introduction of scene-painting is likewise ascribed to Æschylus. The machinery requisite for theatrical performances must have attained a high degree of perfection under him, on account of his frequent introduction of the gods and other supernatural beings upon the stage. Every thing, in fine, of importance to the performance of the drama was thus either perfected or introduced by Æschylus, who left to those who succeeded him nothing but to complete the work which he had commenced.

It is stated that Æschylus wrote seventy tragedies and several satyric dramas. Five were ascribed to him on doubtful authority. All these productions were written within forty-four years, from 500 to 456 B.C. Of their general excellence we may judge from the fact that he gained the prize of tragedy thirteen times. It is a very questionable point whether the tragedies of Æschylus were always so arranged as to form trilogies, that is, great dramatic compositions consisting of three distinct tragedies, each of which was in some degree entire in itself, and yet formed, as it were, only one of the three acts of a greater drama, and could not be properly understood unless viewed in its connection with the others. Welcker, by a careful examination of the extant plays, and of the fragments and titles of those which are lost, has endeavored to show that all the works of Æschylus were such trilogies; but although it is beyond doubt that many were intended to form trilogies, there is not sufficient evidence to show this of all; and as regards the "Persæ," it is perfectly certain that it was not part of a trilogy. The few fragments of many of the lost pieces, moreover, scarcely enable us to form an accurate idea of their contents. The only specimen of a trilogy which is preserved entire is the "Orestea," consisting of the "Agamemnon," the "Choëphoræ," and the "Eumenides." The three other pieces which we possess entire, namely, the "Seven against Thebes," the "Suppliants," and the "Prometheus," are undoubtedly likewise parts of trilogies. The earliest among the seven extant plays is the "Persæ," which was first acted at Athens in B.C. 472, and forms an exception to the other plays of Æschylus, inasmuch as the subject is taken from the history of the poet's own time. A year after the "Persæ," the "Seven against Thebes" was brought out. The latest is the Orestean trilogy, which, as already stated, was brought upon the stage in B.C. 458. The "Suppliants" and the "Prometheus" came in the period between this year and that in which the "Persians" was brought out, but the exact time is not known. From allusions, however, in the "Suppliants," it has been inferred, with some probability, that it was written about B.C. 461, during the time that Athens was allied with Argos.[1]

[1] *Biograph. Dict. of Soc. for Diff. of Useful Knowledge*, vol. i., p. 408.

The performance of each trilogy of Æschylus was followed by that of a satyric drama, which, together with the three tragedies, formed a tetralogy, and the subject of which was in some cases connected with that of the trilogy. The name of the satyric drama connected with the "Orestea" was the "Proteus." We know the names of eight others of these burlesque dramas of Æschylus, but none are preserved. The ancients state that Æschylus was as great a master in the satyric drama as in tragedy. As regards the artistic character of the tragedies of Æschylus, to which we have already in part alluded, we have few observations of the ancients themselves. Sophocles, who is reported to have said that Æschylus always composed his poems as he ought, without being conscious of it, has expressed in the best manner the fact that Æschylus was a great poet. All that Sophocles, Aristophanes, and other ancient writers object to in Æschylus refers merely to form, and not to the artistic plan and structure of his work; it is only the pompous grandiloquence and the boldness of his imagery which they find fault with. These are, indeed, very striking features in the dramas of Æschylus, but he himself seems not only to have been aware of it, but to have thought it necessary that his gods and heroes, being so far above the human standard, should also speak a language above that of ordinary mortals.

Although the Greeks at all times had great reverence for the father of their tragedy, yet the further they were removed from his age, the less were they able to appreciate him. In fact, the most extraordinary power of his master genius, the artistic construction of a trilogy, is scarcely noticed by them, and its discovery and right appreciation belong altogether to modern times, and more especially to Welcker, whose researches on this point have been followed up by Droysen, Gruppe, and others. Soon after the death of Æschylus, the Greeks began to perform his single plays separately, and thus gradually forgot that they were only acts of greater dramas. The plan of a tragedy of Æschylus is always extremely simple, and without any complicated plot; the action proceeds smoothly, but rapidly, and the poet does not anxiously concern himself to lay open to his audience every link by which the parts of the action are connected; he draws his pictures only in bold outline, which he leaves to the imagination of his hearers to fill up. But it is this very simplicity of his design which constitutes his grandeur and sublimity.

One leading idea of the dramas of Æschylus is a struggle between the free will of man and the power of destiny, to which the gods themselves must submit, and to which man must fall a victim if he presumes to oppose it. Such an idea is both religious and ethical, and intended to impress upon man the necessity of submitting to higher powers, and of humbly recognizing his own weakness. Another leading idea which appears in some of his plays is, that crime, by a moral necessity, leads to farther crime, and so to calamity, which is its punishment, or, as Droysen has expressed it, that "whoever acts must suffer." Æschylus represents to us the piety of the age to which he belonged, an age which could not conceive that its own great works were accomplished without the aid of the gods. He himself was, as we have said, initiated in the Eleusinian mysteries, and well acquainted with the philosophical inquiries which then began to be carried on in Greece; and these circumstances undoubtedly contributed to the earnestness with which he looked upon man, and his relation to higher powers.[1]

EDITIONS OF ÆSCHYLUS.[2]

The tragedies of Æschylus which have come down to us have, with the exception of the "Prometheus," suffered more from the carelessness of transcribers than many other remains of ancient literature. The first edition was printed at Venice, 1518, 8vo, by Aldus; but considerable parts of the "Agamemnon" and of the "Choëphoræ" are not contained in this edition; and, what is still more surprising, the printed part of the Agamemnon is attached to the Choëphoræ, and both are made up into one play; so that thus this edition contains six plays merely. Robortellus, in his edition, Venice, 1552, 8vo, corrected the error, and separated the Agamemnon from the Choëphoræ; and in the same year he also published the Greek scholia, and the Greek "Life of Æschylus," in 2 vols. 8vo. The first complete edition of the seven tragedies is that by H. Stephens, Paris, 1557, 4to. One of the best among the subsequent editions is that of Stanley, London, 1663, fol., which contains the scholia, a commentary, and a Latin translation. This was reprinted with some additions by De Pauw, Haag, 1745, 2 vols. 4to, and again by Butler, Cambridge, 1809–1816, with additions from Stanley's unpublished notes, 8 vols. 8vo, and 4 vols. 4to. The edition of Schütz, in 5 vols. 8vo, though of very little value, has gone through three imprints (1782–1809). The first three volumes contain the text and commentary, the other two the fragments of the lost plays and the Greek scholia. The best recent editions are those of Wellauer, Lips., 1823–1830, 3 vols. 8vo, the text and notes in two volumes, and the Lexicon Æschyleum in one; of W. Dindorf, in the *Poetæ Scenici Græci*, reprinted at Oxford, 1832–1841, in 3 vols. 8vo, the last volume in two parts; of Scholefield, Cambridge, 1828, 8vo, reprinted in 1851; of Ahrens, in Didot's *Bibliotheca*, Paris, 1842; and of Hermann, Leipzig, 1852, 2 vols. 8vo. A new edition was commenced, also, by Klausen, Gotha, 1833, 8vo, but was interrupted by his death. Only the Agamemnon and Choëphoræ were published. The editions of single plays, and dissertations upon them, or passages of them, are almost innumerable. The separate plays, except the "Suppliants" and the "Eumenides," have been ably edited in England by Blomfield. Of the separate editions of these plays in Germany, one of the most valuable is that of the "Eumenides," by K. O. Müller. There is also an excellent edition of the "Orestea," by Franz, Leipzig, 1846, 8vo. Welcker's works in relation to Æschylus, and Greek tragedy in general, are also exceedingly valuable. Their titles are: *Die Æschylische Trilogie Prometheus*, Darmstadt, 1824, 8vo; *Nachtrag zur Trilogie*, Frankfort, 1826; and *Die Griechischen Tragoedien*, Bonn, 1840, 8vo. The Lexicon to Æschylus, by Linwood, Lond., 1843, reprinted Lond., 1847, will be found a very useful auxiliary to the student.

---

[1] *Biograph. Dict. of Soc. for Diff. of Useful Knowledge*, vol. i., p. 408.

[2] *Smith, Dict. Biogr.*, *s. v.*

CHAPTER XXIV.

FOURTH OR ATTIC PERIOD—*continued.*

GREEK TRAGEDIANS—*continued.*

I. Sophŏcles (Σοφοκλῆς)[1] was born at Colonus, a demus of Attica, about a mile from the city of Athens, toward the northwest, five years before the battle of Marathon, B.C. 495.[2] He was thirty years younger, therefore, than Æschylus, and fifteen years older than Euripides. His father's name was Sophilus or Sophillus, of whose condition in life we know nothing for certain; but it is clear that Sophocles received an education not inferior to that of the most distinguished citizens of Athens. To both of the two leading branches of Greek education, music and gymnastics, he was carefully trained, and in both he gained the prize of a garland. Of the skill which he had attained to in music and dancing in his sixteenth year, and of the perfection of his bodily form, we have conclusive evidence in the fact that, when the Athenians were assembled in solemn festival around the trophy which they had set up in Salamis to celebrate their victory over the fleet of Xerxes, Sophocles was chosen to lead, naked and with lyre in hand, the chorus which danced around the trophy, and sang the songs of triumph, B.C. 480.[3] The statement of the anonymous biographer of Sophocles, that he learned tragedy from Æschylus, has been objected to on grounds that are perfectly conclusive, if it be understood as meaning any direct and formal instruction; but, from the connection in which the words stand, they appear to express nothing more than the simple and obvious fact, that Sophocles, having received the art in the form to which it had been advanced by Æschylus, made in it other improvements of his own.

His first appearance as a dramatist took place in B.C. 468, under peculiarly interesting circumstances; not only from the fact that Sophocles, at the age of twenty-seven, came forward as the rival of the veteran Æschylus, whose supremacy had been maintained during an entire generation, but also from the character of the judges. The solemnities of the greater Dionysia were rendered more imposing by the occasion of the return of Cimon from his expedition to Scyros, bringing with him the bones of Theseus. Public expectation was so excited respecting the approaching dramatic contest, and party feeling ran so high, that Apsephion, the archon eponymus, whose duty it was to appoint the judges, had not yet ventured to proceed to the final act of drawing the lots for their election, when Cimon, with his nine colleagues in the command, having entered the theatre, the archon detained them at the altar, and administered to them the oath appointed for the judges in the dramatic contests. Their decision was in favor of Sophocles, who received the first prize, the sec-

[1] *Smith, Dict. Biogr., s. v.; Donaldson, Theatre of the Greeks*, p. 81, *seqq.*, 6th ed.; *Müller, Hist. Gr. Lit.*, p. 337, *seqq.*

[2] Clinton, Müller, and others prefer B.C. 496.

[3] *Athen.*, i., p. 20; *Vit. Anon.*

ond only being awarded to Æschylus, who was so mortified at his defeat that, according to the common account, he left Athens in consequence, and retired to Sicily.[1] From this epoch Sophocles held the supremacy of the Athenian stage, until a formidable rival arose in Euripides, who gained the first prize for the first time in 441. The drama which Sophocles exhibited on the occasion of his first victory is supposed, from a chronological computation in Pliny,[2] to have been the Triptolemus, respecting the nature of which there has been much disputation. Welcker, who has discussed the question very fully, supposes that the main subject of the drama was the institution of the Eleusinian mysteries, and the establishment of the worship of Ceres at Athens, by Triptolemus.

The year 440 B.C. is a most important era in the poet's life. In the spring of that year, most probably, he brought out the earliest and one of the best of his extant dramas, the *Antigone*, a play which gave the Athenians so much satisfaction, especially on account of the political wisdom it displayed, that they appointed him one of the ten generals, of whom Pericles was the chief, in the war against the aristocratic faction of Samos, which lasted from the summer of B.C. 440 to the spring of B.C. 439. The anonymous biographer states that this expedition took place seven years before the Peloponnesian war, and that Sophocles was 55 years old at the time. From an anecdote preserved by Athenæus, from the Travels of the poet Ion, it appears that Sophocles was engaged in bringing up the re-enforcements from Chios, and that, amid the occupations of his military command, he preserved his wonted tranquillity of mind, and found leisure to gratify his voluptuous tastes, and to delight his comrades with his calm and pleasant conversation at their banquets. From the same narrative it would seem that Sophocles neither obtained nor sought for any military reputation; he is represented as good-humoredly repeating the judgment of Pericles concerning him, that he understood the making of poetry, but not the commanding of an army.[3]

The period extending from the 56th year of his age to his death was that of his greatest poetical activity, and to it belong, with the exception of the Antigone, all his extant dramas. Respecting his personal history, however, during this period of thirty-four years, we have scarcely any details. The excitement of the Peloponnesian war seems to have had no other influence upon him than to stimulate his literary efforts by the new impulse which it gave to the intellectual activity of the age; until that disastrous period after the Sicilian expedition, when the reaction of unsuccessful war led to anarchy at home. Then we find him, like others of the chief literary men of Athens, joining in the desperate attempt to stay the ruin of their country, by means of an aristocratic revolution; although, according to the accounts which have come down to us of the part which Sophocles took in this movement, he only assented to it as a measure of public safety, and not from any love of oligarchy. As he was then in his 83d year, however, it is not likely that he took an active part in public affairs. One thing, at least, is clear as to his political principles,

[1] *Plut. Cim.*, 8; *Marm. Par.*, 57.
[2] *H. N.*, xviii., 7, 12.
[3] *Ath.*, xiii., p. 603, *seq.*; *Vit. Anon.*; *Plut.*, *Per.*, 8.

that he was an ardent lover of his country. The patriotic sentiments which we still admire in his poems were illustrated by his own conduct; for, unlike Simonides and Pindar, Æschylus, Euripides, and Plato, and others of the greatest poets and philosophers of Greece, Sophocles would never condescend to accept the patronage of monarchs, or to leave his country in compliance with their repeated invitations.

The family dissensions which troubled his last years are connected with a well-known and beautiful story. His family consisted of two sons, Iophon, the offspring of Nicostrate, who was a free Athenian woman, and Ariston, his son by Theoris of Sicyon; and Ariston had a son named Sophocles, for whom his grandfather showed the greatest affection. Iophon, who was, by the laws of Athens, his father's rightful heir, jealous of his love for the young Sophocles, and apprehending that the poet purposed to bestow upon his grandson a large proportion of his property, is said to have summoned his father before the Phratores, who seem to have had a sort of jurisdiction in family affairs, on the charge that his mind was affected by old age. As his only reply, Sophocles exclaimed, "If I am Sophocles, I am not beside myself; and if I am beside myself, I am not Sophocles;" and then he read from his "Œdipus at Colonus," which had been only lately written, and was not yet brought out, the magnificent *parodus* beginning **Εὐίππου, ξένε, τᾶσδε χώρας,** whereupon the judges at once dismissed the case, and rebuked Iophon for his undutiful conduct.[1] Sophocles forgave his son, and it is probable that the reconciliation was referred to in the lines of the "Œdipus at Colonus," where Antigone pleads with her father to forgive Polynices, as other fathers had been induced to forgive their bad children.

Sophocles died soon afterward, in B.C. 406, in his ninetieth year. All the various accounts of his death and funeral are of a fictitious and poetical complexion. According to some writers, he was choked by a grape; another writer related that, in a public recitation of the *Antigone*, he sustained his voice so long without a pause that, through the weakness of extreme age, he lost his breath and his life together; while others ascribed his death to excessive joy at obtaining a dramatic victory.

By the universal consent of the best critics, both of ancient and modern times, the tragedies of Sophocles are not only the perfection of the Greek drama, but they approach as nearly as is conceivable to the perfect ideal model of that species of poetry. The subjects and style of Sophocles are human, while those of Æschylus are essentially heroic. The latter excite terror, pity, and admiration, as we view them at a distance; the former bring those same feelings home to the heart, with the addition of sympathy and self-application. No individual human being can imagine himself in the position of Prometheus, or derive a personal warning from the crimes and fate of Clytemnestra; but every one can, in feeling, share the self-devotion of Antigone in giving up her life at the call of fraternal piety, and the calmness which comes over the spirit of Œdipus when he is reconciled to the gods. In Æschylus, the sufferers are the victims of an inexorable destiny; but Sophocles brings more

[1] *Plut., An seni sit gerend. Resp.*, 3, p. 775, *B.*

prominently into view those faults of their own, which form one element of the destiny of which they are the victims, and is more intent upon inculcating, as the lesson taught by their woes, that wise calmness and moderation, in desires and actions, in prosperity and adversity, which the Greek poets and philosophers celebrate under the name of σωφροσύνη. On the other hand, he never descends to that level to which Euripides brought down the art, the exhibition of human passion and suffering for the mere purpose of exciting emotion in the spectators, apart from the moral end. The difference between the two poets is illustrated by the saying of Sophocles, that he himself represented men as they ought to be, but Euripides exhibited them as they are.[1]

Of the dramatic changes introduced by Sophocles, the most important was the addition of the τριταγωνιστής, or third actor, by which three persons were allowed to appear on the stage at once and take part in the dialogue, instead of only two. This change vastly enlarged the scope of the dramatic action, and appeared, indeed, to accomplish all that was necessary to the variety and mobility of action in tragedy, without sacrificing that simplicity and clearness which, in the good ages of antiquity, were always held to be most essential qualities. By the addition of this third actor, the chief person of the drama was brought under two conflicting influences, by the force of which both sides of his character are at once displayed; as in the scene where Antigone has to contend at the same time with the weakness of Ismene and the tyranny of Creon. Sophocles also introduced some very important modifications in the choral parts of the drama. According to Suidas, he raised the number of choreutæ from twelve to fifteen. At the same time, the choral odes, which still in Æschylus occupied a large space in the tragedy, and formed a sort of lyric exhibition of the subject interwoven with the dramatic representation, were very considerably curtailed. The mode, too, in which the chorus is connected with the general subject and progress of the drama, is different in Sophocles. In the dramas of Æschylus, the chorus is a deeply-interested party, often taking a decided and even vehement share in the action, and generally involved in the catastrophe; but the chorus of Sophocles has more of the character of a spectator, moderator, and judge, comparatively impartial, but sympathizing generally with the chief character of the play, while it explains and harmonizes, as far as possible, the feelings of all the actors. The chorus of Sophocles is cited by Aristotle as an example of his definition of the part to be taken by the chorus.

By these changes, Sophocles made the tragedy a *drama* in the proper sense of the word. The interest and progress of the piece centred almost entirely in the actions and speeches of the persons on the stage. A necessary consequence of this alteration, combined with the addition of a third actor, was a much more careful elaboration of the dialogue; and the care bestowed upon this part of the composition is one of the most striking features of the art of Sophocles, whether we regard the energy and point of the conversations which take place upon the stage,

[1] *Smith, Dict. Biogr., s. v.*

or the vivid pictures of actions occurring elsewhere, which are drawn in the speeches of the messengers. It must not, however, be imagined for a moment that, in bestowing so much care upon the dialogue, and confining the choral parts within their proper limits, Sophocles was careless as to the mode in which he executed the latter. On the contrary, he appears as if determined to use his utmost efforts to compensate in the beauty of his odes for what he had taken away from their length.

Another alteration of the greatest consequence, which, though it perhaps did not originate with Sophocles, he was the first to convert into a general practice, was the abandonment of the trilogistic form, in so far at least as the continuity of subject was concerned. In obedience to the established custom at the Dionysiac festivals, Sophocles appears generally to have brought forward three tragedies and a satyric drama together; but the subjects of these four plays were entirely distinct, and each was complete in itself. Among the merely mechanical improvements introduced by Sophocles, the most important was that of scene-painting, in which he availed himself of the aid of the Athenian artist Agatharchus, and improved upon the perspective painting which the same artist had previously executed for Æschylus.

The number of plays ascribed to Sophocles was 130, of which, however, according to Aristophanes of Byzantium, seventeen were spurious. He contended not only with Æschylus and Euripides, but also with Chœrilus, Aristias, Agathon, and other poets, among whom was his own son Iophon; and he carried off the first prize twenty or twenty-four times, frequently the second, but never fell to the third.[1] It is remarkable, as proving his growing activity and success, that of his 113 dramas eighty-one were brought out in the second of the two periods into which his career is divided by the exhibition of the *Antigone*, which was his thirty-second play;[2] and also that all his extant dramas, which of course, in the judgment of the grammarians, were his best, belong to the latter of these two periods. By comparing the number of his plays with the sixty-two years over which his career extended, and also the number belonging to each of the two periods, Müller obtains the result that he at first brought out a tetralogy every three or four years, but afterward every two years, at least; and also that in several of the tetralogies the satyric dramas must have been lost, or never existed, and that among those 113 plays there could only have been, at the most, twenty-three satyric dramas to ninety tragedies. The titles and fragments of the lost plays of Sophocles will be found collected in the chief editions, and in Welcker's *Griechischen Tragoedien*, Bonn, 1840. In addition to his tragedies, Sophocles is said to have written an elegy, pæans, and other poems, and a prose work on the chorus in opposition to Thespis and Chœrilus.

The following is most probably the chronological order in which the seven extant tragedies of Sophocles were brought out: 1. Antigone; 2. Electra; 3. Trachiniæ; 4. Œdipus Tyrannus; 5. Ajax; 6. Philoctetes; 7. Œdipus at Colonus. The last of these was brought out after the death of the poet by his grandson, as has already been stated.

---

[1] *Vit. Anon.; Suid., s. v.*

[2] *Aristoph. Byz., Argum. ad Antig.*

ANCIENT COMMENTATORS ON SOPHOCLES.

In the *scholia*, the commentators are quoted by the general title of οἱ ὑπομνηματισταί, or οἱ ὑπομνηματισάμενοι. Among those cited by name, or to whom commentaries on Sophocles are ascribed by other authorities, are Aristarchus, Praxiphanes, Didymus, Herodianus, Horapollon, Androtion, and Aristophanes of Byzantium. The question of the value of the *scholia* is discussed by Wunder, *De Schol. in Soph. auctoritate*, 1838, 4to, and Wolff, *De Sophoclis Scholiorum Laur. Variis Lectionibus*, Lips., 1843, 8vo.[1]

EDITIONS OF SOPHOCLES.

The *Editio Princeps* is that of Aldus, 1502, 8vo, and there were numerous other editions printed in the 16th century, the best of which are those of H. Stephanus, Paris, 1568, 4to, and of Canterus, Antwerp, 1579, 12mo, both founded on the text of Turnebus. None of the subsequent editions deserve any particular notice, until we come to those of Brunck, in 4 vols. 8vo, Strasburg, 1786–1789, and in 2 vols. 4to, Strasburg, 1786; both editions containing the Greek text with a Latin version, and also the scholia and indices. The text of Brunck, which was founded on that of Aldus, has formed the foundation of all the subsequent editions, of which the following are the most important: that of Musgrave, with scholia, notes, and indices, Oxford, 1800, 1801, 2 vols. 8vo, reprinted Oxford, 1809, 1810, 3 vols. 8vo; that of Erfurdt, with scholia, notes, and indices, Leipzig, 1802–1825, 7 vols. 8vo, completed by Heller and Doederlein; that of Bothe, who re-edited Brunck's edition, but with many rash changes in the text, Leipzig, 1806, 2 vols. 8vo, last edition, 1827, 1828; that of Hermann, who completed a new edition, which Erfurdt commenced, but only lived to publish the first two volumes, Leipzig, 1809–1825, 7 vols. small 8vo; Hermann's entirely new revision of Brunck's edition, with additional notes, &c., Leipzig, 1823–1825, 7 vols. 8vo; the edition of Schneider, with German notes and a Lexicon, Weimar, 1823–1830, 10 vols. 12mo; the London reprint of Brunck's edition, with the notes of Burney and Schaefer, 1824, 3 vols. 8vo; the edition of Elmsley, with the notes of Brunck and Schaefer, Lexicon Sophocleum, &c., Oxford, 1826, 2 vols. 8vo, reprinted Leipzig, 1827; that of the text alone by Dindorf, in the *Poetæ Scenici Græci*, Leipzig, 1830, 2d ed. 1847, reprinted at Oxford, 1832–1836, with the scholia and a volume of notes, 3 vols. 8vo; that of Benloew and Ahrens, in Didot's Bibliotheca, Paris, 1842; that of Mitchell, Lond., 1841–2, 2 vols. 8vo; and lastly, by far the most useful editions for the ordinary student are, that of Neue, Leipzig, 1831, 8vo; that of Linwood, Lond., 1846, 8vo; and more particularly that of Wunder, in Jacob and Rost's *Bibliotheca Græca*, containing the text, with critical and explanatory notes, and introductions, Gotha and Erfurdt, 1831–1846, 2 vols. 8vo, in 7 parts, and with a supplemental part of emendations to the Trachiniæ, Grima, 1841, 8vo. The editions of separate plays are, as may be supposed, exceedingly numerous. Among the number the following are deserving of especial mention: the "Ajax," by Lobeck, Leipzig, 1835, 2d ed., and with English notes by Pitman, London, 1830; the "Œdipus Coloneus," by Reisig, Jena, 1820, and by Elmsley, London, 1823, 8vo; and the "Antigone" by Wex, Leipzig, 1829–31, 2 vols. 8vo, and by Boeckh with a German version and notes, Berlin, 1843, 8vo. A very useful and learned commentary on Sophocles is contained in the valuable "*Lexicon Sophocleum*" of Ellendt, Königsberg, 1835, 2 vols. 8vo.

II. Euripides[2] (Εὐριπίδης) was the son of Mnesarchus and Clito, and is said to have been born at Salamis, B.C. 480, on the very day that the Greeks defeated the Persians off that island, whither his parents had fled from Athens on the invasion of Xerxes. Müller regards, however, the account of his having been born on the day of the battle as a mere legend,[3] and other scholars also look with suspicion on the way in which it was thus contrived to bring the three great tragic poets of Athens into connection with the most glorious day in her annals.[4] Thus it has been said that while Euripides then first saw the light, Æschylus, in the maturity of manhood, fought in the battle, and Sophocles, a beautiful boy of

---

1 *Smith, Dict. Biogr., s. v.*

2 *Ibid.*

3 *Müller, Hist. Gr. Lit.*, p. 358.

4 *Hartung, Eurip. Restitut.*, p. 10.

fifteen, led the chorus in the festival which celebrated the victory. According to another account, he received his name in commemoration of the battle of Artemisium, which took place near the Euripus, not long before he was born, and in the same year; but Euripides was not a new name, and had already belonged to an earlier tragic writer mentioned by Suidas. Some writers relate that the parents of Euripides were in mean circumstances, and his mother is represented by Aristophanes as an herb-seller, and not a very honest one either;[1] but much weight can not be accorded to these statements. It is more probable that his family was respectable.[2] We are told that the poet, when a boy, was cup-bearer to a chorus of noble Athenians at the Thargelian festival, an office for which nobility of blood was requisite.[3] We know, also, that he was taught rhetoric by Prodicus, who was certainly not moderate in his terms for instruction, and who was in the habit of seeking his pupils among youths of high rank.[4] It is said that the future distinction of Euripides was predicted by an oracle, promising that he should be crowned with "sacred garlands," in consequence of which his father had him trained to gymnastic exercises; and we learn that, while yet a boy, he won the prize at the Eleusinian and Thesean contests, and offered himself, when seventeen years old, as a candidate at the Olympic games, but was not admitted because of some doubt about his age.[5] Some trace of his early gymnastic pursuits has been remarked in the detailed description of the combat between Eteocles and Polynices in the Phœnissæ.[6]

Soon, however, abandoning these pursuits, he studied the art of painting,[7] not, as we learn, without success; and it has been observed that the veiled figure of Agamemnon in the Iphigenia of Timanthes was probably suggested by a line in Euripides' description of the same scene.[8] To philosophy and literature he devoted himself with much interest and energy, studying physics under Anaxagoras, and rhetoric, as we have already seen, under Prodicus. We learn also from Athenæus that he was a great book-collector, and it is recorded of him that he committed to memory certain treatises of Heraclitus, which he found hidden in the temple of Diana, and which he was the first to introduce to the notice of Socrates.[9] His intimacy with the latter is beyond a doubt, though we must reject the statement of Gellius, that he received instruction from him in moral science, since Socrates was not born till B.C. 468, twelve years after the birth of Euripides. Traces of the teaching of Anaxagoras have been remarked in many passages both of the extant plays and of the fragments, and were impressed especially on the lost tragedy of "Melanippa the Wise."[10]

Euripides is said to have written a tragedy at the age of eighteen; but the first play which was exhibited in his own name was the *Peliades*, when he was twenty-five years of age (B.C. 455). In B.C. 441 he gained,

[1] *Aristoph.*, *Acharn.*, 454; *Thesm.*, 387, 456; *Plin.*, *H. N.*, xxii., 22. [2] *Suid.*, *s. v.*
[3] *Athen.*, x., p. 424, *E.* [4] *Plat.*, *Apol.*, p. 19, *E; Stallb. ad loc.*
[5] *Œnom. ap. Euseb.*, *Præp. Evang.*, v. 33; *Gell.*, xv., 20. [6] v. 1392, *seqq.*
[7] *Thom. Mag.*, *Vit. Eur.; Suid.*, *s. v.* [8] *Iph. in Aul.*, 1550. [9] *Athen.*, i., p. 3, *A.*
[10] *Orest.*, 545, 971; *Pors. ad loc.; Fragm. Melanipp.*, ed. *Wagner*, p. 255.

for the first time, the first prize, and he continued to exhibit plays until B.C. 408, the date of the "Orestes." Soon after this he left Athens for the court of Archelaus, king of Macedonia, his reasons for which step can only be matter of conjecture. Traditionary scandal has ascribed it to his disgust at the intrigue of his wife with Cephisophon, and the ridicule which was showered upon him in consequence by the comic poets. But the whole story has been refuted by modern writers.[1] Other causes must, therefore, have led him to accept an invitation from Archelaus, at whose court the highest honors awaited him. The attacks of Aristophanes and others had probably not been without their effect; and he must have been aware that his philosophical tenets were regarded with considerable suspicion. He died in Macedonia in B.C. 406. Most testimonies agree in stating that he was torn in pieces by the king's dogs, which, according to some, were set upon him through envy by Arrhidæus and Crateuas, two rival poets. The Athenians sent to ask for his remains, but Archelaus refused to give them up, and buried them in Macedonia with great honor. The regret of Sophocles for his death is said to have been so great, that, at the representation of his next play, he made his actors appear uncrowned. The statue of Euripides in the theatre at Athens is mentioned by Pausanias. The admiration felt for him by foreigners, even in his lifetime, may be illustrated not only by the patronage of Archelaus, but also by what Plutarch records, that many of the Athenian prisoners in Sicily regained their liberty by reciting his verses to their masters, and that the Caunians, on one occasion, having at first refused to admit into their harbor an Athenian ship pursued by pirates, allowed it to put in when they found that some of the crew could repeat fragments of his poems.[2]

We have already intimated that the accounts which we find in Athenæus and others of the profligacy of Euripides are mere idle scandal, and scarcely worthy of serious refutation.[3] Nor does there appear to be any better foundation for that other charge, which has been brought against him, of hatred to the female sex. This is said to have been occasioned by the infidelity of his wife, but, as has already been remarked, this tale does not deserve credit. Euripides, like his master Anaxagoras, was a man of serious temper and averse to mirth,[4] and it was in consequence of this that the charge probably originated. It is certain that the poet who drew such characters as Antigone, Iphigenia, and, above all, Alcestis, was not blind to the gentleness, the strong affection, the self-abandoning devotedness of woman. With respect to the world and the Deity, he seems to have adopted the doctrines of his master, not unmixed apparently with pantheistic views.[5] To class him with atheists, as some have done, is undoubtedly unjust. At the same time, it must be confessed that we look in vain in his plays for the high faith of Æschylus; nor can we fail to admit that the pupil of Anaxagoras could not sympathize with the popular religious system around him, nor throw himself cordially into it. He frequently, also, altered in the most arbitrary manner the ancient

[1] *Hartung*, p. 165, *seqq.*
[2] *Smith, l. c.*
[3] *Athen.*, xiii., p. 557, *E*; p. 603, *E*.
[4] *Gell.*, xv., 20; compare *Æl.*, *V. H.*, viii., 13.
[5] *Valck. Diatr.*, p. 4, *seqq.*; *Hartung*, § 47.

legends. Thus, in the "Orestes," Menelaus comes before us as a selfish coward; in the "Helena," the notion of Stesichorus is adopted that the heroine was never carried to Troy at all, and that it was a mere εἴδωλον of her for which the Greeks and Trojans fought.[1]

With Euripides tragedy is brought down into the sphere of every-day life. Men are represented, according to the remark of Sophocles, not as they ought to be, but as they are. Under the names of the ancient heroes, the characters of his own times are set before us; it is not Iphigenia, or Medea, or Alcestis, that is speaking, but a daughter, a mother, or a wife.[2] All this, indeed, gave fuller scope, perhaps, for the exhibition of passion, and for those scenes of tenderness and pathos in which Euripides especially excelled; and it will serve also to account, in a great measure, for the preference given to his plays by the practical Socrates, who is said to have never entered the theatre unless when they were acted, as well as for the admiration felt for him by Menander and Philemon, and other poets of the new comedy. The most serious defects in his tragedies, artistically speaking, are his constant employment of the "*Deus ex machina;*" the disconnection of his choral odes from the subject of the play; the extremely awkward and formal character of his prologues; and the frequent introduction of frigid γνῶμαι and of philosophical disquisitions, making Medea talk like a sophist, and Hecuba like a free-thinker, and aiming rather at subtilty than simplicity. On the same principles on which he brought his subjects and characters to the level of common life, he adopted also in his style the every-day mode of speaking, and Aristotle commends him as having been the first to produce an effect by the skillful employment of words from the ordinary language of men, peculiarly fitted, it may be observed, for the expression of the gentler and more tender feelings. Euripides was held in high estimation by Cicero and Quintilian, the latter of whom says that he is worthy of being compared with the most eloquent pleaders of the Forum;[3] while Cicero so admired him that he is said to have had in his hand his tragedy of the "Medea" at the time of his murder.[4]

According to some accounts, Euripides wrote, in all, 75 plays; according to others, 92. Of these, 18 are extant, if we omit the "Rhesus," the genuineness of which has been defended by Vater and Hartung, while Valckenaer, Hermann, and Müller have, on good grounds, pronounced it spurious. To what author, however, or to what period it should be assigned, is a disputed point.[5] A list is here subjoined of the extant plays of Euripides, with their dates, ascertained or probable: 1. *Alcestis,* B.C. 438. This play was brought out as the last of a tetralogy, and stood, therefore, in the place of a satyric drama, to which, indeed, it bears, in some parts, great similarity, particularly in the representation of Hercules in his cups. 2. *Medea,* B.C. 431. 3. *Hippolytus Coronifer,* B.C. 428, gained the first prize. 4. *Hecuba.* Exhibited before B.C. 423. 5. *Her-*

[1] Compare *Herod.*, ii., 112, *seqq.*
[2] *Keble, Prælect. Acad.*, p. 596.
[3] *Cic., Ep. ad Fam.*, xvi., 8; *Quint., Inst. Or.*, x., 1.
[4] *Ptol. Hephæst.*, v., 5.
[5] *Valck., Diatr.*, 9, 10; *Herm., De Rheso trag., Opusc.*, vol. iii.; *Müller, Hist. Gr. Lit.*, p. 380, note.

aclidæ, about B.C. 421. 6. *Supplices*, about B.C. 421. 7. *Ion*, of uncertain date. 8. *Hercules Furens*, of uncertain date. 9. *Andromache*, about B.C. 420–417. 10. *Troades*, B.C. 415. 11. *Electra*, about B.C. 415–413. 12. *Helena*, B.C. 412. 13. *Iphigenia among the Tauri*, of uncertain date. 14. *Orestes*, B.C. 408. 15. *Phœnissæ*, of uncertain date. 16. *Bacchæ*. This play was apparently written for representation in Macedonia, and therefore at a very late period of the life of Euripides. 17. *Iphigenia at Aulis*. This play, together with the Bacchæ and the Alcmæon, was brought out at Athens, after the poet's death, by the younger Euripides. 18. *Cyclops*, of uncertain date. It is interesting as the only extant specimen of the Greek satyric drama.

Besides the plays, there are extant five letters, purporting to have been written by Euripides, but they are spurious. They are generally appended to the editions of the entire plays, and are also given in the Collection of Greek letters by Aldus and others. Three of these letters are addressed to King Archelaus, and the other two to Sophocles and Cephisophon respectively. Among those who deny their authenticity may be named Bentley. Barnes declares in their favor!

EDITIONS OF EURIPIDES.

The *Editio Princeps* of Euripides contains the *Medea*, *Hippolytus*, *Alcestis*, and *Andromache*, in capital letters. It is without date or printer's name, but is supposed, with much probability, to have been edited by J. Lascaris, and printed by De Alopa, at Florence, toward the end of the 15th century. In 1503, an edition was published by Aldus, at Venice; it contains 18 plays, including the "Rhesus," and omitting the "Electra." Another, published at Heidelberg in 1597, contained the Latin version of Æmilius Portus, and a fragment of the Danaë, for the first time, from some ancient MSS. in the Palatine library. Another was published by P. Stephens, Geneva, 1602. In that of Barnes, Cambridge, 1694, whatever be the defects of Barnes as an editor, much was done toward the correction and illustration of the text. It contains also many fragments, and the spurious letters. Other editions are that of Musgrave, Oxford, 1778, 4 vols. 4to; of Beck, Leipzig, 1778–88, 3 vols. 8vo; of Matthiæ, Leipzig, 1813–1829, 9 vols. 8vo; a variorum edition, published at Glasgow in 1821, 9 vols. 8vo; the edition of Dindorf, the text merely, contained in his *Poetæ Scenici Græci*, reprinted at Oxford, 1832–40, 4 vols. 8vo, with a commentary; that of Pflugk, in the *Bibliotheca Græca* of Jacobs and Rost, Lips., 1829, &c., continued after Pflugk's death by Klotz, still in a course of publication; and that of Fix, in Didot's *Bibliotheca*, Paris, 1840. The fragments have been edited in a separate form by Wagner, Wratislaw, 1844, reprinted in Didot's *Bibliotheca*. Of separate plays there have been numerous editions; but the most important and valuable are those by Porson, Elmsley, Valckenaer, Monk, and Hermann. Porson edited four plays, the *Hecuba*, *Orestes*, *Phœnissæ*, and *Medea*, with critical notes, and valuable prefatory matter. His work was reprinted at Leipzig, under the supervision of Schaefer. Elmsley edited the *Medea*, *Heraclidæ*, and *Bacchæ;* Valckenaer edited the *Phœnissæ* and *Hippolytus;* Monk, the *Alcestis* and *Hippolytus;* and Hermann, the *Hecuba*, *Phœnissæ*, *Helena*, *Andromache*, *Iphigenia among the Tauri*, *Iphigenia at Aulis*, *Cyclops*, and the *Orestes*.

CHAPTER XXV.

FOURTH OR ATTIC PERIOD—*continued.*

THE OTHER TRAGIC POETS.[1]

I. We may consider ourselves fortunate in possessing, as specimens of Greek tragedy, master-pieces by those poets whom their contemporaries and all antiquity unanimously regarded as the heroes of the tragic stage. Æschylus, Sophocles, and Euripides are the names which continually recur whenever the ancients speak of the height which tragic poetry attained at Athens; the state itself distinguished them by founding institutions the object of which was to preserve their works pure and unadulterated, and to protect them from being interpolated at the caprice of the actors. According to a law proposed by the orator Lycurgus, authentic copies of the works of the three great tragic poets were kept in the archives at Athens, and it was the duty of the public secretary (γραμματεὺς τῆς πόλεως) to see that the actors delivered this text only.[2]

II. Their contemporaries among the tragic writers must be regarded as, for the most part, far from insignificant poets, inasmuch as they maintained their places on the stage beside them, and not unfrequently gained the tragic prize in competition with them. Yet, though their *separate* productions may have been in part happy enough to merit most fully the approbation of the public, the *general* character of these poets must have been deficient in that depth and peculiar force of genius by which the great tragic poets were distinguished. If this had not been the case, their works would assuredly have attracted greater attention, and have been read more frequently in later times.

III. Neŏphron (Νεόφρων) or Neŏphon (Νεοφῶν), of Sicyon, appears to have been one of the most ancient of these poets, and is placed by Clinton before the age of Euripides. In the scholia to the "Medea" of the latter, we have two fragments of a play written on the same subject by Neophron, one of four lines at verse 668, and another of five lines at verse 1354. Besides these, we have fifteen lines quoted by Stobæus from the same tragedy. Suidas states that he wrote 120 tragedies, that the "Medea" of Euripides was sometimes attributed to him, and that he was the first to introduce on the stage the παιδαγωγός, and the examination of slaves by torture. In one particular, namely, that the "Medea" of Euripides was sometimes attributed to him, Suidas is confirmed by Diogenes Laertius; but when the former adds that Neophron was involved in the fate of Callisthenes, and put to death by Alexander the Great, he violates chronology, and evidently confounds Neophron with a later tragedian named Nearchus.[3] As far as we can judge from the fragments of Neophron already mentioned, Euripides may have borrowed his

[1] *Müller, Hist. Gr. Lit.*, p. 381. [2] *Plut., Vit. Decem Orat.*, p. 841, *seqq.*
[3] *Elms. ad Eurip., Med.*, p. 68; *Diog. Laert.*, ii., 134.

plot and characters from him, but certainly not his style.[1] The fragments are given in Wagner's collection, in Didot's *Bibliotheca Græca.*

IV. Ion (Ἴων), of Chios, was one of the five Athenian tragic poets of the canon. He lived at Athens in the time of Æschylus and Cimon, and in the fragments of his writings speaks of the events of their day as from personal knowledge. He was a very comprehensive writer, and, what was very uncommon in ancient times, a prose author as well as a poet. He wrote a history, entitled Χίου κτίσις, in the dialect and after the manner of Herodotus, except that he paid more attention to the private life of distinguished individuals. This work was probably the same with the συγγραφή, which is quoted by Pausanias.[2] Another prose work was entitled Κοσμολογικός, identical probably with the philosophical work named τριαγμός (or τριαγμοί), which seems to have been a treatise on the constitution of things according to the theory of triads, and which some ancient writers ascribed to Orpheus. Another work, entitled ὑπομνήματα, seems to have contained either an account of his own travels, or of the visits of great men to Chios.[3]

Ion did not come forward as a tragedian until B.C. 452, after the death of Æschylus, whose place, it seems, he expected to fill on the stage. The materials of his dramas were in a great measure taken from Homer; they may have been connected in trilogies like those of Æschylus; the few remains, however, hardly allow us to trace the connection of these trilogical compositions. He is mentioned as third in competition with Euripides and Iophon in Ol. 87, 4 (B.C. 429–428); and he died before B.C. 419, as appears from the "Peace" of Aristophanes,[4] which was brought out in that year. Only one victory of Ion's is mentioned, on which occasion, it is said, having gained the dithyrambic and tragic prizes at the same time, he presented every Athenian with a pitcher of Chian wine.[5] Hence it would seem that he was a man of considerable wealth. The number of his tragedies is variously stated at twelve, thirty, and forty. We have the titles and a few fragments of eleven. Longinus describes the style of Ion's tragedies as marked by petty refinements and want of boldness, and he adds an expression, which shows the distance that there was, in the opinion of the ancients, between the great tragedians and the best of their rivals, that no one in his senses would compare the value of the "Œdipus" with that of all the tragedies of Ion taken together. Nevertheless, he was greatly admired, chiefly, it would seem, for a sort of elegant wit. There are some beautiful passages in the extant fragments of his tragedies. Commentaries were written upon him by Arcesilaus, Batton of Sinope, Didymus, Epigenes, and even by Aristarchus. Besides his tragedies, we are told by the scholiast on Aristophanes that Ion also wrote lyric poems, comedies, epigrams, pæans, hymns, scolia, and elegies. Respecting his comedies a doubt has been raised, on account of the confusion between comedy and tragedy, which is so frequent in the writings of the grammarians; but, in the case of so universal a writer as Ion, the

---

1 *Elms., l. c.; Smith, Dict. Biogr., s. v.*

2 *Pausan.*, vii., 4, 8.

3 *Bentley, Ep. ad Mill.; Opusc.*, p. 494, *seqq.*, ed. *Lips.*

4 *Aristoph., Pax*, 830.

5 *Schol. ad Aristoph., l. c.; Athen.*, i., p. 3, F.

probability seems to be in favor of the scholiast's statement. Of his elegies we have still some remnants in the Greek Anthology,[1] which are given also in the collections of Schneidewin and Bergk. The fragments of Ion have been published, with an account of his life, &c., by Nieberding, Lips., 1836, and Köpke, Berol., 1836. They are contained also in Wagner's *Fragm. Trag. Græc.*

V. Aristarchus (Ἀρίσταρχος), of Tegea, was contemporary with Euripides, and flourished about 454 B.C. He lived to the age of a hundred. Out of seventy tragedies which he exhibited, only two obtained the prize.[2] Nothing remains of his works except a few lines,[3] and the titles of three of his plays, namely, the Ἀσκληπιός, which he is said to have written and named after the god in gratitude for his recovery from illness; the Ἀχιλλεύς, which Ennius translated into Latin;[4] and the Τάνταλος.[5] The fragments are contained in Wagner's *Fragm. Trag. Græc.*

VI. Achæus (Ἀχαιός), of Eretria, in Eubœa, was born B.C. 484, the year in which Æschylus gained his first victory, and four years before the birth of Euripides. In B.C. 447, he contended with Sophocles and Euripides, and though he subsequently brought out many dramas, according to some as many as thirty or forty, he nevertheless only gained the prize once. The fragments of Achæus contain much strange mythology, and his expressions were often forced and obscure.[6] Still, in the satyrical drama, he must have possessed considerable merit, for in this department some ancient critics thought him inferior only to Æschylus.[7] The titles of seven of his satyrical dramas and ten of his tragedies are still known. The extant fragments of his pieces have been collected and edited by Urlichs, Bonn, 1834, and are also contained in Wagner's *Fragm. Trag. Græc.* This Achæus must not be confounded with a later tragic writer of the same name, a native of Syracuse, who, according to Suidas and Phavorinus, wrote ten, but, according to Eudocia, fourteen tragedies.[8]

VII. Carcĭnus (Καρκίνος), of Athens, was a very skillful scenic dancer,[9] and is occasionally alluded to by Aristophanes.[10] His dramas, of which no fragments have come down to us, seem to have perished at an early day. Another tragic poet of the same name appears to have been a grandson of the first, and is probably the same as the one who spent a great part of his life at the court of Dionysius the younger at Syracuse.[11] The tragedies which are referred to by the ancients under the name of Carcinus probably all belong to the younger one. Suidas attributes to him 160 tragedies, but we possess the titles and fragments of nine only, and some fragments of uncertain dramas. His style is said by some of the ancient writers to have been marked by studied obscurity; though in the fragments extant we can scarcely perceive any trace of this obscurity, and their style bears a close resemblance to that of Euripides.[12] The fragments of the younger Carcinus are given in Wagner's *Fragm. Trag. Græc.*

1 *Smith, Dict. Biogr., s. v.*
2 *Suid., s. v.; Euseb., Chron. Armen.*
3 *Stob.*, tit. 63, § 9; tit. 120, § 2; *Athen.*, xiii., p. 612, *F.*
4 *Festus, s. v. prolato ære.*
5 *Stob.*, ii., 1, § 1.
6 *Athen.*, x., p. 451, *C.*
7 *Diog. Laert.*, ii., 133.
8 *Smith, Dict. Biogr., s. v.*
9 *Athen.*, i., p. 22.
10 *Aristoph., Nub.*, 1263; *Pax*, 794.
11 *Diog. Laert.*, ii., 7.
12 *Meineke, Hist. Crit. Com. Græc.*, p. 505, *seqq.; Smith, Dict. Biogr., s. v.*

VIII. Agăthon (Ἀγάθων) was born about B.C. 447, and sprung from a rich and respectable Athenian family. He was contemporary with Socrates and Alcibiades, and the other distinguished characters of their age, with many of whom he was on terms of intimate acquaintance. Among these was his friend Euripides. He was remarkable for the handsomeness of his person, and his various accomplishments.[1] He gained his first victory at the Lenæan festival in B.C. 416, when he was a little above thirty years of age; in honor of which Plato represents the symposium or banquet to have been given, which he has made the occasion of his dialogue so called. The scene is laid at Agathon's house, and among the interlocutors are Apollodorus, Socrates, Aristophanes, Diotima, and Alcibiades. Plato was then fourteen years of age, and a spectator at the tragic contest in which Agathon was victorious.[2] When Agathon was about forty years of age (B.C. 407), he visited the court of Archelaus, king of Macedonia,[3] where his old friend Euripides was also a guest at the same time. He is generally supposed to have died about B.C. 400, at the age of forty-seven.[4]

The poetic merits of Agathon were considerable, but his compositions were more remarkable for elegance and flowery ornaments, than force, vigor, or sublimity. They abounded in antithesis and metaphor, and he is said to have imitated in verse the prose of Gorgias the philosopher. The style of his verses, and especially of his lyric compositions, is represented by Aristophanes as affected and effeminate, corresponding with his personal appearance and manner.[5] In another play, however, acted five years afterward, Aristophanes speaks of him in high terms both as a poet and a man. In some respects Agathon was instrumental in causing the decline of tragedy at Athens. He was the first tragic poet, according to Aristotle,[6] who adopted the practice of inserting choruses between the acts, the subject-matter of which was unconnected with the story of the piece, and which were, therefore, called ἐμβόλιμα, or intercalary, as being merely lyrical or musical interludes. Agathon also wrote pieces, the story and characters of which were the creations of pure fiction. One of these was called the "Flower" (Ἄνθος);[7] its subject-matter was neither mythical nor historical, and therefore probably neither seriously affecting nor terrible. We can not but regret the loss of this work, which must have been both amusing and original. The titles of only four of his tragedies are known with certainty; they are the "Thyestes," the "Telephus," the "Aërope," and the "Alcmæon." A fifth, which is ascribed to him, is of doubtful authenticity. The opinion that Agathon also wrote comedies has been refuted by Bentley, in his Dissertation upon the Epistles of Euripides.[8] The fragments of Agathon are given in Wagner's *Fragm. Trag. Græc.*

IX. About this time the tragic stage received a great influx of poets, which, however, does not prove that a great advance had taken place in

1 *Plat., Protag.*, p. 156, *B.* 2 *Athen*, v., p. 217, *A.* 3 *Ælian, V. H.*, xiii., 4.
4 *Bode, Gesch. d. Dram. Dichtk.*, i., p. 553. 5 *Aristoph., Thesmoph.*, p. 191.
6 *Aristot., Poët.*, 18, § 22. 7 *Ibid.*, 9, § 7.
8 *Ritschl, Comment. de Agathonis vita*, &c., Halis, 1829, 8vo; *Smith, s. v.*

the art of tragic poetry.[1] Aristophanes speaks of thousands of tragedy-making babblers, more garrulous by a good deal than Euripides. He calls their poems muses' groves for swallows, comparing their trifling and insignificant attempts at polite literature with the chirping of birds. Happily these dilettanti were generally satisfied with presenting themselves *once* before the people as tragic poets. There was such a taste for the composition of tragedies, that we find, among those who wrote for the stage, men of the most different pursuits and dispositions; such as CRITIAS, the head of the oligarchical party at Athens, and DIONYSIUS the elder, tyrant of Syracuse, who often came forward as a competitor for the tragic prize, and had the satisfaction of receiving the crown once before he died. Such men were fond of availing themselves of tragedy, in the same way that Euripides did, as a vehicle for bringing before the public, in a less suspicious manner, their speculations on the political and social interests of their auditors. In the drama called *Sisyphus* (which is, perhaps, more rightly ascribed to Critias than to Euripides), there was a development of the pernicious doctrine of the sophists, that religion was an ancient political institution, designed to sanction the restraints of law by superadding the fear of the gods; and we are told that Dionysius wrote a drama against Plato's theory of the state, which was called a tragedy, but had rather the character of a comedy. It is well known, too, that PLATO also composed a tetralogy in his younger days, which he committed to the flames when he had convinced himself that dramatic poetry was not his vocation.[2]

X. The families of the great poets contributed in a considerable degree to continue the tragic art after their death. As the great poets not only felt themselves called upon by their own taste to devote themselves to dramatic poetry, and to bring out plays and teach the chorus year after year, but really practiced this art as an ostensible profession, we can not wonder that this, like other employments and trades, was transmitted by a regular descent to their sons and grandsons. Æschylus was followed by a succession of tragedians, who flourished through several generations. His son EUPHORION, as we have before remarked, sometimes brought out plays of his father's which had not been represented before, sometimes pieces of his own, and he gained, as we have seen, the tragic prize in competition with both Sophocles and Euripides. Similarly, Æschylus' nephew, PHILOCLES, gained the prize against the "King Œdipus" of Sophocles, a piece which, in the opinion of modern times, is not to be surpassed. Philocles must have had a good deal of his uncle's manner. MORSIMUS, the son of Philocles, seems to have done but little honor to the family; but, after the Peloponnesian war, the Æschyleans gained new lustre from ASTYDAMAS, who brought out 240 pieces, and gained fifteen victories. From these numbers we see that Astydamas in his time supplied the Athenian public with new tetralogies almost every year at the Lenæa and great Dionysia, and that, on an average, he gained the prize once every four contests.[3]

XI. With regard to the family of Sophocles, IOPHON was an active and

[1] *Müller, Hist. Gr. Lit.*, p. 384. [2] *Müller, l. c.* [3] *Id. ib.*

popular tragedian in his father's lifetime, and Aristophanes considers him as the only support of the tragic stage after the death of the two great poets. We do not know, however, in what manner a later age answered the comedian's doubtful question, whether Iophon would be able to do as much by himself, now that he was deprived of the benefit of his father's counsel and guidance. Some years later, the *younger* SOPHOCLES, the grandson of the great poet, came forward, at first with the legacy of unpublished dramas which his grandfather had left him, and soon after with plays of his own. As he gained the prize, according to one statement, twelve times, he must have been one of the most prolific poets of the day He was undoubtedly the most considerable rival of the Æschylean Astydamas. He did not begin to exhibit his own dramas until B.C. 396. He had previously, in B.C. 401, brought out the "Œdipus Coloneus" of his grandfather, followed very probably by other plays of the latter.[1]

XII. A younger EURIPIDES also gained some reputation by the side of these descendants of the other two tragedians. He stands on the same footing in relation to his father as Euphorion to Æschylus, and the younger Sophocles to his grandfather; he first brought out plays by his distinguished parent, and then tried the success of his own productions. Suidas mentions also a nephew of the great poet of the same name, to whom he ascribes the authorship of three plays, "Medea," "Orestes," and "Polyxena," and who, he tells us, gained a prize with one of his uncle's tragedies, after the death of the latter. It is probable, however, that the son and the nephew have been confounded by him.

XIII. By the side of these successors of the great tragedians others from time to time made their appearance, and in them we may see more distinct traces of those tendencies of the age, which were not without their influence on the others. In them tragic poetry appears no longer as independent, and as following its own object and its own laws, but as subordinated to the spirit which had developed itself in other branches of literature. The lyric poetry and the rhetoric of the time had an especial influence on the form of tragic poetry.

XIV. How much CHÆRĒMON (Χαιρήμων), who flourished about B.C. 380, was possessed with the spirit of the lyric poetry of his time, is clear from all that is related of him. The contemporary dithyrambic poets were continually making sudden transitions in their songs from one species of tones and rhythms to another, and sacrificed the unity of character to a striving after metrical variety of expression. But nobody went farther than Chæremon in this, for, according to Aristotle, he mixed up all kinds of metres in his Κένταυρος, which seems to have been a most extraordinary compound of epic, lyric, and dramatic poetry. His dramatic productions were rich in descriptions, which did not, like those of the old tragedians, belong to the pieces, and contribute to place in a clearer light the condition, the relations, the deeds of some person engaged in the action, but sprung altogether from a fondness for delineating subjects which produce a pleasing impression on the senses. No tragedian could be compared with Chæremon in the number of his charming pictures of female

[1] *Müller*, p. 387.

beauty, in which the serious muse of the great tragedians is exceedingly chaste and retiring; the only counterpoise to this is his passion for the multifarious perfumes and colors of flowers, in the description of which he luxuriates. With this mixture of foreign ingredients, tragedy ceases to be a *drama*, in the proper sense of the word, in which every thing depends on the causes and developments of actions, and on manifestations of the will of man. Accordingly, Aristotle calls this Chæremon, in connection with the dithyrambic poet Licymnius, *poets to be read* (ἀναγνωστικοί), and says of the former, in particular, that he is exact, that is, careful and accurate in detail, like a professed writer, whose sole object is the satisfaction of his readers.[1] The fragments of Chæremon have been collected by Bartsch, Mogunt., 1843, 4to, and are also contained in Wagner's *Fragm. Trag. Græc.*

XV. But this later tragedy was still more powerfully affected by the *rhetoric* of the time, that is, the art of speaking as taught in the school. Dramatic poetry and oratory were so near one another from the beginning, that they often seem to join hands over the gap which separates poetry from prose. The object of oratory is to determine by means of argument the convictions and the will of other men; but dramatic poetry leaves the actions of the persons represented to be determined by the development of their own views and the expression of the opinions of others. The Athenians were so habituated to hear long public speeches in their courts and assemblies, and had such a passion for them, that their tragedy, even in its better days, admitted a greater proportion of speeches on opposite sides of a question than would have been the case had their public life taken another direction. But, in process of time, this element was continually gaining upon the others, and soon transcended its proper limits, as we see even in Euripides, and still more in his successors. The excess consists in this, that the speeches, which in a drama should only serve as a means of explaining the thoughts and frame of mind of the actors, and of influencing their convictions and resolves, became, on their own account, the chief business of the play, so that the situations and all the labor of the poet were directed toward affording opportunities for the display of rhetorical sparring. And as the practical object of real life was, naturally enough, wanting to this stage-oratory, and as it depended on the poet alone how he should put the point of dispute, it is easy to conceive that this theatrical rhetoric would, in most cases, make a display of the more artificial forms, which, in practical life, were thrown aside as useless, and would approximate rather to the scholastic oratory of the sophists than to the eloquence of a Demosthenes, which, possessed by the great events of the time, raised itself far above the trammels of a scholastic art.[2]

XVI. Theodectes (Θεοδέκτης),[3] of Phaselis, the chief specimen of this class of writers, flourished about B.C. 356, in the time of Philip of Macedon. Rhetoric was his chief study, although he also applied himself to philosophy. He belongs to the scholars of Isocrates,[4] another of whom,

[1] *Müller, Hist. Gr. Lit.*, p. 387; *Smith, Dict. Biogr.*, *s. v.*
[2] *Müller, Hist. Gr. Lit.*, p. 388. [3] *Id. ib.* [4] *Pseudo-Plut.*, *Vit. Isocr.*, 10, p. 837, *D.*

a son of Aphareus, also left the rhetorical school for the tragic stage. Theodectes never gave up his original pursuits, but came forward both as an orator and tragedian. At the splendid funeral feast which the Carian queen, Artemisia, instituted in honor of Mausolus,[1] the husband whom she mourned for so ostentatiously, Theodectes, in competition with Theopompus and other orators, delivered a panegyric on the deceased, and at the same time produced a tragedy, the *Mausolus*, the materials for which were probably borrowed from the mythical traditions or early history of Caria, but which had also in view, of course, the exaltation of the prince of the same name just deceased. In the competition of oratory, on this occasion, Theodectes was defeated by Theopompus; but his tragedy gained the prize, and was extant down to the time of Gellius.[2] Theodectes, indeed, had so hit the taste of the age in his tragedies, that he obtained eight victories in thirteen contests. Aristotle, who was his friend, and, according to some, his teacher also, made use of his tragedies as furnishing him with examples of rhetoric. For excellence in the art of rhetoric, indeed, as it was practiced by the school of Isocrates, Theodectes appears to have possessed the highest qualifications. Dionysius places him with Aristotle, at the head of the writers on the art of rhetoric.[3] Some even appear to have believed the "Rhetoric" of Aristotle to be the work of Theodectes; but this is a manifest error.[4]

CHAPTER XXVI.

FOURTH OR ATTIC PERIOD—*continued*.

GREEK COMEDY.

I. Comedy (Κωμῳδία) took its rise at the vintage festivals of Bacchus.[5] It originated, as Aristotle[6] remarks, with those who led off the phallic songs of the *comus* (κῶμος) or band of revellers, who, at the vintage festivals of Bacchus, gave expression to the feelings of exuberant joy and merriment which were regarded as appropriate to the occasion, by parading about, partly on foot, partly in wagons, singing a wild, jovial song in honor of Bacchus and his companions. These songs were commonly interspersed with or followed by petulant, extemporaneous witticisms, with which the revellers assailed the by-standers. This origin of comedy is indicated by the name *κωμῳδία*, which undoubtedly means "the song of the Comus" (*κώμου ᾠδή*). This appears both from the testimony of Aristotle, that it arose out of the phallic songs, and from the language of Demosthenes,[7] in whom we find mentioned together *ὁ κῶμος καὶ οἱ κωμῳδοί*.[8] Other derivations of the name were, however, given even in antiquity. The Megarians, conceiving it to be connected with the word

---

1 *Suid.*, *s. v.*; *Aul. Gell.*, x., 18.
2 *Gell.*, *l. c.*
3 *Dion. Hal.*, *De Comp. Verb.*, 2; *De vi dic. in Dem.*, 48.
4 *Quintil.*, ii., 15, 10; *Spalding*, *ad loc.*; *Smith*, *Dict. Biogr.*, *s. v.*
5 *Smith*, *Dict. Ant.*, *s. v.*
6 *Poët.*, 4.
7 *c. Mid.*, p. 517.
8 *Müller*, *Hist. Gr. Lit.*, vol. ii., p. 4; *Dor.*, iv., 7, 1.

κώμη, "a village," and to mean "village-song," appealed to the name as an evidence of the superiority of their claim to be regarded as the originators of Comedy over that of the Athenians.[1] This derivation was also adopted by several of the old grammarians, and has the sanction of Bentley, W. Schneider, and even of Bernhardy.[2]

II. It was among the Dorians that comedy first assumed any thing of a regular shape. The Megarians, both in the mother country and in Sicily, claimed to be considered its originators, as we have just remarked; and so far as the comedy of Athens is concerned, the claim of the former appears well founded. They were always noted for their coarse humor,[3] and their democratical constitution, which was established at an early period, favored the development of comedy in the proper sense of the word. In the aristocratical states, the mimetic impulse, as connected with the laughable or the absurd, was obliged to content itself with a less unrestrained mode of manifestation.

III. Among the Athenians, the first attempts at comedy, according to the almost unanimous accounts of antiquity, were made at Icaria, an Attic demus, by Susarion, a native of Tripodiscus, in Megaris.[4] Icaria was the oldest seat of the worship of Bacchus in Attica,[5] and comus processions must undoubtedly have been known there long before the time of Susarion. From the jests and railleries directed by the Bacchic comus, as it paraded about, against the by-standers, or any others whom they selected, arose the proverb τὰ ἐξ ἁμάξης.[6]

IV. It was B.C. 578 that Susarion introduced at Icaria comedy, in that stage of development to which it had attained among the Megarians.[7] It is not easy, however, to decide in what his improvements consisted. Of course there were no actors besides the chorus or comus; whatever there was of drama must have been performed by the latter. The introduction of an actor separate from the chorus was an improvement not yet made in the drama. According to one grammarian, he was the first who adopted the metrical form of language for comedy.[8] It is not, however, to be inferred that the comedies of Susarion were written. Bentley has shown that the contrary is probably true. He no doubt merely substituted for the more ancient improvisations of the chorus and its leader, premeditated compositions, though still of the same general kind. There would also seem to have been some kind of poetical contest, for we learn that the prize for the successful poet was a basket of figs and a jar of wine.[9] It was also the practice of those who took part in the comus to smear their faces with wine-lees, either to prevent their features from being recognized, or to give themselves a more grotesque appearance. Hence comedy came to be called τρυγῳδία, or "lees-song," though others connected the name with the circumstance of a jar of new wine

---

1 *Aristot.*, *Poët.*, 3.

2 *Grundriss der Griech. Lit.*, vol. ii., p. 892.

3 *Aristoph.*, *Vesp.*, 57; *Schol. ad loc.*; *Suid.*, *s. v.* γέλως.

4 *Schol. ad Dion. Thrac.*, in Bekker's *Anecd. Græc.*, ii., p. 748.

5 *Athen.*, ii., p. 40.

6 *Schol. ad Aristoph.*, *Equit.*, 544; *Nub.*, 296.

7 *Smith*, *Dict. Ant.*, *s. v.*

8 *Schol. ad Dion. Thrac.*, in Bekker's *Anecd. Gr.*, ii., p. 748.

9 *Marm. Par.*, ep. 40; *Böckh*, *Corp. Inscript.*, vol. ii., p. 301; *Bentley*, *Phal.*, vol. i., p. 259, ed. *Dyce.*

(τρύξ) being the prize for the successful poet.[1] The comedies of Susarion were, according to the common account, acted upon wagons. But Meineke has rendered the truth of this assertion extremely doubtful. His plays very probably partook of that petulant, coarse, and unrestrained personality for which the Megarian comedy was noted. For entertainments of such a character the Athenians were, however, not yet prepared. It required the freedom of a democracy. Accordingly, comedy was discouraged, and for eighty years after the time of Susarion we have nothing of it in Attica.

V. It was, however, in Sicily that comedy was earliest brought to something like perfection. The Greeks in Sicily always exhibited a lively temperament, and the gift of working up any occurrence into a spirited, fluent dialogue.[2] This faculty finding its stimulus in the excitement produced by the political contests, which were so frequent in the different cities, and the opportunity for its exercise in the numerous rustic festivals connected with the worship of Ceres and Bacchus, it was natural that comedy should early take its rise among them. Yet before the time of the Persian wars, we only hear of iambic compositions, and of a single poet, Aristoxenus. The performers were called αὐτοκάβδαλοι, or improvisatori,[3] and subsequently ἴαμβοι, and their entertainments, being of a choral character, were doubtless accompanied by music and dancing. Afterward, the comic element was developed partly into travesties of religious legends, partly into delineations of character and manners; the former in the comedy of Epicharmus, Phormis, and Dinolochus; the latter in the mimes of Sophron and Xenarchus. Epicharmus is very commonly called the inventor of comedy by the grammarians and others; this, however, is true only of that more artistical shape which he gave it.[4] We will treat more fully of this writer in a subsequent part of the present work.

VI. In Attica, the first comic poet of any importance whom we hear of after Susarion is Chionides, who is said to have brought out plays in B.C. 487, about eight years before the second Persian war. Such, at least, is the account of Suidas. On the other hand, according to a passage in the *Poëtic* of Aristotle,[5] Chionides was *long after* Epicharmus. On the strength of this passage, Meineke thinks that Chionides can not be placed much earlier than B.C. 460, and, in confirmation of this date, he quotes from Athenæus[6] a passage from a play of Chionides, the Πτωχοί, in which mention is made of Gnesippus, a poet contemporary with Cratinus. But we also learn from Athenæus that some of the ancient critics considered the Πτωχοί to be spurious, and with respect to the passage from Aristotle, Ritter has brought forward some very strong arguments against its genuineness.[7] We have some titles and fragments remaining of the pieces of Chionides. They are given by Meineke, in the *Comic. Græc.*

---

1 *Athen.*, ii., p. 40; *Anon.*, *De Com.*, *ap. Meineke*, p. 535, &c.

2 *Cic.*, *Verr.*, iv., 43; *Orat.*, ii., 54.

3 *Athen.*, xiv., p. 622; *Etym. Mag.*, *s. v.* αὐτοκάβδ.

4 *Smith*, *Dict. Ant.*, *s. v.*

5 *Poët.*, 3.

6 *Athen.*, xiv., p. 638, *A.*

7 *Ritter*, *Comm. in Aristot. Poët.*, 3; *Smith*, *Dict. Biogr.*, *s. v.*

Fragm., vol. i., p. 3, *seqq.*, *ed. min.* The only other writer of this period deserving of mention is MAGNES, a native of Icaria, in Attica.[1] He is mentioned by Aristotle in such a manner as to imply that he was contemporary, or nearly so, with Chionides;[2] and from this and other statements of the ancient writers it has been inferred that he flourished about B.C. 460 and onward. There appears to have been a great deal of coarse buffoonery in his pieces.[3] According to Suidas and Eudocia, he exhibited nine plays, and gained two victories; a statement obviously at variance with what Aristophanes says of him. An anonymous writer on comedy assigns to him eleven victories, and states that none of his dramas were preserved, but that nine were falsely ascribed to him. It is worthy of notice that Magnes is the earliest comic poet of whom we find any victories recorded. Only a few titles of his works remain, together with some fragments scarcely exceeding half a dozen lines.[4] The fragments are given by Meineke, *Comic. Græc. Fragm.*, vol. i., p. 5–6, *ed. min.*

VII. That branch of the Attic drama which was called the *Old Comedy* begins properly with Cratinus, who was to comedy very much what Æschylus was to tragedy. As in the Attic drama there can plainly be traced various stages of progress before it arrived at that which in modern times is considered the true form of comedy, namely, the comedy of character or manners, it has been customary to divide it into three species, which are termed the *Old*, *Middle*, and *New* comedy. These divisions are of course arbitrary, and, as the advance from one stage to another took place gradually, it is somewhat difficult to determine accurately the epoch when each species gave place to the succeeding one. The middle comedy, however, is considered by the best modern authorities to have commenced about B.C. 375, with Eubulus, and to have continued until about B.C. 330, when Philemon and Menander, the authors of the New Comedy, began to exhibit.[5]

OLD COMEDY.

VIII. The characteristic feature of the *Old Comedy* is personality. It has been described as the comedy of caricature, and such indeed it was, but it was also a great deal more. Real personages were exhibited on the stage, and the shafts of the poet's ridicule were fearlessly directed against them. As it appeared in the hands of its great masters, Cratinus, Hermippus, Eupolis, and especially Aristophanes, its main characteristic was that it was throughout *political.* Every thing that bore upon the political or social interests of the Athenians furnished materials for it. It assailed every thing that threatened liberty, religion, and the old established principles of social morality and taste, and tended to detract from the true nobleness of the Greek character. It performed, in short, the functions of a public censorship.[6] Though merely personal satire, having no higher object than the sport of the moment, was by no means excluded, though the secrets of domestic life were laid open, its sanctity

---

1 *Suid.*, *s. v.*
2 *Aristot.*, *Poët.*, 3.
3 *Diomedes*, iii., p. 486.
4 *Smith*, *Dict. Biogr.*, *s. v.*
5 *Clinton*, *Fast. Hell.*, vol. ii.; *Introd.*, p. xxxvi., *seqq.*
6 *Hor.*, *Serm.*, i., 4, 1, *seqq.*; *Isocr.*, *De pace*, p. 161.

violated, and the faults of private character held up to odium or ridicule, yet commonly it is on political or general grounds that individuals are brought forward and satirized. A ground-work of reality usually lay at the basis of the most imaginative forms which its wild license adopted. All kinds of fantastic impersonations and mythological beings were mixed up with those of real life. With such unbounded stores of materials for the subject and form of comedies, complicated plots were of course unnecessary, and were not adopted.

IX. All this abuse and slander, and caricature and criticism, were conveyed in the most exquisite and polished style; it was recommended by all the refinements of taste and the graces of poetry. It was because of this exquisite elegance and purity which distinguished the style of the Attic comedy, as well as its energetic power, that Quintilian recommends an orator to study, as the best model next to Homer, the writings of the Old Attic comedy. Doubtless it abounded in grossness and impurity, such as would not for a moment be tolerated in dramatic exhibitions of the present day. But an age in which man was not softened by the influence of good female society, and in which the virtuous of the female sex were not educated so as to fit them for being companions of man, was necessarily a gross one. The comic poet, therefore, was not the corruptor of his countrymen. The worst that can be said against him is, that he did not stem the tide of corruption, that he pandered to a degraded popular taste, instead of using his best endeavors to mould it to a higher standard.[1]

X. The old comedy was to the Athenians the representative of many influences which exist in the present day. It was the newspaper—the review—the satire—the pamphlet—the caricature—the pantomime of Athens. Addressed to the thousands who flocked to the theatre to witness the representation of a new comedy, most of whom were keenly alive to every witty allusion and stroke of satire, and who took a deep interest in every thing of a public nature, because each individual was personally engaged in the administration of state affairs, the old comedy must have been a powerful engine for good or for evil. There can be little doubt that, scurrilous and immoral as it was, the good nevertheless predominated. Gross and depraved as the Athenians were already, notwithstanding their refinement, it is not likely that comedy corrupted their morals in this respect. The vices which prevailed would have existed without it, and were neither increased nor fostered by it. But the comic poet seems, generally speaking, to have been on the side of that which was good in taste, in education, in politics. Fostered as the free satire of comedy was by the unbounded license of a democracy, and owing its vigor, as well as its existence, to the patronage of a sovereign people, it neither spared the vices, nor flattered the follies of its patrons. Like those of the court-fool in the Middle Ages, its most biting jests were received with good humor, and welcomed as acceptable by its supporters, although they themselves were the object of them.[2]

XI. Notwithstanding, however, the favor with which the old comedy

[1] *Browne, Hist. Class. Lit.*, vol. ii., p. 20, *seq.*

[2] *Id. ib.*, p. 21, *seq.*

was viewed by the people, its extreme personality sometimes provoked the interference of the law. In B.C. 440, a law was passed τοῦ μὴ κωμῳδεῖν,[1] which remained in force for three years, when it was repealed. Some understand the law to have been a prohibition of comedy altogether;[2] others,[3] a prohibition merely against bringing forward individuals in their proper historic personality, and under their own name, in order to ridicule them (μὴ κωμῳδεῖν ὀνομαστί). During the period when this law remained in force, the comic chorus, as Horace[4] tells us, "*turpiter obticuit, sublato jure nocendi.*" To this same period probably belongs the law, that no Areopagite should write comedies.[5] About B.C. 415, apparently at the instigation of Alcibiades, whose vanity, ambition, and support of the new systems of philosophy and education had drawn upon him the enmity of the comic poets, the law of B.C. 440, or, at all events, a law μὴ κωμῳδεῖν ὀνομαστί, was again passed, but this law only remained in force for a short time. The nature of the political events in the ensuing period would of itself act as a check upon the license of the comic poets. With the overthrow of the democracy in B.C. 411, comedy would of course be silenced, but on the restoration of the democracy it revived. It was doubtless again restrained by the Thirty tyrants. During the latter part of the Peloponnesian war, also, it became a matter of difficulty to get choragi; and hinderances were sometimes thrown in the way of the comic poets by those who had been attacked by them. Agyrrhius, for instance, though when is not known, got the pay of the poets lessened.

XII. The Old Attic comedy lasted, as has already been remarked, until B.C. 375, ending with Theopompus. The whole number of poets belonging to this division was, according to Clinton, fifty-two. Some, less accurately, make the old comedy to have ended in B.C. 404, and the number of poets to have been forty-one.

XIII. It was not usual for comic poets to bring forward more than one or two comedies at a time; and there was a regulation according to which a poet could not bring forward comedies before he was of a certain age, which is variously stated at thirty or forty years.[6] To decide on the merits of the comedies exhibited, five judges were appointed, which was half the number of those who adjudged the prize for tragedy.[7] The chorus in comedy, as before remarked, consisted of twenty-four. The dance of the chorus was the κόρδαξ, the movements of which were capricious and licentious, consisting partly in a reeling to and fro, in imitation of a drunken man, and partly in various unseemly and immodest gestures. For a citizen to dance the κόρδαξ sober, and without a mask, was looked upon as the height of shamelessness.[8] Aristophanes, however, and probably other comic poets also, frequently dispensed with the κόρδαξ.[9] The most important of the choral parts was the *Parabasis*, already described, when, the actors having left the stage, the chorus turned round from fac-

1 *Schol. ad Aristoph., Acharn.*, 67.
2 *Clinton, Fast. Hell., s. a.*
3 *Meineke, Hist. Crit. Com. Græc.*
4 *Ep. ad Pis.*, 284.
5 *Plut., De Glor. Ath.*, p. 348, *c.*
6 *Aristoph., Nub.*, 530; *Schol. ad loc.*
7 *Schol. ad Aristoph., Av.*, 445.
8 *Theophrast., Charact.*, 6.
9 *Aristoph., Nub.*, 537, *seqq.*

ing the performers, and, advancing toward the spectators, delivered an address to them in the name of the poet, either on public topics of general interest, or on matters which concerned the poet personally, criticising his rivals and calling attention to his own merits; the address having nothing whatever to do with the action of the play.[1]

XIV. From the hints furnished by Aristophanes (for we have a great want of special information on the subject), his comic actors must have been very unlike the performers of the new comedy, of Plautus and Terence.[2] Of the latter we know, from some very valuable and instructive paintings in ancient manuscripts, that they adopted, on the whole, the costume of every-day life, and that the form and mode of their tunics and palliums were the same as those of the actual personages whom they represented. The costume of Aristophanes' players must, on the other hand, have resembled rather the garb of the farcical actors whom we often see depicted on vases from Magna Græcia, namely, close-fitting jackets and trowsers striped with divers colors, reminding us of the modern harlequin; to which were added great bellies and other disfigurations purposely extravagant, the grotesque form being, at the most, but partially covered by a little mantle. Then there were masks, the features of which were exaggerated even to caricature, yet so that particular persons, when such were brought upon the stage, might at once be recognized. The costume of the chorus in a comedy of Aristophanes went farthest into the strange and fantastic. His choruses of birds, wasps, &c., must not, of course, be regarded as having consisted of birds, wasps, &c., actually represented, but, as is clear from numerous hints from the poet himself, of a mixture of the human form with various appendages borrowed from the creatures we have mentioned; and in this the poet allowed himself to give special prominence to those parts of the costume which he was most concerned about: thus, for example, in the "Wasps," which are designed to represent the swarms of Athenian judges, the sting was the chief attribute, as denoting the *stylus*, with which the judges used to mark down the number of their division in their wax tablets. These waspish judges were introduced humming and buzzing up and down, now thrusting out, and now drawing in an immense spit, which was attached to them by way of a gigantic sting.[3]

XV. That the prevalent form of the dialogue should be the same in tragedy and comedy, namely, the *iambic trimeter*, was natural, notwithstanding the opposite character of the two kinds of poetry; for this common organ of dramatic colloquy was capable of the most varied treatment, and was modified by the comic poets in a manner most suitable to their object. The avoidance of spondees, the congregation of short syllables, and the variety of the cæsuras, impart to the verse of comedy an extraordinary lightness and spirit, and the admission of anapæsts into all places of the verse but the last, opposed as this is to the fundamental form of the trimeter, proves that the careless, voluble recitation of comedy treated the long and short syllables with greater freedom than the tragic art

---

[1] *Schol. ad Aristoph., Nub.*, 518; *Pac.*, 733. [2] *Müller, Hist. Gr. Lit.*, vol. ii., p. 9, *seq.*
[3] *Müller*, vol. ii., p. 10.

permitted. In order to distinguish the different styles and tunes, comedy employed, besides the trimeter, a great variety of metres, which we must suppose were also distinguished by different sorts of gesticulation and delivery, such as the light trochaic tetrameter, so well suited to the dance; the lively iambic tetrameter; and the anapæstic tetrameter, flaunting along in comic pathos, which had been used by Aristoxenus of Selinus, an old Sicilian poet, who lived before Epicharmus. In all these things comedy was just as inventive and refined as tragedy. Aristophanes had the skill to convey by his rhythms sometimes the tone of romping merriment, at others that of festal dignity; and often, in jest, he would give to his verses and his words such a pomp of sound that we lament he is not in earnest.[1]

MIDDLE COMEDY.

XVI. The old comedy was replaced by one of a somewhat different style, which was known as the *Middle Comedy*, the age of which lasted from the end of the Peloponnesian war to the overthrow of liberty by Philip of Macedon. During this period, the Athenian state had the form, but none of the spirit of its earlier democratical constitution, and the energy and public spirit of earlier years had departed. The comedy of this period, accordingly, found its materials in satirizing *classes* of people instead of individuals, in criticising the systems and merits of philosophers and literary men, and in parodies of the compositions of living or earlier poets, and travesties of mythological subjects. It formed a transition from the old to the *new* comedy, and approximated to the latter in the greater attention paid to the structure of plots, which seem frequently to have been founded on amorous intrigues, and in the absence of that wild grotesqueness which marked the *old* comedy.[2]

XVII. As regards external form, the plays of the middle comedy, generally speaking, had neither *parabasis* nor chorus. The absence of the chorus was occasioned, partly by the change in the spirit of comedy itself, partly by the increasing difficulty of finding persons capable of undertaking the duties of choragus. As the change in comedy itself was gradual, so it is most likely that the alterations in form were brought about by degrees. At first, showing the want of proper musical and orchestic training, the chorus was at last dropped altogether. Some of the fragments of pieces of the middle comedy, which have reached us, are of a lyrical kind, indicating the presence of a chorus. The poets of this school of comedy seem to have been extraordinarily prolific. Athenæus says that he had read above 800 dramas of the middle comedy. Only a few fragments, however, are now extant. Meineke gives a list of thirty-nine poets of the middle comedy.[3] Clinton makes the number thirty-five.[4] The most celebrated were Antiphanes and Alexis.

---

[1] *Müller*, vol. ii., p. 13, *seq.*

[2] *Bode, Gesch. d. Hell. Dichtk.*, vol. iii., p. 396; *Müller*, vol. ii., p. 46; *Smith, Dict. Ant.*, *s. v.* [3] *Hist. Crit. Com. Gr.*, p. 303. [4] *Fast. Hell.*, vol. ii., p. xlii., *seqq.*

NEW COMEDY.

XVIII. The *New* Comedy was a farther development of the last-mentioned kind. It answered as nearly as may be to the modern comedy of manners or character. Dropping for the most part personal allusions, caricature, ridicule, and parody, which, in a more general form than in the old, had maintained their ground in the middle comedy, the poets of the *new comedy* made it their business to reproduce, in a generalized form, a picture of the every-day life of those by whom they were surrounded. This new comedy might be described, in the words of Cicero, as "*imitationem vitæ, speculum consuetudinis, imaginem veritatis*."[1] The frequent introduction of sententious maxims was a point of resemblance with the later tragic poets.[2]

XIX. In the new comedy there was no chorus, and the dramas were commonly introduced by prologues, spoken by allegorical personages, such as Ἔλεγχος, Φόβος, &c. The new comedy flourished until B.C. 289, if, with Clinton, we close the list with Posidippus. But others give B.C. 260. The number of poets belonging to the new comedy was estimated in antiquity at sixty-four, but, as Bernhardy remarks, it is now impossible to find even the half of this number. Clinton gives the names of twenty, beginning with Philippides, and ending, as before remarked, with Posidippus.[3]

CHAPTER XXVII.

FOURTH OR ATTIC PERIOD—*continued.*

POETS OF THE OLD COMEDY.

I. Cratīnus (Κρατῖνος),[4] one of the most celebrated poets of the old comedy, and who witnessed its rise and complete perfection during a life of ninety-seven years, was born B.C. 519, but did not exhibit till B.C. 454, when he was sixty-five years of age.[5] He exhibited twenty-one plays, and gained nine victories. He was *the poet* of the old comedy. He gave it its peculiar character, and he did not, like Aristophanes, live to see its decline. Before his time the comic poets had aimed at little beyond exciting the laughter of their audience: it was Cratinus who first made comedy a terrible weapon of personal attack, and the comic poet a severe censor of public and private vice. He did not even, like Aristophanes, in such attacks unite mirth with satire, but, as an ancient writer says, he hurled his reproaches in the plainest form at the bare heads of the offenders.[6] Still, like Aristophanes with respect to Sophocles, he sometimes bestowed the highest praise, as upon Cimon.[7] Pericles, on the other hand, was the object of his most persevering and vehement abuse. Besides what Cratinus thus did to give a new character and

1 *Cic.*, *De Rep.*, iv., 11. 2 *Smith*, *Dict. Ant.*, *s. v.* 3 *Clinton*, p. xlv., *seq.*
4 *Smith*, *Dict. Biogr.*, *s. v.* 5 *Euseb.*, *Chron.*, *s. a.*; *Syncell.*, p. 339.
6 *Platonius*, *De Com.*, p. xxvii.; *Christod.*, *Ecphras.*, v. 357. 7 *Plut.*, *Cim.*, 10.

power to comedy, he is said to have made changes in its outward form, so as to bring it into better order, especially by fixing the number of actors, which before had been indefinite, at three. On the other hand, however, Aristotle asserts that no one knew who made this and other such changes.

The character of Cratinus as a poet rests upon the testimonies of the ancient writers, as we have no complete play of his extant. These testimonies are most decided in placing him in the very first rank of comic poets. By one writer he is compared to Æschylus.[1] His style seems to have been somewhat grandiloquent, and full of tropes, and altogether of a lyric cast. He was very bold in inventing new words, and in changing the meaning of old ones. His choruses especially were very much admired, and were for a time the favorite songs at banquets.[2] It was perhaps on account of the dithyrambic character of his poetry that he was likened, as we have said, to Æschylus. His metres seem to have partaken of the same lofty character. He sometimes even used the epic verse. In the invention of his plots, he was most ingenious and felicitous, but his impetuous and exuberant fancy was apt to derange them in the progress of the play.[3] In his later years, Cratinus became much addicted to drinking, and Aristophanes and the other comic poets began to sneer at him as a drivelling old dotard, whose poetry was fuddled with wine.[4] This at length roused the spirit of the veteran dramatist, who brought out, in consequence, his comedy of the Πυτίνη, or "bottle," in which he acknowledged the charge of habitual intemperance, but at the same time treated the subject in so amusing a way as to bear off the prize over the *Connus* of Amipsias, and the *Clouds* of Aristophanes himself.[5] In the following year Cratinus died, at the age of ninety-seven. His fragments are given by Meineke, *Comic. Græc. Fragm.*, vol. i., p. 7, *seqq.*, *ed. min.* They were also edited separately by Runkel, Lips., 1827, 8vo.

II. Crătes (Κράτης),[6] an Athenian, was a younger contemporary of Cratinus, in whose plays he was the principal actor before he betook himself to writing comedies.[7] He began to flourish in B.C. 449, and is spoken of by Aristophanes in such a way as to imply that he was dead before the comedy of the *Knights* was acted, B.C. 424. It would appear from a passage in Aristotle,[8] which has been misunderstood by some, that, instead of making his comedies vehicles of personal abuse, he chose such subjects as admitted of a more general mode of depicting character. His great excellence is attested by Aristophanes, though in a somewhat ironical tone,[9] and also by the fragments of his plays. He excelled chiefly in mirth and fun, which he carried so far as to bring intoxicated persons on the stage, a thing which Epicharmus had done, but which no Attic comedian had ventured on before.[10] His example was followed by Aristophanes and by later comedians; and with the poets of the new comedy it became a very common practice.[11] Like the other great comic

---

1 *Anon.*, *De Com.*, p. xxix. 2 *Aristoph.*, *Equit.*, 526. 3 *Platonius*, p. xxvii.
4 *Aristoph.*, *Equit.*, 531, *seqq.* 5 *Arg. Nub.* 6 *Smith*, *Dict. Biogr.*, *s. v.*
7 *Diog. Laert.*, iv., 23; *Aristoph.*, *Equit.*, 536, *seqq.* 8 *Poët.*, 5. 9 *Aristoph.*, *l. c.*
10 *Athen.*, x., p. 429, *A.* 11 *Dion Chrysost.*, Orat. 32, p. 391, *B.*

poets, he was made to feel strongly both the favor and the inconstancy of the people. The scholiast on Aristophanes says that Crates used to bribe the spectators, a charge which Meineke thinks may have been taken from some comic poet who was an enemy of his. There is much confusion among the ancients about the number and titles of his plays. Some grammarians assign to him seven and eight comedies respectively. The result of Meineke's analysis of the statements of the ancient writers is in favor of eight. Of these eight plays fragments are still extant. There are also several fragments which can not be assigned to their proper plays. The language of Crates is pure, elegant, and simple, with very few peculiar words and constructions. He uses, however, a very rare metrical peculiarity, namely, a spondaic ending to the anapæstic tetrameter. The fragments are given by Meineke, *Comic. Græc. Fragm.*, vol. i., p. 78, *seqq.*, *ed. min.*

III. HEGĒMON (Ἡγήμων),[1] a native of Thasos, but established at Athens, was more celebrated for his parodies than his regular comic pieces. Aristotle makes him the inventor of parody. He was nicknamed Φακῆ, on account of his fondness for that kind of pulse. Hegemon lived in the time of the Peloponnesian war, and was contemporary with Cratinus, when the latter was an old man, and with Alcibiades. His parody of the *Gigantomachia* was the piece to which the Athenians were listening when the news was brought to them in the theatre of the total failure of the expedition to Sicily, and when, in order not to betray their feelings, they remained in the theatre to the end of the performance. The only comedy of his which is mentioned is the Φιλίνη, of which one fragment is preserved by Athenæus, who also gives some amusing particulars respecting him.[2]

IV. PHRYNĬCHUS (Φρύνιχος), of Athens, not to be confounded with the tragic poet of the same name, already mentioned, began to exhibit B.C. 435.[3] He was ranked by the grammarians among the most distinguished poets of the old comedy,[4] and the elegance and vigor of his extant fragments confirm this judgment. Aristophanes, indeed, attacks him, together with other comic poets, for the use of low and obsolete buffoonery,[5] but the scholiast on the passage asserts that there was nothing of the sort in his extant plays. He was also charged with corrupting both language and metre, and with making use of the labors of others. These accusations, however, are probably to be regarded rather as indications of the height to which the rivalry of the comic poets was carried, than as the statement of actual truths. On the subject of metre we are informed that Phrynichus invented the *Ionic a minore catalectic* verse, which was named after him.[6] His language is generally terse and elegant, but he sometimes uses words of peculiar formation. The celebrated grammarian Didymus, of Alexandrea, wrote commentaries on Phrynichus.[7]

---

1 *Smith, Dict. Biogr.*, *s. v.*

2 *Athen.*, i., p. 5, *B*; *Aristot.*, *Poët.*, 2; *Ritter, ad loc.*

3 *Smith, Dict. Biogr.*, *s. v.*, where B.C. 429 is thought the more probable date, and Suidas, who gives B.C. 435, is supposed to be in error. Compare *Clinton*, *s. v.*

4 *Anon.*, *De Comoed.*, p. xxviii.

5 *Ran.*, 14.

6 *Marius Victor*, p. 2542, *Putsch.*

7 *Athen.*, ix., p. 371, *F*; *Smith, Dict. Biogr.*, *s. v.*

The number of his comedies is given at ten. We have the fragments in Meineke, *Com. Græc. Frag.*, vol. i., p. 228, *seqq.*, *ed. min.*

V. Eupŏlis (Εὔπολις)[1] was born about B.C. 446, and is said to have exhibited his first drama in his seventeenth year, B.C. 429, two years before Aristophanes, who was nearly of the same age with him.[2] The date of his death is uncertain. The common story was, that Alcibiades, when sailing to Sicily, B.C. 415, threw Eupolis into the sea, in revenge for an attack which he had made upon him in his Βάπται. But, to say nothing of the improbability of even Alcibiades venturing on such an outrage, or the still stranger fact of its not being alluded to by Thucydides, or any other trustworthy historian, the answer of Cicero is conclusive, that Eratosthenes mentioned plays produced by Eupolis after the Sicilian expedition.[3] There is also a fragment still extant, in which the poet applies the title *στρατηγός* to Aristarchus, whom we know to have been *στρατηγός* four years later than the date at which the common story fixed the death of Eupolis.[4] He probably died in B.C. 411.

The chief characteristic of the poetry of Eupolis seems to have been the liveliness of his fancy, and the power which he possessed of imparting its images to his audience. This characteristic of his genius influenced his choice of subjects, as well as his mode of treating them, so that he not only appears to have chosen subjects which other poets might have despaired of dramatizing, but we are expressly told that he wrought into the body of his plays those serious political views which other poets expounded in their *parabases*, as in the Δῆμοι, in which he represented the legislators of other times deliberating on the administration of the state. To do this in a genuine Attic old comedy, without converting the comedy into a serious philosophic dialogue, must have been a great triumph of dramatic art.[5] The introduction of deceased persons on the stage appears to have given to the plays of Eupolis a certain dignity, which would have been inconsistent with the comic spirit had it not been relieved by the most graceful and clever merriment. In elegance he is said to have even surpassed Aristophanes,[6] while in bitter jesting and personal abuse he emulated Cratinus. Among the objects of his satire was Socrates, on whom he made a bitter, though less elaborate attack than that in the *Clouds* of Aristophanes.[7] The dead were not even exempt from his abuse, for there are still extant some lines of his in which Cimon is most unmercifully treated.[8] A close relation subsisted between Eupolis and Aristophanes, not only as rivals, but as imitators of each other. Cratinus attacked Aristophanes for borrowing from Eupolis, and Eupolis, in his Βάπται, made the same charge, especially with reference to the *Knights*. The scholiasts specify the last parabasis of the *Knights* as borrowed from Eupolis.[9] On the other hand, Aristophanes, in the second (or third) edition of the *Clouds*, retorts upon Eupolis the charge of imitating the

[1] *Smith, Dict. Biogr.*, *s. v.*
[2] *Anon.*, *De Com.*, p. xxix.
[3] *Cic.*, *Ep. ad Att.*, vi., 1.
[4] *Schol. Victor. ad Il.*, xiii., 353.
[5] *Platon.*, p. xxvi.
[6] *Id. ib.*
[7] *Schol. ad Aristoph.*, *Nub.*, 97, 180.
[8] *Plut.*, *Cim.*, 15; *Schol. ad Aristid.*, p. 515.
[9] *Schol. ad Aristoph.*, *Equit.*, 528, 1288.

Knights in his *Maricas*,[1] and taunts him with the further indignity of jesting on his rival's baldness. The number of the plays of Eupolis is stated by Suidas at seventeen, and by another authority at fourteen. The extant titles exceed the greater of these numbers, but some of them are very doubtful. The fragments of Eupolis have been edited by Runkel, *Pherecratis et Eupolidis Fragm.*, Lips., 1829, and are also given by Meineke, *Fragm. Comic. Græc.*, vol. i., p. 158, *seqq.*, *ed. min.*

VI. Aristophănes (Ἀριστοφάνης),[2] the prince of the old comedy, was born about B.C. 444, and probably at Athens. His father, Philippus, had possessions in Ægina, and may originally have come from that island, whence a question arose whether Aristophanes was a genuine Athenian citizen. His enemy Cleon brought against him more than one accusation to deprive him of his civic rights, but without success, as, indeed, they were merely the fruit of revenge for his attacks on that demagogue. He had three sons, Philippus, Ararōs, and Nicostratus, called also by some Philetærus, but of his private history we know nothing. He probably died about B.C. 380.

The comedies of Aristophanes are of the highest historical interest, containing, as they do, an admirable series of caricatures on the leading men of the day, and a contemporary commentary on the evils existing at Athens. Indeed, the caricature is the only feature in modern social life which at all resembles them. Aristophanes was a bold, and often a wise patriot. He had the strongest affection for Athens, and longed to see her restored to the state in which she was flourishing in the previous generation, and almost in his own childhood, before Pericles became the head of the government, and when the age of Miltiades and Aristides had but just passed away. The first great evil of his own time against which he inveighs is the Peloponnesian war, which he regards as the work of Pericles, and even attributes it[3] to his fear of punishment for having connived at a robbery said to have been committed by Phidias on the statue of Minerva in the Parthenon, and also to the influence of Aspasia.[4] To this fatal war, among a host of evils, he ascribes the influence of vulgar demagogues like Cleon at Athens, of which also the example was set by the more refined demagogism of Pericles. Another great object of his indignation was the recently adopted system of education, which had been introduced by the Sophists, acting on the speculative and inquiring turn given to the Athenian mind by the Ionian and Eleatic philosophers, and the extraordinary intellectual development of the age following the Persian war. The new theories introduced by the Sophists threatened to overthrow the foundations of morality, by making persuasion, and not truth, the object of man in his intercourse with his fellows, and to substitute a universal skepticism for the religious creed of the people. The worst effects of such a system were seen in Alcibiades, who combined all the elements which Aristophanes most disliked, heading the war party in politics, and protecting the sophistical school in philosophy and also in literature. Of this latter school, the literary and poetical sophists, Euripides was the chief, whose works are full of that

[1] *Nub.*, 544, *seqq.* [2] *Smith, Dict. Biogr.*, *s. v.* [3] *Pax*, 606. [4] *Acharn.*, 500.

μετεωροσοφία which contrasts so offensively with the moral dignity of Æschylus and Sophocles, and for which Aristophanes introduces him as sitting aloft to write his tragedies. In the comedy of the *Clouds*, however, the sophistical principles in general are attacked at their very source, and as their representative he selects Socrates, whom he depicts in the most odious light. The selection of Socrates for this purpose is doubtless to be accounted for by the supposition that Aristophanes observed the great philosopher from a distance only, while his own unphilosophical turn of mind prevented him from entering into Socrates' merits, both as a teacher and a practicer of morality; and also by the fact that Socrates was an innovator, the friend of Euripides, the tutor of Alcibiades, and pupil of Archelaus, and that there was much in his appearance and habits in the highest degree ludicrous. The philosopher who wore no under-garments, and the same upper robe in winter and summer, who generally went barefoot, and appears to have possessed one pair of dress-shoes which lasted him for life,[1] who used to stand for hours in a public place in a fit of abstraction—to say nothing of his snub-nose and extraordinary figure and physiognomy—could hardly expect to escape the license of the old comedy. The invariably speculative turn which he gave to the conversation, his bare acquiescence in the stories of Greek mythology, which Aristophanes would think it dangerous even to subject to inquiry,[2] had certainly produced an unfavorable opinion of Socrates in the minds of many, and explain his being set down by Aristophanes as an arch-sophist, and represented even as a thief.

Another feature of the times was the excessive love for litigation at Athens, the consequent importance of the dicasts, and the disgraceful abuse of their power; all of which are made by Aristophanes direct objects of attack. But, though he saw what were the evils of the times, he had not wisdom to find a remedy for them, except the hopeless and undesirable one of a movement backward; and therefore, though we allow him to have been honest and bold, we must deny him the epithet of great.

The merits of Aristophanes as a poet and humorist can not be fully understood without an actual study of his works. We have no means of comparing him with his rivals Cratinus and Eupolis, though he is said to have tempered their bitterness, and given to comedy additional grace; but to have been surpassed by Eupolis in the conduct of his plots.[3] Plato called the soul of Aristophanes the temple of the Graces, and has introduced him into his Symposium. His works contain snatches of lyric poetry which are quite noble, and some of his choruses, particularly one in the *Knights*, in which the horses are represented as rowing triremes in an expedition against Corinth, are written with a spirit and humor unrivalled in Greek, and are not very dissimilar to English ballads. Aristophanes was a complete master of the Attic dialect, and in his hands the perfection of that glorious instrument of thought is wonderfully shown. No flights are too bold for the range of his fancy: animals of every kind

[1] *Böckh, Public Econ. of Athens*, vol. i., p. 150.
[2] Compare *Plat.*, *Phædr.*, p. 299.
[3] *Platonius, l. c.*

are pressed into his service: frogs chaunt choruses; a dog is tried for stealing a cheese; and an iambic verse is composed of the squeakings of a pig. Words are invented of a length which must have made the speakers breathless.

Suidas tells us that Aristophanes was the author, in all, of fifty-four plays. Of these we have only eleven remaining. In the year B.C. 427, the poet brought out his first play, entitled Δαιταλεῖς, or "the Feasters," which gained the second prize of the contending pieces. His chief object in this play was to censure the system of education and manners then prevalent at Athens, and to advocate a return to the habits of former times. In it he held up to public contempt the character of the spendthrift. This play was brought out in the name of Callistratus, not in his own. Some have thought that this was done because the poet was under thirty years of age, and because an express law, as they maintain, forbade a poet to exhibit a drama in his own name while he was under thirty. But Bergk has shown that such a law is a mere fiction of the commentators; for Æschylus, Sophocles, and Euripides are all known to have brought out plays in their own name while they were under thirty. The true reason for the step is given by Aristophanes himself in the *parabasis* of the "Knights,"[1] where he states that he had pursued this course, not from want of thought, but from a sense of the difficulty of his profession, and from a fear that he might suffer from that fickleness of taste which the Athenians had shown toward other poets, as Magnes, Crates, and Cratinus. It was the dread of this same fickleness that induced him, even when his fame was established, to have recourse to the same expedient in the case of many of his other plays.[2] The ancient grammarians state that he transferred to Callistratus the political dramas, and to Philonides those which belonged to private life.

The next year he brought out the "Babylonians," also in the name of Callistratus. In this play he ridiculed some of the democratical institutions of Athens, especially the system of appointing to office by lot, and attacked Cleon, the most powerful demagogue of the day, in the presence of the allies and foreign ambassadors. Cleon brought an action, not against Callistratus, in whose name the play appeared, but against Aristophanes himself, on the ground of his having calumniated the government and its officers in the presence of foreigners. The action failed, and the poet was the more encouraged to pursue the course he had begun. In the following play, the "Acharnians," B.C. 425, again exhibited by Callistratus, he renewed the attack upon Cleon, and followed up the attack subsequently in the "Knights."

The following is a list of the extant comedies of Aristophanes, with the year in which they were performed: 1. *Acharnians*, B.C. 425. Produced, as we have said, in the name of Callistratus. It gained the first prize. The poet in this play exhorts his countrymen to peace. 2. *Knights* (or *Horsemen*), B.C. 424. The first play produced in the name of Aristophanes himself. It gained the first prize, Cratinus being second. This

[1] v. 514. Compare *Nub.*, 530.

[2] Compare *Bergk*, in *Meineke's Fragm. Com. Græc.*, p. 939.

play, as just remarked, was directed against Cleon, whose power at this time was so great that no one was bold enough to make a mask to represent his features; so that Aristophanes performed the character himself,[1] with his face smeared with wine-lees. 3. *Clouds*, B.C. 423. This play, though perhaps its author's master-piece, met with a complete failure in the contest for prizes, owing probably to the intrigues of Alcibiades; nor was it more successful when altered for a second representation, if indeed the alterations were ever completed, which Süvern denies. The play, as we have it, contains the parabasis of the second edition.[2] 4. *Wasps*, B.C. 422.[3] This is a pendant to the *Knights*. In the latter, the poet had attacked the sovereign assembly, and here he aims his battery at the courts of justice, the other strong-hold of party violence and the power of demagogues. It gained the second prize. 5. *Peace*, B.C. 419. Gained the second prize, Eupolis carrying off the first. This play is a return to the subject of the Acharnians. 6. *Birds*,[4] B.C. 414. Gained the second prize, Amipsias being first. This piece is intended to discourage the disastrous Sicilian expedition. 7. *Lysistrata*,[5] B.C. 411. The old subject of the Peloponnesian war. 8. *Thesmophoriazusæ*. Exhibited during the oligarchy. This is the first of the two great attacks on Euripides, and contains some inimitable parodies on his plays, especially the "Andromeda," which had just appeared. It is almost wholly free from political allusions. 9. *Plutus*, B.C. 408. 10. *Frogs*,[6] B.C. 405. Gained the first prize, Phrynichus being second, and Plato third. In this play, Bacchus descends to Hades in search of a tragic poet—those then alive being worthless—and Æschylus and Euripides contend for the prize of resuscitation. Euripides is at last dismissed by a parody on his own famous line, ἡ γλῶσσ' ὀμώμοχ', ἡ δὲ φρὴν ἀνώμοτος, "My tongue took an oath, but my mind is unsworn." Æschylus accompanies Bacchus, the tragic throne in Hades being given to Sophocles during his absence. 11. *Ecclesiazusæ*, B.C. 392. Written in ridicule of the political theories of Plato, which were based on Spartan institutions. In B.C. 388, the second edition of the Plutus appeared. The last two comedies of Aristophanes were the *Æolosicon* and *Cocalus*, produced about B.C. 387 (date of the peace of Antalcidas), by Araros, one of his sons. They are both lost.

EDITIONS OF ARISTOPHANES.

The *Editio Princeps* of Aristophanes is that of Aldus, Venice, 1498, published without the *Lysistrata* and *Thesmophoriazusæ*. Of subsequent editions the most deserving of mention are, that of Kuster, Amsterdam, 1710, fol.; that of Brunck, Strasburg, 1783, 6 vols. 8vo, which would be more complete did it contain the scholia; that of Invernizzi, completed by Beck and Dindorf, 13 vols. 8vo, Lips., 1794–1826; that of Bekker, 5 vols. 8vo, London, 1829, with a Latin version, the scholia, and a very copious but ill-digested body of notes, embracing the remarks of numerous preceding commentators; that of Dindorf (the text merely), in the *Poetæ Scenici Græci*, reprinted at Oxford, with the addi-

[1] This, however, though the generally-received account, is denied by *Bergk*, *l. c.*

[2] Bergk (p. 913, *seq.*) thinks it probable that the "Clouds" was brought out in the name of Philonides.

[3] Brought out in the name of Philonides.

[4] Brought out in the name of Callistratus.

[5] Brought out in the name of Callistratus.

[6] Brought out in the name of Philonides.

tion of the scholia and a commentary, in 7 vols. 8vo; that of Bothe, 4 vols. 8vo, Lips., 1828–1830, forming part also of his *Poetæ Scenici Græci* (vol. v.–viii.); that of Thiersch, Lips., 1830, &c., of which only the first volume, containing extensive prolegomena, and the comedy of the *Plutus*, and the first part of the sixth volume, containing the *Ranæ*, have appeared; that in Didot's *Bibliotheca Græca*, with a revised text by Dindorf, and the Scholia by Dübner, 2 vols., Paris, 1838–42; and a new edition with critical text by Enger, Bonn, 1844, of which 2 vols., the *Lysistrata* and *Thesmophoriazusæ*, have appeared. There is also a valuable edition by Mitchell, of the *Acharnians*, *Wasps*, *Knights*, *Clouds*, and *Frogs*, with English notes, 5 vols. 8vo, London, 1835–39, and he has also translated the *Acharnians*, *Wasps*, and *Knights*, with great ability, into English verse. Of editions of separate plays there is a large number, among which we may particularly mention that of the *Acharnians*, by Elmsley, London, 1830; of the *Wasps*, by Conz, Tubing., 1823; of the *Clouds*, by Hermann, Leipzig, 1830; of the *Thesmophoriazusæ*, and of the *Ranæ* by Fritzsche, the former at Leipzig, 1838, the latter at Zurich, 1845; of the *Plutus*, by Hemsterhuis, Harl., 1744, 8vo; of the same, by Dobree, Lond., 1820; and by Cookesley, Lond., 1834, with useful notes in English; and that of the *Birds* and *Frogs*, by Cookesley, Lond., 1834, 1837, also with English notes. The Essay of Süvern on the plot of the *Birds*, in the Transactions of the Royal Academy of Sciences of Berlin (1827), and translated by Hamilton, is well worth perusal. A copious index verborum to Aristophanes, by Caravella, was issued from the Clarendon press, Oxford, 1822.

VII. Pherecrătes[1] (Φερεκράτης), of Athens, was contemporary with Cratinus, Crates, Eupolis, Plato, and Aristophanes, being somewhat younger than the first two, and somewhat older than the others. He gained his first victory B.C. 438, and he imitated the style of Crates, whose actor he had been.[2] Crates and Pherecrates very much modified the coarse satire and vituperation of which the old comedy had previously been the vehicle, and constructed their comedies on the basis of a regular plot, and with more dramatic action. Pherecrates did not, however, abstain altogether from personal satire, for we see by the fragments of his plays that he attacked Alcibiades, the tragic poet Melanthius, and others.[3] He invented a new metre, which was named after him the *Pherecratean* or *Pherecratic*, and which may be best explained as a choriambus, with a spondee for its base, and a long syllable for its termination. The metre is very frequent in the choruses of the Greek tragedians, and in Horace, as, for example, *Grato Pyrrha sub antro.* The extant titles of his plays amount to eighteen, which Meineke reduces to fifteen. The fragments of Pherecrates are given, with those of Eupolis, by Runkel, and also by Meineke, *Comic. Græc. Fragm.*, vol. i., p. 87, *seqq.*, *ed. min.*

VIII. Plato (Πλάτων),[4] of Athens, one of the chief poets of the old comedy, was contemporary with Pherecrates and the others whom we have just mentioned, and flourished from B.C. 428 to 389. From the language of the grammarians, and from the large number of fragments which are preserved, it is evident that his plays were only second in popularity to those of Aristophanes. Purity of language, refined sharpness of wit, and a combination of the vigor of the old comedy, with the greater elegance of the middle and the new, were his chief characteristics. Though many of his plays had no political reference at all, yet it is evident that he kept up the spirit of the old comedy in his attacks on the corruptions and corrupt persons of his age. Among the chief objects of his attacks were the

---

1 *Smith, Dict. Biog.*, *s. v.*

2 *Anon.*, *De Com.*, p. xxix.

3 *Athen.*, viii., p. 343, *C*; xii., p. 538, *B*.

4 *Smith, Dict.*, *s. v.*

demagogues Cleon, Hyperbolus, Cleophon, and the orators Cephalus and Archinus, for, like Aristophanes, he regarded the art of rhetoric as one of the worst sources of mischief to the commonwealth. Plato seems to have been one of the most diligent of the old comic poets. Suidas gives the titles of thirty of his dramas, to which number another is to be added, not mentioned by the lexicographer. The fragments of Plato are given by Cobet, Amsterdam, 1840, and also by Meineke, *Comic. Græc. Frag.*, vol. i., p. 357, *seqq.*, *ed. min.*

IX. Philonides (Φιλωνίδης), an Athenian, better known on account of his connection with the literary history of Aristophanes than from his comic productions. It is generally stated that Philonides was an actor of Aristophanes, who is said to have committed to him and to Callistratus his chief characters; but the best modern critics have shown that this is an erroneous statement, and that the true state of the case is, that several of the plays of Aristophanes were brought out in the names of Callistratus and Philonides.[1] The fragments of Philonides are given by Meineke, *Comic. Græc. Frag.*, vol. i., p. 156, *seqq.*, *ed. min.*

CHAPTER XXVIII.

FOURTH OR ATTIC PERIOD—*continued.*

WRITERS OF SICILIAN COMEDY.

I. We have already stated that comedy was earliest brought to something like perfection in Sicily. It will not be amiss, therefore, to give a brief account of some of the principal comic poets of the Sicilian school before proceeding to the writers of the middle and new comedy of the Athenians. The flourishing period of Sicilian comedy was that in which *Phormis*, *Epicharmus*, and *Dinolochus* wrote for the stage. To these may be added, though not coming strictly under the denomination of a comic poet, *Sophron*, the composer of *Mimes*.

II. Phormis (Φόρμις),[2] less correctly Phormus (Φόρμος),[3] came originally from Mænalus in Arcadia, and, having removed to Sicily, became intimate with Gelon, whose children he educated. He distinguished himself as a soldier, both under Gelon and Hiero his brother, who succeeded B.C. 478. Though the matter has been called in question, there seems to be little or no doubt that this is the same person who is associated by Aristotle with Epicharmus as one of the originators of comedy, or of a particular form of it. We have the names of eight comedies written by him, in Suidas, who also states that he was the first to introduce actors with robes reaching to the ankles, and to ornament the stage with skins dyed purple—as drapery, it may be presumed. From the titles of the plays, we may safely infer that he selected the same mythological subjects as Epicharmus.[4]

---

1 *Smith, Dict.*, *s. v. Philonides.*

2 *Aristot.*; *Pausan.* Bentley is in favor of this as the more correct form. *Phal.*, vol. i., p. 252, ed. Dyce.

3 *Athen.*; *Suid.*

4 *Smith, Dict. Biogr.*, *s. v.*

III. Epicharmus (Ἐπίχαρμος), the chief comic poet among the Dorians, was born in the island of Cos, about B.C. 540. At the age of three months, he was carried to Megara, in Sicily, or, according to the account preserved by Suidas, he went thither at a much later period, with Cadmus, the tyrant of Cos, when the latter resigned his power and emigrated to that island, about B.C. 488. Thence he removed to Syracuse, with the other inhabitants of Megara, when the latter city was destroyed by Gelon (B.C. 484 or 483). Here he spent the remainder of his life, which was prolonged throughout the reign of Hiero, at whose court Epicharmus associated with the other great writers of the time, and among them with Æschylus, who seems to have had some influence on his dramatic course.[1] He died at the age of ninety (B.C. 450), or, according to Lucian,[2] ninety-seven (B.C. 443). Epicharmus was a Pythagorean philosopher, and spent the earlier part of his life in the study of philosophy, both physical and metaphysical. He is said to have followed for some time his father's profession of medicine, and it appears that he did not commence writing comedies until his removal to Syracuse.[3]

Comedy, as we have already remarked, had for some time existed at Megara in Sicily, which was a colony from Megara, near the isthmus of Corinth, the latter of which two towns disputed, it will be remembered, with the Athenians the invention of comedy. But the comedy at the Sicilian Megara, before Epicharmus, seems to have been little more than a low buffoonery. It was he, together with Phormis, who gave it a new character, and introduced a regular plot. The number of his comedies is differently stated at 52 or at 35. There are still extant thirty-five titles. The majority of them refer to mythological subjects, that is, travesties of the heroic myths, and these plays no doubt very much resembled the satyric dramas of the Athenians. But, besides mythology, Epicharmus wrote pieces on other subjects, political and moral, relating to manners and customs, and, it would seem, even to personal character. Those, however, of his comedies which belong to the last head are rather general than individual, and resembled the writings of the new comedy, so that when the ancient writers enumerated him among the poets of the old comedy, they must be understood as referring rather to his antiquity in point of time, than to any close resemblance between his works and those of the old Attic comedians. A considerable number of fragments remain.[4] Müller has observed that the painted vases of Lower Italy often enable us to gain a complete and vivid idea of those theatrical representations of which the plays of Epicharmus are the type.

The style of his pieces appears to have been a curious mixture of the broad buffoonery which distinguished the old Megarian comedy, and of the sententious wisdom of the Pythagorean philosopher. His language was remarkably elegant; he was celebrated for his choice epithets; his plays abounded, as the extant fragments prove, with γνῶμαι, or philosophical and moral maxims, and long speculative discourses, on the instinct of animals, for example. In proof of the high estimation in which he was held by the ancients, it may be enough to refer to the notices of him by

1 *Diog. Laert.*, viii., 78. 2 *Macrob.*, 25. 3 *Smith, Dict., s. v.* 4 *Id. ib.*

Plato and Cicero. It is singular, however, that he had no successor in his peculiar style of comedy, except his son or disciple Dinolochus. He had, however, distinguished imitators in other times and countries. Plautus, for instance, is said by Horace to have made him his model, "*Plautus ad exemplar Siculi properare Epicharmi.*"[1] The parasite, which forms so conspicuous a character in the plays of the new comedy, is first found in Epicharmus.

The fragments of Epicharmus are printed in the collections, of Morellius, *Sententiæ Vet. Comic.*, Paris, 1553, 8vo; of Hertelius, *Collect. Frag. Comic.*, Basil., 1560, 8vo; of H. Stephens, *Poesis Philosophica*, 1573, 8vo; of Grotius, *Excerpt. ex Trag. et Com.*, Paris, 1626, 4to; by Ahrens, in his *De Linguæ Græcæ Dialectis*, vol. ii., p. 435, *seqq.*; and separately by Kruseman, Harlem, 1834. Additions have been made by Welcker (*Zeitschrift für die Alterthumsw.*, 1835, p. 1123) and others. The most important modern work on Epicharmus is that of Grysar, *De Doriensium Comœdia*, Colon., 1828. The second volume, however, containing the fragments, has never appeared.

IV. Dinolŏchus (Δεινόλοχος), of Syracuse or Agrigentum, was, according to some, the son, according to others, the disciple of Epicharmus. He lived about B.C. 488, and wrote fourteen plays in the Doric dialect, about which we only know, from a few titles, that some of them were on mythological subjects.[2]

V. Sōphrōn (Σώφρων),[3] of Syracuse, was the principal writer, and, in one sense, the inventor of that species of composition called the *Mime* (μῖμος), which was one of the numerous varieties of the Dorian comedy. He flourished about B.C. 460–420. When Sophron is called the inventor of mimes, the meaning is, that he reduced to the form of a literary composition a species of amusement, which the Greeks of Sicily, who were preeminent for broad humor and merriment, had practiced from time immemorial at their public festivals. Whether the term μῖμος originally included any kind of imitation without words, we are not sufficiently informed; but it is clear that the mimes of Sophron were ethical, that is, they exhibited not only incident, but characters. Moreover, as is implied in the very fact of their being a literary composition, words were put into the mouths of the actors, though still quite in subordination to their gestures; and in proportion as the spoken part of the performance was increased, the *mime* would approach nearer and nearer to a *comedy*. Of all such representations instrumental music appears to have formed an essential part.

One feature of the mimes of Sophron, which formed a marked distinction between them and comic poetry, was the nature of their rhythm. There is some difficulty, however, in determining whether they were in mere prose, or in mingled poetry and prose, or in prose with a peculiar rhythmical movement, but no metrical arrangement. Suidas expressly states that they were in prose (καταλογάδην);[4] and the existing fragments confirm the general truth of this assertion, for they defy all at-

[1] *Epist.*, ii., 1, 58.
[2] *Suid.*, *s. v.*; *Grysar, De Dor. Com.*, p. 81.
[3] *Smith, Dict. Biogr.*, *s. v.*
[4] *Suid.*, *s. v.*

tempts at scansion. Nevertheless, they frequently fall into a sort of rhythmical cadence or swing, which is different from the rhythm of ordinary prose.[1] This prosaic structure of the mimes of Sophron has given rise to a doubt whether they were ever intended for public exhibition, a doubt which ought never to have been entertained. The dialect of Sophron is the old Doric, interspersed with Sicilian peculiarities. The character of these compositions, as we have said above, appears to have been ethical; that is, the scenes represented were those of ordinary life, and the language employed was intended to bring out more clearly the characters of the persons exhibited in those scenes, not only for the amusement, but also for the instruction of the spectators. Plato was a great admirer of Sophron, a fact which shows that there must have been something of sound philosophy in these productions, and he is said to have been the first who made the mimes known at Athens. The serious purpose which was aimed at in the works of Sophron, was always, as in the Attic comedy, clothed under a sportive form; and it can easily be imagined that sometimes the latter element prevailed even to the extent of grossness, as some of the extant fragments and the parallel of the Attic comedy combine to prove.[2] The best collection of the fragments of Sophron is by Ahrens, *De Græcæ Linguæ Dialectis*. They have also been collected by Blomfield, in the *Classical Journal* for 1811, No. 8, p. 380, *seqq*., and more fully in the *Museum Criticum*, vol. ii., p. 340, *seqq*., Cambridge, 1826.

CHAPTER XXIX.

FOURTH OR ATTIC PERIOD—*continued.*

WRITERS OF THE MIDDLE COMEDY.

I. EUBŪLUS (Εὔβουλος) was a very distinguished poet of the middle comedy, and flourished about B.C. 376. His plays were chiefly on mythological subjects. Several of them contained parodies of passages from the tragic poets, and especially from Euripides. There are a few instances of his attacking eminent individuals by name, as Philocrates, Cydias, Callimedon, Dionysius the tyrant of Syracuse, and Callistratus. He sometimes ridiculed classes of persons, as the Thebans in his Ἀντιόπη. His language is simple and elegant, and generally pure, containing few words which are not found in writers of the best period. Like Antiphanes, he was extensively pillaged by later poets, as, for example, by Alexis, Ophelion, and Ephippus. Suidas gives the number of his plays at 104, of which there are extant more than 50 titles.[3] The fragments of Eubulus are given by Meineke, *Comic. Græc. Frag.*, vol. i., p. 594, *seqq.*, *ed. min.*

II. ARĀRŌS (Ἀραρώς), son of Aristophanes, was first introduced to public notice by his father as the principal actor in the second Plutus, B.C. 388, the last play which Aristophanes exhibited in his own name. The father wrote two more comedies, the Κώκαλος and the Αἰολοσίκων,

[1] *Herm. ad Aristot., Poet.*, i., 8. [2] *Smith, Dict. Biogr., s. v.* [3] *Id. ib.*

which were brought out in the name of Araros,[1] probably very soon after the above date. Araros first exhibited in his own name, B.C. 375.[2] He is charged with frigidity by Alexis,[3] who, however, was his rival. Suidas mentions six comedies of his. The fragments are given in Meineke, *Comic. Græc. Frag.*, vol. i., p. 630, *seqq.*, *ed. min.*

III. Anaxandrĭdes (Ἀναξανδρίδης) was the son of Anaxander, a native of Camirus, in Rhodes. He began to exhibit comedies in B.C. 376, and 29 years later he was present, and probably exhibited at the games celebrated by Philip at Dium. Aristotle held him in high esteem.[4] He is said to have been the first poet who made love-intrigues a prominent part of comedy. He gained ten prizes, the whole number of his comedies being sixty-five. Though he is said to have destroyed several of his plays in anger at their rejection, we still have the titles of thirty-three.[5] The fragments are given by Meineke, *Frag. Comic. Græc.*, vol. i., p. 574, *seqq.*, *ed. min.*

IV. Antiphănes (Ἀντιφάνης) was the most highly-esteemed writer of the middle comedy, excepting Alexis, who shared that honor with him. He was born about B.C. 404, and died B.C. 330. The parentage and birth-place of Antiphanes are doubtful. As his birth-place are mentioned Cios on the Propontis, Smyrna, Rhodes, and Larissa; but the last statement deserves little credit.[6] The fragments which remain of his pieces prove that Athenæus was right in praising him for the elegance of his language, though he uses some words and phrases which are not found in older writers. He was one of the most fertile dramatic authors that ever lived, for his plays amounted, on the largest computation, to 365, on the least to 260. We still possess the titles of about 130. It is probable, however, that some of the comedies ascribed to him were by other writers, for the grammarians frequently confound him with other comic poets. Some of his plays were on mythological subjects, others had reference to particular persons, others to characters, personal, professional, and national, while others seem to have been wholly occupied with the intrigues of private life.[7] The fragments of Antiphanes are given by Meineke, *Frag. Comic. Græc.*, vol. i., p. 491, *seqq.*, *ed. min.*

V. Nicostrătus (Νικόστρατος), the youngest of the three sons of Aristophanes, called by some *Philetærus*. He is ranked by Athenæus expressly among the poets of the middle comedy,[8] though some of his pieces, as, for instance, the Ὀρνιθευτής, belonged rather to the new comedy. Some of the characters also which he introduced in other dramas demonstrate the same. In his Βασιλεῖς, he introduced a boasting soldier;[9] in his Τοκιστής, an avaricious money-lender, and a vaunting cook. Photius has got a story that Nicostratus, through unrequited love, leaped off the Leucadian rock. The titles of nineteen of his plays have come down to us.[10] The fragments are given by Meineke, *Frag. Comic. Græc.*, vol. i., p. 632, *seqq.*, *ed. min.*

---

1 *Arg. ad Plut.*, iv., *Bekker.* 2 *Suid.*, *s. v.* 3 *Athen.*, iii., p. 123, *E.*
4 *Rhet.*, iii., 10, *seqq.*; *Eth. Nicom.*, vii., 10. 5 *Smith, Dict. Biogr.*, *s. v.*
6 *Meineke*, i., 308. 7 *Smith, Dict. Biogr.*, *s. v.* 8 *Athen.*, xiii., p. 597, *D.*
9 *Id.*, vi., p. 230, *D.* 10 *Smith, Dict. Biogr.*, *s. v.*

VI. Alexis (Ἄλεξις) was a native of Thurii, in Magna Græcia, but admitted subsequently to the privileges of an Athenian citizen. He was the uncle and instructor of Menander,[1] was born about B.C. 394, and lived to the age of 106.[2] He appears to have been rather addicted to the pleasures of the table.[3] According to Plutarch, he expired upon the stage while being crowned as victor.[4] By the old grammarians he is commonly called a writer of the middle comedy, and fragments and titles of many of his plays confirm this statement. Still, for more than thirty years, he was contemporary with Philippides, Philemon, Menander, and Diphilus, and several fragments show that he also wrote pieces which would be classed with those of the new comedy. He was a remarkably prolific writer. Suidas says he wrote 245 plays, and the titles of 113 have come down to us. In some of his pieces he ridiculed Plato, in others he satirized Demosthenes. As might have been expected in a person who wrote so much, the same passage frequently occurred in several plays; nor did he scruple sometimes to borrow from other poets, as, for example, from Eubulus. His wit and elegance are praised by Athenæus,[5] whose testimony is confirmed by the extant fragments. His plays were frequently translated by the Roman writers.[6] A considerable list of peculiar words and forms employed by him is furnished by Meineke,[7] who has also given the fragments of his pieces, *Frag. Comic. Græc.*, vol. ii., p. 688, *seqq.*, *ed. min.*

CHAPTER XXX.

FOURTH OR ATTIC PERIOD—*continued.*

WRITERS OF THE NEW COMEDY.

I. Philippĭdes (Φιλιππίδης), of Athens, is mentioned as one of the six principal poets of the new comedy, these six being Philemon, Menander, Diphilus, Philippides, Posidippus, and Apollodorus. He flourished about B.C. 335. Philippides seems to have deserved the rank assigned him, as one of the best poets of the new comedy. He attacked the luxury and corruption of the age, defended the privileges of his art, and made use of personal satire with a spirit approaching to that of the old comedy.[8] Plutarch eulogizes him highly.[9] His death is said to have been caused by excessive joy at an unexpected victory. It appears from Gellius that he lived to an advanced age. The number of his dramas is stated by Suidas at forty-five; there are fifteen titles extant. Some of the ancient critics charge Philippides with infringing upon the purity of the Attic dialect, and Meineke produces several words from his fragments as examples. The fragments are given by the scholar just mentioned, *Frag. Comic. Græc.*, vol. ii., p. 1116, *seqq.*, *ed. min.*[10]

II. Philēmon (Φιλήμων),[11] one of the most eminent poets of the new

[1] *Suid.*, *s. v.* [2] *Plut.*, *Defect. Orac.*, p. 420, *E.* [3] *Athen.*, viii., p. 344.
[4] *An sen. ger. resp.*, p. 785, *B.* [5] *Athen.*, ii., p. 59, *F.* [6] *Aul. Gell.*, ii., 23.
[7] *Meineke*, *Fragm. Com.*, vol. i., p. 374, *seqq.* [8] *Id.*, *Hist. Crit.*, p. 437, *seqq.*
[9] *Plut.*, *Demetr.*, 12. [10] *Smith*, *Dict. Biogr.*, *s. v.* [11] *Id. ib.*

comedy, ranking next to Menander. He was the son of Damon, and a native of Soli, in Cilicia; or, according to some, of Syracuse. He came to Athens at an early age, and there subsequently received the rights of citizenship. He flourished in the reign of Alexander, a little earlier than Menander, whom, however, he long survived, having lived nearly 100 years. The manner of his death is differently related; some ascribing it to excessive laughter at a ludicrous incident,[1] others to joy at obtaining a victory in a dramatic contest;[2] while another story represents him as quietly called away by the goddesses, whom he served, in the midst of the composition or representation of his last and best work. Philemon is regarded by some modern scholars as the first poet of the new comedy in order of time, a place, however, which we have preferred, with others, assigning to Philippides. Although there can be no doubt that Philemon was inferior to Menander as a poet, yet he was a greater favorite with the Athenians, and often conquered his rival in the dramatic contests.[3] Gellius ascribes these victories to the use of unfair influence, and tells us that Menander was accustomed to ask Philemon himself whether he did not blush when he conquered him. We have other proofs of the rivalry between Menander and Philemon in the identity of some of their titles.

Philemon was, however, sometimes defeated; and it would seem that on one such occasion he went into exile for a time.[4] At all events, he undertook a journey to the East, either from this cause or by the desire of King Ptolemy, who appears to have invited him to Alexandrea; and to this journey ought, no doubt, to be referred his adventure with Magas, tyrant of Cyrene, the brother of Ptolemy Philadelphus. Philemon had ridiculed Magas for his want of learning, in a comedy, copies of which he took pains to circulate; and the arrival of the poet at Cyrene, whither he was driven by a storm, furnished the king with an opportunity of taking a contemptuous revenge, by ordering a soldier to touch the poet's throat with a naked sword, and then to retire politely without hurting him; after which he made him a present of a set of child's playthings, and then dismissed him.[5]

Philemon seems to have been inferior to Menander in the liveliness of his dialogue, for his plays were considered, on account of their more connected arguments and longer periods, better fitted for reading than for acting.[6] The extant fragments display much liveliness, wit, elegance, and practical knowledge of life. His favorite subjects seem to have been love-intrigues, and his characters were the standing ones of the new comedy, with which Plautus and Terence have made us familiar. The jest upon Magas, already mentioned, is a proof that the personal satire which formed the chief characteristic of the old comedy was not entirely relinquished in the new. The number of Philemon's plays was ninety-seven. The extant titles, after the doubtful and spurious ones are rejected, amount to about fifty-three; but it is very probable that some of

[1] *Suid.*, *s. v.*; *Val. Max.*, ix., 12, *extr.* 6.
[2] *Plut. an Sen.*, &c., p. 785, *B.*
[3] *Aul. Gell.*, xvii., 4.
[4] *Stob.*, *Serm.*, xxxviii., p. 232.
[5] *Plut.*, *De cohib. ira*, p. 458, *A.*
[6] *Demetr. Phal.*, *De Eloc.*, § 193.

them should be assigned to the younger Philemon.[1] The fragments of Philemon are printed, with those of Menander, by Meineke, Berlin, 1823, 8vo, and in his *Frag. Comic. Græc.*, vol. ii., p. 821, *seqq.*, *ed. min.* They are given also by Dübner, at the end of the Aristophanes in Didot's *Bibliotheca Græca*, Paris, 1839. (Cf. editions of Menander on p. 226.)

III. Menander (Μένανδρος),[2] of Athens, the most distinguished poet of the new comedy, was born B.C. 342, and flourished in the time of the successors of Alexander. His father, Diopithes, commanded the Athenian forces on the Hellespont in the year of his son's birth. Alexis, the comic poet, was the uncle of Menander, on the father's side; and we may naturally suppose that the young Menander derived from his uncle his taste for the comic drama, and was instructed by him in its rules of composition. His character must have been greatly influenced and formed by his intimacy with Theophrastus and Epicurus, of whom the former was his teacher and the latter his intimate friend. His taste and sympathies were altogether with the philosophy of Epicurus; and in an epigram he declared that "as Themistocles rescued Greece from slavery, so did Epicurus from unreason."[3] From Theophrastus, on the other hand, he must have derived much of that skill in the discrimination of character which we so much admire in the Χαρακτῆρες of the philosopher, and which formed the great charm of the comedies of Menander. His master's attention to external elegance and comfort he not only imitated, but, as was natural in a man of an elegant person, a joyous spirit, and a serene and easy temper, he carried it to the extreme of luxury and effeminacy. The moral character of Menander is defended by modern writers against the aspersions of Suidas and others. Thus much is certain, that his comedies contain nothing offensive, at least to the taste of his own and the following ages, none of the purest, it must be admitted, as they were frequently acted at private banquets.

Of the actual events of Menander's life we know but little. He enjoyed the friendship of Demetrius Phalereus, whose attention was first drawn to him by admiration of his works.[4] This intimacy was attended, however, with danger as well as with honor, for when Demetrius Phalereus was expelled from Athens by Demetrius Poliorcetes, Menander became a mark for the public informers, and would have been put to death but for the intercession of Telesphorus, the son-in-law of Demetrius.[5] The first Greek king of Egypt, Ptolemy, the son of Lagus, was also one of his admirers; and he invited the poet to his court at Alexandrea; but Menander seems to have declined the proffered honor.[6] Suidas mentions some letters to Ptolemy as among the works of Menander.

The time of his death is differently stated. The same inscription which gives the date of his birth, adds that he died at the age of fifty-two years, in the archonship of Philippus, in the thirty-second year of Ptolemy Soter. Clinton shows that these statements refer to the year B.C. 292–1; but to make up the fifty-two years, we must reckon in both extremes, 342 and 291. The date is confirmed by Eusebius, by the anonymous writer on

[1] *Smith, Dict. Biogr.*, *s. v.*
[2] *Id. ib.*
[3] *Anth. Pal.*, vii., 72.
[4] *Phædrus*, i., 11.
[5] *Diog. Laert.*, v., 80.
[6] *Plin.*, *H. N.*, vii., 29.

comedy, who adds that Menander died at Athens; by Apollodorus;[1] and by Aulus Gellius.[2] Respecting the manner of his death, all that we know is that an old commentator on Ovid[3] applies the line "*Comicus ut mediis periit dum nabat in undis*" to Menander, and tells us that he was drowned while swimming in the harbor of Piræeus, and we learn from Alciphron[4] that Menander had an estate at that place. He was buried by the road leading out of Piræeus toward Athens. There are two epigrams upon him in the Greek Anthology.

Notwithstanding Menander's fame as a poet, his public dramatic career, during his lifetime, was not eminently successful; for, though he composed upward of a hundred comedies, he gained the prize only eight times.[5] His preference for elegant exhibitions of character above coarse jesting may have been the reason why he was not so great a favorite with the common people as his principal rival, Philemon, who is said, moreover, as we have already remarked, to have used unfair means of gaining popularity.[6] Menander appears, however, to have borne the popular neglect very lightly, in the consciousness of his own superiority. The Athenians erected his statue in the theatre; but this was an honor too often conferred upon very indifferent poets to be of much value: indeed, according to Pausanias, he was the only distinguished comic poet of all whose statues had a place there.[7] The neglect of Menander's contemporaries, however, has been amply compensated by his posthumous fame. His comedies retained their place on the stage down to the time of Plutarch,[8] and the unanimous consent of antiquity placed him at the head of the new comedy, and on an equality with the great masters of the various kinds of poetry. The grammarian Aristophanes assigned him the second place among all writers, after Homer alone;[9] and to the same grammarian is ascribed the happy saying, *Ὦ Μένανδρε, καὶ βίε, πότερος ἄρ' ὑμῶν πρότερον ἐμιμήσατο;*[10] "O Menander and life, which one of you, pray, first imitated (the other)?" Among the Romans, besides the fact that their comedy was founded chiefly on the plays of Menander, we have the celebrated phrase of Julius Cæsar, who addresses Terence as "*dimidiate Menander*,"[11] or "halved Menander." The imitations of Menander are at once a proof of his reputation, and an aid in appreciating his poetic character. Among the Greeks, Alciphron and Lucian[12] were, in various degrees, indebted to his comedies. Among the Romans, Cæcilius, Afranius, and more particularly Terence, are well known to have drawn largely on his rich stores.

Menander is remarkable for the elegance with which he threw into single verses or short sentences the maxims of that practical wisdom in the affairs of common life which forms so important a feature in the new comedy. Various "Anthologies" of such sentences were compiled by the ancient grammarians from his works, of which there is still extant a very

1 *Ap. Aul. Gell.*, xvii., 4. 2 xvii., 21. 3 *Ibis*, 593. 4 *Epist.*, ii., 4.
5 *Aul. Gell.*, xvii., 4. 6 *Id. ib.* 7 *Paus.*, i., 21, 1.
8 *Comp. Men. et Arist.*, p. 854, *B.* 9 *Brunck, Anal.*, vol. iii., p. 269.
10 Or, according to Scaliger's correction, ποτερὸν ἀπεμιμήσατο.
11 *Donat. Vit. Terent.*, p. 754. 12 *Meincke*, p. xxxv.

P

interesting specimen, in the collection of several hundred lines, under the title of *γνῶμαι μονόστιχοι*. The number of Menander's comedies is stated at a few more than a hundred; 105, 108, and 109, according to different authorities.[1] We know with certainty the date of only one of the plays, namely, the Ὀργή, which was brought out in B.C. 321, when Menander was only in his twenty-first year. We have fragments of or references to plays, amounting in all to nearly ninety titles. There are also about 500 fragments which can not be assigned to their proper places. To these must be added the *γνῶμαι μονόστιχοι*, some passages of the *γνῶμαι* (or *σύγκρισις*) Μενάνδρου καὶ Φιλιστίωνος, and two epigrams, one in the Greek Anthology, and one in the Latin version of Ausonius.[2] Of the letters to Ptolemy, which Suidas mentions, nothing survives, and it may fairly be doubted whether they were not, like the so-called letters of other great men of antiquity, the productions of the later rhetoricians. Suidas ascribes to him some orations, a statement of which there is no confirmation; but Quintilian tells us that some ascribed the orations of Charisius to Menander.[3] There were several commentaries on Menander among the ancients, and one in particular by the grammarian Aristophanes, whose admiration of the poet we have already mentioned.

The first attempt at a complete critical edition of Menander, after several previous editions of the poet, was the following: *Menandri et Philemonis Reliquiæ, quotquot reperire potuerunt, cum notis Hug. Grotii et Joh. Clerici*, Amst., 1709, 8vo. This edition was reprinted in 1732, 1752, 1771, and 1777, but has been very generally condemned. Its only merit is that it gave occasion to Bentley's emendations on 323 passages of the fragments. (Cf. *Monk's Life of Bentley*, p. 211.) Since the publication of that work there has been no edition of Menander worthy of notice, except that his *γνῶμαι* have had a place in the various collections of the gnomic poets, until the appearance of Meineke's *Menandri et Philemonis Reliquiæ*, Berol., 1823, 8vo. This admirable edition contains, besides the fragments, dissertations on the lives and writings of the two poets, and also Bentley's emendations of the fragments. The fragments were reprinted by Meineke (with the annotations somewhat condensed), in his larger (1841) and smaller (1847) editions of the *Fragmenta Comicorum Græcorum*. In the larger edition they are given in vol. iv., p. 69, *seqq.*, in the smaller, p. 867, *seqq.*, vol. ii. Meineke's collection has been reprinted (carefully revised) by Dübner, as an Appendix, along with those of Philemon, to the *Aristophanes* of Didot's *Bibliotheca*, Paris, 1839.[4]

IV. Diphĭlus (Δίφιλος), a contemporary of Menander and Philemon, was a native of Sinope.[5] He is said to have exhibited one hundred plays, and sometimes to have acted himself. Though, in point of time, Diphilus belonged to the new comedy, his poetry seems to have had more of the character of the middle. This is shown, among other indications, by the frequency with which he chooses mythological subjects for his plays, and by his bringing on the stage the poets Archilochus, Hipponax, and Sappho.[6] His language is simple and elegant, but contains, at the same time, many departures from Attic purity. The Roman comic poets borrowed largely from Diphilus. The *Casina* of Plautus is a translation of his Κληρούμενοι.[7] His Συναποθνήσκοντες was translated by Plautus in the lost play of the

---

1 *Suid.*, *s. v.*; *Anon.*, *De Com.*, p. xii.; *Donat. Vit. Terent.*, p. 753; *Aul. Gell.*, xvii., 4.
2 *Epig.*, 139.
3 *Quint.*, x., 1, 70.
4 *Smith*, *Dict. Biogr.*, *s. v.*
5 *Strab.*, xii., p. 546; *Anon.*, *De Com.*, p. xxx., *seq.*
6 *Athen.*, xi., p. 487, *A*; xiii., p. 599, *D.*
7 *Plaut.*, *Cas. Prolog.*, 31.

Commorientes, and was partly followed by Terence in his *Adelphi.*[1] The *Rudens* of Plautus is also a translation of a play,[2] but the title of the Greek piece is not known. The fragments of Diphilus are given by Meineke, *Fragm. Comic. Græc.*, vol. ii., p. 1066, *seqq.*, *ed. min.*

V. Posidippus (Ποσείδιππος) was a native of Cassandrea, in Macedonia, and one of the six principal poets of the new comedy.[3] He began to exhibit dramas in the third year after the death of Menander, that is, in B.C. 289, so that his time falls just at the era in Greek literary history which is marked by the accession of Ptolemy Philadelphus.[4] Of the events in the poet's life nothing is known; but his portrait is preserved to us in the beautiful sitting statue in the Vatican, which, with the accompanying statue of Menander, is esteemed by Winckelmann and others as among the finest works of Greek sculpture that have come down to us.[5] According to Suidas, he wrote forty plays, of which eighteen titles are preserved. In his language Meineke has detected some new words, and old words in new senses, totally unknown to the best Attic writers. Gellius mentions him among the Greek comedians who were imitated by the Latin poets. It seems from the titles that some of his plays were of a licentious character. The fragments are given by Meineke, *Fragm. Græc.*, vol. ii., p. 1141, *seqq.*, *ed. min.*[6]

VI. Apollodōrus (Ἀπολλόδωρος), a native of Carystus, in Eubœa, was the last in the canon of the six principal poets of the new comedy. It was from him that Terence took his *Hecyra* and *Phormio.* According to Suidas, Apollodorus wrote forty-seven comedies, and gained the prize five times. We know the titles and possess fragments of several of his plays. The fragments are given by Meineke, *Fragm. Comic. Græc.*, vol. ii., p. 1101, *seqq.*, *ed. min.*[7]

CHAPTER XXXI.

FOURTH OR ATTIC PERIOD—*continued.*

OTHER POETS OF THIS PERIOD.[8]

I. The drama was so well adapted to reflect the thoughts and feelings of the people of Attica in the mirror of poetry, that other sorts of metrical composition fell comparatively into the background, and for the public in general assumed the character rather of isolated and momentary gratifications than of a poetic expression of prevailing sentiments and principles.

II. Still, however, some names occur well deserving of mention, especially in the two departments of *Elegiac* and *Epic* verse, and to a brief consideration of these we will devote the present chapter, before proceeding to the more enlarged field of prose composition.

---

1 *Terent.*, *Prol. Adelph.*, 10.
2 *Plaut.*, *Rud. Prol.*, 32.
3 *Anon.*, *De Com.*, p. xxx.
4 *Clinton*, *Fast. Hell.*, *s. a.*
5 *Visconti*, *Mus. Pio-Clem.*, vol. iii., p. 16, *seqq.*; *Winckelmann*, *Vorläuf. Abhand.*, c. iv., § 126.
6 *Smith*, *Dict. Biogr.*, *s. v.*
7 *Id. ib.*, *s. v.*
8 *Müller*, *Hist. Gr. Lit.*, vol. ii., p. 56, *seqq.*

I. ELEGIAC POETRY.

III. The *Elegy* still continued a favorite poetical amusement while Attic literature flourished; it remained true to one of its particular designations, to enliven the banquet and to shed the gentle light of a higher poetic feeling over the convivialities of the feast. Consequently, the fragments of elegies belonging to this period, by Ion of Chios, Dionysius of Athens, Euenus, the sophist, of Paros, and Critias of Athens, all speak much of wine, of the proper mode of drinking, of dancing and singing at banquets, of the cottabus-game, which young people were then so fond of, and of other things of the same kind, and they took as their subject the joys of the banquet, and the right measure to be observed at it.[1]

IV. This elegiac poetry proceeds on the principle that we should enjoy ourselves in society, combining the pleasures of the senses with intellectual gratifications, and not forgetting our higher calling in the midst of such enjoyments. As, however, the thoughts easily passed from the festal board to the general social and political interests of the times, the elegy had political features also, and statesmen often expressed in this form their opinions on the course to be adopted for Greece in general, and for the different republics in particular. This must have been the case with the elegies of Dionysius, who was a considerable statesman of the time of Pericles, and led the Athenians who settled at Thurii in the great Hellenic migration to that place.

V. The political tendency appeared still more clearly in the elegies of Critias, the son of Callæschrus, in which he said bluntly that he had recommended in the public assembly that Alcibiades should be recalled, and had drawn up the decree. The predilection for Lacedæmon, which Critias had imbibed as one of the Eupatridæ, and as a friend of Socrates, declares itself in his commendations of the old customs which the Spartans kept up at their banquets.[2]

VI. From this elegiac poetry, however, which was cultivated in the circle of Attic training, we must carefully distinguish the elegies of Antimachus,[3] which we may term a revival of the love-sorrows of Mimnermus. Antimachus was a native of Claros. He is usually, however, called a Colophonian, probably only because Claros belonged to the dominion of Colophon. He flourished during the latter period of the Peloponnesian war.[4] Antimachus was in general a reviver of ancient poetry; one who, keeping aloof from the stream of the new-fashioned literature, applied himself exclusively to his own studies, and on that very account found little sympathy among the people of his own time, as, indeed, appears from the well-known story that, when he was reciting his *Thebaïs*, all his audience left the room, with the single exception of Plato, then a young man.[5] This want of sympathy, however, in the case of the *Thebaïs* at least, must have been greatly increased by the voluminous nature of his poem, since we are told that he had spun out his work so much, that in the twenty-fourth book his seven heroes had not yet arrived at

[1] *Müller, l. c.* [2] *Id. ib.* [3] *Smith, Dict. Biogr., s. v.*
[4] *Diod. Sic.*, xiii., 108. [5] *Müller, l. c.*

Thebes.[1] According to Quintilian, Antimachus was unsuccessful in his description of passion, his works were not graceful, and were deficient in arrangement.[2] His style also had not the simple and easy flow of the Homeric poems. He borrowed expressions and phrases from the tragic writers, and frequently introduced Doric forms.[3]

But the work which brings him under the present head was his elegiac poem called *Lyde*, which was dedicated to the remembrance of a Lydian maid of that name, whom Antimachus had loved and early lost. This elegy was very celebrated in antiquity. It was very long, and consisted of accounts of the misfortunes of all the mythical heroes, who, like the poet, had become unfortunate through the early deaths of those whom they loved.[4] It thus contained vast stores of mythical and antiquarian information, and it was chiefly for this, and not for any higher and poetical reason, that Agatharchides made an abridgment of it.[5]

From what has here been stated concerning him, it will be seen that Antimachus was one of the forerunners of the poets of the Alexandrine school, who wrote more for the learned, and a select number of readers, than for the public at large. The Alexandrine grammarians assigned to him the second place among the epic poets, and the Emperor Hadrian preferred his works even to those of Homer. The numerous fragments of this poet have been collected and published by Schellenberg, Halle, 1786, re-edited with Blomfield's corrections by Giles, London, 1838. Some additional fragments are contained in Stoll's *Animadversiones in Antimachi Fragm.*, Götting., 1840. The epic fragments, or those belonging to the *Thebaïs*, are collected in Duntzer's "*Die Fragm. der Episch. Poes. der Griech. bis auf Alexander*," p. 99, *seqq.*; and by Dübner in the *Poetæ Epici Minores*, in Didot's *Bibliotheca Græca*, Paris, 1840.

II. EPIC POETRY.

VII. The mention of Antimachus and his *Thebaïs* has in some degree anticipated the present head, and no further notice of that work need here be taken. The only other epic poets deserving of mention are *Panyasis* and *Chœrilus*.

VIII. PANYĀSIS (Πανύασις) was a native of Halicarnassus,[6] and probably the maternal uncle of Herodotus. He began to be known about B.C. 489, continued in reputation till B.C. 467, in which year he is placed by Suidas, and was put to death by Lygdamis, tyrant of Halicarnassus, probably about the same time that Herodotus left his native city, that is, about B.C. 457.[7] Ancient writers mention two poems by Panyasis. Of these the most celebrated was entitled *Heracleia* (Ἡράκλεια) or *Heracleias* (Ἡρακλειάς), and gave a detailed account of the exploits of Hercules. It consisted of fourteen books and nine thousand verses, and appears, as far as we can judge from the references to it in ancient writers, to have

---

[1] *Porph. ad Horat., Ep. ad Pis.*, 146.
[2] *Quint.*, x., 1, 53. Compare *Dion. Hal., De Verb. Comp.*, 22.
[3] *Schol. ad Nicand., Theriac.*, 3.
[4] *Plut., Consol. ad Apollon.*, p. 106, *B.*
[5] *Phot., Bibl.*, p. 171, ed. *Bekker*.
[6] *Pausan.*, x., 8, 5; *Clem. Alex., Strom.*, vi., 2, 52.
[7] *Clinton, Fast. Hell., sub annis* 489, 457.

passed over briefly the adventures of the hero which had been related by previous poets, and to have dwelt chiefly upon his exploits in Asia, Libya, &c. An outline of the contents of the various books, as far as they can be restored, is given by Müller, in an appendix to his work on the Dorians.[1] The other poem of Panyasis bore the name of *Ionica* (Ἰωνικά), and contained seven thousand verses. It gave the history of Neleus, Codrus, and the Ionic colonies. Suidas says it was written in pentameters; but it is improbable that, at so early a period, a poem of such a length was written simply in pentameters; still, as no fragments have come down to us, we have no certain information on the subject.

We do not know what impression the poems of Panyasis made upon his contemporaries and their immediate descendants, but it was probably not great, since he is not mentioned by any of the great Greek writers. But in later times his works were extensively read, and much admired. The Alexandrine grammarians ranked him with Homer, Hesiod, Pisander, and Antimachus, as one of the five principal epic poets, and some even went so far as to compare him with Homer.[2] Panyasis occupied an intermediate position between the later cyclic poets and the studied efforts of Antimachus, who is stated to have been his pupil. From two of the longest fragments which have come down to us, it appears that Panyasis kept close to the old Ionic form of epic poetry, and had imbibed no small portion of the Homeric spirit.[3] The fragments of the *Heraclea* are given in the collections of the Greek poets by Winterton, Brunck, Boissonade, and Gaisford; in Düntzer's Fragments of Greek epic poetry; in Tzschirner's *De Panyasidis Vita et Carminibus Dissertatio*, Vratisl., 1836; and in Funcke's *De Panyasidis Vita ac Poesi Dissertatio*, Bonn, 1837.

IX. Chœrĭlus (Χοιρίλος) or Chœrillus (Χοίριλλος),[4] a native of Samos, was born about B.C. 470, and died at the court of Archelaus, king of Macedonia, consequently not later than B.C. 399, which was the last year of Archelaus. Suidas says that Chœrilus was a slave at Samos, and was distinguished for his beauty; that he ran away, and resided with Herodotus, from whom he acquired a taste for literature; and that he turned his attention subsequently to poetry. Athenæus states that Chœrilus received from Archelaus, after having taken up his residence at his court, four minæ a day,[5] and spent it all upon good living (ὀψοφαγίαν). Chœrilus was the author of an epic poem on the wars of the Greeks with Darius and Xerxes. The exact title of the work, however, is not known. It may have been Περσικά. It is remarkable as the earliest attempt to celebrate in epic verse events which were nearly contemporary with the poet's life. Of its character we may form some conjecture from the connection between the poet and Herodotus. There are also fragments preserved by Aristotle from the Prooemium;[6] by Ephorus, from the description of Darius's bridge of boats, in which the Scythians are mentioned;[7] by Josephus, from the catalogue of the nations in the army of Xerxes,

---

[1] vol. i., p. 532, Eng. transl.

[2] Compare *Suid.*, *s. v.; Dionys.*, *De Vet. Script. Cens.*, c. 2, p. 419, ed. Reiske.

[3] *Smith, Dict. Biogr.*, *s. v.*

[4] *Id. ib.*

[5] *Athen.*, viii., p. 345, *E.*

[6] *Aristot.*, *Rhet.*, iii., 14.

[7] *Strab.*, xii., p. 303.

among whom were the Jews;[1] and other fragments, the place of which is uncertain. The chief action of the poem appears to have been the battle of Salamis. The high estimation in which Chœrilus was held is proved by his reception into the epic canon; from which, however, he was again expelled by the Alexandrine grammarians, and Antimachus was put in his place, on account of a statement which was made on the authority of Heraclides Ponticus, that Plato very much preferred Antimachus to Chœrilus.[2] The great inferiority of Chœrilus to Homer in his similes is noticed by Aristotle. Chœrilus must not be confounded with the worthless poet of the same name, a native of Iasos, and one of the train of Alexander the Great, of whom Horace makes mention. The fragments of Chœrilus are given by Näke, "*Chœrili Samii Fragmenta,*" Lips., 1817.

CHAPTER XXXII.

FOURTH OR ATTIC PERIOD—*continued.*

PROSE WRITINGS.[3]

I. We have seen both tragedy and comedy, in their latter days, gradually sinking into prose; and this has shown us that prose was the most powerful instrument in the literature of the time, and has made us the more curious to investigate its tendency, its progress, and its development.

II. The cultivation of prose belongs almost entirely to the period which intervened between the Persian war and the time of Alexander the Great. Before this time every attempt at prose composition was either so little removed from the colloquial style of the day, as to forfeit all claim to be considered as a written language, properly so called; or else owed all its charms and splendor to an imitation of the diction and the forms of words found in poetry, which attained to completeness and maturity many hundred years before the rise of a prose literature.

III. In considering the history of Attic prose, we propose to give a view of the general character of the works of the prose writers, and their relation to the circumstances and intellectual energy of the Athenian people. And, in order to effect this in the clearest and most satisfactory manner, we will divide the remainder of the present period into three great branches, namely, the School of History, the School of Eloquence, and the School of Philosophy, giving an account of the most prominent individuals connected with each.

I. SCHOOL OF HISTORY.

IV. Thucydĭdes (Θουκυδίδης),[4] the great Athenian historian, was the son of Olorus[5] or Orolus[6] and Hegesipyle. According to a statement of Pamphila, a female historian in the time of Nero, and who is cited by Gellius,

[1] *Joseph. c. Apion.*, i., 22; vol. ii., p. 454, ed. Hav.
[2] *Proclus, Comm. in Plat. Tim.*, p. 28.
[3] *Müller, Hist. Gr. Lit.*, vol. ii., p. 66.
[4] *Smith Dict. Biogr.*, *s. v.*
[5] *Thucyd.*, iv., 104.
[6] *Marcell.*, *Vit. Thucyd.*

he was forty years of age at the commencement of the Peloponnesian war, or B.C. 431, and, accordingly, he was born B.C. 471. Krüger attempts to show, indeed, on the authority of Marcellinus, that Thucydides was only about twenty-five years of age at the commencement of the war; but he relies too much on his own interpretation of certain words of Thucydides, which are by no means free from ambiguity (*αἰσθανόμενος τῇ ἡλικίᾳ*).[1] He is said to have been connected with the family of Cimon, and we know that Miltiades, the conqueror at Marathon, married Hegesipyle, the daughter of a Thracian king named Olorus,[2] by whom she became the mother of Cimon; whence it has been conjectured, with much probability, that the mother of Thucydides was a grand-daughter of Miltiades and Hegesipyle.

There is a story in Lucian[3] of Herodotus having read his history at the Olympic games to the assembled Greeks; and Suidas adds, that Thucydides, then a boy, was present, and shed tears of emulation; a presage of his own future historical distinction. This story, of which we have already made mention in the account given by us of Herodotus, has been discussed most completely by Dahlmann,[4] as we there remarked, and been rejected as a mere fable. Thucydides is said to have been instructed in oratory by Antiphon, and in philosophy by Anaxagoras, but whether these statements are to be received can not be determined. It is certain, however, that, being an Athenian of a good family, and living in a city which was the centre of Greek civilization, he must have had the best possible education. That he was a man of great ability and of cultivated understanding, his work itself clearly shows. He informs us that he possessed gold mines in that part of Thrace which is opposite to the island of Thasos, and that he was a person of the greatest influence among those in that quarter.[5] This property, according to some accounts, he had from his ancestors; according to other accounts, he married a rich woman of Scaptesyle, and received these mines as a portion with her.

Suidas says that Thucydides left a son, called Timotheus; and a daughter also is mentioned, who is said to have written the eighth book of the history. Thucydides was one of those who suffered from the great plague of Athens, and one of the few who recovered.[6]

We have no trustworthy evidence of Thucydides having distinguished himself as an orator, though it is not unlikely that he did, for his oratorical talent is shown by the speeches which he has inserted in his history. He was, however, employed in a military capacity, and was in command of an Athenian squadron of seven ships at Thasos, B.C. 424, when Eucles, who commanded in Amphipolis, sent for his assistance against Brasidas, who was before that town with an army. Brasidas, fearing the arrival of a superior force, offered favorable terms to Amphipolis, which were readily accepted, for there were few Athenians in the place, and the rest did not wish to make resistance. Thucydides arrived at Eion, at the mouth of the Strymon, on the evening of the same day on which Amphipolis sur-

1 *Thucyd.*, v., 26; *Poppo, ad loc.*
2 *Herod.*, vi., 39.
3 *Lucian, Herod. s. Aët.*, i., *seqq.*
4 *Life of Herodotus*, p. 8, *seqq.*, Eng. transl.
5 *Thucyd.*, iv., 105.
6 *Id.*, ii., 48.

rendered; and though he was too late to save Amphipolis, he prevented Eion from falling into the hands of the enemy.[1] In consequence of this failure, Thucydides became an exile, probably to avoid a severer punishment, that of death, for such appears to have been the penalty of a failure like his, though he may have done the best that he could. According to Marcellinus, Cleon, who was at that time in great favor with the Athenians, excited popular suspicion against the unfortunate commander. Thucydides simply says that he lived in exile twenty years after the affair of Amphipolis,[2] but he does not say whether it was a voluntary exile or a punishment.

There are various untrustworthy accounts as to his places of residence during his exile; but we may conclude that he could not safely reside in any place which was under Athenian dominion, and, as he kept his eye on the events of the war, he must have lived in those parts which belonged to the Spartan alliance. His own words certainly imply that, during his exile, he spent much of his time either in the Peloponnesus or in places which were under Peloponnesian influence;[3] and his work was the result of his own experience and observations. His minute description of Syracuse and the neighborhood leads to the probable conclusion that he was personally acquainted with the localities; and, if he visited Sicily, it is probable that he also saw some parts of Southern Italy; indeed, an anonymous biographer speaks of his having been at Sybaris. But it is rather too bold a conjecture to make, as some have done, that Olorus and his son Thucydides went out in the colony to Thurii, B.C. 443, which was joined by Herodotus, and the orator Lysias, then a young man. Thucydides says that he lived in exile twenty years;[4] and as his exile commenced in the beginning of B.C. 423, he may have returned to Athens in the beginning of B.C. 403, about the time when Thrasybulus liberated Athens. Thucydides is said to have been assassinated at Athens soon after his return; but other accounts place his death in Thrace. There is a general agreement, however, among the ancient authorities that he came to a violent end. His death can not be placed later than B.C. 401.

The time when he composed his work has been a matter of dispute. He himself informs us that he was busy in collecting materials all through the war, from the beginning to the end,[5] and, of course, he would register them as he got them. Plutarch says that he wrote the work in Thrace; and his words mean the whole work, as he does not qualify them; but the work, in the shape in which we have it, was certainly not finished until after the close of the war; and he was probably engaged upon it at the time of his death.

A question has also arisen as to the authorship of the eighth and last book of Thucydides, which breaks off in the twenty-first year of the war, B.C. 411. It differs from all the other books in containing no speeches, and it has also been supposed to be inferior to the rest as a piece of composition. Accordingly, several ancient critics supposed that the eighth book was not by Thucydides; some attributed it to his daughter, and some to Xenophon or Theopompus, because both of them continued the history.

[1] *Thucyd.*, iv., 102 *seqq.* [2] *Id.*, v., 26. [3] *Id. ib.* [4] *Id. ib.* [5] *Id.*, i., 22.

The words with which Xenophon's *Hellenica* commence (μετὰ δὲ ταῦτα) may chiefly have led to the supposition that he was the author, for his work is made to appear as a continuation of that of Thucydides; but this argument is in itself of little weight; and, besides, both the style of the eighth book is different from that of Xenophon, and the manner of treating the subject, for the division of the year into summers and winters, which Thucydides has observed in his first seven books, is continued in the eighth, but is not observed by Xenophon. The rhetorical style of Theopompus also, which was the characteristic of his writing, renders it improbable that he was the author of the eighth book. It seems the simplest supposition to consider Thucydides himself as the author of this book, since he names himself as the author twice (viii., 6, 60); but it is probable that he had not the opportunity of revising it with the same care as the first seven books. It is stated by an ancient writer that Xenophon made the work of Thucydides known, which may be true, as he wrote the first two books of his *Hellenica*, or the part which now ends with the second book, for the purpose of completing the history.

The work of Thucydides, from the commencement of the second book, is chronologically divided into winters and summers, and each summer and winter make a year.[1] His summer comprises the time from the vernal to the autumnal equinox, and the winter comprises the period from the autumnal to the vernal equinox. The division into books and chapters was probably made by the Alexandrine critics. There is nothing in the work itself which gives the least intimation that the division into books was part of the author's design; and, in fact, this same division into books is made in a very arbitrary and clumsy way. For instance, the seventh book ought to end with the sixth chapter of the eighth book; and the seventh chapter of the eighth book ought to be the first. There was a division of the work also into nine books,[2] and a still later division into thirteen books. The title of the work, as well as the division into books, is probably the act of the critics or grammarians. The titles vary in the MSS., but the simple one of Συγγραφή is that which is most appropriate to the author's own expression, Θουκυδίδης Ἀθηναῖος ξυνέγραψε τὸν πόλεμον, κ. τ. λ.[3]

The history of the Peloponnesian war opens the second book of Thucydides, and the first is introductory to the history. He begins his first book by observing that the Peloponnesian war was the most important event in Grecian history, which he shows by a rapid review of the history of the Greeks, from the earliest periods to the commencement of the war (i., 1–21). After his introductory chapters, he proceeds to explain the alleged grounds and causes of the war. The real cause was, he says, the Spartan jealousy of the Athenian power. His narrative is interrupted (c. 89–118), after he has come to the time when the Lacedæmonians resolved on war, by a digression on the rise and progress of the power of Athens; a period which had been either omitted by other writers, or treated imperfectly, and with little regard to chronology, as by Hellanicus in his Attic history (c. 97). He resumes his narrative (c. 119) with the negotiations which preceded the war; but this leads to another

[1] *Thucyd.*, ii., 1. [2] *Diod. Sic.*, xii., 37. [3] *Thucyd.*, i., 1

digression of some length on the treason of Pausanias (c. 128–134) and the exile of Themistocles (c. 135–138). He concludes the book with the speech of Pericles, who advised the Athenians to refuse the demands of the Peloponnesians; and his subject, as already observed, begins with the second book.

A history, intended by its author as "an eternal possession," which treats of so many events that took place at remote spots, could only be written, in the time of Thucydides, by a man who took great pains to ascertain facts by personal inquiry. In modern times, facts are made known by printing as soon as they occur; and the printed records of the day, newspapers and the like, are often the only evidence of many facts which become history. When we know the careless way in which facts are now reported and recorded by very incompetent persons, often upon very indifferent and hearsay testimony, and compare with such records the pains that Thucydides took to ascertain the chief events of a war with which he was contemporary, in which he took a share as a commander, the opportunities which his means allowed, his great abilities, and serious earnest character, it is a fair conclusion that we have a more exact history of a long, eventful period by Thucydides than we have of any period in modern history, equally long and equally eventful. His whole work shows the most scrupulous care and diligence in ascertaining facts, while his strict attention to chronology, and the importance that he attaches to it, are additional proofs of his historical accuracy. His narrative is brief and concise: it generally contains bare facts expressed in the fewest possible words; and when we consider what pains it must have cost him to ascertain these facts, we admire the self-denial of a writer who is satisfied with giving facts in their naked brevity, without ornament, without any parade of his personal importance, and of the trouble that his matter cost him. A single chapter must sometimes have represented the labor of many days and weeks. Such a principle of historical composition is the evidence of a great and elevated mind. The history of Thucydides only makes an octavo volume of moderate size; many a modern writer would have spun it out to a dozen volumes, and so have spoiled it. A work that is for all ages must contain much in little compass.[1]

Thucydides seldom makes reflections in the course of his narrative. Occasionally he has a chapter of political and moral observations, animated by the keenest perceptions of the motives of action and the moral character of man. Many of his speeches are political essays, or materials for them: they are not mere imaginations of his own for rhetorical effect; they contain the general sense of what was actually delivered as nearly as he could ascertain, and in many instances he had good opportunities of knowing what was said, for he heard some speeches delivered.[2] His opportunities, his talents, his character, and his subject all combined to produce a work that stands alone, and in its kind has neither equal nor rival. His pictures are sometimes striking and tragic, an effect produced by severe simplicity and minute particularity. Such is the de-

[1] *Smith, Dict. Biogr., s. v.*

[2] *Thucyd.*, i., 22.

scription of the plague of Athens. Such also is the incomparable history of the Athenian expedition to Sicily, and its melancholy termination.

A man who thinks profoundly will have a form of expression which is stamped with the character of his mind; and the style of Thucydides is accordingly concise, vigorous, and energetic. We feel that all the words were intended to have a meaning: none of them are idle. Yet he is sometimes harsh and obscure; and probably he was so even to his own countrymen. Some of his sentences are very involved, and the connection and dependence of the parts are often difficult to seize. Cicero, undoubtedly a good Greek scholar, found him difficult:[1] he says that the speeches contain so many obscure and impenetrable sentences as to be scarcely intelligible; and this, he adds, is a very great defect in the language of political life (*in oratione civili*).

TEXT AND EDITIONS OF THUCYDIDES.

The first thing that is requisite in reading Thucydides is to have a good text, established on a collation of the MSS., and this we owe to Bekker. Those who were accustomed to read Thucydides in such a text as Duker's can estimate their obligations to Bekker. For the understanding of the text, a sound knowledge of the language, and the assistance of the best critics are necessary, and perhaps nearly all has been done in this department that can be done. But, after all, a careful and repeated study of the original is necessary in order to understand it. For the illustration of the text a great mass of geographical and historical knowledge is requisite; and here also the critics have not been idle. To derive all the advantage, however, from the work that may be derived for political instruction, we must study it; and here the critics give little help, for *Politik* is a thing they seldom meddle with, and not often with success. Here, then, a man must be his own commentator; but a great deal might be done by a competent hand in illustrating Thucydides as a political writer.[2]

The Greek text was first published by Aldus, Venice, 1502, fol., and the scholia were published in the following year. The first Latin translation, which was by Valla, was printed before 1500, and reprinted at Paris, 1513, fol., and frequently after that date. The first edition of the Greek text accompanied by a Latin version was that of H. Stephens, 1564, fol., the Latin version being that of Valla, revised by Stephens. This well-printed edition contains the scholia, the life of Thucydides by Marcellinus, and an anonymous life of the historian. The edition of Bekker, Berlin, 1821, 3 vols. 8vo (reprinted Oxford, 3 vols. 8vo, 1824), forms an epoch in the editions of Thucydides, and, as regards the text, renders it unnecessary to consult any which are of prior date. Among the best editions since the appearance of Bekker's we may mention that of Poppo, Leipzig, 10 vols. 8vo, 1821–38, of which two volumes are filled with Prolegomena; of Haack, with selections from the scholia, and short notes, Leipz., 1820, 2 vols. 8vo, reprinted Lond., 1823, 2 vols. 8vo; of Göller, Leipz., 1826, 2 vols. 8vo; 2d edit., 1836, 2 vols. 8vo; the first edition of which was reprinted at London, 1835, in 1 vol. 8vo; of Arnold, Oxford, 1830–35, 3 vols. 8vo; 2d edit., Oxford, 1840–42, 3 vols.; 3d edit., with copious indexes, Oxford, 1847, 3 vols.; of Bloomfield, Lond., 1830, 3 vols. small 8vo (school edition), enlarged and reprinted, Lond., 1842, 2 vols. 8vo; of Hase, in Didot's *Bibliotheca*, Paris, 1839; of Krüger, with grammatical and brief explanatory notes, for schools, Berlin, 1846, 2 vols. 8vo; and of Poppo (school edition), with brief notes, Erfurt and Gotha, 1843–48, still incomplete. To these may be added the edition of Gail, containing the Greek text, the scholia, the variations of thirteen manuscripts of the Bibliothèque du Roi, a Latin version corrected, and a French version, with notes, historical and philological, Paris, 1807–8, 12 vols. 8vo.

Among the subsidiary works for the study of Thucydides may be mentioned "*Untersuchungen über das Leben des Thucydides*," Berlin, 1832, by Krüger, and Dodwell's "*Annales Thucydidei et Xenophontei*," Oxford, 1702, 4to.

---

[1] *Cic.*, *Orator*, c. 9.

[2] *Smith*, *Dict. Biogr.*, *s. v.*

V. Xenophon (Ξενοφῶν),[1] the Athenian, was the son of Gryllus, and a native of the demus of Ercheia. The only extant biography of him is by Diogenes Laertius, which, as usual, is carelessly written; but this biography and the scattered notices of ancient writers, combined with what may be collected from Xenophon's own works, are the only materials for his life. There is no direct authority either for the time of Xenophon's birth or death, but these dates may be approximated to with reasonable probability. Laertius and Strabo[2] state that Socrates saved Xenophon's life at the battle of Delium, B.C. 424, a fact which there seems no reason for rejecting, and from which it may be inferred that Xenophon was born about B.C. 444. In his *Hellenica*, he mentions the assassination of Alexander of Pheræ,[3] which took place B.C. 357,[4] and Xenophon, of course, was alive in that year. This agrees well enough with Lucian's statement,[5] that Xenophon attained the age of above ninety. There has been much discussion, also, as to the age of Xenophon at the time of his joining the expedition of the younger Cyrus, B.C. 401; and the dispute turns on the point whether he was then a young man, between twenty and thirty, or a man of forty and upward. Those who make him a young man must reject the evidence as to the battle of Delium; but they rely on an expression in the Anabasis,[6] where he is called νεανίσκος. In this passage, however, the best MSS. read "Theopompus" in place of "Xenophon;" and it may also be remarked that the term νεανίσκος was not confined to young men, but was sometimes applied to men of forty at least. Moreover, Xenophon seemed to Seuthes[7] old enough to have a marriageable daughter. The most probable conclusion, then, seems to be, that Xenophon was not under forty at the time when he joined the army of Cyrus.

Xenophon is said to have been a pupil of Socrates at an early age, which is consistent with the intimacy which might have arisen from Socrates saving his life. Philostratus states that he also received instruction from Prodicus of Ceos, during the time that he was a prisoner in Bœotia, but nothing is known of this captivity of Xenophon from any other authority. Photius[8] states that he was also a pupil of Isocrates, which may be true, though Isocrates was younger than Xenophon, having been born in B.C. 436. Another question connected with the life of Xenophon is that which has reference to the statement of Diogenes Laertius, namely, that Xenophon made known the books of Thucydides, which were then unknown. This point, however, has been already considered in the sketch we have just given of the life of Thucydides.

In B.C. 401 Xenophon went to Sardes, to Cyrus the younger, the brother of Artaxerxes Mnemon, king of Persia. He tells us himself, in the *Anabasis*,[9] the circumstances under which he went. Proxenus, Xenophon's friend, was then with Cyrus, and he invited Xenophon to come, and promised to introduce him to Cyrus. Xenophon took the advice of Socrates, who, fearing that Xenophon might incur the displeasure of the

[1] *Smith, Dict. Biogr.*, *s. v.* [2] *Strab.*, p. 403. [3] *Hellen.*, vi., 4, 35.
[4] *Diod. Sic.*, xvi., 14. [5] *Macrob.*, 21. [6] ii., 1, 12. [7] *Anab.*, vii., 2, 8.
[8] *Biblioth. Cod.*, cclx. [9] iii., 1.

Athenians if he attached himself to Cyrus, inasmuch as Cyrus was supposed to have given the Lacedæmonians aid in their recent wars against Athens, advised Xenophon to consult the oracle of Delphi. Xenophon went to Delphi, and asked Apollo to what gods he should sacrifice and make his vows in order to secure success in the enterprise which he meditated. The god gave him his answer, but Socrates blamed him for not asking whether he should undertake the voyage or not. However, as he had obtained an answer from the god, Socrates advised him to go, and accordingly Xenophon set out for Sardes, where he found Cyrus and Proxenus just ready to leave the city on an expedition. This story is characteristic both of Socrates and Xenophon.

It was given out by Cyrus that his expedition was against the Pisidians, and all the Greeks in the army were deceived, except Clearchus, who was alone in the secret. The real object of Cyrus was to dethrone his brother, and, after advancing a short distance, this became apparent enough to his Grecian followers, who, however, with the exception of a few, determined to accompany him. After a long march through Asia Minor, Syria, and the sandy tract east of the Euphrates, Cyrus met the vast army of the Persians in the plain of Cunaxa, about forty miles from Babylon. In the affray that ensued, for it was not a battle, Cyrus lost his life, his barbarian troops were dispersed, and the Greeks were left alone on the wide plains between the Tigris and Euphrates. It was after the treacherous massacre of Clearchus, and other of the Greek commanders, by the Persian satrap Tissaphernes, that Xenophon came forward. He had held no command in the army of Cyrus, nor had he, in fact, served as a soldier. He introduces himself to our notice, at the beginning of the third book of the "*Anabasis*," in that simple manner which characterizes the best writers of antiquity. From this time, Xenophon became one of the most active leaders, and under his judicious guidance the Greeks effected their retreat northward, across the high lands of Armenia, and arrived at Trapezus (*Trebisond*), a Greek colony, on the southeastern coast of the Euxine. From Trapezus the troops were conducted to Chrysopolis, which is opposite to Byzantium. The Greeks were in great distress, and some of them under Xenophon entered the service of Seuthes, king of Thrace, who wanted their aid, and promised to pay for it. The Greeks performed what they had agreed to do, but Seuthes was unwilling to pay, and it was with great difficulty that Xenophon got from him part of what he had promised. The description which Xenophon gives of the manners of the Thracians is very curious and amusing.[1] As the Lacedæmonians under Thimbron were now at war with Tissaphernes and Pharnabazus, Xenophon and his troops were invited to join the army of Thimbron, which was done. Before, however, they joined Thimbron, Xenophon, who was very poor, led them on an expedition into the plain of the Caicus, to plunder the house and property of a Persian named Asidates. The Persian, with his women, children, and all his movables, was seized; and Xenophon, by this robbery, replenished his empty pockets.[2] He tells the story himself, as if he were not ashamed of it.

---

[1] *Anab.*, vi., 3, *seqq.*

[2] *Ib.*, vii., 8, 23.

It is uncertain what Xenophon did after giving up the troops to Thimbron. He remarks, just before he speaks of leading the troops back into Asia, that he had not yet been banished; but as it is stated by various authorities that he was banished by the Athenians because he joined the expedition of Cyrus against the Persian king, who was then on friendly terms with Athens, it is most probable that sentence of banishment followed soon after. It is not certain what he did after the troops joined Thimbron. The assumption of Letronne that he went to Athens is unsupported by evidence.

Agesilaus, the Spartan king, was sent with an army into Asia, B.C. 396, and Xenophon was with him during the whole, or a part at least, of this Asiatic expedition. Agesilaus was recalled to Greece B.C. 394, and Xenophon accompanied him on his return,[1] and he was with Agesilaus in the battle against his own countrymen at Coronea.[2] According to Plutarch, he accompanied Agesilaus to Sparta, after this last mentioned battle, and shortly after settled himself at Scillus,[3] in Elis, near Olympia, on a spot which the Lacedæmonians gave him, and here, it is said, he was joined by his wife and children. This was his second wife, named Philesia, and he had probably married her in Asia. On the advice of Agesilaus,[4] he sent his sons to Sparta to be educated. Thus Xenophon had become an exile from his country for an act of treason, or what was equivalent to treason: he had received a present of land from the Lacedæmonians, the enemies of the Athenians; and he was educating his children in Spartan usages.

From this time Xenophon took no part in public affairs. His time, during his long residence at Scillus, was employed in hunting, entertaining his friends, and in writing some of his later works. Diogenes Laertius states that he wrote here his histories, by which he must mean the "Anabasis" and the "Hellenica," and probably the "Cyropædia." Here also he probably wrote the treatise on "Hunting," and that on "Horsemanship." The history of the remainder of his life is somewhat doubtful. Diogenes says that the Eleans sent a force against Scillus, and, as the Lacedæmonians did not come to the aid of Xenophon, they seized the place. Xenophon's sons, with some slaves, made their escape to Lepreum, a town of Elis, near the confines of Arcadia and Messenia. Xenophon himself first went to Elis, the capital, for what purpose it is not said, and then to Lepreum to meet his children. At last he withdrew to Corinth, and probably died there. The time of his expulsion from Scillus is uncertain. Krüger conjectures that the Eleans took Scillus not earlier than B.C. 371, in which year the Lacedæmonians were defeated at Leuctra. Letronne, however, fixes the date at B.C. 368, and considers it very probable that the Eleans invaded Scillus at the time when the Lacedæmonians were most engaged with the Theban war, which would be during the invasion of Laconia by Epaminondas. Xenophon must have lived above twenty years at Scillus, if the date of his expulsion from that place is not before the year B.C. 371.[5]

[1] *Anab.*, v., 3, 6. [2] *Plut.*, *Ages.*, 18. [3] *Anab.*, v., 3, 7.
[4] *Plut.*, *Ages.*, 20. [5] *Smith*, *l. c.*

The sentence of banishment against Xenophon was revoked by a decree proposed by Eubulus; but the date of this decree is uncertain. Before the battle of Mantinea, in B.C. 362, the Athenians had joined the Spartans against the Thebans. Upon this Xenophon sent his two sons, Gryllus and Diodorus, to Athens, to fight on the Spartan side against the Thebans. Gryllus fell in the battle of Mantinea, in which the Theban general Epaminondas also lost his life, and, according to one account, by the hand of Gryllus himself. No reason is assigned by any ancient writer for Xenophon's not returning to Athens; for, in the absence of direct evidence as to his return, we must conclude that he did not. Several of his works were written or completed after the revocation of his sentence: the "Hipparchicus," the Epilogus to the Cyropædia, if we assume that his sentence was revoked before B.C. 362; and the treatise on the "Revenues of Athens." Stesiclides, quoted by Diogenes, places the death of Xenophon in B.C. 359; but there is much uncertainty on this head. Probably he died a few years after B.C. 359.[1]

The extant works of Xenophon may be divided into four classes: *Historical*, comprising the "Anabasis," the "Hellenica," the "Cyropædia" (which, however, is not strictly historical), and the "Life of Agesilaus." *Didactic*, comprising the "Hipparchicus," the treatise on "Horsemanship," and that on "Hunting." *Political*, comprising the works on the "Republics of Sparta and of Athens," and the "Revenues of Athens." *Philosophical*, comprising the "Memorabilia of Socrates," the "Œconomicus," the "Symposium or Banquet," the "Hiero," and the "Apology of Socrates." There are also extant certain letters attributed to Xenophon, but, like many other ancient productions of the same class, they are not genuine. The works of Xenophon, as enumerated by Diogenes, agree exactly with those which are extant, and we may therefore conclude that we have at least as many works as Xenophon published, though all of them may not be genuine. It is true that Diogenes[2] says that Xenophon wrote about forty books (βιβλία), but he adds that they were variously divided, from which expression, and the list that he gives, it is certain that by the word βιβλία he intends to reckon the several divisions or books, as we call them, of the Anabasis, Hellenica, Cyropædia, and Memorabilia, as distinct βιβλία, and thus we have in the whole the number of thirty-eight, which is near enough to forty.

We will now proceed to give a more particular account of the several works of Xenophon already mentioned, observing the same order that has just been given.

HISTORICAL WORKS OF XENOPHON.

1. The *Anabăsis* (Ἀνάβασις), in seven books, is the work by which Xenophon is best known. It contains the history of the expedition of the younger Cyrus against his brother Artaxerxes Mnemon, and the retreat of the Greeks who formed part of his army. The first book comprises the march of Cyrus to the neighborhood of Babylon, and ends with his death at the battle of Cunaxa. The six remaining books contain the

[1] *Smith, l. c.*

[2] *Diog. Laert.*, ii., 6, 57.

account of the retreat of the "Ten Thousand," as the Greek army is often called. The work is written in an easy, agreeable style, and gives a great deal of curious information respecting the country traversed by the Greeks, and the manners of the people. It is full of interest also as being a minute detail by an eye-witness of the hazards and adventures of the army in their difficult march through an unknown and hostile country. The impression which it makes is favorable to the writer's veracity and his practical good sense; but as a history of military operations it is as much inferior to the only work of antiquity with which it can be compared, the "Commentaries of Cæsar," as the writer himself falls short of the lofty genius of the great Roman commander. Indeed, those passages in the Anabasis which relate directly to the movements of the retreating army are not always clear, nor have we any evidence that Xenophon did possess any military talent for great operations, whatever skill he may have had as a commander of a division.

2. The *Hellenĭca* (Ἑλληνικά), or Greek history, divided into seven books, and comprehending the space of forty-eight years, from the time when the history of Thucydidės ends to the battle of Mantinea, B.C. 362. As, however, the assassination of Alexander of Pheræ, which took place B.C. 357, is mentioned in this work,[1] some have supposed that a portion of the Hellenica was written at a later period than the rest, and perhaps not published till after Xenophon's death, by his son Diodorus, or his grandson Gryllus. There is no need, however, of any such hypothesis, since the mention of the death of Alexander of Pheræ would only prove that Xenophon had the work a long time under his hands. The "Hellenica" has little merit as a history. The author was altogether deficient in that power of reflection and of penetrating into the motives of action which characterize the great work of Thucydides. It is, in general, a dry narrative of events, and contains little to move or affect, with the exception of a few incidents which are given with more than the usual detail. The parts also are not treated in their due proportions, and many important events are passed over briefly. This, the only proper historical work of Xenophon, does not entitle him to the praise of being a good historical writer. It may be urged that the work was only a kind of *Mémoires pour servir*, as some have supposed; but if it is to be taken as a continuation of Thucydides, it is a history, and as such it has been regarded both in ancient and modern times.

3. The *Cyropædĭa* (Κύρου παιδεία), in eight books, is a kind of political romance, in which the ethical element prevails; but, since it is based upon the history of Cyrus, the founder of the Persian monarchy, it is commonly ranked among the historical works of Xenophon. Its object is to show how citizens can be formed to be virtuous and brave, and to exhibit also a model of a wise and good governor. Xenophon chooses for his exemplar Cyrus, the founder of the Persian empire, and the Persians are his models of men who are brought up in a true discipline. The work has no authority whatever as a history, nor is it even authority for the usages of the Persians, some of which we know, from other writers,

[1] vi., 4, 35.

to have been different from what they are represented to be by Xenophon. The writer borrows his materials from the Grecian states, and especially from Lacedæmon, and the "Cyropædia" is one of the many proofs of his aversion to the usages and the political constitution of his native city. The genuineness of the Epilogus, or conclusion of the work, has been doubted by some critics. Its object is to show that the Persians had greatly degenerated since the time of Cyrus. The "Cyropædia" is one of the most labored of Xenophon's works, and contains his views on the training of youth, and of the character of a perfect prince. It is an agreeable exposition of principles under the form of a history, and, like Xenophon's other treatises, it contains more of plain, practical precepts, founded on observation and supported by good sense, than any profound views. The dying speech of Cyrus is worthy of a pupil of Socrates.[1]

4. The *Agesilāus* (Ἀγησίλαος) is a panegyric on Xenophon's friend, the Lacedæmonian king, and forms another proof of his Spartan predilections. Cicero[2] says that he has in this panegyric surpassed all the statues that have been raised in honor of kings. Some modern critics, however, do not consider the extant work as deserving of high praise, to which it may be replied that it will be difficult to find a panegyric which is. It is a kind of composition in which failure can hardly be avoided. However true it may be, it is apt to be insipid, and to appear exaggerated.

DIDACTIC WORKS OF XENOPHON.

1. The *Hipparchicus* (Ἱππαρχικός) is a treatise on the duties of a commander of cavalry (ἵππαρχος), and contains many military precepts, especially for the choice of cavalry men. One would be inclined to suppose that it was written at Athens, but this conclusion, like many others from internal evidence, is not satisfactory. A strain of devotion runs through the treatise, called forth, as the writer himself states in the conclusion of the work, by a view of the many dangers with which the career of arms is beset.

2. The treatise on *Horsemanship* (Ἱππική) was written after the "Hipparchicus," to which reference is made at the end of the present work. The author says that he has had much experience as a horseman, and is therefore qualified to give instruction to others. He speaks at the beginning of a work on the subject by Simon, in whose opinions he coincides, and he professes to supply some of his omissions. This Simon was a writer on horses, to whom several ancient authors refer, and in such a way as to show that he was quite an authority in such matters. His exact date is not known, but he was not earlier than the painter Micon, who lived about B.C. 460, for he criticised the works of that artist.

3. The *Cynegeticus* (Κυνηγετικός) is a treatise on hunting, an amusement of which Xenophon was very fond; and on the dog, and the breeding and training of dogs, on the various kinds of game, and the mode of taking them. It is a treatise written by a genuine sportsman, who loved the exercise and the excitement of the chase, and it may be read with delight by any sportsman who deserves the name.

[1] *Cyrop.*, viii., 7. Compare *Cic.*, *De Sen.*, 22.

[2] *Ep. ad Fam.*, v., 12.

4. Two treatises on the "Republics of Sparta and of Athens" (Λακεδαιμονίων Πολιτεία, Ἀθηναίων Πολιτεία). These were not always recognized as genuine works of Xenophon even by the ancients. They pass, however, under his name, and there is nothing in the internal evidence that appears to throw any doubt upon the authorship. The writer clearly prefers the Spartan to the Athenian institutions.

5. A treatise on the "Revenues" of Athens (Πόροι, ἢ περὶ Προσόδων). This has for its object to show how the revenues of Athens, and especially those derived from the mines, may be improved by better management, and made sufficient for the maintenance of the poor citizens, and for all other purposes, without requiring contributions from the allies and subject states. The matter of this treatise is discussed by Böckh, in his work on the Public Economy of Athens.

PHILOSOPHICAL WORKS OF XENOPHON.

1. The *Memorabilia of Socrates* (Ἀπομνημονεύματα Σωκράτους), in four books, contains a defence of the memory of Socrates against the charge of irreligion, and of corrupting the Athenian youth.[1] Socrates is represented as holding a series of conversations, in which he develops and inculcates moral doctrines in his peculiar fashion. It is entirely a practical work, such as we might expect from the practical nature of Xenophon's mind, and it professes to exhibit Socrates as he taught. It is true that it may exhibit only one side of the Socratic argumentation, and that it does not deal in those subtleties and verbal disputes which occupy so large a space in some of Plato's dialogues. Xenophon was a hearer of Socrates, an admirer of his master, and anxious to defend his memory; and hence, as he certainly had no pretensions himself to originality as a thinker, we may assume that the matter of the "Memorabilia" is genuine, that the author has exhibited a portion of the moral and intellectual character of Socrates, such part as he was able to appreciate, or such as suited his taste, and that we have in this work as genuine a picture of Socrates as his pupil Xenophon could make. That it is a genuine exhibition of the man is indisputable, and it is the most valuable memorial that we have of the practical philosophy of Socrates. On the other hand, the "Memorabilia" will always be undervalued by the lovers of the transcendental, who give to an unintelligible jargon of words the name of philosophy. It comes too near the common understanding (*communis sensus*) of mankind to be valued by those who would raise themselves above this common understanding, and who have yet to learn that there is not a single notion of philosophy which is not expressed or involved by implication in the common language of life.[2]

2. The *Œconomicus* (Οἰκονομικός) is a dialogue between Socrates and Critobulus, in which Socrates begins by showing that there is an art called *Œconomic* (Οἰκονομική), which relates to the administration of a household and of a man's property. Socrates, when speaking in praise of agriculture, quotes the instance of the younger Cyrus, who was fond of horticulture, and once showed to the Spartan Lysander the gardens

[1] *Mem.*, i., 1.

[2] *Smith, l. c.*

which he had planned, and the trees which he had planted with his own hands. Cicero copies this passage in his treatise on Old Age.[1] In answer to the praises of agriculture, Critobulus speaks of the losses to which the husbandman is exposed from hail, frost, drought, and other causes. The answer of Socrates is, that the husbandman must trust in Heaven, and worship the gods. The seventh chapter is on the duty of a good wife, as exemplified in the case of the wife of Ischomachus. This is one of the best treatises of Xenophon.

3. The *Symposium* (Συμπόσιον), or Banquet of Philosophers, contains a delineation of the character of Socrates. The speakers are supposed to meet at the house of Callias, a rich Athenian, at the celebration of the great Panathenæa. Socrates, Critobulus, Antisthenes, Charmides, and others, are the speakers. The accessories of the entertainment are managed with skill, and the piece is interesting as a picture of an Athenian drinking party, and of the amusement and conversation with which it was diversified. The nature of love and friendship is discussed. Some critics think that the *Symposium* is a juvenile performance, and that the *Symposium* of Plato was written after that of Xenophon; but it is an old tradition that the *Symposium* of Plato was written before that of Xenophon.

4. The *Hiero* (Ἱέρων ἢ Τυραννικός) is a dialogue between King Hiero and Simonides, in which the king speaks of the dangers and difficulties incident to an exalted station, and the superior happiness of a private man. The poet, on the other hand, enumerates the advantages which the possession of power gives, and the means which it affords of obliging and doing services. Hiero speaks of the burden of power, and answers Simonides, who wonders why a man should keep that which is so troublesome, by saying that power is a thing which a man can not safely lay down. Simonides offers some suggestions as to the best use of power, and the way of employing it for the public interest. It is suggested by Letronne that Xenophon may have been induced to write this treatise by what he saw at the court of Dionysius, since there is a story of his having visited Sicily in the lifetime of the tyrant of Syracuse.

5. The *Apology of Socrates* (Ἀπολογία Σωκράτους πρὸς τοὺς δικαστάς) is not, as the title imports, the defence which Socrates made on his trial, but it contains the reasons which determined him to prefer death rather than to humble himself by asking for his life from his prejudiced judges. Valckenaer and others do not allow this to be Xenophon's work, because they consider it to be unworthy of him. But, if a man is to lose the discredit of a bad work simply because he has written better, many persons may disown their own books. The "Apology" is certainly a trivial performance, but Xenophon did write an "Apology," according to Diogenes Laertius, and this may be it.

A man's character can not be entirely derived from his writings, especially if they treat of exact science. Yet a man's writings are some index of his character, and, when they are of a popular and varied kind, not a bad index. From the brief sketch which we have given here of his life and writings, some estimate may be easily formed of the general

[1] *De Senect.*, 17.

character of Xenophon. As we know him from his writings, he was a humane man, at least for his age; a man of good understanding and strong religious feelings: we might call him, indeed, superstitious, if the name superstition had a well-defined meaning. Some modern critics find much to object to in Xenophon's conduct as a citizen. He did not like Athenian institutions altogether; but a man is under no moral or political obligation to like the government under which he is born. His duty is to conform to it, or to withdraw himself. There is no evidence that Xenophon, after his banishment, acted against his native country, even at the battle of Coronea. If his preference of Spartan to Athenian institutions is matter for blame, he is blamable indeed. His philosophy was the practical: it had reference to actual life, and in all practical matters, and every thing that concerns the ordinary conduct of human life, he shows good sense and honorable feeling.[1]

As a writer, he deserves the praise of perspicuity and ease, and for these qualities he has in all ages been justly admired. As an historical writer, he is infinitely below Thucydides: he had no depth of reflection, no great insight into the fundamental principles of society. His *Hellenica*, his only historical effort, would not have preserved his name, except for the importance of the facts which this work contains, and the deficiency of other historical records. His mind was not adapted for pure philosophical speculation: he looked to the practical in all things, and the basis of his philosophy was a strong belief in a divine mediation in the government of the world. His belief only required a little correction and modification to allow us to describe it as a profound conviction that God, in the constitution of things, has given a moral government to the world, as manifestly as he has given laws for the mechanical and chemical actions of matter, the organization of plants and animals, and the vital energies of all beings that live and move.[2]

EDITIONS OF XENOPHON.

There are numerous editions of the whole and of the separate works of Xenophon. The *Hellenica*, the first of Xenophon's works that appeared in type, was printed at Venice, 1503, fol., by the elder Aldus, with the title of *Paralipomena*, and as a supplement to Thucydides, which had been printed the year before. The first general edition is that of Boninus, printed by Giunta, and dedicated to Leo X., Florence, 1516, fol.; but this edition does not contain the "Agesilaus," the "Apology," and the treatise on the "Revenues of Athens." A part of the treatise on the "Athenian Republic" is also wanting. This edition of Giunta is a very good specimen of early printing, and useful to an editor of Xenophon. The edition by Andrea of Asola, printed by Aldus, at Venice, 1525, fol., contains all the works of Xenophon, except the "Apology;" though the "Apology" was already edited by Reuchlin, Hagenau, 1520, 4to, with the "Agesilaus and Hiero." The Basle edition, printed by Brylinger, 1545, fol., is the first edition of the Greek text with a Latin translation. The edition of H. Stephens, 1561, fol., contains an amended text, and the edition of 1581 has a Latin version. After these editions we may name the following: that of Leunclavius, or Loewenklau, Basle, 1569, reprinted at the same place in 1572, and at Frankfort in 1694, fol.; of Wells, Oxford, 5 vols. 8vo, with Dodwell's *Chronologia Xenophontea;* reprinted with additions, Lips., 1763–64, 4 vols. 8vo, under the editorial care of Thieme, with a preface by Ernesti; and again in 1801–4, under the superintendence of Sturz; of Weiske, Leipzig, 1798–1804, 6 vols. 8vo; of Schneider, Leipzig, 1815, 6 vols. 8vo (of which the first, second, and fourth volumes have been re-edited

[1] *Smith, l. c.*

[2] *Id. ib.*

and much improved by Bornemann, containing, the first, the *Cyropædia*, Leipzig, 1838; the second, the *Anabasis*, 1825; the fourth, the *Memorabilia*, 1829; and the sixth, containing the *Opuscula politica, equestria, venatica*, by Sauppe, 1838); of Dindorf, in Didot's *Bibliotheca*, Paris, 1838. An edition was commenced in the *Bibliotheca Græca* of Jacobs and Rost, Gotha, 1828, of which there have appeared, vol. i., *Cyropædia*, by Bornemann, 1828; vol. ii., *Memorabilia*, by Kühner, 1841; vol. iii., *Anabasis*, by Kühner, 1852; and vol. iv., *Œconomicus, Agesilaus*, and *Hiero*, by Breitenbach, 1842, *seqq*. The most pretending edition of the works of Xenophon is that of Gail, with a Latin and a French version, critical and explanatory notes, maps and plans, &c., Paris, 1797–1814, 7 vols. 4to. The seventh volume consists of three parts, one of which (published in 1808) contains the various readings of three MSS.; a second (1814) contains the notices of the MSS., and observations literary and critical; and the third an atlas of maps and plans. Letronne, an excellent judge, as all scholars know, bestows very moderate praise upon this edition. Gail has kept to the old text, and has made no use of his various readings for improving it. The notes, however, are generally useful for the understanding of Xenophon.

The best editions of detached portions of the works of Xenophon are the following: of the *Cyropædia*, by Poppo, Leipzig, 1821, 8vo, and by Jacobitz, Leipz., 1843; of the *Anabasis*, by Lion, Göttingen, 1822, 2 vols. 8vo; by L. Dindorf, Leipzig, 1826, 8vo; by Krüger, Halle, 1826, 8vo, last (3d) school edition, 1851; by Poppo, Leipzig, 1827, 8vo; by Constantine Matthiæ, Quedlinburg, 1852, 8vo (school ed.); of the *Symposium* and *Apologia*, by Bornemann, Leipzic, 1824, 8vo; of the *Symposium*, by Herbst, Halle, 1830; by Mehler, Lugd. Bat., 1850; of the *Memorabilia*, by Sauppe, Leipz., 1834; by Herbst, Halle, 1827, 8vo; by Kühner, Gotha, 1841, 8vo; of the *De Republica Lacedæmoniorum*, by Haase, Berlin, 1833; of the *Hellenica*, from the text of Dindorf, with selected notes, at the University press, Oxford, 1831; of the *Hiero* and *Agesilaus*, by Hanow, Halle, 1835; of the *Agesilaus*, by Baumgarten-Crusius, Leipzig, 1812 (new ed.). There is also a separate volume of commentary on the *Cyropædia* by Fischer, edited by Kuinoel, Leipzig, 1803. As a very useful auxiliary in the perusal of Xenophon, we may mention the *Lexicon Xenophonteum* of Sturz, 4 vols. 8vo, Leipzig, 1801–1804.

III. Ctesias (Κτησίας)[1] was a native of Cnidus, in Caria, and a contemporary of Xenophon. He was by profession a physician, and belonged to the caste or family of the Asclepiadæ, whose principal seats were at Cnidus and Cos. Ctesias lived for seventeen years in Persia, at the court of Artaxerxes Mnemon, as private physician to the king.[2] Diodorus says that he was made prisoner by the king, and that, owing to his great skill in medicine, he was afterward drawn to the court, and was highly honored there.[3] When he was thus made prisoner we are not informed; some critics think that it was at the battle of Cunaxa, B.C. 401; but if Ctesias remained seventeen years in Persia, as Diodorus says, and if, as the same writer informs us, he returned to his native country in B.C. 398, it follows that he must have gone to Persia long before the battle of Cunaxa, that is, about B.C. 415. How long he survived his return to his native city is unknown.

During his stay in Persia, Ctesias gathered all the information that was attainable in that country, and wrote, 1. A great work on the history of Persia, entitled Περσικά, with the view of giving his countrymen a more accurate knowledge of that empire than they possessed, and to refute the errors current in Greece, which had arisen partly from ignorance and partly from the national vanity of the Greeks. The materials for his history, so far as he did not describe events of which he had been an eyewitness, he derived, according to the testimony of Diodorus, from the

[1] *Smith, Dict. Biogr., s. v.* [2] *Strab.*, xiv., p. 656. [3] *Diod. Sic.*, ii., 32.

Persian archives (διφθέραι βασιλικαί), or the official history of the Persian empire, which was written in accordance with a law of the country. This important work of Ctesias was written, like that of Herodotus, in the Ionic dialect, and consisted of twenty-three books. The first six contained the history of the great Assyrian monarchy, down to the foundation of the kingdom of Persia. It is for this reason that Strabo speaks of Ctesias as συγγράψας τὰ 'Ασσυριακὰ καὶ τὰ Περσικά.[1] The next seven books contained the history of Persia down to the end of the reign of Xerxes, and the remaining ten carried the history down to the time when Ctesias left Persia, that is, to the year B.C. 398.[2] The form and style of this work were of considerable merit, and its loss may be regarded as one of the most serious for the history of the East.[3] All that is now extant of it is a meagre abridgment in Photius,[4] and a number of fragments which are preserved in Diodorus, Athenæus, Plutarch, and others. Of the first portion, which contained the history of Assyria, there is no abridgment in Photius, and all we possess of that part is contained in the second book of Diodorus, which seems to be taken almost entirely from Ctesias. There we find that the accounts of Ctesias, especially in their chronology, differ considerably from those of Berosus, who likewise derived his information from Eastern sources. These discrepancies can only be explained by the fact that the annals used by the two historians were written in different places and under different circumstances. The chronicles used by Ctesias were written by official persons, and those used by Berosus were the work of priests; both, therefore, were written from a different point of view, and neither was, perhaps, strictly true in all its details.

The part of Ctesias's work which contained the history of Persia, that is, from the sixth book to the end, is somewhat better known from the extracts which Photius made from it, and which are still extant. Here, again, Ctesias is frequently at variance with other Greek writers, especially with Herodotus. To account for this, we must remember that he is expressly reported to have written his work with the intention of correcting the erroneous notions about Persia prevalent in Greece; and if this was the case, the reader must naturally be prepared to find the accounts of Ctesias differing from those of others. It is, moreover, not improbable that the Persian Chronicles were as partial to the Persians, if not more so, as the accounts written by Greeks were to the Greeks. These considerations may fairly account for the differences existing between the statements of Ctesias and the other writers; and there would seem to be no good reason for charging him, as some have done, with wilfully falsifying history. It is at least certain that there can be no positive evidence for such a serious charge. The court chronicles of Persia appear to have contained chiefly the history of the royal family, the occurrences at the court and the seraglio, the intrigues of the women and eunuchs, and the insurrections of satraps to make themselves independent of the great monarch. Suidas mentions that Pamphila made an abridgment of the work of Ctesias, probably the Persica, in three books.

[1] *Strab.*, *l. c.* [2] *Diod. Sic.*, xiv., 46. [3] *Dion. Hal.*, *De Comp. Verb.*, 10. [4] *Cod.*, 72.

Another work, for which Ctesias also collected his materials during his stay in Persia, was, 2. A treatise on India, entitled Ἰνδικά, in one book, of which we likewise possess an abridgment in Photius, and a great number of fragments preserved in other writers. The description refers chiefly to the northwestern parts of India, and is principally confined to a description of the natural history, the produce of the soil, and the animals and men of India. In this description, truth is to a great extent mixed up with fables, and it seems to be mainly owing to this work that Ctesias was looked upon in later times as an author who deserved no credit. But if his account of India is looked upon from a proper point of view, it does not in any way deserve to be treated with contempt. Ctesias himself never visited India, and his work was the first in the Greek language that was written upon this country; he could do nothing more than lay before his countrymen that which was known or believed about India among the Persians. His *Indica* must, therefore, be regarded as a picture of India, such as it was conceived by the Persians. Many things, moreover, in his description, which were formerly looked upon as fabulous, have been proved by the more recent discoveries in India to be founded on facts.

Ctesias also wrote several other works, of which, however, we know little more than their titles: they were, 3. Περὶ ὀρῶν, which consisted of at least two books.[1] 4. Περίπλους Ἀσίας,[2] which is perhaps the same with the Περιήγησις, of which Stephanus Byzantinus[3] quotes the third book. 5. Περὶ ποταμῶν;[4] and, 6. Περὶ τῶν κατὰ τὴν Ἀσίαν φόρων. It has been inferred from a passage in Galen[5] that Ctesias also wrote on medicine, but no account of his medical works have come down to us.[6]

The abridgment which Photius made of the *Persica* and *Indica* of Ctesias were printed separately by H. Stephens, Paris, 1557 and 1594, 8vo, and were also added to his edition of Herodotus. After his time it became customary to print the remains of Ctesias as an appendix to Herodotus. The first separate edition of those abridgments, together with the fragments preserved in other writers, is that of Lion, Göttingen, 1823, 8vo, with critical notes and a Latin translation. A more complete edition, with an introductory essay on the life and writings of Ctesias, is that of Bähr, Frankfort, 1824, 8vo. An edition of Photius, with a revised text, formed on a collation of four MSS., was published by Bekker, 2 thin vols. 4to, Berlin, 1824–5. It has, however, neither version nor notes.

IV. Philistus (Φίλιστος), a Syracusan, was one of the most celebrated historians of antiquity, though, unfortunately, only a few fragments of his works have come down to us. He was born probably about B.C. 435. Philistus assisted Dionysius in obtaining the supreme power, and stood so high in the favor of the tyrant that the latter intrusted him with the charge of the citadel of Syracuse.[7] At a later period, however, he excited the jealousy of the tyrant by marrying, without his consent, one of the daughters of his brother Leptines, and was in consequence banished from

[1] *Plut.*, *De Fluv.*, 21; *Stob.*, *Floril.*, c. 18.
[2] *Steph. Byz.*, *s. v.* Σίγυνος.
[3] *s. v.* Κοσύτη.
[4] *Plut.*, *De Fluv.*, 19.
[5] v., p. 652, ed. Basle.
[6] *Smith*, *l. c.*
[7] *Diod. Sic.*, xiv., 8, *seqq.*

Sicily. He at first retired to Thurii, but afterward established himself at Adria, where he composed the historical work which has given celebrity to his name.[1] But he always bore his exile with impatience, and he is accused both of indulging in abject lamentations over his hard fate and fallen fortunes, and of base and unworthy flattery toward Dionysius, in hopes of conciliating the tyrant, and thus obtaining his recall.[2] These arts, however, failed in producing any effect during the lifetime of the elder Dionysius, but after his death and the accession of his son, those who were opposed to the influence which Dion and Plato were acquiring over the young despot persuaded the latter to recall Philistus from banishment, in hopes that from his age and experience, as well as his military talents, he might prove a counterpoise to the increasing influence of the two philosophers. The plan succeeded; he was recalled from exile, and quickly gained so great an influence over the mind of Dionysius as to alienate him from his former friends, and eventually cause Plato to be sent back to Athens, and Dion to be banished.[3] Philistus was absent from Sicily when Dion first landed in the island, and made himself master of Syracuse, B.C. 356. Afterward, however, he raised a powerful fleet, with which he gave battle to the Syracusans, but having been defeated, and finding himself cut off from all hopes of escape, he put an end to his own life to avoid falling into the hands of his enraged countrymen.

Philistus wrote a history of Sicily, which was one of the most celebrated historical works of antiquity, though unfortunately only a few fragments of it have come down to us. It consisted of two portions, which might be regarded either as two separate works, or as parts of one great whole, a circumstance which explains the discrepancies in the statements of the number of books of which it was composed. The first seven books comprised the general history of Sicily, commencing from the earliest times, and ending with the capture of Agrigentum by the Carthaginians, B.C. 406. Diodorus tells us that this portion included a period of 800 years and upward. He began with the mythical times, and the alleged colonies in Sicily, founded by Dædalus and others before the Trojan war. He appears, besides, to have entered at some length into the origin and migrations of the original inhabitants of the island, the Sicani and Siculi.[4] The second part, which formed a regular sequel to the first, contained the history of the elder Dionysius in four books, and that of the younger in two: the latter was necessarily imperfect, a circumstance which Dionysius of Halicarnassus absurdly ascribes to his desire to imitate Thucydides. As it ended only five years after the accession of the younger tyrant, it is probable that Philistus had not found time to continue it after his own return from exile.[5]

Suidas enumerates several other historical works by Philistus, especially a history of Egypt, in twelve books, one of Phœnicia, and another

[1] *Diod. Sic.*, xv., 7; *Plut.*, *Dion*, 7. [2] *Plut.*, *Timol.*, 15; *Paus.*, i., 13, 9.
[3] *Plut.*, *Dion*, 11, *seqq.*; *Pseud. Plat.*, *Ep.*, 3, p. 671.
[4] *Dion. Hal.*, *Ant. Rom.*, i., 22; *Diod. Sic.*, v., 6.
[5] *Diod. Sic.*, xiii., 103; xv., 89; *Suid.*, *s. v.*

of Libya and Syria. As no traces, however, of any of these works are to be found in any other authority, it has been doubted by some whether the whole statement is not erroneous,[1] while others suppose that these writings are to be attributed to a second Philistus, a native of Naucratis, in Egypt, which would account also for the error of Suidas, who calls our historian Ναυκρατίτης ἢ Συρακούσιος.[2]

In point of style, Philistus is represented by the concurrent testimony of antiquity as imitating and even closely resembling Thucydides, though still falling far short of his great model. Cicero[3] calls him "*capitalis, creber, acutus, brevis, pæne pusillus Thucydides;*" Quintilian[4] also terms him "*imitator Thucydidis, et, ut multo infirmior, ita aliquatenus lucidior.*" This qualified praise is confirmed by the more elaborate judgment of Dionysius of Halicarnassus,[5] who censures Philistus also for the unskillful arrangement of his subject, and the monotony and want of art displayed in his ordinary narrative. Longinus,[6] who cites him as occasionally rising to sublimity, intimates, at the same time, that this was far from being the general character of his composition. His conciseness, also, led him not unfrequently into obscurity, though in a less degree than Thucydides; and this defect caused many persons to neglect his works even in the days of Cicero.[7] Dionysius of Halicarnassus, however, associates his name with those of Herodotus, Thucydides, Xenophon, and Theopompus,[8] as the historians most deserving of study and imitation; but his writings seem to have been almost wholly neglected by the rhetoricians of a later period; and Hermogenes[9] passes over his name, in common with those of Ephorus and Theopompus, as wholly unworthy of attention. It is more remarkable that he does not appear to have been included by the Alexandrine critics in their canon of historical authors.[10] But the reputation that he enjoyed in Greece itself shortly before that period is attested by the fact that his history was among the books selected by Harpalus to send to Alexander in Upper Asia.[11]

The gravest reproach to the character of Philistus as an historian is the charge brought against him by many writers of antiquity, that he had sought to palliate the tyrannical deeds of Dionysius, and give a specious color to his conduct, in order to pave the way for his own return from exile. Plutarch calls him a man eminently skilled in inventing specious pretences and fair speeches to cloak unjust actions and evil dispositions. He was severely censured on the same account by Timæus.[12]

The fragments of Philistus have been collected, and all the circumstances transmitted to us concerning his life and writings fully examined and discussed by Göller, in an appendix to his work *De Situ et Origine Syracusarum* (Lips., 8vo, 1816); the fragments are also given in the *Fragm. Histor. Græc.* of C. and Th. Müller, vol. i., p. 185, *seqq.*, forming part of Didot's *Bibliotheca Græca*, Paris, 1841.

1 *Wesseling, ad Diod. Sic.*, xiii., p. 615; *Göller, De Orig.*, &c., *Syrac.*, p. 106, 124.
2 *Bayle, Dict. Crit., s. v. Philist., not. C.*
3 *Ad Q. fr.*, ii., 13.
4 *Inst. Or.*, x., 1, 74.
5 *Ep. ad Pomp.*, 5, p. 779, *seqq.*
6 *De Subl.*, 40.
7 *Cic., Brut.*, 17.
8 *Ep. ad Pomp.*, p. 767.
9 *De Formis*, p. 396.
10 *Creuzer, Hist. Kunst d. Griechen*, p. 225.
11 *Plut., Alex.*, 8.
12 *Smith, Dict. Biogr., s. v.*

V. THEOPOMPUS (Θεόπομπος)[1] of Chios, a celebrated Greek historian, was born about B.C. 378. He accompanied his father Damasistratus into banishment, when the latter was exiled on account of his espousing the interests of the Lacedæmonians, but he was restored to his native country in the forty-fifth year of his age (B.C. 333), in consequence of the letters of Alexander the Great, in which he exhorted the Chians to recall their exiles.[2] In what year Theopompus quitted Chios with his father is uncertain; but we know that, before he left his native country, he attended the school of rhetoric which Isocrates opened at Chios, and that he profited so much by the lessons of his great master as to be regarded by the ancients as the most distinguished of all his scholars.[3] Ephorus the historian was a fellow-student with him, but was of a very different character; and Isocrates used to say of them, that Theopompus needed the bit, and Ephorus the spur.[4] In consequence of the advice of Isocrates, Theopompus did not devote his oratorical powers to the pleading of causes, but gave his chief attention to the study and composition of history.[5] Like his master Isocrates, however, he composed many orations of the kind called *Epideictic* by the Greeks, that is, speeches on set subjects, delivered for display, such as eulogiums on states and individuals. Thus, in B.C. 352, he contended at Halicarnassus, with Naucrates and his master Isocrates, for the prize of oratory, offered by Artemisia in honor of her husband's memory, and gained the victory.[6] On his return to Chios in B.C. 333, Theopompus, who was a man of great wealth as well as learning, naturally took an important position in the state, but his vehement temper and his support of the aristocratical party soon raised against him a host of enemies. Of these, one of the most formidable was the sophist Theocritus. As long, however, as Alexander lived, his enemies dared not take any open proceedings against Theopompus; and even after the death of the Macedonian monarch he appears to have enjoyed for some years the protection of the royal house. But when he lost this support, he was expelled from Chios as a disturber of the public peace. He fled to Egypt, to Ptolemy,[7] about B.C. 305, being at the time about seventy-three years old. Ptolemy, however, not only refused to receive Theopompus, but would even have put him to death as a dangerous busybody, had not some of his friends interceded for his life. Of his farther fate we have no particulars, but he probably died soon afterward.

The following is a list of the works of Theopompus, none of which have come down to us. We have merely some fragments remaining. 1. Ἐπιτομὴ τῶν Ἡροδότου ἱστοριῶν. "*An Epitome of the History of Herodotus.*" This work is mentioned by Suidas, and in a few passages of the grammarians, but it has been questioned by Vossius whether it was really drawn up by Theopompus, on the ground that it is improbable that a writer of his attainments and skill in historical composition would have engaged in such a task. It is, however, not impossible that Theopompus may have made the Epitome at an early period of his life as an exercise

[1] *Smith, Dict. Biogr.*, *s. v.*
[2] *Phot.*, *Cod.*, 176, p. 120, *B*, ed. *Bekker.*
[3] *Plut.*, *Vit. Dec. Orat.*, p. 837, *B.*
[4] *Cic.*, *Brut.*, 56; *Ep. ad Att.*, v., 1, 12.
[5] *Cic.*, *De Orat.*, ii., 13, 22.
[6] *Aul. Gell.*, x., 18.
[7] *Phot.*, *Cod.*, 176.

in composition. 2. Ἑλληνικαὶ ἱστορίαι, or Σύνταξις Ἑλληνικῶν. "*A History of Greece*," in twelve books, and a continuation of the history of Thucydides. It commenced B.C. 411, at the point where the history of Thucydides breaks off, and embraced a period of seventeen years, down to the battle of Cnidus,[1] in B.C. 394. Only a few fragments of this work are preserved. 3. Φιλιππικά, also called Ἱστορίαι (κατ' ἐξοχήν). "*The History of Philip*," father of Alexander the Great, in fifty-eight books, from the commencement of his reign (B.C. 360) to his death (B.C. 336). This work contained numerous digressions, which, in fact, formed the greater part of the whole work, so that Philip V., king of Macedonia, was able, by omitting them, and retaining only what belonged to the proper subject, to reduce the work from fifty-eight books to sixteen. Fifty-three of the fifty-eight books of the original were extant in the ninth century of the Christian era, and were read by Photius, who has preserved an abstract of the twelfth book. 4. *Orations*, which were either panegyrics,[2] or what the Greeks called Συμβουλευτικοὶ λόγοι. Of the latter kind, one of the most celebrated was addressed to Alexander on the state of Chios. 5. Κατὰ Πλάτωνος διατριβή. Perhaps a digression in his *Philippica*. 6. Περὶ Εὐσεβείας. Another digression, probably, in the same work.

Theopompus is praised by Dionysius of Halicarnassus, as well as by other ancient writers, for his diligence and accuracy; but he is, at the same time, blamed by most writers for the extravagance of his praises and censures. He is said, however, to have taken more pleasure in blaming than in commending; and many of his judgments respecting events and characters were expressed with such acrimony and severity, that several of the ancients speak of his malignity, and call him a reviler.[3] It would seem that the vehemence of the temper of Theopompus frequently overcame his judgment, and prevented him from expressing himself with the calmness and impartiality of an historian. The ancients also blame him for introducing innumerable fables into his history.[4] The style of Theopompus was formed on the model of Isocrates, and possessed the characteristic merits and defects of his master. It was pure, clear, and elegant, but deficient in vigor, loaded with ornament, and, in general, too artificial. It is praised in high terms by Dionysius of Halicarnassus, but it is spoken of in very different language by other critics.[5]

The fragments of Theopompus have been published by Wichers, "*Theopompi Chii Fragmenta, collegit*, &c., *R. H. Eyssonius Wichers*, Lugd. Bat., 1829; and by C. and Th. Müller, *Fragm. Histor. Græc.*, vol. i., p. 278, *seqq.*, in Didot's *Bibliotheca Græca*, Paris, 1841. The following works may also be consulted respecting him: *Aschbach, Dissert. de Theopomp.*, Francof., 1823; *Pflugk, De Theopomp. vita et scriptis*, Berol., 1827.

VI. Ephŏrus (Ἔφορος)[6] of Cyme, in Æolis, a celebrated Greek historian, was a contemporary of Philip and Alexander, and flourished about B.C. 340. He studied rhetoric under Isocrates, of whose pupils he and

---

1 *Diod. Sic.*, xiii., 42.
2 *Theon, Progymn.*, p. 19, 103; *Suid.*, *s. v.*
3 *Corn. Nep.*, *Alcib.*, c. 11; *Clem. Alex.*, i., p. 316.
4 *Cic.*, *De Leg.*, i., 1; *Ælian, V. H.*, iii., 18.
5 *Longin.*, *De Subl.*, 43; *Demetr. Phal.*, περὶ ἑρμ., 75.
6 *Smith, Dict. Biogr.*, *s. v.*

Theopompus were considered the most distinguished. From Seneca[1] it might almost appear that Ephorus began the career of a public orator. Isocrates, however, dissuaded him from that course, for he well knew that oratory was not the field on which he could win laurels, and he exhorted him to devote himself to the study and composition of history. As Ephorus was of a more quiet and contemplative disposition than Theopompus, Isocrates advised the former to write the early history of Greece, and Theopompus to take up the later and more turbulent periods of history.[2] Plutarch relates[3] that Ephorus was among those who were accused of having conspired against the life of Alexander, but that he successfully refuted the charge when he was summoned before the king. This is all that is known of his life.

The most celebrated of all the works of Ephorus was a *History* (Ἱστορίαι), in thirty books, which began with the return of the Heraclidæ, and came down to the siege of Perinthus, in B.C. 341. It treated of the history of the barbarians as well as of the Greeks, and was thus the first attempt at writing a universal history that was ever made in Greece. It embraced a period of 750 years, and each of the thirty books contained a compact portion of the history, which formed a complete whole by itself. Each also contained a special preface, and might bear a separate title, which either Ephorus himself or some later grammarian seems actually to have given to each book, for we know that the fourth book was called Εὐρώπη.[4] Ephorus himself did not live to complete his work, and it was finished by his son Demophilus. Diyllus began his history at the point at which the history of Ephorus left off. Ephorus also wrote a few other works of less importance, of which the titles only are preserved by the grammarians. We possess only isolated fragments of the history. It was written, as might be expected from a scholar of Isocrates, in a clear, lucid, and elaborately-polished style, but at the same time diffuse, and deficient in power and energy, so that Ephorus is by no means equal to his master. As an historian, Ephorus appears to have been faithful and impartial in the narration of events; but he did not always follow the best authorities, and in the latter part of his work he frequently differed from Herodotus, Thucydides, and Xenophon, on points on which they are entitled to credit. Diodorus Siculus made great use of his work. Polybius[5] praises him for his knowledge of maritime warfare, but adds that he was utterly ignorant of the mode of warfare upon land. Strabo[6] acknowledges his merits by saying that he separated the historical from the geographical portions of his work; and, in regard to the latter, he did not confine himself to mere lists of names, but he introduced investigations concerning the origin of nations, their constitution and manners, and many of the geographical fragments which have come down to us contain lively and beautiful descriptions.[7]

The fragments of Ephorus were first collected by Marx, Carlsruhe, 1815, 8vo, who afterward published some additions in Friedemann and

[1] *De Tranq. An.*, 6.
[2] *Suid., s. v.; Cic., De Orat.*, iii., 9; *Phot., Cod.*, 176, 260.
[3] *De Stoic. Repugn.*, 10.
[4] *Diod. Sic.*, iv., 1; v., 1; *Polyb.*, v., 33; *Strab.*, vii., p. 302.
[5] xii., 25.
[6] viii., p. 332.
[7] *Smith, l. c.*

Seebode's *Miscellan. Crit.*, ii., 4, p. 764, *seqq.* They are also contained in C. and Th. Müller's *Fragm. Histor. Græc.*, vol. i., p. 234, *seqq.*, forming part of Didot's *Bibliotheca Græca*, Paris, 1841.

HISTORIANS OF ALEXANDER THE GREAT.

I. Several works existed among the ancients relative to the expeditions of Alexander in the course of his Eastern conquests, most of them composed by individuals who had either followed in his train or had served under his command. We must guard, however, against the common error of making the number of these writers a large one, an error not confined merely to modern times, but into which even Cicero himself[1] has fallen, when he says, with far more of oratorical embellishment than of historical truth, "*quam multos scriptores rerum suarum magnus ille Alexander secum habuisse traditur!*"[2]

II. A careful examination of the whole subject will limit the list of the writers in question to the following individuals; namely, of those who followed in the train of Alexander, *Anaximenes*, *Callisthenes*, and perhaps *Clitarchus*, and of the monarch's companions in arms, *Ptolemæus*, *Aristobulus*, *Onesicritus*, *Nearchus*, *Chares*, *Ephippus*, *Marsyas*, *Androsthenes*, and *Medius*. To these we may add, though not strictly falling under the denomination of *historians* of Alexander, *Eumenes* and *Diodotus*, authors of Ἐφημερίδες Ἀλεξάνδρου, and *Bæton* and *Diognetus*, who measured distances in the marches of Alexander, and wrote each a work on the subject, the title of Bæton's book having been Σταθμοὶ τῆς Ἀλεξάνδρου πορείας.[3]

III. As the works of all these writers are lost, and some scattered fragments alone remain, our account of them will be necessarily brief.

1. ANAXIMĔNES[4] (Ἀναξιμένης) was a native of Lampsacus, and pupil of Zoilus and Diogenes the Cynic. He was a contemporary of Alexander, whom he is said to have instructed, and whom he accompanied on his Asiatic expedition.[5] He wrote three historical works: 1. A *history of Philip of Macedonia*, consisting of at least eight books.[6] 2. A *history of Alexander the Great*,[7] the second book of which is quoted by Harpocration. 3. A *history of Greece*, in twelve books, from the earliest mythical ages down to the battle of Mantinea and the death of Epaminondas. The histories of Anaximenes, of which only a very few fragments are now extant, are censured by Plutarch for the numerous prolix and rhetorical speeches which he introduced into them. The fact that we possess so little of his histories shows that the ancients did not think highly of them, and that they were more of a rhetorical than an historical character. He enjoyed some reputation as a teacher of rhetoric and as an orator, and what renders him a person of the highest importance in the history of Greek literature is the fact that he is the only rhetorician whose scientific treatise on rhetoric, prior to that of Aristotle, is now extant. This is the so-called Ῥητορικὴ πρὸς Ἀλέξανδρον, which is usually printed

---

[1] *Or. pro Arch.*, c. 10. Compare *Sainte-Croix*, *Ex. Crit.*, &c., p. 33.

[2] *Geier*, *Hist. Scrip. Alex. M.*, *Prolegom.*, c. 2, p. xvii. Geier's work is far more worthy of reliance than Sainte-Croix's.

[3] *Geier*, *l. c.*

[4] *Smith*, *Dict. Biogr.*, *s. v.*

[5] *Suid.*, *s. v.*; *Eudoc.*, p. 51.

[6] *Harpocrat.*, *s. v.* Καβύλη.

[7] *Diog. Laert.*, ii., 3.

among the works of Aristotle, to whom, however, it can not belong, as all critics agree. The treatise on rhetoric was edited separately by Spengel, Turici, 1844. The fragments of the history of Alexander are given by Geier, in his "*Scriptores Historiarum Alexandri M. ætate suppares*," Lips., 1844, p. 285, *seqq.*, and by C. Müller, in the appendix to Dübner's Arrian, in Didot's *Bibliotheca Græca*, p. 35, *seqq.*

2. Callisthĕnes[1] (Καλλισθένης) of Olynthus, a relation and pupil of Aristotle, accompanied Alexander the Great to Asia. In his intercourse with the monarch he was arrogant and bold, and took every opportunity of showing his independence. He expressed his indignation at Alexander's adoption of Oriental customs, and especially at the requirement of the ceremony of adoration. He thus rendered himself so obnoxious to the king that he was accused of being privy to the plot of Hermolaus to assassinate Alexander, and, after being kept in chains for seven months, was either put to death or died of disease. Callisthenes wrote an account of Alexander's expedition; a history of Greece, in ten books, from the peace of Antalcidas to the seizure of the Delphic temple by Philomelus (B.C. 387–357), and other works, all of which, except a few fragments, have perished. The fragments of the history of Alexander are given by Geier, *Script. Hist. Alex. M.*, &c., Lips., 1844, p. 232, *seqq.*, and by C. Müller, in the appendix to Dübner's Arrian, in Didot's *Bibliotheca Græca*, p. 1, *seqq.* Some MSS. are still extant, professing to contain writings of Callisthenes, but they are spurious.[2]

3. Clitarchus[3] (Κλείταρχος), son of the historian Dinon,[4] accompanied Alexander in his Asiatic expedition, and wrote a history of it. Such, at least, is the commonly received account, although considerable doubt has recently been thrown upon the assumed fact of his having accompanied the monarch. The work of Clitarchus has been erroneously supposed by some to have formed the basis of that of Quintus Curtius, who is thought to have closely followed, even if he did not translate it. We find Curtius, however, in one passage, differing from Clitarchus, and even censuring him for his inaccuracy. Cicero also speaks very slightingly of the production in question. Quintilian says that his ability was greater than his veracity; and Longinus condemns his style as frivolous and inflated. The fragments of Clitarchus are given by Geier, *Script. Hist. Alex. M.*, p. 160, *seqq.*, Lips., 1844, and by C. Müller, in the appendix to Dübner's Arrian, p. 77, *seqq.*

4. Ptolemæus (Πτολεμαῖος), son of Lagus, first Greek king of Egypt, not content with the praise of an enlightened patron and friend of literature, sought for himself also the fame of an author, and composed an historical narrative of the wars of Alexander, in which he had borne part. His work is frequently cited by later writers, and is one of the chief authorities which Arrian made the ground-work of his history. That author repeatedly praises Ptolemy for the fidelity of his narrative, and the absence of all fables and exaggerations, and justly pays the greatest defer-

---

1 *Smith, Dict. Biogr.*, *s. v.*

2 Müller has given the *Pseudo-Callisthenes* in his appendix to Dübner's Arrian, p. 1–152.

3 *Smith, Dict. Biog.*, *s. v.*

4 *Plin.*, *H. N.*, x., 49.

ence to his authority, on account of his personal acquaintance with the events which he relates. No notice of his style has been preserved to us, from which we may probably infer that his work was not so much distinguished in this respect as for its historical value. Arrian expressly tells us that it was composed by Ptolemy after he was established on the throne of Egypt, and probably during the latter years of his life.[1] The fragments of this work are given by Geier, *Script. Hist. Alex. M.*, p. 5, *seqq.*, Lips., 1844, and by C. Müller, as above, p. 87, *seqq.*

5. Aristobūlus (Ἀριστόβουλος) of Cassandrea (of which, however, consistently with chronology, he could not have been a native) was one of the companions of Alexander the Great in his Asiatic conquests, though not named among his generals. He wrote a history of Alexander, which was one of the chief sources used by Arrian in the composition of his work. Aristobulus lived to the age of ninety, and did not begin to write his history until he was eighty-four.[2] His work is frequently referred to by Athenæus.[3] Lucian[4] relates an anecdote relative to Alexander and Aristobulus, tending to prove that the latter had written his work in a spirit of gross adulation toward the monarch, but many modern scholars think that the story ought to be referred to Onesicritus, and that the error arose from the copyists. Schneider and Geier, however, dissent from this opinion. The fragments of Aristobulus are given by Geier, *Script. Hist. Alex. M.*, p. 31, *seqq.*, Lips., 1844, and by C. Müller, as above, p. 94, *seqq.*

6. Onesicrĭtus[5] (Ὀνησίκριτος) was, according to some writers, a native of Astypalea, one of the Sporades; according to others, of Ægina;[6] and it was probably to this island-origin that he was indebted for the skill in nautical matters which afterward proved so advantageous to him. Onesicritus accompanied Alexander on his campaigns in Asia, and wrote a history of them, which is frequently cited by ancient authors. We have no account of the circumstances which led him to accompany Alexander into Asia, nor does it appear in what capacity he attended on the conqueror; but during the expedition into India he was sent by the king to hold a conference with the Indian philosophers or Gymnosophists, the details of which have been transmitted to us from his own account of the interview.[7] When Alexander constructed his fleet on the Hydaspes, he appointed Onesicritus to the important station of pilot of the king's ship, or chief pilot to the fleet (ἀρχικυβερνήτης), a post which he held not only during the descent of the Indus, but throughout the long and perilous voyage from the mouth of that river to the Persian Gulf. In this capacity, he discharged his duties so much to the satisfaction of Alexander, that, on his arrival at Susa, he was rewarded by that monarch with a crown of gold, at the same time as Nearchus. Yet Arrian blames him for want of judgment, and on one occasion expressly ascribes the safety of the fleet to the firmness of Nearchus in overruling his advice.[8]

1 *Arrian, Anab.*, i., *proœm.*
2 *Lucian, Macrob.*, 22.
3 ii., p. 43, *D*; vi., p. 251, *A*; x., p. 434, *D*, &c.
4 *Quomodo Hist. conscrib.*, c. 12.
5 *Smith, Dict. Biogr.*, *s. v*
6 *Diog. Laert.*, vi., 75; *Arrian, Ind.*, 18.
7 *Strab.*, xv., p. 715; *Plut.*, *Alex.*, 65.
8 *Arrian*, vii., 20; *Ind.*, 32.

We know nothing of his subsequent fortunes; but, from an anecdote related by Plutarch, it seems probable that he attached himself to Lysimachus, and it was perhaps at the court of that monarch that he composed his historical work,[1] though, on the other hand, a passage of Lucian[2] might lead us to infer that this was at least commenced during the lifetime of Alexander himself. Such is the opinion of Geier, among others.

We learn from Diogenes Laertius[3] that the history of Onesicritus comprised the whole life of Alexander, including his youth and education; but it is most frequently cited in relation to the campaigns of that prince in Asia, or to the geographical description of the countries that he visited. Though an eye-witness of much that he described, it appears that he intermixed many fables and falsehoods with his narrative, so that he early fell into discredit as an authority. Still, his work appears to have contained much valuable information concerning the remote countries for the first time laid open by the expedition of Alexander. In particular, he was the first author that mentioned the island of Taprobane.[4] He is said to have imitated Xenophon in his style, though he fell short of him, as a copy does of the original.[5] Onesicritus, when advanced in years, turned his attention to the Cynic philosophy, of which he became an ardent votary. The fragments of Onesicritus are given by Geier, *Script. Hist. Alex. M.*, p. 83, *seqq.*, Lips., 1844, and by C. Müller, in Didot's *Bibliotheca Græca*, p. 47, *seqq.*, Paris, 1846.

7. NEARCHUS (Νέαρχος) was a native of Crete, but settled at Amphipolis,[6] and one of the most distinguished of the officers and friends of Alexander. He accompanied the king to Asia, and in B.C. 325 was intrusted by Alexander with the command of the fleet which he had caused to be constructed on the Hydaspes.[7] Upon reaching the mouth of the Indus, Alexander resolved to send round his ships by sea from thence to the Persian Gulf, and he gladly accepted the offer of Nearchus to undertake the command of the fleet during this long and perilous navigation. Nearchus set out on the 21st of September, B.C. 326, and arrived at Susa in safety in February, B.C. 325. He was rewarded with a crown of gold for his distinguished services. Nearchus left a history of the voyage, the substance of which has been preserved to us by Arrian, who has derived from it the whole of the latter part of the "Indica." The fragments of the work of Nearchus are given by Geier, *Script. Hist. Alex. M.*, p. 117, *seqq.*, Lips., 1844, and by C. Müller, at the end of Dübner's Arrian, Paris, 1846, p. 60, *seqq.* There is also a valuable translation of the voyage of Nearchus (from Arrian) by Vincent, Oxford, 1809, 4to.

8. CHARES (Χάρης) was a native of Mytilene, and an officer at the court of Alexander, whose duty it was to introduce strangers to the king (εἰσαγγελεύς). He wrote a history, or, rather, a collection of anecdotes concerning the campaigns and the private life of Alexander, in ten books, fragments of which are preserved by Athenæus and Plutarch. Pliny appears to have drawn largely from him. Chares was regarded as a writer

[1] *Plut., Alex.*, 46. [2] *Quomodo Hist. conscr.*, c. 40. [3] vi., 84.
[4] *Strab.*, xv., p. 691; *Plin., H. N.*, vi., 24. [5] *Diog. Laert.*, vi., 84.
[6] *Arrian, Ind.*, 18; *Diod. Sic.*, xix., 19. [7] *Arrian, Anab.*, iv., 7, 4, &c.

of high authority, and pleasing in style. The fragments are given by Geier, *Script. Hist. Alex. M.*, p. 293, *seqq.*, and by C. Müller, as above, p. 114, *seqq.*

9. Ephippus (Ἔφιππος), of Olynthus, was also an historian of Alexander. Mention is made in a passage of Arrian of an Ephippus who was appointed, along with Æschylus the Rhodian, superintendent (ἐπίσκοπος) of Egypt. It has been supposed that this Ephippus is the same with the historian. From the few fragments still extant, it would appear that Ephippus described more the private and personal character of his heroes than their public careers. The fragments are given by Geier, p. 312, *seqq.*, and by C. Müller, p. 125, *seqq.*

10. Marsyas[1] (Μαρσύας) was a native of Pella, in Macedonia, and, according to Suidas, was educated along with Alexander, whom he afterward accompanied into Asia. We find him, after the death of that monarch, appointed by Demetrius to command one division of his fleet in the great sea-fight off Salamis, in the island of Cyprus,[2] B.C. 306. His principal literary work was a history of Macedonia, in ten books, commencing from the earliest times, and coming down to the wars of Alexander in Asia, when it terminated abruptly with the return of that monarch into Syria, after the conquest of Egypt and the foundation of Alexandrea. It is repeatedly cited by Athenæus, Plutarch, Harpocration, and other writers. Suidas also speaks of a history of the education of Alexander (αὐτοῦ τοῦ Ἀλεξάνδρου ἀγωγήν) as a separate work by Marsyas. He is often confounded with another and younger Marsyas, a native of Philippi. The fragments of Marsyas are given by Geier, p. 325, *seqq.*, and by C. Müller, p. 42, *seqq.*

11. Androsthĕnes (Ἀνδροσθένης), of Thasus, was one of Alexander's admirals, and sailed with Nearchus. He was also sent by Alexander to explore the coast of the Persian Gulf. He wrote an account of this voyage, and also a Τῆς Ἰνδικῆς παράπλους. The fragments of Androsthenes are given by Geier, p. 345, *seqq.*, and by C. Müller, p. 72, *seqq.*

12. Medius (Μήδιος)[3] was a native of Larissa, in Thessaly, and a friend of Alexander's. He is mentioned as commanding a trireme during the descent of the Indus,[4] but, with this exception, his name does not appear in the military operations of the king. He appears, however, to have enjoyed a high place in the personal favor of the monarch, and it was at his house that Alexander supped just before his last illness. Hence, according to those writers who represented the king to have been poisoned, it was at this banquet that the fatal draught was administered, and not without the cognizance, as it was said, of Medius himself. Plutarch speaks in very unfavorable terms of Medius, whom he represents as one of the flatterers to whose evil counsels the most reprehensible of the actions of Alexander were to be ascribed.[5] But no trace of this is to be found in the better authorities.

After the death of Alexander, Medius followed the fortunes of Antigonus, whose fleet we find him commanding in B.C. 314. The following

[1] *Smith, Dict. Biogr.*, *s. v.* [2] *Diod. Sic.*, xx., 50. [3] *Smith, Dict. Biogr.*, *s. v.*
[4] *Arrian, Ind.*, 18. [5] *Plut.*, *De Adul. et Amic.*, 24.

year he took Miletus. In B.C. 312 he was dispatched by Antigonus, with a fleet of 150 ships, to make a descent on Greece, and landed a large army in Bœotia. At a subsequent period, he accompanied Antigonus on his unsuccessful expedition against Egypt, but after this we hear no more of him. He wrote an historical work, as plainly appears from Strabo, but whether it related to the campaigns of Alexander or of his successors, is uncertain. The fragments are given by Geier, p. 351, and by C. Müller, p. 128.

13. The fragments of the Ἐφημερίδες of Eumenes and Diodotus are given by Geier, p. 360, *seqq.*, and by C. Müller, p. 121, *seqq.*; and those of the Σταθμοὶ τῆς Ἀλεξάνδρου πορείας of Bœton and Diognetus, by Geier, p. 367, *seqq.*, and C. Müller, p. 134, *seq.*

CHAPTER XXXIII.

FOURTH OR ATTIC PERIOD—*continued.*

GEOGRAPHICAL WRITERS.

I. In connection with the writers composing the school of history, we propose to consider briefly the geographical authors of this same period, as far as their date can be correctly ascertained through the investigations of modern scholars. Geography and history are so naturally connected, that a separation of them would only tend to produce confusion and consequent obscurity.

II. The geographical writers, however, that will here require our attention are very few in number, namely, *Scylax* of Caryanda, and *Pytheas* of Massilia, as a fit introduction to whose labors we will first give a sketch of the discoveries of the Carthaginian navigator Hanno, the more especially as they are known to us through the medium of the Greek translation of the Punic work in which the account was originally written.

III. Hanno (Ἄννων)[1] was a Carthaginian navigator, as already stated, under whose name we possess a Περίπλους, or a short account of a voyage round a part of Africa. This work was originally written in the Punic language, and what has come down to us is a Greek translation of the original. The work is often referred to by the ancients, but we have no statement containing any direct information, by means of which we might identify its author, Hanno, with any of the many other Carthaginians of that name, or fix the time at which he lived. Pliny[2] states that Hanno undertook the voyage when Carthage was in a most flourishing condition. Some call him king, and others *dux* or *imperator* of the Carthaginians, from which we may infer that he was invested with the office of *Suffete.*[3] In the Periplus itself Hanno says that he was sent out by his countrymen to undertake a voyage beyond the Pillars of Hercules, and to found Libyphœnician towns, and that he sailed accordingly with sixty penteconteres, and a body of men and women, to the number of 30,000, and provisions and other necessaries. On his return from his voyage, he dedicated an

---

[1] *Smith, Dict. Biogr.*, *s. v.*

[2] *H. N.*, ii., 67; v., 1, 36.

[3] *Solin.*, 56; *Hanno, Peripl.*, *Introd.*

account of it, inscribed on a tablet, in the temple of Saturn, or, as Pliny says, in that of Juno.[1] It is therefore presumed that the *Periplus* which has come down to us is a Greek version of the contents of that Punic tablet.

These vague accounts, leaving open the widest field for conjecture and speculation, have led some critics to place the expedition as early as the Trojan war, or the time of Hesiod, while others bring it down to the reign of Agathocles. Others, again, as Falconer, Bougainville, and Gail, with somewhat more probability, place Hanno about B.C. 570. But it seems preferable to identify him with Hanno, the father or son of Hamilcar, who was killed at Himera B.C. 480. The fact of such an expedition at that time has nothing at all improbable, for in the reign of the Egyptian king Necho, a similar voyage had been undertaken by the Phœnicians, and an accurate knowledge of the western coast of Africa was a matter of the highest importance to the Carthaginians. The number of colonists, 30,000, is undoubtedly an error either of the translator or of later transcribers. This circumstance, as well as many fabulous accounts contained in the Periplus, and the difficulties connected with the identification of the places visited by Hanno, and with the fixing of the southernmost point to which he penetrated, are not sufficient reasons for denying the genuineness of the Periplus, or for regarding it as the product of a much later age, as Dodwell did. The best opinion appears to be that Hanno passed considerably south of the *Senegal* River, but hardly farther than the coast of *Sierra Leone*.

The first edition of Hanno's Periplus appeared at Basle, 1534, 4to, as an appendix to Arrian, by Gelenius. This was followed by the editions of Boecler and Müller, Strasburg, 1661, 4to; Berkel, Leyden, 1674, 12mo; and Falconer, London, 1797, with an English translation, two dissertations, and maps. It is also printed in Hudson's *Geographi Græci Minores*, Oxford, 1698–1712, 4 vols. 8vo, with Dodwell's dissertation "*De vero Peripli, qui Hannonis nomine circumfertur, tempore*," in which he attacks the genuineness of the work; but his arguments are satisfactorily refuted by Bougainville (*Mem. de l'Acad. des Inscript.*, xxvi., p. 10, *seqq.*; xxviii., p. 260, *seqq.*), and by Falconer in his second dissertation. The Periplus is also given in Gail's *Geographi Græci Minores*, Paris, 1826–1831, 3 vols. 8vo, and separately by Kluge, Lips., 1829, 8vo.

IV. Scylax (Σκύλαξ) of Caryanda, in Caria, was sent, according to Herodotus, by Darius Hystaspis, on a voyage of discovery down the Indus. Setting out from the city of Caspatyrus and the Pactyican district, Scylax and his companions sailed down the river to the east and the rising of the sun, till they reached the sea; whence they sailed westward through the Indian Ocean to the Red Sea, performing the whole voyage in thirty months. Thus far Herodotus.[2] We have still extant a brief description of certain countries in Europe, Asia, and Africa, which bears the name of Scylax of Caryanda, and is entitled Περίπλους τῆς θαλάσσης οἰκουμένης Εὐρώπης καὶ Ἀσίας καὶ Λιβύης. This little work was supposed by Holstenius, Fabricius, Sainte-Croix, and others, to have been written by the Scylax mentioned by Herodotus; other writers, on the contrary, such as G. Vossius, J. Vossius, and Dodwell, regarded the author as the contemporary of Panætius and Polybius; but most modern scholars are dis-

[1] Compare *Pomp. Mela*, iii., 9; *Athen.*, iii., 83.

[2] *Herod.*, iv., 44.

posed to follow the opinion of Niebuhr, who supposes the writer to have lived in the first half of the reign of Philip of Macedon, the father of Alexander the Great (Philip began to reign B.C. 360). Niebuhr shows from internal evidence that the Periplus must have been composed long after the time of Herodotus; while, from its omitting to mention any of the cities founded by Alexander, such as Alexandrea in Egypt, as well as from other circumstances, we may conclude that it was drawn up before the reign of Alexander. It is probable, however, that the author, whoever he was, may not have borne the name of Scylax himself, but prefixed to his work that of Scylax of Caryanda, on account of the celebrity of the navigator in the time of Darius Hystaspis. Aristotle is the first writer who refers to Scylax;[1] but it is evident from his reference, as well as from the quotations from Scylax in other ancient writers,[2] which refer to matters not contained in the *Periplus* that has come down to us, that we possess only an abridgment of the original work.[3]

The *Periplus* of Scylax was first published by Hoeschel, with other minor Greek geographers, Augsburg, 1600, 8vo; next by Is. Vossius, Amsterdam, 1639, 4to; subsequently by Hudson, in his *Geographi Græci Minores*, Oxford, 1698–1712, 4 vols. 8vo; by Gail, in his *Geogr. Græc. Min.*, Paris, 1826–1831, 3 vols. 8vo; and separately by Klausen, attached to his edition of the fragments of Hecatæus, Berlin, 1831, 8vo. The following works may be consulted with profit in relation to the work under consideration: *Niebuhr, Ueber das Alter des Küstenbeschreibers Skylax von Karyanda*, in his *Kleine Schriften*, vol. i., p. 105, *seqq.*, translated in the *Philological Museum*, vol. i., p. 245, *seqq.*, and *Ukert, Geogr. der Gr. und Röm.*, vol. i., pt. ii., p. 285, *seqq.*, as also the dissertations prefixed to Klausen's edition.

V. Pytheas (Πυθέας) of Massilia, in Gaul, a celebrated Greek navigator, sailed to the western and northern parts of Europe, and wrote a work containing the results of his discoveries. We know nothing of his personal history, with the exception of the statement of Polybius that he was a poor man.[4] The time at which he lived can not be determined with accuracy; as he is quoted, however, by Dicæarchus, a pupil of Aristotle, and by Timæus, he probably lived in the time of Alexander the Great, or shortly afterward. It would appear from Pytheas's own statement, as related by Polybius, that he undertook two voyages. In one he visited Britain and Thule, and of this voyage he appears to have given an account in his work "*On the Ocean*" (Περὶ τοῦ Ὠκεανοῦ). In a second, undertaken after his return from his first voyage, he coasted along the whole of Europe from Gadira (now *Cadiz*) to the Tanais, and the description of this second voyage probably formed the subject of his *Periplus* (Περίπλους, or, as it is termed by the scholiast on Apollonius Rhodius, Γῆς περίοδος). There has been much dispute as to what river we are to understand by the Tanais. The most probable conjecture appears to be, that, upon reaching the Elbe, Pytheas concluded he had arrived at the Tanais, separating Europe from Asia.[5]

1 *Polit.*, iii., 14. 2 *Philostr.*, *Apollon.*, iii., 47; *Harpocrat.*, p. 174, ed. *Gronov.*
3 *Smith, Dict. Biogr.*, *s. v.* 4 *Ap. Strab.*, ii., p. 104. 5 *Smith, Dict. Biogr.*, *s. v.*

The works of Pytheas are frequently referred to by the ancient writers; some, as, for example, Eratosthenes and Hipparchus, regarding them as worthy of belief; but other writers, especially Polybius and Strabo, regard them as of no value at all. Polybius says that it is incredible that a private man, and one who was also poor, could have undertaken such long voyages and journeys;[1] and Strabo, on more than one occasion, calls him a great liar, and regards his statements as mere fables, only deserving to be classed with those of Euhemerus and Antiphanes.[2] Most modern writers, however, have been disposed to set more value upon the narrative of Pytheas. It would appear from the extracts which have been preserved from his works, that he did not give simply the results of his own observations, but added all the reports which reached him respecting distant countries, without always drawing a distinction between what he saw himself and what was told him by others. His statements, therefore, must be received with caution and some mistrust. It is equally uncertain how far he penetrated. Some modern writers have regarded it as certain that he must have reached Iceland, in consequence of his remark that the day was six months long at Thule; while others have supposed that he advanced as far as the Shetland islands. But either supposition is very improbable, and neither is necessary; for reports of the great length of the day and night in the northern parts of Europe had already reached the Greeks before the time of Pytheas.[3]

Pytheas cultivated science. He appears to have been the first person that ascertained the latitude of a place from the shadow of the sun, and it is expressly stated that he determined the position of Massilia by observing the shadow of the sun by the gnomon.[4] He also paid considerable attention to the phenomena of the tides, and was well aware of the influence of the moon upon them.

The voyages of Pytheas have been discussed by a large number of modern writers. Among the most important works on the subject we may name *Bougainville, Sur l'Origine et sur les Voyages de Pythéas*, in the *Mem. de l'Acad. des Inscript.*, vol. xix., p. 146, *seqq.; D'Anville, Sur la Navigation de Pythéas à Thule, ibid.*, vol. xxxvii., p. 436, *seqq.; Ukert, Bemerkungen über Pytheas*, in the *Geogr. der Gr. und Röm.*, vol. i., pt. i., p. 298, *seqq.; Fuhr, De Pythea Massiliensi dissertatio*, Darmstadt, 1835; *Lelewel, Pytheas und die Geographie seiner Zeit*, &c., Leipzig, 1838. The fragments of Pytheas have been edited by Arwedson, Upsala, 1824, 8vo.

[1] *Polyb. ap. Strab.*, ii., p. 104.

[2] *Strab.*, i., p. 63; ii., p. 102; iii., p. 148, &c.

[3] *Smith, l. c.*

[4] *Strab.*, ii., p. 71, 115.

CHAPTER XXXIV.

FOURTH OR ATTIC PERIOD—*continued.*

II. SCHOOL OF ELOQUENCE.

INTRODUCTORY REMARKS.[1]

I. If we take an extensive view of ancient and modern literature, and compare their several departments, in order to form an accurate estimate of their relative merit, the palm of oratory seems confessedly conceded to the former. A review of modern history presents to our observation few who deserve the name of orators, even among those nations whose governments would seem likely to facilitate the growth of eloquence, by admitting to a share in its Legislature such assemblies as may be supposed to lie under the dominion of its influence. Indeed, the slightest acquaintance with the records of antiquity is sufficient to teach us, that the style and character of the eloquence of the ancients is materially different from our own; and, before we proceed to give any account of the productions of the Greek orators, or to introduce a sketch of their respective lives, it will not be amiss to make some preliminary observations on the causes of their vast and acknowledged superiority.

II. Without inquiring into the extent of that influence which climate may exercise over national character, it may be remarked that the geographical situation of Greece was eminently favorable to the development of intellectual power, and to that peculiarly nice organization by which delicacy of feeling is refined even to fastidiousness. That the Athenians did possess this exquisite susceptibility, we know as well by several historical anecdotes as by the direct and explicit testimony of Cicero. Speaking of this extraordinary people, he says, "*Sincerum fuit eorum judicium, nihil ut possent nisi incorruptum audire atque elegans.*"[2] So faultless was their judgment, that they would listen to nothing but what was pure and elegant. A tribunal, then, whose discrimination was so keen, whose taste was so fastidious, and from whose authority there was no appeal, would, by the very severity of its decisions, call forth productions of finished excellence from those who were conscious of talents which deserved approbation, and were stimulated by ambition to pursue it. Such a tribunal, though it might intimidate and abash minds of inferior calibre, would urge to active industry and unwearied perseverance those more eminent abilities which no difficulties can alarm, and no disappointment effectually retard.

III. Accordingly, we find that among the ancients the study of eloquence was, as it were, almost the occupation of life, and the splendor of their success is only proportionate to the vigor of their exertions. The laborious diligence of Demosthenes, his careful correction of natural defects, his seclusion from society, and his earnest zeal in preparing him-

[1] *Ottley, Greek Orators, Encyc. Metropol.*

[2] *Cic., De Orat.*, viii., 25.

self for the career of a public speaker, are familiar to every one. The moderns may have the same powers of genius, and the same indefatigable application as orators—both parties must have aimed at persuasion; but some of the means which one employed are either above or beneath the other. In fact, our *scholastic* pursuits were an Athenian's leisure occupation (σχολή); his business was politics; literature was his recreation, and he found both in the speeches of the public orator. These were allied to politics by their subject, to music by their rhythm, and by attitude, gesture, and action to the drama. Hence some of their beauties, expected and admired by an Athenian audience, would be thrown away upon a modern assembly; they would be too visibly artificial to be persuasive. Legislative assemblies at the present day are too practical, too intent generally on business, to care much about the rhythmical structure of sentences. As, on the one hand, modern orators could not, perhaps (a few rare cases excepted), copy the vehement reasoning, the energy, and earnest boldness of Demosthenes, there are, on the other hand, beauties of style in the structure of his sentences which they would not copy if they could. So, again, Dionysius of Halicarnassus praises the dignity and magnificence with which the funeral oration of Pericles opens; then he accounts for these excellencies by remarking that the first period contains three spondees, then an anapæst, then a spondee, then a cretic, "all dignified feet" (ἅπαντες ἀξιωματικοί).[1] Praise of this kind does not occur to any one who enjoys or recommends a speech of Burke or of Fox, of Clay or of Webster; yet, no doubt, these dignified feet were important beauties to the ears of the Athenian assembly, and the supply was adjusted to the demand.

IV. Cicero, in his celebrated treatise "*De Oratore*,"[2] has left us much valuable information respecting the Greek orators. From them he learned the graces which eloquence is capable of assuming, and the deep and durable impression which it makes on the minds both of the learned and the illiterate. His estimate of what an orator ought to be was formed by what the Greeks had actually done; and we may therefore learn, in some measure, from his precepts, the nature and extent of their exertions in the prosecution of their favorite pursuit. After enumerating some exercises, such as speaking extempore, and from memory, or repeating, in Latin, orations which had been read in Greek—exercises, the habitual practice of which was necessary to the attainment of eloquence —he contends that an almost universal knowledge is essentially requisite to perfection in this noble art, enumerating, among other things, an acquaintance with the poets, or, as we would say, a full course of belles-lettres studies; a thorough knowledge of history, of the principles and constitution of the republic, of law in general and the municipal code in particular, of philosophy and the moral nature and habits of men.

V. If, then, such were the earnestness and zeal with which the ancients cultivated the art of eloquence, and so wide the range of learning which they brought to bear upon it; if the audience, to whose judgment their speeches were submitted, were so alive to the perception of beau-

[1] *Dion. Hal.*, *De Verb. Comp.*, § xviii., p. 114, ed. *Reiske*.

[2] *Cic.*, *De Orat.*, i., 34.

ties, and so keen in discovering defects, we need not wonder that the superior excellence of the Greek orators is so vast and indisputable. As the prize for which these intellectual gladiators contended was valuable, so the weapon they employed combined the highest polish with the greatest strength. Those who are familiar with the Greek language need not to be reminded of its unrivalled copiousness of expression, its majesty, elegance, and compactness, its unlimited range of compound words, and the flexible ductility with which it lends itself to convey every variety of meaning. The power of such an instrument was only to be surpassed by the skill of those who wielded it. The democratic government of Athens, its foreign wars and domestic discord, furnished the Greek orators with ample materials for the employment of their eloquence; and successful exertions were crowned, not only with the pleasing tribute of popular applause, but the more profitable reward of political power.

VI. Such, then, were some of the causes which promoted the growth and secured the celebrity of eloquence in Greece, or, to speak more properly, at Athens. Oratory, in fact, flourished only at Athens; and while other states arrest attention by occasional periods of military glory—while Sparta excites astonishment by the extreme austerity of its national manners, and the singularity of its political institutions, history does not inform us that these republics produced any individual whose eloquence elevated him to importance during his life, or secured his posthumous renown.[1]

HISTORY OF ELOQUENCE AMONG THE GREEKS.[2]

I. Public speaking had been common in Greece from the earliest times. Long before popular assemblies had gained the sovereign power by the establishment of democracy, the ancient kings had been in the habit of addressing their people, sometimes with that natural eloquence which Homer ascribes to Ulysses, at other times, like Menelaus, with concise but persuasive diction. Hesiod assigns to kings a muse of their own—Calliope—by whose aid they were enabled to speak convincingly and persuasively in the popular assembly and from the seat of judgment. With the farther development of republican constitutions after the age of Homer and Hesiod, public officers and demagogues without number had spoken in the public meetings, or in the deliberative councils of the numerous independent states, and no doubt they often spoke eloquently and wisely; but these speeches did not survive the particular occasion which called them forth.

II. Turning to Athens, the native soil of oratory, the first great name that arrests our attention in the department of public speaking is that of Pericles. It is manifest, from the whole political career of this eminent statesman, that while, on the one hand, he presupposed in the Athenian people a power of governing themselves, so, on the other, he wished to prevent the state from becoming a mere stake, to be played for by ambitious demagogues; for he favored every institution which gave the poorer

[1] *Cic., Brut.*, 13; *Vell. Paterc.*, i., 18.

[2] *Müller, Hist. Gr. Lit.*, vol. ii., p. 67.

citizens a share in the government; he encouraged every thing which might contribute to extend education and knowledge; and by his astonishing expenditure on works of architecture and sculpture, he gave the people a decided fondness for the grand and beautiful. And thus the appearance of Pericles on the bema (which he purposely reserved for great occasions) was not intended merely to aid the passing of some law, but was, at the same time, calculated to infuse a noble spirit into the general politics of Athens, to guide the views of the Athenians in regard to their external relations, and all the difficulties of their position; and it was the wish of this true friend of the people that all this might long survive himself. This is obviously the opinion of Thucydides, whom we may consider as in many respects a worthy disciple of the school of Pericles; and this is the representation which he has given us of the oratory of that statesman in the three speeches (all of them delivered on important occasions) which he has put into his mouth.[1]

III. This wonderful triad of speeches forms a beautiful whole, which is perfect and complete in itself. The *first* speech proves the necessity of a war with the Peloponnesians, and the probability that it will be successful; the *second*, delivered immediately after the first successes obtained in the war, under the form of a funeral oration, confirms the Athenians in their mode of living and acting. It is half an apology for, half a panegyric upon Athens: it is full of a sense of truth, and of noble self-reliance, tempered with moderation. The *third*, delivered after the calamities which had befallen Athens, rather through the plague than through the war, and which had nevertheless made the people vacillate in their resolutions, offers the consolation most worthy of a noble heart, namely, that up to that time fortune, on which no man can count, had deceived them, but they had not been misled by their own calculations and convictions; and that these would never deceive them, if they did not allow themselves to be led astray by some unforeseen accidents.[2]

IV. No speech of Pericles has been preserved in writing. It may seem surprising that no attempt was made to write down and preserve, for the benefit of the present and future generations, works which every one considered admirable, and which were regarded as, in some respects, the most perfect specimens of oratory. The only explanation of this that can be offered is, that in those days a speech was not considered as possessing any value or interest, save in reference to the particular practical object for which it was designed. It had never occurred to people that speeches and poems might be placed in one class, and both preserved without reference to their subjects, on account of the skill with which the subjects were treated, and the general beauties of the form and composition. Only a few emphatic and nervous expressions of Pericles were kept in remembrance; but a general impression of the grandeur and copiousness of his oratory long prevailed among the Greeks.[3]

V. We have said that Athens was the native soil of oratory, a remark that must not, however, be construed so strictly as to prove any disparagement to the Sicilian Greeks, and especially the Syracusans, whose

[1] *Müller, l. c.* [2] *Id. ib.* [3] *Id. ib.*

lively disposition and natural quickness raised them, more than any other Dorian people, to a level with the Athenians, and who had commenced, even earlier than the people of Attica, the study of an artificial rhetoric useful for the discussions of the law-courts. The situation of Syracuse, at the time of the Persian war, had contributed a good deal to awaken their natural inclination and capacity for such a study; especially by the impulse which the abolition of arbitrary government had given to democratic sentiments, and by the complicated transactions which sprang up from the renewal of private claims long suppressed by the tyrants.[1]

VI. At this time, Corax, who had been highly esteemed by the tyrant Hiero, came forward in a conspicuous manner, both as a public orator and as a pleader in the law courts. His great practice led him to consider more accurately the principles of his art; and at last it occurred to him to write a work on the subject. This book, like the innumerable treatises which succeeded it, was entitled Τέχνη Ῥητορική, "the Art of Rhetoric," or simply Τέχνη, "the Art." This work is worthy of notice as the first of its kind, not only among the Greeks, but perhaps also in the whole world. All that we know of it is, that it laid down a regular form and regular divisions for the oration, which, above all, was to begin with a distinct prooemium, calculated to put the hearers in a favorable train, and to conciliate their good-will at the very opening of the speech. According to some, Corax would seem not to have been a pleader in the law courts, but merely a composer of speeches for others, since it is doubtful whether there was an establishment of *patroni* and *causidici* at Syracuse as at Rome, or whether every one was compelled to plead his own cause, as at Athens, in which case he was always able to get his speech made for him by some professed rhetorician.[2]

VII. Tisias was first a pupil, and afterward a rival of Corax. He also was known not only as a public speaker, but likewise as the author of a Τέχνη. Gorgias,[3] again, was the pupil of Tisias, and followed closely in his steps. Gorgias was a native of Leontini, a Chalcidian colony in Sicily. He was somewhat older than the Attic orator Antiphon (born in B.C. 480 or 479), and lived to such an advanced age (some say 105, and others 109 years), that he survived Socrates, though probably only a short time. According to the common account, he was sent by his fellow-citizens, when advanced in years (B.C. 427), as ambassador to Athens, for the purpose of soliciting its protection against the threatening power of Syracuse. Another account makes Tisias to have been his colleague on the occasion. Through Gorgias this artificial rhetoric obtained more fame and glory than fell to the share of any other branch of literature. The Athenians, to whom this Sicilian rhetoric was still a novelty, though they were fully qualified and predisposed to enjoy its beauties, were quite enchanted with it, and it soon became fashionable to speak like Gorgias. The impression produced by his oratory was greatly increased by his stately appearance, his well-chosen and splendid costume, and the self-possession and confidence of his demeanor. Besides, his rhetoric rested on a basis of philosophy, which taught that the sole aim of the orator is

1 *Müller*, *l. c.*, p. 75. 2 *Id. ib.* 3 *Id.*, p. 73; *Smith*, *Dict. Biogr.*, *s. v.*

to turn the minds of his hearers into such a train as may best consist with his own interests; that, consequently, rhetoric is the agent of persuasion, the art of all arts, because the rhetorician is able to speak well and convincingly on every subject, even though he has no accurate knowledge respecting it.[1]

In accordance with this view of rhetoric, Gorgias took little pains with the subject-matter of his speeches; he only concerned himself about this so far as to exercise himself in treating of general topics, which were called *loci communes*, and the proper application and management of which have always helped the rhetorician to conceal his ignorance. The chief study of Gorgias, however, was directed to the form of expression. His oratory was chiefly calculated to tickle the ear by antitheses, by combinations of words of similar sound, by the symmetry of its parts and similar artifices, and to dazzle by metaphors, allegories, repetitions, apostrophes, and the like; by novel images, poetical circumlocutions, and high-sounding expressions, and sometimes also by a strain of irony. He, lastly, tried to charm his hearers by a symmetrical arrangement of his periods. But as these artifices, in the application of which he is said to have often shown real grandeur, earnestness, and elegance, were made use of too profusely, and for the purpose of giving undue prominence to poor thoughts, his orations did not excite the feelings of his hearers, and, at all events, could produce only a momentary impression. This was the case with his oration addressed to the assembled Greeks at Olympia, exhorting them to union against their common enemy, and with the funeral oration which he wrote at Athens, though he probably did not deliver it in public; and a fragment of which is preserved by the scholiast on Hermogenes.[2]

Gorgias seems to have returned to Leontini, but only for a short time, and to have spent the remaining years of his vigorous old age in the towns of Greece proper, especially at Athens and the Thessalian Larissa, enjoying honor every where as an orator and teacher of rhetoric. Besides Polus, of Agrigentum, his favorite scholar and devoted partisan, who is described in such lively colors in the *Gorgias* of Plato, such men as Alcibiades, Critias, Alcidamas, Æschines, and Antisthenes, are called either pupils or imitators of Gorgias. We will return to this individual in our remarks on the Sophists.

Two declamations have come down to us under the name of Gorgias, viz., the *Apology of Palamedes*, and the *Encomium on Helena*. Their genuineness is maintained by Reiske, Geel, and Schönborn, and doubted by Voss and others. It is difficult to give any decisive opinion on the subject, since the characteristic peculiarities of the oratory of Gorgias, which appear in these declamations, especially in the former, might very well have been imitated by a skillful rhetorician of later times. These declamations are given by Reiske in the eighth volume of his *Oratores Græci*; by Bekker, in the fifth volume of his *Oratores Attici*; and by Mullach, Berlin, 1845.

[1] *Müller, Hist. Gr. Lit.*, vol. ii., p. 77.

[2] *Id. ib.*

ATTIC ORATORS.

VIII. The cultivation of the art of oratory among the Athenians is due to a combination of the natural eloquence displayed by the Athenian statesmen, and especially by Pericles, with the rhetorical studies introduced by Gorgias. The first person in whom the effects of this combination were fully shown was *Antiphon*, who was both a practical statesman and man of business, and also a rhetorician of the schools.[1] The *canon* of Attic orators, as settled in a later age by the Alexandrine grammarians, commences therefore with his name. This canon contains ten names, given in chronological order, as follows: *Antiphon, Andocides, Lysias, Isocrates, Isæus, Æschines, Lycurgus, Demosthenes, Hyperīdes*, and *Dinarchus*. These ten are known by the appellation of the *Ten Attic Orators*, and we shall proceed to consider them in the order in which they have been named.

1. ANTĪPHON (Ἀντιφῶν),[2] the most ancient of the ten Attic orators in the Alexandrine canon, was a son of Sophilus the sophist, and born at Rhamnus, in Attica, B.C. 480.[3] He was a man of eminent talent and firm character,[4] and is said to have been educated partly by his father and partly by Pythodorus, while, according to others, he owed his education to no one but himself. When he was a young man, the fame of Gorgias was at its height. The object of Gorgias's sophistical school of oratory, as already remarked, was more to dazzle and captivate the hearer by brilliancy of diction and rhetorical artifices, than to produce a solid conviction based upon sound arguments. Antiphon perceived this deficiency, and formed a higher and more practical view of the art to which he devoted himself; that is, he wished to produce conviction in the minds of the hearers by means of a thorough examination of the subjects proposed, and this not with a view to the narrow limits of the school, but to the courts and the public assembly. Hence the ancients call Antiphon the inventor of public oratory, or state that he raised it to a higher position.[5] Antiphon was thus the first who regulated practical eloquence by certain theoretical laws, and he opened a school in which he taught rhetoric.

Thucydides the historian, a pupil of Antiphon, speaks of his master with the highest esteem, and many of the excellences of his style are ascribed by the ancients to the influence of Antiphon.[6] At the same time, Antiphon occupied himself with writing speeches for others, who delivered them in the courts of justice; and as he was the first who received money for such orations—a practice which subsequently became quite general—he was severely attacked and ridiculed, especially by the comic writers Plato and Pisander.[7] These attacks, however, may also have been owing to his political opinions, for he belonged to the oligarchical party. This

---

[1] *Müller, Hist. Gr. Lit.*, vol. ii., p. 79.
[2] *Smith, Dict. Biogr.*, *s. v.*
[3] *Plut., Vit. Dec. Orat.*, p. 832, *B.*
[4] *Thucyd.*, viii., 88; *Plut., Nic.*, 6.
[5] *Philostr., Vit. Soph.*, i., 15, 2; *Hermog., De Form.*, ii., p. 498.
[6] *Schol. ad Thucyd.*, iv., p. 312, ed. *Bekker.*
[7] *Philostr., l. c.; Plut., Vit. Dec. Orat.*, p. 833, *C.*

unpopularity, together with his own reserved character, prevented his ever appearing as a speaker, either in the courts or in the assembly; and the only time he spoke in public was in B.C. 411, when, on the overthrow of the oligarchical government, Antiphon was brought to trial for having attempted to negotiate peace with Sparta, and was condemned to death. His speech in defence of himself is stated by Thucydides[1] to have been the ablest that was ever made by any man in similar circumstances. It is now lost, but was known to the ancients, and is referred to by Harpocration, who calls it λόγος περὶ μεταστάσεως. His property was confiscated, his house razed to the ground, and on the site of it a tablet was erected with the inscription "Antiphon the Traitor." His remains were not allowed to be buried in Attic ground; his children, as well as any one who should adopt them, were punished with *atimia.*

As an orator, Antiphon was highly esteemed by the ancients. Hermogenes[2] says of his orations that they were clear, true in the expression of feeling, and faithful to nature, and consequently convincing. Others say that his orations were beautiful but not graceful, or that they had something austere or antique about them. The want of freshness and gracefulness is very obvious in the orations still extant, but more especially in those actually spoken by Antiphon's clients. His language is pure and correct, and the treatment and solution of the point at issue are always striking and interesting.[3]

The ancients possessed sixty orations of different kinds which went by the name of Antiphon, but Cæcilius, a rhetorician of the Augustan Age, declared twenty-five to be spurious.[4] We now possess only fifteen orations of Antiphon, three of which were written by him for others. The remaining twelve were composed as specimens for his school, or exercises on fictitious cases. They are a peculiar phenomenon in the history of ancient oratory, for they are divided into three tetralogies, each of which consists of four orations, two accusations and two defences on the same subject. The subject of the first tetralogy is a murder, the perpetrator of which is yet unknown; that of the second an unpremeditated murder; and that of the third a murder committed in self defence. The clearness which distinguishes his other three orations is not perceptible in these tetralogies, which arises in part from the corrupt and mutilated state in which they have come down to us. A great number of the orations of Antiphon, and in fact all those which are extant, have for their subject the commission of a murder, whence they are sometimes referred to under the name of λόγοι φονικοί.[5] The three real speeches—the tetralogies must be left out of the question here—contain more information than any other ancient writings respecting the mode of proceeding in the criminal courts at Athens. Besides the orations, the ancients ascribe to Antiphon, 1. A treatise on "*Rhetoric*" (Τέχνη ῥητορική), in three books. This work is occasionally referred to by ancient rhetoricians and grammarians, but is now lost. 2. Προοίμια καὶ Ἐπίλογοι. These seem to have been model-speeches or exercises, for the use of himself or his

[1] viii., 68. [2] *De Form.*, p. 497. [3] *Dionys., Jud. de Thucyd.*, 51; *Phot.*, p. 485.
[4] *Plut., Vit. Dec. Orat.*, p. 833, *B.* [5] *Hermog., De Form.*, p. 496, *seqq.*

scholars; and it is not improbable that his tetralogies may have belonged to them.

The orations of Antiphon are printed in the collections of the Attic orators, edited by Aldus (Venice, 1513, fol.), H. Stephens (Paris, 1575, fol.), Reiske (Leipzig, 1770–75, 12 volumes 8vo), Bekker (Oxford, 1822–3, 4 volumes 8vo; reprinted Berlin, 1823–4, 5 volumes 8vo), Dobson (London, 1828, 16 volumes 8vo), Baiter and Sauppe (Zürich, 1838–45, 4to), and others. The best separate editions are those of Baiter and Sauppe (the text merely), Zürich, 1838, 16mo, and Mätzner, Berlin, 1838, 8vo, the last with critical notes and commentary. The best modern works on Antiphon are, P. Van Spaan (Ruhnken), *Dissertatio de Antiphonte, Oratore Attico*, Leyden, 1765, 4to, reprinted in Ruhnken's *Opuscula*, and in Reiske's and Dobson's Greek Orators; Taylor, *Lect. Lysiac.*, vii., p. 848, *seqq.*, ed. Reiske; and Westermann, *Geschichte der Griech. Beredtsamkeit*, § 40, *seq.* The student may consult also Dobree's "*Annot. in Antiphontem*," in Scholefield's edition of Dobree's Adversaria, Cambridge, 1831, and in Dobson's Attic Orators.

2. Andocĭdes (Ἀνδοκίδης)[1] was born at Athens in B.C. 467. He belonged to a noble family,[2] and was a supporter of the oligarchical party at Athens, and through their influence obtained, in B.C. 436, together with Glaucon, the command of a fleet of twenty sail, which was to protect the Corcyreans against the Corinthians.[3] After this he seems to have been employed on various occasions as ambassador to Thessaly, Macedonia, Molossia, Thesprotia, Italy, and Sicily;[4] and, although he was frequently attacked for his political opinions, he yet maintained his ground, until in B.C. 415, when he became involved in the charge brought against Alcibiades for having profaned the mysteries and mutilated the Hermæ. It appeared the more likely that Andocides was an accomplice in the latter of these crimes, which was believed to be a preliminary step toward overthrowing the democratical constitution, since the Hermes standing close to his house was among the very few which had not been injured.[5] Andocides was accordingly seized and thrown into prison, but after some time recovered his liberty by a promise that he would reveal the names of the real perpetrators of the crime; and, on the suggestion of one Charmides or Timæus,[6] he mentioned four, all of whom were put to death. He is said to have also denounced his own father, but to have rescued him again in the hour of danger. But as Andocides was unable to clear himself from the charge, he was deprived of his rights as a citizen, and left Athens.[7]

He returned to Athens on the establishment of the government of the Four Hundred in 411, but was soon obliged to fly again.[8] In the following year he ventured once more to return to Athens, and it was at this time that he delivered the speech still extant, *On his Return* (Περὶ τῆς ἑαυτοῦ καθόδου), in which he petitioned for permission to reside at Athens, but in vain. He was thus driven into exile a third time, and went to reside at Elis.[9] In B.C. 403 he again returned to Athens, upon the overthrow of the tyranny of the Thirty by Thrasybulus, and the proclamation of the general amnesty. He was now allowed to remain quietly at Athens for the next three years, but in B.C. 400 his enemies accused him

[1] *Smith, Dict. Biogr.*, *s. v.*
[2] *Plut.*, *Vit. Dec. Orat.*, p. 834, *B.*
[3] *Thucyd.*, i., 51; *Plut.*, *l. c.*
[4] *Andoc. c. Alcib.*, § 41.
[5] *Plut.*, *l. c.*; *Nepos.*, *Alcib.*, 3.
[6] *De Myst.*, § 48; *Plut.*, *Alcib.*, 21.
[7] *De Red.*, § 25.
[8] *Lys. c. Andoc.*, § 29.
[9] *Plut.*, *Vit. Dec. Orat.*, p. 835, *A.*

of having profaned the mysteries. He defended himself in the oration still extant, *On the Mysteries* (Περὶ τῶν Μυστηρίων), and was acquitted. In B.C. 394 he was sent as ambassador to Sparta, to conclude a peace, and on his return, in 393, he was accused of illegal conduct (παραπρεσβείας) during his embassy. He defended himself in the extant speech *On the Peace with Lacedæmon* (Περὶ τῆς πρὸς Λακεδαιμονίους εἰρήνης), but was found guilty, and sent into exile for the fourth time. He seems to have died soon afterward in exile.

Andocides appears to have left no issue, since at the age of seventy he had no children,[1] though the scholiast on Aristophanes mentions Antiphon as a son of Andocides. This was probably owing to his wandering and unsteady life, as well as to his dissolute character.[2] The large fortune which he inherited from his father, or acquired in his commercial undertakings, was greatly diminished in the latter years of his life.[3] Andocides has no claim to the esteem of posterity either as a man or as a citizen. Besides the three orations already mentioned, which are undoubtedly genuine, there is a fourth, against Alcibiades (Κατὰ Ἀλκιβιάδου), said to have been delivered by Andocides in B.C. 415, but it is in all probability spurious, though it appears to contain genuine historical matter. Taylor ascribed it to Phæax, while others think it more probable that it is the work of some one of the later rhetoricians, with whom the accusation or defence of Alcibiades was a standing theme. Besides these four orations we possess only a few fragments, and some very vague allusions to other orations.

As an orator Andocides does not appear to have been held in very high esteem by the ancients, as he is seldom mentioned, though Valerius Theon is said to have written a commentary on his orations. We do not hear of his having been trained in any of the sophistical schools of the time, and he had probably developed his talents in the practical school of the popular assembly. Hence his orations have no mannerism in them, and are really, as Plutarch says, simple, and free from all rhetorical pomp and ornament. Sometimes, however, his style is diffuse, and becomes tedious and obscure. The best among the orations is that on the Mysteries; but, for the history of the time, all are of the highest importance.

The orations are printed in the collections of the Greek orators mentioned at the end of the article on Antiphon. The best separate editions are those of Schiller, Leipzig, 1835, 8vo, and of Baiter and Sauppe, Zürich, 1838, 8vo. The most important works on the life and orations of Andocides are: Sluiter, *Lectiones Andocideæ*, Leyden, 1804, reprinted at Leipzig, 1834, with notes by Schiller; a treatise of A. G. Becker, prefixed to his German translation of Andocides, Quedlinburg, 1832, 8vo; Ruhnken, *Hist. Crit. Orat. Græc.*, p. 47, *seqq.*; Westermann, *Gesch. der Griech. Beredtsamkeit*, § 42, *seq.*

3. Lysias (Λυσίας) was born at Athens in B.C. 458. He was the son of Cephalus, who was a native of Syracuse, and had taken up his abode at Athens on the invitation of Pericles.[4] When he was little more than fifteen years old, in B.C. 443, Lysias and his two (some say three) brothers joined the Athenians who went as colonists to Thurii, in Italy. He

[1] *De Myst.*, § 146, § 148. [2] *Ib.*, § 100. [3] *Ib.*, § 144.
[4] *Dionys.*, *Lys.*, 1; *Plut.*, *Vit. Dec. Orat.*, p. 835.

there completed his education under the instruction of two Syracusans, Tisias (already mentioned by us) and Nicias, and afterward enjoyed great esteem among the Thurians, and even seems to have taken part in the administration of the young republic. From a passage of Aristotle,[1] we learn that he devoted some time to the teaching of rhetoric, though it is uncertain whether he entered upon this profession while yet at Thurii, or did not commence till after his return to Athens, where we know that Isæus was one of his pupils.[2] In B.C. 411, when he had attained the age of forty-seven, after the defeat of the Athenians in Sicily, all persons, both in Sicily and in the south of Italy, who were suspected of favoring the cause of the Athenians, were exposed to persecutions; and, accordingly, Lysias, together with 300 others, was expelled by the Spartan party from Thurii as a partisan of the Athenians. He now returned to Athens; but there, too, great misfortunes awaited him; for, during the rule of the Thirty tyrants, after the battle of Ægospotami, he was looked upon as an enemy of the government, his large property was confiscated, and he was thrown into prison with a view to being put to death. But he escaped from Athens, and took refuge at Megara.[3] His attachment to Athens, however, was so great, that when Thrasybulus, at the head of the patriots, marched from Phyle to liberate their country, Lysias joyfully sacrificed all that yet remained of his fortune, for he sent the patriots 2000 drachmas and 200 shields, and engaged a band of 302 mercenaries. Thrasybulus procured him the Athenian franchise as a reward for his generosity; but Archinus afterward induced the people to declare it void, because it had been conferred without a probouleuma; and Lysias henceforth lived at Athens as an *isoteles*, occupying himself, as it appears, solely with writing judicial speeches for others, and died in B.C. 378, at the age of eighty.[4]

Lysias was one of the most fertile writers of orations that Athens ever produced, for there were in antiquity no less than 425 orations which were current under his name, though the ancient critics were of opinion that only 230 of them were genuine.[5] Of these orations only thirty-five are extant, and even among these some are incomplete, and others are probably spurious. Of fifty-three others we possess only a few fragments. Most of these orations, only one of which (that against Eratosthenes, B.C. 403) he delivered himself in court, were composed after his return from Thurii to Athens. There are, however, some among them which probably belong to an earlier period of his life, when Lysias treated his art more from a theoretical point of view, and they must therefore be regarded as rhetorical exercises. But from the commencement of the speech against Eratosthenes, we must conclude that his real career as a writer of orations began about B.C. 403. Among the lost works of Lysias we may mention a manual of rhetoric (τέχνη ῥητορική), probably one of his early productions, which, however, is lost.

How highly the orations of Lysias were valued in antiquity may be inferred from the great number of persons that wrote commentaries upon them. All the works, however, of these critics have perished. The only

[1] *Ap. Cic. Brut.*, 12. [2] *Plut., l. c.; Phot., Cod.*, p. 490, *A*. [3] *Plut., Phot., ll. cc.*
[4] *Dionys., Lys.*, 12; *Plut.*, p. 836. [5] *Dionys., Lys.*, 17; *Plut.*, p. 836.

criticism of any importance upon Lysias that has come down to us is that of Dionysius of Halicarnassus, in his Περὶ τῶν ἀρχαίων ῥητόρων ὑπομνηματισμοί, the τῶν ἀρχαίων κρίσις, and in his account of Lysias; to which we may add the remarks of Photius. According to the judgment of Dionysius, and the accidental remarks of others, which are borne out by a careful examination of the orations still extant, the diction of Lysias is perfectly pure, and may be looked upon as the best canon of the Attic idiom. His language is natural and simple, but, at the same time, noble and dignified;[1] it is always clear and lucid; the copiousness of his style does not injure its precision, nor can his rhetorical embellishments be considered as impairing the charming simplicity of his manner of expression.[2] His delineations of character are always striking and true to life. But what characterizes his orations above those of all other ancients, is the indescribable gracefulness and elegance which pervade all of them, without in the least impairing their power and energy; and this gracefulness was considered so peculiar a feature in all the productions of Lysias, that Dionysius thought it a fit criterion by which the genuine works of this orator might be distinguished from the spurious productions which went by his name.[3] The manner in which Lysias treats his subjects is equally deserving of high praise. It is therefore no matter of surprise to hear that, among the many orations he wrote for others, two only are said to have been unsuccessful.[4]

The extant orations of Lysias are contained in the collections of the Greek orators mentioned at the close of the article on Antiphon. Among the separate editions we may mention those of Taylor, London, 1739, 4to, with a full critical apparatus, and the emendations of Markland; of Auger, Paris, 1783, 4to, and 8vo, 2 vols.; of Bremi, in Jacobs' and Rost's *Biblioth. Græc.*, Gotha, 1826 ("*Lysiæ et Æschinis Orationes Selectæ*"); of Baiter and Sauppe, Zürich, 1838; of Foertsch, Leipzig, 1829; of Franz, Münich, 1831; and the *Select Orations* of Rauchenstein, in Haupt and Sauppe's Collection, Leipzig, 1850. The following modern works in relation to Lysias deserve also to be mentioned here: Franz, *Dissertatio de Lysia Oratore Attico Græce scripta*, Nurimb., 1828, 8vo; Hoelscher, *De Lysiæ oratoris vita et dictione*, Berlin, 1836, 8vo; and Westermann, *Gesch. der Griech. Beredtsamkeit*, § 46, *seqq.*; *Beilage*, iii., p. 278, *seqq.*

4. Isocrătes (Ἰσοκράτης)[5] was born at Athens in B.C. 436. His father, Theodorus, was a man of considerable wealth, and had a manufactory of flutes or musical instruments, for which the son was often ridiculed by the comic poets of the time; but the father made a good use of his property, in procuring for the young Isocrates the best education that could be obtained. The most celebrated sophists are mentioned among his teachers, such as Tisias, Gorgias, and Prodicus.[6] Socrates also is named among his instructors. Isocrates was naturally timid, and of a weakly constitution, for which reasons he abstained from taking any direct part in the political affairs of his country, and resolved to contribute toward the development of eloquence by teaching and writing, and thus to guide others in the path for which his own constitution unfitted him. According, however, to some accounts, he devoted himself to the teaching of

1 *Dionys.*, *Lys.*, 2, 3; *Cic.*, *Brut.*, 82; *Quintil.*, xii., 10, 21.
2 *Dionys.*, *Lys.*, 4, *seqq.*
3 *Id. ib.*, 10, *seqq.*
4 *Plut.*, *Vit. Dec. Orat.*, p. 836.
5 *Smith*, *Dict. Biogr.*, *s. v.*
6 *Dionys.*, *Isocrat.*, 1; *Plut.*, *Vit. Dec. Orat.*, p. 836.

rhetoric for the purpose of ameliorating his circumstances, since he had lost his paternal inheritance in the war against the Lacedæmonians.[1]

Isocrates first established a school of rhetoric in the island of Chios, but his success does not appear to have been very great, for he is said to have had only nine pupils there. He is stated, however, to have exerted himself in another direction, and to have regulated the political constitution of Chios after the model of that of Athens. After this he returned to Athens, and there opened a school of rhetoric. He met now with the greatest success, and the number of his pupils soon increased to 100, every one of whom paid him 1000 drachmas. In addition to this he realized a large income by writing orations. Thus Plutarch[2] relates that Nicocles, king of Cyprus, gave Isocrates twenty talents for the oration πρὸς Νικοκλέα. The orations of Isocrates were either sent thus to the persons to whom they were addressed, for their private perusal, or they were intrusted to others to deliver in public. He is said to have delivered only one himself. In this manner he gradually acquired a considerable property, and he was several times called upon to undertake the expensive trierarchy. This happened first in B.C. 355, but, being ill, he excused himself through his son Aphareus. In B.C. 352 he was called upon again, and, in order to silence the calumnies of his enemies, he performed it in the most splendid manner. The oration περὶ ἀντιδόσεως πρὸς Λυσίμαχον refers to that event, though it was written after it. This is said by Plutarch to have been the only oration that he ever delivered.

Isocrates has the great merit of being the first who clearly saw the great value and objects of oratory in its practical application to public life and the affairs of the state. At the same time, he endeavored to base public oratory upon sound moral principles, and thus to rescue it from the influence of the Sophists, who used and abused it for any and every purpose; for Isocrates, although educated by the most eminent sophists, was the avowed enemy of all sophistry. He was, however, not altogether free from their influence; and what is most conspicuous in his political discourses is the absence of all practical knowledge of real political life, so that his fine theories, though they were unquestionably well meant, bear a strong resemblance to the visions of an enthusiast. The influence which he exercised on his country by his oratory must have been limited, since his exertions were confined to his school, but through his school he had the greatest possible influence upon the development of public oratory; for the most eminent statesmen, philosophers, orators, and historians of the time were trained in it, and afterward developed, each in his particular way, the principles they had imbibed therein. No ancient rhetorician had so many disciples that afterward shed lustre on their country as Isocrates. Hence Cicero[3] beautifully compares his school to the Trojan horse, from which so many leaders (*principes*) came forth.

The great esteem in which the orations of Isocrates were held by the ancient grammarians is attested by the numerous commentaries that were written upon them. All these commentaries, however, are now

---

1 *Plut.*, *l. c.*, p. 837; *Isocrat.*, *De Permut.*, § 172. 2 *l. c.*, p. 838. 3 *De Orat.*, ii., 22.

lost, with the exception of the criticism by Dionysius of Halicarnassus. The language of Isocrates is the most refined Attic, and thus forms a great contrast to the pure and natural simplicity of Lysias, as well as the sublime power of Demosthenes. His artificial style is more elegant than graceful, and more ostentatious than pleasing; the carefully-rounded periods, the frequent application of figurative expressions, are features which remind us of the Sophists; and although his sentences flow very melodiously, yet they become wearisome and monotonous by the perpetual recurrence of the same over-refined periods, which are not relieved by being interspersed with shorter and easier sentences. In saying this, however, we must remember that Isocrates wrote his orations to be read, and not with a view to their recitation before the public. The immense care which he bestowed on the composition of his orations, and the time he spent in working them out and polishing them, may be inferred from the statement that he was engaged for a period of ten, and, according to others, of fifteen years, upon his Panegyric oration.[1] It is owing to this very care and labor that, in the arrangement and treatment of his subject, Isocrates is far superior to Lysias and other orators of the time, and that the number of orations which he wrote is comparatively small.

The politics of Isocrates were conciliatory. He was a friend of peace: he repeatedly exhorted the Greeks to concord among themselves, and to turn their arms against their common enemy, the Persians. He addressed Philip of Macedon in a similar strain after his peace with Athens, B.C. 346, exhorting him to reconcile the states of Greece, and to unite them against Persia. Though no violent partisan, he proved, however, a warm-hearted patriot; for, on receiving the news of the battle of Chæronea, he refused to take food for several days, and thus closed his long and honorable career at the age of ninety-eight, B.C. 338.

There were in antiquity sixty orations which went by the name of Isocrates, but Cæcilius, a rhetorician of the time of Augustus, recognized only twenty-eight of them as genuine,[2] and of these only twenty-one have come down to us. Eight of them were written for judicial purposes in civil cases, and intended to serve as models for this species of oratory. All the others are political discourses, or show-speeches, intended to be read by a large public; they are particularly characterized by the ethical element, on which his political views are based. Of these, the most remarkable is the discourse entitled Πανηγυρικός, *Panegyricus*, or "Panegyrical Oration," that is, a discourse intended to be pronounced before the assembled people. It was published (though not with a view of being delivered) about B.C. 379, in the time of the Lacedæmonian ascendency, and in it he exhorts the Lacedæmonians and Athenians to vie with each other in a noble emulation, and to unite their forces in an expedition against Asia. He descants eloquently on the merits and glories of the Athenian commonwealth, on the services it had rendered to Greece, and on its high intellectual cultivation; while he defends it from the charges, urged by its enemies, of tyranny by sea, and of oppression toward its colonies. In the Ἀρεοπαγιτικός, *Areopagiticus*, one of the best

[1] *Quintil.*, x., 4, 4.

[2] *Plut.*, *l. c.*, p. 838; *Phot.*, *Cod.*, 260.

of his discourses, he declares that he sees no safety for Athens save in the restoration of that democracy which Solon had founded, and Clisthenes had revived.

Besides these entire orations, we have the titles and fragments of twenty-seven other orations, which are referred to under the name of Isocrates. There also exist under his name ten letters, which were written to friends on political questions of the time; one of them, however (the tenth), is in all probability spurious. A scientific manual of rhetoric (τέχνη ῥητορική), which Isocrates wrote, is lost, with the exception of a few fragments, so that we are unable to form any definite idea of his merits in this respect.

The orations of Isocrates are printed in the various collections of the Greek orators already mentioned at the close of the article on Antiphon. Of the separate editions we may mention those of H. Wolf, Basle, 1553, 8vo, and with Wolf's notes and emendations, Basle, 1570, fol.; of Auger, Paris, 1782, 3 vols. 8vo, which is not what it might have been, considering the MSS. he had at his disposal; of Lange, Halle, 1803, 8vo; of Coraes, Paris, 1807, 2 vols. 8vo; of Baiter and Sauppe, Zürich, 1839, 8vo; and of Baiter, in Didot's *Bibliotheca Græca*, Paris, 1846, 8vo. There are also many good editions either of the orations separately, or else of particular orations, among which we may name the *Select Orations*, by Bremi, Gotha, 1831, part i.; the *Panegyricus*, with the notes of Morus, by Spohn, Leipzig, 1817, 2d edition by Baiter, Lips., 1831; by Pinzger, Leipzig, 1825, and by Dindorf, 1826; the *Areopagiticus*, by Benseler, Leipzig, 1832; the *Panegyricus* and *Areopagiticus*, by Rauchenstein, Leipzig, 1849, 8vo, forming part of Haupt and Sauppe's collection; the *Euagoræ Encomium*, by Leloup, Mayence, 1828; and the oration περὶ ἀντιδόσεως, by Orelli, Zürich, 1814.

A useful *Index Græcitatis* was published by Mitchell, Oxford, 1827, 8vo. The following works will also be found worthy of attention: Westermann, *Gesch. der Griech. Beredtsamkeit*, § 48, *seq.*; *Beilage*, iv., p. 288, *seqq.*; Leloup, *Commentatio de Isocrate*, Bonn, 1823, 8vo; and Pfund, *De Isocratis Vita et Scriptis*, Berlin, 1833.

5. ISÆUS (Ἰσαῖος) was a native of Chalcis, or, as some say, of Athens, probably only because he came to the latter city at an early age, and spent the greater part of his life there. The time of his birth and death is unknown, but all accounts agree in the statement that he flourished (ἤκμασε) during the period between the Peloponnesian war and the accession of Philip of Macedonia, so that he lived between B.C. 420 and 348.[1] He was instructed in oratory by Lysias and Isocrates.[2] He was afterward engaged in writing judicial orations for others, and established a rhetorical school at Athens, in which Demosthenes is said to have been one of his pupils. Suidas states that Isæus instructed him gratis, whereas Plutarch relates that he received 10,000 drachmas;[3] and it is further said that Isæus wrote for Demosthenes the speeches against his guardians, or, at least, assisted him in the composition. All particulars about his life are unknown, and were so even in the time of Dionysius, since Hermippus, who had written an account of the disciples of Isocrates, did not mention Isæus at all.

In antiquity there were sixty-four orations which bore the name of Isæus, but fifty only were recognized as genuine by the ancient critics.[4] Of these only eleven have come down to us; but we possess fragments and the titles of fifty-six speeches ascribed to him. The eleven extant are

[1] *Dionys.*, *Isæus*, 1; *Plut.*, *Vit. Dec. Orat.*, p. 839.
[2] *Phot.*, *Cod.*, 263.
[3] *Plut.*, *De Glor. Ath.*, p. 350, C.
[4] *Id.*, *Vit. Dec. Orat.*, *l. c.*

all on subjects connected with disputed inheritances; and Isæus appears to have been particularly well acquainted with the laws relating to inheritance (περὶ κλήρου). Ten of these orations have been known ever since the revival of letters, and were printed in the collections of the Greek orators; but the eleventh, περὶ τοῦ Μενεκλέους κλήρου, was first published from a Florentine MS., by Tyrwhitt, London, 1785, 8vo; and afterward in the *Götting. Biblioth. für alte Lit. und Kunst*, for 1788, part iii., and by Orelli, Zürich, 1814, 8vo. In 1815, Mai discovered the greater part of the oration of Isæus, περὶ τοῦ Κλεωνύμου κλήρου, which he published at Milan, 1815, fol., and reprinted in his *Classic. Auctor. e Cod. Vatican.*, vol. iv., p. 280, *seqq.*

Isæus wrote also on rhetorical subjects, such as a work entitled ἴδιαι τέχναι, which, however, is lost.[1] Though his orations were placed in the Alexandrean canon, still we do not hear of any of the grammarians having written commentaries upon them except Didymus. But we still possess the criticism upon Isæus written by Dionysius of Halicarnassus; and, by a comparison of the orations still extant with the opinions of Dionysius, we come to the following conclusion. The oratory of Isæus resembles in many points that of his teacher Lysias; the style of both is pure, clear, and concise. But while Lysias is, at the same time, simple and graceful, Isæus evidently strives to attain a higher degree of polish and refinement, without, however, in the least injuring the powerful and impressive character of his oratory. The same spirit is visible in the manner in which he handles his subjects, especially in their skillful division, and in the artful manner in which he interweaves his arguments with various parts of the exposition, whereby his orations become like a painting in which light and shade are distributed with a distinct view to produce certain effects. It was mainly owing to this mode of management that he was envied and censured by his contemporaries, as if he had tried to deceive and mislead his hearers. He was one of the first who turned their attention to a scientific cultivation of political oratory; but excellence in this department of the art was not attained till the time of Demosthenes.[2]

The orations of Isæus are contained in the collections of the Greek orators mentioned at the close of the article on Antiphon. A separate edition, with Reiske's and Taylor's notes, appeared at Leipzig, 1773, 8vo, and another by Schäfer, Leipzig, 1822, 8vo. The best separate edition, however, is that by Schömann, Greifswald, 1831, 8vo, with critical notes and a good commentary. There is an English translation of the orations of Isæus by Sir William Jones, London, 1794, 4to, with prefatory discourse, notes critical and historical, and a commentary. This translation will give an English reader a sufficient notion of the orator, but it is somewhat deficient in critical accuracy, and also wanting in force. For farther information concerning Isæus, the student may consult Westermann, *Gesch. der Griech. Beredts.*, § 51, *Beilage*, v., p. 293, *seqq.*, and Liebmann, *De Isæi Vita et Scriptis*, Halle, 1831, 4to.

6. ÆSCHĬNES (Αἰσχίνης)[3] was the son of Atrometus and Glaucothea, and was born B.C. 389. According to Demosthenes, his political antagonist, and who was no doubt in this guilty of exaggeration, his parents were of disreputable character, and not even citizens of Athens. Æs-

[1] *Plut., Vit. Dec. Orat., l. c.* [2] *Smith, Dict. Biogr., s. v.* [3] *Id. ib.*

chines himself, on the other hand, says that his father was descended from an honorable family, and lost his property during the Peloponnesian war. Æschines had two brothers, one of whom, Philochares, was older than himself, and the other, Aphobetus, was the youngest of the three. Philochares was at one time one of the ten Athenian generals, an office which was conferred upon him for three successive years; Aphobetus followed the calling of a scribe, but had once been sent on an embassy to the King of Persia, and was afterward connected with the administration of the public revenue of Athens.[1] All these things seem to contain strong evidence that the family of Æschines, though poor, must have been of some respectability.

In his youth Æschines appears to have assisted his father, who kept a small school; he next acted as secretary to Antiphon, and afterward to Eubulus, a man of great influence with the democratical party, with whom he formed an intimate friendship, and to whose political principles he remained faithful to the end of his life. After leaving the service of Eubulus, he tried his fortune as an actor, for which he was provided by nature with a strong and sonorous voice. He acted the parts of a *τριταγωνιστής*, but was unsuccessful, and, on one occasion, when he was performing in the character of Œnomaus, he was hissed off the stage.[2] After this he left the stage and engaged in military services, in which, according to his own account,[3] he gained great distinction.[4] After sharing in several less important engagements in other parts of Greece, he distinguished himself, in B.C. 362, in the battle of Mantinea. Subsequently, in B.C. 358, he also took part in the expedition of the Athenians against Eubœa, and fought in the battle of Tamynæ, and on this occasion he gained such laurels that he was praised by the generals on the spot, and, after the victory was gained, was sent to carry the news of it to Athens. The Athenians honored him with a crown. Two years before this campaign, the last in which he took part, Æschines had come forward at Athens as a public speaker,[5] and the military fame which he had now acquired established his reputation. His former occupation as a scribe to Antiphon and Eubulus had made him acquainted with the laws and constitution of Athens, while his acting on the stage had been a useful preparation for public speaking.

During the first period of his public career, Æschines was, like all other Athenians, zealously engaged in directing the attention of his fellow-citizens to the growing power of Philip, and exhorted them to check it in its growth. In B.C. 347, he was sent, along with Demosthenes, as one of the ten ambassadors to negotiate a peace with Philip. From this time he appears as the friend of the Macedonian party, and as the opponent of Demosthenes. Shortly afterward, he formed one of the second embassy sent to Philip to receive that monarch's oath to the treaty which had been concluded with the Athenians; but, as the delay of the ambassadors in obtaining the ratification had been favorable to the interests of Philip, Æschines, on his return to Athens, was accused by Timarchus. He evaded the danger, however, by bringing forward a counter-accusation

[1] *Æsch.*, *De fals. Leg.*, p. 48. [2] *Dem.*, *De Coron.*, p. 288. [3] *De fals. Leg.*, p. 50.
[4] Compare *Demosth.*, *De fals. Leg.*, p. 375. [5] *Æsch.*, *Epist.*, 12.

against Timarchus, and by showing that the moral character of his accuser was such that he had no right to speak before the people. The speech in which Æschines attacked Timarchus is still extant. Timarchus was condemned, and Æschines gained a brilliant triumph. As we know little more of the matter than what is contained in the two speeches of Æschines and his accuser, as they have come down to us, we have not the means of forming a proper judgment of the innocence or guilt of Æschines. His simple, clear, and persuasive statement, however, of his own case proves his great abilities ; and, contrasted with the somewhat confused speech of his accuser, leaves a favorable impression of the justice of his defence.

Æschines and Demosthenes at length were at the head of the two parties, into which not only Athens, but all Greece, was divided, and their political enmity created and nourished personal hatred. This enmity came to a head in B.C. 343, when Demosthenes charged Æschines with having been bribed, and having betrayed the interests of his country during the second embassy to Philip. This charge of Demosthenes (*περὶ παραπρεσβείας*) was not spoken, but published as a memorial, and Æschines answered it in a similar memorial on the embassy, which was likewise published, and in the composition of which he is said to have been assisted by his friend Eubulus.[1] The result of these mutual attacks is unknown, but there is no doubt that a severe shock was given to the popularity of Æschines. At the time he wrote his memorial we gain a glimpse into his private life. Some years before that occurrence he had married a daughter of Philodemus, a man of high respectability in his tribe of Pæania, and in B.C. 343 he was father of three little children.[2]

The last great event in the public life of Æschines was his prosecution of Ctesiphon. It seems that after the battle of Chæronea, in B.C. 338, the enemies of Demosthenes made the misfortune of that day a handle for attacking him ; but, notwithstanding the bribes which Æschines had received from Antipater for this purpose, the pure and unstained patriotism of Demosthenes was so generally recognized, that he received the honorable charge of delivering the funeral oration over those who had fallen at Chæronea. Acting upon this same idea, therefore, Ctesiphon proposed that Demosthenes should be rewarded for the services he had done to his country with a golden crown in the theatre, at the great Dionysia. Æschines availed himself of the illegal form in which this reward was proposed to be given to bring a charge against Ctesiphon on that ground. But he did not prosecute the matter till eight years later, that is, in B.C. 330, when, after the death of Philip, and the victories of Alexander, political affairs had assumed a different aspect in Greece. After having commenced the prosecution against Ctesiphon, he is said to have gone for some time to Macedonia. What induced him to drop the prosecution of Ctesiphon, and to take it up again eight years afterward, are questions which can only be answered by conjectures. The speech in which he accused Ctesiphon in B.C. 330, and which is still extant, is so skillfully managed, that, if he had succeeded, he would have totally destroyed all

[1] *Demosth., De fals. Leg.*, p. 337.

[2] *Æsch., De fals. Leg.*, p. 52.

the political influence and authority of Demosthenes. The latter answered Æschines in his celebrated oration "on the crown" (περὶ στεφάνου). Æschines lost his cause, and not having obtained one fifth part of the votes of the judges, he was compelled to leave Athens, being unable to pay the penalty in that case required by the law.

Æschines went to Asia Minor. The statement of Plutarch that Demosthenes provided him with the means of accomplishing his journey is surely a fable. He spent several years in Ionia and Caria, occupying himself with teaching rhetoric, and anxiously waiting for the return of Alexander to Europe. When, in B.C. 324, the report of the death of Alexander reached him, he left Asia and went to Rhodes, where he established a school of eloquence, which subsequently became very celebrated, and occupies a middle position between the grave manliness of the Attic orators and the effeminate luxuriance of the so-called Asiatic school of eloquence. On one occasion, he read to his audience in Rhodes his speech against Ctesiphon, and when some of his hearers expressed their astonishment at his having been defeated, notwithstanding his brilliant oration, he replied, "You would not have been surprised if you had heard Demosthenes." The anecdote is told somewhat differently by Cicero,[1] and in a manner better suited to the purpose to which he applies it.

The conduct of Æschines has been censured by the writers of all ages, and for this many reasons may be mentioned. In the first place, and above all, it was his misfortune to be constantly brought into juxtaposition or opposition to the spotless glory of Demosthenes, and this must have made him appear more guilty in the eyes of those who saw through his actions, while in later times the contrast between the greatest orators of the day was frequently made the theme of rhetorical declamation, in which one of the two was praised or blamed at the cost of the other, and less with regard to truth than to effect. Respecting the last period of his life we scarcely possess any other source of information than the accounts of late sophists, and declamations. Another point to be considered, in forming a just estimate of the character of Æschines, is, that he had no advantages of education, and that he owed his greatness to no one but himself. His occupations during the early part of his life were such as necessarily engendered in him the low desire of gain and wealth; and had he overcome these passions, he would perhaps have been nearly equal to Demosthenes. No ancient writer except Demosthenes charges him with having received bribes from the Macedonians for the purpose of betraying his country; still, however, coming as it does from so true a patriot, the charge can hardly have been an unfounded one, though perhaps in some degree exaggerated by the violence of party. It is impossible to arrive at the complete truth from the perplexing history of a period when the principal authorities are two political rivals, whose statements about the same matter are often in direct contradiction to one another.[2]

But if the integrity of Æschines is suspected, his great abilities both as a popular leader and an orator are undisputed. He was the rival, and,

[1] *De Orat.*, iii., 56. Compare *Plin.*, *H. N.*, vii., 30; *Quintil.*, xi., 3, 6. [2] *Smith*, *l. c.*

in the judgment of Cicero and Quintilian, all but the equal of Demosthenes. In the lucid arrangement of his matter, in the ease and clearness of his narrative, he has never been surpassed; if he falls below Demosthenes in any quality of an orator, it is in powerful invective and vehement passion. The facility and felicity of his diction, the boldness and the vigor of his descriptions, carry away the reader now, as they must have carried away his audience in former times.

Æschines published only three of his numerous orations, namely, the one against Timarchus, that on the embassy, and the oration against Ctesiphon. The ancients, as Photius remarks, designated these three orations as the *Graces*. Photius mentions also nine letters of Æschines, which the ancients in like manner called the *Muses*. At present, besides the three orations, we possess twelve letters ascribed to Æschines, which, however, in all probability, are not more genuine than the so-called epistles of Phalaris, and are undoubtedly the work of late sophists.

The orations and letters are given in all the collections of the Greek orators mentioned at the end of the article on Antiphon. Of separate editions we may mention the following: that by Wolf, Basle, 1572, fol.; by Taylor, Cambridge, 1748–57, 3 vols. 4to; by Schäfer, Leipzig, 1817, 8vo; by Bremi, Zürich, 1823–4, 2 vols. 8vo; by W. Dindorf, Leipzig, 1824, 8vo; by Bremi, *Lysiæ et Æschinis Orationes Selectæ*, in Jacobs' and Rost's *Bibliotheca Græca*, Gotha, 1826, 8vo; by Baiter and Sauppe, Zürich, 1840, 16mo; by Wunderlich (the oration against Ctesiphon), Göttingen, 1810, 8vo; by Franke (the oration against Timarchus), Cassel, 1839, 8vo.

7. LYCURGUS (Λυκοῦργος), namesake of the celebrated Spartan lawgiver, was born at Athens about B.C. 396, and was the son of Lycophron, who belonged to the noble family of the Eteobutadæ.[1] In early life he devoted himself to the study of philosophy in the school of Plato, but afterward became one of the disciples of Isocrates, and entered upon public life at a comparatively early age. He was appointed three successive times to the office of *ταμίας τῆς κοινῆς προσόδου*, or manager of the public revenue, and held his office each time for five years, beginning with B.C. 337. The conscientiousness with which he discharged the duties of this station enabled him to raise the public revenue to the sum of 1200 talents This, as well as the unwearied activity with which he labored, for increasing both the security and splendor of the city of Athens, gained for him the universal confidence of the people to such a degree, that when Alexander the Great demanded, among the other opponents of the Macedonian interest, the surrender of Lycurgus also, who had, in conjunction with Demosthenes, exerted himself against the intrigues of Macedonia even as early as the reign of Philip, the people of Athens clung to him, and boldly refused to deliver him up.[2] He was farther intrusted with the superintendence (*φυλακή*) of the city, and the keeping of public discipline; and the severity with which he watched over the conduct of the citizens became almost proverbial.[3]

Lycurgus had a noble taste for every thing that was beautiful and grand, as he showed by the buildings he erected or completed, both for the use of the citizens and the ornament of the city. His integrity was

[1] *Plut.*, *Vit. Dec. Orat.*, p. 841.
[2] *Phot.*, *Cod.*, 268, p. 496, *seqq.*
[3] *Cic. ad Att.*, i., 13; *Plut.*, *Flamin.*, 12.

so great that even private persons deposited with him large sums of money, which they wished to be kept in safety. He was also the author of several legislative enactments, of which he enforced the strictest observance. One of his laws forbade women to ride in chariots at the celebration of the mysteries; and when his own wife transgressed this law she was fined.[1] Another ordained that bronze statues should be erected to Æschylus, Sophocles, and Euripides, and that copies of their tragedies should be made and preserved in the public archives. The lives of the ten orators ascribed to Plutarch[2] are full of anecdotes and characteristic features of Lycurgus, from which we must infer that he was one of the noblest specimens of old Attic virtue, and a worthy contemporary of Demosthenes. He often appeared as a successful accuser in the Athenian courts, but he himself was as often accused by others, though he always, and even in the last days of his life, succeeded in silencing his enemies. He died while holding the office of ἐπιστατής of the theatre of Bacchus, in B.C. 323. A fragment of an inscription containing an account which he rendered to the state of his administration of the finances is still extant. According to Böckh, Lycurgus was the only statesman of antiquity who had a real knowledge of the management of finance. At his death he left behind him three sons. Among the honors paid his memory it may be mentioned that he received a public funeral, and that a bronze statue was subsequently erected to him in the Ceramicus.

Plutarch[3] and Photius[4] mention fifteen orations of Lycurgus as extant, but we know the titles of at least twenty.[5] With the exception, however, of one entire oration against Leocrates, and some fragments of others, all the rest are lost, so that our knowledge of his skill and style as an orator is very incomplete. Dionysius and other ancient critics draw particular attention to the ethical tendency of his orations, but they censure the harshness of his metaphors, the inaccuracy in the arrangement of his subject, and his frequent digressions. His style is noble and grand, but neither elegant nor pleasing.[6] The extant oration (κατὰ Λεωκράτους) is an accusation of Leocrates, an Athenian citizen, for abandoning Athens after the battle of Chæronea, and settling in another Grecian state. It was delivered in B.C. 330.

The oration against Leocrates is printed in the various collections of the Attic orators mentioned at the close of the article on Antiphon. Among the separate editions the following are most worthy of notice: that of Taylor, Cambridge, 1743, 8vo, printed together with the speech of Demosthenes against Midias; of Heinrich, Bonn, 1821, 8vo; of Pinzger, Leipzig, 1824, 8vo, with a learned introduction, notes, and a German translation; of Becker, Magdeburg, 1821, 8vo; of Baiter and Sauppe, Zürich, 1834, 8vo; and of Mätzner, Berlin, 1836, 8vo. The fragments of the other orations are collected by Kiessling, *Lycurgi Deperd. Orat. Fragmenta*, Halle, 1847. The following works may be consulted in relation to Lycurgus: Blume, *Narratio de Lycurgo Oratore*, Potsdam, 1834, 4to; Nissen, *De Lycurgi Oratoris vita et rebus gestis dissertatio*, Kiel, 1833, 8vo.

8. Demosthĕnes (Δημοσθένης), the greatest of the Greek orators, was the son of Demosthenes, and born in the Attic demus of Pæania. His

[1] *Ælian, V. H.*, xiii., 24. [2] p. 842, *seqq.* [3] *Plut.*, *l. c.*, p. 843.
[4] *Phot.*, *l. c.*, p. 496, B. [5] *Westermann, Gesch. d. Griech. Beredts.*, Beilage, vi., p. 296.
[6] *Dionys.*, *Vet. Script. cens.*, v., 3.

birth-year, according to the most commonly received opinion, was B.C. 385. His father carried on the trade of sword-manufacturer (μαχαιροποιός); his mother was Cleobule, the daughter of Gylon. This Gylon, who had been governor of Nymphæum, an Athenian settlement in the Tauric Chersonesus, betrayed it to the Scythians, and, afterward taking refuge with their chief, married a Scythian woman, who was the maternal grandmother of Demosthenes. This impurity of blood and the misconduct of Gylon, his maternal grandfather, formed a theme for the taunts of Æschines. There is a well-known allusion in Juvenal[1] to the trade of Demosthenes the elder, and hence the opinion so commonly entertained that the father of the orator was a blacksmith. The point of the satirist, however, is somewhat if not altogether lost, when we remember that Plutarch[2] applies to the father a term (καλοκἀγαθός) which expresses all that can be said to the advantage of a man, and also that he had two manufactories (ἐργαστήρια), containing, on the whole, more than fifty slaves.

Demosthenes the elder died when his son was seven years old, leaving him and a sister, younger than himself, to the care of three guardians, Aphobus and Demophon, his first cousins, and Therippides, a friend. The property left by him amounted to fifteen talents. The guardians, however, as we learn from Demosthenes himself, disregarded all his father's injunctions, and, while they neglected to improve the property of which they were trustees, embezzled nearly the whole of it. Plutarch[3] states that they also deprived Demosthenes of proper masters. He himself, however, in a passage where it is his object to magnify all that concerns his own history, boasts of the fitting education which he had received. He is said to have been instructed in philosophy by Plato;[4] but it is very doubtful whether this statement be correct. It may be that Demosthenes knew and esteemed Plato, but this probably is all, and to make him, as some critics have done, a perfect Platonist, is certainly going too far. According to some accounts, moreover, he was instructed in oratory by Isocrates;[5] but this was a disputed point with the ancients themselves, some of whom stated that he was not personally instructed by Isocrates, but only that he studied the τέχνη ῥητορική which Isocrates had written.[6] To this may be added, that Demosthenes himself speaks with contempt of the rhetorical school of Isocrates.[7] The account that Demosthenes was instructed in oratory by Isæus[8] has much more probability; for at that time Isæus was the most eminent orator in matters connected with the laws of inheritance, the very thing that Demosthenes needed. This account is farther supported by the fact that the earliest orations of Demosthenes, namely, those against Aphobus and Onetor, bear so strong a resemblance to those of Isæus, that the ancients themselves believed them to have been composed by Isæus for Demosthenes, or that the latter had written them under the guidance of the former.[9]

---

1 *Sat.*, x., 130. 2 *Plut.*, *Dem.*, 4. 3 *Plut.*, *l. c.*
4 *Plut.*, *Vit. Dec. Orat.*, p. 844; *Dem.*, 5. 5 *Plut.*, *l. c.*
6 *Plut.*, *Vit. Dec. Orat.*, p. 837; *Dem.*, 5. 7 *Dem. c. Lacrin.*, p. 928, 937.
8 *Plut.*, *Dem.*, 5; *Vit. Dec. Orat.*, p. 844.
9 *Plut.*, *Vit. Dec. Orat.*, p. 839; *Liban.*, *Vit. Dem.*, 3.

At the age of eighteen, the termination of his minority, Demosthenes called upon his guardians to render him an account of their administration of his property, but by intrigues they contrived to defer the business for two years. At length, in B.C. 364, Demosthenes accused Aphobus before the archon, and obtained a verdict in his favor.[1] Aphobus was condemned to pay ten talents, Demosthenes having estimated his losses at thirty talents (inclusive of ten years' interest), and having sued him for one third part. He did not, however, succeed in obtaining more than a small part of the sum thus awarded to him. This took place, as already intimated, when Demosthenes was in his twentieth year, or, as he says of himself, when he was quite a boy; but the extant orations against his guardians are evidently not the work of a youth of that age, and, as we have before remarked, were either composed by Isæus or under his direction. Emboldened by his success, Demosthenes ventured to come forward as a speaker in the public assembly. His first effort, however, was a failure, and he encountered the ridicule of his hearers; but he was encouraged to persevere by the actor Satyrus, who gave him instruction in action and declamation; and his efforts were finally crowned with the most brilliant success.

The physical disadvantages under which Demosthenes labored are well known, and the manner in which he surmounted them is often quoted as an example to encourage others to persevere. It should be observed, however, that the authority for some of these stories is but small, and that they rest on the assertions of writers of late date. He was naturally of a weak constitution; he had a feeble voice, an indistinct articulation, and a shortness of breath. From his defective utterance, his inability to pronounce the letter ρ, and his constant stammering, he derived, in fact, the nickname of βάτταλος (or βάταλος), the delicate youth or stammerer. It was only owing to the most unwearied and persevering exertions that he succeeded in overcoming and removing the obstacles which nature had thus placed in his way; and yet the means which he is said to have taken to remedy these defects look very like the inventions of some writer of the rhetorical school, though Plutarch quotes Demetrius Phalereus as saying that he had from the orator's own lips that the account was correct. Among these means we hear of his speaking with pebbles in his mouth, in order to cure himself of stammering; of repeating verses of the poets as he ran up hill, in order to strengthen his voice; of declaiming on the sea-shore, to accustom himself to the noise and confusion of the popular assembly; of his living for months in a cave under ground, engaged in constantly writing out the orations contained in the history of Thucydides, in order to form a standard for his own style. And yet, though these tales are not worthy of much credit, they, nevertheless, attest the common tradition of antiquity respecting the great efforts made by Demosthenes to attain to excellence as an orator.

It was about B.C. 355 that Demosthenes began to obtain reputation as a speaker in the public assembly. It was in this year that he delivered the oration against Leptines, and from this time we have a series of

[1] *Dem. c. Aphob.*, i., p. 828.

his speeches on public affairs. His eloquence soon gained him the favor of the people; and the influence which he acquired he employed for the good of his country, and not for his own aggrandizement. He clearly saw that Philip had resolved to subjugate Greece, and he therefore devoted all his powers to resist the aggressions of the Macedonian monarch. For fourteen years he continued the struggle against Philip, and neither threats nor bribes could turn him from his purpose. It is true he failed; but the failure must not be regarded as his fault. The struggle was brought to a close by the battle of Chæronea, which crushed the independence of Greece. Demosthenes was present in the conflict, and fled like thousands of others. His enemies reproached him with his flight, and upbraided him as the cause of the misfortunes of his country; but the Athenians judged better of his conduct, requested him to deliver the funeral oration upon those who had fallen at Chæronea, and even celebrated the funeral feast in his house. At this time many accusations were brought against him by the adherents of the Macedonian party, one of the most formidable of which was the attack made by Æschines upon Ctesiphon, but which was in reality aimed at Demosthenes himself. The nature and the issue of this prosecution have already been mentioned in the article on Æschines.

Meantime important events had taken place in Greece. The death of Philip, in B.C. 336, roused the hopes of the patriots, and Demosthenes, though he had lost his daughter only seven days before, was the first to proclaim the joyful tidings of the king's death, and to call upon the Greeks to unite their strength against Macedonia. But Alexander's energy, and the frightful vengeance which he took upon Thebes, compelled Athens to submit and sue for peace. Alexander demanded the surrender of Demosthenes and the other leaders of the popular party, and with difficulty allowed them to remain at Athens. During the life of Alexander, Athens made no open attempt to throw off the Macedonian supremacy. But in B.C. 325, Harpalus having fled from Babylon with the treasure intrusted to his care by Alexander, came to Athens, the protection of which he purchased by distributing his gold among the most influential demagogues. The reception of such an open rebel was viewed as an act of hostility against Macedonia itself; and accordingly Antipater called upon the Athenians to deliver up the offender, and to bring to trial those who had accepted his bribes. Demosthenes was one of those who were suspected of having received money from Harpalus. The accounts of his conduct during the presence of Harpalus at Athens are so confused that it is almost impossible to arrive at any certain conclusion respecting his guilt or his innocence. Theopompus,[1] and Dinarchus, in his oration against Demosthenes, state that he did accept the bribes of Harpalus; but Pausanias[2] expressly acquits him of the crime. The authority of his accusers, however, is very questionable; for, in the first place, they do not agree in the detail of their statements, and, secondly, if we consider the conduct of Demosthenes throughout the disputes about Harpalus, if we remember that he opposed the reception of the rebel, and that he volun-

[1] *Theopomp. ap. Plut., Dem.*, 25. Compare *Vit. Dec. Orat.*, p. 846. [2] *Pausan.*, ii., 33, 4.

tarily offered himself to be tried, we must own that it is, at least, highly improbable that he should have been guilty of common bribery, and that it was not his guilt which caused his condemnation, but the implacable hatred of the Macedonian party, which eagerly seized this favorable opportunity to rid itself of its most formidable opponent, who was at that time abandoned by his friends from sheer timidity.

Demosthenes was declared guilty, and thrown into prison, from which, however, he escaped, apparently with the connivance of the Athenian magistrates.[1] Having quitted his country, he resided partly at Trœzene and partly in Ægina, looking daily, it is said, across the sea toward his beloved native land. But his exile did not last long. On the death of Alexander, in B.C. 323, the Greek states rose in arms against Macedonia, Demosthenes was recalled from exile, a trireme was sent to Ægina to convey him to his native land, and his progress to the city was a glorious triumph.[2] It was a triumph, however, of short duration. In the following year, B.C. 322, the confederate Greeks were defeated by Antipater at the battle of Cranon, and were compelled to sue for peace. Antipater demanded the surrender of Demosthenes, who thereupon fled to the island of Calauria, in the Saronic Gulf, off the coast of Argolis, and took refuge in the temple of Neptune. Here he was pursued by the emissaries of Antipater; he thereupon took poison, which he had for some time carried about his person, and died in the temple, B.C. 322.

Thus terminated the career of a man who has been ranked by persons of all ages among the greatest and noblest spirits of antiquity. And this fame will remain undiminished so long as sterling sentiments and principles, and a consistent conduct through life, are regarded as the standard by which a man's worth is measured, and not simply the success —so often merely dependent upon circumstances—by which his exertions are crowned. The very calumnies which have been heaped upon Demosthenes by his enemies and detractors, more extravagantly than upon any other man, have only served to bring forth his political virtues in a more striking and brilliant light. Some points there are in his life which perhaps will never be quite cleared up, on account of the distorted statements which have come down to us respecting them. Some minor charges which are m de against him, and affect his character as a man, are almost below contempt. It is said, for example, that he took to flight after the battle of Chæronea, as if thousands of others had not fled with him;[3] that, notwithstanding his domestic calamity (his daughter had died seven days before), he rejoiced at Philip's death, which shows only the predominance of his patriotic feelings over his personal and selfish ones;[4] and, lastly, that he shed tears on going into exile, a fact for which he deserves to be loved and honored rather than blamed. In his administration of public affairs Demosthenes is perfectly spotless, and free from all the crimes which the men of the Macedonian party committed openly and without any disguise. The charge of bribery, which was so often raised against him by Æschines, must be rejected altogether, and

[1] *Plut., Vit. Dec. Orat.*, p. 846. [2] *Plut., Dem.*, 27; *Vit. Dec. Orat.*, p. 846.
[3] *Plut., Dem.*, 20; *Vit. Dec. Orat.*, p. 845. [4] *Plut., Dem.*, 22; *Æsch. c. Ctes.*, § 77.

is a mere distortion of the fact that Demosthenes accepted subsidies from Persia for Athens, which assuredly stood in need of such aid in its struggles with Macedonia; but there is not the shadow of a suspicion that he ever accepted any personal bribes.[1]

His career as a statesman received its greatest lustre from his powers as an orator, in which he has not been equalled by any man of any country. Our own judgment on this point would necessarily be one-sided, as we can only *read* his orations; but among the contemporaries of Demosthenes there was scarcely one who could point out any definite fault in his oratory. By far the greater part looked up to him as the greatest orator of his time, and it was only men of such over-refined and hypercritical tastes as Demetrius Phalereus who thought him either too plain and simple or too harsh and strong.[2] These peculiarities, however, are far from being faults; they are, on the contrary, proofs of his genius, if we consider the temptations which natural deficiencies hold out to an orator to pursue the opposite course. The obstacles which his physical constitution threw in his way when he commenced his career were so great, that a less courageous and persevering man than Demosthenes would at once have been intimidated, and entirely shrunk from the arduous career of a public orator. Those early difficulties with which he had to contend led him to bestow more care upon the composition of his orations than he would otherwise have done, and produced in the end, if not the impossibility of speaking extempore, at least the habit of never venturing upon it; for he never spoke without preparation, and he sometimes even declined speaking when called upon in the assembly to do so, merely because he was not prepared for it. There is, however, no reason for believing that all the extant orations were delivered in that perfect form in which they have come down to us, for most of them were probably subjected to a careful revision before publication; and it is only the oration against Midias, which, having been written for the purpose of being delivered, and being afterward given up and left incomplete, may be regarded with certainty as a specimen of an oration in its original form. This oration alone sufficiently shows how little Demosthenes trusted to the impulse of the moment.[3]

The first cause of the mighty impression which his speeches made upon the minds of his hearers was their pure and ethical character; for every sentence exhibits Demosthenes as the friend of his country, of virtue, truth, and public decency;[4] and as the struggles in which he was engaged were fair and just, he could without scruple unmask his opponents, and wound them where they were vulnerable, though he never resorted to sycophantic artifices. The second cause was his intellectual superiority. By a wise arrangement of his subjects, and by the application of the strongest arguments in their proper places, he brought these subjects before his hearers in the clearest possible form; doubts that might be raised were met by him beforehand, and thus he proceeded calmly but irresistibly toward his end. The third and last cause was the magic force of his language, which, being majestic and yet simple, rich,

[1] *Smith, l. c.* [2] *Plut., Dem.*, 9, 11. [3] *Smith, l. c.* [4] *Plut., Dem.*, 13.

yet not bombastic, strange and yet familiar, solemn without being ornamented, grave and yet pleasing, concise and yet fluent, sweet and yet impressive, carried away the minds of his hearers. That such orations should, notwithstanding, sometimes have failed to produce the desired effect, was owing only to the spirit of the times.[1]

The ancients[2] state that there existed sixty-five orations of Demosthenes, but of these only sixty-one, and if we deduct the letter of Philip, which is, strangely enough, counted as an oration, only sixty have come down to us under his name, though some of these are spurious, or, at least, of very doubtful authenticity. Besides these orations there are fifty-six *exordia*, or introductions to public orations (Προοίμια δημηγορικά), and six letters which bear the name of Demosthenes, though their genuineness is very doubtful. Confining ourselves to the classification adopted by the ancient rhetoricians, we may arrange all the discourses of Demosthenes under one of three heads: 1. *Deliberative discourses* (λόγοι συμβουλευτικοί), treating of political topics, and delivered before the Senate or the Assembly of the People. 2. *Judicial speeches* (λόγοι δικανικοί), having for their object accusation or defence. 3. *Studied* or *set speeches*, called also *Show-speeches* (λόγοι ἐπιδεικτικοί), intended to censure or praise. Seventeen of the orations of Demosthenes belong to the first of these classes, forty-two to the second, and two to the third.

Of the deliberative or political discourses, the twelve Philippic orations are the most important, and relate to the quarrels between the state and King Philip, and also to the other political movements of that monarch for the increase of his power. In the common arrangement, four of these are specially termed "Philippics," while three others are denominated "Olynthiacs," the object of the former being to urge the Athenians to prosecute the war vigorously against Philip, and of the Olynthiacs, to stimulate the Athenians to succor Olynthus, and prevent its falling into the hands of that monarch. The twelve Philippics were delivered in the following order. The *first* Philippic, B.C. 352; the *three Olynthiacs*, also called the second, third, and fourth Philippics, B.C. 349; the *fifth* Philippic (which, according to some critics, forms part of the first in our present copies), B.C. 347; the *sixth* Philippic, also called the "Oration on the Peace," B.C. 346; the *seventh* Philippic (according to the common arrangement, the second), B.C. 344; the *eighth* Philippic, also called the "Oration concerning Halonesus," B.C. 343; the *ninth* Philippic, also called the "Oration on the Chersonesus," the *tenth* and *eleventh* Philippics (according to the common arrangement, the third and fourth), all in B.C. 342; the *twelfth* Philippic, also called the "Oration against the Letter," B.C. 340. This last is a spurious oration, and so, according to nearly all critics, is the eleventh, which many make to belong, not to B.C. 342, but to 341. The oration concerning Halonesus, also, was suspected by the ancients themselves, and ascribed to Hegesippus. Weiske undertakes to defend it, but is opposed by Becker and Vömel, the latter of whom even published a separate edition of it under the name of Hegesippus in 1833.

Of the judicial discourses, the most important are the oration against

[1] *Smith, l. c.*

[2] *Plut., Vit. Dec. Orat.*, p. 847; *Phot.*, p. 490.

Midias, written B.C. 355, but never delivered; that against Leptines, in the same year; that on the dishonest conduct of Æschines during his embassy to Philip; and especially that on the Crown. The action against Midias was for personal violence offered to Demosthenes during the celebration of the great Dionysia, but it was settled before trial, on Demosthenes receiving from Midias the sum of thirty minæ. The oration against Leptines charged him with having proposed a law taking away all special exemptions from the burden of public charges (ἀτέλειαι τῶν λειτουργιῶν). The subjects of the other two orations have already been referred to.

The ἐπιτάφιος λόγος and the ἐρωτικός are the two show-speeches. But they are both unquestionably spurious. The former belongs to B.C. 338, and is an eloge on those who fell at Chæronea; the latter is written in praise of the beauty of the young Epicrates.

EDITIONS OF DEMOSTHENES.

Most of the critical works that were written upon Demosthenes by the ancients are lost, and, independent merely of many scattered remarks, the only important critical work that has come down to us is that of Dionysius of Halicarnassus, entitled περὶ τῆς τοῦ Δημοσθένους δεινότητος. The acknowledged excellence of Demosthenes' orations made them the principal subjects of study and speculation with the rhetoricians, and called forth numerous commentators and imitators. It is probably owing to these rhetorical speculations, which began as early as the second century B.C., that a number of orations, which are decidedly spurious and unworthy of him, such as the λόγος ἐπιτάφιος and the ἐρωτικός, were incorporated in the collections of those of Demosthenes. Others, such as the speech on Halonesus, the first against Aristogiton, those against Theocrines and Neæra, which are undoubtedly the productions of contemporary orators, may have been introduced among those of Demosthenes by mistake. It would be of great assistance to us to have the commentaries which were written upon Demosthenes by such men as Didymus, Longinus, Hermogenes, and others; but, unfortunately, most of what they wrote is lost, and scarcely any thing of importance is extant, except the miserable collection of scholia which have come down to us under the name of Ulpian, and the Greek *argumenta* to the orations by Libanius and other rhetoricians.

The orations of Demosthenes are contained in the various collections of the Attic orators mentioned in the account of the editions of Antiphon. Of separate editions we may mention that of Wolf, Basle, 1572 (often reprinted); of Auger, Paris, 1790; of Schäfer, with a copious commentary, Leipzig and London, 1822, 9 vols. 8vo, the first two containing the text, the third the Latin version, and the others the critical apparatus, indices, &c. A thin volume containing an *Index verborum, grammaticus*, &c., was added by Seiler, Leipzig, 1833. A good edition of the text is that by W. Dindorf, Leipzig, 1825, 3 vols. 8vo, 2d edition, Leipzig, 1851; and with a revised text and Latin translation, by Voemel, in Didot's *Bibliotheca Græca*, Paris, 1843. But the most elaborate and complete edition is the one recently issued from the Oxford press, edited anew by W. Dindorf, 1847–52, 9 vols. 8vo, the first four volumes containing the text, the fifth, sixth, and seventh the commentary, and the eighth and ninth the scholia, amended and enlarged from MSS.

The orations of Demosthenes have often been edited also in selections or separately. Of these the most valuable for text or commentary are as follows: The *Philippics*, by Bekker, Berlin, 1816, 1825, and 1835; by Rüdiger, Leipzig, 1818, 1829, and 1833; by Voemel, Frankfort, 1829; and by Franke, Leipzig, 1842, 2d edition, 1850. The *Olynthiacs*, by Frotscher and Funkhaenel, Leipzig, 1834. The oration *De Haloneso*, by Voemel, Frankfort, 1830. *De Corona*, by Bekker, with scholia, Halle, 1815, and Berlin, 1825; by Harless, Leipzig, 1814; with other select orations, by Bremi, in 2 parts, Gotha, 1829–33, 2d edition, by Sauppe, 1845–51; by Dissen, Göttingen, 1837. The oration against Leptines, best edition by Wolf, Halle, 1789, re-edited by Bremi, Zürich, 1839, 8vo. The oration against Midias, by Buttmann, Berlin, 1823, 1833, and 1841; by Blume, Sund., 1828; and by Meier, Halle, 1832. The oration against Androtion, by Funkhaenel, Leipzig, 1832, 8vo. The oration against Aristocrates, by Weber, Jena, 1845.

Besides the ancient and modern historians of the times of Philip and Alexander, the following works will be found useful to the student of Demosthenes; Schott, *Vitæ Parallelæ Aristot. et Demosth.*, Antwerp, 1603; Becker, *Demosthenes als Staatsmann und Redner*, Halle, 1816, 2 vols. 8vo; Westermann, *Quæstiones Demosthenicæ*, in four parts, Leipzig, 1830–37; *Geschichte der Griech. Beredtsamkeit*, § 56, *seq.*, and *Beilage*, vii., p. 297, *seqq.*; Böhneke, *Studien auf dem Gebiete der Attischen Redner*, Berlin, 1843.

9. Hyperīdes (Ὑπερείδης or Ὑπερίδης) was the son of Glaucippus, and belonged to the Attic demus of Collytus. He was a friend of Demosthenes, and with him and Lycurgus he was at the head of the anti-Macedonian party. His birth-year is unknown, but he must have been of about the same age as Lycurgus, who was born in B.C. 396.[1] Throughout his public career he joined the patriots with the utmost determination and with his whole soul, and remained faithful to them to the last, through all the dangers and catastrophes by which Athens was weighed down successively under Philip, Alexander, and Antipater. This steadfast adherence to the good cause may have been owing, in a great measure, to the influence which Demosthenes and Lycurgus exercised over him, for he seems to have been naturally a person of a vacillating character; and Plutarch states that he sometimes gave way to his passions, which were not always of the noblest kind.[2] In philosophy he was a pupil of Plato,[3] and Isocrates trained and developed his oratorical talent.[4] He began his career by conducting lawsuits of others in the courts of justice.[5] Our information, however, respecting his life is very meagre. It seems that he first displayed his patriotic feelings in B.C. 358 by the sacrifices which he made for the public good during the expedition against Eubœa, for on that occasion he and his son are said to have equipped two triremes at their own expense. After the death of Alexander (B.C. 323), Hyperides took an active part in organizing that confederacy of the Greeks against Antipater which produced the Lamian war. Upon the defeat of the confederates at the battle of Cranon in the following year, Hyperides fled to Ægina, where he was slain by the emissaries of Antipater.

Hyperides must have appeared before the public on many occasions, both in the courts of justice and in the assembly of the people. The number of orations attributed to him was seventy-seven, but even the ancient critics rejected twenty-five of them as spurious.[6] The titles of sixty-one (for more are not known) are enumerated by Westermann.[7] The most important among them appear to have been the Δηλιακός, the ἐπιτάφιος, and the orations against Aristogiton, Demades, and Demosthenes, especially the last. This speech was the one which he delivered when he accused Demosthenes of corruption in the affair of Harpalus. Plutarch states that Hyperides was found to have been the only man who had not received any money from Harpalus, and it may therefore be that he was compelled to act the part of an accuser, or he may have hoped to give the matter a more favorable turn for Demosthenes by coming forward as accuser. Hyperidės and Demosthenes, however, again, at a

[1] *Plut.*, *Vit. Dec. Orat.*, p. 848, *D*; *Diog. Laert.*, ii., 46.
[2] *Plut.*, *l. c.*, p. 849, *D*.
[3] *Diog. Laert.*, *l. c.*
[4] *Athen.*, viii., p. 342; *Phot.*, *Cod.*, 260, p. 487.
[5] *Plut.*, *l. c.*, p. 448, *E*.
[6] *Id. ib.*, p. 849, *D*.
[7] *Gesch. d. Griech. Beredts.*, p. 307, *seqq.*

subsequent period, stood in friendly relations to each other, and again united against the common foe.

Until the year 1847, we may be said to have had no one of the orations of Hyperides remaining, but merely a considerable number of fragments, few of them of any length. In that year, however, a manuscript of the oration against Demosthenes was discovered at Thebes, in Egypt, on papyrus, which, though it did not give the entire speech, in consequence of its mutilated condition, yet afforded fragments of so great length, that we may almost be said to have the oration entire. Böckh undertook the restitution and arrangement of these fragments in 1848, in the *Hallischer Literaturzeitung*, and afterward in a separate form. A similar attempt was made by Sauppe, somewhat later, in the "Philologus" (vol. iii., p. 610, *seqq.*). About the same time, the fragments, arranged, and with a translation, were published by Sharpe in the transactions of the Philological Society (vol. iv., No. 79, p. 39, *seqq.*); and, finally, an edition was published in 1850, by Babington, London, with preliminary dissertation and notes.[1] The discovery of these fragments renders the accounts of Brassicanus and Taylor more probable than they have been accustomed to be regarded. The former (*Præf. ad Salvianum*), who lived at the beginning of the seventeenth century, states that he himself saw at Ofen, in the library of King Matthias Corvinus, a complete copy of Hyperides, with numerous scholia; and Taylor (*Præf. ad Demosth.*) likewise says that he saw a MS. containing some orations of Hyperides.

As we have, therefore, but little to form an independent opinion upon respecting the merits of Hyperides, we must acquiesce in the judgment which some of the ancients have pronounced upon him. That he was regarded as a great orator is attested by the fact of his speeches being incorporated in the canon of the ten Attic orators, and of several distinguished grammarians having written commentaries upon them. Hyperides did not bind himself to any particular model; his oratory was graceful and powerful, thus holding the middle between the gracefulness of Lysias and the overwhelming power of Demosthenes. His delivery, however, is said to have been wanting in liveliness. His style and diction were pure Attic, though not quite free from a kind of mannerism, especially in certain words. But his orations were distinguished, above all, by their exquisite elegance and gracefulness, which were calculated, however, to produce a momentary rather than a lasting and moral impression.[2]

10. Dinarchus (Δείναρχος),[3] the tenth and least important of the Attic orators, was born at Corinth about B.C. 361.[4] Though a native of Corinth, he lived at Athens from his earliest youth, and devoted himself with great zeal to the study of oratory under Theophrastus, having, at the same time, profited much by his intercourse with Demetrius Phalereus.[5] As he was a foreigner, and did not possess the Athenian franchise, he was not allowed to come forward himself as an orator on the great questions,

[1] *Zeitschrift für die Alterthumswiss.* (*Bergk und Cæsar*), *Achter Jahrgang*, 1850, p. 378.
[2] *Smith, Dict. Biogr.*, *s. v.* [3] *Id. ib.* [4] *Dionys.*, *Dinarch.*, 4.
[5] *Dionys.*, *l. c*, 2; *Plut.*, *Vit. Dec. Orat.*, p. 850.

which then divided public opinion at Athens, and he was therefore obliged to content himself with writing orations for others. He appears to have commenced this career in his twenty-sixth year, about B.C. 336, and as about that time the great Attic orators died away one after the other, Dinarchus soon acquired considerable reputation and great wealth. He belonged to the friends of Phocion, and the Macedonian party, and took a very active part in the disputes as to whether Harpalus, who had openly deserted the cause of Alexander the Great, should be tolerated at Athens or not. The time of his greatest activity is from B.C. 317 to B.C. 307, during which time Demetrius Phalereus conducted the administration of Athens. But when, in B.C. 307, Demetrius Poliorcetes advanced against Athens, and Demetrius Phalereus was obliged to take to flight, Dinarchus, who was suspected on account of his equivocal political conduct, and who was anxious to save his riches, fled to Chalcis, in Eubœa. It was not till fifteen years after, B.C. 292, that, owing to the exertions of his friend Theophrastus, he obtained permission to return to Athens, where he spent the last years of his life, and died at an advanced age. The last event of his life of which we have any record is a lawsuit which he instituted against his faithless friend, Proxenus, who had robbed him of his property; but in what manner the suit ended is unknown.

The number of orations which Dinarchus wrote is uncertain, for Demetrius of Magnesia[1] ascribed to him 160, while Plutarch and Photius speak only of sixty-four genuine ones; and Dionysius is of opinion that, among the eighty-seven which were ascribed to him in his time, only sixty were genuine productions of Dinarchus. Of all these orations only three have come down to us entire, and all three refer to the question about Harpalus. It is, however, not improbable that the speech against Theocrines, which is usually printed among those of Demosthenes, is likewise a production of Dinarchus. The titles and fragments of the orations which are lost are collected by Fabricius,[2] and more completely by Westermann.[3] The ancients, such as Dionysius, who gives an accurate account of the oratory of Dinarchus, and especially Hermogenes,[4] speak in terms of commendation of his orations; but there were others also who thought less favorably of him; some grammarians would not even allow him a place in the canon of the ten Attic orators, and Dionysius mentions that he was treated with indifference by Callimachus and the grammarians of Pergamus. However, some of the most eminent grammarians, such as Didymus of Alexandrea, and Heron of Athens, did not disdain to write commentaries upon him. The orations still extant enable us to form an independent opinion upon the merits of Dinarchus; and we find that Dionysius's judgment is, on the whole, quite correct. Dinarchus was a man of no originality of mind, and it is difficult to say whether he had any oratorical talent or not. His want of genius led him to imitate others, such as Lysias, Hyperides, and more especially Demosthenes; but he was unable to come up to his great model in any point, and was therefore nicknamed Δημοσθένης ὁ ἄγροικος, or ὁ κρίθινος. Even Hermogenes, his great-

[1] *Ap. Dionys.*, *l. c.*, 1.

[2] *Bibl. Gr.*, ii., p. 864, *seqq.*

[3] *Gesch. der Griech. Beredts.*, p. 311, *seqq.*

[4] *De Form.*, ii., 11.

est admirer, does not deny that his style had a certain roughness, whence his orations were thought to resemble those of Aristogiton. Although it can not be denied that Dinarchus is the best among the many imitators of Demosthenes, yet he is far inferior to him in power and energy, in the choice of his expressions, in invention, clearness, and the arrangement of his subjects.[1]

The orations of Dinarchus are contained in the various collections of Attic orators already mentioned. There are two good separate editions, one by Schmidt, Leipzig, 1826, 8vo, and the other by Mätzner, Berlin, 1842, 8vo. There is also a useful commentary on Dinarchus by Wurm, "*Commentarius in Dinarchi Orationes tres*," Nuremburg, 1828, 8vo.

CHAPTER XXXV.

FOURTH OR ATTIC PERIOD—*continued.*

III. SCHOOL OF PHILOSOPHY.

I. OUR remarks on the earlier Greek philosophy closed with a brief sketch of the school of Pythagoras. The period that now comes under consideration embraces some of the most important and singular speculations in which the human mind has ever indulged, and deserves a much more extended examination than our limits will allow us to give. All that we can do will be to enumerate the several schools of philosophy that marked the period under review, and give a brief sketch of the eminent individuals who either founded, enlarged, or adorned them.

II. The different schools or sects which, according to this arrangement, will occupy our attention, are the following: 1. The *Atomic;* 2. The *Sophistic;* 3. The *Socratic;* 4. The *Cyrenaic;* 5. The *Megaric;* 6. The *Eliac* and *Eretriac;* 7. The *Academic;* 8. The *Cynic;* 9. The *Peripatetic;* 10. The *Stoic;* 11. The *Skeptical;* 12. The *Epicurean.*

1. THE ATOMIC SCHOOL.

III. The founder of the Atomic theory of the ancient philosophy is admitted on all hands to have been LEUCIPPUS (Λεύκιππος).[2] Where and when he was born we have no data for deciding, Miletus, Abdera, and Elea having been assigned as his birth-place; the first, apparently for no other reason than because it was the birth-place of several natural philosophers; the second, because Democritus came from that city; the third, because he was looked upon as a disciple of the Eleatic school. The period when he lived is equally uncertain. He is called the teacher of Democritus,[3] the disciple of Parmenides,[4] or, according to other accounts, of Zeno, of Melissus, nay, even of Pythagoras.[5] With regard to his philosophical system it is impossible to speak with certainty, since the writers who mention him either speak of him in conjunction with Democritus, or attribute to him doctrines which are in like manner attributed to Democritus.

---

[1] *Smith, l. c.* [2] *Smith, Dict. Biogr., s. v.* [3] *Diog. Laert.*, ix., 34.
[4] *Simplic., Phys., fol.* 7, *A.* [5] *Simplic., l. c.; Diog. Laert.*, ix., 30, &c.

IV. Democrĭtus (Δημόκριτος)[1] was a native of Abdēra, in Thrace, an Ionian colony of Teos, and was born about B.C. 460. He was thus forty years younger than Anaxagoras, and eight years younger than Socrates. His father, Hegesistratus—or, as others call him, Damasippus or Athenocritus—was possessed of so large a property, that he was able to entertain Xerxes on his march through Abdera. Democritus spent the inheritance which his father left him on travels into distant countries, which he undertook to satisfy his extraordinary thirst for knowledge. He is said to have visited Egypt that he might learn geometry from the Egyptian priests; to have been in Persia with the magi, and with the gymnosophists in India; and to have penetrated to Æthiopia.[2] He sojourned for some time at Athens; but from contempt of notoriety, as it is said, was known to nobody in that city. It is for this reason that Demetrius Phalereus, as cited by Diogenes Laertius,[3] contended that Democritus had never visited Athens. One result of his extensive travels was, as we have already remarked, that he expended all his patrimony, which is said to have exceeded 100 talents. Now it was a law of his native city, that any one who spent his whole patrimony should not be buried within the limits of his country; but Democritus having read his chief work aloud to his fellow-citizens, so impressed them with an admiration of his learning, that he not only obtained a special exemption from the above law, but was presented with 500 talents, and at his death was buried at the public expense. A story substantially the same, though varying somewhat in detail, is given in Athenæus. He is said to have continued travelling till he was eighty years old. He died B.C. 357, at the age of 104, the same year in which Hippocrates is said to have died. There is a story of his having protracted his life for three days after death seemed inevitable, by means of the smell of either bread or honey, in order to gratify his sister, who, had he died when first he seemed likely to die, would have been prevented from attending a festival of Ceres.

Democritus loved solitude, and was wholly wrapped up in study. There are several anecdotes illustrative of his devotion to knowledge, and his disregard of every thing else. They conflict somewhat with one another in their details, but accuracy of detail is not to be looked for, and, tending as they all do to the same point, they prove, which is all that we can expect to know, what character was traditionally assigned to Democritus. Cicero speaks of him as, like Anaxagoras, leaving his lands uncultivated in his undivided care for learning; while, as an instance of how these stories conflict, Diogenes Laertius represents him as having, on the division of the paternal estate with his two brothers, taken his own share entirely in money, as being more convenient than land for a traveller. Valerius Maximus makes him show his contempt for worldly things by giving almost the whole of his patrimony to his country. He is said, too, to have put out his own eyes, that he might not be diverted from thought; but it is more probable that he may have lost his sight by too severe application to study. This loss, however, did not disturb the

[1] *Smith, Dict. Biogr., s. v.*

[2] *Cic., De Fin.*, v., 19; *Strabo*, xvi., p. 703.

[3] *Diog. Laert.*, ix., 34, *seqq.*

cheerful disposition of his mind and his views of human life, which prompted him every where to look at the cheerful and comical side of things, a course of conduct which later writers took to mean that he always laughed at the follies of men.

Of the extent of his knowledge, which embraced not only natural sciences, mathematics, mechanics,[1] grammar, music, and philosophy, but various other useful arts, we may form some notion from the list of his numerous works which is given by Diogenes Laertius,[2] and which, as Diogenes expressly states, contains only his genuine works. The importance which was attached to the researches of Democritus is evident from the fact that Aristotle is reported to have written a work in two books on the problems of this philosopher.[3] His works were composed in the Ionic dialect, though not without some admixture of the local peculiarities of Abdera. They are much praised by Cicero on account of the poetical beauties and the liveliness of their style, and are in this respect compared even with the works of Plato.[4] Unfortunately, not one of his works has come down to us, and the treatise which we possess under his name is considered spurious. Comparatively few fragments have even reached us, and these fragments refer more to ethics than to physical matters.

Democritus followed Leucippus by a very short distance of time, and preceded Epicurus by somewhat less than a century, as an expounder of the atomic or corpuscular philosophy. He viewed all matter as reducible to particles, which are themselves indivisible, and are hence called *atoms* (ἄτομοι, ἀ *priv.* and τομή). He included mind under the head of matter, recognizing only matter and empty space as composing the universe, and viewed mind as consisting of round atoms of fire. Arguing that nothing could arise out of nothing, and also that nothing could utterly perish and become nothing, he contended for the eternity of the universe, and thus dispensed with a creator. He farther explained the difference in material substances (mind, as has been said, being one of them) by a difference in the nature and arrangement of their component atoms, and all material (including mental) phenomena by different motions, progressive or regressive, straight or circular, taking place among these atoms, and taking place of *necessity*. Thus the cosmology of Democritus was essentially atheistic. In psychology he explained sensation, as did Epicurus after him, by supposing particles, εἴδωλα, as he called them, or sensible images, to issue from bodies. He also thought to explain men's belief in gods by the supposed existence of large images of human form in the air. In moral philosophy he announced nothing more than that a cheerful state of mind (εὐθυμία) was the one thing to be sought after, this tranquillity of mind and freedom from fear and passion, from the dread of death and from all apprehension of gods or superstitious emotions, being the fairest fruit of philosophic inquiry.[5]

There is a very good collection of the fragments of Democritus by Mullach, *Democriti*

[1] *Brandis, Rhein. Mus.*, iii., p. 134, *seqq.*
[2] *Diog. Laert.*, ix., 46, *seqq.*
[3] *Id.*, v., 26.
[4] *Cic.*, *De Div.*, ii., 64; *De Orat.*, i., 11.
[5] *Penny Cyclop.*, viii., p. 380; *Smith, Dict. Biogr.*, *s. v.*

Abderitæ Operum fragmenta, Berlin, 1843, 8vo, containing elaborate dissertations on the life and writings of Democritus. The student may also consult Burchardt, *Comment. Crit. de Democriti de sensibus philosophia*, in two programmes, Minden, 1830 and 1839, 4to; Burchardt, *Fragmente der Moral des Demokrit*, Minden, 1834, 4to; Heimsöth, *Democriti de anima doctrina*, Bonn, 1835, 8vo; Orelli, *Opusc. Græc. sent.*, vol. i., p. 91, *seqq.*; Ritter, *Gesch. d. Philos.*, vol. i., p. 559, *seqq.* (vol. i., p. 544, *seqq.*, Eng. transl.), and the article of Brandis in *Smith's Biographical Dictionary*, *s. v.* Concerning the spurious works and letters of Democritus, consult Fabricius, *Bibl. Gr.*, i., p. 683, *seqq.*; ii., p. 641, &c.

II. THE SOPHISTIC SCHOOL.

I. It is well known that the term *σοφιστής* at first had an honorable meaning, and was synonymous with *σοφός*, a sage, a scholar in the widest sense, for even artists were comprehended in it. Protagoras was the first who adopted the name of *σοφιστής*, to distinguish more decidedly one who makes others wise, especially one who taught eloquence, the art of governing, politics, or, in short, any kind of practical knowledge. From that time the word "sophist" acquired that odious meaning which it retains at the present day. Afterward, in the time of the Roman emperors, the name of sophist again became, for a while, an honorable appellation, and was applied to the rhetoricians or teachers of eloquence.[1]

II. The race of Sophists, whose enmity to Socrates, their great opponent, has perhaps been the principal cause of their celebrity, was not without influence on the philosophy and literature of Greece. They were a class of men who went about Greece discoursing and debating, and sometimes educating the youthful sons of rich and noble families. The cause of their success lay in the very nature and habits of the Greek people, who were so much addicted to talk and so little to study, who were so passionately fond of and so easily led by rhetoric; and the easy triumph which a fluent talker can always obtain, by a rapid and artful confusion of words and ideas, must also have operated in their favor.

III. The period at which the Sophists flourished was one of obsolete creeds, one lifeless from the want of some vivifying faith. Religion was attacked by open skepticism; the whole sect of the Eleatics, with the exception of Empedocles, if he, in truth, belonged to them, appear to have handled the history of the gods with arbitrary and allegorizing boldness. Even the pious Pythagorean adopted the old religion merely in a peculiar sense of his own. Heraclitus argued against its probability; Anaxagoras understood it allegorically; and, lastly, Hippo was regarded as an open and avowed atheist. Every thing human and divine had lost its earnest nature, and came to be regarded as an art, a mere exercise of ingenuity. The art of the Sophists was oratory, and their boast was that by it they could make the worse appear the better cause. Their doctrines, indeed, closely resembled those of the Skeptics, since they equally denied the possibility of truth, and even interdicted inquiry into it; but the distinction between these sects consisted in the Sophists' not masking their arrogance under doubt, but boldly and distinctly averring that there was no truth at all, and seeking to communicate this wisdom to others, to save them the trouble of investigation.[2]

[1] *Penny Cyclop.*, xxii., 257. [2] *Ibid.*

IV. That all knowledge is *subjective*, that it is true only for the individual, was the meaning of the celebrated saying of PROTAGORAS *of Abdera*, namely, *πάντων μέτρον ἄνθρωπος.* Protagoras was the first who called himself a sophist, and taught for pay. He made his appearance at Athens in the time of Pericles (about B.C. 444), and for a long time enjoyed a great reputation there, till at last a reaction was caused by the bold skepticism of his opinions, and he was banished from Athens, and his books were publicly burned. Agreeing with Heraclitus in regard to the doctrine of a perpetual motion, and of a continual change in the impressions and perceptions of men, he deduced from this that the individual could know nothing beyond these ever-varying perceptions; consequently, that whatever *appeared to be was so* for the individual. According to this doctrine, opposite opinions on the same subject might be equally true; and if an opinion were only supported by a momentary appearance of truth, this was sufficient to make it true for the moment. Hence it was one of the great feats which Protagoras and the other Sophists professed to perform, to be able to speak with equal plausibility *for* and *against* the same positions; not in order to discover the truth, but in order to show the nothingness of truth. It was not, however, the intention of Protagoras to deprive virtue, as well as truth, of its reality, but he reduced virtue to a mere state or condition of the subject—a set of impressions and feelings which rendered the subject more capable of active usefulness.[1]

V. GORGIAS of *Leontini*, whom we have spoken of elsewhere, proceeded from an older philosophic school than Protagoras, but yet there was a great correspondence between the pursuits of the two; and from this we may clearly see how strongly the spirit of the age must have inclined to the form and mode of speculation which was common to them both. Gorgias undertook to prove that nothing exists; that even if any thing did exist, it would not be cognizable, and even if it both existed and were cognizable, it could not be conveyed and communicated by words. The result was that absolute knowledge was unattainable; and that the proper end of instruction was to awaken in the pupil's mind such conceptions as are suitable to his own purposes and interests. The chief distinction between Gorgias and the other sophists consisted in the frankness with which he admitted that he promised and professed nothing else than to make his scholars apt rhetoricians; and the ridicule with which he treated those of his colleagues who professed to teach virtue, a peculiarity which Gorgias shared with all the other Sophists of Sicily. The Sophists in the mother country, on the other hand, endeavored to awaken useful thoughts, and to teach the principles of practical philosophy: thus HIPPIAS of Elis, the contemporary of Socrates, endeavored to season his lessons with a display of multifarious knowledge, and may be regarded as the first Polyhistor among the Greeks, though in other respects remarkable for vanity and boastful arrogance. So, again, PRODICUS of *Ceos*, another contemporary of Socrates, and perhaps the most respectable among the Sophists, used to present lessons of morality under an agreea-

[1] *Müller, Hist. Gr. Lit.*, vol. ii., p. 73.

ble form; such, for instance, as the well-known allegory of the choice of Hercules.[1]

VI. In general, however, the labors of the Sophists were prejudicial alike to the moral condition of Greece and to the serious pursuit of knowledge. The national morality, which drew the line between right and wrong, though not, perhaps, according to the highest standard, yet, at any rate, with honest views, and, what was of most importance, with a sort of instinctive certainty, had received a shock from the boldness with which philosophy had handled it, and could not but be altogether undermined by a doctrine which destroyed the distinction between truth and falsehood. And though Protagoras and Gorgias shrank from declaring that virtue and religion were nothing but empty illusions, their disciples and followers did so most openly, when the liberty of speculation was completely emancipated from all the restraints of traditionary opinions. In the course of the Peloponnesian war, a class of society was formed at Athens which was not without influence on the course of affairs, and whose creed was that justice and belief in the gods were but the inventions of ancient rulers and legislators, who gave them currency in order to strengthen their hold on the common herd, and assist them in the business of government. They sometimes gave this opinion with this far more pernicious variation, that laws were made by the majority of weaker men for their protection, whereas nature had sanctioned the right of the strongest, so that the stronger party did but use his right when he compelled the weaker to minister to his pleasures as far as he could.[2]

VII. If, however, we turn from the influence of the Sophists on the spirit of their age, and set ourselves to inquire what they did for the improvement of written compositions, we are constrained to set a very high value on their services. The formation of an artificial prose style is due entirely to the Sophists, and although they did not at first proceed according to a right method, they may be considered as having laid a foundation for the polished diction of Plato and Demosthenes. The Sophists of Greece Proper, as well as those of Sicily, made language the object of their study, but with this distinction, that the former aimed at *correctness*, the latter at *beauty* of style. Protagoras investigated the principles of accurate composition (ὀρθοέπεια), though practically he was distinguished for a copious fluency, which Plato's Socrates vainly attempted to bridle with his dialectic; and Prodicus busied himself with inquiries into the signification and correct use of words, and the discrimination of synonyms. His own discourses were full of such distinctions, as appears from the humorous imitation of his style in Plato's *Protagoras*.[3]

VIII. The view here taken of the Sophists is the one that is commonly entertained respecting them. It may not be amiss, however, before concluding, to state briefly the sentiments of an eminent historical writer on the subject, and to show the contrast between his views and the popular representation of the Sophists. According to the common notion, they were a sect; according to Grote, they were a class or profession. According to the common view, they were the propagators of demoralizing

[1] *Müller, Hist. Gr. Lit.*, vol. ii., p. 37. [2] *Id. ib.*, p. 74. [3] *Id. ib.*

doctrines, and (what from them are termed) "sophistical" argumentations; according to Grote, they were the regular teachers of Greek morality, neither above nor below the standard of the age. According to the common view, Socrates was the great opponent of the Sophists, and Plato his natural successor in the same combat; according to Grote, Socrates was the great representative of the Sophists, distinguished from them only by his higher eminence, and by the peculiarity of his mode of life and teaching. According to the common view, Plato and his followers were the authorized teachers, the established clergy of the Greek nation, and the Sophists the dissenters; according to Grote, the Sophists were the established clergy, and Plato was the dissenter—the Socialist, who attacked the Sophists (as he attacked the poets and the statesmen), not as a particular sect, but as one of the existing orders of society.[1]

III. THE SOCRATIC SCHOOL.

I. SOCRĂTES (Σωκράτης),[2] the celebrated Athenian philosopher, was born in the demus of Alopece, in the immediate neighborhood of Athens, B.C. 469. His father, Sophroniscus, was a statuary; his mother, Phænarete, was a midwife. In his youth he followed the profession of his father, and attained sufficient proficiency to have executed the group of the Graces, clothed in flowing drapery, which was preserved in the Acropolis, and was shown as his work down to the time of Pausanias.[3] He did not, however, devote himself to this profession; he carried it on so far as to earn a decent subsistence from it, but was content to devote the greater part of his time and talents to the study of philosophy, for which he had a strong natural inclination. While still engaged in statuary, and much more so after he had given it up, he spent a great part of his time in reading all the accessible works of former and contemporary philosophers. Crito supplied him with money to pay the masters who taught various branches at Athens, and he became an auditor of many of the eminent teachers of the day, though he appears, in truth, to have owed very much to his own habits of study and self-examination.

The personal qualities of Socrates were marked and striking. His physical constitution was healthy, robust, and enduring to an extraordinary degree. He was capable of bearing fatigue or hardship, and indifferent to heat or cold, in a measure which astonished all his companions. He went barefoot in all seasons of the year, even during the winter campaign at Potidæa, under the severe frosts of Thrace; and the same clothing sufficed for him in winter as well as in summer.[4] His forbidding physiognomy excited the jests both of his friends and enemies, who inform us that he had a flat nose, thick lips, and prominent eyes, like a satyr or Silenus. To all this was added the protuberance of a Falstaff-stomach, which no necessary hardships, no voluntary exercise could bring down. In his moral character he was most exemplary. In all situations, he ex-

[1] *Quarterly Review*, No. 175, p. 53, note.
[2] *Smith, Dict. Biogr., s. v.; Penny Cyclop.*, xxii., p. 182, *seqq.*
[3] *Pausan.*, ix., 35; compare i., 22; *Diog. Laert.*, ii., 19.
[4] *Plat., Sympos.*, p. 219, *seqq.; Alcib.*, p. 194; *Diog. Laert.*, i., 22, *seq.*

ercised that self-command which is founded on virtuous principles, and strengthened by reflection and habit; and, in acquiring this entire dominion over his passions and appetites, he had the greater merit, as it was not effected without a violent struggle against naturally impetuous appetites.[1]

Of the circumstances of his life we are almost wholly ignorant. With regard, however, to his public career, we know that he served his country faithfully as a soldier, according to the duty of all Athenian citizens. During the Peloponnesian war he made three several campaigns. In the first of these he took part in the long blockade of Potidæa,[2] and Alcibiades, in Plato's *Symposium*, gives a full account of his extraordinary hardihood and valor during this long service. He endured with the greatest indifference hunger and thirst, heat and cold: in one of the skirmishes which took place, Alcibiades fell, wounded, in the midst of the enemy; Socrates rescued him, and carried him off, together with his arms, for which exploit the generals awarded him the prize of valor (τὰ ἀριστεῖα); this, however, he transferred to Alcibiades. The scene of his second campaign was Bœotia, where he fought for his country in the disastrous battle of Delium. Here he saved the life of another of his pupils, Xenophon, whom he carried from the field on his shoulder, fighting his way as he went. In his third campaign he served at Amphipolis. The merit of his civil services was equally conspicuous. As president of the day, when a member of the senate, he refused to put the vote for the iniquitous condemnation of the victors of Arginusæ,[3] and on a subsequent occasion resolutely disobeyed the mandate of the Thirty tyrants for the apprehension of Leon the Salaminian.[4]

Socrates took no part in the concerns of the state. Entertaining, as he did, the most lively conviction that he was called by the Deity to strive, by means of his teaching and life, after a revival of moral feeling, and the laying of a scientific foundation for it,[5] he conceived that an internal divine voice had warned him against participating in political affairs.[6] When it was that he first recognized this vocation, can not be ascertained; and probably it was by degrees that, owing to the need which he felt, in the intercourse of minds, of coming to an understanding with himself, he betook himself to the active duties of a teacher. But he never opened a school, nor did he, like the Sophists of his time, deliver public lectures. Every where, in the market-place, in the gymnasia, and in the work-shops, he sought and found opportunities for awakening and guiding, in boys, youths, and men, moral consciousness, and the impulse after self-knowledge respecting the end and value of our actions. But he only endeavored to aid in developing the germs of knowledge which were already in them, not to communicate to them ready-made knowledge. Unweariedly and inexorably did he fight against all false appearance and conceit of knowledge; and hence, to the mentally proud and the mentally idle he appeared an intolerable bore, and often enough experienced

[1] *Cic.*, *De Fato*, 5; *Alex. Aphrod.*, p. 30, ed. Lond.
[2] *Plat.*, *l. c.*
[3] *Xen.*, *Mem.*, i., 1, 18.
[4] *Plat.*, *Apol.*, p. 32; *Diog. Laert.*, ii., 24.
[5] *Plat.*, *Apol.*, p. 30, 31, 33; *Euthyph.*, p. 2.
[6] *Plat.*, *l. c.*, p. 31, 36; *Xen.*, *Mem.*, i, 6, 15.

their bitter hatred and calumny. Such persons might easily be misled by the "Clouds" of Aristophanes into regarding Socrates as the head of the Sophists, although he was their victorious opponent.

That the condemnation, however, of Socrates was at all connected with the exhibition which Aristophanes makes of him in the "Clouds," is a thing altogether improbable, since the first exhibition of this comedy preceded the prosecution and condemnation of the philosopher by twenty-four years, though it must be confessed that it had produced an unfavorable opinion respecting him. The motive for the production of that comedy, on the part of Aristophanes, does not appear to have been personal enmity, but to have sprung from the conviction that the ancient faith and the ancient manners could be regained only by thrusting aside all philosophy that dealt in subtleties, and hence he represented Socrates, the best known of the philosophers, as the head of that sophistical system which was burying all morals and piety.

Attached to none of the prevailing parties, Socrates found in each of them his friends and his enemies. Hated and persecuted by Critias, Charicles, and others among the Thirty tyrants, who had a special reference to him in the decree which they issued forbidding the teaching of the art of oratory,[1] he was impeached after their banishment and by their opponents. An orator named Lycon, and a poet (a friend of Thrasybulus) named Meletus, had united in the impeachment with the powerful demagogue Anytus, an embittered antagonist of the Sophists and their system.[2] The chief articles of impeachment were, that Socrates was guilty of corrupting the youth, and of despising the tutelary deities of the state, putting in their place other new divinities.[3] At the same time, it had been made a matter of accusation against him that Critias, the most ruthless of the Tyrants, had come forth from his school.[4] Some expressions of his, in which he had found fault with the democratical mode of electing by lot, had also been brought against him;[5] and there can be little doubt that use was made of his friendly relations with Theramenes, one of the most influential of the Thirty, with Plato's uncle Charmides, who fell by the side of Critias in the struggle with the popular party, and also with other aristocrats, in order to irritate against him the party which at that time was dominant. The substance of the speech which Socrates delivered in his defence is probably preserved by Plato in the piece which goes under the name of the "Apology of Socrates." Being condemned by a majority of only six votes, and called upon to speak in mitigation of the sentence, instead of suing for any diminution of punishment, he expressed the conviction that he deserved no punishment at all, but rather to be maintained at the public cost in the Prytaneum, and refused, therefore, to acquiesce in the adjudication of imprisonment, or a large fine, or banishment. He would assent to nothing more than a fine of sixty minæ, on the security of Plato, Crito, and others of his friends. Con-

---

1 *Xen.*, *Mem.*, i., 2, 31, 37.

2 *Plat.*, *Meno*, p. 91.

3 *Plat.*, *Apol.*, p. 23, 24; *Xen.*, *Mem.*, i., 1, 1; *Diog. Laert.*, ii., 40.

4 *Xen.*, *Mem.*, i., 2, 12. Compare *Æschin. c. Timarch.*, § 173, *Bekker*.

5 *Xen.*, *l. c.*, i., 2, 9.

demned to death by the judges, who were incensed by this speech, by a majority of eighty votes, he departed from them with the protestation that he would rather die after such a defence, than live after one in which he had endeavored to excite their pity.

The sentence of death, however, could not be carried into execution until after the return of the vessel which had been sent to Delos on the periodical Theoric mission. The thirty days which intervened between its return and the execution of Socrates were devoted by him, in undisturbed repose, to poetic attempts (the first he had made in his life), and he is said to have composed a hymn in honor of Apollo and Diana, and to have versified a fable of Æsop. He devoted, also, a portion of his time to his usual conversations with his friends. One of these conversations, on the duty of obedience to the laws, Plato has reported in the *Crito*, so called after the faithful follower of Socrates, who had endeavored without success to persuade him to make his escape. In another, imitated or worked up by Plato, in his *Phædo*, Socrates, immediately before he drank the fatal cup, developed the grounds of his immovable conviction of the immortality of the soul. He died with composure and cheerfulness, in his seventieth year, B.C. 399.

The philosophical merits of Socrates are of the highest order. The mere fact that he is made the chief interlocutor in those wonderful dialogues, which contain the whole system of Plato, is sufficient to prove that he exerted no slight influence on that great philosopher, and though he never committed any of his own thoughts to writing, he has left indisputable traces of the important innovations in science, of which he must be considered as the real and first author. We have three authorities for the doctrines of Socrates, namely, Xenophon's "*Memorabilia*," the "*Dialogues*" of Plato, and the strictures of Aristotle. With regard to the first work, we have already expressed the opinion that it is to be viewed merely as a practical treatise, not as a full exposition of the philosophy of Socrates. As to Plato, there can be no doubt that he never meant to pass off as his own the doctrines and speculations which he puts into the mouth of Socrates; but we can not help feeling that the Socrates whom he represents with such dramatic truth must have been a real person, and no creature of the imagination, and that Socrates must have been the philosophical as he is the formal basis of all that Plato has done for science. If, then, we seek to make up for the deficiencies of Plato and Xenophon as exponents of the doctrines which their master actually promulgated, by turning to the criticisms of Aristotle, we shall find that Plato gives us a much truer conception of what he effected by his scientific labors than we could have derived from Xenophon. Aristotle distinctly tells us that Socrates philosophized about virtue, and made some real discoveries with regard to the first principles of science. Now this is just the philosophical basis which we discern in the Socrates of Plato.[1]

We find Socrates, as depicted to us by Plato, always endeavoring to reduce things to their first elements, stripping realities of their pompous garb of words, and striving to arrive at certainty as the standard of

[1] *Penny Cyclop.*, xxii., p. 183.

truth; and we also find that his philosophy is generally applied to ethics rather than to physics. Socrates, indeed, was the first who turned his thoughts and discussions to the subject of ethics, and was the first to proclaim that "the proper study of mankind is man." With the philosophers who preceded him, the subject of examination had been Nature, or the Cosmos, as one undistinguishable whole, blending together cosmogony, astronomy, geometry, physics, metaphysics, and other similar topics. Socrates, on the other hand, appears to have been convinced of the unity of virtue, and to have believed that it was teachable as a matter of science. In fact, with him the scientific and the moral run into one another, for knowledge is the final cause of the will, and good is the final cause of knowledge; hence he who knows what justice is must needs be just, since no one wittingly departs from that which he knows to be good.[1]

Socrates considered it to be his particular vocation to arouse the idea of science in the minds of men. This is clear from the manner in which he is said to have insisted upon the consciousness of ignorance, and also of the use which he made of the Delphian response, *γνῶθι σεαυτόν*, "Know thyself." "For," says Schleiermacher (in his valuable paper on the "Worth of Socrates as a Philosopher"), "if he went about in the service of the god, to justify the celebrated oracle, it is impossible that the utmost point he reached could have been simply to know that he knew nothing; there was a step beyond this which he must have taken, that of knowing what knowledge is. For by what other means could he have been enabled to declare that, which others believed themselves to know, to be no knowledge, than by a more correct conception of knowledge, and by a more correct method founded upon that conception?" In all the isolated particulars which are recorded of Socrates, this one object is every where discernible. His antagonistic opposition to the Sophists is one very strong feature of this. They professed to know every thing, without having the idea of science, or knowledge of what knowledge is, and as he had that idea without the mass of acquirements on which they prided themselves, he was naturally their opponent, and his strife with them is carried on entirely in this way, that he endeavors to nullify the effects of their acquired knowledge by shifting the ground from the objects to the idea of science, whereby he generally succeeds in proving their deficiency in the one thing needful to the philosopher. His *irony*, as it is called, is another remarkable proof of his devotion to his vocation as an awakener of the idea of science. The irony of Socrates has been well described as the co-existence of the idea of science in him, with the want of clear and complete views on any objects of science—in a word, as the knowledge of his ignorance. With this is intimately connected the indirect dialogical method which he invariably adopted, and which may be considered as his method of extracting scientific truth from the mass of semblances and contradictions by which it was surrounded.[2]

His *δαιμόνιον*, or secret monitor, which was a great puzzle to his contemporaries, as it has been to many of the moderns, seems to have been little more than a name which he gave to those convictions on practical

[1] *Penny Cyclop.*, xxii., p. 183.

[2] *Ibid.*

subjects which sprung up spontaneously in his mind, and for which he could not find any satisfactory means of accounting, though he felt himself constrained to follow in the course which they prescribed, as when he felt convinced of the issue of an undertaking, or was restrained by some secret misgiving from taking a certain route on his retreat from a disastrous battle.[1]

Such are the leading outlines of the philosophy of Socrates, so far as they are capable of being established with any certainty. The importance of his doctrines is most clearly perceived when we consider them as they were developed and applied by the various schools which acknowledged him as their founder, and especially as they were carried out by Plato. In all these schools we find, along with the purely Socratic element, some foreign admixture, which constitutes the diagnosis of the different systems, and it is not a matter of wonder that no school of Socratic philosophy merely adopted the principles and method of its great founder. A thoroughly original man like Socrates would naturally gather around him all the original and thinking men who fell in his way, and his business was best done by making them all think for themselves, and work by themselves, on the idea of science which he had awakened in their minds. The Socratic impulse being once communicated, it would take a different direction according to the character and natural bias of the subject on which it operated; and, though Socrates may be considered the basis of the whole superstructure, he can have no more claim to the whole merit of the Platonic philosophy than he is entitled to be blamed for the singular views entertained by some of his followers.[2]

The followers of Socrates may be divided into three classes. The *first class* consists of such as were neither philosophers by profession nor addicted to the study of philosophy, but attended upon Socrates as a moral preceptor. Among these were several young men of the first rank in Athens, particularly Alcibiades and Critias. In this class may also be placed the poet Euripides and the orator Isocrates. The *second class* included all those who, after his death, became founders of particular sects; and, though they differed from each other greatly, were united under the general appellation of Socratic philosophers. These were *Aristippus*, the founder, as he is called, of the Cyrenaic sect; *Phædon*, of the Eliac; *Euclides*, of the Megaric; *Plato*, of the Academic; and *Antisthenes*, of the Cynic. The *third class* comprehends those disciples of Socrates who, though their names are found in the catalogue of philosophers, did not institute any new sect. Among these, the most distinguished were *Xenophon*, *Æschines*, *Simon*, and *Cebes*.[3] Xenophon has already been mentioned under the head of the historical writers. We will give brief sketches of the other three.

1. Æschĭnes (Αἰσχίνης),[4] the namesake of the orator, and commonly called in literary history, for distinction' sake, *Æschines Socraticus*, "Æs-

---

[1] Lelut, *Du Démon de Socrate*, &c., Paris, 1836, ranks the belief which Socrates entertained respecting a divine and secret monitor under the head of mental hallucination.

[2] *Penny Cyclop.*, xxii., p. 184.

[3] *Enfield's History of Philosophy*, vol. i., p. 186.

[4] *Smith, Dict. Biogr.*, *s. v.*

chines the Socratic," was an Athenian of low birth, son of a sausage-seller,[1] and a disciple, although by some of his contemporaries held an unworthy one, of Socrates. From the account of Diogenes Laertius, he appears to have been the familiar friend of his great master, who said that "the sausage-seller's son alone knew how to honor him." The same writer has preserved a tradition that it was Æschines, and not Crito, who offered to assist Socrates in his escape from prison. The greater part of his life was spent in abject poverty, which gave rise to the advice of Socrates to him, "to borrow money of himself by diminishing his daily wants." After the death of his master, according to the charge of Lysias,[2] he kept a perfumer's shop with borrowed money, and, soon becoming bankrupt, was obliged to leave Athens. Whether from necessity or inclination, he followed the fashion of the day, and retired to the Syracusan court, where the friendship of Aristippus might console him for the contempt of Plato. He remained there until the expulsion of the younger Dionysius, and, on his return, finding it useless to attempt a rivalry with his great contemporaries, he gave private lectures. One of the charges which his opponents delighted to repeat, and which, by association of ideas, constituted him a sophist in the eyes of Plato and his followers, was that of receiving money for his instructions. Another story was invented that the dialogues published by him were really the work of Socrates; and Aristippus, either from joke or malice, publicly charged Æschines with the theft while he was reading them at Megara. Plato is related by Hegesander[3] to have stolen from him his solitary pupil Xenocrates.

The dialogues attributed to Æschines,[4] which bore the stamp of the Socratic method, were seven, according to Diogenes Laertius; namely, *Alcibiades*, *Axiochus*, *Aspasia*, *Callias*, *Miltiades*, *Rhinon*, and *Telauges*. Lucian says that Æschines got into the favor of Dionysius by reading to him his *Miltiades* (according to Diogenes, the worst of the seven), and that thenceforth he became one of his parasites, and forgot all the precepts of Socrates. But no critic takes Lucian's anecdotes for more than he intended them to be taken; and here his business is not to write biography. There are now extant, under the name of Æschines, three dialogues, respectively entitled, "On Virtue, whether it can be an Object of Instruction" (Περὶ 'Αρετῆς, εἰ διδακτόν); "Eryxias, or, on Wealth" ('Ερυξίας, ἢ περὶ Πλούτου); and "Axiochus, or, on Death" ('Αξίοχος, ἢ περὶ Θανάτου). These dialogues are not without merit as respects the language, though it savors of the late rhetorical school; but the best critics do not allow them to be genuine. Æschines was one of those followers of Socrates who did not aim at founding a sect. We can not collect that he professed to do more than to expound his master's doctrine, a circumstance which would increase the value of any genuine fragment of his writings. The *Axiochus* is mentioned by several ancient writers, and particularly by Athenæus,[5] in such terms as to show that it can hardly be the dialogue now extant under that name. Hermogenes considers

---

1 *Diog. Laert.*, ii., 60. 2 *Ap. Athen.*, xiii., p. 611, *E, F.* 3 *Ibid.*, xi., p. 507, *C.*
4 *Dict. Biogr. Soc. Usef. Knowl.*, vol. i., p. 406. 5 *Athen.*, p. 220, ed. *Casaub.*

Æschines superior to Xenophon in elegance and purity of style. There is a fragment of the *Aspasia* in Cicero,[1] part of which is quoted from Cicero by Quintilian.[2]

The three extant dialogues attributed to Æschines appear in almost all the editions of Plato. They were edited separately by Fischer, Leipzig, 1753, 1766, 1786, 1788, the third and fourth editions of which are the best, containing the *Testimonia Veterum*, the criticisms of Wolf, and the Fragments. The *Eryxias* and *Axiochus* are also in Böckh's edition of Simon Socraticus (*Simonis Socratici, ut videtur, dialogi* iv., &c.), Heidelberg, 1810, 8vo. There is extant a letter attributed to Æschines in the collection of Orelli, Leipzig, 1815.

2. SIMON (Σίμων)[3] was a native of Athens, a disciple of Socrates, and by trade a leather-cutter (σκυτοτόμος), which is usually Latinized *coriarius*. Socrates was accustomed to visit his shop and converse with him on various subjects. These conversations Simon afterward committed to writing, as far as he could remember them; and he is said to have been the first who recorded, in the form of conversations, the words of Socrates. His philosophical turn attracted the notice of Pericles, who offered to provide for his maintenance if he would come and reside with him; but Simon refused, on the ground that he did not wish to surrender his independence. The favorable notice of such a man as Pericles may be considered as overbalancing the unfavorable or sneering judgment of those who characterized his *Dialogues* as "leathern." He reported thirty-three conversations, Διάλογοι, *Dialogi*, which were contained in one volume. Diogenes Laertius,[4] from whom we derive our knowledge of Simon, enumerates the subjects, the variety of which shows the activity and versatility of Simon's mind. The twelfth of the so-called *Socratis et Socraticorum Epistolæ* is written in the name of Simon, and professes to be addressed to Aristippus. The concluding passage of it is cited by Stobæus. Böckh has given an edition of four spurious Platonic dialogues, ascribed to Simon (*Simonis Socratici, ut videtur, dialogi* iv., &c.), Heidelberg, 1810, 8vo, but the genuine dialogues are lost.

3. CEBES (Κέβης),[5] a native of Thebes, was also a disciple of Socrates, and connected with him by the ties of intimate friendship.[6] He is introduced by Plato as one of the interlocutors in the Phædon, and as having been present at the death of Socrates.[7] He is said at the advice of Socrates to have purchased Phædon, who had been a slave, and to have instructed him in philosophy.[8] Diogenes Laertius and Suidas ascribe to him three works, namely, Πίναξ, Ἑβδόμη, and Φρύνιχος. The last two are lost, but the Πίναξ is still extant, and is referred to by several ancient writers. This Πίναξ is a philosophical explanation of a *tablet*, on which the whole of human life, with its dangers and temptations, was symbolically represented, and which is said to have been dedicated by some one in the temple of Saturn at Athens or Thebes. The author introduces some youths contemplating the tablet, and an old man who steps among them undertakes to explain its meaning. The whole drift of the little book is to show that only the proper development of our mind and the possession

1 *De Invent.*, i., 31.
2 *Inst. Or.*, v., 11.
3 *Smith, Dict. Biogr.*, *s. v.*
4 *Diog. Laert.*, ii., 122, *seq.*
5 *Smith, Dict. Biogr.*, *s. v.*
6 *Xen.*, *Mem.*, i., 2, 28; *Plat.*, *Crit.*, p. 45, *B.*
7 *Phæd.*, p. 59, *C.*
8 *Gell.*, ii., 18; *Macrob.*, *Sat.*, i., 11.

of real virtues can make us truly happy. Suidas calls this πίναξ a διήγησις τῶν ἐν Ἅιδου, an explanation which is not applicable to the work now extant, and some have therefore thought that the πίναξ to which Suidas refers was a different work from the one which we possess. This and other circumstances have led some critics to doubt whether our πίναξ is the work of the Theban Cebes, and to ascribe it to a later Cebes of Cyzicus, a Stoic philosopher of the time of Marcus Aurelius.[1] But the πίναξ which is now extant is manifestly written in a Socratic spirit and on Socratic principles, so that, at any rate, its author is much more likely to have been a Socratic than a Stoic philosopher. There are, it is true, some few passages (*e. g.*, c. 13) where persons are mentioned belonging to a later age than that of the Theban Cebes, but there is little doubt that this and a few similar passages are interpolations by a later hand, which can not surprise us in the case of a work of such popularity as the πίναξ of Cebes; for, owing to its ethical character, it was formerly extremely popular, and the editions and translations of it are very numerous. The best modern editions are those of Schweighäuser, in his edition of Epictetus, Lips., 1799–1800, 5 vols. 8vo; and also separately printed (Strasburg, 1806, 12mo), and of Coraes, in his edition of Epictetus, Paris, 1826, 8vo.

The inferior sects which sprang from the teachings of Socrates were the *Cyrenaic*, the *Megaric*, and the *Eliac* or *Eretriac*. Those of higher celebrity were the *Academic* and the *Cynic*, from which former sprang the *Peripatetic* and the *Stoic*.

IV. THE CYRENAIC SCHOOL.

I. The *Cyrenaic* sect was founded by Aristippus, and took its name from his native city *Cyrēne*, the capital of *Cyrenaïca*, in Northern Africa.

II. Aristippus (Ἀρίστιππος)[2] was a native, as we have just said, of the Greek colony of Cyrene, in Northern Africa, and belonged to a rich family. The year of his birth is unknown, but his period is sufficiently fixed by the fact that he came to Athens when a young man to listen to Socrates,[3] and was one of his hearers till his death. Aristippus, it is said, was in the island of Ægina at the time when Socrates was executed: he was certainly not present on the occasion, as we learn from the Phædon of Plato. It is, however, rather difficult to give so much significance to the words of Plato, in which this fact is barely stated, as some ancient and modern writers have done. He was still living in the year B.C. 366,[4] but the time of his death is not recorded.

The life of Aristippus, by Diogenes Laertius, is very barren of information concerning him, and it is chiefly filled with anecdotes of his sharp sayings and repartees. According to the scanty and scattered notices of him, he rambled to various countries, and was a visitor at the court of the younger Dionysius of Syracuse at the same time with Plato. He also visited Asia, where he fell into the hands of Artaphernes, the Persian satrap who drove the Spartans from Rhodes.[5] He appears, howev-

1 *Athen.*, iv., p. 156. 2 *Smith, Dict. Biogr.*, *s. v.* 3 *Plut.*, *De Curios.*, 2.
4 *Diod. Sic.*, xv., 76. 5 *Id.*, xiv., 79. Compare *Brucker*, *Hist. Crit. Phil.*, ii., 2, 3.

er, to have returned at last to Cyrene, and there to have spent his old age. The brief notices that we have of Aristippus represent him as a man who viewed pleasure as the object of life, and showed by his example that he considered the enjoyments of sense as part of a wise man's pursuit. He indulged in the luxuries of the table, and frequented the company of prostitutes. Among his favorites was the notorious Lais. He made himself as happy as he could in all circumstances. His philosophy suited the views of Horace in his maturer age, who characterizes the versatility of his character by one happy line;[1] and in another passage[2] he represents Aristippus as trying to subject circumstances to himself, and not submitting to circumstances; where, as Wieland observes, Horace intends to mark the opposition between the Cyrenaic and the Stoic systems.

Aristippus is called the founder of the Cyrenaic sect, but there is no clear proof that he left behind him any systematic exposition of his doctrines. If he did leave any written system, it would appear to have attracted little attention, for, as Ritter observes, Aristotle makes no mention of Aristippus in his Nicomachean Ethics, though he there examines the subject of pleasure, and the various opinions upon it. Yet he is said to have had hearers, and he was the first of the Socratics who received pay for his instructions, with which he is reproached, though without his name being mentioned, by Xenophon. Xenophon disliked Aristippus, and accordingly, as Diogenes Laertius observes, he makes Socrates direct his discourse on temperance against him. Aristotle called him a sophist, partly, as would seem, because he took pay for his teaching, but mainly in reference to his doctrines. The school of Aristippus derives its name from Cyrene, not simply because the founder was born and perhaps taught there in his old age, but because his successors also lived there, or in the neighboring parts. Aristippus taught his daughter Arete and Antipater of Cyrene. Arete taught her son, the younger Aristippus, who is called the "Mother-taught" (Μητροδίδακτος), and is said to have systematized his grandfather's doctrines. Diogenes Laertius,[3] on the authority of Sotion (B.C. 205) and Panætius (B.C. 143), gives a long list of books whose authorship is ascribed to Aristippus, though he also says that Sosicrates of Rhodes (B.C. 255) states that he wrote nothing. Among these are treatises Περὶ Παιδείας, Περὶ Ἀρετῆς, Περὶ Τύχης, and many others. Some epistles attributed to him are deservedly rejected as forgeries by Bentley.[4]

The Cyrenaics despised Physics, and limited their inquiries to Ethics, though they included under that term a much wider range of science than can fairly be reckoned as belonging to it. So, too, Aristippus neglected mathematics, as being a study not concerned, in any way, with good and evil;[5] which is consistent with the doctrines of Socrates, who set little value on pursuits that had not a moral object. They divided philosophy into five parts, namely, the study of (1) Objects of desire and aversion; (2) Feelings and Affections; (3) Actions; (4) Causes; (5)

[1] *Epist.*, i., 17, 23. [2] *Ib.*, i., 1, 18. [3] *Diog. Laert.*, ii., 65.
[4] *Dissertation on Phalaris*, p. 104. [5] *Metaphys.*, ii., 2.

Proofs. Of these, (4) is clearly connected with Physics, and (5) with Logic.

1. The first of these five divisions of science is the only one in which the Cyrenaic view is connected with the Socratic. Socrates considered happiness (i. e., the enjoyment of a well-ordered mind) to be the aim of all men, and Aristippus, taking up this position, pronounced pleasure the chief good, and pain the chief evil; in proof of which he referred to the natural feelings of men, children, and animals; but he wished the mind to preserve its authority in the midst of pleasure. Desire he could not admit into his system, as it subjects men to hope and fear: the τέλος of human life was momentary pleasure (μονόχρονος, μερική). For the present only is ours, the past is gone, and the future is uncertain; present happiness, therefore, is to be sought, and not εὐδαιμονία, which is only the sum of a number of happy states, just as he considered *life* in general the sum of particular states of the soul. In this point the Cyrenaics were opposed to the Epicureans. All pleasures were held equal, though they might admit of a difference in the degree of their purity. So that a man ought never to covet more than he possesses, and should never allow himself to be overcome by sensual enjoyment. It is plain that, even with these concessions, the Cyrenaic system destroys all moral unity, by proposing to a man as many separate τέλη as his life contains moments.

2. The next point is to determine what is pleasure and what pain. Both are positive, that is, pleasure is not the gratification of a want, nor does the absence of pleasure equal pain. The absence of either is a mere negative inactive state, and both pleasure and pain are motions of the soul (ἐν κινήσει). Pain was defined to be a violent, pleasure a moderate motion, the first being compared to the sea in a storm, the second to the sea under a light breeze, the intermediate state of no-pleasure and no-pain to a calm, a simile not quite apposite, since a calm is not the middle state between a storm and a gentle breeze. In this denial of pleasure as a state of rest we find Aristippus again opposed to Epicurus.

3. Actions are in themselves morally indifferent, the only question for us to consider being their result; and law and custom are the only authorities which make an action good or bad. This monstrous dogma was a little qualified by the statement that the advantages of injustice are slight.

4. There is no universality in human conceptions; the senses are the only avenues of knowledge, and even these admit a very limited range of information. For the Cyrenaics said that men could agree neither in judgments nor notions, in nothing, in fact, but names. We have all certain sensations, which we call *white* or *sweet*, but whether the sensation which A calls *white* is similar to that which B calls by that name, we can not tell; for by the common term *white* every man denotes a distinct object. Of the causes which produce these sensations we are quite ignorant; and from all this we come to the doctrine of modern philological metaphysics, that truth is what each man troweth. All states of mind are motions; nothing exists but states of mind, and they are not the same

to all men. True wisdom consists, therefore, in transforming disagreeable into agreeable sensations.

5. As to the Cyrenaic doctrine of proofs no evidence remains. In many of these opinions we recognize the happy, careless, selfish disposition which characterized their author; and the system resembles in most points those of Heraclitus and Protagoras, as given in Plato's Theætetus. The doctrines that a subject only knows objects through the prism of the impressions which he receives, and that man is the measure of all things, are stated or implied in the Cyrenaic system, and lead at once to the consequence that what we call reality is appearance; so that the whole fabric of human knowledge becomes a fantastic picture. The principle on which all this rests, namely, that knowledge is sensation, is the foundation of Locke's modern ideology, though he did not perceive its connection with the consequences to which it led the Cyrenaics. To revive these was reserved for Hume.[1]

V. THE MEGARIC SCHOOL.

I. The *Megaric* sect was instituted by EUCLĪDES (Εὐκλείδης) of *Megara*, and took its name from the place which gave birth to its founder. From its disputatious character, it also received the appellation of *Eristic* (Ἐριστική, from ἐρίζειν, "to contend"); and it was likewise termed the *Dialectic*, not because it gave rise to dialectics or logical debates, which had before this time exercised the ingenuity of philosophers, particularly in the Eleatic school, but because the discourses and writings of this class of philosophers commonly took the form of a dialogue.

II. EUCLIDES[2] was a native of Megara, the capital of the district of Megaris. According to some less probable accounts, he was born at Gela, in Sicily. He was one of the chief disciples of Socrates, but, before becoming such, he had studied the doctrines, and especially the dialectics of the Eleatics. Socrates on one occasion reproved him for his fondness for subtle and captious disputes.[3] On the death of Socrates, Euclides, with most of the other pupils of that philosopher, took refuge in Megara, and there established a school which distinguished itself by the cultivation of dialectics. The doctrines of the Eleatics formed the basis of his philosophical system. With these he blended the ethical and dialectical principles of Socrates. The Eleatic dogma, that there is one universal, unchangeable existence, he viewed in a moral aspect, calling this one existence the *Good*, but giving it also other names (as Reason, Intelligence, &c.), perhaps for the purpose of explaining how the real, though one, appeared to be many. He rejected demonstration, attacking not so much the premises assumed as the conclusions drawn, and also reasoning from analogy. He is said to have been a man of a somewhat indolent and procrastinating disposition. Euclides was the author of six dialogues, no one of which, however, has come down to us. He has frequently been erroneously confounded with the mathematician of the same name.

Euclides introduced new subtleties into the art of disputation, several of which, though often mentioned as examples of great ingenuity, deserve

[1] *Smith, Dict. Biogr.*, s. v.   [2] *Id. ib.*   [3] *Diog. Laert.*, ii., 30.

only to be remembered as proofs of egregious trifling. Of these sophistical modes of reasoning, called by Aristotle Eristic syllogisms, a few examples may suffice. 1. The *Lying* sophism: If, when you speak the truth, you say, you lie, you lie: but you say you lie, when you speak the truth; therefore, in speaking the truth, you lie. 2. The *Occult:* Do you know your father? Yes. Do you know this man who is veiled? No. Then you do not know your father, for it is your father who is veiled. 3. The *Sorites:* Is one grain a heap? No. Two grains? No. Three grains? No. Go on, adding one by one; and, if one grain be not a heap, it will be impossible to say what number of grains make a heap. In such high repute were these silly inventions for perplexing plain truth, that Chrysippus wrote six books upon the first of these sophisms; and Philetas, a Coan, died of consumption, which he had contracted by the close study that he had bestowed upon it.

III. The only other member of the Megaric school deserving of being mentioned here is STILPON (Στίλπων),[1] also a native of Megara. According to one account, he engaged in dialectic encounters with Diodorus, nicknamed Cronus, at the court of Ptolemy Soter; while, according to another, he did not comply with the invitation of the king to visit Alexandrea. He acquired great reputation, and so high was the esteem in which he was held, that Demetrius, the son of Antigonus, spared his house at the capture of Megara. He is said to have surpassed all his contemporaries in inventive power and dialectic art, and to have inspired almost all Greece with a devotion to the Megaric philosophy. A number of distinguished men, too, are named, whom he is said to have drawn away from Aristotle, Theophrastus, and others, and attached to himself; among others, Crates the Cynic, and Zeno, the founder of the Stoic school. Not less commendation is bestowed upon his political wisdom, his simple, straightforward disposition, and the equanimity with which he endured the fate of being the father of a degenerate daughter. Of the nine dialogues which were ascribed to him, and which are said to have been of a somewhat frigid kind, we learn only the titles, two of which seem to point to a polemical disquisition on Aristippus and Aristotle. In like manner, we obtain exceedingly scanty disclosures respecting his doctrines in the few propositions and sayings of his which are quoted, torn as they are from their connection. Only we can scarcely fail to recognize in them the direction which the Megaric philosophy took, to demonstrate that the phenomenal world is unapproachable to true knowledge. He seems, however, especially to have made the idea of virtue the object of his consideration, and to have placed in a prominent point of view the self-sufficiency of it. He maintained that the wise man ought not only to overcome every evil, but not even to be affected by any, not even to feel it.

VI. THE ELIAC AND ERETRIAC SCHOOL.

I. The *Eliac* school is represented by PHÆDON (Φαίδων),[2] a native of Elis. He was of high birth; but was taken prisoner in his youth, and

[1] *Smith, Dict. Biogr., s. v.*

[2] *Id. ib.*

became a slave at Athens. According to Diogenes Laertius, he ran away from his master to Socrates, and was ransomed by one of the friends of the latter.[1] Phædon then attached himself to Socrates, and was present at the death of the philosopher while yet quite a youth.[2] He appears to have lived in Athens some time after the death of Socrates, and then returned to Elis, where he became the founder of a school of philosophy.[3] He was succeeded by Plistanus,[4] after whom the Eliac school was merged in the Eretriac, by Menedemus. Of the doctrines of Phædon nothing is known, except as they made their appearance in the philosophy of Menedemus. None of his writings have come down to us. They were in the form of dialogues. The celebrated dialogue of Plato on the immortality of the soul is named after Phædon.

II. MENEDĒMUS (Μενέδημος),[5] a native of Eretria, though of noble birth, was poor, and worked for a livelihood either as a builder or a tent-maker. According to one story, he seized the opportunity afforded by his being sent on some military service to Megara to hear Plato, and abandoned the army to addict himself to philosophy; but it may be questioned whether he was old enough to have heard Plato before the death of the latter. According to another story, he and his friend Asclepiades got their livelihood as millers,[6] working during the night that they might have leisure for philosophy during the day. The two friends afterward became disciples of Stilpon at Megara. From Megara they went to Elis, and placed themselves under the instruction of some disciples of Phædon. On his return to Eretria, Menedemus established a school of philosophy, which was called the Eretriac. He did not, however, confine himself to philosophical pursuits, but took an active part in the political affairs of his native city, and came to be the leading man in the state. He went on various embassies to Lysimachus, Demetrius, and others; but, being suspected of the treacherous intention of betraying Eretria into the hands of Antigonus, he quitted his native city secretly, and took refuge with Antigonus in Asia. Here he starved himself to death, in the seventy-fourth year of his age, probably about B.C. 277.

Of the philosophy of Menedemus little is known, except that it closely resembled that of the Megaric school. Its leading feature was the dogma of the oneness of the *Good*, which he carefully distinguished from the *Useful*. All distinctions between virtues he regarded as merely nominal. The Good and the True he looked upon as identical. In dialectics, he rejected all merely negative propositions, maintaining that truth could be predicated only of those which were affirmative, and of these he admitted only such as were identical propositions. He was a keen and vehement disputant, frequently arguing, if we may believe Antigonus Carystius, as quoted by Diogenes Laertius, till he was black in the face. He never committed any of his doctrines to writing.

[1] *Diog. Laert.*, ii., 105. [2] *Plat.*, *Phæd.*, c. 38. [3] *Diog. Laert.*, ii., 126.
[4] *Id.*, ii., 105. [5] *Smith*, *Dict.*, *s. v.* [6] *Athen.*, iv., p. 168.

VII. THE ACADEMIC SCHOOL.

I. The *Academic* school, or *Academy*, as it is more familiarly termed, derived its name from the *Academia* (Ἀκαδημία), a public grove or garden in the suburbs of Athens, where Plato established his school.

II. The Academy was divided into the *Old*, the *Middle*, and the *New*. The *Old Academy* consisted of those followers of Plato who taught the doctrines of their master without admixture or corruption. The *Middle Academy* commenced with Arcesilaus or Arcesilas, and brought in the skeptical doctrine of *uncertainty;* in other words, it taught that every thing is uncertain to the human understanding, and that all confident assertions are unreasonable, and to be avoided. The *New Academy* was established by Carneades, who introduced what has been termed the doctrine of *probabilities;* namely, that although the senses, the understanding, and the imagination frequently deceive us, and therefore can not be infallible judges of truth, still that, from the impressions which we perceive to be produced on the mind by means of the senses, we infer *appearances* of truth, or *probabilities*. We will now give a sketch of the philosophers of the Old Academy, reserving the Middle and the New Academy for the Alexandrine and Roman periods respectively.

OLD ACADEMY.

I. Plato (Πλάτων),[1] the celebrated founder of the Old Academy, was born, according to the most consistent accounts, in B.C. 429. His father was Ariston, the son of Aristocles, and Plato is said to have been originally called Aristocles, after his grandfather, according to a custom very common among the Greeks. The old anecdote-collectors have thought it necessary to find some explanation of the second name, by which he is now known, as, for instance, that he was so called from the breadth of his style (διὰ τὴν πλατύτητα τῆς ἑρμηνείας), or from his expansive forehead (ὅτι πλατὺς ἦν τὸ μέτωπον);[2] but this seems quite idle, as the name Plato was of common occurrence among the Athenians of that time. The philosopher's mother was Perictione, to whom later writers attribute a lineal descent from Execestides, the father of Solon. As might have been expected from the high standing of his family, Plato received the best education that Athens could furnish. He was even sufficiently skilled in wrestling to contend at the Pythian and Isthmian games; and his first literary attempts, namely, the composition of dithyrambic, lyric, and tragic poems, showed that he had profited by the instructions of his teachers in music and literature. He is also said to have applied himself to painting.

Plato's connection with Socrates is said to have commenced in B.C. 410. He had previously become acquainted, through Cratylus, with the doctrines of Heraclitus,[3] and through other instructors, or by means of writings, with the philosophical dogmas of the Eleatics and of Anaxagoras. The intimacy of the relation between Socrates and himself is attested, better than by hearsay accounts and insufficient testimonies, by

[1] *Smith, Dict. Biogr., s. v.*

[2] *Diog. Laert.*, iii., 4; *Vita Platonis*, p. 6, *B.*

[3] *Aristot., Metaph.*, i., 6.

the enthusiastic love with which Plato not only exhibits Socrates as he lived and died—in the Banquet and Phædon—but also glorifies him by making him the leader of the investigations in the greater part of his dialogues; not as though he had thought himself secure of the assent of Socrates to all the conclusions and developments which he had himself drawn from the few though pregnant principles of his teacher, but in order to express his conviction that he had organically developed the results involved in the Socratic doctrine. It is therefore probable enough that, as Plutarch[1] relates, at the close of his life he praised that dispensation which had made him a contemporary of Socrates. At the death of the latter, he betook himself, with others of the Socratics, as Hermogenes had related, in order to avoid threatened persecutions,[2] to Euclides, at Megara, who, of all his contemporaries, had the nearest mental affinity with him. That Plato, during his residence in Megara, composed several of his dialogues, especially those of a dialectical character, is probable enough, though there is no direct evidence on the subject.[3]

Friendship for the mathematician Theodorus (though this, indeed, does not manifest itself in the way in which the latter is introduced in the Theætetus) is said to have led Plato next to Cyrene.[4] Through his eagerness for knowledge, he is said to have been induced to visit Egypt, Sicily, and the Greek cities in Lower Italy.[5] Others, however, in inverted order, make him travel first to Sicily and then to Egypt,[6] or from Sicily to Cyrene and Egypt, and then again to Sicily. As his companion, we find mentioned Eudoxus,[7] or Simmias,[8] or even Euripides. The more distant journeys of Plato into the interior of Asia, to the Hebrews, Babylonians, and Assyrians, to the Magi and Persians, are mentioned only by writers on whom no reliance can be placed. That Plato, during his residence in Sicily, became acquainted, through Dion, with the elder Dionysius, but very soon fell out with the tyrant, is asserted by credible witnesses. But more doubt attaches to the story which relates that he was given up by the tyrant to the Spartan ambassador Pollis, by him sold into Ægina, and set at liberty by the Cyrenean Anniceris. Plato is said to have visited Sicily when forty years old, consequently in B.C. 389.

After his return, he began to teach, partly in the gymnasium of the Academia and its shady avenues, between the Ceramīcus and the hill Colōnus Hippius, partly in his garden, which was situated at Colonus.[9] Respecting the acquisition of this garden, and the circumstances of Plato as regards property generally, we have conflicting accounts, which need not here be examined into. Plato taught gratuitously,[10] and, agreeably to his maxims,[11] without doubt mainly in the form of lively dialogue; yet on the more difficult parts of his doctrinal system he probably also delivered connected lectures. The more narrow circle of his disciples (the number of them, which can scarcely have remained uniform, is stated at

[1] *Marius*, 46. Compare *Lactant.*, *Div. Inst.*, iii., 19.
[2] *Diog. Laert.*, ii., 106; iii., 16.
[3] *Ast, vom Leben, &c., des Plato*, p. 51.
[4] *Diog. Laert.*, iii., 6.
[5] *Cic.*, *De Rep.*, i., 10; *De Fin.*, v., 29.
[6] *Quintil.*, i., 12, 15; *Diog. Laert.*, iii., 6.
[7] *Strab.*, xvii., 29.
[8] *Plut.*, *De Dæm. Socr.*, 7.
[9] *Timon. ap. Diog. Laert.*, iii., 7; *Plut.*, *De Exil.*, c. 10, *seqq.*
[10] *Diog. Laert.*, iv., 2.
[11] *Phæd.*, p. 275; *Protag.*, p. 329; *Gorg.*, p. 449.

twenty-eight) assembled themselves in his garden at common, simple meals,[1] and it was probably to them alone that the inscription, said to have been set up over the vestibule of the house, "Let no one enter who is unacquainted with geometry,"[2] had reference. From this house came forth his nephew Speusippus, Xenocrates of Chalcedon, Aristotle, Heraclides Ponticus, Hestiæus of Perinthus, Philippus the Opuntian, and others, men from the most distant parts of Greece. To the wider circle of those who, without attaching themselves to the more narrow community of the school, sought instruction and incitement from him, such distinguished men as Chabrias, Iphicrates,[3] Timotheus,[4] Phocion, Hyperides, Lycurgus, and Isocrates[5] are said to have belonged. Whether Demosthenes was of the number is doubtful. Even women are said to have attached themselves to him as his disciples.

Plato's occupation as an instructor was twice interrupted by his voyages to Sicily: first, when Dion, probably soon after the death of the elder Dionysius, persuaded him to make the attempt to win the younger Dionysius to philosophy;[6] the second time, a few years later (about B.C. 360), when the wish of his Pythagorean friends, and the invitation of Dionysius to reconcile the disputes which had broken out between him and his step-uncle Dion, brought him back to Syracuse. His efforts were both times unsuccessful, and he owed his own safety to nothing but the earnest intercession of Archytas.[7] That Plato cherished the hope of realizing, through the conversion of Dionysius, his idea of a state in the rising city of Syracuse, was a belief generally spread in antiquity,[8] and which finds some confirmation in the expressions of the philosopher himself, and of the seventh Platonic letter, which, though spurious, is written with the most evident acquaintance with the matters of which it treats. With the exception of these two visits to Sicily, Plato was occupied, from the time when he opened the school in the Academy, in giving instruction and in the composition of his works. He died in the eighty-second year of his age, B.C. 347. He is said by some to have died while writing, by others at a marriage-feast.

According to his last will, his garden remained the property of the school,[9] and passed, considerably increased by later additions, into the hands of the New Platonists, who kept as a festival his birth-day, as well as that of Socrates.[10] Athenians and strangers honored his memory by monuments. Yet he had no lack of enemies and enviers, and the attacks which were made upon him, partly by contemporary comic poets, partly by one-sided Socratics, as Antisthenes, Diogenes, and the later Megarics,[11] found a loud echo among Epicureans, Stoics, certain Peripatetics, and later writers eager for detraction. Thus, even Antisthenes and Aristoxenus charged him with sensuality, avarice, and sycophancy;[12] and others with vanity, ambition, and envy toward other Socratics.[13] Others,

---

1 *Athen.*, i., 7; xii., 69; x., 14.
2 *Tzetzes*, *Chiliad.*, viii., 972.
3 *Aristid.*, ii., p. 325.
4 *Athen.*, x., 14.
5 *Diog. Laert.*, iii., 46.
6 *Plat.*, *Epist.*, vii., p. 327; iii., p. 316, *C.*
7 *Id. ib.*, vii., p. 339.
8 *Plut.*, *Philos. e princ.*, c. 4; *Diog. Laert.*, iii., 21.
9 *Diog. Laert.*, iii., 43.
10 *Damasc. ap. Phot.*, cod. ccxlii.
11 *Diog. Laert.*, iii., 35; vi., 7, &c.
12 *Id.*, iii., 29.
13 *Athen.*, xi., p. 507, *D*; *Diog. Laert.*, vi., 3. 7, 24, 26, &c.

again, accused him of having borrowed the form and substance of his doctrine from earlier philosophers, as Aristippus, Antisthenes,[1] Protagoras,[2] Epicharmus,[3] and Philolaus. But, as the latter accusation is refuted both by the contradiction which it carries in itself, and by a comparison of the Pythagorean doctrines with those of Plato, so is the former, not only by the weakness of the evidence brought forward in its favor, but still more by the depth and purity of moral sentiment, which, with all the marks of internal truth, is reflected in the writings of Plato.

WRITINGS OF PLATO.[4]

These writings have come down to us complete, and have always been admired as a model of the union of artistic perfection with philosophical acuteness and depth. They are in the form of dialogue; but Plato was not the first writer who employed this style of composition for philosophical instruction. Zeno the Eleatic had already written in the form of question and answer. Alexamenus the Teian, and Sophron in the Mimes, had treated ethical subjects in the form of dialogue. Xenophon, Æschines Socraticus, Antisthenes, Euclides, and other Socratics, had also made use of the dialogistic form; but Plato has handled this form not only with greater mastery than any one who preceded him, but, in all probability, with the distinct intention of keeping, by this very means, true to the admonition of Socrates, not to communicate instruction, but to lead to the spontaneous discovery of it.

The dialogues of Plato are closely connected with one another, and various arrangements of them have been proposed. Schleiermacher's division appears, on the whole, to be the best. He divides the works of Plato into three series or classes. In the *first* he considers that the germs of dialectic and of the doctrine of ideas begin to unfold themselves in all the freshness of youthful inspiration; in the *second*, those germs develop themselves further by means of dialectic investigations, respecting the difference between common and philosophical acquaintance with things, respecting notion and knowledge (δόξα and ἐπιστήμη); in the *third* they receive their completion by means of an objectively scientific working out, with the separation of ethics and physics. The first series embraces, according to Schleiermacher, the *Phædrus*, *Lysis*, *Protagoras*, *Laches*, *Charmides*, *Euthyphron*, and *Parmenides;* to which may be added, as an appendix, the *Apologia*, *Crito*, *Ion*, *Hippias Minor*, *Hipparchus*, *Minos*, and *Alcibiades II.* The second series contains the *Gorgias*, *Theætetus*, *Meno*, *Euthydemus*, *Cratylus*, *Sophistes*, *Politicus*, *Symposium*, *Phædon*, and *Philebus;* to which may be added, as an appendix, the *Theages*, *Erastæ*, *Alcibiades I.*, *Menexenus*, *Hippias Major*, and *Clitophon*. The third series comprises the *Republic*, *Timæus*, *Critias*, and the *Laws*.[5]

The genuineness of several of the dialogues has been questioned, but, for the most part, on insufficient grounds. The *Epinomis*, however, is probably to be assigned to a disciple of Plato; the *Minos* and *Hipparchus* to a Socratic. The second *Alcibiades* was attributed by ancient critics

[1] *Theopomp. ap. Athen.*, xi., p. 508, *C.* [2] *Diog. Laert.*, iii., 37. [3] *Id.*, iii., 9.
[4] *Smith*, *Dict. Biogr.*, *s. v.* [5] *Schleiermacher's Plato*, *Einleitung*, &c., p. 45, *seqq.*

to Xenophon. The *Erastæ* and *Clitophon* are probably of much later origin. The Platonic letters were composed at different periods; the oldest of them, the seventh and eighth, probably by disciples of Plato. These letters, some of which are of considerable length, have reference to the visits made by Plato to Sicily, and to the intrigues of which this island was the theatre, in consequence of the tyranny of the younger Dionysius and the movements of Dion. The correspondence in question appears to have been published by some of the followers of Plato, with the view of exculpating their master from the charge of fomenting troubles in Syracuse. The dialogues *Demodocus*, *Sisyphus*, *Eryxias*, *Axiochus*, and those on justice and virtue, were with good reason regarded by ancient critics as spurious; and with them may be associated the *Hipparchus*, *Theages*, and the *Definitions*. The genuineness of the first *Alcibiades* seems doubtful. The *smaller Hippias*, the *Ion*, and the *Menexenus*, on the other hand, which are assailed by many modern critics, may very well maintain their ground as occasional compositions of Plato.[1]

No one can be conversant with the writings of Plato without perceiving every where the strong tincture of that poetical spirit which he displayed in his earliest productions. This is the principal ground of those lofty encomiums which both ancient and modern critics have passed upon his style, and particularly of the high estimation in which it was held by Cicero, who, treating of the subject of diction, says, that "if Jupiter were to speak in the Greek tongue, he would use the language of Plato." The accurate Stagirite describes it as "a middle species of diction, between prose and verse." Some of his dialogues are elevated by such sublime and glowing conceptions, are enriched with such copious diction, and flow with so harmonious a rhythm, that they may truly be pronounced to be highly poetical. Even in the discussion of abstract subjects, the language of Plato is often clear, simple, and full of harmony. At other times, however, he becomes turgid and swelling, and involves himself in obscurities which were either the offspring of a lofty fancy, or borrowed from the Italic school.[2]

PHILOSOPHY OF PLATO.[3]

The attempt to combine poetry and philosophy (the two fundamental tendencies of the Greek mind) gives to the Platonic dialogues a charm which irresistibly attracts us, though we may have but a deficient comprehension of their subject-matter. Plato, like Socrates, was penetrated with the idea that wisdom is the attribute of the godhead; that philosophy, springing from the impulse *to know*, is the necessity of the intellectual man, and the greatest of the blessings in which he participates.[4] When once we strive after Wisdom with the intensity of a lover, she becomes the true consecration and purification of the soul, adapted to lead us from the night-like to the true day.[5] An approach to wisdom, however, presupposes an original communion with *Being*, truly so called;

[1] *Schleiermacher's Plato, Einleitung*, &c.
[2] *Smith, l. c.*
[3] *Id. ib.*
[4] *Phædr.*, p. 278, *D*; *Lysis*, p. 218, *A*; *Apolog.*, p. 23.
[5] *De Rep.*, vii., p. 521, *D*; vi., p. 485, *B*.

and this communion, again, presupposes the divine nature or immortality of the soul, and the impulse to become *like* the Eternal. This impulse is the love which generates in Truth, and the development of it is termed *Dialectics*. Out of the philosophical impulse which is developed by *Dialectics*, not only correct knowledge, but also correct action, springs forth.

Socrates's doctrine respecting the unity of virtue, and that it consists in true, vigorous, and practical knowledge, is intended to be set forth in a preliminary manner in the *Protagoras*, and the smaller dialogues attached to it. They are designed, therefore, to introduce a foundation for ethics, by the refutation of the common views that were entertained of morals and of virtue; for although not even the words ethics and physics occur in Plato, and even dialectics are not treated of as a distinct and separate province, yet he must rightly be regarded as the originator of the three-fold division of philosophy,[1] inasmuch as he had before him the decided object, to develop the Socratic method into a scientific system of dialectics, that should supply the grounds of our knowledge as well as of our moral action (physics and ethics), and, therefore, he separates the general investigations on knowledge and understanding, at least relatively, from those which refer to physics and ethics. Accordingly, the *Theætetus*, *Sophistes*, *Parmenides*, and *Cratylus* are principally dialectical; the *Protagoras*, *Gorgias*, *Politicus*, and *Philebus* principally ethical; while the *Timæus* is exclusively physical. Plato's dialectics and ethics, however, have been more successful than his physics.

Plato's doctrine of *ideas* was one of the most prominent parts of his system. The great object of the dialectician is to establish what are those general terms which are the object of the mind when a man thinks. It is clear that they can not be objects of sense, for these are in a continual state of transition.[2] They must, therefore, be of the number of those things which we know by means of reflection (διάνοια), through the understanding (λογισμός, νοῦς, νόησις), for these things being fixed, belong to οὐσία, and can become the objects of science, or certain knowledge.[3] Every thing of this kind is an εἶδος, that is, a general term,[4] or quiddity.[5] Consequently, there is an *idea*, or εἶδος, of every thing that is called by a general name. Hence the formula for the universal is neither ἕν only, as the Eleatics said, nor πολλά only, as the Heracliteans asserted, but ἓν καὶ πολλά, "the one and the many," *i. e.*, the subject of which many predicates may be asserted, and which, therefore, appears as manifold.[6] From all this, it will appear that Plato regarded philosophy as an undressing of the world, as the means of discovering the certainty and eternity which are in this world hidden and wrapped up in the garb of the mutable and the temporal. For if the sensible is true, which he maintains against the Eleatics, it is true only through the essence of which it partakes; and therefore the object of philosophy must be to strip off this garment of the sensible, and ascend to the *superior idea* which contains

[1] *Aristocles, ap. Euseb. Præp. Ev.*, xi., 33.
[2] *Parmenid.*, p. 152, *A*.
[3] *Parmen.*, p. 129, *E*; *Phædr.*, p. 65, *C*.
[4] *De Rep.*, x., p. 596, *A*; *Leg.*, x., p. 835.
[5] *Phædr.*, p. 237, *B*.
[6] *De Rep.*, v., p. 476, *A*; *Sophist.*, p. 251, *A*.

all the subordinate ones, and which has nothing in it capable of being apprehended by the senses, for individual ideas are but hypothetical notions, for which a true ground can only be given by a higher hypothesis; and thus God is the common standard of all things, and not the individual man, as Protagoras said.[1]

The nature of the human soul, according to Plato, is the same as that of the soul of the universe; but as, until death separates them, the human soul is connected with a mortal body, it stands in a relation to the sensible or perishable, as well as to the ideal or eternal. So far as it is related to the sensible, it participates in the changeable and transitory properties of the sensible; hence in the soul there is a mortal as well as immortal element. The one is divine and the seat of the reason, the other the seat of the passions. But when subordinate to the divine reason, keeping the passions in check, delighting in pure aspirations, striving after the real and beautiful, it is the link between the divine and human nature, both of which are combined in man. This link between the divine and the human, the ideal and the sensible, has two antagonistic tendencies. That which is in the direction of the divine is represented by θυμός, which, though untranslatable, implies spirit, heart, zeal, courage, love, hope, earnestness—in a word, what we understand by the term emotions. The tendency, on the other hand, toward the objects of sense is represented by ἐπιθυμία, appetite, or concupiscence, which is capable of control and of right direction. The soul, therefore, may be considered as a state in which the reason or divine soul is the governing power, and the θυμός and ἐπιθυμία are the subordinate members. When, therefore, the reason does not demand more than is right, or the other parts refuse their just obedience, that constitutional state results which, according to Plato, constitutes virtue.[2]

Immortality is the property of the rational soul alone, and the following are the principal Platonic statements and arguments which refer to this great doctrine. Most of these will be found in the *Phædon*, a dialogue which has for its principal subject-matter the proof of this doctrine. 1. Whatever comes into existence proceeds from its contrary, and as from life comes death, so from death comes life. Therefore, the phenomena which we call death is the passing into life, and our souls exist in the unseen world, or Ἀΐδης. 2. It is an invariable law of nature that nothing perishes; if, therefore, the soul existed previous to its union with the body, it necessarily follows that it is immortal. 3. Nothing can be dissolved or dissipated unless it be compounded. Now the soul is simple, uncompounded, not cognizable by the senses, and therefore not capable of dissolution, but endued with properties of existence independent of the body. 4. The soul is not, as has been held by some, a mere harmonious adjustment of the parts of the body, which is destroyed when those parts decay; for harmony can not coexist with discord, and the soul, when deranged by vice, presents an appearance of discord rather than of harmony. 5. All knowledge is the recollection of truth which was revealed

[1] *Leg.*, iv., p. 716, *C*; *Penny Cyclop.*, xviii., p. 235.

[2] *Browne's Hist. Class. Lit.*, vol. ii., p. 250.

to us in a former state of being, for there is nothing real but the idea, to which we can not attain in this life. As, therefore, the soul has lived before, so it will again, after it is set free from the body. 6. The number of immortal beings is a constant quantity; if the living died and remained in that state, a universal death would absorb all nature. 7. The body is the great cause of error, and experience proves that the more we can abstract ourselves from the influence of it, the more free and powerful are the energies of the soul. This approximation, therefore, or tendency toward a perfect state, proves that the natural state of the soul, that in which it is best fitted for intellectual energy, is one of independence of the body.[1]

From this brief and necessarily imperfect sketch of Plato's philosophy we may form, notwithstanding, some idea of the catholic spirit of this great writer, and the grand and original conceptions by which he endeavored to unite in one great system all that was true in the results of previous investigations. Plato was the greatest of all philosophers, because he was the first who adopted a true method, and followed it out in all its bearings and applications. It would not be easy to overrate the influence which Plato's works have exercised upon the speculations of all subsequent inquirers. Although his name has not been so much bandied about for good or for ill as that of his scholar Aristotle, his intellectual empire has been neither less extensive nor less durable. Coleridge has said that all men are born disciples of either Aristotle or Plato; a saying which, as far as it goes, is perfectly true. It means that the doctrines which Plato was the first to proclaim to the world will always be adopted by those who come to the hearing of them with minds akin to his; otherwise they will have recourse to the modification of those doctrines which was propounded by Aristotle, whose mind was no less repugnant than their own to the spirit of Platonism.[2]

POLITICAL THEORIES OF PLATO.[3]

The political theories which Plato based upon his ethical system will require only a brief notice. His views tended decidedly toward oligarchy, or, as he would have called it, aristocracy. He had a great admiration for Dorian institutions, and a great aversion to democracies, especially to that of Athens. His connection with the chief agents in the oligarchical revolution at Athens may have had some share in this, and it is certainly some proof of the intimate connection between his political opinions and those of the party to which we refer, that the interlocutors in the great trilogy of dialogues, which contains the *Republic*, the *Timæus*, and the *Critias*, are, besides Socrates, the Syracusan Hermocrates, the deadliest foe of Athens, Critias, the head of the Thirty Tyrants, and Timæus, the speculative Locrian legislator. From a set of dialogues managed by such persons as these we should hardly expect any thing different in politics from what we find in them; an attempt, namely, to recommend, by argument and fiction, a system of government based upon

---

[1] *Browne's Hist. Class. Lit.*, vol. ii., p. 250.

[2] *Penny Cyclop.*, xviii., p. 241.

[3] *Ibid.*, p. 239.

Dorian and immediately upon Lacedæmonian institutions. There is something eminently unfeeling in the manner in which Plato, after the manner of the Lacedæmonians, considers marriage in a gross and physical light, and subordinates all the better sentiments of human nature to the harsh jurisdiction of an uncompromising aristocracy.

It has been supposed by Morgenstern[1] that one of the later comedies of Aristophanes, the *Ecclesiazusæ*, is directed against this Λακωνομανία of the great philosopher. Stallbaum[2] has opposed this conjecture with some chronological arguments, which Meineke does not consider satisfactory. Meineke[3] thinks that Plato's scheme for a community of property and wives is undoubtedly ridiculed in the *Ecclesiazusæ*, and adduces, as an additional argument for this, the satirical remarks of Aristophanes upon one Aristyllus,[4] whose name Meineke, following some old grammarians, regards as a diminutive form of Aristocles, Plato's original name.

EDITIONS OF PLATO.

The first edition of the works of Plato was that published by Aldus, Venice, 1513, fol.; the next, that published at Basle, in 1534, by Oporinus. The more important subsequent editions are, that of H. Stephens, 1578, 3 vols. fol.; the Bipont edition, 1781–86, 11 vols. 8vo, to which should be added the "*Dialogorum Platonis Argumenta exposita et illustrata a D. Tiedemann*," Biponti, 1786, 8vo; by Imm. Bekker (with the Latin version of Ficinus[5] restored to its original form), Berlin, 1816–18, 8 vols. 8vo, to which were added two volumes of critical commentary and scholia, Berlin, 1823; this edition was reprinted with the notes of Ast, Heindorf, Wyttenbach, and others, by Priestley, London, 1826, 11 vols. 8vo (edited by Burges); by Ast, Leipzig, 1819–32, 11 vols. 8vo, incomplete, the tenth and eleventh volumes containing annotations on only four dialogues; by Stallbaum, a critical edition of the text in 8 vols. 8vo, Leipzig, 1821–25, completed by four additional volumes of various readings and other critical apparatus, Leipzig, 1824–25; a reprint of the text of the foregoing edition, by Stallbaum, 8 vols. 12mo, 1826; a more elaborate edition, with valuable commentary, was commenced by the same editor, Gotha, 1827, in Jacobs' and Rost's *Bibliotheca Græca*, not yet completed, 9 vols., thus far, having been published; an edition of the text, with the scholia collected by Ruhnken, in Tauchnitz's Classics, Leipzig, 1829, 8 vols. 16mo, the last edition revised by Stallbaum, Leipzig, 1850, 8 vols.; by Baiter, Orelli, and Winckelmann, 4to, Zürich, 1839–42, and a text-reprint of the same in 21 vols. 16mo, Zürich, 1839–46; again edited by Stallbaum, 1 vol. small folio, Leipzig, 1850; a critical recension of the text has been commenced by C. F. Hermann, in the new issue of Teubner's *Bibliotheca Classica*, of which three volumes have thus far appeared; and, lastly, with Latin translation, in Didot's *Bibliotheca Græca*, 8vo, of which one volume has appeared, edited by Schneider.

The most important and valuable editions of separate works are the following: *Dialogi Selecti* (12), by Heindorf, Berlin, 1802–10, 4 vols. 8vo, the first and second re-edited by Buttmann, Berlin, 1827–29; *Dialogi Selecti* (11), by Fischer, Leipzig, four separate volumes, 1770, 74, 76, 83; *Dialogi* iv., by Buttmann, Berlin, fifth edition, 1830; *Charmides*, from the text of Heindorf, by Buttmann, Leipzig, 1839, 8vo; *Cratylus*, by Fischer, Leipzig, 1792–99, 8vo; the doubtful pieces *Eryxias* and *Axiochus* (already mentioned under the account of Æschines Socraticus), by Böckh, at the end of his *Dialogi* iv., Heidelberg, 1810; *Euthyphro*, by Stallbaum, Leipzig, 1823, 8vo; *Euthydemus* and *Gorgias*, by Routh, Oxford, 1774; *Euthydemus*, by Winckelmann, Leipzig, 1833; *Gorgias*, by Findeisen, Gotha, 1796; by Coraes, Paris, 1825; *Io*, with prolegomena, &c., by Nitzsch, Leipzig, 1822, 8vo; *Leges*, by Ast, Leipzig, 1814, 2 vols. 8vo; *Menexenus*, by Loers, Colon., 1825, 8vo; *Meno*, by Stallbaum, Leipzig, 1827, 1839; *Parmenides*, by Stallbaum, with prolegomena, &c., Leipzig, 1839, 1848; *Phædon*, by Wyttenbach, Leyden, 1810, reprinted and enlarged,

[1] *Comment. de Republ.*, p. 73, *seqq.*
[2] *Prolegom. ad Plat. Remp.*, p. 68, *seqq.*
[3] *Hist. Crit. Com. Græc.*, p. 289.
[4] *Eccles.*, 646; *Plut.*, 313.
[5] *Marsilio Ficino*, born at Florence A.D. 1433.

Leipzig, 1825; with the notes of Heindorf, Berlin, 1810; *Phædrus*, by Ast, Leipzig, 1810; *Phædrus* and *Symposium*, translated, with copious notes in German, by Ast, Jena, 1817; *Philebus*, by Stallbaum, Leipzig, 1820, 1826; *Politia*, or *De Republica*, by Ast, Leipzig, 1814; by Schneider, Breslau, 1841, 3 vols. 8vo; *Protagoras*, by Ast, Leipzig, 1831; *Symposium* and *Alcibiades I.*, by Ast, Landishut, 1809; *Symposium*, by Rückert, Leipzig, 1829; with critical and exegetical notes, by Wolf, Leipzig, 1782, 1828.

Useful aids, also, for the student are *Timæi Lexicon*, by Ruhnken, Leyden, 1754, 1789, 8vo, reprinted, with additions, Leipzig, 1828 and 1833; Ast, *Lexicon Platonicum*, 3 vols. 8vo, Leipzig, 1834–38; Mitchell, *Index Græcitatis Platonicæ*, Oxford, 1832, 2 vols. 8vo.

Among the numerous works written in illustration of Plato, the following may be particularly mentioned: Tiedemann's *Platonis Dialogorum Argumenta, &c.*, already referred to; *System der Platonischen Philosophie*, by Tennemann, Leipzig, 1792–95, 4 vols. 8vo; *Initia Philosophiæ Platonicæ*, by Van Heusde, Leyden, 1842; *Platons Leben und Schriften*, by Ast, Leipzig, 1816; *Geschichte und System der Platonischen Philosophie*, by C. F. Hermann, Heidelburg, 1838; *Platonis de Ideis et numeris Doctrina ex Aristotele illustrata*, by Trendelenburg, Leipzig, 1826; *Platonische Studien*, by Zeller, Tübingen, 1839; Schleiermacher's *Introductions to the Dialogues of Plato*, translated by Dobson, Cambridge, 1836, 8vo; Sewell's *Introduction to the Dialogues of Plato*, London, 1841, 12mo.

II. Speusippus (Σπεύσιππος),[1] the successor of Plato, was a native of Athens, and a nephew of the philosopher on the sister's side.[2] We hear nothing of his personal history till the time when he accompanied his uncle Plato on his third journey to Syracuse, where he displayed considerable ability and prudence, especially in his amicable relations with Dion.[3] He succeeded Plato as president of the academy, but was at the head of the school for only eight years (B.C. 347–339). He died, as it appears, of a lingering paralytic illness, having resigned the chair of instruction to Xenocrates. Speusippus wrote many philosophical works which are now lost, but which Aristotle thought sufficiently valuable to purchase at the expense of three talents.[4] Aristotle, indeed, appears to have deemed Speusippus most, of all his academic antagonists, worthy of the honor of being refuted. From the few fragments that remain of his writings, it appears that Speusippus adhered very closely to the doctrine of his great master, with the exception, however, of certain points where he introduced a modification of Plato's views, especially with regard to the "ultimate principium," which he designated, indeed, like Plato, as the absolutely *one*, but would not have it to be regarded as an *existing* entity, since all definitude can only be the result of development.[5] For the fragments, and a more extended account of the doctrines of Speusippus, the student may consult the treatise of Ravaisson, *Speusippi de Primis Rerum Principiis Placita*, Paris, 1838, 8vo.

III. Xenocrătes (Ξενοκράτης),[6] the successor of Speusippus in the academic chair, was a native of Chalcedon.[7] He was born B.C. 396, and died B.C. 314, at the age of eighty-two. He attached himself first to Æschines the Socratic,[8] and afterward, while still a youth, to Plato, whom he accompanied to Syracuse. After the death of Plato, he betook himself, with Aristotle, to Hermias, tyrant of Atarneus;[9] and, after his return, at a subsequent period, to Athens, he was repeatedly sent on em-

[1] *Smith, Dict. Biogr.*, *s. v.* [2] *Diog. Laert.*, iv., 1. [3] *Plut.*, *Dion.*, c. 22, 17.
[4] *Diog. Laert.*, iv., 5; *Aul. Gell.*, iii., 17. [5] *Arist.*, *Met.*, xii., 7.
[6] *Smith, Dict. Biogr.*, *s. v.* [7] *Cic.*, *Acad.*, i., 4; *Athen.*, xii., p. 530, *D.*
[8] *Athen.*, ix., p. 507, *C.* [9] *Strab.*, xii., p. 610.

bassies to Philip of Macedon, and at a later period to Antipater, during the Lamian war. He is said to have wanted quick apprehension and natural grace;[1] but these defects were more than compensated by persevering industry, pure benevolence, freedom from all selfishness, and a moral earnestness which obtained for him the esteem and confidence of the Athenians of his own time. Yet he is said to have experienced the fickleness of popular favor, and, being too poor to pay the protection-money (μετοίκιον), to have been saved only by the courage of the orator Lycurgus[2] from being sold, or even to have been actually purchased by Demetrius Phalereus, and then emancipated.[3] He became president of the academy on the resignation of Speusippus, who was bowed down by sickness, and he occupied that post for twenty-five years. The importance of Xenocrates is shown by the fact that Aristotle and Theophrastus wrote upon his doctrines, and that Panætius and Cicero entertained a high regard for him as a writer on philosophy. Of his numerous works only the titles have come down to us. With regard to the doctrines of Xenocrates, the student may consult the work of Van de Wynpersee, *Diatribe de Xenocrate Chalcedonio*, Lugd. Bat., 1822, 8vo, and the review of the same by Brandis, in the *Heidelberger Jahrbücher*, 1824, p. 275, *seqq*.

IV. Polĕmo (Πολέμων),[4] the successor of Xenocrates in the academic chair, was a native of Athens and of a wealthy and distinguished family. In his youth he was extremely profligate; but one day, when he was about thirty, on his bursting into the school of Xenocrates at the head of a band of revellers, his attention was so arrested by the discourse, which chanced to be upon temperance, that he tore off his garland and remained an attentive listener; and having from that day adopted an abstemious course of life, he continued to frequent the school, of which, on the death of Xenocrates, he became the head,[5] B.C. 315. He died B.C. 273, at a very advanced age. Polemo esteemed the object of philosophy to be to exercise men in things and deeds, not in dialectic speculations; his character was grave and severe, and he took pride in displaying the mastery which he had acquired over emotions of every sort. He was a close follower of Xenocrates in all things, and an intimate friend of Crates and Crantor, who were his disciples, as well as of Zeno and Arcesilas. Crates was his successor in the academy. In literature he most admired Homer and Sophocles, and he is said to have been the author of the remark, that Homer is an epic Sophocles, and Sophocles a tragic Homer. He left, according to Diogenes Laertius, several treatises, none of which were extant in the time of Suidas. Polemo placed the *summum bonum* in living according to the laws of nature.[6]

VIII. THE CYNIC SCHOOL.

I. Antisthĕnes (Ἀντισθένης), the founder of the Cynic sect, was a native of Athens; his father was an Athenian citizen, his mother is said to have been a Thracian. He distinguished himself in youth at the battle

[1] *Diog. Laert.*, iv., 6.
[2] *Plut.*, *Flamin.*, c. 12; *Vit. Dec. Orat.*, 7.
[3] *Diog. Laert.*, iv., 14.
[4] *Smith, Dict. Biogr.*, *s. v.*
[5] *Diog. Laert.*, iv., 16, *seqq.*
[6] *Diog. Laert.*, *l. c.*

of Tanagra (B.C. 426), when he must have been about twenty years of age. He was at first a hearer of Gorgias, from whom he learned the rhetorical style which he adopted in his dialogues and other writings. He afterward attached himself to Socrates, and recommended his own disciples, for he had already a large number of followers, to do the same. His dwelling was in the Piræeus, and he used to walk daily the forty stadia (above four miles) to hear his new master, to whom he faithfully adhered to the end of his life. The time of his death is not mentioned; he is said to have reached his seventieth year. Antisthenes is reckoned among those who preserved at least a portion of their master's doctrines and manner of teaching. He was a man of stubborn character, and he carried his opinions to extremes; yet he was an agreeable companion, according to Xenophon, and distinguished by temperance in all things. He is mentioned, in the *Phædon*, as one of those present at the death of Socrates.[1] After this event, he established a school in the gymnasium of Cynosarges, adjoining the temple of Hercules, which he selected apparently for two reasons: the Cynosarges was the gymnasium for those Athenians who were not of genuine Attic stock, and Hercules was the ideal model of manly excellence to Antisthenes, and formed the subject of at least one of his treatises.

The followers of Antisthenes were first called *Antisthenēi*, and afterward *Cynics* (κυνικοί), a term that had reference either to the name *Cynosarges*, or to the Greek word κύων, "a dog," which may have been given to the disciples of Antisthenes on account of the coarseness of their manners, and their dog-like neglect of all forms and usages of society.[2] Many sayings of Antisthenes are recorded by Diogenes. They are marked by a sententious brevity, a play upon words, and a caustic humor, which may have contributed to affix on him and his followers the appellation of Cynic or snarling. His doctrines had chiefly a moral and a practical end. It is not possible to state them in any thing like a systematic form from such evidence as we have. He had probably no great originality as a thinker; and the best part of his moral philosophy harmonizes with that of Socrates. But, as in other like cases, many things may have been attributed to Antisthenes as the founder of a sect, which belong to the later Cynics.

Antisthenes placed the *summum bonum* in a life according to virtue—virtue consisting in action, and being such, that when once obtained it is never lost, and exempts the wise man from the chance of error; that is, it is closely connected with reason, but, to enable it to develop itself in action, and to be sufficient for happiness, it requires the aid of energy (Σωκρατικὴ ἰσχύς), so that we may represent him as teaching that the *summum bonum*, ἀρετή, is attainable by teaching (διδακτόν), and made up of φρόνησις and ἰσχύς. But here he becomes involved in a vicious circle, for when asked what φρόνησις is, he could only call it an insight into good, having before made the good to consist in φρόνησις.[3] His philosophy was directed to enforce a simple mode of life in opposition to the increasing luxury of the age. He condemned pleasure which was sought purely for

[1] *Phæd.*, § 59. [2] *Schol. in Aristot.*, p. 23, *Brandis.* [3] *Plat.*, *De Repub.*, vi., p. 505.

its own sake, and which enfeebled the mind and body; but he approved of those healthy pleasures which followed or were consequent upon labor. The doctrines of the Cynics then did not reject pleasure; they sought pleasure in their own way. The *Physicus* of Antisthenes contained a theory of the nature of the gods,[1] in which he contended for the unity of the Deity, and that man is unable to know him by any sensible representation, since he is unlike any being on earth. He probably held just views of providence, showing the sufficiency of virtue for happiness by the fact that outward events are regulated by God so as to benefit the wise. Such, at least, was the view of his pupil, Diogenes of Sinope, and seems involved in his own statement, that all which belongs to others is truly the property of the wise man.

Antisthenes, after he had established a school of his own, never had many disciples, which annoyed him so much that he drove away those who did attend his teaching, except Diogenes, who remained with him till his death. His staff, and wallet, and mean clothing were only proofs of his vanity, which Socrates told him he saw through the holes of his tunic. His philosophy was evidently thought worthless by Plato and Aristotle, to the former of whom he was personally hostile. His school is classed by Ritter among the imperfect Socraticists. After his death, his disciples wandered farther and farther from all scientific objects, and plunged more deeply into fanatical extravagances. Perhaps some of their exaggerated statements have been attributed to their master.

The fragments which remain of his writings have been collected by Winckelmann, *Antisthenis Fragmenta*, &c., Zürich, 1842, and this small work, with the account of him by Ritter (*Gesch. der Philosophie*, vii., 4), will supply all the information that can be desired.

II. Diogĕnes (Διογένης),[2] a celebrated member of the Cynic school, was a native of Sinope, in Pontus, and born about B.C. 412. His father was a banker, named Icesias or Icetas, who was convicted of some swindling transaction, in consequence of which Diogenes quitted Sinope and went to Athens. His youth is said to have been spent in dissolute extravagance; but at Athens his attention was arrested by the character of Antisthenes, who at first drove him away. Diogenes, however, could not be prevented from attending him even by blows, but told him that he would find no stick hard enough to keep him away. Antisthenes at last relented, and his pupil soon plunged into the most frantic excesses of austerity and moroseness. In summer he used to roll in the hot sand, and in winter to embrace statues covered with snow; he wore coarse clothing, lived on the plainest food, slept in porticoes or in the street, and finally, according to the common story, took up his residence in a tub belonging to the Metroum, or temple of the mother of the gods. The truth of this latter tale, however, has been reasonably disputed.[3]

In spite of his strange eccentricities, Diogenes appears to have been much respected at Athens, and to have been privileged to rebuke any thing of which he disapproved. He seems to have ridiculed and despised all

[1] *Cic., N. D.*

[2] *Smith, Dict. Biogr., s. v.*

[3] Consult the authorities quoted by Stahr in *Smith's Dict. Biogr., s. v.*

intellectual pursuits, which did not directly and obviously tend to some immediate practical good. He abused literary men for reading about the evils of Ulysses, and neglecting their own; musicians for stringing the lyre harmoniously, while they left their minds discordant; men of science for troubling themselves about the moon and stars, while they neglected what lay immediately before them; orators for learning to say what was right, but not to practise it. Various sarcastic sayings of the same kind are handed down to us as his, generally showing that unwise contempt for the common opinions and pursuits of men which is so unlikely to reform them. On a voyage to Ægina, he was taken prisoner by pirates, and carried to Crete, to be sold as a slave. Here, when he was asked what business he understood, he answered, "How to command men." He was purchased by Xeniades of Corinth, over whom he acquired such influence that he soon received from him his freedom, and was intrusted with the care of his children, and passed his old age in his house. During his residence at Corinth, his celebrated interview with Alexander the Great is said to have taken place. Diogenes died at Corinth, at the age of nearly ninety, B.C. 323.

With regard to the philosophy of Diogenes there is little to say, as he was utterly without any scientific object whatsoever. His system, if it deserve the name, was purely practical, and consisted merely in teaching men to dispense with the simplest and most necessary wants;[1] and his whole style of teaching was a kind of caricature upon that of Socrates, whom he imitated in imparting instruction to persons whom he casually met, and with a still more supreme contempt for time, place, and circumstances. Hence he was sometimes called "the mad Socrates." He did not commit his opinions to writing, and therefore those attributed to him can not be certainly relied on. The most peculiar, if correctly stated, was, that all minds are air, exactly alike, and composed of similar particles, but that in the irrational animals and in idiots they are hindered from properly developing themselves by the arrangement and various humors of their bodies. This resembles the Ionic doctrine, and has been referred by Brucker[2] to Diogenes of Apollonia.

Diogenes died in the same year with Alexander, and, as Plutarch tells us, both died on the same day. If so, this was probably the 6th of Thargelion.

IX. PERIPATETIC SCHOOL.

I. Aristotĕles (Ἀριστοτέλης),[3] the celebrated founder of this school, was born at Stagīra, a town in Chalcidice, in Macedonia, B.C. 384. His father, Nicomachus, was physician in ordinary to Amyntas II., king of Macedonia, and the author of several treatises on subjects connected with natural science. His mother, Phæstis (or Phæstias), was descended from a Chalcidian family.[4] The studies and occupation of his father account for the early inclination manifested by Aristotle for the investigation of nature, an inclination which is perceived throughout his whole life.

[1] *Diog. Laert.*, vi., 70.
[2] *Hist. Crit. Phil.*, ii., 2, 1, § 21.
[3] *Smith, Dict. Biogr.*, s. v.
[4] *Dionys., De Demosth. et Arist.*, 5.

He lost his father before he had attained his seventeenth year, and he was intrusted to the guardianship of one Proxenus, of Atarneus, in Mysia, who was settled in Stagira. In B.C. 367, when seventeen years of age, he went to Athens to pursue his studies, and there became a pupil of Plato, upon the return of the latter from Sicily, about B.C. 365. Plato soon distinguished him above all his other disciples. He named him "the intellect of his school" (νοῦς τῆς διατριβῆς),[1] and his house the house of the "reader" (ἀναγνώστης). Aristotle lived at Athens for twenty years, till B.C. 347. During the whole of this period the good understanding which subsisted between teacher and scholar continued, with some trifling exceptions, undisturbed, for the stories of the disrespect and ingratitude of the latter toward the former are nothing but calumnies invented by his enemies. During the last ten years of his first residence at Athens, Aristotle gave instruction in rhetoric, and distinguished himself by his opposition to Isocrates, at that time the most distinguished teacher of rhetoric. Indeed, he appears to have opposed most decidedly all the earlier and contemporary theories of rhetoric.[2] His opposition to Isocrates, however, led to most important consequences, as it accounts for the bitter hatred which was afterward manifested toward Aristotle and his school by all the followers of Isocrates. It was the conflict of profound philosophical investigation with the superficiality of stylistic and rhetorical accomplishment, of which Isocrates might be looked upon as the principal representative, since he not only despised poetry, but held physics and mathematics to be illiberal studies, cared not to know any thing about philosophy, and looked upon the accomplished man of the world and the clever rhetorician as the true philosophers. On this occasion Aristotle published his first rhetorical writings. That during this time he continued to maintain his connection with the Macedonian court is intimated by his going on an embassy to Philip of Macedonia on some business of the Athenians.[3] Moreover, we have still the letter in which his royal friend announces to him the birth of his son Alexander.[4]

After the death of Plato, which occurred during the above-mentioned embassy of Aristotle, the latter left Athens, though we do not exactly know for what reason. Perhaps he was offended by Plato's having appointed Speusippus as his successor in the Academy.[5] At the same time, it is more probable that, after the notions of the ancient philosophers, he esteemed travels in foreign parts as a necessary completion of his education. He first repaired to his friend Hermias, at Atarneus. A few years, however, after the arrival of Aristotle, Hermias, through the treachery of Mentor, a Grecian general in the Persian service, fell into the hands of the Persians, of whom he had made himself independent, and was put to death. Aristotle, who had married Pythias, the adopted daughter of Hermias, fled with his wife to Mytilene. A poem on his unfortunate friend, which is still preserved, testifies the warm affection which he had felt for him. He afterward caused a statue to be erected to his memory at Delphi.[6]

---

[1] *Philopon., De Æternit. Mund.*, vi., 27. [2] *Aristot., Rhet.*, i., 1, 2. [3] *Diog. Laert.*, v., 2.
[4] *Aul. Gell.*, ix., 3. [5] *Diog. Laert., l. c.*; iv., 1. [6] *Id. ib.*, v., 6, *seq.*

Two years after his flight from Atarneus (B.C. 342), he accepted an invitation from Philip of Macedonia to undertake the instruction of his son Alexander, then thirteen years of age.[1] At the court of this monarch he was treated with the most marked respect; his native city, Stagira, which had been destroyed by Philip, with many other Grecian cities in the same quarter, was rebuilt at his request, and the monarch caused a gymnasium to be erected there, in a pleasant grove, expressly for Aristotle and his pupils. Plutarch informs us that several other noble youths enjoyed the instruction of Aristotle along with Alexander,[2] among whom we may mention Cassander, the son of Antipater,[3] Marsyas of Pella (brother of Antigonus, afterward king), and Ptolemy, the future monarch of Egypt. Alexander attached himself with such ardent affection to the philosopher, that the youth, whom no one yet had been able to manage, soon valued his instructor above his own father. Aristotle spent seven years in Macedonia, but Alexander enjoyed his instruction without interruption for only four. But with such a pupil even this short period was sufficient for a teacher like Aristotle to fulfill the highest purposes of education, to aid the development of his pupil's faculties in every direction, to awaken susceptibility and lively inclination for every art and science, and to create in him that sense of the noble and great which distinguishes Alexander from all the conquerors who have only swept like a hurricane through the world. According to the usual mode of Grecian education, a knowledge of the poets, eloquence, and philosophy were the principal subjects into which Aristotle initiated his royal pupil. Thus we are even informed that he prepared a new recension of the Iliad for him,[4] that he instructed him in ethics and politics,[5] and disclosed to him the abstrusities of his own speculations, of the publication of which by his writings Alexander afterward complained.[6]

On Alexander's accession to the throne, in B.C. 335, Aristotle returned to Athens. Here he found his friend Xenocrates president of the Academy. He himself had the Lycēum, a gymnasium sacred to Apollo Lycēus, assigned him by the state. He soon assembled around him a large number of distinguished scholars, to whom he delivered lectures in philosophy, in the shady walks (περίπατοι) which surrounded the Lyceum, while walking up and down (περιπατῶν), and not sitting, which last was the general practice of the philosophers. From one or other of these circumstances the name *Peripatetic* is derived, which was afterward given to his school. He gave two different courses of lectures every day.[7] Those which he delivered in the morning (ἑωθινὸς περίπατος), to a narrower circle of chosen and confidential (*esoteric*) hearers, and which were called *acroamatic* or *acroatic*, embraced subjects connected with the more abstruse philosophy (theology), physics, and dialectics. Those which he delivered in the afternoon (δειλινὸς περίπατος), and intended for a more promiscuous circle (which, accordingly, he called *exoteric*), extended to rhetoric, sophistics, and politics. He appears to have taught not so much in the

1 *Plut.*, *Alex.*, 5; *Quintil.*, i., 1.
2 *Apophth. Reg.*, vol. v., p. 683, ed. *Reiske*.
3 *Plut.*, *Alex.*, 74.
4 *Wolf*, *Prolegom.*, p. clxxxi.
5 *Plut.*, *Alex.*, 7.
6 *Gell.*, xx., 5.
7 *Id. ib.*

way of conversation as in regular lectures. His school soon became the most celebrated in Athens, and he continued to preside over it for thirteen years (B.C. 335–323). During this time he also composed the greater part of his works. In these labors he was assisted by the truly kingly liberality of his former pupil, who not only presented him with 800 talents, but also caused large collections of natural curiosities to be made for him, to which posterity is indebted for one of his most excellent works, the *History of Animals*.[1]

Meanwhile, various causes contributed to throw a cloud over the latter years of the philosopher's life. In the first place, he felt deeply the death of his wife Pythias, who left behind her a daughter of the same name: he lived subsequently with a friend of his wife's, the slave Herpyllis, who bore him a son, Nicomachus.[2] But a source of still greater grief was an interruption of the friendly relation in which he had hitherto stood to his royal pupil. This was occasioned by the conduct of Callisthenes, the nephew and pupil of Aristotle, who had vehemently and injudiciously opposed the changes in the conduct and policy of Alexander. Still, Alexander refrained from any expression of hostility toward his former instructor, although their previous cordial connection no longer subsisted undisturbed. The story that Aristotle had a share in poisoning the king is a fabrication of a later age, and, moreover, it is most probable that Alexander died a natural death. After the death of this monarch (B.C. 323), Aristotle was looked upon with suspicion at Athens as a friend of Macedonia; but as it was not easy to bring any political accusation against him, he was accused of impiety (ἀσεβείας) by the hierophant Eurymedon. He withdrew from Athens before his trial, and escaped, in the beginning of B.C. 322, to Chalcis, in Eubœa, where he died in the course of the same year, in the sixty-third year of his age, of a chronic disease of the stomach. His body was transported to his native city, Stagira, and his memory was honored there, like that of a hero, by yearly festivals. He bequeathed to Theophrastus his well-stored library, and the originals of his writings.

In person, Aristotle was short and of slender make, with small eyes, and a lisp in his pronunciation, using L for R, and with a sort of sarcastic expression in his countenance. He exhibited remarkable attention to external appearance, and bestowed much care upon his dress and person. He is described as having been of weak health, which, considering the astonishing extent of his studies, shows all the more the energy of his mind. The whole demeanor of Aristotle was marked by a certain briskness and vivacity. His powers of eloquence were considerable, and of a kind adapted to produce conviction in his hearers, a gift which Antipater praises highly in a letter written after Aristotle's death.

WORKS OF ARISTOTLE.

The numerous works of Aristotle may be divided into the following classes, according to the subjects of which they treat. We only mention the most important in each class.

[1] *Plin.*, *H. N.*, viii., 17.

[2] *Diog. Laert.*, v., 1; v., 13.

I. DIALECTICS AND LOGIC.[1]

The extant logical writings are comprehended as a whole under the title *Orgănon* (Ὄργανον, i. e., instrument of science). They are occupied with the investigation of the method by which man arrives at knowledge. An insight into the nature and formation of conclusions, and of proof by means of conclusions, is the common aim and centre of all the separate six works composing the *Organon*. These separate works are: 1. Κατηγορίαι, *Prædicamenta*, or "Categories," in which Aristotle treats of the ten comprehensive generic ideas, under which all the attributes of things may be subordinated as species. These are, *Substance, Quantity, Quality, Relation, Where, When, Position* (κεῖσθαι), to *Have*, to be *Active*, to be *Passive*. The doctrine of the Categories has been important to philosophy, for a great question is there propounded, and an insight is opened into the most essential notions of the mind. The Stoics in ancient, and Kant in modern times, have occupied themselves very much with this subject; and the progress of the modern German logic is connected with the inquiry, from what principles the Categories are developed in the thought, and what authority they have. 2. Περὶ ἑρμηνείας, *De interpretatione*, concerning the expression of thought by means of speech. In this work Aristotle examines the judgment and its various forms, the general, the particular, and the indefinite judgment; the model-forms, as they appear in the judgment, of reality, possibility, chance, and necessity; the value and the relations of these forms; and he discusses the subject of contraries. The mode of treating these matters is so acute and subtle, but yet so difficult, that the ancients said that Aristotle, when he wrote this book, dipped his pen in intellect. 3, 4. Ἀναλυτικὰ πρότερα and ὕστερα, *Analytica Priora* and *Posteriora*, each in two books, on the theory of conclusions, so called from the resolution of the conclusion into its fundamental component parts. The *Analytica Priora* are specially occupied about the syllogism, and therein Aristotle shows a wonderful, one might say a mathematical, combination of all possible relationship, and a comprehensive view of the internal nature of the syllogism, especially of the middle term. The *Analytica Posteriora* go farther, inasmuch as they have for their object to ascertain how science is established through the conclusions of the syllogism. Accordingly, they treat of proof, and the general and particular principles of the sciences. 5. Τοπικά, *De Locis*, in eight books, of the general points of view (τόποι) from which conclusions may be drawn. 6. Περὶ σοφιστικῶν ἐλέγχων, concerning the fallacies which only apparently prove something. This work contains an examination and solution of sophistical fallacies, especially those of the Megaric school.—There is generally prefixed to the *Organon* the Introduction of Porphyry, entitled Πορφυρίου εἰσαγωγή, or Περὶ τῶν πέντε φωνῶν, "On the Five Voices," which is a treatise on the logical notions of genus and species, differences, proper or peculiar, and accident. It is an introduction to the Aristotelian logic, and was much used in the Middle Ages.

[1] *Smith, l. c.; Trendelenburg, Biog. Dict., Soc. U. K.*, vol. iii., p. 457, *seqq.*

II. THEORETICAL PHILOSOPHY.[1]

This consists of *Metaphysics*, *Mathematics*, and *Physics*, on all of which Aristotle wrote works. 1. The *Metaphysics* (τὰ μετὰ τὰ φυσικά), in fourteen books. The first part of Theoretical Philosophy, according to Aristotle, is metaphysic. He calls it the "First Philosophy" (πρώτη φιλοσοφία, *Philosophia Prima*), because it treats of Being as Being, and considers the general principles in which the objects of the other sciences, as particular parts of Being, have their foundation. In ancient times, as, for instance, in Plutarch's "Life of Alexander," the books which contain the First Philosophy are called "Metaphysic" (μετὰ τὰ φυσικά), or that which comes after the physical writings. This term, which with us has become the name of the science, does not denote any relation of the two subjects, as has sometimes been supposed, contrary to the usage of the preposition μετά, as if it denoted that which, as being above, lies beyond Nature, or lies beyond Nature as the hidden power. The fact is, that the title has merely an accidental origin, as the old commentators expressly say. When the ancients were arranging the works of Aristotle, they placed the First Philosophy after the books on Physics, and expressed this fact by the title μετὰ τὰ φυσικά, or metaphysics. 2. In *Mathematics* we have two treatises by Aristotle: (I.) Περὶ ἀτόμων γραμμῶν, i. e., concerning "indivisible lines," which treats of the infinite divisibility of magnitudes. (II.) Μηχανικὰ προβλήματα, or Mechanical Problems, a treatise of which Vitruvius has made some use.

3. In *Physics*[2] we have, (I.) *Physics* (φυσικὴ ἀκρόασις, called also by others περὶ ἀρχῶν). It consists of eight books, in which Aristotle develops the general principles of natural science (Cosmology). One of the most remarkable parts of this work is the subtle and exhaustive discussion of the nature of Space and Time, in the fourth book; and in the eighth book, in a discussion which corresponds to one in the Metaphysic, Aristotle, by inferring a principle which is at rest, the unmoved, which produces motion, has given the first indication of the celebrated cosmological proof of the existence of God as the prime mover. (II.) *Concerning the Heavens* (περὶ οὐράνου), in four books. The heavens, according to Aristotle, extend from the extreme limits of the world to the moon, and they move, according to their nature, in a circular direction about the earth, which is in the centre at rest. Aristotle, in the second book, speaks of a passage of the moon over the disk of Mars, which he observed himself; Kepler calculated that this phænomenon took place in the year B.C. 357, and, consequently, the observation would belong to the time of Aristotle's first residence at Athens, when he was closely connected with Plato. (III.) *On Production and Destruction* (περὶ γενέσεως καὶ φθορᾶς), in two books, developing the general laws of production and destruction. (IV.) *On Meteorology* (Μετεωρολογικά), in four books, treating of the operation of the elements as shown in ætherial phænomena, and especially of fiery meteors, and of the phænomena produced on the earth by means of water. To this division of Aristotle's writings belongs the work on

[1] *Smith, l. c.; Trendelenburg, Biog. Dict., Soc. U. K.*, vol. iii., p. 457, *seqq.* [2] *Id. ib.*

the local names of the various winds (ἀνέμων θέσεις καὶ προσηγορίαι), which is all that is preserved of the larger work entitled περὶ σημείων χειμώνων, or "On the Signs of Storms." (V.) *On the Universe* (περὶ κόσμου, *De Mundo*), a letter to Alexander, treating the subject of the last two works in a popular style and rhetorical tone altogether foreign to Aristotle. The whole is probably a translation of a work with the same title by Appuleius. (VI.) *The History of Animals* (περὶ ζώων ἱστορία), in ten books. This work contains no proper system of zoology; but animals are classed according to various principles of division, for the purpose of subjecting to examination their parts, their functions, their active energies, and their mode of life. Pliny drew largely from this work in his Natural History. Many discoveries of Aristotle have been made again in recent times; for instance, the smooth shark (γαλεὸς λεῖος). This great work, partly the fruit of the kingly liberality of Alexander, has not reached us quite complete. On the other hand, respecting a tenth book, appended in the MSS., which treats of barrenness in the female, scholars are not agreed. The observations in this work are the triumph of ancient sagacity, and have been confirmed by the results of the most recent investigations. (VII.) *On the parts of Animals* (περὶ ζώων μορίων), in four books, in which Aristotle, after describing the phænomena in each species, develops the causes of these phænomena by means of the idea to be formed of the purpose which is manifested in the formation of the animal. (VIII.) *On the generation of Animals* (περὶ ζώων γενέσεως), in five books, treating of the generation of animals and the organs of generation. (IX.) *On the progression of Animals* (περὶ ζώων πορείας), or *De incessu animalium*, treating of the instruments by which change of place is effected. (X.) *On the Soul* (περὶ ψυχῆς), in three books. After he has criticised the views of earlier investigators, he himself defines the soul to be "the internal formative principle of a body which may be perceived by the senses and is capable of life."

Several *anatomical* works of Aristotle have been lost. He was the first person who, in any special manner, advocated anatomical investigations, and showed the necessity of them for the study of the natural sciences. He frequently refers to investigations of his own on the subject.

III. PRACTICAL PHILOSOPHY OR POLITICS.[1]

All that falls within the sphere of practical philosophy is comprehended in three principal works: the *Ethics*, the *Politics*, and the *Œconomics*. 1. The *Nicomachēan Ethics* (Ἠθικὰ Νικομάχεια), in ten books. Aristotle here begins with the highest and most universal end of life, for the individual as well as for the community in the state. This is happiness (εὐδαιμονία); and its conditions are, on the one hand, perfect virtue, exhibiting itself in the actor; and, on the other hand, corresponding bodily advantages and favorable external circumstances. Virtue is the readiness to act constantly and consciously according to the laws of the rational nature of man (ὀρθὸς λόγος). The nature of virtue shows itself in its appearing as the medium between two extremes. In accordance with

[1] *Smith, l. c.; Trendelenburg, Biog. Dict., Soc. U. K.*, vol. iii., p. 457, *seqq.*

this, the several virtues are enumerated and characterized. The authenticity of the work, which an ancient tradition ascribes to Nicomachus, the son of Aristotle, is indubitable, though there is some dispute as to the proper arrangement of the several books. Why these writings were called *Nicomachean*, we can not tell; whether the father so named them as a memorial of his affection for his young son, or whether they derived their title from being afterward edited and commented on by Nicomachus. 2. The *Eudemēan Ethics* ('Ηθικὰ Εὐδήμεια), in seven books, of which only books i., ii., iii., and vii. are independent, while the remaining books, iv., v., and vi. agree word for word with books v., vi., and vii. of the Nicomachean ethics. This ethical work is, perhaps, a recension of Aristotle's lectures, edited by Eudemus. 3. The *Great Ethics* ('Ηθικὰ μεγάλα), or *Magna Moralia*, in two books. Pansch has lately endeavored to show that this is not a work of Aristotle's, but an abstract, and one, too, not made by a very skillful hand; while another critic looks upon it as the authentic first sketch of the larger work. 4. *Politics* (Πολιτικά), in eight books. The Ethics conduct us to the Politics. The connection between the two works is so close, that in the Ethics, by the word ὕστερον, reference is made by Aristotle to the Politics; and in the latter, by πρότερον, to the Ethics. The Politics show how happiness is to be attained *for the human community in the state;* for the object of the state is not merely the external preservation of life, but "happy life," as it is attained by means of virtue (ἀρετή, perfect development of the whole man). Hence, also, *ethics* form the first and most general foundation of political life, because the state can not attain its highest object if morality does not prevail among its citizens. The house, the family, is the element of the state. Accordingly, Aristotle begins with the doctrine of domestic economy, then proceeds to a description of the different forms of government, after which he gives a delineation of the most important Hellenic constitutions, and then investigates which of the constitutions is the best (the ideal of a state). The doctrine concerning education, as the most important condition of this best state, forms the conclusion. 5. *Œconomics* (οἰκονομικά), in two books, of which only the first is genuine.

IV. WORKS ON ART.[1]

These have for their object the exercise of the creative faculty or art, and to them belong the *Poetics* and *Rhetoric*. 1. The *Poetics* (περὶ ποιητικῆς). Aristotle penetrated more deeply than any of the ancients into the essence of Hellenic art. He is the father of the *æsthetics of poetry*, as he is the completer of Greek rhetoric as a science. The greatest part of the treatise contains a theory of tragedy; nothing else is treated of, with the exception of the epos; comedy is merely alluded to. The treatise itself is undoubtedly genuine, but the explanation of its present form is still a problem of criticism. Some, as, for instance, G. Hermann and Bernhardy, look upon it as the first sketch of an uncompleted work; others as an extract from a larger work; others, again, as the notes taken by some hearer of lectures delivered by Aristotle. Thus much, however,

[1] *Smith, l. c.*

is clear, that the treatise, as we have it at present, is an independent whole, and, with the exception of a few interpolations, the work of one author. 2. The *Rhetoric* (τέχνη ῥητορική), in three books. Rhetoric, as a science, according to Aristotle, stands side by side with dialectics. The only thing which makes a scientific treatment of rhetoric possible is the argumentation which awakens conviction. He, therefore, directs his chief attention to the theory of oratorical argumentation. The second main division of the work treats of the production of that favorable disposition in the hearer, in consequence of which the orator appears to him to be worthy of credit. The third part treats of oratorical expression and arrangement.

According to a well-known tradition,[1] Aristotle bequeathed his library and MSS. to Theophrastus, his successor in the Peripatetic school. On the death of Theophrastus, the libraries and MSS. of both Aristotle and Theophrastus are said to have come into the hands of his relation and disciple, Neleus of Scepsis, in Troas. This Neleus sold both libraries to Ptolemy II., king of Egypt, for the Alexandrean library; but he retained for himself, as an heir-loom, the original MSS. of the works of these two philosophers. The descendants of Neleus, who were subjects of the King of Pergamus, knew of no other way of securing them from the search of the Attali, who wished to rival the Ptolemies in forming a large library, than by concealing them in a cellar (κατὰ γῆς ἐν διώρυχί τινι), where, for a couple of centuries, they were exposed to the ravages of damp and worms. It was not till the beginning of the century before the birth of Christ that a wealthy book-collector, the Athenian Apellicon of Teos, traced out these valuable relics, bought them from the ignorant heirs, and prepared from them a new edition of Aristotle's works, causing the manuscripts to be copied, and filling up the gaps and making emendations, but without sufficient knowledge of what he was about. After the capture of Athens, Sulla, in B.C. 84, confiscated Apellicon's collection of books, and had them conveyed to Rome. From this story an error arose, which has been handed down from the time of Strabo to the present day. It was concluded, from this account, that neither Aristotle nor Theophrastus had published their writings, with the exception of some exoteric works, which had no important bearing on their system, and that it was not till two hundred years later that they were brought to light by the above-mentioned Apellicon, and published to the philosophical world. That, however, was by no means the case. Aristotle, indeed, did not prepare a complete edition, as we call it, of his writings. Nay, it is certain that death overtook him before he could finish some of his works, and put the finishing hand to others. Nevertheless, it can not be denied that Aristotle destined all his works for publication, and published several in his lifetime. This is indisputably certain with regard to the exoteric writings. Those which had not been published by Aristotle himself were given to the world by Theophrastus and his disciples in a complete form.[2]

[1] *Strab.*, xiii., p. 608. [2] *Smith, l. c.*

LEADING FEATURES OF ARISTOTLE'S PHILOSOPHY.[1]

We can not fully comprehend the peculiar character of Aristotle's doctrines without contrasting them with those of Plato. Plato and Aristotle occupy the central place in the philosophy of the Greeks, and the investigations of the present day must always recur to them, if our object be to ascertain the principles by which we may form a view of the whole of things. The axis around which philosophical speculation turns is centered in the minds of Plato and Aristotle. The investigations of the earlier philosophers reached only to parts, though important parts, of the universe, and they regarded these parts as the whole. Pythagoras made number and harmony the principle of his philosophy; the Ionian physical speculation adopted a material first principle; and the philosophy of Socrates had for its basis that which was good with reference to man. The greatness of Plato and Aristotle consisted in binding together the several parts of philosophy in one governing comprehensive unity, and in creating one intellectual antitype of the Universal, a self-conscious entirety of thoughts—a system in the proper sense of the term. Yet they constructed their respective systems from a different point of view. Plato's was the Ideal: he spiritualized our cognition. Aristotle's was the Real: he established it on realities. Plato contemplated the world with the eyes of the Greek artist, and he clothed his conceptions in the vesture of the beautiful: his ideas are the spiritual forms, according to which God, like an artificer, fashions the world and all things. Aristotle stripped off this vesture: he sought to discover the notions which are at the bottom of all sensuous impressions, and these notions are only objects of thought. He examined facts, and endeavored to subject them to the notion which we have of them. But it is a misrepresentation to say that Aristotle was an Empiric, according to whom the mind is a mere *tabula rasa,* on which experience, sensation, and reflection impress ideas. According to Aristotle, the understanding is also that creative activity which conceives principles and apprehends them in phænomena.

Aristotle is an unfathomable intellect. There is nothing too great or too small for his observation; nothing which his understanding could not grasp. He not only mastered all the sciences of his day, but he carried them farther; he extended them in detail, he fitted the parts together, and formed them into a consistent whole. In philosophy we observe a two-fold tendency, which is seldom united in the same person; a tendency toward the infinite variety of individual things, to the inexhaustible mass of material; and the opposite tendency to the universal thought, which masters this variety and pervades this mass. Seldom, if ever, have these two tendencies been so nearly balanced, and seldom have they so mutually co-operated with each other as in Aristotle. In this union consists his astonishing greatness. Plato is more ideal, but Aristotle more universal. In the writings of Plato, the genius of the artist, of the poet, is always felt; but Aristotle is the man of prose, and the investigation of bare realities is his province. In place of the charm of plastic art, we

[1] *Trendelenburg, Biog. Dict., Soc. U. K.,* vol. iii., p. 452.

find in Aristotle greater power of observation, and more acute analysis and investigation. In nearly all the sciences Aristotle opened new paths. He created Logic, and laid down the laws which govern our conclusions. What existed before his time was no more than unconnected attempts. Kant observes, that "Logic, since the time of Aristotle, like pure Geometry, since the time of Euclid, is a finished science, which in all essentials has received neither improvement nor alteration."

With profound thought he investigated the nature of the mind, and explained its development in his wonderful Psychology: he was thus the first to create a science of Mind. In his Ethics he considered new questions, as, for example, the freedom of the will and responsibility. Plato planned the ideal of a state, yet, with all the depth of his philosophy, he could not discover the means of adapting his ideal to real life. Aristotle examined the constitutions and positive usages of existing states in detail, and with his mind matured by this practical experience, he wrote his "Politic," in which work he examines and passes judgment on existing political forms, according to their several internal characters.

Lastly, by his investigation of ultimate principles, which is comprised in his "First Philosophy," he gave to metaphysics its proper direction. Aristotle's method is characterized by sound criticism: before giving his own views, he never neglects to examine the doctrines of his predecessors in philosophy. He shows wherein they are defective, and at the same time states how far they are true; and thus he prepares the way for his own theory. This peculiarity makes his writings an authority for the history of philosophy, and Aristotle may be considered the founder of this science also. Aristotle does not belong to the national mind of Greece. The period of genuine Greek antiquity, which has perpetuated itself in the beautiful creations of poetry and eloquence, of sculpture and architecture, was already past, and Aristotle could only contemplate it at a distance; he reflects upon it as on a subject foreign to his age. The whole direction of his philosophy is rather toward that which belongs to mankind in general, and to the rational, than to that which is peculiarly Greek. This character of universality made Aristotle's works intelligible even in the Middle Ages, and it rendered his philosophy susceptible of an intimate union with Christian theology.[1]

EDITIONS OF ARISTOTLE.

The most important editions of the entire works of Aristotle are the following: 1. The *editio princeps*, by Aldus Pius Manutius, Venice, 1495–98, 5 vols. fol. (called, also, *Aldina major*). For the criticism of the text, this is still the most important of all the old editions. 2. The third Basle edition, 1550, 2 vols. fol., with several variations from, and some essential improvements upon, the *editio princeps*. The first and second Basle editions, which appeared in 1531 and 1539, are nothing but reprints of the *editio princeps*. 3. The edition of Camotius, sometimes called *Aldina minor*, Venice, 1551–53, 6 vols. 8vo. 4. The edition of Sylburgius, Frankfort, 1584–87, 11 vols. 4to. This edition surpassed all the previous ones, and even the critics of the present day can not dispense with it. 5. The edition of Isaac Casaubon, Leyden, 1590, 2 vols. fol., reprinted in 1597, 1605, 1646. This is the first Greek and Latin edition of the entire works of Aristotle, but prepared hastily, and now worthless. The same may be said of, 6. The edition of Du Val, Paris,

1 *Trendelenburg*, *l. c.*

1619 and 1629, 2 vols. fol.; 1639, 4 vols. fol. Much more important is, 7. The Bipont edition (not completed), by Buhle, 1791–1800, 5 vols. 8vo. It contains only the Organon, and the rhetorical and poetical writings. The continuation was prevented by the conflagration of Moscow, in which Buhle lost the materials which he had collected. The first volume, which contains, among other things, a most copious enumeration of all the earlier editions, translations, and commentaries, is of great literary value. The critical remarks contain chiefly the variations of older editions. Little is done in it for criticism itself and exegesis. 8. The edition of Bekker, Berlin, 1831–40, 4 vols. 4to. The text is in two volumes, the Latin translation occupies a third volume, and the fourth is a volume of scholia, edited by Brandis, which is to be followed by another volume of scholia that has not yet appeared. This is the first edition founded on a diligent, though not always complete comparison of ancient MSS. It forms the commencement of a new era for the criticism of the text of Aristotle. Unfortunately, there is still no notice given of the MSS. made use of, and of the course in consequence pursued by the editor, which occasions great difficulty in making a critical use of this edition. The text of Bekker's edition has been reprinted at Oxford, in 11 vols. 8vo, with the indices of Sylburg. Besides these, there is a stereotype edition published by Tauchnitz, Leipzig, 1832, 16 vols. 16mo, but it is an uncritical one, and the pointing is so bad as to destroy the sense. The very same text has been repeated under the title of a new edition: "*Aristotelis Opera Omnia quæ exstant. Cura Car. Herm. Weise*," Leipzig, 1841, &c., 1 vol. 4to. What is added upon the order of Aristotle's writings shows a want of all sound knowledge of the subject, and it is incredible how such a production could venture to make its appearance in Germany after Bekker's edition.[1]

The most important editions of the separate works are as follows: *Aristotelis Organon*, by Pacius, with an analytical commentary, Frankfort, 1597, 4to; by Bekker, Berlin, 1843, 2 vols. 8vo; best edition by Waitz, Leipzig, 1844–46, 2 vols. 8vo. *Metaphysica*, with critical text, by Brandis, in "*Aristotelis et Theophrasti Metaphysica*," &c., ed. C. A. Brandis, Berlin, 1823, 1 vol.; the "*Scholia Græca in Aristot. Metaphysica*," by Brandis, Berlin, 1837, form the second part to this edition; with a German translation, and copious commentary by Schwegler, Tübingen, 1846–48, 3 vols. 8vo; with critical text and commentary by Bonitz, Bonn, 1848–49, 2 vols. 8vo. Of the Mathematics, *Aristotelis* περὶ ἀτόμων γαμμῶν, by H. Stephens, Paris, 1557, 8vo; and the Μηχανικά, by Van Capelle, Amsterdam, 1812. Of the Physics, *Aristotelis Physica*, by Bekker, Berlin, 1843; *De Cœlo*, by Morelli, Lyon, 1563; and by Havenreuter, Frankfort, 1605. Περὶ γενέσεως καὶ φθορᾶς, Venice, 1520, fol.; by Pacius, Frankfort, 1601, with the books *De Cœlo* and others. Of the *Meteorologica*, by Vicomeratus, Paris, 1556; by Bekker, Berlin, 1832, 8vo; by Ideler, with Latin version and a learned commentary, Leipzig, 1834–36, 2 vols. 8vo.

Of the *Historia Animalium*, with the commentary of Scaliger and translation of Maussac, Toulouse, 1619, fol.; by Camus, with French translation, Paris, 1783, 2 vols. 4to; by Schneider, Leipzig, 1811, 4 vols. 8vo; and by Bekker, Berlin, 1832, 8vo. Of the *De Anima*, by Pacius, Frankfort, 1596, 8vo; by Trendelenburg, Jena, 1833, 8vo; the *De Anima, De Sensu, De Memoria*, and several minor treatises, by Bekker, Berlin, 1829, 8vo. Of the *De Coloribus*, by Portius, Florence, 1548, 4to. Of the *Physiognomica*, in Frantz's *Scriptores Physiognomici Veteres*, Altenburg, 1780, 8vo. Of the Πολιτεῖαι, or constitutions of states, &c., the fragments by Neumann, Heidelberg, 1827, 12mo. Of the Ethics, *Ethica Nicomachea*, by Wilkinson, Oxford, 1715, 4th ed., 1818, 8vo; by Zell, Heidelberg, 1820, 2 vols. 8vo; by Coraes, Paris, 1822, 8vo; by Cardwell, Oxford, 1828, 2 vols. 8vo, by Michelet, Berlin, 1828–35, 2 vols. 8vo, 2d ed., 1848; by Bekker, Berlin, 1845; *Ethica Eudemia (sive Eudemi Rhodii Ethica)*, by Fritzsche, Ratisbon, 1851, 8vo. Of the *Politica*, by Schneider, Frankfort on the Oder, 1809, 2 vols. 8vo; by Coraes, Paris, 1821, 8vo; by Göttling, Jena, 1824; by Stahr, with a German version, Leipzig, 1837; by Barthelemy St. Hilaire, with a French translation, Paris, 1837. Of the *Rhetoric*, by Victorius, Basle, 1549, fol.; Oxford, 1759, without accents, 8vo; by Reiz, Leipzig, 1772, 8vo; with a Latin version and commentary, Oxford, 1820, 2 vols. 8vo; by Bekker, Berlin, 1843, 8vo. Of the *Poetics*, by Robortellus, Florence, 1548, fol.; by Heinsius, 1610, 1611; by Tyrwhitt, Oxford, 1794, 4to and 8vo; by G. Hermann, Leipzig, 1802, 8vo; by Graefenhan, Leipzig, 1821, 8vo; by F. Ritter, Cologne, 1839; and by Bekker, with the Rhetoric, Berlin, 1832, 8vo. Of the *De Admirandis Narrationibus*, by Beckmann, Göttingen, 1786, 4to;

[1] *Bonitz, Die Neue Jenaische Literaturzeitung*, 1842.

and by Westermann, in the *Paradoxographi Græci*, Brunswick, 1839. Of the *Œconomicus*, by Schneider, Leipzig, 1815, 8vo; by Goettling, Jena, 1830.

II. Theophrastus (Θεόφραστος),[1] a celebrated Greek philosopher, and the successor of Aristotle in the Peripatetic school, was a native of Eresus, in Lesbos,[2] and studied philosophy at Athens, first under Plato, and afterward under Aristotle.[3] He became the favorite pupil of Aristotle, who is said to have changed his original name of Tyrtamus to Theophrastus (or the Divine speaker), to indicate the fluent and graceful address of his pupil;[4] but the story is scarcely credible. It is much more likely that the proper name itself, which occurs elsewhere,[5] suggested the idea of connecting it with the eloquence which so eminently distinguished the Eresian. Aristotle named Theophrastus his successor in the presidency of the Lyceum, and in his will bequeathed to him his library and the originals of his own writings. Theophrastus was a worthy successor of his great master, and nobly sustained the character of the school. He is said to have had two thousand disciples, and among them such men as the comic poet Menander.[6] He was highly esteemed by the kings Philippus, Cassander, and Ptolemy, and was not the less an object of regard to the Athenian people, as was decisively shown when Agonis ventured to bring an impeachment against him on the ground of impiety;[7] for he was not only acquitted, but his accuser would have fallen a victim to his calumny, had not Theophrastus generously interfered to save him. Nevertheless, when the philosophers were banished from Athens, in B.C. 305, according to the law of Sophocles, Theophrastus also left the city, until Philo, a disciple of Aristotle, in the very next year, brought Sophocles to punishment, and procured the repeal of the law.[8] From this time Theophrastus continued to teach at Athens without any farther molestation till his death. He died in B.C. 287, after having presided over the Lyceum about thirty-five years. His age is differently stated. According to some accounts, he lived eighty-five years;[9] according to others, one hundred and seven years. He is said to have closed his life with the complaint respecting the short duration of human existence, that it ended just when the insight into its problems was beginning. The whole population of Athens took part in his funeral obsequies. He bequeathed his library to Neleus of Scepsis.

Theophrastus exerted himself to carry out the philosophical system of Aristotle, to throw light upon the difficulties contained in his books, and to fill up the gaps in them. With this view he wrote a great number of works, the main object of which was the development of the Aristotelian philosophy. Unfortunately, most of them have perished. The following are alone extant: 1. *Charactēres* (Ἠθικοὶ χαρακτῆρες), in thirty chapters, containing descriptions of vicious or ridiculous characters. Schneider, one of the editors of Theophrastus, has been led to form the opinion that the "Characters," as we now have them, are only extracts from different

---

1 *Smith*, *l. c.*
2 *Strab.*, xiii., p. 618.
3 *Diog. Laert.*, v., 36, *seqq.*
4 *Strab.*, *l. c.*; *Diog. Laert.*, v., 38; *Cic.*, *Orat.*, 19.
5 *Steph.*, *Thesaur. Ling. Græc.*
6 *Diog. Laert.*, v., 36, *seq.*
7 *Id. ib.*; *Ælian*, *V. H.*, iv., 19.
8 *Diog. Laert.*, v., 38; *Menag. ad loc.*
9 *Id.*, v., 40.

moral works published by the philosophers, and extracts, too, made at different times and by different persons. This opinion, however, has found many opponents. More unanimity prevails among critics relative to the spuriousness of the preface. The "Characters" stand very high as a classic work, on account of the purity and precision of the style, and the exactness and fidelity of the portraits. Among their numerous imitators, La Bruyère stands most conspicuous. 2. A Treatise on sensuous perception and its objects (Περὶ αἰσθήσεως καὶ αἰσθητῶν). 3. A fragment of a work on metaphysics (τῶν μετὰ τὰ φυσικά). 4. *On the History of Plants* (Περὶ φυτῶν ἱστορίας), in nine books, with a fragment of a tenth, one of the earliest works on Botany that have come down to us. As the philosopher of Stagira is the father of Zoology, so is Theophrastus to be regarded as the parent of Botany. His vegetable physiology contains some very just arrangements: he had even a glimpse of the sexual system of plants. 5. *On the Causes of Plants* (Περὶ φυτῶν αἰτιῶν), originally in eight books, of which only six have come down to us. It is a system of botanical physiology. 6. *Of Stones* (Περὶ λίθων). This work proves that, after the time of Theophrastus, mineralogy retrograded. We have also other treatises of his on *Odors*, *Winds*, *Prognostics of the Weather*, &c. All these fragments have been preserved for us by Photius.

Of the earlier editions of the entire works of Theophrastus we may mention the Aldine, Venice, 1498, fol.; that of Basle, 1541, fol.; and that by D. Heinsius, Leyden, 1613, fol. Much superior, however, to the older ones is that by Schneider, Leipzig, 1818–21, 5 vols. 8vo. Still, this needs itself a careful revision, since the piecemeal manner in which the critical apparatus came into Schneider's hands, and his own ill health, compelled him to append supplements and corrections, twice or thrice, to the text and commentary. Wimmer has published the first volume of a new and much improved edition of Theophrastus, containing the history of plants, Breslau, 1842, 8vo. No other volumes, however, have as yet appeared. Of the separate works, we may mention the following editions: the *Characteres*, by Needham, Cambridge, 1712, 8vo; by Fischer, Coburg, 1763, 8vo, one of the best; by Goez, Nuremburg, 1798, 8vo; by Schneider, Jena, 1799, 8vo; by Coraes, Paris, 1799, 8vo; by Ast, Leipzig, 1816, 8vo. The *History of Plants*, by Bodæus à Stapel, Amsterdam, 1644, fol.; by Stackhouse, Oxford, 1813, 2 vols. 8vo; and by Wimmer, mentioned above. *On Stones*, by De Laet, Leyden, 1647, 8vo; and by Hill, with an English version and notes, London, 1746, 8vo.

III. Straton (Στράτων),[1] of Lampsacus, a distinguished Peripatetic philosopher, and tutor of Ptolemy Philadelphus, succeeded Theophrastus as head of the school in B.C. 288, and, after presiding over it eighteen years, was succeeded by Lycon.[2] He devoted himself especially to the study of natural science, whence he obtained, or, as it appears from Cicero, himself assumed the appellation of φυσικός (*Physicus*). Cicero, while speaking highly of his talents, blames him for neglecting the most necessary part of his philosophy, that which has respect to virtue and morals, and giving himself up to the investigation of nature.[3] In the long list of his works given by Diogenes, several of the titles are upon subjects of moral philosophy, but the great majority belong to the department of physical science. From the few notices of his tenets which we find in the ancient writers, Straton appears to have held a pantheistic system, the specific character of which, however, can not be determined. He seems

[1] *Smith, Dict. Biogr*, *s. v.* [2] *Diog. Laert.*, v., 58. [3] *Acad. Quæst.*, i., 9; *De Fin.*, v., 5.

to have denied the existence of any god out of the material universe, and to have held that every particle of matter has a plastic and seminal power, but without sensation or intelligence; and that life, sensation, and intellect are but forms, accidents, and affections of matter. Some modern writers have regarded Straton as a forerunner of Spinoza, while others see in his system an anticipation of the hypothesis of monads. He has been charged with atheism by Cudworth, Leibnitz, Bayle, and other distinguished writers, and warmly defended by Schlosser, in his *Spicilegium historico-philosophicum de Stratone Lampsaceno*, &c., Vitemberg, 1728, 4to. For an account of the controversy to which the tenets of Straton have given rise among modern scholars, the student should consult Harless, in his edition of Fabricius. Compare, also, Nauwerck, *De Stratone Lampsaceno Phil. Disquis.*, Berlin, 1836, 8vo.

The heads of the Peripatetic school who followed Theophrastus and Straton, namely, *Lycon*, *Ariston* of Ceos, *Critolaus*, &c., were of less importance, and seem to have occupied themselves more in carrying out some separate dogmas, and commenting on the works of Aristotle. Attention was especially directed to a popular rhetorical system of ethics. The school declined in splendor and influence; the more abstruse writings of Aristotle were neglected, because their form was not sufficiently pleasing, and the easy superficiality of the school was deterred by the difficulty of unfolding them. Thus the expression of the master himself respecting his writings might have been repeated, "that they had been published, and yet not published." Extracts and anthologies arose, and satisfied the superficial wants of the school, while the works of Aristotle himself were thrust into the background. In Rome, before the time of Cicero, we find only slender traces of an acquaintance with the writings and philosophical system of Aristotle. They only came there with the library of Apellicon, which Sulla, as we have said, had carried off from Greece.

X. THE STOIC SCHOOL.

I. ZENO (Ζήνων),[1] the celebrated founder of the Stoic philosophy, was a native of Citium, in Cyprus. He began at an early age to study philosophy through the writings of the Socratics, which his father, who was a merchant, was accustomed to bring back from Athens when he went thither on trading voyages. At the age of twenty-two, or, according to others, of thirty years, having been, while pursuing the vocation of his father, shipwrecked in the neighborhood of the Piræeus,[2] Zeno was led to settle in Athens, and to devote himself entirely to the study of philosophy. According to some writers, he lost all his property in the shipwreck; according to others, he still retained a large fortune;[3] but, whichever of these accounts is correct, his moderation and contentment became proverbial, and a recognition of his virtues shines through even the ridicule of the comic poets. The weakness of his health is said to have first determined him to live rigorously and simply; but his desire to make himself independent of all external circumstances chiefly led him to

[1] *Smith, Dict. Biogr.*, *s. v.* [2] *Diog. Laert.*, vii., 2, *seqq.* [3] *Id.*, vii., 13.

attach himself to the Cynic Crates. In opposition to the advice of Crates, he studied under Stilpo, of the Megaric school; and he subsequently received instruction from the two other contemporary Megarics, Diodorus Cronus and Philo, and from the Academics Xenocrates and Polemo. The period which Zeno thus devoted to study is said to have extended to twenty years. At its close, and after he had developed his peculiar philosophical system, he opened his school in the porch (*στοά*, *stoa*) adorned with the paintings of Polygnotus, and hence denominated *στοὰ ποικίλη* (*Stoa Poecĭle*), which, at an earlier period, had been a place where poets met.[1] From this place his disciples were called *Στωϊκοί*, or *οἱ ἐκ τῆς στοᾶς*, that is, *Stoics*, or *men of the porch*. They were previously styled *Zenonians*.

Among the warm admirers of Zeno was Antigonus Gonatas, king of Macedonia; and he is said also to have attracted the attention of the Egyptian monarch Ptolemy. Much more honorable, however, was the confidence and esteem which the Athenians showed toward him, stranger as he was; for although the well-known story that they deposited the keys of the Acropolis with him, as the most trustworthy man,[2] may be a later invention, there seems no reason for doubting the authenticity of the decree of the people, by which a golden crown and a public burial in the Ceramicus were awarded to him, because, during his long residence in Athens, by his doctrines, and his life spent in accordance with them, he had conducted the young men who attached themselves to him along the path of virtue and discretion. The Athenian citizenship, however, he is said to have declined, that he might not become unfaithful to his native land, where, in return, he was highly esteemed. We do not know the year either of Zeno's birth or death. He is said to have presided over his school for fifty-eight years, and to have died at the age of ninety-eight. He was still alive, according to the ordinary account, in B.C. 260.

Zeno wrote numerous works; but the writings of Chrysippus and the later Stoics seem to have obscured those of Zeno, and even the warm adherents of the school appear seldom to have gone back to the books of its founder. Hence it is difficult to ascertain how much of the later Stoic philosophy really belongs to Zeno. His successors in the Stoic school were as follows: *Cleanthes*, *Chrysippus*, *Zeno* of Tarsus, *Diogenes* of Babylon, *Antipater* of Tarsus, *Panætius* of Rhodes, and *Posidonius*.

Zeno's doctrines were mainly directed to the moral part of philosophy, and he approached nearer to the Cynics than his followers. It would appear, from the fact of his disciples separating into different parties, that his system was either not completely developed, or that it possessed too little originality to unite all his followers. Chrysippus is said to have been the one who gave to the Stoical system its full development, and fixed its doctrines; and hence the saying, "If there had been no Chrysippus, there would have been no Stoa." The Stoics made three divisions of philosophy, which Plutarch calls the Physical, Ethical, and Logical (*λογικόν*), of which, however, our word Logical is not a translation. But other Stoics made different divisions. The triple division was made by

[1] *Diog. Laert.*, vii., 5.

[2] *Id.*, vii., 6.

Zeno himself. The logical part of the Stoical system comprehended their metaphysics. They made a distinction between truth (ἀλήθεια) and true (ἀληθές); truth implied body (σῶμα), but true was without body, and was merely in opinion. They attributed to things an absolute existence in themselves. Their system, so far as we can learn what it was, was obscure, and they were certainly not well agreed among themselves on their metaphysical doctrines. They cultivated logic, rhetoric, and grammar. In their physical doctrines they assumed two first principles, the Active and the Passive. The Passive was οὐσία, or matter, the first substance of which all things were made; the Active was God, who was one, though called by many names. The universal belief in a Deity, or in many deities, they considered one of the evidences of God's existence.[1]

All the universe, says Seneca, according to our Stoical doctrines, consists of two things, cause and matter. The cause, which puts matter in motion, is conceived as pervading it, but it is rational; the motions produced are not the effect of chance, and all the harmony and beauty of the visible world are a proof of design. It followed from their general doctrines that the soul (ψυχή) is corporeal, for they defined all things to be body, which produce any thing or are produced. They argued thus: nothing that is without body sympathizes with body, nor does body sympathize with that which is not body, but only body with body. The body and the soul sympathize, for they are both bodies. Death is the separation of the soul and the body. The soul is a spirit (πνεῦμα) that is born with us; consequently it is body, and it continues after death; still, it is perishable; but the soul of all things, of which the souls of animals are parts, is imperishable. As to the duration of the soul there were different opinions: Cleanthes thought that all souls lasted to the general conflagration; Chrysippus thought that the souls of the wise only lasted so long.[2]

The ethical doctrines of the Stoics have attracted most attention as exhibited in the lives of distinguished Greeks and Romans. To live according to nature was the basis of their ethical system; but by this it was not meant that a man should follow his own particular nature; he must make his life conformable to the nature of the whole of things. This principle is the foundation of all morality; and it follows that morality is connected with philosophy. To know what is our relation to the whole of things, is to know what we ought to be and to do. To live according to nature is virtue, and virtue is itself happiness. Every man having within himself a capacity of discerning and following the law of nature, has his happiness in his own power, and is a divinity to himself. Wisdom consists in distinguishing good from evil. Good is that which produces happiness according to the nature of a rational being. As the order of the world consists in an invariable conformity to the law of fate, so the happiness of man is that course of life which flows in an uninterrupted current according to the law of nature. Since those things alone are truly good which are becoming and virtuous, and since virtue, which is seated in the mind, is alone sufficient for happiness, external things

[1] *Smith, l. c.*

[2] *Id. ib.*

contribute nothing toward happiness, and therefore are not in themselves good. The wise man will only value riches, honor, beauty, and other external enjoyments as means and instruments of virtue; for, in every condition, he is happy in the possession of a mind accommodated to nature. Pain, which does not belong to the mind, is no evil. The wise man will be happy in the midst of torture. All external things are indifferent, since they can not affect the happiness of man; nevertheless, some of these are conducive, others unfavorable to the life which is according to nature, and, as such, are proper objects of preference or rejection, προηγμένα ἢ ἀποπροηγμένα. Every virtue being a conformity to nature, and every vice a deviation from it, all virtues and vices are equal.[1]

The Stoics advanced many extravagant assertions concerning their wise man. For example, that he feels neither pain nor pleasure; that he exercises no pity; that he is free from faults; that he is divine; that he can neither deceive nor be deceived; that he does all things well; that he alone is noble, great, ingenuous; that he alone is free; that he is a prophet, a priest, a king, and the like. These paradoxical vauntings are humorously ridiculed by Horace. In order, however, to conceive the true notion of the Stoics concerning their wise man, it must be clearly understood that they did not suppose such a man actually to exist, but that they framed in their imagination an image of perfection, toward which every man should continually aspire. All the extravagant things which are to be met with in their writings on this subject may be referred to their general principle of the entire sufficiency of virtue to happiness, and the consequent indifference of all external circumstances. It is one of the boasts of the Stoics that their wise man is perfectly free, and can do whatever he pleases without restraint or compulsion; and yet nothing is more certain than that they understood this freedom to consist merely in the superiority of virtue to all external circumstances; for, according to the fundamental doctrine of the Porch, the human mind is bound by the indissoluble chain of nature, and subject to the eternal law of fate; and all human actions are a necessary consequence of that order, by which all beings in nature are irresistibly impelled.[2]

For a fuller exposition of the doctrines of the Stoics, the student is referred to the article on Zeno by Brandis, in Smith's *Dictionary of Biography*, and to the works of Brucker (*Hist. Crit. Philosoph.*, pt. ii., book ii., ch. ix., p. 893, *seqq.*) and Ritter (*Hist. Philos.*, vol. iii., p. 449, *seqq.*, Eng. transl.).—It remains to give a brief notice of *Cleanthes* and *Chrysippus*, reserving *Panætius* and *Posidonius* for the Roman period.

II. Cleanthes (Κλεάνθης)[3] was a native of Assos, in Troas, and born about B.C. 300. He entered life as a boxer, but had only four drachmas of his own when he felt himself impelled to the study of philosophy. He first placed himself under Crates, and then under Zeno, whose faithful disciple he continued for nineteen years. In order to support himself and pay Zeno the necessary fee for his instructions, he worked all night at drawing water, as a common laborer, in the public gardens; but as he spent the whole day in philosophical pursuits, and had no visible means

[1] *Enfield, Hist. Philos.*, vol. i., p. 346. [2] *Id. ib.*, p. 347. [3] *Smith, Dict. Biogr.*, *s. v.*

of support, he was summoned before the Areopagus to give an account of his manner of living. The judges were so delighted by the evidence of industry which he produced, that they voted him ten minæ, though Zeno would not permit him to accept them. He was naturally slow, but his iron industry overcame all difficulties; and, on the death of Zeno, Cleanthes succeeded him in his school. He died about B.C. 220, at the age of eighty, of voluntary starvation. His physician had recommended him to abstain from food two days, in order to cure an ulcer in his mouth, and at the end of the second day he said that, having now advanced so far on the road to death, it would be a pity to have the trouble over again. He, therefore, still refused all nourishment, and died, as we have said, of starvation.

The names of the numerous treatises of Cleanthes preserved by Diogenes Laertius present the usual catalogue of moral and philosophical subjects: περὶ ἀρετῶν, περὶ ἡδονῆς, περὶ θεῶν, &c. A hymn of his to Jove is still extant, and contains some striking sentiments. It was edited by Sturz, 1785, re-edited by Merzdorf, Lips., 1835.

The doctrines of Cleanthes were almost exactly those of Zeno. There was a slight variation between his opinion and the more usual Stoical view respecting the immortality of the soul. Cleanthes taught that all souls are immortal, but that the intensity of existence after death would vary according to the strength or weakness of the particular soul, thereby leaving to the wicked some apprehension of future punishment; whereas Chrysippus considered that only the souls of the wise and good were to survive death. Again, with regard to the ethical principle of the Stoics, "to live in unison with nature," it is said that Zeno only enunciated the vague direction, ὁμολογουμένως ζῆν, which Cleanthes explained by the addition of τῇ φύσει. By this he meant the universal nature of things, whereas Chrysippus understood by the nature which we are to follow, the particular nature of man as well as universal nature.[1]

III. Chrysippus (Χρύσιππος) was born at Soli, in Cilicia, B.C. 280. When young, he lost his paternal property and went to Athens, where he became the disciple of the Stoic Cleanthes. Disliking the academic skepticism, he became one of the most strenuous supporters of the principle that knowledge is attainable, and may be established on certain foundations. Hence, though not the founder of the Stoic school, he was the first who based its doctrines on a plausible system of reasoning, so that it was said, as we have already stated, that if Chrysippus had not existed, the Porch could not have been.[2] He died in B.C. 207, aged seventy-three. Chrysippus possessed great acuteness and sagacity, and his industry was so great that he is said to have seldom written less than five hundred lines a day, and to have left behind him seven hundred and five works. Though none of them are extant, yet numerous fragments remain, which have been collected by Baguet, "*De Chrysippi Vita et Reliquiis*," Louvaine, 1822, 4to. His erudition was profound, and he appears to have overlooked no branch of study except mathematics and natural philosophy, which were neglected by the Stoics till the time of Posidonius.

[1] *Diog. Laert.*, vii., 89.

[2] *Id.*, vii., 183.

XI. THE SKEPTICAL OR PYRRHONIC SCHOOL.

I. The leading characteristic of this school was to call in question the truth of every system of opinions adopted by other sects, and to hold no other settled opinion save that every thing is uncertain.

II. On account of the similarity of the opinions of this sect and those of the Middle Academy, many of the real followers of the former chose to screen themselves from odium by adopting the name of Academics. The founder of the skeptical school was Pyrrho, whence it has also been called the Pyrrhonic.

III. PYRRHO (Πύῤῥων) was a native of Elis, in the Peloponnesus. He is said to have been poor, and to have followed at first the profession of a painter.[1] He is then said to have been attracted to philosophy by the writings of Democritus,[2] to have attended the lectures of Bryson, a disciple of Stilpon, to have attached himself closely to Anaxarchus, and with him to have joined the expedition of Alexander the Great. During the greater part of his life he dwelt in retirement, and endeavored to render himself independent of all external circumstances. His disciple Timon extolled his divine repose of soul, and his indifference to pleasure or pain.[3] It is said, moreover, that his fellow-citizens, through their admiration of him, made him their high-priest, and erected a monument to him after his death.[4] The Athenians also, as we are told, conferred upon him the rights of citizenship. These accounts, however, are to be received with great caution, since it is highly improbable that a half-insane man, such as his biographer Antigonus of Carystus depicts him, would ever have been invested with the high-priesthood, or made an Athenian citizen. We know little respecting the principles of his skeptical philosophy. He asserted that certain knowledge on any subject was unattainable, and that the great object of man ought to be to lead a virtuous life. It is related[5] of this philosopher that he acted upon his own principles, and carried his skepticism to such a ridiculous extreme, that his friends were obliged to accompany him wherever he went, that he might not be run over by vehicles, or fall down precipices. Pyrrho wrote nothing except a poem addressed to Alexander, which was rewarded by the latter in so royal a manner, that the statements respecting the poverty of the philosopher's mode of life are not easily reconcilable with it. His philosophical system was first reduced to writing by his disciple Timon. He reached the age of ninety years, but we have no mention of the year either of his birth or his death.

IV. TIMON (Τίμων)[6] was a native of Phlius, and flourished in the reign of Ptolemy Philadelphus, about B.C. 279,[7] and onward. Strictly speaking, therefore, he belongs to the succeeding or Alexandrine period of literature; but, from his peculiar connection with the establishment of the Pyrrhonic school, we prefer considering him here. He first studied philosophy at Megara, under Stilpon, and then returned home and married.

[1] *Diog. Laert.*, ix., 61, *seqq.* [2] *Id.*, ix., 69. [3] *Id.*, ix., 65, *seqq.*
[4] *Pausan.*, vi., 24, 5. [5] *Diog. Laert.*, ix., 62. [6] *Smith, Dict. Biogr.*, *s. v.*
[7] *Clinton, Fast. Hell.*, vol. iii., *s. a.*, 279, 272.

He next went to Elis with his wife, and heard Pyrrhon, whose tenets he adopted. Driven from Elis by straitened circumstances, he spent some time on the Hellespont and Propontis, and taught at Chalcedon, as a Sophist, with such success that he realized a fortune. He then removed to Athens, where he passed the remainder of his life, with the exception of a short residence at Thebes. He died at the age of almost ninety.[1]

Timon appears to have been endowed by nature with a powerful and active mind, and with that quick perception of the follies of men which betrays its possessor into a spirit of universal distrust both of men and truths, so as to make him a skeptic in philosophy and a satirist in every thing. He wrote numerous works both in prose and poetry. The most celebrated of his poems were the satiric compositions called *Silli* (σίλλοι), a word of somewhat doubtful etymology, but which undoubtedly describes metrical compositions of a character at once ludicrous and sarcastic. The invention of this species of poetry is ascribed to Xenophanes of Colophon. The *Silli* of Timon were in three books, in the first of which he spoke in his own person, and the other two were in the form of a dialogue between the author and Xenophanes of Colophon, in which Timon proposed questions, to which Xenophanes replied at length. The subject was a sarcastic account of the tenets of all philosophers, living and dead—an unbounded field for skepticism and satire. They were in hexameter verse, and, from the way in which they are mentioned by the ancient writers, as well as from the few fragments of them which have come down to us, it is evident that they were very admirable productions of their kind. The fragments are collected by Wölke, *De Græcorum Sillis*, Warsaw, 1820; and by Paul, *Dissertatio de Sillis*, Berlin, 1821.

XII. THE EPICUREAN SCHOOL.

I. The *Epicurĕan* school, so called from its founder *Epicurus*, was properly a branch of the Eleatic. In strictness, it belongs, like the preceding, to the Fifth or Alexandrine period; but it may be more conveniently considered in the present place.

II. Epicurus (Ἐπίκουρος)[2] was the son of Neocles and Charestrata, and was born B.C. 342, in the island of Samos, where his father had settled as one of the Athenian cleruchi; but he belonged to the Attic demus of Gargettus, and hence is sometimes called the Gargettian.[3] At the age of eighteen he came to Athens, having spent the previous part of his life in Samos and Teos. We are told that he had begun to study philosophy when only fourteen, having been incited thereto by a desire, which the teachers to whom he had applied had failed to satisfy, of understanding Hesiod's description of Chaos; and that he began with the writings of Democritus. In Samos, also, he is said to have received lessons from Pamphilus, a follower of Plato. At the time when Epicurus arrived in Athens, Xenocrates was teaching in the Academy, and Theophrastus in the Lyceum; and we may suppose that he did not fail to avail himself of the opportunities of instruction which were thus within his reach.

[1] *Diog. Laert.*, ix., 12, *seqq.*

[2] *Smith, Dict. Biogr.*, *s. v.*

[3] *Cic.*, *Ep. ad Fam.*, xv., 16.

Indeed, it is actually stated by Demetrius Magnes that Epicurus was a pupil of Xenocrates. After a short stay at Athens, owing to the outbreak of the Lamian war, he went to Colophon, and subsequently resided at Mytilene and Lampsacus, in which places he was engaged for five years in teaching philosophy, namely, one year in Mytilene and four years in Lampsacus. In B.C. 306, when he had attained the age of thirty-five, he again came to Athens, where he purchased for eighty minæ a garden —the famous κῆποι Ἐπικούρου—in which he established his philosophical school. Here he spent the remainder of his life, surrounded by numerous friends and pupils, and by his three brothers, Neocles, Charidemus, and Aristobulus, who likewise devoted themselves to the study of philosophy. His mode of living was simple, temperate, and cheerful; and the aspersions of comic poets and of later philosophers, who were opposed to his doctrines, and who describe him as a person devoted to sensual pleasures, do not seem entitled to the least credit. He took no part in public affairs. He died in B.C. 270, at the age of seventy-two, after a long and painful illness, which he endured with truly philosophic patience and courage.[1]

Epicurus appears to have been one of the most prolific of all the ancient Greek writers. Diogenes Laertius, who calls him πολυγραφώτατος,[2] states that he wrote about 300 volumes (κύλινδροι). His works, however, are said to have been full of repetitions and quotations of authorities. A list of the best of his works is given by Diogenes, among which we may particularly mention the one *On Nature* (Περὶ Φύσεως), in thirty-seven books. Of his epistles, four are preserved in Diogenes. The first is very brief, and was addressed by Epicurus, just before his death, to Idomeneus. The three others are of far greater importance: the first of them is addressed to one Herodotus, and contains an outline of what were termed *Canonics*, and of the *Physics* also; the second, addressed to Pythocles, contains his theory about meteors; and the third, which is addressed to Menœceus, gives a concise view of his *Ethics;* so that these three epistles, the genuineness of which can scarcely be doubted, furnish us with an outline of his whole philosophical system. They were edited separately by Nürnberger, in his edition of the tenth book of Diogenes Laertius, Nürnberg, 1791, 8vo. The letters to Herodotus and Pythocles were edited by Schneider, Leipzig, 1813, 8vo. These letters, together with the Κύριαι δόξαι, that is, forty-four propositions containing the substance of the ethical philosophy of Epicurus, which are likewise preserved in Diogenes, must be our principal guides in examining and judging of the Epicurean philosophy. All the other works of Epicurus have perished, with the exception of a considerable number of fragments. Some parts of the work Περὶ Φύσεως, especially of the second and eleventh books, which treat of the εἴδωλα, have been found among the rolls at Herculaneum, and are published in Corsini's *Volumin. Herculan.*, vol. ii., Naples, 1809, from which they were reprinted separately by Orelli, Leipzig, 1818, 8vo. Some fragments of the tenth book of the same work have been edited by Kreyssig, in his *Comment. de Sallust. histor. Fragm.*, p. 237, *seqq.*

[1] *Diog. Laert.*, x., 13, *seqq.*

[2] *Id.*, x., 26.

If we may judge of the style of Epicurus from these few remains, it must be acknowledged that it is clear and animated, though it is not distinguished for any other peculiar merits.

Epicurus divided the whole field of knowledge into three parts, to which he gave the names respectively of *Canonics*, *Physics*, and *Ethics*.[1] The first two were subordinate to the third. The end of all knowledge, of ethics directly or immediately, of canonics and physics indirectly or mediately through ethics, was, according to Epicurus, to increase the happiness of man. *Canonics*, which formed a subject altogether introductory both to physics and ethics, treated of the means by which knowledge, both physical and ethical, was obtained, and of the conditions or (as they were called by Epicurus) *criteria* of truth. These conditions or *criteria* were, according to him, sensations (αἰσθήσεις), ideas, or imaginations (προλήψεις), and affections (πάθη). From these three sorts of consciousness we get all our knowledge. What Epicurus then called *canonics*, viewed in relation to physics and ethics, is, when viewed absolutely or in itself, psychology. Epicurus seems to have explained rightly the dependence of ideas upon sensations;[2] but, in accounting for sensations, he, like Democritus, left the path of sound psychology, and introduced the fanciful hypothesis of emanations from bodies.

In the physical part of his philosophy he followed the atomistic doctrines of Democritus, though priding himself on being independent of all his predecessors. His views are well known from Lucretius's poem, *De Rerum Natura.* According to Epicurus, as also to Democritus and Leucippus before him, the universe consists of two parts, matter and space, or vacuum, in which matter exists and moves; and all matter, of every kind and form, is reducible to certain indivisible particles, called, from this circumstance, atoms, which are eternal in their nature. These atoms moving, according to a natural tendency, straight downward, and also obliquely, have thereby come to form the different bodies which are found in the world, and which differ in kind and shape according as the atoms are differently placed in respect of one another. We obtain our knowledge and form our conceptions of things, according to Epicurus, through εἴδωλα, that is, images of things which are reflected from them, and pass through our senses into our minds. Such a theory, however, is clearly destructive of all absolute truth, and a mere momentary impression upon our senses or feelings is substituted for it. But the deficiencies of his system are most striking in his views concerning the gods, which drew upon him the charge of atheism. His gods, like every thing else consisted of atoms, and our notions of them are based upon the εἴδωλα, which are reflected from them and pass into our minds. They were and always had been in the enjoyment of perfect happiness, which had not been disturbed by the laborious business of creating the world; and, as the government of the world would interfere with their happiness, he conceived them as exercising no influence whatever upon the world or man.[3]

His ethical theory was based upon the dogma of the Cyrenaics, that pleasure constitutes the highest happiness, and must consequently be the

[1] *Penny Cyclop.*, ix., p. 472. [2] *Diog. Laert.*, x., 33. [3] *Smith, l. c.*

end of all human exertions. Epicurus, however, developed and ennobled this theory in a manner which constitutes the real merit of his philosophy, and which gained for him so many friends and admirers both in antiquity and in modern times. Pleasure with him was not a mere momentary and transitory sensation, but he conceived it as something lasting and imperishable, consisting in pure and noble mental enjoyments, that is, in ἀταραξία and ἀπονία, or freedom from pain and from all influences which disturb the peace of our mind, and thereby our happiness, which is the result of it. The *summum bonum*, according to him, consisted in this peace of mind; and this was based upon φρόνησις, which he described as the beginning of every thing good, as the origin of all virtues, and which he himself, therefore, occasionally treated as the highest good itself.[1]

The number of pupils of Epicurus was very great; but his philosophy received no farther development at their hands, except, perhaps, that in subsequent times his lofty notion of pleasure and happiness was reduced to that of material and sensual pleasure. His immediate disciples adopted and followed his doctrines with the most scrupulous conscientiousness. They were attached and devoted to their master in a manner which has rarely been equalled either in ancient or modern times. Their esteem, love, and veneration for him almost bordered upon worship. They are said to have committed his works to memory. They had his portrait engraved upon rings and drinking vessels, and celebrated his birth-day every year. Athens honored him with bronze statues. But, notwithstanding the extraordinary devotion of his pupils and friends, whose number, says Diogenes, exceeded that of the population of whole towns, there is no philosopher in antiquity who has been so violently attacked, and whose ethical doctrines have been so much misunderstood as Epicurus. The cause of this was partly a superficial knowledge of his philosophy, of which Cicero, for example, is guilty to a very great extent; and partly, also, the conduct of men who called themselves Epicureans, and who, taking advantage of the facility with which his ethical theory was made the handmaid of a sensual and debauched life, gave themselves up to the enjoyment of sensual pleasures. At Rome, and during the time of Roman ascendency in the ancient world, the philosophy of Epicurus never took any firm root; and it is then and there that, owing to the paramount influence of the Stoic philosophy, we meet with the bitterest antagonists of Epicurus.[2]

III. Metrodōrus (Μητρόδωρος) was the most distinguished of the disciples of Epicurus. He was a native, according to some accounts,[3] of Lampsacus, according to others, of Athens, and lived with Epicurus on terms of the closest friendship, never having left him from the time that he became acquainted with him, except for six months on one occasion, when he paid a visit to his home. He died in B.C. 277, in the fifty-third year of his age, seven years before Epicurus, who would have appointed him his successor had he survived him. He left behind him a son named Epicurus, and a daughter, for whom Epicurus the elder provided by will out of the property which he left behind him. The philosophy of Metro-

[1] *Smith, l. c.* [2] *Id. ib.* [3] *Strab.*, xiii., p. 589; *Cic.*, *Tusc. Disp.*, v., 37.

dorus appears to have been of a more grossly sensual kind than that of Epicurus. Perfect happiness he made, according to Cicero's account, to consist in having a well-constituted body, and knowing that it would always remain so. Diogenes Laertius enumerates several of his works, and Athenæus makes mention of his letters. No remains of his writings have come down to us.[1]

CHAPTER XXXVI.

FOURTH OR ATTIC PERIOD—*continued.*

MATHEMATICS.—ASTRONOMY.—MEDICINE.

I. MATHEMATICS.—ASTRONOMY.

I. We have already made incidental mention of the progress of mathematical and astronomical knowledge among the Greeks in our accounts of some of the schools of ancient philosophy. Mathematics, however, were not cultivated as a distinct and regular science until the establishment of the Alexandrean school. Previously to this period a few individuals merely had distinguished themselves by the pursuit of mathematical and astronomical knowledge, of whom we will now give a brief notice.

II. The names, when arranged in chronological order, are, *Hippocrates*, of Chios; *Theodorus*, of Cyrene; *Meton*, of Athens; *Archytas*, of Tarentum; and *Eudoxus*, of Cnidus.

1. Hippocrătes (Ἱπποκράτης), the namesake of the celebrated physician, was a native of Chios, and a Pythagorean philosopher, and lived about B.C. 460. He is mentioned chiefly as a mathematician, and is said to have been the first who reduced geometry to a regular system. He seems to have been also engaged in researches respecting the square of the circle; but we have no means of judging accurately of his mathematical merits. Aristotle states that in every other respect he was a man not above mediocrity.

2. Theodōrus (Θεόδωρος), of Cyrene, was a Pythagorean philosopher, of the age of Pericles. According to Proclus, he was a little younger than Anaxagoras,[2] and was eminent as a mathematician. Appuleius[3] and Diogenes Laertius[4] both state that Plato went to Cyrene to study geometry under a Theodorus of that place, the same probably with the one whom we are here considering.

3. Meton (Μέτων) was an astronomer of Athens, who, in conjunction with Euctemon, introduced the cycle of nineteen years, by which he adjusted the course of the sun and moon, since he had observed that 235 lunar months correspond very nearly to nineteen solar years.[5] The commencement of this cycle has been placed B.C. 432. We have no details of Meton's life, with the exception that he feigned insanity to avoid sailing for Sicily in the ill-fated expedition of which he is stated to have had an evil presentiment.[6]

---

1 *Smith, l. c.* 2 *Procl. in Euclid. Elem.*, 1. 3 *De Dogm. Plat.*, lib. i., *prope init.*
4 *Diog. Laert.*, iii., 6. 5 *Ælian, V. H.*, x., 7; *Diod. Sic.*, xii., 36. 6 *Ælian, V. H.*, xiii., 12.

4. Archytas (Ἀρχύτας),[1] of Tarentum, a distinguished Pythagorean philosopher, mathematician, general, and statesman, probably lived about B.C. 400 and onward, so that he was contemporary with Plato, whose life, as we have before stated, he is said to have saved by his influence with the tyrant Dionysius.[2] Like the Pythagoreans in general, he paid much attention to mathematics. Horace[3] calls him "*maris et terræ numeroque carentis arenæ Mensorem.*" He solved the problem of the doubling of the cube,[4] and invented the method of analytical geometry. He was the first, also, who applied the principles of mathematics to mechanics. To his theoretical science he added the skill of a practical mechanician, and constructed various machines and automatons, among which his wooden flying dove, in particular, was the wonder of antiquity.[5] He also applied mathematics with success to musical science, and even to metaphysical philosophy. The fragments and titles of works ascribed to Archytas are very numerous, but the genuineness of many of them is greatly doubted. Most of them are found in Stobæus. They have been published in part by Gale, *Opusc. Mythol.*, Cambridge, 1671; Amst., 1688; and more fully by Orelli, *Opusc. Sentent. et Moral.*, vol. ii., p. 234, *seqq.*

5. Eudoxus (Εὔδοξος),[6] of Cnidus, was, according to Diogenes Laertius, an astronomer, geometer, physician, and legislator. It is only in the first capacity, however, that his fame has descended to our day, and he has more of it than can be justified by any account of his astronomical science now in existence. As the probable introducer of the sphere into Greece, and perhaps the corrector, upon Egyptian information, of the length of the year, he enjoyed a wide reputation. According to Diogenes Laertius,[7] Eudoxus went to Athens at the age of twenty-three (he had been the pupil of Archytas in geometry), and heard Plato for some months, struggling at the same time with poverty. Being dismissed by Plato, but for what reason is not stated, his friends raised some money, and he sailed for Egypt, with letters of recommendation to Nectanabis, who, in his turn, recommended him to the priests. With them he remained sixteen months, with his chin and eyebrows shaved. After a time he came back to Athens, with a band of pupils, having in the mean time taught philosophy in Cyzicus, on the Propontis. The fragmentary notices of Eudoxus are numerous. Strabo mentions him frequently, and states that the observatory of Eudoxus at Cnidus was existing in his time, from which he was accustomed to observe the star Canopus;[8] so that Eudoxus, before returning to Athens, must have spent some time also in his native place. Strabo, moreover, informs us that he remained in Egypt thirteen years (differing in this from Diogenes), and attributes to him the introduction of the odd quarter of a day into the value of the year. Seneca states that he first brought the motions of the planets (a theory on this subject) from Egypt into Greece. Aristotle[9] says that he made separate spheres for the stars, sun, moon, and planets. According to Archimedes, he made the diameter of the sun nine times as great as

1 *Smith, Dict. Biogr., s. v.* 2 *Diog. Laert.*, viii., 79, *seqq.* 3 *Od.*, i., 28, 1.
4 *Vitruv.*, ix., *præf.* 5 *Gell.*, x., 12. 6 *Smith, Dict. Biogr., s. v.*
7 *Diog. Laert.*, iii., 86, *seqq.* 8 *Strab.*, xvii., p. 806. 9 *Metaph.*, xii., 8.

that of the moon. Vitruvius attributes to him the invention of a solar dial.

But all we positively know of Eudoxus is from the poem of Aratus, and the commentary of Hipparchus upon it. From this commentary we learn that Aratus was not himself an observer, but was merely the versifier of the *Φαινόμενα* of Eudoxus, of which Hipparchus has preserved fragments for comparison with the version of Aratus. The result is, that though there were by no means so many or so great errors in Eudoxus as in Aratus, yet the opinion which must be formed of the work of the former is, that it was written in the rudest state of the science by an observer who was not very competent even to the task of looking at the risings and settings of the stars. Delambre[1] has given a full account of the comparison made by Hipparchus of Aratus with Eudoxus, and of both with his own observations. He can not bring himself to think that Eudoxus knew any thing of geometry (though it is on record that he wrote geometrical works), in spite of the praises of Proclus, Cicero, Ptolemy, Sextus Empiricus (who places him with Hipparchus), and others. Eudoxus, as cited by Hipparchus, neither talks like a geometer, nor like a person who had seen the heavens he describes: a bad globe, constructed some centuries before his time in Egypt, might, for any thing that appears, have been his sole authority. But supposing, which is likely enough, that he was the first who brought any globe at all into Greece, it is not much to be wondered at that his reputation should have been magnified. Eudoxus is said to have written several works, but none of them have come down to us.

II. MEDICINE.[2]

I. The earliest records of the practice of medicine are extremely obscure. Among the Jews, it appears to have been entirely confined to the priests, and the whole art seems to have consisted in the prevention of contagion by isolation and cleanliness, and the administration of a few uncertain remedies. The Egyptians, according to the account of Herododotus, must have made some little progress; cathartics and emetics were well known to them, and much used; and such was the subdivision of labor, that there were physicians for every separate complaint: some for the eyes, others for the head, others for the teeth, others for the abdominal parts, and others for diseases which did not manifest themselves by any outward, visible symptoms.[3] It appears, however, that in the time of Darius Hystaspis the Greeks possessed more skill than the Egyptians.[4] The Greeks probably derived their knowledge of medicine, with that of many other arts, from Egypt, whence, according to one account, the centaur Chiron, who plays so conspicuous a part in some of their legends, is said to have introduced it among them.

II. ÆSCULAPIUS (Ἀσκληπιός), the pupil of Chiron,[5] so much improved the healing art that he was deified; and his sons, MACHAON and PODA-

---

1 *Hist. Astr. Anc.*, vol. i., p. 107.
2 *Penny Cyclop.*, xv., p. 57.
3 *Herod.*, ii., 84.
4 *Id.*, iii., 129.
5 *Pausan.*, ii., 26, 5; *Apollod.*, iii., 10, 3.

LIRIUS,[1] accompanied the Grecian army to the siege of Troy. From circumstances mentioned in the Iliad, it would appear that their practice was almost entirely confined to the treatment of wounds, and that charms and incantations formed a considerable portion of the means which they employed. The descendants of Æsculapius, as they called themselves, but, in reality, an order or caste of priests, under the name of *Asclepiadæ* (Ἀσκληπιάδαι), were for many years the chief practitioners of medicine, and the knowledge of the healing art was thus, for a long period, intimately connected with religion. This knowledge, in fact, was regarded as a sacred secret, which was transmitted from father to son in the families of the *Asclepiadæ*.

III. In the sixth century before the Christian era, medicine, with other sciences, began to be more philosophically studied in Greece, and among the first of those who devoted much of their time to the investigation of the structure and functions of the animal body may be ranked Pythagoras. Democritus and Heraclitus appear also to have added considerably both to anatomy and to practical medicine, and their contemporary Herodicus first introduced the practice of gymnastic exercises, which afterward formed so large a part of medical treatment. But the most remarkable man in the history of Grecian medicine was Hippocrates.[2]

IV. HIPPOCRĂTES (Ἱπποκράτης)[3] was born in the island of Cos, about B.C. 460. He belonged to the caste or order of the Asclepiadæ, and was the son of Heraclides, who was also a physician. He was instructed in medical science by his father and by Herodicus, and he is said to have been also a pupil in rhetoric of Gorgias of Leontini. He wrote, taught, and practiced his profession at home; travelled in different parts of the continent of Greece; and died at Larissa, in Thessaly, about B.C. 357, at the age of 103. He had two sons, Thessalus and Dracon, and a son-in-law, Polybus, all of whom followed the same profession, and who are supposed to have been the authors of some of the works in the Hippocratic collection. These are the only certain facts which we know respecting the life of Hippocrates; but to these later writers have added a large collection of stories, many of which are clearly fabulous. Thus he is said to have stopped the plague at Athens by burning fires throughout the city, by suspending chaplets of flowers, and by the use of an antidote, the composition of which is preserved by Joannes Actuarius. It is also related that Artaxerxes Longimanus, king of Persia, invited Hippocrates to come to his assistance during a time of pestilence, but that Hippocrates refused his request on the ground of his being the enemy of his country.

The writings which have come down to us under the name of Hippocrates were composed by several different persons, and are of very different merit. They are more than sixty in number, but of these only a few are certainly genuine. These few are as follows: 1. Προγνωστικόν, *Prænotiones* or *Prognosticon*. 2. Ἀφορισμοί, *Aphorismi*. 3. Ἐπιδημίων Βιβλία, *De Morbis Popularibus* (or *Epidemiorum*). 4. Περὶ Διαίτης Ὀξέων, *De Rati-*

[1] *Il.*, ii., 731; iv., 194; xi., 518.

[2] *Penny Cyclop.*, *l. c.*

[3] *Greenhill*, in *Smith, Dict. Biogr.*, *s. v.*

one victus in Morbis Acutis, or *De Diæta Acutorum.* 5. Περὶ Ἀέρων, Ὑδάτων, Τόπων, *De Aëre, Aquis, et Locis.* 6. Περὶ τῶν ἐν κεφαλῇ τρωμάτων, *De Capitis Vulneribus.* Some of the other works were perhaps written by Hippocrates, but the great majority were composed by his disciples and followers, many of whom bore the name of Hippocrates. The work by which Hippocrates is most popularly known is the one termed Ἀφορισμοί, or *Aphorisms*, and which appears to have been the production of his old age. It consists of extracts from his other works, to which were afterward added other sentences taken from later authors.

Hippocrates is mentioned or referred to by no less than ten persons anterior to the foundation of the Alexandrean school, and among them by Aristotle and Plato. At the time of the formation of the great Alexandrean library, the different treatises which bear the name of Hippocrates were diligently sought for and formed into a single collection; and about this time commences the series of commentators, which has continued through a period of more than two thousand years to the present day. The first person who is known to have commented on any of the works of the Hippocratic collection is Herophilus, who lived at Alexandrea under the first Ptolemy. The most ancient commentary still in existence is that on the treatise "*De Articulis*," by Apollonius Citiensis. By far the most voluminous, and, at the same time, by far the most valuable commentaries that remain, are those of Galen, who wrote several works in illustration of the writings of Hippocrates, besides those which we now possess. The other ancient commentaries that remain are those of Palladius, Joannes Alexandrinus, Stephanus Atheniensis, Meletius, Theophilus Protospatharius, and Damascius; besides a spurious work attributed to Oribasius, a glossary of obsolete and difficult words by Erotianus, and some Arabic commentaries that have never been published. The writings of Hippocrates were held in the highest esteem by the ancient Greek and Latin physicians, and most of them also were translated into Arabic. In the Middle Ages, however, they were not so much studied as those of some other authors, whose works are of a more practical character, and better fitted for being made a class-book and manual of instruction. In more modern times, on the contrary, the works of the Hippocratic collection have been valued more according to their real worth, while many of the most popular writers of the Middle Ages have fallen into complete neglect.[1]

Hippocrates divides the causes of disease into two principal classes; the one comprehending the influence of seasons, climates, water, situation, &c., and the other consisting of more personal and private causes, such as result from the particular kind and amount of food and exercise in which each separate individual indulges himself. The modifications of the atmosphere, dependent on different seasons and climates, is a subject which was successfully treated by Hippocrates, and which is still far from being exhausted by all the researches of modern science. He considered that while heat and cold, moisture and dryness, succeeded one another throughout the year, the human body underwent certain

[1] *Greenhill, l. c.*

analogous changes, which influenced the diseases of the period; and on this basis was founded the doctrine of pathological constitutions, corresponding to particular conditions of the atmosphere, so that, whenever the year or the season exhibited a special character in which such or such a temperature prevailed, those persons who were exposed to its influence were affected by a series of disorders all bearing the same stamp. How plainly the same idea runs through the *Observationes Medicæ* of Sydenham, the "English Hippocrates," need not be pointed out to those who are at all familiar with his works. The belief in the influence which different climates exercise on the human frame follows naturally from the theory just mentioned; for, in fact, a *climate* may be considered as nothing more than a *permanent season*, whose effects may be expected to be more powerful, inasmuch as the cause is ever at work upon mankind. Accordingly, Hippocrates attributes to climate both the conformation of the body and the disposition of the mind—indeed, almost every thing; and if the Greeks were found to be hardy freemen, and the Asiatics effeminate slaves, he accounts for the difference of their characters by that of the climates in which they lived.[1]

With respect to the second class of causes producing disease, he attributed all sorts of disorders to a vicious system of diet, which, whether excessive or defective, he considered to be equally injurious; and in the same way, he supposed that when bodily exercise was either too much indulged or entirely neglected, the health was equally likely to suffer though by different forms of disease. Into all the minutiæ of the "Humoral Pathology" (as it was called), which kept its ground in Europe as the prevailing doctrine of all the medical sects for more than twenty centuries, it would be out of place to enter here. It will be sufficient, however, to remark, that the four fluids or humors of the body (blood, phlegm, yellow bile, and black bile) were supposed to be the primary seat of disease; that health was the result of the due combination (or *crasis*) of these, and that when this crasis was disturbed, disease was the consequence; that in the course of a disorder which was proceeding favorably, these humors underwent a certain change in quality (or *coction*), which was the sign of returning health, as preparing the way for the expulsion of the morbid matter, or *crisis;* and that these crises had a tendency to occur at certain stated periods, which were hence called critical days.[2]

The medical practice of Hippocrates was cautious and feeble, so much so that he was in after times reproached with letting his patients die, by doing nothing to keep them alive. It consisted chiefly in watching the operations of nature, and promoting the critical evacuations mentioned above; so that attention to diet and regimen was the principal and often the only remedy which he employed. Several hundred substances have been enumerated which are used medicinally in different parts of the Hippocratic collection; of these, by far the greater portion belong to the vegetable kingdom, as it would be in vain to look for any traces of chemistry in these early writings. In surgery he is the author of the frequently quoted maxim, that "what can not be cured by medicine is cured by

[1] *Greenhill, l. c.*

[2] *Id. ib.*

the knife, and what can not be cured by the knife is cured by fire." The anatomical knowledge displayed in different parts of the Hippocratic collection is scanty and contradictory, so much so, that the discrepancies on this subject constitute an important criterion in deciding the genuineness of the different treatises.[1]

With regard to the personal character of Hippocrates, though he says little or nothing about himself, yet it is impossible to avoid drawing certain conclusions from the characteristic passages scattered throughout his writings. He was evidently a person who not only had had great experience, but who also knew how to turn it to the best account, and the number of moral reflections and apophthegms that we meet with in his pages, some of which (as, for example, "Life is short, and Art is long") have acquired a sort of proverbial notoriety, show him to have been a profound thinker. He appears to have felt the moral obligations and responsibilities of his profession, and often tries to impress upon his readers the duties of care and attention, and kindness toward the sick, saying that a physician's first and chief consideration ought to be the restoring of his patient to health. The style of the Hippocratic writings, which are in the *Ionic* dialect, is so concise as to be sometimes extremely obscure; though this charge, which is as old as the time of Galen, is often brought too indiscriminately against the whole collection, whereas it applies, in fact, especially only to certain treatises, which seem to be merely a collection of notes, such as *De Humoribus*, *De Alimento*, *De Officina Medici*, &c. In those writings, which are universally allowed to be genuine, we do not find this excessive brevity, though even these are, in general, by no means easy.[2]

EDITIONS, ETC., OF HIPPOCRATES.

The works of Hippocrates first appeared in a Latin translation by Fabius Calvus, Rome, 1525, fol. The first Greek edition is the Aldine, Venice, 1526, fol., which was printed from MSS., with hardly any correction of the transcriber's errors. The first edition that had any pretensions to being called a critical edition was that by Hieron. Mercurialis, Venice, 1588, fol., Greek and Latin; but this was much surpassed by that of Foësius, Frankfort, 1595, fol., Greek and Latin, which continues to the present day to be the best *complete* edition. Van der Linden's edition, published at Leyden, 1665, 2 vols. 8vo, Greek and Latin, is neat, and commodious for reference, from his having divided the text into short paragraphs. Chartier's edition of the works of Hippocrates and Galen, Paris, 1639–79, 13 vols. fol., is also a very useful and neat one. It contains the whole of the works of Hippocrates and Galen, mixed up together, and divided into thirteen classes, according to the subject-matter. This vast work was undertaken by René Chartier (*Renatus Charterius*), a French physician, who published in 1633 (when he had already passed his *sixtieth* year) a programme, entitled *Index Operum Galeni, quæ Latinis duntaxat typis in lucem edita sunt*, &c., begging the loan of such Greek MSS. as he had not an opportunity of examining in the public libraries of Paris. The first volume appeared in 1639; but Chartier, after impoverishing himself, died in 1654, before the work was completed: the last four volumes were published after his death, at the expense of his son-in-law, and the whole work was at length finished in 1679, forty years after it had been commenced. This edition contains a Latin translation and a few notes and various readings. It is, however, very far from what it might have been, and its critical merits are very lightly esteemed. An edition of Hippocrates has also been given by Kühn, in his collection of the works of the Greek medical authors, Leipzig, 1825–27,

[1] *Greenhill, l. c.*

[2] *Id. Ib.*

3 vols. 8vo, the whole collection being in twenty-eight volumes. Kühn's edition, however, has very small claims to real critical merit, its principal advantages being its commodious form, the reprint of Ackermann's *Histor. Liter. Hippocr.* (from Harles's edition of Fabricius's *Bibliotheca Græca*) in the first volume, and the noticing on each page the corresponding pagination of the editions of Foësius, Chartier, and Van der Linden. By far the best edition, however, in every respect, is one which is now in the course of publication at Paris, under the superintendence of E. Littré, of which the first volume appeared in 1839, and the seventh in 1850. It contains a new text, founded upon a collation of the MSS. in the Royal Library at Paris; a French translation, an interesting and learned general introduction, and a copious argument prefixed to each treatise, together with numerous scientific and philological notes. It is a work quite indispensable to every physician, critic, and philologist who wishes to study in detail the works of the Hippocratic collection, and it has already done much more toward settling the text than any edition that has preceded it; but at the same time it must not be concealed, that the editor does not always seem to have made the best use of the materials that he has had at his command, and that the classical reader can not help now and then noticing a manifest want of a critical, and even at times of grammatical scholarship.[1]

Of some of the separate works we may notice the following editions: *Prognostica*, in Greek, with a French translation, notes, &c., by M. De Mercy, Paris, 1815, 12mo. *Aphorismi*, in Greek, with a French translation, notes, &c., by M. De Mercy, Paris, 1811, 8vo; by Hecker, Greek and Latin, Berlin, 1822, 12mo; by De Bergen, Greek and Latin, Leipzig, 1841, 8vo; by Menke, in Greek, with a German version, Bremen, 1844, 8vo. *Epidemia*, in Greek, with a French version, notes, &c., by M. De Mercy, Paris, 1815, 8vo; by Freind, Greek and Latin, London, 1717, 4to. *De Diæta Acutorum*, in Greek, with a French version, notes, &c., by M. De Mercy, Paris, 1818, 12mo. *De Aere, Aquis et Locis*, in Greek, with a French version, notes, &c., by Coraes, Paris, 1800, 2 vols. 12mo; by M. De Mercy, Paris, 1818, 12mo; by Petersen, Hamburg, 1833, 8vo.

Among the great number of works published on the subject of the Hippocratic collection, or as aids for the perusal of Hippocrates, may be mentioned *Foësii Œconomia Hippocratis*, a very copious and learned lexicon to Hippocrates, published in folio, Frankfort, 1588, and Geneva, 1662; Sprengel, *Apologie des Hippokr. und seiner Grundsätze*, Leipzig, 1789, 1792, 2 vols. 8vo; Ermerius, *De Hippocr. doctrina a Prognostice oriunda*, Leyden, 1832, 4to; Houdart, *Etudes Histor. et Crit. sur la vie et la doctrine d'Hippocrate*, Paris, 1836, 8vo; Petersen, *Hippocr. nomine quæ circumferuntur scripta, ad temporis rationes disposita*, Hamburg, 1839, 4to; Meixner, *Neue Prüfung der Aechtheit und Reihefolge sämmtlicher Schriften Hippokr.*, München, 1836, 1837, 8vo.

---

[1] *Greenhill; Smith, Dict. Biogr., s. v.* Hippocrates.

CHAPTER XXXVII.

FIFTH OR ALEXANDRINE PERIOD.

INTRODUCTORY REMARKS.[1]

I. THE *Fifth* or *Alexandrine* period of Greek literature may be dated from the foundation of Alexandrea, and ends with the fall of the Græco-Egyptian empire under the power of Rome. We have already, in a few instances, anticipated the commencement of this period, especially as regards the subject of Grecian philosophy, though not, it is hoped, to such a degree as at all to mar the leading features of our arrangement.

II. In the previous period, Athens, as we have seen, was the chief seat of letters and the arts. In the one on which we are now entering,that distinction is enjoyed by the new capital of Egypt. The admirable situation which it possessed for commercial operations, its great wealth, and, above all, the munificent patronage of the first Ptolemies, all tended to make Alexandrea the centre of refinement, and the chief resort of literary and scientific men. But though an asylum was thus afforded for the peaceful culture of literature and science, away from the turbulent and distracting scenes of the mother country, and though many and rich appliances were brought to bear upon this great end by the generous liberality of the first three monarchs of the house of Lagus, yet nothing could replace the taste, and the genius, and the true intellectual spirit which had shone so conspicuously in the productions of the previous or Attic age. Study was now called in to supply what nature no longer furnished. The circle of acquirements was now carefully traced, by the mastering of which alone one could aspire to the title of a literary man. Men of genius were now few, men of learning became numerous.

III. It was during this same period that a taste for verbal criticism arose, which was applied in the first instance to the poems of Homer, and wholly confined to them, but subsequently extended to the productions of later ages. All these furnished an inexhaustible subject for explanations, illustrations, commentaries, and scholia; and in this way history and fable, chronology and inscriptions, the manners and the customs of earlier times, all were laid under contribution for the purpose of clearing up passages and words that might present any difficulty, or that might afford an opportunity of making a display of varied acquirements. Researches were also made into the Greek tongue; what the usage and authority of the great masters had consecrated was now reduced to the form of principles; collections were made of words either little used, or employed in a peculiar sense; the dialects were distinguished from one another, and their characteristics noted; in a word, philology, a science before unknown, now first arose; and criticism began to trace out the

[1] *Matter, Histoire de l'Ecole d'Alexandrie*, &c., Paris, 1840–44, 2 vols. 8vo, 2e ed.; Schoell, *Hist. de la Littérature Grecque Profane*, tome iii., p. 38, *seqq.*

limits beyond which the imagination was forbidden to soar, as well as the rules by which her flight was to be directed.

IV. This, too, was the period of the so-called *seven liberal arts*, an appellation under which were comprehended *Grammar*, *Rhetoric*, *Dialectics*, *Arithmetic*, *Geometry*, *Astronomy*, and *Music*. In proportion, however, as erudition extended her domain, and men began to reason about the principles of the beautiful, literature declined, and the chaste simplicity, unaffected grace, and energy of expression that had marked the purer ages of Grecian composition gave place to studied imitation or far-fetched conceits; to affectation, false refinement, and vain display of erudition. There were, it is true, some striking exceptions to this, but they were mere exceptions, exercising little if any influence on the vicious taste of the age.[1]

V. A peculiar invention of this erudite age was the canon of classical authors, as it was termed, arranged by Aristophanes of Byzantium, curator of the Alexandrean library in the reign of Ptolemy Euergetes, and his celebrated disciple Aristarchus. The daily increasing multitude of books of every kind had now become so great that there was no expression, however faulty, for which some precedent might not be found; and as there were far more bad than good writers, the authority and weight of numbers was likely to prevail, and the language, consequently, to grow more and more corrupt. It was thought necessary, therefore, to draw a line between those classic writers to whose authority an appeal in matters of language might be made and the common herd of inferior authors.[2] The canon of the Alexandrean grammarians, then, was as follows:

ALEXANDRINE CANON.

1. EPIC POETS. The Epic poets contained in the canon were HOMER, HESIOD, PISANDER, PANYASIS, and ANTIMACHUS, arranged, like the other writers to be mentioned under the different heads, in the order of time.

2. IAMBIC POETS. These were ARCHILOCHUS, SIMONIDES, and HIPPONAX.

3. LYRIC POETS. These were nine in number: ALCMAN, ALCÆUS, SAPPHO, STESICHORUS, PINDAR, BACCHYLIDES, IBYCUS, ANACREON, and SIMONIDES.

4. ELEGIAC POETS. Four in number: CALLINUS, MIMNERMUS, PHILETAS, and CALLIMACHUS.

5. TRAGIC POETS. Of these they made two classes. In the first class were ÆSCHYLUS, SOPHOCLES, EURIPIDES, ION, ACHÆUS, and AGATHON. In the second class, ALEXANDER *the Ætolian*, PHILISCUS *of Corcyra*, SOSITHEUS, HOMER *the younger*, ÆANTIDES, SOSIPHANES, and LYCOPHRON. As the poets of this second class were seven in number, they were also called the TRAGIC PLEIADES, from the number usually assigned to those stars.

6. COMIC POETS. The poets of the *Old Comedy* comprehended in the canon were EPICHARMUS, EUPOLIS, ARISTOPHANES, PHERECRATES, and PLA-

[1] *Schoell*, p. 41. [2] *Moore, Lectures on Gr. Lang. and Lit.*, p. 55; *Schoell*, p. 185, *seqq.*

TO. Of the *Middle Comedy*, ANTIPHANES and ALEXIS. Of the *New Comedy*, MENANDER, PHILIPPIDES, DIPHILUS, PHILEMON, and APOLLODORUS.

7. HISTORIANS. These were HERODOTUS, THUCYDIDES, XENOPHON, THEOPOMPUS, EPHORUS, PHILISTUS, ANAXIMENES, and CALLISTHENES.

8. ORATORS. These were ten in number: ANTIPHON, ANDOCIDES, LYSIAS, ISOCRATES, ISÆUS, ÆSCHINES, LYCURGUS, DEMOSTHENES, HYPERIDES, and DINARCHUS.

9. PHILOSOPHERS. These were PLATO, XENOPHON, ÆSCHINES *Socraticus*, ARISTOTLE, and THEOPHRASTUS.

A list was subsequently made of seven distinguished poets of this same period, who were contemporaries, and were called, from their number, the POETIC PLEIADES. Their names were APOLLONIUS *Rhodius*, ARATUS, PHILISCUS, HOMER *the younger*, LYCOPHRON, NICANDER, and THEOCRITUS.

VI. Of the *seventy-five* authors included in this list there are but *twenty-five* of whom we now possess any remains that deserve mention. As regards the list or canon itself, while it can not be denied that it contributed to preserve for some time the purity of the language, it must at the same time be acknowledged that it operated injuriously in excluding a large number of writers who might have furnished us with valuable materials for becoming better acquainted with the actual condition of Greece at the time, as well as the state of her literature, but whose works have perished in consequence of the neglect occasioned by their exclusion from the canon. Some of them, indeed, were in all likelihood justly entitled to a place in the canon itself.[1]

VII. The founder of the Alexandrine school was Ptolemy I., commonly called *Soter*. It was this monarch who first established the famous *library*, and erected the *Museum*, with its theatre for lectures and public assemblies, connected with one another, and with the palace of the Ptolemies by long colonnades of the most costly marble from the Egyptian quarries, and adorned with obelisks and sphinxes taken from the Pharaonic cities. The library contained, according to one account, 700,000 volumes; according to another, 400,000.[2] Part, however, of this unrivalled collection was lodged in the temple of Serapis, in the quarter of Alexandrea called *Rhacotis*. Here were deposited the 200,000 volumes collected by the kings of Pergamus and presented by Antony to Cleopatra. The library of the Museum was destroyed during the blockade of Julius Cæsar in the Brucheum; that in the temple of Serapis was frequently injured by the civil broils of Alexandrea, and especially when that temple was destroyed by the Christian fanatics in the fourth century of our era. The collection begun by Ptolemy Soter was augmented by his successors, for the worst of the Lagidæ were patrons of literature, but more particularly by his two immediate successors, Philadelphus and Euergetes. The portion that remained after the time of Cæsar was respected, if not increased by the Roman emperors, who, like their predecessors, appointed and salaried the librarians and professors of the Museum. The Ptolemies replenished the shelves of the library zealously

[1] *Schoell*, p. 187.

[2] *Joseph.*, *Antiq.*, xii., 2; *Athen.*, i., p. 3.

but unscrupulously, since they laid an embargo on all books, whether public or private property, which were brought to Alexandrea, retained the originals, and gave copies of them to their proper owners. In this same spirit Ptolemy Euergetes (B.C. 246–221) is said to have got possession of authentic copies of the works of Æschylus, Sophocles, and Euripides, and to have returned transcripts of them to the Athenians, from whom they had been borrowed, with an accompanying compensation of fifteen talents.[1]

VIII. The Museum succeeded the once-renowned college of Heliopolis as the University of Egypt. It contained a great hall or banqueting-room (*οἶκος μέγας*), where the professors dined in common; an exterior peristyle, or corridor (*περίπατοι*), for exercise and ambulatory lectures; a theatre where public disputations and scholastic festivals were held; chambers for the different professors; and it possessed a botanical garden, which Ptolemy Philadelphus enriched with tropical flora and a menagerie. It was divided into four principal sections—poetry, mathematics, astronomy, and medicine—and enrolled among its professors or pupils the illustrious names of Euclid, Ctesibius, Callimachus, Aratus, Aristophanes, and Aristarchus, the two Heros, Ammonius Saccas, Polemo, Clemens, Origen, Athanasius, Theon and his celebrated daughter Hypatĭa, with many others. Amid the turbulent factions and frequent calamities of Alexandrea, the Museum maintained its reputation until the Saracen invasion in A.D. 640. The Roman emperors of the West and East, like their predecessors the Ptolemies, kept in their own hands the nomination of the president of the Museum, who was considered one of the four chief magistrates of the city.[2]

IX. Alexandrea, however, did not continue, during all the period which we are now considering, the exclusive seat of letters. The city of Pergamus, in Mysia, the capital of the kingdom of the same name, also attained to high rank as a place of literary culture, under the fostering care of Eumenes II., who came to the throne in B.C. 197. It was here that he founded the celebrated library, which rose to be a rival even to that of Alexandrea. The jealousy which this excited showed itself in a decree prohibiting the exportation of papyrus from Egypt, passed in the reign of Ptolemy Epiphanes.[3] The kings of Pergamus were obliged, therefore, to substitute what, either from their use of it in this way, or from some improvement in the mode of preparing it at Pergamus, was called *περγαμηνή* (scil. *χάρτη*), *Charta Pergamena*, or parchment. We must guard, however, against the error of some, who make Eumenes II. to have been the inventor of this, since Herodotus expressly mentions writing on skins as common in his time, and says that the Ionians had been accustomed to give the name of skins (*διφθέραι*) to books.[4] To the court of Pergamus, now, the learned were, by the liberality of its princes, attracted from every quarter; and its school might have vied with that of Alexandrea, but for the check it received from the bequest by Attalus of his kingdom to the Romans. After this transfer it did but languish

[1] *Matter*, vol. i., p. 43, *seqq.*; *Smith, Dict. Geogr.*, *s. v.* Alexandrea, p. 97.
[2] *Smith, Dict. Geogr.*, *l. c.* [3] *Plin.*, *H. N.*, xiii., 21. [4] *Herod.*, v., 58.

feebly, until Antony struck it a death-blow by removing thence the noble collection of 200,000 volumes left by Attalus, and transporting them to Alexandrea, where, as already remarked, they were deposited in the temple of Serapis.

X. Another rival of Alexandrea rose, at a somewhat later period, in Tarsus, a city of Cilicia, the birth-place of St. Paul. The people of Tarsus were celebrated for their mental power, their readiness in repartee, and their fondness for the study of philosophy; and their schools in this department, as well as in the whole circle of the sciences, were not less famous than those of Athens and Alexandrea. Strabo, indeed, says, with somewhat of exaggeration, that they even surpassed them.

XI. In giving an account of the writers of the Alexandrine period, we will consider them under the two general heads of *Poetry* and *Prose*.

CHAPTER XXXVIII.

FIFTH OR ALEXANDRINE PERIOD—*continued.*

POETRY.

I. The poets who flourished during the period on which we have now entered were, generally speaking, learned men, but deficient in imagination, and often also in good taste. The former of these defects they sought to hide beneath singularity of idea, and novelty and extravagance of expression, while the bad taste of some of them displayed itself in their choice of subjects still more than their manner of treating them. It was during this period, also, that several new kinds of poetry came into vogue, if it is permitted us to apply the name of poetry to such things as anagrams, *jeux de mots*, and other frivolities, which correct taste condemns, but which were then admired as efforts of genius.

II. Still, in the midst of this general corruption of taste, a small number of poets remained faithful, in a great degree, to the ancient models; and although it was impossible for them to rise in all things above the influence of the age, yet their productions are marked by a purity of diction, and a certain air of elegance, which places them at a wide distance from their contemporaries, as well as from their successors.[1]

III. The poetry of the period now under review will be considered as follows: 1. Epic Poetry, subdivided into the *Heroic Epos* and the *Didactic Epos*. 2. Lyric Poetry, in the more general acceptation of the term, embracing both *Elegiac* and *Melic* composition. 3. Bucolic Poetry, forming a new species of poetic writing, in part possessing an epic element, and therefore composed in hexameters, and in part marked by a dramatic character. 4. Dramatic Poetry.

---

[1] *Schœll*, p. 84.

I. EPIC POETRY.

(A.) THE HEROIC EPOS.

The most distinguished Epic poets of the heroic school belonging to this period are *Rhianus*, *Apollonius*, and *Euphorion*.

I. Rhiănus (Ῥιανός),[1] an Alexandrean poet and grammarian, was a native of Crete, and flourished about B.C. 222. He was first, as Suidas informs us, a slave and keeper of a palæstra, but afterward, having been instructed, he became a grammarian. The statement of Suidas, that he was contemporary with Eratosthenes, not only indicates the time at which he lived, but suggests the probability that he lived at Alexandrea in personal and literary connection with Eratosthenes. On the ground of this statement, Clinton fixes the age of Rhianus at B.C. 222, as we have given it above. He wrote several epic poems, the subjects of which were taken either from the old mythology, or from the annals of particular states and countries. Of the former class were his Ἡράκλεια, and of the latter his Ἀχαϊκά, Ἠλιακά, Θεσσαλικά, and Μεσσηνιακά. For a full account of the extant fragments of his poems, and for a discussion of their subjects, the student is referred to Meineke's essay on Rhianus, in his *Analecta Alexandrina*. Like most of the Alexandrine poets, Rhianus was also a writer of epigrams. Ten of his epigrams are preserved in the Palatine Anthology, and one by Athenæus. They treat of amatory subjects with much freedom, but they all excel in elegance of language, cleverness of invention, and simplicity of expression. He had a place in the garland of Meleager. The epic poems of Rhianus, however, were those of his works to which he chiefly owed his fame. His poems are mentioned by Suetonius as among those productions of the Alexandrean school which the Emperor Tiberius admired and imitated. Respecting his grammatical works, we only know that he is frequently quoted in the *Scholia* on Homer as one of the commentators on that poet.

The fragments of Rhianus have been printed in most of the old collections of the Greek poets, and in Gaisford's *Poetæ Minores Græci*. They are separately edited by Saal, in an excellent monograph, Bonn, 1831, 8vo (a review of which by Schneidewin is contained in Jahn's *Jahrbücher* for 1833, vol. ix., p. 129, *seqq.*); and, as already mentioned, by Meineke in his *Analecta Alexandrina*, Berlin, 1843, 8vo.

II. Apollonius Rhodius (Ἀπολλώνιος ὁ Ῥόδιος),[2] a poet and grammarian, was born at Alexandrea,[3] or, according to one account, at Naucratis,[4] on the eastern bank of the Canopic branch of the Nile, and flourished in the reigns of Ptolemy Philopator and Ptolemy Epiphanes (B.C. 222–181). In his youth he was instructed by Callimachus, but they afterward became bitter enemies. The most probable cause of this hatred appears to be, that Apollonius, in his love of the simplicity of the ancient poets of Greece, and in his endeavor to imitate them, offended Callimachus, or perhaps even expressed contempt for his poetry. The love of Apollonius for the ancient epic poetry was indeed so great, and it had such fascinations for him, that even when a youth (ἔφηβος) he began himself an epic

[1] *Smith, Dict. Biogr.*, *s. v.*
[2] *Id. ib.*
[3] *Strab.*, xiv., p. 655.
[4] *Athen.*, vii., p. 283; *Ælian, Hist. An.*, xv., 23.

poem on the expedition of the Argonauts. When at length the work was completed, he read it in public at Alexandrea, but it did not meet with the approbation of the audience. The cause of this may, in part, have been the imperfect character of the work itself, which was only a youthful attempt; but it was more especially owing to the intrigues of the other Alexandrine poets, and, above all, of Callimachus, for Apollonius was, in some degree, opposed to the taste which then prevailed at Alexandrea in regard to poetry. Apollonius was deeply hurt at this failure, and it is not improbable that the bitter epigram on Callimachus, which is still extant,[1] was written at that time. Callimachus, in return, wrote an invective poem, called "*Ibis*," against Apollonius, of the nature of which we may form some idea from Ovid's imitation of it in a poem of the same name. Disheartened by these circumstances, Apollonius left Alexandrea and went to Rhodes, where he taught rhetoric with so much success that the Rhodians honored him with their franchise and other distinctions. Here, also, he revised his poem and read it to the Rhodians, who received it with great approbation. Apollonius now regarded himself as a Rhodian, and the surname *Rhodius* (Ῥόδιος) has at all times been the one by which he has been distinguished from other persons of the same name.

Notwithstanding these distinctions, however, he afterward returned to Alexandrea; but it is not known whether he did so of his own accord or in consequence of an invitation. He is said to have now read his revised poem to the Alexandreans, who were so delighted with it, that he at once rose to the highest degree of fame and popularity. According to Suidas, Apollonius succeeded Eratosthenes as chief librarian of the museum of Alexandrea, in the reign of Ptolemy Epiphanes, about B.C. 194. Farther particulars about his life are not mentioned, but it is probable that he held his office in the museum until his death, and one of his biographers states that he was buried in the same tomb with Callimachus.

The poem on the expedition of the Argonauts, entitled Ἀργοναυτικά, is still extant. It consists of four books. The materials for it were collected by Apollonius from the rich libraries of Alexandrea, and his scholiasts are always anxious to point out the sources from which he derived this or that account. The poem gives a straightforward and simple description of the adventure, and in a tone which is equal throughout. Hence Longinus,[2] in his treatise on the Sublime, calls Apollonius ἄπτωτος, an expression that is well elucidated by the remark of Quintilian on this same writer: "Non contemnendum edidit opus, *æquali quadam mediocritate.*"[3] He never rises to the sublime, but, at the same time, never descends to the vulgar and lowly. The episodes, which are not numerous, and which contain particular mythi or descriptions of countries, are sometimes very beautiful, and give life and color to the whole poem. The character of Jason, although he is the hero of the poem, is not sufficiently developed to win the interest of the reader. The character of Medea, on the other hand, is beautifully drawn, and the gradual growth of her love is described with a truly artistic moderation. The language is an imitation of that of Homer; but it is more brief and concise, and

[1] *Anthol. Græc.*, xi., 275. [2] *De Subl.*, 33. [3] *Quint.*, 10, 1, 54.

has all the symptoms of something that is studied and not natural to the poet. The Argonautica, in short, is a work of art and labor, and thus forms, notwithstanding its many resemblances, a contrast with the easy and natural flow of the Homeric poems. On its appearance, the work seems to have made a great sensation, for even contemporaries, such as Charon, wrote commentaries upon it. Our present scholia are abridgments of the commentaries of Lucillus of Crete, Sophocles, and Theon, all of whom seem to have lived before the Christian era. The common scholia on Apollonius are called the Florentine scholia, because they were first published at Florence, and to distinguish them from the Paris scholia, which were first published in Schaefer's edition of the Argonautica, and consist chiefly of verbal explanations and criticisms. Among the Romans the Argonautica was much read, and P. Terentius Varro Atacinus acquired great reputation by his translation of it. The Argonautica of Valerius Flaccus is a free imitation of the poem of Apollonius.

Besides the Argonautica, Apollonius wrote epigrams (of which we possess only the one on Callimachus), and also several other works which are now lost. Two of them, Περὶ Ἀρχιλόχου and Πρὸς Ζηνόδοτον, were probably grammatical works, and the latter may have had reference to the recension of the Homeric poems by Zenodotus, for the scholia on Homer occasionally refer to Apollonius. A third class of Apollonius's writings were his κτίσεις, that is, poems on the origin or foundation of several towns. These poems were of an historico-epic character, and most of them seem to have been written in hexameter verse. A few lines only are preserved.

The first edition of the Argonautica is that of Florence, 1496, 4to, by Lascaris, which contains the scholia. The next is the Aldine, Venice, 1581, 8vo, which is little more than a reprint of the Florentine edition. The first really critical edition is that of Brunck, Strasburg, 1780, 4to and 8vo. The edition of Beck, Leipzig, 1797, 8vo, is incomplete, and the only volume which appeared of it contains the text, with a Latin translation, and a few critical notes. Schaefer published an edition, Leipzig, 1810–13, 2 vols. 8vo, which is an improvement upon that of Brunck, and is the first in which the Paris scholia are printed. The best edition is that of Wellauer, Leipzig, 1828, 2 vols. 8vo, containing the various readings of thirteen MSS., the scholia, and short notes. The edition of Lehrs, in Didot's *Bibliotheca Græca*, containing merely the text and a Latin version, is based upon that of Wellauer, though occasionally exhibiting better readings. For farther information on the subject of Apollonius, the student may consult Gerhard, *Lectiones Apollonianæ*, Leipzig, 1816, 8vo, and Weichert, *Ueber das Leben und Gedicht des Apollonius von Rhodus*, Meissen, 1821, 8vo.

III. EUPHORION (Εὐφορίων),[1] of Chalcis, in Eubœa, was an eminent grammarian and poet, and was born about B.C. 274. He became the librarian of Antiochus the Great, B.C. 221, and died in Syria, either at Apamea or Antioch. Euphorion wrote numerous works, both in poetry and prose, relating chiefly to mythological history. The following were poems in heroic verse: 1. Ἡσίοδος, probably an agricultural poem. 2. Μοψοπία, so called from an old name of Attica, the legends of which country seem to have been the chief subject of the poem. From the variety of its contents, which Suidas calls συμμιγεῖς ἱστορίαι, it was also termed Ἄτακτα, a title frequently given to the writings of that period. 3. Χιλιά-

[1] *Smith, Dict. Biogr*, *s. v.*

δες, a poem written against certain persons who had defrauded Euphorion of money which he had intrusted to their care. It probably derived its title from each of its books consisting of a thousand verses. Euphorion was an epigrammatist as well as an epic poet. He had a place in the *Garland* of Meleager, and the Greek Anthology contains two epigrams by him. His epigrams appear to have been mostly erotic, and were imitated by Propertius, Tibullus, and Gallus, as also by the Emperor Tiberius, with whom he was a favorite writer. He composed, also, many historical and grammatical works. Euphorion seems to have carried to excess some of the worst faults of the Alexandrean school. He was particularly distinguished by an obscurity, arising, according to Meineke, from his choice of the most out-of-the-way subjects, from the cumbrous learning with which he overloaded his poems, from the arbitrary changes which he made in the common legends, from his choice of obsolete words, and from his employment of ordinary words with a new meaning of his own. Only some fragments remain of his numerous works, collected by Meineke in his *Analecta Alexandrina*, Berlin, 1843.

(B.) THE DIDACTIC EPOS.

I. The epic form of verse was not confined to heroic themes, but was often employed in the elucidation of subjects of a scientific nature, as, for example, geography, astronomy, agriculture, and other similar topics. The scientific material was always, of course, regarded as of primary importance, but still the writer strove, at the same time, after a pleasing form of poetical expression. And yet, after all, many of these so-called poems deserve rather to be regarded as a species of versified text-books than regular works of art.

II. The didactic epic poets of the Alexandrine period most deserving of notice are *Aratus* and *Nicander*.

1. ARĀTUS (Ἄρατος)[1] was a native of Soli, afterward Pompeiopolis, in Cilicia, or (according to one authority) of Tarsus, and flourished B.C. 270. He was invited to the court of Antigonus Gonatas, king of Macedonia, where he spent all the latter part of his life. His chief pursuits were physic (which is also said to have been his profession), grammar, and philosophy, in which last he was instructed by the Stoic Dionysius Heracleotes. Several poetical works on various subjects, as well as a number of prose epistles, are attributed to him, but none of them have come down to us except two astronomical poems. These have generally been joined together as if parts of the same work, but they seem to be distinct poems. The first, called Φαινόμενα, consists of 732 verses; the second, entitled Διοσημεῖα (*Prognostica*), of 422. Eudoxus, of whom we have already made mention, about a century earlier, had written two prose works, Φαινόμενα and Ἔνοπτρον, which are both lost; but we are told by the biographers of Aratus that it was the desire of Antigonus to have them turned into verse, which gave rise to the Φαινόμενα of the latter writer; and it appears, from the fragments of them preserved by Hipparchus,[2] that Aratus has, in fact, versified, or closely imitated, parts of them

[1] *Smith, Dict. Biogr., s. v.*

[2] *Petav. Uranolog.*, p. 173, *seqq.*, ed. Paris, 1630.

both, but especially of the first. The design of the poem is to give an introduction to the knowledge of the constellations, with the rules for their risings and settings; and of the circles of the sphere, among which the Milky Way is reckoned. The positions of the constellations north of the ecliptic are described by reference to the principal groups surrounding the north pole (the Bears, the Dragon, and Cepheus), while Orion serves as a point of departure for those to the south. The immobility of the earth, and the revolution of the heavens about a fixed axis, are maintained; the path of the sun in the zodiac is described, but the planets are introduced merely as bodies having a motion of their own, without any attempt to define their periods; nor is any thing said about the moon's orbit. The opening of the poem asserts the dependence of all things upon Jove, and contains the passage τοῦ γὰρ καὶ γένος ἐσμέν, quoted by St. Paul (Aratus's fellow-countryman) in his address to the Athenians.[1] From the general want of precision in the descriptions, it would seem that Aratus was neither a mathematician nor observer,[2] or, at any rate, that in this work he did not aim at scientific accuracy. He not only represents the configurations of particular groups incorrectly, but describes some phenomena which are inconsistent with any one supposition as to the latitude of the spectator, and others which could not coexist at any one epoch. These errors, however, are partly to be attributed to Eudoxus himself, and partly to the way in which Aratus has used the materials supplied by him

The Διοσημεῖα consists of prognostics of the weather from astronomical phænomena, with an account of its effects upon animals. It appears to be an imitation of Hesiod, and to have been imitated in turn by Virgil in some parts of the Georgics. The materials are said to be taken almost wholly from Aristotle's *Meteorologica*, from the work of Theophrastus on the "Signs of waters, winds, and storms," and from Hesiod.[3] Nothing is said in either poem of *Astrology*, in the proper sense of the word.

The style of these two poems is distinguished by the elegance and accuracy resulting from a study of ancient models; but it wants originality and poetic elevation, and variety of matter is excluded by the nature of the subjects.[4] Still, however, the poems in question were very popular in both the Grecian and Roman world. As one proof of the consideration which he enjoyed, we may cite the monument which his fellow-countrymen erected to his memory, and which became famous by reason of a physical phænomenon which Mela mentions: "*Juxta in parvo tumulo Arati poetæ monumentum; ideo referendum quia, ignotum quam ob causam, jacta in id saxa dissiliant.*"[5] Ovid also passes a high eulogium on Aratus: "*Cum sole et luna semper Aratus erit;*"[6] but this exaggerated compliment was very probably owing to the circumstance of no other poet having taken the astronomic sphere for his theme prior to Aratus. Another proof of the popularity of this writer is afforded by the number of commentaries and Latin translations. The Introduction to the Φαινόμενα, by Achilles

[1] Acts, xvii., 28. [2] *Cic.*, *De Orat.*, i., 16. [3] *Buhle*, vol. ii., p. 471.
[4] Compare *Quintil.*, x., 1. [5] *Mela*, i., 13. [6] *Amor.*, i., 15.

Tatius, the Commentary of Hipparchus, in three books, and another, attributed by Petavius to Achilles Tatius, are printed in the Uranologium, with a list of other commentators (p. 267, *seqq.*), which includes the names of Aristarchus, Geminus, and Erastosthenes. Parts of three poetical translations are preserved: one written by Cicero, when very young; one by Cæsar Germanicus, the grandson of Augustus; and one by Festus Avienus.

The earliest edition of Aratus is that of Aldus, Venice, 1499, fol. The principal later ones are that of Grotius, Leyden, 1600, 4to, headed "*Syntagma Arateorum*," and containing the Greek text, the versions, and valuable notes, with copperplates of the constellations, copied from some old manuscript; that of Fell, Oxford, 1672, 8vo, styled by Fabricius "*editio perquam nitida et castigata*," containing also the scholia; that of Buhle, Leipzig, 1793–1801, 2 vols. 8vo, with the three Latin versions mentioned above; that of Matthiæ, Frankfort, 1817, 8vo; of Voss, Heidelberg, 1824, 8vo, with a German poetical version; of Buttmann, Berlin, 1826, 8vo; and of Bekker, Berlin, 1828, 8vo. The Διοσημεῖα, or *Prognostica*, were edited by Foster, London, 1813, 8vo.

2. Nicander (Νίκανδρος),[1] a physician, poet, and grammarian, of whose life very few particulars are found in ancient authors, and even these few are doubtful and contradictory. It seems most probable, upon the whole, that he lived about B.C. 135,[2] in the reign of Attalus III., the last king of Pergamus, to whom he dedicated one of his poems, which is no longer extant. His native place, as he himself informs us, was Claros,[3] a city of Ionia, near Colophon, whence he is commonly called *Colophonius*,[4] and he succeeded his father as hereditary priest of Apollo Clarius. He appears to have been rather a voluminous writer, as the titles of more than twenty of his works have been preserved; but of all these we possess at present only two in a perfect state, with a few fragments of some of the others. Both are poems. The longer one of these poems is entitled Θηριακά, and consists of nearly a thousand lines in hexameter verse. It is dedicated to a person named Hermesianax, who must not be confounded with the poet of that name. It treats (as the name imports) of venomous animals, and the wounds inflicted by them, and contains some curious and interesting zoological passages, together with numerous absurd fables. His other poem, called Ἀλεξιφάρμακα, consists of more than six hundred lines, written in the same measure. It is dedicated to a person named Protagoras, and treats of poisons and their antidotes.

Among the ancients, Nicander's authority in all matters relating to toxicology seems to have been considered high. Galen several times quotes him, and Dioscorides, Aëtius, and other medical authors have made frequent use of his works. Plutarch, Diphilus, and others, wrote commentaries on his *Theriaca*; Marianus paraphrased it in iambic verse; and Eutecnius wrote a paraphrase in prose of both poems, which is still extant. Among the moderns, on the other hand, Haller has passed a very severe judgment on both productions. To counterbalance, however, in some degree, his unfavorable opinion, it ought in justice to be stated, that the knowledge of natural history possessed by Nicander appears to be at least equal to that of other writers of his own or even a later age.

1 *Smith, Dict. Biogr.*, *s. v.*

2 Compare *Clinton, Fast. Hell.*, vol. iii., *s. a.*

3 *Theriaca, in fine.*

4 *Cic., De Orat.*, i., 16.

Dr. Adams, the translator of Paulus Ægineta, remarks of Nicander's general treatment of cases, that it appears to be founded on very rational principles, and that, in some instances, the correctness of his physiological views is such as can not but command our admiration, considering the age in which he lived.

On the subject of his poetical merits the ancient writers were not well agreed; for, though a writer in the Greek Anthology compliments Colophon on having been the birth-place of Homer and Nicander,[1] and although Cicero praises the poetical manner in which, in his "Georgics," he treated a subject of which he was wholly ignorant,[2] Plutarch, on the other hand,[3] says that the *Theriaca*, like the poems of Empedocles, Parmenides, and Theognis, have nothing in them of poetry but the metre. Modern critics have differed equally on this point; but, *practically*, the judgment of posterity has been pronounced with sufficient clearness, and his works are now scarcely ever read as *poems*, but merely consulted by those who are interested in points of zoological and medical antiquities. In reference to his style and language, Bentley calls him, with great truth, "*antiquarium, obsoleta et casca verba studiose venantem, et vel sui sæculi lectoribus difficilem et obscurum.*"[4]

A list of Nicander's lost works is given by Fabricius. Among them we may mention, 1. **Γεωργικά**, a poem in hexameter verse on husbandry, consisting of at least two books, of which some long fragments remain. 2. **Ἑτεροιούμενα**, a poem in hexameter verse, in five books, mentioned by Suidas, and quoted by Athenæus, Antoninus Liberalis, and other writers. It was perhaps in reference to this work that Didymus applied to Nicander the epithet of "*fabulosus*." 3. **Θηβαϊκά**, in at least three books, mentioned by the scholiast on the *Theriaca*. 4. **Περὶ ποιητῶν**, probably the work in which Nicander tried to prove that Homer was a native of Colophon. 5. The **Προγνωστικά** of Hippocrates, paraphrased in hexameter verse. 6. **Σικελία**, of which the tenth book is quoted by Stephanus Byzantinus.

Nicander's poems have generally been published together, but sometimes separately. They were first published in Greek at the end of Dioscorides, Venice, 1499, fol., by Aldus, and by the same in a separate form, Venice, 1523, 4to. The Greek paraphrase of both poems, by Eutecnius, first appeared in Bandini's edition, Florence, 1764, 8vo. The most complete and valuable edition that has hitherto appeared is Schneider's, who published the *Alexipharmaca* in 1792, Halle, 8vo, and the *Theriaca* in 1816, Leipzig, 8vo; containing a Latin translation, the scholia, the paraphrase by Eutecnius, the editor's annotations, and the fragments of Nicander's lost works. The latest edition is that of Lehrs, in Didot's *Bibliotheca Græca*, Paris, 1846, printed along with Oppian and others, and containing the Greek text, a Latin version, and the fragments. The text is emended from the "*curæ posteriores*" of Schneider, and the conjectures of Lobeck, Meineke, and Naeke. The *Theriaca* were published in the Cambridge "*Museum Criticum*" (vol. i., p. 370, *seqq.*), with Bentley's emendations, copied from the margin of a copy of Gorræus's edition, which once (apparently) belonged to Dr. Mead, and is now preserved in the British Museum. The scholia on Nicander have been published in Didot's *Bibliotheca Græca*, along with those on Theocritus and Oppian, under the supervision of Dübner and Bussemaker.

---

1 *Anthol. Græc.*, ix., 213.
2 *Cic.*, *De Orat.*, i., 16.
3 *De aud. poet.*, c. 2, vol. i., p. 36, ed. *Tauchn.*
4 *Cambridge Museum Criticum*, vol. i., p. 371.

They have been carefully collated with the MSS. in the "Bibliothèque Nationale," and some portions have been hitherto unedited.

DIDACTIC POETS NOT EPIC.

The didactic poets of the period under review did not always confine themselves to hexameter versification, but employed likewise other measures. The iambic trimeter, for instance, was adopted by two who remain to be noticed by us, namely, *Apollodorus* and *Scymnus*.

I. Apollodōrus (Ἀπολλόδωρος),[1] a grammarian of Athens, was a pupil of Aristarchus, and flourished about B.C. 140, a few years after the fall of Corinth. Farther particulars are not mentioned respecting him. He is best known by his prose work entitled Βιβλιοθήκη, and he will, therefore, more properly be noticed by us among the prose writers of this period. At present we will merely consider some of his poetical productions. Among his other works, Apollodorus wrote, 1. Γῆς περίοδος, κωμικῷ μέτρῳ, that is, a *Universal Geography*, in iambic verse (trimeters), such as was afterward written by Scymnus of Chios, and by Dionysius. 2. Χρονικά, or Χρονικὴ σύνταξις, a *Chronicle*, in iambic trimeters, comprising the history of 1040 years, from the destruction of Troy (B.C. 1184) down to his own time, B.C. 143. This work was a sort of continuation of the Bibliotheca. Of how many books it consisted is not quite certain. In Stephanus Byzantinus the fourth book is mentioned; but if Syncellus refers to this work, it must have consisted of at least eight books. The loss of this work is one of the severest that we have to lament in the historical literature of antiquity.

II. Scymnus (Σκύμνος),[2] of Chios, wrote a *Periegēsis*, or description of the earth, which is referred to in a few passages of Stephanus Byzantinus,[3] and other later writers. A brief Periegesis, written in iambic metre, and consisting of nearly 1000 lines, has come down to us under his name. This poem, as appears from the author's own statement, was written in imitation of the similar work in iambic verse, composed by the Athenian Apollodorus, and already alluded to. It is dedicated to King Nicomedes, whom some modern writers suppose to be the same as Nicomedes III., king of Bithynia, who died B.C. 74; but this is quite uncertain. A portion of this poem was first published by Hoeschel, under the name of Marcianus Heracleotes, along with other Greek geographers, Augsburg, 1600, 8vo; and again by Morell, also under the name of Marcianus, Paris, 1606, 8vo. But Lucas Holstenius and Is. Vossius maintained that the poem in question was written by Scymnus of Chios, and is the work referred to in the passages of the ancient writers mentioned above. Their opinion was adopted by Dodwell, and the poem was accordingly printed under the name of Scymnus by Hudson and by Gail, in the *Geographi Græci Minores*, as well as by B. Fabricius, in his recent edition of the work, Leipzig, 1846. Meineke, however, maintains, and, in the opinion of some, has proved, in his edition of the poem, published shortly after that of Fabricius (Berlin, 1846), that the Periegesis of Scymnus of Chios,

---

1 *Smith, Dict. Biogr., s. v.*

2 *Id. ib.*

3 *Steph. Byz., s. v.* Πάρος, Ἑρμώνασσα, Ἀγάθη, &c.

quoted by the ancient writers, was written in prose, and was an entirely different work from the extant poem, the author of which is quite unknown, according to him. The best edition is Meineke's, just mentioned.

II. LYRIC POETRY.

I. Of the different kinds of Lyric Poetry, considered in its most general acceptation, the writers of the Alexandrine Age especially cultivated *Elegiac* composition. Of *Melic* poetry, strictly so termed, but few traces present themselves to our notice.

II. The elegiac writers of this period most deserving of notice are *Philetas*, *Hermesianax*, *Phanocles*, and *Callimachus*.

1. PHILĒTAS (Φιλητᾶς), a native of Cos, was a distinguished poet and grammarian,[1] and flourished during the earlier years of the Alexandrine school, at the period when the earnest study of the classical literature of Greece was still combined, in many scholars, with considerable power of original composition. The chief period of his literary activity was during the reign of the first Ptolemy, who appointed him tutor to his son Ptolemy II. Philadelphus. Clinton calculates that his death may be placed about B.C. 290,[2] but he may possibly have lived some years longer, as he is said to have been contemporary with Aratus, who flourished B.C. 270. He was the instructor, if not formally, at least by his example and influence, of Theocritus and Zenodotus of Ephesus. Theocritus expressly mentions him as the model which he strove to imitate.[3] Philetas seems to have been naturally of a very weak constitution, which at last broke down under excessive study. He was so remarkably thin as to become an object for the ridicule of the comic poets, who represented him as wearing leaden soles to his shoes, to prevent his being blown away by a strong wind; a joke which Ælian takes literally, sagely questioning, however, if he was too weak to stand against the wind, how he could be strong enough to carry his leaden shoes.[4] We learn from Hermesianax that a bronze statue was erected to his memory by the inhabitants of his native island, his attachment to which during his lifetime he had expressed in his poems.

The poetry of Philetas was chiefly elegiac.[5] Of all the writers in that department, he was esteemed the best after Callimachus, to whom a taste less pedantic than that of the Alexandrean critics would probably have preferred him, for, to judge by his fragments, he escaped the snare of cumbrous, learned affectation.[6] These two poets formed the chief models for the Roman elegy; nay, Propertius expressly states in one passage that he imitated Philetas in preference to Callimachus.[7] The elegies of Philetas were chiefly erotic, and many of them were devoted to the praises of a female named Bittis, or, as the Latin poets give it, Battis.[8] It seems very probable that he wrote a collection of poems specially in praise of Bittis, and that this was the collection which was known

[1] *Strab.*, xiv., p. 657. [2] *Clinton, Fast. Hell.*, vol. iii., App. 12, No. 16.
[3] *Theocrit.*, *Id.*, vii., 39; *Schol. ad loc.* [4] *Ælian, V. H.*, ix., 14; x., 6.
[5] *Suid.*, *s. v.* [6] *Quintil.*, x., 1, 58. [7] *Propert.*, ii., 34, 31; iii., 1, 1; iv., 6, 2.
[8] *Ovid, Trist.*, i., 6, 1; *ex Ponto*, iii., 1, 57.

and is quoted by Stobæus under the name of Παίγνια.[1] There are also two other poems of Philetas quoted by Stobæus, the subjects of which were evidently mythological, as we see from their titles, Δημήτηρ and Ἑρμῆς. From the fragments that remain of the former, it appears to have been in elegiac metre, and its subject to have been the lamentation of Ceres for the loss of her daughter. The latter poem Meineke suggests may have been in hexameters. Besides his poems, Philetas wrote in prose on grammar and criticism. He was one of the commentators on Homer, whom he seems to have dealt with very freely, both critically and exegetically; and in this course he was followed by his pupil Zenodotus. Aristarchus wrote a work in opposition to Philetas.[2] But his most important grammatical work was that which Athenæus repeatedly quotes under the title of Ἄτακτα. Nothing is left of it except a few scattered explanations of words, from which, however, it may be inferred that Philetas made great use of the light thrown on the meaning of words by their dialectic varieties.

The fragments of Philetas have been collected by Kayser, *Philetæ Coi Fragmenta, quæ reperiuntur*, Götting., 1793, 8vo; by Bach, *Philetæ Coi, Hermesianactis Colophonii, atque Phanoclis Reliquiæ*, Halle, 1829, 8vo; and in the editions of the Greek Anthology (Brunck, *Anal.*, vol. i., p. 189; ii., p. 523; iii., p. 234; *Jacobs' Anth. Græc.*, vol. i., p. 121, *seqq.*). The most important fragments are also contained in Schneidewin's *Delectus Poes. Græc.*, vol. i., p. 142, *seqq.*

Hermesiănax (Ἑρμησιάναξ)[3] of Colophon, a distinguished elegiac poet, the friend and disciple of Philetas, lived in the time of Philip and Alexander the Great, and seems to have died before the destruction of Colophon by Lysimachus, B.C. 302.[4] His chief work was an elegiac poem, in three books, addressed to a female, whose name, *Leontium* (Λεόντιον), formed the title of the poem, like the *Cynthia* of Propertius. A great part of the third book is quoted by Athenæus.[5] The poem is also cited by Pausanias,[6] by Parthenius,[7] and by Antoninus Liberalis.[8] We learn from another quotation in Pausanias that Hermesianax wrote an elegy on the centaur Eurytion.[9] It is somewhat doubtful whether the Hermesianax who is mentioned by the scholiast on Nicander, and who wrote a poem called Περσικά, was the same or a younger poet.

The fragment of Hermesianax has been edited separately by Ruhnken (*Append. ad Epist. Crit.*, ii., p. 283, *Opusc.*, vol. ii., p. 615); by Weston, London, 1784, 8vo; by Ilgen (*Opusc. Var. Philol.*, vol. i., p. 247, Erfurdt, 1797, 8vo); by Rigler and Axt, Cologne, 1828, 16mo; by Hermann (*Opusc. Acad.*, vol. iv., p. 239); by Bach (*Philet. Hermes. et Phanoc. Reliq.*, Halle, 1829, 8vo); by Bailey, with a critical epistle by Burges, London, 1839, 8vo; and by Schneidewin (*Delect. Poes. Eleg.*, p. 147). Compare, also, Bergk, *De Hermesianactis Elegia*, Marburg, 1845.

Phanŏcles (Φανοκλῆς), one of the best of the later elegiac poets, probably lived in the time of Philip and Alexander the Great. He seems to have written only one poem, entitled Ἔρωτες ἢ Καλοί.[10] We still possess a considerable fragment from the opening of it, which is esteemed by

1 *Jacobs, ad Anthol. Græc.*, vol. i., pt. i., p. 388, *seqq.*
2 *Schol. Venet. ad Il.*, ii., 111.
3 *Smith, Dict. Biogr.*, *s. v.*
4 *Pausan.*, i., 9, 8.
5 *Athen.*, xiii., p. 597.
6 *Pausan.*, vii., 17, 5; viii., 12, 1.
7 *Erot.*, 5, 22.
8 *Metam.*, 39.
9 *Pausan.*, vii., 18, 1.
10 *Clem. Alex.*, *Strom.*, vi., p. 750.

Ruhnken and other critics as one of the most perfect and beautiful specimens of elegiac poetry which have come down to us, and as superior even to Hermesianax in the simple beauty of the language and the smoothness of the verse.

The fragments of Phanocles have been edited by Ruhnken (*Epist. Crit.*, ii., *Opusc.*, vol. ii., p. 636); by Bach (*Philetæ, Hermesianactis, atque Phanoclis Reliquiæ*); and by Schneidewin (*Delect. Poes. Græc.*, p. 158). The large fragment and another distich are contained in the Greek Anthology.

CALLIMĂCHUS (Καλλίμαχος),[1] a native of Cyrene, one of the most celebrated Alexandrine grammarians and poets, was, according to Suidas, a son of Battus and Mesatme, and belonged to the celebrated family of the *Battiadæ*, whence Ovid and others call him simply *Battiades*. He was a disciple of the grammarian Hermocrates, and afterward taught at Eleusis, a suburb of Alexandrea. He was highly esteemed by Ptolemy Philadelphus, who invited him to a place in the Museum.[2] Callimachus was still alive in the reign of Ptolemy Euergetes, the successor of Philadelphus.[3] It was formerly believed, but is now established as an historical fact, that Callimachus was chief librarian of the famous library at Alexandrea. This fact leads us to the conclusion that he was the successor of Zenodotus, and that he held this office from about B.C. 260 until his death, about B.C. 240.[4] This calculation agrees with the statement of Aulus Gellius,[5] that Callimachus lived shortly before the first Punic war. He was married to a daughter of Euphrates of Syracuse, and had a sister Megatime, who was married to Stasenorus, and had a son Callimachus, who is distinguished from his uncle by being called the younger, and is said by Suidas to have been the author of an epic poem, Περὶ νήσων.

Callimachus was one of the most distinguished grammarians, critics, and poets of the Alexandrine period, and his celebrity surpassed that of nearly all the other Alexandrine scholars and poets. Several of the most distinguished men of that period, such as his successor Eratosthenes, Philostephanus, Aristophanes of Byzantium, Apollonius Rhodius, Ister, and Hermippus, were among his pupils. Callimachus was one of the most fertile writers of antiquity; and, if the number in Suidas be correct, he wrote 800 works, though we may take it for granted that most of them were not of great extent, if he followed his own maxim, that a great book was a great evil.[6] The number of his works of which the titles or fragments are known to us amounts to upward of forty. But what we possess is very little, and consists principally of poetical productions, apparently the least valuable of all his works, since Callimachus, notwithstanding the reputation he enjoyed for his poems, was not a man of real poetical talent: labor and learning are with him the substitutes for poetical genius and talent. His prose works, on the other hand, which would have furnished us with some highly important information concerning ancient mythology, history, literature, &c., are completely lost.

The poetical productions of Callimachus still extant, either in whole or

[1] *Smith, Dict. Biogr.*, *s. v.*
[2] *Suid.*, *s. v.*; *Strab.*, xvii., p. 838.
[3] *Schol. ad Callim.*, *Hymn.*, ii., 26.
[4] *Ritschl, Die Alexandrin. Biblioth.*, p. 19, 84.
[5] *Aul. Gell.*, xvii., 21.
[6] *Athen.*, iii., p. 72.

in part, are: 1. *Hymns*, six in number, of which five are written in hexameter verse, and in the Ionic dialect, and one on the bath of Pallas, in distichs, and in the Doric dialect. These hymns, which bear greater resemblance to epic than to lyric poetry, are the productions of labor and learning, like most of the poems of this period. Almost every line furnishes some curious mythical information, and it is, perhaps, not saying too much to assert, that these hymns are more overloaded with learning than any other poetical productions of that time. Their style has nothing of the easy flow of genuine poetry, and is evidently studied and labored. There are some ancient Greek scholia on these hymns, which, however, have no great merit. 2. Seventy-three *epigrams*, which belong to the best specimens of this kind of poetry. The high estimation they enjoyed in antiquity is attested by the fact that Archibius the grammarian, who lived, at the latest, one generation after Callimachus, wrote a commentary upon them, and that Marianus, in the reign of the Emperor Anastasius, wrote a paraphrase of them in iambics. They were incorporated in the Greek Anthology at an early period, and have thus been preserved. 3. *Elegies*. These are lost, with the exception of some fragments; but there are imitations of them by the Roman poets, the most celebrated of which is the "*De Coma Berenices*" of Catullus. If we may believe the Roman critics, Callimachus was the greatest among the elegiac poets,[1] and Ovid, Propertius, and Catullus took him for their model in this species of poetry. 4. *Fragments* of other poetical works, among which we may mention, 1. The Αἴτια, an epic poem in four books, on the causes of the various mythical stories, religious ceremonies, and other customs. This work is often referred to, and was paraphrased by Marianus; but the paraphrase is lost, and of the original we have only a few fragments. 2. An epic poem, entitled Ἑκάλη, which was the name of an old woman who had received Theseus hospitably when he went out to fight against the Marathonian bull. This work was likewise paraphrased by Marianus, and we still possess some fragments of the original.

It appears that there was scarcely any kind of poetry in which Callimachus did not try his strength, for he is said to have written comedies, tragedies, iambic and choliambic poems. An account of his poem *Ibis* has been given in the sketch of Apollonius Rhodius.

Of his numerous prose works not one is extant entire, though there were among them some of the highest importance. The one of which the loss is most to be lamented was entitled Πίναξ παντοδαπῶν συγγραμμάτων, or πίνακες τῶν ἐν πάσῃ παιδείᾳ διαλαμψάντων, καὶ ὧν συνέγραψαν, in 120 books. This work was the first comprehensive history of Greek literature. It contained, systematically arranged, lists of the authors and their works. The various departments of literature appear to have been classified, so that Callimachus spoke of the comic and tragic poets, of the orators, lawgivers, philosophers, &c., in separate books, in which the authors were enumerated in their chronological succession. It is natural to suppose that this work was the fruit of his studies in the libraries of Alexandrea, and that it mainly recorded such authors as were contained in

[1] *Quintil.*, x., 1, 58.

those collections. His pupil, Aristophanes of Byzantium, wrote a commentary upon it. Among his other prose works was one entitled Μουσεῖον, which is usually supposed to have treated of the Museum of Alexandrea and the scholars connected with it.

The first edition of the six hymns of Callimachus appeared at Florence in 4to, probably between 1494 and 1500. It was followed by the Aldine, Venice, 1513, 8vo; but a better edition, in which some gaps are filled up, and the Greek scholia are added, is that of Gelenius, Basle, 1532, 4to, reprinted at Paris, 1549, 4to. A more complete edition than any of the preceding ones is that of H. Stephens, Paris, 1566, fol., in the collection of "*Poetæ Principes Heroici Carminis.*" This edition is the basis of the text which from that time has been regarded as the vulgate. A second edition by H. Stephens, Geneva, 1577, 4to, is a great improvement on the previous one. It contains the Greek scholia, a Latin translation, thirty-three epigrams of Callimachus, and a few fragments of his other works. Henceforth scarcely any thing was done for the text, until Th. Grævius undertook a new and comprehensive edition, which was completed by his father, J. G. Grævius. It appeared at Utrecht, 1697, 2 vols. 8vo. It contains the notes of the previous editors, of Bentley, and the famous commentary of Spanheim. This edition is the basis of the one edited by Ernesti, Leyden, 1761, 2 vols. 8vo, which contains the whole of the commentary of Grævius's edition, a much improved text, a more complete collection of the fragments, and additional notes by Hemsterhuis and Ruhnken. Still, Ernesti did not completely satisfy the wishes of the learned in the use which he made of the last-mentioned *subsidia*. Among subsequent editions we need only mention those of Loesner, Leipzig, 1774, 8vo; of Volger, Leipzig, 1817, 8vo; of Schaefer, Leipzig, 1817, 8vo; and of Blomfield, London, 1815, 8vo. The fragments of the Elegies, with the notes of Valckenaer, were given by Luzac, Leyden, 1798, 8vo; an edition of the Fragments generally was given by Naeke (*Opusc. Philol.*, ed. *Welcker*, vol. ii.), Bonn, 1844, large 8vo.

MELIC POETRY.

I. With the exception of the *Scolia*, or convivial songs, to which we have already alluded, the melic productions of this period were comparatively few in number. The writer most deserving of mention under this head is MELINNO (Μελιννώ), a lyric poetess, author of an ode on Rome (εἰς Ῥώμην), in five Sapphic stanzas, which is commonly ascribed to Erinna of Lesbos, as an ode on valor (εἰς ῥώμην). Nothing is known of Melinno with certainty, except what the ode itself shows, namely, that she lived in the flourishing period of the Roman empire. The ode is printed, with an admirable essay upon it, by Welcker, in Creuzer's *Meletemata*, 1817, p. 1, and in Welcker's *Kleine Schriften*, vol. ii., p. 160, *seqq.*

II. Some of the melic poets of this period occasionally indulged in a singular species of trifling. They composed, namely, short poems of that fantastic species called *griphi* (γρῖφοι), or *carmina figurata*; that is, pieces in which the lines are so arranged as to make the whole poem resemble the form of some object. SIMMIAS of Rhodes,[1] who flourished under the early Ptolemies, was one of these writers, and three short poems of his, constructed in this way, have come down to us, along with six epigrams, in the Greek Anthology. The first of these poems is called, from its form, the *Wings* (πτέρυγες); the second, the *Egg* (ᾠόν); the third, the *Hatchet* (πέλεκυς). There are several other poems of the same species in the Anthology, such as the *Pan-pipes* (σῦριγξ) of Theocritus, the *Altar* (βωμός) of Dosiadas, and the *Egg* and *Hatchet* of Besantinus.

[1] *Smith, Dict. Biogr.*, *s. v.*

III. BUCOLIC POETRY.

I. *Bucolic Poetry* (*τὰ βουκολικὰ ποιήματα*), called also *Pastoral*, is a species of poetic composition, the interlocutors in which are herdsmen, shepherds, &c., and the scenes portrayed are drawn from rural life. Theocritus was the creator of bucolic poetry as a branch of Greek, and, through imitators, such as Virgil, of Roman literature. The germ of this species of poetry may be discovered, at a very early period, among the Dorians both of Laconia and Sicily, especially at Tyndaris and Syracuse in the latter, when the festivals of Diana were enlivened with songs, in which two shepherds or herdsmen, or two parties of them, contended with one another, and which gradually grew into an art, practiced by a class of performers called *Lydiastæ* and *Bucolistæ*, who flourished extensively in Sicily and the neighboring districts of Italy.

II. The subjects of the songs sung by this class of performers were popular mythical stories, and the scenes of country life; the beauty, love, and unhappy end of Daphnis, the ideal of the shepherd, who was introduced by Stesichorus into his poetry, and of Diŏmus, who was named by Epicharmus; the melancholy complaints of the coy huntsman Menalcas, and other kindred subjects. These songs were still popular in the time of Diodorus. Theocritus, however, was the first who reduced this species of poetry to such a form as to constitute it a branch of regular literature; and, in so doing, he followed not merely the impulse of his own genius, but, to a great extent, the examples of Epicharmus and of Sophron, especially the latter.[1]

III. The bucolic poets that will here require our attention are three in number; namely, *Theocritus*, *Bion*, and *Moschus*.

1. THEOCRITUS (Θεόκριτος),[2] the celebrated bucolic poet, was a native of Syracuse, and the son of Praxagoras and Philinna. He visited Alexandrea during the latter part of the reign of Ptolemy Soter, where he received the instruction of Philetas and Asclepiades, and began to distinguish himself as a poet. His first efforts obtained for him the patronage of Ptolemy Philadelphus, who was associated in the kingdom with his father, Ptolemy Soter, in B.C. 285, and in whose praise, therefore, the poet wrote the fourteenth, fifteenth, and seventeenth idylls. At Alexandrea he became acquainted with the poet Aratus, to whom he addressed his sixth idyll. Theocritus afterward returned to Syracuse, and lived there under Hiero II. It appears from the sixteenth idyll that Theocritus was dissatisfied both with the want of liberality on the part of Hiero in rewarding him for his poems, and with the political state of his native country. It may, therefore, be supposed that he devoted the latter part of his life almost entirely to the contemplation of those scenes of nature and of country life, on his representation of which his fame chiefly rests.

Theocritus, as we have already remarked, was the creator of bucolic poetry, and was influenced, to a great extent, by the examples of Epicharmus and Sophron. His bucolic idylls are of an essentially dramatic

1 *Welcker, über den Ursprung des Hirtenlieds, Kleine Schriften*, vol. i., p. 402, *seqq.*

2 *Smith, Dict. Biogr.*, *s. v.*

and mimetic character. They are pictures of the ordinary life of the common people of Sicily, whence their name, εἴδη, εἰδύλλια. The pastoral poems and romances of later times are a totally different sort of composition from the bucolics of Theocritus, who knows nothing of the affected refinement, the pure innocence, the primeval simplicity, or even the worship of nature, which have been ascribed to the imaginary shepherds of a fictitious Arcadia; nothing of the distinction between the country and the town, the description of which has been made a vehicle of bitter satire upon the vices of civilized communities. He merely exhibits simple and faithful pictures of the common life of the Sicilian people, in a thoroughly objective, although truly poetical spirit. He abstains from all the mere artifices of composition, such as fine imagery, high coloring, and pathetic sentiment. He deals but sparingly in descriptions, which he introduces only as episodes, and never attempts any of those allegorical applications of the sentiments and adventures of shepherds which have made the bucolics of Virgil a signal failure. Dramatic simplicity and truth are impressed upon the pictures exhibited in his poems, into the coloring of which he has thrown much of the natural comedy which is always seen in the common life of a free people. His fifteenth idyll, the *Adoniazusæ*, is a master-piece of the mimetic exhibition of female character, rendered the more admirable by the skill with which he has introduced the praises of Arsinoë and Berenice, without sacrificing any thing of its genuine dramatic spirit. The form of these poems is in perfect keeping with their object. The symmetrical arrangement and the rapid transitions of the lively dialogue, the varied language and the sweetly musical rhythms, the combination of the prevailing epic verse and diction with the forms of common speech, all contribute much to the general effect. In short, as Theocritus was the first who developed the powers of bucolic poetry, so he may also be said to have been the last who understood its true spirit, its proper objects, and its natural limits.

The poems of Theocritus, however, are by no means all bucolic. The collection which has come down to us under his name consists of thirty poems, called by the general title of *Idylls*, a fragment of a few lines from a poem entitled *Berenice*, and twenty-two epigrams in the Greek Anthology, besides one upon the poet himself, the production probably of Artemidorus. The Greek author of a few sentences on the characteristics of the poetry of Theocritus, prefixed to his works, says that all poetry has three characters, the διηγηματικός, the δραματικός, and the μικτός, and that bucolic poetry is a mixture of every form. Bergk has recently classed the poems of Theocritus under the heads of *Carmina bucolica, mimica, lyrica, epica,* and *epigrammata.*[1]

Of the thirty so-called idylls, the last is a late Anacreontic of scarcely any poetic merit, and has no claim to be regarded as a work of Theocritus. Of the others, only ten belong strictly to the class of poems which the ancients described by the specific names of βουκολικά, ποιμενικά, αἰπολικά, or by the first of these words used in a generic sense, *Bucolics*, or, as we say, *Pastoral* poems. But, taking the term *idyll* in the wider sense,

[1] *Rhein. Mus.*, 1838–39, vol. vi., p. 16, *seqq.*

we must also include under it several of the poems which are not bucolic, but which are pictures of the life of the common people of Sicily. In this general sense, the *idylls*, properly so called, are the first eleven, the fourteenth, fifteenth, and twenty-first, the last of which has a special interest, as being the only representation we possess of the life of Grecian fishermen; the second and fifteenth are evidently pretty close imitations of the mimes of Sophron. Those idylls of which the genuineness is most doubtful are the twelfth, seventeenth, eighteenth, nineteenth, twentieth, twenty-sixth, twenty-seventh, twenty-ninth, and thirtieth.

The metre chiefly employed in these poems is the heroic hexameter, adapted to the purposes of Theocritus by having a more broken movement substituted for the sustained and stately march of the Homeric verse. In a few cases other metres are employed. The dialect of Theocritus has given the grammarians considerable trouble. The ancient critics regarded it as a modification of the Doric dialect, which they called "new Doric" (*νέα Δωρίς*); and some of the modern editors have carried this notion so far as to try to expunge all the epic, Æolic, and Ionic forms which the best MSS. present. The fact, however, is, that Theocritus purposely employed a mixed or eclectic dialect, in which the new or softened Doric predominates.[1]

The *editio princeps* of Theocritus, in folio, containing also the *Works* and *Days* of Hesiod, is without place or date, but is believed to have been printed at Milan about 1481. There is another very early edition in 8vo, without place or date. The next earliest edition is that of Aldus, containing the *Idylls*, and a vast mass of other matter, Venice, 1495, fol. The chief among the more recent editions are those of Reiske, Vienna, 1765, 2 vols. small 4to; of Warton, Oxford, 1770, 4to; of Brunck, in the *Analecta;* of Valckenaer, Leyden, 1779–81, 8vo; reprinted under the revision of Schaefer, Leipzig, 1810, fol.; of Heindorf, Berlin, 1810, 8vo; of Gaisford, in his *Poetæ Minores Græci*, Oxford, 1823; of Kiessling, Leipzig, 1819, 8vo, reprinted with Bion and Moschus, London, 1829, 2 vols. 8vo; of Briggs, in his *Bucolici Græci*, Cambridge, 1821, 8vo; of Meineke, Leipzig, 1825, 12mo; of Wüstemann, in Jacobs and Rost's *Bibliotheca Græca*, Gotha, 1830, 8vo; of Wordsworth, Cambridge, 1844, 8vo; of Ziegler, Tubingen, 1844, 8vo; and of Ameis, in Didot's *Bibliotheca Græca* (*Poetæ Bucolici et Didactici*), Paris, 1846, large 8vo. Most of the editions above enumerated contain also Bion and Moschus.

2. Bion (*Βίων*)[2] was a native of Smyrna, or, rather, of a small place called Phlossa, on the River Meles, near Smyrna.[3] All that we know about him is the little that can be inferred from the third idyll of Moschus, who laments his untimely death. The time at which he lived can be pretty accurately determined by the fact that he was older than Moschus, who calls himself the pupil of Bion.[4] His flourishing period, therefore, may have very nearly coincided with that of Theocritus, and may be fixed at about B.C. 280. Moschus states that Bion left his native country, and spent the last years of his life in Sicily, cultivating bucolic poetry, the natural growth of that island. Whether he also visited Macedonia and Thrace, as Moschus intimates,[5] is uncertain, since it may be that Moschus mentions those countries only because he calls Bion the Doric Orpheus. He died of poison, which had been administered to him by several persons, who afterward received their well-deserved punishment

[1] *Jacobs, Præf. ad Anth. Pal.*, p. xliii.
[2] *Smith, Dict. Biogr., s. v.*
[3] *Suid., s. v.* Θεόκριτος.
[4] *Mosch.*, iii., 96, *seqq.*
[5] *Id.*, iii., 17.

for the crime. With respect to the relation of master and pupil between Bion and Moschus, we can not say any thing with certainty, except that the resemblance between the productions of the two poets obliges us to suppose, at least, that Moschus imitated Bion; and this may, in fact, be all that is meant when Moschus calls himself a disciple of the latter.

The subjects of Bion's poetry were the songs of shepherds and love songs, and are beautifully described by Moschus;[1] but we can now form only a partial judgment on the spirit and style of his poetry, on account of the fragmentary condition in which his works have come down to us. Some of his idylls are extant entire, but of others we have only fragments. Their style is very refined; the sentiments are soft and sentimental; and his versification, which is exclusively the hexameter, is very fluent and elegant. In the selection and management of his subjects he is superior to Moschus; but in strength and depth of feeling, and in the truthfulness of his sentiments, he is much inferior to Theocritus. This is particularly visible in the largest of his extant poems, the Ἐπιτάφιος Ἀδώνιδος. He is usually reckoned among the bucolic poets; but it must be remembered that this name is not confined to the subjects it really indicates; for, in the time of Bion, bucolic poetry also embraced that class of poems in which the legends about gods and heroes were treated from an erotic point of view. The dialect of Bion is, like that of Theocritus, a mixed Doric.

In the first editions of Theocritus the poems of Bion are mixed with those of the former, and the first who separated them was Mekerch, in his edition of Bion and Moschus, Bruges, 1565, 4to. In most of the subsequent editions of Theocritus the remains of Bion and Moschus are printed at the end, as in those of Valckenaer and others, already mentioned under the head of Theocritus. Among the separate editions may be mentioned those of Harles, Erlangen, 1780, 8vo; of Jacobs, Gotha, 1795, 8vo; of Teucher, Leipzig, 1793, 8vo; of Manso, Leipzig, 1807, 8vo, 2d ed., containing an elaborate dissertation on the life and poetry of Bion, a commentary, and a German translation; and of Hermann, Leipzig, 1849.

Moschus (Μόσχος),[2] a grammarian and bucolic poet, a native of Syracuse. He lived about the close of the third century B.C., and, according to Suidas,[3] was acquainted with Aristarchus. He calls himself a pupil of Bion in the idyll in which he bewails the death of the latter; but, as already remarked in an account of that poet, this may merely mean that Moschus imitated Bion. Of his compositions we have extant four idylls: 1. Ἔρως δραπέτης. 2. Εὐρώπη. 3. Ἐπιτάφιος Βίωνος. 4. Μεγάρα. The first three are written in the mixed or new Doric; the last in the Ionic dialect, with a few Dorisms. Besides these we have three small pieces, also called idylls by the commentators, but not entitled to the name, an epigram or inscription, and two fragments, called by some epigrams. The idylls of Moschus were at first intermixed with those of Theocritus, and one or two of those ascribed to Theocritus have been, though without sufficient reason, supposed to be the productions of Moschus. Eudocia[4] ascribes to Theocritus the third of the idylls of Moschus; but a careful separation has been made on the authority of MSS. and quotations in Stobæus. To judge from the pieces which are extant, Moschus was

[1] *Mosch.*, iii., 82. [2] *Smith, Dict. Biogr.*, *s. v.* [3] *s. v.* Μόσχος. [4] *Eudocia*, p. 408.

capable of writing with elegance and liveliness; but he is inferior to Bion, and comes still farther behind Theocritus. His style labors under an excess of polish and ornament. The elegy on Bion is remarkable for sweetness of numbers and luxuriance of imagery, but is perhaps too labored for real sorrow.

The idylls of Moschus are generally printed with those of Theocritus and Bion. An account of the editions may be seen under those heads.

IV. DRAMATIC POETRY.

I. The Alexandrean grammarians, in arranging their canon, made, it will be remembered, two classes of tragic writers, the first containing the great masters who flourished prior to the death of Alexander the Great, and the second consisting of what were denominated the "*Tragic Pleiades.*"

II. The seven poets forming the class denominated the "*Tragic Pleiades*" were, as we have already mentioned, *Alexander* the Ætolian, *Philiscus* of Corcyra, *Sositheus*, *Homer* the younger, *Æantides*, *Sosiphanes*, and *Lycophron.*

III. The dramatic works, however, of the poets of the Alexandrine school differed in a very important particular from those produced during the Attic period. The tragedies now composed were no longer exhibited before the people in the public theatre, but were meant for the closet, being written for the amusement of princes and their courtiers, and for a small circle of connoisseurs.

IV. We will now give a brief sketch of each of these poets in the order in which they have been enumerated.

1. Alexander Ætōlus (Ἀλέξανδρος ὁ Αἰτωλός),[1] a Greek poet and grammarian, lived in the reign of Ptolemy Philadelphus. He was a native of Pleuron, in Ætolia, but spent the greater part of his life at Alexandrea. He had an office in the library at Alexandrea, and was commissioned by the king to make a collection of all the tragedies and satiric dramas that were extant. He spent some time, together with Antagoras and Aratus, at the court of Antigonus Gonatas.[2] Notwithstanding the distinction which he enjoyed as a tragic poet, he appears to have had greater merit as a writer of epic poems, elegies, and epigrams. Of his elegies some beautiful fragments are still extant. All the fragments of this writer are collected by Capellmann, Bonn, 1829, 8vo. Compare Welcker, *Die Griech. Tragödien*, p. 1263, *seqq.*; Düntzer, *Die Fragm. der Episch. Poesie der Griechen, von Alexander dem Grossen*, &c., p. 7, *seqq.*

2. Philiscus (Φιλίσκος) of Corcyra, a distinguished tragic poet, was also a priest of Bacchus, and in that character was present at the coronation procession of Ptolemy Philadelphus,[3] in B.C. 284. Pliny[4] states that his portrait was painted in the attitude of meditation by Protogenes, who is known to have been still alive in B.C. 304. It seems, therefore, that the time of Philiscus must be extended to an earlier period than that assigned to him by Suidas, who merely says that he lived under

[1] *Smith, Dict. Biogr.*, *s. v.*
[2] *Aratus, Phænom.*, ii., p. 431, 433, &c., ed. *Buhle.*
[3] *Athen.*, v., p. 198, *C.*
[4] *Plin.*, *H. N.*, xxx., 10, 36.

Ptolemy Philadelphus. He wrote forty-two dramas, of which we know nothing. The choriambic hexameter verse was named after Philiscus, on account of his frequent use of it.[1] There is much dispute whether the name should be written Φιλίσκος or Φίλικος, but the former appears to be the true form, though he himself, for the sake of the metre, used the latter.

3. Sosithĕus (Σωσίθεος),[2] of Syracuse or Athens, or, rather, according to Suidas, of Alexandrea in the Troad, was the antagonist of the tragic poet Homer. He flourished about B.C. 284, and wrote both in poetry and prose.[3] The remains of his works consist of two lines from his Ἄθλιος, and a considerable fragment of twenty-four lines from his Δάφνις or Λιτυέρσας, which appears to have been a drama pastoral in its scene, and in its form and character very similar to the old satyric dramas of the Attic tragedians. The remains of Sositheus are given by Wagner, *Frag. Trag. Græc.*, in Didot's *Bibliotheca Græca*, p. 149, *seqq.*

4. Homer (Ὅμηρος), a grammarian and tragic poet of Byzantium, flourished in the time of Ptolemy Philadelphus, about B.C. 280. The number of his dramas is differently stated at forty-five, forty-seven, and fifty-seven. His poems are entirely lost, with the exception of one title, *Eurypyleia.*[4] Compare Welcker, *Die Griech. Tragöd.*, p. 1251, *seqq.*

5. Æantĭdes (Αἰαντίδης), a tragic poet of Alexandrea, of whom nothing particular is known. He lived in the time of Ptolemy Philadelphus.

6. Sosiphănes (Σωσιφάνης), a native of Syracuse, according to Suidas, exhibited seventy-three dramas, and gained seven victories. He was born at the end of the reign of Philip, or, as others stated, in that of Alexander, between B.C. 340 and B.C. 330. Of his plays, the only remains are one title, Μελέαγρος, and a very few lines from it and other plays.[5] These are contained in Wagner's *Frag. Trag. Græc.*, in Didot's *Bibliotheca Græca*, p. 157.

7. Lycŏphron (Λυκόφρων),[6] a celebrated Alexandrean grammarian and poet, was a native of Chalcis, in Eubœa. He lived at Alexandrea under Ptolemy Philadelphus, who intrusted to him the arrangement of the works of the comic poets contained in the Alexandrean library. In the execution of this commission Lycophron drew up a very extensive work on comedy (περὶ κωμῳδίας), which appears to have embraced the whole subject of the history and nature of the Greek comedy, together with accounts of the comic poets, and, besides this, many matters bearing indirectly upon the interpretation of the comedians.[7] Nothing more is known of his life. Ovid states that he was killed by an arrow.[8] As a poet, Lycophron obtained a place in the Tragic Pleiades; but there is scarcely a fragment of his tragedies extant. Suidas gives the titles of twenty of his tragedies; while Tzetzes[9] makes their number forty-six or sixty-four. Four lines of his Πελοπίδαι are quoted by Stobæus.[10] He also wrote a satyric drama entitled Μενέδημος, in which he ridiculed his fellow-countryman, the philosopher Menedemus, of Eretria,[11] who nevertheless high-

[1] *Hephæst.*, p. 53. [2] *Smith, Dict. Biogr.*, *s. v.* [3] *Suid.*, *s. v.* [4] *Id. ib.*
[5] *Clinton, Fast. Hell.*, vol. iii., *s. aa.* 278, 259, p. 502, 504. [6] *Smith, Dict. Biogr.*, *s. v.*
[7] *Meineke, Hist. Crit. Com. Græc.*, p. 9, *seqq.* [8] *Ovid, Ibis*, 533.
[9] *Schol. in Lyc.*, 262, 270. [10] *Stob.*, cxix., 13. [11] *Athen.*, x., p. 420; *Diog. Laert.*, ii., 140.

ly prized the tragedies of Lycophron.[1] He is said to have been a very skillful composer of anagrams, of which he wrote several in honor of Ptolemy and Arsinoe.

The only one of his poems which has come down to us is the *Cassandra* or *Alexandra*. This is neither a tragedy nor an epic poem, but a long iambic monologue of 1474 verses, in which Cassandra is made to prophesy the fall of Troy, the adventures of the Grecian and Trojan heroes, with numerous other mythological and historical events, going back as far as the Argonauts, the Amazons, and the fables of Io and Europa, and ending with Alexander the Great. The work has no pretensions to poetical merit. It is simply a cumbrous store of traditional learning. Suidas calls it *σκοτεινὸν ποίημα*, "the dark poem," and its author himself obtained the epithet of *σκοτεινός*. Its stores of learning and its obscurity alike excited the efforts of the ancient grammarians, several of whom wrote commentaries on the poem. Among these were Theon, Dection, and Orus. The only one of these works which survives is the scholia of Isaac and John Tzetzes, who flourished about A.D. 1150, which are far more valuable than the poem itself. Lycophron, indeed, purposely enveloped his poem in the deepest obscurity. There is no artifice to which he does not resort to prevent his being clearly understood. He never calls any one by his true name, but designates him by some circumstances or event in his history. He abounds in unusual constructions, separates words which should be united, uses strange terms more or less obsolete, forms the most singular compounds, and indulges in the boldest and most startling metaphors.

A question has been raised respecting the identity of Lycophron the tragedian, and Lycophron the author of the Cassandra. From some lines of the poem (1226, *seqq.*; 1446, *seqq.*) which refer to Roman history, Niebuhr was led to suppose that the author could not have lived before the time of Flamininus (about B.C. 190); but Welcker, in an elaborate discussion of the question, has shown very conclusively that these lines are interpolated.

The *editio princeps* of Lycophron was the Aldine, printed with Pindar and Callimachus, Venice, 1513, 8vo; the next was that of Lacisius, with the scholia, Basle, 1546, fol. Of the later editions, the most deserving of mention are those of Potter, Oxford, 1697, fol., reprinted 1702; of Reichard, Leipzig, 1788, 8vo; and of Bachmann, Leipzig, 1830, 2 vols. 8vo (of which only the first has appeared), to which must be added the admirable edition of the scholia, by C. G. Müller, Leipzig, 1811, 3 vols. 8vo.

Φλυακογραφία.

I. The *Middle* and *New Comedy* having been already treated of in our account of the *Fourth* or *Attic* Period, it remains merely to notice a species of dramatic composition termed by the Greeks *φλυᾶκογραφία* or *ἱλαροτραγῳδία*.

II. This was a species of burlesque drama, or a parody of tragedy, and may be described as an exhibition of the subjects of tragedy in the spirit and style of comedy. It appears to have existed for a long time prior to the Alexandrine period as a popular amusement among the Greeks of

[1] *Diog. Laert.*, ii., 133.

Southern Italy and Sicily, and especially at Tarentum. At the head of the writers in this department stands *Rhinthon.*

Rhinthon (Ῥίνθων) was a native of Syracuse or Tarentum, and flourished in the reign of Ptolemy I. of Egypt. Suidas places him at the head of the composers of the burlesque drama, by which is meant that he was the first to develop it in a written form, and to introduce it into Greek literature, since it had already, as we have remarked, existed as a popular amusement. It would appear from the fragments of Rhinthon that the comic license extended to the metres also, which are sometimes even more irregular than in the Attic comedians.[1] Rhinthon is said to have written thirty-eight dramas.[2]

CHAPTER XXXIX.

FIFTH OR ALEXANDRINE PERIOD—*continued.*

PROSE COMPOSITION.

I. The peculiarities of the Alexandrine period displayed themselves also in prose composition, and in the degree of importance attached to learning and scientific acquirement. Great attention was also paid to the productions of earlier writers, and they were frequently made the subject of commentary and illustration, but the pure and correct taste which distinguished these productions was rarely imitated. Philosophy, however, and the practical sciences, were vigorously cultivated, and the latter, in particular, with important results.

II. The Attic dialect, modified under Macedonian influence and by local circumstances, had now become the common language of prose literature, and the employment of different dialects was discontinued.

I. HISTORY.

In our account of the historical writers of this period will be found some who do not strictly belong to a course of Grecian literature, but who, nevertheless, from certain circumstances connected with them, or from the nature of the subjects on which they wrote, can not well be passed over. The whole number of writers is as follows: *Hecatæus* of Abdera, *Berosus, Abydenus, Manetho, Diocles* of Peparethus, *Timæus, Aratus* of Sicyon, *Phylarchus, Ister,* and *Polybius,* to whom may be added the mythological writer *Apollodorus.*

I. Hecatæus (Ἑκαταῖος)[3] of Abdera, often confounded with Hecatæus of Miletus, was a contemporary of Alexander the Great and Ptolemy, the son of Lagus, and appears to have accompanied the former on his Asiatic expedition as far as Syria. He was a pupil of the skeptic Pyrrho, and is himself called a philosopher, critic, and grammarian.[4] From the manner in which he is spoken of by Eusebius,[5] we must infer that he was a man of great reputation, on account of his extensive knowledge, as well as for

---

1 *Hephaest.*, p. 9, ed. *Gaisf.* 2 *Suid., s. v.* 3 *Smith, Dict. Biogr., s. v.*
4 *Suid., s. v.; Joseph. c. Apion.*, i., 22. 5 *Præp. Evang.*, ix., p. 239.

his practical wisdom (περὶ τὰς πράξεις ἱκανώτατος). In the reign of the first Ptolemy, he travelled up the Nile as far as Thebes. He was the author of several works, of which, however, only a small number of fragments have come down to us. 1. *A History of Egypt.*[1] 2. A work on the *Hyperboreans.*[2] 3. *A History of the Jews*, of which the book on Abraham, mentioned by Josephus,[3] was probably only a portion. This work is frequently referred to by the ancients, but it was declared spurious, even by Origen,[4] and modern critics are divided in their opinions. The fragments of Hecatæus have been collected by Zorn, *Hecatæi Abderitæ Fragmenta*, Altona, 1730, 8vo; by F. Creuzer, in his *Hist. Græc. Antiq. Fragm.*, Heidelberg, 1806, 8vo; and by C. Müller, in his *Fragm. Histor. Græc.*, vol. ii., p. 384, *seqq.*, in Didot's *Bibliotheca Græca*, Paris, 1848, 8vo.

II. Berōsus (Βηρωσός or Βηρωσσός),[5] a priest of Belus, at Babylon, and an historical writer. His name is usually considered to be the same as *Bar* or *Ber Oseas*, that is, "son of Oseas."[6] He was born in the reign of Alexander the Great, and lived till that of Antiochus II., surnamed Θεός (B.C. 261–246), in whose reign he wrote his history of Babylonia.[7] Respecting his personal history scarcely any thing is known; but he must have been a man of education and extensive learning, and was well acquainted with the Greek language, which the conquests of Alexander had diffused over a great part of Asia. His history was in three books, and is sometimes called Βαβυλωνικά, and sometimes Χαλδαϊκά, or Ἱστορίαι Χαλδαϊκαί. The work itself is lost; but we possess several fragments of it, which are preserved in Josephus, Eusebius, Syncellus, and the Christian Fathers, who made great use of the work, for Berosus seems to have been acquainted with the sacred books of the Jews, whence his statements often agree with those of the Old Testament. From the fragments extant we see that the work embraced the earliest traditions about the human race, a description of Babylonia and its population, and a chronological list of its kings down to the time of Cyrus the Great. The history of Assyria, Media, and even Armenia, seem to have been constantly kept in view also. There is a marked difference, in many instances, between the statements of Ctesias and those of Berosus; but it is erroneous to infer from this, as some have done, that Berosus forged some of his statements. The difference appears sufficiently accounted for by the circumstance that Ctesias had recourse to Assyrian and Persian sources, while Berosus followed the Babylonian, Chaldæan, and the Jewish, which necessarily placed the same events in a different light, and may frequently have differed in their substance altogether.

Berosus is also mentioned as one of the earliest writers on astronomy, astrology, and similar subjects; but what Pliny, Vitruvius, and Seneca have preserved of him on these subjects does not give us a high idea of his astronomical or mathematical knowledge. Pliny relates[8] that the

[1] *Diod. Sic.*, i., 47; *Phot. Cod.*, 244.
[2] *Schol. ad Apollon. Rhod.*, ii., 675; *Diod. Sic.*, ii., 47.
[3] *Joseph.*, *Ant. Jud.*, i., 7.
[4] *Orig. c. Cels.*, i., 15.
[5] *Smith, Dict. Biogr.*, *s. v.*
[6] *Scalig.*, *Animadv. ad Euseb.*, p. 248.
[7] *Tatian, adv. Gent.*, 58.
[8] *Plin.*, *H. N.*, vii., 37.

Athenians erected a statue to him in a gymnasium, with a gilt tongue to honor his extraordinary predictions. Vitruvius[1] attributes to him the invention of a semicircular sun-dial (*hemicyclium*), and states that, in his later years, he settled in the island of Cos, where he founded a school of astrology.

The fragments of the Βαβυλωνικά are collected at the end of Scaliger's work, *De Emendatione Temporum*, and, more complete, in Fabricius, *Bibl. Græc.*, xiv., p. 175, *seqq.*, of the old edition. They are also given by Richter, *Berosi Chald. Historiæ quæ supersunt, cum Comment. de Berosi vita*, &c., Leipzig, 1825, 8vo, and by C. Müller, in the *Fragm. Histor. Græc.*, vol. ii., p. 495, *seqq.*, in Didot's *Bibliotheca Græca*, Paris, 1848, 8vo. The work entitled *Berosi Antiquitatum libri quinque, cum commentariis Joannis Annii*, which appeared at Rome in 1498, fol., and was afterward often reprinted, and even translated into Italian, is one of the many fabrications of Giovanni Nanni, a Dominican monk of Viterbo, better known under the name of Annius of Viterbo, who died in 1502.

III. Abydēnus (Ἀβυδηνός), a Greek historian of uncertain date, according to some, the contemporary and pupil of Berosus, according to others, as late as the second or third century of our era. He wrote a history of Assyria (Ἀσσυριακά). We know that he made use of the works of Megasthenes and Berosus, and Cyrillus states[2] that he wrote in the Ionic dialect. Several fragments of his work are preserved by Eusebius, Cyrillus, and Syncellus. It was particularly valuable for chronology. An important fragment, which clears up some difficulties in Assyrian history, has been discovered in the Armenian translation of the Chronicon of Eusebius.[3] The fragments of his history have been published by Scaliger, in his work *De Emendatione Temporum;* by Richter, *Berosi Chaldæorum Historiæ*, &c., Leipzig, 1825; and by C. Müller, in his *Fragm. Histor. Græc.*, vol. iv., p. 278, *seqq.*, in Didot's *Bibliotheca Græca*, Paris, 1851, 8vo.

IV. Manētho (Μανεθώς or Μανεθών),[4] an Egyptian priest of the city of Sebennytus, who lived in the reign of Ptolemy I., and probably also in that of his successor, Ptolemy Philadelphus. His original Egyptian name is differently given by modern scholars. According to Bunsen,[5] it was *Manethōth*, that is, *Má-en-thôth*, or "the one given by Thoth," which would be expressed by the Greek Hermodotus or Hermodorus. According to Lepsius, however, it was *Maí-en-thôth*,[6] or "beloved by Thoth," while Fruin makes it to have been *Má-net* or *Má-Neith*, i. e., "*qui Neith deam amat.*"[7]

Manetho had in antiquity the reputation of having attained to the highest possible degree of wisdom,[8] and it seems to have been this very reputation which induced later impostors to fabricate books, and publish them under his name. The fables and mystical fancies which thus became current as the productions of the Egyptian sage were the reason why Manetho was looked upon, even by some of the ancients themselves, as a half-mythical personage, like Epimenides of Crete, of whose personal existence and history no one was able to form any distinct notion. The consequence has been that the fragments of his genuine work did not

---

1 *Vitruv.*, ix., 4; x., 7, 9. 2 *Cyrill. adv. Julian.*, p. 8, *seq.* 3 *Smith, Dict. Biogr.*, *s. v.*
4 *Id. ib.*, *s. v.* 5 *Egypt's Place in Universal History*, vol. i., p. 59, Eng. trans.
6 *Lepsius, Chron.*, i., p. 405; *Plutarch, Isis and Osiris*, p. 180, ed. *Parthey.*
7 *Fruin, Maneth. Reliq.*, 1847, p. xxviii.
8 *Syncell., Chronogr.*, p. 32, ed. *Dindorf; Plut.*, *De Is. et Os.*, 9.

meet, down to the most recent times, with that degree of attention which they deserved, although the inscriptions on the Egyptian monuments furnish the most satisfactory confirmation of some portions of his work that have come down to us. There can be no doubt that Manetho belonged to the class of priests, but whether he was high-priest of Egypt is uncertain, since we read this statement only in some MSS. of Suidas, and in one of the productions of the pseudo-Manetho. Respecting his personal history scarcely any thing is known beyond the fact that he lived in the reign of the first Ptolemy, with whom he came in contact in consequence of his wisdom and learning. The circumstance to which Manetho owes his great reputation in antiquity, as well as in modern times, is, that he was the first Egyptian who gave in the Greek language an account of the doctrines, wisdom, history, and chronology of his country, and based his information upon the ancient works of the Egyptians themselves, and more especially upon their sacred books. The object of his works was thus of a two-fold nature, being at once theological and historical.[1]

The work in which he explained the doctrines of the Egyptians concerning the gods, the laws of morality, the origin of the gods and the world, seems to have borne the title of Τῶν φυσικῶν ἐπιτομή.[2] Various statements, which were derived either from this same or a similar work, are preserved in Plutarch's treatise *De Iside et Osiri*, and in some other writers, who confirm the statements of Plutarch.

Suidas mentions a work on *Cyphi* (κῦφι), or the sacred incense of the Egyptians, its preparation and mixture, as taught in the sacred books, and the same is referred to by Plutarch at the end of his above-mentioned treatise. In all the passages in which statements from Manetho are preserved concerning the religious and moral doctrines of the Egyptians, he appears as a man of a sober and intelligent mind, and of profound knowledge of the religious affairs of his own country; and the presumption, therefore, must be, that in his historical works, too, his honesty was not inferior to his learning, and that he ought not to be made responsible for the blunders of transcribers and copyists, or the forgeries of later impostors.

The historical productions of Manetho, although lost, are far better known than his theological works. Josephus[3] mentions the great work under the title of *History of Egypt*, and quotes some passages verbatim from it, which show that it was a pleasing narrative in good Greek.[4] The same author informs us that Manetho controverted and corrected many of the statements of Herodotus. The Egyptian History of Manetho was divided into three parts or books. The *first* contained the history of the country previous to the thirty dynasties, or what may be termed the mythology of Egypt, and also of the first eleven dynasties of mortal kings. The *second* opened with the twelfth and concluded with the nineteenth dynasty; and the *third* gave the history of the remaining eleven dynasties, and concluded with an account of Nectanabis, the last of the

[1] *Euseb.*, *Præp. Ev.*, ii., *init.*
[2] *Diog. Laert.*, *Procem.*, § 10, *seq.*
[3] *Ant. Jud.*, i., 3, 9.
[4] *c. Apion.*, i., 14, *seqq.*

native Egyptian kings. These dynasties are preserved in Julius Africanus and Eusebius (most correctly in the Armenian version), who, however, has introduced various interpolations. According to the calculation of Manetho, the thirty dynasties, beginning with Menes, filled a period of 3555 years. The lists of the Egyptian kings and the duration of their several reigns were undoubtedly derived by him from genuine documents, and their correctness, so far as they are not interpolated, is said to be confirmed by the inscribed monuments which it has been the privilege of our time to decipher.[1]

There exists an astrological poem, entitled Ἀποτελεσματικά, in six books, which bears the name of Manetho; but it is now generally acknowledged that this poem, which is mentioned also by Suidas, can not have been written before the fifth century of our era. A good edition of it was published by Axt and Rigler, Cologne, 1832, 8vo. Whether this poem was written with a view to deception, under the name of Manetho, or whether it is actually the production of a person of that name, is uncertain. But there is a work which is undoubtedly a forgery, and was made with a view to harmonize the chronology of the Jews and Christians with that of the Egyptians. This work is often referred to by Syncellus, who says that the author lived in the reign of Ptolemy Philadelphus, and wrote a work on the Dog-star (ἡ βίβλος τῆς Σώθεος), which he dedicated to the king. The very introduction, however, to this book, which Syncellus quotes, is so full of extraordinary things and absurdities, that it clearly betrays its late author.

The work of the genuine Manetho was gradually superseded: first by epitomizers, by whom the genuine history and chronology were obscured; next by the hasty work of Eusebius, and the interpolations he made for the purpose of supporting his system; afterward by the impostor who assumed the name of Manetho of Sebennytus, and mixed truth with falsehood; and lastly, by a chronicle, in which the dynasties of Manetho were arbitrarily arranged according to certain cycles.

The fragments of Manetho are given by C. Müller, in his *Fragm. Histor. Græc.*, vol. ii., p. 511, *seqq.*, in Didot's *Bibliotheca Græca*, Paris, 1848, 8vo.

V. Dĭŏcles (Διοκλῆς) of Peparethus, a Greek historian of uncertain date, but who belongs to some part of the period which we are considering. He was the earliest Greek historian who wrote about the foundation of Rome, and Q. Fabius Pictor is said to have followed him in a great many points.[2] Diocles was prior, therefore, to B.C. 223, about which time Fabius Pictor flourished. The work in which Diocles made mention of the founding of Rome appears to have been entitled Κτίσεις, and contained accounts of the origin of various states and cities. Whether Diocles, however, is the same also as the author of a work on heroes (περὶ ἡρώων σύνταγμα), which is mentioned by Plutarch,[3] and of a history of Persia (Περσικά), which is quoted by Josephus,[4] is a matter of uncertainty.

The fragments of Diocles are given by C. Müller, in his *Fragm. Histor. Græc.*, vol. iii., p. 74, *seqq.*, in Didot's *Bibliotheca Græca*, Paris, 1849, 8vo.

---

[1] *Schöll, Hist. Lit. Gr.*, vol. iii., p. 215, *seqq.*

[2] *Plut., Rom.*, 3, 8; *Festus, s. v. Romam.* [3] *Quæst. Græc.*, 40. [4] *Ant. Jud.*, x., 11, 1.

VI. Timæus (Τίμαιος)[1] of Tauromenium, in Sicily, the celebrated historian, was the son of Andromachus, tyrant of that place. Timæus attained the age of ninety-six, and though we do not know the exact date either of his birth or death, we can not be far wrong in placing his birth in B.C. 352, and his death in B.C. 256. Timæus received instruction from Philiscus the Milesian, a disciple of Isocrates; but we have no farther particulars of his life, except that he was banished from Sicily by Agathocles, and passed his exile at Athens, where he had lived fifty years when he wrote the thirty-fourth book of his history.[2] The great work of Timæus was a history of Sicily from the earliest times to B.C. 264, with which year Polybius commences the introduction to his work. This history was one of great extent. We have a quotation from the thirty-eighth book, and there were probably many books after this. The work appears to have been divided into several great sections, which are quoted with separate titles, though they, in reality, formed a part of one great whole. The last five books contained the history of Agathocles. Timæus wrote the history of Pyrrhus as a separate work,[3] but as it falls within the time treated of in his general history, it may almost be regarded as an episode of the latter.

The value and authority of Timæus as an historian have been most vehemently attacked by Polybius in many parts of his work. He maintains that Timæus was totally deficient in the first qualifications of an historian, as he possessed no practical knowledge of war or politics, and never attempted to obtain by travelling a personal acquaintance with the places and countries he described; but, on the contrary, confined his residence to one spot for fifty years, and there gained all his knowledge from books alone. Polybius also remarks, that Timæus had so little power of observation, and so weak a judgment, that he was unable to give a correct account even of the things he had seen, and of the places he had visited; and adds, that he was likewise so superstitious, that his work abounded with old traditions and well-known fables, while things of graver importance were entirely omitted. Polybius also charges him with frequently stating willful falsehoods, and of indulging in all kinds of calumnies against the most distinguished men, such as Homer, Aristotle, and Theophrastus. These charges are repeated by Diodorus and other ancient writers, among whom Timæus earned so bad a character by his slanders and calumnies, that he was nicknamed *Epitimæus* (Ἐπιτίμαιος), or the Fault-finder.[4]

Most of the charges of Polybius against Timæus are unquestionably founded upon truth; but from the statements of other writers, and from the fragments which we possess of Timæus's own work, we are led to conclude that Polybius has greatly exaggerated the defects of Timæus, and has omitted to mention his peculiar excellences. Nay, several of the very points which Polybius regarded as great blemishes in his work, were, in reality, some of its greatest merits. Thus it was one of the great merits of Timæus, for which he is loudly denounced by Polybius,

---

1 *Smith, Dict. Biog.*, *s. v.*

2 *Polyb.*, *Exc. Vat.*, p. 389, 393.

3 *Dionys.*, i., 6; *Cic.*, *Ep. ad Fam.*, v., 12.

4 *Athen.*, vi., p. 272, *B.*

that he attempted to give the myths in their simplest and most genuine form, as related by the most ancient writers. Timæus, also, collected the materials of his history with the greatest diligence and care, a fact which even Polybius is compelled to admit. He likewise paid very great attention to chronology, and was the first writer who introduced the practice of recording events by Olympiads, which was adopted by almost all subsequent writers of Greek history. For this purpose he drew up a list of the Olympic conquerors, which is called by Suidas Ὀλυμπιονῖκαι ἢ χρονικὰ πραξίδια. Cicero formed a very different opinion of the merits of Timæus from that of Polybius. He says, "*Timæus, quantum judicare possim, longe eruditissimus, et rerum copia et sententiarum varietate abundantissimus, et ipsa compositione verborum non impolitus, magnam eloquentiam ad scribendum attulit, sed nullum usum forensem.*"[1]

The fragments of Timæus have been collected by Göller, in his treatise *De situ et origine Syracusarum*, Leipzig, 1818, p. 209, *seqq.;* and by C. and Th. Müller, in the *Fragm. Histor. Græc.*, vol. i., p. 193, *seqq.*, in Didot's *Bibliotheca Græca*, Paris, 1841, 8vo.

VII. Arātus (Ἄρατος)[2] of Sicyon, the celebrated general of the Achæans, born at Sicyon B.C. 271, wrote *Commentaries*, being a history of his own times down to B.C. 220, which Polybius characterizes as clearly written and faithful records. But to this latter praise they were not entitled. They formed Plutarch's principal authority for the Life of Aratus. The fragments are given by C. Müller, in the *Fragm. Histor. Græc.*, vol. iii., p. 21, *seqq.*, in Didot's *Bibliotheca Græca*, Paris, 1849, 8vo.

VIII. Phylarchus (Φύλαρχος),[3] a contemporary of Aratus, probably a native of Naucratis, in Egypt, but who spent the greater part of his life at Athens. We may place him at about B.C. 215. His great work was a history in twenty-eight books, embracing a period of fifty-two years, from the expedition of Pyrrhus into the Peloponnesus, B.C. 272, to the death of Cleomenes, B.C. 220. Phylarchus is vehemently attacked by Polybius,[4] who charges him with falsifying history through his partiality to Cleomenes, and his hatred against Aratus and the Achæans. The accusation is probably not unfounded, but it might be retorted with equal justice upon Polybius, who has fallen into the opposite error of exaggerating the merits of Aratus and his party, and depreciating Cleomenes, whom he certainly has both misrepresented and misunderstood.[5] The accusation of Polybius is repeated by Plutarch,[6] but it comes with rather a bad grace from the latter writer, since there can be little doubt, as Lucht has shown, that his lives of Agis and Cleomenes are taken almost entirely from Phylarchus, to whom he is likewise indebted for the latter part of his life of Pyrrhus. The vivid and graphic style of Phylarchus was well suited to Plutarch's purpose. It appears, it is true, to have been too oratorical and declamatory, but at the same time to have been lively and attractive, and to have brought the events of the history vividly before the reader's mind. He was, however, very negligent in the arrangement of his words, as Dionysius has remarked. Suidas mentions other

1 *Cic.*, *De Orat.*, ii., 14; compare *Brut.*, 95.
2 *Smith, Dict.*, *s. v.*
3 *Smith, Dict. Biogr.*, *s. v.*
4 *Polyb.*, ii., 56, *seqq.*
5 *Niebuhr*, *Kleine Schriften*, vol. i., p. 270, note.
6 *Vit. Arat.*, 38.

works of his besides his history, but they were comparatively unimportant.

The fragments of Phylarchus have been collected by Lucht, Leipzig, 1836; by Bruckner, Breslau, 1838, and by C. and Th. Müller, in the *Fragm. Histor. Græc.*, vol. i., p. 334, *seqq.*, in Didot's *Bibliotheca Græca*, Paris, 1841, 8vo.

IX. Ister (Ἴστρος),[1] a Greek historian, who is sometimes called a native of Cyrene, sometimes of Macedonia, and sometimes of Paphos, in the island of Cyprus. These contradictory statements are reconciled by Siebelis, on the supposition that Ister was born at Cyrene, that thence he proceeded with Callimachus to Alexandrea, and afterward lived for some time at Paphos, which was subject to the kings of Egypt.[2] Ister is said to have been at first a slave of Callimachus, and afterward his friend, and this circumstance determines his age, since he accordingly lived in the reign of Ptolemy Euergetes, that is, between about B.C. 250 and B.C. 220. Ister was the author of a considerable number of works, all of which are lost, with the exception of some fragments. The most important of his works was an *Atthis* (Ἀτθίς), or History of Attica, of which the sixteenth book is mentioned by Harpocration.

The fragments of Ister are given by Siebelis, *Fragm. Phanodemi, Demon., Clitodemi et Istri*, Leipzig, 1812, 8vo, and by C. and Th. Müller, in the *Fragm. Histor. Græc.*, vol. i., p. 418, *seqq.*, in Didot's *Bibliotheca Græca*, Paris, 1841, 8vo.

X. Polybius (Πολύβιος),[3] the celebrated historian, was a native of Megalopolis, in Arcadia, and was born about B.C. 204. His father, Lycortas, was one of the most distinguished men of the Achæan league; and Polybius received the advantages of his father's instruction in political knowledge and the military art. He must also have reaped great benefit from his intercourse with Philopœmen, who was a friend of his father's, and on whose death, in B.C. 182, Polybius carried the urn in which his ashes were deposited. In the following year Polybius was appointed one of the ambassadors to Egypt, but he did not leave Greece, as the intention of sending an embassy was abandoned. From this time he probably began to take part in public affairs, and he appears to have soon obtained great influence among his countrymen. After the conquest of Macedonia in B.C. 168, the Roman commissioners, who were sent into the south of Greece, commanded, at the instigation of Callicrates, that one thousand Achæans should be carried to Rome, to answer the charge of not having assisted the Romans against Perseus. This number included all the best and noblest part of the nation, and among them was Polybius. They arrived in Italy in B.C. 167, but, instead of being put upon their trial, they were distributed among the Etruscan towns.

Polybius was more fortunate than the rest of his countrymen. He had probably become acquainted in Greece with Æmilius Paulus, or his sons Fabius and Scipio, and the two young men now obtained permission from the prætor for Polybius to reside at Rome, in the house of their fa-

[1] *Smith, Dict. Biogr.*, *s. v.*

[2] Compare *Plut.*, *Quæst. Gr.*, 43, who calls him an Alexandrean.

[3] *Smith, Dict. Biogr.*, *s. v.*

ther Paulus. Scipio was then eighteen years of age, and soon became warmly attached to Polybius. Scipio was accompanied by his friend in all his military expeditions, and derived much advantage from his experience and knowledge. Polybius, on the other hand, besides finding a liberal patron and protector in Scipio, was able by his means to obtain access to public documents, and to accumulate materials for his great historical work.[1] After remaining in Italy seventeen years, Polybius returned to the Peloponnesus, in B.C. 151, with the surviving Achæan exiles, who were at length allowed by the Senate to revisit their native land. He did not, however, remain long in Greece, but joined Scipio in his campaign against Carthage, and was present at the destruction of that city, in B.C. 146. Immediately afterward he hurried to Greece, where the Achæans were waging a mad and hopeless war against the Romans. He appears to have arrived in Greece soon after the capture of Corinth; and he exerted all his influence to alleviate the misfortunes of his countrymen, and to procure favorable terms for them. His grateful fellow-countrymen acknowledged the great services he had rendered them, and statues were erected to his honor at Megalopolis, Mantinea, Pallantium, Tegea, and other places.[2]

Polybius seems now to have devoted himself to the composition of the great historical work for which he had long been collecting materials. At what period of his life he made the journeys into foreign countries for the purpose of visiting the places which he had to describe in his history, it is impossible to determine. He tells us that he undertook long and dangerous journeys into Africa, Spain, Gaul, and even as far as the Atlantic, on account of the ignorance which prevailed respecting those parts. Some of these countries he visited while serving under Scipio, who afforded him every facility for the execution of his design. At a later period of his life he visited Egypt likewise. He probably accompanied Scipio to Spain in B.C. 134, and was present at the fall of Numantia, since Cicero states that Polybius wrote a history of the Numantine war. He died at the age of eighty-two,[3] in consequence of a fall from his horse, about B.C. 122.

The history of Polybius consisted of forty books. It began B.C. 220, where the history of Aratus left off, and ended at B.C. 146, in which year Corinth was destroyed, and the independence of Greece perished. It consisted of two distinct parts, which were probably published at different times, and afterward united into one work. The first part comprised a period of thirty-five years, beginning with the second Punic war, and the Social war in Greece, and ending with the overthrow of Perseus and the Macedonian kingdom, in B.C. 168. This was, in fact, the main portion of his work, and its great object was to show how the Romans had, in this brief period of thirty-five years, conquered the greater part of the world. But since the Greeks were ignorant, for the most part, of the early history of Rome, he gives a survey of Roman history from the taking of the city by the Gauls to the commencement of the second Punic

[1] *Polyb.*, xxxii., 9, *seqq.*; *Pausan.*, vii., 10.

[2] *Pausan.*, viii., 37, 2; *Polyb.*, xl., 8, *seqq.*

[3] *Lucian*, *Macrob.*, 23.

war in the first two books, which thus formed an introduction to the body of the work. With the fall of the Macedonian kingdom the supremacy of the Roman dominion was decided, and nothing more remained for the other nations of the world than to yield submission to the latter. The second part of the work, which formed a kind of supplement to the former part, comprised the period from the overthrow of Perseus, in B.C. 168, to the fall of Corinth, in B.C. 146. The history of the conquest of Greece seems to have been completed in the thirty-ninth book, and the fortieth book probably contained a chronological summary of the whole work.[1]

The history of Polybius is one of the most valuable works that has come down to us from antiquity. He had a clear apprehension of the knowledge which a historian must possess; and his preparatory studies were carried on with the greatest energy and perseverance. Thus he not only collected with accuracy and care an account of the events that he intended to narrate, but he also studied the history of the Roman constitution, and made distant journeys to become acquainted with the geography of the countries that he had to describe in his work. In addition to this, he had a strong judgment and a striking love of truth, and, from having himself taken an active part in political life, he was able to judge of the motives and actions of the great actors in history in a way that no mere scholar or rhetorician could possibly do. But the characteristic feature of his work, and the one which distinguishes it from all other histories which have come down to us from antiquity, is its *didactic nature.* He did not, like other historians, write to afford amusement to his readers; his object was to teach by the past a knowledge of the future, and to deduce from previous events lessons of practical wisdom. Hence he calls his work a *Pragmateia* (πραγματεία), that is, a systematic history, in which events are put together connectedly, as causes and effects, and not merely a *History* (ἱστορία), where they are given in the order of time.[2] The value of history consisted, in his opinion, in the instruction that might be obtained from it. Thus the narrative of events became, in his view, of secondary importance; they formed only the text of the political and moral discourses which it was the province of the historian to deliver.

Excellent, however, as these discourses are, they materially detract from the value of the history as a work of art. Their frequent occurrence interrupts the continuity of the narrative, and destroys, to a great extent, the interest of the reader in the scenes which are described. Moreover, he frequently inserts long episodes which have little connection with the main subject of his work, because they have a didactic tendency. Thus we find that one whole book (the sixth) was devoted to a history of the Roman constitution; and in the same manner episodes were introduced even on subjects which did not teach any political or moral truths, but simply because his countrymen entertained erroneous opinions on those subjects. The thirty-fourth book, for example, seems to have been exclusively a treatise on geography. Although Polybius was thus enabled to impart much important information, of which we in modern times es-

[1] *Smith, l. c.*

[2] *Polyb.*, i., 1, 3; iii., 32.

pecially reap the benefit, still it can not be denied that such episodes are no improvements to the history, considered as a work of art.

Still, after making these deductions, the great merits of Polybius remain unimpaired. His strict impartiality, to which he frequently lays claim, has been generally admitted by both ancient and modern writers. And it is surprising that he displays such impartiality in his judgment of the Romans, especially when we consider his intimate friendship with Scipio, and the strong admiration which he evidently entertained of that extraordinary people. Thus we find him, for example, characterizing the occupation of Sardinia by the Romans, in the interval between the first and second Punic wars, as a violation of all justice, and denouncing the general corruption of the Roman generals from the time of their foreign conquests, with a few brilliant exceptions. But, at the same time, he does not display an equal impartiality in the history of the Achæan league; and, perhaps, we could hardly expect from him that he should forget that he was a member of it. He describes in far too glowing colors the character of Aratus, the great hero of the Achæan league, and ascribes to the historical work of this statesman a degree of impartiality to which it was certainly not entitled. On the same principle he gives quite a false impression of the political life of Cleomenes, simply because this king was the great opponent of Aratus and the league. He was likewise guilty of injustice in the views which he gives of the Ætolians, in some instances.[1]

Livy did not use Polybius till he came to the second Punic war, but from that time he followed him very closely, though without due acknowledgment; and his history of the events after the termination of that war appears to be little more than a translation of his Grecian predecessor Cicero likewise seems to have chiefly followed Polybius in the account which he gives of the Roman constitution in his *De Republica.* The history of Polybius was continued by Posidonius and Strabo.

The style of Polybius will not bear comparison with the great masters of Greek literature; nor is it to be expected that it should. He lived at a time when the Greek language had lost much of its purity by an intermixture of foreign elements, and he did not attempt to imitate the language of the great Attic writers. He wrote as he spoke, and had too great a contempt for rhetorical embellishments to avail himself of them in the composition of his work. The style of such a man naturally bore the impress of his mind; and as instruction, and not amusement, was the great object for which he wrote, he did not seek to please his readers by the choice of his phrases or the composition of his sentences. Hence the later Greek critics were severe in their condemnation of his style, and Dionysius classes his work with those of Phylarchus and Duris, which it was impossible to read through to the end.[2] But the most striking fault in the style of Polybius arises from his want of imagination. Polybius, with his cool, calm, calculating judgment, was not only destitute of all imaginative power, but evidently despised it when he saw it exercised by others. It is for this reason that his geographical descriptions

[1] *Smith, l. c.*

[2] *Dion. Hal., De Comp. Verb.*, c. 4.

are so vague and indistinct. To this same cause, the want of imagination on the part of Polybius, we are disposed to attribute the apparent indifference with which he describes the fall of his native country, and the extinction of the liberties of Greece. He only sought to relate facts, and to draw the proper reflections from them ; to relate them with vividness, and to paint them in striking colors, was not his calling.[1]

The greater part of the history of Polybius has perished. We possess the first five books entire, but of the rest we have only fragments and extracts, of which some, however, are of considerable length, such as the account of the Roman army, which belonged to the sixth book. There have been discovered, at different times, four distinct collections of extracts from the lost books, to which we will refer more particularly in the account that follows of the editions of Polybius.

EDITIONS OF POLYBIUS.

The first five books were first printed in a Latin translation, executed by Perotti, and issued from the celebrated press of Sweynheym and Pannartz, Rome, 1473, fol. The first part of the work of Polybius, which was printed in Greek, was the treatise on the Roman army, which was published by Ant. de Sabio, Venice, 1529, 4to, with a Latin translation by Lascaris ; and in the following year, 1530, the Greek text of the first five books, with the translation of Perotti, appeared at Hagenau, edited by Obsopæus, but without the treatise on the Roman army, which had probably not yet found its way across the Alps. A few years afterward, a discovery was made of some extracts from the other books of Polybius, but the author of the compilation, and the time at which it was drawn up, are unknown. These extracts contain the greater part of the sixth book, and portions of the following eleven (vii.–xvii.). The manuscript containing them was brought from Corfu, and they were published, together with the first five books, which had already appeared, at Basle, 1549, fol., from the press of Hervagius. The Latin translation of these extracts was executed by Wolfgang Musculus, who also corrected Perotti's version of the other books, and the editing of the Greek text was superintended by Arlenius. A portion of these extracts, namely, a description of the naval battle fought between Philippus and Attalus and the Rhodians, belonging to the sixteenth book, had been previously published by Bayf, in his *De Re Navali Veterum*, Paris, 1536, reprinted at Basle, 1537.

In 1582, Ursinus published at Antwerp, in 4to, a second collection of extracts from Polybius, entitled *Excerpta de Legationibus* (Ἐκλογαὶ περὶ Πρεσβειῶν), which were made in the tenth century of the Christian era, by order of the Emperor Constantinus Porphyrogenitus. These *excerpta* are taken from various authors, but the most important of them came from Polybius. In 1609, Is. Casaubon published at Paris, in folio, his excellent edition of Polybius, in which he incorporated all the *excerpta* and fragments that had hitherto been discovered, and added a new Latin version. He intended, likewise, to write a commentary upon the author, but he did not proceed farther than the twentieth chapter of the first book. This portion of his commentary was published, after his death, at Paris, 1617, 8vo. A farther addition was made to the fragments of Polybius by Valesius, who published, in 1634, another portion of the *excerpta* of Constantinus, entitled *Excerpta de Virtutibus et Vitiis* (περὶ ἀρετῆς καὶ κακίας), containing extracts from Polybius, Diodorus Siculus, and other writers ; and to this collection Valesius added several fragments of Polybius, gathered together from various writers. Gronovius undertook a new edition of Polybius, which appeared at Amsterdam in 1670, in 3 vols. 8vo. The text of this edition is taken almost verbatim from Casaubon's, but the editor added, besides the extracts of Valesius, and the commentary of Casaubon on the first twenty chapters of the first book, many additional notes by Casaubon, which had been collected from his papers by his son, Meric Casaubon, and likewise notes by Gronovius himself. The edition of Gronovius was reprinted under the care of Ernesti, at Leipzig, 1763–64, 3 vols. 8vo, with a *Glossarium Polybianum*. The next edition is that of Schweighaeuser, which

---

[1] *Smith, l. c.*

surpassed all the preceding ones. It was published at Leipzig, 1789–95, in 8 vols. 8vo, of which the first four contain the Greek text, with a Latin translation, and the other volumes a commentary, an historical and geographical index, and a copious "*Lexicon Polybianum*," which is almost indispensable to the student. Schweighaeuser's edition was reprinted at Oxford in 1823, in 5 vols. 8vo, without the commentary, but with the lexicon.

From the time of Valesius no new additions were made to the fragments of Polybius, with the exception of a fragment describing the siege of Ambracia, originally published in the second volume of Gronovius's Livy, until Angelo Mai discovered, in the Vatican library at Rome, the third section of the *Excerpta* of Constantinus Porphyrogenitus, entitled *Excerpta de sententiis* (περὶ γνωμῶν), which, among other extracts, contained a considerable number from the history of Polybius. These excerpta were published by Mai in the second volume of his *Scriptorum veterum nova collectio*, Rome, 1827; but in consequence of the mutilated state of the manuscript from which they were taken, many of them are unintelligible. Some of the errors in Mai's edition are corrected in the reprints of the *Excerpta* published by Geel, at Leyden, and by Lucht, at Altona, in 1830; but these Excerpta appear in a far more correct form in the edition of Heyse, Berlin, 1846, since Heyse collated the manuscript afresh with great care and accuracy. The latest editions of Polybius are that of Bekker, Berlin, 1844, 2 vols. 8vo, who has added the Vatican fragments, and that in Didot's *Bibliotheca Græca*, Paris, 1839, royal 8vo.

Besides the great historical work of which we have been speaking, Polybius wrote, 2. The *Life of Philopœmen*, in three books, to which he himself refers.[1] 3. A *Treatise on Tactics* (τὰ περὶ τὰς Τάξεις ὑπομνήματα), which he also quotes,[2] and to which Arrian and Ælian allude. 4. A *History of the Numantine War*, according to the statement of Cicero;[3] and, 5. A small treatise, *De Habitatione sub Æquatore* (περὶ τῆς περὶ τὸν Ἰσημερινὸν οἰκήσεως), quoted by Geminus;[4] but it is not improbable that this formed part of the thirty-fourth book of the history, which was entirely devoted to geography.

XI. Apollodorus (Ἀπολλόδωρος),[5] a Greek grammarian of Athens, flourished about B.C. 140, a few years after the fall of Corinth. Further particulars are not mentioned respecting him. We know that one of his historical works (the Χρονικά) came down to the year B.C. 143, and that it was dedicated to Attalus II., surnamed Philadelphus, who died in B.C. 138; but how long Apollodorus lived after the year B.C. 143, is unknown. He wrote a great number of works, and on a variety of subjects, which were much used in antiquity; but all of them have perished, with the exception of one, and even this one has not come down to us complete. This work bears the title of Βιβλιοθήκη. It consists of three books, and is by far the best among the extant works of the kind. It contains a well-arranged account of the numerous mythi connected with the mythological and the heroic ages of Greece. The materials are derived from the poets, especially the cyclic poets, the logographers, and the historians. It begins with the origin of the gods, and goes down to the time of Theseus, when the work suddenly breaks off. The part which is wanting at the end contained the stories of the families of Pelops and Atreus, and probably the whole of the Trojan cycle also. The first portion of the work (i., 1–7) contains the ancient theogonic and cosmogonic mythi, which are followed by the Hellenic mythi, the latter being arranged ac-

[1] *Polyb.*, x., 24. [2] *Id.*, ix., 20. [3] *Ep. ad Fam.*, v., 12.
[4] *Gem.*, c. 13; *Petav. Uranolog.*, vol. iii., p. 31, *seqq.* [5] *Smith, Dict. Biogr.*, *s. v.*

cording to the different tribes of the Greek nation. The ancients valued this work very highly, as it formed a running mythological commentary on the Greek poets. To us it is of still greater value, as most of the works from which Apollodorus derived his information, as well as several other works, which were akin to that of Apollodorus, are now lost. Apollodorus relates his mythical stories in a plain and unadorned style, and gives only that which he found in his sources, without interpolating or perverting the genuine forms of the legends by attempts to explain their meaning. This extreme simplicity of the Bibliotheca, more like a mere catalogue of events than a history, has led some modern critics to consider the work, in its present form, either as an abridgment of some larger work of Apollodorus, or as made up out of several of his works. But this opinion is a mere hypothesis without any evidence.

Of the other works ascribed to Apollodorus a considerable number of fragments remain. The most deserving of notice among these works are, 1. Γῆς περίοδος, κωμικῷ μέτρῳ, already mentioned under the head of didactic poets who were not epic. 2. Χρονικά, similarly mentioned. 3. Περὶ Ἐπιχάρμου, either a commentary or a dissertation on the plays of the comic poet Epicharmus, consisting of ten books.[1] 4. Περὶ νεῶν καταλόγου, or περὶ νεῶν, an historical and geographical explanation of the catalogue in the second book of the Iliad. It consisted of twelve books, and is frequently cited by Strabo and other ancient writers. 5. Περὶ Σώφρονος, a commentary on the mimes of Sophron.

The first edition of the *Bibliotheca*, in which the text is in a very bad condition, is by Benedictus Ægius, at Rome, 1555, 8vo. A somewhat better edition is that published at Heidelberg by Commelin, 1599, 8vo, with a more correct text. After various other editions, among which we need mention only those of Tanaquil Faber, Paris, 1661, 8vo, and Gale, in his collection of the "*Scriptores Historiæ Poeticæ*," Paris, 1675, 8vo, there followed the first critical edition, by Heyne, Göttingen, 1782–83, 4 vols. 12mo, of which a second and improved edition appeared in 1803, 2 vols. 8vo. The best among the subsequent editions are those of Clavier, Paris, 1805, 2 vols. 8vo, with a learned introduction, a commentary, and a French translation; of C. and Th. Müller, in the *Fragm. Histor. Græc.*, vol. i., p. 104, *seqq.*, in Didot's *Bibliotheca Græca*, Paris, 1841; and of Westermann, in his *Mythographi, sive Scriptores Poeticæ Histor. Græci*, p. 459, *seqq.*, Braunschweig, 1843, 8vo.

CHAPTER XL.

FIFTH OR ALEXANDRINE PERIOD—*continued.*

GEOGRAPHICAL WRITERS.

I. Geography was one of the branches of knowledge which made most progress during the period under review. The conquests of Alexander, which opened Upper Asia and India to the Greeks, and the maritime enterprises of the Ptolemies, brought into notice communities whose very existence before this had been hardly even suspected.

II. The most important geographical writers of this period were *Dicæarchus*, *Megasthenes*, *Daïmachus*, *Timosthenes*, *Eratosthenes*, and *Polemo*.

1. Dicæarchus (Δικαίαρχος),[2] a celebrated Peripatetic philosopher, ge-

[1] *Porphyr.*, *Vit. Plotin.*, 4.

[2] *Smith*, *Dict. Biogr.*, *s. v.*

ographer, and historian, was born at Messana, in Sicily, though he passed the greater part of his life in Greece Proper, and especially in the Peloponnesus. He was a contemporary of Aristotle[1] and Theophrastus, a disciple of the former and a friend of the latter, to whom he dedicated some of his writings. From some allusions that we meet with in the fragments of his works, we must conclude that he survived the year B.C. 296, and that he died about B.C. 285. Dicæarchus was highly esteemed by the ancients as a philosopher, and as a man of most extensive information upon a great variety of things.[2] His works, which were very numerous, are frequently referred to, and many fragments of them are still extant, which show that their loss is one of the most severe in Greek literature. His works were partly geographical, partly political or historical, and partly philosophical; but it is difficult to draw up an accurate list of them, since many which are quoted as distinct works appear to have been only sections of greater ones. The fragments extant, moreover, do not always enable us to form a clear notion of the works to which they once belonged.

Among his geographical works may be mentioned, 1. *On the heights of mountains.*[3] Suidas mentions καταμετρήσεις τῶν ἐν Πελοποννήσῳ ὀρῶν, but the quotations in Pliny and Geminus show that Dicæarchus's measurements of heights were not confined to the Peloponnesus, and Suidas therefore probably quotes only a section of the whole work. 2. Γῆς περίοδος.[4] This work was probably the text written in explanation of the geographical maps which Dicæarchus had constructed and given to Theophrastus, and which seem to have comprised the whole world, as far as it was then known. 3. Ἀναγραφὴ τῆς Ἑλλάδος. A work with this title, dedicated to Theophrastus, and consisting of 150 iambic verses, is still extant under the name of Dicæarchus, but its form and spirit are both unworthy of him, and it is in all probability the production of a much later writer, who made a metrical paraphrase of that portion of the Γῆς περίοδος which referred to Greece. Buttmann is the only modern critic who has endeavored to claim the work for Dicæarchus, in his "*De Dicæarcho ejusque operibus quæ inscribuntur* Βίος τῆς Ἑλλάδος *et* Ἀναγραφὴ τῆς Ἑλλάδος," Naumburg, 1832, 4to. But his attempt is not very successful, and has been ably refuted by Osann.[5] 4. Βίος τῆς Ἑλλάδος. This was the most important among the works of Dicæarchus, and comprised an account of the geographical position, the history, and the moral and religious condition of Greece. It contained, in short, all the information necessary to obtain a full knowledge of the Greeks, their life, and their manners. It was probably divided into sections; so that when we read of works of Dicæarchus περὶ μουσικῆς, περὶ μουσικῶν ἀγώνων, and the like, we have probably to consider them only as portions of the great work, Βίος τῆς Ἑλλάδος. This work consisted of three books. 5. Ἡ εἰς Τροφωνίου κατάβασις. An account of the degenerate and licentious proceedings of the priests in the cave of Trophonius. The geographical works of Dicæarchus were, according to Strabo, censured in many respects by

[1] *Cic., De Leg.*, iii., 6. [2] *Id., Tusc.*, i., 18; *De Off.*, ii., 5. [3] *Plin., H. N.*, ii., 65.
[4] *Lydus, De Mens.*, p. 98, 17, ed. *Bekker.* [5] *Allgem. Schulzeitung for* 1833, No. 140.

Polybius; and Strabo himself is dissatisfied with his descriptions of Western and Northern Europe, which countries Dicæarchus had never visited.

Among his philosophical works may be mentioned, 1. Λεσβιακοί, in three books, which derived its name from the circumstance that the scene of the philosophical dialogue described in it was laid at Mytilene, in Lesbos. In it Dicæarchus endeavored to prove that the soul was mortal. Cicero refers to it in his Tusculan Disputations. 2. Κορινθιακοί. This likewise consisted of three books, and was a sort of supplement to the preceding one. It is probably the same work which Cicero, on one occasion, calls "*De interitu hominum.*"

The fragments of Dicæarchus have been collected and accompanied by a very interesting discussion by Fuhr, "*Dicæarchi Messenii quæ supersunt, composita, edita et illustrata,*" Darmstadt, 1841, 4to. There is also a valuable dissertation on the writings of Dicæarchus, by Osann, in the *Allgem. Schulzeitung* for 1833, No. 140. The geographical fragments are contained in Gail's *Geographi Græci*, vol. ii.

2. MEGASTHĔNES (Μεγασθένης),[1] a Greek writer, to whom the subsequent Greek writers were chiefly indebted for their accounts of India. Megasthenes was a friend and companion of Seleucus Nicator,[2] and was sent by that monarch as ambassador to Sandrocottus, king of the Prasii, whose capital was Palibothra, a town, probably, near the confluence of the Ganges and Sone, in the neighborhood of the modern Patna.[3] We know nothing more respecting the personal history of Megasthenes, except the statement of Arrian, that he lived with Sibyrtius, the satrap of Arachosia, who obtained the satrapies of Arachosia and Gedrosia in B.C. 323. The time at which he was sent to Sandrocottus, and the reason for which he was sent, are equally uncertain. Clinton[4] places the embassy a little before B.C. 302, since it was about this time that Seleucus concluded an alliance with Sandrocottus; but it is nowhere stated that it was through the means of Megasthenes that the alliance was concluded; and as the latter resided some time at the court of Sandrocottus, he may have been sent into India at a subsequent period. Since, however, Sandrocottus died in B.C. 288, the mission of Megasthenes must be placed previous to that year. We have more certain information, however, respecting the parts of India which Megasthenes visited. He entered the country through the district of the *Pentapotamia*, of the rivers of which he gave a full account; and proceeded thence by the royal road to Palibothra, but appears not to have visited any other parts of India. Most modern writers, from the time of Robertson, have supposed, from a passage of Arrian[5] (πολλάκις δὲ λέγει [Μεγασθένης] ἀφικέσθαι παρὰ Σανδρόκοττον τὸν Ἰνδῶν βασιλέα), that Megasthenes paid several visits to India; but since neither Megasthenes himself nor any other writer alludes to more than one visit, these words may simply mean that he had several interviews with Sandrocottus during his residence in the country.

The work of Megasthenes was entitled τὰ Ἰνδικά, and was probably divided into four books.[6] It appears to have been written in the Attic dialect, and not in the Ionic, as some modern writers have asserted. Me-

1 *Smith, Dict. Biogr.*, *s. v.*
2 *Clem. Alex.*, *Strom.*, i., p. 305, *D.*
3 *Strab.*, ii., p. 70; xv., p. 702.
4 *Fast. Hell.*, vol. iii., p. 482, note.
5 *Anab.*, v., 6.
6 *Athen.*, iv., p. 153, *E.*

gasthenes is repeatedly referred to by Arrian, Strabo, Diodorus, and Pliny. Of these writers, Arrian, on whose judgment most reliance is to be placed, speaks most highly of Megasthenes, but Strabo and Pliny treat him with less respect. Although his work contained many fabulous stories, similar to those which we find in the *Indica* of Ctesias, yet these tales appear not to have been fabrications of Megasthenes, but accounts which he received from the natives, frequently containing, as modern writers have shown, real truth, though disguised by popular legends and fancy. There is every reason for believing that Megasthenes gave a faithful account of every thing that fell under his own observation; and the picture which he presents of Indian manners and institutions is, upon the whole, more correct than might have been expected. Every thing that is known respecting Megasthenes and his work is collected with great diligence by Schwanbeck, Bonn, 1846, 8vo. The fragments are also given by C. Müller, in the *Fragm. Histor. Græc.*, vol. ii., p. 397, *seqq.*, in Didot's *Bibliotheca Græca*, Paris, 1848.

3. DAÏMĂCHUS (Δαΐμαχος), or DEÏMACHUS (Δηΐμαχος),[1] a Greek geographical and historical writer, a native of Platææ, whose age is determined by the fact that he was sent as ambassador to Allitrochades, the son of Sandrocottus, king of the Prasii,[2] which latter died in B.C. 288.[3] He wrote a work on India, consisting of at least two books, having probably acquired, or at least increased, his knowledge of those Eastern countries during his embassy. Strabo, nevertheless, places him at the head of those who had circulated false or fabulous accounts respecting India. We have also mention of a very extensive work on sieges (Πολιορκητικὰ ὑπομνήματα), by one Daïmachus, who is probably the same as the author of the *Indica.* The work on India is lost, but the one on sieges may possibly be still concealed somewhere, since Magirus (in Gruter's *Fax Artium*, p. 1330) states that he saw a MS. of it. The fragments of Daïmachus are given by C. Müller, in the *Fragm. Histor. Græc.*, vol. ii., p. 440, *seqq.*, in Didot's *Bibliotheca Græca*, Paris, 1848.

4. TIMOSTHĔNES (Τιμοσθένης), a native of Rhodes, was admiral of the fleet of Ptolemy Philadelphus, who reigned from B.C. 285 to 247. He may, therefore, be placed about B.C. 282. He wrote a work on harbors (περὶ λιμένων), in ten books, which was copied by Eratosthenes, and which is frequently cited by the ancient writers.[4] We have no remains.

5. ERATOSTHĔNES (Ἐρατοσθένης),[5] a native of Cyrene, was born B.C. 276. He first studied in his native city, and then at Athens. He was taught by Ariston of Chios, the philosopher; Lysanias of Cyrene, the grammarian; and Callimachus, the poet. He left Athens at the invitation of Ptolemy Euergetes, who placed him over the library at Alexandrea. Here he continued till the reign of Ptolemy Epiphanes. He died at the age of eighty, about B.C. 196, of voluntary starvation, having lost his sight, and being tired of life. He was a man of very extensive learning, and wrote on almost all the branches of knowledge then cultivated —geography, astronomy, geometry, philosophy, history, and grammar.

1 *Smith, Dict. Biogr.*, *s. v.* 2 *Strab.*, ii., p. 70. 3 *Justin.*, xv., 4.
4 *Strab.*, ix., p. 421; *Steph. Byz.*, *s. v.* Ἀγάθη. 5 *Smith, Dict. Biogr.*, *s. v.*

His merits as an astronomer and geometer will be considered under a subsequent head ; we will confine ourselves at present to what he did for geography, which was closely connected with his mathematical pursuits. It was Eratosthenes who raised geography to the rank of a science ; for, previous to his time, it seems to have consisted more or less of a mass of information scattered in books of travel, descriptions of particular countries, and the like. All these treasures were accessible to Eratosthenes in the libraries of Alexandrea, and he made the most profitable use of them, by collecting the scattered materials, and uniting them into an organic system of geography in his comprehensive work entitled Γεωγραφικά, or, as it is sometimes, but erroneously, called, Γεωγραφούμενα, or Γεωγραφία.[1]

This work consisted of three books. The *first book*, which formed a sort of introduction, contained a critical review of the labors of his predecessors from the earliest to his own times, and investigations concerning the form and nature of the earth, which, according to him, was an immovable globe. The *second book* contained what is now called mathematical geography. He was the first person who attempted to measure the magnitude of the earth, in which attempt he brought forward and used the method which is employed to the present day. The *third book* contained political geography, and gave descriptions of the various countries, derived from the works of earlier travellers and geographers. In order to be able to determine the accurate site of each place, he drew a line parallel with the equator, running from the Pillars of Hercules to the extreme east of Asia, and dividing the whole of the inhabited earth into two halves. Connected with this work was a new map of the earth, in which towns, mountains, rivers, lakes, and climates were marked according to his own improved measurements. This important work of Eratosthenes forms an epoch in the history of ancient geography. Strabo, as well as other writers, made great use of it. Unfortunately, however, it is lost, and all that has survived consists of fragments quoted by later geographers and historians, such as Polybius, Strabo, Marcianus, Pliny, and others, who often judge of him unfavorably, and controvert his statements ; while it can be proved that, in a great many passages, they adopt his opinions without mentioning his name. Marcianus charges Eratosthenes with having copied the substance of the work of Timosthenes on harbors, to which he added but very little of his own. This charge may be well-founded, but can not have diminished the value of the work of Eratosthenes, in which that of Timosthenes can have formed only a very small portion. It seems to have been the very overwhelming importance of the geography of Eratosthenes that called forth a number of opponents.[2]

Another work of a somewhat similar nature, entitled Ἑρμῆς, was written in verse, and treated of the form of the earth, its temperature, the different zones, the constellations, and the like.[3] Another poem, Ἠριγόνη, is mentioned with great commendation by Longinus.[4] Eratosthenes distin-

[1] *Strab.*, i., p. 29 ; ii., p. 67 ; xv., p. 688

[2] *Smith, l. c.*

[3] *Bernhardy, Eratosthenica*, p. 110, *seqq.*

[4] *De Sublim.*, 33, 5.

guished himself also as a philosopher, historian, and grammarian. His acquirements as a philosopher are attested by the works which are attributed to him. His historical productions were closely connected with his mathematical pursuits. There was also a very important chronological work of his, entitled Χρονογραφία or Χρονογραφιῶν, in which he endeavored to fix the dates of all the important events in literary as well as political history.[1] This work, of which some fragments are still extant, formed a comprehensive chronological history, and appears to have been held in high esteem by the ancients. Another work, likewise of a chronological kind, was the Ὀλυμπιονῖκαι,[2] containing a chronological list of the victors in the Olympic games, and other things connected with them.

Among the grammatical works of Eratosthenes we may mention that *On the Old Attic Comedy* (Περὶ τῆς Ἀρχαίας Κωμῳδίας), a very extensive work, of which the twelfth book is quoted, and which contained every thing that was necessary to arrive at a perfect understanding of those poetical productions. We still possess a considerable number of fragments of this work, and from what he says about Aristophanes, it is evident that his judgment was as sound as his information was extensive.

The fragments of the Geography of Eratosthenes were first collected by Ancher, *Diatribe in Fragm. Geograph. Eratosth.*, Göttingen, 1770, 4to, and afterward by Seidel, *Eratosth. Geograph. Fragm.*, Göttingen, 1789, 8vo. The best collection, however, of all the fragments and remains of Eratosthenes, is that by Bernhardy, *Eratosthenica*, Berlin, 1822, 8vo. The chronological fragments are best given by C. Müller, at the end of Herodotus, in Didot's *Bibliotheca Græca*, Paris, 1844.

6. Polemo (Πολέμων),[3] by citizenship of Athens, but by birth either of Ilium, or Samos, or Sicyon, a Stoic philosopher and an eminent geographer. He was surnamed ὁ περιηγητής, and was a contemporary of Aristophanes of Byzantium, in the time of Ptolemy Epiphanes, at the beginning of the second century B.C.[4] In philosophy he was a disciple of Panætius. He made extensive journeys through Greece to collect materials for his geographical works, in the course of which he paid particular attention to the inscriptions on votive offerings and on columns, whence he obtained the name of Στηλοκόπας[5] (a sort of *Old Mortality*). As the collector of these inscriptions, he was one of the earlier contributors to the Greek Anthology, and he wrote a work expressly, περὶ τῶν κατὰ πόλεις ἐπιγραμμάτων.[6] Athenæus and other writers make very numerous quotations from his various works, the titles of which it is unnecessary to give at length. They are chiefly descriptions of different parts of Greece; some are on the paintings preserved in various places, and several are controversial, among which is one against Eratosthenes.

The fragments of Polemo have been published by Preller, "*Polemonis Periegetæ Fragmenta, collegit, digessit, notis auxit L. Preller,*" Leipzig, 1838, 8vo. For farther information respecting Polemo, consult Vossius, *De Hist. Græc.*, p. 159, *seqq.*, ed. *Westermann*; and Clinton, *Fast. Hell.*, vol. iii., p. 524, where a list of his works is given.

1 *Harpocrat.*, *s. v.* Εὔηνος; *Dion. Hal.*, i., 46.

2 *Diog. Laert.*, viii., 51.

3 *Smith, Dict. Biogr.*, *s. v.*

4 *Suid.*, *s. v.*; *Athen.*, vi., p. 234

5 *Athen.*, *l. c.*

6 *Id.*, x., p. 436, *D*; 442, *E.*

CHAPTER XLI.

FIFTH OR ALEXANDRINE PERIOD—*continued.*

PHILOSOPHY.

I. In considering the philosophy of the Alexandrine period, our attention will be confined to the *Middle* and the *New* Academy, and to the later Stoics, *Diogenes* of Babylon, *Panætius*, and *Posidonius*. The *New Platonic* school will fall under the *Roman* period.

II. The leading distinction between the *Old* and the *Middle* Academy was, as we have already said, that the latter brought in the skeptical doctrine of the *uncertainty* of human knowledge, and taught that every thing is uncertain to the human understanding, and that all confident assertions are unreasonable. The *New* Academy, on the other hand, softened down this bold skepticism, and introduced what has been termed the doctrine of *probabilities;* namely, that although the senses, the understanding, and the imagination frequently deceive us, and therefore can not be infallible judges of truth, still that, from the impressions which we perceive to be produced on the mind by means of the senses, we infer *appearances* of truth, or *probabilities.*

I. MIDDLE ACADEMY.

Arcesilāus (Ἀρκεσίλαος) or Arcesilas (Ἀρκεσίλας),[1] the founder of the *Middle* Academy, flourished toward the close of the third century B.C. He was born at Pitane, in Æolis. He studied at first in his native town, under Autolycus, a mathematician, and afterward went to Athens, where he became the disciple, first of Theophrastus, and next of Polemo and Crantor. Not content, however, with any single school, he left his early masters and studied under skeptical and dialectic philosophers. He was not without reputation as a poet, and Diogenes Laertius[3] has preserved two epigrams of his. Many traits of character are recorded of him, some of them of a pleasing nature. His oratory is described as of an attractive and persuasive kind, the effect of it being enhanced by the frankness of his demeanor. Although his means were not large, his resources being chiefly derived from King Eumenes, many tales were told of his unassuming generosity. But it must be admitted that there was another side to the picture, and his enemies accused him of the grossest profligacy—a charge which he only answered by citing the example of Aristippus; and it must be confessed that the accusation is slightly confirmed by the circumstance of his having died in the seventy-sixth year of his age from a fit of excessive drunkenness; on which event an epigram has been preserved by Diogenes Laertius.

It was on the death of Crates that Arcesilaus succeeded to the chair of the Academy, in the history of which he makes so important an era.

[1] *Smith, Dict. Biogr.*, *s. v.* [2] Compare *Strab.*, i., p. 15. [3] *Diog. Laert.*, iv., 40.

The doctrine of Plato had been that no certain knowledge can be obtained concerning the varying forms of natural bodies, and that *Ideas* are the only objects of science. About the time of Arcesilaus two new sects arose; one founded by Pyrrho, which held the doctrine of universal skepticism; the other under Zeno, which maintained the certainty of human knowledge, and taught with great confidence a system and doctrine essentially different from that of Plato. These sects, especially the latter, became so popular as to threaten the destruction of the Platonic system. In this situation Arcesilaus thought it necessary to exercise a cautious reserve with respect to the doctrine of his master, concealing his opinions from the vulgar under the appearance of doubt and uncertainty. He was more desirous to prevent the progress of other innovators than to become himself the author of a new sect. He, therefore, professed to derive his doctrine concerning the uncertainty of knowledge from Socrates, Plato, and other philosophers. The doctrine of Arcesilaus was, that although there is a real certainty in the nature of things, every thing is uncertain to the human understanding, and consequently, that all confident assertions are unreasonable. In other words, he did not doubt the existence of truth in itself, but only our capacities for obtaining it. Hence he combated most strongly the dogmatism of the Stoics, attacking in every way their doctrine of a convincing conception (καταληπτική φαντασία), as understood to be a mean between science and opinion.[1]

During the interval between the death of Arcesilaus and the appearance of Carneades in the academic chair, or the founding of the New Academy, the Platonic school was under the care successively of Lacydes, Evander, and Hegesinus, none of whom were sufficiently distinguished to merit particular notice. Lacydes presided over the Academy for twenty-six years. The place where his instructions were delivered was a garden, named the Λακύδειον, provided for the purpose by his friend Attalus Philometor, king of Pergamus. He died in B.C. 241, from the effects of excessive drinking.[2] Suidas mentions writings of his under the general name of φιλόσοφα or περὶ φύσεως.

II. NEW ACADEMY.

Arcesilaus had restricted his skepticism to philosophy and science, though his antagonists held them to be essentially subversive of all morality, and maintained that they would produce the dissolution of all the bonds of virtue and religion. Hence his successors found it difficult to support the credit of the Academy; and *Carneades*, one of the disciples of this school, thought it expedient to relinquish, in words at least, some of the more obnoxious tenets of Arcesilaus. From this period the Platonic school took the appellation of the *New Academy*.

I. Carneădes (Καρνεάδης)[3] was born at Cyrene about B.C. 213, and was the founder of the Third or *New* Academy. In B.C. 155, he was sent to Rome by the Athenians, along with Diogenes and Critolaus, to deprecate the fine of 500 talents which had been imposed on the Athenians for the destruction of Oropus. At Rome he attracted great notice

[1] *Cic.*, *Acad.*, ii., 24. [2] *Diog. Laert.*, iv., 60. [3] *Smith*, *Dict. Biogr.*, *s. v.*

from his eloquent declamations on philosophical subjects, and it was here that he first delivered his famous orations on Justice. The first oration was in commendation of the virtue; and the next day, the second answered all the arguments of the first, and showed that justice was not a virtue, but a matter of compact for the maintenance of civil society. Thereupon Cato moved the senate to send the philosopher home to his school, and save the Roman youth from his demoralizing doctrines. Carneades died in B.C. 129, at the age of eighty-five or (according to Cicero) ninety, having lived at Athens twenty-seven years after his return from his embassy. He is described as a man of unwearied industry. He was so engrossed in his studies that he let his hair and nails grow to an immoderate length, and was so absent at his own table (for he would never dine out) that his attendants were constantly obliged to feed him. In his old age he suffered from cataract in his eyes, which he bore with great impatience, and showed, moreover, very little, if any, philosophic resignation to the decay of nature.

Carneades left no writings, and all that is known of his doctrines is derived from his intimate friend and pupil Clitomachus; but so true was he to his own principles of withholding assent, that Clitomachus confesses he never could ascertain what his master really thought on any subject. His general theory was that man did not possess, and never could possess, any criterion of truth. He argued that, if there were a criterion, it must exist either in reason (λόγος), or in sensation (αἴσθησις), or in conception (φαντασία). But then reason itself depends on conception, and this, again, on sensation; and we have no means of judging whether our sensations are true or false, whether they correspond to the objects that produce them, or carry wrong impressions to the mind, producing false conceptions and ideas, and leading reason also into error. Therefore, sensation, conception, and reason are alike disqualified for being the criterion of truth. Still, however, man must live and act, and must have some rule of practical life; therefore, although it is impossible to pronounce any thing as absolutely true, we may yet establish *probabilities* of various degrees. For although we can not say that any given conception or sensation is in itself true, yet some sensations appear to us more true than others, and we must be guided by that which seems the most true. Again, sensations are not single, but generally combined with others, which either confirm or contradict them; and the greater this combination, the greater is the probability of that being true which the rest combine to confirm; and the case in which the greatest number of conceptions, each in themselves apparently most true, should combine to confirm that which also in itself appears most true, would present to Carneades the highest probability, and his nearest approach to truth. But practical life needed no such rule as this, and it is difficult to conceive a system more barren of all help to man than that of Carneades.[1]

II. Clitomăchus (Κλειτόμαχος),[2] a Carthaginian by birth, and called Hasdrubal in his own language, came to Athens in the fortieth year of his age, previously at least to the year B.C. 146. He there became con-

[1] *Smith, l. c.*

[2] *Id., s. v.*

nected with Carneades, under whose guidance he rose to be one of the most distinguished disciples of his school; but he also studied, at the same time, the philosophy of the Stoics and Peripatetics. Diogenes Laertius[1] relates that he succeeded Carneades as the head of the Academy, on the death of the latter, B.C. 129. He continued to teach at Athens until as late as B.C. 111 at all events, since Crassus heard him in that year.[2] Of his works, which amounted to 400 books (βιβλία)[3], only a few titles are preserved. His main object in writing them was to make known the doctrines of his master Carneades, from whose views he never dissented. Clitomachus continued to reside at Athens till the end of his life; but he continued to cherish a strong affection for his native country, and when Carthage was taken in B.C. 146, he wrote a work to console his unfortunate countrymen. This work, which Cicero says he had read, was taken from a discourse of Carneades, and was intended to exhibit the consolation which philosophy supplies even under the greatest calamities.[4] Cicero seems to have paid a good deal of attention to the works of Clitomachus, and speaks in high terms of his industry, penetration, and philosophical talent.[5] Clitomachus appears to have been well known to his contemporaries at Rome, for two of his works were dedicated to illustrious Romans; one to the poet C. Lucilius, and the other to L. Censorinus, consul in B.C. 149.

III. Philo (Φίλων),[6] a native of Larissa, was a disciple of Clitomachus. After the conquest of Athens by Mithradates, he removed thence to Rome, where he settled as a teacher of philosophy and rhetoric. Here Cicero was among his hearers.[7] Through Philo the skepticism of the Academy returned to its original starting-point, as a polemical antagonism against the Stoics, and so entered upon a new course, which some historians have spoken of as that of the *Fourth* Academy.[8] He maintained that, by means of conceptive notions (καταληπτικὴ φαντασία), objects could not be comprehended (ἀκατάληπτα), but were comprehensible according to their nature.[9] How he understood the latter, whether he referred to the evidence and accordance of the sensations which we receive from things, or whether he had returned to the Platonic assumption of an immediate spiritual perception, is not clear.

IV. Antiŏchus (Ἀντίοχος)[10] of Ascalon, the founder, as he is called by some, of a *Fifth* Academy, was a friend of Lucullus, the antagonist of Mithradates, and the teacher of Cicero during his studies at Athens, B.C. 79; but he had a school at Alexandrea also, as well as in Syria, where he seems to have ended his life.[11] He was a philosopher of considerable reputation in his time, for Strabo, in describing Ascalon, mentions his birth there as a mark of distinction for the city,[12] and Cicero frequently speaks of him in affectionate and respectful terms, as the best and wisest of the Academics, and the most polished and acute philosopher of his age.[13]

---

1 *Diog. Laert.*, iv., 67.
2 *Cic.*, *De Orat.*, i., 11.
3 *Diog. Laert.*, *l. c.*
4 *Cic.*, *Tusc.*, iii., 22.
5 *Acad.*, ii., 6, 31.
6 *Smith*, *Dict. Biogr.*, *s. v.*
7 *Cic.*, *Ep. ad Fam.*, xiii., 1; *Acad.*, i., 4.
8 *Sext. Emp.*, *Hypotyp.*, i., 220.
9 *Id. ib.*, i., 235.
10 *Smith*, *Dict. Biogr.*, *s. v.*
11 *Plut.*, *Cic.*, c. 4; *Lucull.*, c. 42.
12 *Strab.*, xiv., p. 579.
13 *Cic.*, *Acad.*, ii., 35; *Brut.*, 91.

His principal teacher was Philo—although he is better known as the adversary than the disciple of Philo; and Cicero mentions a treatise called *Sosus*,[1] written by him against his master, in which he refutes the skepticism of the Academics. Another of his works, entitled *Canonica*, is quoted by Sextus Empiricus, and appears to have been a treatise on logic.[2]

The Academy, as we have already remarked, had fallen into a degree of skepticism which seemed to strike at the root of all truth, theoretical and practical. It was, therefore, the chief object of Antiochus, besides inculcating particular doctrines in moral philosophy, to examine the grounds of our knowledge, and our capacities for discovering truth, though no complete judgment can be formed of his success, as the book in which Cicero gave the fullest representation of his opinions has been lost.[3] He professed to revive the doctrines of the *Old* Academy, or of Plato's school, when he maintained, in opposition to Philo and Carneades, that the intellect had in itself a test by which it could distinguish truth from falsehood; or, in the language of the Academics, discern between the images arising from actual objects and those conceptions that had no corresponding reality. On the whole, Antiochus would appear to have been an eclectic philosopher, and to have attempted to unite the doctrines of the Stoics and Peripatetics, so as to revive the Old Academy.

III. STOIC SCHOOL.

I. Diogenes (Διογένης),[4] surnamed the Babylonian, was a native of Seleucia, in Babylonia, from which he derived his surname, in order to distinguish him from other philosophers of the name of Diogenes. He was educated at Athens, under the auspices of Chrysippus, and succeeded Zeno of Tarsus as the head of the Stoic school at Athens. The most memorable event of his life is the part he took in the embassy which the Athenians sent to Rome in B.C. 155, and which consisted of the three philosophers, Diogenes, Carneades, and Critolaus. These three philosophers, during their stay at Rome, delivered their epideictic speeches at first in numerous private assemblies, and afterward, also, in the senate. Diogenes pleased his audience chiefly by his sober and temperate mode of speaking.[5] According to Lucian, Diogenes died at the age of eighty-eight. He seems to have closely followed the views of his master Chrysippus, especially on subjects of dialectics, in which Diogenes is even said to have instructed Carneades. He was the author of several works, of which, however, little more than the titles is known.

II. Panætius (Παναίτιος),[6] a native of Rhodes,[7] and a celebrated Stoic philosopher, studied first at Pergamus, under the grammarian Crates, and subsequently at Athens, under the Stoic Diogenes the Babylonian, and his disciple, Antipater of Tarsus.[8] He afterward went to Rome, where he became intimate with Lælius and Scipio Africanus the younger. In B.C. 144, he accompanied Scipio on the embassy which he undertook to

[1] *Cic.*, *Acad.*, iv., 4.
[2] *Sext. Emp.*, vii., 201.
[3] *Cic.*, *Ep. ad Fam.*, ix., 8.
[4] *Smith*, *Dict. Biogr.*, *s. v.*
[5] *Aul. Gell.*, vii., 14; *Cic.*, *Acad.*, ii., 45.
[6] *Smith*, *Dict. Biogr.*, *s. v.*
[7] *Suid.*, *s. v.*; *Strab.*, xiv., 968.
[8] *Cic.*, *De Divin.*, i., 3.

the kings of Egypt and Asia in alliance with Rome. Panætius succeeded Antipater as the head of the Stoic school, and died at Athens, at all events, before B.C. 111. The principal work of Panætius was his treatise on the theory of moral obligation (περὶ τοῦ καθήκοντος), from which Cicero took the greater part of his work *De Officiis*. Panætius had softened down the harsh severity of the older Stoics, and, without giving up their fundamental definitions, had modified them so as to make them applicable to the conduct of life, and had clothed them in the garb of eloquence. His work on the philosophical sects (περὶ αἱρέσεων) appears to have been rich in facts and critical remarks; and the notices which we have about Socrates, and on the books of Plato and others of the Socratic school, given on the authority of Panætius, were probably taken from that work. The student may consult, in relation to Panætius, the work of Van Lynden, "*Disputatio Hist. Crit. de Panætio Rhodio*," &c., Leyden, 1802, 8vo.

III. Posidonius (Ποσειδώνιος),[1] a distinguished Stoic philosopher, was a native of Apamea, in Syria.[2] The date of his birth is not known with any exactness, but may be placed about B.C. 135. He studied at Athens under Panætius, after whose death he set out on his travels. After visiting most of the countries on the coast of the Mediterranean, he fixed his abode at Rhodes, where he became the head of the Stoic school. He also took a prominent part in the political affairs of Rhodes, and was sent as ambassador to Rome in B.C. 86. Cicero, when he visited Rhodes, received instruction from Posidonius.[3] Pompey also had a great admiration for him, and visited him twice, in B.C. 67 and B.C. 62.[4] To the occasion of his first visit probably belongs the story that Posidonius, to prevent the disappointment of his distinguished visitor, though severely afflicted with the gout, had a long discourse on the topic that pain is not an evil.[5] In B.C. 51, Posidonius removed to Rome, and appears to have died soon after, at the age of eighty-four. Posidonius was a man of extensive and varied acquirements in almost all departments of human knowledge. Cicero thought so highly of his powers that he requested him to write an account of his consulship.[6] As a physical investigator he was greatly superior to the Stoics generally, attaching himself in this respect rather to Aristotle. His geographical and historical knowledge was very extensive. He cultivated astronomy, also, with considerable diligence. He constructed a planetary machine, or revolving sphere, to exhibit the daily motions of the sun, moon, and planets. His calculation of the circumference of the earth differed widely, however, from that of Eratosthenes. He made it only one hundred and eighty thousand stadia, and his measurement was pretty generally adopted. None of the writings of Posidonius have come down to us entire. His fragments are collected by Bake, Leyden, 1810, 8vo.

1 *Smith, Dict. Biogr.*, *s. v.*
2 *Strab.*, xiv., p. 968; xvi., p. 1093.
3 *Cic.*, *De Nat. Deor.*, i., 3; *De Fin.*, i., 2.
4 *Strab.*, xi., p. 492; *Plut.*, *Pomp.*, 42.
5 *Cic.*, *Tusc.*, ii., 25.
6 *Ep. ad Att.*, ii., 1.

CHAPTER XLII.

FIFTH OR ALEXANDRINE PERIOD—*continued.*

ELOQUENCE.

I. TRUE eloquence, that, namely, which speaks to the heart and the feeling of men, exists only in conjunction with freedom. Under the rule, therefore, of the successors of Alexander, finding no longer an object worthy of itself, it abandoned the scene of public affairs, and took refuge in the schools. Athens, now fallen to the condition of a municipal city, ceased to be the exclusive abode of an art from which, in earlier days, she had derived so fair a lustre. In place of the orators of Attica we now hear of the orators of Asia and the isles of the Ægean, or, rather, from this time forth we hear, not of orators, but of rhetoricians.

II. The most celebrated of these schools of rhetoric was that of Rhodes, which had been founded originally by Æschines. In this and similar institutions the masters gave out themes on which their pupils were required to exercise their talents. These themes were sometimes historical subjects; more frequently, however, the celebrated cases which had occupied the attention of the great masters of antiquity were placed anew before some youthful areopagus.

III. With the change of object, however, a change was also experienced in the very nature of the art itself. The aim of the authors of these oratorical exercises was not to sway the masses, or to bend to the will of the speaker some grave and unimpassioned tribunal, but to distinguish themselves among their fellow-pupils by brilliancy of display, and to gain the suffrages of auditors who did not desire to have their feelings aroused, but merely sought for gratification and literary amusement. Unto such hearers, a style glittering with conceits and overloaded with ornaments would prove far more pleasing than the chaste simplicity of the great masters of eloquence.[1]

IV. This new style of oratory, called the *Asiatic*, or florid, is thus characterized by Quintilian: "*Et antiqua quidem divisio inter Asianos et Atticos fuit, cum hi pressi et integri, contra inflati illi et inanes haberentur, et si his nihil superflueret, illis judicium maxime ac modus deesset. Transitus vero fuit ab Attica ad Asiaticam eloquentiam per Rhodios oratores.*" The faults here referred to were particularly apparent in HEGESIAS of Magnesia, the rhetorician and historian, so much so, in fact, that he was regarded by the ancients as the parent of this Asiatic eloquence, though he himself professed to be an imitator of Lysias. Traces, however, of the decline of oratory were apparent before the time of Hegesias in the productions of DEMETRIUS PHALEREUS (so called from his birth-place, the demus of Phalerum, where he was born, B.C. 345), who was placed by Cassander at the head of the administration of Athens. The orations of this

[1] *Schöll, Hist. de la Litt. Gr.*, vol. iii., p. 239.

individual, who is generally regarded as the last among the Attic orators worthy of the name,[1] bore evident marks of the decline of eloquence. They were soft, insinuating, and effeminate, and altogether deficient in the strength and energy which characterize so forcibly the orations of Demosthenes. Demetrius, however, was a man of the most extensive acquirements, and the author of numerous works, historical, political, philosophical, and poetical. These have all perished; for the work on elocution (περὶ ἑρμηνείας) which has come down to us under his name is probably the work of an Alexandrine sophist, of the name of Demetrius. It is also believed that it was owing to his influence with Ptolemy I. that books were first collected at Alexandrea, and that he thus laid the foundation, in fact, of the great Alexandrine library.

CHAPTER XLIII.

FIFTH OR ALEXANDRINE PERIOD—*continued.*

GRAMMATICAL SCIENCE.—GRAMMARIANS.

I. During the preceding periods the art of criticism and the interpretation of earlier authors had not yet been regarded as a particular science. Grammatical erudition (γραμματικὴ τέχνη) did not properly commence before the third century previous to our era. It was then that those lists of classic authors were compiled to which we have already alluded, and which were comprehended under the general name of the Alexandrean *canon.* It was then that the revision, correction, and explanation of the texts of these writers (διόρθωσις, σημείωσις) became a regular occupation. Commentaries (ὑπομνήματα, ἐξηγήσεις) were then written on entire works; the difficulties of obscure passages were cleared up, and oftentimes difficulties were purposely imagined in order to make a display of sagacity and erudition (ζητήματα, προβλήματα, λύσεις). Those who raised such questions were called ἐνστατικοί, or "difficulty-starters," and those who answered them, λυτικοί or ἐπιλυτικοί, "difficulty-solvers."[2]

II. Some grammarians of this same period employed themselves in explaining words or phrases that had become obsolete, or that belonged to foreign dialects or tongues (γλῶσσαι, λέξεις); others, in collecting together analogous or parallel passages found in different writers; others, again, in composing grammars, or treatises on some particular parts of the language. The works of Homer served as a basis for most of these literary labors.

III. It can not be doubted that the influence which these learned researches had on both the language and literature of Greece was considerable of its kind; and the works of these grammarians or philologists would have been of great assistance to us for the correct understanding of the ancient authors. Unfortunately, however, their successors, instead of pursuing the same path of zealous research, were content with making extracts from the works of their predecessors, and forming all sorts of

[1] *Cic.*, *Brut.*, 8; *Quint.*, x., 1, 80. [2] *Schöll, Hist. de la Litt. Gr.*, vol. iii., p. 182, *seqq.*

new compilations. The result, therefore, has been, that the original works have in a great measure perished, and these meagre compilations have come down to us in their place.[1]

IV. The most celebrated of the grammarians of this period were ZENODOTUS, ARISTOPHANES *of Byzantium*, ARISTARCHUS, AMMONIUS, DEMETRIUS *of Scepsis*, PAMPHILUS *of Alexandrea*, DIONYSIUS THRAX, CRATES *of Mallus*, ARTEMIDORUS, SOSIBIUS, PALÆPHATUS, and DIDYMUS.

1. ZENODŎTUS (Ζηνόδοτος),[2] of Ephesus, a celebrated grammarian, was the first superintendent of the great library at Alexandrea, and flourished under Ptolemy Philadelphus, B.C. 280. Zenodotus was employed by Philadelphus, together with his two distinguished contemporaries, Alexander the Ætolian and Lycophron, to collect and revise all the Greek poets. Alexander, we are told, undertook the task of collecting the tragedies, Lycophron the comedies, and Zenodotus the productions of Homer and the other illustrious poets (*Homeri poemata et reliquorum inlustrium poetarum*). This important statement, preserved by the scholiast on Plautus, from the commentary of Tzetzes on the Plutus of Aristophanes, has given rise to much discussion; but it is now generally conceded that by the words "the other illustrious poets" are meant all the other illustrious poets, both epic and lyric. Zenodotus, however, devoted his chief attention to the Iliad and Odyssey. Hence he is called the first *reviser* (διορθωτής) of Homer, and his recension (διόρθωσις) of the Iliad and Odyssey obtained great popularity. The corrections which Zenodotus applied to the text of Homer were of three kinds. 1. He expunged verses. 2. He marked them as spurious, but left them in his copy. 3. He introduced new readings, or transposed or altered verses.[3] The great attention which Zenodotus paid to the language of Homer caused a new epoch in the grammatical study of the Greek language. The results of his investigations respecting the meaning and the use of words were contained in two works which he published under the title of a *Glossary* (Γλῶσσαι), and a Dictionary of barbarous or foreign phrases (Λέξεις ἐθνικαί). It was probably from his glossary, as Wolf has remarked, that the grammarians took the few explanations of the passages of Homer which they cite under the name of Zenodotus, since it is very doubtful whether he wrote commentaries on the poet. The following works may be consulted in relation to Zenodotus: Heffter, "*De Zenodoto ejusque studiis Homericis*," Brandenburg, 1839; Düntzer, "*De Zenodoti Studiis Homericis*," Göttingen, 1848; Gräfenhan, "*Geschichte der Klassischen Philologie*," vol. i., p. 379, 430, 534; vol. ii., p. 32.

2. ARISTOPHĂNES (Ἀριστοφάνης),[4] of Byzantium, one of the most eminent Greek grammarians at Alexandrea, was a pupil of Zenodotus and Eratosthenes, and teacher of the celebrated Aristarchus. He lived about B.C. 264, in the reign of Ptolemy II. and Ptolemy III., and had the supreme management of the library at Alexandrea. All the ancients agree in placing him among the most distinguished critics and grammarians. He founded a school of his own at Alexandrea, and displayed great merit

[1] *Schöll, Hist. de la Litt. Gr.*, vol. iii., p. 182, *seqq.*
[2] *Smith, Dict. Biogr., s. v.*
[3] Compare *Clinton, Fast. Hell.*, vol. iii., p. 491, *seqq.*
[4] *Smith, Dict. Biogr., s. v.*

in what he did for the Greek language and literature. He and Aristarchus were the principal ones who made out the canon of the classical writers of Greece, in the selection of whom they showed, with a few exceptions, a correct taste and appreciation of what was really good.[1] Aristophanes was the first who introduced the use of accents into the Greek language.[2] The subjects, however, with which he chiefly occupied himself were the criticism and interpretation of the ancient Greek poets, and more especially Homer, of whose works he made a new and critical edition or διόρθωσις. But he, too, like his disciple Aristarchus, was not occupied with the criticism or the explanation of words and phrases only, but his attention was also directed toward the higher subjects of criticism: he discussed the æsthetical construction and the design of the Homeric poems. In the same spirit he studied and commented upon other Greek poets, such as Hesiod, Pindar, Alcæus, Sophocles, Euripides, Anacreon, Aristophanes, and others. The philosophers Plato and Aristotle likewise engaged his attention, and of the former, as of several among the poets, he made new and critical editions.[3] All, however, that we possess of his numerous and learned works consists of fragments scattered through the scholia on the above-mentioned poets, some arguments to the tragic poets, and to some of the plays of Aristophanes, and a part of his Λέξεις, which is printed in Boissonade's edition of Herodian's "Partitiones." Among his other works we may mention, 1. Notes upon the Πίνακες of Callimachus,[4] and upon the poems of Anacreon.[5] 2. An abridgment of Aristotle's work, Περὶ Φύσεως Ζώων, which is, perhaps, the same as the work called Ὑπομνήματα εἰς Ἀριστοτέλην. 3. A work on the Attic hetæræ, consisting of several books.[6] 4. A number of grammatical works, such as Ἀττικαὶ Λέξεις, Λακωνικαὶ Γλῶσσαι, and a work Περὶ Ἀναλογίας, which was much used by M. Terentius Varro. 5. Some works of an historical character, as Θηβαϊκά (perhaps the same as the Θηβαίων ὅροι), and Βοιωτικά, which are frequently mentioned by ancient writers.[7] A collection of all the extant fragments of Aristophanes has been made by Nauck, Halle, 1848, 8vo.

3. Aristarchus (Ἀρίσταρχος),[8] the most celebrated grammarian and critic in all antiquity, was a native of Samothrace. He was educated at Alexandrea, in the school of Aristophanes of Byzantium, and afterward founded himself a grammatical and critical school, which flourished for a long time at Alexandrea, and subsequently at Rome also. Ptolemy Philopator intrusted to him the education of his son Ptolemy Epiphanes, and Ptolemy Physcon, too, was one of his pupils.[9] Owing, however, to the bad treatment which the scholars and philosophers of Alexandrea experienced in the reign of Physcon, Aristarchus, then at an advanced age, left Egypt and went to Cyprus, where he is said to have died, at the age of seventy-two, of voluntary starvation, because he was suffering

1 *Ruhnken*, *Hist. Crit. Orat. Gr.*, p. xcv., *seq.*

2 *Kreuser*, *Griech. Accentlehre*, p. 167, *seqq.*

3 *Schol. ad Hes.*, *Theog.*, 68; *Diog. Laert.*, iii., 61.

4 *Athen.*, ix., p. 408. 5 *Ælian*, *H. A.*, vii., 39, 47. 6 *Athen.*, xiii., p. 567.

7 *Suid.*, *s. v.* Ὁμολώϊος Ζεύς; *Plut.*, *De Mal. Herod.*, 31, 33, &c.

8 *Smith*, *Dict. Biogr.*, *s. v.* 9 *Athen.*, ii., p. 71.

from incurable dropsy. He left behind him two sons, Aristagoras and Aristarchus, who are likewise called grammarians, but neither of them appears to have inherited any thing of the spirit or talents of the father.

The numerous followers and disciples of Aristarchus were designated by the names of *οἱ Ἀριστάρχειοι*, or *οἱ ἀπ' Ἀριστάρχου*. Aristarchus, his master Aristophanes, and his opponent, Crates of Mallus, the head of the grammatical school at Pergamus, were the most eminent grammarians of this period; but Aristarchus surpassed them all in knowledge and critical skill. His whole life was devoted to grammatical and critical pursuits, with the view to explain and constitute correct texts of the ancient poets of Greece, such as Homer, Pindar, Archilochus, Æschylus, Sophocles, Aristophanes, Ion, and others. His grammatical studies embraced every thing which the term in its widest sense then comprised; and he, together with his great contemporaries, are regarded as the first that established fixed principles of grammar, though Aristarchus himself is often called the prince of grammarians (*ὁ κορυφαῖος τῶν γραμματικῶν*, or *ὁ γραμματικώτατος*). Suidas ascribes to him more than 800 commentaries (*ὑπομνήματα*). Besides these, we find mention of a very important work, *περὶ ἀναλογίας*, of which, unfortunately, a very few fragments alone are extant. It was attacked by Crates in a work, *περὶ ἀνωμαλίας*.[1]

All the works of Aristarchus are lost, and all that we have of his consists of short fragments, which are scattered through the scholia on the above-mentioned poets. These fragments, however, would be utterly insufficient to give us any idea of the immense activity, the extensive knowledge, and, above all, of the uniform strictness of his critical principles, were it not that Eustathius, and, still more, the Venetian scholia on Homer (first published by Villoison, Venice, 1788, fol.), had preserved such extracts from his works on Homer as, notwithstanding their fragmentary nature, show us the critic in his whole greatness. As far as the Homeric poems are concerned, he, above all things, endeavored to restore their genuine text, and carefully to clear it of all later interpolations and corruptions. He marked those verses which he thought spurious with an obelus, and those which he considered particularly beautiful with an asterisk. It is now no longer a matter of doubt that, generally speaking, the text of the Homeric poems, such as it has come down to us, and the division of the poems each into twenty-four rhapsodies, are the work of Aristarchus; that is to say, the edition which Aristarchus prepared of the Homeric poems became the basis of all subsequent editions. To restore this recension of Aristarchus has been, more or less, the great object with nearly all the editors of Homer since the days of Wolf, a critic of a kindred genius, who first showed the great importance to be attached to the edition of Aristarchus. Its general appreciation in antiquity is attested by the fact that so many other grammarians, as Callistratus, Aristonicus, Didymus, and Ptolemæus of Ascalon, wrote separate works upon it.

In explaining and interpreting the Homeric poems, his merits were as great as those he acquired by his critical labors. His explanations, as

[1] *Aul. Gell.*, ii., 25.

well as his criticisms, were not confined to the mere detail of words and phrases, but he entered also upon investigations of a higher order, concerning mythology, geography, and on the artistic composition and structure of the Homeric poems. He was a decided opponent of the allegorical interpretation of the poet, which was then beginning, which some centuries later became very general, and which has in later days been carried to the extreme of absurdity. The antiquity of the Homeric poems, however, as well as the historical character of their author, seems never to have been doubted by Aristarchus. He bestowed great care upon the metrical correctness of the text, and is said to have provided the works of Homer and some other poets with accents, the invention of which is ascribed to Aristophanes of Byzantium. A scholiast on Homer declares that Aristarchus must be followed in preference to other critics, even if they should be right; and Panætius[1] called Aristarchus a *μάντις*, to express the skill and felicity with which he always hit the truth in his criticisms and explanations. For farther information respecting this distinguished scholar, the student is referred to Wolf, *Prolegom. in Hom.*, p. ccxvi., *seqq.*, and *Lehrs*, *De Aristarchi studiis Homericis*, Königsburg, 1833, 8vo.

4. Ammonius (*Ἀμμώνιος*),[2] of Alexandrea, was one of the chief teachers in the grammatical school founded by Aristarchus.[3] He wrote commentaries upon Homer, Pindar, and Aristophanes, none of which are extant. He must not be confounded with *Ammonius Grammaticus*, the author of the treatise *On the Differences of Words of like Signification* (*περὶ ὁμοίων καὶ διαφόρων λέξεων*), who lived at the close of the fourth century.[4]

5. Demetrius (*Δημήτριος*) of Scepsis, a Greek grammarian of the time of Aristarchus and Crates.[5] He was a man of good family and an acute philologer.[6] Demetrius was the author of a very extensive work, which is very often referred to, and bore the title of *Τρωικὸς διάκοσμος*. It consisted of at least twenty-six books.[7] This work was an historical and geographical commentary on that part of the second book of the Iliad in which the forces of the Trojans are enumerated. He is sometimes simply called the Scepsian, and sometimes merely Demetrius. The various passages in which he is either mentioned or quoted are collected by Westermann, in his edition of Vossius, *De Historicis Græcis*, p. 179, *seqq.*

6. Pamphĭlus (*Πάμφιλος*), an Alexandrean grammarian of the school of Aristarchus, and the author of a lexicon, which is supposed by some scholars to have formed the foundation of the lexicon of Hesychius. Suidas says that it was in 95 books (other readings give 75, 205, and 405), and that it extended from *ε* to *ω*, the preceding part, from *α* to *δ*, having been compiled by Zopyrion. It was arranged in alphabetical order, and particular attention was paid in it to words peculiar to their respective dialects. Pamphilus appears to have lived, according to some, in the first century of our era, which would throw him into the sixth or Roman pe-

1 *Athen.*, xiv., p. 634.
2 *Smith*, *Dict. Biogr.*, *s. v.*
3 *Suid.*, *s. v.* Ἀμμώνιος.
4 *Matter*, *L'Ecole d'Alexandrie*, vol. i., p. 179, 233.
5 *Strab.*, xiii., p. 609.
6 *Diog. Laert.*, v., 84.
7 *Strab.*, xiii., p. 603.

riod of Greek literature; but it is, in all probability, more correct to assign him an earlier date, and rank him in the present or fifth period.[1]

7. DIONYSIUS (Διονύσιος),[2] surnamed THRAX, or the Thracian, appears to have been so called from the circumstance of his father's being a Thracian. He himself was, according to some, a native of Alexandrea, and, according to others, of Byzantium; but he is also called a Rhodian, because at one time he resided at Rhodes, and gave instruction there.[3] Dionysius also stayed for some time at Rome, where he was likewise engaged in teaching, about B.C. 80. Farther particulars about his life are not known. He was the author of numerous grammatical works, manuals, and commentaries. We possess under his name a τέχνη γραμματική, a small work, which, however, became the basis of all subsequent grammars, and was a standard book in grammar-schools for many centuries. The form, however, in which it has come down to us is not the original one, many interpolations having been made, and the work having been sometimes abridged, and sometimes extended or otherwise modified. These interpolations appear to have been introduced at a very early period, and it was probably owing to them that some of the ancient commentators on the grammar found in it things which could not have been written by a disciple of Aristarchus, and therefore doubted its genuineness. Dionysius did much, also, fcr the explanation and criticism of Homer, as may be inferred from the quotations in the Venetian scholia. He does not, however, appear to have written a regular commentary, but to have inserted his remarks on Homer in several other works. His chief merit consists in the impulse which he gave to the study of systematic grammar, and in what he did for the correct understanding of Homer.

The τέχνη ῥητορική of Dionysius was first printed in the *Bibliotheca* of Fabricius (vol. iv., p. 20, *seqq.*, of the old edition); Villoison (*Anecd.*, ii., 99) then added some excerpta and scholia from a Venetian MS., together with which the grammar was afterward printed in Harles's edition of Fabricius, vol. vi., p. 311, *seqq.*, and somewhat later in Bekker's *Anecdota*, vol. ii., p. 627, *seqq.*

8. CRATES (Κράτης)[4] of Mallus, in Cilicia, is said by Suidas to have been a Stoic philosopher, but is far better known as one of the most distinguished of the ancient Greek grammarians. He lived in the reign of Ptolemy Philometor, and was contemporary with Aristarchus, in rivalry with whom he supported the fame of the school of Pergamus against that of Alexandrea. He was brought up at Tarsus, whence he removed to Pergamus, and there lived under the patronage of Eumenes II. and Attalus II. He was the founder of the Pergamene school of grammar, and seems to have been at one time the chief librarian. About the year 157 B.C., shortly after the death of Ennius, Crates was sent by Attalus as an ambassador to Rome, where he introduced for the first time the study of grammar. The results of his visit lasted a long time, as may be observed especially in the writings of Varro.[5] An accident, by which he broke a leg, gave him the leisure, which his official duties might otherwise have

[1] *Smith, Dict. Biogr.*, *s. v.* [2] *Id.*, *s. v.* [3] *Strab.*, xiv., p. 655; *Athen.*, xi., p. 489.
[4] *Smith, Dict. Biogr.*, *s. v.* [5] *Sueton.*, *De Illustr. Gramm.*, 2.

interrupted, of holding frequent grammatical lectures (ἀκροάσεις). We have no farther particulars of his life.

In the grammatical system of Crates a strong distinction was made between *criticism* and *grammar*, the latter of which sciences he considered as quite subordinate to the former. The office of the critic, according to Crates, was to investigate every thing which could throw light upon literature, either from within or from without; that of the grammarian was only to apply the rules of language, in order to clear up the meaning of particular passages, and to settle the text, the prosody, the accentuation, &c., of the ancient writers. From this part of his system Crates derived the surname of Κριτικός. This title is derived by some from the fact that, like Aristarchus, Crates gave the greatest attention to the Homeric poems; from his labors upon which he was also surnamed Ὁμηρικός. His chief work is entitled Διόρθωσις Ἰλιάδος καὶ Ὀδυσσείας, in nine books, by which we are probably to understand, not a recension of the Homeric poems, dividing them into nine books, but that the commentary of Crates itself was divided into nine books. The few fragments of this commentary which are preserved by the scholiasts and other ancient writers have led Wolf to express a very unfavorable opinion of Crates. As to his emendations, it must be admitted that he was far inferior to Aristarchus in judgment; but it is equally certain that he was most ingenious in conjectural emendations. Several of his readings are to this day preferred by the best scholars to those of Aristarchus. As for his excursions into all the scientific and historical questions for which Homer furnishes an occasion, it was the direct consequence of his opinion of the critic's office that he should undertake them, nor do the results of his inquiries quite deserve the contempt with which Wolf treats them.

Among the ancients themselves Crates enjoyed a reputation little, if at all, inferior to that of Aristarchus. The school which he founded at Pergamus flourished a considerable time, and was the subject of a work by Ptolemy of Ascalon, entitled περὶ τῆς Κρατητείου αἱρέσεως. To this school Wolf refers the catalogues of ancient writers which are mentioned by Dionysius of Halicarnassus. Besides his work on Homer, Crates wrote commentaries on the *Theogony* of Hesiod, on Euripides, on Aristophanes, a work on the Attic dialect, and works on geography, natural history, and agriculture, of all which only a few fragments exist.[1]

The fragments of Crates are collected by Wegener, *De Aula Attalica Litt. Artiumque fautrice*, Havniæ, 1836, 8vo. There is also one epigram by him in the Greek Anthology, upon Chœrilus, though some assign this to an epigrammatic poet of the same name.

9. Artemidōrus (Ἀρτεμίδωρος), surnamed *Aristophanius*, and also *Pseudo-Aristophanius*, from his being a disciple of the celebrated grammarian Aristophanes, of Byzantium, was himself a grammarian, and contemporary of Aristarchus. He is mentioned by Athenæus[2] as the author of a work περὶ Δωρίδος, the nature of which is not clear, and of λέξεις or γλῶσσαι ὀψαρτυτικαί, that is, a dictionary of technical terms and expressions used in the art of cookery.[3] Some MSS. of Theocritus contain, under

[1] *Smith, l. c.* [2] *Athen.*, iv., p. 182. [3] *Id.*, i., p. 5; ix., p. 387.

the name of Artemidorus, an epigram of two lines on the collection of bucolic poems, which perhaps belong to our grammarian.[1]

10. SOSIBIUS (Σωσίβιος), a distinguished Lacedæmonian grammarian, who flourished in the reign of Ptolemy Philadelphus (about B.C. 251), and was contemporary with Callimachus.[2] He was one of those writers who employed themselves in solving the difficulties met with in the ancient authors, and who were therefore called λυτικοί or ἐπιλυτικοί, in opposition to the ἐνστατικοί, who employed their ingenuity in proposing problems for others to solve. Several of his works are mentioned. One of them, but we are not told which, contained information respecting the ancient Dorian comedy. For farther information concerning him, consult Vossius, *De Hist. Græc.*, p. 136, *seqq.*, ed. *Westermann.*

11. PALÆPHATUS (Παλαίφατος),[3] an Egyptian or Athenian, and a grammarian, of uncertain date, but who belongs, very probably, to the period under review. His most celebrated work was entitled *Troica* (Τρωϊκά), and is frequently referred to by the ancient grammarians. It contained, apparently, geographical and historical discussions respecting Asia Minor, and more particularly its northern coasts, and must have been divided into several books. There is extant a small work entitled Παλαίφατος περὶ ἀπίστων, or "Concerning incredible Tales," giving a brief account of some of the most celebrated Greek legends. It is an abstract of a much larger work, which is lost. It was the original work to which Virgil[4] refers, in the line "*Docta Palæphatia testatur voce papyrus.*" Palæphatus adopts the rationalistic interpretation of the myths, according to the semi-historical theory. By various ingenious conjectures, he eliminates from these legends all the incredible circumstances, and leaves to us a string of tales, perfectly credible and commonplace, which we should readily believe, provided a very moderate amount of testimony could be produced in their favor. In other words, we arrive at matters intrinsically plausible, but totally uncertified.[5]

The MSS. of the περὶ ἀπίστων present the greatest discrepancies, in some the work being much longer, and in others much shorter. The printed editions, in like manner, vary considerably. It was first printed by Aldus Manutius, together with Æsop, Phurnutus, and other writers, Venice, 1505, fol., and has since that time been frequently reprinted. The following is a list of the principal editions: by Tollius, with a Latin translation and notes, Amsterdam, 1649; by Brunner, Upsala, 1663, which edition was reprinted with improvements under the care of Paulus Pater, Frankfort, 1685, 1686, or 1687, for these three years appear on different title-pages; by Thomas Gale, in the *Opuscula Mythologica*, Cambridge, 1670, reprinted at Amsterdam, 1688; by Dresig, Leipzig, 1735, which edition was frequently reprinted under the care of Fischer, who improved it very much, and who published a sixth edition at Leipzig, 1789; by Ernesti, for the use of schools, Leipzig, 1816. The best edition of the text is by Westermann, in the "Μυθογράφοι: *Scriptores Poeticæ Historiæ Græci*," Brunswick, 1843, p. 268, *seqq.*

12. DIDYMUS (Δίδυμος),[6] a celebrated Alexandrean grammarian of the time of Cicero and the Emperor Augustus, and who belongs therefore, in fact, partly to the present period and partly to the succeeding one. He was a disciple, or, rather, a follower of the school of Aristarchus,[7] and

1 *Smith, Dict. Biogr.*, *s. v.* 2 *Athen.*, xi., p. 493, *F;* iv., p. 144.
3 *Smith, Dict. Biogr.*, *s. v.* 4 *Ciris*, 88. 5 *Grote, Hist. of Greece*, vol. i., p. 553, *seqq.*
6 *Smith, Dict. Biogr.*, *s. v.* 7 *Lehrs, De Aristarchi stud. Homer.*, p. 18, *seqq.*

was himself the teacher of Apion, Heraclides Ponticus, and other eminent men of the time. He is commonly distinguished from other grammarians of the name of Didymus by the surname χαλκέντερος, "of brazen-bowels," which he is said to have received from his indefatigable and unwearied application to study. But he also bore the nickname of βιβλιολάθας, for, owing to the multitude of his writings, it is said it often happened to him that he forgot what he had stated, and thus in his later productions contradicted what he had said in his earlier ones. The sum total of his works is stated by Athenæus[1] to have been 3500, and by Seneca,[2] 4000. In this calculation, however, single books or rolls seem to be counted as separate works, or else many of them must have been very small treatises. The most interesting among his productions, all of which are lost, would have been those in which he treated of the Homeric poems, the criticism and interpretation of which formed the most prominent portion of his literary pursuits. The greater part of what we now possess under the name of the minor scholia on Homer, which were at one time considered the work of Didymus, is taken from the several works which Didymus wrote upon Homer. Among them was one on the Homeric text as constituted by Aristarchus, a work which would be of the greatest importance to us, as he entered into the detail of the criticisms of Aristarchus, and revised and corrected the text which the latter had established.

But the studies of Didymus were not confined to Homer, for he wrote also commentaries on many other poets and prose writers of the classical times of Greece. We have mention of works of his on the lyric poets, and especially on Bacchylides and Pindar, and the better and greater part of our scholia on Pindar is taken from the commentary of Didymus.[3] The same is the case with the extant scholia on Sophocles. In the scholia on Aristophanes, too, Didymus is often referred to, and we farther know that he wrote commentaries on Euripides, Ion, Phrynichus, Menander, and others. The Greek orators, Demosthenes, Isæus, Hyperides, Dinarchus, and others, were likewise commented on by Didymus. Numerous other works of his are mentioned, and among them a collection of Greek proverbs in thirteen books, from which is taken the greater part of the proverbs contained in the collection of Zenobius. Didymus, in fact, stands at the close of the period in which a comprehensive and independent study of Greek literature prevailed, and he himself must be regarded as the father of the scholiasts who were satisfied with compiling or abridging the works of their predecessors. The *scholiasts* themselves properly belong to the succeeding or *Roman* period of Grecian literature, and will there be treated of by us.

[1] *Athen.*, iv., p. 139. [2] *Senec.*, *Ep.*, 88. [3] *Böckh, Præf. ad Schol. Pind.*, p. xvii., *seq.*

CHAPTER XLIV.

FIFTH OR ALEXANDRINE PERIOD—*continued.*

MATHEMATICS.—ASTRONOMY.—MECHANICS.

The most distinguished mathematicians during this period were Euclides, Archimedes, and Apollonius of Perga. The most eminent astronomers, Conon, of Samos; Aristarchus, of the same island; Eratosthenes (distinguished also as a geometer), and Hipparchus. To these we may add the mechanicians Ctesibius, Hero, Athenæus, Biton, and Philo of Byzantium.

I. MATHEMATICIANS.

I. Euclīdes (Εὐκλείδης), of Alexandrea, was a celebrated mathematician, who has almost given his name to the science of geometry in every country in which his writings are studied, but of whose private history we know next to nothing. The place of his birth is uncertain. He lived at Alexandrea in the time of the first Ptolemy, B.C. 323–283,[1] and was the founder of the Alexandrean mathematical school. He was of the Platonic sect, and well read in its doctrines. It was he who, when asked by Ptolemy if geometry could not be made easier, replied that there was no royal road to it (*μὴ εἶναι βασιλικὴν ἄτραπον πρὸς γεωμετρίαν*). Of the numerous works attributed to Euclid the following are still extant. 1. *Στοιχεῖα*, "the Elements," consisting of thirteen books, with a fourteenth and fifteenth added by Hypsicles, of Alexandrea, about 170 A.D. The first four and the sixth are on plane geometry; the fifth is on the theory of proportion, and applies to magnitude in general; the seventh, eighth, and ninth are on arithmetic; the tenth is on the arithmetical characteristics of the divisions of a straight line; the eleventh and twelfth are on the elements of solid geometry; the thirteenth (and also the fourteenth and fifteenth) are on the regular solids, which were so much studied among the Platonists as to bear the name of Platonic, and which, according to Proclus, were the objects on which the Elements were really meant to be written. This, however, can not be a correct assertion. The author of the Elements could hardly have considered them a mere introduction to a favorite speculation: if he were so blind, we have every reason to suppose that his own contemporaries could have set him right. From various indications, it can be collected that the fame of the Elements was almost coeval with their publication; and by the time of Marinus we learn from that writer that Euclid was called *κύριος στοιχειωτής*.[2]

Next in order, and to be mentioned in connection with the Elements are, 2. The *Data* (*Δεδομένα*) of Euclid. This is a book containing a hundred propositions of a peculiar and limited intent. It is the most valuable

[1] *Proclus, Comm. in Eucl.*, ii., 4.

[2] *De Morgan; Smith, Dict. Biogr., s. v.*

specimen which we have left of the rudiments of the geometrical analysis of the Greeks. Before a result can be found, it should be known whether the given hypotheses are sufficient to determine it. The application of algebra settles both points; that is, ascertains whether one or more definite results can be determined and determines them. But in geometry it is possible to propose a question which is really indeterminate, and in a determinate form, while, at the same time, the methods of geometry which give one answer may not give the means of ascertaining whether the answer thus obtained is the only one. Thus the two following questions seem, to one not versed in geometry, equally to require one specific answer: Given the area of a parallelogram, and the ratio of its sides; required the lengths of those sides: and, Given the area of a parallelogram, the ratio of its sides and one of its angles; required the lengths of the sides. The first question admits of an infinite number of answers, and the second of only one; or, in the language of Euclid, if the area, ratio of sides, and an angle of a parallelogram be given, the sides themselves are given. The same process by which it may be shown that they are given serves to find them; so that the *Data* of Euclid may be looked upon as a collection of geometrical problems, in which the attention of the reader is directed more to the question of the sufficiency of the hypothesis to produce one result, and one only, than to the method of obtaining the result. A preface to this book was written by Marinus of Naples.[1]

Besides the Elements and Data we have, 3. Εἰσαγωγὴ Ἁρμονική, a *Treatise on Music*; and, 4. Κατατομὴ Κανόνος, the *Division of the Scale*. One of these works, most likely the former, must be rejected. 5. Φαινόμενα, the *Appearances* (of the heavens). 6. Ὀπτικά, on *Optics*; and, 7. Κατοπτρικά, on *Catoptrics*. Proceeding on the supposition that rays of light are carried *from the eye to the object*, the first of these two books demonstrates some relations of apparent magnitude, and shows how to measure an unknown height by the well-known law of reflected light. In the second, an imperfect theory of convex and concave mirrors is given.

The only complete edition of all the reputed works of Euclid is that published at Oxford, 1703, fol., Greek and Latin, by David Gregory, then Savilian professor, with the title Εὐκλείδου τὰ σωζόμενα. The *Elements* and the *Data* were published in Greek, Latin, and French, in 3 vols. 4to, Paris, 1814–18, by Peyrard. The most convenient edition for scholars of the Greek text of the Elements is the one by August, Berlin, 1826, 8vo.

II. Archimēdes (Ἀρχιμήδης),[2] the most celebrated of ancient mathematicians, and one of the few men whose writings form a standard epoch in the history of the progress of knowledge, was born at Syracuse B.C. 287. Of his family little is known. Plutarch calls him a relation of King Hiero, but he would seem rather to have been merely a friend of that monarch, and not of elevated origin.[3] In the early part of his life he travelled into Egypt, where he is said, on the authority of Proclus, to have studied under Conon the Samian, a mathematician and astronomer, who lived under the Ptolemies, Philadelphus and Euergetes, and for whom he test-

[1] *Penny Cyclop.*, xi., p. 153.

[2] *Donkin; Smith, Dict. Biogr.*, s. v.

[3] Compare *Cic.*, *Tusc.*, v., 23.

ifies his respect and esteem in several places of his works. Livy calls Archimedes a distinguished astronomer, "*unicus spectator cœli siderumque*,"[1] a description the truth of which is made sufficiently probable by his treatment of the astronomical questions occurring in his work entitled the *Arenarius* (ὁ Ψαμμίτης). He was popularly best known as the inventor of several ingenious machines; but Plutarch,[2] who, it should be observed, confounds the application of geometry to mechanics with the solution of geometrical problems by mechanical means, represents him as despising these contrivances, and only condescending to withdraw himself from the abstractions of pure geometry at the request of Hiero. Certain it is, however, that Archimedes did cultivate not only pure geometry, but also the mathematical theory of several branches of physics, in a truly scientific spirit, and with a success which placed him very far in advance of the age in which he lived. His theory of the lever was the foundation of statics till the discovery of the composition of forces in the time of Newton, and no essential addition was made to the principles of the equilibrium of fluids and floating bodies, established by him in his treatise "*De Insidentibus*," till the publication of Stevin's researches on the pressure of fluids, in 1608.[3]

Archimedes constructed for Hiero various engines of war, which, many years afterward, were so far effectual in the defence of Syracuse against Marcellus as to convert the siege into a blockade, and delay the taking of the city for a considerable time.[4] The accounts of the performances of these engines are evidently exaggerated; and the story of the burning of the Roman ships by the reflected rays of the sun, though very current in later times, is probably a fiction, since neither Polybius, Livy, nor Plutarch gives the least hint of it. The earliest writers who speak of it are Galen[5] and his contemporary Lucian,[6] who (in the second century) merely allude to it as a thing well known. Zonaras (about A.D. 1100) mentions it in relating the employment of a similar apparatus, contrived by a certain Proclus, when Byzantium was besieged in the reign of Anastasius; and gives Dion as his authority, without referring to the particular passage. The extant works of Dion contain no allusion to it. Tzetzes[7] (about 1150) gives an account of the principal inventions of Archimedes, and among them of this burning-machine, which, he says, set the Roman ships on fire, when they came within a bow-shot of the walls; and consisted of a large hexagonal mirror, with smaller ones disposed round it, each of the latter being a polygon of twenty-four sides. The subject has been a good deal discussed in modern times, especially by Cavalieri and Buffon. The latter writer actually succeeded in igniting wood at a distance of 150 feet by means of a combination of 148 plane mirrors. The most probable conclusion seems to be, that Archimedes had on some occasion set fire to a ship or ships by means of a burning-mirror, and that later writers falsely connected the circumstance with the siege of Syracuse.

---

1 *Liv.*, xxiv., 2.

2 *Plut.*, *Marcell.*, 14.

3 *Lagrange*, *Mec. Anal.*, vol. i., p. ii., 176.

4 *Id. ib.*, 15, *seqq.*

5 *Galen*, *De Temper.*, iii., 2.

6 *Lucian*, *Hippias*, c. 2.

7 *Tzetz.*, *Chil.*, ii., 103, *seqq.*

But, whatever we may think of the story of the mirrors, one thing is certain, that the military engines of Archimedes, generally, were a powerful means of defence to the beleaguered city. Polybius states that catapults and balistæ of various sizes were successfully used against the enemy; that in their nearer approach they were galled by arrows shot not only from the top of the walls, but through port-holes constructed in numerous places; that machines which threw masses of stone or lead, of a weight not less than ten talents, discharged their contents on the Roman engines, which had been previously caught by ropes; that iron hands (*manus ferreæ*) or hooks, attached to chains, were thrown so as to catch the prows of the vessels, which were then overturned by the besieged, and that the same machines were used to catch the assailants on the land side, and dash them to the ground.

After the storming of Syracuse, Archimedes was killed by a Roman soldier, who did not know who he was. Marcellus, it is said, had given strict orders to preserve him alive. According to Valerius Maximus, when the soldier asked who he was, Archimedes, being intent upon a problem, begged that his diagram might not be disturbed; upon which the soldier put him to death. According to another account, he was in the act of carrying his instruments to Marcellus, when he was killed by some soldiers, who suspected that the box which he was carrying contained treasure which he was endeavoring to remove. At his own request, expressed during his life, a sphere inscribed in a cylinder was engraved on his tomb, in memory of his discovery that the solid content of a sphere is exactly two thirds of that of the circumscribing cylinder. By this mark it was afterward found, covered with weeds, by Cicero, when quæstor in Sicily.

The following additional instances of the skill of Archimedes in the application of science may here be mentioned. He detected the mixture of silver in a crown which Hiero had ordered to be made of gold, and determined the proportion of the two metals by a method suggested to him by the overflowing of the water when he stepped into a bath. When the thought struck him, he is said to have been so much pleased, that, forgetting to put on his clothes, he ran home, shouting εὕρηκα, εὕρηκα. The particulars of the calculation are not preserved, but it probably depended upon a direct comparison of the weights of certain volumes of silver and gold with the weight and volume of the crown; the volumes being measured, at least in the case of the crown, by the quantity of water displaced when the mass was immersed. It is not likely that Archimedes was at this time acquainted with the theorems demonstrated in his hydrostatical treatise concerning the *loss of weight* of bodies immersed in water, since he would hardly have evinced such lively gratification at the obvious discovery that they might be applied to the problem of the crown; his delight must rather have arisen from his now first catching sight of a line of investigation which led immediately to the solution of the problem in question, and ultimately to the important theorems referred to.[1]

He superintended the building of a ship of enormous size for Hiero, of

[1] *Smith, Dict. Biogr., s. v.*

which a description is given in Athenæus,[1] where he is also said to have moved it to the sea by the help of a screw. According to Proclus, this ship was intended by Hiero as a present to Ptolemy; and it may possibly have been the occasion of Archimedes' visit to Egypt. He invented, also, a machine called, from its form, *Cochlea*, and now known as the water-screw of Archimedes, for pumping the water out of the hold of this vessel; it is said to have been also used in Egypt by the inhabitants of the Delta in irrigating their lands.[2] The Arabian historian Abulpharagius attributes to Archimedes the raising of the dikes and bridges used as defences against the overflowing of the Nile.[3] Tzetzes and Oribasius[4] speak of his *Trispast*, a machine for moving large weights; probably a combination of pulleys, or wheels and axles. A hydraulic organ is mentioned by Tertullian, which Pliny, however, attributes to Ctesibius. An apparatus called *loculus*, apparently somewhat resembling the *Chinese puzzle*, is also attributed to Archimedes. His most celebrated performance, however, was the construction of a *sphere*, a kind of orrery, representing the movements of the heavenly bodies, of which we have no particular description. The apophthegm attributed to him, that if he had a point to stand upon he could move the world (δὸς πoῦ στῶ, καὶ τὸν κόσμον κινήσω), arose from his knowledge of the possible effects of machinery, and, however it might astonish a Greek of his day, would now be admitted to be as theoretically possible as it is practically impossible.

Of the general character of Archimedes we have no direct account. But his apparently disinterested devotion to his friend and admirer Hiero, in whose service he was ever ready to exercise his ingenuity upon objects which his own taste would not have led him to choose (for there is doubtless some truth in what Plutarch says on this point); the affectionate regret which he expresses for his deceased master Conon, in writing to his surviving friend Dositheus (to whom most of his works are addressed); and the unaffected simplicity with which he announces his own discoveries, seem all to afford probable grounds for a favorable estimate of it. That his intellect was of the very highest order is unquestionable. He possessed, in a degree never exceeded, unless by Newton, the inventive genius which discovers new provinces of inquiry, and finds new points of view for old and familiar objects; the clearness of conception which is essential to the resolution of complex phænomena into their constituent elements; and the power and habit of intense and persevering thought, without which other intellectual gifts are comparatively fruitless. It may be noticed that he resembled other great thinkers in his habit of complete abstraction from outward things when reflecting on subjects which made considerable demands on his mental powers. At such times he would forget to eat his meals, and required compulsion to take him to the bath. The success of Archimedes in conquering difficulties seems to have made the expression πρόβλημα Ἀρχιμήδειον proverbial.[5]

The following works of Archimedes have come down to us: 1. A

---

[1] *Athen.*, v., p. 206, *D.*

[2] *Diod. Sic.*, i., 34; *Vitruv.*, x., 11.

[3] *Pope-Blount*, *Censura*, p. 32.

[4] *De Mach.*, xxvi.

[5] Compare *Cic.*, *Ep. ad Att.*, xiii., 28; *pro Cluent.*, 32.

treatise on *Equilibrium and Centre of Gravity of Planes* (Ἐπιπέδων ἰσοῤῥοπικῶν ἢ κέντρα βαρῶν ἐπιπέδων), in which the theory of the equilibrium of the straight lever is demonstrated, both for commensurable and incommensurable weights; and various properties of the centres of gravity of plane surfaces bounded by three or four straight lines, or by a straight line and a parabola, are established. 2. The *Quadrature of the Parabola* (Τετραγωνισμὸς παραβολῆς), in which it is proved that the area cut off from a parabola by any chord is equal to two thirds of the parallelogram of which one side is the chord in question, and the opposite side a tangent to the parabola. This was the first real example of the quadrature of a curvilinear space; that is, of the discovery of a *rectilinear* figure equal to an area not bounded entirely by straight lines. 3. A treatise on the *Sphere and Cylinder* (Περὶ τῆς Σφαίρας καὶ Κυλίνδρου), in which various propositions relative to the surfaces and volumes of the sphere, cylinder, and cone were demonstrated for the first time. Many of them are now familiarly known; for example, those which establish the ratio ($\frac{2}{3}$) between the volumes, and also between the surfaces of the sphere and circumscribing cylinder; and the ratio ($\frac{1}{4}$) between the area of a great circle and the surface of the sphere. They are easily demonstrable by the modern analytical methods; but the original discovery and geometrical proof of them required the genius of Archimedes. Moreover, the legitimacy of the modern applications of analysis to questions concerning curved lines and surfaces can only be proved by a kind of geometrical reasoning, of which Archimedes gave the first example.[1]

4. A work on the *Dimension of the Circle* (Κύκλου μέτρησις), consisting of three propositions. 1st. Every circle is equal to a right-angled triangle, of which the sides containing the right angle are equal respectively to its radius and circumference. 2d. The ratio of the area of the circle to the square of its diameter is nearly that of eleven to fourteen. 3d. The circumference of the circle is greater than three times its diameter by a quantity greater than $\frac{10}{71}$ of the diameter, but less than $\frac{1}{7}$ of the same. The last two propositions are established by comparing the circumference of the circle with the perimeters of the inscribed and circumscribed polygons of ninety-six sides. 5. A treatise on *Spirals* (περὶ Ἑλίκων), containing demonstrations of the principal properties of the curve, now known as the Spiral of Archimedes, which is generated by the uniform motion of a point along a straight line, revolving uniformly in one plane about one of its extremities. It appears from the introductory epistle to Dositheus that Archimedes had not been able to put these theorems in a satisfactory form without long-continued and repeated trials; and that Conon, to whom he had sent them as problems along with various others, had died without accomplishing their solution. 6. A treatise on *Obtuse Conoids* and *Spheroids* (περὶ ἀμβλυγωνίων κωνοειδέων καὶ σχημάτων σφαιροειδέων), relating chiefly to the volumes cut off by planes from the solids, so called; those, namely, which are generated by the rotation of the conic sections about their principal axes. Like the work last described, it was the result of laborious and at first unsuccessful attempts.

[1] Compare *Lacroix*, *Diff. Cal.*, vol. i., p. 63 and 431.

7. The *Arenarius* (ὁ Ψαμμίτης) is a short tract, addressed to Gelo, the eldest son of Hiero, in which Archimedes proves that it is possible to assign a greater number than that of the grains of sand, which would fill the sphere of the fixed stars. This singular investigation was suggested by an opinion which some persons had expressed, that the sands on the shores of Sicily were either, or, at least, would exceed any numbers which could be assigned for them; and the success with which the difficulties caused by the awkward and imperfect notation of the ancient Greek arithmetic are eluded, by a device identical in principle with the modern method of logarithms, affords one of the most striking instances of the great mathematician's genius. Having briefly discussed the opinions of Aristarchus upon the constitution and extent of the universe, and described his own method of determining the apparent diameter of the sun, and the magnitude of the pupil of the eye, he is led to assume that the diameter of the sphere of the fixed stars may be taken as not exceeding 100 million of millions of stadia; and that a sphere one δάκτυλος in diameter can not contain more than 640 millions of grains of sand; then, taking the stadium, in round numbers, as not greater than 10,000 δάκτυλοι, he shows that the number of grains in question could not be so great as 1000 myriads multiplied by the eighth term of a geometrical progression, of which the first term was unity, and the common ratio a myriad of myriads; a number which, in our notation, would be expressed by unity with sixty-three ciphers annexed.[1]

8. The treatise on *Floating bodies* (περὶ τῶν Ὀχουμένων), in two books, containing demonstrations of the laws which determine the position of bodies immersed in water, and particularly of segments of spheres and parabolic conoids. These books are extant only in the Latin version of Commandine, with the exception of a fragment, περὶ τῶν ὕδατι ἐφισταμένων, in Mai's collection, vol. i., p. 427. 9. The treatise called *Lemmata*, a collection of fifteen propositions in plane geometry. It is derived from an Arabic MS., and its genuineness has been doubted.

The works of Archimedes are written in Doric Greek, the prevailing dialect in Sicily. The text is, for the most part, in tolerably good preservation; the style is clear, and has been considered better than that of any of the other Greek geometers. The demonstrations are long but rigorous, and Peyrard, in calling Archimedes the Homer of geometry, has made a simile which is perfectly admissible as to the strength of praise it conveys, if in no other point. Eutocius of Ascalon, about A.D. 600, wrote a commentary on the treatises on the *Sphere and Cylinder*, on the *Dimensions of the Circle*, and on *Centres of Gravity*.

There are some Arabic manuscripts which profess to contain writings of Archimedes, and there are said to be lost the following works: Ἀρχαί, Ἐφόδιον, Περὶ Ζυγῶν, Μηχανικά (though it is doubted whether this be not the same with the treatise on *Equiponderants*, &c., already mentioned), Περὶ Σφαιροποιΐας, also a work on the inscription of a heptagon in a circle, and another (very doubtful) on conic sections. Proclus mentions the Σφαιροποιΐα, and says it described an *imitation* of the celestial motions. Archimedes was an observer of the heavens, and his observations of the solstices are mentioned with praise by Ptolemy.

[1] *Donkin, l. c.*

All the extant works of Archimedes, together with the commentary of Eutocius, were brought from Constantinople, in manuscript, on the fall of that city, and were conveyed first into Italy, and then into Germany, by Regiomontanus, who made many emendations. The first edition was printed at Basle, 1544, Greek and Latin, by Hervagius, edited by Gechauff, called Venatorius. The commentaries of Eutocius, Greek and Latin, are also added. After this we have Rivault's edition, Paris, 1615, fol. It is, however, all in Latin, except that the Greek is added to the enunciations throughout, and to the whole of the *Arenarius*. The scholia are often taken from Eutocius, but that commentator is not added complete. The best edition by far, however, is that of Torelli, Oxford, 1793, fol., containing all the extant works of Archimedes, together with the commentaries of Eutocius. The University of Oxford purchased this edition of the executors of Joseph Torelli, of Verona. It was founded upon the Basle edition, except in the case of the *Arenarius*, the text of which is taken from that of Dr. Wallis, who published this treatise and the one on the *Dimension of the Circle*, with a translation and notes, Oxford, 1679. They are reprinted in vol. iii. of his works. A French translation of the works of Archimedes, with notes, was published by Peyrard, Paris, 1807, 4to, and 1808, 2 vols 8vo. There is also a German version, with critical and explanatory notes, by Nizze, Stralsund, 1824, 8vo.

III. Apollonius (Ἀπολλώνιος),[1] surnamed *Pergæus*, from Perga, in Pamphylia, his native city, a celebrated mathematician, educated at Alexandrea, under the successors of Euclid. He was born in the reign of Ptolemy Euergetes,[2] and died under Philopator, who reigned B.C. 222–205.[3] He was, therefore, probably about forty years younger than Archimedes. Eutocius, his commentator, states that while living he was called "the great geometer,"[4] on account of his discoveries in conic sections. This title belongs rather to Archimedes; but Apollonius lived in Alexandrea, the geometrical capital, and Archimedes in Sicily, the "*Ultima Thule*" of all science. Nothing more is known of his life. Apollonius is also mentioned by Ptolemy as an astronomer, and he is said to have been called by the sobriquet of ε (*epsilon*), from his fondness for observing the moon, the shape of which was supposed to resemble that letter. Ptolemy has preserved his theorems on the stationary points of the planets, and we must suppose that he was the first who solved the problem of finding the stationary points, and the arc of retrogradation, on the epicyclic hypothesis, which, though it now bears the name of Ptolemy, had been struck out by Hipparchus.

Apollonius's most important work, the only considerable one which has come down to our time, was a treatise on conic sections, in eight books. Of these the first four, with the commentary of Eutocius, are extant in Greek, and all but the eighth in Arabic. The eighth book seems to have been lost before the date of the Arabic versions. We have, also, introductory lemmas to all the eight by Pappus. The first four books probably contain little more than the substance of what former geometers had done; they treat of the definitions and elementary properties of the conic sections, of their diameters, tangents, asymptotes, mutual intersections, and so forth. But Apollonius seems to lay claim to originality in most of what follows. The fifth treats of the longest and shortest right lines (in other words, the *normals*) which can be drawn from a given point to the curve. The sixth of the equality and similarity of conic sections;

[1] *Donkin; Smith, Dict. Biogr., s. v.*
[2] *Eutocius, Comm. in Ap. Con.*, lib. i.
[3] *Hephæst. ap. Phot.*, Cod. cxc.
[4] *Eutoc., l. c.*

and the seventh relates chiefly to their diameters, and rectilinear figures described upon them.[1]

We learn from Eutocius[2] that Heraclius, in his life of Archimedes, accused Apollonius of having appropriated to himself in this work the unpublished discoveries of that great mathematician. However this may have been, there is truth in the reply quoted by the same author from Geminus, that neither Archimedes nor Apollonius pretended to have invented this branch of geometry, but that Apollonius had introduced a real improvement into it. For whereas Archimedes, according to the ancient method, considered only the section of a *right* cone by a plane perpendicular to its side, so that the species of the curve depended upon the angle of the cone; Apollonius took a more general view, conceiving the curve to be produced by the intersection of *any* plane with a cone generated by a right line passing always through the circumference of a fixed circle and *any* fixed point.

Apollonius was the author of several other works. The following are described by Pappus, in the seventh book of his "Mathematical Collections."

1. Περὶ λόγου ἀποτομῆς, and περὶ χωρίου ἀποτομῆς, in which it was shown how to draw a line through a given point so as to cut segments from two given lines: 1st, in a given ratio; 2d, containing a given rectangle. Of the first of these an Arabic version is still extant, of which a translation was edited by Halley, with a conjectural restoration of the second, Oxford, 1706. 2. Περὶ διωρισμένης τομῆς. To find a point in a given straight line such that the rectangle of its distances from two given points in the same should fulfill certain conditions. A solution of this problem was published by Robert Simson. 3. Περὶ τόπων ἐπιπέδων. "A treatise in two books on Plane *Loci*. Restored by Robert Simson," Glasgow, 1749. 4. Περὶ ἐπαφῶν, *De Tactionibus*, in which it was proposed to draw a circle fulfilling any three of the conditions of passing through one or more of three given points, and touching one or more of three given circles and three given straight lines. Or, which is the same thing, to draw a circle touching three given circles whose radii may have any magnitude, including zero and infinity. There is an edition of the remains of this work by Camerer, *Apollonii de Tactionibus quæ supersunt*, Gotha and Amst., 1795, 8vo. 5. Περὶ νεύσεων, *De Inclinationibus*. To draw through a given point a right line so that a given portion of it should be intercepted between two given right lines. Restored by Horsley, Oxford, 1770. Proclus, in his commentary on Euclid, mentions two treatises, *De Cochlea* and *De Perturbatis Rationibus*. Eutocius, in his commentary on the *Dimensio Circuli* of Archimedes, mentions an arithmetical work called Ὠκυτόβοον (see Wallis, *Op.*, vol. iii., p. 559), which is supposed to be referred to in a fragment of the second book of Pappus, edited by Wallis.[3] This word has puzzled the commentators. Apollonius, in the work in question, extended the quadrature of the circle given by Archimedes.

Up to the middle of the seventeenth century nothing of Apollonius was known except-

[1] *Donkin, l. c.* [2] *Comm.*, in lib. i. [3] *Op.*, vol. iii., p. 597.

ing the first four books of the Conic Sections, which had come down in Greek, with the commentary of Eutocius in the same language. Of these, one Latin translation had appeared at Venice in 1537, by J. B. Memus; another, by Commandine, at Bologna, in 1566; and a third, of little note, by the Jesuit Claude Richard, at Antwerp, in 1655. Translations had been made into Arabic, which were to be found in European libraries, but had not been looked for. About the middle of that century, James Golius, professor of Oriental languages at Leyden, returned from the East with abundance of Oriental manuscripts, and, among others, with seven books of the Conic Sections. But it so happened that, in 1658, before Golius had published any thing, Alfonso Borelli found, among the manuscripts which had been removed by purchase from the Medicean library to that of Florence, an Arabic writing with the Latin title "*Apollonii Pergæi Conicorum Libri Octo.*" This manuscript, which professed to be a translation by Abalphat of Ispahan, on being examined, by the assistance of some Maronites then at Florence, turned out to agree with the Greek in the four books which were common to both, and was accordingly acknowledged as a genuine translation. But it only contained seven books, and a note on the manuscript which Golius brought to Europe stated that no Arabian translator had ever found more than seven books. But (according to Golius, as cited by Mersenne) Aben Eddin, a learned bibliographer, states that he had seen a part of the eighth book in Arabic, and also that he had seen, in the same language, all the works of Apollonius mentioned by Pappus, and more. The Maronites above mentioned recommended that the translation should be intrusted to Abraham Ecchellensis (so his name, whatever it was, had been Latinized), another Maronite then at Rome, and a distinguished teacher of Oriental languages. Accordingly, Borelli and Ecchellensis completed the translation of the fifth, sixth, and seventh books, and published it at Florence in 1661. Ravius also published a translation of the same, from the Arabic of one Abdu-l-malek, at Kiel (Kilonium), in 1669. This translation Halley terms barbarous.[1]

But the best edition of Apollonius, and the only one which contains the Greek as far as it goes, is the folio published at Oxford in 1710, by Halley. Gregory, who began it, died before much progress had been made. Halley had previously, as we have before stated, published at Oxford, in 1706, 8vo, from the Arabic, the treatise περὶ λόγου ἀποτομῆς. The edition of 1710 contains the four books and the commentary of Eutocius, in Greek and Latin; the fifth, sixth, and seventh books, in Halley's translation from the Arabic; and Halley's attempt at a restitution of the eighth book from the preliminary lemmas given by Pappus. It also contains the two books of Serenus on the cone and cylinder. Some of the editions, or attempted restorations of individual works, have already been mentioned.[2]

II. ASTRONOMERS.

I. Conon (Κόνων),[3] a native of Samos, a mathematician and astronomer, lived in the time of the Ptolemies, Philadelphus and Euergetes (B.C. 285–222), and was the friend and probably the teacher of Archimedes, who survived him. None of his works are preserved. His observations are referred to by Ptolemy, in his φάσεις ἀπλανῶν, and in the historical notice appended to that work they are said to have been made in Italy,[4] in which country he seems to have been celebrated.[5] According to Seneca,[6] he made a collection of the observations of solar eclipses preserved by the Egyptians. Apollonius Pergæus mentions his attempt to demonstrate some propositions concerning the number of points in which two conic sections can cut one another. Conon is said to have given its name to the constellation called *Coma Berenices*, on the authority of an ode of Callimachus, translated by Catullus, a fragment of the original of which is preserved by Theon in his scholia on Aratus. It is doubtful,

---

[1] *Dict. Biog.*, *Soc. D. U. K.*, vol. iii., p. 174.
[2] *Ibid.*
[3] *Donkin; Smith, Dict. Biogr.*, *s. v.*
[4] *Petav.*, *Uranolog.*, p. 93.
[5] Compare *Virg.*, *Eclog.*, iii., 40.
[6] *Nat. Quæst.*, vii., 3.

however, whether this constellation was really adopted by the Alexandrean astronomers.

II. ARISTARCHUS (Ἀρίσταρχος),[1] of Samos, a distinguished astronomer of the Alexandrean school. We know little of his history except that he was living between B.C. 280 and 264. His name is preserved by one remaining work, containing one true method, and by a report that he maintained the motion of the earth. The work in question, on which Pappus has left a commentary, is entitled περὶ μεγεθῶν καὶ ἀποστημάτων ἡλίου καὶ σελήνης, "On the Magnitudes and Distances of the Sun and Moon." The method proves that Aristarchus had a correct idea of the cause of the moon's phases. When the moon appears exactly halved, the line joining the eye and the moon's centre is at right angles to that joining the centres of the sun and moon. In the triangle E M S, then (E being the spectator's eye, M the moon's centre, and S the sun's centre), the angle E M S is a right angle, and the angle M E S is that known by the name of the elongation of the moon from the sun, and can be measured at any time when both luminaries are above the horizon. Hence, two angles of the triangle being known, the triangle can be constructed in species, and the ratio of the distances of the sun and moon from the eye can be found.[2]

Vitruvius makes Aristarchus the inventor of the *scaphe* (σκάφη), a dial, in which the style throws its shadow on a hemisphere whose centre is the top of the style; and also of another which he calls "*discus in planitia.*" Censorinus attributes to Aristarchus the invention of the "*annus magnus,*" a period of two thousand four hundred and eighty-four years.

In the application of his excellent idea on the distances of the sun and moon, Aristarchus was not very fortunate, as his means of measurement did not enable him to get the elongation correctly. Accordingly, he makes the sun's distance only about twenty times that of the moon, instead of about four hundred times, as it should be. His result, even on his own data, is not so accurate as it might have been made from a ruler and compasses; and he appears to have had no idea whatever of any trigonometrical table or process. His notions on the apparent diameters of the luminaries are very inaccurate, as given in his own work, though Archimedes attributes to him much more exact values than his own.

It has been the common opinion, at least in modern times, that Aristarchus agreed with Philolaus and other philosophers of the Pythagorean school in considering the sun to be fixed, and attributing a motion to the earth. It is probable, however, that Aristarchus adopted this opinion rather as an *hypothesis* for particular purposes than as a statement of the actual system of the universe. In fact, Plutarch, in another place, expressly says that Aristarchus taught it only hypothetically. It appears from a passage in the *Arenarius* that Aristarchus had much juster views than his predecessors concerning the extent of the universe. He maintained, namely, that the sphere of the fixed stars was so large that it bore to the orbit of the earth the relation of a sphere to its centre. What he meant by the expression is not clear: it may be interpreted as an antici-

[1] *Donkin; Smith, Dict. Biogr., s. v.* [2] *Dict. Biog., Soc. D. U. K.*, vol. iii., p. 409.

pation of modern discoveries, but in this sense it could express only a conjecture, which the observations of the age were not accurate enough either to confirm or refute, a remark which is equally applicable to the theory of the earth's motion. Whatever may be the truth on these points, it is probable that even the opinion, that the sun was nearly twenty times as distant as the moon, indicates a great step in advance of the popular doctrines.[1]

The editions of Aristarchus are, 1. In Latin, by Geo. Valla, Venice, 1498, fol., in a volume containing the "Logica" of Nicephorus, and other matters. 2. In Latin, by Commandine, with the commentary of Pappus, Pesaro, 1572. 3. In Greek and Latin, with the commentary of Pappus, by Wallis, Oxford, 1688, reprinted in the third volume of his works, Oxford, 1699. There is a French translation of Aristarchus "On the Magnitude and Distances of the Sun and Moon," by Fortia d'Urban, Paris, 1823, 8vo. This translation had previously appeared at Paris in 1810, with the Greek text, which is described as, together with the scholia, having been amended by the aid of some MSS. This work is entitled "*Histoire d'Aristarque de Samos, suivie de la traduction de son ouvrage sur les distances du Soleil de la Lune*," &c.[2]

III. Eratosthenes.[3] We have already spoken of this individual as a geographer, philosopher, historian, and grammarian; we will now consider him as a geometer and astronomer. It is supposed that Eratosthenes suggested to Ptolemy Euergetes the construction of the large *armillæ*. or fixed circular instruments, which were long in use in Alexandrea, but only because it is difficult to imagine to whom else they are to be assigned; for Ptolemy (the astronomer), though he mentions them, and incidentally their antiquity, does not state to whom they were due. In these circles each degree was divided into six parts. We know of no observations of Eratosthenes in which they were probably employed, except those which led him to the obliquity of the ecliptic, which he must have made to be 23° 51′ 20″; for he states the distance of the tropics to be eleven times the eighty-third part of the circumference. This was a good observation for the time: Ptolemy (the astronomer) was content with it, and, according to him, Hipparchus used no other. According to Nicomachus, he was the inventor of the *κόσκινον*, or *Cribrum Arithmeticum*, as it has since been called, being the well-known method of detecting the prime numbers, by writing down all odd numbers which do not end with 5, and striking out successively the multiples of each, one after the other, so that only prime numbers remain.

We still possess, under the name of Eratosthenes, a work entitled Καταστερισμοί, giving a slight account of the constellations, their fabulous history, and the stars composing them. It is, however, acknowledged on all hands that this is not a work of Eratosthenes. It has been shown by Bernhardy[4] to be a miserable compilation made by some Greek grammarian from the *Poëticon Astronomicon* of Hyginus. There is, besides this, a letter of Eratosthenes to Ptolemy on the duplication of the cube, for the mechanical performance of which he had contrived an instrument, of which he seems to contemplate actual use in measuring the contents of vessels. He seems to say that he has had his method engraved in

[1] *Donkin, l. c.*

[2] *Biog. Dict., Soc. D. U. K., l. c.*

[3] *De Morgan; Smith, Dict. Biogr., s. v.*

[4] *Eratosthenica*, p. 110, *seqq.*

some temple or public building, with some verses which he adds. Eutocius has preserved this letter in his comment on book ii., prop. 2, of the Sphere and Cylinder of Archimedes.

The greatest work, however, of Eratosthenes, and that which must always make his name conspicuous in scientific history, is the attempt which he made to measure the magnitude of the earth, in which he brought forward and used the method which is employed to this day. Whether or no he was successful can not be told, as we shall see; but it is not the less true that he was the originator of the process by which we now know, very nearly indeed, the magnitude of our own planet. At Syene, in Upper Egypt, which is supposed to be the same as, or near to the town of *Assouan* (lat. 24° 10′ N., long. 32° 59′ E. of Greenwich), Eratosthenes was told (that he observed is very doubtful) that deep wells were enlightened to the bottom on the day of the summer solstice, and that vertical objects cast no shadows. He concluded, therefore, that Syene was on the tropic, and its latitude equal to the obliquity of the ecliptic, which, as we have seen, he had determined: he presumed that it was in the same longitude as Alexandrea, in which he was out about three degrees, which, however, is not enough to produce what would at that time have been a sensible error. By observations made at Alexandrea, he determined the zenith of that place to be distant by the fiftieth part of the circumference from the solstice, which was equivalent to saying that the arc of the meridian between the two places is 7° 12′. The result of his computations is 250,000 stadia for the circumference of the earth, which he altered into 252,000, that his result might give an exact number of stadia for the degree, namely, 700; this, of course, should have been $694\frac{4}{9}$. Pliny calls this 31,500 Roman miles, and therefore supposes the stadium to be the eighth part of a Roman mile, or takes for granted that Eratosthenes used the Olympic stadium. It is likely enough that the Ptolemies naturalized this stadium in Egypt; but, nevertheless, it is not unlikely that an Egyptian stadium was employed. If we assume the Olympic stadium ($202\frac{1}{4}$ yards), the degree of Eratosthenes is more than seventy-nine miles, upward of ten miles too great.[1]

According to Plutarch, Eratosthenes made the sun to be 804 millions of stadia from the earth, and the moon 780,000; according to Macrobius, he made the diameter of the sun to be twenty-seven times that of the earth.

We have already spoken of Bernhardy's edition of the fragments of Eratosthenes. The Καταστερισμοί have been often printed separately; in Dr. Fell's, or the Oxford, edition of Aratus, 1762, 8vo; by Gale, in the *Opuscula Physica et Ethica*, Amsterdam, 1688, 8vo; by Schaubach, with notes by Heyne, Göttingen, 1795, 8vo; by Matthiæ, in his Aratus, Frankfort, 1817, 8vo; and more recently by Westermann, in his *Scriptores Historiæ poeticæ Græci*, p. 239, *seqq.*

IV. Hipparchus (Ἵππαρχος),[2] a celebrated Greek astronomer, was a native of Nicæa, in Bithynia, and flourished B.C. 160–145. He resided both at Rhodes and Alexandrea. He raised astronomy to that rank among the applications of arithmetic and geometry which it has always

[1] *Donkin, l. c.*

[2] *De Morgan; Smith, Dict. Biogr., s. v.*

since preserved. He was the first who gave and demonstrated the means of solving all triangles, rectilinear and spherical. He constructed a table of chords, of which he made the same sort of use as we make of our sines. He made more observations than his predecessors, and understood them better. He invented the planisphere, or the mode of representing the starry heavens upon a plane, and of producing the solutions of problems of spherical astronomy. He is also the father of true geography, by his happy idea of marking the position of spots on the earth, as was done with the stars, by circles drawn from the pole perpendicularly to the equator; that is, by latitudes and longitudes. His method of eclipses was the only one by which differences of meridians could be determined. The catalogue which Hipparchus constructed of the stars is preserved in the Almagest of Ptolemy. Hipparchus wrote numerous works, which are all lost, with the exception of his commentary on the *Phænomena* of Aratus. This work has always been received as the undoubted work of Hipparchus, though, beyond all question, it must have been written before any of his great discoveries had been made. The comparison of Eudoxus and Aratus, which runs throughout this work, constitutes the best knowledge we have of the former. This work has been twice published, once by P. Victor, Florence, 1567, fol., and again by Petavius, in his *Uranologion*, Paris, 1630, fol.[1]

III. MECHANICIANS.

I. CTESIBIUS (Κτησίβιος),[2] celebrated for his mechanical inventions, was born at Alexandrea, and lived probably about B.C. 250, in the reigns of Ptolemy Philadelphus and Euergetes, though Athenæus[3] says that he flourished in the time of the second Euergetes. His father was a barber, but his own taste led him to devote himself to mechanics. He is said to have invented a *clepsydra*, or water-clock, a hydraulic organ (ὕδραυλις), and other machines, and to have been the first to discover the elastic force of air and apply it as a moving power. Vitruvius mentions him as an author, but none of his works remain.

II. HERON (Ἥρων),[4] of Alexandrea, was a pupil of Ctesibius, and lived in the reigns of the Ptolemies, Philadelphus and Euergetes, B.C. 285–222. Of his life nothing is known; on his mechanical inventions we have but some scattered parts of his own writings, and some scattered notices. The common pneumatic experiment called *Hero's Fountain*, in which a jet of water is maintained by condensed air, has given a certain popular celebrity to his name. This has been increased by the discovery in his writings of a *steam-engine*, that is, of an engine in which motion is produced by steam, and which must always be a part of the history of that agent. This engine acts precisely on the principle of what is called *Barker's Mill:* a boiler with arms having lateral orifices is capable of revolving around a vertical axis; the steam issues from the lateral orifices, and the uncompensated pressure upon the parts opposite to the orifices turns the boiler in the direction opposite to that of the issue of the steam.

1 *De Morgan, l. c.*

2 *Donkin; Smith, Dict. Biogr., s. v.*

3 *Athen.*, iv., p. 174.

4 *De Morgan; Smith, Dict. Biogr., s. v.*

Heron's engine is described in his Pneumatics, presently mentioned; as also a double forcing-pump used for a fire-engine, and various other applications of the elasticity of air and steam. It is, however, but recently that the remarkable claims of Heron to success in such investigations have received any marked notice. In the "*Origine des Découvertes attribuées aux Modernes*" (third edition, 1796), by M. Dutens, who tries with great learning to make the best possible case for the ancients, the name of Heron is not even mentioned.

The remaining works, or, rather, fragments of Heron, of Alexandrea, are as follows: 1. Χειροβαλλίστρας κατασκευὴ καὶ συμμετρία, *De constructione et mensura Manubalistæ.* First published in Greek, by Baldi, at the end of the third work, presently noted. Also (Greek and Latin) by Thevenot, Boivin, and Lahire, in the "*Veterum Mathematicorum, Athenæi, Apollodori, Philonis, Heronis, et aliorum opera,*" Paris, 1693, fol. 2. "*Barulcus, sive de Oneribus trahendis Libri tres,*" a treatise brought by J. Golius from the East in Arabic, not yet translated or published.[1] 3. Βελοποιϊκά, or Βελοποιητικά, on the manufacture of darts. Edited by Bernardino Baldi (Greek and Latin), with notes and a life of Heron, Augsburg, 1616, 4to, also in the *Veter. Mathemat.*, &c., above mentioned. 4. Πνευματικά, or *Spiritalia*, the most celebrated of his works. Edited by Commandine (Latin), with notes, Urbino, 1575, 4to, Amsterdam, 1680, 4to, and Paris, 1683, 4to. It is also (Greek and Latin) in the *Veter. Mathemat.*, &c., already mentioned. It first appeared, however, in an Italian translation by Bernardo Aleotti, Bologna, 1547, 4to, Ferrara, 1589, 4to; and there is also an Italian translation by Alessandro Giorgi, of Urbino, 1592, 4to; and by J. B. Porta, Naples, 1605, 4to. There is a German translation by Agathus Cario, with an appendix by Solomon de Caus, Bamberg, 1687, 4to, Frankfort, 1688, 4to. 5. Περὶ αὐτοματοποιητικῶν, *De Automatorum fabrica, libri duo.* Translated into Italian by B. Baldi, Venice, 1589, 1601, 1661, 4to, also (Greek and Latin) in the *Veter. Mathemat.*, &c. 6. A fragment on Dioptrics (Greek) exists in MS., and two Latin fragments on military machines are given by Baldi at the end of the work on darts. The following lost works are mentioned: Τὰ περὶ ὑδροσκοπειῶν, by Proclus, Pappus, and Heron himself; Περὶ μετρικῶν, by Eutocius; Περι τροχιωδιῶν, by Pappus; and a work, Περὶ Ζυγίων, mentioned by Pappus, and supposed to be by Heron.

III. Athenæus (Ἀθήναιος), a contemporary of Archimedes, and the author of an extant work, Περὶ Μηχανημάτων, "On warlike Engines," addressed to Marcellus (probably the conqueror of Syracuse). He is perhaps the same with Athenæus of Cyzicus, mentioned by Proclus[2] as a distinguished mathematician. The work is printed in Thevenot's *Mathematici Veteres*, Paris, 1693.

IV. Biton (Βίτων),[3] the author of a work called Κατασκευαὶ πολεμικῶν ὀργάνων καὶ καταπελτικῶν, on military machines. His history and place of birth are unknown. He is mentioned by Hesychius, by Heron the younger[4] (who is supposed to have lived under Heraclius, A.D. 610–641), and perhaps by Ælian,[5] under the name of Βίων. The treatise consists of descriptions: 1. Of a πετρόβολον, or machine for throwing stones, made at Rhodes by Charon the Magnesian. 2. Of another at Thessalonica, by Isidorus the Abydenian. 3. Of a ἑλέπολις, an apparatus used for besieging cities, made by Posidonius of Macedon for Alexander the Great. 4. Of a *Sambuca*, made by Damius of Colophon. 5. Of a γαστραφέτης (an engine somewhat resembling a cross-bow, and so named from the way in which it was held in order to stretch the string), made by Zopyrus of Tarentum at Miletus, and another, by the same, at Cumæ, in Italy. The

[1] *Ephem. Litt. Götting. ann.* 1785, p. 625, *seqq.* [2] *In Euclid.*, p. 19. [3] *Donkin; Smith, Dict. Biogr.*, *s. v.* [4] *De Mach. Bell., proœm.* [5] *Tact.*, c. i.

Greek text, with a Latin version, is printed in the collection of ancient mathematicians by Thevenot, already mentioned, Paris, 1693, fol., p. 105, *seqq.* Biton mentions a work of his own on *Optics*, which is lost.

V. PHILO (Φίλων), of Byzantium,[1] a celebrated mechanician, and a contemporary of Ctesibius, flourished about B.C. 146. He wrote a work on military engineering, of which the fourth and fifth books have come down to us, and are printed in Thevenot's Collection of the Ancient Mathematicians, Paris, 1693, fol. The fourth book is headed Ἐκ τῶν Φίλωνος Βελοποιϊκῶν, and the general subject is the manufacture of missiles. In the fifth book we are shocked to find, that while recommending a besieging army to devastate the open country on the approach of an enemy, he advises them to poison the springs and the grain which they can not dispose of (p. 103); and, what renders this the worse, he mentions his having treated of poisons in his book on the preparations that should be made for war. What principally attracted attention to this work in modern times is his notice of the invention of Ctesibius (p. 77, *seqq.*). The instrument described by him, named ἀερότονος, acted on the property of air when condensed, and is evidently, in principle, the same with the modern air-gun. According to Montucla, Philo was well skilled in geometry, and his solution of the problem of the two mean proportionals, although the same in principle with that of Apollonius, has its peculiar merits in practice. We learn from Pappus that he wrote a treatise on mechanics, the object of which was nearly the same as Heron's.

To Philo of Byzantium is attributed another work, Περὶ τῶν ἑπτὰ θεαμάτων, "*On the Seven Wonders of the World.*" But Fabricius thinks it impossible that an eminent mathematician like Philo of Byzantium could have written this work, and conjectures that it was written by Philo of Heraclea. It is more probable, however, that it is the production of a later rhetorical writer, who gave it the name of Philo of Byzantium, as that of a man who, from his life and writings, might be supposed to have chosen it as a subject for composition. The wonders treated of are the *Hanging Gardens*, the *Pyramids*, the *Statue of Jupiter Olympius*, the *Walls of Babylon*, the *Colossus of Rhodes*, the *Temple of Diana at Ephesus*, and, we may presume from the prooemium, the *Mausoleum;* but the last is entirely wanting, and we have only a fragment of the description of the Ephesian temple. The style, though not wholly devoid of elegance, is florid and rhetorical.[2]

This last-mentioned work exists only in one MS., which, originally in the Vatican, was in 1816 in Paris, No. 389. It was first edited by Allatius, Rome, 1640, with a loose Latin translation, and desultory, though learned notes. It was re-edited from the same MS. by *Dionysius Salvagnius Boessius*, ambassador from the French court to the pope, and included in his *Miscella*, printed at Leyden, 1661. This edition has a more correct translation than that of Allatius, but abounds in typographical errors, there being no fewer than 150 in fourteen pages. Gronovius reprinted the edition of Allatius in his *Thesaurus Antiquitatum Græcarum* (vol. vii., p. 2645, *seqq.*). It was finally reprinted at Leipzig, 1816, edited by J. C. Orelli. This edition, which is undoubtedly the best, contains the Greek, with the translations of both Allatius and Boessius (with the exception of a fragment of a mutilated chapter, reprinted from the translation of L. Holstein, which originally appeared in Gronovius, vol. vii., p. 389), the notes of Allatius and others,

[1] *Smith, Dict. Biogr.*, *s. v.*

[2] *Id. ib.*

along with some passages from other writers, who had treated of the same or similar subjects, the fragments of the sophist Callinicus and Adrian the Tyrian, and an *Index Græcitatis*.

CHAPTER XLV.

FIFTH OR ALEXANDRINE PERIOD—*continued.*

MEDICAL SCIENCE.

I. The two most important medical sects during the period under review were the *Dogmatici* and *Empirici*. The former of these had been founded as early as B.C. 400, by Thessalus, the son, and Polybus, the son-in-law of Hippocrates, and were so called because they went by general principles. The school of the *Dogmatici* retained its influence until the rise of the *Empirici*, a sect founded by Philinus of Cos and Serapion of Alexandrea, in the third century B.C., and so called because they professed to derive their knowledge from experience (ἐμπειρία) only; after which time every member of the medical profession, during a long period, ranged himself in one of these two sects.

II. In the first century B.C., Themison founded the sect of the *Methodici*, who held doctrines nearly intermediate between those of the two sects already mentioned. About two centuries later, the *Methodici* were divided into numerous sects, as the doctrines of particular physicians became more generally received. The chief of these sects were the *Pneumatici* and the *Eclectici;* the former founded by Athenæus about the middle or end of the first century A.D.; the latter about the same time, either by Agathinus of Sparta, or his pupil Archigenes.

III. We will now proceed to notice some of the most prominent members of the two sects of the *Dogmatici* and *Empirici*.

DOGMATICI.

I. Diocles *of Carystus* (Διοκλῆς ὁ Καρύστιος),[1] a very celebrated Greek physician, was born at Carystus, in Eubœa, and lived in the fourth century B.C., not long after the time of Hippocrates, to whom Pliny says he was next in age and fame.[2] He wrote several medical works, of which only the titles and some fragments remain, preserved by Galen, Cælius Aurelianus, Oribasius, and other ancient writers. The longest of these is a letter to King Antigonus, entitled Ἐπιστολὴ Προφυλακτική, "A Letter on preserving Health," which is inserted by Paulus Ægineta at the end of the first book of his medical work, and which, if genuine, was probably addressed to Antigonus Gonatas, king of Macedonia, who died B.C. 239, at the age of eighty, after a reign of forty-four years. It resembles in its subject-matter several other similar letters, ascribed to Hippocrates, and treats of the diet fitted for the different seasons of the year. It is published in the various editions of Paulus Ægineta, and also in several other works, as, for example, in Greek, in Matthaei's edition of Rufus Ephesius, Moscow, 1806, 8vo; in Greek and Latin, in the twelfth volume of

---

1 *Greenhill; Smith, Dict. Biogr., s. v.*

2 *Plin., H. N.*, xxvi., 6.

the old edition of Fabricius's *Bibliotheca Græca;* and in Mich. Neander's *Syllogæ Physicæ*, Leipzig, 1591, 8vo; and in Latin with Alexander Trallianus, Basle, 1541, fol.; and Meletius, Venice, 1522, 4to, &c. Some persons have attributed to Diocles the honor of first explaining the difference between the veins and arteries; but this does not seem to be correct, nor is any great discovery connected with his name. Further information respecting him may be found in Fabricius, *Biblioth. Græc.*, vol. xii., p. 584, of the old edition; and in Kühn, *Opuscula Academica, Med. et Philolog.*, Leipzig, 1827, vol. ii., p. 87.

II. Praxagŏras (Πραξαγόρας),[1] of Cos, a celebrated physician, who lived in the fourth century B.C. He belonged to the order of the Asclepiadæ,[2] and was celebrated for his knowledge of medical science in general, and especially for his attainments in anatomy and physiology. He was one of the chief defenders of the humoral pathology, placing the seat of all diseases in the humors of the body.[3] Many of his anatomical opinions have been preserved, which show that he was in advance of his contemporaries in this branch of medical knowledge. On the other hand, several curious and capital errors have been attributed to him, as, for instance, that the heart was the source of the nerves (an opinion which he held with Aristotle), and that the ramifications of the artery which he saw issue from the heart were ultimately converted into nerves as they contracted in diameter. Some parts of his medical practice appear to have been very bold, as, for instance, his venturing, in cases of ileus, when attended with introsusception, to open the abdomen in order to replace the intestine.[4] He wrote several medical works, of which only the titles and some fragments remain, preserved by Galen, Cælius Aurelius, and other writers.

III. Herophilus (Ἡρόφιλος),[5] one of the most celebrated physicians of antiquity, who is best known on account of his skill in anatomy and physiology, but of whose personal history few details have been preserved. He was a native of Chalcedon,[6] and lived at Alexandrea under the first Ptolemy, who reigned B.C. 323–285. Here he soon acquired a great reputation, and was one of the early founders of the medical school in that city, which afterward eclipsed in celebrity all the others, so much so, that, in the fourth century after Christ, the very fact of a physician having studied at Alexandrea was considered to be a sufficient guarantee of his ability.[7] He seems to have given his chief attention to anatomy, which he studied not merely from the dissection of animals, but also from that of human bodies, as is expressly asserted by Galen. He is even said to have carried his ardor in his anatomical pursuits so far as to have dissected criminals alive—a well-known accusation, which it seems difficult entirely to disbelieve, though most of his biographers have tried to explain it away, or to throw discredit on it. He was the author of several medical and anatomical works, of which nothing but the titles and a few fragments

[1] *Greenhill; Smith, Dict. Biogr., s. v.*
[2] *Galen, De Meth. Med.*, i., 3.
[3] *Id., Introd.*, c. 9, p. 699.
[4] *Cæl. Aurel., De Morb. Acut.*, iii., 17, p. 244.
[5] *Greenhill; Smith, Dict. Biogr., s. v.*
[6] *Galen., Introd.*, vol. xiv., p. 683, ed. *Kühn.*
[7] *Amm. Marcell.*, xxii., 16.

remain. These have been collected by Marx, and published in a dissertation entitled "*De Herophili Celeberrimi Medici Vita, Scriptis, atque in Medicina Meritis*," Göttingen, 1840, 4to. Several of the names which he gave to different parts of the human frame still remain in common use, under a Latin form, to this day; as the "*Torcular Herophili*," the "*Calamus Scriptorius*," and the "*Duodenum*." He is the first person who is known to have commented on any of the works of Hippocrates.[1] He was also the founder of a medical school which produced several eminent physicians. Of the physicians who belonged to this school, perhaps the following were the most celebrated: Andreas, Apollonius Mus, Aristoxenus, Baccheius, Callianax, Callimachus, Demetrius, Dioscorides Phacas, and others.

IV. Erasistrătus (Ἐρασίστρατος),[2] one of the most celebrated physicians and anatomists of antiquity, is generally supposed to have been born at Iulis, in the island of Ceos.[3] He was a pupil of Chrysippus of Cnidos, of Metrodorus, and apparently of Theophrastus. Erasistratus flourished from B.C. 300 to B.C. 260. He lived for some time at the court of Seleucus Nicator, king of Syria, where he acquired great reputation by discovering the cause of the malady of Antiochus, the king's eldest son, namely, his love for his mother-in-law, the young and beautiful daughter of Demetrius Poliorcetes, whom Seleucus had lately married.[4] Erasistratus is said to have received 100 talents for being the means of restoring the young prince to health, which (supposing the Attic standard to be meant, and the talent to be equal to £243 15*s*.) would amount to £24,375, one of the largest medical fees on record. Erasistratus afterward lived at Alexandrea, then beginning to be a celebrated medical school, and gave up practice in his old age that he might pursue his anatomical studies without interruption.[5] He prosecuted his experiments and researches in this branch of medical science with great success, and with such ardor that he is said to have dissected criminals alive.[6] He appears to have died in Asia Minor, as Suidas mentions that he was buried near Mount Mycale, in Ionia. The exact date of his death is not known, but he probably lived to a good old age, as, according to Eusebius, he was alive B.C. 258. He had numerous pupils and followers, and a medical school bearing his name continued to exist at Smyrna, in Ionia, nearly till the time of Strabo, about the beginning of the Christian era. He wrote several works on anatomy, practical medicine, and pharmacy, of which only the titles remain, together with a great number of short fragments, preserved by Galen, Cælius Aurelianus, and others. These, however, are sufficient to enable us to form a tolerably correct idea of his opinions both as a physician and anatomist. It is in this latter character that he is most celebrated, and perhaps there is no one of the ancient physicians who did more to promote that branch of medical science. He appears, from a passage preserved by Galen, to have been very near

1 *Littré, Œuvres d'Hippocrate*, vol. i., p. 83.

2 *Greenhill; Smith, Dict. Biogr.*, *s. v.*

3 *Suid.*, *s. v.*; *Strab.*, x., 5.

4 *Appian, De Rebus Syr.*, c. 59, *seqq.*; *Galen, De Prænot. ad Epig.*, c. 6.

5 *Galen, De Hippocr. et Plat. Decr.*, vii., 3.

6 *Cels., De Medic.*, i., præf., p. 6.

the discovery of the circulation of the blood. Of his mode of cure, the most remarkable peculiarity was his aversion to blood-letting and purgative medicines: he seems to have relied chiefly on diet and regimen, bathing, exercise, friction, and the most simple articles of the vegetable kingdom. In surgery he was celebrated for the invention of a catheter that bore his name, and was of the shape of a Roman S.[1]

II. EMPIRICI.

I. PHILĪNUS (Φιλῖνος), of Cos, was the reputed founder of the Empiric sect of physicians.[2] He was a pupil of Herophilus, and probably lived in the third century B.C. He wrote a work on part of the Hippocratic collection directed against Bacchius, and also one on botany, neither of which is now extant. A parallel has been drawn between Philinus and the late Dr. Hahnemann, in a dissertation by Brisken, entitled "*Philinus et Hahnemannus, seu veteris sectæ Empiricæ cum hodierna secta Homœopathica comparatio,*" Berlin, 1834, 8vo.

II. SERAPION (Σεραπίων),[3] a physician of Alexandrea, who lived in the third century B.C. He so much extended and improved the system of Philinus, that the invention of it is by some authors attributed to him. Serapion wrote against Hippocrates with much vehemence, but neither this nor any one of his other works is now extant. He is several times mentioned and quoted by Celsus, Paulus Ægineta, and Nicolaus Myrepsus, who have preserved some of his medical formulæ, which are not, however, of much value. This Serapion must not be confounded with either of the two later Arabic physicians of the same name.

III. HERACLĪDES (Ἡρακλείδης), of Tarentum, lived probably in the third or second century B.C. He belonged to the sect of the Empirici, and wrote some works on Materia Medica which are very frequently quoted by Galen, but of which only a few fragments remain. Galen speaks of him in high terms of praise, saying that he was an author who could be entirely depended upon, as he wrote in his works only what he had himself found from his own experience to be correct.[4] He was also one of the first persons who wrote a commentary on all the works in the Hippocratic collection. A farther account of his lost works, and of his medical opinions, so far as they can be found out, may be found in two essays by Kühn, inserted in the second volume of his *Opuscula Academica, Medica et Philologica*, Leipzig, 1827–8, 2 vols. 8vo.[5]

---

[1] *Greenhill, l. c.*

[2] *Cramer, Anecd. Græc. Paris.*, vol. i., p. 395.

[3] *Greenhill; Smith, Dict. Biogr., s. v.*

[4] *Galen, De Compos. Medic. sec. Gen.*, iv., 7.

[5] *Greenhill; Smith, Dict. Biogr., s. v.*

CHAPTER XLVI.

SIXTH OR ROMAN PERIOD.

INTRODUCTORY REMARKS.

I. The *Sixth* or *Roman* period extends, as we have already remarked, from the fall of the Græco-Egyptian empire (B.C. 30) to the foundation of Constantinople (A.D. 330), and derives its name from the circumstance of Rome's becoming the centre, not only of wealth and power, but of science, literature, and the arts.

II. Greek literature now began rapidly to decline. The total absence of political independence, which marked the rule of the Cæsars, operated prejudicially, of course, not only upon the spirit of the nation, but upon literary efforts of every kind; originality, whether in the domain of poetry or of prose composition, became every day of rarer occurrence, and learned and scientific studies alone were pursued with any degree of spirit and success.

III. One principal cause of the successful cultivation of these last-mentioned studies was the establishment at Rome of public libraries, in which Augustus and several of his successors imitated the example which had been set by the Ptolemies. These became in time so numerous, that, besides many private collections of great extent and value, there were in Rome twenty open to the public, and furnished, at the emperor's expense, with all that could be required by such as had occasion to consult them.[1]

IV. The emperors, however, did not content themselves with accumulating these literary treasures; they were careful, also, to form in the principal cities of their dominions public schools, or, as we would term them, universities, for the education of youth. At Rome, the Capitol was assigned to professors, salaried by the state, for delivering courses of instruction. There were ten for grammar or philology in the Greek and Roman languages respectively; three Latin rhetoricians and five Greek; one instructor in philosophy, and two in jurisprudence. Similar establishments existed at Mediolanum (*Milan*), Massilia (*Marseilles*), and, above all, at Carthage. In the eastern part of the empire the principal schools of this kind were at Athens and Alexandrea. The school at the former place was particularly devoted to rhetorical studies; that of Alexandrea to mathematics, philosophy, and medicine; for it must be remarked that this latter city, having recovered from a temporary depression, became again, and continued for several centuries after the Christian era, an important seat of science and letters; boasting such divines as *Clement*, *Origen*, *Athanasius*, and *Cyrill*, and such mathematicians as *Diophantus*, *Pappus*, *Theon*, *Proclus*, and others.[2]

V. Antioch and Berytus, also, were celebrated for their schools, the

[1] *Schöll, Hist. Lit. Gr.*, vol. iv., p. 1, *seqq.; Moore, Lectures*, &c., p. 66. [2] *Schöll, l. c*

latter having become, from the middle of the third century, the principal rendezvous of those who were pursuing the study of jurisprudence. At Antioch there was a public library, placed in the temple of Trajan, to which, according to Suidas, the Emperor Jovian set fire, by an impulse of fanaticism.

VI. Before entering on our more immediate subject, it may not be amiss to take a general view of the situation of the literary Greeks under the Roman dominion. The habits and tastes of the Greeks and Romans were so different that they produced a feeling of antipathy in the two nations. The Roman writers, from prejudice and jealousy, of which they were themselves perhaps unconscious, have transmitted to us a very incorrect picture of the state of the Greeks during the first centuries of the empire. They did not observe with attention the marked distinction between the Asiatic and Alexandrine Greeks and the natives of Hellas. The European population, pursuing the quiet life of landed proprietors, or engaged in the pursuits of commerce and agriculture, were considered by Roman prejudice as unworthy of notice. The Greek character was estimated from the conduct of the adventurers who thronged from the wealthy and corrupted cities of the East, in order to seek their fortunes at Rome; and who, from motives of fashion and taste, were unduly favored by the Roman aristocracy.[1]

VII. The most distinguished of these Greeks were literary men, professors of philosophy, rhetoric, grammar, mathematics, and music. Great numbers were engaged as private teachers; and this class were regarded with some respect by the Roman nobility, from their intimate connection with their families. The great mass of the Greeks residing at Rome were, however, employed in connection with the public and private amusements of the capital, and were found engaged in every profession, from the directors of the theatres and opera-houses down to the swindlers who frequented the haunts of vice. The testimony of the Latin authors may be received as sufficiently accurate concerning the light in which the Greeks were regarded at Rome, and as a not incorrect portraiture of the Greek population of the capital.

VIII. The expressions of the Romans, when speaking of the Greeks, often display nothing more than the manner in which the proud aristocracy of the empire regarded all foreigners, those even whom they admitted to their personal intimacy. The Greeks were confounded with the great body of strangers from the Eastern nations in one general sentence of condemnation; and not unnaturally, for the Greek language served as the ordinary means of communication with all foreigners from the East. The magicians, conjurers, and astrologers of Syria, Egypt, and Chaldea were naturally mixed up, both in society and public opinion, with the adventurers of Greece, and contributed to form the despicable type which was unjustly enough transferred from the fortune-hunters at Rome to the whole Greek nation.[2]

IX. It is hardly necessary to observe that Greek literature, as cultivated at Rome during this period, had no connection with the national feel-

[1] *Finlay, Greece under the Romans*, p. 77, *seqq.*

[2] *Id., l. c.*

ings of the Greek people. As far as the Greeks themselves were concerned, learning was an honorable and lucrative occupation to its successful professors; but in the estimation of the higher classes at Rome, Greek literature was merely an ornamental exercise of the mind, a fashion of the wealthy. This ignorance of Greece and the Greeks induced Juvenal to draw his conclusive proof of the utter falsity of the Greek character, and of the fabulous nature of all Greek history, from his own doubts concerning a fact which is avouched by the testimony of Herodotus and Thucydides; but, as a retort to the *Græcia mendax* of the Roman satirist, the apter observation of Lucian may be cited, that the Romans spoke truth only once in their lives, and that was when they made their wills.[1]

X. The division of the Greek nation which occupied the most important social position in the empire consisted of the remains of the Macedonian and Greek colonies in Egypt, Syria, and Mesopotamia. These countries were filled with Greeks; and the cities of Alexandrea and Antioch, the second and third in the empire in size, population, and wealth, were chiefly peopled by Greeks. The influence of Alexandrea alone on the Roman empire, and on European civilization, would require a long treatise in order to do justice to the subject. Its schools of philosophy produced modifications of Christianity in the East. Those feuds between the Jews and Christians which its municipal disputes first created were by its powerful influence bequeathed to following centuries, so that, in Western Europe, we still debase Christianity by the admixture of those prejudices which had their rise in the amphitheatre of Alexandrea.[2]

XI. Antioch and the other Greek cities of the East had preserved their municipal privileges; and the Greek population in Egypt, Syria, and Mesopotamia remained every where completely separated from the original inhabitants. Their corporate organization often afforded them an opportunity of interfering with the details of the public administration, and their bold and seditious spirit enabled them to defend their own rights and interests. When the free population of the provinces acquired the rights of Roman citizenship, the Greeks of these countries, who formed the majority of the privileged classes, and were already in possession of the principal share of the local administration, became soon possessed of the whole authority of the Roman government. They appeared as the real representatives of the state, placed the native population in the position of a party excluded from power, and consequently rendered it more dissatisfied than formerly. In the East, therefore, after the publication of Caracalla's edict, the Greeks immediately became again the dominant people.[3]

XII. We will now proceed to consider the literary productions of this period under the two general heads, as we have done in previous instances, of poetic and prose composition.

[1] *Finlay, l. c.* [2] *Id. ib.* [3] *Id. ib.*

I. POETRY.

I. During the period on which we are entering, poetry in general experienced a complete decline. Nothing shows more plainly the bad taste of the age than the choice of scientific subjects made by the poets of the time, in order to cover, under an appearance of erudition, their want of imagination. Frequently, also, in order to hide their own sterility of ideas, they appropriated to themselves entire verses and sentences taken from the earlier poets.

II. There was one department, however, in which the poets of the day employed themselves with more success, namely, *epigrammatic* composition. We have given an historical sketch of the *Greek Anthology* in an earlier part of the present volume; we will now give a brief sketch of the principal epigrammatic poets of the present period.

(A.) EPIGRAM.

I. Antipater (Ἀντίπατρος), of Sidon, the author of several epigrams in the Greek Anthology, is commonly supposed, from a passage in Cicero,[1] to have been contemporary with Q. Catulus, who was consul B.C. 102, but in all probability he belongs to a somewhat later period. Many minute references are made to him by Meleager, who also wrote his epitaph. He lived to a very advanced age.

II. Meleăger (Μελέαγρος),[2] a celebrated writer and collector of epigrams, was a native of Gadara, in Palestine, and lived about B.C. 60, so near, in fact, to the commencement of the present period, that he may, without any great impropriety, be ranked under it. There are 131 of his epigrams in the Greek Anthology, written in a good Greek style, though somewhat affected, and marked by sophistic acumen and amatory fancy.[3] They have been published separately by Manso, Jena, 1789, 8vo, and by Meineke, Leipzig, 1811, 8vo.

III. Philodēmus (Φιλόδημος),[4] of Gadara, an Epicurean philosopher and epigrammatic poet, was contemporary with Cicero, who makes a violent attack upon him, though without mentioning his name, as the abettor of Piso in all his profligacy,[5] although elsewhere[6] he speaks in high terms of him; and, indeed, in the former passage, while attacking his character, he praises his poetical skill and elegance, his knowledge of philosophy, and his general information, in the highest terms. His epigrams were included in the Anthology of Philip of Thessalonica, and he seems to have been the earliest poet who had a place in that collection. The Greek Anthology contains thirty-four of his pieces, which are chiefly of a light and erotic character, and quite bear out Cicero's statements respecting the licentiousness of his matter and the elegance of his manner. Of his prose writings, Diogenes Laertius[7] quotes from the tenth book τῆς τῶν φιλοσόφων συντάξεως, and a MS. has been discovered at Herculaneum containing a work by him on music, περὶ μουσικῆς.

---

1 *Cic., De Orat*, iii., 50.
2 *Smith, Dict. Biogr., s. v.*
3 *Brunck, Anal.*, vol. i., p. 1, *seqq.*
4 *Smith, Dict. Biogr., s. v.*
5 *Cic. in Pis.*, 28, *seq.*
6 *Id., De Fin.*, ii., 35.
7 *Diog. Laert.*, x., 3.

IV. Alphēus (Ἀλφεῖος),[1] of Mytilene, the author of about twelve epigrams in the Greek Anthology, some of which seem to point out the time when he wrote. In the seventh epigram he refers to the state of the Roman empire, as embracing almost all the known world; in the ninth he speaks of the restored and flourishing city of Troy; and in the tenth he alludes to an epigram by Antipater of Sidon. Hence it is not improbable that he wrote under Augustus.

V. Crinagŏras (Κριναγόρας),[2] a Greek epigrammatic poet, a native of Mytilene, among the eminent men of which he is mentioned by Strabo, who speaks of him as a contemporary.[3] There are several allusions in his epigrams which refer to the reign of Augustus, and on the authority of which Jacobs believes him to have flourished from B.C. 31 to A.D. 9. We may also collect from his epigrams that he lived at Rome,[4] and that he was richer in poems than in worldly goods.[5] Crinagoras often shows a true poetical spirit. We have about fifty epigrams of his in the Greek Anthology.

VI. Antipăter (Ἀντίπατρος),[6] of Thessalonica, the author of several epigrams in the Greek Anthology, lived, as we may infer from some of them, in the latter part of the reign of Augustus (B.C. 10 and onward), and perhaps till the reign of Caligula (A.D. 38). He is probably the same poet who is called, in the titles of several epigrams, "*Antipater Macedo.*"

VII. Philippus (Φίλιππος),[7] of Thessalonica, an epigrammatic poet, who, besides composing a large number of epigrams himself, compiled one of the ancient Greek anthologies. The whole number of epigrams ascribed to him in the Greek Anthology is nearly ninety, but of these six (Nos. 36–41) ought to be ascribed to Lucillius, and a few others are manifestly borrowed from earlier poets, while others, again, are mere imitations. They include nearly all the different classes of subjects treated of in Greek epigrammatic poetry. Various allusions in these epigrams prove that he lived after the time of Augustus.

VIII. Antiphĭlus (Ἀντίφιλος),[8] of Byzantium, lived about the time of the Emperor Nero, as appears from one of his epigrams, in which he mentions the favor conferred by that emperor upon the island of Rhodes. The number of his epigrams still extant is upward of forty, and most of them are superior in conception and style to the majority of these compositions. Reiske, in his notes on the Anthology of Cephalus, was led by the difference of style in some of the poems bearing the name of Antiphilus to suppose that there were two or three poets of this name, and that their productions were all, by mistake, ascribed to the one poet of Byzantium. But there is not sufficient ground for such an hypothesis.

IX. Lucillius (Λουκίλλιος),[9] a poet of the Greek Anthology, edited two books of epigrams. In the Anthology 124 epigrams are ascribed to him, but of these the Vatican MS. assigns the 118th to Lucian, and the 96th and 124th to Palladas. This authority, therefore, removes the foundation for the inferences respecting the poet's date, which Lessing and Fa-

[1] *Jacobs, Anth. Græc.*, xiii., p. 839. [2] *Id. ib.*, p. 876, *seqq.* [3] *Strab.*, xiii., p. 617. [4] *Ep.* 24. [5] *Ep.* 23. [6] *Jacobs, Anth. Græc.*, xiii., p. 848, *seq.* [7] *Id. ib.*, p. 934, *seqq.* [8] *Id. ib.*, p. 851, *seqq.* [9] *Id. ib.*, xiii., p. 912, *seqq.*

bricius drew from the mention of the physician Magnus, in the 124th epigram. But, on the other hand, the Vatican MS. assigns to Lucillius the 16th epigram of Ammianus, the 36th and 41st of Philip, the 108th anonymous, and the 23d of Leonidas of Alexandrea. From the last epigram (which is also far more in the style of Lucillius than of Leonidas) it appears that the poet lived under Nero, and that he received money from this emperor. Nearly all his epigrams are sportive, and many of them are aimed at the grammarians, who at that time abounded at Rome.

X. LEONIDAS (Λεωνίδας),[1] of Alexandrea, was born, as he informs us, on the banks of the Nile, whence he went to Rome, and there taught grammar for a long time, without attracting any notice, but ultimately he became very popular, and obtained the patronage of the imperial family. His epigrams show that he flourished under Nero, and probably down to the reign of Vespasian. In the Anthology, forty-three epigrams are ascribed to him; but some of these belong to Leonidas of Tarentum, who appears to have lived in the time of Pyrrhus. Several of his epigrams are marked by the petty conceit of having an equal number of letters in each distich; these are called ἰσόψηφα ἐπιγράμματα. Consult Meineke, "*Prolusio ad utriusque Leonidæ carmina*," Leipzig, 1791.

XI. AMMIANUS (Ἀμμιανός),[2] a Greek epigrammatist, but probably a Roman by birth. The Greek Anthology contains twenty-seven epigrams by him, to which must be added another contained in the Vatican MS., and another which is placed among the anonymous epigrams, but which some MSS. assign to Ammianus. They are all of a facetious character. He was contemporary with the epigrammatist Lucillius, who lived under Nero. We find also from some of his epigrams that he was contemporary with the sophist Antonius Polemo, who flourished under Trajan and Hadrian.

XII. MESOMĒDES (Μεσομήδης), a lyric and epigrammatic poet under Hadrian and the Antonines. He was a native of Crete, and a freedman of Hadrian, whose favorite, Antinous, he celebrated in a poem.[3] A salary which he had received from Hadrian was diminished by Antoninus Pius.[4] Three poems of his are preserved in the Anthology, one of which is a short hymn to Nemesis. This hymn was published for the first time, with the ancient musical notes, by Fell, at the end of his edition of Aratus, Oxford, 1672, 8vo; afterward by Burette, in the fifth volume of the *Mémoires de l'Académie des Inscr. et Belles Lettres*; by Brunck, in his *Analecta*, vol. ii., p. 292; by Snedorf, "*De hymnis veterum Græcorum*," Hafniæ, 1786, 8vo; and by Bellermann, along with those of Dionysius, Berlin, 1840.

XIII. NESTOR (Νέστωρ),[5] of Laranda, in Lycia, according to Suidas; in Lycaonia, according to Strabo and Stephanus Byzantinus. He lived in the reign of the Emperor Severus, between A.D. 194 and 211. Four fragments of his writings are inserted in the Anthology.[6] The fourth of these has point, and rebukes men for attempting poetry who are unskilled in the art. He is mentioned by Suidas as an epic poet also. We

[1] *Jacobs, Anthol. Græc.*, p. 908, *seq.* [2] *Id. ib.*, xi., p. 312, *seqq.* [3] *Suid.*, *s. v.*
[4] *Capitol.*, *Ant. Pius*, 7. [5] *Smith, Dict. Biogr.*, *s. v.* [6] Vol. iii., p. 54, ed. *Jacobs.*

infer from Stephanus Byzantinus that he wrote a poem called Ἀλεξανδρείας, "On the Deeds of Alexander," to which Suidas probably refers. This last-mentioned writer also informs us that Nestor composed an Iliad, omitting in each book the letter indicating its number, as, in the first book, the letter α, in the second the letter β, and so on with the rest through the whole twenty-four books. The epithet applied to such singular productions is λειπογράμματος, this being called an Ἰλιὰς λειπογράμματος. He wrote also a poem entitled Μεταμορφώσεις.

XIV. Strato (Στράτων), of Sardis, an epigrammatic poet, and the compiler of an anthology, composed of epigrams from the earlier anthologies of Meleager and Philip (to which we have referred in another part of this work), and from other sources, and some from the pen of Strato himself. The whole number of poems in the collection is 258, of which ninety-eight are by Strato. Some of the epigrams of Strato are elegant and clever, but nothing can redeem the disgrace attaching to the moral character of his compilation.[1]

XV. Diogenes Laertius (Διογένης ὁ Λαέρτιος or Λαερτιεύς, sometimes also written Λαέρτιος Διογένης), to whom we shall presently come in our account of the prose writers of this period, was also a writer of epigrams. Many of these are interspersed in his biographies. They were collected together in a separate work, and divided into several books. The collection bore the title of πάμμετρος. The remains which we have at the present day are below mediocrity, and not only insipid, but generally deficient in good taste.

(B.) DIDACTIC POETRY.

The most worthy of notice among the didactic poets of this period are Dionysius, surnamed *Periegētes* (ὁ Περιηγητής), Oppianus, and Marcellus *Sidētes*.

I. Dionysius (Διονύσιος),[2] surnamed *Periegetes*, from his being the author of a περιήγησις τῆς γῆς, in hexameter verse, and still extant. Respecting his age and country the most different opinions have been entertained, though all critics are agreed in placing him after the Christian era, or in the time of the Roman emperors, as must, indeed, be necessarily inferred from passages of the *Periegesis* itself, such as v. 355, where the author speaks of his ἄνακτες, that is, his sovereigns, which only apply to the emperors. But the question which emperor or emperors Dionysius there alludes to has been answered in the most different ways. Some writers have placed him in the reign of Augustus, others in that of Nero, and others, again, under Marcus Aurelius and L. Verus, or under Septimius Severus and his sons. Eustathius, his commentator, was himself in doubt about the age of his author. But these uncertainties have been removed by Bernhardy, one of the most recent editors of Dionysius, who has made it highly probable, partly from the names of countries and nations mentioned in the *Periegesis*, partly from the mention of the Huns in v. 730, and partly from the general character of the poem, that its author must have lived either in the latter part of the third, or in the begin-

1 *Jacobs, Anth. Græc.*, vol. iii., p. 68, *seqq.*

2 *Smith, Dict. Biogr.*, *s. v.*

ning of the fourth century of our era. Eustathius[1] and the scholiast[2] expressly call him a native of Africa. Suidas infers, without much foundation for it, that he was born at Byzantium.

The *Periegesis* of Dionysius contains a description of the whole earth, so far as it was known in his time, in hexameter verse, and the author appears chiefly to follow the views of Eratosthenes. It is written in a terse and neat style, and enjoyed a high degree of popularity in ancient times, as we may infer from the fact that two translations or paraphrases of it were made by Romans, one by Rufus Festus Avienus, and the other by the grammarian Priscian. Eustathius wrote a very valuable commentary upon it, which is still extant, and we farther possess a Greek paraphrase and scholia. Besides the Periegesis, Eustathius states that other works also were attributed to Dionysius, namely, λιθικά, ὀρνιθικά, and βασσαρικά, the latter term meaning the same as Διονυσιακά.

The first edition of the *Periegesis* appeared at Ferrara, 1512, 4to, with a Latin translation. Aldus Manutius next brought out an edition of it, Venice, 1513, 8vo, together with Pindar, Callimachus, and Lycophron. H. Stephens incorporated it in his "*Poetæ Principes Heroici Carminis*," Paris, 1566, fol. One of the most useful among the subsequent editions is that of Thwaites, Oxford, 1697, 8vo, with the commentary of Eustathius, the Greek scholia, and paraphrase. It is also printed in the fourth volume of Hudson's *Geogr. Minor.*, Oxford, 1712, 8vo, from which it was reprinted separately, Oxford, 1710, and 1717, 8vo; edited also by Passow, Leipzig, 1825, 12mo. But all the previous editions are superseded by that of Bernhardy, Leipzig, 1828, 8vo, which forms vol. i. of a contemplated collection of the minor Greek geographers. It is accompanied by a very excellent and learned dissertation, and the ancient commentators.

II. Oppianus (Ὀππιανός).[3] Under this name there are extant two Greek hexameter poems, one on fishing, entitled Ἁλιευτικά, and the other on hunting, Κυνηγετικά; as also a prose paraphrase of a third poem on hawking, Ἰξευτικά. These were, till toward the end of the last century, universally attributed to the same person; an opinion which not only made it impossible to reconcile with each other all the passages relative to Oppian that are to be found in ancient writers, but also rendered contradictory the evidence derived from the perusal of the poems themselves. At length, in the year 1776, I. G. Schneider, in his first edition of these poems, threw out the conjecture that they were not written by the same individual, but by two persons of the same name, who have been constantly confounded together; an hypothesis which, if not absolutely free from objections, certainly removes so many difficulties, and, moreover, affords so convenient a mode of introducing various facts and remarks, which would otherwise be inconsistent and contradictory, that it will here be adopted.

The writer of the "*Halieutica*" is said by probably all authorities to have been born in Cilicia, though they are not so well agreed as to the name of his native city. Suidas says Corycus, and this appears to be confirmed by Oppian himself.[4] Respecting his date there has been equal difference of opinion. Athenæus says that he lived shortly before his own time, which will make him to have flourished about A.D. 180. The

1 *Ad.* v. 7.

2 *Ad.* v. 8.

3 *Greenhill; Smith, Dict. Biogr.*, *s. v.*

4 *Opp.*, *Hal.*, iii., 205, *seqq.*

"*Halieutica*" consists of about 3500 hexameters, divided into five books, of which the first two treat of the natural history of fishes, and the other three of the art of fishing. The author displays in parts considerable zoological knowledge, but inserts also several fables and absurdities. In this respect, however, he was not more credulous than most of his contemporaries, and many of his stories are copied by Ælian and other writers. Among the zoological points in the poem that are most worthy of notice, we may mention the following. He mentions (i., 217, *seqq.*) the story of the remora or sucker (ἐχενηΐς) being able to stop a ship when under full sail by sticking to the keel; he was aware of the peculiarity of the *cancellus* or hermit-crab (καρκινάς), which is provided with no shell of its own, but seizes upon the first empty one it can find (i., 320, *seqq.*); he gives a beautiful and correct description of the nautilus (i., 338, *seqq.*); he notices the numbness caused by the touch of the torpedo (νάρκη), and the black fluid emitted by the sepia or cuttle-fish, by means of which it escapes its pursuers (iii., 156, *seqq.*): he several times mentions the dolphin; calls it, for its swiftness and beauty, the king among fishes; and relates an anecdote, similar to those mentioned by Pliny, of its attachment to a little boy.

In point of style and language, as well as poetical embellishment, the "*Halieutica*" is so much superior to the "*Cynegetica*," that Schneider (as we have seen) considers this fact to furnish the strongest proof in favor of his hypothesis; and it is probable that the greater part of the praise that has been bestowed upon Oppian, in a poetical point of view, should be considered as referring to this poem only. A paraphrase of the "*Halieutica*" in Greek prose, bearing the name of Eutecnius, is still in existence in several European libraries, but has never been published.

The author of the "*Cynegetica*" was a native of Apamea or Pella, in Syria, as he himself plainly tells us.[1] The poem is addressed to Caracalla, probably after he had been associated with his father in the empire, A.D. 198, and before the death of the latter, A.D. 211. The "*Cynegetica*" consist of about 2100 hexameters, divided into four books. The last of these is imperfect, and perhaps a fifth book may also have been lost, as the anonymous author of the life of Oppian says the poem consisted of that number of books, though Suidas mentions only four. The following zoological points mentioned in the poem are perhaps the most interesting. He says expressly that the tusks of the elephant are not teeth, but horns (ii., 491); that the bear brings forth her cubs half formed, and licks them into shape (iii., 159); he gives a very spirited description of the giraffe (iii., 461), the exactness of which is in some points remarkable. That the animal must have been seen alive by Oppian is evident from his remark on the brilliancy of the eyes, and the halting motion of the hinder limbs. In style, language, and poetical merit, the "*Cynegetica*" is far inferior to the "*Halieutica*."[2]

With respect to the poem on hawking, Ἰξευτικά, if it is to be attributed to either of the Oppians, it probably belongs to the younger; but Schneider considers that it is more probably the work of Dionysius. The

[1] *Opp.*, *Cyneget.*, ii., 125, *seqq.*

[2] *Greenhill, l. c.*

poem itself, which is said to have consisted of five books, is no longer extant, but there is a Greek prose paraphrase of three books by Eutecnius.

The *Halieutica* and *Cynegetica* are usually published together. The earliest edition of *both* poems is the Aldine, Venice, 1517, 8vo, containing the Greek text, with the Latin translation of the *Halieutica*, by Lippius. The most complete edition that has hitherto been published is that by Schneider, Strasburg, 1776, 8vo, Greek and Latin, with copious and learned notes, containing also the Greek paraphrase of the 'Ἰξευτικά. The editor published some additional notes and observations in his *Analecta Critica*, Frankfort, 1777, 8vo. This edition was executed when Schneider was a young man, in conjunction with Brunck, who assisted him in the *Cynegetica*; and accordingly it exhibits many bold corrections of the text, which he withdrew in his second edition, published in 1813, Leipzig, 8vo. This edition is unfinished, and contains only the Greek text of the two poems, Peifer's Latin translation of the *Cynegetica*, some short notes relating to the text, and a preface in which Schneider repeats his conviction that the *Halieutica* and *Cynegetica* were written by two different persons, and replies to the objections of Belin de Ballu. The latest edition of the two poems is that published in Didot's *Bibliotheca Græca*, together with Nicander, Marcellus Sidetes, &c., edited by F. S. Lehrs, with a preface by K. Lehrs, who completed the work after his brother's early death. It contains the Greek text with a Latin prose translation, and also the Greek paraphrase of the 'Ἰξευτικά, with a Latin version. The scholia on the two poems were published in a separate volume of the *Bibliotheca Græca* (Paris, 1849), along with those on Theocritus and Nicander, under the editorial supervision of Bussemaker.

The *Halieutica* were published separately by Junta, Florence, 1515, 8vo (a book valuable not only for its rarity, but also for the correctness of the text), and by Plantin, under the editorial care of Rittershusius, Leyden, 1597, 8vo. The earliest edition of the Greek text of the *Cynegetica*, apart from the *Halieutica*, appeared in 1549, 4to, Paris, ap. Vascosanum. It was also published by Belin de Ballu, Strasburg, 1786, Greek and Latin, with learned notes, too often deformed by personal controversy with Schneider. The editor intended to publish the *Halieutica* in a second volume, but of this only forty pages were printed, which are rarely to be met with.

III. Marcellus Sidētes (Μάρκελλος Σιδήτης),[1] a native of Side, in Pamphylia, was born toward the end of the first century after Christ, and lived in the reigns of Hadrian and Antoninus Pius, A.D. 117–161. He wrote a long medical poem in Greek hexameters, consisting of forty-two books, which was held in such estimation that it was ordered by the emperors to be placed in the public libraries at Rome. Of this work only two fragments remain, one Περὶ Λυκανθρώπου, "*De Lycanthropia*," and the other 'Ἰατρικὰ περὶ ἰχθύων, "*De remediis ex piscibus*." Of these the former is preserved (but in *prose*) by Aëtius,[2] and is curious and interesting. The second fragment is less interesting, and consists of 101 verses. It was first published in a separate form, in Greek and Latin, by Morell, Paris, 1591, 8vo. The latest edition is that contained in Didot's *Bibliotheca Græca*, with Nicander, Oppian, &c., edited by Lehrs, Paris, 1846, 8vo.

In connection with didactic poetry, the subject of *Fable* naturally presents itself. This whole subject, however, has been discussed in an earlier part of the present volume, where a sketch is also given of *Babrius*, the most distinguished writer of fable during the period under review. We will therefore pass to *epic poetry*.

---

[1] *Greenhill; Smith, Dict. Biogr., s. v.*

[2] *Aët.*, ii., 2, 11, p. 254. Compare *Paul. Ægin.*, iii., 16; *Adams, ad loc.*

(C.) EPIC POETRY.

Quintus Smyrnæus (Κόϊντος Σμυρναῖος),[1] commonly called Quintus Calăber, from the circumstance that the first copy through which his poem became known was found in a convent at Otranto, in Calabria, was the author of a poem in fourteen books, entitled τὰ μεθ' Ὅμηρον, or παραλειπόμενα Ὁμήρῳ. Scarcely any thing is known of his personal history; but from the metrical and poetic characteristics of his poem, as compared with the school of Nonnus, it appears most probable that he lived toward the middle of the fourth century after Christ, or about the close of the present period. From a passage in his poem (xii., 308-313), it would seem that even in early life he made trial of his poetic powers, while engaged in tending sheep near a temple of Diana, in the territory of Smyrna. The matters treated of in his poem are the events of the Trojan war, from the death of Hector to the return of the Greeks. It begins rather abruptly with a description of the grief and consternation at the death of Hector which reigned among the Trojans, and then introduces Penthesilea, queen of the Amazons, who comes to their aid. In the second book we have the arrival, exploits, and death of Memnon; in the third the death of Achilles. The fourth and fifth books describe the funeral games in honor of Achilles, the contest about his arms, and the death of Ajax. In the sixth book Neoptolemus is sent for by the Greeks, and Eurypylus comes to the aid of the Trojans. The seventh and eighth books describe the arrival and exploits of Neoptolemus; the ninth contains the exploits of Deïphobus, and the sending for Philoctetes by the Greeks. The tenth, the death of Paris and the suicide of Œnone, who had refused to heal him. The eleventh book narrates the last unsuccessful attempt of the Greeks to carry Ilium by storm; the twelfth and thirteenth describe the capture of the city by means of the wooden horse; the fourteenth, the rejoicing of the Greeks, the reconciliation of Menelaus and Helen, the sacrifice of Polyxena at the tomb of Achilles, the embarkation of the Greeks, the scattering of their ships, and the death of the Oïlean Ajax.[2]

In phraseology, similes, and other technicalities, Quintus closely copied Homer. The materials for his poem he found in the works of the earlier poets of the epic cycle. But not a single poetical idea of his own seems ever to have inspired him. He was incapable of understanding or appropriating any thing except the majestic flow of the language of the ancient epos. His gods and heroes are alike devoid of character; every thing like pathos or moral interest was quite beyond his powers. Of similes (not very original in their character) he makes copious use. With respect to chronology, his poem is as punctual as a diary. But his style is clear, and marked, on the whole, by purity and good taste, without any bombast or exaggeration. There can be little doubt that the work of Quintus Smyrnæus is nothing more than an amplification or remodelling of the poems of Arctinus and Lesches. It is clear that he had access to the same sources as Virgil, though there is nothing from which it would ap-

[1] *Smith, Dict. Biogr., s. v.*

[2] *Id., l. c.*

pear that he had the Roman poet before his eyes. He appears, however, to have made diligent use of Apollonius.

The first edition of Quintus was published by Aldus Manutius, in 1504 or 1505, from a very faulty MS. Rhodomannus, who spent thirty years upon the correction and explanation of the text of Quintus, published an improved edition in 1604. The standard edition, however, for a long time, was that of Tychsen, Strasburg, 1807, 8vo, founded on a collation of all the extant MSS. Recently, an edition of Quintus has appeared in Didot's *Bibliotheca Græca*, Paris, 1840, by Lehrs, along with Hesiod, Apollonius, &c. The text of this edition is very much improved. The latest and best edition, however, is that of Köchly, Leipzig, 1850, 8vo.

II. PROSE.

The prose writers of this period are numerous, and may be classified as follows: 1. *Historians.* 2. *Rhetoricians* and *Sophists.* 3. Writers of *works of fiction.* 4. *Grammarians* and *Lexicographers.* 5. *Philosophers.* 6. *Mathematicians.* 7. *Geographers.* 8. *Medical writers.*

(A.) HISTORIANS.

I. Castor (Κάστωρ),[1] either a native of Rhodes, of Massilia, or of Galatia, was a contemporary of Cicero and Julius Cæsar, and received the surname of Φιλορώμαιος, on account of his partiality toward the Romans. He wrote, according to Suidas, 1. Ἀναγραφὴ τῶν θαλασσοκρατησάντων, in two books. 2. Χρονικὰ ἀγνοήματα, referred to also by Apollodorus. 3. Περὶ ἐπιχειρημάτων, in nine books. 4. Περὶ πειθοῦς, in two books. 5. Περὶ τοῦ Νείλου. 6. Τέχνη ῥητορική, of which a portion is still extant, and printed in Walz's *Rhetores Græci* (iii., p. 712, *seqq.*). To these productions Clinton[2] adds a great chronological work (Χρονικά or Χρονολογία), in six books, which is referred to several times by Eusebius, though it is not certain whether this is not the same work as the Χρονικὰ ἀγνοήματα mentioned above. He is frequently referred to as an authority in historical matters, though no strictly historical work is specified, so that those references may allude to any of the above-mentioned works. Neither is it known where he showed his partiality for the Romans, though it may have been in a work mentioned by Plutarch,[3] in which he compared the institutions of the Romans with those of Pythagoras. Müller, however, refers it to his conduct in the Mithradatic war of Pompey. None of his works are extant, except some fragments, collected by C. Müller, at the end of Herodotus, in Didot's *Bibl. Græca*, Paris, 1844.

II. Theophănes (Θεοφάνης),[4] of Mytilene, in Lesbos, a learned Greek, and one of the most intimate friends of Pompey,[5] who presented to him the Roman franchise in the presence of his army, after a speech in which he eulogized his merits. He came to Rome with Pompey, and, on the breaking out of the civil war, he accompanied his patron to Greece. After the battle of Pharsalia, he fled with Pompey from Greece, and it was owing to his advice that the latter went to Egypt.[6] After the death

[1] *Smith, Dict. Biogr.*, *s. v.*
[2] *Fast. Hell.*, iii., p 546.
[3] *Quæst. Rom.*, 10, 76.
[4] *Smith, Dict. Biogr.*, *s. v.*
[5] Compare *Cæs.*, *Bell. Civ.*, iii., 18; *Strab.*, xiii., p. 617; *Cic.*, *Ep. ad Att.*, ii, 5, 12, 17.
[6] *Plut.*, *Pomp.*, 76, 78.

of his patron, Theophanes took refuge in Italy, and was pardoned by Cæsar. He wrote the history of Pompey's campaigns, in which he represented the exploits of his hero in the most favorable light, and did not hesitate, as Plutarch more than hints, to invent a false tale for the purpose of injuring the reputation of an enemy of the Pompeian family. He was still alive in B.C. 44, as we see from one of Cicero's letters,[1] and may therefore, without any impropriety, be ranked, like Castor, under the present period. His work is lost.

III. TIMAGENES (Τιμαγένης),[2] a rhetorician and historian, was a native of Alexandrea, whence he was carried as a prisoner to Rome, B.C. 55, where he was first employed as a slave in menial offices; but being liberated by Faustus Sulla, the son of the dictator, he opened a school of rhetoric, in which he taught with great success. The Emperor Augustus induced him to write a history of his exploits; but, having offended the monarch by sarcastic remarks upon his family, he was forbidden the palace; whereupon he burned his historical works, gave up his rhetorical school, and retired to the house of his friend Asinius Pollio, at Tusculum. After he had discontinued writing a long while, he resumed his pen, and composed several historical works, upon which his fame was founded. He afterward went to the East, and died at Dabanum, in Mesopotamia. The works of Timagenes mentioned by the ancient writers are, 1. Περίπλους, from which Strabo, on one occasion, is supposed to quote. 2. Περὶ βασιλέων, which appears to have contained a history of Alexander the Great and his successors. 3. A work on the Gauls. All his works are lost.

IV. JUBA (Ἰόβας),[3] king of Mauritania, son of Juba, king of Numidia, was a mere child at his father's death, was carried a prisoner to Rome by Cæsar, and compelled to grace the conqueror's triumph.[4] He was brought up in Italy, where he received an excellent education, and applied himself with such diligence to study that he turned out one of the most learned men of the day. After the death of Antony, B.C. 30, Augustus conferred on Juba his paternal kingdom of Numidia, and at the same time gave him in marriage Cleopatra, otherwise called Selene, the daughter of Antony and Cleopatra.[5] At a subsequent period (B.C. 25), Augustus gave him Mauritania in exchange for Numidia, which was reduced to a Roman province. He continued to reign in Mauritania till his death, which happened about A.D. 19. He was beloved by his subjects, among whom he endeavored to introduce the elements of Greek and Roman civilization. Juba wrote a great number of works in almost every branch of literature. They are all lost, with the exception of a few fragments. They appear to have been all written in Greek. The most important of them were, 1. A *History of Africa* (Λιβυκά), in which he made use of Punic authorities. 2. *On the Assyrians* (Περὶ Ἀσσυρίων), in two books, in which he followed the authority of Berosus. 3. A *History of Arabia*, which he addressed to C. Cæsar, the grandson of Augustus, when that prince was about to proceed on his expedition to the East, B.C. 1.

[1] *Ad Att.*, xv., 19. [2] *Smith, Dict. Biogr.*, *s. v.* [3] *Id. ib*
[4] *Appian, B. C.*, ii., 101; *Plut., Cæs.*, 55. [5] *Dio Cass.*, li., 15

It appears to have contained a general description of the country, and all that was then known concerning its geography, natural productions, &c. It is cited by Pliny[1] as the most trustworthy account of those regions which was known to him. 4. A *Roman History* (Ῥωμαϊκὴ Ἱστορία), cited repeatedly by Stephanus Byzantinus. Numerous statements quoted by Plutarch from Juba, without mentioning any particular work, but relating to the early history and antiquities of Rome, are evidently derived from this treatise. 5. Θεατρικὴ Ἱστορία.[2] A general treatise on all matters connected with the stage, of which the fourth book related to musical instruments in particular. It was a voluminous work, as the seventeenth book is mentioned by Photius. 6. Περὶ γραφικῆς, or Περὶ ζωγράφων, seems to have been a general history of painting. He wrote, also, two botanical treatises, and a grammatical work. The few fragments of his historical works still extant are collected in C. Müller's *Fragm. Histor. Græc.*, vol. iii., p. 465, *seqq.*

V. Diodōrus (Διόδωρος),[3] surnamed Siculus, or the Sicilian, was a contemporary of Cæsar and Augustus. He was born in the town of Agyrium, in Sicily, where he became acquainted with the Latin language, through the great intercourse between the Romans and Sicilians. In order to collect materials for his history, he travelled over a great part of Europe and Asia, and lived a long time at Rome. He spent altogether thirty years upon his work. It was entitled Βιβλιοθήκη ἱστορική, *The Historical Library*, and was a universal history, embracing the period from the earliest mythical ages down to the beginning of Cæsar's Gallic wars. The time at which he wrote his history may be determined pretty accurately from internal evidence: he not only mentions Cæsar's invasion of Britain, and his crossing the Rhine, but also his death and apotheosis; he farther states that he was in Egypt in Ol. 190, that is, B.C. 20; and Scaliger has made it highly probable that Diodorus wrote his work after the year B.C. 8, when Augustus corrected the calendar and introduced the intercalation every fourth year.

The work of Diodorus consisted of forty books. It was divided, as he himself informs us, into three great sections. The *first section*, which consisted of the first six books, contained the history of the mythical times previous to the Trojan war. The *second section*, which consisted of eleven books, contained the history from the Trojan war down to the death of Alexander the Great. The *third section*, which contained the remaining twenty-three books, treated of the history from the death of Alexander down to the beginning of Cæsar's Gallic wars. Of this work only the following portions are extant entire. The first five books, containing the early history of the Eastern nations, the Egyptians, Ethiopians, and Greeks; and from book eleven to book twenty, containing the history from the second Persian war, B.C. 480, down to B.C. 302. Of the remaining portions there are extant a number of fragments and the *Excerpta*, which are preserved partly in Photius,[4] and partly in the *Eclogæ* made at the command of Constantine Porphyrogenitus.

---

[1] *H. N.*, vi., 26, 28, 30; xii., 31.

[2] *Athen.*, iv., p. 175, *D.*

[3] *Smith, Dict. Biogr.*, *s. v.*

[4] *Bibl. Cod.*, 244.

The work of Diodorus is constructed upon the plan of annals, and the events of each year are placed by the side of one another without any internal connection. In composing his Bibliotheca, Diodorus made use, independent of his own observations, of all sources which were accessible to him; and had he exercised any criticism or judgment, or, rather, had he possessed any critical powers, his work might have been of incalculable value to the student of history. But Diodorus did nothing but collect that which he found in his different authorities: he thus jumbled together history, mythus, and fiction; he frequently misunderstood or mutilated his authorities, and not seldom contradicts in one passage what he has stated in another. The absence of criticism is manifest throughout the work, which is, in fact, devoid of all the higher requisites of a history. But, notwithstanding all these drawbacks, the extant portion of this great compilation is to us of the highest importance, on account of the great mass of materials which are there collected from a number of writers whose works have perished. Diodorus frequently mentions his authorities, and in most cases he has undoubtedly preserved the substance of his predecessors. His style is, on the whole, clear and lucid, but not always equal, which may be owing to the different character of the works which he used or abridged. His diction holds the middle place between the refined Attic and the vulgar Greek which was spoken in his time.

The work of Diodorus was first published in Latin translations of separate parts, until Obsopæus published the Greek text of books sixteen to twenty, Basle, 1539, 4to, which was followed by H. Stephens' edition of books one to five, and eleven to twenty, with the *excerpta* of Photius, Paris, 1559, fol. The next important edition is that of Rhodomannus, Hanover, 1604, fol., containing a Latin translation. The great edition of Wesseling, with an extensive and very valuable commentary, as well as the *Eclogæ* of Constantine Porphyrogenitus, as far as they were then known, appeared at Amsterdam, 1746, 2 vols. fol This edition was reprinted, with some additions, Bipont (Deuxponts), 1793, &c., in 11 vols. 8vo. An excellent edition was published by L. Dindorf, Leipzig, 1828, 6 vols. 8vo The new fragments discovered and published by Mai were edited, with many improvements, in a separate volume, by Dindorf, in the same year. The latest edition of Diodorus is that by C. Müller, in Didot's *Bibl. Græca*, with all the fragments inserted in their proper places, 2 vols. 8vo, Paris, 1842–44. Some of the editions contain sixty-five Latin letters attributed to Diodorus. They had been first published in Italian, in Pietro Carrera's *Storia di Catana*, 1639, fol., and were then printed in a Latin version, by Preiger, in Burmann's *Thesaurus Antiq. Sicil.*, vol. x., and in the old edition of Fabricius, *Bibl. Gr.*, vol. xiv., p. 229, *seqq.* The Greek original of these letters has, however, never been seen by any one, and there can be little doubt that they are a forgery, made after the revival of letters.

VI. Dionysius (Διονύσιος)[1] of Halicarnassus, a celebrated writer, not only in rhetoric and criticism, but also in history. He was born, according to the calculations of Dodwell, between B.C. 78 and 54. Strabo[2] calls him his own contemporary. His death took place soon after B.C. 7, the year in which he completed and published his great work on the history of Rome. Respecting his parents and education we know nothing, nor any thing about his position in his native place before he emigrated to Rome, though some have inferred, from his work on rhetoric, that he enjoyed a great reputation at Halicarnassus. All that we know for certain is the information which he himself gives us in the introduction to his history of Rome (i., 7), and a few more particulars which we may glean from his

[1] *Smith, Dict. Biogr.*, *s. v.*

[2] *Strab.*, xiv., p. 656.

other works. According to his own account, he went to Italy immediately after the termination of the civil wars, about B.C. 29. Henceforth he remained at Rome, and the twenty-two years which followed his arrival at that capital were mainly spent by him in making himself acquainted with the Latin language and literature, and in collecting materials for his great work on Roman history. We may assume that, like other rhetoricians of the time, he had commenced his career as a teacher of rhetoric at Halicarnassus, and his works bear strong evidence of his having been similarly occupied at Rome. There he lived on terms of friendship with many distinguished men, such as Q. Ælius Tubero, and the rhetorician Cæcilius; and it is not improbable that he may have received the Roman franchise, but his Roman name is not mentioned any where.

All the works of Dionysius, some of which are completely lost, must be divided into two classes. The first contains his rhetorical and critical treatises, all of which probably belong to an earlier period of his life (perhaps to the first years of his residence at Rome), than his historical works, which constitute the second class. We will consider merely his historical works at the present time, reserving an account of his other productions for the head of Rhetoricians and Sophists.

Historical Works of Dionysius.—In this class of compositions, to which Dionysius appears to have devoted his later years, he was less successful than in his critical and rhetorical essays, inasmuch as we every where find the rhetorician gaining the ascendency over the historian. The following historical works of his are known: 1. Χρόνοι or Χρονικά. This work, which is lost, probably contained chronological investigations, though not concerning Roman history. 2. Ῥωμαϊκὴ Ἀρχαιολογία, which Photius[1] styles Ἱστορικοὶ λόγοι. This is the great historical work of Dionysius. It consisted of twenty books, and contained the history of Rome from the earliest or mythical times down to the year B.C. 264, in which the history of Polybius begins with the Punic wars. The first nine books alone are complete; of the tenth and eleventh we have the greater part; and of the remaining nine we possess nothing but fragments and extracts, which were contained in the collections made at the command of the Emperor Constantine Porphyrogenitus, and were first published by Mai, from a MS. in the library at Milan (1816, 4to), and reprinted at Frankfort, 1817, 8vo.

Dionysius treated the early history of Rome with great minuteness. The eleven books extant do not carry the history beyond B.C. 441, so that the eleventh book breaks off very soon after the decemviral legislation. This peculiar minuteness in the early history, however, was, in a great measure, the consequence of the object he had proposed to himself, and which, as he himself states, was to remove the erroneous notions which the Greeks entertained with regard to Rome's greatness. Dionysius had no clear notions of the early constitution of Rome, and was led astray by the nature of the institutions which he saw in his own day; and he thus makes innumerable mistakes in treating of the history of the constitution. He introduces numerous speeches in his work, which, though

[1] *Phot., Bibl. Cod.*, lxxxiv.

written with artistic skill, nevertheless show that Dionysius was a rhetorician, not an historian, and still less a statesman. Still, however, his work is one of the greatest importance to the student of Roman history, since he discusses carefully every thing relating to the religion, laws, and private life of the Romans. His style is very good, and, with a few exceptions, his language may be called perfectly pure.[1]

The first complete edition of the Ἀρχαιολογία and the rhetorical works together is that of Sylburg, Frankfort, 1586, 2 vols. fol., reprinted at Leipzig, 1691, 2 vols. fol. Another reprint, with the introduction of a few alterations, was edited by Hudson, Oxford, 1704, 2 vols. fol., which, however, is a very inferior performance. A new and much improved edition, though with many bad and arbitrary emendations, was published by Reiske, Leipzig, 1774, *seqq.*, in 6 vols. 8vo, the last of which was edited by Morus.

VII. Nicolāus Damascēnus (Νικόλαος Δαμασκηνός),[2] a celebrated Greek polyhistor, who lived in the time of Herod the Great and the Emperor Augustus, with both of whom he was connected by intimate friendship. He was, as his name indicates, a native of Damascus, and his parents were distinguished no less for their personal character than for their wealth, his father Antipater having been a highly esteemed orator, and not only invested with the highest magistracies in his native place, but also employed on several embassies. Nicolaus showed great talents, even before he attained the age of puberty, and gained at this time the reputation of being the most accomplished among the youths of his age. At that early age, he composed tragedies and comedies, which met with general applause. But he soon abandoned these poetical pursuits, and devoted himself to rhetoric, music, mathematics, and the philosophy of Aristotle. Herod carried on his philosophical studies in common with Nicolaus, and the amicable relation between the two men was strengthened by these common pursuits. In a conversation with Herod, Nicolaus once directed his attention to the advantages which a prince might derive from history, and the king, who was struck by the truth of the observation, entreated Nicolaus to write a history. The latter complied with the request, and compiled a most voluminous work on ancient history. In B.C. 13, when Herod went to Rome to pay Augustus a visit, he took Nicolaus with him. On this occasion, Nicolaus made Augustus a present of the finest fruit of the palm-tree, which Augustus henceforth called *Nicolai*, a name by which that fruit was known down to the Middle Ages. Nicolaus rose so high in the favor of Augustus, that he was, on more than one occasion, of great service to Herod when the emperor was incensed against the latter. On the death of Herod, Archelaus succeeded to the throne, chiefly through the exertions of Nicolaus. We have no account of what became of Nicolaus after this event, and how long he survived it.

Nicolaus wrote a large number of works, of which the most important were, 1. *A Life of Himself*, of which a considerable portion is still extant. 2. *A Universal History*, already referred to, consisting of one hundred and forty-four books, of which we have only a few fragments. As far as we can judge from these remains, it treated chiefly of the history of the Asiatic nations. It appears, however, to have been a hurried compilation, in which Nicolaus, without exercising any criticism, incorporated what-

[1] *Smith, l. c.*

[2] *Stahr; Smith, Dict. Biogr., s. v.*

ever he found written by earlier historians. 3. *A Life of Augustus*, from which we have some extracts, made by command of Constantine Porphyrogenitus. These *excerpta* show that the author was not much concerned about accuracy, and that the biography was more of a eulogy than a history. 4. *A Life of Herod.* 5. Ἠθῶν παραδόξων συναγωγή, that is, a collection of singular customs among the various nations of the earth. Stobæus has preserved many passages from it. He also wrote commentaries on Aristotle and other philosophical works, and was the author of several tragedies and comedies. Stobæus has preserved a fragment of one of his comedies, extending to forty-four lines.

The best and most complete edition of the fragments of Nicolaus, before that of Müller, with Latin translations by Valesius and Grotius, is that of Orelli, Leipzig, 1804, 8vo. It contains, also, a good dissertation on the life and writings of the author, by the Abbé Sevin, which originally appeared in the *Mémoires de l'Acad. des Inscript.*, &c., vol. vi., p. 486, *seqq.* In 1811, Orelli published a supplement to his edition, which contains notes and emendations by Coraes, Creuzer, Schweighaeuser, and others. The most complete collection of the remains is that of C. Müller, in his *Fragmenta Historicorum Græcorum*, in Didot's *Bibliotheca Græca*, vol. iii., p. 343, *seqq.*

VIII. Memnon (Μέμνων),[1] a native probably of Heraclea Pontica. He wrote a large work on the history of that city, especially of the tyrants under whose power Heraclea had at various times fallen. Our knowledge of this work is derived from Photius. Of how many books it consisted we do not know. Photius had read from the ninth to the sixteenth inclusive, of which portion he has made a tolerably copious abstract. The first eight books he had not read, and he speaks of other books after the sixteenth. The ninth book begins with an account of the tyrant Clearchus, the disciple of Plato and Isocrates. The last event mentioned in the sixteenth book was the death of Brithagoras, who was sent by the Heracleans as ambassador to Julius Cæsar, after the latter had obtained the supreme power. From this Vossius supposes that the work was written about the time of Augustus; in the judgment of Orelli, not later than the time of Hadrian or the Antonines. It is, of course, impossible to fix the date with any precision, as we do not know at all down to what time the entire work was carried. The style of Memnon, according to Photius, was clear and simple, and the words were well chosen. The *excerpta* of Photius, however, contain numerous examples of rare and poetical expressions, as well as a few which indicate the decline of the Greek language. These *excerpta* were first published separately, together with the remains of Ctesias and Agatharchides, by H. Stephens, Paris, 1557. The best edition now is that of Orelli, Leipzig, 1816, 8vo, containing, together with the remains of Memnon, a few fragments of other writers on Heraclea. They are also given by C. Müller, in his *Fragm. Hist. Græc.*, vol. iii., p. 525, *seqq.*

IX. Pamphĭla (Παμφίλη),[2] a female historian of considerable reputation, who lived in the reign of Nero. According to Suidas, she was an Epidaurian; but Photius describes her as an Egyptian, by birth or descent. These two statements, however, may be reconciled by supposing that she was a native of Epidaurus, and that her family came from Egypt. She

[1] *Smith, Dict. Biogr., s. v.*

[2] *Id. ib.*

related in the preface to her work, for an account of which we are indebted to Photius, that, during the thirteen years she had lived with her husband, from whom she was never absent for a single hour, she was constantly at work upon her book, and that she diligently wrote down whatever she heard from her husband, and from the many other learned men who frequented their house, as well as whatever she herself read in books. Hence we can account for the statement of Suidas, that some authorities ascribed her work to her husband. The principal work of Pamphila is cited by various names, but its full and correct title seems to have been the one preserved by Photius, namely, *συμμίκτων ἱστοοικῶν ὑπομνημάτων λόγοι.* This title gives a general idea of the nature of its contents, which are still farther characterized by Photius. The work was not arranged according to subjects, or according to any settled plan, but it was more like a commonplace book, in which each piece of information was set down as it fell under the notice of the writer, who stated that she believed this variety would give greater pleasure to the reader. Photius considered the work as one of great use, and supplying important information on many points of history and literature. The estimation in which it was held in antiquity is shown, not only by the judgment of Photius, but also by the references to it in the works of Aulus Gellius and Diogenes Laertius, who appear to have availed themselves of it to a considerable extent. Modern scholars are best acquainted with the name of Pamphila, from a statement in her work, preserved by Aulus Gellius,[1] by which is ascertained the birth-year of Hellanicus, Herodotus, and Thucydides respectively, though this account, which is received by most scholars, is, as we have already seen, rejected by Krüger, in his life of Thucydides, on account of the little confidence which, according to him, can be placed in Pamphila's authority.

The history of Pamphila was divided into many books. Photius speaks of only eight, but Suidas says that it consisted of thirty-three. The latter must be correct, since we find Aulus Gellius[2] quoting the eleventh and twenty-ninth, and Diogenes Laertius[3] the twenty-fifth and thirty-second. Perhaps no more than eight books were extant in the time of Photius. Besides the historical work just mentioned, Pamphila wrote several other works, the titles of which are given by Suidas. 1. An *Epitome of Ctesias*, in three books. 2. *Epitomes* of histories and of other works, *ἐπιτομαὶ ἱστοριῶν τε καὶ ἑτερῶν βιβλίων.* 3. *Περὶ ἀμφισβητήσεων.* 4. *Περὶ ἀφροδισίων.*

The fragments of the works of Pamphila are collected by Müller, in his *Fragmenta Hist. Græc.*, vol. iii., p. 520, *seqq.*

X. Josephus, Flavius (Φλάβιος 'Ιώσηπος),[4] the celebrated Jewish historian, son of Matthias, is well known not only as a writer, but also as a warrior and statesman. He is himself our main authority for the events of his life, a circumstance obviously not without its drawbacks, especially as he is by no means averse to self-laudation. He was born at Jerusalem, in A.D. 37, the first year of Caligula's reign, and the fourth

[1] *Aul. Gell.*, xv., 23.
[2] *Id. ib.*
[3] *Diog. Laert.*, iii., 23; v., 36.
[4] *Elder; Smith, Dict. Biogr.*, *s. v.*

after our Lord's ascension. On his mother's side he was descended from the Asmonean princes, while from his father he inherited the priestly office. He enjoyed an excellent education, and at the age of twenty-six went to Rome to plead the cause of some Jewish priests, whom Felix, the procurator of Judæa, had sent thither as prisoners. After a narrow escape from death by shipwreck, he safely landed at Puteoli; and, being introduced to Poppæa, he not only effected the release of his friends, but received great presents from the empress.[1] On his return to Jerusalem he found his countrymen eagerly bent on a revolt from Rome, from which he used his best endeavors to dissuade them, but, failing in this, he professed to enter into the popular designs. He was chosen one of the generals of the Jews, and was sent to manage affairs in Galilee.[2] When Vespasian and his army entered Galilee, Josephus threw himself into Jotapata, which he defended for forty-seven days. When the place was taken, the life of Josephus was spared by Vespasian, through the intercession of Titus. Josephus thereupon assumed the character of a prophet, and predicted that the empire should one day be his and his son's.[3] Vespasian treated him with respect, but did not release him from captivity till he was proclaimed emperor,[4] nearly three years afterward (A.D. 70). Josephus was present with Titus at the siege of Jerusalem, and afterward accompanied him to Rome. He received the freedom of the city from Vespasian, who assigned him as a residence a house formerly occupied by himself, and treated him honorably to the end of his reign. The same favor was extended to him by Titus and Domitian. He assumed the name of Flavius as a dependent of the Flavian family. His time at Rome appears to have been employed mainly in the composition of his works.

The date of his death can not be fixed with accuracy, but we know[5] that he survived Agrippa II., who died in A.D. 97, so that his own decease may probably have taken place about A.D. 100. His first wife, whom he took at Vespasian's desire, was a *captive;* his marriage with her, therefore, since he was a priest, was contrary to the Jewish law, according to his own statement;[6] and his language[7] may imply that, when he was released from his bonds, and had accompanied Vespasian to Alexandrea, he divorced her. At Alexandrea he took a second wife, whom he also divorced, from dislike to her character, after she had borne him three sons, one of whom, Hyrcanus, was still alive when he wrote his life. His third wife was a Jewess of Cyprus, of noble family, by whom he had two sons, Justus and Simonides, surnamed Agrippa.[8]

With respect to the character of Josephus, we have already noticed his tendency to self-laudation, so that he himself is by no means free from the vanity which he charges upon Apion. Again, to say nothing of the court he paid to the notorious Agrippa II., his profane flattery of the Flavian family, "so gross (to use the words of Fuller) that it seems not limned with a pencil, but daubed with a trowel,"[9] is another obvious and

[1] *Vit.*, 3. [2] *Ibid.*, 4, *seqq.; Bell. Jud.*, ii., 20, *seq.*
[3] *Vit.*, 74, *seqq.; Bell. Jud.*, iii., 7, *seq.;* vi., 5, &c. [4] *Bell. Jud.*, iv., 10.
[5] *Vit.*, 65. [6] *Ant.*, iii., 12, § 2. [7] *Vit.*, 75. [8] *Ibid.*, 76.
[9] Compare *Wordsworth's Discourses on Public Education*, Disc. xx.

repulsive feature in the character of Josephus. His early visit to Rome, and introduction to the sweets of court favor, must have brought more home to him the lesson he might have learned, at all events, from the example of Herod the Great and others—that adherence to the Roman cause was the path to worldly distinction. And the awe with which the greatness and power of Rome inspired him lay always like a spell upon his mind, and stifled his patriotism. He felt pride, indeed, in the antiquity of his nation and in its ancient glories, as is clear from what are commonly called his books against Apion; neither do we find in him any want of sympathy with his country's misfortunes. But the fault of Josephus was that (as patriots never do) he despaired of his country. Again, holding, in the main, the abstract doctrines of a pharisee, but with the principles and temper of an Herodian, he strove to accommodate his religion to heathen tastes and prejudices, and this by actual omissions, no less than by a rationalistic system of modification. Thus he speaks of Moses and his law in a tone which might be adopted by any disbeliever in his divine legation. He says that Abraham went into Egypt, intending to adopt the Egyptian views of religion, should he find them better than his own. He intimates a doubt of there having been any miracle in the passage of the Red Sea. Numerous other instances of a similar nature our limits forbid us to specify.

The celebrated passage in which mention is made by him of the founder of our religion is now generally regarded as an interpolation.[1]

The writings of Josephus have always been regarded, and with justice, as indispensable for the theological student. For the determination of various readings, both in the Hebrew text of the Old Testament and in the Septuagint version, they are by no means without their value. But their chief use consists in such points as their testimony to the striking fulfillment of our Savior's prophecies, their confirmation of the canon, facts, and statements of Scripture, and the obvious collateral aid which they supply for its elucidation. The character of a faithful historian is claimed by Josephus for himself, and has been pretty generally acknowledged, though, from what has been said of his anxiety to conciliate his heathen readers, it can not be admitted without some drawbacks. The language of Josephus is remarkably pure, though we meet occasionally with unclassical, or, at least, *unusual* expressions and constructions, in some of which instances, however, the readings are doubtful. The speeches which he introduces have much spirit and vigor; and there is a graphic liveliness in his descriptions which carries our feelings along with it, and fully justifies the title of the *Greek Livy* applied to him by St. Jerome.[2]

The works of Josephus are as follows: 1. *The History of the Jewish War* (Περὶ τοῦ Ἰουδαϊκοῦ πολέμου ἢ Ἰουδαϊκῆς ἱστορίας περὶ ἁλώσεως), in seven books. Josephus tells us that he wrote it first in his own language, and then translated it into Greek, for the information of European readers.[3] The Hebrew copy is no longer extant. The Greek was published about A.D. 75, under the patronage and with the especial recommendation of

[1] *Elder, l. c.*

[2] *Hieron. ad Eustoch., De Cust. Virg. Ep.*, xviii.

[3] *Procem. ad Bell. Jud.*, 1.

Titus. It was admitted into the Palatine library, and its author was honored with a statue at Rome. It commences with the capture of Jerusalem by Antiochus Epiphanes, in B.C. 170, runs rapidly over the events before Josephus's own time, and then gives a detailed account of the fatal war with Rome. 2. *The Jewish Antiquities* (Ἰουδαϊκὴ Ἀρχαιολογία), in twenty books, completed about A.D. 93. The work extends from the creation of the world to A.D. 66, the twelfth year of Nero, in which the Jews were goaded to rebellion by Gessius Florus. 3. His own life, in one book. This is an appendage to the Antiquities. 4. A treatise on the antiquity of the Jews, or Κατὰ Ἀπίωνος, in two books. It is in answer to such as impugned the antiquity of the Jewish nation on the ground of the silence of Greek writers respecting it. The title "Against Apion" is rather a misnomer, and is applicable only to a portion of the second book (§ 1–13). This treatise exhibits considerable learning. 5. Εἰς Μακκαβαίους, ἢ περὶ αὐτοκράτορος λογισμοῦ. Probably spurious, though referred to as a work of Josephus by Eusebius, St. Jerome, Philostorgius, and others. It is an extremely declamatory account of the martyrdom of Eleazar (an aged priest), and of seven youths and their mother, in the persecution under Antiochus Epiphanes. Its title has reference to the zeal for God's law displayed by the sufferers in the spirit of the Maccabees.[1]

The invaluable but posthumous edition of Josephus, by Hudson, containing all the works, in Greek and Latin, came out at Oxford in 1720, 2 vols. fol. The Latin version was new; the text was founded on a most careful and extensive collation of MSS., and the edition was farther enriched by notes and indices. Havercamp's edition, Amsterdam, 1726, 2 vols. fol., is more convenient for the reader than creditable to the editor. That of Oberthür, in 3 vols. 8vo, Leipzig, 1782–1785, contains only the Greek text, most carefully edited, and the edition remains, unfortunately, incomplete. Another was edited by Richter, Leipzig, 1826, as part of a *Bibliotheca Patrum*. The latest edition, with probably the best text, is that of Dindorf, 2 vols. large 8vo thus far, in Didot's *Bibliotheca Græca*, Paris, 1845–7. It contains, also, the fragments relative to Jewish history contained in Photius, and fragments by C. Müller, hitherto unedited, of Polybius, Dionysius of Halicarnassus, Polyænus, Dexippus, and Eusebius.

XI. Plutarchus (Πλούταρχος),[2] the biographer and philosopher, was born at Chæronea, in Bœotia. The year of his birth is not known, but we learn from Plutarch himself that he was studying philosophy under Ammonius at the time when Nero was making his progress through Greece, in A.D. 66, from which we may assume that he was a youth or a young man at the time. He spent some time at Rome, and in other parts of Italy;[3] but he tells us that he did not learn the Latin language in Italy, because he was occupied with public commissions, and in giving lectures on philosophy, and it was late in life before he busied himself with Roman literature. He was lecturing at Rome during the reign of Domitian; but the statement of Suidas, that Plutarch was the preceptor of Trajan, ought to be rejected. Plutarch spent the later years of his life at Chæronea, where he discharged various magisterial offices, and held a priesthood. The time of his death is unknown. The work which has immortalized Plutarch's name is his *Parallel Lives* (Βίοι Παράλληλοι) of forty-six Greeks and Romans. The forty-six lives are arranged in pairs;

[1] *Elder, l. c.* [2] *Long; Smith, Dict. Biogr., s. v.* [3] *Vit. Demosth.*, 3

each pair contains the life of a Greek and a Roman, and is followed by a comparison, σύγκρισις, of the two men: in a few pairs the comparison is omitted or lost. He seems to have considered each pair of lives and the parallel as making one book (βιβλίον). When he says that the book of the lives of Demosthenes and Cicero was the fifth, it is the most natural interpretation to suppose that it was the fifth in the order in which he wrote them. It could not be the fifth in any other sense, if each pair composed a book. We have also the lives of Artaxerxes Mnemon, Aratus, Galba, and Otho, which are placed in the editions after the forty-six lives. A life of Homer is also attributed to him, but it is not printed in all the editions. The following lives by Plutarch are lost: Epaminondas, Scipio, Augustus, Tiberius, Caligula, Claudius, Nero, Vitellius, Hesiod, Pindar, Crates the Cynic, Daïphantus, Aristomenes, and the poet Aratus.

The authorities for Plutarch's Lives are incidentally indicated in the lives themselves. He is said to quote 250 writers, of whom about eighty are those whose works are either entirely or partially lost. The question of the sources of Plutarch's Lives has been examined by Heeren.[1] Plutarch must have had access to a good library, and if he wrote all his Lives during his old age at Chæronea, we must infer that he had a large stock of books at command. Being a Greek, and an educated man, he could not fail to be well acquainted with all the sources for his Greek Lives; and he has indicated them pretty fully. His acquaintance with the sources for his Roman Lives was less complete, and his handling of them less critical. Perhaps no work of antiquity has been so extensively read in modern times as Plutarch's Lives. The reason of their popularity is that Plutarch has rightly conceived the business of a biographer: his biography is true portraiture. Other biography is often a dull, tedious enumeration of facts in the order of time, with perhaps a summing up of character at the end. The reflections of Plutarch are neither impertinent nor trifling; his sound good sense is always there; his honesty of purpose is transparent; his love of humanity warms the whole. His work is and will remain, in spite of all the fault that can be found with it by plodding collectors of facts and small critics, the book of those who can nobly think, and dare and do.

Plutarch's other writings, above sixty in number, are placed under the general title of *Moralia*, or ethical works, though some of them are of an historical and anecdotical character, such as the essay on the malignity (κακοήθεια) of Herodotus, which neither requires nor merits refutation, and his *Apophthegmata*, many of which are of little value. Eleven of these essays are generally classed among Plutarch's historical works. Among them, also, are his Roman Questions or Inquiries, his Greek Questions, and his Lives of the Ten Orators. But it is likely enough that several of the essays which are included in the Moralia of Plutarch are not by him. At any rate, some of them are not worth reading. The best of the essays included among the Moralia are of a different stamp. There is no philosophical system in these essays: pure speculation was

[1] *De Fontibus*, &c., *Vit. Parallel.*, &c., Göttingen, 1820, 8vo.

not Plutarch's province. His best writings are practical, and their merits consist in the soundness of his views on the ordinary events of human life, and in the benevolence of his temper. His "Marriage Precepts" are a sample of his good sense and of his happiest expression. He rightly appreciated, also, the importance of a good education, and he gives much sound advice on the bringing up of children.

The first edition of all the works of Plutarch is that of H. Stephens, Geneva, 1572, 13 vols. 8vo. An edition of the Greek text, with a Latin version, appeared at Leipzig, 1774–1782, 12 vols. 8vo, and it is generally called Reiske's edition, but Reiske died in 1774. Hutten's edition appeared at Tübingen, 1791–1805, 14 vols. 8vo. A separate edition of the Lives first appeared in Latin, at Rome, about 1470, 2 vols. fol. The version was made by several hands, and was the foundation of the Spanish and Italian versions. The first edition of the Greek text of the Lives was that printed by Giunta, Florence, 1517, fol. The edition of Bryan, London, 1729, 5 vols. 4to, with a Latin version, was completed by Moses du Soul, after Bryan's death. There is an edition by Coraes, Paris, 1809–1815, with notes, in 6 vols. 8vo; one by Schaefer, Leipzig, 1825–30, 6 vols. 8vo, with notes original and selected; one by Sintenis, Leipzig, 1839–1846, 4 vols. 8vo; and one by Doehner, 2 vols. large 8vo, in Didot's *Bibliotheca Græca*, Paris, 1846. The best of these editions is that of Sintenis. The first edition of the Moralia, which is said to be very incorrect, was printed by the elder Aldus, Venice, 1509, fol.; and afterward at Basle, by Froben, 1542, fol., 1574, fol. The best edition, however, is that of Wyttenbach, the labor of four-and-twenty years. It was printed at Oxford in 4to. It consists of four parts, or six volumes of text (1795–1800) and two volumes of notes (1810–1821). It was also printed at the same time in 8vo, 14 vols. There is also a Leipzig edition of the notes of Wyttenbach, 1820–34, 3 vols. 8vo. An edition of the Moralia, by Dübner, 2 vols. large 8vo, forms part of Didot's *Bibliotheca Græca*, Paris, 1841, and claims to have a text superior to that of Wyttenbach. A useful *Index Græcitatis*, from the papers of Wyttenbach, was published at Oxford, 2 vols. 8vo, 1830, reprinted at Leipzig, 1843.

XII. ARRIANUS (Ἀῤῥιανός),[1] a native of Nicomedia, in Bithynia, born about A.D. 90, was a pupil and friend of Epictetus, and first attracted attention as a philosopher by publishing at Athens the lectures of his master. In A.D. 124, he gained the friendship of Hadrian during his stay in Greece, and received from the emperor the Roman citizenship. From this time he assumed the name Flavius Arrianus. In A.D. 136, he was appointed prefect of Cappadocia, which was invaded the year after by the Alani or Massagetæ, whom he defeated. Under Antoninus Pius, in A.D. 146, Arrian was consul; and about A.D. 150, he withdrew from public life, and from this time lived in his native town of Nicomedia, as priest of Ceres and Proserpina. He died at an advanced age, in the reign of Marcus Aurelius. Arrian was one of the best and most active writers of his time. He was a close imitator of Xenophon, both in the subjects of his works and in the style in which they were written. He regarded his relation to Epictetus as similar to that of Xenophon to Socrates,[2] and it was his endeavor to carry out that resemblance. With this view he published, 1. The *Philosophical Lectures* of his master (Διατριβαὶ Ἐπικτήτου), in eight books, the first half of which is still extant. 2. An *Abstract* of the practical philosophy of Epictetus (Ἐγχειρίδιον Ἐπικτήτου), which is still extant. This celebrated work maintained its authority for many centuries with both Christians and pagans. He also published other works relating to Epictetus, which are now lost. His original works are, 3. A *Treatise on the Chase* (Κυνηγετικός), which forms a kind of supple-

[1] *Smith, Dict. Biogr.*, *s. v.*

[2] *Photius*, p. 17, *B*, ed. *Bekker*; *Suid.*, *s. v.*

ment to Xenophon's work on the same subject, and is printed in most editions of Xenophon's works. 4. The *History of the Asiatic Expedition of Alexander the Great* (Ἀνάβασις Ἀλεξάνδρου), in seven books, and the most important of Arrian's works. This great work reminds the reader of Xenophon's Anabasis, not only by its title, but also by the ease and clearness of the style. It is also of great value for its historical accuracy, being based upon the most trustworthy histories written by the contemporaries of Alexander, especially those of Ptolemy, son of Lagus, and of Aristobulus, the son of Aristobulus. The work likewise shows that Arrian possessed a thorough practical knowledge of military affairs. 5. *On India* (Ἰνδική, or τὰ Ἰνδικά), which may be regarded as a continuation of the Anabasis. This work is written in the Ionic dialect, in imitation, probably, of Ctesias, whose work on the same subject Arrian wished to supplant by a more trustworthy and correct account. 6. A *Description of a Voyage around the Coasts of the Euxine* (Περίπλους πόντου Εὐξείνου), which had undoubtedly been made by Arrian himself during his government of Cappadocia. This Periplus has come down to us, together with a Periplus of the Erythræan, and a Periplus of the Euxine and Palus Mæotis, both of which also bear the name of Arrian, but belong undoubtedly to a later period. 7. A *Work on Tactics* (Λόγος τακτικός, or Τέχνη τακτική), of which we possess at present only a fragment. Arrian wrote also numerous other works which are now lost. These were principally of an historical nature, and composed during the latter part of his life. Among them we may mention, 1. *A History of the Successors of Alexander the Great* (Τὰ μετὰ Ἀλέξανδρον), in ten books, of which an abstract, or, rather, an enumeration of contents, is preserved in Photius. 2. *A History of the Parthians* (Παρθικά), in seventeen books, the main subject of which was their wars with the Romans, especially under Trajan. 3. *A History of Bithynia* (Βιθυνικά), in eight books. This work began with the mythical age, and carried the history down to the time when Bithynia became united with the Roman empire, and in it the author mentioned several events connected with his own life. 4. *A History of the Alani* (Ἀλανική, or τὰ κατ' Ἀλανούς). He had defeated this people when præfect of Cappadocia, in A.D. 136.

The Διατριβαὶ Ἐπικτήτου were first printed by Trincavelli, 1535, and afterward, together with the Ἐγχειρίδιον and Simplicius's commentary, with a Latin translation, by H. Wolf, Basle, 1560. The best editions are in Schweighaeuser's *Epicteteæ Philosophiæ Monumenta*, vol. iii., and in Coraes' Πάρεργα Ἑλλην. Βιβλιοθ., vol. viii. The Ἐγχειρίδιον was first published in a Latin translation by Politian, Rome, 1493; and 1496, by Beroaldus, at Bologna. The Greek original, with the commentary of Simplicius, appeared first at Venice, 1528, 4to. This edition was soon followed by numerous others. The best among the recent editions are those of Schweighaeuser and Coraes, in the collections above mentioned. The Κυνηγετικός is contained in Zeune's *Opuscula Minora* of Xenophon; in Schneider's edition of Xenophon, vol. vi., best in Sauppe's revision of Schneider, vol. vi.; and, as already remarked, in many other editions of Xenophon. The best editions of the *Anabasis* are by Ellendt, Regimontii, 1832, 2 vols. 8vo; by Krüger, Berlin, 1835–48, 2 vols. 8vo. The Ἰνδική is usually printed at the end of the Anabasis; separately by Schmieder, Halle, 1798, 8vo. The *Peripluses* are contained in the collection of the minor works of Arrian by Blancard, Amsterdam, 1683 and 1750, and also in Hudson's *Geographi Minores*, and in Gail's and Hoffmann's collections of the minor geographers. The work on *Tactics* is printed in Blancard's collection. The best and most complete edition of the entire works of Arrian is by Dübner and C. Müller, in Didot's *Bibliotheca Græca*, Paris, 1846, 8vo.

XIII. Appianus (Ἀππιανός),[1] a native of Alexandrea, lived at Rome during the reigns of Trajan, Hadrian, and Antoninus Pius, as we gather from various passages in his work. We have hardly any particulars of his life, for his autobiography, to which he refers at the end of the preface to his history, is now lost. In the same passage he mentions that he was a man of considerable distinction at Alexandrea, and afterward removed to Rome, where he was engaged in pleading causes in the courts of the emperors. He further states that the emperors considered him worthy to be intrusted with the management of their affairs, which Schweighaeuser and others interpret to mean that he was appointed to the office of procurator or præfectus of Egypt. There is, however, no reason for this supposition. We know, from a letter of Fronto, that it was the office of procurator which he held; but whether he had the management of the emperor's finances at Rome, or went to some province in this capacity, is quite uncertain.

Appian wrote a Roman history (Ῥωμαϊκά, or Ῥωμαϊκὴ Ἱστορία), in twenty-four books, on a plan different from that of most historians. He did not treat the history of the Roman empire as a whole, in chronological order, following the series of events; but he gave a separate account of the affairs of each country, from the time that it became connected with the Romans till it was finally incorporated in the Roman empire. The first foreign people with whom the Romans came in contact were the Gauls; and consequently his history, according to his plan, would have begun with that people. But, in order to make the work a complete history of Rome, he devoted the first three books to an account of the early times, and of the various nations of Italy which Rome subdued. The subjects of the different books were: 1. The kingly period. 2. Italy. 3. The Samnites. 4. The Gauls or Celts. 5. Sicily and the other islands. 6. Spain. 7. Hannibal's wars. 8. Libya, Carthage, and Numidia. 9. Macedonia. 10. Greece, and the Greek states in Asia Minor. 11. Syria and Parthia. 12. The war with Mithradates. 13–21. The civil wars (Ἐμφύλια), in nine books, from those of Marius and Sulla to the battle of Actium. The last four books, also, had the title of τὰ Αἰγυπτιακά. 22. Ἑκατονταετία, comprising the history of a hundred years, from the battle of Actium to the beginning of Vespasian's reign. 23. The wars with Illyria. 24. Those with Arabia.

We possess only eleven of these complete, namely, the sixth, seventh, eighth, eleventh, twelfth, thirteenth, fourteenth, fifteenth, sixteenth, seventeenth, and twenty-third. There are also fragments of several of the others. The Parthian history, which has come down to us as part of the eleventh book, has been proved by Schweighaeuser to be no work of Appian, but merely a compilation from Plutarch's lives of Antony and Crassus, probably made in the Middle Ages. Appian's work is a mere compilation. In the early times he chiefly followed Dionysius, as far as the latter went, and his work makes up, to a considerable extent, for the

[1] *Smith, Dict. Biogr.*, *s. v.*

books of Dionysius which are lost. In the history of the second Punic war, Fabius seems to have been his chief authority, and subsequently he made use of Polybius. His style is clear and simple; but he possesses few merits as an historian, and he frequently makes the most absurd blunders. Thus, for instance, he places Saguntum on the north of the Iberus, and states that it takes only half a day to sail from Spain to Britain.

Appian's history was first published in a barbarous Latin translation, by Candidus, at Venice, in 1472. A part of the Greek text was first published by Carolus Stephanus, Paris, 1551; which was followed by an improved Latin version, by Gelenius, put forth, after the death of the latter, at Basle, 1554. The Greek text of the portion of the work relating to Spain and Hannibal's wars was published for the first time by H. Stephanus, Geneva, 1557. Ursinus published some fragments at Antwerp, 1582. The second edition of the Greek text was edited, with the Latin version of Gelenius, by H. Stephanus, Geneva, 1592. The twenty-third book of Appian, containing the wars with Illyria, was first published by Hoeschelius, Augsburg, 1599, and some additional fragments were added by Valesius, Paris, 1634. The third edition of Appian's work was published at Amsterdam in 1670, and is a mere reprint of the edition of H. Stephanus. The work bears on the title-page the name of Alexander Tollius, but he did absolutely nothing for the work, and allowed the typographical errors to remain. The fourth edition, and infinitely superior to all that went before, is that of Schweighaeuser, Leipzig, 1785, 3 vols. 8vo. A few new fragments of Appian were published by Mai, in the second volume of his *Nova Collectio Vet. Script.* They are reprinted in "*Polybii et Appiani Historiarum Excerpta Vaticana*," &c., edited by Lucht, Altona, 1830. Mai also discovered a letter of Appian to Fronto (p. 229 in Niebuhr's edition of Fronto). The latest, and probably the best edition of the text of Appian, is that forming part of Didot's *Bibliotheca Græca*, in which the text and Latin version of Schweighaeuser have been corrected from the private memoranda of that editor. It contains, also, the fragments discovered by Mai.

XIV. Dion Cassius Cocceianus,[1] the celebrated historian of Rome, probably derived the gentile name of Cassius from one of his ancestors, who, on receiving the Roman franchise, had been adopted into the Cassia gens; for his father, Cassius Apronianus, had already borne it. He appears to have adopted the cognomen of Cocceianus from Dion Chrysostomus Cocceianus the orator, who, according to Reimarus, was his grandfather on the mother's side. Dion Cassius was born about A.D. 155, at Nicæa, in Bithynia. His father was a Roman senator. He was educated with great care, and was trained in the rhetorical schools of the time, and in the study of the classical writers of ancient Greece. He accompanied his father to Cilicia, of which the latter had the administration, and after his father's death he went to Rome, about A.D. 180. He was straightway made a senator, and frequently pleaded in the courts of justice. He was ædile and quæstor under Commodus, and prætor under Septimius Severus, A.D. 194. He accompanied Caracalla on his journey to the East; was appointed by Macrinus to the government of Pergamus and Smyrna, A.D. 218; was consul about A.D. 220; proconsul of Africa, A.D. 224, under Alexander Severus, by whom he was sent as legate to Dalmatia in A.D. 226, and to Pannonia in the following year. In the latter province he restored strict discipline among the troops, which excited the discontent of the prætorians at Rome, who demanded his life of Alexander Severus. But the emperor protected him, and raised him to his second consulship, A.D. 229. Dion, however, retired to Campania, and

[1] *Smith, Dict. Biogr., s. v.*

shortly afterward obtained permission from the emperor to return to his native town Nicæa, where he passed the remainder of his days.

Dion wrote several historical works, but the most important was a *History of Rome* (Ῥωμαϊκὴ Ἱστορία), which alone has come down to us, though in a sadly mutilated state, only a comparatively small portion having reached us entire. It consisted originally of eighty books, and was farther divided into decades, like Livy's Roman history. It embraced the whole history of Rome from the earliest times; that is, from the landing of Æneas in Italy down to A.D. 229, the year in which Dion quitted Italy and returned to Nicæa. Of the first thirty-four books we possess only fragments; but since Zonaras, in his annals, chiefly followed Dion Cassius, we may regard the annals of Zonaras as, to some extent, an epitome of Dion Cassius. Of the thirty-fifth book we possess a considerable fragment, and from the thirty-sixth book to the fifty-fourth the work is extant complete, and embraces the history from the wars of Lucullus and Pompey against Mithradates, down to the death of Agrippa, B.C. 10. Of the remaining books we have only the epitomes made by Xiphilinus and others. Dion Cassius himself intimates that he treated the history of republican Rome briefly, but that he endeavored to give a more minute and detailed account of those events of which he had himself been an eye-witness.[1]

Notwithstanding the great losses which the work has experienced, we still possess a sufficient portion to enable us to form a correct estimate of its value. It contains an abundance of materials for the later history of the republic, and for a considerable period of the empire, for some portions of which it is our only source of information. In some of the fragments published by Mai, and to which we shall again allude in our account of the editions of the work, Dion distinctly states that he had read nearly every thing which had been written on the history of Rome, and that he did not, like a mere compiler, put together what he found in other writers, but that he weighed his authorities, and exercised his judgment in selecting what he thought fit for a place in his work. This assertion of the author himself is perfectly justified by the nature and character of his history, for it is manifest every where that he had acquired a thorough knowledge of his subject, and that his notions of Roman life and Roman institutions were far more correct than those of some of his predecessors, such as Dionysius of Halicarnassus. Whenever he is led into error, it is generally owing to his not having access to authentic sources, and to his being obliged to satisfy himself with secondary ones. It must also be borne in mind, as Dion himself observes, that the history of the empire presented many more difficulties to the historian than that of the republic. In those parts in which he relates contemporary events, his work forms a sort of medium between real history and mere memoirs of the emperors. His object was to give a record as complete and as accurate as possible of all the important events; but his work is not, on that account, a dry chronological catalogue of events, for he endeavors, like Thucydides, Polybius, and Tacitus, to trace the events to their causes, and to

[1] *Smith, l. c.*

unfold the motives of men's actions. Indeed, in his endeavor to make us see the connection of occurrences, he sometimes even neglects the chronological order, like his great models.

But with all these excellences, Dion Cassius is the equal neither of Thucydides nor of Tacitus, though we may admit that his faults are, to a great extent, rather those of his age than of his individual character as an historian. He had been trained in the schools of the rhetoricians, and the consequences of it are visible in his history, which is not free from a rhetorical tinge, especially in the speeches which are introduced in it. In the formation of his style he appears to have endeavored to imitate the classic writers of ancient Greece; but his language is, nevertheless, full of peculiarities, barbarisms, and Latinisms, probably the consequence of his long residence in Italy; and the praise which Photius bestows upon him for the clearness of his style must be greatly modified, for it is often harsh and heavy, and Dion seems to have written as he spoke, without any attempt at elegance or refinement.

The first edition of Dion Cassius in the original Greek is that of R. Stephens, Paris, 1548, fol., which contains from book thirty-five to sixty. H. Stephens then gave a new edition, with a Latin translation by Xylander, Geneva, 1591, fol. The epitome of Xiphilinus, from book sixty to eighty, was first printed in the edition of Leunclavius, Frankfort, 1592, and Hanau, 1606, fol. After the fragments and *eclogæ* collected by Ursinus and Valesius had been published, Fabricius formed the idea of preparing a complete and comprehensive edition of Dion Cassius; but his death prevented the completion of his plan, which was carried out by his son-in-law Reimarus, who published his edition at Hamburg, 1750–52, in 2 vols. fol. The Greek text is not much improved in this edition, but the commentary and the indexes are of very great value. The Latin translation which it contains is made up of those of Xylander and Leunclavius. A more recent edition is that of Sturz, in 9 vols. 8vo, Leipzig, 1824, the ninth volume of which (published in 1843) contains the "*Excerpta Vaticana*," which had been first discovered and published by Mai (*Script. Vet. Nov. Collect.*, vol. ii., p. 135, *seqq.*). These *excerpta* were published from a Vatican MS., and bear, indeed, the name of Dion Cassius, but are, in all probability, taken from the work of some Christian writer, who continued the work of Dion. They belonged, in fact, to a work containing the history, from the time of Valerian down to that of Constantine the Great. A few more fragments were published by Haase (Bonn, 1840, 8vo), who found them in a Paris MS.

XV. Herodianus (Ἡρωδιανός),[1] a writer on Roman history. He was a Greek, though he appears to have lived for a considerable period in Rome, but without holding any public office. From his work, which is still extant, we may gather that he was still living at an advanced age in the reign of Gordian III., who ascended the throne A.D. 238. Beyond this we know nothing respecting his life. His history extends over the period from the death of M. Aurelius (A.D. 180) to the commencement of the reign of Gordian III. (A.D. 238), and bears the title Ἡρωδιανοῦ τῆς μετὰ Μάρκον βασιλείας ἱστοριῶν βιβλία ὀκτώ. He himself informs us that the events of this period had occurred in his own lifetime. Photius gives an outline of the contents of the work, and passes a flattering encomium on the style of Herodian, which he describes as clear, vigorous, and agreeable, preserving a happy medium between an utter disregard of art and elegance, and a profuse employment of the artifices and prettinesses which were known under the name of Atticism, as well as between boldness and

[1] *Smith, Dict. Biogr.*, s. v.

bombast, adding that not many historical writers are his superiors. He appears to have had Thucydides before him, to some extent, as a model, both for style and for the general composition of his work, like him, introducing here and there speeches wholly or in part imaginary. In spite of occasional inaccuracies in chronology and geography, his narrative is, in the main, truthful and impartial, though Julius Capitolinus and others charge him with partiality.

The best editions of Herodian are that by Irmisch, Leipzig, 1789–1805, 5 vols. 8vo; by F. A. Wolf, Halle, 1792, 8vo; and by Bekker, Berlin, 1826.

XVI. ÆLIANUS CLAUDIUS (Κλαύδιος Αἰλιανός)[1] was born, according to Suidas, at Præneste, in Italy, and lived at Rome. He calls himself a Roman,[2] as possessing the rights of Roman citizenship. He was particularly fond of the Greeks, and of Greek literature and oratory.[3] He studied under Pausanias the rhetorician, and imitated the style of Dion Chrysostom, but admired Herodes Atticus more than all. He taught rhetoric at Rome in the time of Hadrian, and hence was called ὁ σοφιστής. So complete was the command which he acquired over the Greek language, that he could speak it as well as a native Athenian. That rhetoric, however, was not his forte, may easily be inferred from the style of his works; and he appears to have given up teaching for writing. He lived to about sixty years of age.

There are two considerable works of his remaining: one a collection of miscellaneous history (Ποικίλη Ἱστορία), in fourteen books, commonly called his "*Varia Historia*," and the other a work on the peculiarities of animals (Περὶ Ζώων Ἰδιότητος), in seventeen books, commonly called his "*De Animalium Natura.*" The former work contains short narrations and anecdotes, historical, biographical, antiquarian, &c., selected from various authors, generally without their names being given, and on a great variety of subjects. Its chief value arises from its containing many passages from works of older authors which are now lost. The latter work is of the same kind, scrappy and gossiping. It is partly collected from older writers, and partly the result of his own observations. This book would appear to have become a popular and standard work on zoology, since, in the fourteenth century, Manuel Philes, a Byzantine poet, founded upon it a poem on animals. The similarity of plan in the two works, with other internal evidences, seems to show that they were both written by the same Ælian, and not, as Voss and Valckenaer conjecture, by two different persons. In both works he seems desirous to inculcate moral and religious principles, and he wrote some treatises expressly on philosophical and religious subjects, especially one on "Providence" (Περὶ Προνοίας), in three books, and one on the "Divine Manifestations" (Περὶ Θείων Ἐνεργειῶν), directed against the Epicureans. There are also attributed to him twenty letters on husbandry and such like matters, which are by feigned characters, are written in a rhetorical, unreal style, and are of no value.

The best editions of the *Varia Historia* are by Perizonius, Leyden, 1701, 8vo; by Gronovius, Leyden, 1731, 2 vols. 4to, and by Kühn, Leipzig, 1780, 2 vols. 8vo. The *De Ani-*

[1] *Smith, Dict. Biogr., s. v.* [2] *V. H.*, xii., 25. [3] *V. H.*, ix., 32; xii., 25.

malium Natura was edited by Gronovius, London, 1744, 2 vols. 4to, and by J. G. Schneider, Leipzig, 1784, 2 vols. 8vo. The last edition is that by Jacobs, Jena, 1832, 2 vols. 8vo. This contains the valuable materials which Schneider had collected and left for a new edition. The letters were published apart from the other works by Aldus Manutius, in his "*Collectio Epistolarum Græcarum*," Venice, 1499, 4to.

XVII. Dexippus, Publius Herennius,[1] a Greek rhetorician and historian, was a native of Attica, and lived in the third century after Christ, in the reigns of Claudius Gothicus, Aurelian, Tacitus, and Probus, until about A.D. 280.[2] He was regarded by his contemporaries and by later writers as a man of most extensive learning, and he was honored at Athens with the highest offices in the state. He distinguished himself also in fighting against the Goths, when they invaded Greece in A.D. 262. He was the author of three historical works: 1. Τὰ μετὰ Ἀλέξανδρον, a history of Macedonia from the time of Alexander, in four books. By way of introduction, the author prefixed a sketch of the preceding history, from the time of Caranus to Alexander. 2. Σύντομον ἱστορικόν, a chronological history, from the Mythical Ages down to the accession of Claudius Gothicus, A.D. 268. It consisted of twelve books, and is frequently referred to by the writers of the Augustan History. 3. Σκυθικά, an account of the war of the Goths or Scythians, in which Dexippus himself had fought. It commenced in the reign of Decius, and was brought to a close by Aurelian. We have only fragments remaining of his works, which show, however, that his style has all the faults of the late Greek rhetoricians. These fragments, which have been greatly increased by the discoveries of Mai, have been collected by Bekker and Niebuhr, in the first volume of the *Scriptores Historiæ Byzantinæ*, Bonn, 1829, 8vo.

XVIII. Phlegon (Φλέγων),[3] a native of Tralles, in Lydia, was a freedman of the Emperor Hadrian, and not of Augustus, as has been erroneously asserted by some writers on the authority of Suidas. Phlegon probably survived Hadrian, since his work on the Olympiads came down to Ol. 229, that is, A.D. 137, which was the year before the death of that emperor. He wrote the following works: 1. Περὶ θαυμασίων, a small treatise on wonderful events, which has come down to us, but the beginning of which is wanting. It is a poor performance, full of the most ridiculous tales. 2. Περὶ μακροβίων, likewise extant, consisting of only a few pages, and giving a list of persons in Italy who had attained the age of a hundred years and upward. It was copied from the registers of the censors (ἐξ αὐτῶν τῶν ἀποτιμήσεων), is a bare enumeration of names, and is not worthy to be compared with the work on the same subject ascribed to Lucian. At the end there is an extract from the Sibylline oracles of some sixty or seventy lines. These two are the only works of Phlegon that have come down to us. 3. Ὀλυμπιονικῶν καὶ χρονικῶν συναγωγή, quoted under the title of Χρονογραφίαι or Ὀλυμπιάδες, in seventeen books, and giving an account of the Olympiads from Ol. 1 (B.C. 776) to Ol. 229 (A.D. 137). This was by far the most important of the works of Phlegon. The commencement of the book is preserved in the MSS. of the other works of Phlegon, and an extract from it, relating to the 177th

[1] *Smith, Dict. Biogr.*, *s. v.* [2] *Eunap.*, *Vit. Porphyr.*, p. 21. [3] *Smith, Dict. Biogr.*, *s. v.*

Olympiad, is given by Photius, but with these exceptions, and a few references to it in Stephanus Byzantinus, Eusebius, Origen, and others, the work is entirely lost. 4. Ὀλυμπιάδες ἐν βιβλίοις ή, a sort of abridgment of the preceding. 5. A life of Hadrian, really written by the emperor himself, though published as the work of Phlegon. 6. Γυναῖκες ἐν πολεμικοῖς συνεταὶ καὶ ἀνδρεῖαι, a small treatise, first published by Heeren (*Bibl. d. Alten Literat. und Kunst*, part. vi., Göttingen, 1789), by whom it is ascribed to Phlegon; but Westermann, who has also printed it, with the other works of Phlegon, thinks that it was not written by him. There were, besides these, two or three other unimportant works.

The *editio princeps* of Phlegon was edited by Xylander, along with Antoninus Liberalis, Antigonus, and similar writers, Basle, 1568. The next edition was by Meursius, Leyden, 1620, which was reprinted by Gronovius, in his Thesaurus of Greek Antiquities, vols. viii. and ix. The third edition was by Franz, 1775, of which a new edition appeared in 1822, Halle, with the notes of Bast. The most recent edition is by Westermann, in his Παραδοξογράφοι, *Scriptores Rerum Mirabilium Græci*, Brunswick, 1839. The fragments on the Olympiads are given in the Oxford edition of Pindar, 1697, fol., and in Krause's *Olympia*, Vienna, 1838.

XIX. Africanus Sextus Julius,[1] a Christian writer at the beginning of the third century, called by Suidas a Libyan, but who passed the greater part of his life at Emmaus, in Palestine, where, according to some, he was born.[2] He went to Alexandrea to hear the philosopher Heraclas, who was afterward bishop of that city. The later Syrian writers state that he was subsequently made bishop himself. He was one of the most learned of the early Christian writers. Socrates[3] classes him with Origen and Clement. His chief work was a *Chronicon*, in five books (Πεντάβιβλον χρονολογικόν), from the creation of the world, which he placed in B.C. 5499, to A.D. 221, the fourth year of the reign of Elagabalus. The work is lost, but a considerable part of it is extracted by Eusebius in his "Chronicon," and many fragments of it also are preserved by Georgius Syncellus, Cedrenus, and in the "Paschale Chronicon." The fragments of this work are given by Gallandi (*Bibl. Pat.*) and Routh (*Reliquiæ Sacræ*). Africanus wrote a letter to Origen impugning the authority of the book of Susanna, to which Origen replied. This letter is extant, and has been published, together with Origen's answer, by Wetstein, Basle, 1674, 4to. It is also contained in De la Rue's edition of Origen. He also wrote a letter to Aristides on the genealogies of Christ in Matthew and Luke, of which some extracts are given by Eusebius.

There is another work attributed to Africanus, entitled Κεστοί, that is, embroidered girdles, so called from the celebrated κεστός of Venus. According to Suidas, it contained twenty-four books; but according to Photius, fourteen; and according to Syncellus, nine. It treated of a vast variety of subjects—medicine, agriculture, natural history, the military art, &c., and seems to have been a kind of commonplace book, in which the author entered the results of his reading. Some of the books are said to exist still in manuscript. Some extracts from them are published by Thevenot, in the "*Mathematici Veteres*," Paris, 1693, and also in the *Geoponica* of Cassianus Bassus.

1 *Smith, Dict. Biogr., s. v.* 2 *Hieron., De Vir. Ill.*, 63. 3 *Hist. Eccl.*, ii., 35.

CHAPTER XLVII.

SIXTH OR ROMAN PERIOD—*continued.*

SOPHISTS AND RHETORICIANS.

INTRODUCTORY REMARKS.[1]

I. THE term *Sophist*, which in the time of Socrates and Plato had been a title of reproach, became under the Roman emperors an honorary appellation, and designated a particular class of literary men. The name was now given to those who, independently of the talent of public speaking and extemporaneous discourse, occupied themselves with what we call belles-lettres studies, but with the exception of poetry.

II. As some of this class of individuals, however, devoted themselves more particularly to public speaking and the composition of discourses, and others to writing on the theory of the art, or what we term rhetoric, it will be convenient to make a division of them into *sophists* and *rhetoricians*, and to consider each class in succession.

III. In the period which we are at present considering, public speaking was confined to the bar, public lectures, and the schools, in the last of which imaginary causes were pleaded or set themes discussed. The lectures, which were merely a species of public declamation, became in time extremely popular, and proved a source of both honor and riches. Sometimes, however, they were merely essays, intended to be read to a chosen few. The subjects were generally of a moral, philosophical, or political character, and the aid of mythology and history was frequently called in to render these oratorical displays more interesting and showy.

IV. It was during this epoch of the decline of eloquence that various specific terms began to be applied to the different kinds of oratorical composition which were then in vogue. Such, for instance, were the following: Μελέτη, Σύστασις, Λόγος, Λαλιά, ΠροςΛαλιά, Σχεδίασμα, Διάλεξις, Ἐπίδειξις.

V. By Μελέτη was meant a declamation, carefully prepared and reduced to writing, in which the author, assuming the character of some personage of antiquity, or of some mythological individual, treated of an imaginary subject as if really existing. The Σύστασις was a short discourse, by which the speaker sought to recommend himself to some protector. The term Λόγος was generic, and denoted every kind of composition or discourse, but chiefly a harangue on some important subject. The Προτρεπτικὸς Λόγος was, in particular, a discourse addressed to a public assembly, exhorting them to form some resolve, or, as was oftentimes the case, a moral exhortation. The Λαλιά was what we would call a complimentary address. It was termed ΠροςΛαλιά when it served as an exordium to a public lecture. The Σχεδίασμα designated an off-hand or extemporaneous speech. The Διάλεξις was what we would call a disser-

[1] *Schöll, Hist. Lit. Gr.*, vol. iv., p. 207, *seqq.*

tation. The Ἐπίδειξις was a show-speech, intended for some formal occasion.[1]

VI. We will now proceed to give a brief account of the more important individuals in the two classes just referred to.

I. SOPHISTS.

I. Lesbōnax (Λεσβῶναξ),[2] a philosopher and sophist, who lived in the time of Augustus. He was the father of Polemon, who is known as the teacher and friend of the Emperor Tiberius. Suidas says that he wrote several philosophical works, but does not mention that he was an orator or rhetorician, although there can be no doubt that he is the same as the Lesbonax of whom there were extant in the time of Photius[3] sixteen political orations. Of these orations only two have come down to us, one entitled περὶ τοῦ πολέμου Κορινθίων, and the other a προτρεπτικὸς λόγος, both of which are not unsuccessful imitations of the Attic orators of the best times. They are printed in the collections of the Greek orators published by Stephens, Reiske, Bekker, &c. A separate edition was published by Orelli, Leipzig, 1820, 8vo.

II. Dion Chrysostŏmus (Δίων Χρυσόστομος),[4] that is, Dion the Golden-mouthed, a surname which he owed to his great talents as an orator. He also bore the surname of Cocceianus, which he derived from the Emperor Cocceius Nerva, with whom he was connected by intimate friendship.[5] Dion Chrysostom was born at Prusa, in Bithynia, about the middle of the first century of our era, and belonged to a distinguished equestrian family. He received a careful education, increased his knowledge by travelling in different countries, and came to Rome in the reign of Vespasian; but, having incurred the suspicion of Domitian, he was obliged to leave the city. On the advice of the Delphic oracle, it is said, he put on the attire of a beggar, and with nothing in his pocket but a copy of Plato's Phædon, and the oration of Demosthenes on the Embassy, he visited Thrace, Mysia, Scythia, and the country of the Getæ, and, owing to the power and wisdom of his orations, he met every where with a kindly reception, and did much good.[6] When Domitian was murdered, Dion used his influence with the army stationed on the frontier in favor of his friend Nerva, and seems to have returned to Rome immediately after his accession.[7] Trajan, Nerva's successor, also entertained the highest esteem for him, and showed him the most marked favor, for he is said to have often visited him, and even to have allowed him to ride by his side in his triumphal car. Dion died at Rome about A.D. 117.

Dion Chrysostom is the most eminent of the Greek sophists and rhetoricians in the time of the Roman empire. There are extant eighty of his orations; but they are more like essays on political, moral, and philosophical subjects than real orations, of which they have only the form. We find among them λόγοι περὶ βασιλείας, or λόγοι βασιλικοί, four orations addressed to Trajan on the virtues of a sovereign; Διογένης ἢ περὶ τυραν-

[1] *Himerii Opera*, ed. *Wernsdorff*, p. 20.
[2] *Smith, Dict. Biogr.*, *s. v.*
[3] *Phot.*, *Bibl. Cod.*, 74, p. 52.
[4] *Smith, Dict. Biogr.*, *s. v.*
[5] Orat. xlv., p. 513.
[6] Orat. xxxvi., p. 74.
[7] Orat. xlv., p. 202.

νίδος, on the troubles to which men expose themselves by deserting the path of nature, and on the difficulties which a sovereign has to encounter; essays on slavery and freedom; on the means of attaining eminence as an orator; political discourses, addressed to various towns; on subjects of ethics and practical philosophy; and, lastly, orations on mythical subjects, and epideictic or show-speeches. Besides these eighty orations, we have fragments of fifteen others. There are extant also five letters under the name of Dion, and addressed to one Rufus. They are published in Boissonade's *Marini Vit. Procl.*, p. 85, *seqq.*, and some critics are inclined to consider them as productions of Dion Chrysostom.

All the extant orations of Dion Chrysostom are distinguished for their refined and elegant style. The author most successfully imitated the classic writers of Greece, such as Plato, Demosthenes, Hyperides, and Æschines. His ardent study of those models, combined with his own eminent talents, his firm and pleasing voice, and his skill in extempore speaking, raised him at once above all contemporary rhetoricians and sophists. His style is throughout clear, and, generally speaking, free from artificial embellishment, though he is not always able to escape from the influence of the Asiatic school of rhetoric. His sentences are often interrupted by the insertion of parenthetical clauses, and his proœmia are frequently too long in proportion to the other parts of his discourses. Still, as Niebuhr remarks, he was an author of uncommon talent, and it is much to be regretted that he belonged to the rhetoricians of this unfortunate age.

Passing over the editions of separate orations of Dion Chrysostomus, we mention only those which contain all of them. The first was edited by Paravisinus, at Milan, 1476, 4to, and was followed by that of Aldus Manutius, Venice, 1551, 8vo. The next edition of importance is that of Morel, Paris, 1601, which was reprinted in 1623, with a Latin translation of Naogeorgius, and notes by Morel. A very good critical edition is that of Reiske, Leipzig, 1784, 2 vols. 8vo. The best edition, however, is that of Emperius, Brunswick, 1844, 8vo.

III. Polĕmon (Πολέμων),[1] a highly celebrated sophist and rhetorician, who flourished under Trajan, Hadrian, and the first Antoninus, and was in high favor with the two former emperors.[2] He is placed at the sixteenth year of Hadrian, A.D. 133, by Eusebius. He was born of a consular family at Laodicea, but spent the greater part of his life at Smyrna. His most celebrated disciple was Aristides. Among his imitators in subsequent times was Gregory Nazianzen. His style of oratory was imposing rather than pleasing, and his character was haughty and reserved. During the latter part of his life he was so tortured by the gout, that he resolved to put an end to his existence. He had himself shut up in the tomb of his ancestors, at Laodicea, where he died of hunger, at the age of sixty-five. The only extant works of Polemon are the funeral orations for Cynægirus and Callimachus, generals who fell at Marathon, which are supposed to be pronounced by their fathers, each extolling his own son above the other. Philostratus mentions several others of his rhetorical compositions, the subjects of which are chiefly taken from Athenian history, and an oration which he pronounced, by command of Hadrian, at the dedication of the temple of Jupiter Olympius at Athens, in A.D. 135.

[1] *Smith, Dict. Biogr.*, *s. v.*

[2] *Philostr.*, *Vit. Sophist.*, ii., 25, p. 530, *seqq.*

His λόγοι ἐπιτάφιοι were first printed by H. Stephens, in his collection of the Declamations of Polemon, Himerius, and other rhetoricians, Paris, 1547, 4to; and were afterward published by themselves in Greek, from the same press, Paris, 1586, 4to; and in Greek and Latin, Toulouse, 1637, 8vo. The latest and best edition is that of Caspar and Conrad Orelli, Leipzig, 1819, 8vo.

IV. Herōdes Atticus, Tiberius Claudius,[1] a celebrated Greek sophist and rhetorician, born about A.D. 104, at Marathon, in Attica. His father, whose name was likewise Atticus, discovered on his estate a hidden treasure, which at once made him one of the wealthiest men of his age. His son afterward increased this wealth by marrying the rich Annia Regilla. Old Atticus left in his will a clause, according to which every Athenian citizen was to receive yearly one mina (about $17 60) out of his property; but his son entered into a composition with the Athenians to pay them, once for all, five minas each. As Herodes, however, in paying the Athenians, deducted the debts which some citizens owed to his father, they were exasperated against him, and, notwithstanding the great benefits he conferred upon Athens, bore him a grudge as long as he lived. Herodes received a very careful education from some of the best instructors of the day; and, after completing his studies, opened a school of rhetoric at Athens, and subsequently at Rome also, where Marcus Aurelius Antoninus, who ever afterward entertained a high esteem for him, was among his pupils. In A.D. 143, the Emperor Antoninus Pius raised him to the consulship; but as Herodes cared more for his fame as a rhetorician than for high offices, he afterward returned to Athens, whither he was followed by a great number of young men, and whither L. Verus also was sent as a pupil by the Emperor M. Aurelius Antoninus.

The wealth and influence of Herodes Atticus did not fail to raise up enemies. His public and private life were attacked in various ways, and these annoyances at last appear to have induced him to retire from public life, and to spend his remaining years in his villa near Marathon, surrounded by his pupils. The Emperor M. Aurelius sent him a letter, in which he assured him of his unaltered esteem. In the case of Herodes the Athenians drew upon themselves the just charge of ingratitude, for no man had ever done so much to assist his fellow-citizens, and to embellish Athens at his own expense. Among the great architectural works with which he adorned the city, we may mention a race-course (stadium) of white Pentelic marble, of which ruins are still extant, and the magnificent theatre of Regilla, with a roof made of cedar-wood. His liberality, however, was not confined to Attica. At Corinth he built a theatre, at Olympia an aqueduct, at Delphi a race-course, and at Thermopylæ a hospital; and he also restored, with his ample means, several decayed towns in various parts of Greece. His wealth, generosity, and, still more, his skill as a rhetorician, spread his fame over the whole Roman world. He is believed to have died at the age of 76, in A.D. 180.[2]

If we look upon Herodes Atticus as a man, it must be owned that there scarcely ever was a wealthy person who spent his property in a more generous, noble, and disinterested manner. His greatest ambition, however, was to shine as a rhetorician; and this ambition, indeed, was so

[1] *Smith, Dict. Biogr., s. v.*

[2] *Smith, l. c.*

strong, that, on one occasion, in his early life, when he had delivered an oration before the Emperor Hadrian, who was then in Pannonia, he was on the point of throwing himself into the Danube, because his attempt at speaking had been unsuccessful. This failure, however, appears to have proved a stimulus to him, and he became the greatest rhetorician of his century. His success as a teacher is sufficiently attested by the great number of his pupils, most of whom attained some degree of eminence. His own orations, which were delivered extempore and without preparation, are said to have excelled those of all his contemporaries by the dignity, fullness, and elegance of their style. Philostratus praises his oratory for its pleasing and harmonious flow, as well as for its simplicity and power. The loss of the works of Herodes renders it impossible for us to form an independent opinion. Among his numerous productions, the following only are specified by the ancients: 1. Λόγοι αὐτοσχέδιοι, or extemporaneous speeches. 2. Διαλέξεις, treatises or dialogues. 3. Ἐφημερίδες, or diaries. 4. Ἐπιστολαί. All these works are now lost. There exists an oration, περὶ πολιτείας, in which the Thebans are called upon to join the Peloponnesians in preparing for war against Archelaus, king of Macedonia, and which has come down to us under the name of Herodes, but its genuineness is very doubtful. It is printed in the collections of the Greek orators, and by Fiorillo in *Herodis Attici quæ supersunt*, Leipzig, 1801.

V. Adrianus (Ἀδριανός),[1] a Greek sophist and rhetorician, born at Tyre, in Phœnicia, and who flourished under the emperors M. Antoninus and Commodus. He was the pupil of the celebrated Herodes Atticus, and obtained the chair of philosophy at Athens during the life-time of his master. His advancement does not seem to have impaired their mutual regard. Herodes declared that the unfinished speeches of his scholar were "the fragments of a Colossus," and Adrianus showed his gratitude by a funeral oration which he pronounced over the ashes of his master. He appears, notwithstanding, to have been a very vain and conceited man. His first lecture commenced with the modest encomium on himself, πάλιν ἐκ Φοινίκης γράμματα, while, in the magnificence of his dress and equipage, he affected the style of the hierophant of philosophy. The visit of Antoninus to Athens made him acquainted with Adrianus, whom he invited to Rome, and honored with his friendship. After the death of that emperor, he became the private secretary of Commodus. His death took place at Rome, in the eightieth year of his age, not later than A.D. 192. Of the works attributed to him by Suidas, three declamations only are extant.

The declamations of Adrianus of Tyre have been edited by Leo Allatius, in the *Excerpta Varia Græcorum Sophistarum ac Rhetoricorum*, Rome, 1641, and by Walz, in the *Rhetores Græci*, vol. i., p. 526, *seqq.*, Stuttg., 1832.

VI. Aristīdes, P. Ælius (Ἀριστείδης),[2] surnamed Theodorus, one of the most celebrated Greek sophists and rhetoricians of the second century after Christ, was born at Adriani, in Mysia, in A.D. 129, according to some, but more correctly, according to others, in A.D. 117. He studied

[1] *Smith, Dict. Biogr., s. v.* [2] *Id. ib., s. v.*

under Herodes Atticus at Athens, and subsequently travelled through Egypt, Greece, and Italy. The fame of his talents and acquirements was so great, that monuments were erected to his honor in several towns which he had visited.[1] Shortly before his return, he was attacked by an illness which lasted thirteen years, but which, notwithstanding, did not prevent him from prosecuting his studies. He subsequently settled at Smyrna, and when this city was nearly destroyed by an earthquake in A.D. 178, he used his influence with the Emperor M. Aurelius Antoninus to induce him to assist in rebuilding the place. The Smyrneans showed their gratitude to Aristides by offering him various honors and distinctions, most of which he refused. He accepted only the office of priest of Æsculapius, which he held until his death, about A.D. 180.

The works of Aristides which have come down to us are fifty-five orations and declamations (including those which were discovered by Morelli and Mai), and two treatises on rhetorical subjects, of little value, namely, περὶ πολιτικοῦ λόγου, and περὶ ἀφελοῦς λόγου. Some of his orations are eulogies on the power of certain divinities; others are panegyrics on towns, such as Smyrna, Cyzicus, Rome. One among them is a Panathenaïcus and an imitation of that of Isocrates. Others, again, treat of subjects connected with rhetoric and eloquence. The six orations called ἱεροὶ λόγοι are a sort of diary of his long illness and recovery, and he relates in them that he was frequently encouraged, by visions in his dreams, to cultivate rhetoric to the exclusion of all other studies. They have attracted considerable attention in modern times on account of the various stories they contain respecting the cures of the sick in temples, and on account of the apparent resemblance between these cures and those said to be effected by mesmerism.[2] Aristides, as an orator, is much superior to the majority of sophists in his time, whose great and only ambition was to shine and make a momentary impression by extempore speeches, and a brilliant and dazzling style; although it must be confessed that, in his panegyric orations, he himself often endeavors to display as much brilliancy of style as he can. On the whole, his manner of expression is brief and concise, but too frequently deficient in ease and clearness. His sentiments are often trivial, and spun out to an intolerable length, which leaves the reader nothing to think upon for himself. His orations remind us of a man who is fond of hearing himself talk. Notwithstanding these defects, however, Aristides is still unsurpassed by most of his contemporaries. Several learned grammarians wrote commentaries on his orations, from which the extant scholia are probably compilations.

The first edition of the orations of Aristides (fifty-three in number) is that published at Florence, 1517, fol. A better edition, with some of the Greek scholia, is that of Jebb, Oxford, 1722, 2 vols. 4to. Many corrections of the text of this edition are contained in Reiske's *Animadversiones in Auctores Græcos*, vol. iii. Morelli published, in [illegible], the oration πρὸς Λεπτίνην ὑπὲρ ἀτελείας, which he had discovered in a Venetian MS. It was afterward edited again by F. A. Wolf, in his edition of Demosthenes's oration against Leptines, Halle, 1789; and by Grauert, in his *Declamationes Leptineæ*, Bonn, 1827, 8vo. This edition of Grauert contains also an oration, πρὸς Δημοσθένη περὶ ἀτελείας, which had been discovered by Mai, and published in his *Nova Collect. Script. Vet.*, vol. i., p. 3.

[1] *Aristid.*, *Orat. Ægypt.*, ii., p. 331, *seqq.*

[2] *Thorlacius*, *Opusc.*, ii., p. 129, *seqq.*

A complete edition of all the works of Aristides, which gives a correct text and all the scholia, was published by W. Dindorf, Leipzig, 1829, 3 vols. 8vo.

VII. LUCIANUS (Λουκιανός),[1] a witty and voluminous Greek writer, whom we may consider under the present head, in consequence of his early pursuits. He was born at Samosata, the capital of Commagene, in Syria, probably about A.D. 120, and he appears to have lived till toward the end of this century. We know that some of his more celebrated works were written in the reign of M. Aurelius Antoninus. Lucian's parents were poor, and he was at first apprenticed to his maternal uncle, who was a statuary. He afterward became an advocate, and practiced at Antioch. Being unsuccessful in this calling, he employed himself in writing speeches for others instead of delivering them himself. But he did not long remain at Antioch; and, at an early period of his life, he set out upon his travels, and visited the greater part of Greece, Italy, and Gaul. At that period it was customary for professors of the rhetorical art to proceed to different cities, where they attracted audiences by their displays, much in the same manner as musicians or itinerant lecturers in modern times. He appears to have acquired a good deal of money as well as fame. On his return to his native country, probably about his fortieth year, he abandoned the rhetorical profession, the artifices of which, he tells us, were foreign to his temper, the natural enemy of deceit and pretension. He now devoted most of his time to the composition of his works. He still, however, occasionally travelled; for it appears that he was in Achaia and Ionia about the close of the Parthian war, A.D. 160–165: on which occasion, too, he seems to have visited Olympia, and beheld the self-immolation of Peregrinus. About A.D. 170, or a little previously, he visited the false oracle of the impostor Alexander, in Paphlagonia. Later in life, he obtained the office of procurator of part of Egypt, which office was probably bestowed upon him by the Emperor Commodus.

The nature of Lucian's writings inevitably procured him many enemies, by whom he has been painted in very black colors. According to Suidas, he was surnamed the *Blasphemer*, and was torn to pieces by dogs as a punishment for his impiety; but on this account no reliance can be placed. Other writers state that Lucian apostatized from Christianity, but there is no proof in support of this charge; and the dialogue called *Philopatris*, which would appear to prove that the author had once been a Christian, was certainly not written by Lucian, but was probably composed in the reign of Julian the Apostate. The scholiast on the *Alexander*, § 47, asserts that Lucian was an epicurean, and this opinion has been followed by several modern critics. But, though his natural skepticism may have led him to prefer the tenets of Epicurus to those of any other sect, it is most probable that he belonged to none whatever. Of Lucian's moral character we have no means of judging except from his writings, a method which is not always certain. Several of his pieces are loose and licentious, but some allowance should be made for the manners of the age. In the *Alexander*, § 54, he seems indignant at the charge of immorality brought against him by that impostor; and that he must at least have

[1] *Smith. Dict. Biogr.*, *s. v.*

avoided any grievous and open scandal, may be presumed from the high office conferred upon him in Egypt.[1]

As many as eighty-two works have come down to us under the name of Lucian, but some of them are spurious. The most important of them are his *Dialogues*. They are of very various degrees of merit, and are treated in the greatest possible variety of style, from seriousness down to the broadest humor and buffoonery. Their subjects and tendency, too, vary considerably; for, while some are employed in attacking the heathen philosophy and religion, others are mere pictures of manners, without any polemic drift. Our limits only allow us to mention a few of the more important of these dialogues. The *Dialogues of the Gods*, twenty-six in number, consist of short dramatic narratives of some of the most popular incidents in the heathen mythology. The reader, however, is generally left to draw his own conclusions from the story, the author only taking care to put it in the most absurd point of view. In the *Jupiter Convicted*, a bolder style of attack is adopted; and the cynic proves to Jupiter's face that, every thing being under the dominion of fate, he has no power whatever. As this dialogue shows Jupiter's want of power, so the *Jupiter the Tragedian* strikes at his very existence, and that of the other deities. The *Auction of Lives*, or *Sale of the Philosophers*, is an attack upon the ancient philosophers. In this humorous piece the heads of the different sects are put up for sale, Mercury being the auctioneer. The *Fisherman* is a sort of apology for the preceding piece, and may be reckoned among Lucian's best dialogues. The philosophers are represented as having obtained a day's life for the purpose of taking vengeance upon Lucian, who confesses that he has borrowed the chief beauties of his writings from them.[2]

The *Banquet*, or the *Lapithæ*, is one of Lucian's most humorous attacks on the philosophers. The scene is a wedding feast, at which a representative of each of the principal philosophic sects is present. A discussion ensues, which sets all the philosophers by the ears, and ends in a pitched battle. The *Nigrinus* is also an attack on philosophic pride; but its main scope is to satirize the Romans, whose pomp, vain-glory, and luxury are unfavorably contrasted with the simple habits of the Athenians.

The more miscellaneous class of Lucian's dialogues, in which the attacks upon mythology and philosophy are not direct, but incidental, or which are mere pictures of manners, contains some of his best. At the head must be placed *Timon*, which may, perhaps, be regarded as Lucian's master-piece. The *Dialogues of the Dead* are, perhaps, the best known of all Lucian's works. The subject affords great scope for moral reflection, and for satire on the subject of human pursuits. Wealth, power, beauty, strength, not forgetting the vain disputations of philosophy, afford the materials. The *Icaro-Menippus* is in Lucian's best vein, and a masterpiece of Aristophanic humor. Menippus, disgusted with the disputes and pretensions of the philosophers, resolves on a visit to the stars, for the purpose of seeing how far their theories are correct. By the mechanical aid of a pair of wings he reaches the moon, and surveys thence the miser-

[1] *Smith, l. c.*

[2] *Id. ib.*

able passions and quarrels of men. Hence he proceeds to Olympus, and is introduced to the Thunderer himself. Here he is witness of the manner in which human prayers are received in heaven. They ascend by enormous vent-holes, and become audible when Jupiter removes the covers. Jupiter himself is represented as a partial judge, and as influenced by the largeness of the rewards promised to him. At the end he pronounces judgment against the philosophers, and threatens in four days to destroy them all. *Charon* is a very elegant dialogue, but of a graver turn than the preceding. Charon visits the earth, to see the course of life there, and what it is which always makes men weep when they enter his boat. Mercury acts as his cicerone. In this piece, however, Lucian has not been very scrupulous about chronology. The whole is a picture of the smallness of mankind when viewed from a philosophic as well as a physical height.[1]

Lucian's *rhetorical* pieces were no doubt, for the most part, the first productions of his pen; for we have already seen that he did not lay aside that profession and apply himself to a different style of writing till he had reached the age of forty. Of all his pieces they are the most unimportant, and betray least of his real character and genius. The pieces, again, which entitle Lucian to be called a *biographer*, are rather anecdotical memoirs, like Xenophon's *Memorabilia*, than regular biographies. Under the head of *Romances* may be classed the tale entitled *Lucius*, or *the Ass*, from which Appuleius is thought to have drawn his story of the *Golden Ass*. Under this same head may be ranked the *Veræ Historiæ*, written to ridicule the authors of extravagant tales, and which would appear to have furnished hints to Rabelais and Swift in modern times, not only from the nature and extravagance of the fiction, but from the lurking satire. We have also some *Poems* by Lucian. These consist of two mock tragedies and about fifty epigrams.[2]

Lucian's merits as a writer consist in his knowledge of human nature, which, however, he generally viewed on its worst side; his strong common sense; the fertility of his invention; the raciness of his humor; and the simplicity and Attic grace of his diction. His knowledge was probably not very profound, and it may be suspected that he was not always master of the philosophy which he attacked. His writings have a more modern air than those of any other classic author; and the keenness of his wit, the richness and extravagance of his humor, the fertility and liveliness of his fancy, his proneness to skepticism, and the clearness and simplicity of his style, present us with a kind of compound between Swift and Voltaire. There was abundance to justify his attacks in the systems against which they were directed. Yet he establishes nothing in their stead. His aim is only to pull down; to spread a universal skepticism. Nor were his assaults confined to religion and philosophy, but extended to every thing old and venerated—the poems of Homer and Hesiod, and the history of Herodotus. Yet writing, as he did, amid the doomed idols of an absurd superstition, and the contradictory tenets of an almost equally absurd philosophy, his works had undoubtedly a beneficial influence on

[1] *Smith, l. c.*

[2] *Id. ib.*

the cause of truth. That they were indirectly serviceable to Christianity, can hardly be disputed; but though Lucian is generally just in his representations of the Christians, we may be sure that such a result was as far from his wishes as his thoughts.

The *Editio Princeps* of Lucian was printed at Florence, 1496, fol. The first Aldine appeared at Venice, 1503, fol. This edition, printed from bad MSS., and very incorrect, was somewhat improved in the second Aldine, 1502, fol., but is still inferior to the Florentine. The Aldine, however, served as the basis of subsequent editions till 1615, when Bourdelot published in Paris a Greek and Latin edition in folio, the text corrected from MSS. and the *Editio Princeps.* This was repeated, with emendations, in the Saumur edition, 1619. Le Clerc's edition, 2 vols. 8vo, Amsterdam, 1687, is very incorrect. In 1730 Hemsterhuis began to print his excellent edition, but dying in 1736, before a quarter of it had been finished, the editorship was assigned to J. F. Reitz, and the book was published at Amsterdam, in 3 vols. 4to, in 1743. In 1746, C. C. Reitz, brother of the editor, printed at Utrecht an Index, or *Lexicon Lucianeum*, in one volume 4to, which, though extensive, is not complete. The edition of Hemsterhuis, besides his own notes, also contains those of Jensius, Kuster, Bos, Vitringa, Du Soul, Gesner, Reitz, and other commentators. An appendix to the notes of Hemsterhuis, taken from a MS. in the Leyden library, was published at that place by Geel, 1824, 4to. Hemsterhuis corrected the Latin version for his edition as far as the *De Sacrificiis;* and of the remainder a new translation was made by Gesner. The reprint by Schmidt, Mittau, 1776–80, 8 vols. 8vo, is incorrect. The Bipont edition, in 10 vols. 8vo, 1789–93, is an accurate and elegant reprint of Hemsterhuis's edition, with the addition of collations of Paris MSS.; but the omission of the Greek index is a drawback to it. A good edition, though disfigured by typographical errors, is that of Lehmann, Leipzig, 1821–31, 9 vols. 8vo. There is also a very good and convenient edition of the text, with a Latin version, by W. Dindorf, forming part of Didot's *Bibliotheca Græca*, Paris, 1840.

VIII. MAXIMUS TYRIUS,[1] a native of Tyre, a Greek sophist and rhetorician, and also a Platonic philosopher, lived during the reigns of the Antonines and of Commodus. Some writers suppose that he was one of the tutors of M. Aurelius Antoninus; but it is more probable that he was a different person from Claudius Maximus, the Stoic, who was the tutor of that emperor. Maximus Tyrius appears to have spent the greater part of his life in Greece, but he visited Rome once or twice. The time of his death is unknown. There are extant forty-one Dissertations (Διαλέξεις) of Maximus Tyrius, on theological, ethical, and other philosophical subjects, written in an easy and pleasing style, but not characterized by much depth of thought. Heinsius thinks that the author arranged them in ten *Tetralogies*, or sets of four each, according to the subjects, and in one of his notes he conjecturally gives what he regards as their correct order. The merits of Maximus Tyrius have been variously estimated. Reiske speaks of him as a tedious and affected writer, who degraded the most elevated and important subjects by his trivial and puerile mode of treating them. But Markland, while admitting and blaming the haste and inaccuracy of Maximus, praises his acuteness, ability, and learning.

The Greek text was first printed by H. Stephens, Paris, 1557, 8vo, accompanied, but in a separate volume, by the version of Paccius. The edition of Heinsius, from a MS. in the king's library at Paris, with a new Latin version, and notes by the editor, was printed at Leyden, 1607, 8vo, and again in 1614, and, without the notes, in 1630. It has been reprinted once or twice since then. The first edition of Davies, fellow of Queen's College, Cambridge, with the version of Heinsius, and short notes, was published at Cambridge, 1703, 8vo; the second and more important edition, in which the text was

[1] *Smith, Dict. Biogr., s. v.*

carefully revised, and a new arrangement of the Dissertations was adopted, was published after the editor's death by Dr. John Ward, the Gresham professor, with valuable notes, by Jeremiah Markland, London, 1740, 4to. This second edition of Davies was reprinted, with some corrections and additional notes, by Reiske, 2 vols. 8vo, Leipzig, 1774–5.

IX. Philostrătus (Φιλόστρατος) Flavius,[1] a celebrated sophist and rhetorician, born probably in Lemnos, about A.D. 182. He studied and taught at Athens, whence he is usually called the Athenian, to distinguish him from a younger namesake. He afterward removed to Rome, where we find him a member of the circle of literary men whom the philosophic Julia Domna, the wife of Severus, had drawn around her. It was at her desire that he wrote the life of Apollonius of Tyăna. He was still alive in the reign of the Emperor Philippus (244–249). The following works of Philostratus have come down to us: 1. The *Life of Apollonius of Tyăna*, the famous impostor. Many of the wonders which Philostratus relates in connection with Apollonius are merely clumsy imitations of the Christian miracles. The work is divided into eight books. 2. The *Lives of the Sophists* (Βίοι Σοφιστῶν), in two books, containing the history of philosophers who had the character of being sophists, and of those who were really sophists. It begins with the life of Gorgias, and comes down to the contemporaries of Philostratus, in the reign of Philippus. 3. *Heroïca*, or *Heroïcus* (Ἡρωικά, Ἡρωικός), in the form of a dialogue, and giving an account of the heroes engaged in the Trojan war. 4. *Imagines* (Εἰκόνες), in two books, containing an account of various paintings. This is the author's most pleasing work, exhibiting great richness of fancy, power and variety of delineation, and a rich exuberance of style. 5. *Epistolæ* (Ἐπιστολαί), seventy-three in number, chiefly specimens of amatory letters.

Of the collected works of Philostratus there is, 1. The edition of Morellius, Paris, 1608, containing all the works above mentioned, along with some of other writers. This edition is of no value. 2. That of Olearius, Leipzig, 1709, 2 vols. fol. Previous to this edition, Bentley and others had contemplated one. Indeed, Bentley had gone so far as to publish a specimen sheet. Unhappily, the design was not executed; but he freely communicated to Olearius both his conjectural criticisms and his notes of various readings. The edition is a very beautiful specimen of typography, and, in spite of many faults, and the accusation that the editor has been guilty of gross plagiarism, which has been repeatedly brought against him, is very valuable, especially for its exegetical notes. 3. The last edition, and, critically, by far the best, is that of C. L. Kayser, Zurich, 1844, 4to. It contains introductory remarks on each book, the Greek text, and notes, which are principally critical. As he had already published several of the treatises of Philostratus separately, the notices and notes are, in some cases, briefer than might have been desired. Philostratus seems to have occupied his attention for years, and scholars in various parts of Europe have aided him, in collecting MSS. Of separate editions, we may mention Kayser's elaborate edition of the *Lives of the Sophists*, Heidelberg, 1838; Boissonade's edition of the *Heroica*, Paris, 1806; and Jacobs' and Welcker's edition of the *Imagines*, Leipzig, 1825.

II. RHETORICIANS.

I. Dionysius of Halicarnassus.[2] We have already made mention of this writer when treating of the historical productions of this age. It now remains to notice briefly his *rhetorical* and *critical* works. All the writings of this class show that Dionysius was not only a rhetorician of the first

[1] *Smith, Dict. Biogr.*, s. v.

[2] *Id. ib.*

order, but also a most excellent critic, in the highest and best sense of the term. They abound in the most exquisite remarks and criticisms on the works of the classical writers of Greece, although they are, at the same time, not without their faults, among which we may mention his hypercritical severity. But we have to remember that they were the productions of an early age, in which the want of a sound philosophy and of a comprehensive knowledge, and a partiality for or against certain writers, led him to express opinions which, at a maturer age, he undoubtedly regretted. The following works of this class are still extant: 1. Τέχνη ῥητορική, *Art of Rhetoric.* The present condition of this work is by no means calculated to give us a correct idea of its merits, and of his views on the subject of rhetoric. It consists of twelve, or, according to another division, of eleven chapters, which have no internal connection whatever, and have the appearance of being put together merely by accident. The treatise, therefore, is generally looked upon as a collection of rhetorical essays by different authors, some of which are genuine productions of Dionysius, who is expressly stated by Quintilian to have written a manual of rhetoric. 2. Περὶ συνθέσεως Ὀνομάτων (*De Compositione Verborum*), written probably in the first year or years of his residence at Rome, and, at all events, previous to any of the other works still extant. It is, however, notwithstanding this, one of high excellence. In it the author treats of oratorical power, and of the combination of words, according to the different species and style of oratory. 3. Περὶ μιμήσεως. Its proper title appears to have been ὑπομνηματισμοὶ περὶ τῆς μιμήσεως. The work, as a whole, is lost, and what we possess under the title of τῶν ἀρχαίων κρίσις is probably nothing but a sort of epitome, containing characteristics of poets, from Homer down to Euripides; of some historians, such as Herodotus, Thucydides, Philistus, Xenophon, and Theopompus; and, lastly, of some philosophers and orators. 4. Περὶ τῶν ἀρχαίων ῥητόρων ὑπομνηματισμοί, containing criticisms on the most eminent Greek orators and historians. The author points out their excellences as well as defects, with a view to promote a wise imitation of the classic models, and thus to preserve a pure taste in those branches of literature. The work originally consisted of six sections, of which we now possess only the first three, on Lysias, Isocrates, and Isæus. The other sections treated of Demosthenes, Hyperides, and Æschines; but we have only the first part of the fourth section, which treats of the oratorical power of Demosthenes, and his superiority over other public speakers. 5. A treatise entitled Ἐπιστολὴ πρὸς Ἀμμαῖον πρώτη, which title, however, does not occur in MSS., and instead of πρώτη, it ought to be called ἐπιστολὴ δευτέρα. This treatise or epistle, in which the author shows that most of the orations of Demosthenes had been delivered before Aristotle wrote his Rhetoric, and that, consequently, Demosthenes had derived no instruction from Aristotle, is of great importance for the history and criticism of the works of Demosthenes. 6. Ἐπιστολὴ πρὸς Γναῖον Πομπήϊον, written with a view to justify the unfavorable opinion which Dionysius had expressed upon Plato, and which Pompeius had censured. The latter part of this treatise is much mutilated, and did not, perhaps, originally belong to it. 7. Περὶ τοῦ Θουκυδίδου χαρακτῆρος, &c., written by Dionysius, at the request of his friend Ælius Tubero, for the purpose of explaining more minutely what he had written on Thucydides. 8. Περὶ τῶν τοῦ Θουκυδίδου ἰδιωμάτων. 9. Δείναρχος, a very valuable treatise on the life and orations of Dinarchus.[1]

The Τέχνη ῥητορική was edited, with very valuable prolegomena and notes, by Schott, Leipzig, 1804, 8vo. Of the treatise περὶ συνθέσεως ὀνομάτων, there are two very good editions, one by Schaefer, Leipzig, 1809, 8vo, and the other by Göller, Jena, 1815, 8vo, in which the text is considerably improved from MSS. The epitome, περὶ μιμήσεως, is printed separately in Frotscher's edition of the tenth book of Quintilian, Leipzig, 1826, p. 271, *seqq*. The three treatises mentioned under Nos. 6, 7, and 8, are given in a very good edition by Krüger, Halle, 1823, 8vo. The editions of the entire works have already been given on page 455.

II. Hermogĕnes (Ἑρμογένης)[2] of Tarsus, one of the most celebrated of the Greek rhetoricians, lived in the reign of the Emperor M. Aurelius Antoninus, A.D. 161–180. He bore the surname of ξυστήρ, that is, the scratcher or polisher, either with reference to his vehement temperament, or to the great polish which he strongly recommended as one of the principal requisites in a written composition. He was, according to all accounts, a man endowed with extraordinary talents, for at the age of fifteen he had already acquired so great a reputation as an orator, that the Emperor M. Aurelius Antoninus desired to hear him, and admired and richly rewarded him for his wonderful ability. Shortly after this, he was appointed public teacher of rhetoric; and, at the age of seventeen, he began his career as a writer, which unfortunately did not last long, for at the age of twenty-five he fell into a mental debility, which rendered him entirely unfit for farther literary and intellectual occupation, and of which he never got rid, although he lived to an advanced age; so that he was a man in the time of his youth, and a child during his maturer years. After his death, his heart is said to have been found covered with hair.[3] If we may judge from what Hermogenes did at so early an age, there can be little doubt that he would have far excelled all other Greek rhetoricians, if he had remained in the full possession of his mental powers. His works, five in number, which are still extant, form together a complete system of rhetoric, and were for a long time used in all the rhetorical schools as manuals. Many distinguished rhetoricians and grammarians wrote commentaries upon them, some of which are still extant; many, also, made abridgments of the works of Hermogenes for the use of schools, and the abridgment of Aphthonius at length supplanted the original in most schools.

The works of Hermogenes are as follows: 1. Τέχνη ῥητορικὴ περὶ τῶν στάσεων, composed by the author at the age of eighteen. The work treats of the points and questions which an orator, in civil cases, has to take into his consideration. It examines every one separately, and thence deduces the rules which a speaker has to observe. The work is a very useful guide for those who prepare themselves for speaking in courts of justice. 2. Περὶ εὑρέσεως (*De Inventione*), in four books, containing instructions about the proper composition of an oration. Every point which Hermogenes here discusses is illustrated, as in the preceding work, by

[1] *Smith, l. c.* [2] *Smith, Dict. Biogr., s. v.* [3] *Philostr., Vit. Soph.*, ii., 7, *Eudoc.*, p. 165.

examples taken from the Attic orators, which greatly enhances the clearness and utility of the treatise. 3. Περὶ ἰδεῶν (*De Formis Oratoriis*), in two books, treating of the forms of oratorical style, and their subdivisions. 4. Περὶ μεθόδου δεινότητος (*De apto et solerti genere dicendi Methodus*), forming a sort of appendix to the preceding work, and containing suggestions for the proper application of the rules there laid down. 5. Προγυμνάσματα, that is, practical instructions in oratory, according to given models. A very convenient abridgment of this work was made by Aphthonius, in consequence of which the original fell into oblivion. But its great reputation in antiquity is attested by the fact, that the learned grammarian Priscian made a Latin translation of it, with some additions of his own, under the title of *Præexercitamenta Rhetorica ex Hermogene.* There were some other works of Hermogenes, but they are now lost. All his extant productions bear strong marks of the youthful age of the author; for it is clear that his judgment and his opinions have not yet become settled. He has not the consciousness of a man of long experience, and his style is rather diffuse, but always clear and unaffected. He is moderate in his judgment and censure of other rhetoricians, has a correct appreciation of the merits of the earlier Greek orators, and every where shows symptoms of a most careful study of the ancients. These excellences, which at once place him on a level with the most distinguished teachers of rhetoric, are reasons enough to make us regret that his brilliant career was cut off so early and so fatally.

The Τέχνη ῥητορική is printed in the *Rhetores* of Aldus, vol. i., p. 1, *seqq.* It was also edited separately at Paris, 1530 and 1538, 4to, *ex off. Wechelii;* by Caselius, Rostock, 1583, 8vo; by Sturm, Strasburg, 1570, with a Latin translation and scholia; by Laurentius, Geneva, 1614, 8vo; and by Corales, Venice, 1799, 4to. The extant scholia are printed in Walz's *Rhetores Græci*, vols. iv., v., vi., and vii. The treatise *De Inventione* is printed in the *Rhetores* of Aldus, in the editions of Laurentius, Wechel, and Sturm, but best in Walz's *Rhetores Græci*, vol. iii. We have also scholia on the work by an anonymous commentator, in Aldus's *Rhetores*, vol. ii., p. 352, *seqq.* The treatise *De Formis Oratoriis* is given in the editions of Aldus and Laurentius, and separately at Paris, 1531, 4to; and with a Latin translation and notes, by Sturm, Strasburg, 1571, 8vo. The best edition, however, is that in Walz's *Rhetores Græci*, vol. iii., who has also published the Greek commentaries by Syrianus and Johannes Siceliota, vols. vi. and vii. The treatise *De apto et solerti genere dicendi Methodus* is printed in the editions of Aldus, Wechel, Laurentius, and Sturm, but best in Walz's *Rhetores Græci*, vol. iii., who has also published the Greek commentaries by Gregorius Corinthius, vol. vii. Priscian's Latin version of the Προγυμνάσματα was for a long time the only edition of the work, until the Greek original was found in a MS. at Turin, from which it was published by Heeren in the *Biblioth. für alte Lit. und Kunst*, parts viii. and ix., Göttingen, 1791, and by Ward in the *Classical Journal*, vols. v.-viii. A separate edition was published by Veesenmeyer, Nürnberg, 1812, 8vo. It is also contained in Krehl's edition of Priscian, vol. ii., p. 419, *seqq.*, but best in Walz's *Rhetores Græci*, vol. i., p. 9, *seqq.*, who has collated six other MSS. besides the Turin one.

III. Aphthŏnius (Ἀφθόνιος),[1] of Antioch, a Greek rhetorician who lived about A.D. 315, but of whose life nothing is known. He is the author of an elementary introduction to the study of rhetoric, and of a number of fables in the style of those of Æsop. The work on rhetoric was constructed on the basis of the *Progymnasmata* of Hermogenes, and became so popular that it was used as the common school-book in this branch of

[1] *Smith, Dict. Biogr., s. v.*

education for several centuries. On the revival of letters it recovered its ancient popularity, and during the sixteenth and seventeenth centuries was used every where, but more especially in Germany, as the text-book for rhetoric. The number of editions and translations which were published during that period is greater than that of any other ancient writer. The last and best edition is that in Walz's collection of the *Rhetores Græci*, vol. i., p. 54, *seqq*. The Æsopic fables of Aphthonius, which are inferior in merit to those of Æsop, are printed in Scobarius's edition of the Progymnasmata, and also in the Paris edition of 1623. De Furia's edition of the Fables of Æsop contains twenty-three of those of Aphthonius.

IV LONGĪNUS DIONYSIUS CASSIUS (*Διονύσιος Κάσσιος Λογγῖνος*),[1] a very distinguished rhetorician and philosopher of the third century of our era. His original name seems to have been *Dionysius*, but either because he entered into the relation of client to some Cassius Longinus, or because his ancestors had received the Roman franchise, through the influence of some Cassius Longinus, he bore the name of Dionysius Longinus, Cassius Longinus, or in the complete form given at the head of this article. He was born about A.D. 213, and was put to death in A.D. 273, at the age of sixty. His native place is uncertain. Some say that he was born at Palmyra, while others call him a Syrian, or a native of Emesa. There is more ground, however, for believing that he was born at Athens, as he was brought up by his uncle Fronto, who taught rhetoric at the latter place. Longinus subsequently visited many countries, and became acquainted with all the illustrious philosophers of his age, such as Ammonius Saccas; Origen, the disciple of Ammonius, not to be confounded with the Christian writer; Plotinus, and Amelius. He was a pupil of the two former, and was an adherent of the Platonic philosophy; but instead of following blindly the system of Ammonius, he went to the fountain-head, and made himself thoroughly familiar with the works of Plato. On his return to Athens he opened a school, which was attended by numerous pupils, among whom the most celebrated was Porphyry. At Athens he seems to have lectured on philosophy and criticism as well as on rhetoric and grammar, and the extent of his information was so great, that Eunapius calls him "a living library" and "a walking museum." But his knowledge was not a dead encumbrance to his mind, for the power for which he was most celebrated was his critical skill, and this was indeed so great, that the expression *κατὰ Λογγῖνον κρίνειν* became synonymous with "to judge correctly."[2]

After having spent a considerable part of his life at Athens, and composed the best of his works, he went to the East, either for the purpose of seeing his friends at Emesa, as some think who make this to have been his native place, or with some other view. It seems to have been on this occasion that he became known to Zenobia, queen of Palmyra, who, being a woman of great talent, and fond of letters and the arts, made him her teacher in Greek literature. On the death of her husband Odenathus, Longinus became her principal adviser, and it was mainly

[1] *Smith, Dict. Biogr., s. v.*

[2] *Hieron., Epist.*, 95.

through his influence that she threw off her allegiance to the Roman empire. On her capture by Aurelian in A.D. 273, Zenobia threw all the blame upon her advisers, and Longinus was in consequence put to death by that emperor.[1]

Longinus was unquestionably by far the greatest philosopher of the time, and stands forth so distinct and solitary in that age of mystic and fanciful quibblers, that it is impossible not to recognize in him a man of excellent sense, sound and independent judgment, and extensive knowledge. He had thoroughly imbibed the spirit of Plato and Demosthenes, from whom he derived not only that intellectual culture which distinguished him above all others, but also an ardent love of liberty, and a great frankness both in expressing his own opinions and exposing the faults and errors of others. His work *On the Sublime* (Περὶ Ὕψους), a great part of which is still extant, surpasses in oratorical power every thing written after the time of the Greek orators. There is scarcely any work in the range of ancient literature which, independent of its excellence of style, contains so many exquisite remarks upon oratory, poetry, and good taste in general. It unfortunately contains many lacunæ, which can not be filled up, since all the MSS. extant are only copies of the one which is preserved at Paris. Notwithstanding his manifold avocations, Longinus composed a great number of works, which appear to have been held in the highest estimation. They have all perished, however, and all that has come down to us consists of the treatise Περὶ Ὕψους, and a number of fragments, which have been preserved as quotations in the works of contemporary and later writers.

The first edition of the treatise περὶ ὕψους is that of Robortello, Basle, 1554, 4to. The next important edition is that of Portus, Geneva, 1569, 8vo, which forms the basis of all subsequent ones until the time of Tollius. We may, however, mention those of Langbaene, Oxford, 1636, 1638, and 1650, 8vo, and of Faber, Saumur, 1663, 8vo. In 1694, there appeared the edition of Tollius, with notes and Latin translation, Utrecht, 4to. It was followed in the editions of Hudson, Oxford, 1710, 1718, 1730, 8vo; Pearce, London, 1724, 4to, often reprinted in 8vo; and Morus, Leipzig, 1769–73, 8vo. A collection of all that is extant of Longinus was published by Toup, with notes and emendations by Ruhnken, of which three editions were published at Oxford, 1778, 1789, and 1806, 8vo. The most recent editions are those of Weiske, Leipzig, 1809, 8vo, and of Egger, forming vol. i. of the *Scriptorum Græc. nova Collectio*, Paris, 1837, 16mo.

V. Apsĭnes (Ἀψίνης)[2] of Gadara, in Phœnicia, a rhetorician and sophist, who flourished in the reign of Maximinus, about A.D. 235. He studied at Smyrna, under Heraclides the Lycian, and afterward at Nicomedia, under Basilicus. He subsequently taught rhetoric at Athens, and distinguished himself so much that he was honored with the consular dignity. He was a friend of Philostratus,[3] who praises the strength and fidelity of his memory, but is afraid to say more for fear of being suspected of flattery or partiality. We still possess two rhetorical works of Apsines: 1. Περὶ τῶν μερῶν τοῦ πολιτικοῦ λόγου τέχνη, which was first printed by Aldus in his *Rhetores Græci*, under the incorrect title τέχνη ῥητορικὴ περὶ προοιμίων, as it is called by the scholiast on Hermogenes. This work, however, is only a part of a greater work, and is so much interpolated that it is scarcely possible to form a correct notion of it. A con-

[1] *Zosimus*, i., 56. [2] *Smith, Dict. Biogr.*, *s. v.* [3] *Vit. Soph.*, ii., 33.

siderable portion of it was discovered by Ruhnken to belong to a work of Longinus on rhetoric, which is now lost, and this portion has consequently been omitted in the new edition of Walz, in his *Rhetores Græci* (vol. ix., p. 465, *seqq.*). 2. Περὶ τῶν ἐσχηματισμένων προβλημάτων, of little importance, and very short. It is printed in Aldus's *Rhetores Græci*, p. 727, *seqq.*, and in Walz, *Rhet. Græc.*, vol. ix., p. 534, *seqq.*

III. WRITERS OF WORKS OF FICTION.[1]

I. The principal works of fiction prior to the time of Alexander the Great appear to have been what were termed the "Milesian Tales" (Μιλησιακά, or Μιλησιακοὶ λόγοι). There is little known of them, except that they were not of a very moral tendency, and were written by an individual named Aristides. They were in prose, and extended to six books at least.[2] They were translated into Latin by Sisenna, the Roman annalist, a contemporary of Sulla, and seem to have become popular with the Romans. Aristides is regarded, in fact, as the inventor of the Greek romance. His age and country are unknown, but he was probably a native of Miletus.

II. The more frequent intercourse, however, which the conquests of Alexander introduced between the Greek and Asiatic nations, opened at once all the sources of fiction. CLEARCHUS,[3] who was a disciple of Aristotle, and who wrote a history of fictitious love adventures, seems to have been the first author who gained any celebrity by this species of composition.

III. Some years after the composition of the fictitious histories of Clearchus, ANTONIUS DIOGENES[4] wrote a more perfect romance than had hitherto appeared, founded on the wandering adventures and the loves of Dinias and Dercyllis, and entitled Τὰ ὑπὲρ Θούλην ἄπιστα, or "The incredible things beyond Thule." This island was not, according to Diogenes, the most distant one of the globe, as he talks of several beyond it. Thule is but a single station for his adventurers, and many of the most incredible things are beheld in other quarters of the world. The idea of the work is said to have been taken from the Odyssey, and, in fact, many of the incidents seem to have been borrowed from that poem. The work of Diogenes was in twenty-four books, and was written in the form of a dialogue. It is highly praised by Photius for the clearness and gracefulness of its descriptions. The epitome preserved by Photius is printed also in the *Corpus Eroticorum Græcorum*, vol. i., edited by Passow, Leipzig, 1824, 8vo.

IV. After the composition of the Dinias and Dercyllis of Diogenes, a considerable period seems to have elapsed without the production of any fictitious narrative deserving the appellation of a romance. LUCIUS, of Patræ,[5] is the next writer of fiction that claims our attention. The period, however, when he flourished is uncertain. He wrote accounts of magical transformations, Μεταμορφώσεων λόγοι διάφοροι, *Metamorphoseon Libri Diversi*, which are now lost, but were extant in the time of Photius,

[1] *Dunlop, History of Fiction.*
[2] *Harpocrat.*, *s. v.* δερμηστής.
[3] *Athen.*, xii., p. 553, F.
[4] *Smith, Dict. Biogr.*, *s. v.*
[5] *Id. ib.*

who has described them. His style was perspicuous and pure, but his works were crowded with marvels; and, according to Photius, he related with perfect gravity and good faith the transformation of men into brutes, and brutes into men. Some parts of his works bore so close a resemblance to the *Lucius sive Asinus* of Lucian, that Photius thought he had either borrowed from that writer, or, as was more likely, Lucian had borrowed from him. The latter alternative appears to have been the true one.

V. Subsequently Iamblichus,[1] the Syrian, who lived in the time of the Emperor Trajan, wrote his *Babylonica* (Βαβυλωνικά). It contained the story of two lovers, Sinonis and Rhodanes, and was in thirty-nine books, according to Suidas; but Photius, who gives an epitome of the work, mentions only seventeen. A perfect copy of the work in MS. existed down to the year 1671, when it was destroyed by fire. A few fragments only are still extant, and a new one of some length has recently been discovered by Mai (*Nov. Collect. Script. Vet.*, vol. ii., p. 349, *seqq.*). The epitome of Photius and the fragments are given in Passow's *Corpus Eroticorum*, vol. i.

VI. After Iamblichus we may mention Xenophon, the *Ephesian.*[2] His age, however, is altogether uncertain. Locella assigns him to the time of the Antonines. Peerlkamp, on the contrary, regards him as the oldest of the Greek romance writers, and thinks that he has discovered in other writers of this class traces of an imitation of Xenophon. He also maintains that Xenophon was not the real name of the author, and that, with the exception of Heliodorus, no Greek romance writer published his productions under his real name. Xenophon's work is entitled *Ephesiaca*, or the Loves of Anthia and Abrocomes (Ἐφεσιακά, τὰ κατὰ Ἀνθίαν καὶ Ἀβροκόμην). The style of the work is simple, and the story is conducted without confusion, notwithstanding the number of personages introduced. The adventures, however, are of a very improbable kind. Suidas is the only ancient writer who mentions Xenophon. There is but a single manuscript of the work known, which is in the monastery of the Monte Cassino. There are also seven epistles attributed to Xenophon, among the forty-one so-called Socratic epistles; but the same remark applies to them as to most of the Greek literary remains of that class; they are mere rhetorical essays.

The early editions of Xenophon Ephesius are of very little value. A very excellent and carefully prepared edition, by Baron de Locella, appeared at Vienna, 1796. He procured a fresh collation of the manuscript, and availed himself of the critical remarks of Hemsterhuis, D'Abresch, and D'Orville, and the labors of Bast, who had made preparations for editing the work. Locella also prepared a new translation and a commentary. The *Ephesiaca* was reprinted by Mitscherlich, in his *Scriptores Erotici Græci*, vol. iv., Biponti (Deuxponts), 1794. Another good edition is that of Peerlkamp, Harlem, 1818. The most recent edition is that of Passow, Leipzig, 1833, in the *Corpus Scriptorum Eroticorum Græcorum.*

VII. We may conclude the present head with the subject of *Epistles*. The writers who pursued this species of writing have nearly all the common fault of running too much after ornaments of style and Attic forms

[1] *Phot., Bibl. Cod.*, 166.

[2] *Smith, Dict. Biogr., s. v.*

of expression. The most eminent among these epistolographers, and the one most free from these faults, was ALCIPHRON.[1] Respecting his life, or the age in which he lived, we possess no direct information whatsoever. Some of the earlier critics, as La Croze and J. C. Wolf, placed him, without any plausible reason, in the fifth century of our era. Bergler, and others who followed him, placed Alciphron in the period between Lucian and Aristænetus, that is, between A.D. 170 and 350, while others, again, assign to him a date even earlier than the time of Lucian. The only circumstance that suggests any thing respecting his age is the fact that, among the letters of Aristænetus, there are two (i., 5 and 22) between Lucian and Alciphron; now as Aristænetus is nowhere guilty of any great historical inaccuracy, we may safely infer that Alciphron was a contemporary of Lucian.

We possess, under the name of Alciphron, 116 fictitious letters, in three books, the object of which is to delineate the characters of certain classes of men, by introducing them as expressing their peculiar sentiments and opinions upon subjects with which they were familiar. The classes of persons which Alciphron chose for this purpose are fishermen, country people, parasites, and hetæræ. All are made to express their sentiments in the most graceful and elegant language, even where the subjects are of a low or immoral kind. The characters are thus somewhat raised above their ordinary standard, without any great violation of the truth of reality. The form of these letters is exquisitely beautiful, and the language is the pure Attic dialect, such as it was spoken in the best times in familiar but refined conversation at Athens. The scene from which the letters are dated is, with a few exceptions, Athens and its vicinity; and the time, wherever it is discernible, is the period after the reign of Alexander the Great. The new Attic comedy was the principal source from which the author derived his information respecting the characters and manners which he describes, and for this reason these letters contain much valuable information about the private life of the Athenians of that time.

The first edition of Alciphron's Letters is that of Aldus, in his Collection of the Greek Epistolographers, Venice, 1499, 4to. This edition, however, contains only those letters which, in more modern editions, form the first two books. Seventy-two new letters were added from a Vienna and a Vatican MS. by Bergler, in his edition, Leipzig, 1715, 8vo, with notes and a Latin translation. These seventy-two epistles form the third book in Bergler's edition. Wagner subsequently published his edition, Leipzig, 1798, 2 vols. 8vo, containing, besides the notes of Bergler, two new letters entire, and fragments of five others. One long letter, which has not yet been published entire, exists in several Paris MSS.

IV. GRAMMARIANS, LEXICOGRAPHERS, AND SHOLIASTS.

I. During the period which we are considering, the term *Grammar* (Γραμματική) comprised all that we now embrace under the head of philological erudition, namely, the study of language along with that of mythology and antiquities. The individuals who devoted themselves to these pursuits were called by the honorary appellation of Γραμματικοί,

[1] *Smith, Dict. Biogr., s. v.*

while they who taught merely the elements of language, or what we would term grammar, were termed Γραμματισταί, and their art or profession *Grammatisticē* (Γραμματιστική).[1]

II. Alexandrea continued to be the chief seat of this species of erudition, and the emperors founded various establishments in it for the purpose of promoting still more this branch of literary culture, as, for instance, the *Museum Claudium.* The difficulty, however, of procuring copies of works in an age when printing was as yet unknown, introduced a custom attended by injurious consequences to literature, that, namely, of abridging or making selections from larger works, and which often was the cause of the neglect and eventual loss of the originals, a loss for which these abridgments and selections, for the most part meagre and incomplete in their nature, could but ill compensate.[2]

III. The most useful productions of this age were the *Lexicons.* The grammarians called by the name of λέξεις those words which were remarkable for any peculiarity of signification: those, again, which had become obsolete or obscure, or which were derived from a foreign idiom, or were removed from common phraseology by some dialectic variety, they termed γλῶσσαι. Hence the different kinds of vocabulary were called *Lexicons* or *Glossaries,* of which the former is, strictly speaking, a more comprehensive title than the latter.[3]

IV. After the decline of Grecian liberty and language, it was natural that many words and phrases should become obsolete, which had been current in the better ages of Attic art and eloquence. These were collected and explained by the grammarians under the above-mentioned titles of Λέξεις and Γλῶσσαι. There were Γλῶσσαι ἰατρικαί, νομικαί, ῥητορικαί, φιλοσοφικαί, θεολογικαί, and Γλῶσσαι βαρβαρικαί, Σκυθικαί, Περσικαί, and the like. There were Homeric lexicons even at an early age. One certainly existed much anterior to that of Apollonius, which last has come down to us. Didymus, as we have already remarked, compiled a species of tragic lexicon in the age previous to the present; Theon, who wrote scholia on Aratus and Apollonius Rhodius, a comic lexicon. Other individuals also became known for similar labors, of whom we shall presently give an account.[4]

V. One of the most important of the ancient vocabularies is that which is commonly called the *Etymologicum Magnum,* the compiler of which is unknown, but is supposed by some to have been a grammarian of the name of *Magnus.* The opinion of Thomasius and others, who suspected that Marcus Musurus, or the two Calliergi, compiled this work, is sufficiently refuted by the fact that it is quoted by Eustathius under the title of Τὸ Μέγα Ἐτυμολογικόν. The date of this compilation is placed by Sylburg in the tenth century. It certainly can not be referred to a higher era, since its author quotes Theognotus, who lived in the ninth century. It is very valuable from the numerous extracts which it contains of older grammarians, some of whose works are still extant in manuscript, while

[1] *Schöll, Hist. Lit. Gr.*, vol. v., p. 1, *seqq.* Compare Gräfenhan, *Gesch. Klass. Philol.*, vol. i., p. 93, *seqq.*

[2] *Schöll, l. c.*

[3] *Quarterly Review*, No. xliv., 1820, p. 304, *seqq.*

[4] *Ibid., l. c.*

others, as, for instance, the *Etymologicum* of *Orion the Theban*, have been not very long ago published for the first time. Considerable expectation had been excited among scholars by a notice, which Kulenkamp published in 1765, of a manuscript etymologicon formerly in the possession of Marquardus Gudius. The entire lexicon was published at Leipzig, 1818, 4to, under the editorial care of Sturz. It turns out to be, however, a mere farrago of etymological nonsense, useful only so far as it serves to correct some passages of other lexicons.[1] An account of the lexicons of *Photius*, *Hesychius*, and *Suidas* will be given under the *Byzantine Period.*

VI. In connection with this part of our subject we may mention the ancient *Scholiasts* (Σχολιασταί),[2] who occupied themselves with the explanation of the earlier writers. Generally speaking, they have merely transmitted to us extracts from previous commentators, but it is precisely this which constitutes their value in our eyes, since most of the commentaries from which they made their selections have perished. By the term *scholium* (σχόλιον) is properly meant an explanatory note in the margin of a manuscript, in contradistinction from a gloss (γλῶσσα), which properly meant a note between the lines. These *scholia* originally appear to have been nothing more than extracts from preceding commentaries, and not to have come from the scholiasts themselves. In process of time, however, when these marginal notes had multiplied in number, and could no longer, for want of room, be placed by the side of the text, they were copied off into a separate codex or MS., and formed, as it were, a species of commentary by themselves. These collections of scholia, however, were not what we would call a regularly interwoven body of comments, but oftentimes opinions more or less opposed to one another, were placed side by side, introduced by such brief expressions as ἤ, ἄλλως, ἢ οὕτως, τινές, and the like. The greater part of these scholia are extracted from the best commentaries of the Alexandrine school. Others, where less care has been exercised in the selection, are of comparatively little value. Very little original matter, therefore, may be expected in either case. The race of scholiasts continued until the fall of the Eastern empire. Some are even found after this, as late as the sixteenth century.[3]

VII. We will now give a brief account of some of the most distinguished *Grammarians*, *Lexicographers*, and *Scholiasts* belonging to the present period, observing the following order: 1. Grammarians who have written upon dialects. 2. Lexicographers. 3. Scholiasts. 4. Grammarians in general.

GRAMMARIANS.—WRITERS ON DIALECTS.

I. TRYPHON (Τρύφων),[4] of Alexandrea, son of Ammonius, lived before and during the reign of Augustus. A long list of his works in almost every department of grammar is given by Suidas. Many of these still exist in MS. His treatise entitled Πάθη λέξεων was published by Con-

[1] *Quarterly Review, l. c.*

[2] *Schöll, Hist. Lit. Gr.*, vol. vi., p. 268; *Gräfenhan, Gesch. Klass. Philol.*, vol. iii., p. 274, *seqq.*

[3] *Gräfenhan, l. c.*

[4] *Smith, Dict. Biogr.*, *s. v.*

stantine Lascaris at the end of his Greek grammar, Milan, 1476, 4to, and in the other editions of the same. Stephens also placed it, translated into Latin, at the end of his Thesaurus, whence it passed into the lexicon of Scapula. A much better edition, however, is that of Blomfield, in the *Museum Criticum*, Cambridge, 1814, vol. i., p. 32, *seqq*. Another treatise, Περὶ Τρόπων, is also given by Blomfield in the same work, p. 43, *seqq*., and by Boissonade, *Anecd. Græc.*, vol. iii., p. 270, *seqq*. There is also an edition by Passow and Schneider, from a Breslau MS., published in 1820, in the first volume of the *Museum Criticum Vratislaviense*. This is the best edition.

II. Phrynichus (Φρύνιχος), a grammarian, described by some as an Arabian, and by others as a Bithynian, lived under M. Aurelius Antoninus and Commodus. His great work was entitled Σοφιστικὴ Προπαρασκευή, in thirty-seven books, of which we still possess a fragment, published by Bekker, in his *Anecdota Græca*, vol. i., p. 1, *seqq*. He also wrote a lexicon of Attic words (Ἐκλογὴ ῥημάτων καὶ ὀνομάτων Ἀττικῶν), which is still extant, and the best edition of which is by Lobeck, Leipzig, 1830.

III. Mœris (Μοῖρις),[1] commonly called Mœris Atticista, a distinguished grammarian, of whose personal history nothing is known. He is conjectured to have lived about the end of the second century of our era. He was the author of a work, still extant, entitled Μοίριδος Ἀττικιστοῦ λέξεις Ἀττικῶν καὶ Ἑλλήνων κατὰ στοιχεῖον, though the title varies somewhat in different MSS. In some MSS. the name of the author is given as *Eumœris* or *Eumœrides*. The treatise is a sort of comparison of the Attic with other Greek dialects; consisting of a list of Attic words and expressions, which are illustrated or explained by those of other dialects, especially the common Greek. It was first published in 1712, at Oxford, edited by Hudson. A much better edition is that of Pierson, Leyden, 1759, reprinted, with some additions, by Koch, Leipzig, 1831. The best text is by Bekker, with Harpocration, Berlin, 1833, 8vo.

LEXICOGRAPHERS.

I. Apollonius (Ἀπολλώνιος),[2] of Alexandrea, an eminent grammarian, lived about the time of Augustus, and was the teacher of Apion, while he himself had been a pupil of the school of Didymus. This, at least, is the statement of Suidas, which Villoison has endeavored to confirm. Other critics, however, as Ruhnken, believe that Apollonius lived after the time of Apion, and that our Apollonius, in his Homeric lexicon, made use of a similar work written by Apion. This opinion seems, indeed, to be the more probable one of the two; but, however this may be, the Homeric lexicon of Apollonius to the Iliad and Odyssey, which is still extant, is to us a valuable and instructive relic of antiquity, if we consider the loss of so many other works of the same kind. It is unfortunately, however, very much interpolated, and must be used with great caution.

The first edition of the lexicon was published by Villoison from a St. Germain MS. belonging to the tenth century, Paris, 1773, 2 vols. fol., with valuable prolegomena, and a Latin translation. It was reprinted the same year at Leipzig, in 2 vols. 4to. Tollius

[1] *Smith, Dict. Biogr.*, *s. v.*

[2] *Id. ib.*, *s. v.*

afterward published a new edition, with some additional notes, but without Villoison's prolegomena and translation, Leyden, 1788, 8vo. The latest edition is by Bekker, Berlin, 1833, 8vo, and is a very useful one.

II. Herodianus, Ælius (Αἴλιος Ἡρωδιανός),[1] one of the most celebrated grammarians of antiquity. He was the son of Apollonius Dyscolus, to be presently mentioned, and was born at Alexandrea. From that place he appears to have removed to Rome, where he gained the favor of the Emperor M. Aurelius Antoninus, to whom he dedicated a work on prosody. No farther biographical particulars are known respecting him. The estimation in which he was held by subsequent grammarians was very great. Priscian styles him *maximus auctor artis grammaticæ.* He was a very voluminous writer, but probably the only one of his works that has come down to us complete is the Περὶ Μονήρους Λέξεως (on monosyllabic words), to be mentioned hereafter, though several extracts from others are preserved by later grammarians. The work most worthy of notice here was the Ἐπιμερισμοί, devoted to the explanation of difficult, obscure, and doubtful words, and of peculiar forms found in Homer.

A meagre compilation from this highly valuable work was published from Paris MSS. by Boissonade, London, 1819. Another abstract, which appears to give a better idea of the original, is published in Cramer's *Anecdota Gr. Oxon.*, vol. i. Several important quotations from this work are also found scattered in different parts of the scholia on Homer.

III. Timæus (Τίμαιος),[2] the sophist, wrote a *Lexicon to Plato*, which is still extant. The time at which he lived is quite uncertain. Ruhnken places him in the third century of the Christian era, which produced so many ardent admirers of the Platonic philosophy, such as Porphyry, Longinus, Plotinus, &c. The lexicon is very brief, and bears the title Τιμαίου σοφιστοῦ ἐκ τῶν τοῦ Πλάτωνος λέξεων, from which it might have been inferred that it is an extract from a larger work, had not Photius (*Cod.* 151), who had read it, described it as a very short work (Βραχὺ ποιημάτιον ἐν ἑνὶ λόγῳ). It is evident, however, that the work, as it stands, has received several interpolations of words occurring in Herodotus. Notwithstanding these interpolations, the work is one of great value, and the explanations of words are some of the very best that have come down to us from the ancient grammarians. The work on *rhetorical arguments*, in sixty-eight books (Συλλογὴ ῥητορικῶν ἀφορμῶν), which Suidas assigns to Timæus of Tauromenium, was more probably written by Timæus, the author of the lexicon to Plato.

The lexicon to Plato was printed for the first time from a manuscript at Paris, edited by Ruhnken, Leyden, 1754, with a very valuable commentary; and again, with many improvements, Leyden, 1789. There are also two more recent editions by Koch, Leipzig, 1828 and 1833.

IV. Among the lexicographers of this period is usually, though perhaps not very correctly, placed Julius Pollux (Ἰούλιος Πολυδεύκης),[3] a Greek sophist and grammarian, and a native of Naucratis, in Egypt. He received instruction in criticism from his father, and afterward went to Athens, where he studied rhetoric under the sophist Adrian. He opened

[1] *Smith, Dict. Biogr.*, s. v. [2] *Id. ib.* [3] *Id. ib.*

a private school at Athens, where he gave instruction in grammar and rhetoric, and was subsequently appointed by the Emperor Commodus to the chair of rhetoric at Athens. He died during the reign of Commodus, at the age of fifty-eight. We may, therefore, assign A.D. 183 as the year in which he flourished. Philostratus praises his critical skill, but speaks unfavorably of his rhetorical powers, and implies that he gained his professor's chair from Commodus simply by his mellifluous voice. He seems to have been attacked by many of his contemporaries on account of the inferior character of his oratory, and especially by Lucian in his Ῥητόρων διδάσκαλος.

Pollux was the author of several works, all of which have perished except the *Onomasticon*, which has come down to us. This work is divided into ten books, each of which contains a short dedication to the *Cæsar* Commodus; and the work was therefore published before A.D. 177, since Commodus became Augustus in that year. The title of the work is explained as follows by Hemsterhuis: "*Onomasticorum munus est commoda rebus nomina imponere, et docere quibus verbis uberiore quadam et florente elegantia rem unam designare possimus. Non enim in Onomasticis tanquam proprio quodam loco de vocum difficilliorum interpretatione agebatur, sed quo pacto propriis res quævis et pluribus insigniri posset verbis.*"

Each book of the *Onomasticon* forms a separate treatise by itself, containing the most important words relating to certain subjects, with short explanations of the meaning of the words, which are frequently illustrated by quotations from the ancient writers. The alphabetical arrangement is not adopted, but the words are given according to the subjects treated of in each book. The object of the work was to present youths with a kind of store-house, from which they could borrow all the words of which they had need, and could, at the same time, learn their usage in the best writers. The contents of each book will give the best idea of the nature of the work. 1. The first treats of the gods and their worship, of kings, of speed and slowness, of dyeing, of commerce and manufactures, of fertility and the contrary, of time and the divisions of the year, of houses, of ships, of war, of horses, of agriculture, of the parts of the plough and the wagon, and of bees. 2. The second treats of man, his eye, the parts of his body, and the like. 3. Of relations, of political life, of friends, of the love of country, of love, of the relation between masters and slaves, of money, of travelling, and numerous other subjects. 4. Of the various branches of knowledge and science. 5. Of hunting, animals, &c. 6. Of meals, the names of crimes, &c. 7. Of the different trades, &c. 8. Of the courts, the administration of justice, &c. 9. Of towns, buildings, coins, games, &c. 10. Of various vessels, &c. In consequence of the loss of the great number of lexicographical works from which Pollux compiled his Onomasticon, this book has become one of the greatest value for acquiring a knowledge of Greek antiquity, and explains many subjects which are known to us from no other source. It has also preserved many fragments of lost writers, and the great number of authors quoted in the work may be seen by a glance at the long list given in Fabricius.

The first three editions of the Onomasticon contain simply the Greek text, without a Latin translation, and with numerous errors. They are by Aldus, Venice, 1502, fol., by Junta, Florence, 1520, fol., and by Grynæus, Basle, 1536, 4to. The first Greek and Latin edition was by Seber, Frankfort, 1608, 4to, with the text corrected from MSS. The Latin translation given in this edition had been previously published by Walther at Basle, 1541, 8vo. The next edition is the very valuable one, in Greek and Latin, by Lederlin and Hemsterhuis, Amsterdam, 1706, fol., containing copious notes by Jungermann, Kühn, and the two editors. An account of this edition will be found in Monk's Life of Bentley, p. 153, *seqq.*, where some curious particulars are stated respecting the effect produced upon Hemsterhuis (then not yet eighteen years of age!) by the masterly emendations of the great English scholar, transmitted to the former after the publication of his edition of Pollux. In 1824, W. Dindorf published an edition, Leipzig, 5 vols. 8vo, containing the labors of the previous commentators. The last edition is by Bekker, Berlin, 1846, which gives only the Greek text, in probably its most correct form.

SCHOLIASTS.[1]

I. At the head of the scholiasts is placed, singularly enough, a prince alternately the persecutor and the patron of letters, namely, Ptolemy VII., or Euergĕtes, whose life was almost one continued succession of crimes and folly, but who still retained in a great degree that love of letters which appears to have been hereditary in the whole race of the Ptolemies. He had in his youth been a pupil of Aristarchus, and not only courted the society of learned men, but was himself the author of a *Commentary on Homer*. He is also named among the διορθωταί of that poet, whether it was that he actually made a recension of the Iliad and Odyssey, or was content to take these two poems as the subject of his critical labors. He also wrote a *Literary History of Egypt*, and a work entitled Ὑπομνήματα, or Memoirs, in twenty-four books, repeatedly cited by Athenæus, and which would seem to have been a sort of general natural history rather than an historical narration of events.

II. Didȳmus (Δίδυμος)[2] has already been mentioned as belonging partly to the present period, and partly to the one which preceded it. An account of his scholia on Homer and other ancient poets has been given elsewhere.

III. Apion (Ἀπίων),[3] a Greek grammarian, was a native of Oasis Magna, in Africa. He studied at Alexandrea, and taught rhetoric at Rome, in the reigns of Tiberius and Claudius. He appears to have enjoyed an extraordinary reputation for extensive knowledge, and versatility as an orator; but the ancients are unanimous in censuring his ostentatious vanity. He is spoken of as the most active of grammarians, and the surname Μόχθος, which he bore, according to Suidas, is usually explained as describing the zeal and labor with which he prosecuted his studies. In the reign of Caligula he travelled about in Greece, and was received every where with the highest honors as the great interpreter of Homer. About the same time, A.D. 38, the inhabitants of Alexandrea sent him, at the head of an embassy, to Caligula, to prefer complaints against the Jews residing in their city. The results of this embassy are unknown; but, if we may believe the account of his enemy Josephus, he died of a disease which he had brought upon himself by his dissolute mode of life.

[1] *Schöll, Hist. Lit. Gr.*, vol. vi., p. 268, *seqq.* [2] *Smith, Dict. Biogr., s. v.* [3] *Id. ib.*

Apion was the author of a considerable number of works, all of which are now lost, with the exception of some fragments. 1. Upon Homer, whose poems seem to have formed the principal part of his studies, for he is said not only to have made the best recension of the text of the poems, but to have written explanations of phrases and words (λέξεις Ὁμηρικαί), and investigations concerning the life and native country of the poet. The best part of his λέξεις Ὁμηρικαί is supposed to be incorporated in the Homeric lexicon of Apollonius. Apion's labors on Homer are often referred to by Eustathius and other grammarians. 2. A work on Egypt (Αἰγυπτιακά), consisting of five books, which was highly valued in antiquity, as it contained descriptions of nearly all the remarkable objects in that country. It also contained numerous attacks upon the Jews. 3. A work against the Jews. A reply to these attacks is made by Josephus, in the second book of his work usually called Κατὰ Ἀπίωνος, and this reply is the only source from which we learn any thing about the character of Apion's work. 4. A work in praise of Alexander the Great. 5. Histories of separate countries, and one or two other works.

The historical fragments of Apion are given by C. Müller, in his *Fragm. Histor. Græc.*, vol. iii., p. 506, *seqq.*; in Didot's *Bibliotheca Græca*, Paris, 1849. For information respecting the other remains of Apion, the student is referred to Lehrs, *Quæst. Ep.*, p. 23, note, p. 33, *seqq.*, and Ritschl, *Die Alex. Bibl.*, p. 142, *seqq.*

IV. Epaphrodītus, Marcus Mettius (Ἐπαφρόδιτος),[1] a native of Chæronea, and one of the most celebrated scholiasts of the first century of our era. He was the disciple of Archias of Alexandrea, and became the slave, and afterward the freedman of Modestus, the præfect of Egypt, whose son Pitelinus had been educated by him. After having obtained his freedom, he went to Rome, where he resided in the reign of Nero, and down to the time of Nerva, and enjoyed a very high reputation for learning. He was extremely fond of books, and is said to have collected a library of 30,000 valuable works. He died of dropsy, at the age of seventy-five. He was the author of several grammatical works and commentaries; for example, on Homer's Iliad and Odyssey, on Hesiod's Shield of Hercules, and on the Αἴτια of Callimachus, which is frequently referred to by Stephanus Byzantinus and the scholiast on Æschylus. He is also mentioned several times in the Venetian scholia on the Iliad. His works are lost.

V. Two scholiasts still remain to be mentioned, namely, Ptolemæus of Alexandrea, a disciple of Aristarchus, who wrote, among other works, a *Commentary on Homer*; and Aristonīcus, of the same city, who is mentioned as the author of several works, most of them relating to the Homeric poems. 1. On the wanderings of Menelaus. 2. On the critical signs by which the Alexandrine critics used to mark the suspected or interpolated verses in the Homeric poems, and in Hesiod's Theogony. 3. On irregular grammatical constructions in Homer, consisting of six books. These and some other works are now lost, with the exception of a few fragments.

[1] *Smith, Dict. Biogr., s. v.*

GRAMMARIANS PROPERLY SO CALLED.

I. Demetrius (Δημήτριος) of Adramyttium, surnamed Ixīon, because he had committed a robbery in the temple of Juno, at Alexandrea,[1] was a Greek grammarian of the time of Augustus, and lived partly at Pergamum and partly at Alexandrea, where he belonged to the critical school of Aristarchus. He is mentioned as the author of the following works: 1. Ἐξήγησις εἰς Ὅμηρον, which is often referred to. 2. Ἐξήγησις εἰς Ἡσίοδον. 3. Ἐτυμολογούμενα, or Ἐτυμολογία. 4. Περὶ τῆς Ἀλεξανδρέων διαλέκτου. 5. Ἀττικαὶ γλῶσσαι, of which a few fragments are still extant. 6. On the Greek verbs ending in μι.

II. Draco (Δράκων), a grammarian of Stratonicea, flourished in the time of Hadrian. Suidas mentions several works of his, of which only one (περὶ μέτρων) is extant. It is said to be an extract from a larger work, and has been edited by Hermann from a copy of the Paris MS. furnished by Bast, Leipzig, 1812, 8vo.

III. Apollonius, surnamed Dyscŏlus[2] (Ἀπολλώνιος Δύσκολος), that is, the ill-tempered, was a native of Alexandrea, where he flourished in the reigns of Hadrian and Antoninus Pius. He was one of the most renowned grammarians of his time, partly on account of his numerous and excellent works, and partly on account of his son, Ælius Herodianus, who had been educated by him, and was as great a grammarian as himself. Apollonius is said to have been so poor that he was obliged to write on shells, as he had no means of procuring the ordinary writing materials, and this poverty created that state of mind to which he owed the surname of *Dyscolus*. Apollonius and his son are called by Priscian, in several passages, the greatest of all grammarians, and he declares that it was only owing to the assistance which he derived from their works that he was enabled to undertake his task. He was the first who reduced grammar to any thing like a system. A list of his works, some of which are lost, is given by Suidas. The following productions of his are still extant: 1. Περὶ συντάξεως τοῦ λόγου μερῶν, "*De Constructione Orationis*," in four books. 2. Περὶ ἀντωνυμίας, "*De Pronomine liber.*" 3. Περὶ συνδέσμων, "*De Conjunctionibus;*" and, 4. Περὶ Ἐπιῤῥημάτων, "*De Adverbiis.*" Among the works ascribed to Apollonius by Suidas there is one, περὶ κατεψευσμένης ἱστορίας, on fictitious or forged histories. A work under this title has come down to us, and has been three times edited, the last edition being by Teucher, Leipzig, 1792, 8vo. The work, however, is merely a collection of wonderful phenomena of nature, gathered from Aristotle, Theophrastus, and others, and, of course, is very different from what the title would lead us to expect. It has been supposed, therefore, with great probability, that the work of Apollonius with this title is lost, and that the one which has been mistaken for it belongs to an Apollonius who is otherwise unknown.

The treatise "*De Constructione Orationis*" was first published by Aldus, Venice, 1495, fol. A much better edition, with a Latin translation and notes, was published by Sylburg, Frankfort, 1590, 4to. The last edition, which was greatly corrected by the assist-

[1] *Suidas, s. v.*

[2] *Smith, Dict. Biogr., s. v.*

ance of four new MSS., is Bekker's, Berlin, 1817, 8vo. The treatise "*De Pronomine*" was first edited by Bekker, in the *Museum Antiq. Stud.*, i., 2, Berlin, 1811, 8vo, and afterward separately, Berlin, 1814, 8vo. The treatise "*De Conjunctionibus*" and that "*De Adverbiis*" are both printed in Bekker's *Anecdota Græca*, vol. ii., p. 477, *seqq.*

IV. Herodianus Ælius, already mentioned under the lexicographers, was the son of the preceding, and one of the most celebrated grammarians of antiquity, as before remarked. The only complete treatise which we possess of the numerous works composed by him is probably the one, περὶ μονήρους λέξεως, on monosyllabic words, published by Dindorf in the first volume of his *Grammatici Græci*, Leipzig, 1823.

V. Nicānor (Νικάνωρ),[1] a celebrated grammarian, who lived during the reign of the Emperor Hadrian. According to Suidas, he was of Alexandrea, but according to Stephanus Byzantinus, he was of Hierapolis. His labors were principally directed to punctuation; hence he received the ludicrous name of Στιγματίας, and from his having devoted much of his time to the elucidation of Homer's writings, through means of punctuation, he is called by Stephanus ὁ νέος Ὅμηρος. He wrote, also, on the punctuation of Callimachus, and a work περὶ καθόλου στιγμῆς. He is copiously quoted in the *Scholia Marciana* on Homer.

VI. Arcadius (Ἀρκάδιος),[2] of Antioch, a Greek grammarian of uncertain date, but who did not live before 200 A.D. He was the author of several grammatical works, some of which are mentioned by Suidas. A work of his on *Accents* (περὶ τόνων) has come down to us, and was first published by Barker from a Paris manuscript, Leipzig, 1820. It is also included in the first volume of Dindorf's *Grammat. Græc.*, Leipzig, 1823.

VII. Hephæstion (Ἡφαιστίων),[3] a Greek grammarian, who instructed the Emperor Verus in Greek, and accordingly lived about the middle of the second century after Christ. Suidas, who mentions several works of his, speaks of one entitled μέτρων πεδισμοί, which is believed to be the same as the Ἐγχειρίδιον περὶ μέτρων, which has come down to us under the name of Hephæstion, and is a tolerably complete manual of Greek metres, forming, in fact, the basis of all our knowledge on that subject. This little work is of great value, not only on account of the information it affords us on the subject it treats of, but also on account of the numerous quotations it contains from other writers, especially poets.

The first edition of the Ἐγχειρίδιον appeared at Florence, 1526, 8vo, together with the Greek grammar of Theodore Gaza. It was followed by the editions of Turnebus, Paris, 1553, 4to (with some Greek scholia), and of De Pauw, Utrecht, 1726, 8vo. The best edition, however, is that of Gaisford, Oxford, 1810, 8vo, reprinted at Leipzig, 1832, 8vo.

VIII. Dosithēus (Δωσίθεος),[4] surnamed Magister, a Greek grammarian, taught at Rome about A.D. 207. He has left behind him, in two manuscripts, a work entitled Ἑρμηνεύματα, divided into three books. The first and second books contain a Greek grammar written in Latin, and Greek-Latin and Latin-Greek glossaries. The first book remains unpublished, and deservedly. The second book, containing the glossaries, was published by H. Stephens, 1573, fol., and has since been several times reprinted. The third book contains translations from Latin authors into

[1] *Smith, Dict. Biogr., s. v.* [2] *Id. ib., s. v.* [3] *Id. ib., s. v.* [4] *Id. ib., s. v.*

Greek, and *vice versa*, the Latin and Greek being placed in opposite columns. This part of the work deserves attention. It consists of six divisions or chapters, the first of which, entitled *Divi Hadriani Sententiæ et Epistolæ*, contains legal anecdotes of Hadrian, his answers to petitioners, a letter written by himself to his mother, and a notice of a law concerning parricide. The third chapter is a fragment relative to the civil law, and is probably an extract from the *Regulæ* of *Paulus*. These chapters have been published separately, but the whole of the third book has been edited by Böcking, 16mo, Bonn, 1832.

IX. Conon (Κόνων),[1] a grammarian of the age of Augustus, the author of a work entitled Διηγήσεις, addressed to Archelaus Philopator, king of Cappadocia. It was a collection of fifty narratives relating to the mythical and heroic period, and especially the foundation of colonies. An epitome of this work has been preserved in the Bibliotheca of Photius, who speaks in terms of commendation of his Attic style. There are separate editions of this abstract in Gale's *Histor. Poet. Script.*, p. 241, *seqq.*, Paris, 1675; by Teucher, Leipzig, 1794 and 1802; by Kanne, Göttingen, 1798; and by Westermann, in his *Scriptores Poeticæ Historiæ Græci*, Brunswick, 1843.

X. Ptolemy (Πτολεμαῖος),[2] of Alexandrea, surnamed *Chermus*, flourished under Trajan and Hadrian. His works were, περὶ παραδόξου ἱστορίας; an historical drama, entitled Σφίγξ; and an epic poem, in twenty-four rhapsodies, entitled 'Ανθόμηρος, and some others. We still possess, in the Bibliotheca of Photius, an epitome of the work of Ptolemy, περὶ τῆς εἰς πολυμαθίαν καινῆς ἱστορίας, in seven books, which, there can be little doubt, is the same as that which Suidas mentions by the title περὶ παραδόξου ἱστορίας. It is a farrago of the most heterogeneous materials. The work περὶ παραδόξου ἱστορίας has been edited, with commentaries by Schottus and Hoeschelius, in Gale's *Historiæ Poeticæ Scriptores*, p. 303, *seqq.*, Paris, 1675, 8vo, with a dissertation upon Ptolemy; by Teucher, along with Conon and Parthenius, Leipzig, 1794, 8vo; and by Westermann, in his *Mythographi*, p. 182, *seqq.*, Brunswick, 1843, 8vo.

XI. Antoninus Liberalis ('Αντωνῖνος Λιβερᾶλις), a Greek grammarian, concerning whose life nothing is known, but who is generally believed to have lived in the time of the Antonines, about A.D. 147. We possess a work under his name, entitled Μεταμορφώσεων συναγωγή, and consisting of forty-one tales about mythical metamorphoses. With the exception of nine tales, he always mentions the sources from which he took his accounts. Since most of the works referred to by him are lost, his book is of some importance to the study of Greek mythology, but in regard to composition and style it is of no value. There are but very few manuscripts of this work, and the chief are that at Heidelberg and the one in Paris.

The first edition from the Heidelberg MS., with a Latin translation, is by Xylander, Basle, 1568, 8vo. There is a good edition by Verheyck, Leyden, 1774, 8vo, with notes by Muncker, Hemsterhuis, and other scholars. The best edition, however, is by Koch, Leipzig, 1832, 8vo, who collated the Paris MS., and added valuable notes of his own.

---

[1] *Smith, Dict. Biogr.*, *s. v.*

[2] *Id. ib.*, *s. v.*

XII. ATHENÆUS (Ἀθήναιος),[1] called by Suidas a γραμματικός, and therefore considered under the present head, for convenience' sake, since he can hardly be said properly to belong to it. He was a native of Naucratis, in Egypt, a city situate on the left side of the Canopic mouth of the Nile. He lived about A.D. 230, first at Alexandrea, and afterward at Rome. His extant work is entitled the *Deipnosophistæ*, i. e., the *Banquet of the Learned*, or else, perhaps, as has lately been suggested, *The Contrivers of Feasts.* It may be considered one of the earliest collections of what are called *Ana*, being an immense mass of anecdotes, extracts from the writings of poets, historians, dramatists, philosophers, orators, and physicians, of facts in natural history, criticisms and discussions, on almost every conceivable subject, especially on gastronomy. It is, in short, a collection of stories from the memory and commonplace book of a Greek gentleman of the third century of our era, of enormous reading, extreme love of good eating, and respectable ability. Some notion of the materials which he had amassed for the work may be formed from the fact, which he tells us himself, that he had read and made extracts from eight hundred plays of the middle comedy only.

Athenæus represents himself as describing to his friend Timocrates a banquet given at the house of Laurentius (Λαρήνσιος), a noble Roman, to several guests, of whom the best known are Galen the physician, and Ulpian the lawyer. The work is in the form of a dialogue, in which these guests are the interlocutors, related to Timocrates—a double machinery, which would have been inconvenient to an author who had a real talent for dramatic writing, but which, in the hands of Athenæus, who had none, is wholly unmanageable. As a work of art the failure is complete. Unity of time and dramatic probability are utterly violated by the supposition that so immense a work is the record of the conversation at a single banquet, and by the absurdity of collecting at it the produce of every season of the year. Long quotations and intricate discussions, introduced apropos of some trifling incident, entirely destroy the form of the dialogue, so that before we have finished a speech we forget who was the speaker. But as a work illustrative of ancient manners, as a collection of curious facts, names of authors, and fragments which, but for Athenæus, would utterly have perished; in short, as a body of amusing antiquarian research, it would be impossible to praise the Deipnosophistæ too highly.

Among the authors whose works are now lost, from whom Athenæus gives extracts, are Alcæus, Agathon the tragic poet, Antisthenes the philosopher, Archilochus, Menander, Epimenides of Crete, Empedocles of Agrigentum, Cratinus, Eupolis, Alcman, Epicurus (whom he represents as a wasteful glutton), and many others whose names are well known. In all, he cites nearly eight hundred authors, and more than twelve hundred separate works. Athenæus was also the author of a lost work, περὶ τῶν ἐν Συρίᾳ βασιλευσάντων, which probably, from the specimen of it in the *Deipnosophistæ*, and the obvious unfitness of Athenæus to be an historian, was rather a collection of anecdotes than a connected history.

[1] *Id. ib., s. v.* Compare *Edinburgh Review*, No. 5, vol. iii., p. 181, *seqq.*

Of the *Deipnosophistæ* the first two books, and part of the third, eleventh, and fifteenth, exist only in an epitome, the date and author of which are unknown. The original work, however, was rare in the time of Eustathius (the latter part of the twelfth century); for Bentley has shown, by examining nearly a hundred of his references to Athenæus, that his only knowledge of him was through the epitome. Perizonius (in his preface to Ælian quoted by Schweighaeuser) has proved that Ælian transferred large portions of the work to his *Various History*, a robbery which must have been committed almost in the lifetime of the pillaged author. The *Deipnosophistæ* also furnished to Macrobius the idea and much of the matter of his *Saturnalia* (end of fourth century); but no one has availed himself so largely of Athenæus's erudition as Eustathius.[1]

Only one original manuscript of Athenæus now exists, called by Schweighaeuser the *Codex Veneto-Parisiensis*. From this all the others which we now possess are copies; so that the text of the work, especially in the poetical parts, is in a very unsettled state. The MS. was brought from Greece by Cardinal Bessarion, and, after his death, was placed in the library of St. Mark at Venice, whence it was taken to Paris by order of Napoleon, and there for the first time collated by Schweighaeuser's son. It is probably of the date of the tenth century. The subscript iota is always placed after, instead of under, the vowel with which it is connected, and the whole is written without contractions. The first edition of Athenæus was that of Aldus, Venice, 1514; a second was published at Basle, 1535; a third by Casaubon, at Geneva, 1597, with the Latin version of Dalechamp, and a commentary published in 1600; a fourth by Schweighaeuser, Strasburg, 14 vols. 8vo, 1801–1807, founded on a collation of the above-mentioned MS., and also of a valuable copy of the epitome; a fifth by W. Dindorf, 3 vols. 8vo, Leipzig, 1827. The last is the best, Schweighaeuser not having availed himself sufficiently of the sagacity of previous critics in amending the text, and being himself apparently very ignorant of metrical laws.

CHAPTER XLVIII.

SIXTH OR ROMAN PERIOD—*continued*.

PHILOSOPHERS.

INTRODUCTORY REMARKS.[2]

I. The Romans, a nation of warriors and conquerors, with whom the interests of their republic outweighed all others, became acquainted with Grecian philosophy, particularly with the Peripatetic, Academic, and Stoic doctrines, only after the conquest of Greece; and more especially through the intervention of the three philosophers whom the Athenians sent to Rome, and of whom we have already made mention. In spite of determined prejudices and reiterated denunciations, one of these doctrines (that of the Academy) daily gained disciples there, especially when Lucullus and Sulla had enriched the Capitol with the libraries of the conquered. The latter, after the capture of Athens, 84 B.C., sent thither the collection of Apellicon, which was particularly rich in the works of Aristotle.

II. The spirit of research in Grecian philosophy, once so original and independent, was now, however, exhausted. Reason had tried every

1 *Smith, Dict. Biogr., s. v.* Compare *Edinburgh Review*, No. 5, vol. iii., p. 181, *seqq.*
2 *Tennemann's Manual of Philosophy*, ed. *Morell*, p. 148, *seqq.*

path, every direction then open to her, without being able to satisfy herself; for she had not penetrated to the fundamental problem, that of the nature of reason, and consequently had continued an enigma to herself. The different philosophic systems had viewed truth only in one of its aspects, and consequently were involved in errors.

III. Indeed, the political, religious, and moral condition of the Roman empire, during the first centuries after the Christian era, was not such as to animate and sustain a spirit of philosophic research. Greece had lost her political existence; Rome her republican Constitution. The characteristic features of the period were a neglect of the popular religion, a preference for foreign rites (of which an incongruous medley was tolerated), a widely prevalent superstition, a disdain of what was natural, a mania for what was strange and extraordinary, a curious prying into the (pretended) occult arts, with an extinction of all sentiments truly great and noble.

IV. Nevertheless, philosophy made at least some apparent progress in extension and, at least apparently, in intensity. In extension, because the Romans and the Jews by this time had made themselves acquainted with the philosophical dogmas of the Greeks, and had produced some philosophical works sufficiently original. Nor does this progress of philosophy appear to have been merely external, inasmuch as skepticism had assumed a more intense character, and gave occasion for a fresh dogmatical system in the school of the Platonists. By imagining a new source of knowledge, the intuition of the absolute; by laboring to combine the old and the new theories of the East and the West, they endeavored to provide a broader basis for dogmatic philosophy, to prop up the established religion, and to oppose a barrier to the rapid progress of Christianity, but eventually lost themselves in the region of metaphysical dreams.

V. We will now proceed to consider the different schools, and to notice the Greek writers who have distinguished themselves therein.

I. EPICUREAN SCHOOL.[1]

I. The doctrine of Epicurus, when first disseminated in their country, attracted among the Romans a crowd of partisans, in consequence of its light and accommodating character, and the indulgence it afforded to the inclinations of all; as, also, because it had the effect of disengaging the mind from superstitious terrors. Very few of the Roman Epicureans distinguished themselves by a truly philosophical character; and even these adhered literally to the doctrines of their master, without advancing a step beyond them. Such, among others, was the Roman Lucretius, who gave a statement of those doctrines in his didactic poem "*De Rerum Natura.*"

II. The principal Greek writers belonging to this school, during the period which we are considering, were *Celsus* and *Diogenes Laertius.*

III. Celsus,[2] the adversary of Christianity, to whom Origen replies, though in his attack he sometimes makes use of Platonic and Stoic weapons, is expressly ranked by Lucian, as well as Origen, among the follow-

[1] *Tennemann*, p. 153, *seqq.*

[2] *Smith, Dict. Biogr.*, *s. v.*

ers of Epicurus; and this supposition best accounts for the violence with which he opposed the Christian religion; for an Epicurean would, of course, reject without examination all pretensions to divine communications or powers. The extracts from his writings preserved by Origen, at the same time that they prove him to have been an inveterate enemy to Christianity, show that he was not destitute of learning or ability. Celsus, besides his book against the Christians, wrote a piece entitled "Precepts of Living Well," and another "Against Magic," but none of his writings are extant, except the quotations made by Origen. Celsus was born toward the close of Hadrian's reign, and was contemporary with Lucian under M. Aurelius Antoninus.

IV. Diogenes Laertius, of whom mention has already been made, is also ranked among the followers of Epicurus. His predilection, indeed, for Epicureanism is shown in the extraordinary pains he has taken to give an accurate summary of the doctrine of Epicurus, and a full detail of his life.

II. STOIC SCHOOL.[1]

I. Next to those of Epicurus, the doctrines of the Stoics obtained the greatest success at Rome, especially among men of a severer character, who had devoted their lives to public affairs. With such men, the Stoic philosophy, being more closely applied to real life, and exercising a marked influence over legislation and the administration of the laws, naturally acquired a more practical spirit, and began to disengage itself, in some degree, from speculative subtleties.

II. But, notwithstanding the general credit which the Stoic doctrine obtained, it met with powerful opposition from several quarters, particularly from the Skeptics, who were indefatigable in their endeavors to overturn every dogmatic system; and from the Alexandrean sect, which, by its destructive plan of coalition, corrupted the genuine doctrine of every other school. From the period when the motley Eclectic system was established, Stoicism began to decline; and in the age of Augustine it no longer subsisted as a distinct sect. It was only during the short space of two hundred years that the Roman school of Zeno was adorned with illustrious names, which claim a place in the history of philosophy. Such the, Athenodorus of Tarsus, who flourished about the time of Christ; Chæremon of *Egypt*, who was one of the preceptors of Nero; Euphrates of *Tyre*, or, according to others, of *Byzantium*, an intimate friend of the younger Pliny; Dio Chrysostom, already mentioned; Epictetus, Arrian, of whom we have already spoken, and the philosophic emperor, Marcus Aurelius Antoninus.

III. Epictētus (Ἐπίκτητος),[2] of Hierapolis, in Phrygia, was a freedman of Epaphroditus, who was himself a freedman of Nero. He lived and taught first at Rome, and, after the expulsion of the philosophers by Domitian, at Nicopolis, in Epirus. Although he was favored by Hadrian, he does not appear to have returned to Rome, for the discourses which Arrian took down in writing were delivered by Epictetus when an old

[1] *Tennemann*, p. 154.

[2] *Smith, Dict. Biogr.*, *s. v.*

man at Nicopolis. Only a few circumstances of his life are recorded, such as his lameness, which is spoken of in various ways, his poverty, and his few wants. Epictetus did not leave any works behind him, and the short manual (*Enchiridion*) which bears his name was compiled from his discourses by his faithful pupil Arrian. Arrian also wrote out the philosophical lectures of his master in eight books, from which, though four are lost, we are enabled to gain a complete idea of the way in which Epictetus conceived and taught the Stoic philosophy. Being deeply impressed with his vocation as a teacher, he aimed in his discourses at nothing else but winning the minds of his hearers to that which was good, and no one was able to resist the impression which they produced. Epictetus gave up the proud self-sufficiency which the Stoic philosopher was expected to show in his relation to the vicissitudes of the world and of man. The maxim "*suffer and abstain*" (from evil), which he followed throughout life, was based with him upon the firm belief in a wise and benevolent government of Providence; and in this respect he approaches the Christian doctrine more than any of the earlier Stoics, though there is not a trace in the *Epictetēa* to show that he was acquainted with Christianity, and, still less, that he had adopted Christianity, either in part or entirely.

IV. Antoninus, Marcus Aurelius,[1] the philosophic emperor, was distinguished for his devotion to philosophy and literature. When only twelve years old, he adopted the dress and practiced the austerities of the Stoics, whose doctrines were imparted to him by the most celebrated teachers of the day—Diognotus, Apollonius, and Junius Rusticus. The principles of composition and oratory he studied under Herodes Atticus and Cornelius Fronto. While yet Cæsar, he was addressed by Justin Martyr as *Verissimus* "the philosopher," an epithet by which he has been commonly distinguished from that period down to the present day, although no such title was ever publicly or formally conferred. Even after his elevation to the purple, he felt neither reluctance nor shame in resorting to the school of Sextus of Chæronea, the descendant of Plutarch, and in listening to the extemporaneous declamations of Hermogenes. With the exception of a few letters, contained in the recently discovered remains of Fronto, the only production of Marcus Aurelius which has been preserved is a volume composed in Greek, and entitled Μάρκου Ἀντωνίνου τοῦ αὐτοκράτορος τῶν εἰς ἑαυτὸν βιβλία ιβ', "*Twelve Books of the Meditations of the Emperor Marcus Antoninus.*" It is a sort of commonplace book, in which were registered, from time to time, the thoughts and feelings of the author upon moral and religious topics, together with striking maxims extracted from the works of those who had been most eminent for wisdom and virtue. There is no attempt at order or arrangement, but the contents are valuable in so far as they illustrate the system of self-examination enjoined by the discipline of the Stoics, and present a genuine picture of the doubts, and difficulties, and struggles of a speculative and reflecting mind.

The *editio princeps* of the *Meditations* was published by Xylander, Zurich, 1558, 8vo,

[1] *Smith, Dict. Biogr., s. v.*

and republished, with improvements, by the same scholar ten years afterward, Basle, 1568, 8vo. The next in order was superintended by Merick Casaubon, London, 1643, 8vo, followed by the edition of Gataker, Cambridge, 1652, 4to, reprinted at London, 1679, with additional notes from the French of And. Dacier, and his life of M. Aurelius, translated into Latin by Stanhope. There are also editions by Wolle, Leipzig, 1729, 8vo; Morus, Leipzig, 1775, 8vo; and Schultz (containing a new recension of the text), Sleswick, 1802, 8vo. This last, however, is still imperfect, only one volume having appeared. The edition of Gataker (the London reprint) is, upon the whole, the most useful and ample.

III. PERIPATETIC SCHOOL.[1]

I. The philosophy of Aristotle was not suited to the practical character of the Roman mind, and such as devoted themselves to the study of it became mere commentators of various merit or demerit. We must account as peripatetics CRATIPPUS, of Mytilene, whom Cicero the younger, and several other Romans, attended at Athens; NICOLAUS DAMASCENUS, already mentioned by us among the historical writers; XENARCHUS, of Seleucia, who, as well as the preceding, gave lessons in the time of Augustus; ALEXANDER, of Ægæ, one of the preceptors of Nero; and more especially the celebrated commentator ALEXANDER, of Aphrodisias, whom we shall proceed briefly to notice.

II. ALEXANDER,[2] of Aphrodisias, in Caria, the most celebrated of the commentators on Aristotle, and hence called, by way of eminence, ὁ ἐξηγητής, or "the commentator," lived about A.D. 200. He taught at Alexandrea, and founded a special exegetical school which bore his name, his followers being called *Alexandreans* and *Alexandrists*. In his work "On the Soul," he departed from Aristotle, and taught that the soul is not a special substance (οὐσία), but simply a form of the organized body (εἶδός τι τοῦ σώματος ὀργανικοῦ), and consequently, that it could not be immortal; and in his treatise "On Destiny," he attacked the fatalism of the Stoics, which he declared irreconcilable with morality. If we view him as a philosopher, his merit can not be rated too highly. His excellences and defects are all on the model of his great master; there is the same perspicuity and power of analysis, united with almost more than Aristotelian plainness of style. About half of his voluminous works were edited and translated into Latin at the revival of literature. There are a few more extant in the original Greek, which have never been printed, and an Arabic version is preserved of several others. His most important treatise is that "On Destiny," mentioned above, the best edition of which is that by Orelli, Zurich, 1824, 8vo.

IV. NEW PYTHAGOREAN SCHOOL.[3]

I. Pythagoras, whose reputation, and even whose philosophy had long been familiar to the Romans, had, at the period of which we are treating, a large number of followers; his exemplary life, and still more, the mysterious character of his history and his doctrines, being the principal causes of the species of enthusiastic reverence with which he was regarded.

II. To the New Pythagoreans we may refer EUXENUS, of Heraclea

[1] *Tennemann*, p. 158. [2] *Smith, Dict. Biogr.*, *s. v.* [3] *Tennemann*, p. 159.

Pontica; Apollonius, of Tyana, in Cappadocia, his pupil, of whom we have already spoken in our account of Philostratus; and Secundus, of Athens, about 120 A.D. Others, for instance Anaxilaus, of Larissa, who flourished under Augustus, and was banished from Italy on a charge of magical practices, applied the principles of Pythagoras to the study of nature; or, like Moderatus, of Gades, who flourished in the time of Nero, and Nicomachus, of Gerasa, endeavored to discover in the Pythagorean doctrine of numbers a sublime and occult science, which they blended with the theories of Plato. Nicomachus must be assigned to the reign of Tiberius. He wrote a Life of Pythagoras, now lost, and composed works also on Arithmetic and Music.

The extant works of Nicomachus are, 1. 'Αριθμητικῆς εἰσαγωγῆς βιβλία β', forming what is called the lesser work on Arithmetic, the larger one being lost. It was printed by Wechel (Gr.), Paris, 1538, 4to; also after the *Theologumena Arithmeticæ*, attributed to Iamblichus, Leipzig, 1817, 8vo. 2. 'Εγχειρίδιον ἁρμονικῆς βιβλία β', a work on Music, first printed (Gr.) by Meursius in his collection, Leyden, 1616, 4to, and afterward in the collection of Meibomius (Gr. and Lat.), Amsterdam, 1652, 4to; and again in the works of Meursius, by Lami, Florence, 1745, fol.

V. ECLECTIC ACADEMICS.[1]

I. In the time of Augustus a new school of Platonists began to form itself, and became popular. The philosophers of this school made it their object to disseminate in a popular form the ethics and religious theory of Plato, and constructed for themselves a system of allegorical interpretation, which connected the doctrines of that system with the ancient religious mysteries. With this they blended much that was derived from the Pythagoreans and Aristotle, and, in the dogmatic manner, pursued the most lofty speculations (the outline of which had been traced in the treatises of Plato), on the Deity, the Creator, the Soul of the World, the Demons, the Origin of the World, and that of Evil. They supposed our conceptions to have a hypostatical existence, and applied their abstract principles to account for phenomena of their own days; for instance, the cessation of oracles.

II. Among the philosophers of this school may be mentioned Thrasyllus, of Mendes, the astrologer, in the time of Tiberius; Theon, of Smyrna, the author of an exposition of Plato, and also a mathematical writer, who lived in the time of Hadrian; Alcinous, who has left us a brief sketch of the Platonic doctrine; Albinus, of Smyrna, the preceptor of Galen, and who has left us an introduction to the dialogues of Plato; Plutarch, of Chæronea, already mentioned, and Maximus Tyrius, the rhetorician, of whom also we have already treated.

Of Theon, of Smyrna, all that we have left is a portion of a work entitled Τῶν κατὰ μαθηματικὴν χρησίμων εἰς τὴν τοῦ Πλάτωνος ἀνάγνωσιν. The portion which now exists is in two books, one on Arithmetic, and one on Music. There was a third on Astronomy; and a fourth, περὶ τῆς ἐν κόσμῳ ἁρμονίας. The best edition is by Gelder, Leyden, 1827, 8vo. Of the Epitome of Alcinous we have an edition by Fell, Oxford, 1667, and another by Fischer, Leipzig, 1783, 8vo. The Introduction of Albinus is given in Fabricius, *Bibl. Græc.*, vol. ii., old edition. It is also prefixed to Etwall's edition of three dialogues of Plato, Oxford, 1771, and to Fischer's four dialogues of Plato, Leipzig, 1783, 8vo.

[1] *Tennemann*, p. 161.

VI. SKEPTICISM OF THE EMPIRIC SCHOOL.[1]

I. ÆNESIDĒMUS,[2] a native of Cnosus, in Crete, and who lived probably a little later than Cicero, settled in Alexandrea, and revived the skepticism which had been silenced in the Academy, wishing to make it serve the purpose of strengthening the opinions of Heraclitus, to which he was inclined; for, in order to know that every thing has its contrary, he maintained that we ought to admit that an *opposite* is presented to each and the same individual. He assumed an external principle of thought, making truth to consist in the universality of the subjective appearance. The boldest attack made by any of the ancient philosophers on the possibility of demonstrative knowledge, was that attempted by Ænesidemus against the reality of the idea of causality. He argued that the notion of causality is without signification, because we can not understand the relations of cause and effect.

II. From the time of Ænesidemus to that of SEXTUS EMPIRICUS followed a succession of skeptics, all of them physicians of the Empiric and Methodic schools, who confined themselves to the observation of facts, and rejected all theory respecting the causes of maladies.

III. SEXTUS EMPIRĬCUS[3] was a physician, and received his name *Empiricus* from his belonging to the school of the *Empirici*. He was a contemporary of Galen, and lived in the first half of the third century of the Christian era. Nothing is known of his life. He put the finishing hand to the philosophy of doubt. While he availed himself of the works of his predecessors, especially Ænesidemus, he contributed much to define the object, end, and method of skepticism. Two of his works are extant. 1. Πυῤῥώνιαι Ὑποτυπώσεις ἢ σκεπτικὰ ὑπομνήματα, containing the doctrines of the Skeptics, in three books. 2. Πρὸς τοὺς μαθηματικοὺς ἀντιῤῥητικοί, against the *Mathematici*, in eleven books. This is an attack upon all positive philosophy. The first six books are a refutation of the six sciences of grammar, rhetoric, geometry, arithmetic, astrology, and music. The remaining five books are directed against logicians, natural philosophers, and ethical writers, and form, in fact, a distinct work, which may be viewed as belonging to the Ὑποτυπώσεις. The two works are a great repository of doubts. The language is as clear and perspicuous as the subject will allow.

The first edition of the Greek text of both works was that of Paris, 1621, fol. The second edition was that of Fabricius, Leipzig, 1718, fol., containing the Latin version which had appeared before the first publication of the Greek text, and also some emendations. A reimpression of this latter edition appeared at Leipzig, 1842, 2 vols. 8vo. A new edition, with an amended text, was published by Bekker, Berlin, 1842.

VII. NEO-PLATONISTS.[4]

I. *Neo-Platonism* had its origin in the much-frequented school of the Platonists at Alexandrea, and was characterized by an ardent and enthusiastic zeal. Its disciples aspired to attain unto the highest pinnacles of science, to acquire a knowlege of the *absolute*, and an intimate union

[1] *Tennemann*, p. 163. [2] *Smith, Dict. Biogr., s. v.* [3] *Id. ib.* [4] *Tennemann*, p. 177.

(ἕνωσις) therewith as the final end of man's being. The way thereto they held to be the intuition of the absolute (θεωρία).

II. The principal causes which led to this new system were, the decline of genuine Grecian philosophy, and the admixture with its remains of the theories of the East, added to a continually-increasing attachment to Oriental exaggeration and enthusiasm, which they confirmed by frequent appeals to celestial revelations, while they depreciated the merit of Plato as a philosopher. The prevailing spirit of the age, and the decline of the Roman empire, contributed to this. To these may be added two other causes: the opposition which the skeptics of the new school continually made to all pretensions to rational knowledge, and the alarm which the victorious progress of Christianity occasioned to the defenders of the old religion, lest it should be utterly overthrown.

III. The importance which Platonism assumed in this conflict between Christianity and polytheism, added to the daily-increasing influence of Oriental notions, caused that philosophy to assume a fresh distinction, its ardent character being aided by the scientific turn of the Greeks, and heightened by the admixture of many other doctrines. PHILO JUDÆUS, NUMENIUS, and ATTICUS had already given specimens of this sort of mystical speculation, and association of Oriental ideas with those of the Platonists. The same is observable in the writings of many of the Greek fathers of the Church; JUSTIN, for instance, CLEMENS of Alexandrea, and ORIGEN, who not unfrequently Platonize. The true founder of the Neo-Platonic school, however, was AMMONIUS SACCAS, who ranked among his pupils LONGINUS, the celebrated critic, PLOTINUS, ORIGEN, and HERENNIUS. We will now proceed to give a brief sketch of some of these, and other Platonists of the time.

1. PHILO JUDÆUS,[1] or Philo the Jew, was born at Alexandrea, and was descended from a priestly family of distinction. He had already reached an advanced age when he went to Rome (A.D. 40), on an embassy to the Emperor Caligula, in order to procure the revocation of the decree which exacted from the Jews divine homage to the statue of the emperor. We have no other particulars of the life of Philo worthy of record. His most important works treat of the books of Moses, and are generally cited under different titles. His great object was to reconcile the sacred Scriptures with the doctrines of the Greek philosophy, and to point out the conformity between the two. He maintained that the fundamental truths of the Greek philosophy were derived from the Mosaic revelation, and, in order to make the latter agree more perfectly with the former, he had recourse to an allegorical interpretation of the books of Moses. On the other hand, he transferred into his system of Platonic philosophy many of the opinions of the East, in return for those which he borrowed from Plato. Hence, in strictness, he may be considered as the first Neo-Platonist of Alexandrea, though, as before remarked, the regular founder of that school was Ammonius Saccas.

To the treatises of Philo contained in the earlier editions have recently been added not only those found by Mai in a Florentine MS. (Milan, 1818), but also the treatises dis-

[1] *Smith, Dict. Biogr., s. v.*

covered by Aucher in an Armenian version, and translated into Latin (Venice, 1822, fol. min.; ibid., 1826). The best edition of Philo is the splendid one of Mangey, London, 1742, 2 vols. fol. Still, without detracting from its merits, it is far from complete; and how much remains to be done in order to make a really good edition, was shown by Valckenaer, Ruhnken, Markland, and others, at an earlier period, and more recently by Creuzer (*Zur Kritik der Schriften des Juden Philo*, in Ullmann's and Umbreit's *Theologischen Studien und Kritiken*, 1832, p. i., *seqq.*). The edition of Pfeiffer, Erlangen, 1785–92, 5 vols. 8vo, contributed but little to the correction of the text, and that of Richter, Leipzig, 1828–30, 8 vols. 12mo, is little more than a reprint of Mangey's, including the pieces discovered in the mean time.

2. Numenius (Νουμήνιος) of Apamea, in Syria, was highly esteemed by Plotinus and his school, as well as by Origen. He probably belongs to the age of the Antonines. His object was to trace the doctrines of Plato up to Pythagoras, and, at the same time, to show that they were not at variance with the dogmas and mysteries of the Brahmins, Jews, Magi, and Egyptians. Considerable fragments of his works have been preserved by Eusebius.

3. Justīnus (Ἰουστῖνος),[1] surnamed the Martyr (ὁ Μάρτυς), or the Philosopher (ὁ Φιλόσοφος), one of the earliest of the Christian writers, was a native of Flavia Neapolis, or the New City of Flavia, which arose out of the ruins, and in the immediate vicinity of the ancient town called Shechem in the Old Testament, and Sychar in the New. He was born about A.D. 103. Justin was brought up as a heathen, and in his youth studied the Greek philosophy with zeal and ardor. He was afterward converted to Christianity. He retained as a Christian the garb of a philosopher, but devoted himself to the propagation, by writing and otherwise, of the faith which he had embraced. He was put to death at Rome, in the persecution under Marcus Aurelius, about 165 A.D. Justin wrote a large number of works in Greek, several of which have come down to us. Of these the most important are, 1. *An Apology for the Christians*, addressed to Antoninus Pius, about A.D. 139. 2. *A Second Apology for the Christians*, addressed to the emperors M. Aurelius and L. Verus. 3. *A Dialogue with Tryphon the Jew*, in which Justin defends Christianity against the objections of Tryphon.

The best edition of the collected works of Justin is by Otto, Jena, 1842–44, 2 vols. 8vo; second edition, Jena, 1848–50, 3 vols. 8vo.

4. Clemens Alexandrīnus,[2] so called from his long residence at Alexandrea, was a native of Athens. His full name was T. Flavius Clemens. In early life he was ardently devoted to the study of philosophy, and his thirst for knowledge led him to visit various countries, such as Greece, Southern Italy, Cœle-Syria, Palestine, and Egypt. His philosophical studies had a great influence upon his views of Christianity. He embraced Christianity through the teaching of Pantænus, at Alexandrea, was ordained presbyter about A.D. 190, and died about A.D. 220. Hence he flourished during the reigns of Severus and Caracalla, A.D. 193–217. His three principal works constitute parts of a whole. In the *Hortatory Address to the Greeks* (Λόγος Προτρεπτικός, &c.), his design was to convince the heathens, and to convert them to Christianity. The

[1] *Smith, Dict. Biogr.*, *s. v.*

[2] *Id. ib.*

Pædagogue (Παιδαγωγός) takes up the new convert at the point to which he is supposed to have been brought by the hortatory address, and furnishes him with rules for the regulation of his conduct. The *Stromata* (Στρωματεῖς) are in eight books. The title means "*Patchwork*," and indicates its miscellaneous character. It is rambling and discursive, but contains much valuable information on many points of antiquity, particularly the history of philosophy. The principal information respecting Egyptian hieroglyphics is contained in the fifth book. The object of the work was to delineate the perfect Christian or *Gnostic*, after he had been instructed by the *Teacher*, and thus prepared by sublime speculations in philosophy and theology.

By far the best edition of Clemens is that of Potter, Oxford, 1715, 2 vols. fol. A very good edition also is that of Klotz, Leipzig, 1830–34, 4 vols. 12mo.

5. ORIGĔNES (Ὠριγένης),[1] usually called ORIGEN, one of the most eminent of the early Christian writers, was born at Alexandrea, A.D. 186. He received a careful education from his father Leonides, who was a devout Christian, and he subsequently became a pupil of Clemens, of Alexandrea. After an active and checkered life, the details of which belong more properly to sacred literature, he died in A.D. 253 or 254, his end having been hastened by the sufferings which he had undergone in the Decian persecution (249–251). The place of his death was Tyre, in which city he was buried. He was in his sixty-ninth year at the time of his decease. The following are the most important of Origen's works: 1. The *Hexapla*, which consisted of six copies of the Old Testament ranged in parallel columns. The first column contained the Hebrew text in Hebrew characters; the second the same text in Greek characters; the third the version of Aquila; the fourth that of Symmachus; the fifth the Septuagint; the sixth the version of Theodotion. Besides the compilation and arrangement of these versions, Origen added marginal notes, containing, among other things, an explanation of the Hebrew names. Only fragments of this valuable work are extant. 2. *Exegetical Works*, which comprehend three classes. (A) *Tomi*, which Jerome renders *volumina*, containing ample commentaries, in which he gave full scope to his intellect. (B) *Scholia*, or brief notes on detached passages. (C) *Homiliæ*, or popular expositions, chiefly delivered at Cæsarea. In his various expositions Origen sought to extract from the sacred writings their historical, mystical or prophetical, and moral significance. His desire of finding continually a mystical sense led him frequently into the neglect of the historical sense, and even into the denial of its truth. This capital fault has at all times furnished ground for depreciating his labors, and has no doubt materially diminished their value. It must not, however, be supposed that his denial of the historical truth of the sacred writings is more than occasional, or that it has been carried out to the full extent which some of his accusers have charged upon him. 3. *De Principiis* (Περὶ ἀρχῶν). This work was the great object of attack with Origen's enemies, and the source from which they derived their chief evidence of his various alleged heresies. It was divided into four books.

[1] *Smith, Dict. Biogr., s. v.*

Of this work some important fragments are extant, and the Latin version of Rufinus has come down to us entire; but Rufinus took great liberties with the original, and the unfaithfulness of his version is denounced in the strongest terms by Jerome. 4. *Exhortatio ad Martyrium* (Εἰς μαρτύριον προτρεπτικὸς λόγος), or *De Martyrio* (Περὶ μαρτυρίου), written during the persecution under the Emperor Maximinus, and still extant. 5. *Contra Celsum Libri VIII.* (Κατὰ Κέλσου τόμοι ή), still extant. In this important work Origen defends the truths of Christianity against the attacks of Celsus.[1]

There is a valuable work entitled *Philocalia* (Φιλοκαλία), which is a compilation by Basil of Cæsarea, and his friend Gregory of Nazianzus, made almost exclusively from the writings of Origen, of which many important fragments have been thus preserved. Few writers have exercised greater influence by the force of their intellect and the variety of their attainments than Origen, or have been the occasion of longer and more acrimonious disputes. Of his more distinctive tenets, several had reference to the doctrine of the Trinity, to the subject of the Incarnation, and to the pre-existence of Christ's human soul, which, as well as the pre-existence of other human souls, he affirmed. He was charged, also, with holding the corporeity of angels, and with other errors as to angels and demons. He held the freedom of the human will, and ascribed to man a nature less corrupt and depraved than was consistent with orthodox views of the operation of Divine grace. He held, moreover, the doctrine of the universal restoration of the guilty, conceiving that the devil alone would suffer eternal punishment.

The best edition of the works of Origen is by Delarue, Paris, 1733–59, 4 vols. fol., reprinted in 25 vols. 8vo, 1831–48, under the editorial care of Lommatsch. The best separate edition of the *Hexapla* is by Montfaucon, Paris, 1714.

6. Ammonius, called Saccas (Ἀμμώνιος Σακκᾶς, i. e., Σακκοφόρος),[2] or sack-carrier, because his employment was carrying the corn landed at Alexandrea, as a public porter (*saccarius*), was born of Christian parents. Porphyry[3] asserts, Eusebius[4] and St. Jerome[5] deny, that he apostatized from the faith. At any rate, he combined the study of philosophy with Christianity, and is regarded by those who maintain his apostasy as the founder of the Neo-Platonic school. Among his disciples are mentioned Longinus, Herennius, and Plotinus. He died A.D. 243, at the age of more than eighty years. The pagan disciples of Ammonius held a kind of philosophical theology. Faith was derived by inward perception; God was three-fold in *essence*, *intelligence* (viz., in knowledge of himself), and *power* (viz., in activity), the two latter notions being inferior to the first. The care of the world was intrusted to gods of an inferior race; below those, again, were demons, good and bad: an ascetic life and theurgy led to the knowledge of the Infinite, who was worshipped by the vulgar only in their national deities. If we are to consider him a Christian, he was, besides his philosophy (which would, of course, then be repre-

1 *Smith, l. c.*
2 *Smith, Dict. Biogr., s. v.*
3 *Porph.*, lib. iii., *adv. Christian. ap. Euseb., H. E.*, vi., 19.
4 *Euseb., l. c.*
5 *Vir. Ill.*, § 55.

sented by Origen, and not by the pagan Alexandrean school, as just described), noted for his writings, especially on the Scriptures. He composed a *Diatessaron* or *Harmony of the Gospels*, which still exists in the Latin version of Victor, bishop of Capua (in the sixth century, who wrongly ascribed it to Tatian), and of Luscinius. He also wrote a treatise, *De Consensu Moysis et Jesu*, which is praised by St. Jerome. A life of Aristotle, prefixed to the Commentary of his namesake on the Categories, has been ascribed to Ammonius, but it is probably the work of John Philoponus.[1]

7. PLOTĪNUS (Πλωτῖνος),[2] the originator, according to some, of the Neo-Platonic system (though not of its fundamental principles), lived so exclusively in speculation that he appeared to be ashamed of his own bodily organization, and would tell neither his parents, his forefathers, his native country, nor even his birth-day, in order to avoid the celebration of it. According, however, to Suidas and others, he was born at Lycopolis, in Egypt, about A.D. 203. The details of his life have been preserved by his disciple Porphyry, in a biography which has come down to us. From him we learn that Plotinus began to study philosophy in his twenty-eighth year, and remained eleven years under the instruction of Ammonius Saccas. In his thirty-ninth year, he joined the expedition of the Emperor Gordian, (A.D. 242) against the Persians, in order to become acquainted with the philosophy of the Persians and Indians. After the death of Gordian he fled to Antioch, and thence to Rome (A.D. 244). For the first ten years of his residence at Rome, he gave only oral instruction to a few friends, but he was at length induced, A.D. 254, to commit his instructions to writing. In this manner, when, ten years later (A.D. 264), Porphyry came to Rome, and joined himself to Plotinus, twenty-one books of very various contents had been already composed by him. During the six years that Porphyry lived with Plotinus at Rome, the latter, at the instigation of Amelius and Porphyry, wrote twenty-three books on the subjects which had been discussed in their meetings, to which nine books were afterward added.

Of the fifty-three books of Plotinus, Porphyry remarks that the first twenty-one books were of a lighter character, that only the twenty-three following were the production of the matured powers of the author, and that the other nine, especially the last four, were evidently written with diminished vigor. The correction of these fifty-three books was committed by Plotinus himself to the care of Porphyry. On account of the weakness of his sight, Plotinus never read them through a second time, to say nothing of making corrections; intent simply upon the *matter*, he was alike careless of orthography, of the division of the syllables, and the clearness of the handwriting. The fifty-three books were divided by Porphyry into six *Enneads*, or sets of nine books.

Plotinus was eloquent in his oral communications, and was said to be very clever in finding the appropriate word, even if he failed in accuracy on the whole. Besides this, the beauty of his person was increased when discoursing; his countenance was lighted up with genius, and cov-

[1] *Smith, l. c.*

[2] *Brandis; Smith, Dict. Biogr., s. v.*

ered with small drops of perspiration. He lived on the scantiest fare, and his hours of sleep were restricted to the briefest time possible. He was regarded with admiration and respect not only by men of science, like the philosophers Amelius, Porphyry, the physicians Paulinus, Eustochius, and Zethus the Arab, but even by senators and other statesmen. He enjoyed the favor of the Emperor Gallienus and the Empress Salonina, and almost obtained from them the rebuilding of two destroyed towns in Campania, with the view of their being governed according to the laws of Plato. He died at Puteoli in A.D. 262.

The philosophical system of Plotinus is founded upon Plato's writings, with the addition of various tenets drawn from the Oriental philosophy and religion. He appears, however, to avoid studiously all reference to the Oriental origin of his tenets; he endeavors to find them all under the veil of the Greek mythology, and points out here the germ of his own philosophical and religious convictions. Plotinus is not guilty of that commixture and falsification of the Oriental mythology and mysticism which is found in Iamblichus, Proclus, and others of the Neo-Platonic school.[1]

The best edition of the Enneads of Plotinus is that of Creuzer, Oxford, 1835, 3 vols. 4to, containing very able critical and exegetical annotations.

8. Porphyrius (Πορφύριος),[2] usually called Porphyry, the celebrated antagonist of Christianity, was born A.D. 233, either in Batanæa, in Palestine, or at Tyre. His original name was *Malchus*, the Greek form of the Syrophœnician *Melech*, a word which signified king. The name *Porphyrius* (in allusion to the usual color of royal robes) was subsequently devised for him by his preceptor Longinus. After studying under Origen at Cæsarea, and under Apollonius and Longinus at Athens, he settled at Rome in his thirtieth year, and there became a diligent disciple of Plotinus. He soon gained the confidence of the latter, and was intrusted by him with the difficult and delicate duty of correcting and arranging his writings. After remaining in Rome six years, Porphyry fell into an unsettled state of mind, and began to entertain the idea of suicide, in order to get free from the shackles of the flesh; but, on the advice of Plotinus, he took a voyage to Sicily, where he resided for some time. It was during his residence in Sicily that he wrote his treatise against the Christian religion, in fifteen books. Of the remainder of his life we know very little. He returned to Rome, where he continued to teach until his death, which took place about A.D. 305 or 306. Late in life he married Marcella, the widow of one of his friends, and the mother of seven children, with the view, as he avowed, of superintending their education.

As a writer Porphyry deserves considerable praise. His style is tolerably clear, and not unfrequently exhibits both imagination and vigor. His learning was most extensive. A great degree of critical and philosophical acumen was not to be expected in one so ardently attached to the enthusiastic and somewhat fanatical system of Plotinus. His attempt to prove the identity of the Platonic and Aristotelian systems would alone be

[1] *Brandis*, l. c.

[2] *Smith*, *Dict. Biogr.*, s. v.

sufficient to show this. Nevertheless, his acquaintance with the authors whom he quotes was manifestly far from superficial. His most celebrated work was his treatise against the Christian religion; but of its nature and merits we are not able to judge, as it has not come down to us. It was publicly destroyed by order of the Emperor Theodosius. The attack was sufficiently vigorous to call forth replies from above thirty different antagonists, the most distinguished of whom were Methodius, Apollinaris, and Eusebius. A large number of his works, however, have come down to us, of which his *Life of Pythagoras* and *Life of Plotinus* are two of the best known. Another work of his deserving of notice is that on the Cave of the Nymphs, described in the Odyssey. It is a fanciful allegorical interpretation of Homer's description of the cave, showing both the ingenuity and the recklessness with which Porphyry and other writers of his stamp pressed writers and authorities of all kinds into their service, as holders of the doctrines of their school.[1]

The *Life of Pythagoras* was edited, along with that of the same philosopher by Iamblichus, with the notes of Holstenius, &c., by Kiessling, Leipzig, 1815. The *Life of Plotinus* is given by Creuzer, in his edition of the works of that philosopher, Oxford, 1835, 3 vols. 4to. The work on the *Cave of the Nymphs* is best edited by Goens, Utrecht, 1765, 4to, reprinted by Rhoer, in his edition of Porphyry's work on *Abstinence from Animal Food*, Leyden, 1792, 4to.

9. Iamblĭchus (Ἰάμβλιχος)[2] was born at Chalcis, in Cœle-Syria. He resided in Syria during the greater part of his life, and died in the reign of Constantine the Great, probably before A.D. 333. He was inferior in judgment and learning to the earlier Neo-Platonists, Plotinus and Porphyry, and he introduced into his system many of the superstitions and mysteries of the East, by which he endeavored to check the progress of Christianity. The extant works of Iamblichus are, 1. Περὶ Πυθαγόρου αἱρέσεως, on the *Philosophy of Pythagoras*. It was intended as a preparation for the study of Plato, and consisted originally of ten books, of which five only are extant. The first book contains an account of the Life of Pythagoras, and though compiled without care, it is yet of value, as the other works from which it is taken are lost. The second book, Προτρεπτικοὶ λόγοι εἰς φιλοσοφίαν, forming a sort of introduction to the study of Plato. The third book, Περὶ κοινῆς μαθηματικῆς ἐπιστήμης, containing many fragments of the works of early Pythagoreans. The fourth book, Περὶ τῆς Νικομάχου ἀριθμητικῆς εἰσαγωγῆς. The fifth book, Τὰ θεολογούμενα τῆς ἀριθμητικῆς. 2. Περὶ μυστηρίων, written to prove the divine origin of the Egyptian and Chaldæan theology. Iamblichus wrote other works which are lost.

The *Life of Pythagoras* was edited by Kuster, Amsterdam, 1707, and by Kiessling, Leipzig, 1815. The *Adhortatio ad Philosophiam*, by Kiessling, Leipzig, 1813, 8vo. The treatise περὶ κοινῆς μαθηματικῆς ἐπιστήμης, by Fries, Copenhagen, 1790. The treatise περὶ τῆς Νικομάχου ἀριθμητικῆς εἰσαγωγῆς, by Tennulius, Deventer and Arnheim, 1668. The *Theologumena Arithmeticæ*, by Ast, Leipzig, 1817, 8vo. The *De Mysteriis*, by Gale, Oxford, 1678, fol.

10. Proclus (Πρόκλος),[3] surnamed *Diadŏchus* (Διάδοχος), or the "Successor," from his being regarded as the genuine successor of Plato in doctrine, was one of the most celebrated teachers of the Neo-Platonic

[1] *Smith, l. c.*   [2] *Id. ib.*   [3] *Smith, Dict. Biogr., s. v.*

school. He was born at Constantinople, A.D. 412,[1] and belongs, therefore, in reality to the succeeding period of Grecian literature; but we prefer considering him here, along with his numerous followers, in order to complete the grouping of the Neo-Platonic school. Proclus was brought up at Xanthus, in Lycia, to which city his parents belonged, and which city he himself regarded as his native place. He studied at Alexandrea under Olympiodorus, and afterward at Athens, under Plutarchus and Syrianus. At an early age his philosophical attainments attracted the attention and admiration of his contemporaries. He had written his commentary on the Timæus of Plato, as well as many other treatises, by his twenty-eighth year. On the death of Syrianus, Proclus succeeded him in his school, and inherited from him the house in which he resided and taught.

Marinus, in his Life of Proclus, records with intense admiration the perfection to which his master attained in all virtues. The highest of these virtues were, in the estimation of Marinus, those of a purifying and ascetic kind. From animal food he almost totally abstained; fasts and vigils he observed with scrupulous exactitude. The reverence with which he honored the sun and moon would seem to have been unbounded. He celebrated all the important religious festivals of every nation, himself composing hymns, in honor not only of Grecian deities, but of those of other nations also. Nor were departed heroes and philosophers excepted from this religious veneration; and he even performed sacred rites in honor of the departed spirits of the entire human race. It was, of course, not surprising that such a man should be favored with various apparitions and miraculous interpositions of the gods. He used to tell how a god had once appeared and proclaimed to him the glory of the city. But the still higher grade of what, in the language of the school, was termed the theurgic virtue, he attained by his profound meditation on the oracles, and the Orphic and Chaldaic mysteries, into the profound secrets of which he was initiated by Asclepigenia, the daughter of Plutarchus, who alone was in complete possession of the theurgic knowledge and discipline. He profited so much by her instructions, as to be able, according to Marinus, to call down rain in a time of drought, to stop an earthquake, and to procure the immediate intervention of Æsculapius to cure the daughter of his friend Archiadas.

Proclus died A.D. 485. During the last five years of his life he had become superannuated, his strength having been exhausted by his fastings and other ascetic practices. As a philosopher, Proclus enjoyed the highest celebrity among his contemporaries and successors; but his philosophical system is characterized by vagueness, mysticism, and want of good sense. He professed that his design was not to bring forward views of his own, but simply to expound Plato, in doing which he proceeded on the idea that every thing in Plato must be brought into accordance with the mystical theology of Orpheus. He wrote a separate work on the coincidence of the doctrines of Orpheus, Pythagoras, and Plato. It was much in the same spirit that he attempted to blend together the logical

[1] *Marini Vita Procli*, c. 6.

method of Aristotle and the fanciful speculations of Neo-Platonic mysticism. Several of the works of Proclus are still extant. The most important of them consist of commentaries on Plato.[1]

There is no complete edition of the extant works of Proclus. The edition of Cousin (Paris, 6 vols. 8vo, 1820–27) contains the treatises on Providence and Fate, on the Ten Doubts about Providence, and on the nature of Evil, the commentary on the first Alcibiades, and that on the Parmenides. Of editions of particular portions of his works, we may mention that of Boissonade, containing parts of a commentary on the Cratylus of Plato, Leipzig, 1820; and that of Creuzer, containing the commentary on the first Alcibiades, and the *Institutio Theologica* (Στοιχείωσις Θεολογική), along with the commentary of Olympiodorus on the Alcibiades, Frankfort, 1820–22, 8vo.

Proclus left behind him a crowd of followers, of whom some were females, such as *Hypatia*, *Sosipatra*, &c. His disciples were of very different degrees of talent, but little distinguished for improving the sort of philosophy which he had bequeathed to them. Among the most considerable were Marinus, of Flavia Neapolis, in Palestine, who succeeded Proclus as a teacher at Athens, and wrote his life (edited by Boissonade, Leipzig, 1814), but who subsequently differed from him in his interpretation of Plato; then Isidōrus of Gaza, who took the place of Marinus at Athens, and afterward removed to Alexandrea, an enthusiastic character, but devoid of originality; and Zenodŏtus, the successor of the latter in what they termed the golden chain; still later, Heliodorus and Ammonius, both the sons of Hermias of Alexandrea, and the latter of whom taught there. The last who taught the Neo-Platonic system in the Academy at Athens was Damascius of Damascus, born about A.D. 480, and who united clearness of understanding to activity of imagination. Among his disciples and those of Ammonius was the celebrated commentator on Aristotle, Simplicius of Cilicia, who, as well as his teacher, endeavored to reconcile Aristotle and Plato. He also wrote a commentary on the *Enchiridion* of Epictetus. Both this and his commentaries on the Categories, on the *De Cœlo*, on the *Physica Auscultatio*, and on the *De Anima*, are still extant. The Emperor Justinian having, by a severe decree, caused the schools of the heathen philosophers to be closed, Damascius, with Isidorus, Simplicius, and others, were obliged to flee into Persia, to the protection of the Persian king Chosroes. They returned, indeed, in A.D. 533, by an express stipulation in the treaty of peace between Chosroes and Justinian, but the ardor of this sect, which had so long and so widely prevailed, and had exerted an insensible influence even over the opinions of the Christian philosophers, was manifestly on the decline.[2]

The only work of Damascius which has been edited is entitled "Doubts and Solutions of the first Principles," by Kopp, Frankfort, 1828, 8vo. There are various editions of the commentaries of Simplicius, but a good one is still a desideratum. The best edition of the commentary on the Enchiridion of Epictetus is that by Schweighaeuser, in his *Epicteteæ Philosophiæ Monumenta*, vol. iv. There is also a good edition in Didot's *Scriptores Ethici Græci*, Paris, 1840.

PHILOSOPHY OF THE FATHERS OF THE CHURCH.[3]

I. The disciples whom Christianity was continually gaining in different countries were imbued with very different principles and feelings, and

[1] *Smith, l. c.* [2] *Tennemann*, p. 193, *seqq.* [3] *Id.*, p. 195, *seqq.*

many of them had also imbibed some philosophical system or other. The knowledge which such had already acquired of the theories of the Greeks; the necessity of replying to the attacks of heathen adversaries; and the desire of illustrating, defining, and substantiating the Christian doctrines, and forming into a whole the solutions which were offered, from time to time, of the questions and cavils of their adversaries—all these causes gradually led to the formation of a species of philosophy peculiar to Christianity, which successively assumed different aspects, as regarded its principles and object. By these means something of the Grecian spirit of philosophy was transfused into the writings of the fathers of the Church, and, in after times, proved the material germ of original speculations.

II. The Christian religion was formed for universality by its simplicity, its close alliance with morality, and the spirit of its worship, at once mild and severe. Its first teachers recognized in it a divine doctrine. Wisdom, which had so long been sought for by human reason, seemed at last found. The limits of truth and of duty had (if mankind would have been satisfied) been at length defined, and the strange dissensions of inquirers after both reconciled. But the fact of the divine origin of the religion gave occasion to various representations, and it was asked how revelation can be established; how it can be ascertained that a doctrine is divine; and what is its true import. Hence the various degrees of authority allowed by different parties to the pretensions of tradition and philosophy.

III. Many of the fathers of the Church, especially the Grecian, considered philosophy as in harmony with the Christian religion (at least partially so), inasmuch as both were derived from the same common source. This source of truth in the heathen philosophy was, according to Justin Martyr, derived from internal revelation by the *Λόγος* and tradition. According to St. Clement and the other Alexandreans, it was drawn from tradition recorded in the Jewish Scriptures. According to St. Augustin, it was simply oral. In the estimation of all these fathers, philosophy was, if not necessary, at least useful for the defence and confirmation of the Christian doctrine.

IV. Other fathers of the Church, especially certain of the Latin, as Tertullian, Arnobius, and his disciple Lactantius, surnamed the Christian Cicero, deemed philosophy a superfluous study, and adverse to Christianity, as tending to alienate man from God. Nevertheless, the party which favored such pursuits gradually acquired strength; and the fathers came to make use, on the *eclectic* system, of the philosophy of the Greeks. Accordingly, Julian thought that he was taking an effectual method of obstructing the Christian religion when he interdicted to its followers the study of that philosophy. Yet *all* the schools of the ancients were far from meeting with a like acceptation on the part of the fathers. Those of Epicurus, the Stoics, and the Peripatetics were little considered, on account of the doubtful manner in which they had expressed themselves with regard to the immortality of the soul, the existence of a Supreme Being and his providence, or the opposition which existed between their views and those of Christianity. The Platonic system, on the other hand, from the degree of affinity they affected to discover in it to the Jewish and Christian revelations, was held in high esteem.

V. Philosophy was at first employed as an auxiliary to the Christian religion, to assist in winning over the more cultivated of the Greeks to whom it was addressed. Subsequently, it was turned to the refutation of heresies; and, lastly, applied to the elucidation and distinct statement of the doctrines of the Church. Through all these successive gradations the relations of religion and philosophy continued always the same; the former being looked upon as the sole source of knowledge, the most exalted and the only *true* philosophy; the latter being regarded as merely a handmaid to the former, and a science altogether earthly. Logic was exclusively devoted to polemics.

VI. The prevailing system, therefore, of the fathers is a supernaturalism, more or less blended with rationalism. The former, however, daily acquired additional predominance in consequence of the perpetual disputes with the heretics, who were inclined to place reason side by side with revelation; and in consequence, also, of the resolution of some Christian teachers to preserve the unity and purity of the faith, revelation came to be regarded not only as the source of all Christian belief, but as the fountain also of all knowledge, speculative and practical.[1]

CHAPTER XLIX.

SIXTH OR ROMAN PERIOD—*continued.*

MATHEMATICIANS, ETC.[2]

I. The mathematical sciences did not make much progress during the period under review, with the exception of astronomy. Serenus of Antissa, who lived in the beginning of the first century after Christ, wrote on *cylindric and conic sections*, in two books. Halley has joined this work to his edition of Apollonius Pergæus, Oxford, 1710, fol.

II. Anatolius (Ἀνατόλιος)[3] of Alexandrea, after having taught the peripatetic philosophy in his native city, was appointed, in A.D. 270, bishop of Laodicea, in Syria. He wrote a work on arithmetic, in ten books, of which we have some fragments remaining in the *Theologumena* of Iamblichus, and also a species of mathematical catechism, of which we have also a fragment. In this last, Anatolius makes the distance of the tropics equal to the side of a pentedecagon, that is to say, twenty-four degrees, while Ptolemy had determined the obliquity of the ecliptic at 23° 51′ 15″. Halma seeks to infer from this the diminution of the obliquity of the ecliptic; but Letronne has shown that Anatolius only wished to employ a round number. Anatolius wrote also a work on the chronology of Easter, a large fragment of which is preserved by Eusebius. The work exists in a Latin translation, which some ascribe to Rufinus, under the title of *Volumen de Paschate*, or *Canones Paschales*, and which

[1] *Tennemann, l. c.* [2] *Schöll, Hist. Lit. Gr.*, vol. v., p. 230, *seqq.* [3] *Id. ib.*, p. 233.

was published by Bucherius, in his *Doctrina Temporum*, Antwerp, 1634. The fragments of the mathematical works are given in Fabricius.

III. Theodosius (Θεοδόσιος) of Tripolis, a mathematician and astronomer of some distinction, appears to have flourished later than the reign of Trajan. He wrote several works, of which the three following are extant, and have been published: 1. Σφαιρικά, a treatise on the properties of the sphere, and of the circles described on its surface. 2. Περὶ ἡμερῶν καὶ νυκτῶν. 3. Περὶ οἰκήσεων.

The work on the Sphere has been several times published, both in a Latin version and in Greek. The latest edition of the Greek text is that of Hunt, Oxford, 1707, 8vo, founded on the edition of Pena, the royal mathematician of France, Beauvais, 1558, 4to. The work Περὶ ἡμερῶν καὶ νυκτῶν was published from a MS. in the Vatican, in Latin only, with ancient scholia, and figures by Auria, Rome, 1591, 4to, the propositions, without demonstrations, having been previously edited by Conrad Dasypodius, Strasburg, 1572, 8vo. The treatise Περὶ οἰκήσεων was published in a Latin version, according to Fabricius, by Auria, Rome, 1587, 4to.[1]

IV. Menelaus (Μενέλαος),[2] a Greek mathematician, a native of Alexandrea, the author of a treatise, in three books, on the Sphere, which is comprised in the mathematical collection called μικρὸς ἀστρονόμος, or μικρὸς ἀστρονομούμενος. Menelaus is mentioned by Pappus, Proclus, and Ptolemæus, who, in his *Magna Syntaxis* (p. 170), says that he made some astronomical observations at Rome, in the first year of the Emperor Trajan (A.D. 98). He is probably the same with the Menelaus introduced by Plutarch in his dialogue *De Facie in Orbe Lunæ* (p. 930). Besides his work on the Sphere, Menelaus wrote a treatise *On the Quantity and Distinction of mixed Bodies*. Both works were translated into Syriac and Arabic.

A Latin translation of the treatise on the Sphere was published at Paris in 1644; and it was also published by Marinus Mersennus, in his *Synopsis Mathematica*, Paris, 1644. This edition contained many additions and interpolations. A more correct edition was published at Oxford by Halley, a reprint of which, with a preface by Costard, appeared at Oxford in 1758, 8vo.

V. Hypsĭcles (Ὑψικλῆς) of Alexandrea, a Greek mathematician, is usually said, on the authority of Suidas, to have lived about A.D. 160, under Marcus Aurelius. There are strong arguments, however, for placing him not earlier than A.D. 550. The only work of his extant is entitled Περὶ τῆς τῶν ζωδίων ἀναφορᾶς, published with the Optics of Heliodorus, at Paris, 1567. He is supposed, however, to have added the fourteenth and fifteenth books to the Elements of Euclid.

VI. Ptolemæus, Claudius (Πτολεμαῖος, Κλαύδιος),[3] a celebrated mathematician, astronomer, and geographer. We will here consider him under the first and second of these characters, reserving the third for the succeeding head. Of Ptolemy himself we know absolutely nothing but his date. He certainly observed in A.D. 139, at Alexandrea, and, since he survived Antoninus, he was alive in A.D. 161. His mathematical and astronomical writings are as follows: 1. Μεγάλη Σύνταξις τῆς Ἀστρονομίας, usually known by its Arabic name of *Almagest*. Since the *Tetrabiblus*, the work on astrology, was also entitled Σύνταξις, the Arabians, to distin-

[1] *Smith, Dict. Biogr.*, *s. v.* [2] *Id. ib.*, *s. v.* [3] *De Morgan; Smith, Dict. Biogr.*, *s. v.*

guish the two, probably called the greater work μεγάλη, and afterward μεγίστη. The title *Almagest* is a compound of this last adjective and the Arabic article. The Almagest is divided into thirteen books. It treats of the relations of the earth and heaven; the effect of position upon the earth; the theory of the sun and moon, without which that of the fixed stars can not be undertaken; the sphere of the fixed stars, and those of the five stars called planets. The seventh and eighth books are the most interesting to a modern astronomer, as they contain a catalogue of the stars. This catalogue gives the longitudes and latitudes of one thousand and twenty-two stars, described by their position in the constellations. It seems that this catalogue is in the main really that of Hipparchus, altered to Ptolemy's own time by assuming the value of the precession of the equinoxes given by Hipparchus as the least which could be; some changes having also been made by Ptolemy's own observations. Indeed, the whole work of Ptolemy appears to have been based upon the observations of Hipparchus, whom he constantly cites as his authority.

2. Τετράβιβλος Σύνταξις, generally called *Tetrabiblon*, or *Quadripartitum de Apotelesmatibus et Judiciis Astrorum.* With this goes another small work called Καρπός, or *Fructus Librorum Suorum*, often called *Centiloquium*, from its containing a hundred aphorisms. Both of these works are astrological, and it has been doubted by some whether they are genuine. But the doubt merely arises from the feeling that the contents are unworthy of Ptolemy. 3. Κανὼν βασιλέων, a catalogue of Assyrian, Persian, Greek, and Roman sovereigns, with the length of their reigns, several times referred to by Syncellus. 4. Φάσεις ἀπλανῶν ἀστέρων καὶ συναγωγὴ ἐπισημασιῶν, *De Apparentiis et Significationibus inerrantium*, an annual list of sidereal phenomena. 5, 6. *De Analemmate*, and *Planisphærium.* These works are obtained from the Arabic. The *Analemma* is a collection of graphical processes for facilitating the construction of sun-dials. The Planisphere is a description of the stereographic projection, in which the eye is at the pole of the circle on which the sphere is projected. 7. Περὶ ὑποθέσεων τῶν πλανωμένων, *De Planetarum Hypothesibus.* This is a brief statement of the principal hypotheses employed in the Almagest, for the explanation of the heavenly motions. 8. Ἁρμονικῶν βιβλία γ′, a treatise on the theory of the musical scale. 9. Περὶ κριτηρίου καὶ ἡγεμονικοῦ, a metaphysical work ascribed to Ptolemy.

It is as an astronomical theorist that Ptolemy has earned the fame which outlasts his system. His much-abused epicycles were no other than a geometrical representation of the process which a modern analyst would have been obliged to follow under the same circumstances. If a periodical magnitude is to be represented, a series of sines or cosines is chosen, the angles of which depend upon the periods of the observed inequalities, and the coefficients upon their extreme magnitudes: this is precisely the algebraical representation of the process of Ptolemy. A question has arisen as to whether he himself believed in the solid crystalline orbs which his followers placed in the heavens. Some of his phrases would imply that he leaned to such a belief, but a much larger number are expressive only of an hypothesis which *saves appearances* (to translate literally), or represents phenomena. Had he really adopted such a material mechanism, he, who could argue that celestial motions must be circular, because circular motions are the most perfect, would not have been without some *à priori* reason for the solidity of his planet-carriages. If he had had a better physical system, the state of mathematics would not have permitted the use of it; and Copernicus himself had no more satisfactory mode of explaining the inequalities of the planetary motions than these same epicycles; nor could a modern astronomer, with new phenomena to represent, and no physical cause to refer them to, do otherwise than adopt the same course, in trigonometrical language instead of geometrical. The methods of Ptolemy are those of a great mathematician; and the explanation of the equation of time, of the evection of the moon, and of the planetary orbits, are, the two first absolutely, and the third, as compared with any thing which preceded, master-pieces of success, the last of which has only lost its glory because the pertinacity of his distant followers led them to put a mathematical explanation in place of a physical one. Delambre sees in the method proposed by Ptolemy for the representation of what we now call the eccentricity of Mercury's orbit, the circumstance which suggested the ellipse to Kepler.[1]

The best edition of the *Almagest*, and some of the other works of Ptolemy, is that of Halma, Paris, 1813–28, 6 vols. 4to. The first two volumes contain the Almagest in Greek and French, with the various readings. The third contains the *Κανὼν βασιλέων*, and the *Φάσεις τῶν ἀπλανῶν* of Ptolemy, together with the Εἰςαγωγή of Geminus. The fourth contains the *Ὑποθέσεις καὶ πλανωμένων ἀρχαι* of Ptolemy, and the *Ὑποτυπώσεις* of Proclus; and the two last, the commentary of Theon on the Manual Tables of Ptolemy, translated by Halma from MSS. in the Royal Library of Paris. In the thirteenth volume of the Memoirs of the Astronomical Society will be found a fully-revised and collated edition of Ptolemy's Catalogue (with others) of the stars, by Baily. The *Tetrabiblus* and *Centiloquium* have been twice printed in Greek with a Latin version, and together, first by Camerarius, Nürnberg, 1535, 4to, and secondly by Melanchthon, Basle, 1553, 8vo. The Ἁρμονικά were first published (Greek and Latin) in the collection of Greek musicians, by Gogavinus, Venice, 1562, 4to; next by Wallis (Greek and Latin), Oxford, 1682, 4to, with various readings and copious notes. This last edition was reprinted (with Porphyry's commentary, then first published) in the third volume of Wallis's works, Oxford, 1699, fol. The treatise *Περὶ κριτηρίου, κ. τ. λ.*, was edited by Bouillaud (Greek and Latin), Paris, 1663, 4to, and, with a new title-page merely, in 1681.

WRITERS ON MILITARY TACTICS AND KINDRED SUBJECTS.

I. ONOSANDER (*Ὀνόσανδρος*),[2] the author of a celebrated work on military tactics, entitled *Στρατηγικὸς λόγος*, and which is still extant. Onosander appears to have lived about the middle of the first century after Christ. His work is dedicated to Q. Veranius, who is generally supposed to be identical with the Q. Veranius Nepos who was consul in A.D. 49. Onosander also remarks in his preface that his work was written in time of peace. It might very well have been written, therefore, between A.D. 49 and A.D. 59. If the consul of A.D. 49 was the person to whom the work was dedicated, it would agree very well with all the other data, that this Veranius accompanied Didius Gallus into Britain, and died before the expiration of a year. All subsequent Greek and Roman writers on the same subject made the work of Onosander their text-book, and in

[1] *De Morgan*, *Penny Cyclopedia*, vol. xxiii., p. 482. [2] *Smith*, *Dict. Biogr.*, *s. v.*

particular the emperors Mauricius and Leon did little more than express in the corrupt style of their age what they found in him. Count Moritz, of Saxony, professed to have derived great benefit from the perusal of a translation of this work. Onosander was a disciple of the Platonic school of philosophy, and, according to Suidas, wrote also a commentary on the Republic of Plato, which is lost. In his style he imitated Xenophon with some success.

The best edition of Onosander is that of Schwebel, Nürnberg, 1761, fol. It contains the French translation of the Baron de Zur-Lauben. In this edition the editor availed himself of the manuscript notes by Jos. Scaliger and Is. Vossius, which are preserved in the library at Leyden. There is also a later edition by Coraes, Paris, 1822, 8vo.

II. Apollodōrus (Ἀπολλόδωρος), a native of Damascus, a celebrated architect, lived under Trajan and Hadrian. The former emperor employed him to build his Forum, Odeum, and Gymnasium at Rome, and also to construct the bridge over the Danube, by which he passed into Dacia. Hadrian, on account of some indiscreet words uttered by Apollodorus, first banished him, and afterward put him to death. Apollodorus has left a work on warlike engines, entitled Πολιορκητικά, which is given in the collection of Thevenot.

III. Arriānus (Ἀῤῥιανός), of whom we have already made mention in our account of the historical writers of this period, composed also a work on *Tactics* (Λόγος τακτικός, or τέχνη τακτική). What we now possess of it, under this name, can have been only a section of the whole work, as it treats of scarcely any thing else than the preparatory exercises of the cavalry; but this subject is discussed with great judgment, and fully shows the practical knowledge of the author. It is printed in Scheffer's collection of ancient works on tactics, Upsala, 1664, but better in Blancard's collection of the minor works of Arrian.

IV. Æliānus Tactĭcus (Αἰλιανὸς Τακτικός),[1] a Greek writer on tactics, not to be confounded with Claudius Ælianus, of whom we have already treated. He lived in Rome, and wrote a work in fifty-three chapters on the *Military Tactics of the Greeks* (Περὶ Στρατηγικῶν Τάξεων Ἑλληνικῶν), which he dedicated to the Emperor Hadrian. He also gives a brief account of the constitution of a Roman army at that time. The work arose, he says, from a conversation he had with the Emperor Nerva at Frontinus's house at Formiæ. He promises a work on *Naval* Tactics also; but this, if it was ever written, is lost.

The first edition of the Tactics (a very bad one) was published in 1532; the next, a much better one, was by Robortellus, Venice, 1552, 4to. It contains a new Latin version by the editor, and is illustrated with many cuts. The best edition is that printed by Elzevir at Leyden, 1613, 8vo.

V. Polyænus (Πολύαινος),[2] the Macedonian, was the author of a work on *Stratagems in War* (Στρατηγήματα), which is still extant. He lived about the middle of the second century of the Christian era. Suidas calls him a rhetorician, and we learn from Polyænus himself that he was accustomed to plead causes before the emperor.[3] He dedicated his work to M. Aurelius and Verus while they were engaged in the Parthian war,

1 *Smith, Dict. Biogr., s. v.* 2 *Id. ib., s. v.* 3 *Præf.*, lib. ii.; lib. viii.

about A.D. 163, at which time he says that he was too old to accompany them in their campaigns.[1] The work is divided into eight books, of which the first six contain an account of the stratagems of the most celebrated Greek generals. the seventh those of barbarous or foreign people, and the eighth of the Romans, and of illustrious women. Parts, however, of the sixth and seventh books are lost, so that of the nine hundred stratagems which Polyænus described, only eight hundred and thirty-three have come down to us. The work is written in a clear and pleasing style, though somewhat tinged with the artificial rhetoric of the age. It contains a vast number of anecdotes respecting many of the most celebrated men in antiquity, and has preserved many historical facts of which we should otherwise have been ignorant; but its value as an historical authority is very much diminished by the little judgment which the author evidently possessed, and by our ignorance of the sources from which he took his statements. Polyænus also wrote several other works, all of which have perished.

The first edition of the Greek text was published by Casaubon, Lyon, 1589, 12mo; the next by Maasvicius, Leyden, 1690, 8vo; the third by Mursinna, Berlin, 1756, 12mo; and the last by Coraes, Paris, 1809, 8vo.

WRITERS ON MUSIC.

I. Alypius (Ἀλύπιος),[2] the author of a Greek musical treatise entitled **Εἰσαγωγὴ Μουσική**. His date is uncertain, but he probably flourished under Julian and his immediate successors. His work consists wholly, with the exception of a short introduction, of lists of the symbols used (both for voice and instrument) to denote all the sounds in the forty-five scales produced by taking each of the fifteen modes in the three genera (Diatonic, Chromatic, Enharmonic). It treats, therefore, in fact, of only one (the fifth, namely) of the seven branches into which the subject is, as usual, divided in the introduction, and may possibly be merely a fragment of a larger work. It would have been most valuable if any considerable number of examples had been left us of the actual use of the system of notation described in it; unfortunately, very few remain, and they seem to belong to an earlier stage of the science. However, the work serves to throw some light on the obscure history of the modes.

The work forms part of the collection of Meibomius, "*Antiquæ Musicæ Auctores Septem*," Amsterdam, 1652. The text, which seemed hopelessly corrupt to Meursius, its first editor ("*Aristoxenus, Nicomachus, Alypius*, ed. Joh. Meursius," Leyden, 1616), was restored, apparently with success, by the labors of Meibomius.

II. Gaudentius (Γαυδέντιος),[3] the author of an elementary treatise on music, but concerning whom no definite information whatever has come down to us. In his theory he follows the doctrines of Aristoxenus, whence it has been inferred that he lived before the time of Ptolemy, whose views seem to have been unknown to him. His treatise bears the title of Εἰσαγωγὴ ἁρμονική. It treats of the elements of music, of the voice, of sounds, intervals, systems, &c., and forms an introduction to the study of music, which seems to have enjoyed some reputation in an-

[1] *Præf.*, lib. i. [2] *Smith, Dict. Biogr.*, *s. v.* [3] *Id. ib.*, *s. v.*

tiquity. Cassiodorus mentions it with praise, and tells us that one of his contemporaries, Mucianus, had made a Latin translation of it for the use of schools. This translation is, however, lost.

The work of Gaudentius is printed, with a Latin version and notes, in the collection of Meibomius, already mentioned.

III. Claudius Ptolemæus, of whom we have already spoken, ought also to be placed among the ancient writers on music, as is shown by his treatise on the theory of the musical scale, entitled Ἁρμονικά, in three books. He has the merit of having reduced to seven the fifteen modes of the ancients. He is believed, also, to have fixed the true relations of certain intervals, and to have thus rendered the diatonic octave more conformable to harmony.

IV. Bacchīus (Βακχεῖος), the author of a short musical treatise in the form of a catechism, called Εἰσαγωγὴ τέχνης μουσικῆς. We know nothing of his history. The work consists of brief and clear explanations of the principal subjects belonging to Harmonics and Rhythm. Bacchius reckons seven modes, corresponding to the seven species of octave anciently called by the same names. Hence Meibomius conjectures that he lived after Ptolemy.

The Greek text of Bacchius was first edited by Marinus Mersennus, in his commentary on the first six chapters of Genesis, Paris, 1623, fol., p. 1887. It also forms part with a Latin version and notes, of the collection of Meibomius.

V. Aristīdes Quintilianus (Ἀριστείδης Κοϊντιλιανός),[1] the author of a treatise, in three books, *On Music* (Περὶ Μουσικῆς). Nothing is known of his history, nor is he mentioned by any ancient writer. But he must have lived after Cicero, whom he quotes (p. 70), and before Martianus Capella, who has made use of his treatise in his work *De Nuptiis Philologiæ et Mercurii* (lib. 9). It seems probable, also, that he must be placed before Ptolemy, since he does not mention the difference between that writer and his predecessors with respect to the number of modes. The work of Aristides is perhaps the most valuable of all the ancient musical treatises. It embraces, besides the theory of music (ἁρμονική) in the modern sense, the whole range of subjects comprehended under μουσική, which latter science contemplated not merely the regulation of sounds, but the harmonious disposition of every thing in nature. The first book treats of *Harmonics* and *Rhythm;* the former subject being considered under the usual heads of Sounds, Intervals, Systems, Genera, Modes, Transition, and Composition (Μελοποιΐα). The second, of the moral effects and educational powers of music; and the third, of the numerical ratios which define musical intervals, and of their connection with physical and moral science generally. Aristides refers to another work of his own, Περὶ Ποιητικῆς, which is lost. He makes no direct allusion to any of the ancient writers on music except Aristoxenus.

The only edition of Aristides is that of Meibomius. It is printed along with the latter part of the ninth book of Martianus Capella, in Meibomius's collection of the ancient writers on music already referred to.

[1] *Smith, Dict. Biogr., s. v.*

CHAPTER L.

SIXTH OR ROMAN PERIOD—*continued.*

GEOGRAPHICAL WRITERS.

I. Străbo (Στράβων),[1] the celebrated geographer, was a native of Amasia, in Pontus. The date of his birth is unknown, but may perhaps be placed about 54 B.C. He lived during the whole of the reign of Augustus, and during the early part, at least, of the reign of Tiberius. He is supposed to have died about A.D. 24. Strabo received a careful education. He studied grammar under Aristodemus, at Nysa, in Caria, and philosophy under Xenarchus, of Seleucia, in Cilicia, and Boethus of Sidon. He lived some years at Rome, and also travelled much in various countries. We learn from his own work that he was with his friend Ælius Gallus in Egypt in B.C. 24. He wrote an historical work entitled Ἱστορικὰ Ὑπομνήματα, in forty-three books, which is lost. It began where the history of Polybius ended, and was probably continued to the battle of Actium.

But his great work was his *Geography* (Γεωγραφικά), in seventeen books, which has come down to us entire, with the exception of the seventh, of which we have only a meagre epitome. Strabo's work, according to his own expression, was not intended for the use of all persons; and, indeed, no complete geographical work can be adapted to those who have not the necessary elementary knowledge. His work was intended for all who had a good education, and particularly for those who were engaged in the higher departments of administration. It was designed to be a work which would give such persons that geographical and historical information about each country which a person engaged in matters political can not do without. Consistently with this view, his plan does not comprehend minute description, except when the place or the object is of great interest or importance; nor is his description limited to the physical characteristics of each country; it comprehends the important political events of which each country has been the theatre, a notice of the chief cities and the great men who have rendered them illustrious; in short, whatever was most characteristic and interesting in every country. His work forms a striking contrast with the geography of Ptolemy, and the dry list of names, occasionally relieved by something added to them, in the geographical portion of the Natural History of Pliny. It is, in short, a book intended for reading, and it may be read; a kind of historical geography.[2]

Strabo's work has a particular value to us of the present day, owing to his method of handling the subject. He has preserved a great number of historical facts, for which we have no other evidence than his work. His language is generally clear, except in those passages where

[1] *Long; Smith's Dict. Biogr., s. v.*

[2] *Long, l. c.*

the text has been corrupted; it is appropriate to the matter, simple, and without affectation.

It is objected to Strabo that he has undervalued Herodotus, and puts him on the same footing as Ctesias. The work of Herodotus was, perhaps, hardly appreciated, as it deserved to be, by any writer of antiquity; and it is a well-grounded complaint against Strabo, that he could not or did not choose to discriminate between the stories which Herodotus tells simply as stories which he heard, and that which is the result of the personal observation of the historian. There are many parts of the geography of Strabo, particularly his description of Greece, for which he could have derived excellent materials from Herodotus. Strabo's authorities are almost exclusively Greek. He had a contempt for the Roman writers generally; and certainly, simply as geographers, there was not one among them who could be called by that name. But the campaigns of the Romans, and their historical writings and memoirs, would have furnished him with many valuable geographical facts, both for his Asiatic and European geography. He made some use of Cæsar's writings for his description of Gallia, the Alps, and Britain, and he used other materials also, as we see from his brief notice of the voyage of Publius Crassus to the Cassiterides. But, with this exception, and the writings of Asinius Pollio, Fabius Pictor, and an anonymous chorographer, he drew little from Roman sources. The use that Strabo made of Homer is another objection to his work, and his description sometimes becomes rather a commentary on Homer than an independent description, based on the actual state of knowledge. That which Homer darkly knew, or half guessed, has no value, except as an index of the state of geographical knowledge at that time, and was entirely useless in the age of Strabo.[1]

It is another defect in Strabo's work that the science of astronomy was not properly applied by him. Though Strabo had some mathematical and astronomical knowledge, he undervalued these sciences as helps to geography, and he did not consider the exact division of the earth into climates, in the sense in which Hipparchus used the term, and the statement of the latitudes and longitudes of places, which in many cases were pretty well determined, as essential to his geographical description.

The first two books of Strabo are an introduction to his geography, and contain his views on the form and magnitude of the earth, and other subjects connected with mathematical geography. In the third book he begins his description. He devotes eight books to Europe, six to Asia, and the seventeenth and last to Egypt and Libya.

The first edition of Strabo was by Aldus, Venice, 1516. The next edition of the text was by Casaubon, who used several MSS., but it is uncertain if they exist. There are two editions of the text by Casaubon, Geneva, 1587, and Paris, 1620, fol., accompanied by a Latin translation and a commentary. The edition of 1620 does not differ materially from that of 1587, and it is that which is generally referred to by the page. The reprint of Casaubon's edition by Almeloveen, Amsterdam, 1707, is useful for the collection of the notes of various critics. The edition of Falconer, Oxford, 1807, 2 vols. fol., is a reprint from Almeloveen, and contains no improvement of the text, though there were means for doing this in the collation of five MSS. by Villebrune, and in other resources.

[1] *Long, l. c.*

The notice of this edition in the Edinburgh Review (vol. xiv., p. 429, *seqq.*) gave rise to an acrimonious literary warfare between that periodical and some Oxford scholars. In 1796 was commenced the edition of Siebenkees, at Leipzig, in 8vo. He only lived, however, to complete the first six books, in 2 vols. The work was then taken up by Tzschucke. Siebenkees did his part very ill, but the edition improved greatly after Tzschucke commenced his labors. Friedemann continued the work after the latter, but it reached only the seventh volume, which contains the commentary of Casaubon on the first three books. This volume was Friedemann's addition, and appeared in 1818. Coraes published an edition of Strabo at Paris, 1815–18, in 4 vols. 8vo. This was really the first critical edition of Strabo that was worthy of the name, though he is perhaps justly blamed for being sometimes too bold in substituting the conjectures of others or his own for MSS. readings which ought not to be rejected. By far the most valuable edition, however, is that of Kramer, Berlin, 1844–52, 3 vols. 8vo. The text of this edition is founded on a new collation of MSS., and is furnished with a critical commentary. There is also a school edition of the same, in 2 vols. 8vo.

A French translation of Strabo appeared at Paris, 1805–19, in five quarto volumes, and accompanied by copious critical and other notes. It was translated by La Porte du Theil and Coraes, with the exception of Du Theil's share, which was left unfinished on his death in 1815, and which was completed by Letronne, who translated the sixteenth and seventeenth books. Gosselin added the geographical explanations, and five maps to illustrate the systems of Eratosthenes, Hipparchus, Polybius, and Strabo, with respect to the inhabited portion of the earth. The best translation of Strabo, however, is the German one of Groskurd, 3 vols. 8vo, Berlin and Stettin, 1831–33. The fourth volume, Berlin, 1834, contains a very complete index, which is adapted to the second edition of Casaubon, and all subsequent editions, except the small Tauchnitz one, the only one that has not the paging of Casaubon's edition in the margin.

II. Isidōrus (Ἰσίδωρος) of Charax, a geographical writer, lived probably under the early Roman emperors. His τῆς Παρθίας περιηγητικός is quoted by Athenæus, and his Σταθμοὶ Παρθικοί (probably a part of it) are printed among the works of the minor Greek geographers in the collections of Höschel (1600), Hudson (1703), and Miller, Paris, 1839.

III. Pausanias (Παυσανίας),[1] the traveller and geographer, was perhaps a native of Lydia. He lived under Antoninus Pius and M. Aurelius, and wrote his celebrated work in the reign of the latter emperor. This work, entitled Ἑλλάδος Περιήγησις, *A Periegēsis* or *Itinerary of Greece*, is in ten books, and contains a description of Attica and Megaris (i.), Corinthia, Sicyonia, Phliasia, and Argolis (ii.), Laconica (iii.), Messenia (iv.), Elis (v., vi.), Achæa (vii.), Arcadia (viii.), Bœotia (ix.), Phocis (x.). The work shows that Pausanias visited most of the places in these divisions of Greece, a fact which is clearly demonstrated by the minuteness and particularity of his description. The work is merely an Itinerary. Pausanias gives no general description of a country or even of a place, but he describes the things as he comes to them. His account is minute; but it mainly refers to objects of antiquity and works of art, such as buildings, temples, statues, and pictures. He also mentions mountains, rivers, and fountains, and the mythological stories connected with them, which, indeed, are his chief inducements to speak of them. His religious feeling was strong, and his belief sure, for he tells many old legends in true good faith and seriousness. His style has been much condemned by modern critics; but if we except some corrupt passages, and if we allow that his order of words is not that of the best Greek writers, there is hardly much

[1] *Smith, Dict. Biogr.*, *s. v.*

obscurity to a person who is competently acquainted with Greek, except that obscurity which is sometimes owing to the matter. With the exception of Herodotus, there is no writer of antiquity, and perhaps none of modern times, who has comprehended so many valuable facts in so small a compass.

The best editions are by Siebelis, Leipzig, 1822–28, 5 vols. 8vo.; by Bekker, Berlin, 1826–7, 2 vols. 8vo; by Schubart and Walz, Leipzig, 1838–40, 3 vols. 8vo; and by L. Dindorf, Paris, 1845, 8vo, forming part of Didot's *Bibliotheca Græca.*

IV. Marīnus (Μαρῖνος)[1] of Tyre, a Greek geographer, lived in the middle of the second century of the Christian era, and was the immediate predecessor of Ptolemy, who frequently refers to him. Marinus was undoubtedly the founder of mathematical geography in antiquity; and we learn from Ptolemy's own statement (i., 6) that he based his whole work upon that of Marinus. The chief merit of Marinus was that he put an end to the uncertainty that had hitherto prevailed respecting the positions of places by assigning to each its latitude and longitude. He also constructed maps for his works on much improved principles. In order to obtain as much accuracy as possible, Marinus was indefatigable in studying the works of his predecessors, the diaries kept by travellers, and every available source. He made many alterations in the second edition of his work, and would have still farther improved it if he had not been carried off by an untimely death.

V. Ptolemæus.[2] We have already spoken of the mathematical and astronomical works of this writer. It now remains to make mention of him as a geographer. Ptolemy's great geographical work, entitled Γεωγραφικὴ Ὑφήγησις, is in eight books, and has reached us entire. This work was the last attempt made by the ancients to form a complete geographical system; it was accepted as the text-book of the science, and it maintained that position during the Middle Ages, and until the fifteenth century, when the rapid progress of maritime discovery caused it to be superseded. It contains, however, very little information respecting the objects of interest connected with the different countries and places; for, with the exception of the introductory matter in the first book, and the latter part of the work, it is a mere catalogue of the names of places, with their longitudes and latitudes, and with a few incidental references to objects of interest. The latitudes of Ptolemy are tolerably correct, but his longitudes are very wide of the truth, his length of the known world, from east to west, being much too great. It is well worthy, however, of remark, in passing, that the modern world owes much to this error; for it tended to encourage the belief in the practicability of a western passage to the Indies, which occasioned the discovery of America by Columbus.

The first book of Ptolemy's work is introductory. The next six and a half books (ii.–vii., 4) are occupied with the description of the known world, beginning with the West of Europe, the description of which is contained in book second. Next comes the East of Europe, in book third; then Africa, in book fourth; then Western or Lesser Asia, in book fifth;

[1] *Smith, Dict. Biogr., s. v.*
[2] *Id. ib.*

then the Greater Asia, in book sixth; then India, the Chersonesus Aurea, Serica, the Sinæ, and Taprobane, in book seventh, chapters one to four inclusive. The form in which the description is given is that of lists of places, with their longitudes and latitudes, arranged under the heads, first, of the three continents, and then of the several countries and tribes. Prefixed to each section is a brief general description of the boundaries and divisions of the part about to be described; and remarks of a miscellaneous character are interspersed among the lists, to which, however, they bear but a small proportion. The remaining part of the seventh and the whole of the eighth book are occupied with a description of a set of maps of the known world. These maps are still extant.[1]

The *editio princeps* of the Greek text is that by Erasmus, Basle, 1533, 4to; reprinted at Paris, 1546, 4to. The text of Erasmus was reprinted, but with a new Latin version, notes, and indices, edited by Montanus, and with the maps restored by Mercator, Amsterdam, 1605, fol; and a still more valuable edition was brought out by Bertius, printed by Elzevir, with the maps colored, and with the addition of the Peutingerian Tables, and other important illustrative matter, Leyden, 1619, fol., reprinted Antwerp, 1624, fol. The work also forms a part of the edition of Ptolemy's works, by the Abbé Halma, but left unfinished at his death, Paris, 1813–28, 4to: this edition contains a French translation of the work. A valuable critical edition, by Wilberg and Grashof, Essen, 1838, *seqq.*, is now in course of publication, to be completed in eight parts, of which six have appeared. A useful little edition of the Greek text is contained in three volumes of the Tauchnitz Classics, Leipzig, 1843, 32mo.

CHAPTER LI.

SIXTH OR ROMAN PERIOD—*continued.*

MEDICAL WRITERS.

I. Toward the close of the preceding period, the Empiric school had attained its highest celebrity by the labors of *Serapion* of Alexandrea. It had also been carried to Rome in the person of Archagathus, who was the first person that made medicine a distinct profession in that city. The individual, however, who practiced in this capital with the most brilliant success, was Asclepiades, of Bithynia,[2] who came to Rome at the beginning of the first century B.C., and lived there to a very great age. It is said that when he first came to Rome he was a teacher of rhetoric, and that it was in consequence of his not being successful in this profession that he turned his attention to the study of medicine. From what we learn of his history and of his practice, it would appear that he may be fairly characterized as a man of natural talents, acquainted with human nature (or, rather, human weakness), possessed of considerable shrewdness and address, but with little science or professional skill. He had the discretion to refrain from the use of very active and powerful remedies, and to trust principally to the efficacy of diet, exercise, bathing, and other circumstances of this nature. A part of the great popularity he enjoyed depended upon his prescribing the liberal use of wine to his patients, and upon his not only attending, in all cases, with

[1] *Smith, l. c.*

[2] *Smith, Dict. Biogr., s. v.*

great assiduity to every thing which contributed to their comfort, but also upon his flattering their prejudices and indulging their inclinations. In justice to him, however, it must be confessed, that he seems also to have possessed a considerable share of acuteness and discernment, which, on some occasions, he employed with advantage. It is probable that to him we are indebted, in the first instance, for the arrangement of diseases into the two great classes of *acute* and *chronic*. Nothing remains of his writings but a few fragments, which have been collected by Gumpert, *Asclepiadis Bithyni Fragmenta*, Weimar, 1794.

II. Dioscorĭdes (Διοσκορίδης),[1] *Pedacius* or *Pedanius* (Πεδάκιος or Πεδάνιος), the author of a celebrated treatise on Materia Medica that bears his name. It is generally supposed that he was a native of Anazarba, in Cilicia Campestris, and that he was a physician by profession. It appears pretty evident that he lived in the first century of the Christian era, and, as he is not mentioned by Pliny, it has been supposed that he was a little posterior to him. He has left behind him a treatise on Materia Medica (Περὶ Ὕλης Ἰατρικῆς), in five books, a work of great labor and research, and which, for many ages, was received as a standard production. The greater correctness of modern science, and the new discoveries which have been made, cause it now to be regarded rather as a work of curiosity than of absolute utility ; but in drawing up a history of the state and progress of medicine, it affords a most valuable document for our information. His treatise consists of a description of all the articles then used in medicine, with an account of their supposed virtues. The descriptions are brief, and not unfrequently so little characterized as not to enable us to ascertain with any degree of accuracy to what they refer; while the practical part of his work is, in a great measure, empirical, although his general principles (so far as they can be detected) appear to be those of the Dogmatic sect. The great importance which was for a long time attached to the works of Dioscorides, has rendered them the subject of almost innumerable commentaries and criticisms, and even some of the most learned of our modern naturalists have not thought it an unworthy task to attempt the illustration of his Materia Medica. Upon the whole, we must attribute to him the merit of great industry and patient research; and it seems but just to ascribe a large portion of the errors and inaccuracies into which he has fallen, more to the imperfect state of the science when he wrote, than to any defect in the character and talents of the writer. With respect to the ancient writers on Materia Medica who succeeded Dioscorides, they were generally content to quote his authority, without presuming to correct his errors or supply his deficiencies. That part of his work which relates to the plants growing in Greece has been very much illustrated in the splendid *Flora Græca* of Sibthorp, &c., 10 vols. fol. Besides the treatise on Materia Medica, a few other works are generally attributed to Dioscorides, some of which, however, are spurious.[2]

The first Greek edition of Dioscorides was published by Aldus Manutius, Venice, 1499, fol., and is said to be very scarce. Perhaps the most valuable edition is that of Sara-

[1] *Greenhill; Smith's Dict. Biogr., s. v.*

[2] *Greenhill, l. c.*

cenus (Greek and Latin), Frankfort, 1598, fol., with a copious and learned commentary. The last edition is that by Sprengel (Greek and Latin), 2 vols. 8vo, Leipzig, 1829–30, with a useful commentary, forming the twenty-fifth and twenty-sixth volumes of Kühn's collection of the Greek medical writers.

III. Themĭson (Θεμίσων),[1] the founder of the ancient medical sect of the Methodici, and one of the most eminent physicians of his time, was a native of Laodicea, in Syria. He was a pupil of Asclepiades of Bithynia, already mentioned, and must have lived, therefore, in the first century B.C. He seems to have been a great traveller. He differed from his master on several points in his old age, and became, as already remarked, the founder of a new sect called the "Methodici," which long exercised an extensive influence on medical science. He wrote several medical works, of which the titles and a few fragments remain, preserved principally by Cælius Aurelianus, in a Latin form. He is, perhaps, the first physician who made use of leeches, and he is also said to have been himself attacked with hydrophobia, and to have recovered.

IV. Thessălus (Θεσσαλός),[2] a native of Tralles, in Lydia, remarkable for his arrogance and effrontery. He lived at Rome in the reign of the Emperor Nero, A.D. 54–68, to whom he addressed one of his works. He was the son of a weaver, and had followed the same employment himself during his youth. This, however, he soon gave up, and, though he had had a very imperfect general education, he embraced the medical profession, by which he acquired, for a time, a great reputation, and amassed a large fortune. He adopted the principles of the Methodici, but modified and developed them so much, that he attributed to himself the invention of them, and, indeed, is always considered one of the founders of the sect. He considered himself superior to all his predecessors, and asserted that none of them had contributed any thing to the advancement of medical science, while he boasted that he himself could teach the art of healing in six months. He is frequently mentioned by Galen, but always in terms of contempt and ridicule. None of his works are extant.

V. Sorānus (Σωρανός), a native of Ephesus, practiced his profession first at Alexandrea and afterward at Rome, in the reigns of Trajan and Hadrian, A.D. 98–138. He belonged to the sect of the Methodici, and was one of the most eminent physicians of that school. There are several medical works extant under the name of Soranus, but whether they were written by the native of Ephesus can not be determined. One of these, περὶ γυναικείων παθῶν, was first published in Greek in 1838, Königsberg, 8vo. It was partly prepared for the press by Dietz, and was finished, after his death, by J. F. Lobeck. It is a valuable and interesting work, consisting of one hundred and twenty-two chapters, with a few lines of the one hundred and twenty-third, and the titles of thirty-eight more.[3]

VI. Arĕtæus (Ἀρεταῖος), one of the most celebrated of the ancient Greek physicians, of whose life, however, no particulars are known. There is some uncertainty respecting both his age and country, but it seems probable that he practiced in the first century after Christ, in the reign of Nero or Vespasian; and he is generally styled "the Cappado-

[1] *Greenhill; Smith's Dict. Biogr., s. v.* [2] *Id. ib.* [3] *Id. ib.*

cian" (Καππάδοξ). He wrote in Ionic Greek a general treatise on diseases, which is still extant, and is certainly one of the most valuable reliques of antiquity, displaying great accuracy in the detail of symptoms, and in seizing the diagnostic character of diseases.[1]

The first Greek edition of Aretæus is that of Goupylus, Paris, 1554, 8vo. In 1723, a magnificent edition in folio was published at the Clarendon press at Oxford, edited by Wigan, containing an improved text, a new Latin version, learned dissertations and notes, and a copious index by Maittaire. In 1731, the celebrated Boerhaave brought out a new edition, of which the text and Latin version had been printed before the appearance of Wigan's, and are of less value than his: this edition, however, contains a copious and useful collection of annotations by Petit and Triller. The last and most useful edition is that of Kühn, Leipzig, 1828, 8vo, forming the twenty-fourth volume of the collection of Greek medical writers.

VII. Galēnus, Claudius (Κλαύδιος Γαληνός),[2] commonly called Galen, a very celebrated physician, whose works have had a longer and more extensive influence on the different branches of medical science than those of any other either in ancient or modern times. He was born at Pergamum in A.D. 130. His father Nicon, who was an architect and geometrician, carefully superintended his education. In his seventeenth year (A.D. 146), his father, who had hitherto destined him to be a philosopher, altered his intentions, and, in consequence of a dream, chose for him the profession of medicine. He at first studied medicine in his native city. In his twentieth year (A.D. 149) he lost his father, and about the same time he went to Smyrna for the purpose of studying under Pelops the physician, and Albinus the Platonic philosopher. He afterward studied at Corinth and Alexandrea. He returned to Pergamum in his twenty-ninth year, A.D. 158, and was immediately appointed physician to the school of gladiators, an office which he filled with great reputation and success. In A.D. 164, he quitted his native country on account of some popular commotions, and went to Rome for the first time. Here he stayed about four years, and gained great reputation from his skill in anatomy and medicine. He returned to Pergamum in A.D. 168, but had scarcely settled there when he received a summons from the emperors M. Aurelius and L. Verus to attend them at Aquileia, in Venetia. From Aquileia, Galen followed M. Aurelius to Rome in A.D. 170. When the emperor again set out to conduct the war on the Danube, Galen with difficulty obtained permission to be left behind at Rome, alleging that such was the will of Æsculapius. Before leaving the city, the emperor committed to the medical care of Galen his son Commodus, who was then nine years of age. Galen stayed at Rome some years, during which time he employed himself in lecturing, writing, and practicing with great success. He subsequently returned to Pergamum, but whether he again visited Rome is uncertain. He is said to have died in the year 200, at the age of seventy, in the reign of Septimius Severus; but it is not improbable that he lived some years longer.[3]

Galen's personal character, as it appears in his works, places him among the brightest ornaments of the heathen world. Perhaps his chief faults were too high an opinion of his own merits, and too much bitter-

[1] *Greenhill; Smith's Dict. Biogr., s. v.* [2] *Id. ib.* [3] *Greenhill, l. c.*

ness and contempt for some of his adversaries, for each of which failings the circumstances of the times afforded great, if not sufficient excuse. He was also one of the most learned and accomplished men of his age, as is proved not only by his extant writings, but also by the long list of his works on various branches of philosophy, which are now lost. All this may make us the more regret that he was so little brought into contact with Christianity, of which he appears to have known nothing more than might be learned from the popular conversation of the day during a time of persecution: yet in one of his lost works, of which a fragment is quoted by his Arabian biographers, he speaks of the Christians in higher terms, and praises their temperance and chastity, their blameless lives, and love of virtue, in which they equalled or surpassed the philosophers of the age.[1]

The works that are still extant under the name of Galen consist of eighty-three treatises acknowledged to be genuine; nineteen whose genuineness has, with more or less reason, been doubted; forty-five undoubtedly spurious; nineteen fragments; and fifteen commentaries on different works of Hippocrates; and, besides these, more than fifty short pieces and fragments (many or most of which are probably spurious) are enumerated as still lying unpublished in different European libraries. Almost all these treat of some branch of medical science, and many of them were composed at the request of his friends, and without any view to publication. Besides these, however, Galen wrote a great number of works, of which nothing but the titles have been preserved; so that, altogether, the number of his distinct treatises can not have been less than five hundred. Some of these are very short, and he frequently repeats whole passages, with hardly any variation, in different works; but still, when the number of his writings is considered, their intrinsic excellence, and the variety of subjects of which he treated (extending not only to every branch of medical science, but also to ethics, logic, grammar, and other departments of philosophy), he has always been justly ranked among the greatest authors that have ever lived. His style is elegant, but diffuse and prolix, and he abounds in allusions to and quotations from the ancient Greek poets, philosophers, and historians.

At the time when Galen began to devote himself to the study of medicine, the profession was divided into several sects, which were constantly disputing with each other. The Dogmatici and Empirici had for several centuries been opposed to each other. In the first century B.C. had arisen the sect of the Methodici; and shortly before Galen's own time had been founded those of the Eclectici, Pneumatici, and Episynthetici. Galen attached himself exclusively to none of these sects, but chose from the tenets of each what he believed to be good and true, and called those persons slaves who designated themselves as followers of Hippocrates, Praxagoras, or any other man. In his general principles, however, he may be considered as belonging to the Dogmatic sect, for his method was to reduce all his knowledge, as acquired by the observation of facts, to general theoretical principles. These principles he indeed professed to

[1] *Greenhill, l. c.*

deduce from experience and observation; and we have abundant proofs of his diligence in collecting experience, and his accuracy in making observations; but still, in a certain sense at least, he regards individual facts and the detail of experience as of little value, unconnected with the principles which he laid down as the basis of all medical reasoning. In this fundamental point, therefore, the method pursued by Galen appears to have been directly the reverse of that which is now considered the correct method of scientific investigation; and yet such is the force of natural genius, that in most instances he attained the ultimate object in view, although by an indirect path.[1]

No one has ever set before the medical profession a higher standard of perfection than Galen, and few, if any, have more nearly approached it in their own person. He evidently appears from his works to have been a most accomplished and learned man, and one of his short essays is written to inculcate the necessity of a physician being acquainted with other branches of knowledge besides merely medicine. Of his numerous philosophical writings the greater part are lost; but his celebrity in logic and metaphysics appears to have been great among the ancients, as he is mentioned in company with Plato and Aristotle by his contemporary Alexander Aphrodisiensis. He was most attached to the Peripatetic school, to which he often accommodated the maxims of the Old Academy.[2]

Some account of the edition of Galen's works, in conjunction with those of Hippocrates, by Chartier, has already been given on page 357 of this volume. The latest and most commodious edition of Galen is that by Kühn, Leipzig, 1821–1833, 20 vols. 8vo. Its real critical merits, however, are very small. For the correction of the Greek text little or nothing has been done by Kühn, except in the case of a few particular treatises, and all Chartier's notes, and various readings, are omitted. Kühn has likewise left out many of the spurious works contained in Chartier's edition, as also the fragments, and those books which are extant only in Latin; but, on the other hand, he has published for the first time the Greek text of the treatise *De Musculorum Dissectione*, the *Synopsis Librorum de Pulsibus*, and the commentary on Hippocrates *De Humoribus*. Upon the whole, the writings of Galen are still in a very corrupt and unsatisfactory state, and it is universally acknowledged that a new and critical edition is much wanted.

VIII. Two treatises have come down to us, which have been ascribed to *Alexander Aphrodisiensis*, of Aphrodisias, in Caria, and the most celebrated of the commentators on Aristotle. The first is entitled Ἰατρικὰ Ἀπορήματα καὶ Φυσικὰ Προβλήματα, or *Quæstiones Medicæ et Problemata Physica;* the second is Περὶ Πυρετῶν, or *De Febribus*. There are very strong reasons, however, for believing both to be the productions of some later writer. By some they are ascribed to *Alexander Trallianus*, who flourished in the sixth century after Christ.

The Greek text of the first of these treatises is to be found in the Aldine edition of Aristotle's works, Venice, 1495, fol., and in that by Sylburgius, Frankfort, 1585, 8vo. It is also inserted in the first volume of Ideler's *Physici et Medici Græci Minores*, Berlin, 1841, 8vo. The Greek text of the second treatise first appeared in the Cambridge *Museum Criticum*, vol. ii., p. 359, *seqq.*, transcribed by Demetrius Schinas, from a manuscript at Florence. It was published, together with Valla's translation, by Passow, Breslau, 1822, 4to, and also in Passow's *Opuscula Academica*, Leipzig, 1835, 8vo. The Greek text alone is contained in the first volume of Ideler's work, already mentioned.

IX. One other physician alone remains to be mentioned here, although

[1] *Greenhill, l. c.*

[2] *Id. ib.*

the work which he has left behind him is only remotely connected with medical science. This is ARTEMIDŌRUS,[1] surnamed, for distinction' sake, *Daldianus*, from the circumstance of his mother having been born at Daldia or Daldis, a small town of Lydia. He lived at Rome in the reign of Antoninus Pius and M. Aurelius, as we may infer from several passages of his work,[2] though some writers have placed him in the reign of Constantine. Artemidorus is the author of a work on the interpretation of dreams, entitled Ὀνειροκριτικά, in five books, which is still extant. He collected the materials for this work by very extensive reading (he asserts that he had read all the books on the subject), on his travels through Asia, Greece, Italy, and the Grecian islands.[3] He himself intimates that he had written several works, and, from Suidas and Eudocia, we may infer that one was called οἰωνοσκοπικά, and the other χειροσκοπικά. Along with his occupations on these subjects, he also practiced as a physician. In his work on dreams, his object is to prove that in dreams the future is revealed to man, and to clear the science of interpreting them from the abuses with which the fashion of the time had surrounded it. He does not attempt, however, to establish his opinion by philosophical reasoning, but by appealing to facts partly recorded in history, partly derived from oral tradition of the people, and partly from his own experience. On the last point he places great reliance, especially as he believed that he was called to the task by Apollo. This makes him conceited, and raises him above all fear of censure. The style of the work is simple, correct, and elegant, and this, together with the circumstance that Artemidorus has often occasion to allude to or explain ancient manners and usages, gives to it a peculiar value. The work has also great interest, because it shows us in what manner the ancients symbolized and interpreted certain events of ordinary life, which, when well understood, throws light on various points of ancient mythology.

The first edition of the *Oneirocritica* is that of Aldus, Venice, 1518, 8vo; the next is that of Rigaltius, Paris, 1603, 4to, containing a valuable commentary, which goes down, however, only to the sixty-eighth chapter of the second book. The last edition is that of Reiff, Leipzig, 1805, 2 vols. 8vo. It contains the notes of Rigaltius, and some by Reiske and the editor. In 1821, Benedict published his "*Notæ criticæ ad Artemidori Oneirocritica*," Schneeberg, 8vo.

---

1 *Smith, Dict. Biogr.*, *s. v.* 2 *Oneirocr.*, i., 28, 66; iv., 1. 3 *Ibid.*, *procem.*, lib. i.

CHAPTER LII.

SEVENTH OR BYZANTINE PERIOD.

INTRODUCTORY REMARKS.[1]

I. The translation of the seat of empire from Rome to Constantinople was the beginning of a new order of things. Christianity, viewed at first with indifference by a people who professed the greatest toleration, but who confounded it with the Jewish worship, the object of their contempt; persecuted and tolerated in turn by successive emperors; and finally raised to the throne in the person of Constantine, had now become the dominant religion of the state. Its influence on all the branches of literature and science gave a new form to most of them, while it produced others entirely new, particularly those connected with theological speculation, into which the nature of our subject, however, does not permit us to enter.

II. Apart from the zealous labors of the Christian writers in their new field of inquiry, literature was now rapidly on the decline, although several of the cities in which it had hitherto flourished still retained, for a time, a portion of their former celebrity. Athens, for instance, still possessed philosophers, who explained in their public lectures the writings of Plato and Aristotle, until the edict of Justinian closed their schools, and drove them into the East. This same city had also its schools of grammarians and rhetoricians. Constantinople had similar establishments for the culture of the liberal arts, and also for jurisprudence; Alexandrea had again become the abode of the sciences; and Berytus flourished with its school of law; but the true spirit of literature had departed, and the fall of the Eastern empire buried the whole fabric in its ruins.[2]

III. At what time the ancient Greek may be said to have ceased as a living language, and the modern or Romaic tongue to have taken its place, is difficult to determine. It may be dated, perhaps, from the seventh and eighth centuries of our era, as far as Greece itself was concerned, when the country was permanently occupied by Sclavonic settlers. The extent of the transformation which ensued is most clearly proved by the number of new names which succeeded to those of the ancient geography. But it is also described by historians in terms which have suggested to many the belief that the native population was utterly swept away, and that the modern Greeks are the descendants of barbarous tribes, which subsequently became subject to the empire, and received the language and religion which they have since retained from Byzantine missionaries and Anatolian colonists. The expression of Constantine Porphyrogenitus[3] is worthy of notice, when he says ἐσθλαβώθη πᾶσα ἡ χώ-

[1] *Schöll, Hist. Lit. Gr.*, vol. vi., p. 1, *seqq.*

[2] *Id. ib.*

[3] *De Them.*, ii., 6. Compare *Thirlwall, Hist. Gr.*, vol. viii., p. 471, note.

ρα, καὶ γέγονε βάρβαρος, "The whole country was *Slavonized*, and became barbarian."

IV. In considering the literature of the present period, we shall confine ourselves to very narrow limits, the more especially as the Christian writers (considered as such) do not fall within the scope of our work. We shall content ourselves, therefore, with an enumeration of the different writers of this period, and a brief sketch merely of the most important among them.

CHAPTER LIII.

SEVENTH OR BYZANTINE PERIOD—*continued.*

POETRY.

I. EPIGRAM.[1]

I. THE epigrammatic poets of this period were quite numerous, though few of them possessed any great degree of merit. The principal ones among them were the Emperor JULIAN, APOLLINARIUS of Laodicea, PALLADAS of Chalcis, PAULUS SILENTIARIUS, and AGATHIAS of Myrina, in Æolis.

II. Of the Emperor JULIAN we have three epigrams remaining, one of them directed against beer (εἰς οἶνον ἀπὸ κριθῆς), as wishing to usurp the place of wine. APOLLINARIUS, probably the friend and correspondent of Libanius, has left us two biting epigrams, one of them on a bad grammarian and rhetorician. PALLADAS is the author of a large number of epigrams in the Anthology, which some scholars consider the best in the collection, while others regard them as almost worthless; but the real characteristic of which is an elegant mediocrity. PAULUS SILENTIARIUS, so called because he was the chief of the *Silentiarii*, or secretaries of the Emperor Justinian, and to whom we shall presently again refer, wrote eighty-three epigrams, given in the Anthology, and among which is improperly numbered a poem *On the Pythian Baths* (εἰς τὰ ἐν Πυθίοις θερμά). Of AGATHIAS, mention has already been made in our account of the Anthologies.

II. OTHER DEPARTMENTS OF POETRY.

III. The other poets of this period were NAUMACHIUS, MAXIMUS, DOROTHEUS, HELIODORUS, NONNUS, PROCLUS, MUSÆUS, COLUTHUS, TRYPHIODORUS, and PAULUS SILENTIARIUS. We shall enlarge on the most important of these.

IV. NONNUS (Νόννος),[2] a native of Panopolis, in Egypt, seems to have lived shortly before the time of Agathias, who mentions him among the recent (νέοι) poets. He must be assigned, therefore, to the sixth century of the Christian era. Respecting the events of his life, nothing is known except that he was a Christian. He was the author of an enormous poem, which has come down to us, under the title of Διονυσιακά or Βασσαρικά, and consists of forty-eight books. As the subject of the poem is a

[1] *Schöll, Hist. Lit. Gr.*, vol. vi., p. 36, *seqq.*

[2] *Smith, Dict. Biogr.*, *s. v.*

pagan divinity, and a number of mythological stories are introduced, some writers have imagined that it was composed by him previous to his conversion to Christianity. There appears, however, to be no good ground for this opinion. The poem itself shows that Nonnus had no idea whatever of what a poetical composition should be, and it is more like a chaos than a literary production, the incidents being patched together with little or no coherence. The style is bombastic and inflated in the highest degree; but the author shows considerable learning and fluency of narration. A second work of Nonnus, which has all the defects of the first, is a paraphrase of the Gospel of St. John, in hexameter verse. There is also a collection and exposition of various stories and fables ascribed to Nonnus, but Bentley has shown that this collection is the production of a far more ignorant person.

The first edition of the *Dionysiaca* is that of Falckenburg, Antwerp, 1569, 4to. In 1605, an octavo edition, with a Latin translation, appeared at Hanau. A reprint of it, with a dissertation by D. Heinsius, and emendations by Joseph Scaliger, was published at Leyden in 1610, 8vo. The latest and best edition, however, is that of Graefe, with a critical commentary, Leipzig, 1819–26, 2 vols. 8vo. Of the Paraphrase of St. John, the best editions are that of D. Heinsius, Leyden, 1627, 8vo, and Passow, Leipzig, 1834, 8vo.

V. Musæus (*Μουσαῖος*), not to be confounded with the earlier bard of the same name, was a poet and grammarian, who, according to the most correct opinion, did not live earlier than the fifth century of our era. He is the author of the poem on the loves of Hero and Leander. The general style of this production is quite different from the simplicity of the older poets, and several individual expressions betray the lateness of its origin.

Numerous editions of this poem have been published. The best are those of Teucher, Leipzig, 1789, Halle, 1801; of Passow, Leipzig, 1810, 8vo; of Schaefer, Leipzig, 1825, 8vo; and of Lehrs, along with Hesiod, Apollonius Rhodius, Tryphiodorus, &c., in Didot's *Bibliotheca Græca*, Paris, 1840.

VI. Colūthus (*Κόλουθος*)[1] was a native of Lycopolis, in Upper Egypt, and flourished under the Emperor Anastasius, at the beginning of the sixth century of our era. He wrote laudatory poems (*ἐγκώμια δι' ἐπῶν*), an heroic poem, in six books, entitled *Καλυδονικά*, and another entitled *Περσικά*. These are all lost; but his poem on "the Rape of Helen" (*Ἑλένης ἁρπαγή*) was discovered, with Quintus Smyrnæus, by Cardinal Bessarion, in Calabria. It consists of three hundred and ninety-two hexameter lines, and is an unsuccessful imitation of Homer.

The best editions of Coluthus are those of Bekker, Berlin, 1816, 8vo; of Schaefer, Leipzig, 1825, 8vo; and of Lehrs, along with Hesiod, Apollonius Rhodius, Tryphiodorus, &c., in Didot's *Bibliotheca Græca*, Paris, 1840.

VII. Tryphiodōrus (*Τρυφιόδωρος*),[2] a poet and grammarian, was a native of Egypt, but nothing is known of his personal history. He is supposed to have lived in the fifth century of the Christian era. The only one of several poems of his that has come down to us is that entitled *Ἰλίου ἅλωσις*, consisting of six hundred and ninety-one lines. From the small dimensions of it, it is necessarily little more than a sketch. It is not, like the poem of Quintus Smyrnæus, a continuation of the Iliad; it is

[1] *Smith, Dict. Biogr.*, *s. v.*

[2] *Id. ib.*

an independent poem, but still a production of very little merit. After a brief indication of the subject, there follows a meagre recapitulation of some of the chief events since the death of Hector, given in the clumsiest and most confused manner. The proper subject of the poem begins with the account of the building of the wooden horse.

The best editions are that of Northmore, Cambridge, 1791, and London, 1804, 8vo; of Schaefer, Leipzig, 1808, fol. maj., a splendid edition, of which only forty copies were printed; and that of Wernicke, Leipzig, 1819, 8vo.

VIII. Paulus Silentiarius, already mentioned as an epigrammatic poet, wrote likewise various other poems, of which the following are extant: 1. Ἔκφρασις τοῦ ναοῦ τῆς ἁγίας Σοφίας, *Description of the Church of St. Sophia*, consisting of one thousand and twenty-nine verses, of which the first one hundred and thirty-four are iambic, the rest hexameter. The description is praised as accurate and clear, and the versification is not deficient in elegance. 2. Ἔκφρασις τοῦ ἄμβωνος, *Description of the Pulpit*, consisting of three hundred and four verses, of which the first twenty-nine are iambic, and the rest hexameter. It is, in fact, a second part of the former.

The best editions of both these poems are that of Graefe, Leipzig, 1822, 8vo, and that of Bekker, in the Bonn edition of the Byzantine historians, 1837, 8vo.

IX. Paulus Silentiarius may be regarded as the last of the poets of this period in whom any spark of true poetic talent displayed itself. Those that remain were mere versifiers, such as Georgius Pisides, Theodorus Diaconus, Constantine Psellus, Theodorus Prodromus, Joannes Tzetzes, Manuel Philes, Joannes Pediasmus. Of these we will notice the principal ones.

X. Georgius Pisĭdes,[1] or George of Pisidia, flourished in the time of the Emperor Heraclius (who reigned from A.D. 610 to 641). In the MSS. of his works he is described as a deacon and Χαρτοφύλαξ, or "record-keeper," and Σκευοφύλαξ, or "keeper of the sacred vessels" of the Church of St. Sophia, at Constantinople. He wrote various poems, some of which have come down to us. Among the latter we may mention "the Expedition of Heraclius against the Persians," in three books, containing one thousand and ninety-eight verses, and composed in iambic trimeters; another "on the Invasion of the Avars," and the attack made by them on Constantinople during the absence of Heraclius. It consists of one book of six hundred and forty-one iambic trimeters; and a third poem, entitled Ἑξαήμερον ἢ Κοσμουργία, "On the Creation," in one thousand nine hundred and ten iambic trimeters. The versification of Georgius is correct and elegant, and inharmonious verses are very rare. But his poems, however polished, are frequently dull.

The poems on the Expedition against the Persians and the Invasion of the Avars are edited by Bekker, in the Bonn reprint of the Byzantine writers. The Hexaëmeron is best edited in the *Bibliotheca Patrum*, 1654, fol., vol. xiv., p. 389, *seqq.*

XI. Constantinus Psellus[2] flourished in the eleventh century of our era. He was born at Constantinople, of a consular and patrician family, A.D. 1020. He studied at Athens, and excelled in all the learning of the

[1] *Smith, Dict. Biogr.*, *s. v.*

[2] *Id. ib.*

age, so that he was a proficient at once in theology, jurisprudence, physics, mathematics, philosophy, and history. He taught philosophy, rhetoric, and dialectics at Constantinople, where he stood forth as almost the last upholder of the falling cause of learning. The emperors honored him with the title of "Prince of the Philosophers" (φιλοσόφων ὕπατος). He was not only the most accomplished scholar, but also the most voluminous writer of the age. His works, a great number of which are still unedited, are both in prose and poetry, on a vast variety of subjects.

We will specify here only a few editions of parts of his poetical works. The *Synopsis legum, versibus iambis et politicis*, &c., is best edited by Zeucher, Leipzig, 1789, 8vo, and in the *Auctores Græci Minores*, vol. ii., Leipzig, 1796. The *Paraphrasis in Cantica Canticorum* was edited by Meursius, Leyden, 1617, 4to, and is also given in the Paris *Bibliotheca Patrum*, vol. xiii., p. 681, *seqq.* The *De Vitiis et Virtutibus*, &c., in iambic verse, appeared with the *Allegories* of Heraclides Ponticus, at Basle, 1544, 8vo. The *Carmen Iambicum in depositionem Joh. Chrysostomi* was given in the *Excerpta* of Leo Allatius, Rome, 1641, 8vo.

XII. Theodōrus Prodrŏmus,[1] a monk, lived in the first half of the twelfth century. He was held in great repute by his contemporaries as a scholar and philosopher. He wrote upon a variety of subjects, philosophy, grammar, theology, history, and astronomy, and, in particular, was a somewhat prolific poet. Among his poetical productions we may mention, 1. A *Metrical Romance*, in nine books, on the loves of Rhodanthe and Dosicles. It is written in iambic verse, and exhibits very little ability. There is no natural progress in the action, no unity in the characters. 2. *Galeomyomachia*, a poem in iambic verse, on "the Battle of the Mice and Cat," in imitation of the *Batrachomyomachia.* 3. A *poem on Friendship*, in iambic senarii. 4. A poem addressed to the Emperor Manuel Comnenus, in which he complains of his poverty. 5. *Epigrammata*, consisting of poetical summaries of the subject-matter of the Pentateuch, the Book of Joshua, &c.

There is only one edition of the Metrical Romance, namely, that of Gaulmin, Paris, 1625. The *Galeomyomachia* is often appended to the editions of Æsop and Babrius. It has also been edited by Ilgen, in connection with the Homeric hymns, Halle, 1796. The poem on Friendship has been frequently appended to the editions of Stobæus. It was also printed separately by Morel, Paris, 1549, as well as by others. The poem to Manuel Comnenus is given in the first volume of Coraes' *Atakta*, Paris, 1828. The *Epigrammata* were published first at Basle, 1536, and afterward at Angers, 1632.

XIII. Joannes Tzetzes,[2] a Greek grammarian and poet of Constantinople, flourished about A.D. 1150. His writings bear evident traces of the extent of his acquirements in literature, science, and philosophy, and not less of the inordinate conceit with which they had filled him. He wrote a vast number of works, of which several are still extant. Of these the two following are the most important: 1. Ἰλιακά (*Iliaca*), consisting properly of three poems, collected into one, with the titles Τὰ πρὸ Ὁμήρου, τὰ Ὁμήρου, καὶ τὰ μεθ' Ὅμηρον. The whole amounts to one thousand six hundred and seventy-six lines, and is written in hexameter verse. The first contains the whole Iliac cycle, from the birth of Paris to the tenth year of the siege, when the Iliad begins. The second consists of an abridgment of the Iliad. The third, like the work of Quintus Smyrnæus,

[1] *Smith, Dict. Biogr.*, *s. v.*

[2] *Id. ib.*

is devoted to the occurrences which took place between the death of Hector and the return of the Greeks. It is a very dull composition; all the merits that are to be found in which should be ascribed to the earlier poets, from whom Tzetzes derived his materials. 2. Χιλιάδες (*Chiliades*), consisting, in its present form, of twelve thousand six hundred and sixty-one lines. The name *Chiliades* was given to it by the first editor, Gerbelius, who divided it, without reference to the contents, into thirteen divisions of one thousand lines, the last being incomplete. Tzetzes himself called it Βίβλος ἱστορική, and divided it into three πίνακες, as he termed them. Its subject-matter is of the most miscellaneous kind, but embraces chiefly mythological and historical narratives, arranged under separate titles, but without any farther connection. The following are a few of them as they occur: Crœsus, Midas, Gyges, Codrus, Alcmæon, the sons of Boreas, Euphorbus, &c. It is written in bad Greek, in what is termed *political*, or popular verse. It contains a great deal of valuable and curious information, though, as Heyne has shown, the bulk of it was obtained by Tzetzes at second hand. The brother of John Tzetzes was Isaac Tzetzes, author of the commentary on the Cassandra of Lycophron.

Of the editions of the *Iliaca* we may mention that of Jacobs, Leipzig, 1793, and that of Bekker, Berlin, 1816. The latter is the more correct, and is reprinted by Lehrs at the end of his edition of Hesiod, Apollonius, &c., in Didot's *Bibliotheca Græca*, Paris, 1840. Of the *Chiliades* the best edition is that of Kiessling, Leipzig, 1826, though much still requires to be done.

XIV. Manuel Philes or Phile, a native of Ephesus, but a resident of Constantinople, was born A.D. 1275, and died about 1340. His poem περὶ ζώων ἰδιότητος (*De Animalium Proprietate*), chiefly extracted from Ælian, and in iambic verse, is edited by De Pauw, Utrecht, 1739, and with a revised text by Lehrs and Dübner, forming part of the volume containing Ameis's edition of the Bucolic poets, in Didot's *Bibliotheca Græca*, Paris, 1846.

CHAPTER LIV.

SEVENTH OR BYZANTINE PERIOD—*continued.*

PROSE.

SOPHISTS,[1] ETC.

I. A few only of the Sophists of this period will require our attention. These are Ulpian of Antioch, Themistius, Libanius, Himerius, the Emperor Julianus, Proæresius, Basilius.

II. Ulpiānus[2] of Antioch lived in the time of Constantine the Great, and wrote several rhetorical works. The name of Ulpianus is prefixed to extant commentaries in Greek, on eighteen of the orations of Demosthenes, and it is usually stated that they were written by Ulpian of Antioch. But Suidas does not mention these commentaries at all; and it is evident that in their present form they are of much later origin. The

[1] *Schöll, Hist. Lit. Gr.*, vol. vi., p. 140, *seqq.* [2] *Smith, Dict. Biogr.*, s. v.

commentaries may originally have been written by one of the sophists of the name (for Suidas mentions also two others, one of Gaza, and the other of Emesa); but they have received numerous additions and interpolations from some grammarian of a very late period. This is the opinion of F. A. Wolf, who remarks that there are scarcely twenty passages in Demosthenes in which the writer throws light upon difficulties, which could not be equally well explained without his aid. These commentaries are given in the different editions of Demosthenes, and also in the collections of the Attic orators.

III. Themistius (Θεμίστιος),[1] a distinguished philosopher and rhetorician, was a Paphlagonian, and flourished, first at Constantinople, and afterward at Rome, in the reigns of Constantine, Julian, Jovian, Valens, Gratian, and Theodosius. He enjoyed the favor of all those emperors, and was promoted by them to the highest honors of the state. After holding various public offices, and being employed on many public embassies, he was made prefect of Constantinople by Theodosius, A.D. 384. So great was the confidence reposed in him by Theodosius, that, though Themistius was a heathen, the emperor intrusted his son Arcadius to the tutorship of the philosopher. The life of Themistius probably did not extend beyond A.D. 390. Besides the emperors, he numbered among his friends the chief orators and philosophers of the age, Christian as well as heathen. Not only Libanius, but Gregory of Nazianzus also, was his friend and correspondent, and the latter, in an epistle still extant, calls him the "king of arguments." The orations (πολιτικοὶ λόγοι) of Themistius, extant in the time of Photius, were thirty-six in number, of which thirty-three have come down to us in the original Greek, and one in a Latin version. The other two were supposed to be lost, until one of them was discovered by Mai in the Ambrosian library at Milan in 1816. His philosophical works must have been very voluminous, for Photius tells us that he wrote commentaries on all the books of Aristotle, and that there were also exegetical labors of his on Plato.

The best edition of the orations is that of Dindorf, Leipzig, 1832, 8vo. The *editio princeps* of the Greek text is that of Aldus, 1534, fol., containing the philosophical works that remain, and also eight orations. There has been no subsequent edition of the whole works.

IV. Libanius (Λιβάνιος),[2] a distinguished sophist and rhetorician, was born at Antioch about A.D. 314. He studied at Athens, where he imbibed an ardent love for the great classical writers of Greece; and he afterward set up a private school of rhetoric at Constantinople, which was attended by so large a number of pupils, that the classes of the public professors were completely deserted.[3] The latter, in revenge, charged Libanius with being a magician, and obtained his expulsion from Constantinople about A.D. 346.[4] He then went to Nicomedia, where he taught with equal success, but also drew upon himself an equal degree of malice from his opponents.[5] After a stay of five years at Nicomedia, he was recalled to Constantinople. Eventually he took up his abode at An-

[1] *Smith, Dict. Biogr., s. v.*
[2] *Id. ib.*
[3] *Liban., De Fort. sua*, p. 29.
[4] *l. c.*, p. 30.
[5] *l. c.*, p. 36, *seqq.*

tioch, where he spent the remainder of his life. Here he received the greatest marks of favor from the Emperor Julian, A.D. 362. In the reign of Valens he was at first persecuted, but he afterward succeeded in winning the favor of that monarch also. The Emperor Theodosius likewise showed him marks of respect; but his enjoyment of life was disturbed by ill health, by misfortunes in his family, and more especially by the disputes in which he was incessantly involved, partly with rival sophists, and partly with the prefects. It can not, however, be denied that he himself was as much to blame as his opponents, for he appears to have provoked them by his querulous disposition, and by the pride and vanity which every where appear in his orations, and which led him to interfere in political questions, which it would have been wiser to have left alone. He was the teacher of St. Basil and Chrysostom, with whom he always kept up a friendly connection. The year of his death is uncertain, but from one of his epistles it is evident that he was alive in A.D. 391,[1] and it is probable that he died a few years after, in the reign of Arcadius.

We still possess a considerable number of the works of Libanius, but how many may have been lost is uncertain. The extant works are, 1. **Προγυμνασμάτων παραδείγματα**, or Models for rhetorical exercises. 2. Λόγοι, or Orations, sixty-seven in number. 3. Μελέται, or Declamations, that is, orations on fictitious subjects, and descriptions of various kinds, fifty in number. 4. A Life of Demosthenes, and arguments to the speeches of the same orator. 5. Ἐπιστολαί, or Letters, of which a large number are still extant. Many of these letters are extremely interesting, being addressed to the most eminent men of his time, such as the Emperor Julian, Athanasius, Basil, Gregory of Nyssa, Chrysostom, and others. The style in all of them is neat and elegant.

As regards the style of Libanius as an orator, some modern critics have called him a real model of pure Attic Greek; but this is carrying praise too far, and even Photius entertained a much more correct opinion of him. There can be no doubt that Libanius is by far the most talented and most successful among the rhetoricians of the fourth century; he took the best orators of the classic age as his models, and we can often see in him the disciple and happy imitator of Demosthenes, and his animated descriptions are often full of power and elegance; but he is not able always to rise above the spirit of his age, and we rarely find in him that natural simplicity which constitutes the great charm of the best Attic orators. His diction is a curious mixture of the pure Old Attic with what may be termed the Modern; and the latter would be more excusable, if he did not so often claim for himself the excellences of the ancient orators. Moreover, it is evident that, like all other rhetoricians, he is more concerned about the form than the substance. As far as the history of his age is concerned, some of his orations, and still more his epistles, are of great value, such as the oration in which he relates the events of his own life, the eulogies on Constantius and Constans, the orations on Julian, several orations describing the condition of Antioch, and those which he wrote against his professional and political opponents.[2]

[1] *Epist.*, 941.

[2] *Smith*, *l. c.*

A complete edition of all the works of Libanius does not yet exist. The best edition of the orations and declamations is that of Reiske, Altenburg, 1791–97, 4 vols. 8vo. The number of orations, however, in Reiske's edition, amounts to only sixty-five. Another oration, Περὶ Ὀλυμπίου, was discovered in a Barberini MS. by Siebenkees, who published it in his *Anecdota Græca*, Nürnberg, 1798, p. 75, *seqq*. A sixty-seventh oration was first published by Mai, in his second edition of Fronto, Rome, 1823, p. 421, *seqq*. So, again, the number of declamations in Reiske's edition is forty-eight, but two additional ones have since been published, one by Boissonade, in his *Anecdota Græca*, vol. i., p. 165, *seqq*. The best edition of the Epistles is that of J. C. Wolf, Amsterdam, 1738, fol.

V. Himĕrius (Ἱμέριος),[1] a celebrated sophist, was born at Prusa, in Bithynia, and belongs, according to the most correct account, to the period from A.D. 315 to 386. He studied at Athens, and was subsequently appointed professor of rhetoric there. In this city he gave instruction to Julian, afterward emperor, and the celebrated Christian writers Bazil and Gregory of Nazianzus. In A.D. 362 the Emperor Julian invited him to his court at Antioch, and made him his secretary. He returned to Athens in A.D. 368, and there passed the remainder of his life. According to Suidas, he died in a fit of epilepsy (ἱερὰ νόσος). Himerius was a pagan, and, like Libanius and other eminent men, remained a pagan, though we do not perceive in his writings any hatred or animosity against the Christians; he speaks of them with mildness and moderation, and seems, on the whole, to have been of an amiable disposition. He was the author of a considerable number of works, a part of which only have come down to us. There were extant in the time of Photius seventy-one orations by Himerius, but of these only twenty-four have reached our time complete. Of thirty-six others we have only extracts in Photius, and of the remaining eleven we have only fragments. In his oratory Himerius took Aristides for his model. His style, however, is obscure, and overladen with ornament, and marked occasionally by turgid and bombastic phraseology. Still, he is not without talent as an orator.

A complete collection of all the extant productions of Himerius was first prepared by Wernsdorf, Göttingen, 1790, 8vo. This is the best edition. One fragment of some length has since been discovered, and is given in Boissonade's *Anecdota Græca*, vol. i., p. 172, *seqq*.

VI. Julianus, Flavius Claudius,[2] usually called Julian, and surnamed the Apostate, was born at Constantinople A.D. 331, and reigned as Roman emperor A.D. 361–363. He wrote a large number of works, many of which are extant. Julian was a man of reflection and thought, but possessed no creative genius. He did not, however, write merely for the sake of writing, like so many of his contemporaries; his works show that he had his subjects really at heart, and that in literature as well as in business his extraordinary activity arose from the wants of a powerful mind, which desired to improve itself and the world. His style is remarkably pure, and is a close imitation of that of the best classical Greek writers, although he sometimes indulges in the exaggerated and over-elaborate diction of his contemporaries. The following are his most important works: 1. *Letters*, most of which were intended for public circulation, and are of great importance for the history of the time. One,

[1] *Smith, l. c.*

[2] *Id. ib.*

which was addressed to the senate and people of Athens, and in which the author explains the motives for his having taken up arms against the Emperor Constantius, is an interesting and most important historical document. 2. *Orations* on various subjects, as, for instance, on the Emperor Constantius, on the worship of the sun, on the mother of the gods (Cybele), on true and false cynicism, &c. 3. *The Cæsars, or the Banquet* (Καίσαρες ἢ Συμπόσιον), a satirical composition, which Gibbon justly calls one of the most agreeable and instructive productions of ancient wit. Julian describes the Roman emperors approaching one after the other to take their seat around a table in the heavens; and as they come up, their faults, vices, and crimes are censured with a sort of bitter mirth by old Silenus, whereupon each Cæsar defends himself as well as he can. 4. MISOPŌGON, or "the enemy of the beard" (Μισοπώγων), called also ANTIOCHICUS, or "the Antiochian" (Ἀντιοχικός), a severe satire on the licentious and effeminate manners of the inhabitants of Antioch, who had ridiculed Julian when he resided in that city on account of his austere virtues, and had laughed at his allowing his beard to grow in the ancient fashion. 5. AGAINST THE CHRISTIANS (Κατὰ Χριστιανῶν). This work is lost, but some extracts from it are given in Cyrill's reply to it, which is still extant.[1]

The latest and best edition of the *Letters* is that of Heyler, Mainz, 1828, 8vo. It contains eighty-three letters, with a Latin translation, and a commentary of the editor. There are, besides, some fragments of lost letters. The best editions of the *Cæsars* are by Heusinger, Gotha, 1736, 8vo, 1741, 8vo, and by Harles, the editor of Fabricius' *Bibliotheca Græca*, Erlangen, 1785, 8vo. The best edition of the collected works of Julian is by Spanheim, Leipzig, 1696, fol.

VII. PROÆRESIUS (Προαιρέσιος),[2] a distinguished sophist and rhetorician, was a native of Armenia, born about A.D. 276. He first studied at Antioch under Ulpian, and afterward at Athens under Julian, then seated in the chair of rhetoric. At a later period he became the chief teacher of rhetoric at Athens, and enjoyed a very high reputation. When Julian promulgated his ill-judged decree, forbidding teachers belonging to the Christian religion to practice their art, we are told that Proæresius was expressly exempted from its operation, but that he refused any immunity not enjoyed by his brethren. From the account of Eunapius, we learn that he was of gigantic stature (Casaubon and Wyttenbach conjecture that he was nine feet high!), and of stately bearing, so vigorous in his old age that it was impossible to suppose him other than in the prime of life. His constitution was of iron strength (σιδηρέον), braving the winter colds of Gaul without shoes, and in light clothing, and drinking unwarmed the water of the Rhine when almost frozen. His style of eloquence seems to have been flowing, and graced with allusions to classic times. He had great powers of extemporaneous speaking, and a prodigious memory. Among his pupils were Basil and Gregory of Nazianzus. We have no account of any works of his.

VIII. BASILĪUS (Βασίλειος),[3] commonly called *Basil the Great*, was born A.D. 329, at Cæsarea, in Cappadocia. He studied at Antioch or Constantinople, under Libanius, and subsequently continued his studies for

[1] *Smith, l. c.* [2] *Id. ib.* [3] *Id. ib.*

four years (A.D. 351–355), chiefly under the sophists Himerius and Proæresius. Among his fellow-students were the Emperor Julian and Gregory of Nazianzus, the latter of whom became his most intimate friend. After acquiring the greatest reputation as a student for his knowledge of rhetoric, philosophy, and science, he returned to Cæsarea, where he began to plead causes, but soon abandoned his profession, and devoted himself to a religious life. He now led an ascetic life for many years. He was elected Bishop of Cæsarea in A.D. 370, in place of Eusebius. He died in A.D. 379. Basil stands conspicuous for learning and eloquence, for his zeal for the Catholic faith against the powerful Arian and semi-Arian bishops in his neighborhood, and for his efforts for church union both in the East and West.

The first complete edition of Basil's works was published at Basle in 1551. The most complete and the best edition, however, is that of Garnier, Paris, 1721–30, 3 vols. fol.; reprinted in 6 vols. royal 8vo, Paris, 1839, *seqq.*

CHAPTER LV.

SEVENTH OR BYZANTINE PERIOD—*continued.*

WRITERS OF WORKS OF FICTION.

I. Five writers claim our attention under this head, namely, Heliodorus, Achilles Tatius, Longus, Chariton, and Eustathius.

II. Heliodōrus[1] was born at Emesa, in Syria, and flourished under the Emperor Theodosius and his sons, about the close of the fourth century of our era. He was bishop of Tricca, in Thessaly; but, before he was raised to this dignity, he wrote a romance in ten books, entitled *Æthiopica* (Αἰθιοπικά), because the scene at the beginning and end of the story is laid in Æthiopia. It relates the loves of Theagenes and Chariclea, and is far superior to the other Greek romances. Though very deficient in those characteristics of modern fiction which appeal to the universal sympathies of our nature, the work is extremely interesting on account of the rapid succession of strange and not altogether improbable adventures, the many and various characters introduced, and the beautiful scenes described. The opening scene is admirable, and the point of the story at which it occurs is very well chosen. The language is simple and elegant, though it is sometimes too diffuse, and often deviates from the pure Attic standard. The work formed the model for subsequent Greek romance writers.

In modern times the *Æthiopica* was scarcely known until, at the sacking of Ofen in 1526, a MS. of the work in the library of Matthias Corvinus, king of Hungary, attracted, by its binding, the attention of a soldier, who brought it into Germany, and at last it came into the hands of Obsopæus, who printed it at Basle, 1534, 4to. Several better MSS. were afterward discovered. The best and latest editions are that of Mitscherlich, in his *Scriptores Græci Erotici*, Strasburg, 1798, of which it forms the second volume, in two parts, and that of Coraes, Paris, 1803, 2 vols. 8vo.

III. Achilles Tatius (Ἀχιλλεὺς Τάτιος),[2] or, as Suidas and Eudocia call him, Achilles Statius, an Alexandrine rhetorician, lived in the lat-

[1] *Smith, Dict. Biogr., s. v.*

[2] *Id. ib.*

ter half of the fifth or the beginning of the sixth century of our era. He is the author of a Greek romance, in eight books, containing the adventures of two lovers, Clitophon and Leucippe, which has come down to us. It bears the title Τὰ κατὰ Λευκίππην καὶ Κλειτοφῶντα. Notwithstanding all its defects, it is one of the best love-stories of the Greeks, ranking next to the *Æthiopica* of Heliodorus. Achilles, like his predecessor Heliodorus, disdained having recourse to what is marvellous and improbable in itself; but the accumulation of adventures, and of physical, as well as moral difficulties, which the lovers have to overcome before they are happily united, is too great, and renders the story improbable, though their arrangement and succession are skillfully managed by the author. The style of the work, on which the author appears to have bestowed his principal care, is thoroughly rhetorical; there is a perpetual striving after elegance and beauty, after images, puns, and antitheses. These things, however, were just what the age of Achilles required, and that his novel was much read is attested by the number of MSS. still extant.

The first edition of the Greek original appeared at Heidelberg, 1601, 8vo, printed together with similar works of Longus and Parthenius. An edition, with a voluminous, though rather careless commentary, was published by Salmasius, Leyden, 1640, 8vo. The best and most recent edition is by Jacobs, Leipzig, 1821, 2 vols. 8vo.

IV. Longus (Λόγγος), a Greek sophist, who is believed to have lived in the fourth or at the beginning of the fifth century of our era. Concerning his history nothing is known, but it is probable that he lived after the time of Heliodorus, for there are some passages in his work which seem to be imitations of Heliodorus of Emesa. Longus is one of the erotic writers whom we meet with at the close of ancient and the beginning of middle-age history. His work bears the title Ποιμενικῶν τῶν κατὰ Δάφνιν καὶ Χλόην, or, in Latin, *Pastoralia de Daphnide et Chloe*. It is written in pleasing and elegant prose, but is not free from the artificial embellishments peculiar to that age.

Among more recent editions we may notice those of Boden, Leipzig, 1777, 8vo; Villoison, Paris, 1778, 2 vols. 8vo and 4to, with a very much improved text; Mitscherlich, Bipont (Deuxponts), 1794, 8vo, forming the third volume of his *Scriptores Erotici Græci*; Schaefer, Leipzig, 1803, 8vo; Passow, Leipzig, 1811, 12mo; and Seiler, Leipzig, 1843, 8vo.

V. Charĭton (Χαρίτων),[1] a native of Aphrodisias, in Caria, was the author of a Greek romance, in eight books, on the loves of Chæreas and Callirhoë. The title of the work is Χαρίτωνος Ἀφροδισιέως τῶν περὶ Χαιρέαν καὶ Καλλιῤῥόην ἐρωτικῶν διηγημάτων λόγοι ή, but the name and native place of the writer are probably feigned (from χάρις and Ἀφροδίτη), as his time and position certainly are. He represents himself as the secretary of the orator Athenagoras, evidently referring to the Syracusan orator mentioned by Thucydides as the political opponent of Hermocrates. Nothing is known respecting the real life or the time of the author, but he probably did not live earlier than the fifth century after Christ. The incidents are natural and pleasing, and the style is simple; but the work, as a whole, is reckoned inferior to those of Achilles Tatius, Heliodorus, Longus, and Xenophon of Ephesus.

[1] *Smith, Dict. Biogr., s. v.*

There is only one known MS. of the work, from which it was printed by D'Orville, Amsterdam, 1750, 3 vols. 4to, generally in one. D'Orville's commentary is esteemed one of the best on any ancient author. It was reprinted, with additional notes by Beck, 1 vol. 8vo, Leipzig, 1783. A very beautiful edition of the text was printed at Venice, 1812, 4to.

VI. Eustăthius (Εὐστάθιος),[1] an erotic writer or novelist, whose name is written in some MSS. *Eumathius*. With regard to his native place, he is called in the MSS. of his work Μακρεμβολίτης, which is usually referred to Constantinople, or Παρεμβολίτης, according to which he would be a native of the Egyptian town of Parembole. He appears to have been a man of rank, and high in office, for the MSS. describe him as πρωτονωβελέσιμος, and μέγας χαρτοφύλαξ, or chief keeper of the archives. The time at which he lived is uncertain, but it is generally believed that he can not be placed earlier than the twelfth century of our era, so that his work would be the latest Greek novel that we know of. Some writers confound him with Eustathius the archbishop of Thessalonica, from whom he must surely be distinguished. The novel which he wrote, and through which alone his name has come down to us, bears the title Τὸ καθ' Ὑσμίνην καὶ Ὑσμινίαν δρᾶμα, and consists of eleven books, at the end of the last of which the author himself mentions the title. It is a story of the love of Hysmine and Hysminias, written in a very artificial style. The tale is monotonous and wearisome; the story is frigid and improbable, and shows no power of invention on the part of the author.

This work was first edited by Gaulmin, Paris, 1617, 8vo. Somewhat improved reprints of Gaulmin's edition appeared at Vienna, 1791, 8vo, and Leipzig, 1792, 8vo.

CHAPTER LVI.

SEVENTH OR BYZANTINE PERIOD—*continued.*

GRAMMARIANS.[2]

I. Constantinople became during this period the seat of grammatical erudition. The founder of this new capital established in it a school which bore some resemblance to a modern university, since instruction, in place of being confined to a single science, was extended over all the branches of human knowledge. He also erected a building, which George Codinus calls a *Tetradisium*,[3] in which resided fifteen professors, all ecclesiastics, who were called Οἰκουμενικοί, *Œcumenics* or *Universals*, and had over them a chief who bore the title of Οἰκουμενικὸς διδάσκαλος, or *Œcumenic instructor*, and had charge of the public library and the ecclesiastical archives. The library was subsequently enlarged by Julian, who incorporated with it his own collection. Valens also attached to it seven antiquaries or philologists, charged with the preparation of manuscripts. This collection increased, in the course of a century and a half, to one hundred and twenty thousand volumes.

II. The Œcumenic professors enjoyed the highest consideration at

[1] *Smith, Dict. Biogr., s. v.*

[2] *Schöll, Hist. Lit. Gr.*, vol. vi., p. 254.

[3] *Georg. Cod., De Orig. Constant.*, ed. Paris, p. 42.

Constantinople; the emperor often consulted them; and their order was regarded as a kind of seminary which furnished archbishops and patriarchs to the Church.

III. In A.D. 476, under the very short reign of Basilicus II., a wing of the Tetradisium became a prey to the flames, together with the volumes contained in it, among which were, it is said, the forty-eight books of the Iliad and Odyssey, written in letters of gold on the intestines of a serpent one hundred and twenty feet long! Zeno, the Isaurian, and his successors, repaired in part this loss; but the new collection had not reached more than thirty-six thousand volumes, when, in A.D. 730, Leo III., the celebrated iconoclast, if we believe the common story, gave orders to burn the library of St. Sophia, as it was called, hoping thereby to prevent his opponents from strengthening their opinions by historical arguments. This, however, in all probability, is merely an idle story, invented by some ignorant monk, and repeated by fanatics. The library would seem, however, to have been actually destroyed by some conflagration, and never to have fully revived.[1]

IV. Grammar, that is to say, philology in all its branches, was one of the sciences which the œcumenic doctors professed; but they gave it a new form. Being more of theologians than grammarians, and living together in a kind of brotherhood, the harmony of which would have been disturbed had they not closed the door on all those philological and critical discussions which formed the delight of the Alexandrean literati, and often divided them into parties and sects, the Byzantine professors reduced grammatical science to a regular and unvarying system. As the basis of their grammatical views, they adopted the theory of Dionysius Thrax, or what passed for such, and his precepts served as a foundation for all grammatical instruction.[2]

V. If this system had its advantages, it served, on the other hand, to disgust all those who were gifted with a critical spirit, and were desirous of indulging in bolder speculations. Hence the number of Byzantine grammarians, whose names and works have reached us, was very limited during the existence of the Tetradisium. It became somewhat augmented in the eighth century and subsequently, but among the writers who thus occupied themselves with an expiring language, few attained to any degree of celebrity. Many of their works still remain in MS. in the libraries of Europe, some of which still possess a certain value from the citations which they contain of productions that are now lost. These are the works that modern scholars occasionally put forth, along with other unpublished productions, under the head of *Anecdŏta.*

VI. Among the grammarians to whom we have just been alluding the following may be named: Helladius, Georgius Chœroboscus, Theodosius of Alexandrea, Michael Syncellus, Theognostus, Manuel Moschopulus, uncle and nephew, Maximus Planudes, Nicephoras Gregoras, and Tricha, who wrote on metres.

[1] *Schöll, l. c.*

[2] *Id. ib.*

CHAPTER LVII.

SEVENTH OR BYZANTINE PERIOD—*continued.*

SCHOLIASTS AND COMMENTATORS.

I. Syrianus (Συριανός),[1] a Greek philosopher of the Neo-Platonic school, was a native of Alexandrea. Of his personal history little is known. He studied with great zeal under Plutarchus, who appointed him his successor. The most distinguished of his own disciples was Proclus, who regarded him with the greatest veneration. Syrianus wrote commentaries on various parts of Aristotle's writings. Of these, a commentary on the Metaphysics is still extant, which is of considerable value. We have remaining, also, a treatise on Ideas, and a commentary on the Στάσεις of Hermogenes, published by Aldus in the second volume of the *Rhetores*, 1509, and by Walz in the fourth volume of his rhetorical collection.

II. Eustăthius,[2] archbishop of Thessalonica, was one of the best scholiasts of this period. He was a native of Constantinople, and lived during the latter half of the twelfth century. The works of Eustathius, which have come down to us, contain the amplest proofs that he was beyond all dispute the most learned man of his age. His writings consist of commentaries on ancient Greek poets, theological treatises, homilies, epistles, &c., the first of which are to us the most important. These commentaries show that Eustathius possessed the most extensive knowledge of Greek literature, from the earliest to the latest times, while his other works exhibit his high personal character, and his great power as an orator, which procured him the esteem of the imperial family of the Comneni. The most important of all his works is his *Commentary on the Iliad and Odyssey* (Παρεκβολαὶ εἰς τὴν Ὁμήρου Ἰλιάδα καὶ Ὀδύσσειαν), or, rather, his collection of extracts from earlier commentators of those two poems. This vast compilation was made, with the most astonishing diligence and perseverance, from the numerous and extensive works of the Alexandrean grammarians and critics, as well as from later commentators; and as nearly all the works from which Eustathius made his extracts are lost, his commentary is of incalculable value to us, for he has preserved at least the substance of their remarks and criticisms. The work, indeed, is extremely deficient in plan and method; the author, however, can not be blamed for these deficiencies, as his title does not lead us to expect a regular commentary (the term παρεκβολαί, though commonly rendered "commentary," denoting merely "a compilation"). He incorporates in it every thing which serves to illustrate his author, whether it refers to the language or grammar, or to mythology, history, and geography. We have also by Eustathius a *Commentary on Dionysius Periegētes*, of the same kind, and of the same diffuseness as the commentary on Homer. Its great value consists in the numerous extracts from earlier writers to

[1] *Smith, Dict. Biogr., s. v.*

[2] *Id. ib.*

illustrate the geography of Dionysius. A commentary on Pindar is also mentioned, which, however, is lost, with the exception of the introduction.

The first edition of the *Commentary on Homer* was published at Rome, 1542–1550, 4 vols. fol., of which an accurate reprint appeared at Basle in 1559–60. The Florence edition by Politus, 1730, 3 vols. fol., contains only the commentary to the first five books of the Iliad, with a Latin translation. A tolerably correct reprint of the Roman edition was published at Leipzig, 1825–28, 7 vols. 4to, the seventh containing the Index. The *Commentary on Dionysius* is given in R. Stephens's edition of Dionysius, Paris, 1547, 4to; in that of H. Stephens, Paris, 1577, 4to, and 1697, 8vo; in Hudson's *Geograph. Min.*, vol. iv.; and, lastly, in Bernhardy's edition of Dionysius, Leipzig, 1828, 2 vols. 8vo. The *Introduction* to the *Commentary on Pindar* was first edited by Tafel, in his *Eustathii Thessalonicensis Opuscula*, Frankfort, 1832, 4to, from which it was printed separately by Schneidewin, Göttingen, 1837, 8vo.

III. We have already mentioned John and Isaac Tzetzes, and the commentary of the latter on the Cassandra of Lycophron. It only remains to notice under the present head Demetrius Triclinius.[1] This individual lived about A.D. 1400. He compiled *scholia* on *Hesiod*, *Pindar*, *Sophocles*, and *Aristophanes*. His treatise on the *Metres of Sophocles* is of little value, and of still less is a treatise on Figures. He was the author, also, of a recension of the tragedies of Sophocles, which formed the basis of the editions of this poet from 1553 to the revolution effected by Brunck.

The *scholia* of Triclinius on Sophocles, and his treatise on the metres of that poet, were published for the first time by Turnebus, in his edition of Sophocles. Brunck has inserted the *scholia* in his edition, but not the treatise on metres, which he regards as of no value whatever.

CHAPTER LVIII.

SEVENTH OR BYZANTINE PERIOD—*continued.*

LEXICOGRAPHERS, ETC.

I. Among the lexicographers of this period the most deserving of notice are Harpocration, Ammonius, Hesychius, Philemon, Photius, Zonaras, and Suidas. To these we may add the writers on dialects, Gregorius Corinthus, Thomas Magister, and Georgius Lecapenus. After whom we will consider the literary collections of Photius, already mentioned as a lexicographer, and the Empress Eudocia.

LEXICOGRAPHERS.

II. Harpocration (Ἁρποκρατίων) Valerius[2] was the author of a Greek lexicon to the works of the ten Attic orators, entitled Περὶ τῶν λέξεων τῶν δέκα ῥητόρων, and which is still extant. It contains not only explanations of legal and political terms, but also accounts of persons and things mentioned in the speeches of the Attic orators. The work is to us of the highest importance, as it contains a vast deal of information on the public and civil code of Athens, and on antiquarian, historical, and literary subjects, of which we should be ignorant but for this dictionary of Harpocration, since most of the works from which the author compiled are

[1] *Schöll, Hist. Lit. Gr.*, vol. vi., p. 273.

[2] *Smith, Dict. Biogr.*, *s. v.*

lost, and appear to have perished at an early period. Hence Suidas, the author of the Etymologicum Magnum, and other late grammarians, derived their information on many points from Harpocration. All we know about his personal history is contained in a line or two in Suidas, who calls him a rhetorician of Alexandrea, and, besides the above-mentioned dictionary, attributes to him an ἀνθηρῶν συναγωγή, which is lost. The period when he flourished is uncertain.

The Leipzig edition, 1824, 2 vols. 8vo, incorporates every thing that has been done by previous editors for Harpocration. The most recent edition of the text (together with the dictionary of Moeris) is that of Bekker, Berlin, 1833, 8vo.

III. Ammōnius (Ἀμμώνιος) Grammaticus, professor of grammar at Alexandrea at the close of the fourth century. He was also priest of the Egyptian Ape. On the vigorous overthrow of idolatry in Egypt by the bishop Theophilus, A.D. 388–391, Ammonius fled to Constantinople, and there resumed his profession. He wrote a work in Greek *On the Differences of Words of like Signification* (περὶ ὁμοίων καὶ διαφόρων λέξεων), which is appended to many lexicons, as, for instance, that of Scapula. It was edited by Valckenaer, Leyden, 1739, 4to, and, with farther notes, by C. F. Ammon, Erlangen, 1787, 8vo; and by Schæfer, Leipzig, 1822, 8vo. There is another work by Ammonius, περὶ ἀκυρολογίας, which has not yet been printed.

IV. Hesychius (Ἡσύχιος),[1] an Alexandrean grammarian, under whose name a large Greek dictionary has come down to us. Respecting his personal history absolutely nothing is known, but he probably lived about A.D. 380. The work is based, as the writer himself tells us, upon the lexicon of Diogenianus, who wrote a Greek lexicon in the time of Hadrian. The investigations of modern scholars have rendered it highly probable that Hesychius was a pagan. This view seems, indeed, to be contradicted by the fact that the work also contains a number of Christian glosses (λέξεις, *glossæ sacræ*), and references to Christian writers; but it is now a generally established belief that these glosses and references are interpolations, introduced into the work by a later hand. The work is one of very great importance, not only on account of its explaining the words of the Greek language, but also from its comprising much literary and archæological information, derived from earlier grammarians and commentators, whose works are lost. It contains, also, a large number of peculiar dialectical and local forms and expressions, and many quotations from other writers. The arrangement of the work, however, is very defective. The author would seem to have been more concerned about the accumulation of matter derived from the most heterogeneous sources, than about a skillful and systematic arrangement; but some of these defects are perhaps not to be put to the account of the original compiler, but to that of the later interpolators.

The first edition is that of Venice, 1514, fol., edited by the learned Greek Musurus, who made many arbitrary alterations and additions, as is clear from the Venetian MS. (the only one as yet known). The edition of Musurus was followed by those of Florence, 1520, fol.; Hagenau, 1521, fol.; and that of C. Schrevelius, Leyden and Amsterdam, 1686, 4to. The best critical edition, however, with a comprehensive commentary, is

[1] *Smith, Dict. Biogr., s. v.*

that of J. Alberti, which was completed after Alberti's death by Ruhnken, Leyden, 1746–1766, 2 vols. fol. A supplement to this edition was published by Schow, Leyden, 1792, 8vo. The *Glossæ Sacræ* have been edited separately, with emendations and notes, by Ernesti, Leipzig, 1785. The *Adversaria Hesychiana* of Bishop Pearson, containing much valuable matter, appeared from the Clarendon press, Oxford, 1844, 2 vols. 8vo.

V. Philēmon (Φιλήμων), the author of a Λεξικὸν τεχνολογικόν, the extant portion of which was first edited, from a MS. preserved in the Royal Library at Paris, by C. Burney, London, 1812, and afterward by Osann, Berlin, 1821. The author informs us, in his preface, that his work was intended to take the place of a similar lexicon by the grammarian Hyperechius, for such is the true reading, and not Hypereschius, as it stands in the text of Philemon. The work of Hyperechius was arranged in eight books, according to the eight different parts of speech. Philemon's lexicon was a meagre epitome of this work, the best parts of which he seems to have omitted. It is, however, not without its value in the department of literary history. It is often quoted in the *Etymologicum Magnum*. The part of it which is extant consists of the first book, and the beginning of the second, περὶ ὀνομάτων. Hyperechius lived about the middle of the fifth century of our era, and Philemon may probably be placed about the seventh.

VI. Photius (Φώτιος),[1] patriarch of Constantinople in the ninth century of our era, played a distinguished part in the political and religious history of his age. After holding various high offices at the Byzantine court, he was, although previously a layman, elected patriarch of Constantinople in A.D. 858, in place of Ignatius, who had been deposed by Bardas, who was all-powerful at the court of his nephew, Michael III., then a minor. The patriarchate of Photius was a stormy one, and full of vicissitudes. The cause of Ignatius was espoused by the Romish Church, and Photius thus became one of the great promoters of the schism between the Eastern and Western churches. In A.D. 867, Photius was himself deposed by the Emperor Basil I., and Ignatius was restored; but on the death of Ignatius in 877, Photius, who had meanwhile gained the favor of Basil, was again elevated to the patriarchate. On the death of Basil in 886, Photius was accused of a conspiracy against the life of the new emperor, Leo VI., and was banished to a monastery in Armenia, where he seems to have remained until his death. Photius was one of the most learned men of his time, and, in the midst of a busy life, found time for the composition of numerous works, several of which have come down to us. His *Myriobiblon* will be more appropriately considered at the close of the present chapter, together with some other of his works; his *Lexicon* alone will here be noticed. It is entitled Λέξεων συναγωγή. Of this lexicon there exist several MSS., but that known as the *Codex Galeanus*, because given by Thomas Gale to the library of Trinity College, Cambridge, is considered to be the archetype from which the others have been transcribed. This MS., however, is itself very imperfect, containing, in fact, not more than half the original work. Nearly the whole of the lexicon known as the *Lexicon Sangermanense*, a portion of which was published in the *Anecdota Græca* of Bekker (vol. i., p. 319,

[1] *Smith, Dict. Biogr., s. v.*

seqq.), appears to have been incorporated in the lexicon of Photius, of which, when entire, it is estimated to have formed a third part.

The lexicon of Photius was first published, from Continental MSS., by Hermann, Leipzig, 4to, 1808. It formed the third volume of a set, of which the first and second volumes contained the lexicon ascribed to Zonaras. The edition of Hermann, however, having failed to satisfy the wants of the learned, an edition from a transcript of the Codex Galeanus, made by Porson, was published after the death of that eminent scholar, London, 1822, 4to and 8vo.

VII. Zōnăras Joannes (Ἰωάννης ὁ Ζωναρᾶς), a celebrated Byzantine historian and theologian, lived in the twelfth century, under the emperors Alexis I. Comnenus and Calo-Joannes. Besides his theological works, and his *Annales* (Χρονικόν), in eighteen books, we have a lexicon entitled Συναγωγὴ λέξεων συλλεγεῖσα ἐκ διαφόρων βιβλίων, κ. τ. λ. It was published for the first time by Tittmann, Leipzig, 1808, 2 vols. 4to.

VIII. Suidas (Σουΐδας),[1] a Greek lexicographer, of whom nothing is known. No certain conclusions as to the age of the compiler can be derived from any passages in the work, since it may have received numerous interpolations and additions. Eustathius, who lived during the latter half of the twelfth century of our era, quotes the lexicon of Suidas; and there are passages in the work referring to Michael Psellus, who lived at the close of the eleventh century. The lexicon of Suidas is a dictionary of words, arranged in alphabetical order, with some few peculiarities of arrangement; but it contains both words which are found in dictionaries of languages, and also names of persons and places, with extracts from ancient Greek writers, grammarians, scholiasts, and lexicographers, and some extracts from later Greek authors. The names of persons comprehend both persons who are mentioned in sacred and profane history, which shows that if the work is by one hand, it is by a Christian; but there is no inconsistency in supposing that the original of the lexicon, which now goes under the name of Suidas, is a work of earlier date even than the time of Stephanus of Byzantium, and that it received large accessions from various hands. No well-conceived plan has been the basis of this work; it is incomplete as to the number of articles, and exceedingly irregular and unequal in the execution. Some articles are pretty complete, others contain no information at all. As to the biographical notices, it has been conjectured that Suidas, or the compiler, got them all from one source, which, it is farther supposed, may be the *Onomatologos* or *Pinax* of Hesychius of Miletus, who flourished about A.D. 540. The work of Suidas, though without merit as to its execution, is valuable both for the literary history of antiquity, for the explanation of words, and for the citations from many ancient writers; and a prodigious amount of critical labor has been bestowed upon it. Many emendations have been made on the text by Toup and others.

The first edition of Suidas was by Demetrius Chalcondylas, Milan, 1499, fol., without a Latin version. The second, by the elder Aldus, Venice, 1514, fol., is also without a Latin version: this edition was reprinted by Froben, Basle, 1544, fol., with some corrections. The first Latin translation of Suidas was made by Hieron. Wolf, Basle, 1564, 1581, fol. The first edition which contained both the Greek text and a Latin version was by Æmilius Portus, Geneva, 1619, 2 vols. fol., and 1630, with a new title. The

[1] *Smith, Dict. Biogr., s. v.*

Latin version is said to be better than Wolf's. The edition of Küster appeared at Cambridge, 1705, 3 vols. folio. The basis of this edition is not the *editio princeps*, but that of Portus. Küster corrected the text with the aid of the MSS., added numerous good notes, and improved the version of Portus. But he dealt with the Greek text rather in an arbitrary way, and rejected all that he considered to be interpolated. The edition of Suidas by Gaisford, in three handsome volumes, folio, appeared at Oxford in 1834. The first two volumes contain the text, without a Latin version, and the notes, which are chiefly selected from Küster and others. The third volume contains *Index Küsterianus Rerum et Nominum Propriorum quæ extra seriem suam in Suidæ Lexico occurrunt; Index Glossarum Personarum Verborumque notatu digniorum;* and *Index Scriptorum a Suida citatorum.* In his preface Gaisford states that he used nearly the same MSS. as Küster, but that Küster was careless in noting the readings of the MSS. Gaisford has given the various readings of the best MSS., and those of the edition of Chalcondylas. The edition of Bernhardy, Halle, 1834–50, 4to (not yet complete), contains a Latin version, and notes. It is founded on the edition of Gaisford.

WRITERS ON DIALECT.

IX. Gregorius (or Georgius) Corinthus,[1] more correctly Gregorius (or Georgius) Pardus, was archbishop of Corinth, whence the name given him in some MSS. of *Corinthus*, which last was long supposed to have been his true name. The time when he lived is uncertain, though he would seem to have been later than the reign of Alexis I. Comnenus (A.D. 1081–1118). His only published work is Περὶ διαλέκτων (*De Dialectis*), frequently printed as an appendix to the earlier Greek lexicons, or in the collections of grammatical treatises. All these earlier editions were made from two or three MSS., and were very defective. But in the last century, Gisbertus Koenius, Greek professor at Franeker, by the collation of fresh MSS., published the work in a more complete form, with a preface and notes, Leyden, 1766, 8vo. An edition by G. H. Schaefer, containing all the matter in Koenius's edition, together with other that was new, appeared at Leipzig in 1811. In this edition is a *Commentatio Palæographica* by Bast.

X. Thomas Magister,[2] a rhetorician and grammarian, flourished about A.D. 1310. He appears to have been a native of Thessalonica, to have lived at the court of Andronicus Palæologus I., and to have held the offices of marshal (*Magister Officiorum*) and keeper of the archives (*Chartophylax*); but he afterward retired to a monastery, where he assumed the name of *Theodūlus*, and devoted himself to the study of the ancient Greek authors. His chief work was a *Lexicon of Attic Words* (κατὰ ἀλφάβητον ὀνομάτων Ἀττικῶν ἐκλογαί), compiled from the works of the elder grammarians, but with very little judgment. The work has some value, on account of its containing much from the elder grammarians which would otherwise have been lost. But when he deserts his guides, he often falls into the most serious errors. He wrote also scholia on Pindar, Euripides, and Aristophanes, the remains of which are merged in the collections of ancient scholia, and also lives of those authors, which are prefixed to some of the editions of their works. His other writings consist of letters and orations.

An excellent edition of the *Attic Lexicon*, with notes by Heinsius, Wolf, and many

---

1 *Smith, Dict. Biogr., s. v.*

2 *Id. ib.*

other scholars, was published by Bernard, Leyden, 1757, 8vo. The work has been recently edited by Ritschl, with valuable *Prolegomena*, Halle, 1832, 8vo. An edition of the *Orations* and *Epistles* was published at Upsala, 1693, 4to, by Laurentius Norrmann. Two additional orations were published in the *Nova Collectio Veterum Scriptorum* of Mai, vol. iii., p. 145, *seqq.*; p. 173, *seqq.*, 1827, 4to.

XI. Georgius Lecapenus, a monk of Thessaly, lived about the middle of the fourteenth century, and wrote, among other things, a lexicon of Attic words, in alphabetical order, extracts from which have been given by Villoison, *Anecdota Græca*, vol. ii., p. 79, and by Matthæi, *Lect. Mosq.*, vol. i., p. 55.

AUTHORS OF BIBLIOGRAPHICAL AND OTHER COLLECTIONS.

XII. Photius,[1] of whose life we have already given a sketch, compiled, among other works, a Μυριόβιβλον ἢ Βιβλιοθήκη (*Myriobiblum seu Bibliotheca*). This is the most important and valuable of his works. It may be described as an extensive review of ancient Greek literature, by a scholar of immense erudition and sound judgment. It is an extraordinary monument of literary energy, for it was written while the author was engaged in his embassy to Assyria, at the request of his brother Tarasius, who was much grieved at the separation, and desired an account of the books which Photius had read in his absence. It thus conveys a pleasing impression, not only of the literary acquirements and extraordinary industry, but of the fraternal affection of the writer. It opens with a prefatory address to Tarasius, recapitulating the circumstances under which it was composed, and stating that it contained a notice of two hundred and seventy-nine volumes. The extant copies contain a notice of two hundred and eighty: the discrepancy, which is of little moment, may have originated either in the mistake of Photius himself, or in some alteration of the divisions by some transcriber. The two hundred and eighty divisions of the *Bibliotheca* must be understood to express the number of volumes (codices) or manuscripts, and not of writers or of works. The works of some writers, as, for instance, of Philo Judæus (Cod. 103–105), occupy several divisions; and, on the other hand, one division (for instance, Cod. 125, *Justini Martyris Scripta Varia*) sometimes comprehends a notice of several different works written in one codex. The writers examined are of all classes: the greater number, however, are theologians, writers of ecclesiastical history, and of the biography of eminent churchmen; but several are secular historians, philosophers, and orators, heathen or Christian, of remote or recent times, lexicographers, and medical writers; only one or two are poets, and those on religious subjects, and there are also one or two writers of romances or love-tales. There is no formal classification of these various writers, though a series of writers or writings of the same class frequently occurs. In fact, the works appear to be arranged in the order in which they were read. The notices of the writers vary much in length: those in the earlier part are very briefly noticed, the later ones more fully. Several valuable works, now lost, are known to us chiefly by the analyses or extracts which Photius has given of them.

[1] *Smith, Dict. Biogr., s. v.*

The first edition of the *Bibliotheca* was put forth by Hoeschelius, Augsburg, 1601, fol. Some of the Epistles were subjoined. There was no Latin version. A Latin version, and scholia, by Schottus of Antwerp, were published in 1606, Augsburg, fol.; but the version is inaccurate, and has been severely criticised. It was, however, reprinted with the Greek text at Geneva, 1612, fol., and Rouen, 1653, fol. This last edition is a very splendid one, but inconvenient from its size. An edition with a revised text, formed on a collation of four MSS., was published by Bekker, Berlin, 1824–25, 2 vols. thin 4to. It is convenient from its size, and the copiousness of its index, but has neither version nor notes.

XIII. Eudŏcia,[1] wife of the emperors Constantine XI. (Ducas) and Romanus IV. (Diogenes), compiled a dictionary of history and mythology, which she called Ἰωνιά, i. e., *Collection* or *Bed of Violets.* It is prefaced by an address to her husband Romanus Diogenes, in which she describes the work as "a collection of genealogies of gods, heroes, and heroines, of their metamorphoses, and of the fables and stories respecting them found in the ancients; containing, also, notices of various philosophers." The sources from which the work was compiled are, in a great degree, the same as those used in the lexicon of Suidas. This work was printed for the first time by Villoison, in his *Anecdota Græca*, vol. i., p. 1, *seqq.*, Venice, 1781.

CHAPTER LIX.

SEVENTH OR BYZANTINE PERIOD—*continued.*

HISTORIANS.

I. Before treating of the historians, properly so called, who belong to the present period, we must make mention of a writer that has rendered the greatest service to a branch of knowledge called, with reason, one of the eyes of history; for without this guide history runs the risk of losing herself amid the chaos of events that crowd around her. The science to which we refer is *Chronology*, and the writer is *Eusebius.*

II. Eusĕbius (Εὐσέβιος),[2] of Cæsarea, took the surname of Pamphili, to commemorate his devoted friendship for Pamphilus, bishop of Cæsarea. He was born in Palestine about A.D. 264, toward the end of the reign of the Emperor Gallienus. He was made Bishop of Cæsarea in A.D. 315, and died about 340. Eusebius was a man of great learning. The work which will here claim our attention is the *Chronicon* (Χρονικὰ παντοδαπῆς ἱστορίας), a work of great value to us in the study of ancient history. It is in two books. The first, entitled Χρονογραφία, contains a sketch of the history of several ancient nations, as the Chaldæans, Assyrians, Medes, Persians, Lydians, Hebrews, and Egyptians. It is chiefly taken from the Πεντάβιβλον χρονολογικόν of Africanus, and gives lists of kings and other magistrates, with short accounts of remarkable events from the creation to the time of Eusebius. The second book consists of synchronological tables, with similar catalogues of rulers and striking occurrences, from the time of Abraham to the celebration of Constantine's *Vicennalia* at Nic-

---

1 *Smith, Dict. Biogr., s. v.*

2 *Id. ib.*

omedia, A.D. 327, and at Rome, A.D. 328. Eusebius's object in writing it was to give an account of ancient history previous to the time of Christ, in order to establish belief in the truth of the Old Testament history, and to point out the superior antiquity of the Mosaic to any other writings. In the course of the work Eusebius gives extracts from Berosus, Sanchoniathon, Polyhistor, Cephalion, and Manetho, which materially increase its value. Some of the other works of Eusebius, although not falling within our limits, may briefly be noticed here. These are, 1. The *Præparatio Evangelica* (Εὐαγγελικῆς ἀποδείξεως προπαρασκευή), in fifteen books, a collection of various facts and quotations from old writers, by which it was supposed that the mind would be prepared to receive the evidences of Christianity. 2. The *Demonstratio Evangelica* (Εὐαγγελικὴ ἀπόδειξις), in twenty books, of which ten are extant, a collection of evidences, chiefly from the Old Testament, addressed principally to the Jews. 3. The *Ecclesiastical History* (Ἐκκλησιαστικὴ Ἱστορία), in ten books, containing the history of Christianity from the birth of Christ to the death of Licinius, A.D. 324.

The Greek text of the *Chronicon* is lost, with the exception of some fragments preserved by George Syncellus in his Chronicle, and by Eusebius himself in his *Præparatio Evangelica*. There is extant, however, part of a Latin translation of it by Jerome, published by Scaliger, Leyden, 1606, of which another and enlarged edition appeared at Amsterdam, 1658. Subsequently, in 1792, an Armenian of Constantinople, named Georgius Johannis, discovered an Armenian translation of the entire work. He made a copy of this, and transmitted it, in 1794, to Dr. Zohrab, at Venice. Of this Armenian version Zohrab and Mai published a Latin translation at Milan, 1818, together with the Greek fragments. In the same year Aucher published at Venice the Chronicon in Armenian, Greek (as far as extant), and Latin. The best edition of the *Præparatio Evangelica* is by Heinichen, Leipzig, 1842, 2 vols. 8vo, and of the *Ecclesiastical History*, by the same, Leipzig, 1827, 3 vols. 8vo.

III. The first historian, properly so called, during the period we are at present considering, was Praxagŏras, a native of Athens, who lived after the time of Constantine the Great, probably under his sons. He wrote, at the age of nineteen, two books on the Athenian kings; at the age of twenty-two, two books on the history of Constantine; and at the age of thirty-one, six books on the history of Alexander the Great. All these works were written in the Ionic dialect. None of them have come down to us, with the exception of a few extracts made by Photius from the history of Constantine. In this work Praxagoras, though a heathen, placed Constantine before all other emperors.

IV. Next in order is Eunapius, a sophist and historian, born at Sardis in A.D. 347, and who seems to have lived till the reign of the Emperor Theodosius the younger. He wrote, 1. *Lives of Sophists*, still extant, containing twenty-three biographies of sophists, most of whom were contemporaries of Eunapius, or had lived shortly before him. Though these biographies are exceedingly brief, and the style is intolerably inflated, yet they supply us with important information respecting a period in the history of philosophy, which, without this work, would be buried in utter obscurity. 2. *A continuation of the History of Dexippus*, in fourteen books. It began with A.D. 270, and went down to 404. Of this work we have only extracts.

The latest and best edition of the Lives of the Sophists, which gives a much improved text, with a commentary and notes by Wyttenbach, is that of Boissonade, Amsterdam, 1822, 2 vols. 8vo. The fragments of the History are best given in the *Corpus Script. Hist. Byzant.* of Bekker and Niebuhr, and in Müller's *Fragm. Hist. Græc.*, vol. iv., p. 7, *seqq.*, forming part of Didot's *Bibliotheca Græca*, Paris, 1851.

V. Olympiodorus,[1] an historical writer, a native of Thebes, in Egypt, lived in the fifth century after Christ. He wrote a work in twenty-two books, entitled Ἱστορικοὶ λόγοι, which comprised the history of the Western Empire under the reign of Honorius, from A.D. 407 to October, A.D. 425. Olympiodorus took up the history from about the point at which Eunapius had ended. The original work is lost, but an abridgment of it has been preserved by Photius, who describes the style of the work as being clear, but without force or vigor, loose, and descending to vulgarity, so as not to merit being called a history. Of this Photius thinks that the author himself was aware, and that for this reason he spoke of his work as not being a history, but a collection of materials for a history (ὕλη συγγραφῆς). It was dedicated to the Emperor Theodosius II. It appears, from what Photius has preserved of his writings, that Olympiodorus was a heathen.

The abridgment of Photius has been several times published. It is best given, however, in the Collection of the Byzantine Historians, by Bekker and Niebuhr, Bonn, 1829, and in Müller's *Fragm. Hist. Græc.*, vol. iv., p. 57, *seqq.*, forming part of Didot's *Bibliotheca Græca*, Paris, 1851.

VI. Zosĭmus (Ζώσιμος)[2] lived in the time of the younger Theodosius. He wrote a history of the Roman Empire, in six books, which is still extant. This work must have been written after A.D. 425, as an event is mentioned in it which took place in that year. The first book comprises a sketch of the history of the early emperors, down to the end of the reign of Dioclesian, A.D. 305. The second, third, and fourth books are devoted to the history of the fourth century, which is treated much less concisely. The fifth and sixth books embrace the period from A.D. 395 to 410, when Attalus was deposed. The work of Zosimus is mainly, though not altogether, an abridgment or compilation of the works of previous historians. His style is concise, clear, pure, and not unpleasing. His chief fault, as an historical writer, is his neglect of chronology. Zosimus was a pagan, and comments severely upon the faults and crimes of the Christian emperors. Hence his credibility has been assailed by several Christian writers. There are, no doubt, numerous errors of judgment to be found in the work, and sometimes (especially in the case of Constantine) an intemperate expression of opinion, which somewhat exaggerates, if it does not distort, the truth; but he does not seem fairly chargeable with deliberate invention or willful misrepresentation.

The best editions of Zosimus are by Reitemeier, Leipzig, 1784, 8vo, and by Bekker, Bonn, 1837, forming part of the Collection of Byzantine Historians.

BYZANTINE HISTORIANS.[3]

VII. This is the name given to a series of Greek historians and writers, who lived under the Eastern or Byzantine emperors between the sixth

[1] *Smith, Dict. Biogr.*, *s. v.* [2] *Id. ib.* [3] *Penny Cyclopædia*, vol. vi, p. 81, *seqq.*

and the fifteenth centuries. They may be divided into two classes: 1. The historians properly so called, whose collected works constitute a complete history of the Byzantine empire from the time of Constantine the Great to the taking of Constantinople by the Turks; and, 2. The general chroniclers, who have attempted to give a chronography of the world from the earliest times.

VIII. The historians are as follows:

1. Joannes Zonăras, of Constantinople, first an officer of the imperial court, and afterward a monk of Mount Athos, lived in the twelfth century, under the Emperors Alexis I. Comnenus and Calo-Joannes. We have already mentioned him under the lexicographers of this period. He wrote a *Chronicon* (Χρονικόν), or "Annals of the World," in eighteen books. In the first part of his work he belongs to the class of general chroniclers or compilers; but from the time of Constantine he treats more particularly of the history of the Eastern empire, which he brings down to the death of Alexis I. Comnenus, in 1118. In the latter part of his work, Zonaras wrote as an eye-witness of the events he describes, but with a brevity which is surprising, considering the many interesting and important occurrences of his time. His deficiencies, however, in this respect, are amply supplied by Anna Comnena, the daughter of the Emperor Alexis. 2. Nicētas Acominātus (Νικήτας Ἀκομινάτος), also called Choniātes, because he was a native of Chonæ, formerly Colossæ, in Phrygia, one of the most important Byzantine historians, was born about the middle of the twelfth century, and filled several high offices at the court of Isaac Angelus (A.D. 1185–1195). He died at Nicæa in 1216. His "History" of the Byzantine emperors, in twenty-one books, begins with 1118 and ends with 1206. 3. Nicephorus Gregoras (Νικηφόρος ὁ Γρηγορᾶς), of Heraclea Pontica, enjoyed the favor of Andronicus Palæologus the elder; but, owing to the controversy between the Palamites and Acindynites, he was confined in a convent by the Patriarch in 1351. He was afterward released, and died in 1359. He wrote a Byzantine, or, as he styles it, a "Roman" history, in thirty-eight books, of which the first twenty-four only have been printed, containing the history of the Byzantine empire from 1204 to 1331. The fourteen remaining in MS. bring the history down to 1359. 4. Laonīcus, or Nicolaus, Chalcondȳles (Λαόνικος, or Νικόλαος, Χαλκονδύλης), of Athens, a Byzantine historian of the fifteenth century, wrote a "History of the Turks, and of the Downfall of the Greek Empire," in ten books, to the year 1462. An anonymous writer has continued the history of the Turks down to 1565.

IX. The four writers mentioned in the preceding paragraph form by themselves an entire history of the Byzantine empire, from the time of Constantine to the Turkish conquest. The following writers have treated of detached periods of the same history, or have written the lives of particular emperors.[1] 5. Procopius (Προκόπιος), of Cæsarea, in Palestine, the most celebrated of the Byzantine writers, was born at the beginning of the sixth century of our era, and wrote the "History of his own Time," in eight books, to the year 545. He also wrote a "Secret History" (*Anec-*

[1] *Penny Cyclopædia, l. c.*

dota) of the reign of Justinian down to the year 553, which, as to the manner in which he speaks of that emperor and his court, contrasts singularly with the panegyrical tone of his former work. 6. Agathias (Ἀγαθίας), of Myrina, in Æolis, a poet as well as historian of the sixth century, well known for his Anthology (of which we have made mention in an early part of the present volume), studied first at Alexandrea, whence he removed to Constantinople in 554, being then about eighteen years of age, and applied himself to the study of the law, in which he became eminent. He was surnamed *Scholasticus*, a word which then meant an advocate. He wrote a history, in five books, of the years 553–59 of Justinian's reign, forming a sequel to Procopius. He died about 582. Agathias is one of the most trustworthy Byzantine historians; inferior to Procopius in talent and information, but superior to him in honesty. The impartial manner in which he speaks of the various parties and sects, and particularly of the two great religious systems which divided the world in his time, has made it a matter of dispute whether he was a Christian or a pagan. His account of the Persians, and their celebrated King Chosroes, or Nushirvan, is much valued for its accuracy and fairness. 7. Menander (Μένανδρος), of Constantinople, surnamed Protector (Προτέκτωρ, i. e., *body-guard*), continued the history of Agathias to the year 582. Menander's history is lost, but fragments of it are found in the works of Constantine Porphyrogenitus, which relate to the history of the Huns, the Avari, and other Northern and Eastern races, and also to the negotiations and missions between Justinian and Chosroes. 8. Joannes, of Epiphanēa, in Syria, flourished toward the close of the sixth century. He wrote a history of the Persian war under the Emperor Maurice, which has never been printed, and the only MS. of it known is in the Heidelberg library. 9. Theophylactus Simocatta, an Egyptian by descent, but a Locrian by birth, lived in the first part of the seventh century, and wrote a history, in eight books, from A.D. 582 until the death of Maurice in 602. 10. Joannes, a monk of Jerusalem, in the eighth century, wrote a brief history of the Iconoclasts, and probably an anonymous work against Constantine IV. 11. Theodosius, a monk of Syracuse, in the ninth century, has left a narrative of the taking of Syracuse by the Spanish Arabs.

12. Constantinus VI., surnamed Porphyrogenĭtus, wrote the life of his grandfather, Basilius the Macedonian, from 867 to 886. He also wrote several other works, which may serve as illustrations of the Byzantine history, such as *De Administrando Imperio*, on the administration of the the state, addressed to his son Romanus; *De Cæremoniis Aulæ Byzantinæ; De Thematibus*, on the military divisions of the empire. He also caused several learned men to compile a kind of historical library out of the works of all previous historians. This great compilation was divided into fifty-three books, of which the titles of twenty-six only are known. One was on the succession of kings, another on the art of generalship, &c. Under each of these heads, passages from the various historians bearing upon the subject were collected. Three books alone, more or less mutilated, have come down to us. One, entitled *De Legationibus*, is an account of the various embassies between the Romans and other nations;

another, *De Sententiis;* and the third, *De Virtute et Vitio.* 13. Genesius, who lived in the middle of the tenth century, wrote a history, in four books, containing the reigns of Leo V., the Armenian; Michael II., the Stammerer; Theophilus; Michael III.; and Basil I., the Macedonian, who died in 886. The work of Genesius is short, and altogether a poor compilation; but as it contains the events of a period of Byzantine history of which we have but scanty information, it is, nevertheless, of importance. 14. Leontius, of Byzantium, called the younger, wrote also a history of the same period, to serve as an introduction to Constantine's Life of Basilius. 15. An anonymous writer has left a continuation of Constantine's Life of Basilius, embracing the lives of Leo VI. and his brother Alexander, of Constantine VI. himself, and his son Romanus. 16. Joannes Cameniāta, of Thessalonica, wrote an account of the taking of that city by the Saracens in 904, of which he was an eye-witness.[1]

17. Leo Diacŏnus, of Kaloë, a town of Asia, near the sources of the Caÿster, born about 950, accompanied Basilius II. in his wars against the Bulgarians, and wrote the lives of Romanus, Nicephorus Phocas, and Tzimisces, from 959 to 975. 18. Michael Constantine Psellus wrote a history from the death of Tzimisces, in 975, till the accession of Constantine Ducas in 1059. It has not yet been published. 19. Nicephorus Bryennius, the husband of Anna Comnena, wrote "Historical Materials," being a kind of memoirs of the Comneni family, to the accession of Alexis I. 20. Anna Comnēna has written the history of her father Alexis. 21. Joannes Cinnămus, who lived toward the end of the twelfth century, was imperial notary at Constantinople. He wrote the lives of John Comnenus and of Manuel his son, from 1118, where Anna Comnena ends, till 1176. Like his predecessors, he is partial against the Latins or Franks, and especially unjust toward Roger I. of Sicily, who was a great man for his time, though an enemy of the Byzantines. 22. Georgius Acropolīta, born in 1220, at Constantinople, filled several important offices under Michael Palæologus, and died in 1282. There are two works under his name, one styled a "Chronography," and the other a "Short Chronicle of the late Events," both referring to the period from 1204, when the Franks took Constantinople, to 1261, when they were finally expelled. Acropolita has also written a general chronicle, from the creation to the taking of Constantinople by the Franks, which is not yet printed. 23. Georgius Pachymĕres (Γεώργιος ὁ Παχυμέρης), one of the most important of the Byzantine writers, was born at Nicæa in 1242. After the recovery of Constantinople by the Greeks, he was raised to high offices in the state. He wrote a "Byzantine History," which forms a continuation to Acropolita's work, and comes down to 1308. Pachymeres is a faithful but dull writer. He wrote, also, several philosophical works, and a history of his own life.[2]

24. Joannes Cantacuzēnus, after his abdication of the empire in 1355, retired to a convent, where he wrote a Byzantine history from 1320 to 1357. Cantacuzenus is, in general, a good authority for the history of that period, in which he acted an important part, though he is, of course, somewhat partial in his own cause. 25. Joannes Ducas, of the imperial

[1] *Penny Cyclopædia, l. c.*

[2] *Ibid.*

family of that name, fled from Constantinople at the time of the Turkish invasion, and took refuge at Lesbos under the Genoese adventurer, Prince Castelluzzi. He wrote a Byzantine history, which begins from Adam, after the fashion of the Chroniclers, and is but a brief general chronicle as far as the year 1341, after which his account becomes more circumstantial, being more especially occupied with the history of the latter period of the eastern empire. It ends with the taking of Lesbos by the Turks in 1462. This latter part, therefore, forms a continuation to Cantacuzenus. 26. Joannes Anagnostes, of Thessalonica, has left an account of the taking of that city by the Turks in 1430. 27. Joannes Cananus has written a history of the war against Sultan Murad II. in 1420. 28. Georgius Phranza, born in 1401, of a family related to the Palæologi, filled some of the highest offices in the state under the last emperors. He was made prisoner by the Turks at the taking of Constantinople, was sold as a slave, recovered his freedom, and took refuge with Thomas Palæologus, prince of Peloponnesus. When the Turks invaded that part of Greece, Phranza escaped to Italy, and at last became a monk, at Corfu, in 1468. There he wrote his "Chronicle," in four books, which begins with 1260 and ends with 1477, embracing the whole history of the Palæologi. The work of Phranza is most valuable, though it is full of digressions upon religious controversies, the origin of comets, &c.[1]

X. The following are the *general chroniclers*, properly so called, who are also included under the general appellation of Byzantine historians: 1. Georgius Syncellus, who lived in the eighth century, wrote a "Chronography," from the beginning of the world to the time of Dioclesian, in which he has availed himself of Eusebius and Africanus. 2. Theophanes Isaacius, of Constantinople, who died about 817, continued the Chronicle of Syncellus from 280 till 813. 3. Joannes of Antioch, called Malalas, a Syrian word, meaning a rhetor or sophist, lived in the ninth century, and wrote a Chronicle from Adam till 566. 4. Joannes Scylitzes, who lived in the eleventh century, wrote a "Short History," or Chronicle, from 811 until 1057, which he afterward recast and continued until 1081. 5. Leo Grammaticus wrote a "Chronography," which is a continuation of Theophanes from 813 to 949. 6. Georgius Monachus also left a Chronicle, embracing the same period as Leo's. 7. The Chronicon Paschale, called also Alexandrean Chronicle, is attributed by some to Georgius, the bishop of Alexandrea, who lived in the seventh century. It is also called *Fasti Siculi*, because the MS. was discovered in Sicily. It extends from the beginning of the world to 1042. 8. Georgius Hamartōlus, an Archimandrite, wrote a Chronicle to the year 842, which is yet unedited. 9. Joannes of Sicily wrote, in the ninth century, a Chronicle from the creation of the world till 866, which is not yet printed. An anonymous continuation of it till 1222 exists in the imperial library at Vienna. 10. Nicephorus, patriarch of Constantinople in the first part of the ninth century, has left a *Breviarium Chronographicum*, or short Chronicle, from the creation to the author's death in 828, giving series of the kings, emper-

[1] *Penny Cyclopædia, l. c.*

ors, patriarchs, bishops, &c. He wrote also a *Breviarium Historicum*, or general history of events from 602 to 770.[1]

11. Julius Pollux, not the author of the Onomasticon, wrote a Chronicle with the title of *Historia Physica*, from the creation to the reign of Valens. A MS. in the National Library at Paris brings it down to the death of Romanus the younger in 963. This Chronicle is chiefly engrossed with church matters. 12. Georgius Cedrēnus, a monk of the eleventh century, wrote a Chronicle, compiled chiefly from the former chronicles of Scylitzes and others. It is mixed up with fictions, and is one of the least valuable in the Byzantine collection. 13. Simeon Metaphrastes filled some high stations at the imperial court in the first part of the tenth century. His Chronicle comes down to 963, and has the merit of being compiled from the works of ten lost writers, who lived between Leo Grammaticus and Michael Psellus. 14. Hippolytus, of Thebes, lived toward the end of the tenth and the beginning of the eleventh centuries. He wrote a Chronicle from the birth of our Savior to his own time. 15. Michael Glykas, whose country and age are not ascertained, wrote a Chronicle from the creation to the year 1118. It is valuable both for its historical and its biblical references. 16. Constantine Manasses, who lived in the twelfth century, has left a Chronicle in verse down to 1081. 17. Ephræmius, believed to be the son of John XII., patriarch of Constantinople, wrote a Chronicle, in iambics, of the emperors, from Julius Cæsar to the restoration of the Byzantine empire after the Frankish invasion. It is followed by a chronology of the patriarchs of Constantinople till 1313. The whole poem contains ten thousand four hundred and ten lines. Mai published it first in his Vatican collection of unedited MSS. 18. Joel wrote a short general Chronicle of the world to the Frankish invasion of Constantinople in 1204. 19. Theodosius, of Melite, has left a Chronicle, which is not yet printed. Professor Tafel, of Tübingen, has published a notice of this writer (Tübingen, 1828), from the MS. of his Chronicle at Tübingen, and which was brought from Constantinople by Gerlach in 1578. 20. Hesychius, of Miletus, who lived under Justinus and Justinian, wrote a history of the world, which is lost, except a valuable fragment on the origin of Constantinople, which has been extracted and preserved by Codinus.[2]

XI. Besides the above historians and chroniclers, there are other Byzantine authors who have written on the statistics, politics, antiquities, &c., of the Roman empire, whose history, properly so called, they serve to illustrate, and who are generally included in the collection of Byzantine historical writers. Among these Procopius stands foremost by his curious work, *De Ædificiis Domini Justiniani* (Κτίσματα), in six books, which contains a brief notice of the towns, temples, convents, bridges, roads, walls, and fortifications built or repaired under the reign of Justinian. 2. Joannes Laurentius, called Lydus, from his being a native of Philadelphia, in Lydia, lived under Justinian, and was both a poet and prose writer. He has left a work "On the Roman Magistrates," which affords valuable assistance for the knowledge of Roman civil history.

[1] *Penny Cyclopædia, l. c.*

[2] *Ibid.*

The MS. was first discovered by Choiseul Gouffier and Villoison in the library of Prince Morousi, at Constantinople, in 1781, and is now in the public library at Paris. In the same MS. was found another work of Lydus, Περὶ διοσημειῶν, or *De Ostentis*, on divination or augury. He wrote also Περὶ μηνῶν συγγραφή, *De Mensibus Liber*, of which there are two epitomes or summaries and a fragment extant. 3. Hieroclés, called the *Grammarian*, to distinguish him from the philosopher of the same name, wrote a *Synecdēmos*, or traveller's guide, in which he describes the sixty-four provinces of the Eastern Empire, and the nine hundred and thirty-five cities or towns contained in it. He appears certainly to have lived previous to the tenth century. 4. Theophylactus, archbishop of Achris, in Bulgaria, in the latter part of the eleventh century, wrote a work "On the Education of Princes," intended for the younger Constantine, the son of Michael VII. Parapinaces. 5. Alexis I. Comnenus wrote *Novum Rationarium*, or inventory of the revenues of the state, in imitation of Augustus. 6. A monk of unknown name, who lived under Alexis I., wrote a book on the Antiquities of Constantinople, which gives a description of its buildings, monuments, &c. 7. Matthæus Blastăres, a monk, wrote, about 1305, an account of the numerous household charges and offices in the imperial palace of Constantinople. 8. Georgius Codīnus, surnamed *Curopalātes*, lived in the latter age of the empire, and wrote "On the Dignities and Offices of the Church and Court of Constantinople." 9. The Emperor Manuel Palæologus wrote a book "on the Education of Princes." He also wrote "a Dialogue with a Turk, held at Ancyra, in Galatia," where Manuel was once stationed in winter quarters with his auxiliary corps, serving under Sultan Bajazet. This work, which is yet unpublished, is said to give an interesting view of the tottering condition of the once mighty empire toward the beginning of the fifteenth century. There are also sixty-six unpublished letters of Manuel in the public library at Paris, which contain interesting allusions to the history of that period.[1]

Most of the Byzantine historians, chroniclers, and other writers, were collected and published in the great edition made by order and at the expense of Louis XIV., in 36 vols. fol., Paris, 1645–1711. The Jesuits Labbe and Maltrait, Petau and Poussines; the Dominicans Goar and Combéfis, Professor Fabrot, Charles du Fresne Seigneur du Cange; Allacci, the librarian of the Vatican; Banduri, librarian at Florence; Boivin, the king's librarian at Paris; and Bouilliaud, a mathematician, were each intrusted with parts of this splendid work. The Greek text is accompanied with a Latin translation and notes. The last volume contains the Arabian Chronicle of Abu Ben Raheb, which serves to illustrate Byzantine history. Another edition was published at Venice, in 23 vols. fol., 1729, and the following years, which contains several works omitted in the Paris edition, such as Phranza, Genesius, and Malalas. Others were published separately afterward as a supplement to the Venice edition: "Opera Georgii Pisidæ, Theodosii Diaconi et Corippi Africani," Rome, 1777, fol.; "Julii Pollucis Historia Sacra," Bologna, 1779, fol.; "Constantini Porphyrogeniti libri ii. De Cæremoniis Aulæ Byzantinæ," 2 vols. fol., Leipzig, 1751; "Leonis Diaconi Caloensis Historia," ed. Hase, Paris, 1819, fol. A new edition of the Byzantine historians was projected by the late B. G. Niebuhr, the first volume of which appeared at Bonn, 1828, 8vo. Since Niebuhr's death it has been carried on by Bekker, Dindorf, and other philologists, some of whom were associated with Niebuhr in the outset. It has already reached nearly fifty volumes, and will be, when completed,

[1] *Penny Cyclopædia, l. c.*

the best and most complete edition. The title is as follows: *Corpus Scriptorum Historiæ Byzantinæ. Editio emendatior et copiosior, consilio B. G. Niebuhrii C. F. instituta, auctoritate Academiæ Litterarum Regiæ Borussicæ continuata*, Bonn, 1828, &c.

CHAPTER LX.

SEVENTH OR BYZANTINE PERIOD—*continued.*

GEOGRAPHERS.

I. MARCIĀNUS (Μαρκιανός),[1] of Heraclea Pontica, a Greek geographer, lived after Ptolemy, whom he frequently quotes, and before Stephanus of Byzantium, who refers to him, but his exact date is uncertain. If he is the same Marcianus as the one mentioned by Synesius (Ep. 103) and Socrates (H. E., iv., 9), he must have lived at the beginning of the fifth century of the Christian era. He wrote a work in prose, entitled "A Periplus of the External Sea, both Eastern and Western, and of the largest Islands in it" (Περίπλους τῆς ἔξω θαλάσσης, ἑῴου τε καὶ ἑσπερίου, καὶ τῶν ἐν αὐτῇ μεγίστων νήσων). The term "External Sea" he used in opposition to the "Mediterranean," which, he says, had been sufficiently described by Artemidorus. This work was in two books, of which the former, on the Eastern and Southern seas, has come to us entire; but of the latter, which treated of the Western and Northern seas, we possess only the last three chapters on Africa, and a mutilated one on the distance from Rome to the principal cities of the world. In this work he chiefly follows Ptolemy, and in the calculation of the stadia he adopts the reckoning of Protagoras. He also made an epitome of the eleven books of the periplus of Artemidorus of Ephesus, but of this epitome we have only the introduction, and the periplus of Pontus, Bithynia, and Paphlagonia. It was not, however, simply an abridgment of Artemidorus, for Marcianus tells us that he made use of the works of other geographers who had written descriptions of coasts. Marcianus also published an edition of Menippus of Pergamum, a geographer who lived in the time of Augustus. Some fragments of this are preserved.

The works of Marcianus are edited by Hudson, in the *Geographi Græci Minores*, vol. i.; by Miller, in his "*Supplément aux dernières éditions des Petits Géographes*," Paris, 1839, 8vo; and separately by Hoffmann, *Marciani Periplus*, &c., Leipzig, 1841, 8vo.

II. STEPHĀNUS,[2] of Byzantium, called also STEPHANUS BYZANTINUS, was the author of a geographical lexicon, entitled *Ethnica* (Ἐθνικά), of which, unfortunately, we possess only an epitome. There are few ancient writers of any importance of whom we know so little as of Stephanus. All that can be affirmed of him with certainty is, that he was a grammarian of Constantinople, and lived after the time of Arcadius and Honorius, and before that of Justinian II. His work was reduced to an epitome by a certain Hermolaus, who dedicated his abridgment to Justinian II. According to the title, the chief object of the work was to specify the gentile names derived from the several names of places and countries in the

[1] *Smith, Dict. Biogr., s. v.*

[2] *Id. ib.*

ancient world. But, while this is done in every article, the amount of information given went far beyond this. Nearly every article in the epitome contains a reference to some ancient writer as an authority for the name of the place; but in the original, as we see from the extant fragments, there were considerable quotations from the ancient authors, besides a number of very interesting particulars, topographical, historical, mythological, and others. Thus the work was not merely what it professed to be, a lexicon of a special branch of technical grammar, but a valuable dictionary of geography. How great would have been its value to us, if it had come down to us unmutilated, may be seen by any one who compares the extant fragments of the original with the corresponding articles in the epitome. These fragments, however, are, unfortunately, very scanty.

The best editions of Stephanus are that of Berkelius, Leyden, 1688, fol., reprinted 1694, fol.; that of Dindorf, Leipzig, 1825, &c., 4 vols. 8vo; that of Westermann, Leipzig, 1839, 8vo; and that of Meineke, Berlin, 1849, &c., 2 vols. 8vo.

III. Cosmas (Κοσμᾶς),[1] commonly called Indicopleustes (Indian navigator), an Egyptian monk, flourished in the reign of Justinian, about A.D. 535. In early life he followed the employment of a merchant, and visited many foreign countries, such as Ethiopia, Syria, Arabia, Persia, and almost all places of the East. Being an attentive observer of every thing that met his eye, he carefully registered his remarks upon the scenes and objects which presented themselves. But a migratory life became irksome. After many years spent in this manner, he bade adieu to worldly occupations, took up his residence in a monastery, and devoted himself to a contemplative life. Here he composed his Τοπογραφία Χριστιανική, *Topographia Christiana*, in twelve books. The last book, as hitherto published, is imperfect at the end. The object of the treatise is to show, in opposition to the universal opinion of astronomers, that the earth is not spherical, but an extended surface. The only value of the work consists in the geographical and historical information which it contains. Its author describes in general, with great accuracy, the situation of countries, the manners of their people, their modes of commercial intercourse, the nature and properties of plants and animals, and many other particulars of a like kind, which serve to throw light upon the Scriptures. His diction is plain and familiar. So far is it from approaching elegance or elevation, that it is even below mediocrity. He did not aim at pompous or polished phraseology; and, in several places, he modestly acknowledges that his mode of expression is homely and inelegant.

The work of Cosmas was first published by Montfaucon from a MS. of the tenth century, in Greek and Latin, in his *Collectio Nova Patrum et Scriptorum Græcorum*, Paris, 1706, fol., vol. ii., p. 113–346, to which the editor prefixed an able and learned preface. This is the best edition. It is also printed in the *Bibliotheca Veterum Patrum*, edited by Gallandi, Venice, 1765, vol. xi., p. 401, *seqq.*

---

1 *Smith, Dict. Biogr.*, *s. v.*

CHAPTER LXI.

SEVENTH OR BYZANTINE PERIOD—*continued.*

MATHEMATICIANS.

I. Diophantus (Διόφαντος),[1] of Alexandrea, is the only Greek writer on Algebra. His period is wholly unknown, which is not to be wondered at, if we consider that he stands quite alone as to the subject which he treated. But, looking at the improbability of all mention of such a writer being omitted by Proclus and Pappus, modern inquirers have felt strongly inclined to place him toward the end of the fifth century of our era at the earliest. He wrote *Arithmetica* (Ἀριθμητικά), in thirteen books, of which only six are extant, and one book, *De Multangulis Numeris*, on polygonal numbers. These books contain a system of reasoning on numbers by the aid of general symbols, and with some use of symbols of operation; so that, though the demonstrations are very much conducted in words at length, and arranged so as to remind us of Euclid, there is no question that the work is algebraical; not a treatise *on algebra*, but an algebraical treatise on the relations of integer numbers, and on the solution of equations of more than one variable in integers. The question whether Diophantus was an original inventor, or whether he received a hint from India, the only country we know of which could then have given one, is of great difficulty. The very great similarity, however, of the Diophantine and Hindu algebra (as far as the former goes) makes it almost certain that the two must have had a common origin, or have come one from the other, though it is clear that Diophantus, if a borrower, has completely recast the subject by the introduction of Euclid's form of demonstration.

The first Greek edition, with Latin version, and original notes (the scholia of the monk Maximus Planudes on the first two books being rejected as useless), is that of Bachet de Meziriac, Paris, 1621, fol. Fermat left materials for the second and best edition (Greek and Latin), in which is preserved all that was good in Bachet, and, in particular, his Latin version, with most valuable comments and additions of his own (it being peculiarly his subject).

II. Pappus (Πάππος),[2] of Alexandrea, one of the later Greek geometers, is said by Suidas to have lived under Theodosius (A.D. 379–395). The writings mentioned as having come from the pen of Pappus are as follows: Μαθηματικῶν συναγωγῶν βιβλία, the celebrated *Mathematical Collections.* This work, as we now have it in print, consists of the last six of eight books. Only portions of these books have been published in Greek. 2. Χορογραφία οἰκουμενική. 3. Εἰς τὰ τέσσαρα βιβλία τοῦ Πτολεμαίου μεγάλης Συντάξεως ὑπόμνημα. 4. Ποταμοὺς τοὺς ἐν Λιβύῃ. 5. Ὀνειροκριτικά. The last four have not reached us. They are mentioned by Suidas, and just as here written down in continuous quotation, headed βιβλία δὲ αὐτοῦ.

[1] *De Morgan; Smith's Dict. Biogr., s. v.*

[2] *Id. ib.*

There are two Latin editions of Pappus: the first by Commandinus, Pesaro, 1588, fol., and the second by Manolessius, Bologna, 1660, fol. There is also a small portion of a short comment on a part of the fifth book of Ptolemy's Syntaxis, which Theon has preserved and commented on (*Syntaxis*, Basle, 1538, p. 235, of Theon's commentary). This may be a part of the work mentioned by us as No. 3; for, though the portion in question is on the *fifth* book, yet perhaps the *four* books mentioned by Suidas are not the *first* four books.

III. THEON (Θέων), the younger, so called to distinguish him from the elder Theon, who lived in the time of Hadrian. Theon the younger was a native of Alexandrea, and father of the celebrated Hypatia. He is best known as an astronomer and geometer, and lived in the time of Theodosius the elder. Both Theons were heathens, a fact which the date of the second makes it desirable to state; and each held the Platonism of his period. Of Theon of Alexandrea the following works have come down to us: 1. Scholia on Aratus. 2. An edition of Euclid. 3. A Commentary on the Almagest of Ptolemy, addressed to his son Epiphanius. 4. A Commentary on the Tables of Ptolemy.

The scholia on Aratus, of which there are at least two sets, are printed in the editions of that poet. In like manner, the commentary on the Almagest is given with many of the editions of Ptolemy. The commentary on the Tables of Ptolemy was published by Halma, in three parts, 1822–25, 4to, Paris.

IV. HYPATĬA (Ὑπατία),[1] a lady of Alexandrea, daughter of Theon, by whom she was instructed in philosophy and mathematics. She soon made such immense progress in these branches of knowledge, that she is said to have presided over the Neo-Platonic school of Plotinus at Alexandrea, where she expounded the principles of his system to a numerous auditory. She appears to have been most graceful, modest, and beautiful, but nevertheless to have been a victim to slander and falsehood. She was accused of too much familiarity with Orestes, prefect of Alexandrea, and the charge spread among the clergy, who took up the notion that she interrupted the friendship of Orestes with their archbishop Cyril. In consequence of this, a number of them, at whose head was a reader named Peter, seized her in the street, and dragged her from her chariot into one of the churches, where they stripped her and tore her to pieces. Theodoret accuses Cyril of sanctioning this proceeding; but Cave holds this to be incredible, though on no grounds except his own opinion of Cyril's general character. Synesius valued Hypatia highly, and addressed to her several letters. Suidas says that she married Isidorus, and wrote some works on astronomy and other subjects.

V. HERON (Ἥρων) the younger, so called to distinguish him from Heron of Alexandrea, already mentioned, is supposed to have lived under Heraclius (A.D. 610–641). The writings attributed to him are, 1. *De Machinis Bellicis*, published by Barocius (Latin), Venice, 1572, 4to. There is one Greek manuscript at Bologna. 2. *Geodesia* (a term used in the sense of practical geometry). It was published (Latin), with the preceding, by Barocius. Montucla notices this as the first treatise in which the mode of finding the area of a triangle by means of its sides occurs. 3. *De Obsidione repellenda* (Ὅπως χρὴ τὸν τῆς πολιορκουμένης πόλεως στρατηγὸν πρὸς

[1] *Smith, Dict. Biogr., s. v.*

τὴν πολιορκίαν ἀντιτάσσεσθαι), published (Greek) in the *Vet. Mathemat. Gr. Opera.* 4. Παρεκβολαὶ ἐκ τῶν στρατηγικῶν παρατάξεων. This treatise exists only in MS. 5. Ἐκ τῶν τοῦ Ἥρωνος περὶ τῶν τῆς Γεωμετρίας καὶ Στερεομετρίας ὀνομάτων, published (Greek and Latin) with the first book of Euclid by Dasypodius, Strasburg, 1671, 8vo. 6. *Excerpta De Mensuris* (Greek and Latin), in the Analecta Græca of the Benedictines, vol. i., Paris, 1688, 4to. 7. Εἰσαγωγὴ τῶν γεωμετρουμένων, existing only in MS.

CHAPTER LXII.

SEVENTH OR BYZANTINE PERIOD—*continued.*

COMPILERS.

I. Joannes Stobæus (Ἰωάννης ὁ Στοβαῖος)[1] derived his surname apparently from being a native of Stobi, in Macedonia. Of his personal history we know nothing. Even the age in which he lived can not be fixed with accuracy, but he must have been later than Hierocles, whom he quotes, and who flourished as a Neo-Platonist about the middle of the fifth century. Probably he did not live very long after him, as he quotes no writer of a later date. We are indebted to Stobæus for a very valuable collection of extracts from earlier Greek writers. He was a man of very extensive reading, in the course of which he noted down the most interesting passages. The materials which he had collected in this way he arranged in the order of subjects, for the use of his son Septimius. This collection of extracts has come down to us divided into two distinct works, of which one bears the title of Ἐκλογαὶ φυσικαὶ διαλεκτικαὶ καὶ ἠθικαί (*Eclogæ Physicæ,* &c.), and the other the title of Ἀνθολόγιον (*Florilegium* or *Sermones*). The *Eclogæ* consist, for the most part, of extracts conveying the views of earlier poets and prose writers on points of physics, dialectics, and ethics. The *Florilegium,* or *Sermones,* is devoted to subjects of a moral, political, and economical nature, and maxims of practical wisdom. Each chapter of the *Eclogæ* and *Sermones* is headed by a title describing its matter. The extracts quoted in illustration begin usually with passages from the poets, after whom come historians, orators, philosophers, and physicians. To Stobæus we are indebted for a large proportion of the fragments that remain of the lost works of the poets. Euripides seems to have been an especial favorite with him. He has quoted above five hundred passages from him in the *Sermones,* one hundred and fifty from Sophocles, and about two hundred from Menander. In extracting from prose writers Stobæus sometimes quotes verbatim, sometimes gives only an epitome of the passage. Photius has given an alphabetical list of above five hundred Greek writers from whom Stobæus has made extracts, the works of the greater part of whom have perished.

The best editions of the *Eclogæ* are by Heeren, Göttingen, 1792–1801, 4 vols. 8vo, and by Gaisford, Oxford, 1850–51, 2 vols. 8vo. The best edition of the *Florilegium* is by Gaisford, Oxford, 1822, 4 vols. 8vo; reprinted, Leipzig, 1823, 4 vols. 8vo.

---

[1] *Smith, Dict. Biogr., s. v.*

II. Cassianus Bassus,[1] surnamed *Scholasticus*, was in all probability the compiler of the *Geoponica* (Γεωπονικά), or work on agriculture, which is usually ascribed to the Emperor Constantine Porphyrogennetus. Cassianus Bassus appears to have compiled it by the command of this emperor, who has thus obtained the honor of the work. Of Bassus we know nothing, save that he lived at Constantinople, and had been born at Maratonymum, probably a place in Bithynia. The work itself, which is still extant, consists of twenty books, and is compiled from various authors, whose names are always given. Bassus has contributed only two short extracts of his own, namely, chapters five and thirty-six of the fifth book. The various subjects treated of in the *Geoponica* will best appear from the contents of the different books, which are as follows: 1. Of the atmosphere, and of the rising and setting of the stars. 2. Of general matters appertaining to agriculture, and of the different kinds of corn. 3. Of the various agricultural duties suitable to each month. 4 and 5. Of the cultivation of the vine. 6–8. Of the making of wine. 9. Of the cultivation of the olive and the making of oil. 10–12. Of horticulture. 13. Of the animals and insects injurious to plants. 14. Of pigeons and other birds. 15. Of natural sympathies and antipathies, and of the management of bees. 16. Of horses, asses, and camels. 17. Of the breeding of cattle. 18. Of the breeding of sheep. 19. Of dogs, hares, deer, pigs, and of salting meat. 20. Of fishes.

The best edition of the *Geoponica* is that by Niclas, Leipzig, 1781, 4 vols. (in one) 8vo.

CHAPTER LXIII.

SEVENTH OR BYZANTINE PERIOD—*concluded.*

MEDICAL WRITERS.[2]

I. Medical science made very little progress during this long period. Alexandrea continued to be the seat of the theory of the art, while Rome and Constantinople furnished to those who exercised it an extended practice and enlarged experience. The science of medicine, however, could hardly be said to exist in its true character, requiring, as it always does, a scrupulous observation of nature, and a philosophic spirit to pursue such investigations, both of which were in a great measure checked by the superstition which exercised so powerful an influence during the greater part of the period under review.

II. If, therefore, during this long interval of comparative darkness, there existed any follower of the medical art who had raised himself above the ordinary level, in place of extending the circle of human knowledge by new discoveries, he contented himself with commenting on the works of Galen, and of other medical writers anterior to him. Such physicians formed what was called the *School of Galen*. The principles which they followed were derived in part from the *Dogmatic*, in part from the *Methodic* and *Empiric* sects; for, in imitation of some of the philosophers

1 *Smith, Dict. Biogr.*, *s. v.*

2 *Schöll, Hist. Lit. Gr.*, vol. vii., p. 247.

of the day, they laid claim to the name of *Eclectics*. We will give a brief account of the most remarkable among them, and principally of those whose works have come down to us.[1]

III. ORIBASIUS (Ὀρειβάσιος or Ὀριβάσιος)[2] was born about A.D. 325, either at Sardis, in Lydia, or at Pergamum, in Mysia. He early acquired a great professional reputation. Oribasius was an intimate friend of the Emperor Julian, with whom he became acquainted several years before his accession to the throne. He was almost the only person to whom Julian imparted the secret of his apostasy from Christianity. He was appointed by the emperor, soon after his accession, quæstor of Constantinople, and sent to Delphi to endeavor to restore the oracle of Apollo to its former splendor and authority; but in this mission he failed, as the only answer he brought back was that the oracle was no more. Oribasius accompanied Julian in his expedition against Persia, and was with him at the time of his death. The succeeding emperors, Valentinian and Valens, were not so favorably disposed toward him, but confiscated his property and banished him. It is probable, however, that his exile did not last long, and that it ended before the year 369. Of the personal character of Oribasius we know little or nothing, but it is clear that he was much attached to paganism and to the heathen philosophy. He was an intimate friend of Eunapius, who praises him very highly, and wrote an account of his life. We possess at present three works of Oribasius, which are generally considered to be genuine. The first of these is called Συναγωγαὶ Ἰατρικαί, *Collecta Medicinalia*, or sometimes Ἑβδομηκοντάβιβλος, and is the work that was compiled at the command of Julian, when Oribasius was still a young man. It contains little original matter, but is very valuable on account of the numerous extracts from writers whose works are no longer extant. More than half of this work is now lost, and what remains is in some confusion, so that it is not easy to specify exactly how many books are at present actually in existence; it is believed, however, that we possess twenty-five, with fragments of two others.

The second work of Oribasius that is still extant was written probably about thirty years after the above, of which it is an abridgment (Σύνοψις). It consists of nine books. This work has never been published in Greek, but was translated into Latin by Rasarius, and printed at Venice, 1554, 8vo. The third work of Oribasius is entitled Εὐπόριστα, *Euporista* or *De facile parabilibus*, and consists of four books. Both this and the preceding work were intended as manuals of medicine.

There is no complete edition of the first of the above-mentioned works. The first fifteen books were first published in a Latin translation by Rasarius (together with the twenty-fourth and twenty-fifth), Venice, 8vo, without date, but before 1555. They were published in Greek and Latin by C. F. Matthæi, Moscow, 1808, 4to, but with the omission of all the extracts from Galen, Rufus Ephesius, and Dioscorides. This edition is very scarce. The first and second books had been previously published in Greek and Latin by Gruner, Jena, 1782, 4to. Books twenty-one and twenty-two were discovered in MS. by Dietz, about fifteen years ago, but have not yet been published either in Greek or Latin. Book forty-four was published in Greek and Latin, with copious notes, by

[1] *Schöll, l. c.*

[2] *Greenhill; Smith's Dict. Biogr., s. v.*

Bussemaker, Groningen, 1835, 8vo, having previously appeared in Greek, together with some other books, in Mai's *Classici Auctores e Vaticanis Codicibus editi*, Rome, 1831, 8vo.

IV. Aëtius (Ἀέτιος),[1] a Greek medical writer, born at Amida, in Mesopotamia, and who lived at the end of the fifth, or the beginning of the sixth century after Christ. His work, entitled Βιβλία Ἰατρικὰ Ἑκκαίδεκα, "Sixteen Books on Medicine," is one of the most valuable medical remains of antiquity, as being a judicious compilation from many authors whose works are lost. The whole of it has never appeared in the original Greek. One half was published at Venice, from the Aldine press, 1534, fol.; the second volume never appeared. Different parts have been published at different times, of which we may mention, some chapters of the ninth book, in Greek and Latin, by Hebenstreit, Leipzig, 1757, 4to; another chapter of the same book, in Greek and Latin, by Tengström, Abo, 1817, 4to; and another extract from the same book, in the Συλλογὴ Ἑλληνικῶν ἀνεκδότων of Mustoxydes and Schinas, Venice, 1816, 8vo. There is a corrupt translation of the whole work into Latin, by Cornarius, Basle, 1542, often reprinted.

V. Alexander Trallianus,[2] one of the most eminent of the ancient physicians, was born at Tralles, in Lydia, whence he derived his surname. His date may be safely put in the sixth century after Christ. He was a man of extensive practice, of very great experience, and of distinguished reputation, not only at Rome, but wherever he travelled in Spain, Gaul, and Italy, whence he was called, by way of eminence, "Alexander the Physician." He is not a mere compiler, like Aëtius, Oribasius, and others, but has more the air of an original writer. He was the author of two extant Greek works, 1. Βιβλία Ἰατρικὰ Δυοκαίδεκα, *Libri Duodecim de Re Medica*; and, 2. Περὶ Ἑλμίνθων, *De Lumbricis*. He seems to have written several other medical works, which are now lost.

The work *De Re Medica* was first edited in Greek by Goupylus, Paris, 1548, fol., a beautiful and scarce edition. It was published in Greek, with a Latin translation, by J. Guinterus Andernacus, Basle, 1556, 8vo, which is a rare and valuable edition. The other extant work, *De Lumbricis*, was first published in Greek and Latin by Mercurialis, Venice, 1570, 4to. It is also inserted in his work *De morbis puerorum*, Frankfort, 1584, 8vo, and in the twelfth volume of the old edition of Fabricius' *Bibliotheca Græca*.

VI. Paulus Æginēta,[3] a celebrated medical writer, of whose personal history nothing is known, except that he was born in the island of Ægina, and that he travelled a good deal, visiting, among other places, Alexandrea. He probably lived in the latter half of the seventh century after Christ. Suidas says he wrote several medical works, of which the principal one is still extant, with no exact title, but commonly called *De Re Medica Libri Septem*. This work is chiefly a compilation from former writers. The sixth book is the most valuable and interesting, and contains, at the same time, the most original matter. His reputation among the Arabian writers seems to have been very great.

The Greek text has been twice published, Venice, 1528, and Basle, 1538. There is an excellent English translation by Adams, London, 1844–47, 3 vols. 8vo.

VII. Theophilus Protospatharius,[4] the author of several Greek medical works, which are still extant, lived probably in the seventh century

[1] *Greenhill; Smith's Dict. Biogr., s. v.* [2] *Id. ib.* [3] *Id. ib.* [4] *Id. ib.*

after Christ. *Protospatharius* was originally a military title, given to the colonel of the body-guards of the Emperor of Constantinople (*Spatharii*), but afterward became also a high civil dignity. After arriving at high professional and political rank, he at last embraced the monastic life. Of his works, the two most important are, 1. Περὶ τῆς τοῦ ἀνθρώπου κατασκευῆς, *De corporis humani fabrica*, an anatomical and physical treatise, in five books, the best edition of which is by Greenhill, Oxford, 1842, 8vo; and, 2. Περὶ οὔρων, *De Urinis*, the best edition of which is by Guidot, Leyden, 1703 (and 1731), 8vo.

INDEX OF PROPER NAMES.

THE END.

www.ingramcontent.com/pod-product-compliance
Lightning Source LLC
LaVergne TN
LVHW021222110826
845150LV00002B/220